# UNDERSTANDING **SOCIETY**

# UNDERSTANDING SOCIETY

## AN INTRODUCTION TO SOCIOLOGY

*Third Edition*

*Caroline Hodges Persell*

NEW YORK UNIVERSITY

1817

**HARPER & ROW, PUBLISHERS, New York**
Grand Rapids, Philadelphia, St. Louis, San Francisco,
London, Singapore, Sydney, Tokyo

Acknowledgments for text and photos can be found at the back of the text, following page 653.

Sponsoring Editor: Alan McClare
Development Editor: Robert Ginsberg/Mary Lou Mosher
Project Editor: Carla Samodulski/Lois Lombardo
Art Direction and Cover Coordination: Teresa J. Delgado
Text and Cover Design: Circa 86, Inc.
Cover Photo: Michael G. Merle
Photo Research: Ilene Cherna Bellovin
Production: Jeanie Berke/Beth Maglione

Understanding Society: An Introduction to Sociology, Third Edition
Copyright © 1990 by Harper & Row, Publishers, Inc.

**Library of Congress Cataloging-in-Publication Data**

Persell, Caroline Hodges.
    Understanding society.

    Including bibliographical references.
    1. Sociology.    I. Title.
HM51.P45   1990          301          89-24573
ISBN 0-06-045127-0 (teacher ed.)
ISBN 0-06-045163-7 (student ed.)

89  90  91  92    9  8  7  6  5  4  3  2  1

*Dedicated to*

*Charlie, Patty, and Steve,*
*who helped more than they'll ever know,*
*with thanks and love,*

*Caroline*

**CONTENTS IN BRIEF**

# CONTENTS

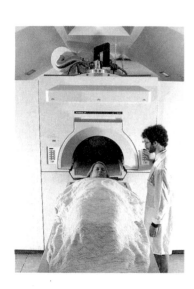

# TO THE INSTRUCTOR

In this third edition of *Understanding Society,* I explore society and how it operates. My goal is to illuminate for students the powerful social forces and patterns that influence their lives and careers. Although the primary focus in the text is generally North American society, there is also much cross-cultural material for contrast. I hope to encourage students to think actively about the issues shaping contemporary society so that they will be in a stronger position to pursue informed choices and actions throughout their lives.

Classic and current sociological theories are used to examine and analyze the major aspects of social life. Each of the primary perspectives—interactionist, functionalist, and conflict—embodies unique insights, and each helps illuminate concepts and trends throughout the text. Although I have made every effort to present the various perspectives in a fair and impartial manner, I believe that texts should have a point of view. I have not hesitated to offer my own assessment of theories and research, and I have tried to provide students with enough information to form their own judgments and even to disagree.

This book tries to entice first-year students into the intriguing world of sociology, in part by linking sociological research to the everyday social world. All too often introductory sociology textbooks seem to underestimate students' capacity to respond to real research. Some of the exciting new research that this edition shares with students includes:

- The sex ratio's effect on male/female relations in light of predictions based on current demographics

- Research on how groups resist unjust authority, based on research by Gamson, Fireman, and Rytina

- Cross-cultural research on work structures and employee services in Japan and the United States by Lincoln and Kalleberg
- Cross-cultural material on murder rates in different societies, and possible sociological explanations for them
- Research on why some persons get longer prison terms than others
- New research on the effect of downward mobility on young people today
- New research on the relative importance of class and ethnicity
- Changing conceptions of masculinity and male sex roles
- New material on occupational sex segregation, and sex segregation in the realm of voluntary organizations and its implications for status differences
- New research on rape and societal supports for it
- New research testing Chodorow's well-known theory about sex role learning
- New research on where marriage and divorce rates are going in the future
- Cohabitation and subsequent marital instability, with cross-cultural evidence
- New research on what are "good jobs" and who gets them
- New research on minority student achievement, educational tracking, and gender and college attendance
- New material on "constructing scientific facts"
- Rational choice theories of why individuals join social movements, as well as structural and ideological explanations
- Recent research on how shared leisure is related to marital stability and quality
- New data, collected by the author, on racial stacking by position in baseball

The third edition retains the thematic unity of the first two editions. It stresses both the significance of understanding how power and inequality operate in varied social contexts and the importance of human action. I hope that students will learn facts, concepts, and theories about the social world that are interesting and important and learn to think sociologically as well.

## NEW TO THE THIRD EDITION

In this edition, Part 2 has been substantially reorganized and culture is treated earlier in the text. A completely reworked Chapter 3 introduces the central ideas of both society and culture.

Chapter 4 considers such elements of social structure as status, role, institution, and social network and discusses the various forms of social interaction. Chapters 5 (socialization), 6 (groups and organizations), and 7 (deviance) complete a shortened, more succinct Part 2. I have retained the effective organization of the other parts of the book.

This edition also features new debates on important social issues. Topics and questions discussed include: Microelectronics: Cultural Transformation for Good or for Ill?; Networking: Pros and Cons About How It Is Done; "Spare the Rod and Spoil the Child?"; Is Women's Liberation Linked to Higher Rates of Female Crime?; Is the United States Becoming a Bipolar Society?; The Underclass: Causes and Proposed Solutions; Do Communications Technologies Promote or Undermine Democracy?; Will Televangelists Hurt Traditional Churches?; Did Panic Behavior Kill Eleven People at the 1979 "Who" Concert in Cincinnati?; and Should Congress Raise the Gasoline Tax?

New illustrated, original summary tables that help organize information for today's more visually oriented students are included in this edition. These tables deal with the strengths and limitations of different methods of collecting data; major social differences in hunting and gathering, agrarian, and industrial societies; changes in American values, class-related life chances and life-styles; and school children's perceptions of life as a member of the opposite sex.

Of course, the most important point about a revised edition is the fresh information it contains. I have added whole new sections on a number of topics including: the sociology of emotions; public policies to support equality (which discusses affirmative action, comparable worth, and family policies in terms of their prospects and their limitations); adult offspring and elderly parents; state terrorism, with extensive cross-cultural examples; the gender gap and class bias in voting; the greenhouse effect; and incest.

I have also added many new topics including, but not limited to, the following:

- Research spending in the United States compared to other industrial societies

- Corporate takeovers and mergers and the role of international investors in the United States economy

- Intergroup relations and ethnic antagonisms

- The current social situation in South Africa

- A new sociological effort to explain juvenile delinquency

- The Family Security Act of 1988 and its social implications

- The sexual revolution and AIDS

- Government medical programs and racial differences in medical care

- The growth of the Pacific Basin and development of the European trading community in 1992

- Changes in the Soviet and Chinese economies
- Self-identification as a homosexual (or not)

## PEDAGOGICAL AIDS

The book is generously illustrated with cartoons, graphs, summary charts, and photographs. The third edition includes many more photographs than previously, almost all of them new to this edition. There are stimulating boxed materials and instructive graphics. All the graphs have legends to guide the student's eyes toward the important trends in the data. Among the aids to student learning in each chapter are an opening outline, a summary of major points, and a list of key terms. Each chapter also contains an annotated list of suggested readings at the end. These provide additional insight into topics and were chosen for their accessibility. They will also be useful to students doing follow-up projects. Key terms are printed in boldface type and defined in the text when they first appear. The key terms are listed at the end of each chapter (and cross-referenced to the text) to help students review the material. All key terms and concepts are collected and defined in the complete glossary at the end of the text. A full alphabetical list of references and both subject and name indexes appear at the end of the book.

## SUPPLEMENTS

The text is especially well-integrated with the *Instructor's Resource Manual,* the student study guide titled *Encountering Society,* and the *Test Bank.*

The expanded *Test Bank,* prepared by Peter Morrill of Bronx Community College, contains 15 true-false, 60 multiple-choice, and 15 fill-in questions, plus 10 essay questions, for each of the 22 chapters. The questions cover major concepts, significant sociological insights and trends, and major figures in the field. For all questions, the level of difficulty and the relevant text reference are given. A computerized version of the *Test Bank* is available. It enables instructors to select and combine questions to produce many different tests of varying length and difficulty. It can be used with the IBM-PC, the Macintosh, and most compatibles.

Mary Bernstein has helped Eleen A. Baumann, Richard G. Mitchell, Jr., and me to prepare the third edition of the *Instructor's Resource Manual* and *Encountering Society,* the student study guide. For each chapter of the text there is a corresponding chapter in the *Instructor's Resource Manual* consisting of: (1) a statement of the goals of the chapter; (2) a chapter outline; (3) teaching suggestions, including in-class exercises, out-of-class projects, community assistance for the teaching process, and a list of films and audiovisual aids; and (4) supplemental materials, including examples or materials that may be used in class discussions or lectures. Available separately is a set of transparency masters that can produce transparencies for use with overhead projectors. Included are copies of all the key tables and figures in the text, so they can be presented and discussed in the classroom.

The student study guide, *Encountering Society,* is keyed to the text. Each chapter includes: (1) a brief summary of the text chapter; (2) a section reviewing what students have learned in the chapter, including review questions and a chance to define major concepts; (3) a section of exercises in which students can apply what they have learned; and (4) a section testing student knowledge that consists of 10 multiple-choice questions, 15 fill-in-the-blanks, and 5 to 10 matching questions, plus answers. The exercises are designed to show how sociology can illuminate students' daily lives. We have successfully used most of these exercises with our own students.

Alan R. Sadovnick, Eleen A. Baumann, Richard G. Mitchell, Jr., and I have also developed a reader to accompany the text. *Exploring Society: A Collection of Readings in Sociology* contains some classic and contemporary sources mentioned in the text so that students and instructors wishing to read primary materials can do so. A test bank for the reader is also available.

## ACKNOWLEDGMENTS

I would like to thank my colleagues and students at New York University for their comments and very helpful ideas and suggestions, especially Mary Bernstein, Peter W. Cookson, Jr., Jo Dixon, Eliot Freidson, Xu Ping Fu, Cynthia Gordon, David Greenberg, Robert Max Jackson, James M. Jasper, Dorothy Nelkin, and Richard R. Peterson.

This edition has benefited considerably from eight expert reviewers who gave detailed comments on specific subjects, suggesting revisions and new sources to consult. I would like to thank them for their generous contributions by listing them here with their areas of expertise:

James E. Blackwell, University of Massachusetts-Boston, *race*

David Greenberg, New York University, *sexuality*

Diana Harris, University of Tennessee, Knoxville, *aging*

Davor Jedlicka, University of Texas at Tyler, *family*

Robert E. Kennedy, Jr., University of Minnesota, *population*

Donald McQuarie, Bowling Green State University, *power and politics*

Richard G. Mitchell, Jr., Oregon State University, *sport and leisure*

Bernice A. Pescosolido, Indiana University, *medicine and health*

I am particularly grateful to the knowledgeable sociologists who either commented on the second edition or who reviewed the manuscript for the third edition. Their comments and suggestions for improvements were invariably helpful:

Peter S. Bearman, University of North Carolina

David Cooperman, University of Minnesota

Pat Johnson, Houston Community College

Hugh Lena, Providence College

Shirley McCorkell, Saddleback Community College

James Orcutt, Florida State University

M.S. Rao, University of Alaska-Fairbanks

Barbara L. Rowland-Mori, California Polytechnic State University

Craig Taylor, Western Kentucky University

Ed Vaughn, University of Missouri-Columbia

Theodore Wagenaar, Miami University

John Zipp, University of Wisconsin

Many people at Harper & Row made this book possible. Alan McClare, the sponsoring editor, maintained his enthusiasm for the book throughout; Robert Ginsberg and Mary Lou Mosher, the development editors, brought thoughtful editing help and attentive management to the project. Carla Samodulski and Lois Lombardo stayed cheerfully on top of a myriad of critically important production details. Ilene Cherna Bellovin added her sharp eye to the photo research; and Teresa Delgado's help with the cover is deeply appreciated.

Helen Lowenhar brought her professional proofreading abilities to my aid at a critical time.

Thank you, one and all.

Caroline Hodges Persell

What should you get out of your study of sociology? As a teacher, I tell my students that sociology both fascinates and informs. Sociology explores society and how it operates. Sociology broadens social insights, fosters critical thinking, trains you in methods of gathering and analyzing data, and can help develop your writing skills. By encouraging you to think actively about the issues facing contemporary society, you will learn to make more informed choices throughout your life.

This book contains an enormous number of topics and issues that will interest you. Here are just a few examples:

- The sociology of emotions
- Adult offspring and elderly parents
- The gender gap and class bias in voting
- Incest
- Intergroup relations and ethnic antagonism
- The sexual revolution and AIDS
- Drug abuse among professional athletes

Other examples come from every area of contemporary social interest, including business (international investment in the United States), ecology (the greenhouse effect), science (controversies on animal testing), sport (declining popularity of exercise), and many more.

This text has a unity of themes. It stresses both the significance of understanding how power and inequality operate in many different social contexts and the importance of human action in those contexts. My hope is you will learn facts, concepts, and theories about the social world that are interesting and important. The goal is to learn to think sociologically.

Physically, the text is organized into five parts. The first part considers social theories and methods, the second examines social concepts and processes, the third treats social inequalities, the fourth analyzes major social institutions, and the fifth explores social changes and issues. Each part is previewed by a part introduction.

To find out more about people who have studied sociology and who find it useful in their daily lives and careers, my interviews with several people who studied sociology are presented in a unique section, *Invitation to the Student,* immediately following. These brief profiles are designed to help you to see that sociology has value in and of itself. I hope you find this book helpful in your course and sociology useful in your life.

Caroline Hodges Persell

As you begin studying sociology, you may be wondering what you can do with it, or what others who have studied it are doing now. What kind of role can a knowledge of sociology play in your life? What are some of the varied and interesting careers being pursued by people who have a B.A., an M.A., or a Ph.D. in sociology? To answer these questions, let's look at the lives and careers of some real people who credit sociology with having a major impact on what they do. These examples include men and women working in business, education, advertising, journalism, media, and law. What they say can show you how sociology can help you enrich your own career and personal life as well.

## A BACHELOR'S DEGREE IN SOCIOLOGY

**Dorothy H. Roberts** is Chairman of the Board of The Echo Design Group, Inc., one of the best-known manufacturers of scarves in the United States. Her father, Edgar C. Hyman, founded the business in 1923, and even as a child she traveled to Europe with her parents on business trips. She attended Carleton College in Minnesota for two years before transferring to Connecticut College, where she earned her B.S. in sociology in 1950. She and her husband, Paul Roberts, joined Echo after college graduation. In 1953 they had a daughter, followed by a son in 1956. Mrs. Roberts worked part-time for a while when they were young, directing advertising, publicity, and special promotions. Her husband became company president, and as the children grew older, Mrs. Roberts became her husband's chief business associate. When he died at age 50 in 1978, Mrs. Roberts became Echo's chief executive.

This is how Mrs. Roberts see the benefits of her sociology major:

*I have always been interested in people—whether in groups or as individuals. This led me to major in sociology and minor in psychology. As I see it, sociology is the study of people in groups, and psychology is the study of people as individuals. My background in sociology has given me a foundation from which to communicate with people around me— whether it be employees, customers, or suppliers.*

*More than ever, through my experience in business, I've learned that to succeed one must care for and be interested in people. The interrelationships between people, and between groups of people as departments, are of primary importance in attaining any goal that an organization sets out to achieve.*

**Denise Richardson** majored in sociology as an undergraduate at Hunter College. She began her media career in 1972 as an employee in the corporate Personnel Department of RKO General Inc. She was the company's first Equal Employment Administrator responsible for the implementation of the company's Affirmative Action programs. While at RKO she had the opportunity to move into journalism by becoming a reporter and Public Affairs Coordinator at WXLO–FM (now KISS–FM), and was responsible for all weekend news and public affairs programming for two years at the RKO–FM radio station. In 1977 she joined the WOR–AM news staff, where she was a street reporter; she also anchored newsbroadcasts and coanchored a public affairs program called *Upfront,* which dealt with minority issues. She was responsible for conceiving, researching, and narrating "The Blue Minority," a 90-minute award-winning program on the day-to-day problems of the New York City street cop. In September 1981 she moved to WOR–TV, where she anchored *News 9: Updates,* served as a general assignment reporter for *News 9: Primetime* and *News 9: At Noon,* and then in 1985 she became the anchor woman for *Straight Talk,* an hour-long, issue-oriented program aired seven days a week. She now works on special projects at WOR–TV. Asked about the value of her major in sociology, Ms. Richardson said.

*A help it is. My understanding of the development of human society sensitizes me to reporting what people do that makes society work.*

**Alvin P. Sanoff** is currently a Senior Editor at *U.S. News & World Report,* where he writes about the media, culture, social issues, and trends. Recent cover stories he has authored include "Who Will Control TV?" and "The New American Male." He also conducts the magazine's "Conversations" series of interviews with scholars, novelists, and social and cultural leaders. He is shown here interviewing Pulitzer prize-winning novelist and poet, Robert Penn Warren. He graduated with an A.B. in sociology from Harvard College in 1963. Asked how he uses sociology in his career, Mr. Sanoff said,

*I think it has helped me to understand specific systems and institutions and how they operate internally, as well as how they affect the lives of individuals who are outside the institutions. It has also helped me to understand the functioning of the broader society, complete with its many subgroups and subcultures.*

## A MASTER'S DEGREE IN SOCIOLOGY

**James L. Castagna** received his B.A. and M.A. in sociology and his J.D. in law from New York University. He worked for five years as a field attorney for the National Labor Relations Board, investigating and litigating unfair labor practice charges. He has served as a media consultant to the Center for the Media Arts, and as an on-camera investigative reporter for two documentary videos dealing with runaway children and the homeless. He has practiced law privately, has taught labor relations, and he has also managed to enjoy a career as a playwright and actor.

Mr. Castagna says,

*Studying sociology increased my awareness of the inequalities in the society and the victimization of certain groups of its people. It has motivated me to investigate further the relationship between the legal system and the society which it attempts to order. As a sociologist, playwright, actor, and lawyer, I have attempted to raise the consciousness of other individuals regarding the society's unfair treatment of poor people and minorities. I believe these attempts have brought about a better protection of basic human rights.*

**Peter Kim** received his B.A., M.A., and M.Phil. in sociology at New York University. As a full-time graduate student he received a Minority Fellowship from the American Sociological Association. He joined J. Walter Thompson USA in 1984 and within a year was promoted to Vice President. He was the principal architect of that firm's "New American Consumer Study." The Consumer Information Department, which he founded, maintains an extensive in-house electronic data archive on consumers drawn from hundreds of different proprietary, syndicated, government, and academic sources. He also lectures on the specific marketing and advertising implications of the current changes in the consumer marketplace for many clients of the agency. He is now a Senior Vice President and Executive Director of the Consumer Behavior Department.

Mr. Kim sees his sociology background as invaluable for what he does. He says,

*Research methodology, survey design, multivariate statistics, and a general understanding of social research are essential tools for today's market researchers. However, the true competitive advantage comes not from tools but from the cultivation of a "sociological imagination" that dwells on ideas, concepts, philosophies, histories, and their interconnect-*

*edness. There is an army of technicians who can massage the numbers, but only a few who can interpret them. The best in the field recognize that the data will never speak, but must be spoken for; it is this that we as sociologists do better than most.*

## A PH.D. IN SOCIOLOGY

The Daily Pennsylvanian

**E. Digby Baltzell** studied sociology at the University of Pennsylvania and at Columbia University, where he completed his doctoral dissertation under the direction of Robert K. Merton. Professor Baltzell began teaching sociology at the University of Pennsylvania in 1947 and retired from there in 1986. During those 39 years he devoted himself fully to every aspect of the University's life and published nationally acclaimed studies of privilege, talent, class structure, and leadership, including *Philadelphia Gentlemen: The Making of a National Upper Class, The Protestant Establishment,* and *Puritan Boston and Quaker Philadelphia.*

In the classroom and beyond, Professor Baltzell has used his understanding of sociology to illuminate social relationships. Distinguishing between "organic relationships" and "mechanistic" ones, he remarks that "suing for damages when a child is killed is mechanistic. The point is that everyone is priceless." Speaking to the graduating class of 1986, he urged them "to be heroes—that's not saying too much," since most of them "have at least one grandparent who was not born in the United States and had to have heroic qualities to undertake a dangerous and uncertain passage to this land." And he urged them to be less afraid of failure. "You will learn from your failures not from your successes."

Sigrid Estrada

**Rosabeth Moss Kanter** received her B.A. from Bryn Mawr College in 1964 and her Ph.D. in sociology from the University of Michigan in 1967, and then served on the faculties of Brandeis, Harvard, and Yale Universities. In 1986 she was named the Class of 1960 Professor of Innovation and Entrepreneurship at the Harvard Business School, the first holder of this new, tenured, full professorship. She is the author of 10 books and more than 100 articles in books and scholarly journals. Her 1977 book, *Men and Women of the Corporation,* received the C. Wright Mills Award in 1978 for the best book of that year on social issues. *The Change Masters: Innovation and Entrepreneurship in the American Corporation* (1983) was a selection of several book clubs and was recently published in Japanese. Her newest book, *When Giants Learn to Dance: Mastering the Challenges of Strategy, Management, and Careers in the 1990s* (1989), is being translated into French, Swedish, Dutch, and Italian. She conceived and directed *A Tale of "O": On Being Different,* an audiovisual production about discrimination, which is used by thousands of organizations worldwide. She is also co-founder (in 1977) and Chairman of the Board of Good-measure, Inc., a consulting firm that has advised such blue chip corporations as Procter & Gamble, BellSouth, Honeywell, General Electric, Apple Computer, International Harvester (now Navistar), Simon & Schuster, Xerox, and Pacific Telesis. She also serves on the Board of the College Retirement Equities Fund (CREF), the largest private pension fund in America; the American Productivity and Quality Center in Houston; the Saatchi & Saatchi Consulting Group; and the Boston Children's Museum.

Dr. Kanter clearly uses her sociological insights on a daily basis. She says,

*Sociological reasoning—a structural, institutional, systemic approach to understanding behavior patterns—is the principal tool I use in helping organizations learn to be more effective. My work focuses on how to organize human effort to create economic and social value. Stimulating innovation, improving productivity, ensuring the success of minorities and women, increasing worker participation and quality of work life—all require knowing how to diagnose organizational problems (data collection and analysis) and solve them.*

**Charles V. Willie** is Professor of Education and Urban Studies, Graduate School of Education, Harvard University. He received his B.A. in sociology from Morehouse College in 1948, his M.A. in sociology from Atlanta University in 1949, and his Ph.D. in sociology from Syracuse University in 1957. He taught at Syracuse University from 1952 to 1974, and since 1974 has been teaching at Harvard. He is the author, coauthor, or editor of 19 books, four research monographs, and of nearly 100 journal articles and chapters in books. His most recent books include *A New Look at Black and White Families, Effective Education,* and *The Caste and Class Controversy in Race and Poverty.* He has been involved since 1974 in the integration of the Boston schools and is the coauthor of the most recent court-approved plan for controlled choice in the Boston school system.

Professor Willie says,

*At work and in the community, I use sociological concepts every day. The major sociological ideas that give direction to my actions are inclusiveness, diversity, and complementarity.*

*As an applied sociologist, I implement these concepts in my daily activities by following five principles. I try (1) to be a person for others, (2) to accept myself as someone significant, (3) to respect the autonomy and integrity of every person, (4) to be generous and magnanimous, and (5) to follow the way of humility. I have invoked these principles in my work as a researcher and teacher of sociology. I have invoked them when serving as a consultant to local and state boards of education on school desegregation planning and to federal agencies such as the President's Commission on Mental Health and the President's Committee on Juvenile Delinquency and Youth Crime. I have also followed these principles as a participant in international conferences on church and society.*

SOCIOLOGY AND YOUR CAREER

Of course sociological degrees are useful for teaching in colleges and universities. But as these examples show, they are also highly useful in an almost unlimited assortment of occupations. Persons with B.A. degrees in sociology often work as social workers, counselors, researchers, teachers, nurses, business managers, sales persons, parole officers, police officers, child care workers, or in other occupations.[1] Even among Ph.D. holders, about one out of five sociologists works outside the academy as a researcher, statistician, analyst, writer, vice president, president, manager, director in federal, state, and local governments, and in corporations and nonprofit organizations.[2]

This book will introduce you to sociology and to some of the many interesting issues that sociologists study. It will help you develop your own sociological insights both by covering important theories and by considering current data and concerns such as the "divorce revolution," the electronic church, and growing poverty among the young.

The text includes numerous features to help you master the material. Chapter outlines and summaries will help you review the main points of each chapter. The boxes are designed to develop or apply the ideas you are learning, and captions illustrate how to interpret the graphs. We have also prepared a student review manual, called *Encountering Society,* that includes a summary of each chapter, review questions, exercises to help you apply the concepts you have learned, and a section of self-test questions to help you identify areas where you may need further study and review.

We hope that your sociology course, and this text, will interest you in the discipline of sociology and show you how sociology can play a role in your life. Like the people described here, you may find the study of sociology fascinating and beneficial, whether you become a sociologist or use its insights in a different career.

CHP

[1] Bettina J. Huber, "Career Possibilities for Sociology Graduates," American Sociological Association, 1722 N Street, N.W., Washington, D.C. 20036. Single copies available free on request.
[2] Bettina J. Huber, "Employment Patterns in Sociology: Recent Trends and Future Prospects." 1985. Washington, D.C.: American Sociological Association.

Chris Den Blaker

Caroline Hodges Persell graduated from Swarthmore College and received her doctorate in sociology from Columbia University in 1971. She has taught at New York University since 1971, where she is currently Professor of Sociology and Chair of the Department of Sociology. In the past she has also served as Director of Undergraduate Studies and Director of Graduate Studies at New York University. She is Chair of the American Sociological Association's Committee on Publications, Chair of the ASA Section on Undergraduate Education, and Vice President of the Eastern Sociological Society.

Dr. Persell has won national awards for both teaching and research. She is the author of numerous scholarly monographs and journal articles, and of two other books: *Quality, Careers, and Training in Educational and Social Research* (1976) and *Education and Ineqality* (1977). In addition, she is the coauthor (with Peter W. Cookson, Jr.) of the well-received *Preparing for Power: America's Elite Boarding Schools* (1985).

Dr. Persell was born in Fort Wayne, Indiana. She is married to Charles Persell, and they have teenage twins, Patricia and Stephen, who are themselves college students. She is an active sportsperson and plays the violin in an amateur chamber ensemble.

# P A R T 1

# SOCIETY
# AND
# SOCIOLOGY

Sociology offers exciting new ways of understanding ourselves, other people, and the social world. Chapter 1 introduces the sociological point of view and shows how sociology differs from related disciplines. Many sociological insights result from the collection and analysis of data, and Chapter 2 examines some of the special techniques, including surveys and social experiments, that sociologists use. It also shows some of the ways social research has influenced governmental policies and has caused people to think differently about social relationships. (To see how sociology has been used by people in their careers, read the Invitation to the Student that precedes this page.)

# Why Study Sociology?

*What is the longest time you have been totally out of contact, in person and by phone, with any other human being? For most of us, it is probably less than twenty-four hours. Although we think of ourselves as individuals, we long for contact with others. Indeed, we cannot survive or become fully human without that contact, since humans are, above all else, social beings.*
**Sociology** *deals with the analysis of patterned social relationships in modern societies. Paradoxically, becoming aware of how social relationships shape our lives may make us freer to be who we want to be.*

## AN INVITATION TO THE SOCIOLOGICAL OUTLOOK

To get a glimpse of how social forces affect us, consider the lives of two very different pairs of young people: Albert and his wife are migrant workers; Alice and her twin brother Alex are heirs to a New Mexican fortune. They spoke to Robert Coles, a social psychiatrist, who has reported on their lives:

*Youth for Albert and his wife was a short-lived time; youth for them was working the way they had done for years as "children." . . . As Albert said, "You stop, you die—that's what we say when we need to remind ourselves about the kind of life we have ahead of us. And if we forget to remind ourselves, the crew leader won't; he won't forget to tell us the score.*

*"He was the one, the crew leader was, who told me I should pick a girl and stay with her. . . .*

*"I listened to his advice; I chose my girl, my wife. She is a good woman. She's always been good. She's nice to be with. She loves me. She tries to be a good mother. I love her. I'd die without her. We'll be moving on up to the next farm, and I'll*

*feel sick. I put my head on her shoulder, and I feel better, all of a sudden; it's like there's been a miracle. She says I make her feel good. She says if it wasn't for me and the children, she'd have died a long time ago."*

*By fifteen, all of [this] had happened to Albert; and by thirteen or fourteen other migrant youths are going through what he described. They are getting ready to surrender a certain exhilaration, a curiosity of mind, a kind of youthful intensity, an inclination to experiment and dream and speak out—and escape. . . .*

*[Albert] tells how he once tried to break away from the crew leader, how he failed to do so. The sheriff came and arrested him for owing money, for disturbing the peace, for drinking too much, for possible thievery. . . . It was all faked, all trumped up, but the point was made, and he was quickly released—into the hands of his accuser and longtime "friend," the crew leader. He was at the time "about fourteen." . . .*

*"If I'd been able to, I would have started on a new life. I would have been my own man and said only what I believed. But maybe you can't have but one kind of life, at least here on this earth—especially if you're like us migrant people. I guess*

3

*Migrant workers and their children occupy a very different position in the social structure than do farm owners and their children.*

those few weeks, when we were dating and figuring out our plan to break away—I guess that was when we were young, when we could hope for a good break." . . .

His wife,[1] who is his age, remembers all of that. . . . "My children ask me questions about what we used to do and where we used to live, a lot of questions. I tell them it's always been the same. They stop asking you if you tell them that. If you let them go, let them ask more and more questions, you'll soon get sad; that's the trouble." [Coles, 1967, pp. 544–546]

Some growers, gas station attendants, and local residents describe the migrants as "animals." Sociologists and other social scientists like Coles who study human behavior do not simply accept other people's descriptions. The sociological outlook requires us to look for possible con-

[1] Coles does not mention Albert's wife's name in his book.

nections between individuals and larger social institutions such as the law and the economic system. It leads us to ask "What else is going on here?" In this case, Coles refused to accept the definition of migrant workers as "animals." Instead, he has shown us the world through the eyes of the migrants themselves.

Coles also gives us a sense of how these individuals are embedded in the world of work, and what their power and resources are. He does the same for two economically privileged young people, Alice and Alex, a girl and a boy who are twins.

*Their parents own a large and beautifully maintained ranch in the so-called North Valley of Albuquerque. . . . The mother collects antiques, the father is a prominent New Mexican . . . and his father . . . is one of the richest men in New Mexico. [Alice] knows that both her father and her grandfather have long been involved in various ways with Indians. The Pueblo people have land, and her family has an interest in land; a willingness to buy it, sell it, build on it, divide it up, display it, advertise it, promote its virtues, and, she knows, overlook (at the very least) its deficiencies. . . . Alex talks of his crusty grandfather's response to Pueblo life: "He said they are nice people, but they don't ever amount to much, because they've got no real fight in them. . . . [Alex] has asked his father whether he thinks the Indians actually suffer, and has been told no, they don't—or don't any more than others do. His father's strongly worded views have (but only tentatively) become his. Every once in a while Alexander has a moment or two of disagreement. . . . Not to his face, however; he tells Alice about his opinions, as against his father's. And she says yes, he ought to stick to his guns, even go speak up to their parents, let them know what one of their children thinks. He has not followed her suggestion, though.*

*He explains why: "My father knows more about the Indians than the teacher. He says he talks to them face-to-face about business, and the teacher only gets her information from books. . . . Alice will probably ask to go to a public school one of these days, just because she likes to argue with Daddy. She tells him she thinks he's wrong sometimes! He smiles and says she's young and she will change her mind later on. She asked him last week what would happen if she didn't change her mind. He said nothing for a while, then he said she* would, even if she thinks she won't. . . . [Alice] asked Daddy about Indians: would he mind if she married one? He said she wouldn't. She said yes, but what if she decided she wanted to. He told her to stop asking him a lot of silly questions. She got upset, because he was really angry with her, and she could tell. That's why I don't want to argue about the Indians with my parents or my grandfather. They think the Indians aren't the same as white people, and we should stay away from them, just like they stay away from us. The teachers have a different opinion; they like the Indians. So does my best friend's father. He's a doctor, and he says the Indians have a lot of diseases, and they should go to the hospital, but they have no money, and the government is supposed to have doctors taking care of Indians, but there aren't enough doctors and its bad to be born an Indian, because you might die very young. I told my mother what he said, and she said it's sad, but it can be the fault of an Indian mother: she doesn't keep a clean house, and she doesn't know the right food to feed her kids, so then they get sick. She said my grandfather is right when he says that the Lord helps the people who try to help themselves."

The boy wonders whether Indians pray to the same God his parents ask him to beseech before going to sleep. His parents are Presbyterians, attend church with the children every Sunday, and encourage in them prayers at the table and upon retiring. . . . Alice will ask the Lord's "kindness" to descend to animals she loves—horses, dogs, cats, a bird—and to "the poor people." So will Alex. He even specifies who they are—"the Indians and the Spanish." . . . The parents say nothing, but the twins know that their concern for the impoverished or the socially and racially "different" is theirs alone at the table. The father has often commented upon how "different" Indians or Spanish-speaking people are. The differences, to him, go quite deep, have to do with what he calls "mentality" as well as social or historical experience, and are ultimately (he has argued) spiritual, hence derived from that hard to comprehend source (for children, certainly, and maybe for grown-ups as well): God's Will. . . .

[Alice] says, "Daddy said he used to worry about the poor Indians and the poor Spanish people, but when you grow up you begin to realize that even if you gave away every penny you have, there would be no change in the world: the rich and the poor would still be there. . . . Maybe if the rich people gave some money to the poor people, Maria [their maid] would be better off. But Alex says he doesn't think they will give enough!" [Coles, 1977, pp. 182–205]

These two examples illustrate that people's personal identities are socially rooted. Albert notes the difficulties they face, "especially if you're like us migrant people." Alex and Alice struggle with the social identity their parents and grandfather try to impose: Are they really "different" from Indians and the Spanish, or not? If all human beings are alike, how can the great inequalities between them be justified? The identities of Alex and Alice are maintained by social relationships with their parents, as Albert's is with the crew leader. These people—parents and employers—mold the young people's lives through affection and through superior power and resources. Their power is rooted in larger social structures, so there is a crucial link between personal feelings and those structures.

One part of the sociological outlook examines how social structures (such as economic institutions and relationships, the family, religion, education) and social inequalities influence the feelings and actions of individuals.

The above examples reveal that people struggle to change their social confinements. Albert and his wife tried to run away. Although they failed, they made the attempt. They also have forged a loving, meaningful relationship with each other despite their hardships. Alex and Alice actively question their parents' views of the world. They ponder how to improve the life of their maid rather than assuming that it should be the way it is. Thus, although bosses, parents, and others seek to define things in certain ways, individuals can resist those definitions to some extent. The sociological outlook also stresses that we can play an active role in our lives even in the face of social influences.

Although most of us are neither as rich as Alice and Alex nor as poor as Albert and his wife, social forces work just as actively in our lives as in theirs. These forces touch us and shape us in various ways. How much we are influenced depends upon our other resources, social supports, and individual personalities. Sociology considers how society affects us as individuals. It also explores how we take parts of society into ourselves—how we may come to believe, feel, think, and act in ways society promotes.

Social forces can be seen as a strong current in an ocean or river. Sometimes such currents are irresistibly strong, and no amount of effort can prevent someone from being pulled out to sea or over a waterfall. At other times, however, swimmers can counteract the force of the current. They can move diagonally across the current rather than directly against it. Or they can decide to flow with the current and use its force to carry them to a better position. Some swimmers are better equipped than others, through training or through natural strength. Others join together to build a raft or boat that can overcome the direction of the current. This comparison illustrates that as conscious, thinking beings, we can make choices or exercise will even in the face of strong social currents.

Clearly our personalities, our styles of life, and the choices available to us would be totally different if we had been born Albert, Alice, or Alex instead of who we are. A major tool sociologists use to see the ways humans create and carry on varied social patterns is the **method of comparison.** We can compare our society or our subgroup within society with other societies or with other subgroups. This method helps determine analytically what factors lead to similarities or differences in behavior. For instance, students cheat more in some colleges than in others. (See, for example, Baird, Jr., 1980; Bowers, 1964; Eve and Bromley, 1981; Harp and Taietz, 1966.)

Are the variations due to personality differences among the students or to social and organizational variations? Sociologists seek to answer such questions by making careful comparisons. Comparing different groups or societies can also reveal how beliefs and ideas are related to social organization and may benefit some people in society more than others. The beliefs about Indians that Alice's and Alex's father holds may be bound up with how he uses their land, for instance.

The sociological outlook is fed by curiosity. Why, we wonder, are individuals and societies so varied? What social forces have shaped different existences? Our quest to understand society has an urgency and importance to it, for if we cannot understand the social world, we are more likely to be overwhelmed by it. Although we may survive without understanding the social world, our chances of influencing social processes without such an understanding are slim indeed. To understand society, we need careful observations and good theories about the way things occur.

The quest for understanding has practical as well as intellectual value. Sociology can help us to understand ourselves better, since it examines how the social world influences the way we think, feel, and act. It can also help with decision making, both our own and that of larger organizations. Sociologists can gather systematic information from which to make a decision, provide insights into what is going on in a situation, and present alternatives. In many people, the desire to understand society is also sustained by the wish to change the way things are. Sociologists themselves differ on this issue. Some see understanding and change as intimately linked; others stress that analysis can occur without commitment to change. These different views are rooted in the values of the people holding them. Some people are unhappy with the way things are; others see no need to change them.

## THE GROWTH OF SOCIOLOGY

### The Social Sciences

Sociology is not the only discipline that studies human behavior and societies. Neighboring disciplines share an interest in some aspect of the social world.

Sociology, economics, anthropology, history, political science, and psychology are neighboring disciplines. One of the characteristics they share is that each has a coherent base of knowledge that is grounded in theory and research. Law, public administration, social medicine, social work, education, and business administration are closely related professional areas that draw upon the social sciences to deal with practical problems. They may also add to our knowledge of social life when they conduct systematic studies. Different historical origins and professional differences of opinion sometimes interfere with relationships among these fields. Despite their differences, however, these specialized subjects all deal with social behavior. All **social sciences,** as these disciplines are called, study human activity and communication, but each discipline separates out certain behaviors as its particular focus of study.

## Economics

The field of economics considers activity relating to the production, distribution, and consumption of goods and services. In studying a factory, an economist tends to see the work force as a "supply of labor." Sociologists consider other aspects of the workers' social makeup that may influence the work situation. They see the work force as made up of individuals of various races, sexes, ages, and cultures. Any or all of these factors may affect the work process.

Because goods and services can easily be counted and measured, economists have been able to use sophisticated mathematical and statistical analyses in their work. But the production, distribution, and consumption of goods and services also occur within a social world. For example, economists predict that energy use will fall if prices rise, and that does happen. But usage drops even more if people *value* energy conservation. The combination of economic and sociological explanations does more to explain human action than does either one alone.

## Political Science

The study of political science emerged after the development of economics and focused on political philosophy and the ideals of good government. In the twentieth century, political science has turned to the study of forms of government in the United States, Great Britain, France, the USSR, and elsewhere. In recent decades political scientists have come to use more numerical data, such as voting records or numbers of people holding certain attitudes. They have also begun to focus on actual political behaviors more than on political philosophies. Today the interests of political scientists and political sociologists overlap to a large degree—for example, in studies of voting behavior, public opinion formation, and state policies toward health insurance.

## Anthropology

Anthropology seeks to describe human variations, both physical and social, since humankind's earliest beginnings. It has a highly comparative, or cross-cultural, perspective. Traditionally, anthropologists have studied remote cultures; they have lived with tribal, exotic, and often preliterate societies that were isolated from the contemporary world. As such untouched societies disappear, anthropologists have begun to study social groups in industrial societies. Thus we begin to see ethnographies (detailed anthropological descriptions) of urban street gangs, peer culture in schools, the transmission of culture among immigrants, and gender-role behavior. These studies closely parallel some of the concerns of sociology.

## History

The study of past societies has only recently attracted the attention of American sociologists, who previously left this field to historians. Some historians claim that history is a series of unique events that can only be described separately and never form patterns or trends. They tend to see history as part of the humanities (along with literature, art, and music) rather than as a social science. Other historians provide comparisons across time or record disappearing styles of life; they resemble sociologists who study the past. A few historians borrow sociological methods for analyzing numerical data, and some sociologists include historical background in their studies of communities, class structures, or organizational change. A sociological study comparing social leadership in Boston and Philadelphia, for example, traces its historical roots to the colonial experience and even back to Europe (Baltzell, 1979).

## Psychology

Psychology explores both the biological and the social origins of human behavior. Physiological psychology considers the physical processes that underlie thinking, feeling, and perceiving. **Social psychology** involves the scientific study of how individual behavior is socially influenced. Social psychologists focus on what happens inside individuals, including personality development, and how people are influenced by the groups, societies, and cultures

*The purpose of social work is to help people with problems.*

to which they belong. Social psychology is well established in both psychology and sociology departments in universities all over the United States.

### Social Work

The professional field of social work is frequently confused with sociology. Sociology is concerned with scientifically analyzing social relationships; its goal is to understand and explain those relationships. Social work, on the other hand, is directed toward helping people who have problems. These problems may stem from public friction or private troubles. Social workers provide a wide variety of services to people in need. For example, among the many activities of social workers would be these: helping families of chronically ill children cope with their situations, administering public assistance to welfare mothers, counseling young people about their personal problems, and helping ex-convicts find jobs. Sociological understanding may assist social workers as they do their work, and sociologists often want their studies to help people.

The difference between the two lies in their primary concerns. One sociologist, Patricia Nash, described it this way: If a man staggered out of a bar and collapsed in a heap, a social worker would go over, try to help him up, and see that he had a place to spend the night. The sociologist would try to understand the social factors affecting alcohol use and abuse and the consequences of alcohol abuse. The social worker provides immediate assistance to one individual; the sociologist might help numerous

people in the long run by gaining insights into the roots and results of certain social behaviors. Similarly, sociology differs from other practical fields such as public administration, public health, education, and management, which draw on theories and research from sociology and other behavioral sciences to try to improve social policies and practices.

## The Nature and Uses of Sociology

Since sociologists study the full range of human social relations, the subject matter of sociology is very broad. It includes, for example, ranking systems in society; the family, religion, and economy; universities, hospitals, and corporations; and social clubs. These social entities may influence how we think, talk, feel, and act.

In trying to describe and explain social behavior, sociologists use a variety of strategies. All of them require that sociologists' ideas be checked against what happens in the social world. This checking is done by systematic observation and analysis. Although these methods aren't perfect, they are more solid than simply guessing how the world is. Sociology is predicated on the assumption that human actions and events do not happen purely by chance. There are certain patterns in social life that can be understood.

The basic substance of sociology is a balance between two views. On the one hand, sociology tries to show how social processes influence the way we think, feel, and behave. On the other hand, there is room in sociology for human choice. As reflective creatures who can think about what we are doing, we make choices that help to shape the social forces we face. Knowledge of the social world combined with the will to act is what makes sociology useful.

The insights of sociology apply in virtually all walks of life, from business to health care to education to criminal justice to community development. Sociology has been useful, for example, to government officials at local, state, and national levels. They use sociological concepts, theories, and findings to orient themselves to problems. Sociology influences the way issues are considered and acted upon in programs such as compensatory education, punishment for alcohol and drug offenses, large-scale public housing, care of the mentally retarded, welfare reform, prepaid health care, child abuse, job training, court reform, and legislative reapportionment (Adams et al., 1984). Throughout this book you will see other examples of the usefulness of sociology.

The usefulness of sociology may sometimes hide the distinction between social problems and sociological research puzzles. For example, the social problem of crime concerns individuals and policy makers who want to prevent it. The sociological researcher might try to analyze why rates of crime are higher or lower under different social conditions. While the research needed to answer such a question could take several years, the knowledge produced might help policy makers to reduce crime more effectively.

## The Birth of Sociology

The social sciences and the professional fields that apply them to practical problems developed in response to a series of social changes and trends. In the sixteenth and seventeenth centuries, Europeans were exploring the world and voyagers returned from Asia, the Americas, Africa, and the South Seas with amazing stories of other societies and civilizations. Widely different social practices challenged the view that European life reflected the natural order of God. People began to think more critically about the European social world as the ways of newly discovered peoples became known.

In the eighteenth and nineteenth centuries, western Europe was rocked by technical, economic, and social changes that forever changed the social order. Science and technology were developing rapidly. James Watt invented the steam engine in 1769, and in 1865 Joseph Lister discovered that an antiseptic barrier could be placed between a wound and germs in the atmosphere to inhibit infection. These and other scientific developments spurred social changes and offered hope that scientific methods might help explain the social as well as the natural world. This trend was part of a more general growth in rationalism.

The industrial revolution began in Britain in the late eighteenth century. By the late nineteenth century, the old order was collapsing "under the twin blows of industrialism and revolutionary democracy" (Nisbet, 1966, p. 21). Mechanical industry was growing, and thousands of people were migrating to cities to work in the new factories. People once rooted to the land they farmed found themselves crowded

*The industrial revolution reorganized work into factories like this cotton mill in Lancashire, England. Such changes undermined the dignity of labor and uprooted workers from family, village, and parish life. The growth of sociology was spurred by such major changes in social relations.*

into cities. The authority of the church, the village, and the family were being undermined by impersonal factory and city life.

Industrialization undermined the dignity of labor by pulling workers out of the protective order of family, village, and parish life and putting them into a commercial relationship. Urban life expanded along with industrialism and was viewed with alarm by those who feared its ills and squalor as well as by those who felt that losing the natural rhythms of country life would destroy European culture and morals. The factory and the machine were seen as additional negative features of industrialization, making people subject to extreme regimentation and turning their minds and hearts into machines (Nisbet, 1966).

All the major figures in sociology in its early years thought about the issue of the "great transformation" from simple, preliterate societies to massive, complex, industrial societies.[2] The German sociologist Ferdinand Tönnies (1887) contrasted these two types. He used the term **gemeinschaft** (ge mine′ shaft), or **community,** to describe a small, traditional society where people have personal, face-to-face relationships with each other and where they value social relationships as ends in themselves. There, people are committed to tradition and group values. The French sociologist Emile Durkheim (1893) felt that people in such a society share common tasks that develop similar values. Nearly everyone plants a crop, harvests it, marries, and has children. These similarities bind them together.

Tönnies characterized urban industrial society as a **gesellschaft** (ge zell′ shaft), or association. An **association** is a group of people bound together by common goals and rules, but not necessarily by close personal ties. People in such societies have more impersonal, distant relationships with each other and tend to use social relationships as a means to an end. Individualism is valued more than group solidarity. More complex societies are held together by webs of trade among otherwise quite different individuals. The farmer and the transportation worker need each other, and both depend on manufacturers and bankers. Personal relationships also exist in urban industrial societies, however.

[2] The term "great transformation" comes from the book *The Great Transformation,* by Karl Polanyi (1944).

Capitalism also grew in western Europe in the nineteenth century. This meant that relatively few people owned the means of production—such as factories—while many others had to sell their labor to those owners. At the same time, relatively impersonal financial markets began to expand. The modern epoch was also marked by the development of administrative state power, which involved increasing concentrations of information and armed power (Giddens, 1987, p. 27).

Even more revolutionary than industrialization were the changes wrought by the French Revolution, beginning in 1789. This revolution was aimed at restructuring the social order and was marked by the ideals of universal liberty and equality. These ideals remain a dynamic force in modern history.

Finally, there was enormous population growth worldwide in this period, due to longer life expectancy and major decreases in child death rates. These massive social changes lent new urgency to the development of the social sciences, as early sociological thinkers struggled with the vast implications of economic, social, and political revolutions.

## THE FIRST SOCIOLOGISTS

### Comte and Spencer

Auguste Comte (1798–1857), a French philosopher, aimed to establish a new social science, which he named "sociology," to be based on the methods of observation and reasoning that had been used so successfully in the natural sciences. Comte also believed that sociology would use the historical method to compare the consecutive states of humanity. He believed that social phenomena are subject to natural law and hoped that the scientific study of the social world would help to improve the human condition. Since he coined the word "sociology" and did a great deal to advance the discipline, Comte has been called the "father of sociology."

Herbert Spencer (1820–1903), an Englishman, contributed several key ideas to the developing science of sociology. Both he and Comte believed that the social world was patterned and could be understood through careful observation, but they differed with respect to how knowledge that comes from social science inquiry should be used. Comte believed social scientists should become a new kind of priestly class that would direct the course of society.

While believing in the value of studying society scientifically, Spencer stressed the complexity of social causes and the interconnection of various parts in society. He also saw social arrangements in biological terms. The oldest of nine children and the only one to survive into adulthood, he coined the term "survival of the fittest" to describe the evolutionary process he saw operating in social systems. He realized that human actions may have unanticipated consequences. Therefore, Spencer argued, society must not be tampered with by governments or reformers. Similar arguments are heard today. For example, U.S. legislators debate whether the government should provide health insurance or whether a free-market model of health care delivery should prevail. The issue of whether we understand society well enough to change it in a rational, planned way is still very much alive.

## Karl Marx

Along with naturalist Charles Darwin and psychologist Sigmund Freud, Karl Marx (1818–1883) is undoubtedly one of the three most influential thinkers of the past century. He did not think of himself as a sociologist, but his sociological insights are profoundly important. Marx thought social scientists should not only describe the world but also change it; his ideas have done both. Today more than one-quarter of the world's people live in societies that are officially linked to Marxist doctrines.

One of Marx's central contributions is the emphasis he placed on material conditions and how they affect social life. Marx wrote: "It is not the consciousness of men that determines their being, but, on the contrary, their social being determines their consciousness" (Marx and Engels, 1846). At the same time, Marx was aware that people make choices—for instance, when he said that we create our own history, but we do not make it in a vacuum. This statement suggests the operation of freedom within a social framework that sets limits. According

*Karl Marx was undoubtedly one of the most influential thinkers of the past century. He urged us not only to describe the world but to change it.*

to Marx, our ideas, feelings, and even the way we perceive reality are influenced by the social relations surrounding economic production. Whoever controls the means of production will also, to a considerable degree, control the ruling ideas of an era, Marx suggests. The organization of production also determines the class structure of a society. According to Marx, there is a built-in antagonism and conflict between classes, and history consists of the struggles between contending classes.

Marx also stressed that capitalism was riddled with contradictions that might prove to be its undoing. For example, as capitalists produced more and more, the market would not necessarily grow at the same rate. In the face of limited markets and increasing competition, capitalists would have to cut prices, driving the rate of profit down and leading to unemployment and economic depression. Such results could disenchant people with capitalism.

In the unequal class structure that exists in capitalist societies, all the major social institutions, including the state, religion, and political economy, are characterized by what Marx called

**alienation.** "Alienation" refers to the separation, or estrangement, of individuals from themselves and from others. For Marx, alienation was a central feature of capitalism and it took several forms. Workers become alienated from what they make because their products are controlled by others. For example, much of the quality of cars is set by designers and managers rather than by workers. Work itself becomes an alien activity that offers no inherent satisfaction. People work only because they need money rather than because they enjoy their work. These two experiences remove the uniquely human quality of productive work, according to Marx. In the process, workers also become alienated from each other. People are increasingly judged by their incomes, for example, rather than by their human qualities (Ollman, 1971). Marx saw alienation as including people's feelings about their situation and the social and economic arrangements of capitalism that produced those feelings.

## Emile Durkheim

If you approve of the existing social order and it is being seriously challenged from within, it is not surprising that your major preoccupation will be with social order, stability, cohesion, integration, authority, and regulation. This was the case with Emile Durkheim (1858–1917), who lived in France during the severe disorders of the Paris Commune and the Third Republic. For both Durkheim and Comte, writing about social change and social conflict must have been like trying to convey the joys of world travel while desperately seasick. Their intellectual problems were rooted in their views of the social issues of their day. Nevertheless, Durkheim's observations about society still have value today. He developed the notion of social functions. **Functions** refer to the consequences of something for the operation of the whole social system or for some part of the system. Certain religions, for instance, teach that a wife should "love, honor, and obey" her husband, thereby stating a view of ideal gender roles in the family that functions to stabilize a **patriarchal** (father-centered) **family.**

*Emile Durkheim, a French sociologist, was particularly interested in how individuals form meaningful bonds with groups and are influenced by their group memberships.*

Durkheim was particularly interested in the social functions of group bonds, and he wondered about the factors that affect the cohesiveness of social groups. One of the forms of social "glue" that caught Durkheim's attention was religion, particularly the role of religious rituals in generating social bonds among group members. Such social bonds, Durkheim argued, are important explanations even for such seemingly personal actions as committing suicide, which cannot be explained simply by psychological or biological causes. Something happens—emerges—when people get together in groups or institutions that differs from what happens to lone individuals. Durkheim called these properties "social facts" and saw them as defining the unique subject matter of sociology.

## Georg Simmel

The German Georg Simmel (1858–1918) viewed society in a somewhat different way. Rather than seeing society as an organic whole, as a "thing" in itself, Simmel saw it as an intricate web of group affiliations. He felt that society was nothing more than all the individuals who compose it, although he stressed that people in different-sized groups—twosomes, threesomes, and larger groups—interact differently.

Like other early sociologists, Simmel believed we can discover underlying uniformities in social life. For example, the social processes of dominance and submission share certain similarities, whether they occur between parent and child, boss and worker, or king and subject. Simmel analyzed such processes as conflict and cooperation, intimacy and distance. He also studied social types, such as the stranger, the adventurer, the mediator, the renegade, the miser, and the spendthrift. Simmel's work helps to prime our own minds to see the social world in new ways.

## Max Weber

Max Weber (1864–1920) was a German scholar whose interests ranged across religion, economics, cities, and music, among other topics. One of his major contributions was the effort to trace connections between religion and other institutions, such as the economy.

One theory of why the industrial revolution developed in England when it did was advanced by Max Weber (1904). He suggested a possible link between what he called the Protestant ethic and the rise of capitalism. Weber stressed that culture, in this case religion, contributed in a major way to the rise of capitalism. Capitalism requires that some portion of an economic surplus be saved and invested rather than consumed immediately. Weber argued that there was a certain compatibility between the religious teachings of Protestantism and the early growth of capitalism.

First, Protestant reformers saw work as noble. One's work in the world was a "calling," with religious significance. The Protestant view of work offered respect and legitimacy to craftspeople and merchants. Second, Protestants believed the world to be a rational and orderly place. Therefore, rational planning of one's life and work was a sensible approach. This "world

view" facilitated both the development of science and the rational planning of business enterprises. Third, the Calvinist view of predestination held that only a few were chosen at birth for salvation. While no one knew for sure if he or she was among the "elect," worldly success was considered a sign that one might be among the favored few. Finally, Protestants practiced thrift and spent little on personal pleasures. These behaviors enabled individuals to accumulate capital that could be invested in business or trade.

Weber has been most severely criticized for failing to consider that economics might have influenced the development of religion: Protestantism might never have emerged if there had not been a merchant class receptive to it. Although Weber stressed the close relationship between capitalism and Protestantism, he was careful not to claim that Protestantism *caused* capitalism. Weber's importance lies in his explanation of how economic traditionalism was replaced by capitalism. In today's world, the virtues of hard work are encouraged by political

*Max Weber, a German scholar, studied many aspects of social life. He was especially interested in relationships among religion, culture, and other institutions such as capitalism.*

ideologies like Marxism-Leninism in the Soviet Union. These ideologies may serve as functional equivalents to Protestantism: "Like Protestantism, they uphold the virtue of the work ethic and extol the importance of service to a higher moral entity through labor, although for them this entity is the state whereas for the Protestants it was God" (Zaret, 1981).

While seeking to identify patterns in human affairs, Weber also stressed the importance of the subjective meanings humans place on their actions. **Subjective meanings** refer to the values and interpretations individuals place on their life situations and experiences.

In this way Weber emphasized two kinds of understanding, the rational observational understanding of actions and an explanatory understanding. Take the case of a student who receives an F in a course. We can get a rational understanding by looking at what the student, teacher, and/or the school did that produced the failure. But Weber's notion of **verstehen**—explanatory understanding—goes further and probes the motives that the individuals in the situation bring to their action. For example, does the student really want to be in school? If not, is the failure viewed as a relief? Does he or she see the failure as a major crisis and feel like committing suicide as a result? What are the teacher's motives? Does the school have a policy that affects rates of failure? *Verstehen* seeks to place social behavior in an understandable and more inclusive context of meaning. Because these meanings are not always the same, social action can be classified into four major types: *instrumentally rational action, value-rational action, affectual action,* and *traditional action.* The same action can be viewed in different ways by various people.

*Instrumentally rational action* involves analyzing objects and people in one's surroundings and using that analysis to try to attain one's own goals. You may be going to college, for example, to earn a degree that will help you to achieve other goals. *Value-rational action* is based on an ethical or religious belief in the value of behaving a certain way, regardless of its chance of success. For instance, you may study Greek in college, even though you see no direct relevance for a future business career, because you value a classical education. *Affectual action* is based on a person's feelings. You may be in college, for

example, because you love learning and studying. *Traditional action* rests on long-standing habits or social patterns. If you are motivated by tradition, you may be in college because many generations of your family have attended college and you do not want to break that pattern. Weber believed virtually all human actions could be characterized as one or more of these four types. Most action contains several of these strands.

Weber carried these types of action into his analysis of the types of authority that operate in the world. He saw three pure types of legitimate authority. In each case, their legitimacy is based on different grounds. What he called *legal authority* rests on a rational belief in the legality of rules and the right of those holding authority under such rules to issue commands. *Traditional authority* rests on an established belief in traditions and the legitimacy of those exercising authority under those valued traditions. *Charismatic authority* rests on devotion to the special heroism, character, or purity of particular persons and upon the willingness of others to follow their teachings.

*Rational-legal authority* tends to prevail in large bureaucratic organizations and rests on the authority of the office. In traditional authority, obedience is owed to the person who occupies the traditionally supported position of authority, such as the tribal chief or feudal lord. Popular political figures and religious cult leaders are likely to have charismatic authority.

### The Formal Study of Society

Although each of these first sociologists had some unique ideas, they may all be seen as responding to the economic, political, and moral turmoil of their times. On the one hand, the old tyrannies of church and king were undermined, granting more independence to individuals. On the other hand, the weakening of religious authority, the growing power of the state, the rupture of community bonds, the rise of unchecked individualism, and excessive rationality all helped to destroy the old order without creating a new one to take its place. Comte, Spencer, Marx, Durkheim, Weber, and Simmel all struggled with these issues, giving birth to sociology, the formal study of society, in the process.

Although its origins were European, sociology made big gains in the United States in the twentieth century. Many Americans who studied in Europe were introduced to the ideas of sociology, and a number of prominent American sociologists have made important contributions to its body of knowledge. These individuals and their ideas are introduced in this and subsequent chapters.

## MAJOR SOCIOLOGICAL APPROACHES

A **theoretical approach** is a set of guiding ideas. Several major theoretical approaches exist in sociology today: Marxian, Weberian, and functionalist approaches, structural analysis, and interpretive approaches. Each of these directs attention to particular aspects of the social world. The existence of seemingly contradictory approaches is not unique to sociology. Even in the scientific field of physics, light appears to act like a wave in some circumstances and like an individual particle in others. Quantum theory puts these two views together into one coherent theory. To maximize our understanding of society, we need the multiple views of society that coexisting outlooks provide, because the social world is easily as complex and varied as light. Since no single perspective adequately explains all of social life, there is no totally "right" approach that makes the others completely "wrong."

### Marxian Approaches

**Marxian approaches** stress the importance of class struggle centered around economic production. Class is the major basis for social conflict. The Marxian approach stresses that "ultimately" or "in the last analysis," the social arrangements flowing out of economic activities are major determinants of social behavior. For Marxians, conflicts result from historically unfolding contradictions. Conflict is not assumed to be inevitable, since it may be resolved at some future time.

Considering the social phenomenon of sports, Marxians might ask what intensifies or cools

*Macro-sociological thinkers in the tradition of Marx and Weber stress that social groups may try to change political and economic arrangements.*

economic conflicts between team owners and players, for instance. Or they might consider whether sports takes people's minds off their economic situations.

### Weberian Approaches

A Weberian approach sees rationalization as a dominant trend in Western societies. **Rationalization** refers to the process of subjecting social relationships to calculation and administration. Marxians noted this tendency in factory life, but Weberians extend it to politics, religion, economic organization, university administration, scientific research, and the arts. Weberians suggest that not only economic factors but also religion and other cultural factors may shape human actions. For example, rationality and the growth of bureaucracy was connected with the expansion of capitalism, according to Weber. The formation of a system of law and the existence of a guaranteed monetary system administered by the state were necessary for the expansion of capitalism on a large scale (Giddens, 1982, p. 90).

For Weberians, membership is different social groups—for example, groups based on race, occupational position, social status, and religion—in addition to the class relations stressed by

Marx, may influence social action. Conflicts are seen as arising between and among groups divided along any and all these lines. As developed in the work of Randall Collins (1975), Ralf Dahrendorf (1959), and Gerhard Lenski (1966), a Weberian approach assumes that humans rationally strive to maximize their own interests in competition with others trying to do the same thing, and that they use whatever resources they possess in order to do so.

A Weberian might ask how various changes in sports reflect the growing rationalization of the enterprise. He or she might also suggest that various sports activities could become membership badges in particular status groups, or that people may use membership in an elite country club to enhance their social status.

Both Marxian and Weberian approaches suggest important ways of looking at the world. Both stress that we should be especially attentive to the historical roots of a social situation, and both might ask, "Who benefits from this situation at any given moment?" Marxians emphasize the importance of economic arrangements and interests and the possibilities of contradictory trends. Weberians stress the growth of rationality in all spheres of social life. These approaches reappear throughout this book because they provide important angles of vision for understanding society.

## Functionalist Approaches

By the 1940s Harvard and Columbia universities had become especially important for American sociology. Returning from graduate study in Germany to teach at Harvard, Talcott Parsons (1902–1979) wove together a number of ideas from Durkheim, Weber, Marx, and others in his influential book *The Structure of Social Action* (1937). Probably more than anyone else, Parsons shifted American sociology toward theory-building. He developed what has come to be called **structural-functional sociology,** a perspective that focuses on how the various parts of society fit together to maintain the equilibrium of the whole.

The functionalist outlook analyzes social phenomena in terms of their *functions* or consequences for other parts of society or for society

as a whole. For example, a functionalist approach to sports in society might consider whether sports create a sense of community among fans that helps to overcome the extreme individualism generated at work. Functionalists might also ask whether sports have taken the place of religion for many people as a way of forging social solidarity through shared rituals. These questions arise from the functionalist assumption that every part of society contributes to the functioning of the whole, thereby creating an **equilibrium,** or balance, in society. A change in any part creates a certain imbalance, which leads to changes in other parts of the system and perhaps eventually to the reorganization of the entire system.

Functional analysts have trouble explaining the original source of change. In the case of sports, for example, functionalists do not suggest why sports changed from a local pastime to a national, highly organized system. Nor are functionalists especially concerned about the relative importance of various parts of society. A change in the organization of sports, for example, is not likely to have as many and as far-reaching consequences for society as a change in the organization of the family or a reorganization of the economy. Critics tend to see functionalism as being concerned about the consequences of something for the entire society rather than considering the possibility that some groups or classes may benefit more than others from a particular arrangement. In a related vein, functionalism has been attacked for its conservative bias, because it is concerned with order more than with change.

One of Parsons' students, Robert K. Merton (1957), addresses some of these issues. He suggests that all parts of a society may not be functional. Some may actually be dysfunctional at some level. A **dysfunction** is any consequence of a social system that disturbs or hinders the integration, adjustment, or stability of the system. For example, parents in developing nations may find that high birth rates are functional for their families as a means of providing support when they are old, but the same high rates may be dysfunctional for the society at large because of the demands they place on food, housing, education, and jobs. Finally, according to Merton, some features of a society may be dispensable or may have **functional equivalents.** For instance, modern singles may find that communal living arrangements offer a functional equivalent to (or substitute for) the family by providing companionship and affectional ties.

Merton also distinguishes between manifest and latent functions. **Manifest functions** refer to the intended functions of something. The manifest function of an automobile, for example, is transportation, to which there are a number of functional alternatives (depending on the distance to be traveled) such as walking, bicycling, or riding a moped, train, bus, or plane. The **latent functions** are the unintended and unrecognized consequences of a social thing or process. The latent functions of a car may be to impress other people, to display one's wealth, or to provide a place to be alone with someone we especially like.

A functionalist sociologist would be likely to ask: What are the consequences, both positive and negative, of what I am examining for the other institutions in society and for society as a whole? What are its latent (unintended) functions as well as its manifest (intended) functions? What functional equivalents, if any, exist for this social arrangement?

Merton (1982, p. 86) stresses that social patterns have many consequences. This means that individuals and groups in a complex society may be affected in different ways. As a result, some groups may benefit from certain consequences more than other groups do. One of Merton's students, Lewis Coser (1956), focused primarily on the *functions* of social conflict rather than on its dysfunctions. Some of his insights were that conflict is not totally disruptive in a group, certain kinds of conflict can bind groups, conflict with external groups can increase the internal cohesion of a group, and conflict may bind enemies.

## Network (or Structural) Approaches

Network (or structural) analysts stress that sociologists should study social structure rather than personal motives (Wellman, 1983; Berkowitz, 1982). By **social structure** they mean patterned relationships among individuals, organizations, nations, or other social units. Social

*Network (or structural) analysts stress the importance of socially structured relationships among individuals, organizations, nations, or other social units.*

networks can support or limit action by structuring access to scarce resources such as information, wealth, or influence. For example, different social networks affect access to jobs (Granovetter, 1974; Boorman, 1975). As a result, structural analysis reveals that various opportunities (whether for meeting a desirable mate or finding an apartment) are unevenly available to people in different sets of social relationships.

### Exchange Theory

**Exchange theorists** also analyze relationships, but usually only those between two people. Exchange theorists may not focus on how the relationships between two people connect with other relationships in a network or examine the nature of those other relationships (Burgess and Huston, 1979; Wellman, 1983, p. 167).

"There is no free lunch, even in social life," according to exchange theorists of social interaction. Everything we do and everything others do has its price, whether the currency is money, time, food, social approval, company, or prestige. People are viewed as active agents who choose which exchanges they wish to make. They weigh the costs and benefits of various social actions and rationally choose the one that is most attractive to them. According to this theory, exchange is a basic principle of social interaction that can explain behavior as diverse as the decision to get divorced, college dating patterns, and the origins of revolutions.

Exchange theorists recognize the exchange of intangibles—like respect, affection, help, and acceptance—as well as the avoidance of pain, embarrassment, or rejection. The exchange of these social rewards and punishments can be quite subtle and unspoken, or it can be very explicit. Grandparents, for instance, may do a great deal for their grandchildren and expect little back. On the other hand, most grandparents hope and even assume that they will receive some love, affection, and gratitude in return.

Exchange theory may go beyond explaining single acts of kindness to explain more complex social phenomena such as the divorce rate. Exchange theorists do not start by considering abstract "factors" such as the women's movement and changing moral values, however. They assume that divorces start with individuals deciding whether or not they will stay married by assessing their "maximum joint profit." The question then becomes why are more people choosing divorce today than in the past? John Scanzoni (1972) suggests that women are more likely to choose divorce today because increased job openings for women, higher salaries, and a mobile population make divorce a more feasible alternative for women than it was in the past. A 35-year-old woman in 1920 had few alternatives to a husband who drank and beat her. A similar woman today could find a job to support herself and any dependent children and choose an alternative to marriage. Or more men may be straying from their marital obligations because the growing number of women relative to men makes men reluctant to commit themselves to just one partner (Guttentag and Secord, 1983).

Changes in market advantage affect the conditions of exchange that are possible to men and women in any given situation. In 1987, for instance, males aged 20 to 29 began to outnumber "marriageable" females aged 18 to 27. Some argue that this shift will lead women to marry sooner, will lower divorce rates, and will lead to more efforts to restrict female sexuality. The average age at first marriage for women began dropping in 1985; in 1987 birth rates rose and divorce rates were at their lowest level in 12 years (Fowles, 1988). Clearly, therefore, some tendency in this direction is already evident.

The fact that not all women and men weigh these factors in the same way does not destroy the value of exchange theory. What is important about this approach is that it examines social behavior in terms of how different people weigh the considerations they face and what choices they make.

Exchange theory would raise certain kinds of questions about sports. For example, it would suggest that athletes continue to participate in sports only as long as the rewards they receive outweigh the costs for them. If psychic and social rewards are included as well as financial ones, it goes a long way toward explaining why professional athletes continue to play after they have passed their prime and often even when they are in great physical pain.

Peter Blau, an early exchange theorist, stated that the theory is suited to analyzing "face-to-face relations and must be complemented by other theoretical principles that focus on complex structures" (Blau, 1968, p. 457). He has since moved in a more structural direction (Blau and Schwartz, 1984).

## Interpretive Approaches

The theoretical approaches just discussed emphasize social structure and human actions. But as a number of important sociologists stress, social life also occurs on an intimate scale between individuals. The **interpretive approach** focuses on how individuals make sense of—or interpret—their world and react to the symbolic meanings attached to social life. The need for both structural and interpretive perspectives can be seen in an analysis of unemployment. Government agencies provide an official "unemployment rate," which is a structural measure of the phenomenon that affects public policies. But the attitude of the unemployed toward their situation affects the way the individual feels and behaves. Moreover, the individual's actions affect the official "rate" because if a person is not *seeking* work, he or she is not counted as unemployed.

Symbolic interaction and ethnomethodology are variants within the interpretive approach. Each of them will be described briefly, but symbolic interaction is stressed here, because considerable work has been done in that tradition.

### Symbolic Interaction

Human behavior differs from that of lower animals because it uses symbols and attaches meanings to those symbols; hence it can be called **symbolic interaction.** Being pregnant, for example, is a biological reality. But how women react to pregnancy, how they feel about it, and what they do about it stem from the symbolic meanings they have learned to attach to that reality (Miller, 1978). Symbolic interaction was developed by George Herbert Mead (1863–1931), a philosopher at the University of Chicago, and Charles Horton Cooley (1864–1929) at the University of Michigan. Mead studied the emergence of a sense of self in individuals and the place of signs and symbols in social life.

According to Mead, the sense of self emerges fully through social interaction. At first, children have relationships with specific individuals. Later on they develop a sense of the "generalized other"—that is, they learn what other people in their social world are like and what they can expect from them in the way of thoughts, feelings, and actions. Individuals shape their own behaviors in light of what they know about others. Language and other symbols play a critical role in this process, as do games and other forms of play. Baseball, for instance, requires each player to be aware of all the other players in the game and to anticipate what they are likely to do under various conditions. Leaders, according to Mead, are those individuals who are best able to see things through the eyes of the other people in a given situation. Mead's work had a major impact on American social thought and inspired the sociological orientation called **symbolic interactionism.** The term "symbolic interactionism" was coined by Herbert Blumer (Stryker, 1980).

*Human behavior uses symbols and attaches shared social meanings to those symbols, hence the term* symbolic interaction.

Mead stressed that we learn meanings through interaction with others and then organize our lives around those socially created meanings. This feature of social life is readily apparent in the case of sexual behavior. Although some see sexual behavior as a biological or perhaps even instinctual process, there is a great deal of social and symbolic content to it. Masters and Johnson (1979) found that bisexuals acted like homosexuals when they were with homosexuals (for example, more communication than heterosexuals usually show) and like heterosexuals while making heterosexual love (for example, by assuming that the male should take the lead). To Masters and Johnson, these actions are clearly a result of "cultural influences"—bisexuals learn different cues for how heterosexuals and homosexuals make love. Clearly these differences in the same people reflect the socially learned, symbolic features of lovemaking.

A second major theme of symbolic interactionism is that society is most usefully viewed as consisting of people interacting with each other (Manis and Meltzer, 1978). This view emphasizes human society as being in process and always changing, rather than as something static and unchanging. At the same time, symbolic interactionists realize that individuals act within networks of other individuals and groups and know that not everyone is equally powerful.

Symbolic interactionism stresses the active role individuals play in guiding their own behavior. Because human beings have the capacity to select and interpret what aspects of their situation they will respond to, they can shape their courses of action. Although they are not totally free agents, humans can try to modify the social influences and limitations they face.

Erving Goffman developed a new perspective on symbolic interaction with his concept of social life as theater. He views humans as busily acting out complex displays designed to communicate images of self, define a situation, or demonstrate social membership. He sees us as actors playing different roles and managing the impressions we give others. Goffman analyzes "front stage" areas of social life, such as the living room of a house or apartment, and "backstage" areas, such as the kitchen, bedroom, or bathroom. This **dramaturgical analysis** raises questions about the roles people play, the props and staging areas needed to support those roles, and the kinds of behavior that are appropriate in the roles. Goffman shows how people wishing to belong to a particular social group adopt the special handshakes, language, clothing, or behaviors of group members, if they can.

Symbolic interactionists ask quite different questions about sports than do structural theorists. They might ask, for example, how people define and interpret the sports they are playing or watching and how the meanings they attach to those activities affect their interactions with others. Do mountaineers stop climbing when they hear about someone who has a fatal accident, or do they interpret the situation in such a way that they feel no such fate awaits them?

### Ethnomethodology

How people make sense of the social world and share their views of it has been explored by a type of sociology called ethnomethodology. **Ethnomethodology** is concerned with how people see, describe, and explain order in the world in which they live (Zimmerman and Wieder, 1970). It is the study of the methods used by individuals (called "ethnics") to communicate and make sense of their everyday lives as members of society (Garfinkel, 1967). Many ethnomethodologists focus on language and conversation, since they see these areas as central to interpreting life in society.

When two people see each other in the morning, for example, and one says, "Last night was wonderful," and the other says "Yes," these words mean much more to them, from their shared experiences and knowledge, than the simple literal content. The talk between them stands for, or indexes, much more than it actually says. This feature of language characterizes much, if not all, social interaction. It underlies communication between bosses and workers, parents and children, blacks and whites, males and females. For ethnomethodologists, the meaning of the interaction, in this case through words, can be explained only through knowledge of the context in which it occurs.

## FOUR LEVELS OF ANALYSIS: AN ASSESSMENT AND SYNTHESIS

You have just encountered Marxian, Weberian, functionalist, network, and interpretive approaches. Several basic features differentiate them.

1. First, they differ in whether they focus primarily on social stability or on social conflict and change. Functionalists tend to stress shared values, which promote social stability, whereas Marxians and Weberians probe the sources of social change. Interactionists emphasize the meanings individuals attach to events and the active role individuals can play in their own lives. Thus they direct attention to social processes and changes rather than to social structures and stability. This relates to a second major difference.
2. The approaches differ in terms of whether they are more interested in objective social structure or in the interpretations people place on their social experiences. Functionalists, Marxians, and network analysts focus on objective structural characteristics of society, whereas Weberians, ethnomethodologists, and symbolic interactionists place more emphasis on subjective meanings.
3. The social world can be conceptually divided into at least four different levels, as shown in Table 1.1.

The **micro level** includes how we feel about the social world and how it affects us subjectively. It also includes how we interact with others and the meanings we attach to the social actions of others. Kanter (1977) found that people's subjective feelings and motivations are influenced by the amount of power they have in an organization.

The **organizational level** treats social life in larger groups and formal organizations, such as colleges or universities, corporations, or the military service. It considers how organizations are structured and how organizational processes affect us.

The structure of higher education, for example, is affected by organizational size. The larger the university is, the more likely it is to develop a "center" that handles critical public relations and financial dealings with outside organizations and the more likely the disciplinary departments and faculty governing boards are to influence educational policy decisions (Boland, 1973). Such a situation affects both students and faculty. Functionalists, Weberian conflict theorists, Marxian theorists, and some symbolic interactionists have studied organizations.

More general than the organizational level is the institutional level. It focuses on social **institutions,** which consist of clusters of patterned activities centered around meeting an important social need, such as obtaining food or raising children. Sociological studies at the institutional level examine the different ways that educational systems are organized in the United States, Great Britain, and France, for example, or com-

**Table 1.1**   *Various Levels for Analyzing the Social World*

| | |
|---|---|
| I. Micro level | How we feel and what we think about the social world. How the social world affects us subjectively. How we interact with others. What meanings we attach to social actions. |
| II. Organizational level | Social life in larger groups and formal organizations. |
| III. Institutional level | The patterned activities that focus on meeting important social needs, such as obtaining food or raising children. How those institutions are related to each other or vary from one society to another or vary over time. |
| IV. Macro level | Entire societies as the unit of analysis. Comparisons across societies or over time. |

pare family structures in industrial and tribal societies. Marxians, Weberians, and functionalists frequently study institutions.

Analysis at the **macro level** seeks to unearth the core features of an entire society by focusing on large-scale institutions, structures, and processes. Much of the work of Marx and Weber as well as that of Durkheim was concerned with macro-level analysis and comparisons between societies. A macro-level analysis was done by Ouchi (1981) when he compared the national cultures, management styles, and organizational productivity of Japan and the United States. He suggests that Japanese society is characterized by greater trust, subtlety, and intimacy .than is American society, and that differences in national culture are reflected in management styles that emphasize lifelong employment rather than short-term employment, job rotation rather than specialization, slow evaluation and promotion practices rather than rapid evaluation and promotion, collective responsibility and decision making rather than individual responsibility and decision making, and a holistic concern rather than an isolated concern with only one aspect of the organization.

The basic features of the five major approaches are summarized in Table 1.2. The first four are structural approaches, while the fifth stresses the interpretations people make about the social world. These approaches can be productively combined. The work of C. Wright Mills, for example, tried to integrate the analysis of social structures with the social psychology of individuals. He studied such topics as white-collar workers, "the power elite," and the causes of war and wanted other sociologists to assume the roles of social critic and activist.

**Table 1.2    Basic Features of the Five Major Theoretical Approaches**

| | Major Theorists | Emphasis on Stability or Change | Stress on Objective or Subjective | Level of Analysis |
|---|---|---|---|---|
| **Marxian Approaches** | Marx | Change | Objective | Organizational, institutional, macro |
| **Weberian Approaches** | Weber Collins Coser Lenski | Change | Objective (but subjective interpretations as well in Weber and Collins) | Organizational, institutional, macro (but micro as well in Collins) |
| **Functionalist Approaches** | Comte Durkheim Parsons Merton | Stability | Objective | Organizational, institutional, macro |
| **Network Approaches** | Wellman Berkowitz | Either | Objective | Organizational, institutional, macro |
| **Exchange Theory** | Blau | Either | Both | Micro, organizational |
| **Interpretive Approaches** **Symbolic Interactionism** | Mead Cooley Goffman | Change | Subjective interpretations | Micro, sometimes organizational |
| **Ethnomethodology** | Garfinkel | Either | Subjective | Micro |

An integrated approach requires an awareness of all four levels of analysis, an alertness to power differences, and a sensitivity to both stability and change. It requires us to understand how social structure can set limits or provide opportunities. At the same time, we need to deal with social definitions, processes, and changes. These are the theoretical strands this book brings to understanding society. Sociologists are becoming increasingly aware that their methodological "bag of tricks" needs to be as diverse as their theoretical one. No single perspective or method can capture the complexity and meaning of social life, but a composite approach that stands on many legs holds the greatest promise.

## SUMMARY

1. Sociology represents a blend of the imaginative and the scientific. It requires us to look at the social world with various lenses. The sociological enterprise is fueled by curiosity and personal urgency and guided by scientific criteria.

2. Sociology has practical value for us as we try to understand how the social world affects us and as we seek to make personal decisions.

3. Related social science fields—economics, anthropology, history, political science, and psychology—share some similarities with sociology but also diverge in their central focus. Sociology differs from practical fields such as social work, public administration, public health, education, and management, which aim to apply knowledge from sociology and other social sciences to deal with important social issues.

4. Sociology includes the broad subject matter of all aspects of social life. It stresses systematic observation and analysis and recognizes the operation of human choices. Sociological insights are widely useful.

5. Sociology developed in western Europe in response to the scientific revolution, industrialization, urbanization, and the French Revolution.

6. Early major sociological thinkers were Comte, Spencer, Marx, Durkheim, Simmel, and Weber. All of them were responding to the industrial, political, and moral turmoil of their times.

7. A variety of sociological approaches exists today: Marxian, Weberian, functionalist, structural (or network), and interpretive approaches. Each of them centers upon certain problems and issues, and each has unique contributions to make to our understanding of society. The most complete understanding of society requires us to draw on all five approaches and to remember the four levels of analysis from micro to macro.

## KEY TERMS

alienation (p. 12)
association (p. 10)
community (p. 10)
dramaturgical analysis (p. 20)
dysfunction (p. 16)
equilibrium (p. 16)
ethnomethodology (p. 20)
exchange theory (p. 17)
functional equivalent (p. 17)
functions (p. 12)
gemeinschaft (p. 10)
gesellschaft (p. 10)
institutions (p. 21)
interpretive approach (p. 18)
latent function (p. 17)
macro level (p. 22)
manifest function (p. 17)
Marxian approach (p. 15)
method of comparison (p. 6)
micro level (p. 21)
organizational level (p. 21)
patriarchal family (p. 12)
rationalization (p. 15)
social psychology (p. 7)
social sciences (p. 7)
social structure (p. 17)
sociology (p. 3)
structural-functional perspective (p. 16)
subjective meanings (p. 14)
symbolic interaction (p. 19)
symbolic interactionism (p. 19)
theoretical approach (p. 15)
verstehen (p. 14)
Weberian approach (p. 15)

## SUGGESTED READINGS

Berger, Peter. 1963. *Invitation to Sociology.* New York: Doubleday/Anchor. A moving personal statement about the reasons for studying sociology.

Coles, Robert. 1977. *Privileged Ones.* Volume V of *Children of Crisis.* Boston: Little, Brown. Sensitive depth interviews with children, including Alex and Alice, who were born into wealthy and privileged families.

Coles, Robert. 1967. *Migrants, Sharecroppers, Mountaineers.* Volume II of *Children of Crisis.* Boston: Little, Brown. Thoughtful and extensive interviews with impoverished young people, including Albert.

Collins, Randall, and Michael Makowsky. 1988. *The Discovery of Society,* 4th ed. New York: Random House. An interesting introduction to some of the classic thinkers who have influenced the development of sociology.

Giddens, Anthony. 1982. *Sociology: A Brief but Critical Introduction.* New York: Harcourt Brace Jovanovich. A brief introduction to the major theoretical views in sociology today.

Huber, Bettina J. 1982. *Embarking upon a Career with an Undergraduate Sociology Major.* Washington, DC: American Sociological Association. A guide to careers that may be pursued with a sociology major.

Mills, C. Wright. 1959. *The Sociological Imagination.* New York: Oxford University Press. A classic statement of what sociology is.

Wallace, Ruth A., and Alison Wolf. 1986. *Contemporary Sociological Theory,* 2nd ed. Englewood Cliffs, NJ: Prentice-Hall. A lucid comparison of the sociological theories discussed in this chapter.

# Doing Social Research

*Emily M. was like many impoverished children growing up in a welfare home in the 1960s. The difference for Emily was that she and a small number of other children were able to attend a preschool educational program. Careful long-term research by several teams of social researchers shows that children from such programs are more likely to graduate from high school and get jobs, or to go for further education, than similar children who did not attend such a program. Children from preschool programs are also less likely to get arrested or get pregnant as teenagers (Deutsch, Jordan, and Deutsch, 1985). The school system operating the program in Ypsilanti, Michigan, saved about $3100 per child because children in the program needed less remedial teaching and other social services. [Fiske, 1984]*

Research studies such as these show how individual lives and society can benefit from particular social programs. Researchers seek to grasp vibrant human issues with scientific procedures. Sociologists do not just sit in their armchairs and spin grand schemes; they go out in the world, observe, talk with people, and systematically analyze existing data to try to understand what is going on and why. This chapter considers some of the ways social researchers do their work. After reading it, you should have a better idea of how social scientists conduct their inquiries; you should be acquainted with a number of important research terms that will reappear in this book; and you should be aware of some of the ethical concerns that confront social researchers. You may also become more aware of your own reasoning processes.

## SCIENCE VERSUS EVERYDAY KNOWLEDGE

Most social researchers make every effort to be scientific in the way they conduct their research. To understand better how they proceed, we need to consider how scientific research differs from everyday knowledge. Our everyday knowledge-gathering strategies suffer from a number of weaknesses. We are not always the most careful observers. Considering your friends, for instance, can you say who is right- and left-handed? Do you know what color clothing your professor wore the last time you went to class? Unless we work consciously to observe and note behaviors or traits, there is much we can overlook. We also tend to "overgeneralize"—that is, to draw conclusions about many based on only a few cases. Suppose you talk with 3 out of 300 student demonstrators on campus and all 3 say they are protesting the food in the dining room. It is tempting but faulty to infer that all 300 are demonstrating for the same reason.

Left to our own devices, we tend to overlook cases that run counter to our expectations. If you think all football players are politically conservative, you may ignore the ones who are not. Or if you notice some exceptions, you may conclude they are not really football players. Often there is an emotional stake in our beliefs about the world that causes us to resist evidence that challenges those beliefs. This tendency may lead to closing one's mind to new information—an "I've made up my mind, don't confuse me with the facts" approach. Research seeks to overcome these pitfalls of everyday inquiry.

Although some people complain that research is simply an expensive way of finding out what everyone already knew, the results sometimes contradict commonsense expectations. Consider the following statements of the "obvious."

1. Social factors have no effect on suicide.
2. Since there was a steady increase in the number of births in the United States between 1976 and 1982, the number of college students preparing to be teachers has increased in anticipation of a teacher shortage in the 1990s.
3. Men engaging in occasional homosexual acts in the bathroom of a public park belong to a highly visible homosexual subculture.
4. When a number of people observe an emergency, they are more likely to go to the aid of the victim than when only one person is a witness (the "safety in numbers" principle).
5. Stress leads to higher IQ scores in children, since it stimulates them to live by their wits.
6. Religious beliefs are less important to Americans than they are to Europeans. (Everyone knows Europeans are more traditional than Americans.)

All these commonsense statements have been contradicted by careful research studies: (1) Durkheim (1897) presented evidence that social integration strongly affects the rate of suicide among different social groups. (2) In 1970, 19 percent of first-year college students planned a career in elementary or secondary school teaching. By 1985, this figure had plunged to just 6 percent (Astin et al., 1985). The career attitudes of college students were still being shaped by memories of the teacher glut of the 1970s. (3) A study conducted by Laud Humphreys (1970) found that many of the men he observed engaging in homosexual acts in the bathroom of a public park were married, had children, and were model citizens in their communities, very few of them belonged to a homosexual subculture. (4) When witnessing an emergency, a single individual has been found more likely than several people together to help the victim, perhaps because he or she is the only one who can do so (Latané and Darley, 1970). (5) Stress leads to lower IQ scores among children (Brown, 1983). (6) Americans are actually much more likely than Europeans to say that their religious beliefs are "very important" to them. In 1975–1976, 56 percent of Americans felt that religion is very important, compared to 36 percent of Italians and 17 percent of Scandinavians (U.S. Department of Commerce, 1980, p. 523).

The existence of research findings that run counter to what we might expect suggests that we should pause before we say "everyone knows that. . . ." Instead, we should ask: "What evidence do we have for believing that to be true?" Social research is concerned with how evidence is gathered and evaluated.

## Science as a Form of Knowing

A central feature of human existence is the desire to know and to understand the world. Knowledge is part of all human cultures, along with strategies for obtaining knowledge and for deciding whether or not something is true. In all cultures the major sources of knowledge are tradition, authority, and observation and reasoning. Cultures differ with respect to how much they emphasize each source. Science flourishes in societies that place relatively greater stress on observation and reasoning. Some societies see the natural and social worlds as caused, patterned, and open to human understanding through observation and logic. Others see the world as mysterious. One way these differences are reflected is in the ways cultures and individuals respond to unknowns. Sometimes they say "We don't know enough yet," as contrasted with "There are many things we will never understand." The former statement reflects a strong faith in science; the latter suggests a more limited view of science.

Social theory and research deal with what is and why it is that way in social life, not with what should be. "Should-be" issues are the concern of philosophy, religion, and ethics, although they invariably color the problems researchers wish to study and the ethical principles they follow in conducting their research. A carefully done research study could add to our understanding, for example, of the social causes and consequences of drug use. How you react to that knowledge depends on your own values. Sometimes personal, religious, or political concerns lead people to deny or ignore unappealing research results. This fact helps explain why research supporting key values or interests tends to be more widely accepted than research that opposes strong values and interests. It also suggests why some research may be utilized by policy makers and other research may not be utilized.

## Assumptions Underlying Social Theory and Research

Social theory and research assume there are patterns in social life. This assumption is sometimes challenged on several grounds. First, there are always individual exceptions. For instance, whereas whites earn more than blacks in the United States in general, some individual blacks earn more than some individual whites. Theory and research generate knowledge about collections of individuals, not about lone individuals. In addition, they make these statements in terms of percentages or probabilities; for example, they say 5 percent of white households had incomes of less than $5000 in 1979, compared to 18 percent of black households, a difference of 13 percent (U.S. Bureau of the Census, 1981, p. 435).

Sociology helps us understand the chances people have of being in certain situations and of behaving in certain ways. Sociologists can make strong statements about the approximate percentage of people who will behave in certain ways, even though they cannot say how *particular individuals* may act. Similarly, life insurance specialists can say with confidence that nonsmokers in general will live several years longer than smokers; they cannot say that any particular nonsmoker will live longer than any specific smoker. Generalizations and predictions are possible when they deal with large numbers of people, but not when they refer to single individuals. Sociological knowledge permits similar kinds of statements. We can say what percentage of people will behave in a certain way if the social conditions around them do not change drastically, but we cannot predict how a specific individual will act. There is no inconsistency in recognizing a measure of choice available at the individual level while finding patterned behaviors at the collective level. We can know the general tendencies about the sex, race, or class

to which we belong and yet still hope that we as individuals will be exceptions to general sociological trends.

The effort to achieve a scientific understanding of human behavior has also been criticized on the grounds that human affairs are extremely complex. Many factors—historical, social, psychological, economic, organizational, societal, and interpersonal—influence human behavior. How can any explanation or prediction take them all into account? No study or theory *can* include every factor, which is the reason sociologists cannot explain every possibility that may occur. But a study or theory can state that one factor is relatively more important than several others or that something will occur more frequently under one set of conditions than another. Although incomplete and imperfect, this is more accurate than uninformed guesses.

The accuracy of general statements in the social sciences depends on how observations are conducted. The social sciences do not consist simply of one person's opinion pitted against that of someone else. There are rules of evidence and inference that social scientists follow. Some evidence is better than other evidence; some conclusions are more supportable than others. The difference lies in the **methodology**—that is, in the rules, principles, and practices that guide the collection of evidence and the conclusions drawn from it.

Research differs from everyday inquiry in that researchers try to be conscious of what they are

*"Would you say Attila is doing an excellent job, a good job, a fair job, or a poor job?"*

Drawing by Chas. Addams; © 1982 The New Yorker Magazine, Inc.

*The sample survey is one of the most important research tools that sociologists have developed. It is for social scientists what the telescope is for astronomers.*

doing, how they are doing it, and what their biases are. **Bias** refers to the way the personal values and attitudes of scientists may influence their observations or conclusions. **Objectivity** refers to the efforts researchers make to minimize distortions in observation or interpretation due to personal or social values. Every research report has a section describing what procedures were followed in order to arrive at the results. That section should be explicit enough that another researcher can duplicate the procedure. Researchers also point out the limitations of their work and highlight questions that remain. However, caution is sometimes lost when results are presented in the popular press. Finally, by publishing their work, researchers allow others to question the quality of their procedures, evidence, and conclusions. These practices help to keep inquiry open to new or better evidence.

## The Uses of Research

Social research has numerous applications, many of which depend on the ingenuity of the people using it. (See the box on *The Divorce Revolution* for an example of how social research provided the facts vital for the passage of key new legislation.) Leaders in education, business, labor, and government, for example, sometimes use existing or commissioned research to help them decide whether a school should be closed in a particular neighborhood; whether a university should be decentralized into minicolleges; how teachers should be trained; where a new manufacturing plant should be located; what type of work organization will maximize productivity and minimize absenteeism; what new products should be developed; or how services can be most effectively distributed. Doctors, nurses, and other health professionals can gain from research showing ethnic differences in responses to pain and medication or research linking social experience and disease (Brown, 1976). In writing this book, I have used a variety of research tools and strategies.[1] Individuals can use research to investigate schools to attend, careers to pursue, or places to live. Throughout this book I will suggest possible applications of the research and theories we will be considering. As you read the book, you might ask yourself— what are the implications of these ideas for my life, my family, my community, and my career?

The general importance of social research is highlighted in a report by the National Academy of Sciences (Adams et al., 1984) that credits social science researchers with inventing information-generating technologies. Of these, the most important is the **sample survey,** which includes household sampling techniques, personal interviews, and questionnaires and data collection in experimental settings. "The sample survey has become for some social scientists what the telescope is to astronomers, the accel-

---

[1]The research strategies used include depth interviews with students, teachers, and researchers; large-scale surveys of instructors; content analysis of research articles and books; social indicator analysis to uncover social trends in American and other societies; and field observation of social life in different states and countries. These types of methods will be described later in the chapter.

## Divorce Revolution Research Plays Key Role in New Legislation

On October 1, 1985, the Congressional Caucus for Women's Issues held a reception in the Capitol to honor the work of Lenore J. Weitzman, then a member of the Stanford University faculty and chair of the ASA's Section on the Sociology of the Family. Not coincidentally, October 1 also marked the effective date of the Child Support Enforcement Amendments, federal legislation which mandates that child support payments be withheld from divorced fathers' pay checks.

In introducing Weitzman, Representative Barbara Kennelly of Connecticut noted that legislation cannot be passed unless information and research are available to show that it is necessary and potentially useful. In the case of the new child support amendments, she continued, Weitzman's research on the effects of the no-fault divorce laws so widely adopted in the 1970s, provided the facts vital for passage of the new legislation. Margaret Heckler, Secretary of Health and Human Services, echoed these sentiments when she commented that Weitzman's book *The Divorce Revolution* "provides a painful portrait of the real life hardship that women and children encounter when child support is not paid. Lenore Weitzman's insights and research were enormously valuable to us as we battled for a federal child support enforcement law with real bite."

Weitzman's book reports the findings of her ten-year study of the impact of the no-fault divorce laws enacted by 49 states since 1970. Her research was supported by NSF, NIMH, and the Ford Foundation and involved analysis of 2500 court records over a ten-year period. She also interviewed lawyers and judges as well as a stratified random sample of several hundred recently divorced men and women.

She found that "divorce is a financial catastrophe for most women." In the first year after a divorce, a woman's standard of living decreases by 73%, while her husband's increases by 42%. In addition, splitting a couple's property equally usually requires selling the family home, thereby forcing the mother and children to leave their neighborhood, friends and system of social support.

According to census figures, only 15% of the 17 million divorced women in this country were awarded any alimony at all. Moreover, Weitzman found that the median child support payment ordered by the courts covers less than half the actual cost of raising children. And in 53% of the cases, women do not receive the court-ordered payments, with men earning incomes of $30,000 to $50,000 a year being no more likely to pay than those earning $10,000.

Today one quarter of all divorces end marriages of 15 years or longer, compared to 4% 25 years ago. The women involved in such marriages often have been full-time homemakers, which severely limits their employment possibilities in midlife. They have been most adversely affected by the new divorce laws, according to Weitzman's research, because the courts' interpretation of "equality" at divorce disregards economic inequities created during marriage (e.g., his career assets and her diminished job prospects).

In practice, the no-fault divorce laws have freed men from many of the financial obligations of the old laws, while simultaneously undermining the security formerly provided to women and children. Weitzman deals with this dilemma by proposing changes in the divorce process which would preserve the no-fault ethic but eliminate its crippling consequences for women and children. Her primary focus is on fairer standards for property division, alimony and child support. . . .

Since 1980, when Ronald Reagan was elected President, the social sciences have been repeatedly called upon to document the value of their research for public policy. This process has provided sociologists with the opportunity to evaluate the role of their research in policy formation. Lenore Weitzman's work on no-fault divorce provides an excellent example of just how vital sociological research can be in the enactment of new legislation. As such, it serves to enhance the image of the discipline in the eyes of lawmakers and the public at large.

*Source:* Huber, 1985, pp. 1, 9.

erator to physicists, and the microscope to biologists—the principal instrument of data collection for basic research purposes."

Social scientists, governments, and many private organizations now use the sample survey as their primary means of collecting information. "The statistical systems of most industrialized nations, which provide information on health, housing, education, welfare, commerce, industry, etc., are constructed largely on the methodology of sample surveys" (Adams et al., 1984, p. 65).

The data and research findings generated by these techniques are useful in many walks of life. "Our notions about ourselves and each other—about racial differences, for example, or the nature of childhood—have been radically transformed by the dissemination of social and behavioral research findings," and "it is fair to say that as a result of such research Americans today have a different view of human behavior and social institutions than their parents did a generation ago" (Adams et al., 1984, p. 89).

Race and ethnicity is probably the area in which behavioral and social science research has caused the greatest change in perception. For example, there has been a dramatic shift through the twentieth century in the *Encyclopaedia Britannica's* description of the mental abilities of blacks. In 1911 the encyclopedia stated: "Mentally, the negro is inferior to the white." By 1929, based on research obtained in the intervening years, it read: "There seem to be no marked differences in innate intellectual power." By 1974 the encyclopedia attributed differences in scores on intelligence tests to environmental influences that "reflect persistent social and economic discrimination" (Adams et al., p. 86).

The National Academy study concludes that basic social science research should be thought of as "a long-term investment in social capital" and that "the benefits to society of such an investment are significant and lasting, although not immediate or obvious. A steep reduction in the investment may produce short-run savings, but it would be likely to have damaging long-term consequences for the well-being of the nation and its citizens" (Adams et al., p. 4).

## TOOLS OF THE TRADE: DEFINITIONS AND PROCEDURES

Part of encountering any new field involves learning the names of some of the "tools of the trade," so that you know what people are talking about. If you are learning to work with wood, for example, it helps to know the difference between a claw hammer and a ball-peen hammer, so that you will use the right one. To understand a piece of social research, you need to know the unit of analysis in a study; what sampling procedures were used; the difference between a descriptive and an explanatory study; what a hypothesis is; and how concepts, variables, operational measures, and relationships between variables are defined. (Additional tools of the trade are presented in the boxes throughout this chapter.)

A second step in exploring a new area involves learning something about the procedures people use to do their work. Certain procedures used in research are very powerful; they enhance our potency in everyday life as well as in social research. At the top of this list are rules for believing that one factor may have caused another one and the steps in doing research.

## Some Research Terms

### Units of Analysis

One of the first things to know about research is the **unit of analysis**—that is, who or what is being studied. Social researchers often look at individuals—at their attitudes or behaviors. Sometimes the unit of analysis that interests us is something larger, like a social group or an organization. For example, studies have found that some hospitals have lower rates of infectious hepatitis among their patients than others (Titmuss, 1971, p. 146). Several summary measures of data are discussed in the box on mean, median, and mode. Although the rates were compiled by adding up the total number of individuals who caught the disease and dividing by the total number of people in the hospital, the unit of analysis was the hospital and the research question was "Why should some hospitals have higher rates than others?" The explanation lay in the sources of blood used by different hospitals rather than in the patients' medical histories. Teaching hospitals received blood for transfusions from volunteer donors, whereas some other hospitals were more likely to purchase blood from private blood banks that paid individuals to give blood. People selling their blood were more likely to have hepatitis than were people giving blood voluntarily. If the unit of analysis had been individuals who contracted hepatitis in the hospital, this research might never have been solved. Looking at the hospitals as the unit of analysis raised new questions and supplied answers.

Units of analysis can also refer to families, ethnic groups, nation-states, or societies, when appropriate. Social artifacts such as books, TV

## Mean, Median, Mode

Suppose you listed on piece of paper all the grades you got last year in school. For illustrative purposes, assume you had the following 11 grades:

4.0  (A)        4.0  (A)
3.0  (B)        2.0  (C)
2.0  (C)        2.0  (C)
1.0  (D)        4.0  (A)
3.0  (B)        2.0  (C)
                1.0  (D)

You can see how even as few as 11 separate pieces of data become difficult to understand. So social researchers use a variety of statistics to summarize data and report general tendencies. There are three ways to present the central tendencies in a set of data.

The **arithmetic mean,** or average, is computed by adding all the items and dividing by the number of grades. In this case the mean grade is 2.55 (or a low B). Many schools use the mean as your grade point average (GPA). The mean is most useful and least misleading when the range of scores is narrow. Otherwise, the average tends to obscure the lower and higher ends of the range. In the case of last year's grades, the range is fairly wide.

The **median** is the score that cuts a distribution of figures in half. In this list of 11 items, it is the sixth one, or 2.0 (C):

1.0, 1.0, 2.0, 2.0, 2.0, 2.0, 3.0, 3.0, 4.0, 4.0, 4.0

The **mode** is the figure that occurs most often, in this case 2.0 (C).

All three of these summary statistics obscure the range of grades received. The **range** is the simplest way to indicate the extent of variation in a set of data. The range can be stated by reporting the lowest and highest examples, in this case 4.0 (A) and 1.0 (D). Someone with a 2.55 GPA based on the grades in this example may be quite a different type of student from someone with a similar GPA but a range of 3.0 (B) to 2.0 (C).

shows, sculptures, songs, scientific inventions, and jokes could all be units of analysis for social research.

### Descriptive and Explanatory Studies

There are two major types of research studies: descriptive and explanatory. In a **descriptive study** the goal is to describe something, whether it is the behavior and values of a religious cult, the culture of an old-age community, or the nature of a national population. Such studies help to outline the social world. **Explanatory studies** seek to explain why or how things happen the way they do in the social world. An explanatory study might seek to explain why crime rates are much lower in Switzerland than in the United States, West Germany, or Sweden or why the birth rate declined in industrial nations in the 1960s and 1970s.

### Hypotheses

A **hypothesis** is a tentative statement—based on theory, prior research, or general observation—asserting a relationship between one factor and something else. A descriptive hypothesis is a tentative statement about the nature or frequency of a particular group or behavior.

For instance, the statement "People find jobs through various means, including answering advertisements and being referred by friends" is a descriptive hypothesis that can be verified by research. An explanatory hypothesis tries to link one variable (such as a behavior) with another variable, as in the statement "How someone finds a job is related to income in that job."

Researchers try to design studies to test whether or not their hypotheses are true and to rule out **rival hypotheses** (that is, explanations that compete with the original hypothesis). They reason the way a detective does in trying to figure out who the murderer is. The data uncovered in a study may support the original hypothesis, refute it, support a rival hypothesis, or suggest conditions under which the hypothesis is supported. This method of reasoning goes beyond the testing of academic social science hypotheses. It is widely used by market researchers to test ideas for designing and selling new products or services, by political candidates seeking to understand public sentiments, and by policy makers developing new social programs.

One source of hypotheses for a research study may be social **theory,** which can be defined as a system of orienting ideas, concepts, and their

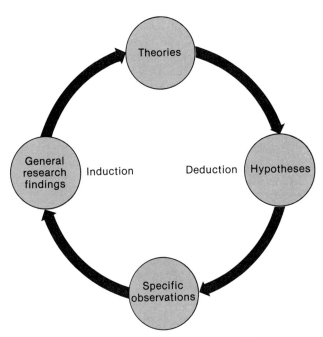

**Figure 2.1   The Continuous Cycle of Science.**

Science develops as theories generate hypotheses that guide specific observations. A number of specific observations begin to form sets of general research findings, which may shape future theories.

*Source:* Adapted from Wallace, 1971, p. 18.

relationships that provide a way of organizing the observable world. The interplay between theory and research is shown in Figure 2.1. In this model, theories suggest hypotheses, which lead to observations, which produce research findings, which, in turn, may modify theories, generate new hypotheses, and so on. Scientists may step into this circle at any point and work to advance knowledge.

**Deduction** refers to reasoning from the general to the specific. A general theoretical statement is confirmed or refuted by testing specific hypotheses deduced from it. **Induction** refers to reasoning from the particular to the general. The truth of a theoretical statement becomes increasingly probable as more confirming evidence is found. There is always the possibility of a disconfirming case, however.

## Concepts and Variables

Suppose you want to investigate the question of whether job-finding strategy is related to income. One of the first steps in any research study is to define the concepts—in this case job-finding strategies and income. A **concept** is a formal definition of what is being studied. Researchers must define what their major concepts include and do not include, what they are like and unlike. In research, concepts are refined further into variables. A **variable** is any quantity that varies from one time to another or one case to another. Variation can be seen in different categories or in different degrees of magnitude. For example, in the United States, the variable "political party membership" includes the categories Democratic, Republican, and others. The variable "income" has different degrees of magnitude depending on its amount in dollars.

A **proposition** is a statement about how variables are related to each other. It is similar to a hypothesis, which is a tentative statement about how variables *might be* related to each other. Usually a hypothesis is stated so that it may be tested empirically (that is, through systematic research and analysis) and verified or rejected.

## Operationalizing Variables

Variables are said to be **operationalized** when we define the procedures used to measure them. One procedure for measuring job-finding strategies would be to follow people around as they looked for a job. But most people do not want researchers hovering around while they look for a job, and such a procedure would take a long time. For these reasons, researchers often use interviews to find out what people do. So we say that the variable, job-seeking strategy, is *operationalized* in terms of one or more questions in an interview.

Mark Granovetter (1974), who did an operationalized study of professional, technical, and managerial workers, asked the following question to learn how people found out about the most recent job they had obtained:

How exactly did you *find out* about the new job listed [above]?
   a. I saw an advertisement in a newspaper (or magazine, or trade or technical journal). _____
   b. I found out through an employment agency (or personnel consultants, "headhunters", etc.). _____

c. I asked a friend, who told me about the job. _____
d. A friend who knew I was looking for something new contacted me. _____
e. A friend who didn't know whether I wanted a new job contacted me. _____
f. Someone I didn't know contacted me and said I had been recommended for the job. _____
g. I applied directly to the company. _____
h. I became self-employed. _____
i. Other (please explain):

He also asked their income in their present job.

### Relationships Between Variables

Frequently hypotheses suggest that a change in one variable causes a change in another variable. If one variable is thought to cause another one, we call the first variable the **independent variable** and the second variable the **dependent variable,** because it is believed to depend on the independent one. Put differently, the independent variable is the hypothesized cause and the dependent variable is the hypothesized effect. In this example, job-finding method is the independent variable and income is the dependent variable.

In Table 2.1, Granovetter's respondents have been grouped according to the method they used to find their jobs. Fifty people used "formal means" such as advertisements, public or private employment agencies, or the placement of-

fices of their colleges. Using formal methods meant that job seekers used the services of an impersonal "go-between" to get in touch with potential employers. The method of "personal contacts" was used by more respondents (154) than any other method. This meant that respondents knew someone personally who told them about their new job or recommended them to an employer, who then contacted them. Respondents had become acquainted with their "personal contacts" in some setting unrelated to the search for job information. "Direct application" was used by 52 respondents. This method meant that respondents went to or wrote directly to an employer, without using any go-betweens and without hearing about a specific opening there from a personal contact. Nineteen people used some other method (Granovetter, 1974, p. 11).

Table 2.1 shows the strong association of income level with job-finding method. Nearly half (45 percent) of those using personal contacts report incomes of $15,000 or more (these interviews were done in 1969, when that represented a much higher income). Among those who used formal means, only one-third reported such high incomes; and among those who applied directly, less than one-fifth reported incomes of $15,000 or more. Another way to summarize these results is to say that there is a correlation between job-finding method and income level. A **correlation** is an observed association between a change in the value of one variable and a change in the value of another variable.

**Table 2.1**    *Level of Income of Respondent in Present Job, by Job-Finding Method Used*

| Income | Method Used | | | | |
|---|---|---|---|---|---|
| | Formal Means | Personal Contacts | Direct Application | Other | Total |
| Less than $10,000 | 28% | 23% | 50% | 5% | 28% |
| $10,000–14,999 | 42% | 32% | 31% | 26% | 33% |
| $15,000–24,999 | 24% | 31% | 15% | 53% | 28% |
| $25,000 or more | 6% | 14% | 4% | 16% | 11% |
| N | 50 | 154 | 52 | 19 | 275 |

Source: Granovetter, 1974, p. 14.

## Inferring Causality

Although we can say that the two variables are correlated, we cannot say at this point that one *caused* the other. Correlation is only the first piece of evidence needed to decide that one factor caused the other one. We also need to know that the independent variable occurred *before* the dependent variable (a time order that is clear in this example), and that no other factors might have caused the observed result. Many other factors—such as age, religious background, or occupational specialty of job seekers—might affect income. Without evidence ruling out alternative explanations for the observed relationship between job-finding method and income level, we cannot infer that the way people found their jobs caused them to earn higher incomes. (Granovetter was not interested in pinpointing the causes of income variation but rather in understanding the dynamics underlying the way people find different kinds of jobs, so he did not pursue an analysis of causes.) In general, social researchers try to rule out alternative explanations by **controlling for** other factors that might be affecting the relationship. In this example, for instance, Granovetter found that religious background had no particular impact on the chances of using a given method, but that age was related—job seekers over 34 were more likely to use personal contacts. You should get from this example a sense of the kind of reasoning social researchers follow when they are testing explanatory hypotheses.

No matter how strong a correlation is, it is important to remember that it does not indicate causality unless time order and the elimination of alternative explanations are also present. We can sharpen our everyday thinking and our critical appraisal of causal claims made by others by asking whether all three of these criteria are being met.

Suppose, for example, you have a job, but you have not received a raise in three years. Can you infer that your boss is not pleased with your work? Applying the research orientation to everyday life suggests a number of questions: Do you have any direct indicators of how your boss feels about your work? Did anyone else where you work get a raise? What else might be affecting whether you get a raise (for exam-

ple, is the boss making money)? What might the boss expect you to do if you do not get a raise? Can the boss replace you with someone as good for the same or less money? What kind of bargaining power do you and other employees have? There are many rival explanations for why you did not get a raise, only one of which consists of the boss's appraisal of your work. Thinking like a researcher can help you assess the evidence for inferring that one factor caused another.

The strongest way to rule out all rival explanations is to conduct a tightly controlled experiment where subjects are randomly assigned to two groups, only one of which is exposed to the independent variable while the other is not. Happily, no experimenter has the power to assign us randomly to groups and then tell us how we must or must not find a job so that the effect on our income can be studied. Many areas of sociological research share these ethical and practical constraints. In such situations we can only try to approximate the logic of experimental designs by controlling for as many rival explanations as possible.

## Steps in the Research Process

Although not all research studies follow the same pattern, it is possible to spell out the steps that occur frequently in the research process.

### Defining the Problem
Defining the problem involves selecting a general topic for research, identifying a research question to be answered, and defining the concepts of interest. Individuals have personal research questions, and social researchers have more general ones. You may wonder, for example, how you will get your first job. On a larger scale, sociologists might ask how people in general find jobs, as Granovetter did (1974).

### Reviewing the Literature
The next step is to review the existing literature to determine what is already known about the problem. Prior work may offer general descriptions, raise some key questions, discuss the strengths and limitations of measures that have already been tried, and suggest profitable lines

of further research. More and more libraries offer computerized literature searches that speed up the review process.

### Devising One or More Hypotheses

Ideally, in their effort to build knowledge, researchers develop several competing hypotheses. Durkheim (1897) did this in his classic study entitled *Suicide*. He considered the possibility that suicide rates varied as a result of heredity, climate, or social factors. He found social factors, such as the presence or absence of cohesion within a social group, to be the most important determinant of suicide.

### Designing the Research

Researchers then decide on a design for the study that will allow them to eliminate one or more of the hypotheses. **Research design** is the specific plan for selecting the unit of analysis; determining how the key variables will be measured; selecting a sample of cases; assessing sources of information; and obtaining data to test correlation, establish time order, and rule out rival hypotheses.

### Collecting the Data

Sociologists gather information in a variety of ways, depending on what they want to investigate and what is available. They may use field observations, interviews, written questionnaires, existing statistics, historical documents, content analysis, or artifactual data. Each of these methods will be discussed briefly in the next section.

### Analyzing the Data

Once the data are collected, they must be classified and the proposed relationships analyzed. Is a change in the independent variable indeed related to a change in the dependent variable? Can time order be established? Are alternative explanations ruled out?[2]

[2] The growing use of computers for social science research has greatly enlarged the statistical analyses that can be performed on data. Although it can speed up the process of data analysis and make complex computations feasible, the computer can do nothing to improve the quality of the data collected. Simply because data were analyzed by computer does not necessarily mean that a study is of high scientific quality. "Garbage in, garbage out" is the maxim that captures the inability of computers to improve on the material fed to them.

*Sociologists are very likely to use computers to analyze large amounts of data because computers can increase the speed and efficiency of data analysis.*

### Drawing Conclusions

Drawing conclusions involves trying to answer such questions as these: Which of the competing hypotheses are best supported by the evidence? Which are not? What limitations in the study should be considered in evaluating the results? What lines of further research does the study suggest? Conclusions rest heavily on the way research is designed and data are gathered.

## DESIGNING STUDIES AND GATHERING DATA

Social researchers study and try to understand the social world. Either they seek to describe some feature of social life or they try to analyze and explain interrelationships among social factors. Various types of data are available for both goals, and those data may be collected in different ways.

### Experiments

Does early childhood education for children living in poverty help them to succeed in school and beyond? In a social experiment, the experimenter tries to see whether a change in the independent variable (in this case, exposure to a preschool program) is related to a change in the dependent variable (school success or failure, criminal arrests, teen pregnancies, unemployment, and the need for welfare), while other conditions are held constant (family and neighborhood).

In an experimental design, the effect of the independent variable is assessed by comparing two groups of people. One group, the **experimental group,** is exposed to the hypothesized independent variable (the preschool program), while another group, the **control group,** is not. To rule out other explanations, the experimental and control groups must be identical in every respect except their exposure to the treatment.

In the Perry preschool study there was an experimental group of 58 and a control group of 65. They were selected for the study at age 3 or 4 on the basis of parents' low educational and occupational status, family size, and children's low IQ (intelligence test) scores. Pairs of children matched on IQ, family socioeconomic status, and gender were split between the two groups. The experimental group attended a preschool program for two years. Studies of the Perry Preschool Program in Michigan and five other preschool programs show significant differences between children in the experimental and control groups in terms of their higher intellectual performance as they began elementary school, their lesser need to repeat a grade or to receive special education, and their lower rates of dropping out of high school. In the Perry preschool study, the two groups were also compared in their early adult lives. Nineteen-year-olds who had attended the program were better off in a variety of ways than the control group. The program seems to have increased the percentage of participants who were literate (from 38 to 61 percent), enrolled in postsecondary education (from 21 to 38 percent), and employed (from 32 to 50 percent). Moreover, the program seems to have reduced the percentage of participants who were classified as mentally retarded during their school years (from 35 to 15 percent), school dropouts (from 51 to 33 percent), pregnant as teenagers (from 67 to 48 percent), on welfare (from 32 to 18 percent), or arrested (from 51 to 31 percent) (Schweinhart and Weikart, 1987, pp. 91–93).

Experiments are strong methods for meeting the three criteria of time order, correlation, and the elimination of rival hypotheses needed for inferring causality. They are limited by the practical and ethical restraints that exclude the study of private or dangerous behavior. Another method—interviews—can help researchers to obtain information about private, personal, or taboo attitudes and behaviors.

## Interviews and Surveys

What kind of gender-role behavior occurs between long-term partners in a relationship? Are there differences in the gender roles people assume when couples are straight (heterosexual) and gay (composed of two homosexual men or lesbian women)? These are some of the research questions posed by Philip Blumstein and Pepper Schwartz (1983), two sociologists at the University of Washington. To investigate these and related issues, they conducted interviews with more than six hundred people living in long-term relationships, and they mailed a written questionnaire to more than ten thousand people who agreed to participate in the study. (See Table 2.2 for a sample of some of the questions that were asked in this study.) Although carefully protecting the identities of the individuals involved, the researchers collected background information on the respondents' educations, occupations, incomes, and ethnicity, as well as considerable information about their relationships with their partners.

The use of interviews and questionnaires enabled them to ask everyone the same questions, so that comparisons could be made between long-term and short-term couples; between gay, lesbian, and straight couples; between couples with children and those without; and so forth. Practical and ethical considerations would have made it impossible to gather such data by observation, and other methods of data collection would have been equally inappropriate. Surveys are useful for describing the characteristics of large numbers of people in an efficient way. In this case, if only a few individuals had been studied, we might think that the results were unique to them and did not occur in the larger population. Surveys of carefully selected samples permit the accurate determination of rates of behavior or the frequency with which certain attitudes are held.

**Table 2.2** *Sample Questions from Blumstein and Schwartz Study of Couples and Their Relationships*

| | Extremely Satisfied | | Not at All Satisfied | Does Not Apply to Our Situation |
|---|---|---|---|---|
| 1. How satisfied are you with these parts of your relationship? | | | | |
| a. Our moral and religious beliefs and practices | 1 | 2 3 4 5 6 7 8 | 9 | |
| b. How my partner's job affects our relationship | 1 | 2 3 4 5 6 7 8 | 9 | X |
| c. How we communicate | 1 | 2 3 4 5 6 7 8 | 9 | |
| d. How my job affects our relationship | 1 | 2 3 4 5 6 7 8 | 9 | X |
| e. My partner's attitudes about having children | 1 | 2 3 4 5 6 7 8 | 9 | |
| f. How the house is kept | 1 | 2 3 4 5 6 7 8 | 9 | |
| g. The amount of influence I have over the decisions we make | 1 | 2 3 4 5 6 7 8 | 9 | |
| h. Our social life | 1 | 2 3 4 5 6 7 8 | 9 | |
| i. The amount of money coming in | 1 | 2 3 4 5 6 7 8 | 9 | |
| j. How we express affection for each other | 1 | 2 3 4 5 6 7 8 | 9 | |
| k. How we manage our finances | 1 | 2 3 4 5 6 7 8 | 9 | |
| l. How we raise the children | 1 | 2 3 4 5 6 7 8 | 9 | X |
| m. Our sex life | 1 | 2 3 4 5 6 7 8 | 9 | |
| 2. How satisfied are you with your relationship in general? | 1 | 2 3 4 5 6 7 8 | 9 | |
| 3. How would your partner rate [his/]her satisfaction with your relationship in general? | 1 | 2 3 4 5 6 7 8 | 9 | |

Source: Blumstein and Schwartz, 1983, p. 609.

## Sampling Procedures

The special sampling procedures researchers have developed are among the most powerful tools in their kit. Properly done, sampling permits conclusions about entire populations (of individuals, groups, organizations, or other aggregates) by studying only a few of them. The key lies in how those few are selected. A **population** is the total number of cases with a particular characteristic. Suppose you were interested in the sexual attitudes of American college students. Do you think you could walk out the door (wherever you are) and select the first ten warm bodies you encountered, interview them, and draw accurate conclusions about the attitudes of all college students? Such a technique is likely to be very unrepresentative. To overcome this problem, researchers use random sampling.

There are many types of scientific samples. In a **random sample,** every element (person, group, organization, or whatever) of the pop-

"*Could you go over that once again, Gene? Just in case any of us don't understand it.*"

Drawing by Weber; © 1979 The New Yorker Magazine, Inc.

ulation must have an *equal* and *known* chance of being selected for inclusion in the sample. There is solid technical knowledge available about sampling, but we cannot cover it all in an introductory sociology text. If you pursue a career in social research, you will learn more about the strengths of sampling techniques. Properly done, sampling allows researchers to judge the likelihood that their results could have occurred by chance.

Surveys work only when respondents are able and willing to report what they know, do, or feel. One of the limitations of survey research is the need to standardize the wording of questions and, in precoded versions, the allowable responses. This may lead to the problem of people not understanding what a standardized question means, or not finding the answer they want to give. Such limitations can be overcome by using open-ended or depth interviews before developing precoded response categories. Field research can also be used prior to designing a survey so as to get a better understanding of what is important to people, what meanings different words have for them, and how social processes unfold. Without depth interviews prior to questionnaire design, it is often impossible to know what questions to ask or how to ask them.

## Observational Research

Field research involves going where people are. It includes observation and sometimes **participant observation,** in which the researcher makes observations while taking part in the activities of the social group being studied. In her study of how policewomen were accepted by others in the force, Martin (1980) worked as an auxiliary policewoman and actually went out on patrol with other officers. She found that policemen developed a closed occupational brotherhood and expressed serious opposition to the entry of policewomen, although some younger and more critical officers were willing to accept women as colleagues. A social researcher can do fieldwork by being a complete participant, only an observer, or anything in between.

The ability to observe in field research can be enhanced by recording devices, just as the ability to listen in interviews can be aided by a tape recorder. Film, still photography, and videotape can add to the ability to record and later note (and code) specific behaviors. Videotape or film is particularly useful for studying interactions. For example, using film that could be studied frame-by-frame, Stern (1977) and others were able to observe in caregiver-child interactions whether the caregiver or the child moved first toward the other. They expected that caregivers

*Observational research by Susan Martin revealed how male police officers reacted when policewomen entered the force.*

would initiate all contacts with babies but found that infants often initiated movement toward the caregiver, who then became involved. To the unaided eye, the movement occurred so fast that it was impossible to unravel without the help of a tool to slow down the process.

Still photography provides a check on visual memory. It allows researchers to record cultural and social events precisely. These records can then be studied by people who were not present when they were made. Cameras share the same limitations that affect all human observation. They are subject to bias or personal projection—in terms of what we select to "see" or "film," how we frame a picture, and what we combine within a picture.

Another potential instance of bias arises when we present interviews on film or videotape. Do researchers select sympathetic and likable people to express certain views, or are the spokespersons unattractice or unsympathetic? Obviously, in such techniques, social research borders on journalism and the mass media. Similar questions can be raised in both: What is being included and what excluded? How representative are the people selected? How were they sampled?

## Other Sources of Data

### *Existing Data and Government Documents*

Government documents are a major source of social statistics. The United States and many other governments spend millions of dollars each year gathering information from residents and private and state sources. World statistics are available through the United Nations *Demographic Yearbook*, which presents births, deaths, and other vital statistics for individual nations of the world.

Governments vary in how carefully they collect social statistics. Crime waves have risen and fallen merely because the crime data were recorded by different administrators. In developing nations, where many babies are still born at home, birth records may be very incomplete. Wealthier nations can afford to spend more money to gather systematic data. The General Social Survey (GSS), for example, done by the National Opinion Research Center (NORC)

*Government documents are a major source of social data. They are freely available to students of society in educational and public libraries.*

with U.S. National Science Foundation support, is an annual social survey of about 1500 Americans that was begun in 1972. It taps beliefs and opinions about public affairs, perceptions of well-being, and reports of social behavior. Such surveys over time (called longitudinal studies) permit the analysis of social trends and changes. The data tapes from surveys such as these are available to persons who want to analyze them further. Many colleges and universities have copies of the NORC GSS data tapes. NORC also publishes an annual "codebook," which lists the questions asked, the answers given by people in the sample, and more information on the sample design.[3]

---

[3] The codebooks are sold (with or without data tapes) by the Roper Public Opinion Research Center, Box U-164R, University of Connecticut, Storrs, CT 06268. Many college libraries already have copies.

# Reading Tables

Sociologists are interested in data from a variety of sources. They often summarize these data in statistical form and present them in tables of numbers. Learning to read a table is like learning to drive a car with a stick shift: you never know when it might be useful. And, there are similar procedures to follow each time you do it. The basics that are worth mastering are these:

1. *Read the title,* which tells what the table is about and how it is presented. Table 2.3, for instance, describes the median income of white, black, and Hispanic families from 1960 to 1987, in 1987 constant dollars (that is, dollars adjusted for the rate of inflation).

2. *Read the headings* that group the data in relevant ways. In Table 2.3, separate vertical columns distinguish whites from blacks and Hispanics. The labels on the horizontal rows indicate the relevant year.

3. *Note the source.* At the bottom of a decent table you should find the source of the data. You can then judge how much confidence you want to place in the table, and you can locate the original data if you want to check them further. In this case the source is the Department of Commerce's Bureau of the Census, one of our best sources of descriptive data about the United States.

4. *Make comparisons.* For any given row (in this case year), compare the income of white, black, and Hispanic families. That is, look at columns A, B, and C in row 1. We can see that white families earned much more than black or Hispanic families in 1975. This difference is quantified in columns D and E, where the table maker has computed a ratio of black or Hispanic to white family income. That number is obtained by dividing the annual median income of black families ($18,538) by the annual median income of white families ($30,129). The ratio tells us that in 1960, black families had a median income that was 55 percent of the median income of white families. By 1987, black families had a median income that was 56 percent of that of white families. Hence the gap in median incomes between blacks and whites has not changed in that time period. The ratio of Hispanic income to that of white families is somewhat higher than that of blacks, but also actually declined between 1975 and 1987.

This conclusion requires us to make several comparisons at the same time—one comparing whites and blacks or Hispanic families (as summarized in the ratio), the other moving down the time rows to compare 1960 with 1987, and to note in passing whether there were any years when this trend did not appear.

In general terms, the rule for making comparisons in tables is to compare columns within rows, and then rows within columns.

5. *Ask what is missing, or what you cannot tell from the table.* For example, in Table 2.3, were both parents working in the family? What might be the effects of age, geographical region, education, or other factors on this correlation between ethnicity and income over time? The table cannot answer these questions, but the probes suggest further data or research that is needed before we can say to what extent ethnicity and income are causally related.

**Table 2.3  *Median Income of Families by Race and Hispanic Origin: 1960–1987 (1987 constant dollars)***

| | | | Families | | |
| | Col. A | Col. B | Col. C | Col. D Ratio of Black Income to White | Col. E Ratio of Hispanic Income to White |
| Year | Whites | Blacks | Hispanics | | |
|---|---|---|---|---|---|
| 1960 | $22,393 | $12,396 | (NA)[a] | 0.55 | (NA) |
| 1965 | $26,119 | $14,383 | (NA) | 0.55 | (NA) |
| 1970 | $29,960 | $18,378 | (NA) | 0.61 | (NA) |
| 1975 | $30,129 | $18,538 | $20,168 | 0.62 | 0.67 |
| 1980 | $30,211 | $17,481 | $20,297 | 0.58 | 0.67 |
| 1981 | $29,388 | $16,578 | $20,495 | 0.56 | 0.70 |
| 1982 | $28,969 | $16,011 | $19,106 | 0.55 | 0.66 |
| 1983 | $29,474 | $16,610 | $19,313 | 0.56 | 0.66 |
| 1984 | $30,294 | $16,884 | $20,606 | 0.56 | 0.68 |
| 1985 | $30,799 | $17,734 | $20,102 | 0.58 | 0.65 |
| 1986 | $31,935 | $18,247 | $20,726 | 0.57 | 0.65 |
| 1987 | $32,274 | $18,098 | $20,306 | 0.56 | 0.63 |

[a] NA means not available.    *Source:* U.S. Bureau of the Census, 1989a, p. 445.

*Strengths and Limitations of Various Methods of Collecting Data*

| Method of Data Collection | Type of Data— Quantitative or Qualitative | Strengths | Limitations |
| --- | --- | --- | --- |
| Participant observation | Qualitative (non-numerical) | Permits processes to be observed as they occur. Good for studying interactions. Helps get at the meanings of words and events for people. May show the range of possibilities that exists. Flexible; focus can shift as research progresses. Relatively inexpensive. Puts primary researcher in direct contact with people being studied. | Hard to tell how typical the observed people are. Difficult to repeat. Close ties between observer and observed may bias results. |
| Surveys and interviews | Either | Standard questions can be asked of randomly selected respondents, giving comparable and representative information about a large population. May be repeated by other researchers. May reveal information about private or illegal behavior that would not have been observed. | People must know the meaning of the questions they are answering. Only works when people are able and willing to report what they know, do, or feel. Generally an expensive method. |
| Existing data and government documents | Quantitative (numerical) | Collects data on nearly everyone in a population or on a carefully drawn, representative sample of the population. Less expensive than gathering data oneself. | Omits certain data such as religion. May not define and measure concepts the way researcher would like (the census defines a place as "urban" if it has more than 2500 people in it). |

| Method of Data Collection | Type of Data—Quantitative or Qualitative | Strengths | Limitations |
|---|---|---|---|
| Comparative historical analysis | Qualitative | Useful for studying large-scale social processes that unfold over decades or centuries. May suggest the causes behind those processes. | Cases that can reasonably be compared may be rare and difficult to find. Requires a great deal of comparative historical knowledge. |
| Content analysis | Either | May catch cultural shifts over time, even when possible respondents are dead. | Tells only about symbolic behavior. Actual behavior may or may not conform to the symbolic portrayals. Does not reveal how the content of various cultural products affects the people exposed to it. |
| Physical traces and artifacts | Either | People do not know they are being studied; therefore they cannot try to influence the results. | Many behaviors and attitudes do not leave physical traces. High "dross rate"; a great deal of garbage must be sifted through to find something useful. |

In Figure 2.2 the same data that appear in Table 2.3 are presented in graphic form. Interpreting a graph involves the same initial steps as reading a table. First, read the title, identify the relevant headings, and note the source. Generally tendencies are more immediately apparent in a chart. We can tell at once that median incomes for everyone were generally rising between 1960 and 1970. In 1980 they began to decline, until 1983. They dipped again in 1987. Although the general trends are more immediately apparent, and differences between black, Hispanic, and white families are readily visible, the ratio numbers that were so useful in Table 2.3 are not presented directly. Instead, the ratios must be sensed from the figure. Ultimately, the purpose for which we will use the data should determine the form in which it is presented. For communication purposes, graphic presentation is usually more effective and efficient than tabular material. Therefore, throughout most of this book, material is presented graphically whenever possible.

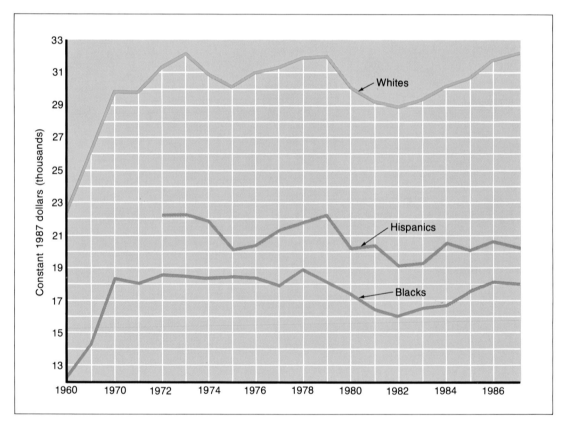

*Source:* U.S. Bureau of the Census, 1989a, p. 445.

**Figure 2.2   Median Income of Families by Race, 1960–1987.**

The median income of blacks, whites, and Hispanics in constant 1987 dollars rose and fell between 1960 and 1987. Whites had the highest median income, followed by Hispanics and trailed by blacks.

## Comparative Historical Methods

In order to make causal inferences, one must study events over time and compare cases that differ in certain key respects but are similar in other important ways. For some problems this is possible only by using historical materials. In her study of revolutions, Theda Skocpol (1979) utilized comparative historical analysis. This method is appropriate for developing explanations of large-scale historical phenomena of which only a few major cases exist (such as revolutions within entire nation-states). Skocpol's problem was to identify and validate the causes of social revolutions. Her strategy was to find a few cases that shared certain basic features. France, Russia, and China were similar in their old regimes, their revolutionary processes, and the revolutionary outcomes. All three revolutions occurred in wealthy and politically ambitious agricultural states, none of which had ever been the colony of another state. All three suddenly faced a military competitor that was more developed economically than itself. External problems combined with widespread peasant rebellions and competing political leaders.

The result in each case was a centralized and bureaucratic nation-state with potential for considerable international power. The analysis of these three cases is an example of the method of agreement, where similar causal chains appear in several situations.

## Unobtrusive Measures: Physical Traces and Artifacts

Some of the methods mentioned so far are limited by the fact that when people know they are being studied, they may try to influence what is learned about them. One solution is to look for nonreactive measures—that is, indicators that do not change because they are being studied. For example, one could assess the amount of drinking that occurs on a "dry" college campus by counting the number of beer, wine, and liquor bottles in the trash rather than by asking people about their drinking behavior (Webb et al., 1966).

## Content Analysis

How can we analyze the mass media? The method, **content analysis,** is used to describe and analyze in an objective and systematic way the content of literature, speeches, or media. It helps to identify cultural themes or trends. Alone it cannot tell us whether people think or behave differently as a result of reading certain stories, but it can measure the ideas that are in circulation.

For example, the reactions of working-class women to the experience of miscarriage and infant death were analyzed by studying the content of articles on the subject that appeared in the magazine *True Story* from 1920 to 1985. Some women blamed themselves for the creation of their own tragedies, and mothers were taught to doubt themselves and rely on male authorities. Other women came to accept death as part of life and learned to enjoy other relationships more fully as well as to validate other women's experiences by their writing (Simonds, 1988).

The preceding discussion of various types of data and data collection suggests that each method has one or more limitations, as well as having particular strengths. Some of these strengths and limitations are summarized in Table 2.4 on pages 2-2, 2-3.

*Sociologists can study changes in popular culture over time by analyzing shifts in the content of popular videos.*

## POLICY RESEARCH AND ETHICAL ISSUES

The conduct of most research involves the participation of the people being studied. One of the justifications for their time and trouble is the possibility that some research will be used to inform public policy. **Policy research** aims to assess alternative possibilities for public or social action in terms of their costs and/or consequences. For example, a cost-benefit analysis of the Perry Preschool Program showed that the total benefits to taxpayers (in constant 1981 dollars) were about $28,000 per participant, nearly six times the annual program operation cost of $5000 per participant (Schweinhart and Weikart, 1987, p. 94). Actual public policy-making is a complex process, however. Research evidence is seldom the sole basis for setting political agendas and actions (Gerstein, Luce, Smelser, and Sperlich, 1988).

Who sees the results of research studies and who decides whether or not they inform public policy are among the ethical issues involved in social research. There are other ethical concerns as well. People cannot and should not be endlessly manipulated by researchers. Certain ethics guide most social researchers. First, subjects should be told as much as possible about the nature of the study without jeopardizing the validity of the information to be gathered.

Having had a research study described to them, subjects should be asked whether they agree to participate. Any research is somewhat of an intrusion into the lives of individuals, and researchers must be as sensitive and delicate as possible when making such intrusions. Potential discomfort to respondents must be weighed against likely scientific gains. One way of protecting respondents is by keeping their individual responses confidential.

Should researchers always reveal their identities, especially when doing participant observation? There are certain groups that may not want researchers in their midst, such as reclusive religious cults, corporate boards, and certain criminal groups. There are ethical and practical dangers in clandestine research, however, and many people do not feel comfortable doing it.

Many research topics can be studied without concealing one's identity as a researcher.

Social researchers must ask whether the same or similar results could have been obtained without deceiving people—without concealing the identity of the researchers. In many cases the answer is yes. Where it is no, researchers must scrutinize the value of the research. In an interview or a written questionnaire, subjects can refuse to answer particular questions they find offensive. Of course, they should be informed of this right at the outset. The right to withhold consent is more difficult to exercise in experiments where one does not know in advance what is going to happen.

A final important ethical issue is who gets studied and who learns the results of the research. Traditionally, the poor and the powerless have been studied most frequently, usually with little or no gain for themselves. Hence we know quite a bit about welfare mothers and children, for example, but rather little about wealthy parents and their children.

Many research projects have provoked controversy over ethical issues, but one of the most prominent ones is Laud Humphreys' (1970) study *Tearoom Trade: Impersonal Sex in Public Places*, about homosexual acts between strangers meeting in the public rest rooms of parks (called "tearooms" by those meeting there). Initial research by Humphreys suggested the hypothesis that the men involved were very often family men who were accepted members of their community. They were not active homosexuals in any other sense. For these reasons, anonymity was very important to them. To avoid hassles with the police, participants always got a third person to serve as lookout (called the "watchqueen") at the door of the "tearoom." Humphreys took this role and was thereby able to observe the behaviors directly. Testing his hypothesis required more information on the social background of participants. To get this, Humphreys quietly noted the car license-plate numbers of participants and traced their names and addresses.

A year later, while conducting a health survey of men in the community, Humphreys was able to add the tearoom men to his sample. He changed his appearance, style of dress, and the car he drove in the days he served as watchqueen and then called on them at home. He reports that none of the respondents recognized him or appeared upset by the interview. They were being treated as normal people, answering survey questions that might be asked of anyone. In this way Humphreys obtained information about their family backgrounds, socioeconomic status, personal health, social history, religious and employment background, social and political attitudes, friendships, and marital and social relationships. He discovered that many participants were married, living with their families, and active in their communities.

Although widely applauded for its ingenuity and success in lifting the veil of stigma that shrouded homosexuality in 1970, Humphreys' work was also roundly criticized for its use of deception, both to observe the sexual encounters and to gain background information on participants. In the second edition of his book, Humphreys agrees with this criticism and says he should have identified himself as a researcher, even if it meant losing some observations. Others suggest that the deception may have been necessary to obtain the information needed to test the hypothesis. And, they add, Humphreys completely protected his respondents' identities. Even so, some participants became nervous when the case made the local papers and called Humphreys in a panic that their lives would be ruined. Besides public exposure, they feared the threat of blackmail. So, even while protected, they suffered personal anguish.

This example raises many of the ethical issues noted earlier. Who gets the results of the research and who benefits? How are the subjects protected from harm? Under what conditions, if any, is deception justified in social research?

Ethical issues such as these suggest that social research need not be a dull, bloodless substitute for life. This fact will become more apparent in the next chapter, which considers how various types of societies survive and change and how sociologists study social structure and culture.

## SUMMARY

1. Science differs from other forms of knowledge in the way it stresses observation and reasoning. Science tries to improve upon everyday inquiry by being systematic and careful and by trying to link observations with more general statements (theories).

2. Social science assumes that social life is patterned and that these patterns occur in collections of individuals on a probability basis. Individual exceptions occur, and general statements rarely apply 100 percent of the time. Although it may be complex, the social behavior of collections of people can be described and understood.

3. Researchers following careful, conscious procedures sometimes make discoveries that contradict commonsense expectations. Such instances remind us to ask, "What evidence do we have for believing something to be the way someone suggests, and how was that evidence obtained?"

4. The systematic nature of good research and the measurement instruments social scientists have developed have made social research useful in business, the courts, education, elections, government, housing, public policy-making, sales, social services, and other areas.

5. The various "tools of the research trade" include units of analysis, descriptive and explanatory studies, hypotheses, concepts and variables, operationalizing variables, relationships between variables, rules for inferring causality, and steps in the research process.

6. A variety of design and data-gathering techniques are used by social researchers. The primary ones are experiments, interviews and surveys, and observational research. Other sources of data include government documents, comparative historical methods, physical traces and artifacts, and content analysis. Each has certain strengths and certain limitations.

7. Research may affect the lives of the people studied, as revealed in a number of ethical issues. Human subjects have the right to informed consent, protection from harm, privacy, and the benefit of the knowledge gained from research.

## KEY TERMS

bias (p. 29)
concept (p. 33)
content analysis (p. 41)
control group (p. 37)
controlling for (p. 35)
correlation (p. 34)
criteria for inferring causality (p. 31)
deduction (p. 33)
dependent variable (p. 34)
descriptive study (p. 32)
experimental group (p. 37)
explanatory study (p. 32)
hypothesis (p. 32)
independent variable (p. 34)
induction (p. 33)
mean, arithmetic (p. 32)
median (p. 32)
methodology (p. 28)
mode (p. 32)
objectivity (p. 29)
operationalization (p. 33)
participant observation (p. 39)
policy research (p. 42)
population (p. 38)
proposition (p. 33)
random sample (p. 38)
range (p. 32)
research design (p. 36)
rival hypothesis (p. 32)
sample survey (p. 29)
theory (p. 32)
unit of analysis (p. 31)
variable (p. 33)

## SUGGESTED READINGS

Adams, Robert McCormick, et al. 1984. *Behavioral and Social Science Research: A National Resource.* Washington, DC: National Academy Press. Shows many of the useful benefits of social research.

Babbie, Earl R. 1983. *The Practice of Social Research,* 3d ed. Belmont, CA: Wadsworth. A clear, interesting, and helpful text on methods of social research.

Bart, Pauline, and Linda Frankel. 1986. *The Student Sociologist's Handbook.* 4th ed. New York: Random House. A useful guide to doing social investigations.

Granovetter, Mark. 1974. *Getting a Job: A Study of Contacts and Careers.* Cambridge, MA: Harvard University Press. A straightforward study of how individuals actually get their jobs.

Melbin, Murray. 1979. "Settling the frontier of night." *Psychology Today* (June): 40–41ff. An intriguing research study, using several different methods, that explores the similarity between the American frontier and nighttime.

U.S. Bureau of the Census. 1987. *Statistical Abstract of the United States 1988.* Washington, DC: U.S. Government Printing Office. An invaluable annual source of data on many aspects of life in the United States.

# SOCIAL CONCEPTS AND PROCESSES

Sociologists study many major features of social life, some of which you will meet in this section. In Chapters 3 and 4, you will look at some of the most fundamental strategies that societies use to survive and see the significance of culture. You will also consider the different roles individuals play in societies, the different ways individuals interact with each other, how individuals form social networks, and the importance of such networks in people's lives. In Chapter 5, you will consider how babies and youths learn to become members of their societies. Since individuals become social beings only by interacting with others, Chapter 6 considers the important effects that groups and organizations have on all of us. Groups and societies inevitably develop ideas about what they consider "deviant" or criminal behavior. Chapter 7 looks at the forms of social control societies use to keep people in line and to guard against deviant behavior.

# Societies and Culture

*"Amanda died on the same day that her father refused to buy her a new pair of rubber boots. In temperatures that dropped to −30 and −40°F, she was still wearing an old and torn pair of sneakers. In the Hudson's Bay store, she approached her father while he was cashing his welfare check. She begged him for new boots because her feet were freezing. In a conversation widely reported around the [community], he apparently replied 'Get out of my way. . . . You don't give me anything, so why should I give you anything? I need the money for myself!' Then he went out drinking in Kenora. When he returned . . . his daughter was dead. She had killed herself with an overdose of tuberculosis pills.*

*"[Her] father was part of the 'broken generation,' a man in his middle thirties, caught between the old and the new ways of life. He worked intermittently at the sawmill, but most of his income came from welfare and unemployment insurance. He was one of the heaviest binge drinkers on the reserve. His house was bare of furniture, and most of his money went to buy liquor and rides to town in taxis. When he felt rich, he ordered a plane to fly him the 60 miles to Kenora. . . ."* [Shkilnyk, 1985, p. 17]

Amanda's suicide was rooted in the disintegration of the community in which she lived—an Ojibwan Indian community in Grassy Narrows, Ontario, Canada, north of the northern Minnesota border. The community life of this Indian band was intact as recently as the 1960s, when they lived by hunting, trapping, fishing, and gathering, sometimes supplementing this by wage labor. They moved seasonally between winter trapping grounds and a summer encampment. They had relatively little contact with white society and, as a result, the band had maintained "considerable stability and continuity with the ancient patterns of Ojibwa life" (Shkilnyk, 1985, p. 2).

In 1963 the Department of Indian Affairs of Canada decided to move this band to a "new reserve," because there they could be reached by road and could have electricity, a school, improved housing, social services, and other benefits of modern life. "The uprooting, however, proved devastating to the Ojibwa way of life. And before the people had time to adjust, to establish new roots, they were hit in 1970 by another blow: the discovery that the river that had sustained them was poisoned by methyl mercury. In little more than a decade, the society that had held together and prospered on the old reserve was in shambles. And the people, finding themselves trapped in a no-man's land, an abyss between two cultures, had begun to self-destruct" (Shkilnyk, 1985, p. 2).

Social life is not random; neither does it reflect the inflexible expression of a natural law. Instead, social life is historically and culturally patterned. Historical experiences, methods of obtaining food, and cultural traditions all influence the nature of a society, including how tasks are assigned, the size of communities, the amount of inequality between individuals, the importance of family ties, and even what people eat. When methods of obtaining food and cultural traditions are violently disrupted, as at Grassy Narrows, it may destroy the sense of community that holds a social group together.

Since the focus of this book is society and how people interact with it, we begin this chapter by defining society. We will consider the problems societies face and the major subsistence strategies they have adopted. Societal adaptations and culture are closely intertwined. The second part of this chapter examines the key phenomenon of culture.

Culture affects almost everything we do, think, and feel. Culture surrounds us like the air we breathe. It shapes our habits, behaviors, language, and interpersonal style. Often it does this in invisible ways—for example, by influencing our ideas about what is "natural," just, or beautiful. Culture affects what we take for granted as well as what we question.

We shall consider what sociologists mean by culture, examine how culture helps to set humans apart from other species, explore common features in the cultures of many societies, analyze changes in American culture and values, look at explanations for cultural variation, consider whether culture smothers individualism, and critically examine sociobiology (a field that stresses the importance of a biological rather than a cultural basis for human behavior).

## SOCIETIES

### What Is Society?

At what point does a cluster of people become a society? The first major feature of a society is that its people share a common heritage, called "culture," consisting of customs, values, ideas, and artifacts. In a society this common cultural heritage is transmitted from one generation to the next. Part of what people in a society share are patterned ways of interacting: ways of raising chidren, forming families, dividing work, making love, greeting one another, and so on.

A **society,** then, is a group of people with a shared and somewhat distinct culture, who live in a defined territory, feel some unity as a group, and see themselves as distinct from other peoples. A society needs to be independent enough

*Cultural heritages such as the one shared by this family in Jodhpur, India, are transmitted from one generation to the next, unless they face drastic social upheavals.*

to avoid being swallowed up by other societies. One test of a society is whether it could survive in a form close to its present one if all other societies in the world disappeared. A society, in short, is a relatively independent collection of people who share a common heritage and common ways of interacting.

## Societal Concerns

To survive, societies need to cope with and find some form of solution to a variety of problems. These include:

1. Subsistence. Living beings have physical needs for air, water, food, warmth, shelter, and sleep that must be met if they are to survive. Meeting subsistence needs usually requires some kind of work to hunt, gather, or produce food and shelter.
2. Distribution. The means of subsistence must be distributed in some way among the members of a society. Very seldom does every member have equal access to the means of subsistence. If nothing else, the babies and young members of a society need others to provide them with an adequate food supply.
3. Biological reproduction. All individuals do not need to reproduce; but for a society to survive, some of its members must reproduce.
4. Cultural transmission. For a society to persist, the customs, values, and ideas of the society must be passed on to new members.
5. Protection. Societal members must avoid destroying one another, and a society as a whole needs protection from external threats, whether physical or social.
6. Communication. To deal with these problems, members must be able to communicate with one another.

How societies address these problems varies widely and seems to depend both on features of the physical environment and on societal and cultural factors. The physical environment includes climate and the variety of available resources (water, animals, plants, soil, sun, minerals, and metals). Physical environment will influence but not completely determine the subsistence strategies followed by a society. Societal

features include a society's subsistence strategies; its social structure, culture, and material products; and its demographic features—that is, the number of people, their age and sex, birth rates, and death rates. (**Demography** is the study of population trends.) These interrelated features shape much of social life in different societies.

## Subsistence Strategies[1]

Examining the subsistence strategies of various societies has intellectual and practical value. Intellectually, such an exploration illustrates how subsistence strategies may influence social structures and culture and gives us a sense of our history as a species. In practical terms, such an analysis helps us to understand societies today, for people still use these strategies to survive. The United States and other industrialized societies have been involved at various times in military, diplomatic, or trade activity with societies using subsistence strategies different from their own. For these reasons, it is valuable to survey some of these strategies.

About thirty thousand years ago, people were seeking protection from the huge masses of ice that covered much of North America and northern Europe. They lived in caves and depended on their abilities as hunters to supply themselves with food and clothing. As the glaciers retreated and people emerged from their caves, there was a gradual shift away from the hunting mode of existence toward farming and stock raising. This shift, which began around 11,000 B.C., may have occurred because the numbers of large animals were reduced by heavier hunting and the changing climate (Harris, 1979). The human population on earth then began to surge, from about 5 million in 8000 B.C. to about 86 million by 4000 B.C. (Deevey, 1960). By the time Jesus was born (A.D. 1) there were an estimated 200 to 300 million people on earth (United Nations, 1972).

During this time farming evolved from the simple use of hoes and sticks, with no animals, to the more effective use of plows using animals to pull them. The use of animal labor increased the agricultural surplus, which, in turn, could

[1] The following discussion benefits from Lenski (1966) and Lenski and Lenski (1978).

support more people in closely settled groupings. The first cities arose. Agricultural surplus also permitted new social arrangements. As irrigation and agricultural techniques developed, social groupings grew larger and more complex, leading to the rise of large nation-states. The industrial revolution, which has shaped contemporary society as we know it, began only 250 years ago. It has brought us to a world of assembly-line factories, nuclear bombs and power plants, supersonic jets, communications satellites, space shuttles, multinational corporations, and computerized banking.

Societies may be grouped according to the subsistence strategies they use or according to size, complexity, and form of political integration. The key questions to ask about subsistence strategies are these: What is a group's food supply? How is it obtained? The answers to those two questions determine whether a social group will settle down permanently or move from place to place, what size group can be maintained, the amount of warfare the group engages in, the kind of culture that develops, and the type of social structure that emerges. In the history of the human species, the four major types of subsistence strategies have given rise to four major types of societies. In their pure forms, these appear as hunting and gathering societies, horticultural societies, agrarian societies, and industrial societies. Considering each of these suggests how subsistence strategies are related to the types of authority and inequity that develop in a society and to its culture, religion, and social interaction.

### Hunting and Gathering Societies

The subsistence strategy used for the longest time in human history was that of hunting animals for meat and gathering berries, nuts, vegetables, and fruit for food. This strategy prevailed until only a few thousand years ago. Today there are still a few hunting and gathering societies around, such as the bush people of Namibia (Southwest Africa) and the Tasaday, who live in a rain forest in the Philippine Islands. Our knowledge of hunting and gathering societies is based on two major types of evidence: archeological remains of early humans and anthropological studies, called **ethnographies,** of remaining hunting and gathering groups.

With the exception of larger fishing societies, **hunting and gathering societies** typically are small bands of 75 to 100 people each (Lee and DeVore, 1968). They may be independent societies in their own right or loosely connected to other bands. Until 1970, for example, the Tasaday apparently had no contact with modern societies. Although the authenticity of the Tasaday has been challenged in a series of political, business, and academic rivalries, Dula, a member of the tribe, testified in Manila in 1987 as to her genuineness as a Tasaday tribeswoman. After her testimony and that of several anthropologists and other experts, the skeptics' case was undermined (Mydans, 1987).

Hunters and gatherers are generally nomads, since they tend to exhaust the supply of food in one area and then move on to another. Activities are divided by age and sex. In some tribes, reaching the age at which he can hunt with the men is a sign of adulthood for a boy. In most hunting and gathering societies, there is a sexual division of labor. Women do most of the gathering and also are responsible for child care. Men do most of the hunting.

Hunting and gathering societies reveal a number of important connections between subsistence strategies and social structure. The major organizing institution is the system of family and kinship. In such societies all individuals have relationships with others that are clearly defined in kinship terms. Virtually everyone is related in some way, and individuals need to know what that relationship is so that they will know how they should behave toward one another (Elkin, 1954). The kinship ties of the family encourage the practice of sharing food, which is especially important because of the uncertainty and variability that marks a hunting and gathering economy.

Despite the uncertainty, hunting and gathering societies have considerable leisure. A study of Bushmen shows they devote between 12 and 17 hours per week to getting food (Lee and DeVore, 1968, p. 35). About a third of the population produces no food because of their age or other limitations (Lee, 1969, p. 67).

Because of their nomadic existence, members of hunting and gathering societies accumulate few possessions or other types of wealth. The tendency not to accumulate a surplus is shown

*Hunters and gatherers catch or find their food rather than producing it.
As a result, their societies are usually smaller than 100 people, are quite
mobile, and have relatively small differences in social rank between individuals.*

by the life of the Tasaday. The first outsiders to
see the Tasaday brought knives as presents,
which they laid out for the Tasaday to take.
Each man took one, and there was one left over.
They explained "Everyone has a knife now," so
they did not need the extra one (Nance, 1975).
Every man can provide for his own material
needs and that of his family to about the same
degree. Every man learns how to make his own

weapons out of available materials and how to
use them. No one has a monopoly over the
means of production. As a result, the headman's
position is based largely on respect and prestige
rather than on superior wealth. It may be that
he is the best hunter, has the best ideas about
how to do things, has a talent for storytelling,
or gives away more food and gifts to other
villagers (Harris, 1979). These behaviors are

likely to gain him respect, prestige, and influence. Nevertheless, there are no major differences in social rank among individuals.

### Horticultural and Pastoral Societies

**Horticultural societies** are societies in which the cultivation of plants is the primary means of subsistence. In simple horticultural societies, people garden with hoes and sticks; in more complex horticultural societies, they use metal tools. Somewhere between 11,000 and 7000 B.C., hunters and gatherers began to shift to farming and animal raising. Even before this they had been harvesting wild grains for food, as the name "gatherers" indicates. The shift from hunting and gathering strategies to simple gardening and animal raising enabled humans to produce food rather than simply to find it.

As a result, cultivators may be able to accumulate surpluses. The existence of a surplus food supply promotes trade and commerce, since the food stored by one group can be traded or sold to another group. Surpluses also permit increasing occupational specialization because they free people to do more than just find food. Plant cultivation also makes possible larger, more permanent settlements with denser populations, since there is less concern about overhunting in an area. Gardening societies can be as large as 150 to 200 inhabitants; occasional settlements with as many as 2000 to 3000 people have been found—for example, in the Sudan region of Africa. The growth of food surplus and of population made possible by cultivation can also contribute to the growth of warfare. Conquest and exploitation of some groups by others may be more attractive and profitable if stored food can be seized.

In dry areas unsuited to farming, hunters began to raise sheep, goats, and cows for their milk, skins, and meat. Such **pastoral societies** still exist today in the Middle East and the drier regions of Africa. They are by necessity **nomadic**—that is, they move their residences from place to place. With the expansion of human and animal populations in a region, warfare increases as groups begin to compete over who will use the land for grazing. Although pastoral communities are fairly small, due to the limited number of herds an area can support, they are tied together into larger societies. The median size of herding communities is 55 people, but they may be grouped into societies of 2000 or more (Murdock, 1967). Their frequent travel, contact with others, and need to band together to protect grazing territories probably account for the considerable degree of trading and political development pastoral societies show. The idea of a supreme being as a shepherd who takes an active interest in his flock emerged in a number of herding societies. So the means of subsistence appears to influence even such "otherworldly" aspects of culture as religion.

One development that separated simple from advanced herding and gardening societies was metallurgy, the extraction of metals from ore. First copper and then bronze were discovered by various simple farming societies. In the beginning, metals were used primarily for weapons, ornaments, and religious artifacts. The specialized knowledge and skill that were necessary to smelt and shape bronze meant that the processes of metalworking tended to be learned and controlled by a few specialists, who were sometimes thought to possess magical qualities. Because making bronze weapons was costly, such weapons tended to be monopolized by the wealthy. Since bronze weapons were sharper and more durable than stone weapons, societies with such weapons had an advantage in warfare against societies without them.

In the more advanced horticultural societies there was more warfare and greater inequality. Wherever there were critical resources that could be monopolized, whether of metallurgy, irrigation facilities, or domestic animals, the concentration of wealth and power began to increase. The advantages that one generation possessed were now more likely than had been the case in hunting and gathering societies to be transmitted to the next generation. Rank came to be based less on personal skills, talents, or behaviors and more on control of technology and wealth.

### Agrarian Societies

**Agrarian societies** are those in which large-scale cultivation takes place. Hunting and gathering and simple gardening societies used labor-efficient techniques, but the yield from a unit of land was small. Therefore these techniques could not support as many people in an area

(Granovetter, 1979b, p. 494). The plow contributed to the efficient use of land. Plowing turned over the soil regularly and brought up buried nutrients. For the first time, people could continue to use the same piece of land for a series of crops. In this period the scale and permanence of food-growing activities changed dramatically.

Then animal power began to be used to supplement human energy to pull plows. This change set the stage for the future development of additional nonhuman energy sources. The period in which the plow came into use, from about 4000 to 3000 B.C., was an extremely creative one, marked by the invention of the wheel for use in wagons and making pottery; by the harnessing of windpower to propel sailboats; and by the development of writing, numbers, and the calendar (Childe, 1964). Human productivity increased greatly as a result.

Technological developments, population pressures, the decline in large game animals, possible interest in trade, and concentrations of political power may all have contributed to a shift in agricultural techniques (Granovetter, 1979b; Harris, 1977; Polgar, 1975). With improved grain production and transportation, cities developed, although most people still lived and worked on the land. Some of these cities had as many as a hundred thousand people by the time of the Roman Empire (first century B.C. to fourth century A.D.). Agricultural surplus and urban concentration allowed ever-greater division of labor and specialization. For example, there were a hundred or more occupational specialties—including tanners, innkeepers, fishermen, sailors, wool dressers, and spicers—in Paris and Barcelona in the fourteenth century (Russell, 1972). Increasing specialization, in turn, was related to the growth of trade, the use of money as a medium of exchange, and the emergence of a new merchant class of traders and shopkeepers.

Political and military organizations became increasingly complex and powerful (Harris, 1977). All the large agricultural civilizations of history—ancient Egypt, Babylonia, Assyria, Persia, Greece, Rome, old India, old China, and pre-Columbian Mexico and Peru—were governed by aristocracies that monopolized military force. A few rulers lived in great splendor. They wore special clothing for each occasion (with servants to care for each type of clothing) and ornaments made from precious metals and jewels. They engaged their own personal entertainers, such as jugglers and musicians. Under the sponsorship of wealthy rulers, architecture and the arts flourished. Such monuments as the Taj Mahal in India and the Egyptian temples and pyramids were built in agrarian societies.

Economic diversity was accompanied by growing institutional specialization. One notable shift involved the gradual separation of religion and kinship. In hunting and gathering societies, religion was closely tied to one's clan—that is, one's extended family. The great world religions, including Buddhism, Christianity, Hinduism, Islam, and Judaism, emerged in the major agrarian societies. They are called world religions because they claim to apply equally to all persons, regardless of family ties.[2] This shift meant that people in different clans might belong to the same religion. Religious beliefs were also transformed in the process, with numerous local deities being replaced by universal religions claiming that one deity ruled the entire world. The tendency to believe in a single deity may have reflected a greater awareness of the world, which arose from trade and military contact with other lands and peoples.

The use of animal power, such as these bulls plowing a rice paddy in Indonesia, increases the amount of land that humans can cultivate, thus enabling fewer people to produce more food.

[2] I am indebted to Zaret (1981) for bringing this idea to my attention.

The combination of rulers, military elites, and surplus is associated with greatly increased warfare and tendencies toward empire building. Empires in Egypt, Rome, China, and elsewhere were claimed by societies with dominant military power. Once conquered, however, new territories posed organizational and administrative problems that rulers sought to handle with a growing number of state officials. The ability to read, write, and count was important for state officials, so that they could collect taxes properly and communicate with the empire's home base. These skills were generally limited to the sons of the wealthy, since they were the only ones who could afford the time and the tutors needed to learn such skills.

In agrarian societies such as those of ancient Egypt (3100 B.C. to 1085 B.C.) and the Roman Empire, the class structure became increasingly complex. Besides the rulers and the ruled, there were a growing array of state officials and military commanders and a thriving class of merchants, who were often more wealthy than even high state officials. Greater complexity in the class structure was reflected in marriage practices. Increasingly, marriage took on political as well as economic significance, as parents tried to solidify their positions in the social structure by making good matches for their children.

The era of agrarian revolution—which began with a number of highly significant innovations, including the plow, the wheel, money, and writing—was followed, almost paradoxically, by a rather stagnant period in human affairs. The social anthropologist Vernon Childe (1964) suggests that this stagnation may have resulted from the structured social inequality in society. Rulers lost touch with the technology of their times, in part because of their scorn for physical labor. The producers, who had the knowledge to make innovations, knew that the benefits would be enjoyed mainly by the rulers. Therefore they had little motivation to try to improve on the processes they were using. Industrialization, however, represented a dramatic return to innovation.

### Industrialized Societies

Industrialization replaces human or animal energy and labor with machines and new energy sources such as water power, steam, electricity, and oil. The industrial revolution began in England in the mid-1700s. Hand spinning wheels and looms were replaced by increasingly efficient mechanical devices for spinning and weaving. By the 1850s, iron, steam, and machine technologies were applied successfully to transportation, and a national railroad network developed in England. It reduced the costs of shipping heavy commodities and facilitated trade. Similar advances were made in water transport.

The combined forces of industrialization and political revolution that shook western Europe in the eighteenth and nineteenth centuries profoundly affected European social structures. The supreme authority of the church was shattered, and family structure was deeply wrenched by the increasing separation of family and work. Whereas the household was once the center of work for most families, industrialization greatly undermined its importance as a center of economic production. The massive size, weight, and cost of steam-powered spinning and weaving machines required that factories be built. Factories needed plentiful supplies of labor living nearby, so more and more factories were built in cities. Cities also sprang up around outlying factories when factory owners built cheap, substandard housing to attract workers. Many rural dwellers moved to cities in the hope of improving their lives.

These developments had their social and human costs, however. The growth of factories and urbanization created new social problems. Migrations to cities cut social ties with kin and village. Individuals who had been well integrated into a kinship and community group at home found themselves without the social support and social control such ties provide. Workers spent long hours under dismal and often dangerous working conditions, and they returned to equally dreary quarters at night. Sickness, drunkenness, crime, and vice were rampant. The immediate benefits of technology and industrialization were invisible to those working in the factories and coal mines in the early years of the industrial revolution.

Once productive machinery was built and owned by a limited number of individuals, other individuals had only their labor to sell in the marketplace. They owned neither land nor the expensive machinery needed to produce cloth or anything else. Owners paid workers very low wages. In Britain, as in the United States later on, industrialization and capitalism went hand in hand. Over time, however, some of the gains came to be shared by workers as well as owners.

The period from 1900 to 1940 in both Europe and the United States witnessed the expansion of the automotive, electrical, oil, telephone, and chemical industries. During and after World War II, the aviation industry expanded, which fanned aluminum production. Plastics, electronics (including computers), and nuclear technology also emerged during this time. By 1969, technical developments had reached the point where a passenger-carrying spacecraft could be launched from the earth, fly to the moon, and circle the moon while a smaller lunar module detached itself from the larger craft and landed on the moon, enabling two American astronauts to get out and walk around. From horse and wagon to lunar module in slightly over three hundred years—such has been the speed and extent of the industrial revolution. Throughout this time, the division of labor became ever more specialized, with new occupations developing steadily. Technical innovations continued, the amount of knowledge and information exploded, and methods of transportation and communication improved.

Some observers suggest that we are on the brink of a new era. The industrial world was able to increase agricultural and manufacturing productivity by tapping a new source of cheap energy. The wealth generated was spread among considerable numbers of the population of industrialized nations at a time when birth rates were declining. The result was a tremendous upsurge in the standard of living of most inhabitants of industrial societies. But that prosperity rested on nonrenewable energy sources. When the price of energy soared in the late 1970s, many people's standard of living declined. Although conservation and new exploration have slowed the trend, the longer-term prospect is that oil production will peak in 1995 and coal production in 2100 (Hubert, 1976). How much this will depress living standards depends on how quickly societies convert to alternative energy sources (Harris, 1977, pp. 282–283). We are entering the computer age, but computers depend on electricity which often depends on fossil fuels. How societies adapt to such changes depends on both technology and culture.

Astronauts flying from the earth to the moon and back represent the extent to which industrialization and technology have magnified the reach of humans into their environment.

## WHAT IS CULTURE?

*A group of Arab oil workers sent to Texas for training found American teaching methods impersonal. Several Japanese workers at a U.S. manufacturing plant had to learn how to put courtesy aside and interrupt conversations when there was trouble. Executives of a Swiss-based multinational couldn't understand why its American managers demanded more autonomy than their European counterparts.*

*Jose Carlos Villates, a business manager for animal health products at American Cyanamid Co., also had a problem with office protocol. Back in Puerto Rico and the Dominican Republic, where he was raised, business people would begin meetings with relaxed chitchat. At the company's headquarters in Wayne, NJ, though, he says he picks up "signals or body language" that Americans find such sociability time wasting. But even after 15 months in the U.S., Mr. Villates feels uncomfortable plunging abruptly into business. "It strikes us as cold-blooded," he says.*

*"Most people think that culture is manners, food, dress, arts and crafts," says Clifford Clarke, president of IRI International, a Redwood City, CA, consulting company. "They don't realize that how you motivate a guy is culturally determined. Every managerial task is culturally determined." [Bennett, 1986, p. 33]*

Even a definition of culture depends on culture. In the German, Scandinavian, and Slavic language groups, the word "culture" tends to mean a particular way of life, whether of a people, a time period, or a group. But in Italian and French, the word refers more to art, learning, and a general process of human development (Williams, 1976a, p. 81). Both meanings exist today as the word is used in English. It is helpful to distinguish so-called high culture (classical music, opera, ballet, art, literature, and so forth) from all processes and products of human activity. High culture is associated with class distinctions and is sometimes put down with the affected pronunciation "culchah" (Williams, 1976). We will use the term culture in its more general social sense to mean the customs of a group or a society.

**Culture** refers to all the symbolic and socially learned aspects of human society. Material culture includes things, technology, and the arts. Nonmaterial culture includes language and other symbols, knowledge, skills, values, beliefs, and customs. Culture has a certain durability. This does not mean it is unchanging; culture changes constantly. Indeed, it is like a living, breathing entity. Only the rate of change varies from one society to another. But there is an important historical dimension to it that cannot be ignored. Culture has a certain coherence, although it may contain contradictions. Ruth Benedict (1934), in her famous book *Patterns of Culture,* referred to "cultural configurations."

When people encounter a new culture, they can see, hear, feel, and otherwise sense the existence of a culture that differs from their own. When such changes are very dramatic, they say they experience "culture shock" from the jolt of so many unfamiliar activities. It takes time to adjust to the different tempo, social styles, food, and activities. Even experienced anthropologists who have made numerous trips to study other cultures report that they feel culture shock when they return home. In the United States, visitors from the North to the South or vice versa also notice differences in tempo, politeness, language, customs, and diet. Northerners may get impatient with the apparent slowness of southern service; southerners may be shocked by what seems like northern rudeness. We tend to take culture for granted until we are confronted with differences or changes.

Although culture and society are intimately bound together, it is possible to separate them, at least conceptually. Society consists of people and their social organizations. Culture is all the socially learned behaviors, beliefs, feelings, and values the members of a group or society experience. It includes customs and language. It affects how people interact, the meanings they place on different interactions, and how interactions are organized. The members of a society are like the actors in a play, and culture is like the script they follow (or do not in some cases).

The capacity to create, transmit, and modify culture dramatically distinguishes humans from animals. Animals appear to depend on instincts, imitative social learning, or trial and error for solving their survival problems. Humans rely much more on cultural prescriptions. If culture distinguishes humans from animals, it is important to consider the similarities between us and animals as well as the unique features of human life.

*Cultural differences in the workplace can lead to misunderstandings unless people learn to understand the special values and customs of others.*

## HUMAN UNIQUENESS

Which biological traits do we share with other animals and which represent unique features? We are born and we die. Unlike humans, most animals appear to be unaware of the fate that awaits them. Humans—like our closest relatives, the great apes—are a sociable species, preferring to live in groups rather than alone. Primate research suggests that socially learned behavior helps apes survive (DeVore, 1965). Like apes, we interact with one another often and enjoy being affectionate. We have unusually large brains, which have grown dramatically in size during the last 3 million years of evolution (Wilson, 1975a). The increasing size of the brain has meant ever-increasing intelligence for members of the species, leading to increasingly complex culture and technology and less reliance on instincts. Many insects and animals inherit instincts for behaving in certain ways. **Instincts** are genetically determined patterns of behavior triggered by certain conditions and over which animals have little or no control. Beavers, for example, have an instinctual response to cut down trees with their teeth. If, however, they cut through the trunk of a tree and it does not fall because its branches are caught in the branches of other trees, the beavers will start chewing all over again. Their instincts tell them to chew until the tree falls. For humans, culture and reasoning greatly outweigh instinctual bases for behavior.

We have very useful hands that are strong, precise, and skillful. Having an opposing thumb means that we can grasp, grip, and manipulate in ways few other species can. This allows us to make and then use all kinds of tools and implements.

Human feet, legs, and backs have evolved in such a way that we can walk and run easily in an upright position, something most animals are unable to do for any length of time. Human females can have sexual intercourse any time during the year, rather than being limited to a particular period of female "heat" or estrus. This year-round potential for sexual activity increases the chances that humans will form relatively lasting social-sexual relationships. These relationships are particularly important in view of the long period of human infant dependency. Human infants need care from others for a number of years to meet their physical needs and to learn their culture. Finally, along with our primate forebears, we are very talkative.

The combination of large brains and useful hands has enabled humans to adapt to widely varying geographical locations. Humans live more widely and more densely than any other mammal species on earth. The inventions of our brains, hands, and tongues can be passed along to our descendants. Each generation, in turn, can adapt or modify existing cultural forms and continue the never-ending process of cultural creation.

## CULTURAL UNIVERSALS

All human societies appear to share certain cultural features, although the particular forms they take differ dramatically. These are called **cultural universals** and include the use of language and other symbols, the existence of norms and values, and the tension between ethnocentrism (the attitude that one's own culture is superior to all others) and cultural relativism (the view that the customs and ideas of a society must be viewed within the context of that society).

### Common Cultural Elements

After comparing 220 societies, anthropologist George Murdock identified cultural elements found in all of them. These universal elements include age grading, athletic sports, cooking, dancing, folklore, hospitality, hygiene, joking, mourning, personal names, and soul concepts. Although these cultural features exist in all the societies studied, their particular content varied widely. Every culture, for example, has symbols and language, but there are many different symbolic meanings and languages.

#### Symbols

More than any other animal, humans fill the physical and social world with symbolic meanings. A **symbol** is any object or sign that produces a shared social response. A piece of rock,

*Kilts worn by Scottish men have never symbolized feminininity, showing the importance of the social meaning of symbols.*

an animal, the moon, a cross, a glance at another person, and a piece of paper wth the word "dollar" on it are all imbued with various meanings and sometimes mythical or magical qualities. The symbolic meaning placed upon something may be separated from its physical aspects.

Symbols share several characteristics. First, they are socially developed. The sun may symbolize strength to you or to me, but unless that meaning is shared with others it will not become a significant symbol. So, one feature of symbols is that they are socially shared. Black symbolizes mourning for many Americans, but New Guinea women paint themselves white to show grief. Second, symbols may have more than one meaning. A stack of hundred-dollar bills can symbolize wealth, happiness, greed, materialism, and a host of other things, depending on the meanings people attribute to it. So all meanings are not equally shared, and a variety of symbols can arise from an object like a stack of bills. Third, there is a certain amount of cultural arbitrariness in the meanings assigned to particular symbols, and symbols may differ in time and place. The skirt, for instance, has traditionally symbolized femininity in Western cultures, although Scottish men proudly wear kilts without being considered feminine. Many women wear pants and are considered no less feminine, and the meaning of long hair on men has varied widely.

One of the features of a highly diverse society such as ours is that people share different sym-

bolic universes. That is, the symbolic meaning your group agrees on for something may not be shared by other groups. Wearing jeans may symbolize that someone is unpretentious, unconcerned with displaying material success, desirous of comfort, unhappy doing laundry, and a host of other meanings you could supply. Designer jeans, however, introduced an element of status competition into casual dressing. In our society there is less and less common meaning attached to cultural symbols. It used to be that driving a large car was a sign of success. But is it still? If you asked 20 different people, I think you would get 20 different responses. The size of one's car no longer means the same thing to everyone in our society.

### Language

Of all the symbols humans use, language is the most highly developed. **Language** consists of spoken or written symbols combined into a system and governed by rules. It enables us to share with others our ideas, thoughts, experiences, discoveries, fears, plans, and desires. Written language extends our capacity to communicate through time and space. Without language, it would be difficult to transmit culture, and culture would develop exceedingly slowly. Language is a critical key to understanding any culture and any society. It is the secret to reaching beyond ourselves, which is the heart of our social existence. A person may be a superb athlete, mechanic, or cook, but teaching or talking about that skill requires language. Otherwise, learning can only come from imitating actions.

Yet the importance of language goes even further. Two American linguists, Edward Sapir and Benjamin Whorf, argue that language shapes the way people think and the way they view reality. If this is the case, it helps to explain why both the civil rights movement and the women's movement have been concerned about the use of language. Contrast the words "boy" and "man" with respect to what they say about a person's role and stature in society. Similarly, use of the words "girl" and "woman" has been important to the women's movement. Not only are roles and statuses reflected in language, but language seems to shape a person's identity and sense of self. Language concepts can raise mental fences around the conceptions of self available to us and to others. The concept of "old" as applied to people in our society, for example, has generally implied that "old" people do not want or need sex, despite recent research showing that they desire and enjoy sexual relations of all kinds (Starr and Weiner, 1980). And by excluding sex as part of the identity of an "old" person, older people and the people around them may not be able to address their sexual needs.

The Sapir-Whorf hypothesis that language characteristics influence thought has been extensively criticized. Some argue that thought and culture shape language. Others hold that the iron grip of language over all our thought categories has not been demonstrated. However, people tend to see natural objects, such as colors, in the terms language provides. An artist may have words for 14 shades of red and "see" them accordingly, whereas the Jale of New Guinea

*Language, especially written language, is the most highly developed form of human symbol. When young people learn to read and write, they become full cultural participants in their society. This is why this young girl in India is struggling to learn to write.*

name and "see" the world only in terms of warm and cold color categories. Even social perceptions seem to be shaped by language, as research on teachers' expectations for "gifted" and "slow" learners suggests. In short, language does in some ways shape how we see the world and makes it difficult, although not impossible, to experience the world in alternative ways. Becoming aware of how language may limit us is the first step toward breaking free of those limits.

Language also provides clues to what a culture considers important. Farmers have many words to describe various types of soil, reflecting its importance to them. Our culture has numerous slang words for money (including "bread," "dough," "jack," "simoleons," "kale," "greenbacks," "bucks," "bones," "wad," "shekels," and "do-re-mi"), suggesting the importance of money in our culture.

Language also identifies the members of a group. If you "know the language," whether of football, electronics, or human physiology, you are a long way toward being "in" the group. If you do not know the language, you probably will not be accepted as part of the inner group and also may not know what is going on. (This applies to sociology as well. You need to learn enough sociological "lingo" to pass the course you are taking.) Finally, language can obscure as well as clarify. For example, the phrase "nuclear events" refers to *accidents* in nuclear power plants but plays down their importance and removes them from the realm of human responsibility.

## Norms

Suppose you were taking a seminar with 20 other students and you circulated a list with each person's name and telephone number on it. Then assume that several members of the seminar began receiving obscene phone calls, apparently from someone in the class. How would you feel if you received a call? Probably you would feel outraged. Your feelings would be intensified because the caller would be violating a social norm. **Norms** refer to shared rules about acceptable and unacceptable social behavior. In this case, the phone numbers were shared to advance the work of the seminar, not to aid obscene phone callers.

All societies have norms, although their content differs from one society to the next. In rural West Africa today, if a stranger knocks on the door in the middle of the night, the norm is to invite the person in and offer food and a place to sleep (if only on the floor). In downtown Chicago, this would not be the normative response to a midnight knock. Norms provide guidelines about what is "acceptable" or appropriate behavior in a given situation. They go beyond suggesting what people *might* do, however, in that they also contain an aspect of what they *ought* to do. Quite often they come to believe that they *should* behave in a certain way. Probably most of us feel that we ought to avoid talking out loud to ourselves in a crowded public place.

Norms apply to more than behavior, however. Even emotions are saddled and bridled by norms, as Hochschild (1983) points out. We think to ourselves, "I ought to feel grateful for all they have done for me," or "I shouldn't have felt so angry," suggesting that we are comparing our feelings to a normative standard. These examples suggest that norms, like other features of culture, slip into people's minds in subtle ways.

We may be unaware of how strongly norms weave together the fabric of social life. In an effort to unearth these normative threads, Harold Garfinkel had his students set out to disrupt the usual flow of social life. He asked them to do such things as go home for dinner with their parents and act as though they were strangers visiting there for the first time: "Yes, thank you, Mrs. Jones, I would like to have some more lima beans." "Mr. Jones, how is your bowling team doing?" It took very little of this "bizarre" behavior for the parents to react: "What's wrong with you? Are you sick? Are you playing games with us? Why are you behaving this way?" Some became rather heated.

In another experiment, researchers Stanley Milgram and John Sabini (1978) asked students to ride a crowded bus or subway during rush hour when there were no seats left. They were to approach a stranger and ask if they could please have his or her seat. This was such counternormative behavior that many students found they could not do it. They simply felt "too awkward." It was easier for them to ask for the seat when they could give a reason: "I

feel dizzy," or "I just got out of the hospital." Other passengers were more likely to give up their seats when presented with a "legitimate" reason. Otherwise, you can imagine the reactions the students received. Part of their discomfort in asking undoubtedly arose from anticipating those reactions. And that discomfort is a clue to the existence of a social norm.

Four kinds of norms can be identified, depending on the degree of conformity that is required. **Folkways** require less conformity; they are social customs to which people generally conform although they feel little pressure to do so. We are expected to wear matching socks (if we wear socks), to wear clothes without holes in them, to speak when introduced to someone, to shake hands when someone offers a hand, and to eat at least some of what is offered us when we are guests at dinner. Violations of folkways do not usually arouse moral outrage. People who do not accept the social customs of the group may be considered odd or sloppy, but they are not likely to be arrested for their behavior.

**Mores,** on the other hand, are strongly held social norms. Their violation arouses a sense of moral outrage. A naked baby on an American beach may be violating a folkway (to some), but a naked man on anything except a nude beach is violating mores and indeed is breaking the law in most communities. Violating mores excites strong public reaction and usually involves legal sanctions as well, since most are written into formal law. **Laws** are norms that have been formally enacted by a political body. Preliterate societies do not usually have formal laws or lawyers. Laws may be enforced by the police, military, or some other state organization.

A **taboo** is a strongly prohibited social practice. It is the strongest form of social norm. The most nearly universal rule in all known human cultures is the **incest taboo**—the prohibition of sexual intercourse between fathers and daughters, mothers and sons, brothers and sisters, and sometimes other relatives as well. The wide appearance of this taboo suggests that it may have developed early in human evolution. Just because something is taboo, however, does not mean it never happens. Indeed, there is growing evidence that the incest taboo is violated fairly frequently (although no definitive statistics exist on how often incest occurs). The taboo nature of incest is evident in the fact that people do not practice it openly. Moreover, they are often embarrassed or ashamed to discuss what happened to them. The existence of such feelings signals the presence of a taboo behavior.

Social norms are supported by sanctions. A **sanction** is a reward or penalty directed at desired or undesired behavior. Negative sanctions include disapproving looks, negative gossip, social shunning, imprisonment, and the electric chair. Positive sanctions include prizes such as the Nobel award, praise, applause, esteem, financial rewards, and smiles. The effectiveness of a sanction depends on how the receiver feels about it and about the people giving it. Electrocution is fairly universal in its negative impact, whereas prizes may mean little or a great deal to the people winning them.

The type of sanction helps us to distinguish between folkways and mores. Violations of folkways usually receive only informal social sanctions, such as stares, snide remarks, or other signs of disapproval. Mores are usually backed up with formal sanctions. Taboos vary as to whether or not they have formal sanctions. Norms may be socially sanctioned, as in the case of norms about appropriate dress, or legally sanctioned, as in the case of norms against beating up people and stealing their money. Norms are rooted in social values.

## Values

Norms are concrete applications of values in everyday life. **Values** are strongly held general ideas people share about what is good or bad, desirable or undesirable. Values are more general than norms in that they do not prescribe specific behaviors for concrete situations. In fact, the same values may support a number of

*Folkways are social customs to which people generally conform, like the styles of dress observed by these girls in a Montana Hutterite community. Hutterites are an Anabaptist sect which fled persecution in Europe to settle in the western United States, where they run collective farms.*

different—or even competing—norms. For example, parents who value their families may be torn between working hard in their occupations and spending more time at home. Both behaviors may be normative expressions of the underlying value of commitment to their families. Examples of values generally held in our society include freedom, justice, and individualism. The normative counterparts to these more general values are freedom of speech, equal justice before the law, and the right to privacy. Religious or humanistic values helped concentration camp prisoners to resist their captors despite the best efforts of their captors to break down their social solidarity (Pawelczynska, 1979).

A society's values are important to understand because they influence the content of both norms and laws. How can we tell what we, our neighbors, or other societies value? Sociologist Robin Williams (1960) suggests a number of indicators of the choices people make that may point to their underlying values. Patterns of money expenditure, directions of interest (in literature, movies, music, and other arts), and direct statements all provide clues to what individuals, groups, or societies value. Some families, for example, spend their extra money on cars, boats, furniture, or clothing, whereas others may spend it on books, education, and concerts. These choices reflect different sets of cultural values. To these can be added time allocation (how much time people spend on various activities) as another indicator of how highly they value the activities or the goals those activities represent. Value statements may reflect what people see as **ideal,** whereas time or money expenditures may be better indicators of their **real values.**

In any given situation more than one value may be operating. A desire for efficiency in business clashes with a growing value on humanizing the work setting. You may value friendship and also value getting your schoolwork done. Often these values compete for one's time and attention. Many societies experience tension and even conflict over competing values. Developing nations often experience conflict over preserving valued traditions and modernizing. Industrialized countries face conflicts between the values of equality and rewarding merit.

## American Culture and Values

One of the earliest studies of U.S. culture and values was conducted by the Frenchman Alexis de Tocqueville (1835). To him, one of the notable features of American life was the emphasis on equality between people. He observed that Americans do not like people who "put on airs" and try to seem better than others. They like people to be like themselves. The anthropologist Clyde Kluckhohn (1954) calls this tendency the "cult of the average man." It is reflected in the use of humor to sanction people who try to be what they are not and also in press stories that carry detailed descriptions of the problems of people in public life. This tendency may be related to the way we personalize issues and achievements, whether they are good or bad. We tend to blame inflation or recession on the president, making him personally responsible. Similarly, if someone gains great wealth, the media analyze the person's character to see what propelled him or her to riches. Despite the emphasis on equality in American life, there is the countertendency to glorify, publicize, and even imitate successful people. Americans are both attracted and repelled by nobility, celebrity, glamour, and the elite. The absence of nobility and the relative equality of position in America leads people to be "forever brooding over advantages they do not possess . . . and restless in the midst of abundance," suggested Tocqueville (1835) in his nineteenth-century observations of the American scene (vol. II, chap. XIII).

Kluckhohn (1954) saw American values as "faith in the rational, a need for moralistic rationalization, an optimistic conviction that rational effort counts, romantic individualism and the culture of the common man, high valuation of change . . . and the conscious quest for pleasure" (p. 199).

Kluckhohn seems to have captured traits that existed in the 1950s. By focusing on a longer time span and on more specific cultural values, other analysts have noted changes in American values during the past 50 years. These changes are summarized in Table 3.1 on pages 3-2, 3-3.

Americans have become obsessed with the self at the expense of public life, suggests Richard Sennett. He sees the source of this shift as lying in changes in capitalism, specifically the

IMAGES OF THE CHANGING AMERICAN EXPERIENCE, 1930s TO 1980s.

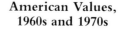

# SUMMARY TABLE
## 3.1

*Changing American Values*

| | American Values, 1930s to 1950s | American Values, 1960s and 1970s | American Values, 1980s |
|---|---|---|---|
| **Content** | Self-denial<br>Emphasis on work<br>Success as something to be achieved<br>Future planning, saving | Focus on self, self-expression<br>Stress on leisure time off the job<br>Success as something to which one is entitled<br>Living for today, loss of confidence in the future | Ethic of commitment<br>Groping toward a balance between competition and cooperation, individualism and commitment<br>Search for deeper relations with people and things, reverential thinking, creation of community, and deepened concern with both past and future |

| | | | |
|---|---|---|---|
| **Origins** | Forged in the austerity of the Depression and the frugality of World War II | Begun in the individualism sparked by the industrial and French revolutions. Fanned by postwar prosperity, advertising, and the rapid inflation of the 1970s | Yearning for meaning and coherence in life, not just achievement<br>Realization that instrumental and individual pursuits alone are not satisfying<br>Realization that the goal of being uniquely successful and admired risks destroying the chance to live in a society that is really worth living in |

| | **American Values, 1930s to 1950s** | **American Values, 1960s and 1970s** | **American Values, 1980s** |
|---|---|---|---|
| **Indicators** | High rates of saving, modest use of debt | Shrinking savings, rising consumer debt, declining public participation in voting and public office-holding | Percent of Americans who are "searching for community" increased from 32 percent in 1973 to 47 percent in the early 1980s (Yankelovich, 1981)<br><br>Revival of religious beliefs and church attendance, especially among the strictest and most demanding denominations, such as southern Baptists<br><br>A slight decline in divorce rates |

Sources: Bell, 1976; Bellah et al., 1985; Lasch, 1979; Naisbitt, 1982; Sennett, 1974; Skelly, 1978; Yankelovich, 1978, 1981.

LOOKING FORWARD INTO THE 1990s.

movements toward mass production and mass retailing, a shift in religious beliefs away from an otherworldly focus to a center on this world, and the loss of boundaries between public and private life. As a result, Sennett believes that Americans have lost the capacity to work with relative strangers in the interests of larger social institutions (Sennett, 1974).

Daniel Bell (1976) echoes the theme of preoccupation with self. He sees the central principle of modern culture as being the "expression and remaking of the self in order to achieve self-realization and self-fulfillment" (p. 13). Capitalism has developed a culture, he argues, that contradicts future capitalist development. By encouraging the push toward individualism that began in the eighteenth century, Western culture and capitalism have encouraged individual self-expression, self-indulgence, and anti-intellectual ways of knowing and experiencing the world. These tendencies run counter to the needs of capitalism for rationality, hierarchy, bureaucracy, efficiency, self-denial, and hard work. These sociologists suggest that cultural values

are shifting in relatively short time periods, and much faster than they did in traditional societies.

In the 1980s a number of social scientists began sensing that a new trend was emerging. Resulting in part from a reaction to the focus on self that proved to be basically unsatisfying and perhaps from a fear of AIDS, people have begun to express a yearning for meaning and coherence in their lives, not just individualistic achievement (Bellah et al., 1985; Yankelovich, 1981). Although limited in their thinking by a language of psychology and individualism, people are beginning to express a need to balance the process of separation and individuation with a renewal of commitment and community, note Bellah (1985) and his associates. Yankelovich (1981) calls this the new ethic of commitment. Some preliminary indicators of the feelings people expressed in their interviews may be the revival of religious belief, church membership and church attendance, and a decline in divorce rates. Whether this cultural trend continues remains to be seen. These changes in American culture and variations in other cultures suggest

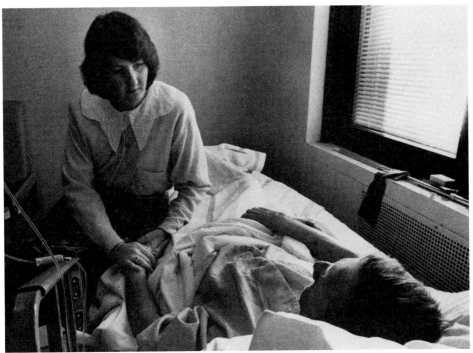

*Several social scientists suggest that there has been a renewal of commitment and community in American culture in recent years. Here a social worker is talking to a blind AIDS patient, helping him to make his burial plans.*

that cultural values and practices may change quite rapidly, especially in an era marked by structural changes and rapid communication.

Even when they have conflicting values, though, most societies have a tendency to see their own values as superior to those of other societies.

## Ethnocentrism

The tendency to see one's own culture as superior to all others is called **ethnocentrism.** At its most extreme, ethnocentrism involves taking one's own culture for granted and being unaware of the existence of any culture, values, behaviors, or beliefs besides one's own. In a somewhat less extreme form, it is the tendency to see one's culture as superior to all other cultures, even though one is aware that other cultures and societies exist. Ethnocentric people tend to judge all other cultures by the standards of their own and to see them as inferior, unnatural, or wrong when they diverge. An American oil company executive, for instance, expressed disgust over the way Arab workers in the desert would stop working for an entire day if someone they knew came along. From the American's ethnocentric viewpoint, work was much more important than being sociable. To the Arab, however, whose cultural values were shaped by centuries of dealing with the dangers of the desert, "a friend in the desert is much more important than work."

*Ethnocentrism is the tendency to see one's own culture as superior to others. In its extreme form it involves hostility to other peoples and cultures. These young Nazi demonstrators in Chicago are asserting white power in a multiracial city and society.*

## Cultural Relativism

**Cultural relativism** is the opposite of ethnocentrism. In this view, no belief, practice, behavior, or custom is assumed to be inherently good or bad, right or wrong. Instead, cultural practices are assessed in terms of how they work within a particular culture as a whole. Do various cultural practices contradict each other? Are the features of the culture highly integrated? What are the major cultural configurations of a particular society? How do they compare with those of other societies? These are some of the sociological questions we can ask about culture.

In a society with numerous ethnic groups, for example, sociologists may try to understand why some groups value large families while others prefer having no children. The sociologist may personally prefer one position and even make a moral judgment about what he or she thinks is better. It is important, however, to try to separate one's analysis of the causes and consequences of a cultural feature from one's moral evaluation of it. By becoming aware of personally held values and norms, we can better understand how they affect our reactions to other cultures. Some people may find cultural practices that appeal to them in other societies—for example, the greater social cooperation shown by Native American children or the sexual permissiveness of the Trobriand Islanders of New Guinea (Wax and Wax, 1971).

## CULTURAL VARIATION

Within the general cultural similarities found in many societies, there are vast differences in what people eat, what they believe, and how they behave. The Dutch, Eskimos, and Japanese eat raw fish; Americans usually eat fish cooked if at all.

The very term "American" is ethnocentric because members of U.S. society have taken for themselves the more general geographic term that also applies to Canadians, Mexicans, Central Americans, and all South Americans. Despite the fact that these other nationalities live in parts of the Americas, we residents of the United States seem to be saying that we are the only "true" Americans.

The Chinese like dog meat but loathe cow milk; we like both cow milk and meat but do not eat dogs. The Masai of East Africa drink both milk and cow blood. Clearly, although hunger is an underlying biological drive, the tastes people develop to satisfy hunger are culturally acquired.

Like eating habits, sexual preferences are culturally influenced. In an extensive survey of cross-cultural sexual practices, Ford and Beach (1951) found that societies ranged from permissive to restrictive in their treatment of sexuality. Restrictive societies try to keep children from learning anything about sex, and they check any spontaneous sexual activities. For example, the Ainaye (a technologically simple, peaceful, monogamous tribe in Brazil) and the Ashanti (a complex society in Ghana) forbid children to masturbate. By contrast, in permissive societies such as those in the Pacific Islands, both boys and girls freely engage in autoerotic and heterosexual play, including oral-genital contacts and imitative coitus (Katchadourian and Lunde, 1972).

Economic activities also vary. Some societies stress acquisition and the display of wealth (perhaps U.S. society more than most). Others, such as the Kwakiutl Indians of the Pacific Northwest, hold great ceremonies (called *potlatches*) for the purpose of giving away their possessions to others. The more they can give away, the higher their status. In some societies, wealth is indicated by the number of wives a man can support or by how fat family members

are. In other societies, wealth is related to how slender family members are or how hefty their bank accounts. Members of Chinese communes and Israeli *kibbutzim* share valued tools, resources, and goods, retaining only a few personal possessions as private property. In other societies, virtually all property is privately owned.

Within the same society, different subcultures may exist. A **subculture** refers to the values, attitudes, behaviors, and life-styles of a social group that is distinct from but related to the dominant culture of a national society. The concept assumes the existence of a clearly identifiable and agreed upon dominant culture, but the fragmentation of contemporary U.S. culture, for example, makes it difficult to identify such a dominant culture. Despite this problem with the concept, sociologists use it to highlight the way many ethnic groups—Japanese-Americans, Italian-Americans, Mexican-Americans, and Jewish-Americans—may have subcultural identities that distinguish them from other ethnic groups in the United States. At the same time, they are also members in various legal and cultural senses of the larger U.S. society.

Sociologists do not agree on how distinctive cultural patterns need to be in order to form a separate subculture. Although most would agree that various ethnic groups have distinctive subcultures, the term has also been used to refer to the social patterns of adolescent street gangs and rock musicians and of various occupations and social classes. The anthropologist Charles Valentine (1971) suggests that many individuals are **bicultural**—that is, they are able to understand and function well in more than one cultural group. Black Americans and Hispanics, for instance, may enjoy the food, music, and speech of their subculture but also understand and function well in the white culture that predominates in the United States.

Some subcultures are not merely different from the larger culture of a society but stand in sharp opposition to it. A **counterculture** is defined as "a set of norms and values of a group that sharply contradicts the dominant norms and values of the society of which that group is a part" (Yinger, 1977, p. 833). Various religious cults (such as the Hare Krishna), drug-oriented groups, or political radicals may all develop a counterculture. Yinger believes that the changes in values and norms desired by countercultures cannot proceed far without parallel changes in social structure and character.

Vast differences in food preferences, sexual behavior, economic activity, and subcultures call for explanations. Three major explanations for cultural variation have been offered: the ecological view, the functionalist view, and the Marxian view.

## The Ecological View

The **ecological view** suggests that climate, food and water supplies, and the presence or absence of threatening enemies influence the evolution of various cultural practices that help people adapt to the environment. More specifically, according to anthropologist Marvin Harris (1979), how people produce food and other necessities explains the origin and development of many cultural practices.

Harris (1974) examined the tribal custom of the potlatch in terms of its ecological significance. The intent of a potlatch was to give away or even to destroy more wealth than one's rival could. The potlatch was a magnificent feast celebrating a major social event such as a marriage. A chief would display urns of food, copper pots, woven mats, smoked fish, whale oil, and anything else of value he had. Then he would press these lavish gifts on his guests, including rival chiefs. The more a chief could give away, the higher his prestige and the more obligated his guests and rivals were. The only way they could get out of his debt was by holding an even more magnificent potlatch themselves (Mauss, 1954).

These competitive feasts were practiced by the Kwakiutl Indians in the Pacific Northwest and by tribes in New Guinea and the Solomon Islands. To prepare for the potlatch, a chief and his supporters caught and dried extra fish, collected berries, and accumulated animal skins, blankets, fish oil, and other valuables. The wealth to be given away was arranged in neat piles and counted by official gift counters. Harris explains this status rivalry as serving the economic system by ensuring that a greater level of wealth was produced and distributed. He believes that when everyone had equal access to the means of subsistence, the competitive feasts

helped keep the labor force from slacking off and being content with levels of productivity that offered no margin of safety for crises such as crop failures. In the absence of political institutions that could integrate separate villages into a viable economic framework, competitive feasting served to pool the productive efforts of a larger population than that of any single village. If one village had a poor year for fishing, its people could benefit from the better luck of another village. The competitive thrust of the feasts assured that food and other valuables would be transferred from richer to poorer villages (Harris, 1974).

Thus an otherwise apparently bizarre custom becomes explainable in terms of how it raises productivity and distributes wealth. Like the functional explanation of cultural variation, the ecological approach runs the risk of concluding that whatever exists must be "right" because it is adaptive or functional for the society. But the sheer range of cultural alternatives suggests that a wide variety of "functional equivalents" can and do exist. Basic needs may be met in a wide variety of ways.

## The Functionalist View

Cultural variations have often been explained in terms of the different functions they serve in the society in which they are found. Basically, the functionalist approach assumes that society has a tendency to maintain a state of equilibrium and that various cultural elements play a role in restoring or maintaining the equilibrium. Early anthropologists such as A. R. Radcliffe-Brown and Bronislaw Malinowski found this view useful in understanding otherwise seemingly strange customs in the isolated societies they studied.

As Malinowski (1926) said, functionalist theory aims to explain social facts by their function in society—that is, by the way they work within the entire system of culture. Anthropologists developing functionalist ideas, however, tended to study nonliterate, tightly knit, rather small societies. It is questionable whether the concept of functional unity can be transferred to more complex, literate societies (Merton, 1957). Religion, for example, may be said to contribute to the functional unity of society by developing common values and ends. But when this function is transplanted from nonliterate, simple societies to literate, complex industrial societies, it tends to overlook the possibility that religion may serve to splinter and divide societies (Merton, 1957). Consider the deep religious conflict in Northern Ireland, conflicts between Christians, Jews, and Muslims in Lebanon, and numerous other examples of religion serving as a basis for cultural and social division within a society. The functionalist view may suggest that some form of religion (or its functional equivalent) will exist in a society to deal with the universal problems of illness, death, and the hope for an afterlife. But the exact form religion takes may vary widely. The functionalist view is not able to explain, for instance, why religion takes such different forms.

## The Marxian View

The Marxian approach to culture differs from functionalism in several important respects. First, Marxians suggest that functionalist sociologists stress the independent importance of culture too much. An extreme version of this view, **cultural determinism,** sees the nature of a society as determined by the ideas and values of the people living in it. This view ignores the origin of those ideas and their possible relation to forms of economic production. Beliefs are treated as far too independent of other aspects of society.

Marxians suggest that culture is created by dominant groups in society who use cultural ideas and values to advance their own interests. Far from being functional for all members of society, culture thus serves as a means of domination for some. Clearly, not all forms of culture fall into this category. It is not a matter of cultural domination, for instance, whether a red or a green light means stop, but only that the same color be consistently and widely used. Nevertheless, although some cultural features are clearly a matter of convenience for all, it is important to consider the question raised by the Marxian perspective: Do certain groups favor particular beliefs or practices especially strongly? For example, the claim that Scholastic Aptitude

Tests (SATs) reflect some kind of basic academic aptitude, rather than cultural and academic exposure, benefits the children of upper- and middle-class families who do well on the tests but does not help students from less advantaged backgrounds. Some cultural elements may be functional for all, whereas others clearly benefit some groups more than other groups.

Finally, functionalist and Marxian views differ in terms of how they explain cultural change. Functionalists see cultural changes as possibly arising from contact with other cultures, inventions, or internal adjustments within a culture. They tend to explain cultural change by saying that it was functional for a society, say, to change its religious practices. But the question remains—why was it functional for a society to change at that time? Functionalist answers to these questions are not always convincing. Marxians suggest that cultural variations evolve as forms of economic production change. Within each form (slavery, feudalism, or capitalism, for example) variations arise through class conflict, internal contradictions, and adaptation. By indicating such mechanisms for change, this approach suggests how cultural changes might occur.

In short, both Marxian and ecological views suggest how and why cultural changes occur. Moreover, they both see cultural change as an expected aspect of social life. Functionalism, on the other hand, tends to view cultural change as disruptive or dysfunctional for the social system. Hence functionalism seems better suited for analyzing how cultural components operate within a relatively static society than for analyzing cultural change.

## Sources of Cultural Change

Cultures may remain relatively constant for long periods of time if their ecological and population context remains relatively stable and if they have little or no contact with other cultures. However, most societies in the "global village" that is now our world are bombarded with stimuli for cultural change. As a result, cultural changes stem from a variety of sources.

1. Structural changes. Structural changes include demographic and economic changes. The

baby boom and the declining birth rates that followed it in U.S. society represent sudden and dramatic changes in the size and shape of the population, as we will see in Chapter 18. Along with major migrations like the ones experienced by the United States around the turn of the century and to a lesser degree since 1950 (see Figure 10.2), such demographic changes can produce notable cultural changes. Economic changes like the shift from a manufacturing to a service economy, the amount of economic growth in a society, and the globalization of the world economy (discussed in Chapter 18) may also promote cultural changes.

2. Invention. **Inventions** are new cultural creations; they are often produced by combining existing cultural elements in new ways. Inventions occur in all areas of material and cultural life, from the observation that corn grows better when dead fish are planted with it to the realization that representative government may work more effectively than dictatorship. Although some people may enjoy invention for its own sake, without regard to its usefulness, the old maxim "necessity is the mother of invention" captures the conditions under which inventions often occur, are adopted, and spread. The rate of invention in industrial societies has taken off in the last century like a jet plane. (See the debate on microelectronics and cultural transformation.)

3. Discovery. **Discovery** involves uncovering something that existed but was unknown. The Pacific Coast Indians discovered the existence of copper, which had both ornamental and hunting value. Imagine when humans discovered fire for the first time and realized what potential it contained. The discovery of new, dangerous, and yet untreatable diseases may lead to cultural changes. For example, sexual norms appear to be becoming more restrictive as a result of increasing concerns over sexually transmitted diseases such as AIDS.

4. Diffusion. When people of different cultures come into contact, useful inventions and discoveries are likely to be **diffused**—that is, spread from one to another group on a voluntary basis. The advantages of using fire, for example, or clay pots to hold water, could readily be seen by observers from other tribes, who could then adopt such techniques themselves.

Today in East Africa, many rural people use large plastic jugs to carry water on their heads. The light weight and unbreakable quality of plastic make it attractive to users despite the longer-term ecological consequences of using plastics. The rate of diffusion has greatly increased because of jet planes, television, and satellite communications.

5. Cultural imposition. Cultures may also be imposed by one group on another—as, for instance, when one society occupies or dominates another one. Systems of taxation, government, language, military service, and religion may then be required of people in the subjugated group. Many former European colonies in South America and Africa retain the colonial language as their official national language, although they have shed colonial rule.

6. Cultural revolution. Cultures may be imposed by some on others; they may also be resisted or opposed, as occurred in the Chinese cultural revolution or in the counterculture in the United States in the 1960s and 1970s. Cultural revolution involves the repudiation of many existing cultural elements and the substitution of new ones.

Cultural changes suggest that culture is not rigid but bends or moves in response to changing conditions and human actions. Hence people help to shape their culture at the same time that it influences them.

## CULTURE, SOCIOBIOLOGY, AND INDIVIDUALISM

### Are Individuals Trapped by Culture?

If culture powerfully influences how people learn to behave, does this mean we are somehow trapped by our culture and lose the chance for independent action? Clearly not. Culture influences us, but we also shape its direction. Culture provides us with valued strategies that have been developed by our ancestors. In this way it may offer opportunities for action as well as limitations on what we can do. But individuals retain the capacity for self-reflection. They do not always accept traditions blindly. Recently observed changes in American values suggest that things need not always be the way they are now. Other factors also help to keep us from being prisoners of culture.

Cultural relativism suggests that ours is not the only way of doing something, nor is it necessarily the best way. Cultural diversity based on the existence of many subgroups, each of which possesses somewhat different values and norms, helps to provide knowledge of alternatives and offers the possibility of finding a comfortable group or subculture. The existence of countercultures or social movements dedicated to encouraging cultural change indicates that cultural features may be changed by conscious actions.

## Sociobiology

Another hotly debated issue in social thought is the degree to which human nature is shaped by culture or is biologically determined. This old "nature versus nurture" controversy took new form with the publication in 1975 of Edward O. Wilson's (1975a) book *Sociobiology*. Wilson defines **sociobiology** as "the systematic study of the biological basis for human behavior" (p. 4). The goal of sociobiologists is to compare societies of animals and humans and to develop and test theories about the degree to which social behavior might be hereditary. Sociobiology is basically the application of Darwinian evolutionary theory to social behavior. Evolutionary theory suggests that individual organisms are selected to maximize their fitness (their ability to reproduce themselves) in a particular environment. This theory can explain a certain amount of behavior, but how can it explain altruism and self-sacrifice? Suppose a set of parents is killed defending their children from a saber-toothed tiger. This behavior, say sociobiologists, increases the chances that their genes will survive, because they have helped relatives who possess their genes to stay alive. One problem with sociobiology is that there are different levels at which behavior may be adaptive. An act may be adaptive for individuals, for their family or kin, for the group to which they belong, for the population, or for the species as a whole.

For example, hoarding the food killed in a hunt may help a hunter and his immediate family to survive, but it may also endanger the other members of his tribe, which could reduce an individual's chances of surviving at some future time. Fighting a tribe that threatens one's own tribe with destruction may lead to an individual's death, but it may also save the lives of his family and tribe. It is difficult to say which of these behaviors would be predicted by sociobiology.

Sociobiology hypothesizes that the powerful emotion underlying altruism, which appears in all human (and some animal) societies, may have evolved genetically by preserving the genes of people willing to help their relatives. Even Wilson (1975b) acknowledges, however, that the "intensity and form of altruistic acts are to a large extent culturally determined" (p. 41). In a similar vein, Wilson suggests that aggression is "an important and widespread organizing technique in human and animal societies" (p. 42). However, the human species exhibits an incredibly broad range of behavior, from peaceful to aggressive. A number of very peaceful societies have been discovered in the world, including the Tasaday of Mindanao, encountered in a dense Philippine rain forest (Nance, 1975); the Hopi Indians of the American Southwest; and the cooperative Arapesh, discovered by Margaret Mead (1935) in the South Seas. At the other end of the spectrum of human behavior are the dangerous Dobuan tribe discovered by Ruth Benedict (1934), the fierce Yanamamö tribe of Brazil (Chagnon, 1968), and the Nazi military machine in Germany during the 1940s.

Sociobiology suggests that humans have the genetic potential for a wide range of possible behaviors on a scale from very peaceful to very aggressive. But it does not claim that the particular notes played on this scale are genetically determined. Given this broad range of possible behaviors, the task for the social sciences is to identify the conditions under which peaceful behavior may be triggered and the conditions under which aggressive behavior is called forth.

Sociobiology hypothesizes very general potentials and possible constraints on human social behavior. Human behavior is widely variable but not infinitely plastic. Sociobiology amplifies the importance of identifying environmental

We are living through a major cultural transformation as a result of microelectronics—those little silicon chips that have replaced transistors, which replaced vacuum tubes. Not since the invention of the steam engine has there been a technological development with such far-reaching potential. Electricity is the closest corollary, but even the development of electric power only continued the process of mechanization initiated by steam power. Although the industrial revolution enormously enhanced the puny muscular power of humans and animals, microelectronics extend human mental capacities, thought, and symbolic communications in ways that are still barely imaginable.

Like those transformations, this new technology has touched off considerable debate about its benefits and costs. Let us consider first some indications of the impact of microelectronics on our lives. In the process, we shall note possible positive and negative consequences.

Language is a vital clue to the importance of a phenomenon. The computer, one of the major users of microelectronics, is replacing the clock and the steam engine as the defining technology and principal technological metaphor of our time, suggests David Bolter (1984) in his book *Turing's Man* (p. 40). If this is the case, we would expect to find many examples of how people use "computer talk" in their everyday lives. More generally, we should find indications that microelectronics influence the way people think about themselves. Many terms from the world of computers have entered our daily lives. For example:

### Microelectronics: Cultural Transformation for Good or for Ill?

My "buffer" is full.
We have to "debug" the plans for the party.
"I'm in an endless loop."
"My system crashed."
I've had a lot of "downtime" this week.
It's like we're "hard-wired" to each other; we understand each other so completely.

Overheard in a restaurant from a young woman who was in the process of getting a divorce, to her friend, "I have to reprogram myself to be single."

This last example suggests more than simply a new word in our language; it suggests a shift in the way we think about ourselves. In the research on people and computers described in her book *The Second Self*, Sherry Turkle (1984) found that people who work with computers begin to think about themselves and their lives in imagery related to computers. As one young woman said, "We're all programmed" (to think and behave in certain ways as a result of our upbringing), but you can always change the program "once you know how." The people Turkle interviewed saw the mind as a machine, and their personalities as programs that could be changed—an optimistic view of the self.

Turkle's path-breaking work suggests that computers are influencing the psychological and social development of children. People once thought that thinking set them apart from animals.

Now some children say that the capacity to feel is what sets them apart from machines (Turkle, 1984).

Besides language and thought, another indicator of cultural change is the formation of new statuses and roles. Two decades ago departments of computer science were small or nonexistent on college campuses. Now they are often quite large. Similarly, the positions of computer programmer, systems analyst, director of electronic data processing, director of data banks, and organizer of computer camps did not exist a short time ago.

Cultural change also affects social interactions. Nearly instantaneous interaction via microelectronics is now possible around the world. Telephones permitted this before, but now much larger amounts of data can be sent, and multiple sources of data may be considered simultaneously. At the interpersonal level, some shy high school and college students have become acquainted with persons they didn't know via computer networks; they have even dated and occasionally married each other.

Many handicapped persons find that new computer technologies help them cope with everyday life. Voice-recognition devices allow paralyzed people to control their living environments by operating appliances, dialing the phone, and writing checks. For the blind, computers can optically scan and "read" written materials and translate them into spoken words through a voice synthesizer (Semler, 1988).

Cultural change affects definitions of deviant or criminal behavior. Is it deviant when a computer hacker breaks into and overloads a university and defense department network with a virus? Is it criminal? Are professors or businesspeople who duplicate copyrighted software programs and give them to their friends deviants or criminals? The need for new definitions of deviant and criminal behavior in these areas suggests the existence of a major cultural change.

Civil libertarians note the increasing potential of computerized systems to sketch detailed electronic profiles of individual citizens. Powerful computers can link the data base of the Internal Revenue Service, credit ratings, criminal records, bank records, telephone calls, medical records, and records of drugs purchased at local pharmacies (Markoff, 1988). The number and kinds of data being computerized have increased faster than the ethics and laws determining access to such data. Computers are a prime example of technological developments outpacing cultural norms.

Other indicators of cultural transformation are the changes in major social institutions such as the family, economy, education, science, and sports. Micros may increasingly be used in families to do homework, do banking, make plane reservations, balance accounts, compute taxes, shop, and so forth. One study found that families tended to re-create their patterns of interaction around the computer. Specifically, families that tended to do many activities together also used their home computers together, whereas those who carried on separate, individual activities tended to use the home computer in independent ways (Giacquinta et al., 1984). More people may be able to work at home because of microelectronics, a change that could have profound implications for the family.

Microelectronics have also changed the economy. Not only has the design and production of new microelectronic devices been a major growth industry, but the application of micros in computer-assisted design and computer-assisted manufacturing (so-called CAD-CAM uses), robotics, political campaigns, media presentations, accounting, inventory control, customer files, and mass mailings permits greater efficiency in both large and small businesses.

In the workplace, the potential for monitoring and controlling workers is greatly enhanced when they use electronic equipment all day. The amount of non-work time can be recorded, as can mistakes. Micro devices have been placed in long-haul trucks to see if drivers speed and how long they stop.

In education, computer-assisted instruction (CAI) helps students to review material at their own pace, and simulations allow them to see on a computer screen, for example, how cell division occurs. High school students can review for the SATs on a computer or search for suitable colleges. Teachers can do their syllabi, update grade books, prepare reading lists, and do other paperwork on them.

In science, desktop computers can analyze scientific data that used to require a multimillion dollar mainframe computer. Researchers can do electronic searches of the research literature and write articles and grant proposals on a word processor. The more rapid production and dissemination of knowledge should spur more discoveries and inventions. Engineers use computers to design new microchips, and so-called artificial intelligence can approximate some of the ways people think about problems. For example, in health care, some systems of artificial intelligence can propose medical diagnoses after a given patient's symptoms are entered into the computer. High-speed computers may also help solve problems in genetic engineering, oil exploration, astronomy, particle physics, and brain functioning.

In sports, at least one manager (Davey Johnson of the New York Mets) uses a computer to form his lineup against each pitcher his team faces, so as to maximize the chances of success. He also stores information on which of his pitchers does better against which teams.

Humor is another indicator of cultural change. Numerous jokes and cartoons deal with computers. People wear T-shirts saying "To err is human, but to really foul up you need a computer." A cartoon shows a sign in a hardware store window that says, "Left to go into software."

Through changes in language, thought, and new statuses and roles, in major social institutions, and humor, we can see a major cultural transformation occurring before our very eyes.

Whether these changes bode good or ill depends on how they are applied and whom they affect. What do you think? What uses of computers have you observed and what is your assessment of their consequences? What do you think should be done about the negative possibilities?

and cultural factors that encourage, inhibit, and shape the expression of particular behaviors, such as altruism or aggression. Sociobiology does *not* suggest that certain genes directly determine particular behaviors. Nor does it suggest that whatever is in nature is adaptive.

Human biological potential and limits are enclosed in many different cultural envelopes. Genes do not tell us how to tell time, write letters, cook dinner, program computers, or do most of what we do. Much more than any other animals, humans can self-consciously modify their environment or adapt themselves to it. We can live in the desert, under the sea, or in space without waiting for natural selection or mutation to modify our biological capacities. Truly it is culture that sets us apart from all other animals.

## Summary

1. A society is a group of people with a shared and somewhat distinct culture who live in a defined territory, feel some unity, and see themselves as distinct from other peoples.

2. To survive, all societies need to solve certain basic problems, including physical subsistence, distribution, reproduction, protection, and communication. These concerns can be met in a wide variety of forms, as the major types of subsistence strategies suggest. The major subsistence strategies found in human societies are hunting and gathering, horticulture, agriculture, and industry.

3. The subsistence strategy employed by a society affects social institutions such as the family, shapes the types of authority and inequality that develop, and influences culture, religion, and social interaction.

4. Even one's definition of culture varies by culture, ranging from the way of life of a group or society to their artistic products. In this book we use the first, more general definition. Culture includes material objects like tools, homes, and art as well as nonmaterial elements such as norms, values, language, and other symbols.

5. Humans share sociability and communication with other primates but have much more highly developed brains, language capacity, and tool-using capabilities.

6. A number of common cultural features appear in all societies. These include the use of symbols and language, the existence of norms and values, and a tension between ethnocentrism and cultural relativism. The forms they take differ, however.

7. Language is one of the most important features of human society. It allows us to share ideas, plans, and feelings. Written language extends communication through time and space. Language may also limit perception of the world, but it is possible to overcome such limitations through conscious effort and analysis. Language provides clues to what a culture values and what it seeks to hide.

8. Norms are shared expectations about desirable and undesirable behavior and contain an "ought to" aspect that affects emotions as well as minds.

9. Values are more general ideas, also strongly held, about what is desirable and undesirable.

10. American cultural values may include individualism, equality, active mastery, involvement with the external world, openness, rationality, and orderliness. Despite these core values, several social observers suggest that American values have changed in recent decades, moving away in the 1960s and 1970s from self-denial, the "work ethic," and future planning toward a new focus on self, leisure, and living for today rather than for the future. In the late 1980s and 1990s, a new trend toward greater commitment and shared community may be emerging.

11. The tendency to see one's own culture, language, norms, and values as superior to others is called ethnocentrism. It may be accentuated by stress or hostility. Cultural relativism, on the other hand, means viewing cultural practices within the context of the culture in which they occur.

12. Cultural variations exist in food preferences, sexual practices, economic activities, and other social behaviors. Three explanations have been offered for these variations. The ecological view suggests that cultural differences emerge from population pressures or other environmental constraints. Functionalist theory explains social facts according to how they work within the integral system of culture. The Marxian view suggests that cultural variations emerge from changing systems of production and benefit dominant groups more than subordinate groups.

13. Rapid social changes may help individuals avoid being trapped in their culture, since things need not always be the way they are. Sources of cultural change include structural changes, invention, discovery, diffusion, cultural imposition, and cultural revolution.

14. The emerging field of sociobiology raises the question of how much of human behavior is genetically determined. While biology provides humans with a wide range of potentialities, environment and culture are the keys to behavioral variations within this range.

## KEY TERMS

agrarian societies (p. 52)
bicultural (p. 65)
counterculture (p. 65)
cultural determinism (p. 67)
cultural relativism (p. 64)
cultural universals (p. 57)
culture (p. 56)
demography (p. 49)
diffusion (p. 68)
discovery (p. 68)
ecological view (p. 66)
ethnocentrism (p. 64)
ethnography (p. 50)
folkways (p. 60)
horticultural societies (p. 52)
hunting and gathering societies (p. 50)
ideal values (p. 62)
incest taboo (p. 60)
industrialized societies (p. 54)

instinct (p. 57)
invention (p. 68)
language (p. 58)
laws (p. 60)
mores (p. 60)
nomadic (p. 52)
norms (p. 59)
pastoral societies (p. 52)
real values (p. 62)
sanction (p. 61)
society (p. 48)
sociobiology (p. 69)
subculture (p. 65)
symbol (p. 57)
taboo (p. 60)
values (p. 61)

## SUGGESTED READINGS

Bell, Daniel. 1976. *The Cultural Contradictions of Capitalism.* New York: Harper & Row. A scholarly analysis of how the conditions behind the expansion of capitalism (including advertising and installment credit) create a set of cultural attitudes that help to undermine the motivation for capital investment.

Bellah, Robert N., Richard Madsen, William M. Sullivan, Ann Swidler, and Steven M. Tipton. 1985. *Habits of the Heart.* Berkeley: University of California Press. A noteworthy study of middle-class Americans' search for meaning and commitment in the 1980s.

Hochschild, Arlie R. 1983. *The Managed Heart.* Berkeley: University of California Press. Explores the way individuals learn culturally prescribed norms to govern feelings as well as behavior.

Shkilnyk, Anastasia M. 1985. *A Poison Stronger Than Love.* New Haven, CT: Yale University Press. A moving account of how the loss of a society's means of subsistence led to the breakdown of its culture and to high rates of alcoholism.

Turkle, Sherry. 1984. *The Second Self: Computers and the Human Spirit.* New York: Simon & Schuster. A study of how computers are changing the self-conceptions of individuals.

# Social Structure, Networks, and Interactions

*When Cheryl and John entered the labor force in 1985, they found it difficult to find "good jobs." John began as a clerical worker, although he had graduated from college. Cheryl worked part time for a while, even though she preferred full-time work. Changes in the social structure of jobs in the 1980s explain their work experiences better than do their individual attitudes and behaviors.*

## SOCIAL STRUCTURE

The term **social structure** refers to patterned relationships. It includes social institutions, the division of labor, and the concepts of status and role. This chapter begins by defining and discussing these central sociological concepts. It continues by examining structured relationships between social positions, or what we call social networks. It concludes by considering the social interactions that develop among people embedded in social institutions and social networks.

### Social Institutions

The survival of every society requires that it address the problems of finding food and shelter, reproducing, protecting and rearing its young, preserving sufficient social order, and transmitting culture and values. Members of all societies develop ways of meeting these needs, and they tend to preserve the successful strategies they find. These strategies are repeated and become patterned.

Sociologists call these patterned responses institutions. An **institution** consists of statuses, roles, and norms centered around an important social concern, such as producing and distributing food or rearing children. A particular institution such as the economy may involve individuals from different families, members of different religions, perhaps even persons of different nationalities, as well as members of labor unions, business organizations, consumer groups, and farm organizations. Despite the social differences that may exist among individuals, an institution like the economy operates to regularize the thoughts and actions of people involved in fulfilling its activities. The institution of religion deals with the mysterious aspects of life through shared rituals and beliefs; the institution of the family channels sexual behavior, reproduction, and child rearing; political institutions address the use of power and force in society; and the institution of education transmits cultural knowledge and skills to young people.

Institutions tend to change slowly. The social practices that become **institutionalized**—that is, well established—have been hallowed by tradition and custom for so long they seem "natural" to members of a society. They feel comfortable, familiar, predictable, and safe. Supports provided by custom and tradition make it difficult to change social institutions.

It is also difficult to change institutions because they are part of a complex web that binds various groups, values, and norms in society. A change in one institution, such as the economy, may have major implications for the family, education, and other institutions. Analyzing insti-

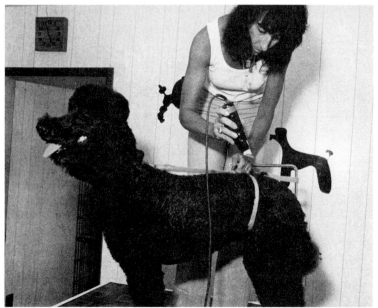

*As societies become more complex, a larger number of distinct occupations develop, and the division of labor increases. Specialized occupations arise devoted to such work as flower arranging, baking, and dog clipping.*

tutional change or stability requires that we consider the relative power of various groups seeking or resisting change. It may be that resistance to institutional change is centered among the most powerful individuals and groups in society. They may be satisfied with the way existing institutions are operating and have no desire to change them. Marginal groups, too, sometimes fight hard to preserve institutions in their traditional forms. Some sociologists suggest, for example, that the economic marginality of the "moral majority" lies behind its efforts to stifle changes in institutions such as religion and the family (Greenberg and Bystryn, 1978). Therefore resistance to change may go beyond the weight of shared custom and include the specific concerns of particular groups or classes in a society.

A major source of both continuity *and* change lies in the way individuals interact—forming networks; transmitting culture; preparing new members to join their groups, organizations, and societies; and exercising social control over people who do not conform. These issues are explored below and in the next two chapters.

## The Division of Labor

As societies develop more complex institutions, more varieties of jobs develop. The **division of labor** refers to the assignment of specialized tasks to various members of a group, organization, community, or society. As societies become more complex, more and more distinct occupations develop, such as hatmaker, pinmaker, watchmaker, baker, and so forth. Today the U.S. Census lists more than 33,000 occupations. In addition, the division of labor means that people become more specialized in what they do.[1] In early societies, family role determined political and occupational positions. In more complex societies, family, politics, and religion become increasingly separate institutions.

[1] Some critics raise the interesting point that occupational differentiation and specialization may not benefit everyone equally. Braverman (1974) stresses that "scientific management" promoted task specialization as a way of limiting the control of workers over the production process while increasing the control of owners and managers (Zaret, 1981).

## Ranking in Society

As positions multiply, some individuals may come to control more key resources (power, money, knowledge) than others. When that happens, rank differentiation develops. **Rank differentiation** refers to the unequal placement and evaluation of various positions in society. As the number of unequally ranked positions increases, there is usually a growing gap between leaders and followers. For example, a chief may have increasing power and privileges, and there may be growing numbers of sub-chiefs. The result may be that the chief has less contact with the rank-and-file members of the group. Different types of rank differentiation—based on property, power, and status—are considered in Chapters 8 and 9. For the moment it is important to note that the amount and basis of social ranking is a prominent feature of social structure.

*The amount and basis of social ranking is a prominent feature of social structure, although rank comes from various sources in different societies. This tribal chief in Ghana clearly occupies a position of high social rank.*

Differences in the division of labor and in rank differentiation are associated with various types of societies, as Table 4.1 on pages 4-2, 4-3 indicates. In simple societies, the division of labor is low; it is based on age and sex and sometimes on kin-group membership.[2] In such a society, functional position would be based almost entirely on ascribed status. An **ascribed status** is acquired at birth—for example, sex or race. In an agrarian society, position in the occupational and status hierarchy would be almost entirely determined by family origins, also an ascribed characteristic. In industrial societies occupational position is based to a somewhat greater degree on achieved traits such as skill and knowledge; although it is also influenced by age, sex, race, and class. An **achieved status** is obtained through an individual's own talents and efforts—for example, in becoming a major league baseball player.

Within the restrictions of age and sex, simple, agrarian, and industrial societies differ considerably with respect to the amount of their rank differentiation. Anthropological studies of existing simple societies suggest that they have less rank inequality than did large agrarian societies of the past, such as ancient Egypt and the Roman and Ottoman empires, or than nineteenth-century China or industrial societies of today.

## Statuses and Roles

Sociologists have several conceptual tools for looking at the social structure of a society. Two key ones are status and role.

### Status: Position and Rank

The term **status** refers to a socially defined position in society. Each position is accompanied by certain prescribed rights, obligations, and expected behaviors, although there is considerable variation in actual behaviors. The status of child, for example, is an identifiable social position in virtually every society, although the age limits vary widely from one society to another. Occupants of that position have certain socially prescribed rights (such as to be fed),

[2] The word "simple" in this context refers to the degree of complexity in social structure.

obligations (say, to obey one's elders), and expected behaviors (for instance, finding firewood and gathering berries or playing with companions). Various children may behave differently even though they all occupy the same status. Given the arrangement of statuses in a particular society, your location within various institutions of society largely determines *with whom* you will interact (in both personal and structural terms) and to a considerable degree the *form* that interaction will take.

The term "status" also connotes *rank*—that is, a position relative to other people in society. Someone is of higher or lower social status than someone else. In virtually all societies, children occupy an inferior status relative to adults, for instance. How is location in the functional and status systems of society determined? Family social status; parental occupation; neighborhood, school, and racial and religious group membership; age; and gender are major determinants of position in the social structure. These features interact with educational experiences to shape aspirations, occupational choices, and goals. Even in complex societies, one status may dominate. A **dominant status** is one that overshadows all others (Hughes, 1945). In the past, race was the dominant status of blacks in the United States. Even if they were doctors or lawyers, people responded to them first in terms of their race. The statuses of female and of child also tend to be dominant.

### Role: Two Views

Functionalists and interactionists define the key concept of **role** differently. Both views are helpful. For functionalists, roles are the culturally prescribed behaviors associated with particular social positions. Roles convey a sense of how people should behave in particular situations, and they may shape personality to some degree. These expectations may be enforced by rewards or punishments. Roles also are socially patterned by societal values, behaviors, and attitudes that influence how people with a given status are expected to behave. A wife in Saudi Arabia, for example, is expected to perform very different roles from those of a wife in Hollywood, California. When you become a college student, there are certain rights and duties associated with that status. These rights and duties

IMAGES OF DIFFERENT TYPES OF SOCIETIES.

*Major Social Differences in Hunting and Gathering, Agrarian, and Industrial Societies*

| | Type of Society | | |
| --- | --- | --- | --- |
| | **Hunting and Gathering** | **Agrarian** | **Industrial** |
| **Food Supply** | May be irregular | Steady; usually surpluses | Steady; surpluses |

| | | | |
| --- | --- | --- | --- |
| **Community Size** | Small (75 to 100) | Wide variation; some towns and cities | Large; many towns and cities |
| **Societal Size** | Small (loosely connected bands) | More than 100,000 | In the millions |

| | Type of Society | | |
|---|---|---|---|
| | **Hunting and Gathering** | **Agrarian** | **Industrial** |
| **Social Relationships** | Face-to-face | Mostly face-to-face | Many impersonal ones |
| **Culture** | Similar; widely shared | Somewhat diverse | Very diverse |
| **Division of Labor** | Low | Medium | High |
| **Basis for Division of Labor** | Age and sex; sometimes kinship | Kinship, age, sex | Skills, knowledge, age, sex, family, kinship |
| **Rank Differentiation** | Low | High | Medium |
| **Basis for Rank Differentiation** | Wit, talent, ideas, age, sex, kinship, gift giving | Family, kinship, age, sex | Wealth, occupation, race, sex, kinship, education, talent, skills, age |
| **Amount of Leisure for Most People** | Quite high | Low | Medium |
| **Social Change** | Slow | Slow to medium | Rapid |

Sources: Elkin, 1954; Lee and DeVore, 1968; Lenski, 1966; Murdock, 1967; Nance, 1975.

**Table 4.2** *Likely Statuses and Role Partners of a College Student*

| Status | Likely Role Partners |
|---|---|
| College student | Professors, deans, classmates, librarians, coaches, roommates, college staff members, friends |
| Daughter or son | Parents, siblings, aunts and uncles, cousins |
| Male or female | Members of the same and of the opposite sex |
| Catholic, Protestant, Jew, other | Clergy, members of the congregation, agnostics, atheists |
| White, black, Hispanic, other | Members of one's own ethnic group; members of other ethnic groups |
| Citizens of the United States or other countries | Fellow citizens; other nationals |
| Employee | Boss; coworkers; perhaps customers or clients |

are often reinforced by the role expectations held by others with whom you interact. Your professors, for instance, expect certain behaviors from you, and the college grants you certain rights. You yourself probably have certain expectations about how you should perform the roles attached to your particular position. Each status has a cluster of role partners and roles attached to it, each with a variety of expectations. Knowing what statuses people occupy helps sociologists predict how people are likely to behave.

To a functionalist, **role performance** refers to the way people perform the behaviors expected in certain roles. Sometimes role behavior is judged quite loosely, as Woody Allen noted when he said "showing up is eighty percent of life." At other times role performance is judged by exacting standards, as in microsurgery. Functionalists, then, stress that roles exist before individuals come along and fill them. Once role performers appear, roles impose their demands on them. This conception of role leaves little room for individual freedom.

Interactionists do not accept a rigid and fixed conception of role. When they speak of role, they stress its interactive nature rather than emphasizing a social role specified by society. The interactive role is an effort to mesh the demands of a social position with one's own personality and identity (McCall and Simmons, 1966). People directing traffic may fill that role like robots or find ways to express their personalities and identities on the job. The interactionist approach, rather than looking at the common aspects of a role, stresses the different ways various individuals express themselves in a role.

Our understanding of social roles is enhanced by using both functionalist and interactionist approaches. Social roles vary from those that are tightly patterned and prescribed to those that are much more flexible. When a priest, minister, or rabbi conducts a religious service, for example, certain attitudes and behaviors are usually expected. The functionalist view may better explain role behavior in this instance. The roles attached to the position of sports announcer, on the other hand, may allow a wider range of feelings, beliefs, and behaviors. The interactive view can explain the variation to be found among people occupying this role.

## Role Expectations

In simple, relatively traditional societies, there may be a smaller range of possible role behaviors and less room for improvisation. In a society like ours, which has many cultural patterns and practices and where considerable social change is occurring, roles associated with particular positions—for example, with being male or female, black or white, old or young—are not universally prescribed. Even in our diverse society, however, there are guidelines for how people should play their roles. These are called **role expectations.** Often these guidelines are not a single prescription but rather an inventory of possible behaviors. There may even be competing prescriptions—for example, should mothers of small children work or stay home with the children? The existence of a range of possible role behaviors gives individuals room for choice. There may even be the chance to improvise new behaviors and add them to the inventory.

Flexibility and improvisation allow for greater individual freedom on the one hand but may create personal and organizational strain on the other. Social changes begin to occur when groups of individuals create new recipes for role behavior. We have witnessed this, for example, in the broader inventory of role behaviors that has recently come to be attached to the status of wife in the United States.

Role expectations are like social recipes that enable us to cook up a number of social interactions with relative ease, rather than having to produce a newly created social behavior each time. Cultural habits in the form of role prescriptions mean that people can buy magazines, borrow library books, cross the street, get married, and engage in many other social acts without first having to work out common ground rules with all the other people in the situation.

The power of expectations is evident not only in that people often behave in expected ways but also in the fact that they often feel the way occupants of their positions are "supposed to feel," just as some actors and actresses feel the emotions of the characters they are playing (Hochschild, 1979, 1983). The fact that role expectations can affect behavior is illustrated by people who are suddenly elevated to leadership positions in civic organizations. They often say they used to be terrified of speaking in public, but that the demands of their roles called forth capacities they did not know they had.

In your status as student you have a **role set**—that is, a cluster of roles to play in relation to professors, other students, roommates, college staff members, friends, and so forth. You also occupy statuses besides that of student. You have one or more family statuses, a gender status (masculine or feminine), a racial status, a religious status, a nationality, and perhaps an occupational status. Table 4.2 on page 4-4 shows some of the statuses and role partners of a "typical" college student.

### Role Conflict and Strain

**Role conflict** refers to the incompatibility between two or more roles, either within a status (as when a parent is torn between playing with the children and cleaning house, for instance) or between statuses (as when your coach expects you to play in an away game and your professor requires you to take an exam at the same time). Role conflict tends to give a person the feeling of being pulled in many different directions at once. Role conflict is particularly acute in situations where there are no socially prescribed guidelines for resolution. Competing demands from various role partners about which status should dominate can also cause role conflict. Do you and your family agree about when studying should take precedence over a family event, for example? The participants in most role relationships tend to feel that their expectations and demands are paramount and should receive priority. Even among professors, you may have noticed that each seems to assume you are taking only one course.

### Role Accumulation

The possibilities for role conflict and strain tend to increase as an individual occupies more statuses. Nevertheless, according to Sieber (1974), **role accumulation,** that is, adding to one's statuses and roles, may be more gratifying than stressful, since it offers the possibility of greater privileges, status security, resources for status enhancement, role performance, personality enrichment, and ego gratification. If Sieber is right, his view helps to explain why women want to hold responsible jobs or take part in

local and national affairs in addition to running households and raising children. Despite possible role conflict and strain, women value the chance to increase their resources (which may enhance their role performance as wives and mothers), gain privileges, and feel a greater sense of personal worth.

Drawing on symbolic interaction theory, Thoits (1983) formulated the concept of social isolation in terms of possessing few social statuses and roles. Using data from a New Haven, Connecticut, community survey, she tested her theories and found evidence to support the view that the more statuses and roles people have, the less likely they are to experience psychological distress.

What happens when people give up or lose a major status in their lives—for example, when people divorce, lose their jobs, or stop being nuns or priests? In traditional societies people generally maintained such positions until they died. But an increasingly common feature of modern societies is the process of losing positions. **Role exit** is the process of leaving a role that was central to one's self-identity and building an identity in a new role while taking the prior one into account (Ebaugh, 1988, p. 1). Most individuals experience several major role exits in their lives, whether from divorce or career change. Ebaugh studied ex-nuns and ex-priests; divorcees; people who had had sex-

*"Role exit" involves leaving a role that was central to one's self-identity and building an identity in a new role (Ebaugh, 1988). Not everyone announces a role exit in as dramatic a way as this couple has, but role exits are becoming increasingly frequent in modern industrial societies.*

change operations; recovered alcoholics; ex-convicts; and people who had stopped being doctors, lawyers, air-traffic controllers, and so on. She found that a patterned sequence of events appears in most role exits. This includes: (1) First doubts, where a person begins to question his or her taken-for-granted role commitment. (2) Seeing and weighing of role alternatives, where a person begins exploring other possibilities. (3) Turning points, which mark the decisions by individuals to leave the roles they occupy. (4) Establishing an ex-role identity, which includes incorporating a previous role identification into a new identity. Role exits are complicated because they disrupt social networks.

## SOCIAL NETWORKS

*When Albert Einstein completed his university studies in 1900 he could not obtain a job appropriate to his training, in part because he had so antagonized his professors that they would neither hire nor help him. After more than a year of searching and temporary employment, Einstein applied for a post at the Swiss Patent Office and was a few months later called to Zurich for an interview with the office director. In spite of an inadequate performance during the interview, Einstein was hired. As it turned out, the director was an intimate friend of the father of Marcel Grossman, a good friend and former classmate of Einstein. The appointment was no doubt a favor from the director to the Grossmans. Einstein's major scientific insights occurred during his several years at the Patent Office. [Fischer et al., 1977, p. 19]*

Einstein's job was a direct result of his informal network of social relationships. Being a genius was not .enough to secure a position. Through his interactions with a friend, Einstein, whether he knew it or not, became part of a social network that included his friend's father.

Growing evidence suggests that most people hear of their jobs through networks rather than through want ads or agencies (Bolles, 1977; Granovetter, 1974). This is one important reason for knowing more about social networks and how they operate.

*Social networks—whether of individuals, organizations, nations, or other social units—create important social relationships and can influence what happens in the social world.*

### Networks Defined

A **social network** is a set of interdependent relations, or links, between individuals, organizations, nations, or other social units. Everyone belongs to some network, if only one based on family ties. Because networks create important social connections, they help to explain why people are not so isolated as early observers of urban industrial life thought. People linked in networks can be relatives; they can like or love each other; they can do things together, such as discuss finances, play tennis, or work together. The more links two people have, the stronger is the bond between them. But the strength of that bond also depends on how often and how intensely they interact.

Organizations belong to networks as well. For example, corporate directorate ties and the flow of resources have been analyzed (Burt, 1983; Levine, 1972; Miller, 1980). Burt found that directorate ties increased market efficiency somewhat, and he found no evidence of systematic abuse of those ties in data from 1957 (1983, p. 177).

Some networks consist of social equals who have a symmetrical relationship. In a symmetrical relationship the exchanges between members are relatively equal (Fischer et al., 1977, p. 36). Not all links are symmetrical, however. In a study of Christmas-card sending behavior, for example, Sheila Johnson (1971) found that almost everyone sent some cards to people above them in social status and fully expected not to receive a card in return. Most people have nonreciprocal, or asymmetrical, relations with certain individuals, often those of higher social status. In most cases in Johnson's study the asymmetry of the relationship indicated the greater status of the receiver. In some cases, however, a person of higher status may send cards to related individuals of lower status. For example, the president of a college or a corporation may send everyone in the organization a card, not expecting one in return from most of them.

## Network Formation

A person's first social network is the one he or she is born into—usually immediate family and other relatives. Parents have social ties with people in the neighborhood; with people where they work; perhaps with people around the world; as well as with those in religious, fraternal, occupational, voluntary, or other associations. Other social links, forged as children grow up, are with other children and adults in the neighborhood, with people in school, perhaps with people in a religious group, and so forth. Through the statuses individuals and their parents occupy, they have certain social, economic, informational, and other resources. To those are added the resources of people with whom individuals and their families form ties. By the time people go to work, they have added many contacts beyond the family members with whom they started. New ties form on the job and in careers. Social statuses such as race, sex, age, social class, and occupation affect the number and types of networks formed. Individuals may be linked with people who have useful information or other resources. In this way networks can help individuals as they pursue their life goals.

*Social networks begin forming early in families, neighborhoods, schools, and colleges. These networks transmit culture, provide information, and preview social futures.*

## How Networks Operate

Social networks operate in a number of ways. People in a network can "put in a good word" for you even with persons who are strangers to you. They can transmit culture (values, norms, and styles of presenting yourself) and provide access to information, money, status, or power. A recent study found that young people obtained considerable help in finding jobs from their social ties, particularly when those ties were with people who had more status and experience than they did. Contact with these helpful links was not accidental, however. The occupational status of the "contact" was highly related to the education and career of the young person's father. Much more of the social status of the "tie" was explained by these parental characteristics than by the young person's talent or experience (Lin, Ensel, and Vaughn, 1981). This research suggests that the nature and operation of networks in social life is an important trail to follow into the forest where individual lives become connected to careers and social status.

Network theory has direct practical applications—for instance, as a valuable means of obtaining information about the world of work. A senior partner in a major New York law firm keeps a notebook with the names, addresses, telephone numbers, and other helpful information on the people in his network (including people he has just met). Thus, when he has a question, needs some information, or needs to know whom to call, he has leads in his notebook. The wisdom of this approach is upheld by Mark Granovetter's research on how people find jobs (1974). Most of the people he studied found their jobs through personal contacts; better-paying and more prestigious jobs were particularly likely to be obtained in this way. The existence and operation of networks is one of the ways individuals manage to survive in bureaucratic organizations and in large urban environments. "Network analysis is a kind of scientific exposé in that one of its most dramatic characteristics is the unmasking of otherwise invisible communication structures" (Kadushin, 1977). People run into each other on the street, in their clubs, at a dinner party or a convention; they telephone each other or they correspond. If, for example, the subject matter of the contact is a job, it is likely that the job will not be visible to 80 percent or more of the people who would be interested in it (Crystal and Bolles, 1974). As that fact makes obvious, news about most job openings runs through networks, rather than in newspapers. Sometimes dubbed the "old boy" network, this system of connecting people with jobs is deplored by advocates of equal employment opportunity. One of the features required under the Equal Employment Opportunity Act, for instance, is the public advertisement of available jobs. From the employers' point of view, however, the network system may be much more efficient. News travels faster that way; networks may provide more reliable information about candidates; and the chances of finding someone appropriate may be enhanced. Hence networks often provide efficient channels of communication and effective methods of screening potential candidates for positions. (See the debate on the pros and cons of social networking.)

Traditionally networks have been heavily used by "old boys"—that is, people in established positions who have school, military, social, or other connections. Women and minorities have usually been excluded. As more women and minorities form their own networks, however, and build bridges to existing networks of insiders, they will begin to benefit from these informal processes as well.

The pattern of links between people is such that at least in the United States, most individuals are connected indirectly to everyone else. Do you doubt that statement? I did the first time I heard it. But some interesting experiments, called "small-world studies," document it.

## Networks in Action: Small-World Studies

If you were given the name of a total stranger living 1500 miles away, do you think you could get a document to him using only a chain of acquaintances? This was the problem Jeffrey Travers and Stanley Milgram (1969) set out to answer. They wanted to know how many people could establish contact with the "target" individual, and how many individuals the document had to go through to reach its target. The target individual was a Boston stockbroker. The senders were 296 volunteers—one a group of general residents from Nebraska, another a set of Nebraska blue-chip stockholders, and the third a set of general Boston residents who responded to an ad for volunteers in a local paper. Participants were not paid or otherwise rewarded for being in the study.

The original volunteers were given the following information about the target person: his name, address, occupation and place of employment, his college and year of graduation, his military service dates, and his wife's maiden name and hometown. They were asked to send the document directly to the target if they personally knew him on a first-name basis. If they did not, they were asked not to contact him directly but to mail the document to a friend,

People disagree about the practice of networking.

## Background

Traditionally "the old boy network" included white males from upper-class, upper-middle-class, and middle-class families. They formed their networks by attending private schools and by joining fraternities, churches, clubs, or lodges, where they met other men. Thus they learned who worked where and what each did. When they needed information or help of various kinds, there were numerous people to ask. What is changing now is that previously excluded groups—particularly blacks and women—have begun to form their own networks (Kleinman, 1981; Lee, 1984; Welch, 1980).

If you want to do networking as well as read about it, you should buy several packages of 3-by 5-inch index cards (suggest Crystal and Bolles, 1974). For each person you know, write down his or her name, address, phone number, when and how you met them, where they work, their interests, and other key facts. Think of all your relatives and in-laws, friends and neighbors; classmates and alumni from all the schools and colleges you attended or are attending; members of your church or synagogue; people that you work with; colleagues in civic associations, political groups, volunteer groups; sports partners; your doctor, lawyer, banker, accountant, and the like, if you have one; current and former teachers; and every other responsible person you know. As you meet new people, you can add them to your network file. Include the names of people whom friends tell you to look up. As you can see in the

*Networking: Pros and Cons About How It Is Done*

diagram, each person in your social network is also embedded in his or her own social network, and in their networks may be just the person you need to meet.

## Adding to Your List

You can join existing organizations, either ones devoted specifically to networking or ones with some other purpose that you share. These might be college clubs, church or synagogue social activities, political or athletic clubs, fraternal or sororal groups, alumni associations, or a personal computer users' group. If there are no groups of interest

to you in your area, you might consider starting one. (See Kleinman, 1980, and Welch, 1980, for ideas on how to do this.) When you meet new people, get their names and addresses. Keep in touch with the people you know and meet. Work with them on civic or professional or trade association tasks; call up and chat with them if you feel inclined.

You may ask them for advice, moral support, and certain kinds of information. You can't expect them to hire you, redecorate your home, or teach you "all about" computers. People seeking information should refine their questions. Asking people how they write a book is a bit like asking architects how they design a building. You might ask, "Do you write from an outline?" Shy people find that it is sometimes

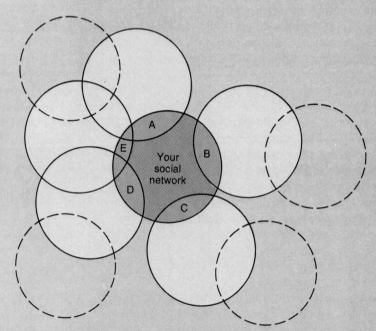

The central circle here represents you and your network. You know persons A, B, C, D, and E. Each of them, in turn, has a network of other people whom he or she knows.

easier to write people letters than to telephone them or meet them in person. Finally, help others if you say you will and thank the people who help you.

**Pros and Cons**

Not everyone supports the idea of networking. Some people feel that networking seems like "using people." Others are shy about meeting new people or are afraid to call up someone they barely know. They feel networks exclude some people and do not allow the most deserving people to get jobs or do business with them.

Others argue that even if opportunities are openly advertised, networking happens anyway. They suggest further that unqualified people will not be hired this way, since networking alone cannot get them a job. Furthermore, proponents say that networking succeeds only if people feel that it is mutually beneficial and if people ask others for legitimate and reasonable information or help.

What do you think? Do you agree with the sociological statement that everyone is in more than one network? If so, do you think the debate hinges on whether those networks should be used consciously and how they should be used?

relative, or acquaintance who "is more likely than you to know the target person" (Travers and Milgram, 1969, p. 184). Out of 296 initial volunteers, 217 actually sent the document on to someone else. Of those sent on, 64, or 29 percent, eventually reached the target person.

How many contacts were needed to link starters with targets? The mean number required was 5.2 links. The Boston group did it with fewer contacts than either Nebraska group, not surprisingly. Those moving the document through Boston business contacts reached the target sooner (through fewer links) than those moving it through the target's hometown of Sharon, Massachusetts. Senders got the document to the town readily, but it sometimes circulated around there before it hit the target's acquaintances. As chains converged on the target, senders used many of the same intermediaries. Twenty-five percent of all the documents reached the target through one intermediate, his neighbor. This fact suggests that chains converge on a few key individuals who have a substantial number of outside personal contacts.

Participants in the study tended to send the document on to individuals who were similar to themselves with respect to occupation, gender, and age. The social similarity of links in a network helps to explain how social inequalities are passed from one generation to the next. Middle-class parents, for example, may be more likely than lower-class parents to know someone who can help their teenagers get a job. In the small-world studies, both senders and target were middle-class, a factor that undoubtedly helped them to make contact. Another small-world study discovered that the number of intermediaries needed to link white and black senders and targets does not differ markedly from that needed to link white senders and targets, despite the need for racial crossover (Korte and Milgram, 1970).

The Travers and Milgram study and other small-world studies have gone a long way toward documenting the existence of personal interconnections in a society of more than 235 million people. They show the existence of far-flung contacts among people. Because the people you know also know other people whom you do not know, there is a good chance you

*Young people are helped in their quest for a job by the networks of their parents and friends, as well as by their own networks.*

can reach a total stranger through a personal contact. In addition to linking people who may be able to help one another, social networks influence whom people meet, whom they marry, where they get jobs, what they know, where they live, how they spend their leisure time, and how they think and behave.

## Networks Influence Feelings and Behaviors

Membership in social networks influences how people think, feel, and behave. How husbands and wives behave toward each other is affected by their social networks. Bott (1971) found that when each partner in a marriage has his or her own close-knit network of people to rely on, a rigid separation of marital roles concerning household tasks and child care was possible because both partners could get help with their tasks from people in their networks. Couples without such close-knit networks put more stress on the importance of shared interests and common activities for a happy marriage. A key difference in their feelings and behaviors was the nature of the social network to which they belonged.

In another example, many of the young people who joined a satanic cult were in a friendship network with someone already in the cult, but it was also true that people who were not heavily involved in other social networks were prime candidates for joining (Bainbridge, 1978). Similarly, people who joined social protest movements were affected not only by their personal dispositions but very much by having close social ties with other members of the movement (Snow et al., 1980).

In large organizations, much of a person's power comes from social networks beyond the work group. Important ties with sponsors, for example, influence a person's chances for success. Sponsors (or mentors) coach young people and help with introductions and advice. Sponsors may also fight for their people, help to cut red tape, and signal others that an individual has powerful backing (Kanter, 1977). If sponsors are important to men, notes Kanter, they are essential to women in organizations but may be

harder to obtain. Some people obtain sponsors because of their good performance, but for others it may be because they "have the right social background or know some of the officers from outside the corporation or look good in a suit" (Kanter, 1977, p. 184). In short, sponsors may be obtained through prior social networks and may increase the range and power of a person's network in an organization.

Networks provide restraints as well as opportunities. People often have and/or form network ties with others whom they do not necessarily like. Such involuntary ties may be with disliked family members, individuals at work, neighbors, or members of one's club. "Despite their involuntary nature, such ties are often important in terms of the time spent on them, the resources that flow through them and the ways in which they constrain other network members' activities . . ." suggests Wellman (1983). People may feel "social pressure" to contribute to the political campaign of a candidate they dislike, to use drugs or alcohol, or attend a boring social event because the members of their network expect it of them.

Networks link organizations as well as individuals into larger structures of social influence. For example, the college counselors at elite private secondary boarding schools have close relationships with the admissions officers at elite private colleges. These networks permit college advisers to obtain useful information about how colleges put their classes together, to establish helpful procedures (such as not ranking students in their high school class), and to lobby in support of their students (Persell and Cookson, 1985).

Networks of organizations are very important in economic life, with banks still at the center of the corporate network (Mintz and Schwartz, 1985; Mizruchi, 1982). Leaders of major corporations are linked by serving on the boards of directors of each other's firms (Useem, 1984). They are also connected through various social networks, such as shared memberships in social clubs, boards of cultural bodies like symphonies and art museums, and governmental advisory boards (DiMaggio and Useem, 1978; Domhoff, 1967; Freitag, 1975; Koenig et al., 1979; Mintz, 1975; Ratcliff, 1980; Salzman and Domhoff,

1979–1980; Soref, 1976; Useem, 1979). In these ways, social networks knit together structures of social stratification.

## SOCIAL INTERACTION

Societies are composed of individuals who interact in various ways with others. Ignoring someone you know, waving enthusiastically when a friend approaches, telephoning, borrowing a book, dancing, or buying a candy bar (from a person, not a machine) are a few examples of social interaction. Exchanges between heads of state, submitting architectural plans for zoning approval, cutting someone's hair, reserving a concert ticket, and having a job interview are also social interactions.

These interactions are considered first. Then a symbolic interactionist approach is used to analyze several vivid types of social interaction.

### Defining Social Interaction

**Social interaction** refers to the ways people behave in relation to one another, using language, gestures, and symbols. Much of what we do each day involves social interactions, which can have profound significance or be quite trivial in their consequences. Even an act you may do alone, like reading this book, may well be done because of your social interactions with others. You may do it because you want to pass the course you are taking or because you want to learn about the social world in which you live or both. Thus, even seemingly solitary acts may be rooted in a fabric of social interactions.

Many species of animals also interact socially. Human interaction, especially, involves the creation and use of complex symbols, including language. These symbols, especially language, can transcend time and space and allow people to communicate with others far away or still unborn. The term **symbolic interaction** is often used to refer to interactions that rely on shared symbols, such as a thumbs-up sign or a wave and a smile. A second unique feature of human interaction is that people attach symbolic meanings to virtually everything in their lives, although these meanings can vary widely. The same event (for example, being pregnant) can mean very different things to different people, as noted in Chapter 1. And the same meaning can be assigned through quite different procedures, as we will see later in the chapter in the

*Sociologists focus on various features of social interaction, including language, gestures, symbols, and behavior.*

discussion of who is declared "dead on arrival" at a hospital and who is not. Interaction is central to social life, and sociologists approach it in several distinct ways.

## Differing Views of Social Interaction

Functionalists stress that shared social standards shape social interaction: for example, how you behave in your role as a son or daughter is largely prescribed by society and by other people. Certain forms of social interaction are considered "appropriate" and are expected in certain circumstances. The functionalist view of social interaction emphasizes its patterned and predictable nature. This view helps us to understand something about how social interaction is possible, even between strangers.

As noted in the discussion of social roles, a functionalist view suggests there is one "right" way to interact socially. Some functionalists acknowledge that different ethnic groups or social classes may prescribe different behaviors, but they hold that the element of prescription still exists and is imposed in some way on the individuals involved. It is this "straitjacket" aspect of cultural prescriptions that led Herbert Blumer and others to stress the creative side of social interaction. They developed the major theoretical approach called symbolic interactionism in response to the neglect they felt human action and social interaction were receiving in sociology. There are no prescribed social behaviors in many situations, suggests Blumer, particularly in such unusual situations as riots, panics, or wild celebrations. Social behaviors in such contexts, therefore, cannot be understood in terms of cultural prescriptions. Instead, we need to understand how people attach meaning to situations and to their own and others' actions within them.

Functionalist and interactionist approaches lead sociologists to understand social interaction in different ways. For instance, Wallace and Wolf have compared and contrasted the behaviors of two sociologists at work:

*During the rallies of the Free Speech Movement at Berkeley (in the 1960s), [Herbert] Blumer could be observed mingling with the crowds, observing from an upper level window, and later talking at length with students involved. As a symbolic interactionist, his approach to explaining students' involvement was to find out how individuals perceived and interpreted events and how they had made the decision to become involved. An illuminating contrast can be found in the work of sociologists such as [Amitai] Etzioni, who are more concerned with "social structure." They approach such an event not by looking at individual decisions and actions that went into making up the Free Speech Movement, but by looking for general social phenomena that explain why the sixties was a period of campus turmoil. [Wallace and Wolf, 1980, p. 248]*

Etzioni looked at social structural factors like the fact that young people constituted a larger proportion of the population than ever before or since. His approach suggests that certain societal conditions may result in greater or lesser amounts of student turmoil. It reflects the interest of functionalists in explaining why patterned social behaviors occur. Blumer's microscopic scrutiny of how individuals behaved and the meaning of those behaviors for them helps to explain why certain individuals rather than others decided to get involved politically and what the consequences of certain symbolic meanings and behaviors were for the way they organized their actions.

## Types of Social Interaction

In keeping with their interest in finding and explaining patterned social behaviors, functionalists have identified and described several major types of interaction, including cooperation, exchange, conflict, competition, negotiation, and coercion. Each type can be considered separately, even though they frequently blend together in social life.

### Cooperation

**Cooperation** refers to a collaborative effort between people to achieve a common goal. It seems to arise most frequently when working with others can produce a desired end more effectively and efficiently than can working alone. In team sports, for example, it is usually difficult for a single football, basketball, or volleyball player to create a winning team. Instead, a group effort is needed. Communities facing natural disasters like floods or earthquakes often respond to the threat with cooperative effort. Cooperation is most likely to arise when individuals assessing a situation conclude that their own chances of winning or surviving will be greater if they work together than if they proceed alone. Cooperation also brings its own social rewards—a sense of sharing a challenge, adversity, or fun with others, a sense of caring about others and of being cared for in return.

### Exchange

**Exchange** represents a more formalized system of cooperation, in which individuals trade valued objects or sentiments. Exchange is commonly noted in economic activities, but it occurs also in love and friendship relationships. Social exchange usually involves intangibles such as respect, affection, acceptance, or help. Members of a family assist one another knowing that they can count on the help of other members when they need it. Neighbors lend each other tools or watch each others' children. Work colleagues provide assistance in return for esteem. Exchange creates and reinforces social bonds between individuals and groups. Trade, for example, increases social contacts and ties between neighboring communities. Similarly, successful social exchanges increase social interactions. Everyday speech reflects the fact that people take this feature into account in sizing up other people—"They have nothing to offer me," or "They do a lot for me."

### Conflict

**Conflict** involves direct struggle between individuals or groups over commonly valued resources or goals. Conflict theorists stress that conflict is significant and frequent in social life. Conflict may involve a relatively insignificant object or a quite important one. Conflict may arise between two children over one television set when they want to see different programs or between nations that seek exclusive fishing rights in the ocean.

Virtually all conflicts occur within certain ground rules that are shared by opponents. Rather than fighting each other to the death, antagonists usually establish certain rules to mediate their conflicts and keep them from being destructive: "First I choose the show; then you get to choose the next one." Even armed conflicts are governed to some extent by norms: "You take care of our prisoners of war (especially officers), and we'll take care of yours."

Conflicts may have positive sociological results, as Simmel (1905) and Coser (1956, 1967) have pointed out. Groups that have a common enemy are drawn closer together. Members of religious sects that were persecuted by other religious groups tended to band together more tightly within their group. Conflict can also clarify values and issues. Labor and management may not realize until they are in open conflict that their interests are essentially dissimilar.

### Competition

**Competition** is a form of conflict in which there is agreement on the means that can be used to pursue an end. More rules and limits are imposed on the interaction than in open conflict, and they are more strictly followed by the participants. At one extreme is the classic case of sports, where the rules are well known, clearly spelled out, and enforced by presumably impartial referees or judges whose decisions are final.

*This fight over a fender bender is an example of social interaction that has reached the stage of open conflict.*

Everyone involved knows what constitutes a "win" or "loss."

Our society seems to produce a number of situations in which people must cooperate and compete at the same time. In trying out for the football team, aspirants are expected to shine individually, but they are also supposed to be good team players. Similarly, junior professors or young associates in a law firm are judged by their seniors in relation to one another. At the same time, they need the social support, help, and cooperation of their peers.

### Negotiation

In **negotiation,** two or more competing parties reach a mutually satisfactory agreement. People may negotiate the terms under which they agree to social exchange, social cooperation, or competition. College roommates, for example, often decide peacefully when their room will be used for entertaining and when for study, whether or not they will smoke in the room, and whether they will compete for members of the opposite sex or adopt a "hands off" attitude toward their roommate's friends.

They do not usually sit down and say, "let's negotiate." Instead, they work out a way of getting along or they change rooms. When negotiations break down, conflict or coercion sometimes occurs.

### Coercion

**Coercion** refers to the process of making someone do something through the use of social pressure or force. At first glance coercion appears to be one-sided. But every act of coercion is at least partially determined by the expected reaction to it. In this sense there is a relationship between the coercer and the coerced. The relationship between master and slave or guard and prisoner is an interactive one, even though very asymmetrical.

Coercion often occurs through the use of physical force—the armed might of the police or a robber, or the greater size and strength of a parent carrying a child to bed. Coercion can involve the use of social sanctions such as ridicule, guilt, excommunication, withholding of love, or failure to grant recognition.

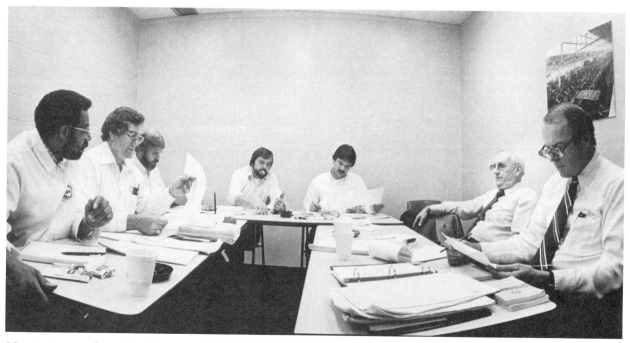

*Negotiation is a form of social interaction between two or more competing parties. Here the United Auto Workers Union is negotiating a new contract with executives from a Ford truck plant in Louisville, Kentucky.*

## Interactional Cues

Social interaction involves a mutual relationship between two or more people, and it includes their actions and responses. They communicate through various cues. Language is a major means, but communication can also occur through facial expression, body movement, visual behavior, the use of space, the social use of time, and speech features (such as tempo).

Language, both spoken and written, is among the most important means of social interaction. It allows remote as well as face-to-face interaction. **Nonverbal communication,** including the use of visual and other symbols, supplements language. Nonverbal behaviors may reveal the underlying feelings of a speaker. A speaker's tone of voice, speed of talking, facial expressions, and bodily movements all convey emotions. People answering questions in class, for example, may twist their hair, a gesture that has nothing to do with what they are saying but which may reveal inner anxiety or self-consciousness. Folding the arms across the body may be a protective move to fend off attack and may contradict a verbal message of trust and openness (Ekman and Friesen, 1969).

Space may be used to indicate social closeness or distance. We move close to and touch people we like or love; we move away from people we dislike. The "unnatural" social closeness that occurs when strangers are pressed together on a crowded elevator or subway is handled by strategies of avoidance. Even though their bodies may be in full contact, they tend to avoid making eye contact, they rarely talk, and in general they act as though the other people were not there. In this way people neutralize the inappropriate closeness of strangers.

Time provides other interactional clues. More powerful people are more likely to keep less powerful people waiting, as Schwartz (1975) noted. People receiving unemployment compensation wait on long lines to get their checks. Attorneys may make every effort not to keep prominent clients waiting. Beyond waiting, the amount of time a person spends with someone else is one nonverbal indicator of value and esteem for that person. This can produce problems if, as happens in many marriages, husbands and wives hold different expectations about how much time together is desirable. The quality of time also makes a difference. If you are always preoccupied when you see someone, that gives a negative impression of your regard for that person.

To understand the significance of social interactions, sociologists consider who initiates contact, how frequently people interact, how intensely they appear to feel about the interaction, and why they interact. In these ways they uncover a number of dynamic aspects of social interaction.

## APPLICATIONS OF THE SYMBOLIC INTERACTIONIST APPROACH

Symbolic interactionists study various aspects of social interaction, including impression management, how individuals reserve a part of themselves from organizations and institutions, and how meanings are constructed in social situations. Symbolic interactionism is also useful for analyzing organizations and institutions.

### Impression Management and Face-Work

Some of the best-known work in the interactionist tradition is that done by Erving Goffman (1959, 1961, 1963, 1967, 1971, 1974). Goffman analyzes factors from everyday life that people might overlook as they interact. He draws parallels, for instance, between the theater and the way individuals perform in their relationships with others. Because people draw inferences and make judgments about one another in their dealings, individuals may try to influence how others come to perceive them. Goffman calls this **impression management** and suggests that it characterizes many types of interactions. A host and hostess giving a party, for example, will try to make their home attractive before the guests arrive. Someone coming to the door may start to smile before the door is opened. Before the party, parents may give children elaborate instructions about how they are to behave. Even the food served may be selected with an eye to the impression it will create or reinforce.

Individuals vary considerably with respect to how much they calculate and try to control the impression they create and how spontaneous or sincere they are in their interactions with others. There is the possibility that part of their impression management is designed to convince others that they are "sincere" or "natural," so they may behave in a way that leads others to form this impression. Politicians and other people running for public office are particularly concerned about impression management. They may hire a publicist or an "image" specialist who will design and project a positive image for them. Although the thought of an "image consultant" may seem somewhat silly, Goffman's work suggests that people serve as their own image managers in many aspects of their daily interactions.

One way impressions are managed in daily interactions is through what Goffman (1967) calls **face-work.** He uses the word "face" to mean a favorable image a person presents to others; "face-work" refers to the actions taken by individuals to make whatever they are doing consistent with the face they are presenting (p. 12). Individuals try to present certain images to others, but their success depends on these others, who decide whether to accept or reject that face. Because face can only be granted by others, it is a social attribute. Face "is only on loan . . . from society; it will be withdrawn unless [a person] conducts himself in a way that is worthy of it. Approved attributes and their relation to face make of every man his own jailer; this is a fundamental social constraint even though each man may like his cell" (Goffman, 1967, p. 10). This statement suggests that people may act to preserve the faces that go along with certain social positions. Teachers, for instance, may not always feel like acting in a dignified way but may realize that if they do not, it may be difficult to reassert their authority and position at a later time. Individuals are always weighing how much they can do and still maintain their face.

One way face is maintained is by avoidance strategies. People avoid situations in which they may lose face. A quarrel between two neighbors or two family members, for example, may be reconciled by a go-between who can save the face of both parties by not having it appear as though either party had lost face by approaching the other one first. People often cooperate in interactions to help save each other's faces. Social customs, for instance, encourage men not to ask women for New Year's Eve dates too early in the year, thereby making it difficult to offer a graceful excuse for refusing (Goffman, 1967, p. 29).

### Reserving Part of the Self

Goffman also suggests that individuals reserve a part of their selves from the hold of the institutions to which they belong. Goffman conducted a number of studies inside **total institutions**—that is, places where people spend 24 hours of every day for an extended part of their lives, cut off from the rest of society, and tightly controlled by the people in charge. Based on his studies inside mental hospitals, he noted how patients in the hospital refused to assume completely the identity the hospital and its staff tried to impose on them. Sometimes they asserted their independence by refusing to play the role of the "good patient," by being incontinent or refusing to get out of their bathrobes for meals, for example. At other times they carved out little areas where they could be free from the surveillance of the staff—clumps of trees outside where they could smoke, little rooms in the basement where they could play poker, or an area with a sink and a radiator where one patient set up his own personal laundry to wash and dry clothes. In these and numerous other ways, even the patients in a total institution retained some independence and autonomy. They did not allow their entire identities to be controlled by the institution in which they were confined. These "distancing" behaviors on the part of inmates, however, were perceived by hospital staff as further evidence that the patients needed to be hospitalized.

A key element of the interactionist perspective is its focus on how individuals can reflect on themselves and their own actions as well as on the behavior of others. We ask ourselves, "What do you suppose he means by that?" or "What am I trying to do here?" We do not need to act in a way that resembles a knee-jerk reflex; we can think about what is being done to us and can choose among several courses of action. This capacity for self-reflection enables us to reserve a part of ourselves from the domination of social organizations and institutions to which we belong.

## Dramaturgical Analysis—The Pelvic Examination

One of the ways people cooperate in protecting the self from potentially embarrassing situations is by the use of stage management and props to manage uncomfortable interactions. Goffman's dramaturgical analysis, which examines social interaction as though it were a series of scenes in a play, is useful for analyzing such situations.

No matter how liberated women become, a pelvic examination, especially the first one, can be an anxiety-provoking experience. In it women are asked to expose what may be the most private part of their bodies to a stranger, often a male. A situation like this, which is potentially embarrassing or sexually suggestive, needs to be socially defined so that it seems as "normal" and comfortable as possible.

The social management of this interaction has been analyzed by James Henslin and Mae Briggs (1971), who drew on Briggs's observations of several thousand pelvic examinations that she legitimately attended as a practicing nurse. They applied Goffman's **dramaturgical analysis,** looking at the examination as a series of scenes in a play. The "prologue" to the play consists of the woman entering the doctor's waiting room, preparing to take on the role of patient. The first "scene" opens when she is called into the consulting room, where she meets the "character" of the competent doctor. He relates to her as another human being and inquires about her medical problems in a polite and professional manner. He may make notes in her file. If the patient needs a pelvic exam, the doctor mentions that he will do one and then leaves the room.

The second "scene" begins with the entrance of the nurse, who helps to stage the following scenes. Her role is to help the patient shed her identity as a woman and to create a new situation in which a depersonalized pelvis is to be clinically inspected. The nurse provides sympathy, and she provides such "props" as a hospital gown or sheet that covers the patient's body. She suggests where the patient may leave underwear and other clothes, so they will not be hanging in the doctor's view. By having the doctor out of the room during this preparation, any resemblance to a sexually suggestive striptease is eliminated and the clinical definition of the situation prevails.

When the doctor returns, the patient has become a covered body lying on the examination table. The nurse's presence underscores the clinical nature of the encounter. The patient may not be able to see the doctor's face as he sits on a low stool below her line of vision. He may raise one or two medical questions, but the patient can mentally disengage herself from the whole scene.

The special language of doctor–patient interactions helps to desexualize their encounter (Emerson, 1970). When speaking to a patient, the doctor refers to "the vagina" rather than "your vagina." The sexually charged statement "spread your legs" is replaced with the neutral instruction "let your knees fall apart" (Emerson, 1970). In such ways as these, language contributes to the staging and sustaining of a medical rather than a sexual definition of the situation.

After the examination, the doctor departs. The nurse may stay on to welcome the patient back into her regular role again, and the patient may say she is glad that the exam is over. In the final scene the patient meets with the doctor, perhaps in his book-lined office, where they return to more usual roles. The doctor treats her in the same professional and polite way that he did before, affirming that nothing unusual has happened and that he views her in the same way that he did before. They discuss her medical situation and agree on whatever course of action is to be followed. The patient then exits, returning to her roles in the outside world.

This analysis helps to explain a social situation in terms of the stage settings, props, and roles called into play to manage potentially embarrassing or ambiguous situations for the purpose of accomplishing some larger goal.

### Defining the Situation—Dead on Arrival

Much of social action concerns defining situations, and social factors influence how situations are defined. **Defining the situation** refers to the socially created perspective that people bring to a situation. Even something as apparently biological as death does not have a single meaning independent of the people involved.

In his research in the emergency room of a county hospital, David Sudnow (1967) found that patients who arrived at the hospital without a heartbeat or not breathing were treated differently by the attending staff depending on the patient's age and appearance. A person aged 20 or younger was not immediately pronounced "dead on arrival." Instead, a long time was spent listening for a heartbeat, inspecting the eyes, stimulating the heart, and giving oxygen and stimulative medications. All this was likely to occur before the patient was pronounced dead. The older the person, Sudnow reported, the less thorough the examination given. Frequently these people were pronounced dead simply on the basis of a stethoscopic examination of the heart. But not only the age of a patient shaped the definition as death or not-yet death: social characteristics such as dress and whether or not alcohol could be smelled on the person also influenced how quickly a patient was pronounced dead (Sudnow, 1967, p. 104).

### Studying Social Services Through Symbolic Interactionism

Symbolic interactionism may also be usefully applied to an understanding of larger social institutions. In social services such as health care or social work, for example, various participants in the situation may challenge prevailing "meanings" that are assigned to the services provided, as Carole Joffe (1979) suggests. For instance, "traditional ways of giving birth . . . are under significant challenge, as natural childbirth enthusiasts, 'birth without violence,' and home-birth advocates confront the practices of obstetricians and hospital maternity ward personnel; at the other end of the life cycle, there are similar confrontations over the most appropriate orga-

nization of death, as a coalition of euthanasia, hospice, and 'death at home' advocates challenge traditional medical practices" (Joffe, 1979, p. 254).

Not only are prevailing meanings being challenged and redefined, but different participants in social service situations have different personal, professional, and political agendas concerning what the social services "are" or should be. These different conceptions may erupt in conflicts—for example, between welfare workers and clients over appropriate client behavior in a welfare office, between doctors and counselors over whether an abortion should occur, among rape counselors over the advantages and disadvantages of working closely with the local police force, or between county health officials and free clinic staff members over the issues of recordkeeping and patient confidentiality (Joffe, 1979, p. 252). Individuals with different concerns do not always see a situation the same way. Thus they behave differently or try to negotiate new definitions of the situation.

Joffe goes one important step further in her application of symbolic interactionism to social services. She suggests that the negotiation of new and different meanings, and the institutionalization of certain practices rather than other ones, may actually transform the larger social order in important ways. As an example, she notes that certain social services—such as crisis centers for battered wives, abortion clinics, and changing adoptive practices for single individuals—may appear to some people to be eroding the foundation of the nuclear family. To others, these changes represent possibly desirable new conceptions of family structure and gender-role behaviors. Thus the definitions that get negotiated within newly emerging social service organizations may redefine family structures and roles in the larger society. Thus interactionists reveal how negotiations and redefinitions may alter major social institutions.

Social interaction, like social life, is both structured and created. Functionalists stress the structured aspects of social interaction. They believe that institutions, statuses, roles, and values impinge strongly on individuals, largely governing their actions, beliefs, and feelings. Blumer and other symbolic interactionists stress the creative role individuals play constructing their own conduct by interpreting, evaluating, defining, and planning their actions. Lasting interactions between individuals begin to form larger units of social structure.

## EVALUATION AND IMPLICATIONS

Interactions and networks between people form the connective tissue of social structure. These socially formed structures develop histories and momentum. As a result, they influence the statuses, roles, interactions, and networks that emerge. In this way, social life is both actively created and tends to become more structured over time. In the face of structural limitations and opportunities, individuals retain a capacity for self-reflection and for actively evaluating, interpreting, and defining their own actions. Individuals do not need to bob passively like corks on the waves of social forces; they can join or form networks pursuing a course they want to follow. There they can strengthen or challenge various social definitions, institutions, and organizations. They can try to avoid networks whose nature or goals they dislike. Individuals can carve out freedom, choice, and initiative within the structural constraints they face. Sociology provides some powerful tools for doing this when we bring together the interactionist and structural approaches. The apparent paradox that social life is both structured and created now takes on new meaning.

### SUMMARY

1. "Social structure" refers to patterned relationships. These include social institutions, the division of labor, statuses and roles, and social networks.

2. Social institutions consist of statuses, roles, and norms clustered around important societal tasks such as producing food and rearing children.

3. The term "division of labor" refers to the assignment of specialized tasks to various members of a group, organization, community, or

society. As societies become more complex, more distinct occupations develop. "Rank differentiation" refers to the unequal evaluation of various positions.

4. The concepts of status and role help us see how individuals are connected to abstract social structures. A social status is a socially defined position in society. It is usually accompanied by certain expectations and privileges. The term "status" also suggests a ranking of positions, with some people occupying positions with greater status, wealth, or power than others.

5. Each status is accompanied by certain roles. Interactionists stress the negotiable quality of roles; functionalists stress the way in which roles impose expectations on individuals. Both views capture an important aspect of social roles.

6. "Role exit" refers to the process of leaving a significant role.

7. Status and role focus on the individual; social networks draw attention to the relationships between individuals. A network is the set of links, or connections, a person has with others. Our first links are with family members, and we gradually add links with other people. Small-world studies suggest that most people could make direct personal contact with someone unknown to them through a chain of personal connections. Nevertheless, social factors affect networks by influencing who is in them and how the people in them interact. Networks provide people with information, introductions, influence, exposure to cultural styles, and access to power, money, or status. They also link organizations in significant ways.

8. Individuals interacting with one another create social life anew every day. Humans have the capacity to reflect on what they and others are doing, and to interpret those actions. Social interaction refers to the ways people behave in relation to one another.

9. Functionalists stress that interaction is patterned by the population, institutions, sta-

tuses, and roles in a society. In contrast, interactionists emphasize the creative aspects of social interaction.

10. Social interaction appears in a variety of forms, including cooperation, exchange, conflict, competition, negotiation, and coercion. Interactions occur through written or spoken communications and through nonverbal cues.

11. Symbolic interactionism has proved useful for analyzing impression management and face-work; the ways in which individuals reserve parts of their selves from institutions; the management of potentially awkward situations; the influence social characteristics have on certain decisions; and the negotiation of new meanings and new structures in social organizations and institutions.

12. Like all aspects of social life, social interaction is both structured and created. Social structures provide limits as well as possibilities for what we can do. At the same time, individuals actively evaluate, interpret, and try to define their own actions.

## KEY TERMS

achieved status (p. 78)
ascribed status (p. 78)
coercion (p. 90)
competition (p. 89)
conflict (p. 89)
cooperation (p. 88)
defining the situation (p. 94)
division of labor (p. 79)
dominant status (p. 78)
dramaturgical analysis (p. 93)
exchange (p. 89)
face-work (p. 92)
impression management (p. 91)
institution (p. 75)
institutionalized (p. 75)
negotiation (p. 90)
nonverbal communication (p. 91)
rank differentiation (p. 77)
role (p. 78)

role accumulation (p. 80)
role conflict (p. 80)
role exit (p. 80)
role expectations (p. 79)
role performance (p. 79)
role set (p. 80)
social interaction (p. 87)
social network (p. 81)
social structure (p. 75)
status (p. 78)
symbolic interaction (p. 87)
total institution (p. 92)

## SUGGESTED READINGS

Crystal, John C., and Richard N. Bolles. 1974. *Where Do I Go from Here with My Life?* New York: Seabury Press. A witty and sensitive approach to career and life planning, including practical applications of social network theories.

Ebaugh, Helen Rose Fuchs. 1988. *Becoming an EX: The Process of Role Exit.* Chicago, IL: University of Chicago Press. An analysis of the process of role exit, based on depth interviews with ex-nuns and ex-priests; divorcees; people who had sex-change operations; recovered alcoholics; ex-convicts; and people who had left their callings as doctors, lawyers, air-traffic controllers, and so on.

Goffman, Erving. 1959. *The Presentation of Self in Everyday Life.* Garden City, NY: Doubleday/Anchor. Develops Goffman's dramaturgical analysis of social interaction and analyzes how people present themselves in social situations.

Persell, Caroline Hodges, and Peter W. Cookson, Jr. 1985. "Chartering and bartering: Elite education and social reproduction." *Social Problems* 33:114–129. A research study showing how college advisers in elite private high schools use social networks to help their students get into college.

Sudnow, David. 1967. *Passing On: The Social Organization of Dying.* Englewood Cliffs, NJ: Prentice-Hall. Considers the socially created nature of death.

# Becoming a Member of Society Through Socialization

**5**

*A girl named Genie was found in the United States in 1970. Genie's father had kept her locked in a room from the age of 20 months until age 13. Genie was harnessed naked to an infant's potty seat and left alone for hours and days through the years. When she was remembered at night, she was put to bed in a homemade straitjacket. There were no radios or televisions in the house, people spoke in hushed tones, and the only language Genie heard was an occasional obscenity from her father. He hated noise, and if Genie made any sound her father would growl at her like a dog or beat her with a stick. As a result of her confinement, Genie could not walk and her eyes could not focus beyond the boundaries of her room. She was malnourished, incontinent, and salivated constantly [Curtiss, 1977].*

*Despite all this, when the psychologist Susan Curtiss first met her, Genie was alert, curious, and intensely eager for human contact. When frightened or frustrated she would erupt into silent frenzies of rage—flailing about, scratching, spitting, throwing objects, but never uttering a sound. Aside from not speaking, her lack of socialization was apparent in her behavior: She would urinate in unacceptable places, go up to someone in a store and take whatever she liked of theirs, and peer intently into the faces of strangers at close range. Although Curtiss worked with her for several years, Genie never developed language abilities beyond those of a 4-year-old, and she ended up being placed in an institution.[1]*

---

The story of Genie shows the importance of socialization in human society. **Socialization** refers to the preparation of newcomers to become members of an existing group and to think, feel, and act in ways the group considers appropriate. Viewed from the group's point of view, it is a process of member replacement.[2]

Such widely diverse situations as child rearing, teaching someone a new game, orienting a new member of an organization, preparing someone who has been in sales work to become a manager, or acquainting an immigrant with the life and culture of a new society are all instances of socialization.

Socialization is a central process in social life. Its importance has been noted by sociologists for a long time, but their image of it has shifted over the last hundred years.[3]

In the early years of American sociology, socialization was equated with civilization. The issue was one of taming fierce individualists so they would willingly cooperate with others on common endeavors. An unruly human nature was assumed to exist prior to an individual's

---

[1] Genie's mother has since sued Curtiss for disclosing confidential information for ''prestige and profit'' (Pines, 1981).

[2] I am grateful for Anne Rankin Mahoney's helpful comments on earlier drafts of this chapter.

[3] I am indebted to Wentworth (1980) for his excellent analysis of the changing conception of socialization through time.

encounter with society. This nature had to be shaped to conform to socially acceptable ways of behaving.

As time went on, however, socialization came to be seen more and more as the end result—that is, as internalization. **Internalization** means taking social norms, roles, and values into one's own mind. Society was seen as the primary factor responsible for how individuals learned to think and behave. This view is evident in the work of functionalist Talcott Parsons, who gave no hint that the result of socialization might be uncertain or might vary from person to person. If people failed to play their expected roles or behaved strangely, functionalists explained this in terms of incomplete or inadequate socialization. Such people were said to be "unsocialized"—they had not yet learned what was expected of them. The trouble is, they might very well know what was expected but simply be rejecting it. Someone who runs a red light, for example, knows perfectly well that one is not supposed to do that but is doing it anyway. The possibility that individuals might have needs, desires, values, or behaviors different from those that society expects (or demands) of them was not seriously considered by functionalists.

As Parsons used the term "internalization," it referred to the tendency for individuals to accept particular values and norms and to conform to them in their conduct. Dennis Wrong (1961) deplored this view of internalization as being an "oversocialized" conception of human beings. It left no room for the "animal" or biological side of human existence, where motivational drives might conflict with the discipline of internalized social norms. Functionalists deny the presence in humans "of motivational forces bucking against the hold that social discipline has over them" (Wrong, 1961, p. 187). Individual drives do sometimes conflict with social expectations, however. For example, a common theme in movies and TV is that of married people becoming involved in sexual relationships with persons other than their spouses. They *know* they are not supposed to have an affair, but they do so anyway.

Undoubtedly as a reaction to the overly determined Parsonian view of socialization, a group of interpretive sociologists has reasserted the independence of individuals. They reject Parsons's view of socialization as internalized values, norms, and habits, and they reject the notion of society as something out there (a given) that affects individuals the way Parsons suggested it did. The interpretive perspective sees socialization as an interactive process. Individuals negotiate their definitions of the situation with others. A couple, for example, may negotiate between themselves a conception of marriage that is sharply different from the view of marriage held by people in the larger society. The interpretive view offers an "undersocialized" view of human behavior, since it tends to minimize the importance of historical social structures and the deep internalization of social values and norms (Wentworth, 1980). But the innovative couple may find that their personally developed conception of marriage is challenged or undermined by friends, in-laws, legal systems, employers, or others.

Both the functionalist and the interpretive views of socialization are incomplete. Each is relevant for understanding some features, but both tend to ignore other important aspects of social life. It is useful to combine the helpful points of each approach into a more complete view of socialization. Wentworth (1980) proposes exactly such a synthesis. He suggests that an adequate view of socialization must leave room for free will and human autonomy,

*A couple may negotiate between themselves a conception of marriage different from that held by others, but they do this within the cultural and economic constraints of their society.*

though noting the patterned social structures and processes that influence individuals. Wentworth's combined view clarifies the socialization that occurs in families, schools, groups, sports teams, organizations, and societies. It may also explain why resocialization programs such as those designed to rehabilitate criminals, drug addicts, alcoholics, or sex offenders often have relatively low rates of success.

We can distinguish three major aspects of socialization:

1. The *context* in which it occurs
2. The actual *content and processes* people use to socialize others
3. The *results* arising from those contexts and processes

The *context* is like the theater or stage in which socialization occurs. Social context includes culture, language, and social structures such as the class, ethnic, and gender hierarchies of a society. Context also includes social and historical events, power and control in social life, and the people and institutions with whom individuals come in contact in the course of their socialization.

The *content and process* of socialization is like the play, the lines, and the actors. It includes the structure of the socializing activity—how intense and prolonged it is, who does it, how it is done, whether it is a total experience or only a partial process, how aware the individual is of alternatives, and how attractive those alternatives are. *Content* refers specifically to what is passed from member to novice. *Processes* are those interactions that convey to new members how they are to speak, behave, think, and even feel. The view of socialization as an interactive process stands in contrast to the deterministic views of how socialization occurs. Old and new members interact, and in the process exercise mutual influence on each other.

*Outcomes* may properly be defined as what happens later, after someone has been exposed to particular content and processes. New members may learn the behaviors, attitudes, and values that old members hoped they would learn. What do these include? First and foremost among humans is learning how to speak and to apply the rules of language to creating new sentences. Like learning to play chess, learning a language involves being shown some of the ways vocabulary and grammer can be combined (like learning how the various pieces can be moved in a chess game), and then creating one's own combinations from those possibilities. Closely related to learning to use a language is gaining a sense of the rules underlying a society's culture. Even learning to walk in an upright position appears to be the result of socialization.

## THE CONTEXT OF SOCIALIZATION

Socialization occurs within biological, psychological, and social contexts. Each of these offers possibilities and limitations that may influence socialization.

*Even babies seek social interaction.*

## The Biological Context

Biological features are regularly suggested as sources of human behavior. Sociobiologists (see Chapter 3) suggest that some human capacities may be "wired into" our biological makeup. For example, even newborn babies seem to strive for maximum social interaction. They move their heads back and forth in burrowing or "rooting" motions looking for milk; they have powerful, grasping fingers that cling tightly to other human fingers or bodies; and they move so as to maximize body contact with their caregivers. These facts suggest that infants are born wanting human contact.

Sociobiologists argue that traits which aid survival and reproduction (like learning not to eat things that induce vomiting) will survive, whereas others (like unusual whiteness in certain animals, which makes them easier prey) will tend to die out. Although this evidence suggests that biological factors clearly play a role in development, it does not show that all human behavior is biologically determined. Biology sets the stage, on which a very broad range of human behavior occurs. Most or all of the important differences between societies are due to social rather than biological factors.

As educators have become more aware of children with "learning disabilities," they have begun to wonder if some conditions, such as those labeled "dyslexia" (that is, the inability to grasp the meaning of something one reads) are due to the incomplete development of certain nerve pathways in the brain that may scramble signals on the way to the brain, making it likely that children will "see" *b*s instead of *d*s, *q*s rather than *p*s, and so forth. Such problems may be part of the biological context of socialization. They may interact in significant ways with psychological and social factors during socialization and have important effects on the outcomes— for example, if children are labeled retarded or develop a sense of worthlessness, they may be less likely to learn.

In short, biology provides rich potential for becoming human and may present general tendencies, such as the tendency to seek out social interaction or to use language, but it does not determine the particular form such social development takes.

## The Psychological Context

### Emotional States and the Unconscious

The primary factor in the psychological context of socialization is the psychological state of the person being socialized. Psychological states include feelings such as fear, anger, grief, love, and happiness or a sense of emotional deprivation. Strongly feeling one or more of these emotions might very well inhibit or promote socialization of a particular kind. Fear may make it difficult for young children to be socialized in school, whereas people in love may learn very quickly what makes their loved ones happy. Emotions can also influence how individuals perceive the content of socialization, whether in becoming a member of a family group or a religious sect. Knowing something about the feelings of the people involved (the psychological context) helps explain the results of the socialization process.

### Cognitive Development Theories

A number of psychologists emphasize the series of stages through which humans progress. Although emotional concerns can be involved, these theorists focus on **cognitive** (intellectual) **development,** which occurs in a systematic, universal sequence through a series of stages. The most influential theorist of intellectual development was the Swiss psychologist Jean Piaget. A sharp observer of children's development, Piaget stressed that children need to master the skills and operations of one stage of intellectual development before they are able to learn something at the next stage.

Whether or not they all agree on the unfolding of specific stages, cognitive development theorists see children as increasingly trying to make sense of their social worlds as they grow up. Children try to see patterns in the way things happen.

## The Social Context

Social contexts influence individual development. Culture exists before the socialization of new members begins. Parents, for example, do not need to decide alone what they are going to teach their children, since much of what they

*Cognitive development theorists see children as trying to make sense of their worlds.*

will pass along they have themselves learned through socialization. Besides culture, individuals are affected by social and historical events and by a number of individuals who actively try to socialize them.

### Social and Historical Events

Major social and historical events can be a force in socializing an entire generation. Such major events as the Great Depression of the 1930s, the Holocaust in Europe during World War II, or the civil rights movement that took shape in the United States in the 1960s have profound implications for individual socialization. Elder (1974) compared children whose families were very poor during the 1930s with others whose families were more comfortable. Those suffering greater deprivation depended less on formal education for their life achievements and more on effort and accomplishment outside of education. Their health as adults tended to be affected negatively by their economic hardships. Finally, they tended to value marriage and family more highly as a result of their economic deprivation (Elder, 1974). Thus individuals who live in extraordinary times appear to be influenced by the historical events around them.

### Participants in Socialization

Obviously, parents and the immediate family of infants are important to their early care and development. Major changes in the family are increasing the importance of other caregivers as well. Teachers and schools transmit formal skills, knowledge, and social values. As infants mature, they have more and more contact with other children their age, called peers. Inevitably, children are affected by the community and nation in which they are reared. Children in the United States today spend a great deal of time with the mass media. Radio, movies, and—most significantly—television have transformed the way we experience the world and what we know about it.

**THE FAMILY.** In rural societies, children have most of their early social contact with the family. Today, however, the family's importance in the child's life is changing. The American family no longer necessarily conforms to the stereotyp-

*Although children growing up in America today will spend much of their time with people other than members of their families, the participation of parents and families in socialization is still very important.*

**Figure 5.1  Primary Child Care Arrangements for Preschool Children in the United States (over 8 million children).**

Of the 8.2 million children under 5 years old whose mothers work, 31 percent were cared for in their own homes (mainly by their fathers); 37 percent were cared for in another home (usually by a nonrelative); and 23 percent were in organized child care facilities, including day-care centers, nurseries, and preschools. Another 8 percent were cared for by their mothers while they were working either at home or away from home.

*Source:* U.S. Bureau of the Census, 1987b.

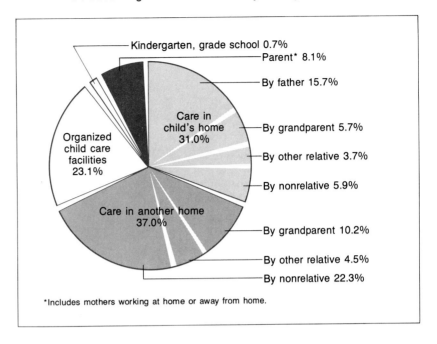

ical nuclear family with two parents and two or more dependent children. Fewer than one family in five consists of a working father, full-time homemaker mother, and at least one child. There are more and more single-parent families, and 56 percent of all mothers with children under 6 years old are working (U.S. Bureau of the Census, 1985a, p. 399). More and more children are receiving their early and primary care from others in addition to their parents. What are the effects on young children of having only one parent in the home? Of having a mother who works outside the home? One study suggests that single parents with adequate financial and emotional support are able to raise their children quite effectively (Monaghan-Leckband, 1978).

Although most children growing up in America today will spend a great deal of time with people other than members of their families, this does not mean that the participation of families in socialization has ended.

On the contrary, the family continues to be a major means of passing on values, attitudes, and behaviors. As we saw in Chapter 1, in the case of Alex and Alice as compared to Albert and his wife, family origin does a great deal to shape a child's social opportunities, resources, and experience. Different social positions may be related to different socialization for children even when they live in the same society.

**DAY CARE.** Nearly 10 million children 5 years old or younger have mothers who work away from home. This includes 48 percent of the mothers of children 3 years old or younger. For these children, day care is an important agent of socialization. In 1982 there were more than 30,000 day-care centers, ranging from informal arrangements at the home of a neighbor to large nurseries run by schools, churches, charities, corporations, and occasionally employers (Lindsey, 1984). Figure 5.1 shows the primary child-care arrangements for children under age 5 whose mothers work outside the home.

When the ratio of staff to children is at least one to ten or lower, when the groups of children are not larger than 20, and when caregivers are trained in early childhood development and are attentive to the children, the children who attend day care do very well (Collins, 1984; Lindsey, 1984). Children from very low income families have benefited considerably over the long term as a result of federally financed Head Start and other early day-care programs (Deutsch et al., 1985; Schweinhart and Weikart, 1987).

**SCHOOLS.** As societies become more complex and there is a greater division of labor, family members cannot spend all day every day teaching children what they need to know to function effectively as adults in society. Therefore, most societies have established schools to teach youngsters certain skills. Schools teach values and attitudes as well. These values and attitudes include, for example, competitiveness or cooperation, conformity or innovation.

Schools try to impress upon children the importance of working for rewards, and they try to teach neatness, punctuality, orderliness, and respect for authority. Teachers are called upon to evaluate how well children perform a particular task or how much skill they have. Thus, in school, children's relationships with adults move from nurture and behavioral concerns to performance of tasks and skills determined by others.

**PEERS.** A **peer group** consists of friends and associates who are about the same age and social status. As children get older, going to school brings them into regular contact with other children of their age. As early as first or second grade, children form social groups. In these early peer groups, children learn to share toys and other scarce resources (such as the teacher's attention). Peers may reinforce behaviors that are stressed by parents and schools—for example, whether it is all right to hit someone else and what are acceptable behaviors for boys and girls. As children move through school, the interests of peer groups may diverge more and more from those of adults. This is particularly true of the United States but seems also to be the case in certain socialist societies today. Youthful concerns may center on popular music and movies, sports, sex, or illegal activities. Par-

*Peers who are about the same age and social status are important socializers of children as they grow up.*

*Day care is important in the socialization of increasing numbers of children.*

ents and teachers, on the other hand, want children to do schoolwork, help at home, and "stay out of trouble." Peer groups may provide social rewards—praise, prestige, and attention—to individuals for doing things adults disapprove of.

In the Soviet Union the peer group is used by authorities to reinforce the behaviors and attitudes they desire. For example, if a child comes to school late, it is not only the teacher who notes this (perhaps by praising children who are on time) but also those in the child's row in the classroom, who may be enlisted to urge the child to come to school on time (Bronfenbrenner, 1970). Peer sanctions (punishments) are particularly effective. In Israel, for instance, in a collective farm group, a child who breaks a rule such as using a tractor when it is not allowed and damaging the machine in the process may be formally ostracized for some time. During this period the other children will not speak to or play with the child. Although effective in achieving social goals, the united effect of peer and official authority is more powerful and painful than official authority alone for the individual who does not conform. In our society, adolescents are heavily influenced by their peers when it comes to dress, musical fads, cheating, and drug use. In making their future life plans, however, they are influenced more by their parents than by their peers (Davies and Kandel, 1981; Kandel and Lesser, 1972; Krosnick and Judd, 1982; Williams, 1972). Girls seem to be somewhat more influenced in their future life plans by peers than are boys (Bush, 1985; Davies and Kandel, 1981; Simmons et al., 1979).

**COMMUNITY AND COUNTRY.** Every society tries to influence how young people grow up. Much of this influence is expressed through parents, schools, and peers, but it is worth considering for a moment how children become exposed to the political and economic ideas that are considered important for citizens of a particular country.

Children learn political information and attitudes rapidly during the elementary school years, particularly between fourth and fifth grades (Hess and Torney, 1967). One of the first things they learn is that they belong to some kind of a political unit. Even very young children develop a sense of "we" in relation to their own country and learn to see other countries in terms of "they." Children also tend to believe that their own country and language are superior to others. This bond may be the most critical socialization feature relating to the political life of the nation (Hess and Torney, 1967). The family helps provide this basic loyalty to country, but the school also shapes the political concepts that expand and develop children's early feelings of attachment. Political orientations develop early and reach nearly adult levels by the end of elementary school, but there are still some critical changes that occur at other points during the life cycle. High school students become more aware of differences between political parties and tend to become more active politically. In the first decade of adult life people modify their political orientations as they take on new occupational and family roles (Jennings and Niemi, 1968).

Children form economic ideas fairly early in life. One study examined how youngsters are socialized into capitalism. When third-graders were compared with twelfth-graders, the older students were found to hold more negative at-

titudes toward labor unions and more favorable attitudes toward business than did the younger children (Cummings and Taebel, 1978), suggesting that, over time, they developed attitudes that were more favorable toward capitalism, perhaps because of what they learned at school, from the media, or at home.

**MASS MEDIA.** The **mass media** include many forms of communication—such as books, magazines, radio, television, and movies—that reach large numbers of people without personal contact between senders and receivers. In the last few decades, children have been dramatically socialized by one source in particular: television. Studies have found that children spend more time watching TV than they spend in school.

It seems unbelievable that in 1945 the pollster George Gallup asked Americans, "Do you know what television is?" Now virtually every American home has at least one television set, and the average set is on almost 7 hours a day (Comstock et al., 1978). How has this transformation affected children? Reports vary, but children in the fifth to eighth grades view an average

*In the Soviet Union the peer group is used by authorities to reinforce behaviors and attitudes they consider desirable.*

of 4 to 6 hours daily (B. S. Greenberg and Dervin, 1970; Lyle and Hoffman, 1972). Most of the research on the effects of television has been on the cognitive and behavioral results of TV watching. The topic most often studied has been the influence of television on antisocial behavior, especially violence. Current research supports the view that seeing violence on television increases the chance that a child will be aggressive (Comstock et al., 1978). No publicly available studies unambiguously relate changes in behavior (such as food habits or drug use) to exposure to television advertising (Comstock et al., 1978).

Research also suggests that young people obtain considerable political and social information from television, but that how they perceive the information depends largely on parental influence (Comstock et al., 1978). For example, during the Vietnam War, television was the most important source of public information about the war. Yet how young people felt about it—whether they favored or opposed it—seemed to be influenced more by their parents than by the opinions presented on television. Those who opposed the war interpreted the news on TV as opposing the war, whereas those favoring it saw the news as favoring it (Comstock et al., 1978).

Most researchers studying the effects of television on children have focused on the content of the programs and not on the total experience of television watching. They argue that there is too much violence and sex on children's programs and that more good educational programs for children are needed.

Winn (1977) suggests that the experience of watching television itself is limiting. When people watch television, no matter what the program, they are simply watchers and are not having any other experience. According to Winn, and many agree, children need to develop family relationships, the capacity for self-direction, and the basic skills of communication (reading, writing, and speaking); to discover their own strengths and limitations; and to learn the rules that keep social interaction alive. Television works against all these goals by putting children in a passive situation where they do not speak, interact, experiment, explore, or do anything else active because they are *watching* a small moving picture on a machine. This research

*Social class affects the way young people are socialized.*

shows the growing importance of television as a medium of socialization, although clearly it is only one among a number of important influences.

## Social Position as Part of the Context

Your family's social class, economic position, and ethnic background—as well as your gender—can affect the ways in which you will be socialized. People in more advantageous positions, like Alice and Alex in Chapter 1, tend to develop higher self-evaluations. As a result, they feel justified in having more resources. Similarly, those in less desired positions tend to have lower self-evaluations and may feel that their lower status is deserved (Della Fave, 1980).

Sociologists ask if children in different social classes are socialized differently. For instance, are middle-class children socialized differently from lower-class children? If so, why and how? Middle-class parents are slightly less likely to use physical punishment than are lower-class parents (Gecas, 1979). Middle-class parents appear to be more concerned about their children's intentions than with the negative consequences of their actions. Thus, if a child breaks a dish, a middle-class parent will be concerned with whether he or she did it "on purpose" or whether it was an accident, and the reaction will vary accordingly. Lower-class parents tend to react in about the same way whatever the intention of the child (Kohn, 1969).

These differences in parental response may stem from the life situations of people in different classes. Different parental experiences in the occupational world color the view of what children need to learn (Kohn, 1969, 1976; Kohn and Schooler, 1983; Pearlin, 1971).

Parents who are closely supervised on the job (more often blue-collar workers) value conformity more than do less supervised parents (usually white-collar workers). Both blue- and white-collar parents increasingly prefer more autonomy in their children, at least in the Detroit area (Alwin, 1984).

Cross-cultural studies show that members of agrarian and herding societies (where food can be accumulated and stored) tend to emphasize compliance in their socialization practices. In societies where food cannot be stored (as in hunting, gathering, or fishing economies), members more often stress individual achievement and self-reliance (Barry, Child, and Bacon, 1959).

Political structure may also be related to socialization practices. Autocratic states tend to have more "severe" socialization, show clear power and deference relationships, and stress obedience (Stephens, 1963). The Soviet Union, for example, works harder to socialize children to conformity than does the United States (Bronfenbrenner, 1970). By way of contrast, tribal societies that lack a centralized or autocratic political system allow children to be less obedient and less conforming (Stephens, 1963).

All these studies suggest that parents value different traits for their children, depending on the economic, political, and social situations they face. In general, when adults have more opportunities for self-determination, they value and try to develop greater self-reliance in their children (Ellis, Lee, and Petersen, 1978). All groups try to socialize their children as well as they can, but they stress different behaviors, depending on what they see as needed in their own situation. Just as different societies may see the need for different behaviors and skills in their children, subgroups within society may do the same thing. They try to prepare their children as well as possible for the positions they are likely to hold.

# THE CONTENT AND PROCESSES OF SOCIALIZATION

We have just seen how one's position in society is related to the content of socialization—that is, to the kind of behavior that is preferred. In this section we consider several theories about how people learn what is valued in their cultures. These ideas include learning theory, social learning theory, the importance of interaction, and how a sense of self emerges through interaction. We then consider a number of case studies that show what happens when these processes are absent.

## Learning Theory

At one time, socialization was considered the same as learning theory. **Learning theory** suggests that specific human behaviors are learned or forgotten as a result of the rewards or punishments associated with them. The focal problem of socialization was how to teach children to become the "right" kind of adults.

James B. Watson, a major American learning theorist, carried on this tradition. Watson argued that human behavior and personalities are completely flexible and can be shaped in any direction. He taught an 11-month-old boy to fear white rats and other furry white objects, such as Santa Claus's beard, by conditioning. Today social learning theorists such as B. F. Skinner and other behaviorists continue Watson's tradition. Skinner stresses that rewards are much more effective conditioners than punishments; he was even able to teach pigeons to play Ping-Pong using this approach.

Behaviorism has been modified by some social psychologists who have advanced a **social learning theory** (Bandura, 1969; Bandura and Walters, 1963). These psychologists study such human behaviors as aggression, sharing, and competitiveness, and are particularly interested in how children imitate or model the behavior they see in others. They argue that people learn through observation, even if they are not always rewarded. Observational learning is more likely to occur in some situations than in others. For example, children are more likely to imitate the

*Social learning theory suggests that children imitate the behavior they see in others they like. This young boy is modeling the behavior of his mother in her college classroom.*

behavior of someone who is more prestigious than that of someone who has less prestige (a sports star more than a bum); more likely to imitate someone like themselves (another child more than a cartoon animal); and more likely to imitate the behavior of models who are rewarded for their actions than that of those who are punished. Social learning theory stresses the vital role played by other people in the socialization process.

## The Importance of Interaction

A newborn child's fussiness, liveliness, or good spirits may affect how people respond to him or her. Whether such traits are genetic or learned, there is growing evidence that people caring for infants react to individual differences in babies (Freedman, 1974). The individual variations that caregivers react to in infants may be social as well as biological and learned. For example, race, class, or gender may influence caregiver reactions as much as crankiness, cuteness, health, or size. There also may be a complex interaction between social and biological traits. A high activity level, for example, may be viewed by some as desirable in a boy but not in a girl.

Infants, in turn, respond differently to similar treatments. This evidence underscores the importance of interaction between new and old members in the process of socialization. Recent observational studies suggest that babies learn early or are born with ways of inviting caregivers to play with them. By 3 months, if not before, infants are well equipped with various behaviors to engage and disengage their caregivers. These include gazing directly into caregivers' eyes, turning their heads or eyes to invite further interaction or to withdraw from it, smiling, and crying (Stern, 1977). In these ways infants present caregivers with signals that enable them to modify their behaviors. Stern's findings suggest that caregivers are reinforced in the attention they offer infants, and therefore are motivated to spend more time interacting with them. They also suggest that infants play an active part in the process. Stern also indicates that infants learn something about sequencing of human interaction, and a sense of "taking turns" in social interaction that develops further as they get older.

## Mead's View of the Self

How interactions affect socialization and development may be illuminated further through George Herbert Mead's concept of the self. Mead (1934) saw the self as composed of two parts, "I" and "me." The "I" portion of the self represents the spontaneous disposition or impulse to act. This part of the self allows for some innovation and creativity on the part of individuals, as well as for some freedom from control by others. The "I" acts when the individual takes the initiative in a situation. This part of the self allows individuals to act on their environment. The "me" portion of the self brings the influence of others into the individual's consciousness. This part of the self includes the views of self an individual learns from others, and it carries the thoughts, norms, and values that the major agents of socialization (family, school, peers, television, and so forth) present.

Charles Horton Cooley (1902), Mead's teacher, used the term the **looking-glass self** to describe how people become aware of who they are from the ideas others have about them.

In his view other people are like mirrors who reflect back to us what they think we are. Just as people get a sense of what they are like from an image in the mirror, so they get a sense of self as they see how others treat them and react to them.

This social nature, or what Mead calls the "me" portion of the self, develops as children grow up and learn to play multiple-person games that require them to take the role of the **generalized other**—that is, to be able to see how each player will behave toward each other player. Ultimately the generalized other expands to include the attitudes of the whole community, of which children come to be aware. This process is continuous, and Mead saw the self as always emerging—that is, constantly developing and changing—rather than being static or fixed. This potential for change is due in part to the way Mead's self can **reflect on itself** and make choices.

The "I" and the "me" parts of one's self can interact with each other in what Mead calls "self-interaction," or making an object out of one's self. For example, people may ask themselves, "Why do you feel so depressed?" or "Why did you stay out so late last night?" They step back and look at their feelings and behaviors the way they would those of another person. In these ways, what people think, feel, and do interacts with what they know others wish or expect them to do. People can decide to give relatively greater weight to one rather than another of these demands, and they can make choices among the competing influences. They can weigh alternatives, take things into account, make choices, and organize themselves for action. In this way Mead's conception of the self allows individuals to participate in their own socialization. They can even "rehearse" mentally for actions they plan to take in the future.

People frequently seem to prepare for certain life roles before they happen. Sociologists call this **anticipatory socialization** and see it as referring to the way people take on the attitudes, values, and behaviors of some status they expect to occupy in the future. One 5-year-old boy, for example, ran to watch his father barbecue dinner outside, saying: "I need to learn how to do this because when I grow up I'll need to do this for my family." This is a good example of

modeling behavior, but the imitation is not immediate. Instead, there is the expectation that certain skills and behavior will be useful or desirable at some fairly distant time in the future. People may want to learn how to read a map or change a tire because someday it might be helpful. The intrinsic motivation for competence combines with an anticipation of what will be useful or fun in the future, stimulating people to internalize certain values or learn new skills.

## Case Studies of Socialization

Socialization contexts and processes inevitably affect the results that occur. Nowhere is this more apparent than in the cases of individuals who receive distorted or deprived childhood experiences. Of course it is unethical and illegal to perform experiments on infants or children that would deprive them of social contact from an early age. However, a number of "natural experiments" have occurred that indicate what happens when infants or children are denied social contact. Some instructive experiments showing the results of denying them contact with a caring adult have also been done with monkeys.

There are numerous reports from the Middle Ages onward about infants whose every physical need was met and yet who failed to grow normally and often grew sick and died (Ross and McLaughlin, 1949; Spitz, 1945). Evidence suggests that to survive and become human, people need certain kinds of social as well as biological sustenance. This evidence comes from accounts of children kept isolated by their own families; studies of children raised in institutions; and experiments on the effects of isolation in monkeys.

### Effects of Early Childhood Isolation

Two cases of extreme childhood isolation in the United States were reported by Kingsley Davis (1940, 1947). Most children who are kept isolated eventually sicken and die, but there is the known case of a girl, named Anna, who did not. She was kept locked in the attic of her family's Pennsylvania farm because she was an illegitimate child and her grandfather was unwilling to acknowledge her presence. The mother was unable to place Anna in a foster home, so she brought her home. Since Anna's grandfather was violently opposed to the child, her mother put her in an attic room, where she stayed. The girl was fed just enough to keep her alive, but she received no social play or affection. When she was discovered by a social worker six years later, Anna was unable to speak, sit up, walk, keep herself clean, or feed herself. She didn't laugh, smile, or seem to care about anything or anyone. The social workers assumed she was mentally retarded, deaf, or both. Placed in a special school, Anna learned to coordinate her body and to communicate. She could speak words and phrases. She also learned how to string beads, to build with blocks, to identify some colors, to wash her hands and brush her teeth, to play with dolls, and to help other children. She learned to walk and even to run clumsily before she died four and a half years later.

A second child, Isabelle, found about the same time as Anna, fared somewhat better. Like Anna, Isabelle was illegitimate and was about 6½ when discovered. Isabelle's grandfather kept her and her deaf-mute mother in a dark room most of the time. Unlike Anna, Isabelle had the advantage of interaction with another human being, but she could not learn conventional language. Instead, she and her mother developed a system of gestures for communicating with each other. When discovered, Isabelle reacted wildly to other people. Because she could utter only strange croaking sounds, she was first thought to be deaf. Specialists declared her feebleminded. Even so, a skilled team of psychologists and doctors began working intensively with her. Her learning began slowly, but suddenly she began racing through the stages of childhood learning that usually occur in the first six years. She went through the stages in the usual order, but far more rapidly. By the age of 8½, she had gone from being "feebleminded" to achieving an apparently normal level of development. She eventually entered school and took part in school activities as normally as other children. Her giant gains seem to have been due to the early interaction she had with her mother and to her skilled trainers.

The cases of Anna, Isabelle, and Genie, who was mentioned at the beginning of the chapter,

reveal that much of the behavior we think of as human does not arise directly from biology. Instead, it seems to depend on the interplay between biological potential and social interaction and affection. Isabelle, although deprived in her early years, did receive affection and had contact with at least one other human. Hence she could, in effect, catch up with other children her age. Isabelle shows that the developmental stages children are thought to go through are *situationally activated*—that is, they may not occur at the expected time unless certain things are happening in the infant's environment. These cases illustrate the complex interaction between "unfolding" human nature and the environment in which a child lives. What children need from this environment is further specified by cases of children raised in institutions.

### Children Raised in Institutions

In two classic studies done in 1945 and 1946, René A. Spitz, a psychologist, compared infants raised in a foundling home (an institution for babies whose mothers could not support themselves and their children) with those cared for in the nursery of a penal institution for delinquent girls. If anything, Spitz suggests that the parents of the foundling home infants had social and intellectual backgrounds that were superior to those of the nursery children's parents. Both institutions were clean; offered well prepared, adequate food; dressed the children similarly; and offered comparable health care. In terms of physical provisions, they were similar.

The 45 babies in the foundling home were cared for by a head nurse and five assistant nurses. Although Spitz reported that the nurses loved the babies, each one had to divide her time among eight babies. As a result, the babies of the foundling home lacked human contact for most of the day. Much of the time there was little going on to attract the babies' attention. Their beds had sheets draped over the sides so that they could see only the ceiling of the room. A quarter of the babies died before they were 3 months old, apparently from lack of social contact.

In contrast, the nursery was run by a head nurse with three assistants, but the care of the children fell to their own mothers, the young women in the penal institution. Each baby had the full-time care of his or her own mother.

Moreover, Spitz indicates that caring for their babies was one of the few sources of solace for the otherwise heavily deprived inmates. So their babies received lavish attention and tenderness. All day long the nursery teemed with social activity. Despite the probably better hereditary background of the foundling children, Spitz suggests, the nursery children actually developed faster and further physically, emotionally, and socially. Good physical care is not sufficient for the healthy physical, emotional, intellectual, and social development of children. They also need social stimulation and sustained human warmth and contact. Similar effects have been found with young monkeys.

### Even Monkeys Need Others

In a series of famous experiments Harry F. Harlow and his associates explored what happens to monkeys raised in isolation or without mothers. He reared the monkeys under different sets of conditions: some only with other baby monkeys, some with terrycloth models of mothers, and some with chicken-wire mothers. All these monkeys developed serious problems

*Harlow's famous experiments with baby monkeys and real mothers, wire mothers, and terry cloth mothers revealed much about how various kinds of interactions affect the development of monkeys. This is the terry cloth mother that Harlow used in his experiments.*

as adults. Most of the mother-deprived monkeys could not play or otherwise interact with other monkeys, socially or sexually. Those few adult females who were successfully impregnated showed completely abnormal maternal behavior. They either avoided their infants completely or they beat them. The monkeys needed both a live mother *and* live peers to develop normally (Harlow, 1963; Harlow and Harlow, 1965; Seay, Alexander, and Harlow, 1964).

Harlow's work suggests that monkeys deprived of needed interpersonal socialization in their youth are unable to reproduce and nurture a new generation. Adequate socialization seems necessary for survival of the species. Of course, we need to be careful about generalizing from other primates to humans, but the fact that humans depend even more than monkeys on social learning suggests the importance of early social interaction. Together these strands of evidence strongly support the assertion that although human potential may be rooted in biological capacities, its full development requires key social experiences. Virtually all theories of human development assume that infants and children receive at least minimal social contact.

Assuming such contact occurs, and an individual begins to develop a conception of self, the Meadian view of self becomes useful. People do "talk to themselves" about what they are doing and what will happen as a result of what they are doing. They can decide to make one choice rather than another. They can weigh the value of various alternatives.

These cases are summarized in Table 5.1. In this brief form, very dramatic relationships appear among context, processes, and results. These patterns dramatize the social nature of socialization and suggest that outcomes depend heavily on social processes rather than solely on innate capacities.

## THE RESULTS OF SOCIALIZATION

### Language Acquisition

One of the results of socialization in virtually every society is that people learn to use the language of their group. The first words children learn are simply labels for persons, things, or

**Table 5.1**    *Socialization Case Studies in Terms of Context, Processes, and Results*

| Case | Context | Processes | Results |
|---|---|---|---|
| **Anna** | Nearly total isolation. | Little or negative contact with others. | Could not speak, sit up, walk, feed herself, laugh, smile, or wash at age 6. Uninterested in anything. |
| **Isabelle** | Locked in a darkened room with a deaf-mute mother. | No exposure to other people, culture, or society. Mother and child developed a system of signs for communicating. | At age 6, she had not learned to speak and she behaved wildly. |
| **Genie** | Nearly total confinement. | Punished for vocalizing. Very little stimulation. | Did not learn language beyond that of 4-year-old. Unsocialized. Could not walk. |
| **Foundling Home Babies** | Sterile hospital environment; one nurse for eight babies. | Little human contact. Physical needs were met, but babies received little play or attention. | Twenty-five percent died by their third month. Others were very slow to develop speech and motor skills. |
| **Prison Nursery Babies** | Early rearing in a prison ward; cared for by their own mothers. | Prison mothers lavished attention and tenderness on their babies. | Babies were curious, very vocal and active. Most walked at 10 months. |
| **Harlow's Monkeys** | Wire "mothers." | No bodily contact or touching. | Could not play or interact with other monkeys socially or sexually. |
| | Live mother and peers. | Much touching and playing. | Able to interact with others, to mate, and to rear their young. |

actions—for example, "Daddy," "juice," "go," or "dog." Children also learn to describe or request things: "stove hot" or "want milk." At this stage, words serve basically as signs—that is, as names that substitute for things themselves. In the early stages of using language, children create sentences that are shorthand versions of adult sentences. For instance, "where is Mommy?" is often expressed as "where Mommy?"

In their second year children begin to attach words to objects. Average 1-year-olds understand only about three words, but at age 2 vocabulary has swelled to nearly three hundred words. Children in the 1970s used longer clauses and sentences and had larger vocabularies than children in the 1940s. This change may be due to television, to the existence of nursery schools, or to the general rise in the level of education in the population. Besides vocabulary, children also need to learn the rules of grammar in their language. It is not fully understood how they learn grammatical rules so early and how they can use these rules to generate totally new sentences. It does not seem to be the result of direct training, since parents seldom systematically reward correct grammar and punish incorrect forms. Nor does simple imitation explain the process, since children can create new sentences.

By the age of 6, the average child has a vocabulary of about 2500 words, assuming the child has interacted regularly with people in a social environment. By this time children have begun learning the symbolic uses of language, and they begin to make jokes and puns. They realize that words have various meanings and that these meanings are appropriate at different times. It may be all right to call a friend who knows it is a joke a "cuckoo-head," but not so nice to call a stranger that name.

Learning to talk and learning to walk are two of the most difficult tasks the growing child must learn. Yet virtually all children succeed in doing both by the age of 5 or 6 unless they are physically impaired or isolated from human contact.

## Sense of Self and Personality

### Freud's Id, Ego, and Superego

Sigmund Freud (1856–1939) was one of the most influential thinkers of this century. In the social realm, Freud saw the individual and society as being at war. According to him, individuals are born with uncontrolled drives, especially for sex and aggression, and society seeks to repress or channel those drives into acceptable outlets. The dictates of society, particularly the Victorian era in which Freud lived, often shaped this suppression in such a heavy-handed way that people became neurotic.

In explaining the conflict that arises between self and society, Freud identified three concepts in the personality structure. The first is the **id**, the unconscious part consisting of instinctual impulses—for instance, aggressive or sexual impulses that seek immediate expression. Newborn babies and very young children are governed almost exclusively by the id. As children mature, a conscious part of the self emerges, which Freud called the **ego**. The ego strives to mediate between the impulses of the id and the rules of society. Parents are the major carriers of societal requirements; they teach their children what is expected and hope that children will come to accept for themselves the values of

their society. The internal regulator that develops in most people is the third personality part proposed by Freud, which he called the **superego.** The superego upholds the norms of society. Freud felt that healthy individuals learned how to accommodate the inherently conflicting desires of the id and the socially prescribed restrictions on expressing those desires. That accommodation represented successful socialization, in Freud's view.

### Locus of Self-Definition

Another way of assessing the results of socialization is by probing an individual's self-conceptions. A method for doing this was developed by Kuhn and McPartland (1954). They asked individuals to give 20 answers to the question "Who am I?" You might try doing this now, before you read further. Simply list on a piece of paper 20 words or phrases that describe who you are. When this question was asked of college students in 1957, most of them (51 percent) gave answers such as "I am a student," "I am an American," and so forth (Hartley, 1968). This type of reply described the self in terms of social roles. In its extreme form the conception of the self as consisting only of all the social roles an individual plays denies the existence of any self separate from the performance of social roles. This view leads to an "oversocialized" view of behavior. Fewer students (31 percent) described themselves in terms of personal qualities such as "I am a happy," "humorous," or "shy person." Fewer still (2 percent) used physical descriptions ("I am blond"), or very general and vague replies like "I am a living person," which did nothing to distinguish the respondent from anyone else (16 percent).

When the same question was asked of college students 12 years later, in 1969, the results were dramatically different. The majority of students (68 percent) described themselves in terms of personal qualities. Whereas earlier students were more likely to say "I am a college student," the later group more often replied with a personal statement, such as "I am a concerned person" (Zurcher, 1977). This trend is consistent with data from national samples that have been collected and analyzed by Florence Skelly (1978). This shift alerted Zurcher (1977) and Turner (1976) to the possibility that the self might have shifted its point of primary anchor from an institutional to an impulse base. In this sense the institutional base refers to social roles. In all these cases it is important to note that one's self-identity is rooted in both the impulse and the institutional realms. What Turner, Zurcher, and others are remarking on is the relative importance of one in relation to the other.

## Sociology of Emotions

Emotions and feelings seem to be clear pyschological phenomena. Yet even emotions are shaped by sociological processes (Averill, 1980; Hochschild, 1975, 1979, 1981; Kemper, 1978, 1981a, 1981b; Shott, 1979). In the Pacific Island of Tahiti, for example, the emotions of fear and shame are expected and encouraged, while sad feelings are made "culturally invisible" (Levy, 1973, pp. 273, 307, 324). Tahitians whose spouses die interpret the "strange" feelings of loss as illness (Levy, 1973, p. 324, cited in Shott, 1979, p. 1320). This and other cross-cultural examples indicate that the way we interpret our emotions and even to some degree *what* we feel is guided by our culture and its feeling rules (Hochschild, 1975, p. 289). *How* emotions are expressed is shaped by cultural expectations. In some cultures, anger is barely allowed any expression; in others, anger may be expressed through calm discussion; in yet others, shouting exchanges are the expected way for anger to be expressed.

The concept of **emotion work** refers to the effort to change an emotion or feeling (Hochschild, 1979, p. 561). It does not simply mean denying or suppressing a feeling; it refers to shaping the way one feels. People may do emotion work if they sense their feelings are inappropriate for the social situation of the moment. In our culture, most people would try not to giggle constantly at a funeral, for example. Socialization of feelings is important because a considerable amount of social control depends upon self-control (Shott, 1979). **Social control** refers to the relatively patterned and systematic ways in which society guides and restrains individual behaviors so that people act in predictable and desired ways. The feelings of guilt, shame, and embarrassment may deter some deviant behavior and encourage altruistic conduct (Shott, 1979). The meaning of these feelings is socially

learned and their expression varies widely in different societies. This approach to the sociology of emotions has been called the *social constructionist* approach, because it stresses the way social and cultural norms shape emotional experiences and expressions. It is close to the symbolic interactionist perspective discussed in Chapter 1. A more positivist approach to the sociology of emotions has also been proposed (Kemper, 1978, 1981a). (The term **positivist** designates an approach to explaining human action that does not need to take into account the person's interpretation of the situation.) In this view, power and status relations produce certain physiological processes, which in turn determine different emotions (Kemper, 1981b, pp. 339, 344). As an example, Kemper says "I see my spouse at a distance and I feel authentic happiness (she is the epitome of the ideal person in how she treats me and others)" (1981b, p. 349). A social constructionist suggests that positivists do not go far enough. We need to understand how people move from objective power and status relationships to their various interpretations of those relationships (Hochschild, 1981, p. 434). Why does a child interpret parental power as domination one day and as love another day? Interpretations and power relations are both important for understanding the sociology of emotions.

## Effective Socialization

All societies socialize new generations reasonably effectively. The only exceptions seem to occur when a society loses its physical means of sustenance. This happened in this century to the Ik tribe in Uganda when it was moved off its hunting lands and could not survive physically. Ik culture and socialization practices broke down, and Ik people tended to ignore their own children (Turnbull, 1972). It also happened to the Ojibwa tribe described at the beginning of Chapter 3. Within any particular society, different families are more or less effective in getting their children to feel and act deeply committed to the values of their group. Why and how do such differences occur?

Certain conditions have been identified as leading to a greater likelihood that individuals will come to resemble their elders. Caregivers who are warm, nurturing, and loving are more likely to reinforce good behavior in children. Also, the withdrawal of approval is seen as a more serious punishment by children when they feel that the adult in question loves and approves of them. A warm, nurturing relationship makes children want to identify with the adults who care for them. When children identify with parents or other significant adults, they seek to be like them; they "take on," or internalize, the behaviors and attitudes of those adults. Children also are more likely to follow their parents' advice or commands if they see their parents as having authority in other areas of their life. If outsiders defer to their parents, if their parents seem to be in charge of their own lives in reasonably successful ways, and if, in general, they seem to know what they are doing, young people are more likely to feel that parental authority should be taken seriously. Several observers have noted that the combination of power and love is particularly influential in a child's life (Goode, 1977).

Relative consistency in the application of rules also helps children to follow them and to see them as fair. If an action is usually treated in the same way and if different children are treated similarly for doing something right or wrong, children are more likely to get a clear idea of what is expected of them. In the application of rewards, some inconsistency tends to reinforce behaviors more effectively than being rewarded for something every time. Called **intermittent reinforcement** by psychologists, this phenomenon has daily applications. If children are sometimes praised or rewarded for particularly good behavior, they are more likely to keep doing it in the hope that this time they will be rewarded or praised. As they get older, they can usually go longer and longer between reinforcements.

Participation in the rule-making process also elicits greater commitment to those rules than does the imposition of rules. Youngsters on a ball team who agree to certain rules of play are very much involved in maintaining and defending those rules, more so than if a teacher or other adult tells them what the rules are. Children and adults who are told what the rules are are more likely to accept the rules if they are told why it is important to follow them. Even quite young children can be persuaded to do something (or not to do it) if they can be led to

see what the likely outcome is and if they value or dislike that consequence. (See the debate on the role of punishment in child rearing.)

## SOCIALIZATION THROUGH THE LIFE COURSE

There is no special age at which people stop growing and being influenced by the social world. Although many earlier theorists saw development as ending in childhood, we now view socialization as continuing throughout the life course. Indeed, sociologists are increasingly applying an approach called **life-course analysis,** which examines how different social stages of life influence socialization and behavior (Elder, 1978; Dannefer, 1984). This sociological approach emphasizes that human development responds to social environments, that social environments are complex and varied, and that social knowledge and human intentions shape development (Dannefer, 1984, pp. 106–107). Take the example of learning an occupational identity. Medical students, for instance, gradually begin to acquire the identity of doctor as they go through the rigors, despairs, exhilarations, and doubts of medical school (Becker et al., 1961). The intense, lengthy, and concentrated training helps to solidify that identity, as do the rewards and status that accompany it.

### Resocialization

It is helpful to distinguish between socialization for something new and **resocialization.** The former refers to such experiences as going to law school or being an apprentice or a management trainee. The latter refers to the process of socializing people away from a group or activity in which they are involved. Resocialization is the goal of programs for alcoholics, drug addicts, delinquents, or criminals. Comparing socialization for something new with resocialization in terms of key differences in their social contexts and processes shows why they tend to have different results (see Table 5.2). The former involves some new, usually attractive goal valued and freely chosen by the individual, rather than simply the giving up of something

## DEBATING SOCIETY'S ISSUES

### *"Spare the Rod and Spoil the Child?"*

One of the most hotly debated issues in child rearing is the effect of punishment on children. "Spare the rod and spoil the child" is a maxim from an earlier era. Today there is little evidence to support the use of corporal punishment on children, but it is not clear that there is less physical harm done to youngsters. One study found that more than 80 percent of American parents had physically punished their children within the past year, and more than 60 percent had done so at least once a week, on the average. Among the college students, 46 percent had been beaten or physically assaulted by a parent during their senior year of high school (Straus et al., 1979).

How do spanking and other forms of physical punishment affect children? In a systematic review of relevant evidence, Gilmartin (1979) reports many negative effects and virtually no positive ones. Children who are frequently spanked tend to become highly resentful and distrustful of authority; they are more likely to develop poor self-images; they are more likely to fight and be aggressive at school and elsewhere; and they are very apt to beat their own children. Even more serious, violent criminals are more likely to have been frequently beaten and otherwise cruelly punished as children than are law-abiding citizens. Furthermore, such criminals seldom received any warmth or respect from their parents or guardians. The authorities in their lives were cruel, callous, hostile, or indifferent to them (Gilmartin, 1979). To the degree that physical punishment makes children nervous and tense, it impedes their ability to learn effectively. Children who are relaxed but alert learn and think better than tense ones. If children misbehave frequently, that should be taken as a sign of unfulfilled and unrecognized needs (Gilmartin, 1979, p. 23). Harsh physical punishment increases the social distance between adult and child and reduces the chance that they will interact on a mutually enjoyable basis. To be most effective, socialization requires one or more adults who care very deeply about the child (White, Kaban, and Attanucci, 1979).

Research seems to suggest that corporal punishment is not good for children. Many experience it and most survive relatively unharmed, but excessive physical punishment can be quite damaging. Two questions are not answered by the research, however. First, how do parents and communities discipline children when they do not behave in desirable ways? To what degree should families be allowed to determine for themselves whether or not to use physical punishment? If they do, how much physical punishment is permissible? Should the state play a role in protecting the health and safety of young children? If so, what role should the state play? Should it pass laws against child abuse? Should it inspect homes for signs of compliance or violation? What do you think?

---

that may be desired by the individual. The process of socialization for something new may itself be interesting or enjoyable; most resocialization processes are not. It is possible that these differences account for the widely different success rates in the two types of socialization.

## Socialization for Death

In many ways socialization for death resembles resocialization. It is not a goal actively sought by most people; it may be seen mainly as socialization away from something (life). Socialization for death has been made more difficult in our society by the way death and dying are treated. Socialization involves interactions that result in socially constructed meanings. But if people have limited interactions in a particular realm, it is difficult to develop socially shared meanings and a sense of how to behave.

This lack is vividly apparent in the way our society deals with death and dying. Death is often a taboo topic in our culture. People don't die, they "pass away." Death is considered too morbid to discuss. It also became unacceptable for people to die at home. Instead of dying comfortably in their own surroundings, people were relegated to hospitals and old age homes. The medical profession's definition of death tended to prevail. Because doctors and nurses are trained to save lives and consider themselves successful when they do, death may represent failure to them. For them to be actively involved

**Table 5.2**   *Socialization for Something New and Resocialization (or Rehabilitation)*

| Socialization for Something New | Resocialization |
| --- | --- |
| Context<br>1. Involves socialization *toward* something (a new status, position, skill, or reward). | Context<br>1. Involves socialization *away from* something (drug use, overeating, alcoholism, criminal or delinquent behavior). |
| 2. This goal is usually chosen and desired by the individual. | 2. This goal may not be desired or chosen by individuals, who may prefer their present behaviors. |
| 3. Sometimes people pay the cost themselves. | 3. Individuals seldom pay the cost themselves. |
| Process<br>4. The process may be interesting and enjoyable. | Process<br>4. The process may be unpleasant or unbearable, physically, psychically, or socially. |
| 5. The connection between the process and the end is clear to the participant. | 5. The connection between the process and any desired end may be completely unclear to the participant. |
| Result<br>6. The process succeeds at a fairly high rate. | Result<br>6. The process fails more often than it succeeds. |

in preparing people for death suggests somehow that they have given up hope for the sick person. Part of being prepared to be a physician ideally involves being trained to deal with and ultimately to accept death, as Coombs and Powers (1975) indicate.

The "denial of death," as Ernest Becker (1973) has called it, begins at an early age in our society. Children under a certain age are not allowed into most hospitals, so they cannot see a sick or

*Resocialization often involves giving up desirable behaviors. As a result, it may require dramatic intervention, as in this Daytop drug treatment encounter group.*

dying person. Sometimes they are even told "Grandma went away" rather than what really happened. Yet when children are in a home where death has struck and are allowed to join in the talk, fear, and grief, they may gain comfort from the shared responsibility and mourning. Gradually they may come to view death as part of life (Kübler-Ross, 1969). Communities that provide opportunities for people to witness death, talk about death and dying, and collectively prepare for it seem to socialize people rather successfully for impending death (Hochschild, 1973b; Marshall, 1975).

A few communities have hospices, which offer an alternative to hospital or home care for the terminally ill. In such an institution it is understood that no heroic efforts will be made to prolong the patient's life (such as resuscitations, use of respirators, or endless operations), although comfort therapy (for example, pain medications and nutrients) will be provided. The aim is to make such an institution as comfortable, pleasant, and unlike a hospital as possible. The knowledge that doctors would treat them as they themselves would want to be treated set to rest many of the worries and fears of people in one retirement community (Marshall, 1975, p. 1139).

Using a facility like a hospice requires, of course, that patients be told how sick they are. Controversy surrounds the issue of how much patients should be told about their condition. Increased discussion of death and dying is one of several social changes that are occurring and that may help people prepare for death. A number of books, including Kübler-Ross's *On Death and Dying* (1969) and Ernest Becker's *Denial of Death* (1973)—as well as numerous articles—have promoted public discussion of death.

After interviewing hundreds of terminally ill patients over a number of years, Kübler-Ross, for instance, began to discern a pattern in their behavior. She noticed that individuals move through five distinct stages in response to their impending deaths. The first stage is one of denial, even for patients who suspect the worst and fight to hear the truth. They may retreat into a self-imposed isolation at this point. Second, patients get angry—at their relatives for being healthy, at nurses for being young, at doctors for doing nothing to help, or at God. After the rage has been expressed, patients enter a third phase in which they try to bargain for their lives. They promise they will mend their ways if only they are allowed to live. In the fourth stage, patients grieve for themselves. They often become quite depressed at this point. Patients who get through this stage often face death more calmly for having been through it. The fifth and final stage, reached only by some, is the acceptance of death. These stages offer psychological preparation for death. But without the social opportunities to share such experiences, individuals may not be able to prepare for death.

After someone has died, there is wide variation in how the event is handled. A few people have private, nearly secret, burials; others have socially shared customs for dealing with death and the ensuing grief. Irish and Italian Catholics have "wakes," or vigils over the corpse before a burial. Jews engage in "sitting shivah." Both practices allow time and space for families and friends to gather to share their mourning and reaffirm their support for one another. This provides people with some preparation for death, as well as help in their time of loss.

Socialization toward death is something most people experience only once. The broader socialization processes that it illustrates, however, occur much more frequently in such life-giving experiences as learning to be a student, joining a team, preparing for parenthood, becoming a citizen, becoming a grandparent, and so forth. The process of being socialized continues throughout life, and individuals continue to play an active part in that process.

## SUMMARY

1. In the last hundred years, the view of socialization has changed from one of civilizing unruly individuals with a focus on the end result of internalization to an interpretive reaction that stresses individual responsibility for creating the social world.

2. Wentworth's synthesis combines aspects from each of these views. He offers a framework for analyzing socialization in terms of contexts, processes, and results.

3. Context consists of biological, psychological, and social factors. People need food, water, warmth, and shelter. Certain behaviors such as grasping, rooting, and sucking are evident at birth, before they could have been socially reinforced.

4. The psychological context of socialization includes emotional states, the unconscious mind, and stages of cognitive development.

5. The social context of socialization is influenced by historical and social events, by the major participants in the situation, and by one's position in the social hierarchies of society. Families, other caregivers, day-care centers, schools and teachers, peers, communities, nations, and the mass media all interact with growing individuals.

6. The process of socialization is an interactive one. Infants with certain innate temperaments or traits interact with their social world and indeed even influence it. The social world and social stimuli, in turn, influence individual development and growth.

7. Mead and Cooley suggest a conception of the self that incorporates individual drives, desires, and initiatives (the "I" portion) with an

internalization of social values, norms, and ideas the individual has learned from others (the "me" part of the self). These two parts can interact, and individuals can make choices among the competing alternatives available to them.

8. Both young people and adults anticipate positions they will occupy and begin thinking and behaving in ways they see as appropriate for their futures.

9. Case studies of extreme social deprivation suggest that infants do not develop into walking, talking, social beings without experiencing social interaction.

10. Learning to use the language of one's group is proof that socialization occurs. Children cannot learn to speak by themselves. They need to learn not only the objects and actions words represent, but also the underlying rules of grammar and syntax that permit those words to be strung together in ways that are meaningful to others.

11. Freud offers a theory of the self as composed of id, ego, and superego. The ego mediates between the impulses of the id and the demands of society.

12. The terms people use to describe their "selves" have shifted in recent decades away from social roles and toward personal traits.

13. Emotions are shaped by social structures and by socially learned interpretations.

14. Effective socialization appears to depend on a reasonably secure food supply, caregivers who love and interact with infants and children, the perceived reasonableness of what is expected, and the encouragement of favored behaviors rather than excessive punishment of undesirable behavior.

15. Socialization continues throughout life as adults learn new roles.

16. Resocialization differs in a number of significant ways from socialization for something new. Such differences may explain why resocialization seems to have only limited results.

17. Socialization for death resembles resocialization in certain respects. Moreover, in the United States death is structured in ways that make it difficult for people to develop socially shared meanings and behaviors in relation to death. Several social changes, including increased discussion and the existence of hospices, contribute to successful socialization for death. Socialization toward death illustrates the processes of socialization that occur in life-giving experiences, such as preparing for parenthood.

## KEY TERMS

anticipatory socialization (p. 109)
cognitive development (p. 101)
ego (p. 113)
emotion work (p. 114)
generalized other (p. 109)
id (p. 113)
intermittent reinforcement (p. 115)
internalization (p. 99)
learning theory (p. 107)
life-course analysis (p. 115)
looking-glass self (p. 108)
mass media (p. 105)
peer group (p. 104)
positivist (p. 114)
resocialization (p. 115)
socialization (p. 98)
social control (p. 114)
social learning theory (p. 107)
superego (p. 113)

## SUGGESTED READINGS

Becker, Howard S., Blanche Geer, Everett C. Hughes, and Anselm L. Strauss. 1961. *Boys in White: Student Culture in Medical School*. Chicago: University of Chicago Press. An interesting study of how medical students learn to become doctors.

Comstock, George et al. 1978. *Television and Human Behavior*. New York: Columbia University Press. A major study of how television affects attitudes and behaviors.

MacLeod, Jay. 1987. *Ain't No Makin' It: Leveled Aspirations in a Low-Income Neighborhood*. Boulder, CO: Westview Press. An ethnographic study of two groups of lower-class adolescent males and how their aspirations and actions are influenced by their families, peers, schools, and communities.

Ogbu, John U. 1978. *Minority Education and Caste.* New York: Academic Press. A significant study of how caste barriers in a society limit the educational efforts of young people and how, when those barriers are removed, young people raise their aspirations and efforts.

Wentworth, William M. 1980. *Context and Understanding: An Inquiry into Socialization Theory.* New York: Elsevier. An important theoretical assessment and synthesis of socialization theory.

Wrong, Dennis. 1961. "The Oversocialized Conception of Man in Modern Sociology." *American Sociological Review* 26: 183–193. Attacks a view of socialization that fails to leave room for the way individuals may reject social norms.

# Groups and Organizations

*In the 1930s, U.S. automobile workers faced management speedups. For example, one employee on a work team would be removed while the same production quota was required. Although they were not yet well organized, workers frequently expressed their grievances through brief sit-down strikes.*

*A typical incident occurred in 1936 in a major General Motors plant in Flint, Michigan, according to Gamson, Fireman, and Rytina (1982, p. 1). When a team of welders came to work, they found that one worker had been removed. Two brothers named Perkins stopped working. When the foreman and superintendent came over, they had a major argument over the speedup. Quite a few car bodies went by on the line before the Perkins brothers went back to work. The next night they were fired.*

*At that time the United Automobile Workers (UAW) had only about 40 members among the 8000 workers at the plant, and the Perkins brothers did not belong. But when some of the union activists heard their story, one of them, named Bud Simons, ran through the welding department and yelled, "The Perkins boys were fired! Nobody starts working." Kraus described the events that followed (1947, pp. 48–54):*

*The whistle blew. Every man in the department stood at his station, a deep, significant tenseness in him. The foreman pushed the button, and the skeleton bodies, already partly assembled when they got to this point, began to rumble forward. But no one lifted a hand. All eyes were turned to Simons who stood out in the aisle by himself.*

*The bosses ran about like mad.*

*"Whatsamatter? Whatsamatter? Get to work!" they shouted.*

*But the men acted as though they never heard them. One or two of them couldn't stand the tension. Habit was deep in them, and it was like physical agony for them to see the bodies pass untouched. They grabbed their tools and chased after them. "Rat! Rat!" the men growled without moving, and the others came to their senses.*

*The superintendent stopped by the "bow-men."*

*"You're to blame for this!" he snarled.*

*"So what if we are?" little Joe Urban, the Italian, cried, overflowing with pride. "You ain't running your line, are you?"*

*That was altogether too much. The superintendent grabbed Joe and started for the office with him. The two went down the entire line, while the men stood rigid as though awaiting the word of command. . . . Simons, a torch-solderer, was almost at the end of the line. He too was momentarily held in a vise by the superintendent's overt act of authority. The latter had dragged Joe Urban past him when he finally found the pesence of mind to call out:*

*"Hey, Teefee, where you going?"*

*It was spoken in just an ordinary conversational tone, and the other was taken so aback he answered the really impertinent question.*

*"I'm taking him to the office to have a little talk with him." Then suddenly he realized and got mad. "Say, I*

*think I'll take you along too!"*

*That was his mistake.*

*"No you won't!" Simons said calmly.*

*"Oh yes I will!" and he took hold of his shirt. Simons yanked himself loose.*

*And suddenly, at this simple act of insurgence, Teefee realized his danger. He seemed to become acutely conscious of the long line of silent men and felt the threat of their potential strength. They had been transformed into something he had never known before and over which he no longer had any command. He let loose of Simons and started off again with Joe Urban, hastening his pace. Simons yelled:*

*"Come on, fellows, don't let him fire little Joe!"*

*About a dozen boys shot out of line and started after Teefee. The superintendent dropped Joe like a hot poker and deer-footed it for the door. The men returned to their places and all stood waiting. . . . The moment tingled with expectancy.*

*When Teefee returned, he was accompanied by the assistant plant manager, Bill Lynch. They approached Simons, who suggested that the workers get a committee together to see the plant manager, and Lynch agreed (Gamson et al., p. 3). This incident shows that collective group action can slow or stop even massive organizations.*

---

This chapter explores features of social groups and organizations of various kinds. Groups are important to individuals from birth on. As we get older, much of what we do occurs in the context of formal groups called organizations. Ours has been called an "organizational society," reflecting the importance of large organizations for much of social life.

Organizations themselves are embedded in larger social structures (such as nation-states and perhaps a world economy). As a result, organizations connect those larger social structures with individuals. For example, auto manufacturers who began to lose business to international competitors in the 1970s and 1980s started to close plants, lay off workers, and/or cut wages. Individuals lost jobs, health insurance,

and perhaps even their homes. What occurs in larger social structures and networks may affect what happens inside those organizations. So organizational policies can have immense effects on individual lives. This is why some groups are pressing for legislation to require advance notice of plant closing for workers and the communities in which firms are located. This represents just one of a number of areas in which groups are calling for increased corporate responsibility. Other areas include the disposal of toxic substances, worker safety, auto safety, the use of animals in laboratory experiments, and stopping investments in South Africa.

The call for corporate responsibility represents an awareness that organizational values and interests may not always coincide with

*People in the same social category share certain social characteristics or statuses, such as being West Point cadets.*

those of individuals and a sense that the power of organizations is so great in relation to individuals that some other organizational body, such as the state or stockholders, ought to influence the organizational power of corporations. Like any competition over power and control, this one elicits controversy and disagreements. But the presence of such controversy serves to underscore the major importance of organizations in social life.

**Groups** are collections of people who share some common goals and norms and whose relationships are usually based on interactions. As a result, they tend to feel a sense of belonging and shared identity. Groups differ from **aggregates,** which are collections of people who do not know each other and who feel no sense of belonging together.

Finally, there are **social categories** of people who may not interact but who share certain social characteristics or statuses. Examples include working women, blacks, millionaires, and teenagers. If members of a social category develop a sense of common awareness and shared purpose, as the workers at the General Motors plant did in 1936, they may develop into a social group, but this does not always happen.

## GROUPS

### Primary and Secondary Groups

**Primary groups** are the first and most important groups to which people belong. They include families and close friends. Primary groups are characterized by frequent face-to-face inter-

action, by the commitment and emotional ties members feel for each other, and by their relative permanence. These early and usually rather intense group ties are critically important for the development of an individual's sense of identity.

In the nuclear family primary group, members see one another often and remain members of the group even when some of them have moved away; they are intimate with one another; and they are committed to one another and to the group aside from any common tasks they may be trying to accomplish. Elementary school classmates, tentmates at an overnight camp, or members of a youth gang may all form primary groups. Like families, these groups have the capacity to offer affection and support as well as to inflict pain and anguish.

People often find it difficult to leave their primary groups. On-duty soldiers, children, or tribespeople are not usually free to leave their platoons, families, or tribes. It may be difficult emotionally or legally for primary group members to break away. Because of bonds with primary groups and because so many parts of people's lives are involved with them, they have a profound influence on feelings, values, and behaviors. People may love and try to maintain what they experience in primary groups, or dislike and reject it, but it is unlikely that they will be indifferent.

*Primary groups such as families are usually characterized by frequent face-to-face interaction, by the commitment and emotional ties members feel for each other, and by their relative permanence.*

**Secondary groups** are less intimate than primary groups. They tend to be more temporary, to have less face-to-face interaction, and to be bound more by common tasks. Your classmates in a large lecture course may become a secondary group. You probably do not see the other members every day; the group will probably disband when the course is completed; and you are unlikely to get to know one another in a wide variety of situations the way you do family members. You share a common task, but you may have little else in common.

People who work together may form secondary groups, or they may become more involved with their co-workers and form primary groups. For most people, college alumni groups, union or professional associations, or consumer cooperatives are examples of secondary groups. Some of the differences between primary and secondary groups are summarized in Table 6.1. Groups often contain a mixture of primary and secondary group characteristics. Whether they act more like one or the other may depend on the surrounding social conditions. In a crisis such as a flood, blackout, or bombing raid, secondary groups tend to become more like primary groups. But once the external crisis lessens, they tend to drift back into secondary groups.

## Distinguishing Features of Groups

Although different in important ways, the members of primary and secondary groups share one or more social statuses in common. For instance, they are members of the same kinship group; they are neighbors; they belong to the same social class; they have the same racial or ethnic background; or they share a common activity. A common social status generates at least some shared values and goals among the members of a group. Shared values and goals tend to emerge from frequent interaction. The members of a basketball team, for example, all share the status of being a team member. They share the goal of trying to win games. The more they interact, especially in the face of a common challenge, the more they feel like a team. The sense of a common identity and purpose is what distinguishes a group from an aggregate. It does

not always work this way, however. Sometimes, the more the individuals in an aggregate interact, the more aware they become of their different interests and values. In such a case they may never form a group.

Group identity is enhanced by a clear sense of group boundaries that delineate members from nonmembers. Often this involves a special form of dress (a football uniform, for example), a badge (safety patrol), or a pin (as in a fraternity or sorority). Some fraternal groups develop special handshakes or greetings to separate members from nonmembers. Some groups require members to cut their social ties with nonmembers and to isolate themselves physically from others as well (for example, the Unification Church).

When group members identify with the group as a whole, there is a tendency for them to see the world in terms of "in group" and "out group" people, or "we" and "they." They may try to claim that all the "right" people belong to one clique or club and set themselves up as social judges to decide who can and cannot become a member. Such processes add the dimension of social ranking to group membership. Sometimes out-group people may feel excluded and hurt by such boundaries. On a campus dominated by fraternities and sororities, for example, individuals may feel devastated if they are not pledged by the house they prefer. In other cases individuals do not care because they happily belong to a group of their own. The New Year's Day Rose Parade in Pasadena, California, for instance, is planned by a socially exclusive committee. Someone from Chicago, however, might not care at all about being on that committee.

Sociologists use the term **reference group** for a group whose standards and opinions are important to us. We compare ourselves to members of reference groups and use them as yardsticks for our own attitudes and behaviors. A positive reference group, like a group of popular, smart athletes on campus, shows valued behaviors and attitudes. A negative reference group illustrates what people do not want to imitate—for instance, a group of drunken bums. Reference groups affect people as they assess themselves and their life situations. Factory workers who have been promoted may compare

**Table 6.1**   *Major Differences Between Primary and Secondary Groups*

| | Primary Groups | Secondary Groups |
|---|---|---|
| **Size** | Relatively small (usually ten or fewer) | May be several dozen or more |
| **Interaction** | Face-to-face | Often indirect |
| **Type of Involvement** | Engages whole personality of individual members | Engages only a limited part of a member's personality |
| **Social Relations** | Emotional | Instrumental (that is, goal-oriented) |
| **Frequency of Interaction** | Frequent | Less frequent |
| **Length of Relationship** | Long-term | Short-term |

themselves with their friends who have not been promoted and feel satisfied, whereas junior managers (even if they have been promoted) may compare themselves with managers above them and be dissatisfied.

It is not always clear why individuals adopt one rather than another group as a reference point. Very often individuals belong to a number of groups that may have competing values and goals, thereby producing potential conflicts. A Catholic woman, for instance, may feel conflict over the issues of birth control and abortion—torn between her religious teachings and her concerns for independence and responsible parenthood. If she belongs to both a women's group and a religious group, she may gradually be drawn more to the one whose view she favors. Although sociologists cannot always say why an individual adopts one rather than another reference group, they do know something about what features of groups influence individuals. One of the most important of these is group size.

## The Effects of Group Size

Group size directly affects the number and type of interaction that can occur within a group. For each person added to a group, the number of possible relationships in the group increases dramatically. With 4 people there are 25 possible relationships among individuals and various subgroups. With 6 people there are 301 possible relationships (see Kephart, 1950, for an explanation). As the size of a group increases, the satisfaction of each individual member with the group tends to decrease. Dissatisfaction may grow because each member has less chance to participate. When groups increase from 5 to 12 members, they are less likely to reach consensus based on group discussion (Hare, 1976). Although it is hard to get a family of 5 to agree on something, it is much more difficult to get a family of 12 to agree.

### Dyads

Two-person groups, or **dyads,** have certain unique characteristics that are not shared by groups of other sizes. Consider the dyad of a couple. Either member can destroy the pair by withdrawing (Simmel, 1950). Because the dyad depends totally on the participation of both members, concern about its existence is accompanied by concern about its termination more than in groups of any other size. Larger groups can more easily survive the loss of one or more members without causing the group to dissolve. Even disagreement threatens the unity of a dyad. There is no majority in a dyad to which a member can appeal for fairness or justice. The only group standards of behavior that are binding are those shared by both members. Many of these unique features of a dyad change with the addition of even one member. A marital relationship changes, for instance, with the birth of a baby.

## Triads

When a third person is added to a dyad, each individual in the newly formed group, called a **triad,** can act as an intermediary between the other two members. As such, the third one can serve to unite the two or to separate them. There is always the possibility that two of the three members of the triad will consider the third an intruder. A close union of two is generally disrupted by a spectator (Simmel, 1950). At the same time, the third person can mediate disputes between the other two. Triads, or triangles as they are popularly termed, contain the potential for the pairing of two members against one. Unless one member is consistently more powerful than the other two, coalitions are possible between A and B against C, between A and C against B, and between B and C against A. Triads are unstable because one of the members of the pair may join the single person. Two roommates out of three, for example, may be in agreement over how neat to keep their room, but one of them may unite with the lone person over what television show they want to watch. Such shifting usually prevents one member from being permanently excluded, which might lead him or her to leave the group altogether.

The power of these coalitions should not be underestimated. Even in the rather unbalanced power relation of a parent and two young children, a firm coalition between the children can diminish parental power. This coalition is most pronounced in the case of identical twins who have genetic and social bonds. Twin observers note a phenomenon called "twin solidarity," which takes the form of shared secrets, behaviors, and sometimes even language. An individual twin's first loyalty is often to the other twin rather than to a parent or older sibling.

In sum, dyads experience certain unique tensions, and triads have a shifting nature. These features of group size operate independently of the personalities of the group members. In groups that exceed three people, two other features of size are worth noting: odd or even numbers and group proportions. Whether there is an odd or an even number of people in a group makes a difference, particularly if the group needs to reach a decision. In groups with an even number of people, there is always the possibility of a deadlock, where the same number

*Couples form a dyad. When a third person, such as a baby, joins them, the newly formed group is a triad. Triads have unique social properties that differ from those of dyads.*

of people will support and oppose some idea or plan. Groups with an odd number contain the potential for one member to break a tie. Groups that are mandated to come up with decisions, such as the U.S. Supreme Court, have an odd number of members or a procedure for breaking ties.

## The Effects of Group Proportions

The relative proportion of different individuals in a group is a structural feature that affects what happens in them. A homogeneous group, for example, where most members are adults rather than children, males rather than females, or blacks rather than whites, differs from a group with a more balanced mixture of statuses. Although Simmel's analysis of dyads and triads refers to absolute numbers, Kanter alerts us to the importance of relative proportions in a group. Suppose we symbolize people in the majority as Xs (whether they be males, whites, adults, or whatever) and those in the minority as Os. Four types of groups can be formed, as shown in Figure 6.1. Homogeneous groups consist only of Xs. In skewed groups, Xs predominate. In tilted groups, with about one-third Os to two-thirds Xs, the minority members begin to be perceived as individuals; they can form alliances with other members, and their type will be noticed and distinguished from the majority type. Finally, when Xs and Os are about even, groups become balanced. The balance is reflected in the interests and activities (the culture) and the interaction of the group (Kanter, 1977).

Skewed groups are typical of many professional and organizational groups today that have recently begun to include women or ethnic minorities as "token" representatives of their social type. Because tokens are proportionately rare, they face certain unique problems of visibility, contrast, and fitting in (Kanter, 1977). Although tokens are sometimes ignored by the majority, more often their minority status makes them stand out. It is impossible, for instance, for tokens to keep a "low profile." They are always noticed. Being in the limelight can aid recognition and promotion, but it can also advertise a token's early mistakes. The presence of tokens may lead dominant members to exaggerate their culture, as in heightened sexual innuendos around token women. Tokens may also be stereotyped by dominant members. Women in a largely male organization, for example, tend to be categorized into one of the following familiar roles: mother, seductress, pet, or "iron maiden." Each of these stereotypes may make it difficult for token members of the group to exhibit fully appropriate behavior in their situation (Kanter, 1977).

| Homogeneous groups | XXXXXXXXXX |
| Skewed groups | XXXXXXXXXO |
| Tilted groups | XXXXXOOOO |
| Balanced groups | XOXOXOXOXO |

**Figure 6.1  Four Types of Proportions That Occur in Groups.**

Homogeneous groups are similar, skewed groups have a token representative from another social group, tilted groups have a few more representatives, and balanced groups have about equal numbers of people with various attributes.

*Source:* Adapted from Kanter, 1977.

## Group Pressures and Conformity

Group pressures by a majority on a minority were observed by Asch (1952) in his famous experiments on conformity and resistance to group pressure. Asch called together groups of college students (usually seven to nine) for what he called an experiment in visual perception. The groups were shown two pictures of lines (see Figure 6.2). One card had a single standard line (line A) on it, the other had three lines— one the same length as the standard one, one longer, and one shorter. The experimenter went around the group, asking each individual to say which line was the same as line A. It sounds easy enough. There was unanimous agreement by the group the first two times the experimenter showed line A. But the third time, seven out of eight students called out line 2 as the one that matched line A. These seven students were in secret partnership with the experimenter, and they all spoke before the real subject of the experiment did.

How did individuals react to having direct evidence from their senses challenged by the other members of an experimental group? They got very upset. They wondered if their eyes were going bad, the light was wrong, or they were losing their minds. About a third of the subjects conformed to the opinion of the majority, yielding even though the group contradicted the evidence of their senses. Part of this **conformity** (that is, going along with the norms or behaviors of a group) occurred because the individuals represented a minority of one against a unanimous majority, a situation comparable to that of the single token analyzed by Kanter. Asch's experiments yield a number of other important results. It is notable that two-thirds of the subjects did not conform, although even those who were confident of their own perceptions still yearned to be in agreement with the group. When group size was reduced to just one other person (making a dyad), subjects almost never went along with the incorrect call of the other person, reinforcing Simmel's distinction between dyads and other groups.

In another variation, Asch introduced an additional group member who selected a different but also incorrect line as the proper match. Even though that person did not agree with the sub-

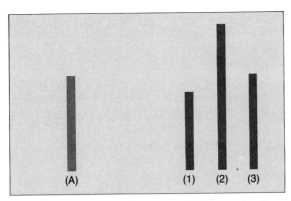

**Figure 6.2   Lines Shown to Subjects in the Asch Experiments.**

The subject was shown line A and asked whether line 1, 2, or 3 most closely matched it in length. The secret partners of the experimenter chose line 2, which is longer, rather than line 3, which is the same length.

*Source:* Adapted from Asch, 1952.

ject in the experiment, the fact that someone else differed from the majority liberated individual subjects, who then felt free to "call it as they saw it." The presence of even one nonconformist in a group breaks the chains of groupthink. **Groupthink** refers to the tendency of individuals to go along with the ideas or actions of a group because they feel a strong loyalty to it and do not want to disagree or raise uncomfortable questions.

While it is sometimes difficult for unaided individuals to resist the power and authority of a group, other research shows how groups may collectively resist what they see as unjust authority. Gamson, Fireman, and Rytina (1982) studied the social conditions leading groups of people to resist an authority who asked them to express opinions they did not hold. They had been told that their statements were being videotaped as evidence of community opinion for use in a courtroom. The researchers identified social processes that influence different types of rebellious reactions. One of the first actions is for someone to call attention to a questionable act by an agent of authority.

The work of Asch, Gamson, Fireman, and Rytina shows how important it is for groups and societies to protect the rights of people who disagree with prevailing views. Even if many of

their ideas seem silly, the presence of such independent thinkers frees other members of a group or a society to say what they think, thereby increasing the creative possibilities available to the group.

## Group Dynamics

### Division of Labor

Groups vary in terms of how much of their time they spend on task behavior—that is, behavior devoted to accomplishing a particular goal, and on socioemotional behavior—that is, managing tensions, building friendships within the group, or being mutually supportive. The roles played by individual members in a group also vary, with some serving more as socioemotional leaders and others more as task-oriented leaders. Certain individuals make the jokes, tease the other members of a group, and mediate conflicts between group members. They are called **expressive leaders** and they help to maintain the stability of the group. Others, called **instrumental leaders,** try to keep the group's effort directed to the task at hand. They may say such things as "Let's see, what we have to do here is this," or "What do you think would be the best way for us to accomplish this?" Considerable research on group life suggests that both kinds of members and activities are needed in groups if they are to operate successfully.

Early work on the division of labor in small groups suggested that instrumental and expressive leadership roles are not usually played by the same person in a small group (Bales and Slater, 1954), in a family (Zelditch, 1955), or in a complex organization (Etzioni, 1965). However, other researchers concluded that expressive and instrumental roles need not be incompatible and may be integrated in the same person (Lewis, 1972). The possibility that expressive and instrumental roles could be played by one person is supported by a study done by Rees and Segal (1980) of two college football teams. They found that some players scored high on both types of leadership, suggesting that leadership roles may be integrated in the same person, at least in some groups. Groups differ with respect to how much attention they devote to

*These people are trying to decide where to go during their visit to Boston. Group decision making often moves through predictable stages.*

task versus expressive activities. One place these differences occur is during decision making.

### Group Decision Making

Recall a group decision you have observed, perhaps a family deciding how to share housekeeping tasks or a club meeting you attended. Every group tends to move through four stages as its members work to arrive at a decision (Bales and Strodbeck, 1951). First, members get oriented to the problem at hand. They gather information, share ideas, and suggest possible solutions. Second, the group debates and weighs available information and suggestions. Tension and conflict increase as a group approaches the third stage, which is actually making a decision about what to do. Different interests, values, goals, and emotional responses tend to surface at this point. After a decision has been made, the group becomes more relaxed again, members begin to joke and laugh, and group solidarity reappears, if only because members have shared a common trial and made a joint decision.

Even if a group has no formal leader, certain individuals tend to assume leadership roles as groups work to arrive at a decision. As exchange theorist George Homans noted in his classic study *The Human Group* (1950), leaders tend to conform most closely to shared standards of behavior in a group. Conformity is related to greater status in a group. Leaders interact more with other group members than do people of

lower status. Interaction, in turn, contributes to friendship between the members of a group, just as friendship tends to be associated with more interaction. Those who participate in pleasurable communal activities with group members tend to become committed to the group and its values. Competition or conflict between one group and another tends to enhance the cohesiveness of a group, as Simmel noted.

### Commitment to a Group

Everyone who cares about and benefits from the existence of a group is concerned about members being committed to it. This includes ministers, business leaders and managers, scout leaders, founders of communes, club owners, and school administrators, for instance. Commitment of group members seems to depend on a balance between what group members want to give to a group and what the group expects or requires of them. Committed group members are loyal and involved; they have a sense of belonging and a feeling that the group is an extension of themselves and they are an extension of the group (Kanter, 1972). According to Kanter, "**Commitment** thus refers to the willingness of people to do what will help maintain the group because it provides what they need" (p. 66). Committed athletic team members will help each other on and off the playing field. Many decisions will be made based on what is in the team's best interest rather than just an individual's interest. Such commitment invariably strengthens a group and often enhances its task performance. Obviously, groups vary widely in terms of the commitment of their members.

An understanding of some of these dynamics of group life puts us in a better position to grapple with a major feature of the social world today—life in organizations.

## ORGANIZATIONS

**Organizations** are social groups deliberately formed to pursue certain goals. How many organizations have you encountered? You were probably born in a hospital, your birth certificate is on file in the records of the community where you were born, you have been inoculated in ways determined by health organizations, you go to school, you may have worked in an organization, you probably have applied for a driver's license, and you may belong to a religious organization. You can undoubtedly add to this list of contacts with formal organizations. In truth, it is becoming ever more difficult to do anything in our society without meeting one or more organizations. Beginning about 1875, the United States started becoming an organization society, marked by large-scale bureaucracies in every social area (Presthus, 1962).

Three features of organizations have profound implications for our lives. First, fewer and fewer jobs exist outside organizations. The number of self-employed workers continues to decline in the United States, having dropped from 11 percent of employed male workers in 1965 to 9 percent in 1981 (U.S. Bureau of the Census, 1982a, p. 385). For females, the rate of self-employment has always been low. In the United States in 1965, only 5.8 percent of women were self-employed, and by 1981 only 5 percent were. These statistics mean that fewer people can work for themselves today than in the past. Second, organizational units are becoming ever larger. The number of government employees, for example, has grown from 2.6 million in 1920 to 16.4 million in 1984, mostly at the state and local levels (U.S. Bureau of the Census, 1985a, p. 294). Third, these ever-larger organizations control a major share of the material and social resources of society. In 1984 the 200 largest manufacturing corporations owned 65 percent of all corporate assets, compared to 48 percent in 1950 (U.S. Bureau of the Census, 1985a, p. 532). These figures point to one of the dominant trends in our society today—namely, the increasing centralization and concentration of power and resources in huge organizations. In fact, we are moving from a society that has organizations in it to an "organizational society" (Perrow, 1979a). It is virtually impossible to live in our society without being affected, on a daily basis, by large and powerful organizations. Therefore it is imperative to know something about how these organizations are structured, how they work, and how they affect people.

Why has the importance of organizations grown so much in modern industrial society? Modern organizations did not exist in hunting and gathering societies. They began to take shape in horticultural societies. Organizations became important in agrarian societies because of the need to manage complex irrigation systems. Weber saw the growth of bureaucratic organizations as part of the growth of rationality in Western civilization. Marxian analysts stress the growth of bureaucratic organizations as useful instruments of control over an economic or agricultural surplus.

Huge gains in industrial and agricultural productivity in less than a century show the effectiveness of organizing work in a rational way. Between 1890 and 1960, for example, national output per worker increased nearly 200 percent in the United States and about 750 percent in Japan (*Encyclopaedia Britannica*, 1977, vol. 15, p. 30). Many organizational innovations introduced in the name of rationality and effectiveness, however, seem to serve mainly to centralize knowledge, control, and profits in the hands of managers and owners, as Marxians suggest. Whatever the reasons for the growth of modern organizations, their importance in our lives today is indisputable.

In this section we examine organizations from several vantage points. First, we examine bureaucratic organizations, including Weber's classic view of them, problems in them, and additional features. Then we consider links between organizations and individuals.

## Bureaucratic Organizations

As noted in Chapter 1, Max Weber described three pure types of legitimate authority: legal, traditional, and charismatic. Modern bureaucracies are organized primarily on the basis of rational-legal authority. Bureaucracy is fully developed only in the modern state, according to Weber. This form of organization appears in most modern armies, government agencies, business corporations, and hospitals. Examples include the telephone company and the department of motor vehicles in a particular state. Authority and activities in bureaucratic organizations are generally ordered by laws or administrative rules.

**Formal organizations** are highly structured groups with specific objectives and usually clearly stated rules and regulations. The most

*Max Weber was the first sociologist to analyze large bureaucratic organizations. Although he realized that bureaucracy was an efficient way to coordinate the efforts of large numbers of people, he also saw that it could operate without regard for the individuals involved. This Crow Indian woman is dealing with her tribal office in South Dakota.*

prevalent form of formal organization in modern society is the bureaucracy. Traditional, rational, and value-oriented action are all associated with types of formal organization. But in modern industrial society the bureaucratic type like the telephone company or the Pentagon is the most common. Since individuals and society are strongly affected by bureaucratic organizations, we need to understand how they work. The ideas of Max Weber are helpful in this regard.

### Weber's View of Bureaucracy

Weber worked as a civil servant in the German government around the turn of the century, so he had a chance for firsthand observations of bureaucracy. He saw both strengths and limitations in bureaucratic organization. He believed that bureaucracy was technically superior to other forms of organization for coordinating the efforts of large numbers of people working toward specific goals. Bureaucratic organizations

could do things with greater precision, speed, and financial efficiency than organizations based on tradition or charisma. Bureaucratic organizations were intended to operate "objectively"—that is, "according to calculable rules and without regard for persons," said Weber (1925a). This meant they sometimes had negative, dehumanizing effects on the individuals who worked in them. Indeed, Weber wondered how to "keep a portion of mankind free from this parcelling out of the soul" demanded by the bureaucratic way of life. Like most social scientists who study bureaucratic organizations, he was aware of their two-sided nature.

Weber developed an "ideal type" or model of **bureaucracy.** (An ideal type is a mental model of something in terms of its essential traits.) Actual organizations can be compared with this model. To him, there were six essential features to the model.

**DIVISION OF LABOR AND SPECIALIZATION.** The total work to be done in an organization is divided up into smaller tasks. Each position is responsible for a limited number of these tasks and has no authority for doing other ones. Thus positions are highly specialized. In the university, for instance, professors do not change light bulbs and the maintenance staff does not teach classes.

**HIERARCHY.** Positions in a bureaucracy are arranged in order of rank—that is, in a hierarchy. People in lower positions are supervised by those in higher positions. Orders and directives are issued from the top down, through a specified chain of command. Those at the top have greater authority over more people and more activities than do those further down. Hierarchy is most visible in the military, but it also appears in corporations and government agencies. Formal authority is limited, however. Corporate bosses can say what time employees must be at work, but they cannot say what time they should go to bed.

**RULES AND REGULATIONS.** Formal, written rules govern most activities in a bureaucracy. Decisions are based on these rules. Explicit procedures are spelled out for all actions. As a result, the organization operates in an orderly, stable, and predictable way. For instance, once you have mastered college registration procedures, you can probably assume they will continue about the same way in the future.

**IMPARTIALITY.** Rules, procedures, and decisions are to be carried out in a rational, nonemotional way, without regard to personal feelings. Clients are viewed as cases; subordinates are thought of as replaceable. Relatives and friends are barred from being considered as job applicants or are treated the same way as everyone else.

**TECHNICAL QUALIFICATIONS.** Occupants of positions are trained specialists. The more complicated the work becomes, the more it demands the "personally detached and strictly 'objective' expert" (Weber, 1925a). Advancement is based on merit and seniority. This ensures that competent people fill organizational positions and helps staff morale.

**RECORDS AND FILES.** Bureaucratic organizations rely heavily on records and files. Originally kept in written form by scribes and then by typists and clerks, they are increasingly stored in computers. One of the transformations

*Any of you who have dealt with college registration know that formal rules govern most actions in such a bureaucratic process.*

of modern bureaucracies has occurred in the way that records sometimes come to be regarded as "official secrets" of the organization. One recent legislative thrust in the United States has been to make some of these organizational records available to individuals through the Freedom of Information Act and credit information laws.

Although useful in suggesting what Weber thought bureaucratic organizations should be like, his pure type is not reflected perfectly in the world of real organizations. Weber's analysis of bureaucracy looked basically at its positive functions for increasing the efficiency and goal attainment of the organization. Weber was well aware of the negative features of bureaucracy, but he did not analyze them as systematically as others have since.

### Problems in Bureaucracies

Observers of bureaucracy have noted a number of their negative features. These include waste, ritualism, and oligarchy.

**ORGANIZATIONAL WASTE.** Because there are many layers in a bureaucratic hierarchy, those at the top may be quite unaware of the ideas, problems, and feelings of those down below. *Organizational waste* of ideas, expertise, money, or materials may contribute to inefficiencies and mistakes.

**RITUALISM.** **Organizational ritualism** occurs when people follow the rules and regulations in a bureaucracy so closely that they forget the purpose of the rules and regulations. Merton describes what he calls the "bureaucratic personality," a person who enforces the rules rigidly, perhaps out of excessive caution (1957). People more concerned with the letter of the law than its spirit can slow things down a great deal in an organization. For example, someone's doctoral diploma was delayed three weeks by one university until the clips holding the dissertation were replaced with a different binding.

**OLIGARCHY.** **Oligarchy** refers to the rule of the many by the few. As coined by Robert Michels (1911), the "iron law of oligarchy" states that in any organization, power tends to become concentrated in the hands of a small group of leaders as those with the most time, energy, and ability take over. Once there, their power and prestige grow, since they have access to information and resources unavailable to non-leaders. This happens even in supposedly democratic organizations like political clubs or labor unions. The main interest of these leaders becomes preserving the organization and their own leadership in it rather than the interests of the members. This may affect rank-and-file members badly. It may also undermine the democratic nature of an organization. Members feel they know less and so they look to the leaders for direction. The result of these tendencies is to make oligarchy inevitable, according to Michels.

In a case study of the United Steel Workers of America labor union, Nyden (1985) found that Michels's "iron law of oligarchy" did not rule out the possibility of organizational democracy, however. Democratic reforms of the union's structure occurred when the group pushing for reform elected their own officers, followed open decision-making procedures, communicated regularly with members, and emphasized a consistent political ideology and longer-term political goals.

Although Michels is correct that power in organizations is greater at the top of the hierarchy, there are usually some legal or political checks on how that power is exercised. There may be several groups contending for leadership in an organization, which may at least lead to a "circulation of elites." Every time a different party takes control of the U.S. Congress, for example, there is at least a partial "circulation of elites" as members of the new majority party take over as chairs of committees. Examples can also be found of deeply entrenched oligarchies—for instance, at various times in the history of the Teamsters Union, the board of directors of General Motors, or the inner circle of the Communist party in the USSR.

### Additional Features of Organizations

Additional significant organizational characteristics include the existence of informal as well as formal organizational structures, the relations between organizations and their environments, and the views of human nature associated with various views of organizations. All these features provide useful sociological insights for people who deal with or work in organizations.

**INFORMAL STRUCTURES WITHIN FORMAL ORGANIZATIONS.** There are informal as well as formal structures of power in organizations. Bureaucratic organizations provide specific job descriptions and indicate lines of authority (often formalized in an organizational chart showing who reports to whom). But once people fill formal organizational slots, they form friendships and find ways to bend or ignore the rules; they develop personal ways of solving problems; and they cut through bureaucratic "red tape" when possible. These informal groups may also affect productivity.

In a classic study of men wiring telephone switchboards at a Western Electric Company plant in Chicago, Roethlisberger and Dickson (1939) found that whatever incentives the company offered to encourage productivity, the men had their own notion of what was a fair day's work: wiring about 6000 terminals. Anyone who did less was a "chiseler," but anyone who did more was condemned as a "ratebuster," "slave," or "speed-king." The latter were semi-playfully punched in the arm by the other workers, who felt they might cause layoffs or higher work requirements for the whole group. Informal rules affected more than productivity. To keep from getting too bored, the men sometimes did each other's tasks, although doing so was against company rules. They also worked very quickly in the morning but much more slowly in the afternoon. No members "squealed" to management about the shortcomings of any other group member. In these ways the informal structure of the group operated independently of the formal organizational structure.

All formal organizations have informal lines of power, influence, and communication (the "grapevine") and informal norms about missing work, tardiness, acceptable amounts of overtime, and practical divisions of labor. Functioning in a large organization, then, requires people to understand both the formal and the informal structures and rules. And just as there is an informal structure, there is also a context within which organizations must function.

**ORGANIZATIONAL CONTEXTS.** One way of looking at organizational contexts is to distinguish between open and closed systems. An **open system** depends on the environment to provide nourishment, raw materials, or resources as well as to absorb products or wastes. There are degrees of openness in a system. A forest fire, for instance, is a fairly open system, being strongly affected in its course by available air, fuel, and water. A mechanical clock, on the other hand, is a relatively closed system once its spring has been wound. An isolated family or tribe living on an island without contact with other humans is in a relatively closed system, whereas a family that entertains foreign visitors is much more open. A system may accept passively what its environment offers (as in the case of the fire), or it may work actively to control its environment. Like humans, organizations that are better able to control their environments stand a better chance of surviving and thriving. For this reason, some business organizations become involved in the political affairs of the country in which they operate.

Rather than assuming just one kind of organizational structure, Lawrence and Lorsch (1967) asked what kind of organizational structure is most useful for dealing with different environmental conditions. They suggested that flexible, humanistic structures may be best for dealing with highly uncertain tasks and environments, such as developing innovative technologies. Uncertainty cannot be handled well through rigid rules.

Organizations use a variety of strategies to manipulate or control uncertain and changing environments so that they can be successful within them. **Multinational corporations,** for example, reduce their dependency on a single environment (whether for labor, raw materials, or markets) by locating in a number of nations. Such arrangements often lead to domination of the environment by the organization. (See Table 13.3 for a list of the top 50 multinational corporations.)

Another effort to control the environment occurs through vertical integration. **Vertical integration** involves an organization assuming control of one or more of its resources or outlets. For example, a photographic company may buy silver mines to ensure an adequate supply of the natural resource it needs (silver) at a predictable price, and it may own photography stores to sell its products. Even educational systems can have some degree of vertical integration. Primary schools may have "feeder" nurs-

ery schools that send them children, and they, in turn, may supply specific secondary schools with students. Oil companies use vertical integration to control the production, refining, and distribution of gasoline and related products.

Certain forms of vertical integration have been declared illegal because they destroy competition and lead to monopolies. **Monopoly** refers to the exclusive control of a particular industry, market, service, or commodity by a single organization. The United States began enacting antitrust laws in 1890, with the Sherman Anti-Trust Act. Such laws are designed to restrict business practices considered monopolistic or unfair. In recent years a major antitrust lawsuit was brought against the American Telephone and Telegraph Company (AT&T) by the U.S. Department of Justice. In 1982 AT&T was ordered by the courts to separate from the regional companies it controlled.

Sometimes control is exercised by several large organizations, in which case it is called **oligopoly.** Monopoly and oligopoly eliminate competition in the marketplace. Particularly when a vital product like food or oil is controlled, it means that prices can rise far above production costs. But a monopoly greatly reduces organizational uncertainty.

Without monopoly, organizational uncertainty appears in the distribution and marketing of goods or services. Advertising, publicity, and sales forces are legally accepted ways organizations use to deal with such unknowns. Illegal ways have also been used, however. In the record business, for example, four big firms dominated the industry from 1948 to 1955. They were vertically integrated through long-term contracts with artists and producers, they owned the manufacturing facilities, and they controlled the system of distribution. But for a record to become popular, disc jockeys needed to feature it on the air. Since the big firms did not control all the radio stations, they used bribery (called "payola") to encourage disc jockeys to play their records (Perrow, 1979a). In other instances companies have resorted to illegal price fixing to ensure their share of the market and available profits.

Sometimes the environmental uncertainty organizations face goes beyond labor, raw materials, or markets to include the financial sphere in which they operate (Mintz and Schwartz,

1985; Ratcliff, 1980; Useem, 1984). The practice of interlocking directorates may be used to gain control over these broader environments. **Interlocking directorates** are boards of directors that control two or more separate organizations by overlapping membership. Thus the key officers of a steel company may be on the board of a major bank, and several top bank executives may be on the steel company's board. The links between board members of major industrial corporations and financial institutions (banks) were noted by Levine (1972), who discovered what he called "spheres of influence" among banks and corporations. Morgan Bank, for instance, shares three directors with General Motors and General Electric; two directors with Ford, U.S. Steel, Bethlehem Steel, and Continental Oil; and one common director with Chrysler, Boeing, National Dairy, and Procter and Gamble. The interlocking directorates among them tend to reduce uncertainties in the environments of each.

**ORGANIZATIONAL ANALYSIS AND VIEWS OF HUMAN NATURE.** The analysis of organizations is not simply an empty academic exercise. Instead, the views owners and managers have about organizations and the people in them lead to competing styles of management. In one view, called **Theory X** by McGregor (1960), managers believe that people hate their jobs, want to avoid responsibility, resist change, and do not care about organizational needs. Theory X suggests that people work only when controlled through time clocks and rewards like bonuses or promotions. In contrast, **Theory Y** suggests that people are passive or irresponsible because of their experiences in organizations; that, by nature, people have the desire to work, to be creative, and to take responsibility. Under this set of assumptions, control rests on self-direction. Management's task, in this view, is to organize things so that people can accomplish their own goals while furthering the organization's goals. Few managers totally accept either one of these theories, but tendencies toward one or the other may be identifiable in various organizations.

Another theory of organizational culture is Theory Z, developed by Ouchi (1981). Used in many Japanese corporations but also in some U.S. companies, **Theory Z** corporations value long-term employment, trust, and close personal relationships. Both managers and employees are encouraged to take a long-term orientation toward problems and products. Theory Z sees a work organization as a social creation involving subtle coordination between individuals. Friendships among co-workers are encouraged. For this reason, the worst act at a Theory Z company is untrustworthiness. Managers move around to different positions rather than becoming narrow specialists. They are also encouraged to "manage by walking around" (MBWA), so as to work closely with other employees.

These competing views of human nature, along with various other human and contextual features of organizations, can be added to Weber's description of bureaucracy. For some people, however, features of bureaucracies—such as informal organization, relations with their environments, and assumptions about human nature as well as problems such as waste, ritualism, and oligarchy—are not just intellectual shortcomings. Some people feel that bureaucracy runs counter to their humanistic values as well as being inefficient. They have proposed nonbureaucratic ways of structuring organizations. (See the debate on the pros and cons of different organizational forms.)

## Links Between Organizations and the People in Them

Why is it that some organizations have high employee morale and productivity whereas others do not? Why do people hate to work in some organizations and find others good places in which to work? There are many ways to analyze the links between individuals and organizations, but among the most helpful are the concepts of location, opportunity, and power as developed by Kanter (1977, 1979).

One's *location* with respect to having control over decision making in an organization profoundly affects task performance. Kanter suggests that organizational location is more important for morale and job satisfaction than the task being performed. This was apparent in the reorganization of a Volvo automobile manufac-

*When Volvo reorganized its manufacturing operation, it changed the structure of the work from an assembly line where the workers had no communication or decision-making roles to a work group in charge of making a car. The result was higher employee morale, lower absenteeism, and better work quality and productivity.*

turing plant. The structure of the work was changed from an assembly line where the workers had no communication or decision-making roles to a work group that was charged with building a car. The group organized a system of who would do what and when; they talked with one another and decided how they would do the work. In this case, location was changed by a major restructuring of the work. As a result, employee morale was better, absenteeism was lower, and work quality and productivity was higher (Dickson, 1975).

The concept of *opportunity* also helps to explain the way people behave in organizations. This idea refers to the potential that a particular location contains for the expansion of work responsibilities and rewards. Jobs and job categories tend to be evaluated in terms of the prospects they contain for advancement, aside from the job content, grade level, or salary. In the organization Kanter studied, clerical jobs had low status because they led nowhere, whereas sales jobs were attractive because people were promoted from them into management. Most

people preferred line jobs rather than staff jobs because they offered longer and more varied chains of career opportunity (Kanter, 1977). Originating in the military, the term **line job** refers to positions that involve the actual fighting, selling, manufacturing, production, or whatever, as distinct from the **staff,** comprising those who serve in an advisory or administrative capacity (for example, legal departments, accountants, clerical workers, data processing personnel, and so forth).

In a study of a federal bureaucracy, Kanter's ideas were tested by others. Not surprisingly, people who felt they had poor chances for promotion were likely to be dissatisfied with the promotion system. The other kinds of responses to blocked opportunity that Kanter described were not observed (Markham et al., 1985).

A particular location, then, can be assessed in terms of the opportunities it offers for advancement and mobility, for doing more important tasks, and for gaining responsibility. Hierarchical organizations affect individuals by making advancement within the hierarchy the measure of personal success or failure. In an organization where locations are assessed in terms of the opportunities they offer for advancement, it is not just how well you do your job that matters; the opportunities the job provides for advancement and how rapidly that advancement comes are also significant.

The relative opportunities of a position affect how involved people become in their work. This is especially evident in Kanter's comparison of organizational "movers" and those who were organizationally "stuck." "Movers" took on extra assignments and poured time, energy, and new ideas into their work. They sought to learn skills that would be useful in their journey upward in the company. They zeroed in on what was happening further up in the hierarchy (Kanter, 1977). Sudden opportunities for promotion within an organizational hierarchy could accelerate an individual's aspirations, work commitment, and responsibility. The movers and others with opportunities within the organization tended to form task-oriented groups. If they had a grievance, they were likely to do something about it formally.

*Text continues on page 140.*

**Table 6.2**  *Features of Democratic-Collective Organizations and Bureaucracies*

| Organizational Feature | Democratic-Collective Organizations | Bureaucracies |
|---|---|---|
| Authority. The power to act, with that power seen as legitimate by other participants. | Place authority in collective as a whole. Decisions have authority when everyone participates in making them. Everyone has an equal voice. | Place authority in the position that individuals occupy. Often based on education or experience. Hierarchically organized. |
| Rules | Minimize the use of rules. (One free school had only one rule: "No dope in school.") Make decisions as they are needed. | Rely heavily upon codified, often written rules. Use rules to guide many decisions. Most decisions are predictable. |
| Social control. Needed in some form in all organizations if they are to accomplish their goals. | Use personalistic or moral appeals to secure conformity. Try to recruit new members who share values of existing group members. | Use mainly three types of social control: direct supervision, standardized rules, and selecting people who are similar (Perrow, 1976). |
| Recruitment and advancement. On what basis are people hired and promoted? | Use friendship and shared social-political values. Advancement not an issue, since there is no hierarchy of positions. | Based on credentials and other rationalistic criteria. |
| Incentives. What rewards does the organization offer individuals? | A chance for individuals to fulfill their values and share a sense of community. Members also gain valuable experience and contacts (help in getting into law or medical school). May offer members considerable control over their work. | Stress financial incentives and promotion possibilities. |
| Social stratification. How are positions ranked in the organization? | Egalitarianism is a central value. Reflected in small variations in pay (Bernstein, 1976, pp. 20–21; Perry, 1978; Russell et al., 1977). Try to convey equality of status through dress, informal social relations, terms of address, and task sharing. | Organizational position is consistent with stratifiction by race, sex, age, education, and experience (three-quarters of all managers and administrators are white males). Compensation may range from millions per year for chief executive officers to $8000 for clerks. Use prestige differences to support organizational hierarchy, through office size and decor, titles, executive bathrooms, and company cars. |
| Differentiation. How specialized is the division of labor? | Try to minimize it by keeping work roles as general as possible and by rotating jobs. | Stress maximum division of labor with experts doing very narrow specialized tasks. |

*Source:* Adapted from Rothschild-Whitt, 1976, 1979; Rothschild and Whitt, 1986.

## DEBATING SOCIETY'S ISSUES

Recent decades have witnessed the growth of so-called alternative organizations or **democratic-collective organizations,** such as alternative schools or worker-owned and -controlled firms.[1] Although relatively small in number, such organizations provide an important contrast with bureaucratic organizations. Extreme versions of the two forms may be seen as two ends of a continuum, ranging from a nearly total democratic-collective organization to a highly bureaucratic organization. Many organizations fall somewhere in between these two poles, containing some elements of each type of organization. Some bureaucratic organizations contain democratic-collective elements. Participatory work structures and employee services have been found to raise commitment and morale among employees in both the United States and Japan, but they are more typical of Japanese than U.S. plants (Lincoln and Kalleberg, 1985).

Case studies of democratic-collective organizations permit comparisons between them and bureaucratic organizations. They show that bureaucracy is not necessarily inevitable, but that people can choose to organize their endeavors in alternative ways. And they point out some of the advantages and liabilities of various organizational forms.

If you worked in a democratic-collective organization, you would spend considerable time discussing all major decisions the

[1] This discussion of democratic-collective organizations draws heavily on the work of Rothschild-Whitt (1976, 1979) and Rothschild and Whitt (1986).

*What Are the Pros and Cons of Democratic-Collectivist Versus Bureaucratic Organizations?*

organization had to make. Such decisions might include whom to hire, how to divide work assignments, and how to determine pay scales. You would spend much of your working day in meetings. You would also know a great deal about all phases of the organization's programs, problems, and policies, and you might perform a wide variety of tasks within the organization.

In a bureaucratic organization your actions and behaviors would be shaped by established rules and procedures. You might work alone or with a few other people in a small group. Your tasks would be fairly narrowly defined and relatively specialized. You would not be involved in making decisions about all aspects of the organization's program. Indeed, you might know very little about areas outside your own. Ideas or new proposals would have to go through the "proper channels"—that is, be presented to your boss and perhaps your boss's boss in the organizational hierarchy. Only then might you be authorized to go ahead with innovations. You would probably spend less time in meetings and more time producing goods or services, or in writing or filing letters, memos, and reports. Table 6.2 compares seven features of democratic-collective organizations and bureaucracies. These features spotlight some of the major differences in organizational types.

1. One way of assessing democratic-collective and bureaucratic organizations is in terms of the tasks or activities they perform. Some tasks, such as making plastic garbage bags, are clear, predictable, routine, and repetitive. For such tasks, a bureaucratic structure may be the more efficient one. But nonroutine tasks, such as teaching children with learning disabilities or inventing new technologies, are more difficult to accomplish in a bureaucracy. Personnel in such organizations require more discretion and will depend more on experience or professional expertise than on rules for making decisions. Hence fewer activities can be covered by bureaucratic procedures.

2. Bureaucratic organizations may limit the damage that a relatively incompetent person can do; democratic-collective organizations may find it more difficult to contain the havoc that one clearly unsuited person can wreak. On the other hand, a bureaucratic organization may also restrict the contribution that a particularly original and/or unorthodox individual can make.

3. One of the major social costs of democratic-collective organizations is the time it takes to make decisions. For instance, an alternative newspaper spent more than fifteen hours in meetings to plan one systematic job rotation. As a result, less time remained to do the tasks of the organization. Although two-way communication seems to generate higher morale, more innovative ideas, and creative solutions to complex problems, it is undeniably slow (Leavitt, 1964).

Many bureaucratic organizations are adopting some features

of democratic-collective organizations, including two-way communication, task rotation, collective decision making on some issues, and even partial worker ownership. It is important to realize, however, that ownership and control do not always go together. Some large corporations—such as IBM, for example—enable workers to purchase the company's stock at below-market prices. But although employees may share in some of the profits this way, they do not necessarily influence the way their work is organized.

Certain social conditions seem to help democratic-collective organizations persist and survive. These include banking resources available only to firms with democratic-collective structures (Johnson and Whyte, 1977), active sponsorship of the state, as in Yugoslavia, and U.S. laws governing employee stock ownership plans (ESOPs) (Rothschild and Russell, 1986, p. 324).

What do you think are the relative advantages of democratic-collective and bureaucratic organizations? In which type would you rather work? Why? On what basis do you think a decision to organize in one way rather than another should be made? Some possible criteria might include efficiency, philosophical grounds, personal preferences, and legal and financial constraints. Can you think of how each of these criteria might be used to argue for one rather than another organizational form?

The organizationally "stuck" contrasted vividly with the movers. These were people on short career ladders and those who had no further career possibilities. They had reached a dead end in the organization. Structurally blocked from moving and lacking opportunity in a system where success was measured by mobility, they behaved in many ways opposite to the "fast trackers." They tended to see fewer chances to use their skills and indeed used fewer skills; they were less involved in their work and less attached to it. They invested their energies outside their jobs and dreamed of escaping. Individuals blocked from opportunities for advancement within the organization tended to form strong peer bonds. These peer groups were openly critical of organizational superiors. Kanter (1977) found that members of such closed peer groups experienced pressure to stay loyal to their co-workers. Leaving the group, even when they were promoted, was seen as "disloyal." People on high-mobility tracks tend to develop commitment to their work, high ambitions, and an orientation toward their superiors that fuels future success. Those on low-mobility or blocked tracks tend to withdraw or become indifferent, thereby seeming to "prove" to their superiors that they are not able to handle opportunities (Kanter, 1977).

Just as the structure of opportunities within an organization appears to influence individuals, the structure of *power* can also shape their behavior. "Power," suggests Kanter, refers not just to the capacity of one individual to dominate or control others. It also refers to the capacity to get things done or to mobilize resources. Organizational locations vary in terms of their productive power. Organizational sources of power include access to supply lines, information sources, and lines of support. The marketing and the finance divisions of most corporations are strong because they control the vital supplies of customers and money.

The amount of power in a position affects the way authority is exercised. Those in positions of authority who lack real power tend to become coercive, petty, and rule-minded; they frequently oversupervise their subordinates. Since they have no real power to delegate, they are afraid to delegate anything (Kanter, 1977, 1979). This situation may apply to organizations as well as to individuals. Government agencies with little legislated power may operate in a particularly petty way. Kanter's concepts of location, opportunity, and power within organizations offer interesting examples of how structural features of organizations can affect the individuals working within them.

## SUMMARY

1. Primary groups, including family and close friends, are characterized by frequent face-

to-face contact, commitment and emotional ties among members, and relative permanence.

2. As people get older, they join more secondary groups—a school class or a work group—that are more limited and task-oriented than primary groups.

3. Group members share a common social location; they tend to share values and goals; and they interact frequently. These characteristics may generate a sense of common identity.

4. Group boundaries may be strengthened by external conflict or by greater internal conformity.

5. Reference groups are groups whose standards or behaviors we accept or reject for our life situations.

6. Dyads (two-person groups) and triads (three-person groups) have unique characteristics resulting from their numbers.

7. Groups are affected by the relative proportion of individuals of different types they possess. Token minority members of a group face certain unique problems. Group size and unanimity affect the amount of pressure to conform felt by individuals in the group.

8. Organizations are growing in size and influence. There is very little we can do in society today without dealing with one or more organizations.

9. Weber's model of bureaucratic organizations stressed six distinctive features: division of labor and specialization, hierarchy, rules and regulations, impartiality, technical qualifications, and records and files.

10. Bureaucracy sometimes shows the negative features of waste, ritualism, and oligarchy.

11. Organizations reveal patterns of informal social relations and standards, and many organizations depend heavily on their environment for success and survival. Assumptions about hu-

man nature may affect organizational structures and styles of management.

12. Some of the links between organizations and individuals can be explored by using the concepts of location, opportunity, and power.

## KEY TERMS

aggregate (p. 124)
bureaucracy (p. 132)
commitment (p. 130)
conformity (p. 128)
democratic-collective organization (p. 139)
dyad (p. 126)
expressive leader (p. 129)
formal organizations (p. 131)
groups (p. 124)
groupthink (p. 129)
instrumental leader (p. 129)
interlocking directorates (p. 136)
line job (p. 137)
monopoly (p. 135)
multinational corporation (p. 135)
oligarchy (p. 133)
oligopoly (p. 135)
open system (p. 134)
organization (p. 130)
organizational ritualism (p. 133)
primary group (p. 124)
reference group (p. 125)
secondary group (p. 125)
social category (p. 124)
staff job (p. 137)
Theory X (p. 136)
Theory Y (p. 136)
Theory Z (p. 136)
triad (p. 127)
vertical integration (p. 135)

## SUGGESTED READINGS

Gamson, William A., Bruce Fireman, and Steven Rytina. 1982. *Encounters with Unjust Authority*. Homewood, IL: Dorsey. Describes a series of experimental situations designed to see how a small group of people would react to the unjust exercise of authority.

Kanter, Rosabeth Moss. 1977. *Men and Women of the Corporation*. New York: Basic Books. Analyzes how individual behavior is shaped by corporate structures and opportunities and how men and women face different opportunities.

Ouchi, William. 1981. *Theory Z: How American Business Can Meet the Japanese Challenge*. New York: Avon. A readable account of the organizational methods used by many Japanese corporations.

Patchin, Robert I. 1983. *The Management and Maintenance of Quality Circles*. Homewood, IL: Dow Jones-Irwin. A short introduction to "quality circles" in organizations—what they are, how they began, and how they work.

Weber, Max. 1925a/1958. *From Max Weber: Essays in Sociology*. New York: Oxford University Press. A classic selection of Max Weber's writings. Chapter 8 contains his analysis of bureaucracy.

# Deviance, Crime, and Social Control

*When Betty and her friend Desirée want to relax, they go to an abandoned building in their neighborhood. They give the guard at the door a password and enter a candlelit room, since the electricity has long since been turned off in the building. The room is filled with low couches. The building is a ''free-base'' house where people heat up cocaine and inhale the vapors. To Betty and Desirée, such behavior seems ''normal.'' To many, it may seem very deviant.*

All societies and organizations work to shape and control the behavior of people in them. One way this happens is through the emergence of social norms. When clear-cut and widely shared norms exist, people who violate those norms may be defined as deviant or criminal. In this chapter we consider how sociologists define deviance and crime and the explanations that have been offered for behaviors that are defined as criminal or deviant. Then we analyze various processes of social control, including law and prisons.

## DEFINING DEVIANCE

Nothing is intrinsically deviant. The same personal characteristics or behavior can be considered deviant in one instance but not in another. Burping after a meal, tattooing one's face, having intercourse with one's cousin, picking one's nose in public, and piercing one's ears are all behaviors considered deviant in some societies but practiced widely by members of other societies. The determining factor is whether a sig-

nificant expectation or norm is being violated by the behavior or trait. Furthermore, other people or groups must see and react negatively to the behavior or trait. As Durkheim noted, an action does not offend society because it is deviant. Instead, it is deviant because it offends society.

Behaviors that offend society the most are those that violate strongly held norms. There is a strongly held prohibition against child molesting, for example. Not only is such action illegal, but it arouses moral indignation as well. Because different norms are considered important by various societies and social groups, deviance is a matter of degree rather than an ''all-or-nothing'' characteristic (Schur, 1979). Child molesting may be considered quite deviant, whereas littering may be considered only mildly deviant or not deviant at all.

Deviance is relative to the time and place in which a particular behavior occurs. A drug user may be considered highly deviant by some people but not by others. A man who is considered a communist by his conservative friends at the bank where he works may be considered a reactionary conservative by his friends at a liberal political club, although his politics remain unchanged in both situations. A guerrilla band may be viewed as a liberation army by some groups in a society and as dangerous terrorists by others. It is particularly important to stress the relative aspect of deviance in a pluralist society such as that of the United States. One group's definition of what is deviant may not be shared by other social groups. Take smoking as an example. Once people who smoked did so wherever it was not expressly prohibited. In recent years, however, designated nonsmoking areas have appeared in airplanes, restaurants, and offices. As the health hazards for nonsmokers have been publicized, smokers have become more likely to ask others for permission to smoke. In short, smoking has moved from being thought a socially neutral behavior to a somewhat more deviant behavior. Similarly, a couple living together before marriage used to be considered sinful or deviant by many people, and in some parts of the country such behavior may still be viewed this way. In other regions, however, it is considered perfectly normal, at least by some people.

These examples demonstrate that norms may be *ambiguous*. People may not always know if what they or someone else is doing will arouse a negative reaction. Even within a group, there may be little agreement about whether or not a particular behavior violates a norm. Is smoking marijuana viewed as deviant? By whom? Is oral sex deviant, or jaywalking, "borrowing" someone's car to take it for a spin, beating a child, or cheating on an exam? Is a woman surgeon, a male nursery-school teacher, a school superintendent who "flashes," or a college drug dealer a deviant? If you asked 100 college students around the country which of these activities and people they considered deviant, it is likely that you would receive a wide variety of responses.

One study asked a sample of respondents to name people or behaviors they considered deviant. The list of replies included homosexuals, prostitutes, drug addicts, radicals, and criminals; it also included liars, reckless drivers, atheists, Christians, suburbanites, the retired, priests, executives, divorcees, motorcycle gangs, smart-aleck students, and know-it-all professors (Simmons, 1969). This variation in responses suggests the inherently social nature of deviant behavior. An action will not be defined as deviant unless other people know about it and react negatively to it. This reaction generally includes the feeling that something should be done about the behavior, usually to change or stop it (Erikson, 1966).

Finally, an important aspect of deviance is the fact that certain social groups have relatively greater power and resources to use in getting their own definition of deviance to prevail and perhaps even to be written into law. As Becker (1973) has suggested, middle-class definitions of marijuana use as deviant held sway through the 1940s and 1950s and may have been in part a reaction to the use of marijuana by lower-class minority subcultures. As we see later in this chapter, the definition of homosexuality as a sickness was successfully challenged in the 1970s, as gay-rights groups mobilized political and intellectual resources to support their point of view. These examples illustrate some of the essential features of deviant behavior. **Deviance** is relative to time and place; it results from social and political processes; it depends on the existence of social organization and norms; and it provokes a negative response.

## DEFINING AND MEASURING CRIME

*When I was a very little child, oh, about six or seven, I had a habit of walking down [the street]. . . . As I walked I would look at the cars and in my mind I would buy them, but they only cost nickels or dimes. Big ones a dime, little ones a nickel, some that I liked a whole lot would cost a quarter. So as I got older this became a habit. For years I bought cars with the change that was in my pocket, which in those times wasn't very much.*

*Now this was a kind of wish, but more than that it was a way of looking at things—an unrealistic way—it's like I wanted things to be easy, and misguidedly tried to make everything that way, blinded then to the fact that nothing good or worthwhile comes without serious effort. What I'm trying to say is that while I was walking through life I had a distorted view of how I wanted things to be rather than how they really were or are. Always wanted things to be easy; so instead of dealing with things as they were, I didn't deal with them at all. I ducked hard things that took effort or work and tried to have fun, make a party, 'cause that was always easy. [Wideman, 1984, p. 3]*

In his book, *Brothers & Keepers*, John Wideman captures his younger brother's recollection of how he started down a path of looking for the easy way, which ended with his serving a life term in prison for killing a man in an armed robbery. Sociologists offer a number of explanations for deviant and criminal behavior, explanations that try to weave together personal histories and social settings.

A **crime** is a behavior that is prohibited by law. Although many crimes are considered deviant, not every crime is considered deviant by all groups. Smoking marijuana, for example, is a crime in many states, but it is not considered deviant by the Rastafarians, a religious sect from the island of Jamaica. And not all deviance is a crime. For instance, not wearing a shirt when it is 30°F outside or performing a sexual act with a plant might be considered deviant by many, but it is not illegal. Indeed, in some cases, crimes may be committed in an effort to control what

is considered deviant (Black, 1983). For example, in some cultures a person may avenge a humiliation to a family member by trying to kill the offender.

## Measuring Criminal Activity

Federal law defines more than 2800 acts as crimes, and this number is swelled still further by state and local statutes. Literally thousands of activities have been defined as illegal. Eight of these are considered very serious crimes; they are called "index offenses": rape, robbery, murder, aggravated assault, burglary, larceny (theft of $50 or more), arson, and auto theft. These index offenses are used by the Federal Bureau of Investigation to compute changes in the rate of serious crimes.

In the United States, crime rates generally declined between 1981 and 1984, but increased since 1984, as reflected in FBI data shown in Figure 7.1. These figures are compiled by the FBI using police reports from all over the country. Because not all crimes are reported, the

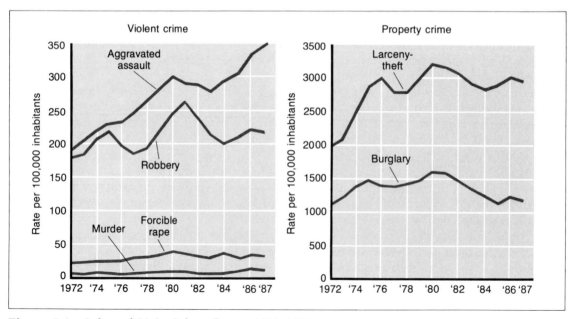

**Figure 7.1    Selected U.S. Crime Rates: 1972–1987.**

Property crime rates have increased slightly in recent years, as have aggravated assault rates. Other crime rates show small variations but no dramatic changes.

*Source:* U.S. Bureau of the Census, 1986a, p. 156; 1987a, p. 159; 1989a, p. 167.

**Table 7.1**   *Crime Rates in the U.S. per 100,000 Inhabitants, Based on FBI Data and Victim Reports*

|  | FBI Rate | Reported by Victims |
|---|---|---|
| Forcible rape | 37 | 70 |
| Robbery | 213 | 510 |
| Aggravated assault | 351 | 790 |
| Burglary | 1,330 | 6,150 |
| Larceny-theft | 3,081 | 13,490 |
| Motor vehicle theft | 529 | 1,500 |

*Sources:* U.S. Department of Justice, 1987; Flanagan and Jamieson, eds., *Sourcebook of Criminal Justice Statistics—1987,* 1988, p. 214.

government conducts surveys in which it asks if a person has been the victim of a crime. These surveys give a crime rate based on reports by victims (see Table 7.1).

As is apparent from comparing the columns in Table 7.1, the rate of all crimes reported by victims is much higher than the rate based on FBI data. The rate of theft reported by victims, for example, is more than four times as high as the FBI rate (Ennis, 1967; Hindelang, 1976). Why do FBI figures and reports from victims differ so widely? People say they do not report crimes to the police because they think it will not do any good. Some say they do not want to get the offender in trouble or they fear revenge if they report the crime. (As far as rape is concerned, underreporting is associated with the fact that sexual abuse often occurs within families or that rape victims may be stigmatized.) These reasons may explain why some people do not report crimes to the police.

In 1980 the proportion of families victimized by crime fell slightly to 30 percent (from 32 percent in 1979), according to reports from victims. The proportion of violent crimes stayed the same, at about 6 percent. This relative stability flies in the face of FBI reports that the crime rate is skyrocketing. The FBI's figures for the same period show that the proportion of reported crimes rose 10 percent nationally in 1980, whereas violent crimes increased 13 percent.

Both victim reports and FBI data omit many crimes, however. First, they represent only efforts to count index offenses. Yet only a small portion of criminal acts are in the crime index. Second, surveys of victims fail to ask about crimes against business, such as burglaries or robberies. Third, what Edwin Schur (1965) calls "crime without victims"—including gambling, homosexuality, and prostitution—is not included in these crime counts. Fourth, crime statistics do not include much of the substantial white-collar crime that occurs.

**White-collar crime** refers to violations of the law by high-status, otherwise respectable persons in the course of their occupations or financial pursuits (Coleman, 1987; Sutherland, 1983). It includes embezzling money, evading taxes, stealing computer time or data, forging checks, or printing counterfeit money. At the corporate level, white-collar crime includes fraudulent advertising, price-fixing, illegal payoffs to politicians, unlawful monopolies, and disregard for the health of consumers and the safety of products or wastes. Governments also commit white-collar crimes when they spy on citizens, do unauthorized wiretapping, perform political assassinations, or deny due process. A considerable amount of white-collar crime is concealed because it may occur while people practice their occupations. Some, such as mail-order frauds or stock market manipulations, may go undetected even by the victims. For all these reasons, then, both FBI data and crimes reported by victims represent a serious undercount of criminal activity in the United States.

The biggest differences in rates of crimes such as murder are found among nations (Figure 7.2). There are several explanations for this, including income inequality (Messner, 1982; Braithwaite and Braithwaite, 1980) and cultural differences (Jencks, 1987). Much more systematic cross-cultural research is needed before we can identify the causal mechanisms that produce such differences.

## Who Commits Crimes?

The types of crimes people commit vary by the race, social class, age, and sex of offenders. White middle-class males are more likely than lower-class males to commit such white-collar

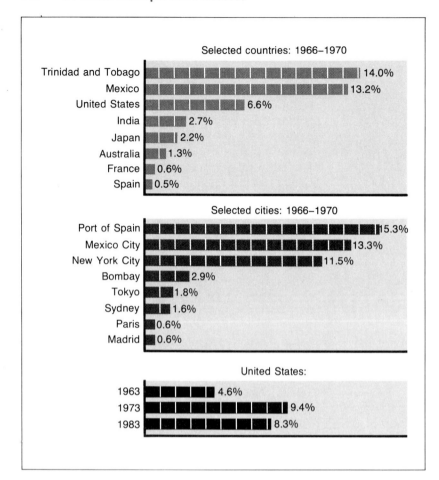

**Selected countries: 1966–1970**

| | |
|---|---|
| Trinidad and Tobago | 14.0% |
| Mexico | 13.2% |
| United States | 6.6% |
| India | 2.7% |
| Japan | 2.2% |
| Australia | 1.3% |
| France | 0.6% |
| Spain | 0.5% |

**Selected cities: 1966–1970**

| | |
|---|---|
| Port of Spain | 15.3% |
| Mexico City | 13.3% |
| New York City | 11.5% |
| Bombay | 2.9% |
| Tokyo | 1.8% |
| Sydney | 1.6% |
| Paris | 0.6% |
| Madrid | 0.6% |

**United States:**

| | |
|---|---|
| 1963 | 4.6% |
| 1973 | 9.4% |
| 1983 | 8.3% |

**Figure 7.2 Murders per 100,000 Inhabitants in Selected Years and Places.**

The biggest differences in rates of crime such as murder occur among nations.

*Source:* Jencks, 1987; U.S. Department of Justice, *Sourcebook of Criminal Justice Statistics—1984;* and Dane Archer and Rosemary Gartner, *Violence and Crime in Cross-National Perspective* (Yale University Press, 1984).

crimes as forgery, embezzlement, and computer theft as well as corporate crimes such as price-fixing or illegal waste disposal. Arrest rates for these types of crimes are fairly low, however. Lower-class males are more likely than middle-class males to commit violent crimes and burglaries, according to official arrest rates as well as self-reports by offenders (Elliott and Ageton, 1980). This relationship is particularly strong for blacks (Thornberry and Farnworth, 1982).

Arrest records show major differences by race, age, and sex, with blacks, persons under 20, and males arrested more frequently than whites, persons 20 or older, and females (see Table 7.2). Some sociologists argue that arrest and sentencing records show more about bias in the way the police and the courts process offenders than they show about who commits crimes. This position is supported by a number of studies that find little or no significant correlation between social class, for instance, and

self-reported crimes (Akers, 1964; Hirschi, 1969; Nye et al., 1958; Tittle et al., 1978; Voss, 1966). Tittle and Villemez (1977) found that all social classes commit thefts and assaults and that all classes use marijuana, with the middle classes more likely to gamble or cheat on their taxes than the highest or the lowest social classes.

Although there may well be biases in the way police and courts handle offenses, such biases do not explain completely the variations in crime rates by race, social class, age, and sex. Instead, considerable research suggests that when the seriousness of an offense and prior record are taken into account, the possible role of class bias in the generation of official data is quite small (Braithwaite, 1979, 1981; Hindelang et al., 1979; Hohenstein, 1969; Liska and Tausig, 1979; Terry, 1967). With respect to race, whites comprise 85 percent of the population, but only 71 percent of those arrested in 1986 were white (Flanagan and Jamieson, 1987). Victim studies corroborate racial differences in official arrest records. In personal and business victimizations, offenders were twice as likely to be perceived as black or of other minority status than their proportion in the population would predict (Hindelang, 1976).

How a person's prior record gets developed may depend on social background, however. A study of Seattle, Washington, showed that when the frequency and type of self-reported delinquency were comparable, police were less likely to arrest and book juveniles in higher-class neighborhoods than in lower-class neighborhoods (Sampson, 1986). Higher-class individuals were also less likely than lower-class individuals to be sent to court. This was not true for serious crimes such as robbery or homicide. It was true, however, of the much more frequent juvenile offenses like fighting, vandalism, burglary, and drug violations (Sampson, 1986, p. 884). Thus it is possible that class bias enters into the way that social control is exercised in a society.

### Sentencing and Social Background

Once people have been arrested, what affects the types of criminal sentences they receive? Black murderers were less likely than white ones to receive a death sentence or be executed except in the South, where they faced considerable discrimination, according to one major study (Kleck, 1981). When black defendants committed crimes other than murder against black victims, they tended to receive more lenient sentences than did white offenders who committed similar crimes against white victims. Kleck suggests that one explanation for these lighter sentences may be the undervaluing of black victims by the criminal justice system.

In drug-related crimes, race was related to sentencing in different ways, depending on the size of the crime. Black "big dealers" were treated more harshly than white ones, whereas nonwhite small offenders were considered to be victims and received the same sentences as their white counterparts (Peterson and Hagan, 1984). Racial bias in the processing of juvenile offenders seems to occur more in the way the police handle cases than in court decisions (Dannefer and Schutt, 1982).

Both occupation and race influence the length of time that prisoners are held in jail before trial as well as the length of prison sentence, according to other research. The amount of bail that is set depends on the severity of the crime committed and the judge's estimate that the individual charged with a crime will appear in court for trial. An individual's ability to pay bail may depend on the amount of bail and on financial status. Laborers and nonwhites receive longer sentences than white-collar workers and whites, even when prior arrests and seriousness of crimes are the same (Hagan, 1974, 1975; Lizotte, 1978).

People of higher social status received more severe sentences than those of lower status, according to a study of the sentences given out by federal district court judges to offenders convicted of white-collar crimes (Wheeler et al., 1982). This surprising result may have occurred because, in the post-Watergate era, managers may have been more likely to be prosecuted than they had been before (Hagan and Parker,

The types of crimes people commit vary by the social class, age, and sex of offenders. This man is being arrested on suspicion of drunk driving after driving his truck into the swimming pool of a California motel.

**Table 7.2**    *A Comparison of Race, Age, Socioeconomic Status, and Sex Among Offenders in the United States*

|  | **Arrest Records: Official Criminal Behavior** | **Self-report Data: Law-violating Behavior** | **Victimization Studies: Perception of Victims** |
| --- | --- | --- | --- |
| **Race** | Blacks are arrested proportionately more often than whites (Hindelang et al., 1981). | Frequency of law violations among black males is only slightly higher than it is among white males (Gold, 1970; Hirschi, 1969; Institute for Juvenile Research, 1972; Williams and Gold, 1972). However, male black youths are more likely than white youths to commit serious offenses, resulting in greater personal injury to others (Illinois Institute for Juvenile Research, 1972, pp. 23–24; Williams and Gold, 1972, p. 217. | Offenders are twice as likely to be perceived as black or of another minority than their proportion in the population would suggest (Hindelang, 1976, p. 455). |
| **Age** | Majority of arrests involve young persons under the age of 20. Young people are twice as likely to be arrested for index offenses than their proportion in population suggests (U.S. Department of Justice, 1987). | Extent of juvenile law-breaking is far greater than extent of official delinquency (Empey, 1978, p. 163). Same may be true of adults, but data are rare. | One-third of lone offenders and one-half of multiple offenders were perceived to be 12 to 20 years old (Hindelang, 1976, p. 453). |
| **SES** | Lower-class persons are more likely than middle-class persons to be arrested (Wolfgang et al., 1972). | Some studies suggest little or no correlation between social class and self-reported crimes (Akers, 1964; Hirschi, 1969; Nye et al., 1958; Tittle et al., 1978; Voss, 1966; Williams and Gold, 1972). When prior record and seriousness of offense are considered, lower-class persons report more numerous and more serious crimes than middle-class persons (Braithwaite, 1979, 1981; Elliott and Ageton, 1980; Hardt, 1968; Smith, 1975). | Victims cannot tell the socioeconomic status of offenders. |

|  | Arrest Records: Official Criminal Behavior | Self-report Data: Law-violating Behavior | Victimization Studies: Perception of Victims |
|---|---|---|---|
| **Sex** | Females are much less likely than males to be arrested. | Females generally report fewer offenses than males, but their offenses are similar to those of males (Hindelang et al., 1981; Jensen and Eve, 1976; Smith and Visher, 1980; Williams and Gold, 1972; Wise, 1967). | Lone offenders were perceived to be female 4 percent of the time and to be multiple offenders 3 percent of the time (Hindelang, 1976, p. 456). |

1985). These managers would be considered high-status in the study by Wheeler and his associates. Thus the greater severity of sentences for managers and other high-status offenders may reflect the judges' reactions to what they perceived as the excesses of Watergate.

Another explanation is that the federal court districts studied by Wheeler et al. have larger case loads, are more urbanized, and are more racially mixed than the average district. These factors, rather than post-Watergate morality, may explain the surprising finding that higher social status resulted in more severe sentences (Benson and Walker, 1988).

Black Americans and lower-class unemployed workers are more likely than white Americans to perceive criminal injustice. When class and race are considered together, black members of the professional and managerial class perceive much more criminal injustice than white members (Hagan and Albonetti, 1982), a finding that is consistent with the lower political trust of blacks who are high in the occupational structure.

Other factors may also influence the length of sentences people receive. These include the jurisdiction (federal or state, lower or superior court), the nature of the offense, and the race of the victim (Zatz, 1982).

The sex of an offender has no clear-cut relation to the sentences received. Existing research shows mixed results by sex. A number of states give women longer or more indeterminate sentences than men for the same crimes (Temin, 1979). In other states women offenders may get lighter sentences than men except with regard to offenses such as running away from home or promiscuity (Martin, 1982). There may also be an interaction between sex and type of offense; a woman who uses a gun, for example, may be sentenced more harshly than a man (Zatz, 1982).

### Self-Reports by Offenders

Is race or social class related to crime? Those who argue that it is not rely heavily on self-reports of offenders. One problem with such studies is that middle-class youths report more of their offenses than do lower-class youths (Braithwaite and Braithwaite,1978; Hardt, 1968; Smith, 1975). Another limitation is that such studies lump respondents who report three or more offenses together with those who report dozens of offenses (Elliott and Ageton, 1980). Virtually all youths report some delinquent activities on a self-report measure—for example, destroying property, lying to get into the movies, jumping on a bus without paying, failing to return extra change, making obscene phone calls, or skipping classes without an excuse. For most young people, though, these acts are neither very frequent nor very serious. When the frequency and seriousness of offenses are considered, those at the upper end of the scale on self-reports have the same social class and racial characteristics as those in police reports. Lower-class respondents report four times as many ''predatory crimes against persons'' and twice as many ''predatory crimes against property'' as do middle-class respondents (Elliott and Ageton, 1980).

With respect to sex, 84 percent of those arrested in 1978 were male and only 16 percent were female, a ratio of more than 4 to 1, although more than half the U.S. population is female (Hindelang et al., 1981). Self-reports of delinquent behavior, however, suggest that the ratio of males to females is only about 2 or 3 to 1. Females apparently commit more crimes than arrest records suggest. Moreover, the number of crimes committed by females appears to be rising in recent years—particularly with respect to larceny-theft, embezzlement, and fraud (Simon, 1979)—perhaps because of increasing financial need or growing access to the financial resources of a business.

Finally, both official arrest records and self-reports show that crime rates drop dramatically with age. Arrests for property crimes and vandalism peak at age 15 to 16, drop in half in two to four years, and continue to decline rapidly thereafter. Arrests for assaulting another person (homicide, forcible rape, aggravated assault, robbery) reach their highest rates at age 19 to 21 and then decline, although more slowly than property crimes do (Greenberg, 1977a).

As the rate of crime has been increasing, it is not surprising that people's fear of crime has grown. Crime is rated by urban residents as their most severe problem. More than 70 percent of urban dwellers rated it as a severe problem, compared to 20 percent or less for suburban, small-town, or rural dwellers. Crime was also perceived by more people as a serious problem than drugs, unemployment, or other problems.

## EXPLANATIONS OF DEVIANCE AND CRIME

Deviance and crime arouse strong reactions and concerns, and many social thinkers have tried to explain why such behaviors occur. Physical and psychological explanations have been offered (Lombroso, 1911; Goring, 1913; Witkin et al., 1976; Wilson and Herrnstein, 1987; Bandura, 1969, 1977). But here we focus on sociological explanations. These include the anomie theory of functionalists; differential association and labeling theory, which are influenced by the symbolic interactionist approach; Marxian ex-

planations of crime; and economic and deterrence theories.

## Anomie Theory

**Anomie theory** was first proposed by Emile Durkheim (1893) to explain different rates of suicide among people with different religious and marital statuses. **Anomie** refers to a social condition marked by the breakdown of norms governing behavior. (Married persons and Catholics and Jews had the lowest rates of suicide, Protestants the highest.) Durkheim believed that human desires and aspirations, if unchecked by social values and norms, were virtually limitless. In social life, groups usually develop norms that regulate and set limits on human aspirations. But in times of revolution, extreme prosperity, or economic depression, the power of social norms breaks down and people are in the state of normlessness Durkheim called anomie, in which life lacks meaning. As a result, people become more aggressive or depressed, resulting in higher rates of homicide and suicide.

The American sociologist Robert K. Merton (1957) adapted Durkheim's concept of anomie to a theory of deviant behavior. He suggested that deviance occurs when there is a mismatch between the normative goals of a society—for example, being successful and wealthy—and the allowable means for achieving those goals—getting a good job, for instance. If the goal of success is held out to everyone but only some people have access to legitimate means for achieving that goal, some people may become deviant.

Merton notes five types of responses that people make to the culturally prescribed goals and means in a society. These are presented schematically in Table 7.3. *Conformists* accept both conventional ends and means, even though they may be only partially successful in achieving the ends. They are the only ones who do not deviate in some way. *Innovators* accept the social goals but reject the approved ways of achieving them. They substitute theft, drug selling, or prostitution as an alternative means of trying to achieve their goals. They may also reject approved ways of doing something and yet still try to stay within the law, as in "creative" accounting. *Rit-*

**Table 7.3** *Merton's Types of Deviance*

| | Response to | |
| --- | --- | --- |
| | **Culturally Approved Goals** | **Culturally Approved Means** |
| Conformist | Acceptance | Acceptance |
| Innovator | Acceptance | Rejection |
| Ritualist | Rejection | Acceptance |
| Retreatist | Rejection | Rejection |
| Rebel | Substitution of new goals | Substitution of new means |

*Source:* Merton, 1957, p. 140.

*ualists* reject big views of success but conform closely to prescribed means. Office bureaucrats embody ritualism when they religiously follow the rules of their organization but lose sight of its goals.

*Retreatists* abandon both means and goals; they become drug addicts, alcoholics, or bums. *Rebels* reject culturally valued means and goals and substitute their own instead. They may become political revolutionaries or live modest lives dedicated to religion or to serving other people. Although it is possible to measure what proportion of a society adopts one or another of these responses, we can say little about why particular individuals react in one or another way.

Applied to crime, anomie theory offers a direct explanation of theft and perhaps an indirect explanation for murder, rape, and vandalism if the latter are assumed to arise at least in part out of frustration over failing to attain culturally valued goals. One application of this theory has been made by Messner (1980), who found that a measure of income inequality in 39 countries, including the United States, was associated with murder rates; whereas economic production, population, population density, and urbanization were not. He suggests that industrial and industrializing nations have a certain commitment to the value of equality and that this is violated when income is very unequally distributed. The resulting discrepancy between social expectations about how income should be distributed and how it actually is, he argues, undermines respect for social rules. It is this break-

down in the normative order that he believes is reflected in the high murder rates of nations with great income inequality. Additionally, short-term economic fluctuations, as reflected in unemployment rates, may also be related to changing criminal behavior (Brenner, 1973).

The relationship between unemployment rates and crime rates depends on the type of crime, with higher unemployment related to property crimes (Cantor and Land, 1985). An experimental study of 2000 ex-prisoners found that induced unemployment was related to increased arrests for property and nonproperty crimes; modest welfare payments to ex-prisoners were related to lower arrest rates for property and nonproperty crime (Berk et al., 1980). For ex-offenders at least, unemployment and poverty do cause individual criminal acts (Berk et al., 1980).

Unemployment rates are related to arrest rates in Canada (Greenberg, 1977b) and in the United States as well (Yaeger, 1979). When studied over time, the relationship between unemployment and criminal involvement appears to be reciprocal; that is, unemployment affects crime, and crime, in turn, is related to later unemployment (Thornberry and Christenson, 1984).

Anomie theory looks at deviance as a rational adaptation to the discrepancy between culturally approved goals and means. As Table 7.2 shows, lower-class individuals are more likely to report that they commit crimes and are more likely to be arrested than are middle-class individuals, findings consistent with Merton's anomie theory of criminal activity. The theory may thus

*Areas with higher rates of unemployment have higher rates of property crime, perhaps because legitimate means of acquiring desired goods are unavailable to the unemployed. However, not everyone without a job commits crimes, showing the importance of distinguishing between overall rates for an area and individual behaviors.*

explain certain types of deviance, especially theft and robbery, but it does little to explain insanity, for example, and a number of other acts that are often termed deviant.

## Differential Association

Another group of sociologists has focused on why one rather than another behavioral response is followed. These sociologists suggest that people learn responses from those with whom they associate. People whose parents and friends are conformists, they suggest, are more likely to become conformists themselves; those surrounded by innovators or retreatists are more likely to choose one of those approaches. The theory of **differential association** attempts to explain how deviant behavior, including criminal activity, is transmitted from one generation to another and from one ethnic group to a new one that may replace it in an urban neighborhood. Yet everyone is surrounded by a number of different types of people, some who are retreatists and others who are innovators, ritualists, conformists, or rebels. Why does a person choose to model behavior after one rather than another type? Is it the appeal and attractiveness of the people, their apparent success, or their similarity to the observer?

The prestige of the person in the eyes of other people is relevant to the influence that person

has (Sutherland and Cressey, 1978). This process is evident in Shaw's classic study *The Jack-Roller* (1930). One youngster told Shaw:

*Stealing in the neighborhood was a common practice among the children and approved by the parents. Whenever the boys got together they talked about robbing and made more plans for stealing. I hardly knew any boys who did not go robbing. The little fellows went in for petty stealing, breaking into freight cars, and stealing junk. The older guys did big jobs like stick-ups, burglary, and stealing autos. The little fellows admired the "big shots" and longed for the day when they could get into the big racket. Fellows who had "done time" were big shots and looked up to and gave the little fellows tips on how to get by and pull off big jobs. [Shaw, 1930, p. 54]*

Deviant or criminal behavior is learned, just like language, religion, or baseball, according to Edwin Sutherland (1937). He suggests that people who have an intense emotional relationship at an early age with individuals who hold favorable attitudes toward breaking the law are more likely to break the law themselves. Conversely, people who grow up surrounded by family and friends who do not favor breaking the law (or any other form of deviant behavior) are much less likely to be lawbreakers or deviants themselves.

Further research supports differential association theory. For both black and white youths in the United States, the relationship between delinquency, broken homes, and attachment to parents and friends is influenced by learned attitudes toward delinquency (Matsueda and Heimer, 1987). Attitudes were measured by agreement or disagreement with statements such as "It is all right to get around the law if you can get away with it" and "To get ahead you have to do some things which are not right."

David Matza (1969) suggests that becoming deviant is usefully understood in terms of the notion of "causal drift," which falls between free will and total determinism. Becoming deviant involves being converted to a particular way of life, which occurs in several steps. First, people must be willing to try an action defined as deviant (say, smoking marijuana), and they must actually try it. The next question is whether or not the experience seems satisfying. Does it fit with what people expected and wanted from it? If so, they may become converted. If not, they may walk away from the experience and decide not to try it again.

The theory of differential association suggests that deviant behaviors are transmitted from one generation to another, as younger people model the behaviors of older people around them.

Although every deviant situation contains a dare that is intimidating, it would be a mistake, Matza suggests, to say that people convert to deviance simply because they cave in to pressure from others. The people offering a deviant experience may be attractive or admired for reasons that go beyond that experience. Their influence may be considered by those individuals who take group pressure into account. But they also consider the nature of the experience itself. Before deciding to convert, people consider themselves in relation to a particular activity. They may choose to say no and pass the joint on, or they may take another drag. In short, people form a picture of themselves that may or may not include certain deviant actions, and they act accordingly.

One's choice is shaped by the situation one is in and by the attractions of the experience itself, suggests Matza. But he seems to assume that all individuals are equally likely to find themselves in similar situations. His view contains no conception of social structure, in which some people are more likely to be exposed to certain opportunities than others. The theory of differential association begins to explain how deviant or criminal behavior is learned. It does not, however, suggest how the behavior originated, who gets exposed to it, or how it came to be defined as deviant. Indeed, both differential association and anomie theories assume that everyone agrees on what deviant behavior is. Labeling theory challenges this assumption by stressing that deviance and crime are socially defined by various groups and are relative.

## Labeling Theory

In his book, *Outsiders*, Howard Becker (1963) rejected the view of deviance as similar to sickness. Treating deviance as a sickness for which causes and cures can be found ignores the critical role played by power and politics in the definition of deviance. Deviance, according to Becker, is created when some groups are able to impose their definitions and rules on others. Sociologists ask: Who is controlling whom, by what means, under what circumstances, and for what reasons? (Schur, 1980.)

By making rules whose infraction constitutes

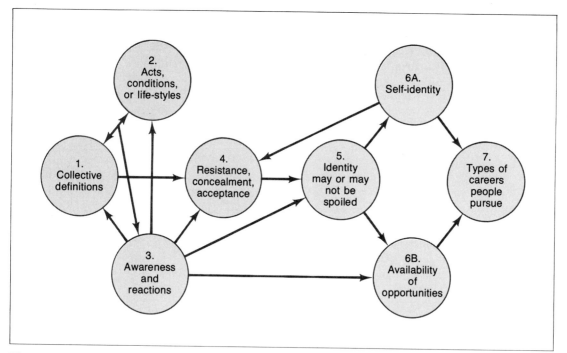

**Figure 7.3    The Labeling Process.**

A series of processes is involved in labeling. Within each process there is a range of possible experiences, and each may have a variety of consequences.

1. *Collective definitions* are socially created with respect to a wide variety of acts, conditions, lifestyles, or omissions. Collective definitions refer to the broad characterizations in a whole society of certain types of behavior or conditions (Schur, 1979). Some of these are defined as deviant to varying degrees. This is what Becker (1963) meant when he said groups create deviance by making rules, which may then be violated. Labeling theorists like Schur raise questions such as these: How are collective definitions made? What is the relative power of various groups in the process? What resources are mobilized in what ways in this process? Some collective definitions are formally stated as laws; others are negotiated more informally. Even laws, however, may be changed through political processes.

2. Individuals *perform acts, exhibit conditions, or pursue certain life-styles* (for example, stealing a candy bar, being handicapped, or living openly as a gay person) that may be defined to varying degrees as deviant if they are known to other people.

3. If other people become aware of certain behaviors or conditions, they may react to them as deviant through some formal means like a trial or informally through many small interpersonal expressions of revulsion or rejection. These reactions may help to create the collective definitions of something as relatively deviant, depending on

where the boundaries get set. The relative power of the people who are reacting is an important factor in this process. Finally, the reactions of others may change the behaviors or life-styles of those being stigmatized.

4. The persons being labeled may try to resist or fend off the efforts to stigmatize them (for example, by trying to get the charges against them dropped, by concealing behaviors or conditions that might be stigmatized, or by trying to change the negative collective definitions of particular physical conditions or life-styles). Their success in changing collective definitions depends in part on their own rejection of those definitions and on their relative power. On the other hand, they may accept the collective definition of their behavior as deviant (as do some rapists or alcoholics when they decide to seek help).

5. Depending on the strength of the collective definitions and the capacity of those being labeled to resist being stigmatized, one's identity may be spoiled to a greater or lesser degree. Child molesters face much more social consensus about the "deviantness" of their condition than do people who spray paint on public property. Conditions or behaviors differ with respect to how easily they may be concealed. Sadomasochists, for example, may be better able to conceal their predilections than transvestites; blind persons may be less able than epileptics to hide their condition.

6. The degree to which a person's identity is spoiled may affect that person internally and externally.

6A. Internally, people vary in the degree to which they accept or reject the stigmatized defini-

**156**

tion of themselves and incorporate it into their identities. Thus, for instance, they may see themselves as "nothing but a common thief," as a "pervert," or as a persecuted minority.

6B. Externally, being stigmatized may close off future opportunities for individuals (for example, for legal employment or for acceptance by people who have not been stigmatized, and so forth) (Cohen, 1966). Such a limitation of opportunities may make people who have been stigmatized more likely to pursue *deviant careers*. The term "deviant career" refers to the regular pursuit of activities that are regarded by individuals and by others as deviant.

7. Self-identities and the availability of nonstigmatized opportunities may affect the degree to which individuals pursue relatively deviant or nondeviant careers (Cohen, 1966). For example, individuals may conclude, "there's nothing else I can

do but be a full-time thief," or "I may be a dwarf, but I can still do worthwhile things with my life." Thus individuals can be deviant in some ways without necessarily accepting a spoiled identity. In addition, deviant identities do not necessarily involve people on a full-time basis. Someone may be a reputable banker in the daytime and spend the evenings snorting cocaine. By concealing behavior that might be stigmatized, people may be able to pursue two careers, one that might be labeled by many as deviant and another that many people would not see as deviant. It is also possible that people might abandon behavior, life-styles, or conditions that are considered deviant.

*Sources:* Schur, 1979, 1982; Cohen, 1966; Becker, 1963. I am particularly indebted to my colleague Ed Schur for his helpful comments in the course of preparing this figure.

---

deviant behavior, some social groups label particular people as outsiders. **Labeling theory,** then, describes the ability of some groups to impose a label of "deviant" on certain other members of society. It focuses attention on the process by which individuals are labeled as deviant rather than on the nature of their behavior.

Everyone behaves in ways that might be considered deviant, but most of us are not labeled as deviant because the behavior is invisible to others, short-lived, or unimportant. Such behavior is called **primary deviance.** Examples include such actions as running a red light, stealing a candy bar, flirting with one's cousin, or screaming obscenities out a car window at a stranger. If people do not notice or comment on such behavior, the persons doing it are not viewed as deviant by others, nor are they likely to see themselves as deviant. But if someone else discovers and makes such acts public, **secondary deviance** may occur: the behavior may be publicly labeled as deviant and the person, being treated as a deviant, may possibly begin to see himself or herself as deviant.

Such labeling may involve a "degradation ceremony" (Garfinkel, 1956), in which a person is publicly accused, berated and punished, and forced to admit wrongdoing. The person is labeled "sinner," "queer," "crazy," "junkie," "slut." Sometimes called **stigmatization,** this process involves spoiling someone's identity by labeling him or her in a negative way. (Figure

7.3 shows how this multipart process occurs.) For example, suppose an individual exhibits a certain behavior, such as theft. Other people may feel threatened or displeased with that particular behavior, and they may begin to label that person or behavior in an effort to control what they find objectionable.

The police, for example, have ideas about "typical" juvenile behavior and of who are "good kids" or "punks," partly depending on family background. Later actions by youngsters, the nature of their family life, their school adjustment, psychiatric evaluations, and other evidence are all weighed by juvenile authorities as they decide whether or not someone is delinquent (Cicourel, 1968). Groups vary with respect to how well they can resist official definitions. Middle-income families, for example, mobilize resources to fight the definitions law enforcement officials try to impose. These families are routinely able to generate or command resources for neutralizing or changing probation and court recommendations, particularly with respect to putting youngsters in detention centers. A juvenile justice official's relationship to juveniles influences the immediate disposition of their cases and has long-range career consequences for the youths. Having spent time in a juvenile facility or detention center is a serious negative feature of juveniles' records and may hurt their futures (Cicourel, 1968).

If police officers are in a position to impose

their judgment on the situation, as teachers can sometimes impose the label of "retarded" on a child or psychiatrists can impose the label of "mentally ill" on an individual, then their social typing may lead to the label being accepted by others or by the individual. The accused may incorporate the label into his or her self-image and begin to behave accordingly. The person may then associate only with others who share the stigmatized identity, which leaves little chance to practice other forms of behavior. One feature of stigmatization is its cumulative negative effect in a person's life, just as high social status can have a cumulative positive effect.

Thus the process of labeling may produce **deviant careers.** Other people interpret the present and even the past behavior of stigmatized individuals in terms of their new identities. Someone caught cheating on a test is assumed not to have written the excellent paper turned in earlier. Sexual relations experienced with someone later labeled a prostitute may lose their former personal significance.

In addition, stigmatized individuals bear the pain and shame of being viewed solely in terms of the stigmatized trait or behavior. All other aspects of their personalities and behavior may be ignored by other people, making it difficult or impossible for them to form normal social relationships with others. People with physical handicaps, for example, often report the experience of being stigmatized. People rush to help them when they fall, stare at their handicaps, or constantly bring up the topic in conversation. All these actions make it more difficult for someone with a handicap to have normal social relationships (Goffman, 1963a).

At the interpersonal level, stigmatizing occurs when people engage in vicious gossip about someone, with or without regard to the facts in the situation. Stigmatizing processes continue when someone is avoided at the water fountain or the coffee shop, or is not invited to social gatherings. At the organizational level, stigmatizing may occur when a bad evaluation is placed in a personnel file, when a person is fired, when a computer shows negative credit information, or when someone is required by organizational authorities to go for psychological counseling. At the societal level, someone who has been imprisoned, hospitalized for mental illness, dishonorably discharged from the armed services,

treated for cancer, or who has worked for an unpopular political organization may find it difficult or impossible to obtain employment, housing, insurance, or credit.

The process is very close to that of **scapegoating,** whereby someone who is different or weaker is picked out and blamed for the problems of a larger group, regardless of the person's part in those problems. Hitler did this in the 1930s when he blamed the Jews for the structural social and economic problems Germany faced. Stigmatizing some individuals or behaviors may temporarily increase the cohesiveness of a group, but it also has several grave costs. First, it creates undeserved pain and suffering in the individuals who are stigmatized. Second, their contributions to the group are often lost because they are excluded or demoralized. Third, individuals in the larger group often cannot feel really secure, since they may be the next to be stigmatized. In addition, scapegoating involves a misplaced grievance. Many problems have their roots in social structural causes that are difficult to pinpoint. It is easier to blame some weak yet visible group for these problems than to link them to structural causes.

Besides providing temporary emotional relief and unity to those doing the labeling, the process of stigmatization may unify and mobilize the stigmatized individuals. They may organize to change the way their behavior is defined. This struggle over whose definition will prevail has been called "the politics of deviance" (Schur, 1980) and is discussed in the next section.

The labeling explanation of crime suggests that crime rates may not vary much from one country to another or from one time to another. Instead, what changes is whether or not people define acts as crimes and how police departments and other officials record crimes. Unquestionably there are variations in crime statistics because of the way acts are defined and the way records are kept. Sometimes the murder rate in a country leaps from one year to the next when a new and more efficient set of public bureaucrats begins keeping records. Societies do vary with respect to what they consider to be crimes. Prostitution, for example, is legal in some societies. And even where it is illegal, the number of arrests made for prostitution may swing wildly, depending on the political pressure put on the police at any given time. It is important to realize that social factors influence the definitions of crimes, the number of people who are arrested for those crimes, and the care with which records are kept. But even a social constructionist would have trouble maintaining that all differences in crime rates can be explained by social definitions.

## Conflict and Marxian Explanations

### The Politics of Deviance

A conflict perspective on deviance and crime emphasizes the relative power of different groups in a social situation and their capacity to impose rules and definitions on others. When, for example, is a particular behavior—like drinking liquor or smoking pot—defined as deviant or illegal and when is it viewed as an "alternative life-style" that individuals are free to accept or reject? Formal and informal social power play major roles in this definitional process.

The social conflict surrounding the definition of behavior as deviant or not, legal or illegal, is well illustrated by the case of the gay-rights movement. Members of this movement mobilized themselves politically in an effort to change the American Psychiatric Association's definition of homosexuality as a sickness and to change laws in many states that discriminate against homosexuals in hiring, housing, or credit. By openly challenging the label other groups in society were trying to pin on homosexuals, the gay-rights movement has been rather successful. Behavior that had been considered sinful, criminal, perverse, or sick has come increasingly to be defined as simply a sexual variation or an alternative life-style. By the middle of the twentieth century, a growing body of social science literature was suggesting that a wide range of sexual practices falls within the range of "normative" human behavior. Moreover, the distinction began to be made between sexual behavior on the one hand and how that behavior is defined on the other. In the 1960s a growing number of publications and organizations grew up in response to efforts to gain equal rights for homosexuals. The term "homosexual" was increasingly replaced with the term "gay," which represents an alternative definition of a particular orientation and life-style (Conrad and Schneider, 1980; Spector and Kitsuse, 1977; Teal, 1971).

A police raid on a gay bar in Greenwich Village in 1969 became one of the rallying points for the gay-rights movement. When the police raided the bar, allegedly on the charge of a liquor license violation, the patrons resisted the attack with fists, bottles, and fire. A number of people were injured, and the police had to summon reinforcements. For perhaps the first time the patrons of a gay bar refused to be harassed by police and society. The incident mobilized the gay community: the results included public protests, demonstrations, and the organization of the gay-rights movement. By 1972, more than a thousand local gay organizations existed in the United States; by 1980, 26 states had decriminalized private consensual same-sex acts between adults (Conrad and Schneider, 1980).

Besides political and legal mobilization and change, removing the definition of a behavior as deviant requires changing the definitions used by public definers of behavior. This case involved modifying the way research and writings on same-sex behavior was classified in American libraries and changing the American Psychiatric Association's definition of homosexuality as sickness. In 1970 the American Library Association formed a Task Force on Homosexuality to remove the topic of homosexuality from its file location under "Sexual Perversion" (Spector and Kitsuse, 1977). After a heated political and scientific controversy within the American Psychiatric Association, that organization voted in 1973 to remove homosexuality as a psychiatric condition from the APA's *Diagnostic and Statistical Manual*. People disturbed by their sexual orientation or wishing to change it are considered to have a "sexual orientation disturbance" and can receive psychiatric treatment for it. But anyone who accepts his or her preference for same-sex partnerships is no longer, according to the diagnostic manual, considered "sick."

Although the gay-rights movement has made major gains in changing the way important groups in society define same-sex behavior, it has done less to change the way that preference is viewed in the larger society. About three-quarters of the general public in 1981 believed homosexuality to be morally wrong. On the other hand, more than two-thirds of the leaders in the news media, government, education, law, justice, and science viewed homosexuality or lesbianism as not morally wrong. Gay-rights activists have made some gains with respect to changing the legal and medical definitions that others place on their behavior, but they have not yet had the same success in changing what the general public thinks about that behavior. In 1985 there was some antigay backlash in some parts of the country, focused around reactions to acquired immune deficiency syndrome (AIDS).

New political and legal battles are raging over AIDS; at issue are the rights of infected persons as opposed to those who are free from AIDS, the amount and type of research to be supported, when blood testing should be done, how insurance coverage should be handled, and other matters.

This example suggests that the definition of something as deviant or illegal may depend quite heavily on the social and political resources of groups favoring such a definition. Groups opposing such definitions may sometimes mobilize successfully. Thus the definition of something as deviant may result from the social and political resources and strategies of contending groups. This theory would explain uneven rates of deviance in various societies in terms of what definitions prevailed in which societies.

### Marxian Criminology

Some Marxian criminologists explain deviance and crime in terms of the relative powerlessness of different groups. They suggest that capitalism may produce conditions that generate deviant or criminal behavior. Thus they explain much of lower-class crime as a substitute for revolutionary activity. As such, criminals are actually rebels against a repressive capitalist system that uses the law, courts, prisons, mental institutions, and juvenile centers as weapons for controlling ever-larger numbers of rebellious members (Taylor, Walton, and Young, 1973). They see law as a tool of the powerful used to maintain social relations, especially class relations (Chambliss, 1969; Quinney, 1970, 1974).

Marxian criminology provides valuable insights into the place of law in capitalist societies, but it tends to overlook several important features of crime. There is, for example, considerable social agreement about the major crime categories. Most people, regardless of their class

background, are offended by and opposed to murder, rape, assault, armed robbery, breaking and entering, and arson. Moreover, ghetto residents and members of the working classes are among the most concerned in society about being victimized by crime (Greenberg, 1976), perhaps because they are more likely to be victims.

### Economic and Deterrence Theories

#### Increasing the Costs of Crime

Whatever the social conditions that encourage criminal acts and however people learn to do them, the possibility remains that criminals are sufficiently rational to respond to the certainty and severity of punishments imposed by law. Regardless, then, of what causes crime, one way to try to reduce it is to catch and punish offenders. A number of policy analysts argue that increasing the certainty and severity of punishment should lead to lower crime rates when other things are equal (Becker, 1968; Reynolds, 1971; Sjoquist, 1971; Tullock, 1974; Van den Haag, 1975).

Economic and deterrence theories of crime extend economists' analysis of choice in an effort to explain variations in crime rates. This approach suggests that people will commit crimes if they feel they will gain more by doing so than they would by using their time and resources in some other way (Becker, 1968). Some people become criminals and others do not because the costs and benefits differ. For example, burglars may believe that the economic or other benefits of stealing outweigh their feelings about committing an illegal act or their fears of being caught and punished. Sociologists who accept this economic explanation stress, in addition, that people have different costs and benefits depending on their locations in the social structure, their wealth, prior offenses, and the other opportunities available to them. As a result, everyone is not equally likely to commit crimes.

The general population tends to think about crime in terms that are compatible with economic and deterrence explanations. One-third of the respondents in a Gallup poll indicated that people commit crimes because of "the high cost of living or unemployment." The second most frequently mentioned reason also fits into a cost-

*The poor and urban dwellers are frequently victims of crimes and are more likely than other groups in society to call for stiff penalties for criminals.*

benefit analysis. One-quarter of the respondents said that the "court system is too lenient," suggesting they believe that the costs of criminal activity are not high enough (cited in Flanagan et al., 1982, p. 192).

At the societal level, an economic explanation for crime indicates that the number of offenses depends on the probability of conviction, the punishment if convicted, income available from legal and illegal activities, and an individual's willingness to commit an illegal act (Becker, 1968). The focus, then, is on the probabilities of being caught and the severity of punishment. Even murder is deterred by punishment, according to several research studies (Ehrlich, 1974, 1975, 1977). A study of reported crime and arrest rates for 98 cities from 1964 to 1970, however, failed to show that a greater chance of being arrested reduced the rate of crime (Greenberg, Kessler, and Logan, 1977).

Despite the absence of a relationship between crime and arrest rates, Greenberg feels that this evidence does not invalidate deterrence effects on crime. These records show only arrests, not punishments. Moreover, numerous reports from former juvenile offenders, as well as in-

trospection, point to the importance of punishment as a deterrent to crime. For example, if it were possible to steal $100,000 from a bank and be sure of never getting caught, many people would do so. Some people would not because they have internal controls against stealing, believing that it is deeply wrong. Others do not find stealing incompatible with their self-image and do not have deeply held convictions against doing it. Some of them are deterred from stealing, however, by the possibility of being caught and then embarrassed or punished. The punishment need not be a severe one to be a deterrent. In the Scandinavian countries, the Netherlands, and Switzerland, punishments are quite mild, yet those countries have very low rates of crime (Greenberg, 1981).

### Does the Death Penalty Deter Homicide?

Capital punishment (the death penalty) is one of the most hotly debated issues in social policy. Punishment by death is an ancient practice. In the last two or three hundred years, societies began to develop a rational justification for using the death penalty, which rests on deterrence theory. **Deterrence theory** asserts that qualities of punishment—for example, its certainty, swiftness, and severity—will help prevent others from committing that particular offense. Deterrence theory suggests that increasing the severity of the penalty for an offense will reduce the chances that it will occur. Thus, according to deterrence arguments, punishing by death people who are convicted of homicide will reduce homicides. If deterrence theory is correct that capital punishment more effectively deters murder than does long imprisonment (an alternative punishment), then the abolition of capital punishment should lead to higher rates of homicide. A good research design to test this hypothesis requires data over time from many countries around the world. Such a study has been done using data from 1900 to 1970 from 110 national and 44 urban centers (Archer and Gartner, 1984). Of those 154 centers, 14 had abolished capital punishment. Did their homicide rates increase? No. After one year, after five years, or in relation to other crimes, homicide rates did not increase. Often they decreased after the death penalty was abolished (Archer and Gartner, 1984, chap. 6). Supporters of capital punishment may argue for it because they favor the idea of retribution or because of the economic costs of long-term punishment. But the best available evidence does not support deterrence theory (see also Bowers, 1974; Bowers and Pierce, 1980; Joyce, 1961).

For some groups of offenders, perceptions of risks fail to deter other forms of lawbreaking as well. For such offenders, perceptions of criminal opportunities and positive attitudes toward criminal acts seem to influence decisions to commit crimes (Piliavin, Gartner, Thornton, and Matsueda, 1986). In sum, while deterrence may reduce the chances of some people committing certain types of crimes, it does not deter everyone. Moreover, the existence of capital punishment does not affect homicide rates.

## Integration and Evaluation

The potential of several of these theories of crime can be seen by applying them to the task of explaining variations in crime rates by age. Using a strand from anomie theory, Greenberg (1977a) argues that the structural position of juveniles in American society puts a great deal of pressure on them to realize highly valued immediate goals. Strong age segregation (which makes youths particularly dependent on peers for approval) and the rise of a clear "teenage market" for records, entertainment, clothes, makeup, cigarettes, alcohol, drugs, and other goods have combined to generate consumer "needs" in teenagers. When tastes were less expensive, parents or part-time employment could support such consumer desires. The growing costs of adolescent life-styles, along with the persistent decline in employment opportunities for young people, present teenagers with a gap between the wish for activities and purchases and the legitimate means to pay for them.

Considerable qualitative evidence supports this explanation of teenage theft; money and goods are stolen because they are strongly desired. As teenagers grow older, their chances of getting jobs increase and their growing involvement in other institutions such as the family and work may reduce their dependence on peers for self-esteem at the same time that it provides legal sources of income. Thus Merton's version of anomie theory predicts a rapid decline in theft, which is what happens.

Schools may contribute to such delinquent acts as vandalism in that they shackle teen autonomy, publicly evaluate student performance, and sometimes humiliate students before their peers. Some acts of seeming bravado may stem from anxieties over gender identity that are certainly not helped by the absence of paid employment and being humiliated in school. This explanation draws on the insights of labeling theory.

A third explanatory strand stems from the growing seriousness of being caught, a form of deterrence theory. As offenders get older, their behavior is no longer so likely to be viewed as simply "childish pranks" by parents or police. Judges are likely to be more severe with older offenders, and the penalties may be harsher. Some former delinquents say they stopped committing crimes because they were unwilling to risk stiffer penalties as they grew older. By drawing on these theoretical threads, Greenberg (1977a) has woven a composite theory that explains different types of criminal acts and fits the way criminal behavior declines with age.

This theory and its supporting evidence have been hotly debated in the sociological literature (Greenberg, 1985; Hirschi and Gottfredson, 1983, 1985), suggesting the kind of sparks that may fly when sociological ideas clash. Models combining age structure, business cycles, criminal opportunities, and rates of imprisonment explain most of the variation in yearly rates of homicide and car theft from 1946 through 1986 (Cohen and Land, 1987).

An interesting theory of juvenile delinquency has integrated a Marxian notion of alienation with the socialization theory and research, differential association, and Merton's anomie theory. Colvin and Pauly (1983) suggest that parents who have little ownership or control over the means and ends of production are more likely to experience a "coercive workplace control structure" (that is, they are more likely to get fired than be talked to if they "mess up"). These workers are less likely to feel a positive bond to their work, to the authorities at their workplace, and to the organization where they work.

As parents, such people probably stress conformity to external authority when they raise their children (here Colvin and Pauly draw on Kohn's socialization research, which is discussed

**Table 7.4**   *Foci of Various Theoretical Approaches to Deviance and Crime*

| Theoretical Orientation | Macro Level | Institutional Level | Group Level | Individual Level |
|---|---|---|---|---|
| **Functionalist Approach** **Anomie Theory** | Discrepancy between culturally approved means and ends. | | | Individual acts of deviance or crime. |
| **Interactionist Approaches** **Differential Association** | | | People learn deviant behavior from parents, peers, or subgroups. | |
| **Labeling** | | Reactions of institutions to behavior labels it deviant. | | Individuals continue to pursue acts once they have been labeled deviant. |
| **Weberian Conflict Approach** | Political and legal groups define deviance or crime. | Institutional definitions reflect powerful groups. | | |
| **Marxian Approach** | Capitalism produces conditions that generate deviance or crime. | Capitalism may undermine forms of communal life such as family. | Peer groups develop that foster various forms of delinquent behavior. | Individuals develop different evaluations of deviant or criminal behavior. |
| **Deterrence Theories** | | Severity, certainty, and swiftness of punishment reduces likelihood of crime. | | Rational choice (cost-benefit analysis) by individuals affects crime rates. |

in Chapter 5), whereas parents who have greater decision-making power put more value on "internalized self-control," initiative, and creativity in their children. Coercive family control structures make juveniles feel alienated from their families. Alienated juveniles are likely to be put into "coercive school control structures" (that is, schools with harsh rules and few resources), which increases their level of alienation yet again. The more alienated an individual juvenile is, the more likely he or she is to associate with other alienated peers, and to form strong peer-group control structures.

These peer groups must deal with the limited opportunities that their social class, community, or ethnic group makes available to them. In juvenile groups with coercive control structures, members in all probability show violent delinquent behavior. If they make money through illegitimate means, they may develop a "utilitarian control structure," which contributes to a pattern of instrumental delinquent behavior (for example, drug-dealing or car theft) rather than violent patterns of delinquency.

Thus Colvin and Pauly's hypothesis weaves together a number of strands of theory and re-

## D E B A T I N G   S O C I E T Y ' S   I S S U E S

*Is Women's Liberation Linked to Higher Rates of Female Crime?*

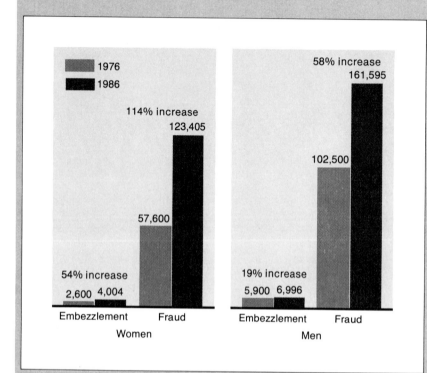

**1976**
**1986**

114% increase
123,405

57,600

54% increase
2,600  4,004

Embezzlement        Fraud

**Women**

58% increase
161,595

102,500

19% increase
5,900  6,996

Embezzlement        Fraud

**Men**

**Figure 7.4   Number of Women and Men Arrested for Embezzlement and Fraud in the United States, 1976 and 1986, and the Percentage Increase over That Time.**

While the percentage of women arrested for embezzlement and fraud has increased much faster than has the percentage of men, the total number of men arrested for these crimes is still larger than the total number of women arrested for the same crimes. One reason may be the increased willingness of firms to have small-time female offenders arrested compared to big-time male offenders (Burrough, 1987).

*Source:* U.S. Bureau of the Census, 1987, 1979.

### Yes

1. There is a "rising tide of recorded female crime" (Adler, 1975); but much of her data were from case studies, and it is not clear that they are generalizable.

2. In 1975, 15.7 percent of persons *arrested* in the United States for all crimes were female; in 1987, the figure was 17.7 percent. So there has been a slight increase. This meant that the figure for females went from 1.2 million arrested to 1.9 million arrested, while for males it went from 6.8 million to 8.9 million (U.S. Department of Justice, 1987, p. 181).

3. There is an increase in the number of women involved in fraud and embezzlement, and the percentage increase for women was much greater than that for men between 1976 and 1987 (see Figure 7.4).

### No

1. Female property offenses have increased faster than male offenses, but crimes of violence have not. The former is due to nonoccupational frauds such as shoplifting rather than to job-related thefts (Box and Hale, 1983, p. 36; Steffensmeier, 1978, p. 580).

2. Women's crimes used to be nearly invisible because the numbers were so small. When the numbers rose slightly, it was deemed a "sudden dramatic increase" because the percentage change was relatively large. Women still have much lower rates than men.

3. Men steal much bigger amounts than do women. According to one study of white-collar crime, men stole an average of ten times more money than did women (Burrough, 1987).

## DEBATING SOCIETY'S ISSUES

| Yes | No |
|---|---|
| 4. These increases in white-collar crime are correlated with increasing percentages of women in the work force. | 4. Firms may be more willing to crack down on small-time female offenders than on networks of big-time male offenders who are more embarrassing to their firms (Burrough, 1987). |
| | 5. If certain arrest rates are increasing, it may not be the liberation of women that is the cause but the increasing financial obligations of larger numbers of single women. |

What needs to be explained is the "moral panic over new, aggressive female criminals" (Heidensohn, 1985, p. 159). Why has this happened? Several explanations have been offered: (1) the small increase in crime may be used as ammunition by those opposed to the women's movement, (2) the hue and cry about crime deflects attention from problems in the criminal justice system, and (3) excessive concern about their role in crime might be seen as another attempt to keep women subordinated to men (Chesney-Lind, 1980, p. 28).

search into a proposed explanation for delinquent groups participating in violence or theft.

Another integrated effort to explain juvenile delinquency appears in the book *Adolescent Subcultures and Delinquency* (Schwendinger and Schwendinger, 1985). The book suggests that the roots of upper-middle-class "socialite delinquents" and tough street gangs are similar in both industrialized countries and developing nations. The political and economic changes that accompany capitalism produce different class conditions. These lead to changes in families and other forms of communal life. They also create different types and proportions of peer groups, who show different rates and types of delinquent behavior (Schwendinger and Schwendinger, 1985).

In evaluating the various theoretical approaches to crime and deviance that have been presented here, we should not conclude that some are "correct" and others are not. Instead, the different approaches allow us to consider somewhat different questions and address those questions several ways. Physical and psychological explanations, anomie theory, differential association, conflict, and Marxian views are all useful approaches to the question of who is relatively more likely to commit crimes. If we want to consider such questions as why crime rates vary at different times or in different societies, or why crime rates vary by age, then anomie, economic, conflict, Marxian, and labeling theory are all helpful viewpoints. Labeling theory is well suited to considering how acts, conditions, or life-styles are reacted to in ways that stigmatize them as deviant. (See Table 7.4 for a summary of the foci of various theories.)

## Women and Crime

Women consistently have a much lower rate of officially recorded crimes than men do, at least in the United States and Great Britain (Heidensohn, 1985; Leonard, 1982; Simon, 1975), although women may be taking a somewhat larger part in crime now than they did in the past. (See the debate "Is Women's Liberation Linked to Higher Rates of Female Crime?")

Existing theories of deviance and crime do very little to explain female crime. An adequate theory of crime and delinquency must be able to explain gender differences in crime rates (Heidensohn, 1985, p. 143). Greater delinquency by men results from the class structure of modern patriarchal families, suggest Hagan, Simpson, and Gillis (1987). In such families, daughters are much more tightly controlled than sons and are also much less delinquent. In more balanced, egalitarian families or in female-headed households, daughters gain more freedom and gender differences in delinquency decline (Hagan et al., 1987, p. 813).

# SOCIAL CONTROL AND LAW

## Social Control

Deviance and crime, like other social behaviors, are defined and shaped by the forms of social control in a society. **Social control** refers to the relatively patterned and systematic ways in which society guides and restrains individual behaviors so that people act in predictable and desired ways. An essential means of social control is socialization, through which children learn the values and norms of their social group. Once social rules are learned, many people comply with them out of habit or because they are committed to certain social values. But sometimes individual desires clash with social expectations, and people behave in ways that violate social norms or values.

Societies usually then use other means to ensure conformity. Chief among these are **sanctions**—the rewards or punishments issued by individuals, organizations, or societies in an effort to secure conformity of behavior. Sanctions that are seen as rewards for desirable behavior are called **positive sanctions;** those that are meant to deter unwanted behavior are **negative sanctions.** At the interpersonal level, sanctions include smiles, scowls, praise, complaints, favors performed or withheld, and numerous other ways humans have devised for making life pleasurable or miserable for people they wish to influence. Organizations also have an extensive repertory of rewards and punishments. Higher organizational authorities can manipulate pay, hours worked, type of work done, size and location of workers' offices, opportunities for promotion, and chances for internal and external acclaim or blame. Depending on how such elements are handled within the organization, they can serve as rewards or punishments. Clear neg-

ative sanctions include being disgraced within the organization or being fired.

Most societal rewards and sanctions are filtered through individuals or organizations. Certainly an organization's sanctioning power is enhanced by the degree of prestige that society assigns to the money, title, and power the organization can confer upon individuals within it. Newscasters, for example, face stiff competition to attain anchor positions on the evening news. Because of the public recognition and high financial rewards the major networks can offer, the networks also hold considerable sanctioning power. Broadcasters are readily fired or demoted, thereby immediately losing all the advantages of their position. Through local, state, and federal laws, society can also exercise negative sanctions resulting in fines, arrests, or imprisonment for certain behaviors.

In primary groups and small communities, most social control is exercised through **informal sanctions,** through the immediate responses of people whose reactions matter very much to an individual in the group. **Formal sanctions** are embedded in such institutional forms as the law or in procedures for granting awards. Table 7.5 offers examples of positive and negative formal and informal sanctions. All four types of sanctions operate in many social

*Informal sanctions involve immediate responses to persons in primary groups or small communities. The Ku Klux Klan uses negative, illegal sanctions to control (and terrorize) people whose race or beliefs they don't like.*

**Table 7.5**  *Types of Social Sanctions and How They Are Administered*

| | Form of Administration | |
| --- | --- | --- |
| | **Formal** | **Informal** |
| **Positive sanctions** | Money, diplomas, medals, awards, prizes, promotions | Praise, admiration, approval, smiles, kisses, "pats on back" |
| **Negative sanctions** | Fines, imprisonment, banishment, death | Ridicule, ostracism, criticism, threats, name-calling ("weirdo," "fink," "nut," "nerd," "geek") |

situations to ensure social control. Consider, for example, an individual teacher in a classroom who wants the students to be quiet or to do the assignment.

If social control is not formalized, the teacher has only personal charm, wit, smiles, scowls, or praise to draw on in exercising social control (Swidler, 1979). Many educators—and parents—feel that this is an insufficient and chancy basis for social control in the classroom; hence more formal methods exist in most schools. Schools grant teachers the power to grade (including the power to flunk students), and authority to send pupils to the detention center or the principal's office. School systems have the formal authority (through law and accreditation organizations) to grant or withhold diplomas, certificates, degrees, and honors. These credentials have a certain value in the marketplace, and withholding them can have negative economic and status effects on individuals. In this way, through the effect of positive and negative formal and informal sanctions, one individual teacher becomes part of a larger system of social control.

Functionalists tend to define social control as the means and processes used by a group or a society to ensure that members conform to its expectations. This definition assumes that a society or group agrees on the expectations held for members—for example, that adultery is not only illegal but also a sin. A conflict view of social control suggests that groups with relatively greater power and legitimacy are most likely to get their power formalized. In a pluralistic society with many competing groups and interests, it is impossible for all views to be fully expressed in the law. So to some degree law and

social control are arbitrary in such societies (Toby, 1981). This is evident, for instance, in statutes against loitering in certain neighborhoods.

In the interactionist view, social control emerges out of interactions between individuals rather than being something that always exists ready-made, needing only to be exercised in various ways at particular times. Norms and rules are created or defined as they are applied (Schur, 1979), and we can only become aware of what those norms or rules are after we see how they have been applied. For example, in a study of mental illness, Yarrow et al. (1955) found that wives tended to "normalize" the erratic behavior of their husbands for quite a while before coming to the conclusion that their husbands were mentally ill. When they "couldn't take it any longer," they concluded the behavior was not normal. As Schur (1979) suggests, the process of defining "mental disturbance" has at least two parts—the husband's behavior and the wife's reaction to that behavior. This example illustrates that rules and norms do not simply exist "out there," waiting for someone to come along and apply them. Instead, they emerge out of behaviors and the reactions to those behaviors.

Like rules and norms, social control emerges from an ongoing process of struggle and negotiation. Various participants bring unequal resources to bear in this process. Formal systems of social control include formal agents of social control. Every system of formal social control needs control agents. Becker (1963) distinguished two kinds of control agents: rule creators and rule enforcers. Rule creators such as lawmakers shape the rules, norms, or laws for a group, organization, or society. Rule enforcers like police officers try to keep people in line through various processes. In practice, however, the distinction between rule making and rule enforcement is a matter of degree rather than kind, as the interactionist approach reminds us. For example, police officers exercise discretion on the street.

In brief, functionalism points to the universality of social control in all societies, whereas the interactionist perspective emphasizes that rules are negotiated in social interactions. Conflict theory suggests that some groups may gain greater control over the negotiations that define what is to be socially controlled and how those definitions are enforced. All three outlooks contribute to our understanding of social control.

One of the major mechanisms of social control in modern societies is the law.

## Law as a Means of Social Control

One of the central differences between modern industrial societies and simple tribal societies is the reliance of modern societies on law and formal legal systems to manage social processes that were once handled by tradition, the family, or tribal customs. In general, the less a society uses other forms of social control, the more it relies on law (Black, 1976). This is true about what behavior is defined as deviant as well as about other social practices. An American returning from Upper Volta (now Burkina Faso), in West Africa, remarked that he could leave his bicycle on the ground in a village and it would still be there a year later. Bicycles are valuable in Upper Burkina Faso, but tribal customs dictate what you may and may not do with something that belongs to someone else. In a pluralistic and highly complex society like ours, however, there is no one custom dictating how things should be done. Moreover, the binding quality of tradition works in a highly cohesive society where people see each other often on a face-to-face basis and can reward or sanction one another for their behavior. Tradition or personal honor is deeply undermined in a society where strangers do business and people have different goals, interests, and customs. In a transitory, diverse, and highly complex society, growing reliance is placed on law rather than on other

methods to establish procedures, resolve disputes, and uphold rights and duties.

**Law** is a system of formalized rules established for the purpose of controlling or regulating social behavior. Even in a modern society, however, law is like an empty sack if it tries to stand up for a principle that is largely at odds with widely held mores and values. For example, in the 1920s the Prohibition Amendment did not stop people who wanted to drink from doing so, and today the speed limits of 55 or 65 miles per hour are widely violated on many highways. Thus the law is a social beast. Social processes and social relations shape the content of law, and the law at any given moment affects society and social life. (See the box for a summary of how functionalists and conflict theorists view the law.)

Law also touches on politics. Laws are enacted through political procedures, and they are interpreted and enforced by political authorities rather than purely according to custom. In modern societies, the body of law that controls and regulates social behavior consists of two types—criminal and civil.

**Criminal law** is concerned with wrongs against society. It is enacted by recognized political authorities; it prohibits or requires certain behaviors and provides specific punishment, administered by designated authorities, for violators. Criminal offenses may be grouped into three broad types: (1) acts of physical violence such as murder, rape, and assault; (2) infringe-

*Persons accused of serious criminal offenses have the right to trial by a jury of peers, such as the one being sworn in here.*

# *How Functionalists and Conflict Theorists View the Law*

Law has tremendous potential to protect people and property. It also has the potential to oppress. Functional and conflict views of the law stress different sides of this double-edged blade.

## Functionalists See the Law as Functioning:

1. To maintain public order, by defining crime and criminal activity and empowering agents to regulate it. Law may be called into play to settle disputes (such as broken contracts), marital disagreements, or differences over property boundaries. Law can take the place of screaming contests, fistfights, or murder.

2. To establish and uphold rights and duties. The law functions to interpret constitutional and other legal precedents for rights and duties. It also supports or denies an individual's rights or obligations in certain situations. For example, there are laws that affirm a handicapped person's right to access to a public building and that state parents' obligations to support their children.

3. To establish procedures for doing certain things. The laws surrounding wills, for example, ensure the protection and disposal of property.

4. To confer legitimacy. The law operates to confer legitimacy on political leaders, on the heads of publicly chartered organizations such as universities, on religious leaders, and on corporate business leaders. Legal systems also operate as a major means of keeping records in a society. Births, deaths, marriages, citizenship—all these and other details of modern life need to be recorded in a legally binding and legitimate way.

5. To redistribute or innovate. Government agencies seek to use the legal system for social planning. Health care delivery, for instance, is affected by a system of laws that regulates what services are and are not covered by government medical insurance, by permissible fee schedules, and so forth.

6. To permit and protect certain rights and actions, such as First Amendment rights to freedom of religion, speech, assembly, or foreign travel.

7. To advance the interests of virtually all members or groups in a society. Stability and predictability, supported by law, facilitate the conduct of production, commerce, and education. Another benefit for the vast majority of citizens stems from laws that are designed expressly to limit the power of rulers. This was a major concern of those drafting the Constitution of the United States. They set up legal procedures enabling Congress to overrule or impeach the president, allowing the president to veto laws, and establishing the Supreme Court's right to declare laws unconstitutional.

## Conflict Theorists Suggest That:

1. Law may operate to maintain a highly unjust or unequal social order.

2. The more powerful members of society may define the rights and duties that laws uphold in ways that benefit them. For example, doctors may influence legislation requiring influenza vaccine and then benefit from the added business it gives them.

3. Some people may benefit more than others from particular procedures. Lawyers in the state legislature of New York have made the procedures surrounding wills complicated enough so that people cannot handle their relatives' estates themselves. The procedures in California are much simpler and make it possi-ble for many people to handle the estates of their relatives.

4. More powerful classes or groups may influence who is defined as legitimate. Deciding on the criteria to be used to confer legitimacy is often the real point where power is exercised. What criteria determine who is to be granted state, federal, or local scholarship aid for college?

5. Who should be making social planning decisions? In the case of health care delivery, for example, it is obvious that older citizens who receive services, the medical profession, and taxpayers have different views of how social engineering should be conducted, or even if it should occur.

6. The legal system is inevitably bound up with a society's system of stratification (Schur, 1968). The most extreme cases of law being used in the interests of dominant groups occur in Nazi Germany or South Africa today. There the ruling group shapes the legal system to serve its aims. But even in more democratic societies, "law invariably reflects and influences the ordering of social strata within a society" (Schur, 1968, p. 88).

The functionalist and conflict views together show the law's potential for both oppression and protection. They alert us to the possibility that a legal system or particular set of laws may be more beneficial for some members of society than for others. To youths who like to hang out on street corners, antiloitering laws seem oppressive and discriminatory, whereas home-owners may see the same laws as their only way of controlling strangers who may be planning burglaries. One's actual (or hoped for) position in a society's system of privilege and property goes a long way toward explaining one's view of the law.

ments on property rights, including theft, fraud, and burglary; and (3) a broad range of actions labeled crimes against health, morals, and public safety, including prostitution, gambling, pornography, drug use, and drunkenness. In a serious criminal case the state initiates legal proceedings, often beginning with a police arrest. The rules of evidence are strict; a person is presumed innocent until proven guilty; a defendant must be found guilty "beyond a reasonable doubt"; and the court decides whether to acquit or convict the person charged. A crucial element in a criminal violation is the existence of criminal intent by the lawbreaker, who is thereby thought to deserve punishment, deterrence, or rehabilitation. Within criminal law, *felonies* are major crimes such as murder, arson, or rape. *Misdemeanors* are minor offenses under the law, such as breaking a municipal ordinance.

**Civil law,** which developed from Roman law, largely deals with private wrongs; that is, wrongs against the individual. Such actions as defamation of character, the invasion of privacy, selling defective goods, trespass, and negligence are violations of civil law. Civil cases are initiated by private citizens. The alleged wrongdoer receives a summons to appear in a civil court. The claim against him or her must be established by a "preponderance of the evidence" rather than the rule of "beyond a reasonable doubt." The court decision is termed a finding or a judgment, and violators are not usually punished.

Instead, the victim is "made whole" (that is, compensated for any losses), or competing claims are resolved by further legal proceedings (Sykes, 1978).

The uniform commercial code is an example of a civil law that has been adopted in a number of states. This group of laws operates to standardize the law surrounding business practices such as the sale of goods, negotiable instruments such as checks, the loan of money, or documents of title such as a bill of sale.

## Prisons as a Form of Social Control

When the law fails as a form of social control, prisons may be called on to perform that function. Prisons are intended to contain criminals so that they cannot harm more people and to punish wrongdoers. At the same time, they are charged with treating or rehabilitating criminals so that they may return to society. An unintended result of prisons is that they may teach new criminal behaviors by providing contact between novices and hardened criminals.

### Do Crimes Lead to Prison?

What happens when someone commits a crime? Not all crimes are reported, as we have already seen. For those crimes that are reported, there is a wide variation in the percentage that result in arrests, as Figure 7.5 shows. Murder is

*When law fails to control people's behavior, prisons serve as a more severe form of social control.*

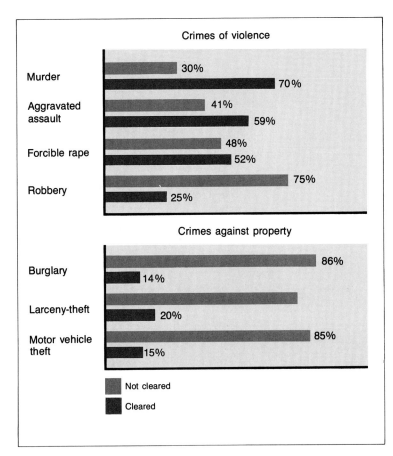

**Figure 7.5   U.S. Crimes Cleared by Arrest, 1986.**

Crimes of violence are much more likely to be cleared by someone being arrested than are property crimes, with about two-thirds of murder crimes being cleared by arrest. Less than one out of five crimes against property are cleared by arrest.

*Source:* Flanagan and Jamieson, 1988, p. 392.

most likely to result in the arrest of a suspect (in 76 percent of the cases), whereas motor vehicle theft is least likely to lead to arrest (only 14 percent of the cases).

Of those arrested for criminal acts, 40 percent are imprisoned, 10 percent are fined, and 31 percent are placed on probation. About 19 percent are not convicted (U.S. Bureau of the Census, 1989a, p. 180). Figure 7.6 illustrates these data.

Arrested adults face a prosecutor who decides whether the evidence warrants prosecuting the case. The prosecutor may offer to "plea bargain" with the offenders—that is, to charge them with lesser offenses if they agree to plead guilty to the lesser charge. "Copping a plea," as it is known in the courts, was ruled legal by the Supreme Court in 1969. It reduces the overload faced by the courts and cuts the expense of a lengthy trial. People who cannot afford a lawyer to try the case are more likely to plea bargain. Those who insist on going to trial for the orig-

inal offense face the threat of longer sentences, if they are found guilty, than those who plea bargain. The outcome of a trial can be acquittal for those found not guilty, or a suspended sentence, probation, or jail sentence for those found guilty. Some states have mandatory penalties for certain crimes; others leave the length of a prison sentence to the discretion of the judge.

Juveniles, those under the age of 18 in most states, are processed through a juvenile court. They may be acquitted, put on probation, returned to the care of their parents, placed in a foster or group home if the family situation is considered undesirable, placed in a community rehabilitation program, or sentenced to a juvenile correctional facility. Both adult and juvenile offenders may be released on parole after they have served some portion of their sentences.

In 1987 there were 557,256 people imprisoned in federal and state prisons in the United States and more than 325,000 on parole (U.S. Bureau of the Census, 1989a, pp. 184–185).

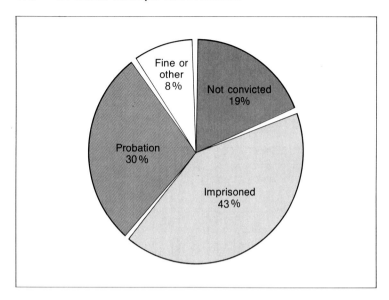

**Figure 7.6 Disposition of Criminal Cases in U.S. District Courts, 1987.**

Half of the defendants in U.S. District Court criminal cases in 1987 were imprisoned or fined, about one-third were put on probation and one in five was not convicted.

*Source:* U.S. Bureau of the Census, 1989, p. 180.

Public expenditures for operating jails totaled nearly $15 billion in 1986. (U.S. Bureau of the Census, 1989a, p. 177). In New York City the cost of keeping one person in jail for a year was $40,000 in 1983 (Blair, 1984), a figure considerably above the average annual family income.

People get put in jail who have been arrested for a crime, are awaiting trial, and are unable to raise the money required for their bail. Given the delays in the court systems of many cities today, poor people who cannot raise bail may stay in jail for months awaiting trial, without ever having been convicted of committing a crime. The rest of the jailed population consists of people who have been arrested, tried, convicted, and sentenced to serve a jail term.

### Effects of Prison on Guards and Prisoners

Sociologists note that treatment and custody are different and competing goals in prisons. But even when prison officials say their goal is treatment, such a statement may not always be taken at face value, since treatment programs can be used to achieve the aims of custody and control as well. Drugs, psychotherapy, and even lobotomies have been used to control prisoner militance, particularly when public attention prohibits the use of more obvious violence (Greenberg, 1977c; Speiglman, 1977).

The potential abuse of power exists in any situation where power differences between participants are very large and where there is little chance for outsiders to know what is going on. This situation is pronounced in prisons, and reports of prisoners being murdered by guards, beaten, drugged, unlawfully put into solitary confinement, and not protected from attack or rape by other prisoners confirm the possibility that power can be abused in prisons.

The role of prison guards seems to call forth stern, harsh, or cruel actions, even from mild-mannered college students in an experimental situation. The social psychologist Philip Zimbardo (1972) simulated a prison in the basement of his office at Stanford University. He advertised for paid volunteers to participate in a study and screened more than 70 young men who applied for his experiment before selecting about two dozen for the study. Those selected were mature, stable, normal, intelligent college students from middle-class homes throughout the United States and Canada. By flipping a coin, Zimbardo assigned half of the volunteers to be prisoners and half to be guards. The guards made up their own rules, and were assigned to eight-hour, three-man shifts. The Palo Alto police arrested the "prisoners" at unexpected times and places, such as their homes, and brought them to jail, where they were stripped, deloused, put into uniforms, given numbers, and put into cells with two roommates. They were expected to stay there for two weeks.

The motivation of prisoners and guards alike had been the same—to make money (they were paid $15 per day). But the roles of prisoner and guard took over the values and personalities of the individuals involved and dehumanized them both. In Zimbardo's words:

*At the end of only six days we had to close down our mock prison because what we saw was frightening. It was no longer apparent to most of the subjects (or to us) where reality ended and their roles began. The majority had indeed become prisoners or guards, no longer able to clearly differentiate between role playing and self. There were dramatic changes in virtually every aspect of their behavior, thinking and feeling. In less than a week the experience of imprisonment undid (temporarily) a lifetime of learning; human values were suspended, self-concepts were challenged and the ugliest, most base, pathological side of human nature surfaced. We were horrified because we saw some boys (guards) treat others as if they were despicable animals, taking pleasure in cruelty, while other boys (prisoners) became servile, dehumanized robots who thought only of escape, of their own individual survival and of their mounting hatred for the guards. [Zimbardo, 1972, pp. 4–8]*

Although the results of the study were startling, we should be careful about generalizing Zimbardo's study. One problem in doing so is that the college students were new to the game of being a prison guard. In a real prison a guard enters an existing structure that has been set up to be repressive. In such a situation individual guards may not be required to be as tyrannical as they were in Zimbardo's experiment.

Because prisons are "total institutions" in the sense that Goffman uses the term, meaning a place where people conduct all aspects of their lives (sleep, work, relaxation) under the same authority, with the same group of other people, and on a tightly scheduled and regimented basis, individuals are cut off from the outside social world and lose most of their capacity to be self-determining. One result is that prisons tend to develop their own subcultures, although these subcultures are influenced by the wider society. For instance, racial hostilities that exist in the larger society may get acted out inside prison.

Groups of inmates may form informal understandings with prison guards whereby certain inmates receive special privileges, such as extra rations of cigarettes or greater freedom of movement, in return for keeping things "under control" inside the prison (Barton and Anderson, 1966; McCleery, 1966). Inmate subculture forbids open cooperation with prison authorities and prohibits "squealing" or "ratting" to the authorities about anything. "Square Johns" are middle-class people who never become part of the criminal subculture; "right guys" avoid contact with prison officials and other inmates; "outlaws" disrupt life for inmates and guards alike; and "dings" behave inconsistently and tend to avoid others completely, according to one study (Garabedian, 1963).

### Do Prisons Reduce Crime?

Prisons fail to accomplish most of the major goals society assigns to them. Since so few crimes actually result in arrest, conviction, or sentencing, the goal of restraining crime by keeping people out of circulation is only partially realized. Few offenders actually mend their ways and follow the "straight and narrow" after they are released, partly because once someone is labeled as an ex-convict it becomes difficult to find a legitimate job. Moreover, many criminals learn new tricks in jail. Prisons are often called "schools for crime."

Numerous surveys of different correctional programs, including rehabilitation and treatment programs, suggest that most programs do not prevent people from returning to crime (Greenberg, 1977c; Lipton et al., 1975; Martinson, 1974). Some programs show modest success, particularly those that offer educational opportunities or vocational training. Existing rehabilitation programs rest on the assumption that individual behaviors are entirely responsible for crime and ignore the social effects of opportunity structures and differential association. Since prisons deal only with individuals and not with the social conditions that might cause or increase crime, and they do this with mixed purposes, it is not surprising that they do little to prevent repeat offenses. But although prisons may do little to prevent new offenses by former prisoners, their existence may serve as a deterrent to members of the larger society.

## SUMMARY

1. Deviance is socially defined and varies by time, place, and social group. Behavior that is defined as deviant violates strongly held social norms. Certain groups have more power than other groups to get their definitions of what is deviant accepted.

2. Crimes are acts that are prohibited by law. More than 2800 acts have been defined as crimes by federal law, but only eight are termed "index offenses": rape, robbery, murder, aggravated assault, burglary, larceny, auto theft, and arson.

3. Crime rates in the United States are high, but they have declined in recent years. Interviews with victims suggest that crime figures are higher than the FBI statistics suggest.

4. White middle-class males are more likely to commit white-collar crimes such as embezzling, tax evasion, price-fixing, or illegal waste disposal than are blacks or females. Lower-class and black males are more likely to commit violent crimes and burglaries than are middle-class whites or females. The way the police and the courts handle and record offenses explains part, but not all, of the variation in criminal rates by race, age, social class, and sex. Differences do exist, and they need to be explained by social theory.

5. Various sociological theories of deviance and crime have been offered. The four major ones are anomie theory, differential association, labeling theory, and conflict and Marxian theories.

6. Anomie theory suggests that when there is a tension between the goals a society holds out for individuals and the available means for achieving those goals, some people may become frustrated and deviate from either the goals or the acceptable means for achieving those goals.

7. The theory of differential association asserts that deviant or criminal behavior is learned by associating with people who have already been labeled as deviants or criminals.

8. Labeling theory challenges a relatively fixed view of deviance. Most people engage in a variety of unusual behaviors in their lives but are never labeled deviants because either no one observes the unusual behavior or they choose to ignore it. The process of labeling a behavior as deviant may stigmatize individuals and stimulate further deviant behavior.

9. "The politics of deviance" refers to the way the differential power of various groups in society helps determine which social rules get imposed and on whom they are imposed. The struggle of the gay-rights movement to change the definitions of deviance imposed on homosexuals by the American Psychiatric Association, the law, and the American Library Association reveals the political nature of these definitional conflicts over what is defined as deviant.

10. Marxian criminologists suggest that criminal behavior grows out of capitalist social relations, in which one class exploits the labor of another class. Different class conditions change family and community relations, create new types of peer groups, and generate new attitudes toward delinquency.

11. Economic and deterrence theories grow out of the economic assumption that people will commit crimes if they feel they will gain more by doing so than they would by using their time and resources in some other way. In these theories the certainty and severity of punishment are expected to influence criminal behavior. While deterrence may reduce the chances of some people committing certain types of crimes, it does not deter everyone. Capital punishment does not affect homicide rates.

12. The usefulness of several theories together is apparent in Greenberg's explanation of

why youthful crime rates drop dramatically as youths reach their early twenties. The various theoretical views of crime and deviance provide useful approaches to different types of questions, including which individuals are most likely to commit crimes, why crime rates vary, and how particular acts or conditions are stigmatized.

13. Functionalism stresses the universality of social control in all societies. The interactionist perspective emphasizes how rules are negotiated in social interactions. Conflict theory suggests that some groups may have more control over the processes that define what is to be socially controlled and how such rules are enforced. The various theories focus on different aspects of the social world.

14. Law, socialization, and sanctions are some of the ways societies and social groups try to get their members to conform to social expectations. Positive sanctions like smiles and praise as well as negative sanctions such as scowls or scolds operate on the individual level. Organizations and legal entities can bestow rewards or punishments as well.

15. Modern industrial societies rely heavily on the law and legal systems rather than on custom and tradition to define deviance, maintain public order, establish the rights and duties of members, set procedures, confer legitimacy, and resolve disputes.

16. Functionalists tend to focus on the purposes law serves for the whole society. Conflict theorists suggest that some interests might benefit more than others from particular legal arrangements. Each view captures part of the double-edged nature of law in society: law can both oppress and protect individuals.

17. Less than half of all reported index crimes are cleared by arresting a suspect, and of those arrested only about 30 percent are found guilty as charged. The charge being leveled against someone may be reduced by the process of plea bargaining. As a result, most people are not brought to trial for the actual crimes that they commit.

18. Prisons are designed to contain criminals to prevent their harming other people; they are meant to punish wrongdoers; and they may be expected to treat or rehabilitate prisoners so they are fit to return to society.

19. Prison life takes its toll on prisoners, guards, and taxpayers. Zimbardo's experiment (1972) shows how even "normal" college students took on the roles of prisoners and guards in a very short time. There are nearly half a million people in federal, state, and local prisons in the United States. Public expenditures on jails exceeded $2 billion in 1983.

20. Surveys of correctional programs suggest that such programs often do not prevent people from returning to crime. They may, however, serve as deterrents to people who might otherwise commit crimes.

## KEY TERMS

anomie (p. 152)
anomie theory (p. 152)
civil law (p. 170)
crime (p. 146)
criminal law (p. 168)
deterrence theory (p. 161)
deviance (p. 145)
deviant career (p. 158)
differential association (p. 154)
formal sanctions (p. 166)
informal sanctions (p. 166)
labeling theory (p. 157)
law (p. 168)
negative sanctions (p. 166)
positive sanctions (p. 166)
primary deviance (p. 157)
sanctions (p. 166)
scapegoating (p. 158)
secondary deviance (p. 157)
social control (p. 166)
stigmatization (p. 157)
white-collar crime (p. 147)

## SUGGESTED READINGS

Becker, Howard. 1963. *Outsiders*. New York: Free Press. An original statement of the labeling perspective on deviant behavior.

Goffman, Erving. 1963. *Stigma: Notes on the Management of Spoiled Identity*. Englewood Cliffs, NJ: Prentice-Hall. An intriguing account of the social processes of stigmatization.

Heidensohn, Frances. 1985. *Women and Crime*. New York: New York University Press. A discussion of women's contribution to criminal behavior. It reviews recent research, includes accounts women themselves have given of their experiences with crime, and treats recent theoretical developments about women and crime.

Schur, Edwin M. 1984. *Labeling Women Deviant: Gender, Stigma, and Social Control*. New York: Random House. A thoughtful analysis of how gender behavior is controlled by the process of stigmatizing behaviors and individuals who are considered undesirable.

Schwendinger, Herman, and Julia Siegel Schwendinger. 1985. *Adolescent Subcultures and Delinquency*. New York: Praeger. Comprehensive research and analysis that traces the relationship between delinquency and changes in the political economy. It develops new analytic and linguistic categories for distinguishing adolescent subcultures.

# P A R T 3

# SOCIAL INEQUALITY

Structured inequality, or stratification, is a fundamental aspect of the social world. Social inequalities may be rooted in ethnic differences or in the distribution of property or power, although as Chapter 8 shows, the three are often intertwined. Chapter 8 also examines social processes that tend to maintain stratification systems. Chapter 9 considers social class and poverty in the United States and compares the life-styles of the different classes. Chapters 10 and 11 examine structured inequalities by race and gender, suggesting some of the reasons such stratification occurs. These chapters also consider the social conditions necessary for greater equality.

# Social Stratification

*A 14-year-old boy sits in a little tailor shop down the street from Eton, one of England's most prestigious "public schools." He is sewing the long-tailed "morning coat" worn to class by Eton boys. His own schooling has ended, and he is now an apprentice to a tailor. If he stays on course, he will be a tailor for the rest of his life. Meanwhile, up the street his counterparts are preparing to enter Oxford, Cambridge, and other distinguished English universities, as part of their lives as members of England's upper class. Patterned social inequalities in England and other societies influence the lives of individuals in many different ways.*

All of us have experienced the effects of social stratification. Our personal tastes, leisure activities, friends, individual aspirations for life and work, health, life expectancy, where we live, work, and go to school are all directly influenced by social stratification. This statement holds true for most societies.

**Social stratification** is the fairly permanent ranking of positions in a society in terms of unequal power, prestige, or privileges. "Stratification" refers to patterned or structured social inequalities among whole categories of people, not just individuals. **Social inequalities** refer to the unequal opportunities or rewards for people in different social positions. Stratification systems contain social inequalities, but the term "stratification" goes beynd inequality in several key respects. First, "stratification" refers to differences in social groupings; "inequality" refers to differences among individuals. Stratification is relatively permanent and may be handed down from one generation to another; inequalities are less likely to be passed from one individual to another. The proportion of the U.S. population that is poor, for example, remains fairly constant from one year to the next, even

though each year some new individuals fall into poverty and some who were poor escape to a higher standard of living. Systems of stratification are relatively permanent because they are systematically linked with other important institutions in society, such as the economy, the family, religion, politics, and education.

The life of the English 14-year-old noted above illustrates the differences between stratification systems and inequality. Such young people show individual differences in personality, appearance, and speech style, but those personal differences are not what cause their starkly different lives. Instead, they occupy positions in a system of social stratification based on class, status, and power that profoundly affects virtually every aspect of their lives—whom they know; when, where, and how they start working; and what alternatives are open to them.

Social stratification affects the life chances of individuals in the various social groupings of a society. **Life chances** refers to an individual's odds for obtaining various opportunities in his or her society. Sociologists often use the term to include, for example, chances of earning a college degree, having a healthy and long life, getting a good job, or living in pleasant surroundings.

Societies around the world differ with respect to their systems of stratification. Western capitalist countries tend to have relatively greater equality with respect to political rights and fairly high levels of economic inequality. Many communist countries reduce the degree of economic inequality but concentrate a great deal of political power in the hands of state and party officials.

In this chapter we consider first why stratification is important; analyze the roots of stratification—class, status, and power; examine three types of stratification systems; and, finally, analyze why stratification exists, how it is maintained, and what the potential for changing systems of stratification is.

## THE ROOTS OF STRATIFICATION

Where social stratification exists, members of privileged groups (usually families) are generally able to transmit their positions of superior power and resources to other family members regardless of their personal qualities. For example, a wealthy family seeks to protect the wealth given to inept family members by establishing trust arrangements and legal and financial advisers. Young people who want to become doctors but are not admitted to an American medical school may go to other countries to study medicine if their parents have the knowledge and money to help them do so. Systems of social stratification are firmly grounded in three major interrelated sources: class, status, and power.

### Class

Max Weber and many subsequent sociologists include two central elements in the concept of social class, namely property ownership and market situation. Property includes the ownership or control of productive resources, whether land, water, industrial equipment, ideas, or technology. The concept of **property** includes the rights and obligations of a group or individual in relation to an object, resource, or activity. Private property in the United States includes the right to occupy a home that you own, to dig for oil on your own land, and to receive available interest or dividends on money you have invested. Ownership of productive resources—rather than consumer goods or "collectibles" such as paintings or diamonds—constitutes socially significant property in the long run. The people who own productive resources not only get whatever income those resources generate but also make decisions that may affect the lives of many other people. People owning real estate may decide where they will build an apartment building, to whom they will rent units, and how much they will charge (within legal and market limits). People owning a factory may decide to close it or to move it somewhere else, thus dramatically affecting the lives of those who work there. For these reasons, control of productive property has a much greater effect on other people than do inequalities of income or prestige. It is significant that in the United States, Canada, and western Europe, inequalities of wealth are much greater than inequalities of income. (These differences are discussed further in the next chapter.)

Societies vary widely in terms of what property individuals own. Many societies, especially hunting and gathering societies, regard land as something no individual can "own." Instead, the right to use land for certain purposes is shared by the entire community. Social ranking begins to occur when surpluses are generated and when some individuals own or control appreciably more productive resources than others. Those who own more gain higher rank.

Market situation affects the class position of the vast majority of people in an industrial society who do not own significant productive property. Such persons must sell their talents and labor in the marketplace. Individuals and groups have various advantages and disadvantages in that process. Some have relative monopolies over the labor or service they can provide, while others face considerable competition. For example, only a few people in the world have the skill, knowledge, and facilities to perform microsurgery. Many people are able to sweep a floor, however. As a result, microsurgeons and sweepers fare differently in the marketplace. Status-group membership and political power may also influence market advantage.

## Status

You have already learned that "status" refers to social position. Status can also imply social honor, rank, recognition, respect, admiration, and difference. In different societies and even within different groups in the same society, status may be accorded to individuals for the possession or achievement of very different traits. In some circles in the United States, family and "breeding" are still considered more important for status than newly acquired wealth.

Even monks in a religious order who have taken vows of poverty and have completely equal physical living conditions may experience some inequality in their social rank based on how well they comply with community ideals of love, friendliness, simplicity, humility, spir-

*A status group refers to people who share a social identity based on similar values and life-styles.*

ituality, and integrity (Della Fave and Hillery, 1980).

Weber (1920) touched on such differences when he used the term **status group** to describe people who share a social identity based on similar values and life-styles. Members of the same status group are likely to belong to the same clubs and associations, enjoy social activities together, and consider it appropriate to intermarry.

In American sociology status has been studied with a variety of indicators and by using occupation alone. In a famous study of Newburyport, Massachusetts, researchers Warner, Meeker, and Eels (1949) described social status within the community. They suggested there were six classes based on social reputation, lifestyle, occupation, and wealth. The six classes were upper upper class, lower upper class, upper middle class, lower middle class, upper lower class, and lower lower class. In Newburyport, the tiny upper upper class was composed of rich families with old wealth, usually made at sea. The lower upper class comprised wealthy families with new money made in shoes or textiles. They had less social status than the upper upper class. The upper middle class consisted of professionals and owners of smaller stores and businesses. They aspired to join upper-class status groups but seldom succeeded. They worked actively in civic life, generally advancing the interests of the upper class. The top three classes made up about 13 percent of the population of that city.

The lower middle class consisted of clerks, white-collar workers, small tradespeople, and highly skilled workers. This group represented about 28 percent of the population. The upper lower class consisted of "poor but honest workers" who made up 34 percent of the population. Members of the lower lower class were alleged by others to be shiftless, improvident, and sexually promiscuous. Warner found them to be simply poor and lacking in ambition. Although Warner and his associates asserted the independent importance of status differences, the distinctions they observed were actually rooted in economic positions consolidated over generations (Rossides, 1976). This example reveals that status does not exist in a vacuum: it has economic and cultural sources. As Weber noted, propertied and propertyless people can belong to the same status group. Such equality of social esteem is shaky over time, however, and may not last for generations.

The status of various occupations has also been studied. The ranking of occupations is based on the income, educational level, nature of the work, clothing worn to work (particularly white-collar versus blue-collar), and the social or political influence that an occupation commands (Hatt and North, 1947; Hodge, Siegel, and Rossi, 1966; Hodge, Treiman, and Rossi, 1966; and Treiman, 1977). (See Table 9.2.) Over the last two decades, Americans have been fairly consistent in the way that they ranked occupations, and these rankings are fairly constant in other industrialized and nonindustrialized societies as well (Hodge, Treiman, and Rossi, 1966; Treiman, 1977).

## Power

Individuals and groups vary in terms of how much political or military power they possess. **Power** is the ability to get others to obey your commands. To be most effective, the exercise of power needs to be seen as **legitimate** by those affected; that is, they need to accept the authority of those exercising power and to feel that those with power have the right to exercise that power. Legitimate power (authority) is being exercised when the librarian asks to see your card when you check out a book. When a person with a gun asks for your wallet, that represents an illegitimate use of power.

Social ranking enters the picture when some individuals or groups have more military or political power, more influence, or more authority than others. In most modern industrial societies, the military power of individuals has been severely limited by the state. Although it is still possible in some states for individuals to buy dynamite, machine guns, rifles, and handguns, it is certainly illegal for them to be used in most situations. So military power is more frequently used to compare nations than individuals. Political power is important to both individuals and groups. Their goal usually is to influence the selection, election, and behavior of important political figures. Groups seeking to change or

to maintain the legal order seek to maximize their political power, and they differ widely with respect to how much political influence they have.

Power is the central basis for stratification in a totalitarian society, where there are few limits on the power of the state. The state extends its control to all features of social life, without regard for individual rights. The term "totalitarian" was coined to refer to political regimes that use every conceivable control mechanism, such as party machines, police, terror, torture, the destruction of all opposition, control of the mass media, and even youth groups that report on "disloyal" parents. Expensive and sophisticated technologies increase and concentrate the instruments of oppression available to nations today. These include electronic surveillance equipment, computerized data banks, physically and psychologically sophisticated methods of torture, and elaborate weaponry.

The importance of occupational and organizational power, rather than state power is stressed by the sociologist Ralf Dahrendorf (1959). He underscores the importance of authority in the working world for determining one's position in society. Individuals with authority over large numbers of subordinates frequently have greater power, income, and status than individuals who do not have such authority.

The three roots of stratification—class, status, and power—very often go together. Sometimes they do not, as in the case of sports figures or movie stars who may have high incomes and high status of a certain kind but little power, or federal judges who have considerable power and status but are not highly paid. And sometimes it is possible to distinguish one or another as the primary foundation for a particular stratification system.

## THREE TYPES OF STRATIFICATION SYSTEMS

Certain types of societies have stratification systems based on one or another major source. Great Britain, for example, is mainly a class society based on property distinctions, although status distinctions are highly refined and important. The caste society of South Africa is an example of a society stratified by racial dominance. In a caste society, the law and police power are used to harden the boundaries between status groups. Nazi Germany was stratified by power. Differences in social status or power may therefore result in restricted human rights, freedoms, and opportunities for certain groups.

## Class Systems—The Case of Great Britain

In a **class system** stratification is based primarily on the unequal ownership and control of economic resources. One gains power, position, and prestige by controlling productive wealth. Generally it is difficult to pass along status or political power to a second generation without owning productive property. Popular rock singers, sports stars, or politicians occasionally get rich, but if their money is not invested in economically productive ways, their positions will be neither influential nor lasting. If newly rich folk heroes spend their money on consumer goods—houses, Rolls Royces, fur bedspreads, and so on—they may change their life-styles but not their social class, because they have no control over productive resources. Their high incomes may disappear over time, as happened to Mohammed Ali, the world-champion boxer.

The stratification of society along class lines is more apparent in Great Britain than in most other industrial societies. Political leaders are drawn almost exclusively from privileged families and upper-status occupations. Business leaders are drawn from even more privileged backgrounds (Putnam, 1976). Britain has a very small upper class comprising families with "old wealth." The top 1 percent owns 25 percent of the nation's wealth, the richest 5 percent owns nearly 50 percent, and the wealthiest 10 percent owns more than 60 percent (according to a 1980 Royal Commission report). The upper class retains many of the trappings of a feudal hierarchy, with earldoms, knighthoods, and peerages still bestowed upon people and reflected in titles of social address, such as Lady Bellamy or Sir Henry. Originally, English wealth was based on land ownership, but since the industrial rev-olution it has branched into industrial ownership as well. In addition to controlling the wealth and being addressed in distinctive ways, the upper class is notable for its accent and speech. In fact, differences in accent are a rather precise indication of social class membership in Britain. Over time class differences are usually converted into status and cultural distinctions as well. These status distinctions may be more evident to casual observers than are class differences.

Beneath the upper class, Britain has a small upper middle class of professionals, a rather large lower middle class of skilled white-collar workers, and a big working class comprising more than half the total population.

Until the Tories won the election in 1979, the upper class had been getting poorer and the poor had been making small gains. But Margaret

*The British class system is highly stratified. Although more than half the population is working class and has limited resources for housing and entertainment, political and economic power is concentrated heavily in the hands of upper-class families, who can afford luxurious hobbies.*

Thatcher reversed the trend by cutting taxes at the top and reducing services at the bottom. In two years, as many as 4 million people sank into poverty, increasing the total already there to 15 million (Newman, 1985). Profound differences in inherited wealth also divide the classes in England.

Besides inherited wealth and accent, class divisions in Britain are maintained by a system of private boarding schools (called "public schools"). The children of the top 5 percent attend these exclusive and expensive schools, where they receive rigorous academic preparation for Oxford and Cambridge, the nation's two elite universities. The majority of public school graduates attend "Oxbridge," as it is called (Cookson and Persell, 1985a). They are virtually assured a high position in business, religion, the media, or political life upon graduation. Exclusive men's clubs keep members of the national elite in contact with one another, forming what has been dubbed "the establishment" or "the magic circle," a rather vivid example of social networks in operation. The magic circle is a closed circle to most outsiders, and rates of upward mobility in Britain are lower than in the United States (Treiman and Terrell, 1975; Covello, 1979).

Rates of mobility are lower primarily because of differences in the occupational structures in the two countries. There are more professional and managerial workers in the United States than in Britain and more operatives (for example, truck drivers) in Britain than in the United States (Kerckhoff et al., 1985). Interestingly, individuals in the United States perceive their class positions just as clearly as do people in Great Britain (Vanneman, 1980).

## Caste Systems—The Case of South Africa

Suppose the government told you where you could and could not live and that you could not vote in regional or national elections. That is exactly the situation of nonwhites in South Africa today, despite the fact that they comprise more than four out of five persons in the total population. They live in the most complete caste system in the world. Because the system is not considered legitimate by blacks, it has to be maintained by force.

### Defining Caste

A **caste system** is a closed system of social stratification based on heredity that determines a person's occupation, prestige, residence, and social relationships. The term "caste" originally referred to religiously sanctioned social categories in India, where there was a priestly Brahmin caste at the top and an "untouchable" outcaste group at the bottom of society, with a number of other castes in between. A caste system is established by custom and/or law and is supported by religious or other ideologies.

Because social contacts between members of different castes are restricted, most caste systems require that one's caste be immediately visible. Racial or other physical differences often form an important basis for stigmatizing certain individuals as belonging to a lower caste and serve as boundary markers for caste groups. Caste systems, then, are very likely to be based on racial or ethnic differences. Besides the traditional caste system in India, caste systems of social stratification have developed in certain horticultural and agrarian societies. Features of a caste society were evident in the southern part of the United States during and after the period of slavery, when blacks were denied the right to vote or to use public facilities such as restaurants and were required to use deferential terms of address such as "Sir," "Ma'am," "Mr.," and "Mrs." (However, they were never addressed that way themselves.) Similarly, Native Americans were treated in castelike ways when they were barred from political participation and moved off their land. Since the caste system in South Africa is the most intact one in the world today, it is worth considering in more detail.

### South Africa: A Case Study

The Republic of South Africa represents a contemporary caste system that is supported by the religious, legal, and law enforcement apparatus of that country. One of the notable features of South Africa is the fact that it has not always been a caste society. It is only within this century that nonwhites lost their rights to own property, vote, and obtain legal protections. South African history from 1910 to the present reflects the reaction of the early Dutch settlers, called Afrikaaners, to their economic situation, and their use of a racially based caste system to try to catch up with the more privileged British members of white society. Their strategy was to gain control of the state and its legal apparatus. Between 1924 and 1929, legislation was passed to protect white workers from African competition. Certain better-paying and more desirable jobs were simply reserved for whites.

In 1948 the Afrikaaner National Party won electoral control over the South African government. That election was fought over both racial and class issues. One of the issues was governmental policies for white supremacy. The "pass laws" (requiring Africans to have passes for being anywhere off their reserves), color bars to jobs, and the legal prohibition of African trade unions contributed greatly to the rapid growth of the white standard of living, whereas that of nonwhites remained effectively level for decades. During these years there was a policy to erode the rights of nonwhites. Multiracial political parties were outlawed in 1968. Under the policy of separate development, nonwhites were denied national and provincial political participation in exchange for the establishment of their own separate political institutions. As opposition to white domination mounted, many nonwhites (the numbers are not even reported) were detained without trial.

Between 1984 and 1986, open insurrections swept many black townships. In 1986 the government declared a state of emergency. Under emergency rule, the government has used tough security measures to try to control the revolutionary climate. White or black persons who oppose apartheid have been publicly silenced by jailings, stiff press censorship, and the banning of mass political rallies and public funerals (Reiss, 1988). In June 1988, black labor unions staged a national walkout, in which 1½ million people took part. This took about one-quarter of the black workers away from their jobs. In response, the government extended the state of emergency. Former President Botha of South Africa had a "total strategy" for resisting revolution. He aimed to crush all opposition and then to win "hearts and minds" among blacks. About 30,000 people were rounded up after the walkout, and about 2,500 were detained without trial (Reiss, 1988). These detainees were threatened, beaten, humiliated, and tortured (Lelyveld, 1985, p. 203). Any member of the opposition who was not arrested was forced underground. Botha hoped to buy the support of other blacks by spending more money on housing, schools, and roads in black townships. For those blacks who cooperate, Botha said he would create new community groups, sports clubs, and other organizations. He also suggested that blacks might be brought into his cabinet and be allowed to form a new multiracial national council (Reiss, 1988). Many blacks doubted such promises because Botha had broken his word before—for example, in relation to neighboring Mozambique (Maren, 1988). It remains to be seen whether his successor will keep control over the black majority.

Unequal rights are also apparent in education, which is free and compulsory for all whites aged 7 to 16; it includes free books and equipment. For nonwhites, education is neither free nor compulsory and parents must pay for some books and equipment. The average per capita expenditure for primary and secondary education varies widely, with the expenditure for whites being more than ten times that for blacks. University enrollments are also unbalanced. Although whites comprise only 18 percent of the total population, they make up 80 percent of university enrollments. Africans, who constitute about 70 percent of the national population, represent only 9 percent of university students. The other 11 percent consists of "coloreds"—that is, East Indians and other nonwhites.

The vastly unequal distribution of income in South Africa is assured by job and geographical restrictions, the banning (until very recently) of any union representation, the absence of political and legal rights, and low pay. Whites earn nearly five times what other Africans earn.

South Africa spends a great deal on police and prisons. Police activities are coordinated with military defense for any perceived antiguerrilla activities. Nonwhites serve in the police and armed forces, but they are not allowed to carry guns.

Along with the economic, political, legal, and educational inequalities that whites impose on blacks in South Africa, there is a religious and political ideology that attempts to legitimate that inequality. The Dutch Reformed Church supports the "policy of racial separation and guardianship of whites over the native" (Moodie, 1975, p. 261). Political and military power as well as economic control play a critical role in maintaining caste systems.

South Africa operates as a caste society, but it has strong elements of a class society, with whites owning and controlling all the major productive resources, including diamond, gold, and other mines; most of the land; and all the manufacturing concerns. Within the white population, there are class divisions between those who own or control a great deal and those who control very little. Resentment over these class inequalities is undoubtedly reduced by the caste society, which enables whites to feel superior to nonwhites. There are few class divisions within the black population, since blacks do not own or control significant resources.

Particularly since whites are in such a minority in South Africa, they have used political, state, legal, police, and military means to retain social control and to advance the policy of racial separation called *apartheid*. They have also used the power of the state to influence the ideology and ideas that circulate within the society. There is close censorship of all publications appearing in the country. Religious leaders, authors, and other ideological trend setters run the risk of being banned from the country if their views are unacceptable to the authorities. Thus in all realms—intellectual, religious, social, economic, and political—the South African state uses its resources, backed by its tremendous police and military apparatus, to enforce the policy of apartheid. In the way it uses state-sanctioned

In South Africa, the policy of apartheid, or formal racial separation, is maintained by political, state, legal, police, and military means.

force South Africa resembles Nazi Germany and other totalitarian societies.

## Stratification by Power—Nazi Germany

Some systems of stratification are based primarily on political power and force. This becomes particularly apparent in an **autocracy,** where power is concentrated in a single ruler or group of leaders who are willing to use force to maintain control. The contemporary and most complete form of autocracy is called **totalitarianism,** and it involves the use of state power to control and regulate all phases of life. Divergent views are treated as threats to the state, and conformity is enforced by propaganda, censorship, regimentation, and force. Stratification occurs in this system when rank, prestige, and material resources as well as political power are controlled by the state. Stratification by political power is evident to some degree in such state-socialist countries as the Soviet Union, Poland, Hungary, and Czechoslovakia (Lenski, 1979). Nazi Germany under the rule of Adolf Hitler was perhaps the most extreme example of stratification by power.

Hitler was appointed chancellor of Germany in 1933. Through a series of maneuvers, he succeeded in obtaining the authority to issue decrees without the approval of the general legislative body or the president. He also appointed a Nazi party member to the cabinet position of minister of public enlightenment and propaganda. Having gained control of the state apparatus, Hitler proceeded to build an alliance with business leaders and the army. With the army's support, the offices of president and chancellor were merged, making Hitler supreme commander of the armed forces.

From 1934 to 1939 the Nazi totalitarian police state extended its power. Dissidents were controlled by the dreaded SS police and security system. Education, art, media, science, and religion were all required to conform to Nazi dictums. The compulsory Hitler Youth Movement aimed to indoctrinate the young. Although politically under Hitler's control, the army and the foreign service remained relatively independent until 1939. By attacking their private lives, Hitler succeeded in removing the commander in chief and the minister of defense. He also retired 16 senior generals, thereby gaining full control of the army. Individuals and groups, particularly Jews, were persecuted, arrested, had their property seized, and were imprisoned. Eventually millions were killed. Institutionalized inequality was taken to its outer limit.

## WHY DOES STRATIFICATION EXIST?

Why do various systems of stratification exist? There are several competing explanations. Some suggest that people "get what they deserve"; others maintain that advantaged members of society use their superior power, wealth, and influence to maintain their privileged positions. The former include functionalists who stress that merit and achievement lead to social position; they consider occupational position, status, and sometimes earnings. The latter, who are conflict theorists, focus on unequal wealth, power, and control. Functionalists and conflict theorists stress different features of stratification.

### Functionalist Explanations

Functionalists begin with the assumption that unstratified societies do not exist. Their first goal, therefore, is to explain why stratification is necessary in all social systems. They see stratification as necessary because all societies need to place and motivate individuals in social positions. If many people have the necessary talents and it is easy to fill a particular position, then it does not need to be heavily rewarded, even though it is functionally important. Sometimes talent is abundant, but a long and difficult training process scares people away. Davis and Moore (1945) feel, for example, that many people have the mental capacity to become doctors, but that the burdensome and expensive process of medical education would discourage most from even trying to be doctors if that goal did not carry rewards equal to the sacrifice. Functionalist explanations are supported to a degree by cross-national research which finds that occupations are ranked very similarly in 60 indus-

*Hitler used the power of the state to persecute, imprison, and kill millions of Jewish citizens in Germany and in other countries that Germany invaded. These men, women, and children are being led off by Nazi storm troops during the destruction of Warsaw, Poland, in 1943.*

trial and agricultural countries (Treiman, 1977). They are not all equally rewarded financially, however.

Because positions vary in their importance, attractiveness, and the talents or training they require, functionalists argue that a society "must have" rewards it can offer as incentives to lure people into vital positions. Rewards include unequal economic, symbolic, and aesthetic benefits. University presidents, for instance, are paid more than professors; usually have large offices and ample secretarial help; and often have substantial travel and entertainment budgets, high prestige in the wider community, and a university house in which to live.

For functionalists, the rank of a position is determined by how important the position is for society and by the scarcity of people with the talent or skill for filling the position. In short, functionalists feel that stratification is "an unconsciously evolved device by which societies

ensure that the most important positions are conscientiously filled by the most qualified persons" (Davis and Moore, 1945). The functional view of stratification held sway over American sociology for nearly 20 years, despite the existence of vigorous arguments against it. Five major criticisms have been leveled against this view.

1. Rewards are not associated with importance. Although no fully objective measure of importance is possible, various observers note that rewards often are poorly correlated with jobs that appear to have societal importance. Sports or rock stars who earn six- or seven-figure salaries do not seem more important than garbage collectors. Similarly, people who inherit their wealth may do nothing socially important for society. Moreover, there is a connection between the amount of protection a group can gain for itself and the income of its members. Unionized auto workers earn much

more than nonunion textile workers, but clothes are as important as cars. The reason doctors are scarce and highly paid is that medical school admissions are limited. Other occupations restrict the number of practitioners by strict licensing practices that may or may not be relevant to performing well in the occupation. The most important and responsible positions in government, education, the judicial system, and religion are not nearly so highly rewarded as comparable positions in private industry. Are they really so much less important for society? Numerous discrepancies between rewards and social significance seriously undercut the functional argument.

2. The functionalist view justifies the status quo. Functional theories support the status quo because they suggest that the existing stratification system is necessary and indeed desirable (Dahrendorf, 1958; Simpson, 1956; Tumin, 1953). The view suggests that people who do important and difficult jobs deserve the rewards they get. Thus the theory operates as an ideology that legitimates existing social inequalities and says they exist for the benefit of society as a whole.

3. Talent is only imperfectly utilized. Stratification may actually restrict the development of scarce talents, rather than being necessary to place people effectively in various positions. The assumption that stratification is based on functional criteria overlooks the existence of stratification by race, sex, social class, or inheritance. Such stratification limits the size of the pool that may be tapped as a source of talent. In this way stratification may restrict rather than enhance the development of special talents.

4. Unequal rewards are not the only way to motivate people. The extremes of inequality that exist in the United States are neither functional nor inevitable (Tumin, 1953). In worker cooperatives, people work hard for the same rewards or for very small differentials. Therefore it remains an open question how much inequality is required to generate maximum effort. Some people work for pleasure, challenge, and excitement as well as for external rewards, so it is possible that individuals could be motivated more by intrinsic rewards than they currently are. Finally, how does the functional theory address the problem of motivating "the masses"? Can a society survive if they are not motivated? A vastly unequal system of rewards may not be productive for the many people who fill "unimportant" positions in society. People seeing others who work no harder than they do yet receive much greater rewards may become angry, withdrawn, unconcerned, or deliberately sabotage the work they are doing. Such a reaction is hardly functional for society in general.

5. The functionalist view fails to explain changes in rewards. The functional theory is unable to explain why certain positions may change with respect to the rewards they receive. Teachers' salaries went up during the 1970s, although there was a surplus of teachers. Clearly other factors, such as unionization and strikes, operate to change the rewards particular positions receive.

## Conflict Theories

Whereas functionalists see stratification as inevitable and necessary for the "good" of society, conflict theorists see it as resulting from the competition of various interest groups or classes. Groups use the power and resources they control to advance and protect their own positions in relation to other groups. Institutionalized inequality developed with the concept of private property, and the creation of an economic surplus along with a belief in private property set the conditions for some individuals or groups to obtain more wealth than others. First, through force or legitimating ideologies, some groups gained privileged positions. Once they had a relatively permanent material base, those positions could be passed along to their heirs. Inequalities of wealth arose and then became a resource that could be used to retain superior advantages. Conflict theories try to explain human behavior in terms of how individuals seek to realize their interests in a world marked by inequality, threats, and sometimes violence.

"Conflict theorists" is an umbrella term that includes a number of scholars who emphasize issues of conflict and dominance in stratification systems. Since Karl Marx and Max Weber approached stratification differently, their views are worth considering separately.

### Marxian Theory

According to Marx and others using his ideas, stratification develops through the following steps:

1. When the economy produces a surplus that can be controlled by those who own the means of production, classes develop.
2. With their economic power, owners dominate and exploit those who do not own property.
3. Dominant groups use the state, religion, education, and ideas to legitimize the system that benefits them.
4. Those being exploited may be unaware, unorganized, or viciously suppressed. Therefore conflict and resistance are controlled.
5. Potential contradictions may occur within the production process. Potential contradictions may undermine the development of capitalism. For example, bringing workers together in urban areas where they can recognize their common plight may intensify class conflict and lead to revolutionary change.

Marxian class theory has been criticized on several grounds. First, critics argue that societies reflect more than simply economic interests (Turner, 1978). The state, the military, and even the education system may sometimes operate independently of the economy. This is particularly true in the state-socialist societies of eastern Europe, where party leaders may become a new elite strata.

Second, the last step in Marx's theory has rarely occurred. Class conflict has not always led to revolutionary change, perhaps because Marx failed to predict the shift from individual capitalists to large corporations; underestimated the growth in size and importance of the middle class, which tends to buffer conflict between the upper and lower classes; and did not anticipate the rise of labor unions. Also, he failed to predict the enormous economic development that raised the living standard of middle- and working-class members alike.

These criticisms question Marx's theory of class conflict, but they should not persuade us to overlook the usefulness of a Marxian approach. As Zeitlin (1967) suggests, anyone wanting to understand a particular society should consider the economic order first, and see whether changes in it affect unemployment rates, the distribution of workers in the economy, or social relationships at work. The next step would be to try to identify the major economic classes and determine their objective economic interests, level of class consciousness, and extent of class conflict. How is the dominant class related to major social institutions? What coalitions develop between classes and political parties? How strong or powerless are the subordinate classes? Zeitlin concludes that questions like these make Marx's work very relevant to contemporary social inquiry.

### Weberian Theory

Weber's explanation of social stratification differs from Marx's because Weber considered other sources of inequality and stratification besides economic ones. Stratification could also be based on status groups or on political and organizational power that might sometimes be independently based. Weber shared Marx's view that property and market relations are extremely important, and he noted that status groups with class cleavages were unstable over time. Weber, however, suggested that the state could have power that was independent of economic production, whereas Marx felt that the state was subordinate to the economy in capitalist societies.

Marx and Weber also differ with respect to the role of ideas in the social world. Marx wrote that in any era, the ruling ideas were the ideas of the ruling class. Writing within the Marxian tradition, for example, Karier (1973) suggests that the rise of intelligence testing in the 1920s reflected the interests of the corporate liberal state. It did this by helping to create a more orderly corporate state. Weber, on the other hand, felt that ideas could influence economic behavior, for instance, in the way Protestantism encouraged people to save and invest their money. Although ideas cannot change the world on their own, they can encourage people to act.

A particular interest group or stratum may have some vague feelings about the way the world is, and a set of ideas may come along that captures what they have been thinking. Thus, by creating a particular world image in someone's mind, ideas may help push action along one rather than another track. But despite such differences of emphasis in Marx and Weber, they share a number of ideas about how and why stratification exists.

### Common Themes in Weber and Marx

Major themes shared by Marx and Weber include the following:[1]

1. Social stratification emerges as the result of the domination of one or more groups by other groups. This domination may be based on differing control over property, goods, and services, and the unequal market value of different occupations.
2. Because stratification is based on dominance and coercion, the potential for opposition, resistance, and hostility on the part of the subordinated groups is always present.
3. Members of the dominant class are faced with the crucial problem of controlling the subordinate classes. A number of mechanisms, however, may be employed to keep the lower classes in line. (These methods are discussed in the next section of this chapter and in the next chapter.)

### Criticisms of Conflict Theory

Two steps are needed to confirm conflict theory. First, the dominant class must be shown to play a major role in formulating actions and ideologies. Second, those actions and ideologies must be shown to serve the interests of the dominant class but not those of other classes. Numerous studies of local school boards, for example, have documented that their members overwhelmingly represent the community's upper or upper middle class. But evidence has not been presented to show that they operate in their

own interests rather than in those of the community at large (Charters, 1974). Further evidence is needed on both points.

Further complexity arises because conflict does not always result in change. Sometimes it contributes to social order by establishing relationships, reaffirming values, resolving disagreements, or reasserting power (Coser, 1956; Simmel, 1956). Children who were previously strangers, for instance, may fight over the use of a toy and later play happily together with it. They have established a relationship through conflict. In some instances the relatively equal strength of two competing parties can serve as an effective deterrent to conflict, but their respective strengths may be detectable only through conflict.

Both functional and conflict theories have been modified but not demolished by their critics. The general themes in each have been compared by Stinchcombe (1963), as shown in Table 8.1. This comparison provides a useful backdrop to the efforts that have been made to synthesize the two theories (Horowitz, 1962; Lenski, 1966; Ossowski, 1963; van den Berghe, 1963; Williams, 1966).

## A Synthesis

Perhaps the most complete attempt to synthesize the functionalist and conflict views of stratification is the one offered by Lenski (1966), who tried to explain both conflict and order in society. He began with the assumption that humans are selfish beings who need to live and cooperate socially with others. Forced to choose, most individuals will opt for their own or their group's self-interest rather than for the interests of all other humans, although they may try to hide this choice from themselves and others. Self-interest is particularly apparent with regard to the rewards and resources that are in relatively short supply—especially power and privileges. People will struggle for these scarce rewards. In that struggle some will be better endowed by their social locations, resources they already control, and their natural talents. The result is social inequality. Power—rather

---

[1] This and the next section have benefited considerably from Vanfossen, 1979, pp. 43–46.

**Table 8.1   *Two Views of Social Stratification***

| The Functional View | The Conflict View |
|---|---|
| 1. Stratification is universal, necessary, and inevitable. | 1. Stratification may be universal without being necessary or inevitable. |
| 2. Social organization (the social system) shapes the stratification system. | 2. The stratification system shapes social organization (the social system). |
| 3. Stratification arises from society's need for integration, coordination, and cohesion. | 3. Stratification arises from group conquest, competition, and conflict. |
| 4. Stratification facilitates the optimal functioning of society and the individual. | 4. Stratification impedes the optimal functioning of society and the individual. |
| 5. Stratification is an expression of commonly shared social values. | 5. Stratification is an expression of the values of powerful groups. |
| 6. Tasks and rewards are equitably allocated. | 6. Tasks and rewards are inequitably allocated. |
| 7. The economic dimension is subordinate to other dimensions of society. | 7. The economic dimension is paramount in society. |
| 8. Stratification systems generally change through evolutionary processes. | 8. Stratification systems may change through revolutionary processes. |

*Source:* Arthur L. Stinchcombe, "Some Empirical Consequences of the Davis-Moore Theory of Stratification." *American Sociological Review*, 28 (October 1963), p. 808. Reprinted by permission of the American Sociological Association.

than need, usefulness, or merit—is the primary source of major social inequalities. Some of these inequalities may be functional for society—for example, giving the best hunter the best weapons—but inequalities tend to last long after they cease to be useful. The relative stability of the stratification system is explained, in Lenski's view, by the fact that humans are creatures of habit who are strongly influenced by custom and tradition.

An approach that combines both functional and conflict elements may explain many social inequalities. Treiman (1977) does this in his explanation of why occupations are ranked so similarly in many different societies. He suggests that the division of labor is functional for a society. Once such a division occurs, however, occupational groups are able to convert their command of scarce resources—such as skill and knowledge, economic power, and authority—into additional material and social advantages. They can do this because their control of scarce resources improves their market position and can be used to manipulate the system that allocates additional power and resources (Treiman, 1977). As a result, the more powerful occupations gain more prestige and privileges in all societies.

The most complete sociological answer to the question of why stratification exists involves an interplay between functional specialization and power. People perform certain roles in society, whether because of skill, training, or interest. They also tend to use the positions, power, and resources they control to maximize their own advantages. In this way inequalities widen and become relatively permanent systems of stratification. Such systems do not exist unless they are maintained, however. A number of institutions and social processes help to maintain systems of stratification, but sometimes internal conflicts lead to changes.

Adding an interactionist view here suggests that self-evaluation (that is, people's views of their own worthiness) may be shaped by their position in a system of social stratification. People with more feel they deserve what they have, whereas those with less do not see themselves as deserving any better (Della Fave, 1980). Such self-evaluations tend to form one basis for legitimating a system of inequality. Other processes also contribute to at least some degree of conformity with a system of stratification.

## HOW ARE STRATIFICATION SYSTEMS MAINTAINED?

The mechanisms used to maintain stratification are most apparent in a country such as South Africa, but all stratification systems use a variety of social processes to maintain and re-create themselves. Crucial links with the economy, the family, religion, ideology, and the state tend to support the position of dominant groups. In addition, several key processes (described here) work to sustain stratification. These processes include hopes of upward mobility for one's self or children (Chinoy, 1955; Form, 1976; Lane, 1962; Lopreato and Hazelrigg, 1972); fear of losing one's standard of living (Mankoff, 1970); a feeling of powerlessness (Wright, 1976); and the inability to imagine an egalitarian alternative model of society (Dahl, 1967; Mann, 1970; Moore, 1978; Sallach, 1974; Sennett and Cobb, 1973; all cited in Della Fave, 1980).

## Institutional Links

### The Economic Roots of Stratification

Although the economic basis for stratification was discussed earlier in this chapter, it is worth repeating that every system of stratification is related to the economy. Either the original position of the dominant groups in society is rooted in economic advantages (control or ownership of productive resources) or, as in the case of priests or military leaders who achieve dominant positions, powerful positions in other realms tend to be converted to economic advantage over time. The raising of educational credentials for entry to occupations is an excellent example of how privileged groups seek to reserve more desirable positions for themselves by raising the cultural and economic "capital" required for their attainment. The economic basis for stratification is very often handed down in families through the inheritance of wealth.

### The Family's Role in Re-Creating Stratification

In some societies (and in some communities), family name is important, usually because it alerts people to the fact that an individual is a member of a wealthy or powerful family. In many societies but by no means all, if a family has material wealth, the laws and customs of the society allow it to pass along that wealth to its descendants (or to whomever else the family wishes). But material wealth alone (whether ownership of land, factories, money, or other resources) is rarely enough to ensure that the position of family members is maintained. New generations must be taught to think, believe, feel, and behave in ways that will be appropriate to the family's position. Families with positions or assets they wish to protect work to enhance their children's development in particular directions. An international business family, for example, may arrange for its children to live in various countries during their young adulthood so that they will learn several languages and build their own international networks.

Child-rearing practices are related to social stratification and vary with parental life situations, as we saw in Chapter 5. When adults have a degree of autonomy in their work and political life, they tend to value self-reliance and try to teach it to their children. Similarly, if adults view most of the authorities in their lives with deference, they may try to teach their children the same respectful attitudes. On the other hand, if children grow up seeing their parents behave in a superior way while others respond to them with respect, they are likely to believe that is how one interacts with people. These cultural and interactional features of social life within a system of stratification enable some families to transmit cultural and social advantages to their children.

### How Religion and Ideology Work to Legitimate Stratification

Virtually every stratification system is accompanied by religious or ideological beliefs that aim to legitimize the existing state of affairs. Feudal monarchies propounded the "divine right of kings"; caste societies advance the genetic and/or moral inferiority of subordinate groups; modern industrial societies rely on an ideology of equal opportunity and "merit" that claims to reward superior talent, training, and skills (rather than luck or unscrupulousness); to-

*Jesse Jackson's presidential candidacy represented an effort to bring those who feel excluded from the American dream back into the political process. If people feel shut out, they will not see the political and economic order as legitimate.*

talitarian societies advance the claim that people are rewarded because of their "service" or loyalty to the state or punished for its absence. Even the Afrikaaner dominance over blacks in South Africa, which is so overtly political and military, is sugar-coated with an ideology of separatism that has the approval of some religious as well as secular authorities.

**Ideology** is a system of ideas that reflects and justifies the interests of those who believe it. An ideology makes existing inequalities seem more "natural" or taken for granted. An important feature of ideology is that it bears some slight resemblance to reality, which makes it all the more difficult to combat. For example, the ideology of equal opportunity is just closely enough related to reality—everyone knows at least someone who has risen from poverty to prominence—that it cannot be rejected as totally false. The problem is that it is only partially true. The examples that are cited are the exceptions.

Since 1945 in the United States, this ideology served many people well as they sought to improve their standard of living. Social structural changes including economic growth and the expansion of white-collar jobs led to some upward mobility for many, even if relatively few became millionaires. Everyone's chances for mobility were not equal, however. Social characteristics, such as class, ethnicity, or gender, affect an individual's chances. Those who lack opportuni-

ties are more likely to reject the dominant ideologies.

For those lacking opportunities, ideology probably does little to restrain their anger, alienation, and resistance to a system that offers them little hope. Karl Marx pointed out that the dominant ideas of a society are the ideas of the ruling class and serve to justify their economic interests. As groups become aware of the legitimating role of certain ideas, they seek alternative belief systems to explain their life situations. Peasants, workers, and new political parties all work to rally supporters to their cause with ideas that serve their interests and perhaps the interests of those they seek to mobilize. As a result, growing numbers of people are exposed to competing ideas. Ruling groups in various societies no longer monopolize the belief systems of society. Growing literacy, the mass media, and rapid communications have begun to broaden the spread of competing ideas.

### The Role Played by the Law, the State, the Police, and the Military

When ideology falters, any stratification system that is going to maintain itself needs to be backed by the state, law, police, and military, as the South African case shows. Without the potential for coercion, whether legal or physical, no stratification system will last for long. As noted in Chapter 7, functionalists see the law and legal order as serving the needs of the whole society, whereas conflict sociologists see the legal order as operating to protect and enhance the rights and property of more powerful members of society. Because the goal of the legal system is to preserve order and to maintain the status quo, legal systems in all societies tend to operate in ways that support and maintain the advantages of more powerful members of society. In caste systems the legal order is called upon to make caste boundaries into legal boundaries, with penalties for violations. Jobs are legally reserved for members of some castes rather than others. Intermarriage between castes is prohibited by law. Caste systems can break down only when these laws are eliminated or ignored. Totalitarian political regimes also use the law and legal machinery to legitimate their police and military actions, as in Nazi Germany.

In order to persist, dominant groups must

influence the law and the legal structure of a society. One reason that ex-President Richard Nixon did not remain in office was that he could not completely dominate the law and the legal structure. Certain procedures and processes had been developed by the legal system, and he could not quickly change them. The process of gaining influence over the legal structure of a society is usually a gradual and subtle one, especially if it is to be perceived as legitimate by members of society.

The potential for armed intervention by the state and the police underlies all legal systems. Very often the use of force is viewed as legitimate, at least by some members of society, as when the police use force to quell an urban riot. Norms govern the conditions under which force may be used legitimately. Even when political protestors are trespassing, say, on the property of a nuclear power plant, the police are not supposed to beat them up.

The use of force and violence can backfire, particularly if it is used by authorities in ways that are seen as unjust and illegitimate by most people. Those who once believed in the legitimacy of the authorities can be "radicalized" by witnessing what seems to be an illegitimate use of force by those authorities. This happened in 1969 when Columbia University students occupied buildings in a dispute over social and political issues. Many students were opposed or indifferent to the issues until the city police were called in. When they witnessed the police beating students, dragging them downstairs by the feet with their heads banging on the stone steps, and saw their blood all over the floors and walls, many who had been indifferent came to believe that the authorities were unjust and that the demonstrating students were right. Dominant groups may feel that the use of police force is less effective for maintaining stratification than more subtle social processes of control, such as cooptation.

## Social Processes

### Cooptation

**Cooptation** is one of the key social processes used to maintain any stratification system, whether societal or organizational. It involves bringing new people into the leadership or policy-making structure of an organization or a society, specifically people who might otherwise threaten its stability or existence. The term was first used by Philip Selznick (1948), who noted that the real trick for an organization or society is to share the symbols and burdens of authority without transferring real power. Stated this way, the essence of cooptation as a mechanism of control becomes apparent. For instance, granting token representation on presidential commissions or corporate boards to blacks, women, or labor unions is the first step in the process of cooptation. The second step involves making sure no major changes are made. Selznick observes that "it therefore becomes necessary to insure that the coopted elements do not get out of hand, do not take advantage of their formal position to encroach upon the actual arena of decision. Consequently, formal cooptation requires informal control over the coopted elements lest the unity of command and decision be imperiled" (1966, p. 261).

These informal controls include social favors—inviting people for lunch or dinner, playing golf or other sports with them, and so forth. During such times newly coopted individuals are oriented to "the way things are." If new members refuse to go along with the way things have always been done, they may be socially ostracized, meetings may be set at times when they cannot attend, they may be publicly embarrassed, or other negative sanctions may be applied (Kerr, 1964). From Kerr's case study we cannot tell how widespread these sanctions are, but we can see some of the forms they take.

In short, the process of cooptation may occur when dominant groups in a society or existing leaders in an organization identify the brighter, more energetic, more vocal, and more ambitious members of subordinate groups; share with them some of the symbols and rewards of power, position, or authority; and at the same time, ensure that no major changes will be made. The process of cooptation has occurred in the labor movement and in various poor people's movements (Piven and Cloward, 1977). It may be helped by the "principle of cumulative advantage," which operates in favor of dominant group members and increasingly to the benefit of individuals being coopted into the system.

### The Matthew Effect and the Principle of Cumulative Advantage

"For unto every one that hath shall be given, and he shall have abundance: but from him that hath not shall be taken away even that which he hath." This passage from the Gospel of Matthew (13:12) has been identified by Robert K. Merton as describing the operation of the reward system in science. It takes longer for people who are relatively unknown to receive credit for their ideas, and if they collaborate with a highly esteemed scientist, the famous one tends to be credited with the work. Furthermore, recognition for excellent scientific work can be converted into improved resources and facilities for doing scientific work. Thus, concludes Merton, the operation of the reward system in science "provides a stratified distribution of chances" to scientists (1968).

As developed by Merton, the term "Matthew effect" refers to the enhancement of the position of already eminent individuals, for example, scientists. He uses a related term, the **principle of cumulative advantage,** to describe a similar process that occurs in institutions. For example, recognized centers of scientific training and discovery tend to gain resources (such as research grants and bright doctoral students) at a rate that makes other centers become relatively poorer (Merton, 1973b, p. 457).

The **Matthew effect** is a social process whereby one advantage an individual or organization has is likely to lead to other advantages. An advantaged berth in the ship of life provides access to multiple resources—financial, legal, political, police, military, informational, and human. These can be applied to an individual's goals, whatever they are. Several examples illuminate the process in operation. Lawyers in large firms and officers of major corporations often receive preferential treatment from banks for loans or home mortgage money. This is one small instance of how a favorable position in one field may be converted into an asset in another. People who vacation with the rich and powerful may gain inside information, influence, or other valued resources that may heighten differences in wealth, power, or status (Domhoff, 1974).

Maintaining a system of stratification involves major social institutions such as the family and active processes, such as cooptation. It is possible, however, that these institutions and processes may contain contradictions and the potential for change.

## CONFLICT, CONTRADICTIONS, AND POTENTIAL CHANGE

Whenever some people have more than others, the possibility exists for conflict over those inequalities. As a result, those with more power, wealth, income, or prestige may try to control those with less and also try to reduce conflict. Those with less may resist or try to change a system that offers them less. In order to assess the amount of conflict over social stratification, we need to clarify what constitutes conflict. Certain actions are fairly clear instances—the seizure of privately held land and its redistribution among many people or a political campaign with that aim. It is less clear whether strikes, crime rates, income tax cheating, parking violations, and vandalism may also be viewed as conflict over social stratification.

Conflict and resistance occur even in the most repressive of societies. The forms of conflict, protest, and resistance vary, depending on the society in which they occur. Reactions and efforts to control conflict and protest also differ. What forms of resistance or conflict are available, for example, in a caste and police society like South Africa? Work stoppages are criminal offenses; weapons are prohibited to nonwhites; and suspected "troublemakers" can be arrested and held indefinitely without trial. These features make resistance more difficult.

What happens? Do people passively accept their situations and go along with their oppressors? Despite all the restrictions, there *is* a tremendous amount of resistance among the black population in South Africa. Slowdowns, sit-downs, and school strikes by children are some of the forms of protest that have been used. In class societies such as that of Great Britain, conflict over inequality appears in mass demonstrations, political reforms, labor unionization, strikes, and urban riots and violence.

Some reasonably successful protest movements in the United States include the civil

*Sociologist Robert Merton noted a process he called the "Matthew effect," whereby a favorable position in one area of life may be converted into an advantage in another area.*

rights movement in the 1960s and the reawakening of the women's movement in the 1970s. Sometimes such movements benefit their leaders more than the masses. The civil rights movement, for example, may have developed a black elite with a stake in the system. On a limited basis this strategy is being pursued by the South African government at the time of this writing. It is seeking to coopt a black elite by offering sufficient economic and social rewards to a few who will help to keep the caste system functioning. This elite minority of blacks is also meant to serve as a buffer between the dominant whites and the mass of blacks. The very process of cooptation, however, is a double-edged sword. It may be a first step toward changing the system, because efforts to contain reform-minded new leaders may fail and the process of cooptation may have unintended consequences. It may also be the case that the South African government makes too few concessions too late, and that those advocating violence and revolution will "carry the day."

Virtually all systems of stratification contain some contradictions and potential for change.

Probably the most important are historical changes in the technological, economic, military, or political realms. In the United States in the 1960s and 1970s, as more women began working outside the home, their growing economic independence increased pressure for social equality. Such structural changes undercut existing ideologies (such as "a woman's place is in the home") and marshall support for alternative ideas ("equal pay for equal work"), which provide footholds for social change. There have always been ideological contradictions between democracy and capitalism, democracy and racial inequality, and democracy and sexual inequality.

Ideological tensions may appear to individuals who occupy two or more unequal statuses in a society (a phenomenon called **status inconsistency**). Usually the various dimensions of inequality (wealth, power, and status) are closely correlated, but sometimes an individual of relatively low social status (a minority group member or a woman, for instance) holds relatively high educational or occupational status (for example, as a doctor). Individuals occupying such inconsistent statuses may become more aware than most people of the discrepancy between their treatment in one status compared with that in another one.

Because people develop networks surrounding each of their statuses, their ideas may cross-pollinate. A member of a low status group may, by virtue of occupational position, religious group membership, or cooptation, come in contact with members of dominant groups. Depending on how willing the members of the dominant group are to include lower-status members, they may learn skills, information, or cultural styles that they can transmit to members of their own group. Again, depending on how well received they are, the lower-status people may be able to change the minds or behaviors of those in the dominant group to some degree.

## SUMMARY

1. Social stratification affects life chances.

2. Social inequality is less permanent than social stratification.

3. The three major sources of stratification are class, status, and power.

4. Class societies like Great Britain rest heavily on economic stratification.

5. Extreme stratification by power occurs in totalitarian states such as the one Hitler built in Nazi Germany. Conformity and domination are enforced by propaganda, censorship, the secret police, and force.

6. "Caste" refers to a permanent, hereditary, religiously sanctioned system of social ranking that affects all forms of daily interaction between differing groups. South Africa is a caste society that relies heavily upon military power and the legal system to try to maintain control.

7. Sociologists have offered two major answers to the question of why stratification exists. Functionalists stress that stratification is necessary to motivate people to fill important positions in society. Six major criticisms have been leveled at the functionalist view of stratification.

8. The conflict view sees stratification as growing out of the unequal power and resources of various groups in society. Marx saw stratification developing when an economic surplus was produced. When a limited number of people control the means of production and the resulting economic surplus, classes develop. Weber suggested that stratification can also be based on political, military, or organizational power that may sometimes operate independently of economic wealth. Conflict theory has also received a number of criticisms.

9. Several efforts have been made to combine a functionalist and a conflict view of stratification. Such a synthesis suggests that stratification involves an interplay between functionalist specialization and power. Social status affects the chances people have to develop their talents. Skill and training may help people to obtain certain positions. Once there, people and groups tend to use their positions and other resources to maintain or advance themselves.

10. Several institutional connections serve to pass on stratification from one generation to the next, including the inheritance of economic wealth, family socialization and connections, the existence of ideologies (systems of ideas) that help make existing inequalities seem more natural or taken for granted, and the use of the law and police to maintain the existing order.

11. The Matthew effect and cooptation are social processes that tend to preserve systems of stratification.

12. All systems of stratification contain conflict, contradictions, and other potential for change.

## KEY TERMS

autocracy (p. 187)
caste system (p. 184)
class system (p. 183)
cooptation (p. 195)

ideology (p. 174)
legitimate (p. 182)
life chances (p. 179)
Matthew effect (p. 196)
power (p. 182)
principle of cumulative advantage (p. 196)
property (p. 180)
social inequality (p. 179)
social stratification (p. 179)
status group (p. 181)
status inconsistency (p. 197)
totalitarianism (p. 187)

## SUGGESTED READINGS

Cookson, Peter W., Jr., and Caroline Hodges Persell. 1985. "English and American Residential Schools: A Comparative Study of the Reproduction of Social Elites." *Comparative Education Review* 29:283–298. A field study of how very elite boarding schools in two societies teach their students to become members of the upper strata.

Davis, Kingsley, and Wilbert E. Moore. 1945. "Some Principles of Stratification." *American Sociological Review* 10:242–249. A classic statement of the functionalist theory of stratification that widely influenced American sociology in the 1950s and 1960s.

Della Fave, L. Richard, and George A. Hillery, Jr. 1980. "Status Inequality in a Religious Community: The Case of a Trappist Monastery." *Social Forces* 59:62–84. Shows how competition for prestige may occur in a variety of realms, including the religious.

Lelyveld, Joseph. 1985. *Move Your Shadow*. New York: Times Books. A moving account by a journalist of how conditions in South Africa have been changing during the last 25 years.

Tumin, Melvin. 1953. "Some Principles of Stratification: A Critical Analysis." *American Sociological Review* 18:387–394. A sharp rebuttal to the Davis and Moore functionalist theory of stratification.

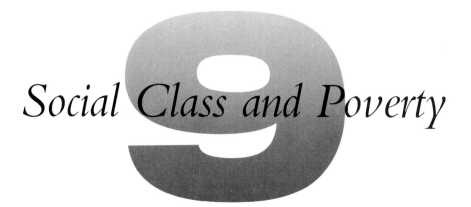

# Social Class and Poverty

*In his research on the children of the rich and the poor, Robert Coles asked the children to draw pictures of themselves with crayons. He found that poor children often do a hasty and incomplete job, drawing an unflattering picture. "Sometimes they are unwilling to complete what they have begun—as if they are unsure of life itself," notes Coles. A migrant child once told him, very matter-of-factly, that he didn't think he would live beyond the age of 20. Coles felt that this was simply a child who knew the score for someone in his situation. The children of business executives, doctors, and lawyers also know the score for themselves, reflecting this in their carefully drawn pictures of themselves, their homes, and their surroundings. (Coles, 1977, p. 386 and passim)*

Although sociologists differ in the way they define social class, they agree on its importance in the lives of individuals and societies. In this chapter we begin by examining some of the ways social class has been defined and measured; then we analyze how class differences affect life chances and life-styles. The third section explores poverty, how it is defined, what causes it, and how it responds to social policies. The next section considers class consciousness and social mobility, and the last section addresses the question: Are classless industrial societies possible?

## DEFINING AND MEASURING SOCIAL CLASS

One of the single most important ideas for understanding society is social class. **Social class,** as widely used by U.S. sociologists, refers to economic position and social status. It includes strong elements of social status, meaning place in a social hierarchy and indicated by the willingness of various groups to interact socially with other individuals and groups. Although Warner, Meeker, and Eels (1949) mentioned occupation and wealth, their primary emphasis was on prestige and on whether or not Americans would associate with one another as social equals. As noted in Chapter 8, their emphasis was on shared values, life-styles, and behavior (indicated by who socialized with whom), with little attention to the social locations that shaped those behaviors.

### Major Views of Class

Weber (1920) focused on the market position of individuals and groups. By this he meant how well they fared at the economic bargaining table, which was affected by their power, knowledge, skill, and scarcity. Weber's focus adds occupation and property to social status. He certainly was aware of the important role played by property in social stratification, but it was Karl Marx who suggested a theory of classes based on property ownership or nonownership.

The modern theorist Ralf Dahrendorf adds a third dimension to status and economic position. He stresses the importance of one's position in a bureaucratic structure—for example, as vice president for marketing or deputy director of a city housing agency (1959). Position in the class structure is influenced by the significance of the decisions one makes at work and by how many people are affected by those decisions. Since class is based on one's position in an organization, class would change at retirement, when one no longer possesses authority within an organization. This view stresses the growth and importance of organizations (already noted in Chapter 6) for class position, while it plays down the importance of market position and property.

These theoretical positions may be summarized by saying they are concerned primarily with status, economic life chances, ownership of productive resources, and organizational po-

sition. These different definitions of class are important because they influence the way class has been measured in research studies, and the concepts and measures used affect the conclusions people draw about the significance of social class in the United States.

## Research Conceptions of Class

Most American researchers characterize someone's **socioeconomic status (SES)** by using the person's occupation, education, and income. As you can see, this index of SES touches on several of the dimensions noted in the theoretical views of class, but it ignores distinctions based on property and position in the relations of production. (The various ways social class has been measured are summarized in Table 9.1.)

**Table 9.1** *How Social Class Has Been Measured*

| Concept | Measure | Comments |
|---|---|---|
| "Objective" measures of socioeconomic status | Father's occupation, father's education | Based on ranking of occupations according to their prestige |
| | | Treats the class structure as an unbroken band rather than viewing classes as separate groupings |
| | Income (whether earned or from investments) | May classify individuals logically, but people with the same incomes may have widely different life-styles. Difficult to distinguish groups rather than points on an unbroken band |
| | Wealth (need to distinguish between productive property and personal property) | May confer control over production and may produce income without working |
| Class | Position in the social relations of production | Sees classes as distinct groups that are in relation to one another |
| Subjective indicators of social class membership | An individual's subjective evaluation of the class group to which he or she belongs | Most people end up seeing themselves as "middle-class." Self-classification depends a lot on how the question is asked |

Let's look more closely at occupation and income to see if they capture the central inequalities of our society; then let us consider whether adding the concept of property adds to an understanding of social class in the United States.

## Occupational Rankings

How is it possible to classify the thousands of different occupations in the United States? Different scholars focus on different features of occupations. Some distinguish occupations on the basis of whether they involve mainly mental or physical work; whether people spend most of their time on the job giving orders or taking orders; in terms of access to useful knowledge and information, opportunity for advancement, degree of autonomy, or degree of exposure to occupational hazards; and finally in terms of their prestige. In all these approaches, someone assesses a particular occupation and assigns a rank to it.

In a study designed to measure occupational prestige, the National Opinion Research Center (NORC) asked a random sample of the population to give "their personal opinion of the general standing" of selected occupations. Re-

*Sociologists study many different occupations, including those of forklift operator and judge, in terms of the nature of the work, opportunity for advancement, rewards, and other features.*

## Table 9.2    *Prestige Ranking of 90 Occupations in the United States*

In Table 9.2, selected occupations in the United States have been ranked according to the scores they were given by various respondents in the United States in 1947, 1963, and 1983. The scores and the relative ranks of most occupations have changed little since 1963. Occupations are ranked in quite similar ways in 60 other industrial and agricultural countries as well.

| Occupation | 1947 | 1963 | 1983[a] | Occupation | 1947 | 1963 | 1983[a] |
|---|---|---|---|---|---|---|---|
| U.S. Supreme Court justice | 96 | 94 | NA[b] | International labor union official | 75 | 77 | NA |
| Physician | 93 | 93 | 82 | Railroad engineer | 76 | 76 | 51 |
| Nuclear physicist | 86 | 92 | 74 | Electrician | 73 | 76 | 47 |
| Scientist | 89 | 92 | 68 | Owner-operator of a printing shop | 74 | 75 | NA |
| Government scientist | 88 | 91 | NA | Trained machinist | 73 | 75 | 48 |
| State governor | 93 | 91 | NA | Farm owner and operator | 76 | 74 | NA |
| Federal cabinet member | 92 | 90 | NA | Undertaker | 72 | 74 | NA |
| College professor | 89 | 90 | 78 | Welfare worker for a city government | 73 | 74 | NA |
| U.S. representative in Congress | 89 | 90 | NA | Newspaper columnist | 74 | 73 | NA |
| Chemist | 86 | 89 | 69 | Policeman | 67 | 72 | 48 |
| Lawyer | 86 | 89 | 76 | Reporter on a daily news-paper | 71 | 71 | 51 |
| Diplomat in U.S. Foreign Service | 92 | 89 | NA | Bookkeeper | 68 | 70 | 48 |
| Dentist | 86 | 88 | 74 | Insurance agent | 68 | 69 | 47 |
| Architect | 86 | 88 | 71 | Carpenter | 65 | 68 | 40 |
| County judge | 87 | 88 | 76 | Manager of a small store in a city | 69 | 67 | NA |
| Psychologist | 85 | 87 | 71 | A local official of a labor union | 62 | 67 | NA |
| Minister | 87 | 87 | 69 | Mail carrier | 66 | 66 | 42 |
| Member of the board of directors of a large corporation | 86 | 87 | NA | Traveling wholesale sales-man | 68 | 66 | 40 |
| Mayor of a large city | 90 | 87 | NA | Plumber | 63 | 65 | 41 |
| Priest | 86 | 86 | 69 | Automobile repairman | 63 | 64 | 37 |
| State gov't. department head | 87 | 86 | NA | Playground director | 67 | 63 | 49 |
| Civil or electrical engineer | 84 | 86 | 68 | Barber | 59 | 63 | 38 |
| Airline pilot | 83 | 86 | 70 | Machine operator in a factory | 60 | 63 | 32 |
| Banker | 88 | 85 | 72 | Owner-operator of a lunch stand | 62 | 63 | NA |
| Biologist | 81 | 85 | 68 | Corporal in the regular army | 60 | 62 | NA |
| Sociologist | 82 | 83 | 66 | Garage mechanic | 62 | 62 | 37 |
| Captain in the regular army | 80 | 82 | NA | Truck driver | 54 | 59 | 32 |
| Accountant for a large business | 81 | 81 | 57 | Fisherman who owns his own boat | 58 | 58 | 30 |
| Public school teacher | 78 | 81 | 61 | Clerk in a store | 58 | 56 | 29 |
| Factory owner (about 100 people) | 82 | 80 | NA | Lumberjack | 53 | 55 | 26 |
| Building contractor | 79 | 80 | NA | Restaurant cook | 54 | 55 | 26 |
| Exhibited artist | 83 | 78 | 56 | Singer in a nightclub | 52 | 54 | NA |
| Musician in a symphony orchestra | 81 | 78 | 46 | Night watchman | 47 | 50 | 22 |
| Author of novels | 80 | 78 | 60 | | | | |
| Economist | 79 | 78 | 57 | | | | |

| Occupation | 1947 | 1963 | 1983[a] | Occupation | 1947 | 1963 | 1983[a] |
|---|---|---|---|---|---|---|---|
| Coal miner | 49 | 50 | 26 | Bartender | 44 | 48 | 20 |
| Restaurant waiter | 48 | 49 | 20 | Clothes presser in a laundry | 46 | 45 | 18 |
| Taxi driver | 49 | 49 | 22 | Garbage collector | 35 | 39 | 17 |
| Janitor | 44 | 48 | 16 | | | | |

[a] In general, more recent rankings of occupations have been lower than in earlier years, although the relative rank of different occupations has stayed about the same over time.
[b] NA means not available.
*Sources:* 1947, 1963: Hodge, Siegel, and Rossi, 1966; 1983: adapted from Davis, 1983.

spondents graded each occupation on a five-point scale from "excellent" to "poor." The results of the original study in 1947, and restudies in 1963 and 1983, appear in Table 9.2. As you can see, the relative rankings remained quite constant over time. The best predictors of the rank of an occupation are the educational level and income of workers in it (Reiss et al., 1961). Both efforts to rank occupations view the American class structure as a continuous band rather than as composed of separate categories. The prestige of an occupation seems to involve the averaging of two distinct dimensions: people's perceptions of the rewards of an occupation and its value to society (Hope, 1982).

### Measuring Class with Income

**Income** equals the sum of money wages and salaries, income from self-employment, and income other than earnings. Notice that total money income thus includes money you worked for—earnings—and income other than earnings. Income other than earnings includes money income from estates, trusts, stock dividends, interest on savings or bonds, rental income—in short, income from money invested in your name. Families have incomes that are higher and more equally distributed than do single individuals, as Figure 9.1 indicates. This occurs because family incomes are often based on the incomes of more than one individual.

Income poses certain problems for research. People tend to be more reluctant to reveal their incomes than their occupations, and they may not always be reporting the same thing. (Are they reporting gross income before taxes or net income after taxes?) There are other problems with using income alone as an indicator of social

class. The gap between manual and nonmanual workers is declining in terms of what they earn and how they spend it. In the United States, unlike Great Britain, it is difficult to judge the exact "social class" of many people on the basis of their speech, appearance, or cars except at the extremes of the class structure. Both upper- and lower-class individuals can usually be identified by appearance and clothing, but the great majority in the middle are not so distinguishable.

Although people can be categorized by income, those categories may have little or no shared social meaning. An electrician and a salesperson may earn similar incomes in a year but have widely different life-styles and attitudes. Thus income may not be the only element that distinguishes social classes. Class differences appear to be rooted in more basic underlying disparities, such as wealth.

### Differences in Wealth

Although differences in occupation and income do exist, Marxian sociologists argue that a more fundamental cleavage underlies all capitalist industrial societies. This division is one of property, not income. And property, or wealth, is obtained primarily through inheritance or luck rather than through occupation or income (Thurow, 1975). Wealth differs from income. Wealth is the total value (minus debts) of what is owned. It includes consumer goods (such as houses and cars) as well as assets (stocks, bonds, real estate, factories).

The top fifth of the population in the United States (about 45 million people) owns or controls three-quarters of the nation's wealth (Figure 9.1). In stark contrast, the remaining four-fifths (or about 181 million people) share the

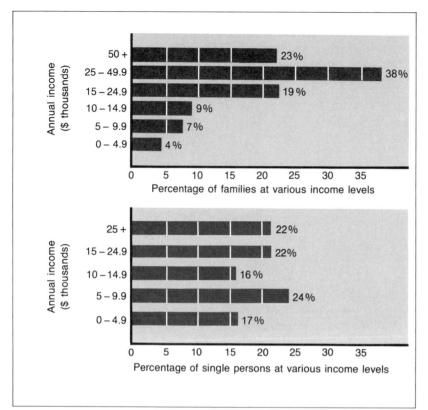

**Figure 9.1  Percentage of Families and Single Persons at Various Income Levels in the United States, 1987.**

Large percentages of single persons earn relatively low annual incomes, with 41 percent earning less than $10,000 per year in 1987. The annual income of families is somewhat higher, with only 11 percent earning less than $10,000 per year and 57 percent of families earning between $15,000 and $49,999 per year in 1987.

*Source:* U.S. Bureau of the Census, 1989b, pp. 38–39.

remaining one-quarter. This vast majority owns little beyond their own personal property—clothing, furnishings, a car, and perhaps a house. For these people, property means something quite different from what it means for the very wealthy. It means a few possessions, many of which are still being paid for. This property does not usually produce income for the owner (except in the case of a traveling salesperson, whose car may help to produce income). The bottom fifth of the population owns less than 0.2 percent of the nation's wealth (Thurow, 1975). This group has more debts than assets.

Thus, as Figure 9.2 illustrates, the differences in the amount of wealth owned by the top and bottom fifths of the American population are enormous. Some individuals control fortunes exceeding $500 million, whereas millions of people have only their debts. Differences in income are considerable, but not nearly so great as differences in wealth. As Figure 9.2 reveals, the top fifth of American families earned 43.7 percent of all the income earned in 1987, whereas the bottom fifth earned 4.6 percent—a

difference of 39 percent, compared to the 76 percent difference in wealth.

The distinction between earnings and income from property holdings is crucial to understanding social class structure and to reconciling competing explanations for the existence of inequality. Holding property is important for about 5 percent of the total American population. This 5 percent, however, represents more than 10 million people, and property is very important for them. It affects their income, power, status, self-image, and life-style. It provides resources to the top 5 percent that are not available to the other 95 percent. These are financial resources that may be converted to power, that tend to confer status, that can command knowledge and information, and that enable them to advance ideologies consistent with their interests in the world. Moreover, the property they control affects the social arena within which the other 95 percent of the population operates. Corporate owners, for example, may decide to close a plant in a town, thus putting more than half the population out of work.

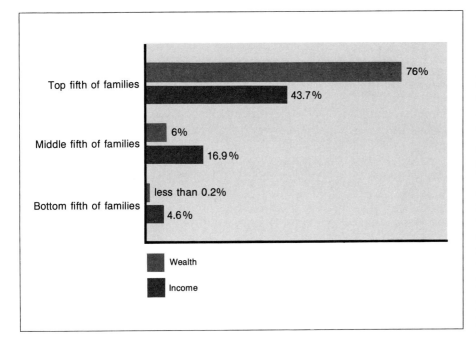

**Figure 9.2  Distribution of Family Wealth and After-Tax Income**

Wealth and income are very differently distributed among families in the United States. The top fifth of families owns more than three-quarters of all wealth while earning less than half of all income. The bottom fifth of families owns no wealth and earns less than 5 percent of the total income.

*Source:* Thurow, 1975; U.S. Bureau of the Census, 1989a, p. 446.

### Social Class as Position in the Social Relations of Production

A Marxian concept of class is related to both ownership and income (Wright and Perrone, 1977). This conception emphasizes the position of individuals in the social relations of production. Four criteria are used to pinpoint an individual's position in the **social relations of production:**

1. The ownership of the means of production
2. The purchase of the labor power of others
3. The control of other people's labor power
4. The sale of one's own labor power

These four criteria are used in Table 9.3 to assign individuals to one of four classes. Capitalists are defined as the class that owns the means of production, buys and controls the labor of others, and does not need to sell its own labor. Managers are considered a separate class even though they supervise others and may own some stock in the corporation. They are not capitalists unless they own a controlling interest. They also need to sell their own labor. The class position of workers is set by their situation of selling their own labor and not having any control over the labor of others. The last class, called the "petty bourgeoisie," consists of small

**Table 9.3  *Wright and Perrone's Expanded Marxian Criteria for Class***

| Class | Criteria for Class Position | | | |
|---|---|---|---|---|
| | Ownership of the Means of Production | Purchase of the Labor of Others | Control of the Labor of Others | Sale of One's Own Labor |
| Capitalists | Yes | Yes | Yes | No |
| Managers | No | No | Yes | Yes |
| Workers | No | No | No | Yes |
| Petty bourgeoisie | Yes | No | No | No |

*Source:* Wright and Perrone, 1977, p. 34.

businesspeople and shopkeepers who own their own stores but do not buy or control the labor of others in any major way.

The class categories in Table 9.3 represent an entirely different way of viewing class structure. When occupational differences are examined, classes are seen as a ladder with many rungs. Small steps exist between positions, but it is difficult to say which rungs comprise a distinct class. "Occupation" represents an effort to classify the substantive content of jobs, whereas "class" refers to the social relations of control within which occupational activities are conducted. This means, for example, that certain people supervise others and that certain classes receive profits while others do not. There is some relationship between occupational position and class position, but it is by no means perfect. Employers are much more likely to be managers, proprietors, and officials than to hold any other occupation, and they are much more likely to hold those occupations than are the members of other classes. Workers are likely to hold such jobs as truck drivers, clerks, or craft workers. The total number of employers and petty bourgeoisie is rather small. The vast majority of the working population (almost 90 percent) are workers or managers. As a result, a small group occupies the dominant position in the social relations of production, a feature that is nearly invisible when we consider only occupational categories.

In later research Wright et al. (1982) added more criteria to those in Table 9.3, including degree of participation in decision making, authority over others at work, and the degree of autonomy and self-direction people have in their work. Their findings are as follows:

1. The working class is the largest class in the class structure of the United States.
2. Nearly half of all the positions in the class structure have a "contradictory character." By this they mean that the positions share features of several classes; for example, a position may have a high degree of autonomy but involve no ownership. The fact that there are relatively few "pure" class positions means that class polarization is lessened.
3. Lower-status white-collar occupations share many of the features of manual occupations;

therefore it makes little sense to call such occupations "middle-class."
4. A sizable majority of the U.S working class consists of women and minorities.

Some argue that class should be measured by occupation rather than by property because of the managerial revolution in American business. This has created a situation where knowledge or other technical criteria are more important than property for one's class position. It is understandable why so much stress is placed on occupation, since the majority of people in the labor force do not possess property. However, whether we want to explain variations in income or in wealth, a Marxian class analysis explains more of these differences than an occupational explanation alone does. Owners consistently have higher incomes than do managers and workers, even when education, occupational status, age, and length of time in the job are comparable. Within the nonpropertied class, managers earn much more than workers, even when education is held constant (Wright and Perrone, 1977). This evidence is more consistent with a class analysis than with a technical skills explanation. Managerial pay scales may go up much more sharply than do worker pay scales, because pay reflects not only productivity but also the exercise of social control within businesses and bureaucracies. The promise of higher salaries may encourage individuals to control themselves and others in ways that are desired by higher-level managers and owners.

Nevertheless, Marxian class categories do not explain all the inequality in job rewards. Considerable inequalities in earnings and job fulfillment are also produced by occupational distinctions (Kalleberg and Griffin, 1980). These findings confirm once again the value of using several theoretical lenses to view and explain the social world. Occupation and class together account for more inequality than does either one alone.

### Subjective Indicators of Class

Assessments of occupation and productive position do not include information about individuals' perceptions of their own class positions, or **subjective social class.** Yet no consideration of social class is complete without taking into account the perceptions of individuals. It could be, for example, that Sam's neighbors consider him to be working class, whereas Sam considers himself to be middle class. Whose judgment do we use in such a situation? Do we follow the neighbor's (or a sociologist's) definition of Sam's social class, or do we accept Sam's self-definition? We cannot ignore Sam's ideas because they are likely to affect his behavior. He may be more likely to have middle-class friends, to follow middle-class recreational and leisure activities, to belong to a middle-class church, and to have middle-class aspirations for his children. Although his beliefs may not coincide completely with his objective class position, they may affect his behavior. So if we want to understand social behavior, we need to know both a person's "objective" social class and his or her subjective class identification.

In the early 1940s pollster Elmo Roper did a nationwide survey for *Fortune* magazine in which Americans were asked whether they belonged to the upper, middle, or lower classes. When 79 percent replied that they were middle class, it was widely asserted that the United States was a middle-class nation. But social psychologist Richard Centers quickly challenged this interpretation. Also using a national sample, Centers added the category "working class" to the possible choices available to respondents. In his survey, half the respondents chose "working class" and only 43 percent said they were middle-class (Centers, 1949). Centers also found a high correlation between subjective class position and position as measured by more objective criteria, such as occupational type. The work by Centers and others who came after him suggests that Americans do not like to describe themselves as lower-class but are quite willing to say they are working-class, which sounds honest and industrious.

Two more recent studies reveal consistency in the percentage who identify themselves as middle-class, but there is some shift away from self-descriptions as upper- or upper-middle-class (Table 9.4). Hodge and Treiman's (1968) results show the same aversion to describing oneself as lower-class that Centers observed. Jackman and Jackman (1982) found that people questioned in 1975 were just about as likely to identify themselves as middle-class and somewhat more likely to say they were working-class or poor. Given the changes in income discussed in the debate "Is the United States Becoming a Bipolar Society?" it will be interesting to see if people's subjective interpretation of their class position changes in the future in the same direction that the income distribution is changing. Occupational standing is the objective socioeconomic factor that is most strongly related to subjective class identification, although education, skill, income, job authority, and freedom to make decisions on the job are also important (Jackman and Jackman, 1982). Fully half of clerical workers identified themselves as working-class or poor, as did 58 percent of craft workers, a result that is consistent with the research of Wright et al. (1982).

These studies are notable because very few people said they did not believe in classes or could not answer, suggesting that nearly everyone is aware that classes exist. Indeed, Jackman and Jackman (1982) report that class rivals race as a source of group identity and that class bonds are especially pronounced among those identifying with the lower classes.

**Table 9.4**  *Percent of People Identifying with Different Social Classes, 1968, 1975*

| 1968 | | 1975 | |
|---|---|---|---|
| **Class** | **Percent** | **Class** | **Percent** |
| Upper class | 2.2% | Upper class | 1.0% |
| Upper middle class | 16.6 | Upper middle class | 8.0 |
| Middle class | 44.0 | Middle class | 43.0 |
| Working class | 34.3 | Working class | 37.0 |
| Lower class | 2.3 | Poor | 8.0 |
| Don't believe in classes | 0.6 | No answer | 3.0 |

*Source:* Hodge and Treiman, 1968; Jackman and Jackman, 1982.

# DEBATING SOCIETY'S ISSUES

Traditionally the United States has had a large middle class. For many families the dream of owning their own house, educating their children, and owning a car came true. Even those with relatively modest incomes hoped their children would do better than they had done. Are the chances of realizing those dreams fading as the middle class shrinks? Is the United States becoming more of a bipolar society where the rich get richer and more members of the middle class become poor?

Between 1968 and 1983, the proportion of the population classified as "middle-class" by income began to shrink (Figure 9.3), whereas the number of high- and low-earning families increased. More and more often,

### Is the United States Becoming a Bipolar Society?

rich families and poor families are replacing the wide expanse of middle-class families. Why have these changes occurred and are they temporary? What are their social consequences?

Economic, political, and demographic changes contribute to this shift. The manufacturing industries that are growing most quickly, such as those in high technology, tend to employ two tiers of workers—some very well paid and others poorly paid—with few in between. This contrasts with the declining "smokestack" industries—such as automobiles, steel, and machine

tools—that employ large numbers of well-paid blue-collar workers. The 20 most rapidly growing occupations paid $100 a week less, on the average, than the 20 most rapidly shrinking occupations. The shift from a manufacturing to a service economy also works to depress wage rates for workers. In 1987 the 35.7 million workers in service industries had an average weekly wage of $149, compared to $220 for the 21.1 million working in manufacturing jobs (U.S. Bureau of the Census, 1989a). Most workers at General Motors, for example, earn about $20,000 per year, whereas at McDonald's executives earn over $30,000 per year and most other employees earn only slightly above the minimum hourly wage (at 1988 rates,

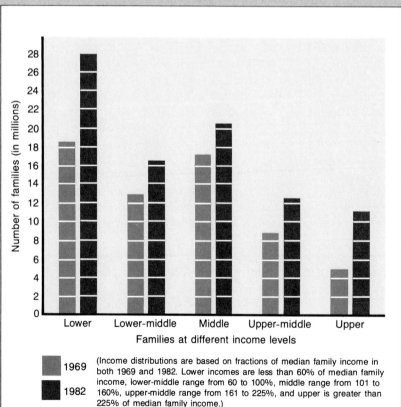

(Income distributions are based on fractions of median family income in both 1969 and 1982. Lower incomes are less than 60% of median family income, lower-middle range from 60 to 100%, middle range from 101 to 160%, upper-middle range from 161 to 225%, and upper is greater than 225% of median family income.)

**Figure 9.3   Number of Families in Different Income Groups, 1969 and 1982.**

Between 1969 and 1982, the number of U.S. families in both the lowest and the highest income categories increased much more than the number of families in the middle three income categories. This suggests that income polarization increased in the United States during that time.

*Source:* Graphed from data in Blackburn and Bloom, 1985, p. 21.

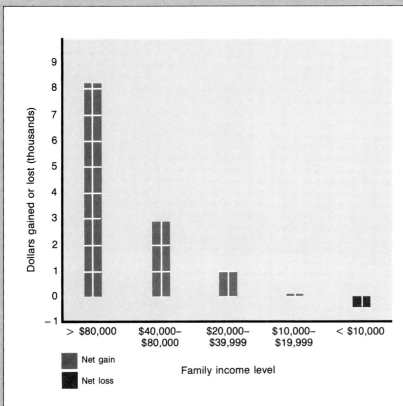

**Figure 9.4   Amount Gained and Lost by Families of Different Incomes from Reagan's Tax Reforms.**

U.S. families earning more than $80,000 per year gained more than $8000 per year as a result of President Reagan's tax reforms, while families earning less than $10,000 per year lost $390 per year, on the average.

*Source:* U.S. Congressional Budget Office, 1984.

this totaled $6968 if someone worked full time for a year). The competitive global economy is also putting downward pressure on wages. Industries hurt the hardest by the American trade deficit include automobiles, steel, and machine tools. When the primary breadwinner loses his or her job in one of these industries, middle-income families are frequently pushed into low-income brackets.

Political decisions have also contributed to the polarization of income in the United States. Reaganomics, with its deep personal income tax cuts and reductions in spending on social programs, has been a boon to the nation's wealthy families and has hurt those that were already poor, concluded the Congressional

Budget Office (1984). The 1981 tax changes meant that households with incomes over $80,000 had a net gain of $8260, whereas households with incomes under $10,000 had a net loss of $390, on the average (Figure 9.4).

Two demographic changes contribute to the bipolar trend, whereas one that is sometimes said to explain it does not. The increasing number of female-headed households (from 8.7 percent of households in 1970 to 16.2 percent in 1987) have lower earnings than male-headed households because of the lower wages of women in general. The median income of full-time, year-round female workers in 1987 was $17,504, compared to $26,722 for full-time male workers (U.S. Bureau of the Census,

1989a). The growth of two-income households, on the other hand, has contributed to the greater number of higher-income households (Figure 9.5).

Some argue that because of the baby boom there are proportionately fewer middle-aged households with middle incomes than in the past, and that therefore the situation will change as the young people in the Baby Boom generation become middle-aged. But there are fewer middle-income households within each age group today compared to the past, suggesting that the baby boom will not change this trend in the future. The trends that caused the middle class to shrink seem likely to persist. What are the probable social effects?

# DEBATING SOCIETY'S ISSUES

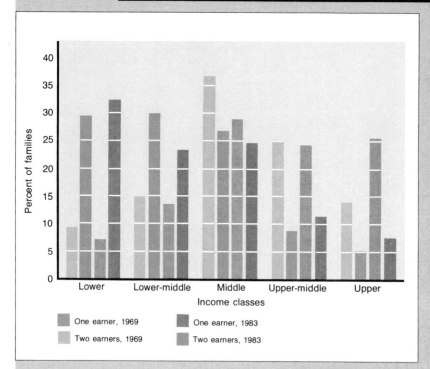

**Figure 9.5   Percent of Families in Different Income Groups, by Number of Earners.**

Growing numbers of two-earner families increased the percent of upper-income families between 1969 and 1983 (Blackburn and Bloom, 1985). At the same time, a larger percent of single-earner families were in the lower-income group in 1983 than in 1969, partly because more single-earner households were headed by women who, in general, earned less than men.

*Source:* Graphed from data in Blackburn and Bloom, 1985, p. 21.

Many of the consequences are already visible. Fewer people are able to buy their own homes. In 1980, 65 percent of Americans owned their own homes, the peak year. Since then the figure has moved downward to 63.8 percent in 1986, the latest year for which figures are available (McQueen, 1988). Since 1979 the fraction of children living in high-income families ($100,000 or more per year) increased by 1 percent, while the fraction of children living in low-income families (under $10,000 per year) increased by 6 percent (Levy, 1988).

The downwardly mobile members of the middle class tend to fill the ranks of the radical right and fundamentalist religious movements as they seek to achieve in political and moral ways what they sense they are losing in economic and social realms. Their anger is leveled at both those above and below them in the class structure. They see those above doing well and feel that those below get too many "handouts."

More children are growing up in poverty today than has been the case since 1959. Many of them are being poorly educated or are dropping out of school. Consequently, they are likely to be unemployed or to be employed at only the lowest wage rates. Their low wages provide less income for goods and services and thus contribute little to economic growth. They also have less taxable income to support state-financed social services.

Such trends are likely to lead us to a dual society in which poor, nonwhite females will form an underclass, whereas rich, white males will dominate from above. The result is likely to be a growing polarization in all aspects of society, reflected in everything from consumer products and retailing to housing, health care, and the emergence of distinct class cultures. We may also expect friction and conflict between social groups. In a number of cities and several states, the underclass will constitute a majority of the population and a potential majority of voters as young people reach adulthood. They will support social movements that promise to improve their situation (Carnoy and Levin, 1985). Their impoverished childhood and neglected educations may create a largely uninformed electorate, unable to deal with complex social, economic, and scientific issues. The poten-

## DEBATING SOCIETY'S ISSUES

tial for serious political conflict and social disruption is great. These consequences will escalate the costs of public assistance and criminal justice, while the economic potential for meeting such costs deteriorates. Such a situation clearly threatens the health of a political democracy.

Traditionally the existence of a large middle class served as a political and economic buffer and fueled people's hopes for social mobility and their commitment to the social, economic, and political order. In contrast, Latin American countries with small middle-class populations invest heavily in police forces to control the underclass. Military dictatorships flourish. The rich live in a state of near siege, in walled compounds surrounded by barbed wire, guard dogs, and armed guards. The poor struggle to feed their children and grow angrier and angrier at a system that offers little hope for improvement. Such conditions are not favorable ones for an open democratic society.

Extreme inequality may generate economic disaster. Each of the four major depressions in U.S. history (in the 1780s, 1840s, 1930s, and 1970s) was preceded by huge and increasing inequalities in wealth and income. The poor and middle classes borrow more to maintain their standard of living, which drives up consumer debt. The rich have so much money that they gamble on risky investments, which generate huge speculative bubbles in the stock and other markets (Batra, 1987).

It is the possibility of social, political, and economic consequences such as these that concern sociologists as they view the trend toward an increasingly bipolar society in the United States.

*Sources:* Blackburn and Bloom, 1985; Carnoy and Levin, 1985; Greenberg and Bystryn, 1978; Hymowitz and O'Boyle, 1984; Kuttner, 1985; Levin, 1985; Palmer and Sawhill, 1984; Scott, 1984; Thurow, 1984; U.S. Bureau of the Census, 1987a; Congressional Budget Office, 1984; and Zonana, 1984.

---

A major problem with the subjective method is that it depends heavily on how the question about class is worded. Also, some individuals may rank themselves higher or lower than their income, occupation, property, and life-style seem to warrant.

"Social class" is the general concept referring to economic position and social status. SES and the Marxian class measure developed by Wright and Perrone are summary measures that tap several dimensions of economic position and social status. Both of these measures are related to the life chances and life-styles of individuals.

## DIFFERENCES IN LIFE CHANCES AND LIFE-STYLES

Undoubtedly class location affects individuals' perceptions of their class position (including subjective definition of class). Table 9.5 on pages 9-1 to 9-8 presents a composite portrait of different classes in terms of their roots, consequences, and life-styles. Use of the term **life-style** requires some qualification, since it suggests more freedom of choice than may actually exist. There are very real consequences of class situations that extend far beyond the style of music one prefers, the furnishings in one's home, and other superficial but highly visible features of life-style. These consequences include access to education, health, life expectancy, and general life chances, factors over which individuals have much less control.

Life-styles and life consequences are clearly influenced by one's position in the economic system. As Zablocki and Kanter (1976) suggest, these positions may be compressed into three basic categories: life-styles that are primarily property-dominated, those that are occupation-dominated, and those that are income- or poverty-dominated. Variations within these three basic categories can be illuminated by relationship to the means of production, income, authority and autonomy at work, and occupational prestige.

In Table 9.5, five socioeconomic groups are designated and their relationships to various criteria are indicated. Because multiple criteria are used, the boundaries of each category are somewhat fuzzy. The categories could be sliced

*Class position dramatically affects a person's life-style and life chances. Some dogs owned by upper-class individuals live in greater comfort than many poor people do. The middle classes tend to assume that everyone in the United States is middle class, while ignoring the extremes.*

somewhat thinner. The upper class, for example, could be divided into the upper upper and the lower upper, depending on the size of the fortune and its age. Further divisions along occupational, income, and authority dimensions could be made within each of these categories. The Marxian perspective is reflected in the full lines dividing the property-holding upper class from those who must work and separating those with fairly regular work and income from the unemployed and poor. If these cleavages are meaningful, they should be reflected in life chances and life-styles, including family, child rearing, education, personal values, personal style, residence, consumer behavior, political and civic behavior, religion, and health. Some of these consequences are summarized in the table.

## Differences in Family, Child Rearing, and Education

Since most property is passed down through families, the property-dominated upper class is very concerned with family identity and kin ties. Extended kin networks are important and useful to the upper class. This concern is reflected in the emphasis members of this class place on rearing and educating their children. Often people who are not family members—such as nurses, governesses, and private-school teachers—play a large role in child rearing, but they are paid by the families and generally perform their duties in ways the parents desire.

The upper middle class values the companionship of marriage. Child rearing stresses the development of individual autonomy and aca-

# A PORTRAIT OF CLASS-RELATED LIFE CHANCES AND LIFE-STYLES

Summary Table 9.5 portrays life chances and life-styles of the five major classes in American society. On each of the following two-page spreads, three variables are portrayed for each class. The classes are listed in order, with the upper class on the top of the left page and the lower class on the bottom of the right page. Photographs illustrate some of the descriptions. By comparing up and down the class scale within each aspect of lifestyle, you will increase your understanding of the importance of class differences. The photographs below vividly illustrate, for example, the different class-related life chances and life-styles of two Americans.

## A Portrait of Class-Related Life Chances and Life-Styles: Class Position, Occupation, and Family

| | Socioeconomic Class Category (and % of total U.S. population in it) | Roots of Class Position | Occupation | Family |
|---|---|---|---|---|
| **Property-dominated** | Upper class (1–3%) | Ownership of productive property (usually inherited). High income (more than $200,000 per year) | Managers, "public servants," philanthropists, professionals, corporate board members | Dynastic alliance. Major source of identity. Women unlikely to have careers. Modified extended family with strong kin ties. Strong elders. Age grading. Low fertility rates |
| **Occupation-dominated** | Upper middle class (5–10%) | Occupational power and prestige. High income ($50,000 to $200,000). Some income from investments or savings | High-level corporate managers, CEOs, professionals, high-level civil servants, academics. Major source of identity. Demanding of time and energy even during private time | Generally stable. Value companionship in marriage. Isolated nuclear family. Marriage important as a rite of passage to adult responsibility and privilege. Male success traditionally required wife serving as a helpmate |
| **Occupation-dominated** | Lower middle class (30–35%) | Lower income ($15,000 to $40,000), less property than upper middle class | Lower professionals, semiprofessionals, sales and clerical workers, small-business proprietors | More egalitarian husband-wife relationships than working class. Wives are increasingly likely to work. Increasing use of institutionalized child care. Drop in fertility rates |

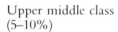

**Table 9.5 (Continued):** *Class Position, Occupation, and Family*

| | Socioeconomic Class Category (and % of total U.S. population in it) | Roots of Class Position | Occupation | Family |
|---|---|---|---|---|
| **Occupation-dominated** | Working class<br><br>(40–45%) | Less occupational power and prestige, lower income ($10,000 to $50,000) and own little property | Skilled laborers (electricians, plumbers, machinists), truck drivers, barbers, semiskilled laborers. Longer hours, less paid vacation | Patriarchal, adult-centered family structure with sharply seg-regated sex roles. Relatives are important. Early marriage and child rearing |

| | | | | |
|---|---|---|---|---|
| **Income- or poverty-dominated** | Lower class<br><br>(20–25%) | High rates of unemployment, poverty-level income (welfare to $9,000). No savings, property, or financial security Unemployment due to health disabilities or lack of work opportunities | Semiskilled or unskilled laborers. Migrant workers. Women raised to believe they should be supported by men, untrained for work, then often deserted | Heavy reliance on kin networks to meet daily domestic needs. Marriage not very important as an institution as it solves no economic problems and may add some. High fertility rate |

## Table 9.5 (*Continued*): *Child Rearing, Education, and Residence*

| | Socioeconomic Class Category | Child Rearing | Education of Children | Residence |
|---|---|---|---|---|
| **Property-dominated** | Upper class | Children raised by nurses and governesses. Confers a sense of "entitlement" | Insulated from other classes at elite private schools, often boarding schools. Attend elite private colleges. Boys and girls study liberal arts. Education imparts sense that privilege is earned and deserved | May have more than one residence. May have long-standing family home, heirlooms, antiques. Often some joint family territory, like a summer compound or estate |
| **Occupation-dominated** | Upper middle class | Emphasizes development of individual autonomy. Generally more permissive than lower classes. Parents may threaten to withdraw love as punishment | Liberal arts education at elite schools, colleges, and graduate or professional schools. Increasingly comparable education for boys and girls | Home location and furnishings are important. Considerable geographical mobility. Home ownership by 83% |

**Table 9.5 (*Continued*):** *Child Rearing, Education, and Residence*

| | Socioeconomic Class Category | Child Rearing | Education of Children | Residence |
|---|---|---|---|---|
| **Occupation-dominated**  | Lower middle class | Emphasizes obedience and docility as well as sociability. More stress on discipline than higher classes | Want schools that stress discipline and respect for adults. Parochial schools are popular with this group. More likely to attend college than working and lower classes but more likely to attend local, public institutions than are higher classes | Home ownership by 67%  |
| **Occupation-dominated** | Working class | Stresses obedience, respect for elders. Emphasizes discipline | Harder to plan for education. More high-school-only graduates than higher classes. Increasing college attendance at community colleges. Some preference for technical and vocational education | Home ownership by 61%. Highly valued and considered an achievement |
| **Income or poverty-dominated**  | Lower class | Slightly more likely to use physical punishment on children, but much less than most people assume. Children help with necessary labor in the home | Highest rates of illiteracy. High dropout rates. Schools in low-income areas tend to be lowest quality, with few alternatives available | Rental or other temporary lodging. Live in oldest, most deteriorated, least desirable housing and neighborhoods. Buildings in poor repair. May lack heat, plumbing; have rats, roaches, leaks. Frequent relocations |

**Table 9.5 (*Continued*):** *Consumer Behavior, Political & Civic Behavior, and Health*

| | Socioeconomic Class Category | Consumer Behavior, Leisure | Political and Civic Behavior | Health |
|---|---|---|---|---|
| **Property-dominated** | Upper class | Discreet. Shun ostentatious displays of wealth, although this depends on age of family fortune | "Behind the scenes" political activity and support. Play high-prestige, often honorary roles | Generally good. The best that money, education, and knowledge can buy. Fairly heavy social drinking |
| **Occupation-dominated** | Upper middle class | Fairly divided between the frugal and the ostentatious, depending on situation. Value culture, books, theater, sports | High sense of civic duty. Active in community groups, political organizations, voluntary associations. Predominantly Republican | Good physical and mental health. Good health insurance plans through their jobs. Drink wine, champagne, and other liquor |
| **Occupation-dominated** | Lower middle class | Frugal | May work as civil servants. Most dissatisfied with their standard of living, jobs, and family incomes | Longer life expectancy than lower classes. Some health insurance through their jobs. More likely to smoke than higher classes, but drink somewhat less |

**Table 9.5 (*Continued*): *Consumer Behavior, Political & Civic Behavior, and Health***

|  | Socioeconomic Class Category | Consumer Behavior, Leisure | Political and Civic Behavior | Health |
|---|---|---|---|---|
| **Occupation-dominated** | Working class | Spectator sports, hunting, fishing, boating, family gatherings, shopping expeditions, television | Mainly Democrats. Less likely to vote than higher classes. Feels politically powerless. More than half belong to unions. Belong to churches, but two-thirds belong to no other community organizations | More exposure to occupational health and safety hazards than higher classes. Some health insurance if a union member and regularly employed. Smoke more than higher classes, drink less wine and more beer |
| **Income- or poverty-dominated** | Lower class | Purchase second-hand clothing and furniture. Shop locally, pay higher prices. Spend about half of income on food, a quarter on rent | Less likely to vote | Poorest mental and physical health. Lower life expectancy. 40% of poor have serious medical problems from malnutrition. Poorer health care. No health insurance. Smoke and drink more than other classes |

*Sources:* Coles, 1977; Cookson and Persell, 1985b; Hacker, 1980; Huber and Form, 1973; Kerbo, 1983; Mitchell, 1983; Ostrander, 1984; Rossides, 1976; Vanfossen, 1979; Zablocki and Kanter, 1976.

demic and interpersonal skills, since the children's future social position will depend heavily upon education and occupation.

The lower middle class is moving toward egalitarian relationships between husband and wife as more wives take jobs. Lower-middle-class families may keep close ties with their extended families, since they are likely to live nearby. They value obedience among their children and want schools that stress discipline and respect for adults, the way parochial schools do. Lower-middle-class children are increasingly likely to attend local public college.

The working class marries earlier than any of the preceding groups, and its family life tends to be patriarchal, with roles segregated by sex. Wives are looking for more emotional sharing than existed in traditional working-class families (Rubin, 1976). Extended kin ties are important, and children are expected to be obedient and to respect their elders. Traditional education that stresses discipline and basic skills is preferred over educational innovations such as "open classrooms." College is more uncertain, and technical and vocational education is more likely in this group.

The lower class has less reason to value the nuclear family, which can solve few of its economic problems. Birth rates are high, however. Extended family relations are important for sharing household and child rearing work. Children are pressed into household service, caring for younger children, going to the store, or doing laundry. Parents value education, particularly that stressing basic skills in reading and arithmetic, although the parents may be illiterate or poorly educated themselves. Schools in poor areas tend to be the lowest-quality in the country, with high teacher and pupil turnover. Families may have little choice about where they can send their children to school. Youths frequently drop out and seldom go to college.

## Differences in Personal Values, Style, Residence, Consumer Behavior, and Leisure

The upper class values tradition and the past and emphasizes "good breeding" (manners and personal style), graciousness, and culture. Members

believe in discreet, understated public displays of wealth, emotions, personality, and leisure behavior. "Playboys" exist but tend to be frowned upon. Upper-class homes are often filled with family heirlooms and antiques, and members may vacation in a family compound at the ocean or in the mountains.

The upper middle class values ability and achievement as well as personal development, effort, and growth. Members of this class emphasize high culture, books, and theater; they may also enjoy sports such as sailing, golf, tennis, football, and baseball. Although they may move more often than the upper class, they value having a nice home and a "good address."

The lower middle class seems most concerned with maintaining the appearance of respectability; hence they value cleanliness, frugality, morality, and stability. Their leisure activities are generally home-based and inexpensive. The working class may identify with other working-class people fairly strongly. They know their work does not get as much public respect as white-collar work does. They value home ownership and enjoy working on their homes, cars, trucks, campers, or boats. They like spectator sports, hunting, fishing, and family gatherings.

The lower class feels somewhat isolated socially. It does not participate fully in either the occupational or the consumer and leisure spheres of society, and most of its income goes for food and rent. Members of the lower class live in the poorest housing in an area and generally feel more miserable than others. Leisure activities such as sports may cut across class lines. Where they do not, cultural interests may reinforce occupational differences.

## Differences in Politics, Religion, and Health

The upper class and the upper middle class may play an active role in political, civic, and religious activities. They are most likely to belong to Protestant denominations. They have the best health that money, education, and knowledge can obtain. For example, they are less likely to smoke than are members of lower classes. The lower middle class may be active in rank-and-file political activities, although they are less often in leadership positions than the upper and upper middle classes. They live longer than the working and lower classes.

Catholics make up a larger proportion of the working class than of other classes. Traditionally members of the working class have voted for the Democratic party, although in recent presidential elections about 50 percent have voted Republican. About half the working class belongs to labor unions. Their work often involves health and safety hazards.

Members of the lower class are less active politically than are the other classes. They often belong to fundamentalist or revivalist religious groups. They have the greatest problems with mental and physical health and are least likely to have health insurance from a union or employer to help them deal with such medical problems. As a group, they have the shortest life expectancy.

Overall, then, class situation is quite strongly associated with different attitudes, behaviors, and life chances. It would be useful if these divisions of the class structure could be compared with people's subjective impressions of where they stand and whether or not they feel a sense of membership with that group. Table 9.5 reveals some of the complexity reflected in social classes and may help to explain why class consciousness is not always clearly formulated along a single dimension such as property, relation to the means of production, or income. Family life, neighborhood, residence, racial and gender differences, religion, leisure activities—all these factors and others influence individuals in the social world and shape their identities and their perceptions of the class structure and their place in it.

# POVERTY

One of the starkest features of the American class structure is the widespread existence of poverty. Poverty means babies dying of lead poisoning, old people freezing to death, people living only on macaroni for a month at a time, stunted hopes, and frustrated lives. In an affluent industrial society, the existence of poverty poses sharp contradictions and challenges. Policy makers concerned with poverty have grappled with the problems of how to define it, who is most likely to be poor, the causes of poverty, and what programs might provide relief.

## Definitions of Poverty

Poverty has been defined in both absolute and relative terms. **Absolute poverty** refers to having too little income to buy the necessities of food, shelter, clothing, or health care. The U.S. government and other agencies use an objective standard of what a person or family needs to subsist. In 1987 the poverty level for a family of four was $11,611. The effects of poverty become apparent when we realize that such a budget allows only about $240 a month for rent for a family of four.

In absolute terms, the number of people below the poverty line has increased, from 24.1 million in 1969 to 32.6 million in 1987 (U.S. Bureau of the Census, 1989a). Since the total population has been increasing during this time, it is important to look at the proportion of the population below the poverty line. In 1969, 12.1 percent of the population was in poverty, and by 1987 the figure was up to 13.5 percent.

**Relative poverty** suggests that people are poor if they have much less than the average person in their society has, even if they can afford the necessities of life. Relative poverty may be more significant socially than absolute poverty. Relative poverty means that people cannot afford the material goods and life-styles that most people take for granted, such as electricity, hot and cold running water, a telephone, no rats in one's home, a TV set, and shoes. These may not be necessary for survival, but they are considered social necessities in most parts of the United States. Some analysts suggest that relative poverty causes such antisocial behavior as delinquency, educational apathy, and attacks on the more affluent. Rainwater (1969) suggests this may occur because individuals do not feel they are part of their society.

Poverty measured in relative terms, as a percentage of all income, for example, has not diminished over the last three decades. In 1950 the poorest 20 percent of all families earned 4.5 percent of all income, whereas in 1987 they earned 4.6 percent of all income (U.S. Bureau of the Census, 1989a).

## Who Is Poor?

Poverty is not evenly distributed throughout the population (Figure 9.6). More than half the poor are under the age of 14 or over 65 and are poor because they are unable to work (Retine and Huber, 1974, p. 102). Although two-thirds of all persons below the poverty level are white, the rates of poverty are much higher for non-whites. Only 11 percent of whites but 33 percent of blacks, 28 percent of Hispanics, and more than 50 percent of Native Americans are below the official poverty level. Poverty is more likely to be found in central cities and rural areas than in suburbs. Families headed by women without husbands had a poverty rate of 46 percent, compared to 7 percent for husband-wife families. In short, the poor are disproportionately young, old, inner city or rural, females, and members of a minority.

## What Causes Poverty?

Poverty in the United States is not due to an overall failure to produce enough goods and services. It is, instead, a question of how wealth is distributed. To some extent the same is true on a worldwide scale. Three types of explanations of poverty have been offered: economic, political, and cultural.

### Economic and Structural Explanations

A major cause of poverty is lack of jobs and low wages paid for many jobs. Half the poor families are headed by someone who works, and one-third of those family heads work full time. Someone working full time and earning the minimum wage in 1988 earned $6968, not enough to bring a family of four above the poverty line. Poverty among those who work is due to lower pay for jobs traditionally filled by unskilled workers, minorities, and women.

Unemployment contributes to poverty, particularly in one-earner families. In 1987 the U.S. unemployment rate was 6.1 percent (with 7.4 million Americans out of work). Unemploy-

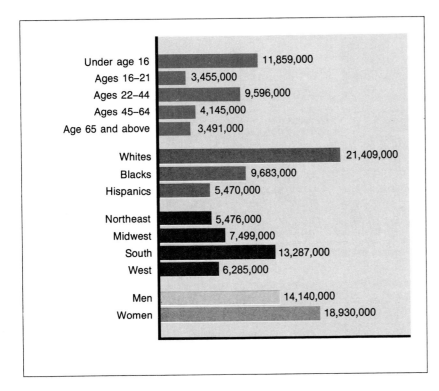

**Figure 9.6   Who Was Poor in 1984?**

Many more of the poor are young rather than old, white rather than black or Hispanic, and women rather than men. They are more likely to live in the South than in other regions, although there are millions of poor people in every region of the United States.

*Source:* U.S. Bureau of the Census, 1987, p. 35; 1989a, p. 454.

*Herbert Gans suggests that the existence of poor people contributes to the comfort of the middle and upper classes, because poor people are willing to do less attractive work that makes the lives of members of the higher classes more pleasant.*

ment is much higher among young people, older people, and minorities. Recent unemployment has been due to extensive layoffs, particularly in manufacturing industries such as automobiles, as well as to the limited number of new jobs. Many people listed as having jobs are actually "underemployed"—for example, more college graduates are filling clerical jobs. Such individuals are not represented in unemployment figures.

Unemployment rates vary among industrial countries. In 1987 the rate was 8.9 percent in Canada, 2.9 percent in Japan, 1.9 percent in Sweden, 6.9 percent in West Germany, and 10.3 percent in Britain (U.S. Bureau of the Census, 1989a). These rate differences may be partly due to economic conditions, such as rates of savings and productivity increases. Political as well as economic causes also lie behind unemployment and poverty. Rates of unemployment that are tolerated in the United States are considered politically unacceptable in Japan, Sweden, and West Germany. Their lower rates result in part from government policies to minimize unemployment.

### Political Explanations

Poverty and chronic unemployment do not appear to be a major political issue in the United States. Except for President Lyndon Johnson's War on Poverty in the 1960s, recent political campaigns have focused more on building military strength and patriotic issues than on redistributing wealth and income in the United States.

The existence of poverty serves the interests of many who are more rich and powerful than the poor, suggests Herbert Gans (1971). Without poverty, much of society's dirty work would not get done; the prices of many goods and services (like housecleaning) would be much higher; many welfare workers, government bureaucrats, pawnbrokers, and police officers would be unemployed; merchants could not unload their shoddy furniture, dented canned goods, or day-old bread; and some group other than the poor would need to bear the costs of change and growth in American society—for example, relocation in the face of a new highway or cultural complex. Thus, suggests Gans, in many direct and indirect ways the existence of poor people contributes to the comfort of the middle and upper classes.[1]

Welfare programs are a major means of regulating the political and economic behavior of the poor, argue Piven and Cloward (1971). They suggest that relief programs expand in periods of mass unemployment and threats to civil disorder. When threats of civil disorder subside, welfare programs become more restrictive and aim more directly at reinforcing work norms. Piven and Cloward do not deny the value of work in all societies. Their point is, however, that welfare policies help to maintain inequities by "defining and enforcing the terms on which different classes" are made to do various kinds of work. In this way the political and economic significance of welfare and unemployment insurance is that it makes some people "do the harshest work for the least reward" (Piven and Cloward, 1971, p. xvii). Many people in our society, however, may be unwilling to view poverty as a political and economic issue and be more likely to "blame the victims" for being poor. This approach is reflected in cultural explanations of poverty.

### Cultural Explanations

Some social scientists suggest that cultural differences between the poor and others in society explain their predicament. Anthropologist Oscar Lewis (1965) suggests that a distinct **culture of poverty** develops as a reaction to political and economic exclusion in a society. This culture is characterized by the unwillingness to delay gratification, especially regarding sex and alcohol; a fatalistic view that one's own efforts are useless and can do nothing to change things; and a weak commitment to family and community. This culture is passed on from one generation to the next, making it difficult or impossible for individuals to break out of the cycle of poverty. "Culture of poverty" explanations suggest that cultural values must change before poverty can be eliminated.

[1] On the other hand, it may be argued that the costs to the middle and upper classes in terms of crime, vandalism, and loss of productive labor, as well as the costs of controlling and regulating the poor, may at some point outweigh the benefits Gans describes. At that point, a rational model would predict that social changes should occur.

Moynihan's (1967) work on the disintegration of the black family shows that it was brought about by slavery and that the resulting "tangle of pathology" passed poverty and problems from one generation of blacks to the next; it has striking similarities to the "culture of poverty" view. Similarly, Banfield (1960) suggests that the cause of poverty is the present rather than future orientation of poor people. In these views, people must change their attitudes if they are to escape poverty. Other anthropologists challenge the idea that the culture of poverty is passed from one generation to the next. They argue that each generation faces the conditions of political isolation and economic deprivation that may create similar behaviors in each succeeding generation. When economic conditions improve, individuals will change their behavior and values and escape poverty. It is these conditions, rather than culture, they say, that explains the poverty of certain groups.

Although many academic social scientists have challenged and qualified the "culture of poverty" explanation, it appears to strike a responsive chord in Americans, who have a strong faith in an "ideology of individualism" (Feagin, 1975). The absence of an entrenched aristocracy

*A cultural explanation of poverty suggests that the attitudes and values of the poor cause poverty to be transmitted from one generation to the next.*

and the existence of free land and economic opportunities in the American past generated a tremendous faith in the value of individual effort. Hard work paid off handsomely for many early settlers. In many people's minds hard work and success were seen as going hand in hand. Therefore it was easy to conclude that the unsuccessful must be lazy or otherwise personally responsible for their poverty.

Despite changes in the availability of free land and economic opportunities in American society and the emergence of a wealthy class, beliefs in hard work and equal opportunity persist, perhaps because they are functional for some individuals even if they inaccurately represent society as a whole. Studies find that Americans still tend to consider individual factors more important for explaining poverty than structural factors like chronic unemployment or fatalistic factors like poor health (Feagin, 1972; Huber and Form, 1973). Huber and Form, however, found that poor people and blacks considered personal qualities less important than did whites, the middle class, and the rich.

Perhaps because of the absence of formally structured inequality in their heritage, Americans tend to avoid searching for structural explanations for either success or failure. This tendency is reflected in the remarkably consistent attitudes of young people in Muncie, Indiana, in 1924 and 1977. Muncie was first described in the famous *Middletown* study conducted by Robert and Helen Lynd in 1924 (published in 1929) and in a 1977 replication study by Theodore Caplow, Howard M. Bahr, and Bruce A. Chadwick. Both teams of investigators asked high school students whether they agreed or disagreed with the statement "It is entirely the fault of a man himself if he does not succeed." In both 1924 and 1977 exactly the same percentage of students (47 percent) agreed with that statement (Caplow and Bahr, 1979). This result suggests that nearly half the young people surveyed still believe in complete individual responsibility for success or failure; they discounted health, race, or social class background as factors.

But a widespread belief in individualistic explanations for poverty does not mean they are correct. Regional and cross-national differences in the rates of poverty strongly support a structural rather than a purely individual explanation.

## Antipoverty Policies

The most far-reaching antipoverty policy would result in full employment at a living wage. This situation has nearly been accomplished in a number of western European countries but has not received wide support in the United States. Instead we have had a series of welfare programs. The poor ordinarily have little influence on government. Therefore the social welfare policies that exist cannot be assumed to serve their best interests (Piven and Cloward, 1971). Old-age pensions and unemployment insurance may benefit some, but only certain people are eligible. You need to have worked at some point and be certified as unneeded in the labor force, either because of old age or because your job ended. Many jobs (for example, some domestic servants and agricultural workers) are denied the benefits of such insurance programs (Piven and Cloward, 1971).

Aside from these programs, the two major types of welfare are Aid to Families with Dependent Children (AFDC) and supplemental security income (SSI). About 15 million Americans receive some form of publicly labeled assistance, or welfare, each year. Nearly three quarters of them receive AFDC; the remaining recipients comprise the aged, blind, or disabled, who are eligibe for supplemental security income. Only about three out of five of those below the poverty line are receiving public assistance.[2] The rest are the working poor or those on private pensions.

In the decade of the 1960s the welfare rolls rose to 2.4 million families, an increase of 225 percent for the decade. By 1979 the figure had reached 3.6 million families. This increase, suggest Piven and Cloward, was due to the government's anti-inflation strategy, the welfare system's high rate of accepting applications, and changing attitudes toward going on welfare. Public assistance had come increasingly to be viewed as a right rather than as something to be

[2] The fact that about 40 percent of the poor do not receive public assistance may not be too surprising if Piven and Cloward (1971) are right in arguing that the growth of modern welfare systems may be due more to the effort to control and silence the poor than to the desire to improve their situations.

*Public assistance has increasingly come to be viewed as a right rather than as something shameful.*

ashamed of. The average monthly payment to families with dependent children was $365 in 1987, or a total of $4380 per year (U.S. Bureau of the Census, 1989a).

Many people do not regard the expansion of the welfare rolls as an acceptable antipoverty policy. After each expansion in the past, suggest Piven and Cloward, there has been a reaction aimed first at imposing work requirements and second at the expulsion of large numbers of people from the relief rolls, pushing them into a labor market with too little work. Those who were allowed to remain on the relief rolls (some blind and aged) were treated in the punitive and degrading way that all past recipients of relief had been (Piven and Cloward, 1971).

The Family Security Act of 1988 requires mothers with pre-school-age children to find jobs and support themselves. If they are not employable, they must finish high school and enter a job-training program. The bill also requires fathers to provide child support. The law allows states to require "blood tests and genetic typing" for suspected fathers. If fathers are unemployed or poorly paid, states may require them to enter training programs. This does not address the problem of fathers without money, such as the 850,000 men in state, federal, and local jails, the drug- or alcohol-addicted, and the homeless. Also, the act does not provide for the estimated 1.5 million new child-care places needed by mothers who would, presumably, be added to the work force (Hacker, 1988). The act

assumes that existing and new job training programs are effective and that new jobs will exist for those required to find work. It removes the option for welfare recipients of caring for their own preschoolers, an option that is open to many women who are not on welfare. In this sense it represents a more coercive policy than AFDC.

Over a ten-year period more than one in four Americans lived in a family that received some income from welfare sources at least once. Short-term welfare use is common, but continuing dependency on welfare is not. Only 2 percent of the U.S. population was persistently and heavily dependent on welfare income for more than seven years out of the ten studied (Duncan, 1983–1984). Thus, the need for welfare persists, but the people who need it change over time.

There is, however, another form of welfare in the United States, although it is not publicly labeled and stigmatized. This form of welfare includes various market subsidies, including government contracts—for example, for computers, airplanes, tanks, or jeeps; price programs for dairy and agricultural products; and export-import policies that place tariffs on goods competing with major U.S. industries. In addition, a series of federal tax loopholes protects those who have some money to invest. These include income exclusions, such as the interest paid on municipal bonds; deductions such as the interest

*The Family Security Act of 1988 requires welfare mothers with preschool children to find jobs and support themselves.*

paid on a home mortgage; and tax credits for business investments.

Many people with modest incomes may depend on such programs or subsidies to stay afloat, and strong arguments can be made to support their economic or social value. People with more money benefit more than people with less money. It is important to realize, however, that such programs represent a form of state subsidy for investors and businesspeople and therefore resemble other social welfare programs.

The unequal effects of such policies is documented by a Brookings Institution study which found that $92 million a year in tax breaks goes to the poorest 6 million families in the United States, whereas $2.2 billion (24 times as much) flows to only 3000 families with incomes of more than $1 million per year (Stern, 1972).

Proposals to reduce absolute poverty in the United States include ideas for tax reform, job programs to reduce unemployment, more public assistance, a guaranteed annual income, and organizing the poor to demand changes. Limited efforts have been made to effect tax reform, extend public assistance, and organize the poor. The guaranteed annual income proposal has never gone beyond the discussion stage. The Reagan administration urged private charity rather than public efforts to overcome poverty. In such a climate, poverty is a long way from being eliminated.

In a controversial book called *Losing Ground,* Charles Murray (1984) suggests that the circumstances of the poor have worsened as a result of the War on Poverty and the programs of the Great Society in the 1960s. Many social scientists have challenged Murray, some quarreling with his choice of data and others disagreeing with his interpretations (Coe and Duncan, 1985; Greenstein, 1985; Jencks, 1985; and McLanahan et al., 1985). A group of researchers at the Institute for Research on Poverty have critically scrutinized Murray's book. They question his general condemnation of the Great Society programs because they find that those programs have achieved at least some of their goals. They agree with him that we need some new approaches to reduce poverty and crime, stabilize families, improve educational achievements, and encourage self-reliance (*Focus,* 1985).

The widespread persistence of poverty might be expected to increase class consciousness and militancy. Although poverty persists at the societal level, however, many individuals move in and out of poverty over the course of their lives. The existence of individual mobility, at both the poverty level and above, seems to play a major role in dampening class consciousness.

## CLASS CONSCIOUSNESS AND SOCIAL MOBILITY

However social class is measured, vast differences exist in ownership, income, and prestige. Why is it, then, that the United States has not witnessed the rise of a class-conscious and militant working class? Compared to other industrial nations such as France, Italy, or Great Britain, the United States has experienced much less unified social and political action directed at changing the existing inequalities. The blurring of class consciousness and a preoccupation with social mobility may explain the lack of unified opposition to the class structure.

### Class Consciousness

**Class consciousness** refers to the sense of common class position and interests. But class differences do not necessarily create class consciousness. The upper class may be most aware of their common class interests and most cohesive in their actions (Baltzell, 1964; Domhoff, 1967; Useem, 1980). The working class is much less cohesive as a class than Marx predicted. Although labor unions represent class interests to a degree, there is no working-class political party in the United States, nor are class issues often expressed in other political ways. There were several protracted and bloody general strikes in the United States between 1870 and 1900, which certainly showed working-class consciousness. Why didn't this militancy continue? Several factors seem to have undermined class consciousness in the American working class. The early twentieth century was marked by waves of new immigrants of different ethnic backgrounds as well as by violent repression of the strikes that did occur. Racial and ethnic rivalries cut across economic similarities in the working class. In recent years the working class has consisted heavily of minorities and women. These social differences may lessen any shared sense of class consciousness.

The importance of class boundaries may be reduced by wide variations in income within the working class and considerable overlap in the incomes and consumer behaviors of the working and middle classes. Although the poor are not highly visible, people know they are there, and their existence may serve to make people in the working and lower middle classes feel relatively better off, compared to the poor. Differences between the working class and the lower middle class are not so great in income terms, although white-collar workers tend to have more job security and benefits. Since the vast majority of the population falls into one of these two social classes and most of their contact is with members of their own or a neighboring class, they have little direct experience with vast class differences. The upper middle class and, to an even greater extent, the upper class keep a low profile and have limited social contact with the lower middle and the working classes. Income differences are justified on the grounds that they are earned (by superior education, experience, and talent), and property differences tend to be buried in corporate holdings. Exclusive residential areas, clubs, and schools keep the wealthy and powerful from being too visible.

In addition, America has been noted since its beginning as a "land of opportunity" where a person could become an *individual* success, regardless of social or economic background. So the ideology of individual success and mobility is part of the national culture and to some extent works against development of a more inclusive class consciousness. In the early years of this nation the availability of land and rich natural resources, a shortage of labor, and a robustly growing economy fed people's hopes that effort and opportunity could create individual progress (at least for white males). In this century, as the white-collar segment of the labor force grew much faster than the blue-collar portion, people had the experience of occupational mobility, if not their own at least that of their children or of people they knew. This mobility could be cited as evidence that opportunities exist for people with "ability" and the willingness to work hard. Social mobility was facilitated by geographical mobility. Individuals could move to a new region where no one knew their families or their social origins.

The development of class consciousness may be further depressed by the way Americans (more than any other nationality) seem to strive for status; that is, they seem to adopt the trappings, symbols, or other material goods of an affluent life-style. A secretary may buy a fur coat, whereas a college professor probably would not. Fads such as particular styles of sneakers may sweep the country, cutting across class lines. In this way status striving and common patterns of consumption may blur class boundaries. Status striving may reflect the ideology of upward mobility, and that ideology may reduce class consciousness and therefore fortify the class structure. Individuals preoccupied with rising or falling in the social hierarchy are not likely to challenge the existence of the class structure. The preoccupation with social mobility in American society is reflected in numerous studies of social mobility by sociologists.

## Social Mobility

"Getting ahead" is a central element in the American dream. As a source of popular concern, it is reflected in the popularity of autobiographies by "self-made men" such as Lee Iacocca and Donald Trump and in TV shows like *The Beverly Hillbillies*. Sociological researchers are also very interested in the subject. They define **social mobility** as the movement from one status to another within a stratified society.

Social mobility in the United States is usually examined in terms of occupation and only occasionally in terms of income. In general terms, **vertical mobility** refers to individual or group movement upward or downward in the social hierarchy, but the possibility of downward mobility is seldom considered. **Horizontal mobility** involves moving from one social status to another of about equal rank, such as changing

*Chrysler Corporation chairman Lee Iacocca wrote a popular autobiography that described his rise from modest circumstances. The theme of "making it" or "getting ahead" has been a central element in American culture.*

from one job to another similar one. Various types of mobility are summarized in Table 9.6. Most researchers focus on mobility from one generation to another. **Intergenerational mobility** refers to a vertical change of social status from one generation to the next. In most studies of mobility, the son's occupational status is compared with his father's in part because relatively few mothers and daughters worked in the 1950s and 1960s.

There is also the chance of mobility within the lifetime of an individual. **Intragenerational mobility** refers to the vertical mobility experienced by a single individual within his or her own lifetime. Someone may rise from a modest beginning to a position of high income or prestige, or aristocrats may lose their property and position in a social revolution. Although they are infrequent, rapid shifts in social location have always captured the American imagina-

tion. The most drastic shifts in social position occur during social revolutions when one class is deposed or foreign rulers are overthrown. This change creates opportunities for different individuals, groups, or classes to rise in the social hierarchy.

Structural changes affect rates of social mobility. With the advent of the industrial revolution, upward mobility became more likely than downward mobility because industrialization meant the expansion of higher-status and better-paid positions, whereas farm jobs continued to shrink. In 1900 there were 10 farm workers for every professional and technical worker (Blau and Duncan, 1967); today there are 2 professionals and technicians for every farmer. Gradual change in the occupational structure—with the expansion of clerical, technical, and professional employment and the decline of manual and farm work—explains a great deal of the upward mobility in Western industrial societies. Besides changes in the occupational structure, upward mobility has been increased by class differences in fertility rates. The upper and upper middle classes tend to have fewer children than lower-class families, thereby possibly creating occupational vacancies that lower-status individuals can fill.

How much mobility has there traditionally been in American society? Faith in the opportunity for individual and intergenerational mobility has always fueled the hopes of Americans. In the nineteenth century, unskilled and semiskilled laborers such as factory workers and farmers did experience some mobility, but generally only a step or two up the occupational ladder (Thernstrom, 1964). In a historical study of business executives, Lipset and Bendix (1959) found that it was about as difficult to move from a working-class background to a business career in the late eighteenth century as it was early in the twentieth century.

Patterns of mobility in the twentieth century are similar. In their massive study of more than 20,000 males and their fathers, Blau and Duncan (1967) found that lifetime and intergenerational mobility was frequent but limited in scope. Most people tended to move up only a step or two, and most moves occurred *within* the white-collar, blue-collar, or farm sectors rather than among those occupational divisions.

**Table 9.6**  *Types of Social Mobility*

| Type of Mobility | Unit Experiencing Mobility | |
| | Individuals | Groups |
| --- | --- | --- |
| Horizontal | No change in the position of the individual in the social hierarchy—a factory worker moves from one factory to another | No change in the position of a group in the social hierarchy. A group of salespeople moves from one organization to another similar one |
| Vertical | Involves a change, upward or downward, of the individual in the social hierarchy | Involves a change in the location of a group in the social hierarchy—the prestige of scientists has risen in industrial societies, whereas that of the clergy has declined |
| Intragenerational | Individuals are vertically mobile within their own adult lifetimes | A group is vertically mobile within the lifetime of its members |
| Intergenerational | Children of individuals are vertically mobile—the child of a truck driver becomes a business executive, the child of a doctor becomes a short-order cook | A group is mobile from one generation to the next. The children of lower-status parents move up or the children of higher-status parents move down |
| Geographical | Individuals move from one place to another | Groups migrate from one region to another |

## Status–Attainment Research

How much mobility is *ascribed* (due to characteristics at birth, such as social class, ethnicity, or gender) and how much is *achieved* (through effort, talent, education, and so forth)?

The intergenerational occupational status of individuals seems to be explained by two major factors—educational level, especially higher education, and family background. By comparing the relative success of brothers, Jencks et al. (1979) found that family background explains nearly half of the difference in occupational status and about a quarter of the difference in annual earnings. Educational background has a comparable effect on occupational status and earnings. Education appears to increase earnings mainly by opening the door to high-status (and high-paying) occupations (Jencks et al., 1979). In short, family background is important, but education also makes a difference.

Extensive research on social mobility has been done within this **status-attainment model,** which was developed initially by Blau and Duncan (1967). It showed the relative importance of father's education, father's occupation, son's education, and son's first job for the status of the son's occupation. (Women were not included because so few women were working when the data were collected.) The model was expanded by Wisconsin researchers, who added several social psychological variables—including mental ability, academic performance, the role of significant others, educational aspirations, occupational aspirations, and educational attainment—as predictors of occupational status (Sewell, Haller, and Ohlendorf, 1970).

The status-attainment model has shed impressive light on how the background and achievement of *individuals* is related to the occupation and earnings they attain. In recent years this model has been usefully supplemented by models that include structural factors as well as individual attributes. The status-attainment model rests within the functionalist theoretical tradition. At least three major limits to the status-attainment model have been noted by scholars working within a conflict (or allocation) perspective. These include the following:

1. The incomplete explanatory power of the model, especially with respect to income. It is less able to explain the income of non-whites and females than of white males (Wright, 1978; Wolf and Fligstein, 1971).
2. By focusing on occupational status, the model overlooks other important dimensions of stratification, including authority, property, and power.
3. The exclusive attention to individuals means that the model does not include important structural factors. These include gender, race, characteristics of the labor market, characteristics of firms, and the nature of the economy. (These factors are discussed in Chapters 10, 11, and 13.)

When social structural and individual attributes are combined, more of the variation in income, for example, is explained (Kalleberg and Griffin, 1980; Wright and Perrone, 1977).

How does recent social mobility in the United States compare with past rates? Research suggests that the rates of intergenerational mobility did not change between 1962 and 1973 but that individuals in their own lifetimes may experience more mobility between their first and their current occupations than was true in the past (Featherman and Hauser, 1978). This finding suggests that individuals now may expect more mobility within their own careers than was the case in 1962, but that rates of intergenerational mobility have changed little.

Social researchers have recently begun discussing a less attractive feature of social mobility, namely downward mobility. In the face of contracting economic opportunities, one in five workers is being pushed down the mobility ladder. They earn less, have fewer prospects for advancement, and suffer a severe loss of status and self-respect (Newman, 1988).

Social mobility may have mixed effects on individuals. At the societal level, however, the possibility and the ideology of social mobility encourages individual striving rather than collective action. In this way it may reduce class consciousness and lessen the chances of changing a society's class structure.

## STRATIFICATION IN OTHER INDUSTRIAL SOCIETIES

How are things in the United States compared to other countries? Is there more or less stratification elsewhere? Is there more or less social mobility?

### Is the USSR a Classless Society?

How much stratification and social mobility exist in a socialist country like the Soviet Union? The Soviet Union does not have private ownership of major productive resources, so there are no huge inequalities based on property that can be passed on from one generation to another. Political and economic authority have merged, and political and economic elites are the same. There are income and prestige differences between occupations, however. High-level administrators in industry and the government are at the top, followed by skilled manual workers, lower-level white-collar workers, and unskilled manual workers. Members of the top level, the so-called white-collar intelligentsia, have joined the Communist party in increasing numbers in recent decades. Although some of their social and economic advantage derives from occupational status, being in the inner party circle gives additional advantages—for example, the capacity to pull strings and get favored treatment with respect to placing one's child in a good school or university, obtaining the best theater tickets, or gaining a better apartment (Lenski, 1979; Parkin, 1971; Zaslavsky, 1980). Persons in such high-ranking positions are able to give their children educational advantages that serve to pass privileges from one generation to the next.

At the same time, several features suggest a less rigid system of stratification than exists in the West (Lenski, 1979; Simirenko, 1972). The less well born also have good chances for social advancement, and their parents have high ambitions; there is less distinction between elite culture and mass culture than in the West; and skilled workers may be taught new skills that enable them to advance.

Income differences are not as great in the Soviet Union as in the United States. But housing, cars, and consumer goods are very scarce. Party officials and other members of the elite have special housing, private transportation, and better medical care; they can also shop at special stores (Matthews, 1978; Yanowitch, 1977). There is a fairly high level of intergenerational social mobility in the Soviet Union (Kerbo, 1983, p. 417).

In addition to the distribution of privileges according to occupational and party positions, state-socialist societies have a totalitarian authority structure in which the party monopolizes the decision-making processes. Although such societies do not appear to have classes based on economic ownership, they do have a system of stratification based on occupational and party positions.

## Countries with Less Social Stratification

Although social inequalities still exist in such countries as Sweden, Denmark, and Norway, those nations do provide free medical care and free preschool care for children. Sweden has a state-controlled medical system that produces abundant numbers of doctors and dentists, so that they almost face an unemployment problem and are paid less well than American medics. Swedish taxpayers, however, receive extensive medical benefits (Kesselman, 1982; Stephens, 1979). The ample number of medical professionals notwithstanding, unemployment in general is very low. The Swedish government operates a job placement service, pays moving expenses, and provides unemployment grants until people are reemployed. Each time a child is born, the family receives a cash payment at the time of the child's birth and a tax-free annual allowance until the child is 16. These allowances are designed to provide adequate support for each child in society regardless of how much money the parents have. Roughly 90 percent of all families have similar incomes. As a result, most Scandinavians are healthy and well fed (Vanfossen, 1979). Extremes of poverty and wealth do not exist to the same extent as in the United States.

In Taiwan, conscious government planning has been aimed at reducing economic inequality. In 1953 the bottom 40 percent of Taiwan's population received only 11 percent of the country's income, whereas the top 20 percent got 61 percent. During the 1950s the government instituted a free public education system through college; it also implemented land-reform programs and took control over the tobacco, oil, and liquor industries. By 1975 the bottom 40 percent of the population was receiving 22 percent of the country's income, whereas the top 20 percent's portion was reduced to 39 percent. These changes in the distribution of income occurred at a time when Taiwan's economy was growing rapidly, so the process may have been less painful for the privileged strata.

Not all countries with such high growth rates have managed to shift income allocations, however. In Brazil and Mexico, which have similar growth rates, the bottom 40 percent of the population earns 10 percent of the income, and the top 20 percent controls more than 60 percent. The Philippines has a similar gap (Butterfield, 1977). These examples suggest that income redistribution is a political rather than an economic question.

Wealth inequalities, however, seem even less susceptible to political reform than income inequalities. Revolution seems to be the major way that property and wealth have been redistributed, as in Cuba, China, and the Soviet Union. Such societies have reduced inequality by wealth, but they have increased the power of the state over individuals. The major base for inequality in such societies has shifted from wealth to the political, administrative, organizational, and police power of the state.

Both Cuba and China have struggled to develop participatory practices and to minimize the advantages conferred by more privilege positions. This suggests that efforts to diminish stratification require conscious analysis, planning, and practices (such as job rotations) designed to neutralize the principle of cumulative advantage. The fact that both the Cuban and Chinese societies are primarily agrarian rather than industrial raises questions about whether such an approach can work in highly industrial societies. The social policies of the Scandinavian countries and Taiwan, however, suggest that many of the worst features of social inequality—grossly unequal health care and life expectancy, educational programs, and family support—can be reduced even in highly industrialized countries. It is clear that income inequality can be reduced if not eliminated. The issue is one of structural stratification rather than economic feasibility.

## SUMMARY

1. Social class has been defined in different ways. American sociologists tend to define class in terms of social status or honor. Weber stressed status-group membership and market position, referring to how successfully one could sell his or her labor in the marketplace. A third view emphasizes position in the authority structure of an organization. Marx saw social classes as rooted in property ownership and the social organization of production. Each approach adds an important dimension.

2. Theoretical ideas of class affect the way class is measured in social research. Some researchers have asked people to rank the prestige, or status, of various occupations. The educational level and income of the people in an occupation are the best predictors of its rank.

3. Sometimes income levels are used to set up class categories. However, people with similar incomes may have widely different life-styles and world views, whereas people with quite different incomes may be fairly similar in outlook. Therefore, other measures of social class are better than income.

4. Marxians stress that economic ownership rather than income lies behind class differences. Wealth is distributed much more unequally than is income. The top fifth of the U.S. population owns or controls three-quarters of the wealth in the nation, whereas the bottom fifth owns less than 0.2 percent of that wealth. In contrast, the top fifth earns 43.7 percent of all income, whereas the bottom fifth earns 4.6 percent.

5. When class is defined as position within the social relations of production, that definition includes aspects of ownership, authority, and market position. Defined this way, class is related to both income and power within an organization.

6. The preceding measures of class depend on so-called objective criteria, but individuals' subjective perceptions of their own class position are also important, particularly for understanding their attitudes and behaviors.

7. A number of these features of class come together when sociologists describe the life chances and life-styles of different classes. In general terms, their greater resources—including wealth, income, education, and knowledge—are reflected in the values and behaviors of the upper classes, whereas the lack of such resources shapes the attitudes and actions of the lower classes.

8. Although designating some people as "poor" is somewhat arbitrary, the existence of large numbers of low-income people in an extremely affluent society warrants examination.

9. The poor are defined in absolute terms as those falling below a certain income level and in relative terms as those having much less than the average person in a society. In the United States, poor people are more likely to be under 14 or over 65, inner-city or rural, and female. The rates of poverty within groups are highest for Native Americans, blacks, and Hispanics.

10. The existence of absolute poverty in the United States is due to the way wealth and income are distributed, since enough goods and services are produced to meet the minimal needs of everyone.

11. Economic and structural explanations for poverty locate its source in the overall shortage of jobs and the existence of many low-paying jobs. Such explanations also emphasize the systematic exclusion of minorities, women, the young, and the old from better-paying and more secure jobs.

12. Political explanations focus on how powerful and privileged groups benefit from the existence of poverty in society. As a result, political pressure to eliminate poverty remains weak.

13. Cultural explanations suggest that the

poor develop a "culture of poverty" that is passed on to future generations and makes it difficult or impossible for individuals to break out of the cycle of poverty. Critics of that view say that when economic and political conditions change, people change their cultures. Focusing on culture as a cause of poverty, however, diverts attention from its underlying structural roots.

14. The largest program for dealing with poverty has been the Aid to Families with Dependent Children (AFDC) or welfare system, although only three out of five of those below the poverty line receive public assistance. Because of a strong tradition of individualism in American society, such public assistance has been stigmatized and given reluctantly in many states.

15. The Family Security Act of 1988 increased requirements for paternal support and work by welfare mothers.

16. Other forms of public assistance—including market subsidies, price programs, import quotas, and tax loopholes—are not stigmatized and are not called welfare, even though the amounts of money involved are very great.

17. Given the existence of poverty and of wide class inequalities, one might expect to find intense class consciousness and conflict in the United States. Instead, class consciousness appears to be relatively low, perhaps because of leisure time diversions, styles of consumption that cross class lines, and a distinctly American ideology of upward mobility.

18. Sociologists have studied social mobility a great deal. Their focus has been on mobility in terms of occupational status rather than in terms of income or ownership.

19. Status-attainment models reveal the individual factors that influence the status of occupations attained by white males. This functionalist approach is usefully supplemented by structural factors such as gender; race; and features of labor markets, firms, or economies.

Income variations are explained better when property and authority features of jobs are added to occupational status and the above structural factors.

20. Major studies indicate that occupational mobility both within an individual's lifetime and between generations is frequent but limited in scope. Most people move up only a step or two with respect to occupational prestige, and most moves are within the major sectors of white-collar, blue-collar, or farm work rather than among those occupational divisions.

21. Most of the individual upward mobility in Western industrial societies has not been due to the replacement of people higher in the social hierarchy with those from lower backgrounds but rather to the expansion of the professional, management, and clerical sectors. Hence most existing mobility is due to structural changes.

22. The same is true of the Soviet Union. It has done away with inequalities based on private property ownership, but it has considerable inequality rooted in occupational and party hierarchies.

23. Several industrialized countries have successfully reduced income inequalities and eliminated the extreme poverty that afflicts 33 million Americans. They have done this with extensive taxation and state subsidies. In a rapidly growing economy such as that of Taiwan, the process of income redistribution may be less painful for the upper strata than it would be in an economy that was growing more slowly. Stratification by wealth has been reduced mainly by social revolutions, such as those in the USSR and Cuba. The result appears to have been to shift the type of stratification from one based on wealth to one rooted in state political power.

24. Nevertheless, the social policies of the Scandinavian countries and Taiwan suggest that the worst features of social stratification (dismal poverty and greatly diminished life chances) can be reduced even in industrialized capitalist countries.

## KEY TERMS

absolute poverty (p. 216)
class consciousness (p. 222)
culture of poverty (p. 219)
horizontal mobility (p. 223)
income (p. 205)
intergenerational mobility (p. 224)
intragenerational mobility (p. 224)
life-style (p. 213)
relative poverty (p. 216)
social class (p. 201)
social mobility (p. 223)
social relations of production (p. 207)
socioeconomic status (SES) (p. 202)
status-attainment model (p. 225)
subjective social class (p. 208)
vertical mobility (p. 223)

## SUGGESTED READINGS

Blackburn, McKinley L., and David E. Bloom. 1985. "What Is Happening to the Middle Class?" *American Demographics* (January): 18–25. Presents data on the shift in the incomes of different groups in the United States.

Kerbo, Harold S. 1983. *Social Stratification and Inequality: Class Conflict in the United States.* New York: McGraw-Hill. Develops a conflict analysis of social stratification in the United States. Brings in cross-cultural comparative work.

Murray, Charles. 1984. *Losing Ground.* New York: Basic Books. A highly controversial book suggesting that the federal government's efforts to lessen poverty over the last two decades have failed.

Piven, Frances Fox, and Richard Cloward. 1982. *The New Class Wars: Reagan's War on the Welfare State and Its Consequences.* New York: Pantheon. A neo-Marxian analysis of the conservative Republican agenda for social change.

# Racial and Ethnic Stratification

*"My fellow immigrants," was the way President Franklin D. Roosevelt once addressed the DAR (Daughters of the American Revolution), a group that prided itself on its early American origins. Roosevelt's remark was intended to remind them that—like current immigrants—their ancestors, too, had come from a place where they may have belonged to an oppressed racial, ethnic, or religious minority.*

Human beings display a wide variety of colors, shapes, and cultures. Even without traveling all over the world, we can witness this variety in any major urban center in North America—Boston, Chicago, Los Angeles, Milwaukee, New Orleans, Phoenix, New York, Mexico City, Montreal, or Toronto. Some of the observable differences among peoples are genetically linked, others are purely cultural. Even where racial differences are genetic, however, the importance attached to such differences is social rather than biological.

Sociologists try to understand the significance of social differences based on ethnic distinctions. They try to explain why relations between ethnic groups are sometimes marked by conflict, hostility, and prejudice and sometimes notable for their peaceful, cooperative, and friendly nature. The United States has much more cultural, racial, and ethnic diversity than most societies. Therefore it provides a fascinating opportunity to observe and understand various forms of intergroup relations.

Before exploring ethnic relations, I shall briefly define race and ethnicity. In the first section of this chapter, we'll consider theoretical explanations for group conflict or peaceful coexistence. The second section analyzes the consequences of ethnic antagonism when it occurs. In light of these theoretical issues, we are then in a position to consider the historical and current situations of major ethnic groups in the United States. The fourth section examines the relative importance of race and class for social behavior. We conclude by assessing current and future prospects for ethnic relations in the United States.

Race and ethnicity are not the same thing. An **ethnic group** is one that shares a common ancestry. Ethnicity is characterized by "shared beliefs, norms, values, preferences, in-group memories, loyalties, and consciousness of kind" (See and Wilson, 1988, p. 224). Membership is inherited, regardless of whether members can currently be physically distinguished (Bonacich, 1972, p. 548). An ethnic group often has its own language and religion, along with distinctive customs.

A racial-ethnic group has race as part of its common ancestry. The sociological concept of **race** refers to a group of people who see themselves and are seen by others as having certain

*Urban scenes in many North American cities reveal ethnic and cultural diversity.*

aspects of racial groups (See and Wilson, 1988, p. 224).

A **minority group** is any racial or ethnic group that suffers from some disadvantage resulting from the action of a dominant group with higher social status and greater privileges. Minority-group members are excluded from full participation in the life of a society. Sometimes a minority group may even constitute a numerical majority, as is the case of blacks in South Africa or French-speaking Canadians in the province of Quebec. The critical point is not numbers but how the group members are treated by the more powerful group or groups in society.

Not all racial and ethnic groups are treated as minority groups in society, even when they are outnumbered. Switzerland, for example, consists of a political confederation of German-speaking, French-speaking, Italian-speaking, and Romansch-speaking ethnic groups. Each has constitutionally and legally protected rights that are codified in institutional policies. No group receives unequal treatment or discrimination at the hands of any other group. Virtually everyone in the society is multilingual, so people are able to communicate with one another. It is possible to observe two Swiss people speaking, one in German, the other in French or Italian, and understanding each other perfectly. Why is it that ethnic groups in Switzerland coexist

distinctive physical traits. It is essential to realize that race is a socially constructed rather than a biological concept. Sometimes individuals belong to the same racial or ethnic social groups; for example, when they share certain physical traits and cultural experiences. The concept of race has been used to classify human beings into several subdivisions based on physical characteristics. There are no biologically pure racial groups, however. Moreover, within each racial cluster, there are wide variations. Race, therefore, is a social rather than a biological concept. Racial groups can be included in the term "ethnic groups." For these reasons, the terms "ethnic group" and "ethnicity," rather than "race," are generally used by social scientists. These are social concepts, and they include the significant

*An ethnic group shares a common ancestry and common beliefs, norms, values, and loyalties. This "bamboo group" from the Philippines is performing in the United States.*

*Not all racial and ethnic groups are treated as minority groups in society, even when their numbers are small. This Slovak bride and groom dancing at their wedding in Brooklyn, New York, belong to an ethnic group, but they may not suffer any of the disadvantages often associated with being members of a minority group.*

peacefully while those in the United States and elsewhere are often locked in bitter conflict?

## A THEORY OF INTERGROUP RELATIONS

### Four Conditions of Racial or Ethnic Antagonism

Sociologists ask: What social conditions contribute to intergroup conflict and prejudice rather than peaceful coexistence? A useful framework has been proposed by Donald Noel (1968), who suggests four conditions that are likely to produce ethnic antagonism. These are (1) the existence of different ethnic groups, (2) distinctive cultural practices or physical traits that make these groups recognizable, (3) competition among these groups for scarce goods or resources, and (4) an unequal distribution of power or resources among these competing groups.

Regions or nations that consist of only one ethnic group will not have ethnic antagonisms. They may have class antagonisms, but they will not have cleavages based on ethnic-group membership.

Diverse ethnic groups must be visible and identifiable by their physical appearance or cul-

tural practices, such as language, before ethnic antagonism can develop. Individuals must be recognizable as belonging to one group rather than another. However, the existence of racial or ethnic-group differences does not by itself generate antagonism.

### Ethnocentrism

Besides being distinct, members of each group need a sense of **ethnocentrism**—that is, they need to feel that their group is the center of the social world and all others are rated and scaled in reference to it. The practice of marrying only members of one's own group is a good indication that ethnocentrism exists. Without ethnocentrism, groups would tend to merge and competition would not be structured along racial or ethnic lines. By itself, however, ethnocentrism does not necessarily lead to ethnic conflict or domination of one group by another. **Racism** is a version of ethnocentrism and exists when one group tries to define itself as a distinct race that is superior to other biologically distinct races. Racism can take both individual and institutional forms. Individual racism is directed at individuals because of their membership in a particular social group. Institutional racism refers to structured relations of subordination and oppression between social groups.

Ethnocentrism or racism in combination with competition over scarce goods and resources tends to result in ethnic or racial conflict. When there is a shortage of land, wealth, status, or jobs along with ethnocentrism or racism, groups may work to enhance their own situation by exploiting other, ethnically or racially distinct groups. (European white settlers, for example, wanted the land already being used by Native American tribes.) Moreover, the total amount of intergroup competition may increase as the percentage of minority group members increases (Blalock, 1967, p. 148).

A double standard of morality has always tended to characterize relations between in- and out-group members, with the result that different standards of morality are permitted in relation to outsiders. This double standard may take the form of exploitative labor relations, distributions of wealth, and sexual relations (since sexual relations may occur with out-group members even when marriage is rare or prohibited).

Unequal power between groups is likely to tip the scale from pluralism to partial or total domination of one group by another (Blalock, 1967; Blauner, 1969; Lieberson, 1961). This can take the form of larger numbers, superior force (weapons or armies), wealth, technology, knowledge, social organization, and the absence of legal protection for the subordinate group.

The relative power of two competing racial or ethnic groups depends on their respective resources (including money, property, authority, natural resources, physical strength, the right to bear arms, voting rights, education, and occupational rights) and the degree to which each is mobilized (Blalock, 1967, p. 113). Since any initial advantage tends to magnify subsequent advantages, even a slight tilt in the scale of power can create a situation of permanent racial or ethnic domination. For example, the Dutch Boers beat the Africans in South Africa by only a small margin. Over time, however, they greatly widened the political and economic gap between themselves and the blacks. When ethnic competition occurs, what are the consequences for a society?

## CONSEQUENCES OF RACIAL OR ETHNIC ANTAGONISM

When racial or ethnic antagonisms occur, certain predictable consequences may follow. Ethnic or racial antagonism may result in one of six patterned types of relations. Moreover, any relationship that develops requires a legitimating ideology to help justify and support it. Finally, certain types of relations and ideologies result in discrimination and prejudice toward various ethnic minorities.

### Types of Ethnic and Race Relations

When ethnic or racial antagonisms exist in a society, a variety of responses have developed, depending on the actions of the group with more power and resources and on the actions of

that or those with less. Simpson and Yinger (1972) identify six major types of policies of ethnic relations that dominant groups have developed, and they also note how minorities may respond to such policies. These may be considered in light of the theoretical view advanced above.

1. **Assimilation** involves the merging of minority and majority groups into one group with a common culture and identity. Forced assimilation requires minority-group members to give up their own religion, language, or customs and take on the culture of the dominant group. They change their ways, although the majority group makes little or no change in values and actions. This was largely the situation faced by Irish-Americans and Italian-Americans when they arrived in the United States. This model of ethnic relations tends to assume the superiority (or at least the domination) of the majority culture. The minority group's cultural customs and language tend to be viewed as inferior and unacceptable by the dominant cultural group. If they are to gain even grudging acceptance by the dominant group, minority-group members are expected to adopt the language, values, lifestyles, and sometimes the religion of the dominant group. Privately they may try to retain the language, culture, and customs of their ethnic background, but publicly they try to assimilate as much as possible.

Any ethnic group that is relatively small in numbers, is not too readily identified by its appearance, and faces a relatively intolerant and mobilized "mainstream" society may find this mode of relations between groups to be the only one that is comfortable. Many white ethnics in America—Irish, Italians, Poles, Jews—have felt they had to pursue this course in relation to the dominant culture. Some individuals go so far as to change their names so that ethnic origin is not discernible; others have plastic surgery, change religions, or deny all traces of their past culture and customs. Forced assimilation such as this involves the one-way absorption of an individual or group into another group. Such changes say more about the unyielding nature of the dominant culture than they do about the individuals and groups pursuing this approach.

Assimilation is not a course that can easily be followed by an ethnic or racial group with distinctive physical traits. It seems most likely among members of groups who are relatively dispersed geographically and lack economic and political resources within a society.

"Anglo-conformity" is the term used by Gordon (1964) to describe the most frequent form of American assimilation. The term suggests "the desirability of maintaining English institutions (as modified by the American Revolution), the English language, and English-oriented cultural patterns as dominant and standard in American life" (Gordon, 1964, p. 88). The "Anglo-conformity" model of assimilation was modified considerably by the "melting-pot" vision of assimilation. In the melting-pot imagery, America was described as "a totally new blend, culturally and biologically, in which the stocks and folkways of Europe were, figuratively speaking, indiscriminately mixed in the political pot of the emerging nation and melted together by the fires of American influence and interaction into a distinctly new type" (Gordon, 1964, p. 115). Such a conception comes closer to an image of reciprocal assimilation, which involves a blending of divergent groups, with each group taking on some of the cultural practices of the others. However, the "melting-pot" model is largely mythical, Gordon suggests.

**Amalgamation** occurs when groups are assimilated biologically as well as culturally—that is, when racial or ethnic groups also intermarry. Brazil has an official policy that favors the blending of different races (except the Indian) into a uniquely Brazilian stock.

2. **Pluralism** may occur when both majority and minority groups value their distinct cultural identities while seeking economic and political unity. Minority-group members cherish their cultural heritage and do not wish to lose it, and the dominant group is willing to accept cultural variations. In such a society, groups live and let live; they respect one another's differences, but no one tries to change anyone else or make them conform to a conception of "correct" culture or life-style. Switzerland appears to exemplify pluralistic equality. As noted earlier, it has four language-ethnic groups (Germanic, French, Italian, and Romansch). Each group is represented in the formal governing structure of the country and receives equal protection under the law. Because the country was formed as a confederation of equal states, it has managed to retain propor-

tional representation for all language-ethnic groups. Pluralism seems most likely when competing ethnic groups have significant economic, political, and social resources and are able to retain some degree of control over economic and political institutions (Lieberson, 1961).

The United States and Canada do not fit completely into either the assimilation or the pluralism pattern. There has been a policy of assimilation. On the other hand, religious puralism exists widely. Religious pluralism has remained because ethnic groups have been able to get and keep control over their own religious institutions.

Linguistic pluralism (bilingualism) has gained considerable support in America and in Canadian national policy. Bilingualism as an educational and national policy has been hotly debated in the United States, since reasonable people differ about whether or not bilingualism and biculturalism are desirable goals. Some see the value of bilingualism in the schools as a necessary stepping stone to fluency in English and proficiency in the dominant Anglo culture. Others see the goal of bilingualism as one of maintaining and advancing biculturalism at a societal level, along the lines of the French-speaking population in Canada.

3. **Legal protection** of minorities may occur in societies where the official policy is one of protecting minority-group members, even though some groups in society may behave in a hostile way toward them. In the United States the Thirteenth, Fourteenth, and Fifteenth

*In the 1980s many Haitians such as this boatload were deported from or fled the island of Haiti. They were not always welcomed, however, by authorities in Miami Beach, Florida.*

amendments to the Constitution aimed to protect minority rights, especially those of blacks, in situations where they were being violated. Equal opportunity legislation has the same goal.

Legal protection of ethnic or racial minorities is more likely to occur in societies where all groups have the right to vote and are able to occupy positions and exert influence within the law enforcement, legislative, and judicial systems.

4. Exclusion or **population transfer** is most likely to occur when minority and majority groups are in open conflict. The dominant group often proposes "solving" the problem by removing the minority group. Fairly often, unwanted ethnic or racial groups have been transferred or removed from land that dominant groups wish to possess. This happened to many tribes of Native Americans, to Japanese-Americans, to blacks in South Africa, and recently to the Chinese who were pushed out of Vietnam after the war ended there in 1975. Some people suggest that urban renewal in U.S. cities might be more appropriately called "urban removal," because it is used to remove the poor, who are often ethnic or racial minorities, from land desired by the more affluent white middle and upper classes.

Population transfer may involve the division of a nation's territory, as when the Muslim section of India was taken out of India and formed into the new state of Pakistan. In 1980 the largely French-speaking Province of Quebec had an election to decide whether or not it would remain part of the Commonwealth of Canada. (The population voted to remain Canadian.) These latter examples suggest the forms that population transfer may take when minority-group members seek secession—that is, both cultural and political independence from the majority group.

A related form of ethnic or racial relations is **population exclusion,** where a society seeks to prevent ethnically different groups from joining it (Bonacich, 1972, p. 548). In the United States this has taken the form of immigration restrictions and quotas. The "white Australia" policy is another example. When employers wanted to import cheaper laborers from India, China, Japan, and the Pacific Islands, white Australian laborers held strikes and boycotts and

circulated petitions (Willard, 1967, pp. 51–57; Bonacich, 1972, p. 555). In this case, the whites were seeking to control better-paying jobs (Bonacich, 1972, p. 554).

5. **Continued subjugation** occurs when the dominant group wants to maintain its position of superiority over a minority group. South Africa's policy of apartheid is aimed directly at maintaining the domination of whites over blacks. Dominant groups will use whatever combination of force and ideology is necessary to maintain control.

A castelike system may develop when ethnic or racial groups are essential to the dominant group and thus cannot be moved or destroyed. The black slave population in the American South until the nineteenth century and the black population in South Africa today are two examples of caste systems. Caste systems may arise as a way of preventing direct occupational competition between higher-paid white workers and lower-paid blacks (Bonacich, 1972). Higher-paid workers try to monopolize the learning of certain essential skills, deny access to general education, and weaken the lower-wage group politically (Bonacich, 1972, pp. 555–556).

6. The domination of one group by another may become so extreme that it leads to the extermination of a minority group by the dominant group. This may occur by cutting a group off from its food supply or by deliberate **genocide**—that is, the destruction of an entire population. Indians separated from the buffalo, Cambodians pushed off their rice fields, and other ethnic or political minorities have lost their food supply and starved in large numbers as a result. The United States destroyed perhaps two-thirds of the Native American population (Simpson and Yinger, 1972). Hitler's Nazi regime in Germany tried to exterminate the Jews between 1933 and 1945. Although many fled or were concealed by non-Jewish friends, more than 6 million Jews were destroyed in concentration camps, gas chambers, and forced-labor camps.

Genocide is more likely to occur when an ethnic or racial group is not needed for its labor but possesses resources (land, money, and so forth) that are coveted by a dominant ethnic group. It requires that the political and legal resources and rights of the minority group be destroyed.

## Legitimating Ideologies

Ethnic domination and racism are invariably accompanied by an ideology attempting to justify the superior position of one ethnic or racial group and the inferior position of another. An **ideology** is a belief system that portrays the status quo as a morally just system. In any system of ethnic domination or racism, a great many myths are circulated and tend to be believed by large numbers of people. One of the results of this myth-making process is prejudice toward the minority group or groups and usually discrimination against them. When discrimination results in less education, lower-paying jobs, and exclusion from decent housing, medical care, and other social benefits, it operates to perpetuate and sometimes even to increase the inequality between groups.

In South Africa an ideology of religious destiny and superiority seeks to legitimize the domination of blacks by whites. In the early years of slavery in the United States, the major rationale for permitting such a condition was religious. In the colonial era, Christians were not allowed to hold other Christians as slaves; but since the Africans were "pagans" or "heathens," it was argued, it was all right to enslave them.

Blacks in the United States were also alleged to be lazy, ignorant, dirty, and unconcerned about the future. These allegations were definitely not true of most blacks. Where they may have been based on observation, such behaviors were situationally determined rather than the result of the genes or "human nature" of black people. It is hard to be energetic when you suffer from debilitating diseases; it is difficult to be informed when you are denied schooling; cannot afford books, magazines, or newspapers; and libraries are closed to you. It is difficult to bathe frequently when you have no indoor running water. And saving money is impossible when there is not enough of it for the basic necessities or when someone may steal any savings you have. These negative allegations about blacks are another example of a legitimating ideology that blames the victims for their plight

rather than seeing behavior as arising in response to prevalent situations (Ryan, 1971).

"Blaming the victim" can take many forms. Sometimes it appears in the way a situation is presented, as in the phrases "the black problem" or "the Jewish problem." The next step is to ask what it is about the "problem" group that might have created its inferior position in society. Two favorite—and flawed—explanations are genetic and cultural deficiencies. After religious arguments lost their potency, the "scientific" assertion that certain races or ethnic groups were genetically inferior was widely used. In the 1920s certain eastern and southern European immigrants were labeled "feebleminded" because of their low scores on culturally biased IQ tests (Kamin, 1974). On the basis of these false beliefs, U.S. immigration quotas were set according to the ethnic composition of the United States in 1890.

More recently, the genetic argument for the possible inferiority of blacks compared to whites has been revived in the debate over race and IQ. Arthur Jensen (1969) noted that black Americans score an average of 10 to 15 points lower on IQ tests than whites do. From this observation, Jensen concluded that genetic factors may be strongly implicated in these differences in intelligence. Although most researchers accept that differences exist between the average black and white scores on IQ tests, they do not agree with Jensen's conclusion that these differences are due to genes rather than environment.

Jensen's interpretation is rejected for several important reasons. First, there are no genetically pure races in the United States. At least 70 percent of black Americans have some white ancestry, and perhaps 20 percent of white Americans have some black ancestry, according to Hunt and Walker (1974). Thus there are no pure black genes that could cause the observed differences. Second, no "IQ gene" has been identified. Instead, it is increasingly clear that IQ tests measure cultural knowledge, which is distributed unevenly in the social world. If tests measure cultural skills, it is logical that social learning and environment must contribute in a major way to test performance. Even when black and white families have similar levels of education, occupation, and income, the widespread prejudice and discrimination they face in society may create different environments (varied neighborhoods, schools, and social networks) that may affect test performance. Indeed, one study of black children who were adopted by white families showed that the IQ differences between black and white children shrank steadily the longer they had been adopted (Scarr-Salapatek and Weinberg, 1975). This evidence suggests that IQ tests reflect cultural and social advantages that are unevenly available to blacks and whites in the United States.

Although most scientists reject Jensen's suggestion that blacks are genetically inferior to whites, many have considered that cultural deficiencies may be at least partially responsible for the lower school achievement of ethnic minorities or lower-class children. Various explanations have been offered, including disorganized family structures, inadequate child rearing, undeveloped language use, inability to delay impulse gratification, and low self-esteem. These assumptions about serious cultural "deficiencies" in the lives of racial or ethnic minorities have been strongly refuted (Baratz and Baratz, 1970; Labov, 1973; Ogbu, 1978; Persell, 1977, 1981). Although existing differences between ethnic groups may be related to lower IQ scores on culturally biased tests, they do not explain unequal school achievement or demonstrate cultural inferiority. Moreover, the differences that do exist appear to be rooted in the economic, political, and ethnic inequalities of society rather than in the failings of individuals, families, or cultures.

Defining and locating the "problem" in the individual minority group member rather than in ethnic and economic discrimination sustains the ideology of ethnic inferiority, thereby contributing to a situation of ethnic domination of one group by another. It does so by indicating that it is the racial or ethnic minority members or group that needs to change, rather than the societal structure of domination, inequality, and discrimination.

It is not only legitimating ideologies that help to maintain domination. Items of popular culture may be used to represent a subordinate racial or ethnic group in degrading, stereotyped ways (Dubin, 1987). For example, salt and pepper shakers, cookie jars, and ashtrays were fashioned into or decorated with images of black people performing common service tasks. Dubin found that these material objects were most popular between about 1890 and the 1950s. Their production declined with the growth of the Civil Rights Movement (1987, p. 130).

## Discrimination and Prejudice

**Prejudice** is a "prejudged" unfavorable attitude toward the members of a group who are assumed to possess negative traits. Prejudice is irrational because it is an attitude that is not based on specific experience with the persons being judged. In fact, being prejudiced may seriously distort people's observations and judgments. They may presume individuals have the negative trait they expect and be unable to tell if they really have it or not. Prejudice often provides the emotional support for discrimination.

**Discrimination** is the unequal and unfair treatment of individuals or groups on the basis of some irrelevant characteristic, such as ethnicity, religion, sex, or social class. Discrimination involves drawing distinctions between people in a way that violates widely accepted values and procedures—for example, by refusing to consider members of an ethnic minority for jobs, even when they have all the required formal qualifications (Simpson and Yinger, 1972). No single statement fully expresses the relationship between prejudice and discrimination. Simpson and Yinger note that all five of the following statements are true:

1. There can be prejudice without discrimination.
2. There can be discrimination without prejudice.
3. Discrimination can be among the causes of prejudice.
4. Prejudice can be among the causes of discrimination.
5. Probably most frequently prejudice and discrimination are mutually reinforcing. (Simpson and Yinger, 1972, p. 29)

Discrimination is most often used to describe the action of a dominant majority in relation to a weak minority. It is the active expression of a negative prejudice toward a person or group.

*Evidence on IQ tests suggests that test scores reflect cultural and social advantages that are not equally available to blacks and whites in the United States. When blacks have the same advantages as whites, their test scores are very close to those of whites.*

Both psychological and sociological factors have been suggested as causes of prejudice. The two major psychological explanations are scapegoating and projection. In **scapegoating,** as viewed by frustration-aggression theory, people who are frustrated in achieving their social and economic goals may be unable to express their anger directly at its cause. They may be afraid (with good reason) to vent their anger against parents or a boss, for example; or they may be unable to express anger directly at such a diffuse source as inflation, war, or a natural calamity. They may, however, be able to find some weaker but innocent individual or group on whom to vent their rage. These substitute opponents are scapegoats for the real source of frustration. Sometimes people who are frustrated at work take out their anger on their spouses or children; sometimes they find an ethnic minority to pick on.

In the process of **projection,** members of a majority group project their own unacceptable feelings or desires onto minority-group members to avoid guilt or self-blame. The fear that

black men lusted after white women, for example, may have arisen from the guilt white men felt for their own sexual feelings and behavior toward black women. Similarly, whites may project great anger onto every black person they see on the street because they know whites have done things that could anger blacks.

Even though these explanations appear to be purely psychological in origin, both arise from the social relations in which people are embedded. Hence, although certain psychological traits may help to explain why some people are prejudiced and others are not, there appear to be certain social conditions under which prejudice is more or less likely to emerge. The social roots of prejudice are revealed in regional variations. Middleton (1976) discovered that in the southern United States, antiblack prejudice was part of the regional subculture in certain areas but less so in others. People who moved away from those regions became less prejudiced over time, and those who moved into those regions became more prejudiced over time. This evidence supports a situational explanation for the origins of prejudice.

Whereas prejudice is an attitude held by individuals, "discrimination" refers to actions by individuals or institutions that disqualify or mistreat people in ways that are rationally irrelevant to the situation (Antonovsky, 1960). Over time, discrimination tends to confirm the negative vicious circle that becomes increasingly difficult for a minority group to escape. As we have seen, when relations between ethnic groups become competitive and one group seeks to dominate others, that domination is likely to become institutionalized and to be accompanied by a legitimating ideology. Institutionalized discrimination and racist ideologies fan the flames of prejudice, which reinforces discrimination, in a bitter vicious circle. Together, prejudice and discrimination may support economic and political interests.

## The Contact Hypothesis

The connection between major group inequalities and prejudice is illustrated by the **contact hypothesis** about racial and ethnic relations. In the 1940s and 1950s some social scientists believed that allowing people of different groups to get to know each other would reduce their prejudiced attitudes toward one another. In his classic book *The Nature of Prejudice* (1958), social psychologist Gordon Allport suggested that contact would reduce prejudice only under certain conditions. If the status of individuals from different groups is wildly unequal, then contact may increase their prejudice toward one another. People who had contact only with persons in subordinate or servant positions did not become less prejudiced. When people having contact were of relatively equal status, however, they were much more likely to become less prejudiced toward members of another ethnic group (Brophy, 1945; Ford, 1973; Merton and Lazarsfeld, 1954). In addition to being of relatively equal status, it was helpful if people of different groups were working cooperatively on common tasks rather than competing with each other for scarce resources or rewards (Kephart, 1957). When persons of relatively equal status work together toward a shared goal, prejudice decreases; but if they have unequal status or are competing with each other, then prejudice may increase.

## EXPERIENCES OF DIFFERENT ETHNIC AND RACIAL GROUPS IN THE UNITED STATES

### White Ethnics and WASPs

More so than a great many societies, the United States is composed of diverse ethnic groups, as shown in Figure 10.1. Until about 1860, however, the U.S. population was relatively similar ethnically, composed mainly of white Protestants from the British Isles and the Netherlands. Even among the Irish immigrants in the United States, most were Protestants. The first large wave of immigration into the United States occurred between 1820 and 1860, when more than 5 million Europeans arrived (see Figure 10.2). Nine out of ten of them were from England, Ireland, or Germany. Except for the Catholic Irish, the early immigrants were readily absorbed into the English Protestant United States. For a long time the descendants of English Protestants were the dominant cultural

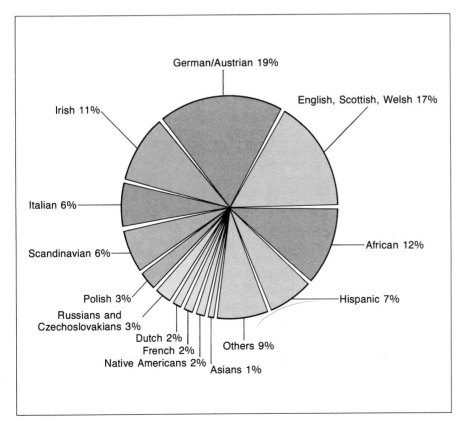

**Figure 10.1 Racial and Ethnic Composition of the United States.**

Although persons of English and German ancestry are the largest segment of the U.S. population, they represent only about one-third of the total population. The other two-thirds include a wide mixture of many different ethnic and national backgrounds, making the United States among the most multiethnic societies in the world. "Other" includes persons from Greece, Hungary, the Philippines, Switzerland, India, Portugal, Lithuania, Yugoslavia, Romania, Belgium, and Arab nations, among others. The Scandinavian category includes Danish, Finnish, Norwegian, and Swedish.

*Source:* U.S. Bureau of the Census, 1985a, p. 34.

German/Austrian 19%
English, Scottish, Welsh 17%
Irish 11%
African 12%
Italian 6%
Scandinavian 6%
Hispanic 7%
Polish 3%
Russians and Czechoslovakians 3%
Dutch 2%
French 2%
Others 9%
Native Americans 2%
Asians 1%

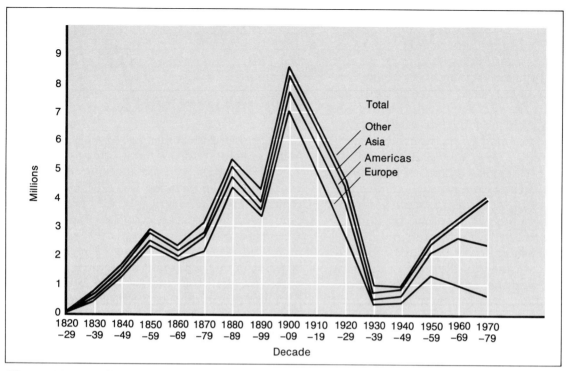

**Figure 10.2   Millions of Immigrants to the United States by Decade and by Continent of Origin, 1820–1979.**

The United States received the largest number of immigrants between 1870 and 1930. The relative effects were also greatest then because the total population was smaller compared to now. Immigration began increasing again after 1950, and the national origin of immigrants changed. Before 1950, most were from Europe; afterward, more came from Central and South America and Asia.

*Source:* U.S. Bureau of the Census, 1982a, p. 87.

group. The so-called WASPs (for White Anglo-Saxon Protestants) still own a great deal of property and wealth in the United States, and they tend to dominant corporate boardrooms, banks, insurance companies, law firms, and educational, cultural, and philanthropic institutions (Baltzell, 1964).

From 1860 to 1920, the United States received some 30 million more immigrants, mostly from central and southeastern Europe, including Italy, Poland, Russia, Greece, and the Balkans. These predominantly Catholic, Greek Orthodox, or Jewish immigrants settled in northern and midwestern cities.

Most of these ethnic groups faced some degree of prejudice and discrimination. They were identifiable culturally if not through their physical appearance. They were often forced to take the lowest-paying jobs. But they arrived in the United States at a time when labor was generally in short supply and they were usually able to find work. Today about 70 percent of their descendants are blue-collar workers, and the rest are mainly in the lower-level white-collar work force. Their children grew up speaking English without a "foreign accent," and their ethnic identity was something they could voluntarily activate or not as they saw fit. Assimilation was an option available to some, as was some degree of ethnic pluralism.

The term **white ethnics** was coined in the 1970s to describe people who value both their U.S. citizenship and their ethnic origins. Some white ethnics still live in "little Italys" or other ethnic enclaves, although moves to outlying suburbs have tended to disperse some of these ethnic concentrations. Moreover, the greatly increased rates of intermarriage across ethnic groups since World War II has led to a mixed ethnic ancestry for the majority of younger white ethnics.

Despite this mixed ancestry, however, a growing number of individuals identify themselves with a single ethnic group, perhaps because they share their cultural backgrounds with neighbors, friends, family members, church members, and co-workers (Alba and Chamlin, 1983). The group identity of white ethnics seems to be based on a partially shared cultural heritage and on their common interests and needs in modern urban America. To the degree that they live in major cities, they are affected by high crime rates and declining municipal services. Like some other Americans, these white ethnics see rising prices and taxes and growing demands for employment from racial minorities and women as possible threats to their livelihoods. At the same time, they view individual effort as the key to success and see poverty as due to the absence of individual effort (Huber and Form, 1973; Kluegel and Smith, 1982). Hence they tend to be impatient with programs and groups that demand changes in the social structure.

## Blacks in the United States

The first boatload of black slaves was brought to the North American colonies in 1619. The shortage of labor and the economic advantages of slavery and the slave trade in the colonial economies fueled the expansion of a practice that violently uprooted and enslaved millions of black Africans. Chained below deck in filthy and overcrowded ships, slaves were auctioned off like livestock at various southern port cities when they arrived. Both on the ships and at the sales, slaves from different tribes and regions, who spoke different languages, were mixed together to minimize the possibility of organized revolts.

During the 250 years that slavery persisted in the United States, there were numerous slave uprisings, contradicting the myth that slaves were content with their lot. Some were brutally beaten by their masters or overseers for not working hard enough, for disobedience, or for insubordination. They were, however, almost never imprisoned for any length of time or hanged (the lynchings came later), because their labor was too valuable. Although many slaves tried to run away, the distance from their tribes and homelands made it impossible for them to return to Africa. The physical and social separation from the slaves' home societies contrasted sharply with the situation of Native Americans. Efforts to enslave individual Native Americans in the United States generally failed. Either their tribesmen came after them and rescued them or they ran away and rejoined their people; they were much closer physically and socially to freedom. Few such options were available to Africans, although the "underground railroad" did help some escape to the North or to Canada.

Until after the Civil War, blacks had no constitutional protection for their civil rights. The Thirteenth to Fifteenth Amendments to the Constitution, passed between 1865 and 1870, provided the first promise of citizenship. The Civil Rights Act of 1875 called for equal accommodations in public facilities (except schools), but by 1883 it was voided. From 1877 on, when the last of the federal troops withdrew from the South, southern conservatives used fraud, the poll tax, violence, and terror to remove the voting rights of blacks and to regain control of their state governments. Secret terrorist organizations like the Ku Klux Klan flourished during this period. Shaking loose from the northern carpetbaggers and freedmen (freed slaves), southern legislatures passed a wave of Jim Crow laws segregating blacks and whites in public transportation facilities, schools, parks, cemeteries, theaters, and restaurants; they also prevented blacks from voting.[1] These "separate but equal" public facilities were upheld by the United States Supreme Court in the 1896 *Plessy* v. *Ferguson* decision.

A caste system of ethnic relations between blacks and whites developed in the South during

---

[1] Jim Crow laws were laws that enforced racial segregation in the American South between the end of the formal Reconstruction period (1877) and the beginning of a strong civil rights movement in the 1960s. Jim Crow was the name of a minstrel routine performed beginning in 1828. The term came to be used as a derogatory word for blacks and as a proper noun referring to their segregated life.

and after slavery. Political, legal, economic, and social restrictions as well as various forms of control and discrimination limited the blacks' access to education and produced elaborate legitimating ideologies. Blacks were physically identifiable and had fewer resources and less power than whites. They also had something, namely cheap labor, that some whites badly needed. Therefore they did not face expulsion or genocide.

It was not until World War II that a number of economic and social changes began to affect the situation of black Americans. During the war discrimination in defense industries was forbidden, and the armed forces were desegregated in 1948. Both the promise of employment in defense industries and the growing mechanization of southern farms spurred the migration of millions of blacks from the rural south to northern cities. Even in the North, however, segregation characterized most social relations between blacks and whites.

Not until the epoch-making *Brown v. Board of Education* decision in 1954 did the Supreme Court rule that separate educational facilities were inherently unequal and therefore unconstitutional. Beginning in 1955, when Mrs. Rosa Parks refused to move to the Negro section of a bus in Montgomery, Alabama, a series of nonviolent civil rights demonstrations and protests galvanized public opinion, the mass media, and the world community. Diplomatic representatives from independent African nations had already encountered segregated facilities in the United States, creating considerable international embarrassment.

During this time the underlying economic, legal, and political contexts of race relations were changing, resulting in a different moral and ideological climate. The tension between equal rights and segregation grew intolerable. Student sit-ins at lunch counters, "freedom riders" trying to desegregate public facilities and transportation, and voter registration drives during the early 1960s involved more than 100,000 blacks and whites. In 1963 Martin Luther King, Jr., led the March on Washington, where he proclaimed to more than 200,000 blacks and whites assembled at the Lincoln Memorial, "I have a dream . . . of an America where blacks and whites can walk together as

*In August 1963, Dr. Martin Luther King, Jr. led a march on Washington, where he proclaimed to more than 200,000 blacks and whites at the Lincoln Memorial, "I have a dream . . . of an America where blacks and whites can walk together as equals."*

equals." President Lyndon B. Johnson was able in 1964 to prod Congress to pass the most far-reaching civil rights bill in the nation's history. It forbade discrimination in public accommodations and threatened to withhold funds from communities that continued to operate segregated schools.

Nevertheless, years of economic frustration and police brutality led to violent reactions. An important reason was that poor black Americans no longer accepted their subordinate status as inevitable or just. Riots erupted in the black ghettoes of major U.S. cities, beginning in the Watts section of Los Angeles in 1965 and causing extensive property damage. The assassination of Martin Luther King, Jr., in 1968 was followed by further riots. A presidential commission investigating the events of 1968 placed most of the blame on "white racism" and declared that "our nation is moving toward two societies, one black, one white—separate and unequal." The commission urged government action at all levels to provide employment, better housing, improved education, and more adequate police protection for ghetto residents.

Since that time, the equal rights movement has aimed for economic and social gains and for increased political officeholding. In 1983, 9.5 percent of the black population had completed four or more years of college, and the median income for all black families was $13,599. Only 2.6 percent of blacks earned $50,000 or more annually, and 36 percent of blacks were below the poverty level. (For more details, see the last section of this chapter.) The number of blacks in elected political offices has increased. In 1989 there were 24 blacks in the U.S. Congress. In 1988 there were 400 blacks in state legislatures, compared to a total of 182 in 1970; and there were 4089 blacks in city and county offices such as mayor, city councillor, and commissioner, compared to 715 in 1970. Despite these gains, however, black elected officials still account for less than 1 percent of all U.S. public officials. Part of the reason for this is the low rate of voting among blacks. Moreover, although the election of black officials is important for symbolic reasons, they tend to lack real power. Black legislators are usually elected in decaying urban districts such as the Bedford-Stuyvesant section of Brooklyn, the long-time district of former U.S. Representative Shirley Chisholm. She describes it as typical of the "shells white leaders leave behind when they abandon an area politically to blacks" (Blum, 1980, p. 1). Black mayors tend to govern cities such as Detroit; Atlanta; Washington; Newark, New Jersey; Oakland, California; Dayton, Ohio; and Gary, Indiana, which face shrinking tax bases, greater dependency on higher levels of government for aid, and large, needy populations heavily weighted toward dependent young people and the very old.

Blacks have long comprised the largest and most visible racial minority group, numbering 29.7 million (or 12.2 percent of the U.S. population) in 1987.

## Hispanics

Some Spanish settlements north of Santa Fe, New Mexico, were founded in 1598, before English settlements along the North American east coast. Only Native Americans and Eskimos lived in what is now the United States before the Spanish arrived. The umbrella term "His-

panic" refers to Mexican-Americans, Puerto Ricans, and all other Spanish-speaking Americans. Hispanics are not a single unified ethnic group but a collection of many distinct ethnic groups who may share a language but differ sharply in culture and behavior. In fact, the term "Hispanic" has served less as a means of self-identification than as a convenient label for government agencies and scholars (Portes and Truelove, 1987, p. 359).

The Bureau of the Census reported 19.4 million Hispanic-Americans, or 8.2 percent of the U.S. population, in 1988. The Hispanic population is growing faster than the black or white populations in the United States, both from higher birth rates and from higher rates of immigration.

About 62 percent of the Hispanics in the United States today are of Mexican origin, living mostly in California, Texas, Arizona, New Mexico, and Colorado. Mexican-Americans are the largest minority group in most states in the American Southwest. More than 90 percent of the Mexican-American population lives in cities or their suburbs such as Los Angeles, California;

Hispanic-Americans include Mexican-Americans, Puerto Ricans, and all other Spanish-speaking people in the United States. Some groups have been in the United States for centuries, whereas others are more recent arrivals who face language and economic obstacles.

San Antonio, Texas; and Santa Fe, New Mexico. They are overrepresented in blue-collar occupations and underrepresented in professional and technical fields. In 1978, the median family income for Mexican-American families was $12,835, compared to $17,912 for non-Mexican-American families. The median number of years of school completed by Mexican-Americans is 9.8, lower than the figure for any other ethnic group except Native Americans (Pachon and Moore, 1981, p. 117).

Several million more Hispanics are from Puerto Rico, a self-governing associated commonwealth of the United States. They live mainly in the Northeast, particularly in and around New York. In recent years the point of origin for Hispanic immigration has shifted from Puerto Rico to South and Central America. Additionally, there are more than 700,000 Cubans, who left their country because of differences with Fidel Castro and settled mainly in Florida. Besides these groups, Hispanics include Dominicans, Ecuadorians, Colombians, Venezuelans, El Salvadorans, and natives of other Latin American countries. Although widely different in their cultural backgrounds, these groups generally share a common language and, often, Roman Catholicism as well. The 1980 U.S. Census was the first to ask specifically about being of Spanish origin.

In some ways Hispanics appear to face less discrimination than blacks. Their median family income was $20,306 in 1988, compared with $32,274 for whites and $18,098 for blacks. Hispanics thus earned 63 percent of what whites earned, whereas blacks earned only 56 percent of what whites earned. For any given level of education or occupation, Hispanics tend to earn less than whites but more than blacks. The span of occupations among persons of Spanish origin is enormous, ranging from migrant farm worker and unskilled laborer to bank president and business entrepreneur. There are real pockets of poverty—for example, among migrant farm workers in the Southwest or new arrivals from Puerto Rico. Hispanic households in the Northeast have a lower average income than do Hispanic households anywhere else in the United States. Politically, Hispanics are still underrepresented at all levels of government.

Hispanics are often culturally distinct. Some have faced competition with whites over land or jobs. They have often filled the lowest-level, lowest-paid, and least desirable jobs (for example as migrant farm workers). This tends to minimize their direct economic competition with white workers. They are sometimes in competition with black workers, however. The resources of different Hispanic groups vary. Cubans arrived with educational, occupational, and organizational assets, and sometimes financial ones as well. These resources helped them to get established economically, occupationally, and politically, as did their large concentrations in certain areas such as Miami, Florida.

## Asian-Americans

Within the past few years, Asian-Americans have become the nation's fastest-growing minority group, through births and legal immigration. Although Asian-Americans still number only about 3.6 million, or 1.6 percent of the total U.S. population, their ranks have grown rapidly since immigration laws were reformed in 1965. (See Figure 10.2.) In 1984 alone, more Asian immigrants—282,000—came to the United States than did in the three decades from 1931 to 1960. About two-thirds of Asian im-

*Within the past decade, Asian-Americans have become the nation's fastest-growing minority group through births and legal immigration.*

migrants live in California. Chinese-Americans are the largest group, followed by Filipino-Americans, Japanese-Americans, Korean-Americans, Vietnamese-Americans, and Asian Indian Americans. Except for the Indochinese refugees, they tend to be well educated and highly skilled immigrants. One indicator of this is the fact that Harvard's freshmen class was 10.9 percent Asian in 1985, the University of California at Berkeley's was 18.9 percent Asian, and Cal Tech's was 18.7 percent Asian (Doerner, 1985).

### Chinese-Americans

In the 1840s the first Chinese were brought to California to work on the railroads and in the gold mines. Between 1850 and 1882, more than 322,000 Chinese entered the United States. They worked in mines and then on the Central Pacific section of the transcontinental railroad, completed in 1869. These migrants were mostly single men who had no plans to stay forever. Their temporary status meant that they kept their Chinese language and customs. When the gold rush ended and jobs grew scarce, they were threatened, beaten, and sometimes even lynched. To protect themselves, the Chinese moved together into "Chinatown" areas where they ran restaurants, laundries, and vegetable stands. About the time of the business crash of 1876 in the United States, newspapers fanned fears of the "yellow peril." "Anti-coolie societies" were formed in opposition to the Chinese in a number of cities, and by 1882 the U.S. Congress had passed the Chinese Exclusion Act, which prohibited Chinese immigration for ten years. In 1902 the act was made permanent until its repeal in 1943.

Labor competition seems to have fueled historical discrimination and exclusionary practices aimed at the Chinese in the United States. Chinese laborers lacked the numbers, political power, and other resources to resist domination by the majority.

Chinese-Americans faced intense discrimination on the West Coast. Housing, schools, theaters, barbershops, hotels, and restaurants were segregated. Interracial marriage was illegal. Toward the end of the nineteenth century, the Chinese began migrating to eastern and midwestern cities to find better economic opportunities. Excluded from many occupations, they entered domestic service and ran laundries and restaurants. Those desiring to open businesses started a kind of rotating credit association. Each person paid a specific sum into a common pool, then participants competed by bid, election, or lot to gain the right to use the entire sum. The next month members would meet again, raise another sum, and those who had not yet won would compete again. They continued until all members of the group had won a chance to use the pool. In this way many small businesses were financed from within the community.

During World War II new job opportunities opened up and the Chinese began to share in the postwar prosperity as well; although, in 1970, 24 percent were still in food and laundry service jobs, more than triple the national average.

Today, few Chinese work in the better-paying blue-collar jobs, but the proportion of Chinese in professional and technical occupations increased from 3 percent in 1940 to 30 percent in 1980. This gain is more than double that made by the general population. Many Chinese have chosen careers in science, technology, engineering, education, and health. By 1980 the median family income for Chinese-Americans was $22,550.

The educational level of Chinese-Americans is rising. Nearly two-thirds complete high school, and more than half of those go on to college. There is a higher proportion of college graduates, 25 percent, than among Americans generally; the national average is 13 percent. One-quarter of Chinese-Americans, however, have not gone beyond elementary school (Kitano, 1981, p. 130). The 1974 Supreme Court decision in the case of *Lau* v. *Nichols* stated that the failure of the San Francisco School District to provide special help to non-English-speaking Chinese students violated the Civil Rights Act of 1964. That ruling had important national implications, since it established the principle of bilingual education not only for Chinese students but also for the estimated 3.5 million other non-English-speaking minority students. In 1981 the U.S. Department of Education ruled that bilingual education could be handled by local districts in any way they chose.

The Immigration Act of 1965 ended the national quota system restricting the number of migrants who could come from different countries; it allowed many Chinese newcomers to enter the United States. Most of them were from Hong Kong or Taiwan. Existing Chinatowns in San Francisco, Los Angeles, and New York lacked adequate facilities for the large numbers of new arrivals, resulting in some problems of overcrowding, substandard housing, and unemployment.

Culturally, many Chinese still observe traditional practices, including the Chinese New Year, Dragon Boat, and Mid-Autumn holidays. Intermarriage with non-Chinese has increased, especially among younger people. In 1970, 30 percent of the men and 22 percent of the women in the 16- to 24-year-old age group in California had non-Chinese spouses.

The Chinese population in the United States is the largest in any nation outside Asia. Most Chinese-Americans live in urban areas. New York has 200,000, and San Francisco and Los Angeles also have large concentrations. Despite their small numbers relative to the total population (about 0.45 percent or an estimated 1.08 million in 1985), the Chinese are an identifiable group with a distinct although not completely homogeneous subculture.

### Filipino-Americans

The Philippine Islands in the Pacific Ocean came under United States rule in 1899 as a result of the Spanish-American War, and for a while Filipinos could enter the United States freely. In 1934 the islands became a commonwealth of the United States and stringent immigration quotas were placed on Filipinos. About 250,000 Filipino-Americans entered the United States between 1966 and 1976, settling mainly in Los Angeles, Chicago, New York, and Honolulu. More than two-thirds of these arrivals qualified as "professional, technical, and kindred workers" whose skills were needed in the United States. Their high levels of education and skill help to explain their high median family income, which was $23,680 in 1980.

Filipinos did not have a strong sense of national identity because of the diverse regional languages in the Islands. For many, family concerns were of the greatest importance (Thernstrom et al., 1980). By 1985 there were an estimated 1.05 million Filipinos in the United States, and within the next 30 years, they are expected to become the largest group of Asian-Americans in the United States.

### Japanese-Americans

The Japanese came to the United States somewhat later than the Chinese, beginning in the 1880s and early 1900s. They found few jobs in the California cities where they landed, so many became farmers. By 1920 they owned about one-eighth of California's irrigated farmland (Lyman, 1977). Throughout the early decades that they were here, Japanese-Americans faced discrimination. To meet their financial needs, they developed mutual-aid financial systems in which individuals pooled their money into a common fund like a credit union. Individuals could earn interest on their savings and borrow money when needed. Such economic cooperation strengthened community cohesion and helped many businesses when regular banks refused to lend them money.

After Japan bombed Pearl Harbor in 1941, a wave of anti-Japanese fear swept the United States and 120,000 Japanese-Americans on the West Coast were herded into internment camps in Arizona, Arkansas, California, Colorado, Idaho, Utah, and Wyoming. The purpose of this roundup was to avoid sabotage, spying, or collaboration with the enemy. Ethnicity was equated with nationality, an unjustified blurring of reality. Many of these Japanese were second- or third-generation Americans. The charges against them were so unfounded that not one of them was ever brought to trial. Critics of the U.S. government's action suggest that the Japanese owned much valuable agricultural land that was then seized by white Americans and only in rare cases returned or paid for. Each Japanese family lost an average of $10,000 from this seizure of property, besides several years of their lives in prison camps (Simpson and Yinger, 1972, p. 121). The Federal Reserve Board estimated in 1942 that a total of about $400 million was lost by all Japanese residents (Masaoka, 1972).

Japanese-Americans faced ethnic competition over a coveted resource, prime agricultural land. However, they had citizenship and legal ownership of that land. Japan's bombing of Pearl Harbor was used to justify the removal of those legal rights.

*In 1942 these and many other U.S. citizens of Japanese origin were forced into internment camps such as this one in Manzanar, California, because their ethnic origins were confused with their national loyalty, an unjustified blurring of reality. Congress recognized this error and authorized compensatory payments in 1988.*

The likelihood that this action against the Japanese was racially and economically based is suggested by the fact that similar actions were not taken against Italian-Americans or German-Americans, even though their ancestral countries were also at war with the United States. German-Americans were, however, required to register and report to government authorities periodically during the war. Along with slavery and the mistreatment of Native Americans by the U.S. government, this internment of a minority group in a concentration camp represents one of the worst breaches of civil rights in American history.[2]

When they were finally allowed to enlist in 1943, more than 33,000 of the nisei, the second-generation Japanese-Americans, joined the armed forces and served honorably, especially in the most highly decorated all-Japanese-American 442d Regimental Combat Team. After the war, those who could returned to their lands, and many others started contract gardening businesses that flourished along with the suburban boom in California. Veterans were able to use the G.I. Bill to attend college. Today Japanese-Americans have the highest high school completion rates of any group, and their college completion rates and occupational achievement are also high. In 1940, 4 percent of Japanese males were professionals; by 1980, 28 percent were managers, professionals, or executives.

Japanese are likely to pursue careers in the fields of medicine, pharmacy, optometry, dentistry, and engineering. Their mean family income in 1980 was $27,350, among the highest for any ethnic group. These gains have not been offset by recent immigration, since the numbers of Japanese migrants have been small and spread out in time and space. The Japanese-American population increased only 19 percent between 1970 and 1980. Today the 766,000 (or 0.3 percent of the population in 1985) Japanese-Americans live mostly in urban areas of Hawaii, California, Washington, New York, and Illinois. In Hawaii they have been a powerful political force since the 1940s, when they comprised over a third of the population.

Several explanations have been offered for the success of Japanese-Americans. These include their strong emphasis on the work ethic and their firm sense of family unity and group orientation, reflected in the polite, consensual behavior expected in social relations. Japanese moral training contains coping strategies drawn from Buddhist teachings and evident in the phrases *gaman* (meaning "don't let it bother you") and *gambatte* (meaning "don't give up"). These precepts reveal the stress placed on continuing to try even in the face of frustration and disappointment, conditions the Japanese have faced repeatedly in their time in the United States.

The high-level occupations and incomes of Japanese-Americans are explained by their educational levels and by the fact that they live in areas with good wages and high living costs. Despite their successes, Japanese-Americans still

[2] In 1980 the U.S. Congress established a commission to consider compensating the Japanese-Americans who spent World War II behind barbed wire. The commission issued its report in 1983, recommending that each of the 120,000 Japanese-American citizens interned during World War II receive $20,000. However, many questions arise about the appropriateness of such an action. Such a blanket award disregards differences in individual suffering or loss. The children of internees would receive nothing under the plan, and other groups, such as blacks and Native Americans who were treated at least as badly, would also receive nothing (Gordon, 1983).

receive lower returns on their educational backgrounds than do white Americans (Hirschman and Wong, 1984; Woodrum, 1981).

### Korean-Americans

Most Korean-Americans have entered the United States since 1968, when the Immigration Act of 1965 went into effect. The largest concentration of Korean-Americans is in Los Angeles, where more than 150,000 live. Many of the recent immigrants are Christians, who are a distinct minority in Korea. About half the adult Korean-American population is college-educated, and many of the migrants were teachers, professionals, or administrators in Korea. In the United States today nearly one in eight Koreans owns a business, and the median family income in 1980 was $20,450. Their occupational and economic success is probably due to their educational levels and to the fact that many families have more than one wage earner.

### Vietnamese-Americans

The most recent group of Asians to enter the United States are the Vietnamese, following the war in their country. By 1985 there were about 634,000 Vietnamese in the United States. About one-third of them settled in California. Many of these families were relocated by private rather than public agencies, although the federal immigration service did modify existing quotas so that more could come into the United States.

Some Vietnamese did face hostility, perhaps because of economic competition. Other communities welcomed them peacefully and were pleased to have them do poorly paid and undesirable work (for example, in restaurants) that no one else was available to do. A survey by the U.S. Department of Health, Education, and Welfare found that 95 percent of the heads of Vietnamese refugee households were employed and their median family income in 1980 was $12,840 (McCarthy, 1980, p. 596).

## Native Americans

At the time of Columbus's arrival in the New World, between 1 and 2 million Native Americans (whom he called "Indians," because he thought he had reached the subcontinent of In-

dia in the Eastern Hemisphere) lived on this continent. Their numbers steadily declined as a result of European invasion. Large numbers were destroyed by European diseases (to which they had no immunity), warfare, massacre, and forced migrations after European settlers arrived. In 1830, for example, 70,000 Indians from five major tribes in the southeastern United States were forced to move westward. On the way, more than 20,000 died. By 1890, when the U.S. Army massacred the Sioux at Wounded Knee, South Dakota, their numbers had been reduced to about 300,000.

After 1890 the Bureau of Indian Affairs made Native Americans wards of the federal government. It required most of them to live on reservations, which were invariably parcels of land that white settlers found undesirable. Ethnic relations between Native Americans and whites were heavily shaped by competition for land. European-Americans used their superior weapons and then their economic, political, legal, and educational institutions to destroy, remove, or dominate Native Americans.

An ideology of European superiority and Indian barbarism and inferiority accompanied this process of genocide, population transfer, and domination. Much of this ideology persists today. In 1980 there were 1.4 million Native Americans concentrated in California, Oklahoma, Arizona, New Mexico, North Carolina, Washington, South Dakota, Michigan, Texas,

*Native Americans faced extensive persecution by European settlers. This Navajo family has retained a traditional dwelling and the crafts of rug-weaving and jewelry-making.*

New York, Montana, and Minnesota, though some also live in Illinois, Wisconsin, Oregon, Alaska, and Utah. Although Native Americans are treated as a single ethnic group, there are actually more than 170 Indian peoples who have different histories, cultures, and identities.

As a group, Native Americans have an average annual family income of $1500 and a 45 percent unemployment rate (American Indian Fund, 1981). More than 40 percent of all Native Americans still live on reservations, where most of the stores are owned by outsiders. The population suffers from high rates of disease, alcoholism, and suicide, and life expectancy is only 46 years (nearly 30 years less than the rest of the U.S. population). Four out of ten Native Americans do not finish high school, and their median level of education is 8 years (compared to a national average of 12.1 years). In 1970 about 14,000 young Indians were attending institutions of higher learning, a figure that is three times as large as the number in 1960. So although their overall educational level is relatively low, it is rising (Thernstrom, 1980, p. 65).

By 1970 the "red power movement" began calling for a reservation-based "tribal nationalism" (Day, 1972, p. 507). They fished in waters that were closed to them; shut down beaches, rivers, highways, and bridges on reservations; and initiated legal actions. In 1973 an angry group of 200 members of the American Indian Movement (AIM) took over the reservation town of Wounded Knee. They held the hamlet for 69 days while under siege by federal marshals. They demanded new tribal leaders, a review of Indian treaties, and a Senate inquiry into the treatment of Native Americans. The occupation of Wounded Knee sparked a national movement to teach languages, crafts, tribal histories, and religious ceremonies to the new generation (Deloria, 1981). Elsewhere a number of tribes have initiated lawsuits to reclaim illegally seized land (in Maine, for example) or to restore their fishing rights (for instance, in Minnesota and Alaska). These lawsuits represent efforts to use the educational and legal institutions of the dominant ethnic group to obtain some measure of justice for the minority ethnic group. Some tribes have been lucky enough to discover valuable minerals under the arid deserts where they were confined, but rich deposits of uranium, coal, or oil have helped only relatively few. Most Native Americans live in abject poverty.

## ETHNIC AND RACE RELATIONS TODAY AND FUTURE PROSPECTS

Both social class and ethnicity are important sources of social identity and behavior. When is one relatively more important than the other? Is ethnicity or race becoming less important in the United States as class becomes more important? Is the problem of a trapped underclass, often heavily peopled by ethnic or racial minorities, becoming more acute? These questions are addressed below. We conclude by considering future prospects for ethnic relations.

### The Relative Importance of Class and Race

What determines whether class or race is the stronger basis for group identity and behavior? Michael Hechter (1978) has developed an interesting theoretical response to this question. He suggests that the relative importance of ethnic compared to class cleavages depends on what he calls the "cultural division of labor" in a society. A **cultural division of labor** develops when individuals having distinct cultural markers (such as ethnicity) take different places in the occupational world. Two features determine variations in the cultural division of labor: (1) the *degree of hierarchy*—that is, the extent to which ethnic groups are unequally distributed in different occupations, and (2) *segmentation*, or the degree to which certain ethnic groups are concentrated in particular occupations. When there is a relatively high degree of hierarchy and segmentation in the cultural division of labor, ethnic identities will be more important for individuals in a society than class identities. For example, under those conditions ethnicity will predict more than will class voting behavior or whether or not someone will marry someone of the same ethnic group. When the cultural division of labor is relatively low, class-based identities will be more important than ethnicity for

*A cultural division of labor is less likely when ethnic diversity is found in the workplace, as is the case in this Boeing factory in Seattle, Washington.*

predicting the behaviors of individuals.

Hechter's theory says nothing about why one rather than another cultural division of labor occurs. Ethnic competition and relative resources may well explain the cultural division of labor that occurs. Also, his theory has been tested with only two kinds of behavior—voting and intermarriage. Despite these limitations, it is a valuable theory because it connects structural differences with the relative influence of class and ethnicity on social behavior.

## Is Race Becoming Less Important in the United States?

In his controversial book *The Declining Significance of Race,* William J. Wilson (1978) declared that although blacks still face barriers in social and institutional arrangements like housing and clubs, "in the economic sphere, class has be-

come more important than race in determining black access to privilege and power." He continued, "it is clearly evident . . . that many talented and educated blacks are now entering positions of prestige and influence at a rate comparable to or, in some situations, exceeding that of whites with equivalent qualifications. It is equally clear that the black underclass is in a hopeless state of economic stagnation, falling further and further behind the rest of society" (p. 2).

For some blacks, educational and occupational opportunities have opened, suggesting the absence of a color-based caste barrier. However, neither Wilson nor the available evidence suggests that all racial inequalities have disappeared. Instead, Wilson suggests that class differences are becoming more important than they have been for blacks, while racial differences are becoming less important. His argument is consistent with Hechter's theory.

Are race and ethnicity losing significance in the United States? Ethnic groups differ with respect to education, occupation, income, and other life chances, as noted earlier. Historically, the educational attainments of all ethnic groups have increased. Blacks still lag behind whites in educational attainment, but they are increasing their educational levels at a faster rate than are whites (see Figure 10.3).

The proportions of blacks and whites in higher-paying occupations has also changed over time. Between 1960 and 1989 the percent of blacks doing white-collar work increased dramatically, from 16 percent to 44 percent, whereas the percentage of white workers in such jobs increased less, from 47 percent to 59 percent (U.S. Department of Labor, 1989a). Moreover, the gap between the percentage of whites and blacks in white-collar jobs has declined from a 31 percent difference in 1960 to a 15 percent difference in 1989.

These are dramatic changes indeed, although their impact is reduced slightly by the realization that the biggest gains of all have occurred in clerical jobs, a category that is at the lower end of the income and prestige hierarchy. When white-collar jobs are subdivided into professional/technical, managers/administrators, salesworkers, and clerical workers, the percentage of black and white clerical workers is equal. The gap between white and black professional spe-

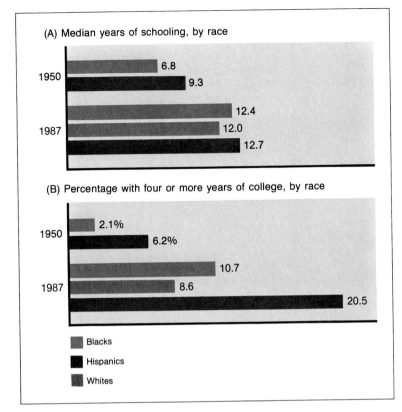

(A) Median years of schooling, by race

1950
6.8
9.3

1987
12.4
12.0
12.7

(B) Percentage with four or more years of college, by race

1950
2.1%
6.2%

1987
10.7
8.6
20.5

Blacks
Hispanics
Whites

**Figure 10.3   Black and White Educational Attainments, 1950 and 1987.**

**Part A:**

Between 1950 and 1987, blacks greatly reduced the gap in median years of schooling between themselves and whites. In 1987 the median years of schooling for Hispanics was somewhat lower than that of both blacks and whites.

**Part B:**

The percentage of blacks and whites with four years of college increased between 1950 and 1987, but the two groups were not yet equal. In 1987 Hispanics had a lower percentage with four years of college than either blacks or whites.

*Source:* U.S. Bureau of the Census, 1985a, p. 133; 1989a, p. 131.

cialty workers has shrunk to 5 percent, and the percentages of black and white salesworkers differ by 6 percent. The gap is largest among managers/administrators (6 percent), which are the most highly paid and prestigious occupations (U.S. Department of Labor, 1989a). In sum, black occupational gains have been considerable, but they do not match the educational gains. At present, the occupational gaps between blacks and whites are still greater than the gaps in educational background, suggesting that race may still have some effect on occupational placement.

Does this mean that blacks and whites are now earning the same incomes? Blacks at every level of education earn less than either whites or Hispanics. Indeed, blacks with some college earn about what whites earn with some high school (U.S. Bureau of the Census, 1989b). So although the number of years of school is related to higher average incomes for all races, it does not have so high a payoff for blacks as it does for Hispanics and whites. Blacks with higher education are younger on the average than

whites with higher education. Therefore age needs to be held constant. When that is done, much of the gap between black and white earnings disappears (Freeman, 1976).

Since black educational gains are not fully reflected in occupational progress, it becomes particularly important to ask if blacks performing the same occupation as whites are earning the same incomes. The closest that blacks come to whites is in blue-collar jobs, where blacks earn 83 percent of what whites in blue-collar jobs earn. Otherwise, blacks earn between 52 percent (among farm workers) and 81 percent (among managers/administrators) of what whites earn in the same occupational category. Furthermore, blacks earn consistently less than Hispanics in every job category except managers/administrators and blue-collar workers. In the Carnegie Commission report *All Our Children* (Keniston, 1977), Rhona Pavis presents data showing that "90 percent of the income gap between blacks and whites is the result . . . of lower pay for blacks with comparable levels of education and experience" (Willie, 1979, p. 59).

In brief, blacks are still less likely than whites to graduate from college; they are somewhat lower on the occupational scale than whites even when they have comparable educations; and they earn considerably less than whites even when they have similar occupations. Three out of 10 black households fall below the official poverty line, whereas only 1 out of 10 white households does. Blacks also have a much higher rate of unemployment than whites. In 1989, 14 percent of black males were unemployed, compared to 6 percent of whites. Among black teenagers aged 16 to 19 in 1987, the rate of unemployment was 35 percent, compared to 14 percent for white 16- to 19-year-olds (U.S. Bureau of the Census, 1989a). Moreover, the gap in teenage unemployment between whites and blacks has been increasing steadily over the past three decades (Mare and Winship, 1984). Finally, with respect to life itself, major differences remain in the life expectancies of blacks and whites. A black male born in 1987 had an average life expectancy of 65 years, compared to 72 years for a white male; a black female's life expectancy was 74 years, compared to 79 years for a white female.

Despite the inequalities that remain, there has been a major increase in the size of the black middle class in recent decades. If middle-class status is defined in terms of employment, education, and real income, about 2 out of 5 black Americans are now middle class, compared to 1 in 20 in 1940. Although the black middle class has increased dramatically, it still lags compared to whites, since 3 out of every 5 white Americans are now middle-class (Landry, 1987; Pettigrew, 1981). Race seems to be less important for determining the disadvantages of black Americans than it was in the past.

Race continues to affect negatively the psychological well-being and quality of life of black Americans—even when social class, marital status, and age are controlled—despite recent political and economic changes (Thomas and Hughes, 1986; Landry, 1987, chap. 3). Wilson does not claim that race has no importance, but he suggests that race is declining in importance. The existence of a growing black middle class and an increasing gulf between that group and a permanent underclass of poor blacks is consistent with Wilson's claim.

## The Urban Underclass

The proportions of black men with annual incomes over $25,000 and those with annual incomes under $5,000 have *both* increased in recent decades. Moreover, inequality of income is now greater among black families than among white families. Fifty-nine percent of black births were to unmarried women, compared to 13 percent of white births. Ten percent of whites, 26 percent of Hispanics, 33 percent of blacks, and more than 50 percent of Native Americans are below the official poverty level. Conservatives and liberals tend to agree that the problem of an urban underclass is serious and growing. They differ in their analysis of what causes this situation and in the solutions they propose. (See the debate "The Underclass: Causes and Solutions.")

## Future Prospects

Competition between ethnic groups seems to shrink in the face of economic growth and prosperity, but it tends to increase in the face of decline and scarcity. Differential power may be reduced by constitutional protection for equal rights, protective legislation, voting rights, or-

*Conservatives and liberals alike agree that the urban underclass has increased in recent decades. They differ in their analysis of what has caused the situation and in the solutions they propose.*

## DEBATING SOCIETY'S ISSUES

Conservatives and liberals disagree about why an urban underclass exists and what should be done about it.

### Suggested Causes

In general conservatives focus on individual-level rather than structural explanations for the rise of an urban underclass. For example, Charles Murray's book *Losing Ground* argues that blacks (whom he equates with the poor) did not gain at all under the Great Society programs (1984). However, the greatest rise in black joblessness and female-headed families occurred during the period (1972–1980) when the real value of Aid to Families with Dependent Children (AFDC) plus food stamps plummeted because states did not peg benefit levels to inflation. Moreover, a study by David Ellwood and Mary Jo Bane of Harvard found that welfare does not significantly affect out-of-wedlock births (1984).

Lawrence Mead's book *Beyond Entitlement: The Social Obligations of Citizenship* suggests that the Great Society programs failed to overcome poverty because the "behavioral problems of the poor" were ignored; that is, people were not told that they must work to get welfare (1986).

The "culture of poverty" explanation, discussed earlier in this chapter, blames the poor for their poverty, suggesting that they do not have the attitudes and values they need to avoid destitution.

In contrast to these individually rooted explanations, liberal analysts offer structural explanations. For example, civil rights leaders tend to focus on racial discrimination as the cause of the urban underclass.

William J. Wilson's recent book *The Truly Disadvantaged:*

### The Underclass: Causes and Proposed Solutions

*The Inner City, the Underclass and Public Policy* (1987) reviews these differing views and suggests a series of structural explanations. First, Wilson challenges the idea of a culture of poverty. He says:

*Cultural values emerge from specific circumstances and life chances and reflect an individual's position in the class structure. They therefore do not ultimately determine behavior. If ghetto underclass minorities have limited aspirations, a hedonistic orientation toward life, or lack of plans for the future, such outlooks ultimately are the result of restricted opportunities and feelings of resignation originating from bitter personal experiences and a bleak future. [1987, p. 158]*

Thus, inner-city social dislocations (for example, joblessness, crime, teenage pregnancies, out-of-wedlock births, families headed by women, welfare dependency, and AIDS) should not be analyzed in cultural terms but should be seen as "symptoms of racial-class inequality" (1987, p. 159; see also Lichter, 1988; Sampson, 1987; and Steinberg, 1981). Wilson believes that changes in the economic and social situations of the ghetto underclass will produce cultural and behavioral changes.

Second, Wilson challenges civil rights advocates by arguing that the existence of racism does not explain why ghetto conditions have deteriorated. While affirmative-action programs are necessary to overcome decades of past discrimination, they help more educated, skilled, and advantaged

blacks while doing little for poor blacks with limited education or training. The agendas of civil rights leaders should be enlarged, states Wilson.

Third, Wilson suggests that structural changes in the economy lie behind the problem. He presents data revealing that (1) substantial job losses have occurred in the very industries in which urban minorities are heavily concentrated and substantial employment gains have occurred in industries that require higher education and which have relatively few minority employees; (2) this mismatch (between the available work force and available jobs) is most severe in the Northeast and Midwest (regions that have had the sharpest increases in black joblessness and female-headed families); and (3) the current growth in entry-level jobs, particularly in the service establishments, is occurring almost exclusively outside the central cities where poor minorities are concentrated. These patterns of change in the economy also enhance the prosperity of better-educated blacks, thereby explaining the increase in the proportion of blacks earning more than $25,000.

Wilson sees a close link between employment prospects and marriage rates. He presents stunning data on the extent to which the declining marriage rates among black women appear to be tied to the sagging economic fortunes and decreased employment rates of young black men. He presents a "black marriageable male index" showing the number of employed black men for every 100 black women in the same age group. In 1960 there were nearly 70 employed black men aged 20 to 24 for every 100 black women that age, while by the early 1980s there were fewer than 50 such men for every 100 women. This pattern holds for other age groups as well. Nationally and regionally, growth in the formation of black female-headed families has largely followed declines in the black marriageable male index.

Fourth, Wilson notes that changes in the black inner-city community have contributed to the problem. As some middle- and stable working-class black families were able to leave the inner cities, those communities changed. Whereas in a more segregated society the black middle, working, and lower classes had lived together, now the inner-city ghettos contain more densely concentrated poverty. Community institutions such as churches, schools, and political organizations that were strengthened by the presence of black middle- and working-class families have become much weaker. This has removed many positive role models for young children and cut off young blacks from the informal job networks and contacts that are available in neighborhoods where adults have jobs.

### Solutions Proposed by Conservatives and Liberals

The conservative solution to the growing urban underclass is workfare—that is, the requirement that persons receiving welfare either work or enter educational or job-training programs designed to make them employable. This solution assumes that those on welfare are not sick or otherwise unfit to work. It also assumes that sufficient jobs with adequate wages exist in the economy.

Wilson's structural analysis focuses on the nature of the economy. He sees full-employment policies as crucial to shrinking the underclass and rejuvenating the inner cities. Using high unemployment as the principal weapon to reduce inflation is unacceptable in his view. Tolerating seven consecutive years of unemployment rates that averaged 7 percent or more for the population as a whole (as we did from 1980 through 1986) led to extremely high unemployment rates for blacks (which averaged about 17 percent for black men during that same period) and greatly harmed the inhabitants of urban ghettos. He suggests the need for policies that favor economic growth and produce a tight labor market.

Wilson emphasizes the importance of training and education initiatives to upgrade the skills of young blacks and connect them with emerging jobs in a changing labor market. He favors a "national labor market strategy" to make the labor force more adaptable to shifts in the economy through, for example, training and retraining programs closely tied to changes in private-sector employment opportunities.

He would move social welfare programs in the direction of European-style "family allowances" (which benefit poor as well as nonpoor families with children) and increase child-support collections from absent fathers, supplementing these payments when they are low. He calls for increased investment in child care.

These economic policies and social programs should be available to the general population, not just to the poor and minorities, in order to build and sustain a broader base of political support, suggests Wilson.

While the costs of such social programs would be considerable, they must be weighed against the economic and social costs of doing nothing. As Levitan and Johnson have pointed out in *Beyond the Safety Net: Reviving the Promising of Opportunity in America,*

*The most recent recession cost the nation an estimated $300 billion in lost income and production, and direct outlays for unemployment compensation totaled $30 billion in a single year. A policy that ignores the losses associated with slack labor markets and forced idleness inevitably will underinvest in the nation's labor force and future economic growth. [1984, pp. 169–170]*

What do you think about this analysis of the problem and the proposed solutions?

ganized political representation, a police force that upholds the law equally for all races, and allies from within the majority group. Obvious legal discrimination is no longer acceptable in American society. Furthermore, Americans increasingly reject racial injustice in principle.

Ethnocentrism seems to be reduced by evidence that shatters ethnic myths and by greater interpersonal contact between relative equals of different groups under nonthreatening conditions. Racial discrimination still exists, however, in subtle forms.

Discrimination may persist because the United States has been an ethnically stratified society, not simply a prejudiced one. Prejudice can be overcome by better contact, communication, and understanding (Blauner, 1972, p. 28). But ethnic stratification is more stubborn. Two decades of efforts to overcome ethnic stratification have not yet produced social and economic equality between blacks and whites. Ethnic stratification creates patterns that not only oppress minority-group members but preserve privileges for the dominant group. Ethnic stratification ensures a large group of people who have no other choice but to do the "dirty work" of society (as janitors, domestics, hospital orderlies, and morgue attendants). Such a system also preserves clean jobs with promotional opportunities for members of the privileged group.

Besides granting economic and occupational advantages, ethnic stratification confers status advantages on the dominant group. Ethnic stratification, in short, goes beyond prejudiced attitudes to encompass all the ways that dominant groups retain their advantages and see that minority groups do not seriously threaten those privileges.

Antiblack prejudice declined in the United States between 1972 and 1984, and this happened in the South as well as in the United States generally (Firebaugh and Davis, 1988). The decline is due to reduced prejudice among younger Americans as well as to changing attitudes among older ones (Firebaugh and Davis, 1988).

The climate of racial and ethnic relations in the United States increasingly rejects injustice in principle. At the same time, there are pockets of strong resistance to school busing, affirmative action, integrated housing, or economic measures that might reduce that injustice (Pettigrew, 1981). Gains have been made, but ethnic and racial equity has not yet been achieved. A gap between values and reality remains.

## SUMMARY

1. An ethnic group shares common ancestry, beliefs, norms, values, and often a common language, religion, and customs. Race is a so-cially constructed concept that refers to a group of people who see themselves and are seen by others as having certain distinctive physical traits.

2. An ethnic or racial group becomes a minority group when its members are singled out for unequal treatment by other groups in society.

3. Certain social conditions must exist to produce intergroup conflict rather than peaceful coexistence. These include ethnic or physical differences, distinguishing characteristics, competition over scarce goods or resources, and unequal power among groups.

4. Ethnocentrism exists when one group feels that it is superior to all others. Racism is a version of ethnocentrism that occurs when one group tries to define itself as a distinct race that is superior to other biologically distinct races.

5. Ethnic or racial antagonism may result in at least six types of intergroup relations: assimilation, pluralism, legal protection of minorities, exclusion or population transfer, subjugation, or genocide.

6. Forceful ethnic domination and racism are accompanied by ideologies designed to legitimate that domination. Domination may also be reflected in and subtly maintained through various aspects of popular culture.

7. Domination may lead to prejudice and discrimination against minority-group members.

8. Contact between racial or ethnic groups reduces prejudice among their members when it involves people of roughly equal social status and when they are cooperating rather than competing with each other.

9. The United States contains a broad mixture of racial and ethnic groups, including WASPs, white ethnics, blacks, Hispanics, Chinese, Filipinos, Japanese, Koreans, Vietnamese, and Native Americans. All of these except the white Anglo-Saxon Protestants have suf-

fered varying degrees of discrimination and domination by others.

10. Hechter's theory suggests that the relative importance of ethnic as compared to class cleavages depends on what he calls the "cultural division of labor" in a society.

11. Wilson argues that race is declining in significance in the United States. The evidence on educational gains supports this argument, but race still appears to be related to the occupations, incomes, psychological well-being, and quality of life of black Americans, even when similarly educated whites and blacks are compared.

12. Both conservatives and liberals see the growing urban underclass as a major problem. They differ in their analysis of its causes and in the solutions they propose.

13. Antiblack prejudice has declined in the United States in recent years, but there is still a gap between the value of ethnic justice and the reality of ethnic stratification.

## KEY TERMS

amalgamation (p. 236)
assimilation (p. 235)
contact hypothesis (p. 240)
continued subjugation (p. 237)
cultural division of labor (p. 251)
discrimination (p. 239)
ethnic group (p. 232)
ethnocentrism (p. 234)
genocide (p. 237)
ideology (p. 238)
legal protection (p. 236)
minority group (p. 233)
pluralism (p. 236)

population exclusion (p. 237)
population transfer (p. 237)
prejudice (p. 239)
projection (p. 240)
race (p. 232)
racism (p. 234)
scapegoating (p. 240)
white ethnics (p. 242)

## SUGGESTED READINGS

DeLoria, Jr., Vine (ed.) 1985. *American Indian Policy in the Twentieth Century*. Norman, OK: University of Oklahoma Press. A series of papers describing and analyzing Indian policy-making at the federal level.

Farley, Reynolds, and Walter R. Allen. 1987. *The Color Line and the Quality of Life in America*. New York: Russell Sage Foundation. An ambitious analysis of economic status and racial identity in American society.

Gardner, Robert W., Bryant Robey, and Peter C. Smith. 1985. *Asian Americans: Growth, Change, and Diversity*. Washington, DC: Population Reference Bureau. Examines the characteristics of Asian-Americans, including their numbers and growth, where they live, and how different groups vary.

Landry, Bart. 1987. *The New Black Middle Class*. Berkeley: University of California Press. A study of blacks who have achieved middle-class status in the last two decades.

Moore, J., and H. Pachon. 1985. *Hispanics in the United States*. Englewood Cliffs, NJ: Prentice-Hall.

Rieder, Jonathan. 1985. *Canarsie*. Cambridge, MA: Harvard University Press. A field study of how Jews and Italians in the Canarsie section of Brooklyn reacted to political, economic, moral, and social changes and pressures in the 1970s.

# *Gender Stratification*

*A normal 7-month-old boy accidentally lost his penis during what was meant to be a routine circumcision operation. For 10 months the parents agonized over what to do. Then they decided to follow available medical advice and agreed to have the boy surgically transformed into a girl. By chance, this baby boy had an identical twin brother. These two children were genetically and hormonally identical. Only their genitals and the way they were raised differed. The parents immediately began treating the new little "girl" differently. The mother let the child's hair grow longer, dressed her in pink slacks and frilly blouses, and encouraged her to wear dresses, bracelets, and hair ribbons. The mother thought the girl was much neater than her brother ("Maybe it's because I encourage it") and found her to be more willing to help with housework. Once when the young son urinated in the front yard the mother laughed, but when the daughter threw her panties over the back fence the mother gave her a little swat on the rear and told her that nice girls do not do that. For Christmas the girl wanted and received dolls, a doll house, and a doll carriage, while the boy asked for and was given a garage with cars, gas pumps, and tools. Although the girl had certain traits her mother saw as tomboyish, such as abundant physical energy, a high activity level, and bossiness among her friends, her mother thought she was not as rough as her brother. [Money and Ehrhardt, 1972]*

The above instance brings out the importance of social interaction for forming gender identity.

The Christmas 1956 issue of *Life* magazine described three possible roles for women—career women, community leader, and total housewife/mother—and clearly rejected the first two as inappropriate. The image in that magazine suggests that the appropriate social role for women and girls 3½ decades ago was to center her life around a husband, children, and a home. A woman's major personal concern was to focus on being as attractive as possible for the sake of her husband and children, whereas men were supposed to succeed in the world outside the family and to be good providers. Many changes in attitudes about women have occurred in the last third of a century.

In this chapter we consider first the gender-role attitudes and behaviors of people in the United States and how they have changed over time. **Gender-role expectations** refer to people's beliefs about how men and women *should* behave. People may *actually* behave differently. You will see that the term **gender** is being used to refer to the traits and behaviors socially designated as "masculine" or "feminine" in a particular culture. These traits include styles of interaction, appearance (for example, hairstyles), patterns of dress, and favored activities and behaviors.

Although in most cultures conceptions of masculinity and femininity are assumed to be linked with biological sex differences, in fact they draw more from social assumptions and customs than from biological determinants. In the West we have traditional ideas about how men and women ought to behave. Margaret Mead, however, studied a tribe in New Guinea, the Tchambuli, where the men reared the children, were the more emotional ones, were artistically creative, and gossiped a great deal. The women in that tribe were the primary breadwinners; they were energetic and domineering; and they wore no jewelry or other ornaments (Mead, 1935). These characteristics contradict our expectations. Similarly, in some periods of history, men's clothing was at least as elaborate as women's clothing, whereas at other periods, such as in the United States generally in recent decades, women's clothing has been more colorful than men's. Such wide cultural variations and marked differences between historical eras suggest that expectations regarding male and female roles and characteristics do not necessarily have a biological basis. **Sex,** on the other hand, refers to the biological distinction of being male or female. It is determined by chromosomes, is reflected in genital and hormonal differences, and is difficult to change (although a few successful sex-change operations have been performed).

Second, we examine the objective status of men and women in the United States today in a number of important areas—education, the economy, political life, and health. Third, we consider explanations for the differences between men and women. The last section of the chapter deals with the prospects for gender equality.

## GENDER-ROLE ATTITUDES AND BEHAVIORS

### Social Conditions Related to Gender Differences

Comparative anthropological work suggests the following conclusions about the social conditions that are related to wider or narrower differences between women and men:

1. Men and women are more alike when they share status and power, when either men or women can do a wide variety of work, and when they work together on similar tasks (Poewe, 1980; Schlegel, 1977).
2. Men are more powerful when they control the resources needed to achieve the group's goals.
3. Gender inequalities may increase when one tribe or nation invades another one and disrupts the traditional economy and culture; they may also become more marked under early industrialization or capitalism (Etienne and Leacock, 1980; Tilly, 1981).
4. Men are likely to be more dominant in societies experiencing environmental stresses, such as an uncertain food supply, chronic warfare, persistent famine, or migration (Friedl, 1975; Harris, 1974; Sanday, 1981).

### Contemporary Views of Gender Roles

Traditional gender roles for men and women in the United States included a rigid division of labor between them, with men being responsible for working outside the home and supporting the family economically, and women being responsible for child care and housekeeping. The traditional male gender role expected men to be strong, decisive, economically successful, sexually skilled, and in control. Such role expectations put tremendous pressure on males to prove themselves at all times, often producing fear of failure and feelings of inadequacy. The denial of feelings often expected of traditional males sometimes closed men off emotionally from their wives and children.

The traditional female role depended on men—first a woman's father, then her husband, and perhaps later her sons—for social status and economic support. Women were expected to devote their lives and energy to nurturing and enhancing the lives of their husbands and children, without regard for their own development or achievement. At the same time, traditional women were allowed more freedom to express their emotions. Most state laws required husbands to support their wives economically, and work did not have the moral imperative for wives that it did for husbands, even when it was economically necessary or personally satisfying. Traditional women felt less pressure to be highly successful if they did work. When traditional roles were prescribed for all women, some women found the lack of autonomy to be unbearable; perhaps for this reason, more women than men were treated and institutionalized for depression and other forms of mental illness (Gove and Tudor, 1973; Rosenfeld, 1980; Scarf, 1980). In short, although traditional gender roles were beneficial for some men and some women, they also had undesirable features for many others.

Sociologists try to gauge people's attitudes by taking social surveys. Recent national surveys have asked about the social qualities that are considered "very important" for a man and a woman. Over time, there has been a steady movement toward valuing the same qualities in both men and women. Figure 11.1 shows that being a good parent, spending time with his or her children, and putting the family before anything else were considered very important qualities for both men and women. Only "being a good provider" was evaluated somewhat differently for men and women.

In a related vein, the percentage of people approving of married women working has risen dramatically, from only 21 percent in 1938 to 81 percent in 1984 (Figure 11.2). In 1978 more than two-thirds of Americans disagreed with the statement "Women should take care of running their homes and leave running the country to men" (NORC, 1978), whereas two-thirds agreed that if the husband in a family wants children but the wife decides that she does not, it is all right for her to refuse (*Public Opinion*, 1980b, p. 34). (This figure does not suggest that two-thirds of the population does not want to have children.) From 1970 to 1979 the percentage of Americans who favored most of the efforts to strengthen and change women's status in society rose from 42 to 65 percent (*Public Opinion*, 1980b, p. 33). These figures suggest that in the past 30 years there has been a dramatic shift in the images of ideal feminine and masculine qualities.

Between the mid-1960s and the early 1970s women's responses to questions on gender roles in five different national surveys in the United States showed a consistent trend toward more egalitarian attitudes (Mason et al., 1976). But that decade was a period of general social protest, economic prosperity, and civil rights activity. Several different studies show that despite a general conservative drift in social sentiments, the trend toward more egalitarian gender-role attitudes continued into the late 1970s and early 1980s (Cherlin and Walters, 1981; Herzog and Bachman, 1982; Thornton et al., 1983) and from 1977 to 1985 (Mason and Lu, 1988).

Young people generally have more egalitarian attitudes than do their mothers, and 18-year-old

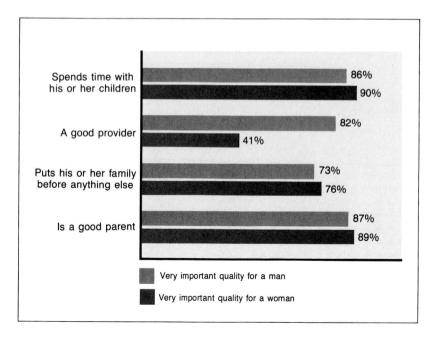

**Figure 11.1    Qualities Considered Important for Men and for Women by a National Sample of Adult Men and Women.**

Spending time with their children, putting their family first, and being a good parent are about equally likely to be considered very important qualities in men and women. Only being a good provider is more likely to be considered very important for men than for women.

*Source:* Survey by Yankelovich, Skelly, and White, cited in *Public Opinion*, 1980, p. 32.

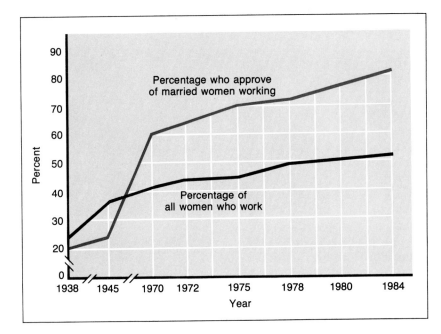

**Figure 11.2 Percentage of U.S. Adults Approving of Married Women Working and Percentage of All Women Who Work, 1938–1984.**

The percentage of U.S. adults who approved of married women working increased dramatically between 1938 and 1984. The percentage approving such behavior has increased even faster than has the percentage of women who work, which has also grown.

*Source: Public Opinion*, 1980, p. 33; 1985, p. 40.

girls have somewhat more egalitarian attitudes than do 18-year-old boys (Thornton et al., 1983). On most questions, more than half the respondents were classified as "nontraditional" in their views of gender roles. The trend toward more egalitarian gender-role attitudes is paralleled by the way men and women, especially younger ones, are more likely to prefer a marriage in which both husband and wife have jobs and both take care of the house and children (Figure 11.3 on page 11-4). Despite this general trend toward more egalitarian gender-role attitudes, however, major attitudinal differences remain.

Some 2000 American students in grades 3 through 12 were recently asked to write their answers to the question: If you were to wake up tomorrow and discover that you were a member of the other sex, how would your life be different? (Baumgartner, 1983). Despite the changes in gender roles during the last two decades, most students were sure that a change in their gender would dramatically change their lives. Boys thought their lives (as girls) would be worse and more limited. Some titled their essays, "The Disaster" or "Doomsday." Girls immediately saw their possibilities as improving. Some of their replies are presented in Table 11.1 on pages 11-2, 11-3. Their perceptions sug-

gest the importance of exploring gender behaviors and differences more fully.

## Contemporary Gender-Role Behaviors

One of the biggest social changes in the last half century has been the dramatic increase in the number of working women, particularly among married women (see Figure 12.3). Clearly gender-role expectations and behaviors have changed regarding women working outside the home.

What we see is a picture of gender-role expectations for women expanding into what were once traditionally male roles. Is the same thing happening for men? Are their role expectations and behaviors expanding to include traditionally feminine role behaviors—such as cooking, child care, housecleaning, laundry, sewing, planning parties, caring for sick and elderly family members, and so forth?

Available evidence suggests that although some fathers are taking a more active part in raising their children and some men have begun to enjoy gourmet cooking, women, even those who work full time, do more of the household work than men (Pleck, 1985; Robinson, 1976).

*Gender role expectations and behaviors have changed dramatically in recent years. This woman helicopter pilot has four years experience in the U.S. army, and men have begun serving as airline stewards.*

Men's share of family work rose from 20 percent in 1965 to 30 percent in 1981 (Pleck, 1985). Husbands who had nontraditional sex-role attitudes and whose wives were employed spent more time with their children than did other men (30 percent compared to 20 percent; Barnett and Baruch, 1987). In a study of 50 dual-career couples with at least one child aged 5 or younger in Indianapolis in 1983, fathers provided 38 percent of the total child care, significantly more than other studies have noted (Jump and Haas, 1987). The majority of fathers were satisfied with the time they spent in child care, and many fathers wished they could spend even more time with their children (Jump and Haas, 1987). These fathers found themselves caught between traditional and more egalitarian models of fatherhood. Their traditional childhood experiences made the integration of new roles difficult at times.

Fathers' involvement with child rearing may enhance the public status of women, at least in certain types of societies, according to a study based on a representative cross-cultural sample of 90 nonindustrial societies (Coltrane, 1988). We know very little about the effects of paternal child care on the status of women in contemporary society. One study found that unlike traditional fathers, who are more likely to stereotype their children according to sex and to engage in rough-and-tumble play, caretaking fathers have more verbal interactions with their children, treat sons and daughters in similar ways, and allow for more self-direction. The

children of such fathers seem to be brighter, to show more empathy, to have fewer sex-stereotyped attitudes, and to be more inner-directed (Radin and Russell, 1983).

Higher-income couples may hire baby-sitters or domestic help, which tends to maintain equality between spouses (Hertz, 1986). This gain in gender equality has the cost of pushing domestic chores outside the household onto another class and often another ethnic group, which is subordinated and may be dehumanized in the relationship (Rollins, 1985).

Berk (1985) found that women do 70 percent of household work, whereas men do 10 to 15 percent. On the average, working women spend 10 to 15 hours more per week than men do on the combined duties of outside work and family work, a difference that adds up to one month per year of additional work done by women as compared to men.

Most of the 335 couples Berk interviewed felt that household work was divided legitimately. Berk's interpretation was that this arrangement produced not only household goods and services but also gender identities. Those identities, according to Berk, involved behavioral demonstrations of dominance and submission.

The concept of masculinity and men's gender-role expectations are also changing (Franklin, 1984; Kimmel, 1987). New role models for men have grown up alongside older ones, "creating a dynamic tension between ambitious breadwinner and compassionate father, between macho seducer and loving companion, between Rambo

IMAGES OF DIFFERENT FAMILIES
AND THE GENDER ROLES WITHIN THEM.

*Schoolchildren's Perceptions of Life as the Opposite Sex*

| | Representative Responses (grade levels in parentheses) |
|---|---|

**As boys, girls would expect to:**

Be more assertive and self-reliant — "I think I would be more outspoken and confident." (tenth)

Show less emotion — "I would have to stay calm and cool whenever something happened." (tenth)

Become more aggressive

"I could beat up people." (sixth)
"I'd probably need to start cussing . . ." (eleventh)
"I'd have to be more (rowdy, macho, smart-alecky, noisy, etc.)" (various)
"I'd kill my art teacher, instead of arguing with him as I do now." (eighth)

Have more freedom — "I could stay out later." (unspecified)
"There would be fewer rules." (unspecified)
"I'd be trusted more when driving." (unspecified)

Think less about appearance — "I wouldn't have to be neat." (fourth)
"I wouldn't have to worry how I look." (sixth)
"If I woke up tomorrow and I was a boy . . . I would go back to bed since it would not take one very long to get ready for school." (tenth)

Be freed from treatment as a sex object — "[I'd no longer have to experience] leers while walking down the street." (eleventh)
(Many girls noted that they would not have to worry about rape.)

Perform different duties at home

"I would take out the garbage instead of doing the ironing." (twelfth)
"I wouldn't have to babysit." (sixth)

Spend more time with and be closer to their fathers

"I could go hunting and fishing with my dad." (sixth)
"My dad would . . . teach me how to work with wood." (sixth)
"My father would be closer because I'd be the son he always wanted." (sixth)
"If I were a boy, my Daddy might have loved me." (third)

| | Representative Responses (grade levels in parentheses) |
|---|---|

**As girls, boys would expect to:**

Be quieter and more reserved

"[I'd have to] . . . wait for others to talk to me first." (tenth)
"I'd have to be (nicer, more polite, goodie-goodie, like a lady, etc.)." (various)

Be less active

"Instead of wrestling with my friends, I'd be sitting around discussing the daily gossip." (unspecified)
"I would play girl games and not have many things to do during the day." (unspecified)
"I would have to hate snakes. Everything would be miserable." (unspecified)
"I couldn't climb trees or jump the creek." (unspecified)

Be more restricted

"I'd have to come in earlier." (unspecified)
"I couldn't have a pocket knife." (unspecified)
"I couldn't throw spit wads." (unspecified)

Worry more about appearance

"I couldn't be a slob any more. I'd have to smell pretty." (eighth)
"I'd have to shave my whole body!" (sixth)
"I would use a lot of makeup and look good and beautiful, knowing that few people would care for my personality . . ." (twelfth)

Be treated as sex objects

"If I were gorgeous, I would be jeered at and hear plenty of comments." (twelfth)
"I'd have to watch out for boys making passes at me." (third)

Worry about violence against females

"I'd have to know how to handle drunk guys and rapists." (eighth)
"I would have to be around other girls for safety." (eleventh)

Perform different duties at home

"I would dust the house instead of vacuuming." (fourth)
"I would be the one who has the kid." (eighth)

Do fewer things with their fathers

"I would not help my dad wash the car or gas up the car." (fourth)
"I would not be able to help my dad fix the car and truck and his two motorcycles." (sixth)

*Source:* Baumgartner, 1983.

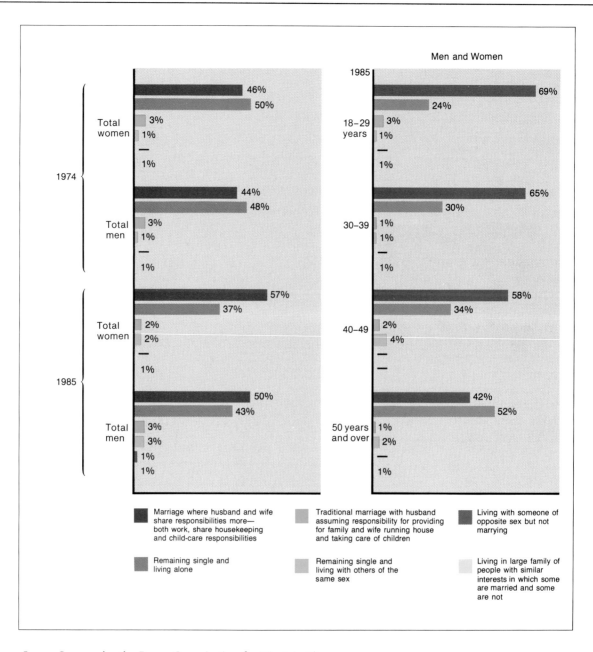

Source: Surveys by the Roper Organization for Virginia Slims,
latest that of March 1985, cited in *Public Opinion,* October/November 1985, p. 47.

**Figure 11.3   Views of What Kind of Marriage Is More Satisfying**

The vast majority of both men and women in the United States think that they
would find being married more satisfying than not being married. Between 1974
and 1985, the percentage of both men and women who preferred a marriage
where both husband and wife work and both share housekeeping and child-care
responsibilities increased, while the desire for a more traditional marriage decreased among women and men, although somewhat more among women than
men. Women under 40 are the most likely to favor a shared marriage; more than
two-thirds of them prefer such an arrangement.

and Phil Donahue" (Kimmel, 1987, p. 9). "We live in an era of transition in the definition of masculinity—what it means to be a real man—not, as some might fantasize, in which one mode comes to replace another mode, but in which two parallel traditions emerge, and from the tension of opposition between them a new synthesis might, perhaps, be born" (Kimmel, 1987, p. 9). Kimmel sees changing definitions of masculinity as reactions to changing definitions of femininity, which in turn reflect structural changes in the organization of the economy, work, and family. Clearly, with respect to gender-role behaviors, women and men are not yet equal.

One attempt to reconcile the discrepancy between gender-role expectations and behaviors may be the ideology of the "superwoman," suggests Hochschild (1985). The superwoman—as portrayed in magazines such as *Working Woman* and *Savvy* and in television characters such as Elyse Keaton in *Family Ties* and Claire Huxtable in *The Cosby Show*—does it all. She has a successful career, a wonderful loving relationship with her husband, thriving children, and an attractive, well-run household. The ideology does not tally the costs—the shortage of time, the lack of leisure, exhaustion, and illnesses such as pneumonia—paid by women seeking "to have it all." Hochschild (1985) suggests that the superwoman ideology offers a degree of comfort to women living in a situation of structured inequality.

The economic inequality women face in the workplace (that is, where they receive less pay than men) and the unequal marriage market (where there are fewer chances for women than men to marry or remarry as they get older) put them at a disadvantage in the negotiations over the division of labor in the home. Many women feel that if they want to stay married, they cannot push their husbands too hard to do more around the home. The women feel they cannot afford to take such a risk—either economically or emotionally (Hochschild, 1985). We shall consider the prospects for gender equality further on. But before doing that we should examine the objective status of men and women in the United States today and consider other explanations of gender stratification.

Changing gender roles have been the center of much social attention in the United States recently. Although they are of interest, it is important to realize that gender roles reflect **gender differences**—variations in the social positions, roles, behaviors, attitudes, and personalities of men and women in a society. A consideration of gender differences does not take into account the question of whether men are ranked more highly than women. A marked focus on differences between men and women may actually serve to strengthen social barriers to gender equality (Epstein, 1988). **Gender stratification,** on the other hand, suggests that men and women and their related gender roles are hierarchically ranked in terms of ownership, power, social control, status, and social rewards.

The existence of gender stratification is revealed in the relative political, economic, and personal power exercised by men and women and in the equality or inequality of the rewards they receive. Their relative status is evident in the amount of personal and sexual freedom women have and in the extent of their informal influence. Exactly what are the life chances of men and women in the United States today?

## DIFFERENCES IN THE LIFE CHANCES OF MEN AND WOMEN TODAY

Life chances are the opportunities a society offers its members. In our society these include educational attainment, labor-market participation, income and wealth, political participation, legal rights and freedom from criminal victimization, physical and mental health, and a normal length of life. In addition, social interaction, including how language is used, is an important interpersonal indicator of equality or inequality. In this section, the status of men and women is compared in these areas of social participation.

### Educational Attainment

By 1993 women are projected to earn at least as many bachelor's and master's degrees as men (Figure 11.4). Women's representation at the advanced degree levels is expected to continue to increase rapidly, as it has in the past decade.

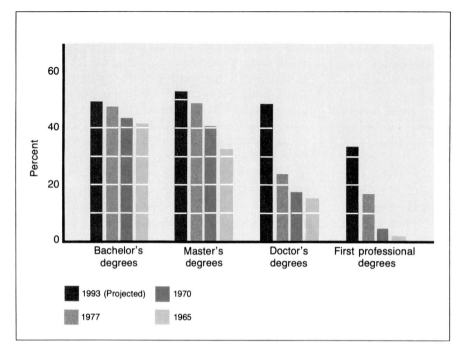

**Figure 11.4   Percentage of Degrees Awarded to Women.**

Women have made major educational gains since 1965. By 1993 women are projected to obtain an equal or greater percentage of bachelor's, master's and doctor's degrees compared to men, and are expected to receive about a third of all first professional degrees awarded in 1993.

*Source:* Plisko and Stern, 1985, pp. 124–128.

Women are expected to earn nearly half of all doctoral degrees in 1993, up from 10 percent in 1965. Women are expected to earn about 34 percent of all first professional degrees (for example, medical, law, or master's in teaching) by 1993, up from 3 percent in 1965. In recent years women have made tremendous gains in educational attainments. Women are, however, somewhat less likely than men to attend four-year or highly selective undergraduate colleges and universities, which may hurt their chances for admission to professional schools or entry into highly paid jobs (Persell, Catsambis and Cookson, 1989).

Men and women still differ somewhat in the disciplines they study as well as in the degrees they earn. In 1982 women were more likely than men to earn degrees at all levels in only four fields—home economics, letters, library science, and foreign languages. In a few more disciplines, women were more likely than men to earn master's degrees. These fields include communications, education, foreign languages, the health professions, home economics, letters, liberal studies, library science, psychology, public affairs, and the visual and performing arts. In all other fields surveyed—agriculture, architecture, biology, business, communications, computer science, engineering, law, mathematics, military science, physical sciences, the social sciences, and theology—men outnumbered women at all three degree levels. Some of these fields were still studied almost exclusively by men, including agriculture, engineering, and military science (Plisko and Stern, 1985, p. 126).

To the extent that employers require degrees in certain disciplines and women lack those degrees, women are less likely to be considered for certain entry-level positions and career paths. Although earning such degrees does not ensure that women will be considered or hired, not having the degree bars them from ever being candidates. The United States has less educational and occupational gender stratification than Japan, however (Brinton, 1988).

## Labor Market Participation

In 1984, 45 percent of the labor force aged 16 and above consisted of women; 57 percent were men. Among the younger (under 45) segments of the population, however, an even larger proportion of women work. This shift is reflected in the fact that in 1988, 73 percent of married women with school-age children were working (U.S. Bureau of the Census, 1989a). By the year 2000, projections suggest that 75 percent of all women will be in the labor force. This prediction represents a new life script, at least for middle-class women growing up today. Gone are the days when a woman could assume that a man would marry her and support her and their children for life. Women have both greater independence and more responsibilities. Men, in turn, have less economic power over their wives but are spared the total responsibility of providing for their families. Men's life scripts are changing also. By 1995 the U.S. Labor Department estimates that only 65 percent of men aged 55 to 64 will be in the labor force (Hacker, 1984). Many will retire early or be unable to find employment in their later years.

Most women will end up working for most of their lives, whether they had planned to or not. Working-class women, after taking time out for child rearing, have always been in the labor force in much larger proportions than their middle-class counterparts. What has changed in the United States since World War II is the record level of middle-class women entering the work force.

Sociological analyses suggest several reasons for the continuance of this trend. Changing economic conditions mean that husbands' incomes alone are increasingly insufficient to support families (Easterlin, 1980). Two "life-cycle squeezes" also put pressure on wives to work: first, the initial costs of setting up a household and, second, the rising costs of rearing older children (Oppenheimer, 1982). Working wives have contributed toward equalizing the incomes among husband-wife families (Treas, 1987, p. 283). One study of a women's college found that many more first-year college women were career-oriented in 1979 than in 1943 (48 percent compared to 12 percent; Komarovsky, 1982). This suggests that younger women are increasingly aware of the changing life scripts they face.

Despite the massive movement of women into the labor market, the amount of occupational sex segregation has changed very little since 1900 (England, 1981). The modern work force remains highly segregated by gender (Baron and Bielby, 1980, 1982; Bridges, 1982). Moreover, men tend to receive greater returns in both status and wages than women do over the paths of their careers (Rosenfeld, 1978, 1980), and sex-specific labor patterns persist over the life course (Blossfeld, 1987). Even in the federal civil service in the mid-1970s, it was harder for women to be promoted from lower- to upper-tier job ladders when other factors were controlled (DiPrete and Soule, 1988).

The concept of **labor-market segmentation** helps to explain women's position in the workplace. The concept refers to the existence of two or more distinct labor markets, one of which is open only to individuals of a particular gender or ethnicity, whereas the other is open to individuals of the other gender or other ethnicities. The fact that men predominate in management, the most prestigious professions, and sales and production jobs; whereas women occupy most of the less prestigious professions, lower-status sales and production jobs, and clerical jobs is explained by employers' hiring and promotion practices. These patterns are found in numerous industrial countries (Roos, 1985). The result is that although the average prestige of all women's occupations is similar to the average prestige of all men's occupations, their jobs differ in earnings and promotion opportunities (Roos, 1985).

Women represent just over half of all professional workers, but that figure needs to be broken down into various occupations (Figure 11.5). Women are overrepresented in the tradi-

*Labor-market segmentation refers to the existence of two or more distinct labor markets, one of which is open only to individuals of a particular gender or ethnicity. The segmented labor market of many large organizations has only recently begun to change.*

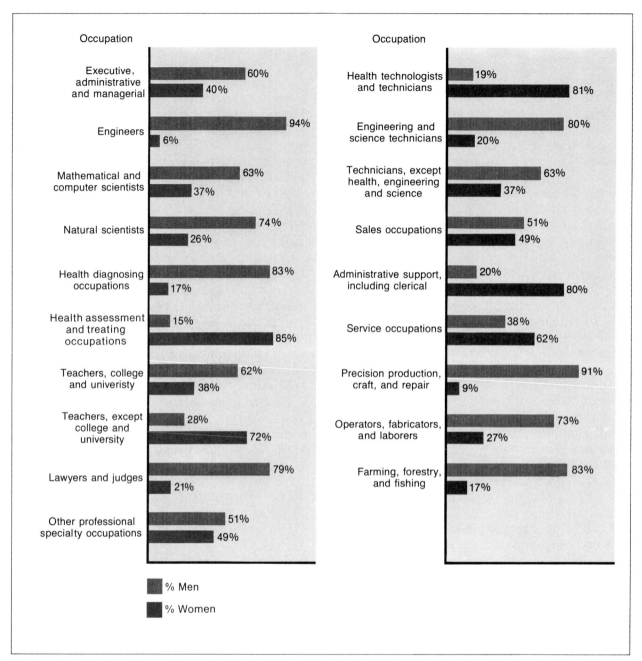

**Figure 11.5  Percentages of Men and Women in Various Occupations, 1989.**

Men and women are not evenly distributed among most occupations.

*Source:* U.S. Department of Labor, 1989a, p. 31–32.

tionally "female" occupations of nursing, library work, teaching, health technology, social work, and educational and vocational counseling as well as in clerical and technician jobs.

Among blacks, 66 percent of all professionals are women; they make up 57 percent of black accountants and auditors (compared to 37 percent for white women), 50 percent of college teachers (compared to 36 percent for white women), and 31 percent of lawyers (compared to 13 percent for white women; Hacker, 1984).

The sex composition of various occupations is not static. As the skills and rewards associated with a particular occupation are upgraded, men tend to enter it in large numbers. This happened in the nineteenth century with respect to health care occupations, as male doctors took over more and more of the work women had been doing (as midwives, for example). Similarly, as skills and rewards decline, the proportion of women in an occupation increases. This happened in the nineteenth century as male clerks were increasingly replaced by women and in education, as female teachers took over from men (Braverman, 1974; Ehrenreich and English, 1978; Reskin and Roos, 1990; Snyder, Hayward, and Hudis, 1979; Tyack and Strober, 1981).

Women today are still only 7 percent of all engineers, 20 percent of lawyers and judges, and 20 percent of doctors. Within the jobs classified as professional and technical, there is a very uneven distribution by sex. Other categories of white-collar work are similarly imbalanced. Women constitute 80 percent of all clerical workers, but only 38 percent of all managers and administrators and 48 percent of sales workers. Men are greatly overrepresented in blue-collar work, particularly in the skilled trades such as precision production, whereas most service workers are women. As long as women do not hold the same occupations as men, the chance of eliminating stratification by sex remains slim. With these major variations by sex, any comparison of the earnings of men and women clearly needs to be done *within* similar occupations.

## Income and Wealth

Across the nation, women earn 65 cents for every dollar men earn (Figure 11.6). In all occupational groups, men earn more than women. In professional, technical, and kindred jobs, women earn about two-thirds of what men do; in sales work they earn about half. Some of this discrepancy may be due to varied educational backgrounds and some to the greater concentration of women in lower-paying jobs within each occupational group. Even in medicine, where

women have the same education as men, in 1978 the average income for women doctors was $39,820, compared to $67,450 for men, a gap of 41 percent (Mattera, 1980, p. 99).

Similarly, a gap of about 40 percent exists in the earnings of men and women business school graduates. Among graduates of Columbia University Graduate School of Business who had been out of school for seven to ten years in 1979, for example, men were earning $48,000, compared to $34,036 for women.

In a major study of gender and earnings among all full-time workers in nine countries, Treiman and Roos (1983) found that women in the United States earned 57 percent of what men earned (a ratio that has remained essentially constant from 1960 to 1978). Considering full-time workers aged 20 to 64, they found the following results regarding female income as a percent of male income: West Germany, 74 percent; Sweden, 69; Finland, 68; Austria, 66; Netherlands, 66; Israel, 65; Norway, 63; Denmark, 57; and the United States, 51.

Four explanations have been offered for these differences:

1. The **human-capital explanation** suggests that women earn less than men because they have less education and less experience, which makes them less productive on the job. As a result, they are paid less than men.
2. **Dual-career responsibilities** suggest that married women may choose lower-paying jobs within occupations and may devote less time and energy to career advancement. The family responsibilities of married women may hamper their chances for pay increases and promotions. This suggests that married women should earn less than never-married women.
3. **Occupational segregation** investigates whether men and women are concentrated in substantially different occupational sectors, with women overrepresented in clerical and service jobs and underrepresented in managerial, craft, and laboring jobs (see Figure 11.5).
4. **Discrimination** based on seniority, sex, age, or race may affect women's earnings. Sometimes these distinctions are regarded as legitimate and sometimes they are considered discrimination.

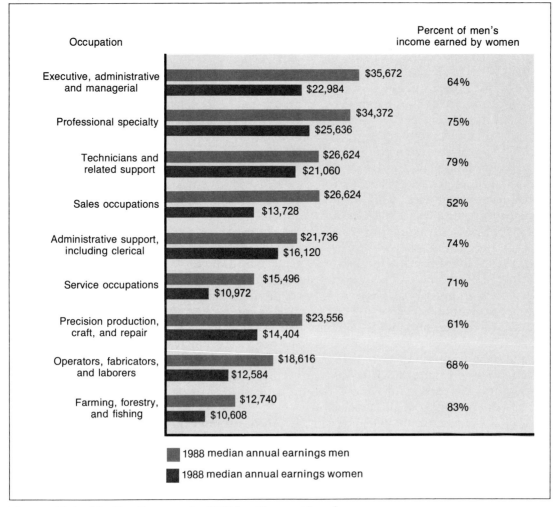

Occupation                                              Percent of men's
                                                        income earned by women

| | | |

**Figure 11.6   Median Income in 1988 by Occupational Group and Sex (Persons 15 years old and over, working year-round, full time).**

In every type of occupation, full-time women workers earn considerably less than full-time men workers, with women earning the lowest percent of men's income among sales workers.

*Source:* U.S. Department of Labor, 1986, p. 212; U.S. Bureau of the Census, 1989a, p. 78.

Treiman and Roos (1983) found the following:

1. Men and women in industrial societies do different work. They are relatively more likely to do similar work in Austria, Norway, Finland, and West Germany, and relatively less likely to do similar work in Sweden. Despite these small differences, there is considerable segregation by sex in all nine countries.

2. Education is positively related to income for men but not for women except in Germany and Norway. This finding calls into question the human-capital explanation of the earnings gap.

3. Regarding marital status, married men earned about 20 percent more than unmarried men when other factors were statistically controlled. This is not explained by their greater experience or generally higher-status occupations. However, employers may prefer to hire

married men, viewing them as more stable and reliable. Married women do not earn less than never-married women in any of the nine countries studied. Remember, however, that this research is confined to full-time workers. These women have made whatever arrangements they needed to make to be able to work full time. Thus the dual-roles argument seems not to apply to full-time workers. It may be that it affects earnings by influencing which women participate in the labor force and the kind of work they do. Women actually put more effort into their work, on the average, than men do, even when men and women with similar family situations and human capital are compared (Bielby and Bielby, 1988).

4. Gender differences in education, experience, marital status, and occupational position do not contribute to the income gap at all. Rather, the gap occurs because women get less payoff on their educations and experience than men do.

Extensive comparison of data from 12 industrialized nations offered more support for using the labor-market-segmentation model to explain widespread differences in occupations and earnings than the human-capital model (Roos, 1985).

A study of 290 firms in California also supports the labor-market-segmentation model. Many firms separate men and women into distinct organizational settings. Even when they employ both sexes in the same occupation, firms typically give them different job titles (Bielby and Baron, 1986). These results suggest that systemic, structural factors play a major role in creating gender differences in occupation and earnings. Both men and women face pay discrimination in predominantly female occupations (England et al., 1988).

Although few would disagree that women earn less than men, some assert that women own or control much of the wealth in the United States. However, only 44 percent of the individuals with personal wealth of $1 million or more are women, and about a quarter of them are widows, most of whom, presumably, inherited their wealth from their deceased husbands (U.S. Bureau of the Census, 1984, p. 462). Very often such wealth is held in trust for the children of such families, so even in this case women do not own or control an equal share of the wealth in America. The figures on wealth ownership are consistent with the existence of stratification by sex in the United States.

## Political and Voluntary Participation

Although women have lower economic status than men, do they also have lower political status? In terms of holding elected office, the answer is yes. In 1989 women held only 25 seats (or 6 percent of the representation) in Congress and 2 Senate seats. In 1988, 16 percent of the 7400 state legislators were women. So women are greatly underrepresented politically. They are running for political office more frequently than in the past, however. Women have also increased their rates of registration and voting in national elections. In 1986 women were just as likely as men to be registered and to vote in national elections (U.S. Bureau of the Census, 1989a).

The political participation of women is increasing, but the number of elected officials is still relatively small, suggesting significant political inequality. These formal indicators of political involvement overlook, of course, such political action as organizing community groups, the women's movement, marches, and the strikes women have participated in. Such activities are no less important than holding an elected office; they are simply more difficult to count. Nevertheless, the participation and power of women in politics has never equaled that of men.

Even though women are as likely as men to join volunteer organizations in general, significant differences between them exist. The organizations men join are three times the size of organizations women join, on the average. The largest differences in size are between fraternal and sororal organizations and in business organizations. Not only are women much less likely to belong to business organizations, but when they do, the organizations they join are much smaller and less prominent. As a result, men occupy positions in the voluntary network that are more likely to offer access to news about possible career opportunities or chances for advancement, whereas women's positions are more likely to provide information about family and neighborhood concerns (McPherson and Smith-Lovin, 1982).

The voluntary sector reflects the sex segregation in our society; it divides men and women into separate domains even more effectively than the occupational structure does. It maintains status differences by creating networks that limit men's and women's information and resources to their traditional domains (McPherson and Smith-Lovin, 1986). For individuals, the typical voluntary organization membership for women generates face-to-face contact with about 29 other members, less than 4 of whom are men. For men, memberships produce contact with an average of more than 37 other members, nearly 8 of whom are women (McPherson and Smith-Lovin, 1986). The fact that men have dominated politics and voluntary business organizations may be related to the subordinate position of women in the legal system, which has been easing only recently.

## Legal Rights and Criminal Victimization

Efforts to improve the legal situation of women in the United States began in 1869, when the National Woman Suffrage Association was founded and started working to get voting rights for women. Women were granted the vote in 1920 by the passage of the Nineteenth Amendment. Even so, all states operate on the basis of an implicit, unwritten marriage contract (Weitzman, 1979). This contract recognizes the husband as the head of the household and holds him responsible for supporting his wife and children; it holds the wife responsible for providing domestic services and child care.

An equal rights amendment (ERA) to the federal Constitution was proposed as early as 1923, when it was introduced into Congress by the National Women's party. Although this amendment was introduced into each Congress after 1923, it was not until 1972, with the support of the women's movement, that the amendment passed both houses of Congress. By January 1982, 35 states, representing 72 percent of the U.S. population, had ratified the ERA. The amendment states: "Equality of rights under the law shall not be denied or abridged by the United States or by any State on account of sex." But later in 1982 the ERA was defeated, despite a strong last-ditch effort by women's groups. In recent years more than half of American men and women supported the ERA, but because many state legislatures are controlled by conservative, rural males, the amendment was not ratified in 3 of the necessary 38 states.

When the Civil Rights Act of 1965 was being considered in Congress, a clause ensuring equal protection under the law regardless of sex was added by a southern congressman as a joke in an effort to get the law defeated. The bill was passed with the clause intact, and its existence has contributed to the legal support available to women seeking equal pay for equal work. Despite the Civil Rights Act, however, women remain unequal before the law in many states.

*On August 28, 1920, two days after the Nineteenth Amendment was passed granting women the right to vote, these women are rallying in support of the Woman Suffrage Party in the United States. Women had already gained the right to vote in Great Britain, New Zealand, and several other countries. As the century progressed, women obtained voting rights in many other countries worldwide.*

Men and women not only have different legal rights, but they are victims of quite different kinds of crimes. Men are more likely than women to report being mugged, robbed, and attacked outside the home. Women face the risk of rape a hundred times more often than men do. In 1987 about one out of every thousand women aged 16 or older in the United States experienced a forcible rape. The United States is among the most rape-prone of all societies (Scully and Marolla, 1985). In 1980 the U.S. rate was 18 times higher than that of England and Wales (West, 1983). Rape may be viewed as an act of violence and social control serving to "keep women in their place" (Scully and Marolla, 1985). Males learn to associate power, dominance, strength, virility, and superiority with masculinity; they link submissiveness, passivity, weakness, and inferiority with femininity (Scully and Marolla, 1985). This cultural context may be seen as a predisposing factor to rape.

In a culture seemingly prone to rape, what do rapists gain from sexual aggression and violence? To address this question, Scully and Marolla interviewed 114 convicted, imprisoned rapists. They found

*that some men used rape for revenge or punishment while, for others, it was an "added bonus" . . . while committing another crime. In still other cases, rape was used to gain sexual access to women who were unwilling or unavailable, and for some it was a source of power and sex without any personal feelings. Rape was also a form of recreation, a diversion or an adventure and, finally, it was something that made these men "feel good." [Scully and Marolla, 1985, p. 254]*

While some rapists may be psychologically disturbed, it is not necessary to use pathological motives to explain rape. Instead, rape can be viewed as an extreme example of more general sexual aggression that rewards men and victimizes women. Most of the rapists interviewed did not expect to go to prison. They saw rape as a rewarding, low-risk act (Scully and Marolla, 1985).

Differences in the rates of rape in different states in the United States are related to gender inequality, social disorganization, the circulation of pornography, economic inequality, and per-

cent unemployed (Baron and Straus, 1987). Campus gang rapes also appear to be increasing (Brozan, 1986).

Rather than recognizing that women are physically more vulnerable than men and trying to compensate for it, the legal system has traditionally made it difficult for women to gain legal protection or recourse—for example, from rape either in or out of marriage. As long as women lack adequate legal protection, equality between the sexes is not a reality.

## Health, Life Expectancy, and Mental Health

Men are three times as likely as women to be murdered and nearly three times as likely to commit suicide. The rate of violent death is much higher for men than for women, even without counting wars. Partly as a result of different rates of violent death, the average life expectancy of women born in 1987 was 78.3 years, whereas that of men was 71.5 years, a difference of 7 years. Women are less likely to get serious diseases than men are. Male death rates compared to female death rates have increased for most causes of death during recent decades, including deaths from heart disease, strokes, accidents, influenza, and pneumonia.

Men have more stress-related illnesses than women, including ulcers, spastic colon, asthma, and migraine headaches. Men are more likely than women to have aggressive or antisocial personality disorders (Rosenfield, 1980), and they are 14 times as likely as women to become alcoholics.[1] These differences suggest that the traditional male gender role, including occupational expectations, has high psychic and physical costs.

Although women have lower death rates than men, they tend to be sick more often. In 1986 women had more infectious and parasitic diseases, respiratory conditions, digestive problems, and other illnesses than men did, whereas

---

[1] When women under the age of 65 do become problem drinkers, it seems to be due to the loss of significant social roles—for example, the lack or loss of marital, employment, and child-rearing roles (Wilsnack and Cheloha, 1987).

men had more injuries (U.S. Bureau of the Census, 1989a).

The key question is how much these differences in life expectancy and health are caused by biological differences between the sexes and how much they are caused by social conditions that may be changing. If the fatal diseases that strike men are due in part to social stresses, then we might expect their rates to drop and the rates among women to increase as responsibilities are shared more evenly. If differential life expectancies are due to social stress factors, they may be seen as one of the costs of sex stratification borne largely by men. The prediction that women would have heart attacks at the same rate as men when they joined the work force has not come true, however (Baruch, quoted in Darnton, 1985).

Socially linked mental health problems, however, seem to bear more heavily on women. Regardless of how mental health is defined, dozens of studies find that married women have more mental health problems than do married men (Gove, 1972; Gove and Tudor, 1973). These differences do not seem to be due to biological sex differences. When Gove compared never-married men to never-married women, divorced men to divorced women, and widowed men to widowed women, the men usually had the higher rates of mental illness (Gove, 1972). Bernard (1972) found that married men were healthier both mentally and physically than single men. To control for some of the factors that may be associated with being single, researchers have compared married clergy with celibate priests and found that the married ones live longer than the single ones. Apparently, something about the structure of gender roles in marriage is helpful to men but not to women.

A wife's traditional responsibilities included living in the home established by her husband; doing the cleaning, cooking, washing; and generally caring for her husband and children. The work done in the housewife's role is generally unpaid, low in outside prestige, and involves restoring or maintaining the status quo rather than creating something new. It isolates a woman from other adults and provides little or no recognition. Although it does provide some flexibility and autonomy during the day (much less if young children need care), it is a role that never ends. Women traditionally have little time

off in the evening, on weekends, or during holidays, whereas men may sit down and relax more at home. These features of sex-role behaviors have not been proved to affect the relative mental or physical health of men and women, but they do warrant further investigation. As long as the work performed by women at home has low status and few rewards, sex status will not be equal. Whenever various forms of sex stratification exist, it seems unlikely that social interaction between men and women will be equal.

## Social Interaction and Language

Studies of conversations between men and women have found that women tend to be more tentative about the statements they make to men. Women often preface their remarks with qualifiers such as, "It seems to me . . ." or "Some people say. . . ." Men tend to assert: "Research shows . . ." or "Everyone knows. . . ." Even men who believe in equal rights for women frequently interrupt women when they are talking.

Men talk more, interrupt more, and ask fewer questions than women do. Are these conversational privileges and duties linked to gender, power, or both? Kollock, Blumstein, and Schwartz (1985) studied couples who shared power equally and couples where one partner had more power than the other. The conversations of male/female, male/male, and female/female couples were tape-recorded and analyzed for the rate of interruptions, questions, and amount of talking time, among other things. Regardless of their gender, the more powerful partner in male/female couples was significantly more likely to do the interrupting. In couples with equal power, there were no gender differences with respect to conversational dominance or support. In short, power can create the conversational dynamics usually considered to be due to gender, and gender by itself has little to do with conversational behavior. This does not deny that power and gender are closely tied in most male/female couples (Kollock et al., 1985).

Men, and older women for that matter, think nothing of addressing a younger to middle-aged woman as "honey" or "dear," but they never use the term when addressing men. The inappropriate use of such endearing terms tends to put down a woman's competence or authority.

Studies of the subtle features of language and gesture in male-female interaction find that women are more likely than men to smile, accept interruptions, and allow others to talk (Goffman, 1979; Thorne, Kramarae, and Henley, 1983). These are the same features of interaction found among members of other groups with lesser power and greater vulnerability.

Male power is reflected in numerous aspects of language. Within existing linguistic conventions, women lack an independent existence apart from men; their identity is presented in terms of men. Women are, it is argued, included in the generic term "man." When two people marry, the wife has traditionally changed her name (e.g., from Jane Smith to Mrs. Robert Jones). Many linguistic practices suggest that females are immature and incompetent, whereas males are complete and capable. For example, men are seldom addressed as "boys" yet women of all ages are often called "girls" or "gals." Women still tend to be described in terms of their sexual attractiveness to men ("chick," "fox," "dog," "a ten") whereas men are described in terms of their sexual prowess ("stud," "dude," "hunk"). In a study of sexual slang, Kramer (1975) counted more than 1000 words and phrases to describe women sexually (sometimes negatively); there were many fewer words for describing men.

Language reveals different gender norms, which may be seen as a means of socially con-

trolling women, suggests Schur (1984). Words may be used to label women deviant, thus contributing to keeping women in their place. Schur notes that a woman's appearance may be characterized as "plain," "unattractive," "masculine," "overweight," "fat," "old," "drab," "poorly made up" *or* "overly made up," "flashy," or "cheap." Similarly, her behavior may be condemned as "oversexed," "nymphomaniacal," "promiscuous," "loose," "cheap," "whore," *or* "dyke," "queer," and so forth (Schur, 1984, p. 53). All of these are judgmental terms that seek to define and limit the roles and behaviors considered appropriate for females (Schur, 1984, pp. 53–54).

Thus the language of our culture reflects many elements of the unequal status of men and women. In addition to being exposed to cultural attitudes through language, Walum (1977) argues that men and women speak differently. Consider the different impact of two reactions to an idea:

"Oh, my—such a lovely idea!"

"Damn, yes—that's a tremendous idea!"

Walum suggests that women may be taught to appear weak, insecure, and dependent on others in the ways they express themselves, whereas Schur's analysis suggests that language is used by men as an instrument of social control. Hence language may force women to conform to the subordinate status in which society places them, therefore reaffirming in their own and others' eyes that they are indecisive or incompetent.

Token representation of women (or other minorities) in a group or organization can produce three responses that hurt their performance: heightened visibility, increased isolation, and stereotyping (Kanter, 1976, 1977a). Studies of women entering male-dominated settings describe the sexual hustles they face (Martin, 1978) and the adaptations they make, such as becoming "one of the boys" (Fine, 1987b). The social attributes of tokens and dominants may be at least as important as their numbers and proportions (Izraeli, 1983; Toren and Kraus, 1987). Organizational tasks and hierarchical structure may also shape the effects of tokenism (Martin, 1985). Too much focus on tokenism may divert attention from the effects of sex stratification in the workplace and in society (Zimmer, 1988). As the next section suggests, stereotyping also

*"How come when a man does the weather forecast, he's called a meteorologist . . . but when a woman does it, she's called a 'weather girl'?"*

appears in apparently scientific theories of the differences between men and women.

## EXPLANATIONS FOR GENDER STRATIFICATION

"Jane did that because she's a girl," "He's all boy." People operate all the time on the basis of implicit theories about why differences exist between men and women. These theories may be boiled down into those that focus on *individuals* and those that focus on *societies*. Theories about individuals attribute different status and life chances to biological differences between the sexes, or they stress the unequal socialization men and women receive. Societal theories suggest that gender differences emerge from the functions they serve in society or result from male power and domination. Considerable evidence allows us to probe both explanations.

### Biological Explanations

There is no denying the biological sex differences between men and women. Three factors define the sexual identity of a newborn baby: chromosomes, sex hormones, and internal sex organs and genitals. The sex of the embryo is decided by one of the 23 pairs of chromosomes (threadlike bodies that contain the genes, the determinants of heredity in all living things). In the fertilized egg cell, the mother always contributes an X chromosome; the father can provide either an X or a Y chromosome. If the father contributes an X, the child has two Xs and is a girl; if he contributes a Y, the child will have an X and a Y and be a boy. The pair of sex chromosomes determines whether the sex glands of the embryo will develop into ovaries or testes. These sex glands secrete hormones (estrogen and progesterone from the female ovaries, and testosterone and other androgens from the male testes). These hormones appear in the fetus after the twelfth week and reappear in puberty, when secondary sex characteristics such as facial hair and body curves develop. In the fetus, these hormones differentiate the internal sex organs and the genitals.

In most infants, chromosomes, sex glands, and hormones work in harmony and produce a consistent sexual identity as a male or a female. Sometimes, however, babies are born as hermaphrodites; that is, their genitals are incompletely formed or they have two sets of genitals, so their sexual identity is unclear. A child may have ovaries and a penis or be genetically male but have genitals like those of normal females. The child may be mislabeled at birth and reared as a boy or a girl, in direct contradiction to the genetic sexual identity. Such cases provide natural experiments that reveal the socially learned nature of gender identity.

In cases of sexual reassignment, Money and Ehrhardt (1972) found that the parents reinforced different behaviors and responses in boys and girls with respect to clothing, general appearance, body movements, play, and the rehearsal of future romantic, family, academic, and vocational roles. Despite a genetic and hormonal sexual identity at odds with gender identity, these children took on the gender identities that had been socially assigned. For most people, biological and social cues interact, and the independent effect of social learning is difficult to detect because gender roles agree with sexual identities. The incongruent cases Money and Ehrhardt analyze, however, uncover the extraordinary influence of child rearing on the emergence of gender identities and behaviors. Clearly the development of gender identity is heavily influenced by social factors. In view of this evidence, it seems unlikely that major status gaps between men and women are caused solely by biological differences.

The power of cultural rather than biological factors is heightened by considerable cross-cultural variations in what gender-role behaviors are deemed appropriate for men and women. In her classic study of three New Guinea tribes, Margaret Mead (1935) found that in one, the Arapesh, both men and women were cooperative, sensitive to the needs of others, and nonaggressive—traits that are usually held to be "natural" to females. In another society, the Mundugumor, Mead found both men and women to be aggressive and unresponsive—characteristics that tend to be labeled masculine in our culture. In a third society, the Tchambuli, Mead found dominant, impersonal, and man-

*Social reinforcement and modeling are two processes that shape gender-role socialization. Parental encouragement for feminine or masculine behaviors plus peer support for certain actions help to explain how children learn gender-specific behaviors.*

aging women living with emotionally dependent men. These cross-cultural variations suggest that cultural values and socialization rather than biological necessity are instrumental in shaping gender role behaviors and personalities. They direct our attention to the content and processes of gender-role socialization.

## Socialization as an Explanation

"Boys don't cry, girls don't swear." All children as they grow up are bombarded with directives about what they should and should not do. The directives come from parents, relatives, neighbors, friends, religious or community groups, books, television, magazines, songs, advertisements, and other aspects of culture. Many of them offer prescriptions for gender-role identities.

### Theories of Socialization

Being *told* what boys and girls do and don't do is only one of a number of processes through which gender role expectations are conveyed. Such information shapes the context within which gender role socialization occurs. The three major theories of socialization are: identification theory, social learning theory, and cognitive development theory.

**Identification theories,** such as Freud's theory of psychosexual development, stress that children tend to identify with and copy the same-sex parent. Nancy Chodorow in *The Reproduction of Mothering* (1978) suggests that because mothers nurture while fathers do not, daughters become nurturing and sons do not. Furthermore, girls never have to separate themselves from their mothers. They are therefore more sensitive and empathetic and are more likely to see issues in terms of contexts and relationships. This theory is consistent with Gilligan's research suggesting that males are more likely to see morality as an issue of rights and justice, whereas females are more likely to see morality as based on relationships, love, and caring (1982, 1985).

Chodorow's theory has been challenged by Jackson (1989), who formulates a mathematical model of the theoretical processes Chodorow proposes. He finds that the model does not explain the greater responsibility of women for child rearing.

**Social learning theory** emphasizes that behaviors that are reinforced or rewarded tend to be repeated more often, whereas those that are ignored or punished tend to occur less often. This theory directs attention to the way children are praised or encouraged for what others consider to be appropriate behavior. "What a pretty, sweet little girl you are,'' or ''My, but you're a strong young man.''

Most social learning theorists feel that other processes besides reinforcement are needed to explain gender-role behavior. They see children as taking on gender-role identities through a process called **modeling**—that is, copying the behavior of people they admire. The admired role models may be older children, adults, or even television and storybook characters. Through their own actions and attitudes, these individuals transmit messages about how members of their gender behave in particular situations.

**Cognitive development theory** suggests that individuals try to pattern their lives and experiences to form a reasonably consistent picture of their beliefs, actions, and values. By the age of 6, boys and girls learn that their gender is permanent (Baker et al., 1980) and that gender is a central organizing principle in social life (Bem, 1983). As a result, they try to figure out the ''proper'' way for people like them to behave. Rewards, punishments, and role models may help to show them the way, but individuals play an active part in searching for patterns in the world and in their own lives.

### Sources of Socialization

As the preceding theories suggest, other people are important sources of socialization. Parents, play and games, schools and books, and television are all significant in the process.

**PARENTS.** Parents seem to be increasingly likely to say that they treat their boy and girl babies the same way. But in an observational study of 11 mothers playing with a 6-month-old baby whom they did not know, researchers noticed that the 6 who were told the baby was a boy named Adam responded differently from the 5 who were told the baby was a girl named Beth. The latter were more likely to offer ''Beth'' the doll to play with, whereas ''Adam'' got the train more often (Will, 1978). Although the study suggests parents treat boy and girl babies differently, the overall body of research on parent-infant exchanges is mixed. Moreover, none of these studies shows that the way mothers behave toward their babies influences the way the child behaves in later life.

Children may be pressured into certain kinds of role behaviors through the jobs they are given to do around the home. For example, in a cross-cultural study of gender differences in children aged 3 through 11, Whiting and Edwards (1973) found that girls were more likely than boys to be asked to care for infants. This difference was related to the expectation of greater nurturing behavior in girls, although when boys were also pressed into baby care, they offered as much help and support as girls did.

**GAMES AND PLAY.** Boys are somewhat more likely than girls to play with building toys such as Legos and Lincoln Logs, toys that are related to the development of spatial-visual abilities among young children (Connor and Serbin, 1977; Serbin and Connor, 1979). Elementary school boys were observed to play outside more than girls did. There they could run around and be more independent. They also played more competitive games in larger groups (Best, 1983). When the boys had a dispute they argued it out, appealed to the rules, or repeated the play that was disputed. Girls often played with a single best friend or in much smaller groups, and if they had a dispute, it tended to end their game (Lever, 1976, 1978). Their play was less competitive and often involved verbal or imaginative activities. Although cause and effect are difficult to untangle, there are patterned differences between the play of boys and girls that may be related to later behaviors—men's work in large organizations and women's skill in sustaining friendships.

**SCHOOLS AND BOOKS.** Elementary and secondary school social studies texts describe a nation created, settled, and led by men (Sadker and Sadker, 1980).

Research on math achievement shows that boys are rewarded more than girls by parents, teachers, and counselors for learning math (Eccles, 1982). Men are more likely than women to teach advanced math classes in high school, yet girls are more likely than boys to be influenced positively or negatively toward science and mathematics by their high school teachers (Lee and Ware, 1985). If male teachers do not take girls seriously as math students, that may reduce girls' interest in that subject.

**TELEVISION AND MEDIA.** By the age of 15 the average teenager has spent more time watching television than attending school. More than three-quarters of the leading characters on television are male (Gerbner and Signorielli, 1979; *Women on Words and Images,* 1975, cited in Tavris and Wade, 1984), and the male characters have more fun (Sternglanz and Serbin, 1974; Mc-Arthur, 1982, cited in Tavris and Wade, 1984). They solve more problems, rescue others, and are rewarded, whereas females more often are only observers. Males are more likely to be "bad guys" and females to be cooperative and affectionate; so the images are mixed, but males are shown to be more important in the shaping of events.

How important is television's influence on people's attitudes and behaviors? Teenagers studied in 1975 and again in 1977 became more sexist over time, especially those who were least sexist in the earlier measures—girls with high IQs. Boys were more sexist than girls whether or not they watched much television, but girls who watched more television became more negative in their attitudes toward women than did girls who watched less television (Morgan, 1982), suggesting that television has some influence on the gender-role attitudes of girls.

### Consequences of Gender-Role Socialization

Socialization has been thought to influence fear of success and lower self-esteem in girls, two consequences that are worth investigating.

**FEAR OF SUCCESS?** "Anne, a medical school student, finds herself at the top of her medical school class at the end of her first semester." Ninety female undergraduates were asked to write a short story about Anne's life. The majority of women (65 percent) wrote stories with negative themes—Anne lost all her friends; she was ugly, unattractive, and lonely; and some even had her dropping out of medical school. Matina Horner (1969), who did this research, termed these themes indicators of the "fear of success" syndrome that plagues bright women. When male undergraduates were asked to complete a comparable story about John instead of Anne, they responded positively. John was portrayed as conscientious and hard-working, with a bright future. Only 9 percent of male students

expressed negative themes. Horner concluded that a huge barrier of anxiety blocks the achievement of many bright women. Knowledge of Horner's research finding based on 200 undergraduates spread rapidly, and many journalists, employers, and academic administrators felt they had an explanation for why women did not achieve as well in graduate and professional school and in the world of work. The fault lay within, not outside of, women themselves.

In the years since Horner did her study, dozens of similar studies have been done in the United States and throughout the world—in Italy, Norway, the West Indies, and Yugoslavia. Criticisms of Horner have appeared, like desert flowers after a flash flood (Condry and Dyer, 1976; Hoffman, 1974; Shaver, 1976; Tresemer, 1974, 1976). Men sometimes fear success as much as women do, reported Tresemer after reviewing 67 studies. And a somewhat later study found only half as many women showing the motive to avoid success (Katz, 1972). Although "success avoidance" appears in both men and women, it seems to take different forms. Women fear social rejection if they succeed; men are more likely to question the value of success as a goal. Rather than reflecting fear of success, respondents' stories may simply reflect a realistic assessment of the results of conforming to or deviating from traditional social roles.

The same young women studied by Horner were studied again nine years later, and their fear of success had declined greatly. Moreover, their earlier fear was not related to their later high levels of achievement (Hoffman, 1977).

**LOWER SELF-ESTEEM?** When males and females evaluate their own abilities, performances, and likelihood of future success, females tend to rank themselves lower (Crandall, 1969; Frieze, 1975; Maccoby and Jacklin, 1974; Parsons et al., 1976). Their evaluations may reflect the lower expectations of women presented in stories, on television, and in other cultural products. As in the case of the "fear of success" syndrome, however, these attitudes may not be related to actual ability, performance, or success. With respect to overall self-esteem, girls and women do not accept for themselves the negative image society presents. Apparently differential self-esteem does not provide a full explanation for the sex differences and stratification in society.

Socialization may help to explain *how* certain gender differences in behaviors or attitudes arise. The problem with focusing primarily on a socialization explanation for gender differences is that it tends to "blame the victims" for their inferior status. As Jessie Bernard (1975) has noted, defenders of the status quo can say, "Sorry, girls, too bad you haven't got what it takes; you're afraid of success and all that. I know it isn't your fault; I know it's the way you were raised; you'd be just as superior as I am if you had played with trucks instead of dolls. But what can I do about it, after all?" What is needed, says Bernard, is to lay bare "the institutional structure which embalms those differences in the form of discrimination against women. The name of the game is power." Stopping with a socialization explanation for gender differences fails to explain *why* different patterns of socialization arise in the first place.

To address the question of why, we need a societal-level explanation. Two possibilities are the functionalist view that the existing division of labor by sex is functional for society, and the conflict view that males dominate through their superior power and control over key resources.

## Functionalist Explanations

Functionalists argue that it was useful in traditional, tribal, and preindustrial societies for men and women to divide the work along sex lines. Mothers who bore and nursed children needed to stay near their young infants. Since they spent much of their time near home, it is likely that they took on domestic duties. The men, who tended to be physically stronger, roamed farther afield, hunting, herding, and protecting the group. In this way a division of labor developed that helped to reproduce and maintain the species.

Talcott Parsons and Robert Bales (1953) have argued that the division of labor by sex is functional for the modern family. They go on to propose that role differentiation and task specialization by sex are universal principles of family organization. They suggest that the family works best when one member, the father, assumes the **instrumental** role of supporting the family and dealing with the outside world, whereas the mother serves in an **expressive** role, providing the love, support, and service that sustains the family. This division of labor requires the male to be dominant and competent and the female to be passive and nurturant.

Considerable contradictory evidence and criticism have been leveled at the functional theory. First, there are findings that challenge the universal principles of task segregation and sex-role differentiation in the family. As to the extent to which instrumental tasks are divided in the family, in nearly half of the societies surveyed by Murdock (1967), women contributed 40 percent or more of the food supply (Aronoff and Crano, 1975). Since providing food is a major instrumental task, this evidence suggests that role sharing rather than role segregation is more characteristic of the family. This undercuts the assertion that the division of labor by sex is universal and functional. If task division is not universally found and therefore not functionally necessary, it may be neither functional nor necessary in modern industrial societies. Today differences in strength are irrelevant in most occupations,[2] and there are fewer families, smaller families, and many more childless families. All these factors increase opportunities for role sharing.

This argument is made by Marwell (1975), who has offered a functional explanation for the origins of sexual differentiation. He begins by asserting that in societies where the family is assumed to be the central economic and social unit, the family must give birth to and socialize new members, produce or earn enough to support itself, and enable husbands and wives to nurture each other. These various tasks are best done by dividing the work. If tasks are assigned on the basis of sex, each family will be assured of having complementary skills. Marwell believes that in certain societies, assigning roles on the basis of sex is functional. These are societies where most people are in male-female family pairs, where the family is central for production and reproduction, and where large numbers of skills are needed to sustain the family. Nowa-

[2] As Gloria Steinem noted, "There are really not many jobs that actually require a penis or a vagina, and all other occupations should be open to everyone."

days, however, according to Marwell, rigid assignment to roles by sex is no longer useful. Society no longer requires that most families produce and raise many children. Economic production is highly specialized and usually occurs outside the family. Fewer skills are needed to maintain families; therefore specialization of tasks and roles within families is no longer functional.

Finally, the rigid assignment of roles by gender may have high personal costs. Although it is unquestionably difficult for both women and men successfully to juggle a combination of career, child care, and housework, the functional theory keeps both men and women "in their places" and denies individual preferences and options. If such a division of labor by sex was ever functional for society, its costs may have long since come to outweigh its benefits. Not all men are happy simply being providers and denying their expressiveness, and not all women are content to suppress their competence and creativity.

The functional division of labor takes a heavy toll on women. Alice Rossi (n.d.) hypothesized that women in their twenties who marry and have children will be more content initially than their age mates who are struggling through graduate school or trying to launch new careers. Sometimes beset by self-doubts, the woman who chooses a career may look longingly at her peers' cozy nests. But a decade later, when the careerist hits her stride and begins to sense her own competence, the housewife feels depressed and envious. Her children are in school and she has no source of external self-esteem. Birnbaum (1975) tested Rossi's predictions with three matched samples of bright college graduates who were housewives, married professional women, and single professional women, all in their thirties. The housewives suffered from the lowest self-esteem and the most doubts about their competence, even with respect to child care and getting along with people. They also felt the least attractive, often felt lonely, and missed the opportunity for challenge and creativity. Perhaps the saddest and most surprising finding was that the married professionals were more likely to be happy in their marriages than the housewives, who devoted all their time to their

*The rigid assignment of roles by gender may have high personal costs for both men and women, since it denies individual preferences and options.*

families. More than half of the housewives (52 percent) saw marriage as burdensome, demanding, and restricting: only 19 percent of married professional women felt this way. This finding hardly suggests an ideal situation for those housewives or their husbands.

A study of Boston-area women found that those who combined both work and family roles felt more satisfied with their lives than did women who had only one of those roles (Baruch and Barnett, 1983).

Although Marwell and other functionalists may explain how sex differences arose in an earlier era, they do not explain sex stratification. Specifically, they do not explain why one set of tasks is considered more valuable and important than another. The functionalist theory of stratification assumes that all societies have certain tasks to perform, and that members of society must be motivated to do those jobs. To explain sex stratification, functionalists must assume that the tasks women do are either less important or easier than the tasks men do. Further, functionalists must show that sex stratification somehow aids the survival, maintenance, or well-being of society. Finally, a functional explanation would have to show how, even when the continuous bearing and raising of children was no longer needed for the biological survival of a group, it was necessary for women to remain in private roles (Nielsen, 1978). Functionalists have not been able to demonstrate these points. They have also been unable to show that the division of labor by sex is universal and therefore necessary for society. If the division of labor was ever functional, its costs today outweigh its benefits for the individual and for society. Functionalist theory may explain the origin of sex differentiation, but it fails to explain sexual stratification. Therefore, we must consider whether sex stratification is explainable in terms of power and dominance.

## Power and Dominance (Conflict) Explanations

Males dominate females because of their superior power and control over key resources, according to a conflict explanation of gender differences. Several theories attempting to explain the origins of male dominance have been offered. Anthropologist Lévi-Strauss (1956) suggests that the inequality of women may have originated in the way they were exchanged among men to build up new families. Another anthropologist, Marvin Harris (1977), suggests that as early tribal societies expanded in size, they began to compete with neighboring tribes for hunting, herding, or agricultural lands. If population pressures continued to build, that competition often took the form of warfare. In the hand combat forms of warfare practiced by those tribes, the greater physical strength of males became a valuable asset for the group. The greater value placed on males was reflected in female infanticide and in male supremacist values and sex roles.

Sociologist Randall Collins (1975) argues that the superior physical strength of men in relation to women is the source of their dominance. In the early years of human life, the theory goes, men dominated women through their physical strength. Women could be beaten, raped, or otherwise forced to do men's will. Once physical domination was established, men began developing ideologies to support their elevated position. These ideologies served to place mental and emotional shackles on women, with the result that they did not always need to be controlled by physical force. The possibility of force was ever-present, however, with both men and women knowing it could be activated any time.

Reports are that physical violence enters as many as half of all domestic relationships between men and women, with more than 95 percent of all spousal assaults being committed by men (Gelles, 1974; Martin, 1988; Straus, 1977–78). This suggests that differences in physical strength may play a role in female subordination—a suggestion that remains valid despite indications that the rate of spousal abuse has declined in recent years (Straus and Gelles, 1986). Some sociologists argue that Collins should not be taken seriously on this point, but his idea does offer one explanation for sexual stratification, since every system of domination ultimately relies on the superior force of the dominant group.

A major consequence of male domination was the exploitation of women by men. Very simply, exploitation means that men and women make unequal exchanges, with men usually getting the better deal. Unequal relations are in the interests of the dominant group, since the subordinate position of women benefits men, who retain greater economic, political, and social power and status. As long as the dominant group benefits from existing arrangements, it has little incentive to change them. In this way gender stratification resembles stratification by class and race.

These types of stratification are also similar in that members of the subordinate group are affected by unequal control of productive resources, wealth, income, political power, and legal and other resources. They have unequal status compared to the dominant group in virtually all spheres of social life. Similarities also arise between race and sex when we address the question of whether the position of women and minorities has improved over the years. For both race and sex we can ask: With respect to what have conditions improved? Do we compare the past and present status of women (or minorities, in which case both appear to have made tremendous progress), or do we compare them to men (or whites, in which case they appear to have made only small gains or to have lost ground)? In a related vein, we can trace the rise of an egalitarian ideology for both minorities and women, but we can distinguish this from the condition of actual equality that may or may not have accompanied the ideology.

A final point of similarity arises in the fact that the balance of power in society—whether based on race, sex, or class—has major implications for personal interactions (Collins, 1975; Etheridge, 1974; Hochschild, 1973a). Subordinates tend to be more sensitive to their superiors—students "psych out" their professors, maids know when their employers are in good moods, children learn to make requests at opportune times, and women learn to "read" the motives of husbands and bosses. Dominants are allowed certain familiarities—touching, first-naming, whistling—which subordinates are not. Dominants also maintain greater social distance and disclose less personal information (Hochschild, 1973a). They might, for instance, ask about the elevator operator's children but would not expect to be asked such a question in return. All these interpersonal differences work to

maintain social inequalities by sex, race, or class. They are similar in that they affect our everyday lives and are difficult to eliminate.

Gender stratification differs from racial stratification, although the lower status of women has sometimes been compared to that of a minority group (Hacker, 1951, pp. 60–69). (Stratification by sex and race are compared in Table 11.2.) Differences also arise from the fact that women are married to men at all levels of the class system, but at any particular level they have less power and status than their male counterparts. At the same time, they may exercise some dominance over men and women in the lower classes. This exercise of dominance may reduce their dissatisfaction with gender inequality. The intimate relation between men and women in marriage may dampen sexual solidarity among women, a feature that does not arise in attempts to change inequalities of class, race, or religion (Rossi, 1972).

### Evaluation of the Four Explanations

Although on the face of it the biological and socialization explanations may seem contradictory and at odds with each other (another version of the old nature-nurture controversy), they actually share a number of common assumptions. They both "blame the victim" for the situation, saying that women are in their predicament because of some deficiency in their own makeup (even if it is not their fault). Furthermore, by focusing only on individuals, both explanations deflect attention from the larger social structures that may create the culture or behavior being observed.

The biological, socialization, and functional explanations all provide a seemingly scientific basis for supporting the status quo; they are legitimating ideologies that appear to be grounded in science. Conflict theory agrees with the functional and socialization theories in stressing that most important sex differences (except for size and strength) are social rather than biological in origin. The functional explanation differs sharply from the conflict theory in the way it suggests that socialization practices arise out of societal "needs" that are functional for society as a whole. The conflict view asserts

**Table 11.2    *Stratification by Gender and by Race***

| Similarities | Differences |
|---|---|
| Difference from the dominant group is usually evident at first sight. | Women are born or marry into all levels of the class structure. At any given level, however, they have less power and status than their male counterparts. |
| Unequal relations are in the interest of the dominant group, which has little incentive to change. | Racial minorities are more likely to be in the lower social classes. |
| Subordinate group has unequal wealth, income, political power, and legal support. | Gender solidarity may be dampened by intimate relations in marriage and by the status differences women derive from their husbands. |
| Inequalities are justified by myths or ideologies, such as the alleged genetic inferiority of blacks or "a woman's place is in the home." | Race does not involve reproductive values and policies. |
| The gap between dominant and subordinate groups has remained fairly large over time. | |
| These inequalities persist despite the existence of a societal ideology of equality. | |
| Inequalities are reflected in personal interactions. Subordinates are more sensitive to dominants; dominants are familiar with subordinates. | |

that socialization practices stem from societal inequalities and the different interests of more powerful people. The theories also differ with respect to the results of socialization. Functionalists stress gender differences, but do not focus on the stratification that accompanies them. Conflict theorists minimize gender differences and focus on sex stratification with respect to status, power, income, and wealth.

These views are not merely topics for an academic debate; they directly affect the lives of men and women in society today. Whatever theory each of us accepts shapes our view of what needs changing and how it might be changed most effectively.

## PROSPECTS FOR EQUALITY BETWEEN THE SEXES

To assess the future of gender roles in the United States, we will consider the forces that have influenced change up to the present, identify the conditions apparently necessary for achieving greater equality between the sexes, and point out possible alternatives. At the outset, we should clarify a point of confusion that frequently arises. Equality does not mean that everyone has to be exactly the *same*. It does mean that groups have equal power and resources that give them the freedom to be different. Not all differences are reflected in stratification by status, power, or wealth. For those who enjoy the variety of different people, and particularly the variety between the sexes, this may be a reassuring distinction.

## Forces That Brought Us to Where We Are Today[3]

Several major factors have contributed to the changing reproductive and productive roles of women in society. These include major female life-cycle changes, improved contraceptive technology, labor-market demands, and social movements pressing for equality without regard to race, creed, or sex. In recent years the female life cycle and reproductive role have been transformed. Childbearing is no longer the central fact of a woman's life. Whereas women once spent most of their adult years bearing and rearing children, they now spend less than 15 percent of their lives doing so. When her youngest child starts school, the average mother still has 40 years of life left (Sullerot, 1971).

### Control over Reproduction

Part of this change is due to the nearly complete control women can exercise over their reproductive potential. They can limit and time their children (or opt not to have any, as increasing numbers of women are doing), yet they need not restrict their sexual activity to do so. This reproductive control makes married women available for work. Although the number of women in the labor force increased steadily since 1870, the demands of the labor market and the shortage of unmarried women workers greatly increased the number of married women who entered the work force since 1960, changing the norms surrounding the employment of married women. These changes in reproductive technology and labor-market participation, along with the civil rights movement, undoubtedly influenced the women's movement.

---

[3] This section and the next have benefited greatly from Etheridge (1974) and from numerous conversations with her.

### The Women's Movement

As noted earlier, women won the right to vote in 1920. In the 1960s a strong women's movement developed again. In 1961 President John F. Kennedy appointed a National Commission on the Status of Women. This group, and similar ones at the state level, documented the current status of women in the United States and developed a network of concerned women. In 1964 Title VII of the Civil Rights Act made discrimination on the basis of sex illegal. However, the members of the Equal Employment Opportunity Commission (the EEOC), the federal agency empowered to enforce the act, did not want to extend it to include sex discrimination. The ensuing confrontation between women and EEOC officials encouraged the formation of the National Organization for Women (NOW). This group constitutes the older branch of the women's movement. It has focused on extending civil rights to all people, including women. Basically reformist in orientation, NOW has aimed at obtaining equal pay for equal work, equality before the law, credit equality, and at opening traditionally male career lines to women. In general, its strategies have included collective efforts to change existing political structures and policies through lobbying, letter writing, political marches, and media coverage.

Meanwhile, activist women were becoming disenchanted with the sexist attitudes and behaviors of the male leaders of the political New Left. Two identifiable groups of younger feminists emerged, the radical feminists and the socialist feminists. The former see sex stratification as rooted in a man's desire to have his ego override that of a women. They call for the elimination of all sex distinctions and especially all male privileges. The socialist feminists see sex stratification as arising from the economic system; that is, women contribute profits by serving as low-paid labor and as a reserve labor force.

Both types of feminists favor a complete social and political restructuring of society. In her analysis of the women's movement, Freeman (1975) suggests that the combined efforts of younger and older feminists contributed to the movement's early success. This success has begun to lay the groundwork for greater equality

*The Women's Movement seeks to change political and cultural practices that contribute to the inequality of women. One focus, for example, takes the form of protests against beauty pagents, such as this Miss California contest in 1988.*

between men and women. At the same time, feminists have made social scientists aware of the need to identify the conditions under which equality is more or less likely to occur.

## Conditions Necessary for Equality

A major way that social analysts work to discover conditions that are critical for a particular social state—in this case equality between the sexes—is by comparing a number of different situations that vary in at least one major respect. Etheridge (1978) used this method in examining family systems in the Oneida community (a utopian community in upstate New York begun in the mid-nineteenth century), Israeli kibbutzim, several U.S. mountain communes, and two-paycheck families in the United States and Great Britain. From this comparative analysis, she was able to discern four conditions necessary for equality between the sexes. First, men and women need to be economically independent. This factor is a necessary but not a sufficient condition, which means that equality will not occur without it, but by itself it is not enough to ensure that equality does occur. Economic independence occurs when men and women have equal access to the productive process and receive equal shares for their contributions. Second, participants need to be committed to an ideology of equality. Without that commitment, there is no will to make the practical arrangements at home and at work that are necessary to ensure the realization of equality.

The third condition is equal task allocation in public and private spheres. It flows directly from the commitment to an ideology of equality and means that men and women need to participate equally in central societal policy-making and administrative positions. This condition is essential for gender equality because people with relatively more information, access to resources, and control over decisions feel—and are, in fact—more powerful in their daily lives (Etheridge, 1978; Kanter, 1977; Kohn and Schooler, 1973, 1978; Miller et al., 1979). Anyone who withdraws into the private world of the family will have less status in society than a partner who is active in the outside world. Public and private tasks need to be equally allocated between men and women; when tasks are assigned on the basis of gender, they become a major means of maintaining different and invariably unequal definitions of "masculine" and "feminine." Fourth, equal sharing of public and private tasks means that both partners will be able to work less or that some form of help with child rearing must exist. Otherwise, parents who are working, caring for children, and keeping house are likely to become overloaded.

We can pursue this line of reasoning further. If these four conditions are the ones necessary to achieve equality between the sexes, how can those conditions be met? The two-earner family has become necessary in many cases. In low-income homes two incomes can ensure that the family is fed and can stay together. In higher-income families, two earners can ensure better housing, education, health care, and recreational opportunities for the family. In periods of unemployment, the two-earner family has more of a cushion than the single-earner family, in which the sole breadwinner may become unemployed.

Farrell (1976) describes other benefits that equality between the sexes may bring to men. Women who have their own lives to control may make less effort to control their husbands' lives. When a man's partner is economically independent, he may be freer to choose a more interesting, lower-paying position instead of a boring, higher-paying job. Men may lose some of the legal burdens that discriminate against them, such as automatic responsibility for alimony, jury duty, and a mandatory later retirement age under social security. All together, Farrell discusses 21 benefits men may obtain from equality between the sexes.

The subordination of women in the United States has been due to their exclusion from the economic and political order and was supported by the resulting patterns of child rearing, sexuality, violence, and ideology. The evolution of the industrial market economy and the political order have been weakening the subordination of women and making gender equality our ultimate destiny, argues Jackson (1990).

## Public Policies to Support Equality

Policies such as affirmative action and pay based on comparable worth aim toward equalizing occupations and incomes by gender. Family policies try to address the child-rearing needs of working parents.

### Affirmative Action

**Affirmative action** requires employers to make special efforts to recruit, hire, and promote qualified members of previously excluded groups, including women and minorities (Giele, 1988). Affirmative action holds the promise of increasing the number of men and women in occupations where they were previously underrepresented (Roos, 1985; Reskin and Hartmann, 1986). Young women in nontraditional occupations are no more likely than young women in other occupations to leave within the first year (Waite and Berryman, 1986). The Reagan administration opposed affirmative action, considering it reverse discrimination. The practice was upheld by the Supreme Court in 1987, however. It is not clear that it has been widely practiced since then. It is important that the Equal Employment Opportunity Commission explore and develop ways of enforcing policies aimed at equitable pay (Reskin and Hartmann, 1986).

### Comparable Worth

Pay on the basis of **comparable worth** aims to equalize the salaries earned by men and women doing similar work in jobs that are labeled differently by sex. For example, men and women prison guards in the state of Washington

were not paid the same wages (Whicker and Kronenfeld, 1986). Comparable worth moves beyond the more individualistic affirmative action strategies aimed at upward mobility toward the goal of collective upward mobility. As such, it has the potential of appealing to large numbers of working women. Sociologists have developed ways of analyzing and evaluating job elements so that equally demanding jobs could receive similar pay (Cain, 1985; Hartmann, Roos, and Treiman, 1985; Ratner, 1980; Treiman and Hartmann, 1981). One scholar estimated that comparable worth would increase women's wages, on average, between 10 and 30 percent, which would go a long way toward eliminating gender stratification in pay and providing economic independence for women (Hartmann, 1987). Actual pay-equity adjustments have fallen far short of these projections, ranging from 5 to 15 percent of salaries (Steinberg, 1987). Ultimately the impact of comparable worth will depend on how solutions are formulated, implemented, and used politically (Brenner, 1987).

Comparable worth addresses the interests of working women in traditional jobs, suggests Blum (1987). Those interests are different from the small numbers of women in well-rewarded positions dominated by men. As a result, comparable worth could contribute to the declining significance of gender, much as the growth of the new black middle class may be related to the declining significance of race. It might do this by bringing clerical workers and semi-professionals up to middle-income levels, while leaving a larger gap between them and under-class women who are unemployed or in peripheral jobs (Blum, 1987). It might also attract men into better-paid women's work, thereby pushing some women out. It sets up antagonism between women and men and fails to attack inequality directly (Blum, 1987). Finally, it could encourage employers to subcontract work, use temporary workers, eliminate jobs, or send work overseas. Despite these possible disadvantages, comparable worth has some potential for improving the life chances of many working women (Blum, 1987).

Reskin (1988) argues that neither integrating jobs by sex nor comparable worth will markedly improve women's employment situation.

It is doubtful that women will advance economically through job integration, according to case studies of a dozen traditionally male occupations where women made big gains during the 1970s (Reskin and Roos, 1990). The researchers found one of two patterns. Either men and women remained highly segregated in supposedly integrated occupations, or women were allowed to enter occupations that were becoming less attractive to men because of changes in the nature of the work, its autonomy, or its rewards (Reskin, 1988). Men may have social as well as economic reasons for preferring gender segregation in the workplace (Wharton and Baron, 1987). Occupational segregation and sex differences in earnings continued despite the growth of service industries (Tienda, Smith, and Ortiz, 1987). Both job integration and comparable worth ignore men's incentive to preserve their advantages and their ability to do so by making the rules that are used to give out rewards. Reskin urges political analyses and political pressure on employers, the regulatory agencies that monitor them, and the branches of government that create and fund those agencies (1988).

### Family Policies

Key family policy proposals are for flexible working schedules, corporate or community-based child care, parental leaves, and family allowances (Bergmann, 1986; Bianchi and Spain, 1986; Giele, 1978; Hewlett, 1986; Kamerman and Kahn, 1978; Kanter, 1977b; Moynihan, 1986; Roos, 1985).

Sweden (Haas, 1980) and most other European countries have already adopted many of these policies (Hewlett, 1986), and they have smaller gender gaps in earnings than does the United States. Further structural and political changes are necessary if gender stratification is to be eliminated.

## SUMMARY

1. In the past 25 years, life scripts for American women have changed dramatically from a sole focus on husband, children, and home to an image of active life choices involving various combinations of family and work. The concept of masculinity and male life scripts are also changing.

2. That shift is reflected in the distinction between sex and gender. Sex indicates one's biological identity as a male or female; gender refers to the traits and behaviors culturally defined as masculine or feminine.

3. Gender-role attitudes and behaviors have changed steadily over the past two decades, mostly in the direction of women taking on roles traditionally belonging to men.

4. Whereas gender differences focus on variations in the social positions, roles, behaviors, and attitudes of men and women in a society, gender stratification refers to the way gender roles are ranked with respect to power and prestige.

5. Sex stratification is revealed in the dramatic differences in the life chances of men and women. Educationally, women are earning about the same number of bachelor's degrees as men, but they still lag somewhat in advanced and professional degrees and they do not study the same fields as men.

6. Although women comprise 45 percent of the labor force, they are still overrepresented in the traditionally "female" occupations of nursing, library science, teaching, and social work and are underrepresented in such "male" occupations as engineering, law, medicine, and the ministry. Today 80 percent of clerical jobs are held by women, compared to only 40 percent of all management and administrative jobs. Labor-market segmentation and other structural factors create gender differences in occupations and earnings.

7. Women earn only 65 cents for every dollar that men earn, and major differences remain even when education, occupation, and experience are the same. Men also control a larger share of wealth.

8. Although women have stepped up their political participation in recent years, they still comprise only a small minority of elected officials. Legally men and women do not have equal rights and responsibilities. Women also join smaller and less prominent voluntary business organizations.

9. Men and women face different forms of criminal victimization. Women face the risk of rape a hundred times more often than men do. Men are more likely to be robbed, mugged, attacked, and murdered. The average life expectancy for men is 71.5 years, compared to 78.3 years for women. Married women have more mental health problems than married men, but unmarried women have fewer mental health problems than unmarried men.

10. Both social interaction and language reveal differences between men and women, although power differentials rather than gender per se may explain conversational dynamics better.

11. Biological, socialization, functional, and conflict theories have been offered to explain sex differences and sex stratification. Cases of children of one biological sex who were reassigned to the other sex and reared as a member of that sex demonstrate the power of socialization in the learning of gender roles. This evidence, along with widely varied gender-linked behaviors in other cultures, suggests that cultural values and socialization rather than biological necessity are the strongest influences on gender behaviors. Socialization occurs through processes such as identification, social learning, and cognitive development, and through such sources as parents, play and games, schools and books, and television and media.

12. Some suggest that "fear of success" among women is one of the consequences of differential gender-role socialization, but the evidence for this fear is mixed and less overwhelming than originally suggested. Research on self-esteem is also mixed.

13. Both functional and conflict explanations go beyond individual-level explanations to societal-level explanations and therefore can help to explain differential gender socialization. Functionalists argue that task specialization by sex is functional for the family and society, with the husband assuming the instrumental bread-winning role and the wife taking on the expressive and nurturant role. Evidence suggests that although combining work and family responsibilities is difficult, the option of doing so is more satisfying for many men and women. Functionalism helps to explain the origin of sex differentiation but not its persistence as sex stratification.

14. The conflict and domination view of sex stratification suggests that men fare better economically and socially than women because of their superior power and resources.

15. Women share certain similarities with minority groups, but they differ in terms of numerical strength, varied class membership, and marriage ties.

16. The changing roles of men and women are related to female life-cycle changes, improved contraception, labor-market demands, the women's movement, and the growing economic necessity for two incomes.

17. To achieve equality between the sexes, men and women need equal access to the productive process, a commitment to an egalitarian ideology, equal participation in public and private life, and help with child care. Without economic equality and equality in the marriage market, equal relations in the home are difficult to achieve.

18. Public policies to support equality include affirmative action, comparable worth, and family policies. They must be passed and enforced if they are to achieve their aims. While comparable worth has increased women's incomes somewhat, it has not raised them as much as expected. Men have the incentive and the capacity to design rules that reward them more, so political pressures are needed, according to Reskin (1988). Family policies are just beginning in the United States, although many European countries have had them for a long time. Their effects remain to be seen. Structural and political changes are needed to end gender stratification.

## KEY TERMS

affirmative action (p. 287)
cognitive development theory (p. 278)
comparable worth (p. 287)
discrimination (p. 269)

dual-career responsibilities (p. 269)
expressive (p. 280)
gender (p. 260)
gender differences (p. 265)
gender-role expectations (p. 260)
gender stratification (p. 265)
human-capital explanation (p. 269)
identification theories (p. 277)
instrumental (p. 280)
labor-market segmentation (p. 267)
modeling (p. 278)
occupational segregation (p. 269)
sex (p. 261)
social learning theory (p. 277)

## SUGGESTED READINGS

Berk, Sarah Fenstermaker. 1985. *The Gender Factory: The Apportionment of Work in American Households.* New York: Plenum. Explores how household work is divided among husbands and wives.

Gerson, Kathleen. 1985. *Hard Choices: How Women Decide about Work, Career, and Motherhood.* Berke- ley: University of California Press. Analyzes how women's decisions respond to social structural opportunities and limitations.

Guttentag, Marcia, and Paul F. Secord. 1983. *Too Many Women? The Sex Ratio Question.* Beverly Hills, CA: Sage. A cross-cultural and historical analysis of how the ratio of men to women affects the gender-role behavior that develops in a society.

Hertz, Rosanna. 1986. *More Equal Than Others: Women and Men in Dual-Career Marriages.* Berkeley: University of California Press. A depth-interview study of husbands and wives who have high-level corporate jobs and of the dilemmas and possibilities they face.

Kimmel, Michael S., ed. 1987. *Changing Men: New Directions in Research on Men and Masculinity.* Beverly Hills, CA: Sage. A series of new studies on the changing nature of male roles and masculinity.

# PART 4

# SOCIAL INSTITUTIONS

Social institutions represent strategies for dealing with important social concerns. The family deals with sexual regulation, reproduction, and child rearing. Chapter 12 considers these traditional functions of the family and explores major changes within the family today. Economy and work address the production and distribution of goods and services. Chapter 13 examines national and international changes in the economy and work and shows how those changes affect individuals' lives. Politics focuses on the use and legitimation of power and authority. Chapter 14 examines theories of power, the structure of power in the United States, and sources of political change. Education develops individual talents, transmits knowledge and social mores to a new generation, and plays an increasingly important part in channeling people into their occupations, as you will see in Chapter 15. Hence education affects the social status of individuals. Religion may promote social unity and help individuals to find meaning beyond themselves. Chapter 16 examines religion in the United States and the world, considers some of the dynamic and changing forms of religious groups, and looks at religion as a source of change as well as stability. Science is a relatively new social institution, devoted to developing new knowledge and technology. Scientists are members of society and of social groups, however, and Chapter 17 analyzes the norms of science, resistance to changing scientific ideas, and the sources of conflict between science and society. These institutions vary in different societies, and some are currently undergoing dramatic changes.

# *The Family* 12

*"I am married to someone who cares about me, who is concerned for my well-being, who gives as much or more than he or she gets, who is open and trustworthy and who is not mired down in a somber, bleak outlook on life" (Lauer and Lauer, 1985, p. 24). In their study of 351 couples married more than 15 years, Lauer and Lauer (1985) found 300 couples who described themselves as happily married. A common theme among happily married couples was the feeling that they had married someone who was caring and giving and had integrity and a sense of humor. They also showed that they believed in marriage as a long-term commitment.*

Historically, marriage was the basis for family life. In recent decades, however, the rising rate of divorce and the growing number of singles and single parents has changed the form of many families, especially in the United States. As a result, everyone is talking about the American family. Some say it is dying, others say it is adapting to social change. Some see it as the center of meaning and intimacy in people's lives, others charge that it is a nest of emotional, social, and physical abuse. These contradictory charges clearly suggest that the family is an important institution for a lot of people and for society. Why else would so many people be giving so much thought to it?

Sociologists point out that some form of the family appears universally in all cultures and societies. On the other hand, they, like other social observers, wonder if the family is declining in U.S. society or simply adapting to social changes. If it is adapting, how and why is it changing?

In the first section of this chapter we examine the functions the family has traditionally filled in society, including sexual regulation, member replacement, care and socialization of the young, and economic functions. Relatively recently in historical terms, love and emotional intimacy have been added to the functions the family is expected to serve.

In the next section we consider some of the major changes in family forms that have emerged in the last 25 years. These include more single-parent households, declining marriage rates, later marriages, more cohabitation without marriage, more childless couples, two-paycheck families, smaller families (fewer children per couple), generally higher divorce rates, and more stepfamilies.

The existence of these changes raises the question: Why have these changes occurred? So in the third section we examine possible causes of these trends, including demographic changes, economic conditions, the "sexual revolution," and cultural attitudes and preferences. Some of the consequences of these trends for family life and for society are analyzed in the fourth section, including changes in family roles and power relations, family violence, and sibling interactions within the family. The societal implications of the increasing "privatization" of the family, and the effects on children of divorce, single-parent families, working mothers, and stepfamilies are also examined.

In light of these trends and their consequences, we return in the final section to the question of whether the family is declining or adapting, and we consider what various groups in society propose doing for and about the family.

The U.S. Bureau of the Census defines a **family** as two or more persons who are related to each other by blood, marriage, or adoption and who live together. Many people would broaden this definition to include the family units of young adult college students who live away from home. Some people feel the definition should be widened further still to include adults who are not relatives but who have made a commitment to each other and want to live together in some sense as a family—for instance, two unrelated old people or homosexual couples. The preceding definition differs from a more traditional conception of the **nuclear family,** which consists of a mother, a father, and their children. Sometimes sociologists and anthropologists use the term **conjugal family** to refer to the same unit.

In the conjugal family, primary emphasis is on the husband-wife relationship rather than on their relationships with blood relatives. The conjugal family may be far removed from its relatives, as when a husband and wife and their unmarried children move to a distant city, away from their families. An **extended family** is one in which relatives from several generations live together. The family is a unit within a larger kinship network. **Kinship** refers to socially defined family relationships, including those based on common parentage, marriage, or adoption.

## THE FUNCTIONS OF THE FAMILY

Traditionally, the family as an institution has served a number of important functions in society, including sexual regulation, biological reproduction, the care and socialization of the young, and the economic functions of providing food, shelter, and warmth for family members. In most societies few institutions filled these functions better than the family. It is worth con-

sidering each of these functions and how they are changing.

### Sexual Regulation

Sex is an important drive in human beings, and it has the potential for disrupting relationships in social groups. For this reason, virtually every society has developed norms governing sexual relations. In all societies, various categories of sexual relations are possible, including marital relations, incest, and homosexual relations, for example. **Marriage** is a social institution that recognizes and approves the sexual union of two or more individuals and includes a set of mutual rights and obligations. Virtually all societies encourage sex within marriage and forbid incest, but how other forms of sexual relations are regulated varies widely. Western societies, at least until recently, have generally forbidden everything except marital sexuality. In the 115 societies around the world that Murdock (1967) studied, however, only three were as strict as Western societies. About 70 percent of them, under certain conditions, allowed sexual freedom prior to marriage.

Some social analysts have suggested that sexual regulation increased when private property and a surplus of food or wealth developed, because the existence of inheritable property made it important to establish the legitimacy of heirs. The desire to regulate reproduction naturally focused on sexual relations.

*Virtually every society has norms governing sexual relations. Many societies encourage marriage and yet at the same time try to regulate marriage.*

## Member Replacement

All societies need to replace their members. The needs of societies, however, vary widely. When people had a relatively short life span and infant mortality was high, it was important for families to have as many children as possible. Societies therefore placed great value on fertility and reproduction. Modern industrial societies show opposite tendencies. Life expectancy has been extended greatly, and infant mortality has declined. As a result, it is no longer widely believed that people should have as many children as possible.

The number of births to unmarried mothers has increased in recent years. In 1986, more than 878,000 babies were born to unmarried women, representing nearly one-quarter of all live births that year. By contrast, in 1950, only 4 percent of all babies were born to unmarried women (U.S. Bureau of the Census, 1985a, p. 62). About one-third of unmarried mothers in 1986 were 19 years old or younger. Teenage mothers are more likely than other mothers to be poor, to live in inner cities or isolated rural areas, and, disproportionately, to be black (Geronimus, 1987).

What are the consequences of teenage pregnancy? Compared to other teenagers, adolescent mothers are (1) less likely to complete high school, (2) more likely to remain in the lower occupational status and income groups, (3) more likely to suffer complications in their deliveries, and (4) more likely to suffer from emotional problems related to sexuality and pregnancy (Kephart and Jedlicka, 1988, p. 279). What about the consequences for their children? Their children are more likely to suffer from complications at delivery, to have below-average birthweights, and to experience serious adjustment problems in their teen years (Kephart and Jedlicka, 1988, pp. 279–280).

## Care and Socialization of the Young

Humans require many years of nurture and socialization before they can become full-fledged members of society. The care and the socialization of the young ensure that a society will

*Every effort is made to teach new members of a society the norms, values, beliefs, and behaviors appropriate for membership in that society. These parents have brought their young son to their college graduation.*

have cultural as well as biological reproduction. Every effort is made to teach new members the norms, values, beliefs, and behaviors appropriate for membership in society. In a fairly simple society, such as that of hunters and gathers, virtually everyone of the same age and sex learns similar norms and values. In more complex societies, however, there is considerable variation in the content of social learning and teaching, in accordance with the class, ethnic group, or nationality of an individual. Such societies and groups transmit their cultures from one generation to the next. Part of the cultural content that is so transmitted may include the social relations between various groups. The family is an important means of such social and cultural transmission.

## Economic Functions

To survive, all societies must meet the subsistence needs of their members; that is they must provide food, clothing, and shelter. The family has been a traditional means for seeing that the dependent members of a society were cared for by other members who were able to produce these basic necessities. With the advent of industrialization, more and more individuals stopped producing food, clothing, and shelter themselves and began working for others in exchange for money. They then used this money to purchase the things that they and their families needed.

In recent years, especially in Western societies, women have been increasingly able to work outside the home. Although they still do not earn as much as men, they are able to meet some of their subsistence needs without depending on a male earner. Some of the economic functions traditionally performed by women in the family—such as cooking, sewing, and canning—have been learned by men or are available in exchange for money. As a result of these and related changes, more and more individuals are able to sustain themselves economically without living in families.

Do family members still provide the basic economic support for their family units? It is difficult to answer this question fully, but sociologists do know that in 1975 one-quarter of U.S. households had no members who worked. By 1990, this will be true of 29 percent of households. Such households include the retired, the widowed, nonworking single parents, and handicapped or infirm single individuals. These families receive income from the government, their kin, private pension plans, and their own savings and investments. The biggest single source of government payments comes from the social security system, which makes old-age, survivor's, and disability payments. That program presumes that at least one member of the family has worked at some earlier time.

Presumably, three-quarters of households have at least one member who works. Some would argue that "two can still live as cheaply as one." One person needed $5778 to be above the government's definition of poverty in 1987, while a second person living with the first was considered to need only an additional $1619 to escape poverty (U.S. Bureau of the Census, 1989a).

Although the family's economic needs are currently being met by work, government programs, and kin, the growth of households without any workers may make it more difficult for such families to meet their needs for food, clothing, shelter, and health care. As a result, we would expect the family's role in meeting economic needs to decrease for some people and the role of the government and outside jobs to increase.

## Emotional Intimacy

In many societies there is little expectation that wives and husbands will be emotionally close. Among the Nayar of India, for example, girls are married before the age of puberty to establish their place in the community. Although they and their ritual husbands are secluded together for four days, they do not necessarily have sexual relations. After that, the ritual husbands and wives have no special relationship except that the ritual wife and any children that she may have must observe rites when the husband dies. The ritual wife and husband may become lovers when they are older if both are willing, but it is not required that they do so. They may or may not be close sexually and emotionally.

In some societies, marriages are arranged by parents, sometimes when the partners are children, and the partners may not even know each other when they get married. More than 2000 arranged marriages occurred in the United States in 1982, when Rev. Sun Myung Moon, leader of the Unification Church, selected partners for 4150 of his young followers and then performed a massive group wedding in New York's Madison Square Garden. Many of these young people had met for the first time only days before. Some did not even speak the same language as their new spouses and could converse only through interpreters. In such situations an individual's needs for emotional intimacy may be met by other family members, such as siblings, parents, or children.

In contemporary Western society there is a fairly strong and widely held expectation that husbands and wives will be intimate emotionally as well as sexually. Although most couples expect intimacy, some can realize their expectations better than others. Lower-income couples may worry less about intimacy than about paying their monthly bills. Blue-collar workers have been found to expect less sharing and emotional intimacy in their marriages than white-collar workers (Komarovsky, 1962). However, Rubin (1976) suggests that these expectations in

*Emotional intimacy is expected by most couples, but the amount of sharing couples experience may vary according to their social-class background. Roseanne Barr and John Goodman play a working-class couple in the television comedy series "Roseanne."*

the working class may be changing as working-class wives come increasingly to look for emotional intimacy in their marriages.

Most adults (78 percent) in a recent national survey said they get a great deal of satisfaction from their family lives; only 3 percent said they get little or none. If they feel their needs are not being met, they may seek a new relationship. Unlike people 25 years ago, they are slower to get married, more likely to live together without marriage, and less likely to have children. Also, they are likely to have fewer children and more likely to get a divorce.

Despite the positive functions of the family for society, the basic role structure of the family may also have some previously overlooked dysfunctions (Komarovsky, 1988). If so, we might expect some changes in family forms and activities.

## CHANGES IN FAMILY FORMS AND ACTIVITIES

Family forms in Western industrial societies have been shifting markedly in recent decades. In the United States, for example, fewer families consist of married couples. In 1970, seven out of ten households consisted of married couples,

and more than half of these had one or more children (Figure 12.1). By 1985, however, less than six out of ten households consisted of married couples. By the year 2000, married couples may represent barely half of all households, according to U.S. Bureau of the Census estimates (Ferriss, 1988).

These shifts are reflected in marriage rates, the increase in the number of singles, birth rates, more working wives, divorce rates, and more stepfamilies.

### Marriage Rates

The **marriage rate** per 1000 single women, representing an average for all age groups, has declined from 90 in 1950 to 57.0 in 1985 (U.S. Bureau of the Census, 1989a, p. 85). This may be due in part to women's increased options outside of marriage (Goldscheider and Waite, 1986). Marriage rates peak for both sexes between the ages of 25 and 29. By age 30, about 90 percent of women and 83 percent of men have married at least once. Figure 12.2 shows the changes over time in the percentage of American women in various age groups who had never married. Some young people are simply postponing marriage while they obtain more education or get established in a career. The age at marriage for both sexes depends heavily on the timing of young men's entry into relatively stable occupational careers, suggests Oppenheimer (1988). Others will not marry at all. The national median age at first marriage reached a low of 20 for women and 23 for men in 1956. After rising steadily, it was 23.0 for women and 24.8 years for men in 1985 (National Center for Health Statistics, 1988).

Despite the rising age at which people marry and the growing number of women who have never married, 88 percent of all women think of marriage as an ideal way of life, according to a 1987 Gallup poll. As recently as 1980, however, 94 percent of women favored marriage as a way of life, so this represents some decline. It is notable that only 33 percent of 18-year-old daughters in 1980 said they would be bothered "a great deal" by not marrying and another 34 percent would be bothered "some," although 97 percent expected they would get married

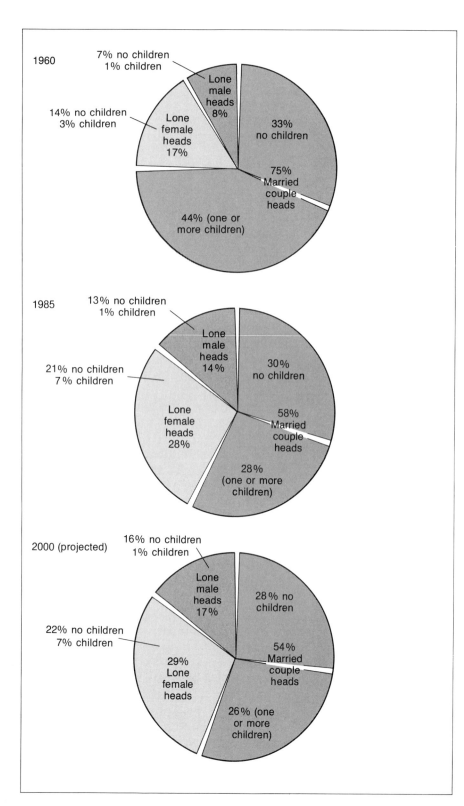

**Figure 12.1   Changing Household Composition in the United States, 1960–2000.**

In 1960, three-quarters of all households consisted of married couples, and more than half of those had children. By 2000, only slightly above half of all households are expected to be married couples, and half of them will have children. The percentage of single male- and female-headed households is increasing markedly.

*Source:* U.S. Bureau of the Census, 1986a, p. 2, and 1986b, p. 2.

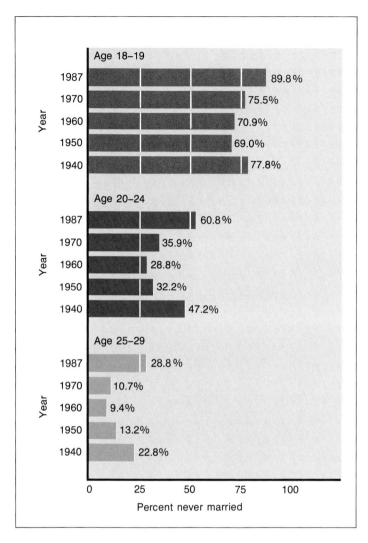

**Figure 12.2  Percentage of Women Who Never Married, in Different Age Groups, 1940–1987.**

Between 1940 and 1960, the percentage of women between the ages of 18 and 29 who had never married declined. Between 1960 and 1987, the percentage who had never married increased to a new high.

*Source:* U.S. Bureau of the Census, 1989a, p. 41.

(Thornton and Freedman, 1982). The nature of the marriage relationship they desire has changed, however. A majority of women (57 percent) feel that marriage responsibilities should be shared equally by both partners, with both earning salaries and sharing family and household activities. Half of men (50 percent) agree. Support for this type of relationship is greatest among younger and college-educated women. Two-thirds of them favor such a marriage (*Public Opinion*, 1985, p. 47).

Even though women overwhelmingly favor marriage as a way of life, they continue to get married at a slower rate today than they did 20 years ago. Several reasons have been offered for this trend. First, women are more likely to pursue higher education today than in the past, a factor that is related to later marriage. Second, there has been a rise in cohabitation among unmarried couples and an increase in same-sex (homosexual and lesbian) relationships.

The number of cohabiting couples has more than quadrupled, from about half a million in 1970 to more than 2 million in 1987. Most of these couples are in the 25 to 44 age range, followed by those under 25; the third largest age group among cohabitors was people who were 45 to 64 years old. Despite the rapid rise in cohabiting couples, they still make up only about 4 percent of all couples living together in the United States (U.S. Bureau of the Census, 1989a). If other countries are any indication, however, this percentage will continue to grow in the United States. In Denmark more than

*The number of cohabiting couples has increased in recent decades. The largest proportion of such couples is in the 25 to 44 age range.*

one quarter of women 18 through 25 live with a man without being married, and in Sweden about 12 percent of all couples (aged 16 to 70) are not married (Westoff, 1978).

One study compared cohabiting cross-sex, homosexual, lesbian, and married couples in terms of how they handled money, occupational responsibilities and housework, and sexual relations (Blumstein and Schwartz, 1983). Stability in their relationship was similar for cross-sex couples, homosexual, and lesbian couples. Those who broke up were likely to have argued about money or work or to include one partner who was more dependent or ambitious than the other (Huber and Spitze, 1988).

Not all cohabiting relationships are the same, however. They differ in terms of motivation and commitment. At least six types of cohabitation have been noted: (1) relations of temporary convenience or mutual benefit; (2) affectionate relationships that are open to other, simultaneous relationships; (3) affectionate monogamous relationships; (4) trial marriage or a conscious test relationship; (5) temporary alternatives to marriage—for example, while awaiting a divorce settlement or graduation; (6) permanent alternatives to marriage (Macklin, 1983).

A majority of college students approve of living together before marriage. In 1987, a national survey of first-year college students showed that 58 percent of men and 47 percent of women approved of living together before marriage (Astin et al., 1987). As compared to a similar survey done in 1974, that represents a 7 percent increase for men and an 8 percent increase for women.

Does cohabitation affect the stability of marriage later on? Two hypotheses have been offered (Bennett, Blanc, and Bloom, 1988). One suggests that cohabitation is a form of trial marriage, with the result that only the most stable of cohabiting couples marry. Thus, cohabiting couples should be better able than noncohabiting couples to avoid marital dissolution. The second hypothesis suggests that those who cohabit are a self-selected group of people whose relationships, both nonmarital and marital, are notable for their lack of commitment and stability. They may also attach less importance to traditional institutions such as marriage. Thus, cohabitors would have higher rates of marital dissolution than married couples who did not cohabit. Research has shown that Swedish women who cohabited before marriage later dissolved their marriages almost 80 percent more often than did women who had not cohabited (Bennett, Blanc, and Bloom, 1988). Women who cohabit for more than three years prior to marriage have marriage dissolution rates that are over 50 percent higher than those of women who cohabit for less time. Cohabitors and noncohabitors whose marriages remained intact for eight years show no differences in their rates of marital dissolution after that time (Bennett, Blanc, and Bloom, 1988). Although they cannot pinpoint the exact cause of higher marital dissolution rates among cohabitors, the researchers see their findings as consistent with the hypothesis that cohabitors may be a select group who tend to lack the "interests" or "values" typically associated with marriage (Bernard, 1982, p. 159, cited in Bennett et al., p. 136). Another indication of the trend is the attitudes of single women, who were twice as likely in 1976 than they were in 1957 to view marriage primarily as a burden and restriction. In 1976 only 17 percent of single women held positive attitudes toward marriage (Bernard, 1981a).

## More Singles

In 1940 fewer than 8 percent of all U.S. households consisted of people living alone, but by 1987 the figure was 24 percent of households. There are 36 million single women and 29 million single men, but their ages are not comparable. One out of every two single women is over age 40, whereas only one out of four single men is. About half of all singles have never been married. Their numbers have increased as the marriage age and divorce rate have risen and as more people choose not to marry at all. Although their life situations and life-styles are quite different, they do share some common satisfactions and frustrations.

The *young singles* are in their twenties and are just out of school and into their first jobs. Although traditionally this group stayed at home with their parents until they married, in recent decades many have been able to afford their own place to live, which they often share with one or more roommates. This group, which may be paying off educational loans, faces the high cost of everything from rent to transportation, clothes, and furnishings. Nevertheless, they may be the most likely to live the "swinging singles" life-style characterized by lots of night life and parties. Their roommates may provide support and friendship, but they may also feel pinched for privacy.

The *divorced* or *never-married middle-aged singles* very often live alone or cohabit with a special partner. If they are divorced, they may have financial, social, and emotional involvements with and obligations toward dependent children. They may be somewhat more established in their work than the young singles and be earning somewhat more. They are likely to have clarified their own likes, dislikes, and interests and to have developed a good circle of friends.

*Singles over the age of 65* are more likely to be women because of their longer life expectancy and because three quarters of husbands are older than their wives. Many are poor and subsist on social security payments and other meager sources of income. Many never worked for income in their own lifetimes and therefore do not receive pensions from their own work. Many are involved in church or other groups that provide a sense of community and friendship.

All singles face the possibility or fear of loneliness. Rather than being socially isolated, many people who live alone compensate by having many more contacts outside their homes than people who live with others (Alwin and Converse, 1984). Some of the younger and middle-aged ones report the pressures of living in a "pro-marriage" environment (Stein, 1976). Many singles who are economically independent say they enjoy their freedom and find that being single provides them with greater variety and more opportunities for personal development.

## More Two-Earner Families

In 1968, 45 percent of all married couples had one wage earner (a male) and 45 percent were two-earner families. (The other 10 percent had either no earners or the husband did not earn.) As noted in the previous chapter, many more wives and mothers are working today than were working in 1970 (see Figure 12.3). As a result, by 1980 two-earner families were 52 percent of all married couples, whereas only 31 percent of

*Many more wives and mothers are working today than were working 25 years ago. Here a four-year-old daughter is emulating her lawyer mother on their way home from day care.*

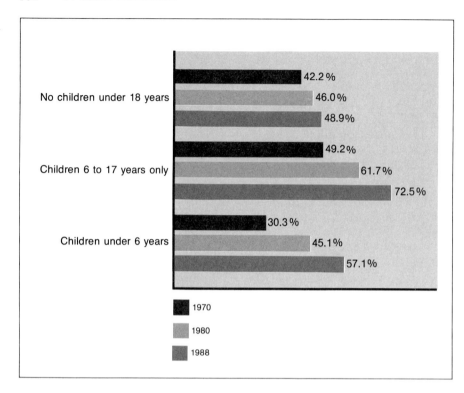

**Figure 12.3   Labor-Force Participation Rates for Married Women Aged 16 to 44 with Husbands Present, by Presence and Age of Children: 1970, 1980, and 1988.**

Between 1970 and 1988, married women who lived with their husbands moved into the labor force in growing numbers. Those with children aged 6 to 17 were most likely to work. But even among those with children under 6, more than half were working in 1988.

*Source:* U.S. Bureau of the Census, 1989a, p. 386.

families had a sole male wage earner. Two-earner families are smaller and younger; the adults have more education and earn more jointly than families with only one male wage earner (Hayghe, 1982, p. 29; see the debate on two-earner families).

About one-quarter of all two-earner families may be characterized as **dual-career families.** These are families in which both husband and wife have occupations that require special training and where they move through a pattern of jobs of increasing prestige (Wilensky, 1961, p. 523).

It is helpful to consider two-earner families in relation to the eight major stages in the family life cycle noted by Duvall (1971). These are:

1. Beginning families (married couples without children).
2. Childbearing families (oldest child under 30 months).
3. Families with preschool children (oldest child 30 months to 6 years).
4. Families with school-age children (oldest child 6 to 13 years).

5. Families with teenagers (oldest child 14 to 20 years).
6. Launching-center families (between the time that the first and last child leaves home).
7. Families in the middle years ("empty nest" to retirement).
8. Aging families (retirement of both spouses; cited in Poloma et al., 1982, p. 180).

Childless women find that marriage does not alter their career development. The major limitation of marriage for wives' careers is the lack of geographic mobility. Among women who have children, many reduce their career involvement in stages 2 and 3 of the family cycle and begin to increase it again in stages 4 and 5. In stages 6 and 7 the professionally employed wife really hits her stride in her career (Astin, 1985; Poloma et al., 1982). Little research has been done about the last stage of family life for dual-career couples.

For men in careers, the pattern is one of professional or graduate school right after college and then an uninterrupted career line that builds to its high point, levels off, and is followed by

Ed is a computer programmer, and his wife Cindy is a teacher. Their children are cared for by his mother three days a week and by a neighbor the other two days. Cindy generally has vacations when their children do. Ed earns about twice what she does.

Kathy earns much more in her job as a television newscaster than Mike, her bank officer husband, does. They both travel a lot, and in some ways their marriage is like the commuter marriages of couples who live apart for days or even weeks at a time for the sake of their jobs. When they had twins, Kathy took a three-month maternity leave. They have a live-in housekeeper and extra help to aid in running the household.

Orlando is a youth worker married to Jenny, who runs a gift shop. He makes dinner on the nights she works late at the store and takes the kids on Saturday outings when she works. She has Mondays off, and on that day she cooks several main dishes for the week's dinners. Orlando and Jenny spend Sundays cleaning the house, doing laundry, and grocery shopping, because they have decided they would rather save the money it would cost to pay someone to come in and do these things for them. They are hoping to save enough to buy their own home. As the children grow older, they are helping more with family chores, becoming "part of the solution rather than part of the problem," as Jenny puts it. When the children were young, they went to a day care center four days a week. Now that they are in grade school, they have after-school sports and activities until 5 o'clock.

Social scientists studying the lives of couples like these point

## Do the Advantages of Two-Earner Families Outweigh the Disadvantages?

out some of the advantages and disadvantages of two-earner families:

### Advantages
1. Two-earner families generally have higher incomes than one-earner families. Having two adults working may provide a cushion for the family if either partner is unemployed for a time.

2. Their good income may help to pay for their children's education, travel, eating out, shows, and other leisure activities.

3. Both partners are more likely to have interesting work lives, since they may be more able to seek jobs they enjoy.

4. They may have more to talk about with each other and may have good insights into each other's worlds.

5. The other spouse and the children may be able to go along on some business trips.

6. Both individuals tend to face challenges and keep growing personally, socially and intellectually.

### Disadvantages
1. Role overload is possible for both husband and wife, particularly if they have children. This sometimes leads to excessive fatigue and illness. Husbands need to help more with children and housework than in traditional families.

2. There may be rather limited time for housework, social life, entertaining, leisure, relaxation, volunteer activities, care of aged relatives, and other things women have traditionally done when they were not working outside the home.

3. Husbands may receive little social support for helping with child care or household tasks.

4. The family needs additional help with child care unless either or both partners have relatively low-key, perhaps even part-time jobs.

5. Sometimes competition flares between husbands and wives when both have careers they consider important.

6. Vacation times of both spouses and children may not always coincide. So even though the family may have the money to vacation together, members may not always have the time to do so.

7. Finding good jobs for both husband and wife in the same area may be difficult, and one may have to take a less desirable job.

What do you think? Do the advantages outweigh the disadvantages? If, as the chapter suggests, more and more families will need two incomes to maintain the standard of living they desire, what could be done to reduce some of the disadvantages?

*Sources:* Aldous, 1982a, 1982b; Hood, 1983; Pepitone-Rockwell, 1980; Rapoport and Rapoport, 1976; Rice, 1979.

retirement (Poloma et al., 1982). Married women's career lines are different from those of most men. Although many young women today report that they want "to have it all"—husband, career, and family—they have very little idea about what "having it all" involves (see, for example, Scarr, 1984; Komarovsky, 1985). Women with children are likely to follow one of four different types of career, depending on how they cope with the various stages of family life. They may follow regular careers, interrupted careers, second careers, or modified second careers (Poloma et al., 1982).

Mothers pursuing regular careers tend to follow the same sequence as men except that they need to fit in the birth and care of one or more children. If they pursue full-time careers, they need considerable help with child care and home responsibilities [see, for example, Epstein's (1981) study of women lawyers]. Part-time regular careers are sometimes pursued by women doctors or lawyers who can set up limited private practices (Poloma et al., 1982). Interrupted careers begin like regular ones but are interrupted for several years, usually for child rearing in stages 2 or 3. They may be resumed in stages 3 or 4. The professional training for second careers may begin in stage 4, after the first career of child rearing is well along, and actual career activities may not begin until stages 5 or 6. A modified second career begins earlier (Poloma et al., 1982). For the two-earner family as for all family forms, a life-cycle perspective illuminates possible strains and ways people compensate for them (Gerson, 1983; Rossi, 1983).

## Divorce Rates

At current rates, 40 percent of today's marriages will end in divorce. (See Figure 12.4 for divorce rates since 1920.) Sociologists have identified social factors that are related to divorce. They also address the question: Will divorce rates continue to increase or will they stay the same?

Three types of factors appear to affect divorce rates: preparation for marriage, investment in it, and economic and marriage markets (Huber and Spitze, 1988). More education may be considered as preparation for marriage and is related to lower divorce rates (Bahr and Galligan, 1984;

Moore and Waite, 1981). People who marry at a somewhat later age are less likely to divorce, perhaps because they are more mature (Thornton, 1978). Children are considered one form of investment in marriage, but their presence has no consistent relationship with divorce (Waite, Haggstrom, and Kanouse, 1985; Cherlin, 1977; Morgan and Rindfuss, 1985), although preschoolers seem to have some deterrent effect. Home ownership, clearly a joint investment, also decreases the likelihood of divorce (Becker, Landes, Michael, 1977; Moore and Waite, 1981), but couples who fear for the stability of their marriage may be less likely to invest (Huber and Spitze, 1988). Remarriages are more divorce-prone than first marriages, especially if there are stepchildren (White and Booth, 1985). One reason may be their greater normlessness (Cherlin, 1978). Another reason may be that people who divorced once may simply have less commitment to permanence in marriage and hence may be more willing to divorce again (Furstenberg and Spanier, 1984). Also, people whose parents divorced have more positive attitudes toward divorce than do others (Greenberg and Nay, 1982).

Market influences on divorce seem to include changes in husbands' socioeconomic level (Cherlin, 1979; Hampton, 1979; Mott and Moore, 1979; Ross and Sawhill, 1975) and wives' employment (Mott and Moore, 1979; Ross and Sawhill, 1975; Cherlin, 1979). Blacks are more likely to experience divorce than whites, even when key variables are controlled (Espenshade, 1983; Moore and Waite, 1981; Thornton, 1978). A major reason may be the lack of good jobs, a market-related factor (Kitson et al., 1985; Patterson, 1982). Although divorce rates for Hispanic groups have risen in recent years (Mirande, 1985), they tend to be lower than those for other groups.

Regarding the future direction of divorce rates, some factors suggest that levels will rise while others suggest they will fall. The number of adults in the most divorce-prone age (between 25 and 40) will not peak until about 1990 (Glick, 1988). Other factors that might push toward higher divorce rates include a continuing low birth rate, a continuing increase in the employment of women, a continuing high level of cohabitation outside marriage, and a continuing

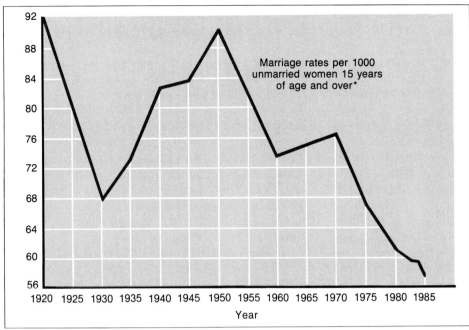

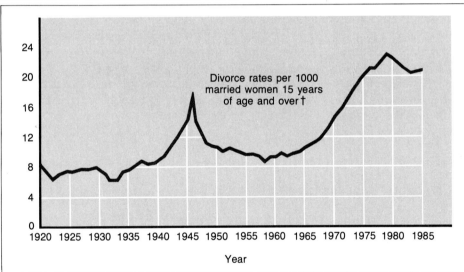

**Figure 12.4  Marriage Rates per 1000 Unmarried Women 15 Years of Age and Over, 1920–1985.**

Marriage rates declined between 1920 and 1930 but increased again between 1930 and 1950. Since 1950 the marriage rate has generally declined except for slight rises in 1965 and 1970.

**Divorce Rates per 1000 Married Women 15 Years of Age and Over, 1920–1985.**

The divorce rate increased dramatically in 1946, as World War II ended. Then it declined until 1958, then climbed to a new high in 1979. At that time it began to stabilize.

* *Source:* National Center for Health Statistics, 1983, p. 1; U.S. Bureau of the Census, 1989a, p. 85.
† U.S. Bureau of the Census, 1975, p. 64; 1989a, p. 85.

acceptance of divorce as a way of resolving marital difficulties (Glick and Norton, 1979). Factors that might tend to lower the divorce rate are the trend toward lower remarriage rates (thus shrinking possible candidates for redivorce), the rising age at marriage, and a "growing fear of consequences of divorce" (Kemper, 1983, cited in Glick, 1986). Another factor in the late 1980s is the relative scarcity of eligible women in the usual age range for first marriage, a condition that has historically tended to promote marital stability (Guttentag and Secord, 1983, cited in Glick and Lin, 1986). The combination of these factors is likely to produce divorce rates that "continue to fluctuate moderately near the current level before reaching a period of relative stability" (Glick and Lin, 1986, p. 745).

What happens to the individuals who divorce? Some research suggests that they are lonelier than the married (Gerstel et al., 1985; Kelly, 1986; Spanier and Thompson, 1984). According to an interview study of 104 women and men (Gerstel, 1988), separated and divorced women were better at maintaining close relationships than were men or than they themselves were while married, but they had a more difficult time making new and casual ties. Men were in a better structural position to activate "instant networks" that provided new, casual ties.

## Birth Rates

Lower marriage rates and higher divorce rates depress birth rates. The long-term trend in this century in the United States, except for the post-World War II "baby boom," has been toward fewer children and smaller families. Figure 12.5 illustrates the rising absolute number of births between 1945 and 1965, the declining number from 1970 to 1975, the upturn since 1975, and another rise in 1988.

The rising number of births between 1975 and 1985 reflects the large number of women of childbearing age, women who are part of the post-World War II baby boom generation. In the 1970s and 1980s there were so many women of childbearing age that the absolute number of babies born rose. The actual rate of births, however, has *dropped* from 118.0 per 1000 women aged 15 to 44 years old in 1960 to 65.4 per 1000 in 1986. It is this decline in birth rates rather than the absolute number of births that sociologists and population counters have tried to explain.

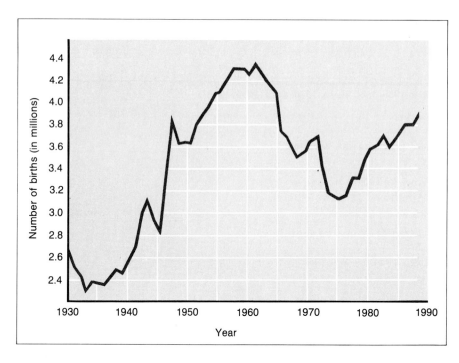

**Figure 12.5   Annual Number of Births in the United States, 1930–1988.**

The absolute annual number of births began increasing enormously in 1946. In 1961, it began a general decline lasting until 1975. For the past decade the number of births generally increased each year until 1983 and 1984, when it dipped slightly. It rose again in 1985, 1987, and 1988.

*Source:* Figures through 1978 from Masnick and Bane, 1980, p. 156; U.S. Department of Health and Human Services, various issues; U.S. Bureau of the Census, 1989a, p. 63; National Center for Health Statistics, 1989, p. 1.

Several factors seem to explain the general trend toward lower birth rates. First, the economic value of children has shifted in this century from being an asset to being a liability. This has resulted from laws against child labor in the early 1900s and from Social Security and other legislation to provide benefits to retired persons. Second, the dramatic growth of women's labor-force participation (Figure 12.3) is related to lower birth rates for several reasons. Outside work increases opportunities for women outside the housewife/mother role. Increased employment opportunities for women mean greater opportunity costs for women (and families) when they choose not to work in the paid labor force. This is consistent with reports from women who do not graduate from high school. Compared to women who graduated from high school or college, they are more likely to report that the benefits of children outweigh the costs (Blake and del Pinal, 1981; Veroff et al., 1981). The opportunity costs of children are lower for such women because they are not able to earn as much outside the home as more educated women can. Outside employment of women may cause role overload and conflict over traditional gender-based divisions of labor, a factor that raises the "costs" of children for women and men (McLanahan and Adams, 1987). More divorce also depresses birth rates, because it is related to the growth of single-parent families, who face numerous forms of stress (Garfinkel and McLanahan, 1986). Single mothers are more likely than married women to say that the costs of children outweigh the benefits (Blake and del Pinal, 1981).

If current birth rates persist, some 30 percent of U.S. women now of childbearing age will never have children. Only once before did so few women have children, and that was during the Great Depression of the 1930s. Even then, only 22 percent of women were childless (Westoff, 1978). Westoff suggests that the decline in births can be seen as both a cause and a consequence of changes in marriage and the family.

All these trends are relected in attitudes about ideal family size, which have changed visibly. Nearly two-thirds of all women in 1941 thought that the ideal family should include three or four children. In 1968 more than half thought that the ideal family size was two children (Roper

Organization, 1980). The other spectacular shift in the 1970s is reflected in the large numbers of young women who plan to have no children at all. In 1978, 11 percent of all women aged 18 to 34 said they planned to have no children; among women 18 to 34 with postgraduate education, 21 percent expected not to have children (Bernard, 1981a). The stigma and pity attached to "childless" marriages in the past has been replaced by the voluntary choice of child-free marriages for many. As a result of these tendencies, the number of children under the age of 5 dropped from 20 million to 18.3 million between 1960 and 1987 (U.S. Census, 1989a).

Birth rates are also declining because people in the United States have been legally able to terminate unwanted pregnancies ever since the 1973 Supreme Court ruling that state laws forbidding abortion were unconstitutional. If many states limit abortion as a result of the Supreme Court's 1989 decision in *Webster* v. *Reproductive Health Services*, birth rates could rise again.

Between 1975 and 1985, 17.5 million American abortions were reported (U.S. Bureau of the Census, 1989a). If these abortions were evenly spread among women of childbearing age in 1980 (which they weren't because younger women are more likely to have abortions than older ones and some women have more than one), then it would represent one abortion for every four women of childbearing age (15 to 44 years of age). Many of these abortions terminated the pregnancies of unmarried teenagers. Most abortions are obtained by younger women (nearly two-thirds are 24 years old or younger and 29 percent are 19 or younger), unmarried women (four out of five are single), and white women (70 percent) (Henshaw et al., 1985, p. 92).

A 1989 *New York Times*/CBS News poll found that 49 percent of American adults favored keeping abortion legal and an additional 39 percent favor legal abortion under certain circumstances.

If these trends toward lower birth rates are seen as representing a social problem, then societal solutions are needed to address the lack of family resources (time and money). Numerous other industrial nations have child allowances and/or subsidized child care (Hewlett, 1986; Kamerman and Kahn, 1978). Public solutions would reduce the economic and psychological strains of childbearing for both men and women (McLanahan and Adams, 1987).

## Growing Numbers of Stepfamilies

More than three-quarters of divorced people remarry, and about half of them do so within three years of their divorces. This means that as divorce rates have increased, the number of stepfamilies has also been increasing. In 1965 there were twice as many marriages as remarriages, but in 1985 the numbers of marriages and remarriages were nearly equal.

Remarriage adds a generally higher male income and help in running and supporting a household. It also adds new and more complex family relationships. The higher divorce rate for remarriages than for first marriages may be due to the complexity and the incomplete institutionalization of remarriage in the United States, suggests Cherlin (1978). He examines language and law as two indicators of incomplete institutionalization. While the term "stepparent" exists, it is still unclear what a child who calls her mother "Mom," should call her stepmother, and whether "Dad" is a term reserved for biological fathers alone. The lack of appropriate terms for parents in remarriage can hurt family functioning and corresponds to the absence of clearly defined roles and relationships in stepfamilies,

*Increasing rates of divorce and remarriage create increasingly complex family relationships. Here children of the bride and groom participate in the wedding of their mother and father, respectively.*

notes Cherlin (1978, p. 643). The law also ignores many of the special problems of stepfamilies. Although all states prohibit marriage and sexual relations between persons closely related by blood, many states do not have laws restricting sexual relations or marriage between other family members in a remarriage—between a stepmother and a stepson, for example, or between two stepchildren (Goldstein and Katz, 1965). Despite the lack of institutionalization for remarriage, many couples and children feel the new marriage is a big improvement over their previous one (Cherlin and Furstenberg, 1983).

## LIKELY CAUSES OF THESE TRENDS

At least four interrelated factors lie behind these changes in family forms, namely, economic conditions, demographic changes, the "sexual revolution," and changing cultural expectations and preferences.

### Economic Conditions

There was a time in the United States when one paycheck could maintain a middle-class family. Today that is no longer possible for most Americans. Over the last two decades, the purchasing power of the dollar has declined, service jobs have replaced many higher-paid manufacturing jobs, and promotions to higher-paying jobs have become more competitive. These factors reduce the ability of one earner to provide for a family. It is not surprising, then, that an increasing number of wives, including those with children, are in the paid labor force. By 1988, 52 percent of women with newborn children were in the labor force, compared to 31 percent a decade earlier (U.S. Bureau of the Census, 1989). When women work, the cost of raising children soars because families must earn the money not only to raise children but also to pay for child care.

Assuming a mother employed full-time, with medium family SES and medium inflation, a first child born in 1981 might cost $184,000 to raise through age 17 (Espenshade, 1984). College costs would be additional. Although every-one is not aware of these numbers, more individuals seem to be sensitive to the financial and personal costs of child rearing.

In the 1950s and 1960s a young man who left his parents' home would quickly catch up to what his father had been earning at the time of his departure. By age 30 he would have been earning one-third more than his father earned. But today a 30-year-old man is earning about 10 percent less than the father earned when the son left home, and the father pays a much lower rate of interest on his home mortgage (Levy and Michel, 1985). In short, as a result of changing economic conditions, families feel the need for two incomes to get along, thus making them more cautious about having children.

The period from 1940 to 1960 was one of rising demand for workers in traditionally female occupations—clerical work and several categories of professional and service work. Moreover, the growing demand for female workers was greatest for more educated women. At the same time, there was a dramatic decline in the number of single women 18 to 34 years old. These younger single women were the ones employers had preferred during the war. As they became increasingly unavailable, employers began turning to older married women to maintain and expand the female labor force. These women, in turn, responded to the expansion of job opportunities and entered the labor force, thus producing the postwar rise in the female work rate (Oppenheimer, 1970).

## Demographic Changes

The extraordinarily large number of young adults from the Baby Boom generation (see box on the "Baby Boom" in Chapter 18, "Population, Health, and Aging") that began looking for jobs and housing in the 1970s contributed to the sense of occupational and economic urgency that they felt. In 1970 only 39 percent of college freshmen felt that "being very well off financially" was "essential" or "very important" in their lives, but by 1987 three-quarters of them felt that way, a change that may be related to reluctance to marry and have children.

Longer life expectancy also affects family forms. Because people live longer in general, there may be a sense that each stage of life can be lengthened—from adolescence, to starting work, to marrying, to having children, and even to retiring later. People may feel less urgency about marrying and having their children quickly when they see a longer life span ahead of them. A new development in this century is the fact that women now outlive men by a wide margin, thus contributing to the growing numbers of older women who become single through being widowed.

The sex ratio of men to women is another demographic factor that may influence family forms. When one sex outnumbers the potential marriage partners of those of the other sex, there is a "**marriage squeeze**." When unattached women outnumber available men, argue Guttentag and Secord (1983), men will seek to shape to their advantage the form that relationships between men and women take. Guttentag and Secord see the decreased willingness of men to commit themselves to an exclusive lifetime relationship with one woman as consistent with the sex ratio imbalance. Some of the trends of the 1970s, including more premarital sex, delayed marriage, more divorce, and a stronger push by women for sexual, economic, and political independence, are consistent with the sex-ratio imbalance.

When men outnumber women, more women marry and at younger ages; that ratio depresses rates of divorce, illegitimacy, and female labor-force participation. Those trends were observed in 117 countries when the level of socioeconomic development of the countries was controlled, and the effect of the sex ratio on women's roles was more pronounced in developed than in developing countries (South and Trent, 1988). Is there any evidence that such a trend is beginning in the United States? In 1987, younger male "baby boomers" began to outnumber their potential marriage partners. Under such conditions, men become more eager to pursue marriage, according to the sex-ratio hypothesis.

For the past three years the average age at first marriage for women has been dropping, a reverse of the previous trend and perhaps an indication that their relative undersupply is being felt. "Between 1986 and 1987, for the first time in 20 years, the number of family households grew faster than the number of non-family households" (Fowles, 1988). In 1975 the birth rate started increasing, for the first time since its long decline began in the late 1950s. Over the next decade, it will be interesting to see what effect a shifting sex ratio has on marriage, divorce, birth rates, and gender roles.

An additional demographic change that affects marriage and families is the "graying of the suburbs" discussed in Chapter 20. Because of high housing costs, many suburban residents are "aging in place," making it difficult for young families to buy homes.

## The Sexual Revolution and AIDS

In an earlier era, sex was supposed to be reserved for married adults. Today about 70 percent of women experience premarital coitus before their twentieth birthday (Forste and Heaton, 1988). Even twenty years ago, most teenage men experienced premarital coitus, whereas fewer than one-third of women had done so (Robinson and Jedlicka, 1982). At that time it was generally considered acceptable for men to have premarital sex but not for women. This dual standard of morality was called the "double standard." One idea of the "sexual revolution" beginning in the 1960s was the notion that premarital sex should be equally acceptable for men and women. Some argued that premarital sex should be unacceptable for both sexes, but that was probably a minority view.

By the late 1980s, more than half of first-year college students agreed that "If two people really like each other, it's all right for them to have sex, even if they've known each other for only a short time" (Astin et al., 1987). Has the emergence of acquired immune deficiency syndrome (AIDS) reduced the rate of premarital coitus? Fear of AIDS appears to have had no effect if we measure sexual activity by the percentage of young people who had engaged in premarital coitus at least once. In the mid-1980s, more college students had premarital coital experience than before AIDS became a public concern (Kephart and Jedlicka, 1988, p. 276). Het-

erosexual college students do not seem to perceive themselves or their partners as being at risk for AIDS, although fear of the disease may reduce the number of partners a sexually active person has. However, a long history of research suggests that moral convictions tend to be more important determinants of sexual behavior than even the fear of a deadly disease (Jedlicka and Robinson, 1987).

When sex becomes more acceptable outside the bonds of marriage, one of the major reasons for getting married is undermined, helping to contribute to lower marriage rates. At the same time, fairly strong prohibitions still exist concerning extramarital sexual relations. About 80 percent of the population feels that infidelity among married men and women is morally wrong (Yankelovich, Skelly, and White, 1977).

These prohibitions, combined with rising expectations that sexual relations in marriage should be satisfying for both partners, may contribute to rising divorce rates.

## Cultural Expectations and Preferences

As already noted, the expectation that marriage should meet one's needs for emotional intimacy and love is a relatively recent idea in social life, as is the idea that one might dissolve a marriage if those needs were not being met.

The generally rising divorce rate over the last two decades should not be taken to mean that people have stopped valuing marriage. It may mean the opposite—namely, that the importance of marriage as a source of emotional satisfaction has increased and that people end marriages that fail to provide such satisfaction. This interpretation is supported by the high remarriage rate for divorced persons.

The remarriage rate for divorced men and women is higher than first-time marriage rates. In 1985, marriage rates were 61.5 and 50.1, respectively, per 1000 single women and men over 15 years of age. In contrast, remarriage rates that year were 81.8 and 121.6, respectively, per 1000 divorced women and men (National Center for Health Statistics, 1988, p. 10). Apparently people are not soured on marriage in general, but only on particular marriages.

Do factors other than degree of happiness influence divorce rates? A model developed by Levinger (1965) suggests an answer to this question. The model identifies three major factors affecting divorce—the attractiveness of the marriage relationship itself, the strength of barriers to marital dissolution, and the attractiveness of alternatives. His model rests on and makes sense of a great many research studies. The attractiveness of a relationship depends on whether the marriage offers emotional, social, and economic rewards to the people in it. These rewards include companionship, good communication with one's spouse, enjoyable sex, shared values, and the social and economic status obtained from a marriage. If people enter marriage largely because they feel they are experiencing a high degree of romantic love, they may find that superficial romantic love declines over time. If they do not share some common life values, companionship, or something else that makes them feel the marriage is rewarding, they may be more likely to get divorced.

Wives who married at an older age, who have been married longer, and whose husbands contribute to the housework are less likely to consider divorce than wives who married younger, have been married for a shorter time, and whose husbands do not help out (Huber and Spitze, 1980). Wives with work experience, whose youngest child is between 6 and 11, and who have egalitarian housework attitudes are more likely to consider divorce than those without work experience, whose youngest child is under 6 or over 11, and who do not have egalitarian housework attitudes (Huber and Spitze, 1980).

In addition to cultural expectations regarding sexual satisfaction and emotional intimacy, people's preferences for different types of marriages vary by age, suggesting a change over time (Figure 11.3). Younger people are more likely than older ones to prefer a marriage of shared responsibility in which husband and wife cooperate on work, homemaking, and child rearing.

Barriers to divorce—the second factor in Levinger's model—exists both within and beyond the individual. They include feelings of obligation to dependent children or of the sanctity of the marriage bond itself. In general, people are much more likely today to believe that separation or divorce is the best solution when marital problems cannot be solved than they were 20 years ago (Thornton, 1985). The size of a husband's earnings and the presence of children are less of a deterrent to considering divorce than they were in the past (Huber and Spitze, 1980).

Marriages between partners of the same religious faith are less likely to end in divorce, perhaps because of their shared views about marriage. Divorce is less likely in marriages where couples attend church together, where they share a common network of friends and kin, and in communities where divorce is stigmatized (Levinger, 1965). The more people there are in a community who are divorced, the greater is the likelihood of divorce (Goode et al., 1971). When barriers to divorce are strong, divorce will be less likely; when they are weak, it will be more likely.

The third set of factors affecting divorce in a major way is the attractiveness of the alternatives to the current marriage. Is there a preferred sex partner outside the marriage? Does the wife have opportunities for independent income? Are there other individuals that one partner finds more compatible with respect to major values and goals? Are there other kin relationships that conflict with the marriage relationship? Has superficial romantic love faded from the marriage but flamed up with someone else? Any of these possibilities might make the alternatives to a marriage more important than the marriage itself.

But none of these factors alone seems to be enough to produce the dissolution of a marriage relationship. It seems more likely that as the appeal of a relationship diminishes, the relatively weak barriers to marital dissolution, combined with increasingly attractive alternatives, increase the chances of divorce.

Booth et al. (1984) found that a wife's employment was related to increased marital instability, especially if she worked more than 40 hours per week. Wives with higher incomes may have been more willing to leave a marriage they found unsatisfactory than wives with lower incomes, but the size of the wife's income was not related to marital happiness. Marital instability increased when disagreements between husbands and wives increased and marital satisfaction declined. The weakening of barriers to divorce and the appeal of alternatives also contribute to marital dissolution.

## IMPLICATIONS OF THESE TRENDS

Shifts in family forms, along with the underlying changes that fostered them, have important implications within the family and for society generally. The roles of men and women within families are changing. Instances of family violence may be increasing and sibling interactions are also changing. Society is being affected by the increasing "privatization of the family" and by the possible effects on children of divorce, single parents, working mothers, and stepfamilies.

### Changing Family Roles

The changing role of married women in the work force is reflected in changing roles in the family. As women have entered the labor market, men have taken more responsibility for rearing children. Some husbands attend natural childbirth classes with their wives, remain in the delivery room during birth, and spend more time caring for the baby than fathers in earlier decades did. Considerable research suggests that men are just as loving and capable caregivers as women (Berman, 1980; Lamb, 1977; Parke, 1981; Sawin and Parke, 1979). Such role changes reflect the capacity of the family to adapt to changing conditions.

Ross et al. (1983) theorize that particular marriage patterns emerged historically in response to macro-level changes in society. They set out to study whether different marital forms were related to the amount of depression experienced by husbands and wives. They suggest that there are four types of marriage: Type I, or what they call **complementary marriage,** is the most traditional type. Here, the wife cares for the home and children and the husband is the breadwinner but plays no part in the housework and child care. Both spouses approve of the arrangement and see their specific gender roles as proper and as part of their identities. In Type I marriages the husbands have greater power and prestige than wives but both are comfortable with the arrangement. This type is consistent with the structural-functional view of marriage and the family. Because male and female roles were tightly prescribed by norms within the functional view, the operation of power and exchange within the family was not a significant research topic. In the nineteenth century a great many marriages may have had tightly structured normative constraints placed on them, partly because there were so few resources and alternatives available to women (Brickman, 1974; Rosaldo and Lamphere, 1974).

Type II begins to reflect changes in the larger society. More wives are employed, but both spouses still feel that a woman's place is in the home and they would prefer that she did not have to work for pay. But in these marriages husbands' and wives' traditional expectations about marital roles are not being met. Hence Ross et al. (1983) hypothesize that the highest levels of depression are here, especially for husbands. The wife in this situation is fully responsible for the housework.

In Type III marriages more wives work, more wives and husbands prefer this arrangement, but wives still do all the housework. Ross et al. (1983) predict lower levels of depression in Type III marriages than in Type II, especially among men. They see Types II and III as transitory stages. Type IV, or what they call **parallel marriage,** is like Type III except that household tasks are shared. Many of the strains found in the transitional types of marriages are gone in Type IV marriages. People's actions and attitudes are in agreement, and working women are no longer faced with full responsibility for the home and the wife no longer has the lower status of wives in Type I marriages. Ross et al. (1983) hypothesize that women will have the lowest levels of depression in Type IV marriages and that the more equitable arrangement may lower tension between husband and wife, thereby leading to lower levels of depression in husbands as well. As a result, they expect to find similar levels of depression among husbands and wives in Type IV marriages.

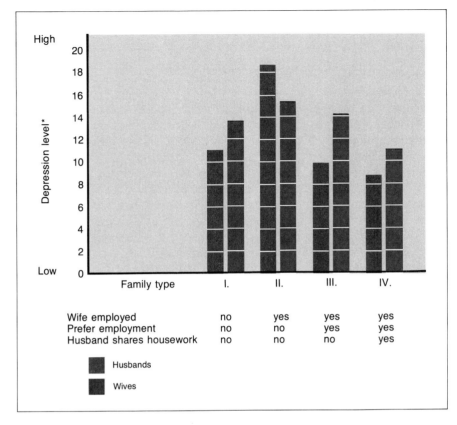

**Figure 12.6 Rates of Emotional Depression\* Among Husbands and Wives in Four Types of Marriages.**

The rates of emotional depression among both husbands and wives were lowest in Type IV marriages where both spouses worked, both spouses preferred that arrangement, and they shared the housework.

*Source:* Adapted from Ross et al., 1983, p. 819.

\* Depression was measured by a modified form of the Center for Epidemiological Studies' Depression scale (CES-D). This scale measures symptoms of depression in community populations rather than diagnosing clinical depression (Ross et al., 1983, p. 813).

Their statistical analysis reveals results consistent with their hypotheses (Figure 12.6). For both men and women, the lowest levels of depression occur in parallel marriages (Type IV), and the second lowest levels occur in complementary marriages (Type I), whereas the highest levels of depression occur in the transitional marriages (Types II and III). This suggests that depression is more likely in situations where people's preferences and behaviors are at odds than in situations where their preferences and behaviors are in agreement. It also indicates that wives are less depressed if their husbands help with the housework, and husbands who help are no more depressed than those who do not (Ross et al., 1983). A related and perhaps also surprising result was reported by Kessler and McRae, Jr. (1982), who found that the mental health of husbands improves as their wives' incomes increase (p. 223).

In marriages where husbands do not help with the housework, women often face role overload as they take on new responsibilities. Help with

their numerous duties has not always been forthcoming from husbands, child-care facilities, or employers. This overload has been documented in both capitalist and communist countries. In the Soviet Union, despite the deliberate expansion of female economic and political participation, wives spend 2.5 times as many hours on housework as their husbands (Lapidus, 1978). Despite the expansion of women's participation outside the home, their home duties have often not been lightened. Child care is the single biggest problem faced by working mothers (Kamerman, 1979).

Despite the prospects of role overload, nearly half of all the women polled by Roper in 1980 would prefer to have a job than to stay at home all the time. As recently as 1974, only about one-third of all women expressed this preference. Moreover, younger and college-educated women are even more likely to want to work. These figures suggest that women's participation in the work force will continue and perhaps increase in the future. At the same time, the majority of women and men feel strongly that more day-care centers should be set up for working women.

The greater economic independence of women that has accompanied these trends has several important implications. First, fewer women need to enter or stay in marriage primarily for economic reasons. From colonial times to the present there is evidence that whenever women had alternatives to unsatisfactory marriages, they used them, as Bernard (1981b) suggests. Moreover, she feels that the widespread wife abuse that has begun to come to light reflects the number of women who may have felt trapped in destructive marriages because they lacked alternatives. Now more women feel they can publicly protest the abuse they are receiving. The growth of jobs for women is one such alternative, at least for some women.

The availability of alternatives to marriage can also influence the type of marriage relationship women enter into. As already noted, women and men increasingly favor more **egalitarian marriages.** For men, this means that both the burden and the social esteem that came from being the sole breadwinner and head of the household may have lessened somewhat. Some men welcome this, others do not. There is still rather limited social support for men who take on primary responsibility for housekeeping or child care, although such support seems to be growing. In 1970 only one out of eight women and one out of five men said they would respect a male homemaker, but by 1980 two out of five women and men said that they would.

Women with higher educational levels and income were more likely to respect a male homemaker than women of lower socioeconomic status (Roper Organization, 1980). Moreover, in 1980 a significant percentage of men were quite willing to help with household chores traditionally performed by women. College-educated men are most likely to help with household tasks. Among all men, more than three-quarters help with grocery shopping and two-thirds help with housecleaning, dishwashing, and cooking. Nearly half help mind the children, whereas two out of five sometimes do laundry. Mending still seems to be a job men

seldom do; three out of five say they never do it (Roper Organization, 1980).

## Family Violence

For a long time the social science literature on the family was filled exclusively with discussions of the functions of the family in society, with little or no attention to violence in the family. Those who did mention it considered only the dramatic extremes, such as homicide.

Various American and British studies reveal that about 90 percent of all parents have used physical punishment at some point in a child's life. Punishment continues into adolescence, with more than half of the student population reporting they have been hit during high school (Bachman, 1967; Steinmetz, 1971, 1974; Straus, 1971). Physical punishment may step over the boundary into what is called child abuse.

Child abuse is defined differently by different people, but most would agree that broken bones, concussions, lost teeth, burns, and serious neglect constitute child abuse. Physical punishment may result in child abuse quite unintentionally when adults do not realize their own strength and hit children too hard or throw them down. Probably most adults do not set out deliberately to abuse a child. They may get so angry they lose control, they may be drunk and not fully aware of what they are doing, or they may unintentionally hit a child harder than they meant to. Because physical punishment of children receives some normative support in our society, this support may contribute to the likelihood of child abuse.

Family violence sometimes leads to murder (Gelles and Straus, 1979). Across the country, family fights are the single most frequent reason for calling the police. This and other evidence suggests that violence is a major feature of family life in America and probably in most other societies as well (Straus, 1976).

Family abuse of all kinds is more prevalent in lower socioeconomic homes and in families where unemployment and economic hardships are serious problems, but it occurs with great frequency in the general population as well (Finkelhor, 1979; Meiselman, 1978; Pelton, 1981;

Straus et al., 1979). The extent of family violence is estimated by national surveys in 1975
and 1985 (Straus, Gelles, and Steinmetz, 1979
and Straus and Gelles, 1986). The encouraging
feature of the second study was that rates of
child abuse and wife beating decreased between
1975 and 1985. However, current rates are still
quite high. A minimum estimate is that more
than a million children aged 3 through 17 in
two-parent households were abused in 1985,
and more than 1½ million wives were beaten
(Straus and Gelles, 1986, p. 475). The researchers think their results probably reflect a combination of changed attitudes and norms and
changes in actual behaviors. The decline may
have been influenced by changes in family structure, such as higher average age at first marriage, fewer children per family, and tendencies
toward more egalitarian marriages; economic
changes such as lower unemployment and less
economic stress; the lessened social acceptability
of family violence and more social control of its
expression; the availability of alternatives for
women; and the availability of treatment and
prevention services (Straus and Gelles, 1986).

Despite the positive direction of change, we
can ask why so much violence still occurs in
families. Is it caused by pathological individuals,
or do social factors encourage the use of violence
in the family? According to conflict theorists,
conflict occurs in all human relationships, including the family. By its very nature, the family is a center of competing interests that result
in conflicts (Sprey, 1969). Violence is one means
of advancing one's interests when other methods fail (Steinmetz and Straus, 1974). In some
families, violence may be the first method
adopted, depending on how individual members have been taught to view violence or depending on the other resources available to individuals.

When individuals lack the resources to influence people around them, they may use violence
(Goode et al., 1971). For example, a husband
who receives little prestige or income from his
job may resort to violence to dominate his family (Gelles and Straus, 1979). Similarly, men
married to women with higher educational and
occupational status than their own are more
likely to use force and violence on family mem-

bers than are men with higher-status occupations (O'Brien, 1971). It may be that given the
cultural pressures on men to dominate in the
family, men lacking the social resources for such
dominance resort to superior physical strength.

This explanation stresses the use of violence
as a resource for domination. Another explanation suggests that stress is a major contributor
to family violence. Straus, Gelles, and Steinmetz
(1979) found that low income, unemployment,
part-time employment, and four or five children
in the home were all related to violence toward
children and between spouses.

A third factor associated with family violence
was the concentration of family decision making
in the hands of only one person, whether husband or wife. There was less violence in families
where a democratic system was used to make
decisions (Gelles, 1974).

## Family Size and Sibling Interaction

The marriage relationship is obviously one key
type of family interaction. In any family that
has children, however, there are other important
interactions. These include parent-child and
child-child interactions (if there is more than one
child in the family). One of the key determinants of family interaction is family size. The
larger the family is, the fewer individual parent-
child interactions there are.

In bigger families, siblings must share family
resources such as parental attention. Family size
is negatively related to IQ, college plans, and
education (Blake, 1981, 1985), but birth order
is not (Hauser and Sewell, 1985). Choosing the
number and spacing of children is a very significant way in which parents can influence the
success of their children (Heer, 1985).

The larger the family, the more sibling interaction there is. Siblings help to socialize each
other. They also increase the complexity of family interactions and conflicts. One of the ways
siblings socialize each other is by performing
pioneering functions for one another. Usually
the older siblings blaze the trail for younger ones
(Bank and Kahn, 1975), although as they get
older, younger siblings sometimes take the lead.
This may happen because each additional child

*Siblings increase the complexity and richness of family interactions.*

tends to open the family more to outside influences (Schvaneveldt and Ihinger, 1979). As a result of the gradual loosening of the family system that occurs with the birth of each new member, the younger siblings tend to be more likely to break with family traditions. This phenomenon may explain why first-born siblings are more sexually conservative than later-born siblings (Reiss, 1967), and younger siblings may pave the way for the greater experimentation of their older brothers and sisters.

In many other areas as well, siblings seem to help each other develop their individual identities through the dual processes of identification and differentiation (Bank and Kahn, 1975). In identification, siblings may identify possibilities for themselves in the actions of their siblings and include some of these alternatives in their own repertory. Learning sexual behavior is a good example of the use of identification. Siblings also help each other to differentiate themselves through the process of recognizing how they differ from each other ("He's that way, but I'm this way"). This helps individuals to define their own unique identities. The processes of individuation may be spurred along by sibling rivalries and conflicts.

One result of such conflict is the greater tendency to form coalitions. Siblings have more chance than only children to form alliances. They may do this to gain greater strength in

relation to their parents or to forge alliances against other sibling coalitions in the family. Same-sex sibling coalitions are most common (Caplow, 1959). First-born siblings may lead a coalition against the parents because other siblings may feel that firstborns have greater power and access to the parents. Tattling, squealing, and shifting coalitions all occur in sibling coalitions.

To the degree that families represent a relatively closed and enduring social system, they need to resolve or at least stalemate the tensions and conflict within them. Sometimes parents mediate the conflicts between competing groups of siblings; at other times the eldest child or one of the sibling coalitions may try to be the peacemaker. Sibling coalitions may produce family isolates, "black sheep," scapegoats, winners, losers, and "pets" within the family (Schvaneveldt and Ihinger, 1979). A family may also direct its unresolved hostilities between its coalitions at a scapegoat or enemy outside the family.

If current trends lead to more single-child families and smaller families, then clearly sibling interactions will be affected. The increasing numbers of children living in stepfamilies will add to the complexity of sibling interactions.

Changing expectations about the family and changing family forms have profound implications for the larger society as well as for the internal life of families. Social observers highlight two major consequences—the increasing privatization of family life and the effects on children of changes in family composition.

## Adult Offspring and Elderly Parents

Longer life expectancy increases the chances that middle-aged adults will have parents living. In 1980, the average 40-year-old couple had nearly the same number of parents and children (2.6 and 2.7 respectively). The trend is toward slightly more parents than children (2.9 and 1.8; Preston, 1984). One result may be more shared households across generations (Hess and Waring, 1978; Troll, Miller, and Atchley, 1979). Care and services are more likely to be provided by women (Brody, 1985; Lopata, 1973; Treas, 1977), an issue that is generally not discussed in studies of the division of household labor. Financial support, on the other hand, is more likely to be provided by sons (U.S. Bureau of the Census, 1988). Fewer than one million parents of providers receive regular cash support payments from people not living with them, representing less than 10 percent of all persons receiving support (U.S. Bureau of the Census, 1988). Most studies have not analyzed the interaction between the care of elderly parents and women's changing role in the labor market. One study found that being employed limited the helping behavior of sons but not daughters (Stoller, 1983). Middle-aged women may also be caught between the needs of elderly parents and those of children, who remain dependent longer (Huber and Spitze, 1988).

These trends mean that more children know their grandparents. Divorce and remarriage complicate relationships with grandparents. For the child, parental divorce and remarriage may beneficially increase the child's network of relatives (Furstenberg and Spanier, 1984). But the grandparents may have to share a grandchild, as low fertility is shrinking the supply (Matthews and Sprey, 1984). Older parents may also receive less help from their divorced daughters, who generally need more child care and money than before their divorce (Cherlin, 1983).

## Increasing Privatization

Observers suggest that the rise of industrialization led to the family being viewed as a retreat from the outside world. The expectation grew that emotional intimacy and love were a primary function of marriage and family. People escaped from the demands of the community and workplace by withdrawing into privacy, domesticity, and intimacy (Hareven, 1982; Lasch, 1979; Laslett, 1974; Zaretsky, 1976). The premodern family had many outside social ties, and families were the foundation of communities, suggests Aries (1962). But the modern family separates itself from the larger community and spends much of its energy helping individual children achieve social mobility. The family no longer works to advance itself as a social unit or to improve the community in which it lives (Aries, 1962).

High expectations for emotional intimacy and withdrawal from larger social circles may place a heavier burden on the family than it can bear. It also pulls family members away from public issues, as they seek private solutions to public problems (such as crime and poor public education). Observers call the tendency of families to turn away from the community and workplace toward a primary focus on domesticity and intimacy **privatization.**

The elderly, for example, increasingly fend for themselves, rather than forging collective responses to the condition of aging. Among women aged 65 or above, four out of ten live alone, and among those without a spouse, two out of three live alone (Michael et al., 1980). Both generations prefer the autonomy that separate households provide (Cherlin and Furstenberg, 1983), but it does represent a noteworthy change. The highly privatized family is particularly vulnerable when it comes to dealing with stressful events like divorce.

## Effects of Divorce on Children

A child's cumulative probability of parental divorce is about 40 percent, with black children's rates much higher than white children's. A child's chances of living at some stage of life in a single-parent family, including those families that result from premarital births, are about 50 percent (Bumpass, 1984a; Bumpass and Rindfuss, 1979; Furstenberg et al., 1983).

In their five-year study of 60 divorcing California families, Wallerstein and Kelly (1980) noted that children went through at least four stages as the divorce proceeded. The *initial period* was very painful for all of the children and many of the parents. *Within a year* children had returned to their usual behavior and were able to do so faster than were their parents. The children were greatly helped if both parents were supportive, understanding, nurturing, and affectionate toward them during the process (Clingempeel and Reppucci, 1982; Little, 1982). Children who were drawn into marital and divorce battles might passively submit, act out their aggressions, or learn to manipulate their parents, all negative consequences for the child (Harris, 1972).

The *transition period* lasted two or three years in most families. Divorce led to changes in social and economic circumstances as well as in relationships within the family. Divorced women and their children suffered a 73 percent drop in their standard of living while ex-husbands enjoyed a 42 percent rise in theirs, according to Weitzman (1985). Nationally, fewer than one child out of five saw the outside parent as often as once a week during the year. Despite the media coverage that joint custody arrangements have received, only 3 percent of all the children of divorce are in such arrangements (Furstenberg, Jr., et al., 1983).

At the *five-year mark* (which was as long as Wallerstein and Kelly studied the families), some parents had made new marriages, whereas others had stabilized the postdivorce family. Some postdivorce families were stable and reflected an improvement in the quality of life for all family members. Others were no happier or were less happy than they had been during the marriage breakdown. The effects of divorce on children are bound up with single-parent homes and stepfamilies.

## Effects of Single-Parent Families on Children

The number of families with children under the age of 18 headed by women has soared in recent years, from about 1.5 million in 1960 to 6.3 million in 1987 (U.S. Bureau of the Census, 1989a). This figure is projected to jump to 6.5 million by 1990 (Masnick and Bane, 1980).

Although the children of divorce may not see their second parent very often, that parent does not become less emotionally important to the child, even as much as five years after the divorce. In fact, the children of divorce would not consider the term "one-parent family" appropriate. The self-images of these children "were firmly tied to their relationship with both parents and they thought of themselves as children with two parents who had elected to go their separate ways," note Wallerstein and Kelly (1980, p. 307).

They also observed that when the burden of child care falls mostly on one parent in a divorced family, that family is more vulnerable to stress. "Chronic emotional and economic overload was frequently intolerable for the custodial parent, and the cumulative effect on the children was all too visible in their unhappiness and depression," write Wallerstein and Kelly (1980, pp. 308–309). They became aware that divorced middle-class families lack social supports. The withdrawal of middle-class families from extended kin networks and community involvement makes such families more isolated and vulnerable when one of the adults in the family leaves. The incidence of depression was higher among children of divorce five years after the divorce than it was 18 months later, suggesting that the initial breakup is but one of a number of stresses that the postdivorce family has to face.

Given the increasing numbers of children born to single parents, however, and the rising divorce rate among very young parents, how are the nearly 14 million children of such families being cared for and socialized? Some single parents do not work, feeling that they should stay home and care for their children. Others share the responsibility for child care with relatives, neighbors, and friends (Kamerman, 1979; Stack, 1974). More children attend preprimary programs than in the past, although higher-income families are more likely than lower-income families to enroll their children in such programs. Slightly more single parents report that they do not have enough time to help their children with their homework in the evenings than do individuals in two-parent families (Dearman and Plisko, 1979). The difficulties of child care and socialization are compounded when parents are themselves very young, lack education, are unable to obtain decent jobs, and are poor.

Research has been conducted to explore the relationship between growing up in single-parent homes and later achievement. Children who grew up in one-parent homes complete fewer years of schooling (Hauser and Featherman, 1976), enter lower-status occupations (Duncan and Duncan, 1969), and have less stability in their own marriages (Bumpass and Sweet, 1972). The lower educational attainment of children from single-parent households is largely explained by the much greater poverty among female-headed families (McLanahan, 1985).

## Effects of Stepfamilies

Remarriage helps to solve the economic problems that face families headed by a single female because it adds the new husband's income to the family. It also adds another adult to help carry the burdens of running a household. But often remarriage also includes combining two families into one. Probably one-fifth of all children living with their mothers share homes with half siblings and face the adjustment problems associated with such arrangements (Bumpass, 1984b).

This can be a difficult process, which is not helped by the lack of clear norms about how to proceed. For example, how much are stepparents supposed to discipline their stepchildren? How many sets of grandparents do you invite to a child's birthday? Even economic obligations may be unclear. How does a father balance the claims of children from previous and current marriages. There are no agreed on ways of answering these questions. When children of divorce were asked who was in their families, the majority of those with stepparents included them, but only half included noncustodial biological parents (Furstenberg and Nord, 1985).

Such combined families can be quite complex. There may be children from each spouse's previous marriage and from the new marriage, and there are multiple sets of grandparents, stepgrandparents, ex-spouses, aunts, uncles, and cousins from prior marriages. Just keeping everyone straight takes heavy concentration. The complexity has long-term consequences as well. For example, will children who barely saw their absent parent while growing up feel responsible for the care of that parent when that parent is older? Many of the consequences of stepfamilies remain to be studied by sociologists.

## Effects of Working Mothers on Children

In the last two decades there has been a steady increase in the proportion of working mothers whose preschool children are cared for outside the home, rising from 33 percent in 1968 to 59 percent in 1988 (U.S. Bureau of the Census, 1989a). Children are not worse off because they spend more time with others besides their mothers (Zinn and Eitzen, 1987). Working mothers can provide quality care "by earmarking time to pay exclusive attention to their children" (Levitan and Belous, 1981, p. 102).

Of paramount importance is the quality of the relationship between mother and children when they are together. Can the children have fun with the mother, can they share confidences with her, do they feel she loves them and cares about them a great deal, even though they cannot be together every moment?

In crisis-ridden families with severe economic problems, mothers may not be able to provide quality care, whether or not they are employed. Equally important is the quality of care children receive from other adults, whether it be from relatives, friends, neighbors, or a day-care center. Are there loving, caring adults with whom the child can have fairly long-term relationships? These two conditions seem to be crucial for the healthy development of children (Bronfenbrenner, 1981).

Not only is employment of the mother by itself not harmful to children, but it appears to have some positive effects. The child of a working mother seems to see the division of household tasks as being more egalitarian (Finkelman, 1966; Hoffman, 1963), to see maternal employment as not threatening to a marriage (King, McIntyre, and Axelson, 1968), to indicate higher esteem for his or her own sex (Vogel et al., 1970), to favor social equality for women (Meier, 1972), and to do more household chores than other children (Rallings and Nye, 1979). Overall, the children of working mothers evaluate female competence more positively, and the daughters of working mothers have higher levels of independence.

One possible negative effect was observed in the sons of working-class mothers. Maternal employment is related to a lower evaluation of their fathers by these boys, perhaps because they see their mothers as having to work and hence consider the fathers to be economically inadequate (Rallings and Nye, 1979). The sons of middle-class working mothers, however, are likely to see their fathers as more nurturant, warm, and expressive individuals (Vogel et al., 1970).

On balance, the negative effects on children of divorce or of a mother working appear to depend heavily on the social conditions surrounding the divorce or the work. When divorce results in a happier family and when a working mother is pleased with her work and with her children, the children may benefit from the situation.

These changes and their consequences do not reflect the death of a narrowly defined American family but rather the emergence of new family forms. The issue for citizens and policy makers is to determine what kinds of social supports all types of families need, so that they can raise their children as well as possible. Ross et al. (1983) suggest that the first and most important starting point is achieving equal pay for women in the workplace, so that they will have sufficient resources to support their children. It should be apparent that the institutions of the family and the economy are closely bound up together.

## SUMMARY

1. Traditionally, the family has been defined as two or more persons who are related by blood, marriage, or adoption and who share a common residence.

2. Generally, the traditional family fulfilled the functions of sexual regulation, member replacement, socialization of the young, meeting economic needs, and sometimes emotional intimacy.

3. These functions have been performed increasingly outside the traditional family as more unmarried people live together, the number of children born to single mothers increases, child care is shared by more people, women enter the work force in growing numbers, and the number of stepfamilies increases.

4. Changing family functions have been paralleled by major changes in family forms and activities. By 2000 only about one in four households in the United States will consist of a married couple with one or more children. The number of couples without children and the number of singles is growing rapidly.

5. Changing family forms are affected by economic conditions, demographic changes such as the Baby Boom, and longer life expectancy. Other factors are the sex ratio of men to women, the sexual revolution, cultural expectations that marriage should meet both spouses' needs for love and intimacy, and increasing acceptance of divorce as the best solution when marital problems cannot be solved.

6. These changes in family forms are related to changes in the roles of men and women in marriage and to possible role overload for women. Moreover, family violence has become an increasingly visible problem. Sibling interactions are affected by shrinking family size and by the growing complexity of stepfamilies.

7. Longer life expectancy increases the chances that adults will have living parents and that children will know at least some of their grandparents. It also increases the complexity of family life.

8. The trend toward increasingly privatized nuclear-family life affects the family's involvement in the larger society and increases its vulnerability to divorce or other stressful events.

9. Divorce is a painful process for almost all children and many parents. The effects last beyond the stress of the initial breakup. The incomes of many divorced women drop dramatically, and children do not see their second parent very often.

10. About one-quarter of all American children live with one rather than two parents. Second parents remain important to children, however, even if they see them infrequently. The lower educational attainment of children from single-parent households appears to be due primarily to the greater incidence of poverty among such families rather than to their social characteristics, the absence of a father figure, or the stress resulting from marital disruption.

11. Stepfamilies are not yet fully institutionalized, as reflected in an incomplete language for the social roles in them and in the legal status of stepfamily relations. Many of their long-term effects remain to be studied.

12. Children do not seem to be worse off because their mothers work, as long as other adults take care of them. Of paramount importance is the quality of the relationship between mother and child when they are together.

## KEY TERMS

complementary marriages (p. 312)
conjugal family (p. 294)
dual-career families (p. 302)
egalitarian marriage (p. 314)
extended family (p. 294)
family (p. 294)
kinship (p. 294)
marriage (p. 294)
marriage rate (p. 297)
"marriage squeeze" (p. 309)
nuclear family (p. 294)
parallel marriage (p. 312)
privatization (p. 317)

## SUGGESTED READINGS

Aldous, Joan (ed.). 1982b. *Two Paychecks: Life in Dual-Earner Families.* Beverly Hills, CA: Sage. A series of papers illuminating aspects of life in two-income families.

Blumstein, Philip, and Pepper Schwartz. 1983. *American Couples: Money/Work/Sex.* New York: Morrow. In this massive study based on interviews with hundreds of couples and questionnaires from hundreds more, the authors analyze how heterosexual and homosexual couples feel about money, work, sex, and their lives together.

Cherlin, Andrew J. 1981. *Marriage, Divorce, Remarriage.* Cambridge, MA: Harvard University Press. A clear discussion of marriage, divorce, and remarriage trends and likely explanations and consequences of those trends. Also considers differences between blacks and whites.

Cherlin, Andrew J., and Frank F. Furstenberg, Jr. *The New American Grandparent: A Place in the Family, A Life Apart.* 1986. New York: Basic Books. Reports on the first representative nationwide study of American grandparents. The authors explore how this traditional relationship is being transformed by the unique tensions of the modern family.

Lasch, Christopher. 1977. *Haven in a Heartless World: The Family Besieged.* New York: Basic Books. An analysis of how the demands being made on the family to provide intimacy and nurture seem to be increasing, although the family as an institution is increasingly unable to meet those needs.

McLanahan, Sara, and Julia Adams. 1987. "Parenthood and Psychological Well-Being." *Annual Review of Sociology,* Vol. 13, pp. 237–257. A thoughtful review of recent research on how parenthood affects the psychological well-being of adults. Includes a good discussion of trends affecting the experience of parenthood.

# *The Economy and Work*

**13**

*Wayne Tarnow puts a question to his high-school economics class: "Who will be leaving La Porte [Indiana] after graduation?" Thirty hands shoot up—everyone in the class. Mr. Tarnow doesn't look surprised. "Kids around here are scared," he explains to a visitor. "The security blanket's not here anymore." During the early 1980s, recession tore a huge gaping hole in northern Indiana's security blanket. Unemployment in tightknit, blue-collar cities such as La Porte, Michigan City, and Gary spiraled past 20%. . . .*

*These days, on the surface at least, things seem better. . . . But while double-digit unemployment is becoming just a bad memory, there is growing uneasiness that something important is missing. . . . What has happened, experts say, is the disappearance of "the ladder": the well-paid, unionized, industrial jobs that have traditionally provided advancement for generations of blue-collar workers into the middle class. [Richards, 1986, p. 1]*

Changes in the social organization of the economy and work are transforming the social lives of many individuals and communities. The human species needs to work to meet basic needs for food, clothing, and shelter. People in all societies, from hunting and gathering tribes to complex industrial nations, participate in the activities that produce and distribute those necessities. In most individuals' lives as well, work occupies a central position. For some, work is drudgery; for others, it is a creative and satisfying process. For all of us, work significantly defines our identities in society and influences whom we meet, how we relate to them, and how we see the world. The pattern of roles, norms, and activities organized around the production, distribution, and consumption of goods and services is the **economic institution.** The nature of that economic institution and the various occupations in it have profound effects on individuals.

One of the striking features of life in this century is the increasingly global nature of the economy. The first section of this chapter explores this trend. National economies vary.

There are capitalist, welfare-state, state socialist, and mixed economies. The second section considers the differences between these admittedly impure types. It also addresses the question of whether the different types are becoming more alike over time. The third section examines where work gets done, while the fourth defines occupations and professions and discusses various types of work. The final section considers some implications of these economic changes for getting jobs, for income, and for unemployment. It also analyzes the social convention of money and explores the growth of the underground economy.

## THE MOVE TOWARD A GLOBAL ECONOMY

A **global economy** is one in which the economic life and health of one nation depends on what happens in the other nations around the world. A number of examples illustrate the move toward an increasingly global economy. These include the changing nature of markets, the internationalization of capital, the growing importance of multinationals, the growth of world trade, and the potential for increasingly important trade partnerships and realignments.

## The Changing Nature of Markets

Markets used to be places where people brought goods to trade or sell. They were located where roads crossed or in major port areas. Take the oil market as an example. Tankers often carried more oil than a particular buyer ordered. That extra oil could be sold "on the spot," when the ship landed. Tankers would go to Rotterdam in the Netherlands because the port was large and well protected. As a result, the "spot" oil market developed in Rotterdam and came to be called the "Rotterdam market." It still is, but the market is no longer confined to Rotterdam. The "market" has become a telex-radio-computer network (Bell, 1987). Brokers operate all over the world, making their trades through the network and sending ships to new ports before they ever get to Rotterdam. Shifts like this in many markets are eliminating specific places of exchange.

## The Internationalization of Capital

In the post-World War II era, the United States dominated the world economy, as Great Britain had from 1875 to 1914 (Block, 1977a). In 1950, the United States was responsible for about 50 percent of the world's production. By 1975 this figure had declined to only about 25 percent, with significantly greater shares coming from Germany and Japan (Miller and Tomaskovic-Devey, 1983). The dominance of a single country had been replaced by that of a number of strong nations.

In the new global capital economy, money moves around very quickly. One day in 1974 at the New York Clearinghouse Interbank Payments System (CHIPS), nearly $43 billion was transferred among banks all over the world

*Markets, such as the Chicago Options Exchange pictured here, have become increasingly international, as communications networks link world trade ever more tightly.*

(Mayer, 1974). CHIPS handles all the U.S. and foreign payments that pass through New York banks. By 1989, an average of $750 million per day was moving through CHIPS.

The global flow of capital is very evident in the surge of purchases of U.S. real estate and corporations by international investors. In recent years, these investors have bought such visible American enterprises as the Exxon headquarters building in Manhattan's Rockefeller Center; Doubleday & Company, book publishers; Carnation milk; Standard Oil of Ohio; Chesebrough-Ponds; the Dunes Hotel and Country Club in Las Vegas; and Smith & Wesson, gun manufacturer. Foreign ownership in the United States rose to $1.33 trillion in 1986, up 25 percent from 1985 (Koepp, 1987). In 1986 U.S. holdings abroad totaled $1.07 trillion, less than the total amount of foreign ownership in the United States. As recently as a decade ago, the situation was reversed, with the United States owning many productive assets in other countries.

Corporate takeovers and mergers, whether national or international, "friendly" or "unfriendly," reflect the growing fluidity of capital. They also reveal the increasing dominance of the financial model of corporate enterprise, where firms are viewed as assets to be bought and sold rather than as collections of people producing products or services (Hirsch, 1986).

## Multinationals

Part of the internationalization of capital results from the growth of multinational corporations. **Multinationals** are corporations that locate their operations in a number of nations. They have work forces, sales, and income from a number of nations rather than primarily from one country.

For a time multinational corporations were overwhelmingly American, but that dominance has been waning. The proportion of the top 100 world firms that are American-based declined from 58 percent in 1971 to 30 percent in 1982. In 1987, 20 of the top 50 were based in the United States. (See Table 13.1 for a list of the top 50.)

The annual income in sales from these multinational corporations often exceeds the total gross national product of many nations. General Motors, the largest multinational industrial corporation in the world in 1987, had sales of $101.8 billion that year, more than the GNP of Saudi Arabia, Pakistan, South Africa, or many other countries.

Committed to growth and maximizing profits and willing to move wherever cheaper production or increased sales can be realized, the multinationals make decisions that affect whether or not people work; what they will eat, drink, and wear; and what is taught in schools (Barnet and Muller, 1974; Vernon, 1977). By pursuing a policy of mobility, they are able to play labor markets off against each other by threatening to move if labor organizes; they can even influence national and international political relations.

Supporters of multinational firms claim that their activities result in greater efficiency, lower prices for consumers, and economic development, including the export of technologies, capital, and jobs for developing nations. Critics such as Barnet and Muller (1974) argue that multinationals are helping to create a social system that is more centralized and hierarchical than anything yet known, and that they try to substitute loyalty to the corporation for more authentic sources of community such as neighborhood, ethnic group, religion, or nation. In the process, they violate human needs for social, ecological, and psychological balance. Both critics and supporters agree that multinational corporations are playing an even more important role in the world and have critical political, economic, and social consequences for people's daily lives.

## World Trade

The growth of international manufacturing and marketing is reflected in the skyrocketing volume of world trade. Cassette players from Hong Kong, Japanese cars, running shoes from Korea, Swiss cheese, Danish beer—you no doubt can add some examples of your own to the list—all illustrate the growth of world trade in recent years. The total volume of U.S. exports and imports soared from $50 billion in 1965 to more than $650 billion in 1987 (U.S. Bureau of the Census, 1989a), an increase of more than 1000 percent.

In 1992 the European Community (E.C.) is scheduled to begin a fully open trade partnership. Its members will have a common currency (the ECU, or European Currency Unit) keyed

*The growth of international manufacturing and marketing is reflected in the skyrocketing volume of world trade. These billboards in New York's Times Square reflect the growth of imports in the United States.*

**Table 13.1**   *50 Largest Multinational Corporations, Ranked by 1987 Sales*

| Rank | Company | Headquarters | Industry | Sales $ Millions |
|------|---------|--------------|----------|------------------|
| 1 | General Motors | Detroit | Motor vehicles | 101,781.9 |
| 2 | Royal Dutch/Shell Group | London/The Hague | Petroleum refining | 78,319.3 |
| 3 | Exxon | New York | Petroleum refining | 76,416.0 |
| 4 | Ford Motor | Dearborn, Mich. | Motor vehicles | 71,643.4 |
| 5 | International Business Machines | Armonk, N.Y. | Computers | 54,217.0 |
| 6 | Mobile | New York | Petroleum refining | 51,223.0 |
| 7 | British Petroleum | London | Petroleum refining | 45,205.9 |
| 8 | Toyota Motor | Toyota City (Japan) | Motor vehicles | 41,455.0 |
| 9 | IRI | Rome | Metals | 41,270.0 |
| 10 | General Electric | Fairfield, Conn. | Electronics | 39,315.0 |
| 11 | Daimler-Benz | Stuttgart | Motor vehicles | 37,535.5 |
| 12 | Texaco | White Plains, N.Y. | Petroleum refining | 34,372.0 |
| 13 | American Tel. & Tel. | New York | Electronics | 33,598.0 |
| 14 | E.I. Du Pont De Nemours | Wilmington, Del. | Chemicals | 30,468.0 |
| 15 | Volkswagen | Wolfsburg (W. Ger.) | Motor vehicles | 30,392.7 |
| 16 | Hitachi | Tokyo | Electronics | 30,332.2 |
| 17 | Fiat | Turin | Motor vehicles | 29,642.8 |
| 18 | Siemens | Munich | Electronics | 27,462.9 |
| 19 | Matsushita Electric Industrial | Osaka | Electronics | 27,325.7 |
| 20 | Unilever | London/Rotterdam | Food | 27,128.8 |
| 21 | Chrysler | Highland Park, Mich. | Motor vehicles | 26,257.7 |
| 22 | Philips' Gloeilampenfabrieken | Eindhoven (Neth.) | Electronics | 26,021.2 |
| 23 | Chevron | San Francisco | Petroleum refining | 26,015.0 |
| 24 | Nissan Motor | Tokyo | Motor vehicles | 25,650.5 |
| 25 | Renault | Paris | Motor vehicles | 24,539.7 |
| 26 | ENI | Rome | Petroleum refining | 24,242.5 |
| 27 | Nestlé | Vevey (Switzerland) | Food | 23,625.9 |
| 28 | BASF | Ludwigshafen (W. Ger.) | Chemicals | 22,383.7 |
| 29 | Philip Morris | New York | Tobacco | 22,279.0 |
| 30 | CGE (Cie Générale D'Électricité) | Paris | Electronics | 21,204.3 |
| 31 | Elf Aquitaine | Paris | Petroleum refining | 21,186.4 |
| 32 | Samsung | Seoul | Electronics | 21,053.5 |
| 33 | Bayer | Leverkusen (W. Ger.) | Chemicals | 20,662.2 |
| 34 | Hoechst | Frankfurt | Chemicals | 20,558.1 |
| 35 | Toshiba | Tokyo | Electronics | 20,378.1 |
| 36 | Amoco | Chicago | Petroleum refining | 20,174.0 |
| 37 | Peugeot | Paris | Motor vehicles | 19,658.2 |
| 38 | Imperial Chemical Industries | London | Chemicals | 18,232.8 |
| 39 | Honda Motor | Tokyo | Motor vehicles | 17,237.7 |
| 40 | United Technologies | Hartford | Aerospace | 17,170.2 |
| 41 | Occidental Petroleum | Los Angeles | Food | 17,096.0 |
| 42 | Procter & Gamble | Cincinnati | Soaps, Cosmetics | 17,000.0 |
| 43 | Atlantic Richfield | Los Angeles | Petroleum refining | 16,281.4 |
| 44 | RJR Nabisco | Atlanta | Tobacco | 15,868.0 |
| 45 | Petrobrás (Petróleo Brasileiro) | Rio De Janeiro | Petroleum refining | 15,640.5 |
| 46 | Boeing | Seattle | Aerospace | 15,355.0 |
| 47 | NEC | Tokyo | Electronics | 15,325.1 |
| 48 | Tenneco | Houston | Petroleum refining | 15,075.0 |
| 49 | Nippon Steel | Tokyo | Metals | 14,639.8 |
| 50 | Volvo | Göteborg (Sweden) | Motor vehicles | 14,576.0 |

*Source: Fortune,* August 1, 1988, pp. D3, D4.

to the currencies of the twelve member nations.[1] As an integrated economy, the E.C. will nearly equal the United States in economic production, and will surpass the combined total of Japan, South Korea, Taiwan, Hong Kong, and Singapore.

Another open question is whether, by the year 2013, the Pacific Basin will be the center of world economic power (Bell, 1987). If so, that would represent an extraordinary historical shift. The initial center of economic development was the European Mediterranean Basin. In the eighteenth century, it shifted to northern European nations and the Atlantic rim. Since 1970, the shift has been toward the Pacific. Currently, the great expansion in U.S. trade is with Pacific Rim countries, which include Japan, China, Southeast Asia, Korea, Taiwan, Hong Kong, and Australia (Bell, 1987). Given the tremendous globalizing tendencies in the economy, it is reasonable to ask whether different types of national economies are becoming more alike.

## ARE NATIONAL ECONOMIES BECOMING MORE ALIKE?

All economic systems, whether capitalist or planned, must address questions concerning the kinds and quantities of goods to be produced, how to coordinate production processes, and how to distribute the fruits of economic activity. How much of total production, for example, will go for consumer goods and how much for research of new equipment? Although such questions deal with economic activities, in fact they are answered in social and political terms.

Economic growth is a recent concern because the idea that an entire society might grow richer within one person's lifetime was inconceivable before the industrial revolution transformed production. Today economic growth is a goal in many industrialized and developing countries. Nations have political and military reasons for seeking economic growth. Politicians know that increasing the prosperity of the populace

may strengthen their own positions, and national defense efforts are fortified by a healthy economy. Economic growth may be measured by assessing changes in an overall measure of economic activity, such as gross national product (GNP). When countries are compared, GNP may be divided by the total number of inhabitants in the country to arrive at a GNP per capita figure.

Societies differ in the degree to which market as opposed to political factors influence economic organization. At least four types of national economies can be distinguished: capitalist market economies, capitalist welfare-state economies, centrally planned economic systems, and hybrid economies. These types illustrate some of the ways that market and political considerations are combined.

## Capitalist Market Economies

**Capitalism** is a form of economic organization in which individuals accumulate and invest capital. Some people own the means of producing and distributing goods and services in a society. Owners keep a portion of the surplus generated. In capitalist private-enterprise economic systems, private investors and their hired managers decide the nature and quantity of goods to produce within a supply-and-demand market framework. The goal in this process is to make a profit for the owners of the corporation. They try to obtain the resources, goods, and services they need for this process, as well as to manage demand through advertising and marketing. If their products are not selling, they may try to eliminate their competition (for example, through tariffs protecting against imports or through price changes) or to change their products so they will be in greater demand.

### Adam Smith and Laissez-Faire Economics

The underlying philosophy of capitalism was articulated by Adam Smith in his *Inquiry into the Nature and Causes of the Wealth of Nations* (1776). He argued that economic wealth develops best when economic actions are regulated only by the free play of market forces. That is, producers and consumers should bargain directly to decide the prices at which they are willing to exchange or buy one another's goods. The government

[1] The nations are Belgium, Britain, Denmark, France, Greece, Ireland, Italy, Luxembourg, the Netherlands, Portugal, Spain, and West Germany.

should provide only those services for which a market price cannot be charged, such as police protection, fire fighting, or flood control. It should not interfere with the operation of free market forces, according to Smith. A **laissez-faire** economic system is one completely free of governmental interference.

Smith believed that each individual, motivated by the self-interest of making a profit, is "led by an invisible hand to promote an end which was not part of his intention"—the interest of society. Until the time he wrote, the English government regulated trade very closely. Smith's work influenced a swing away from government regulation.

### Keynesian Economics

By the nineteenth century, capitalism had become a highly productive economic system. Even Karl Marx (1818–1883), who was critical of capitalism, acknowledged that in just 100 years, capitalists had created more massive and more colossal productive forces than had all preceding generations together. Only the Great Depression of the 1930s really challenged Adam Smith's laissez-faire economic ideology.

**Keynesian economics** took over in Western capitalist economies after the world depression in the 1930s. In his book *The General Theory of Employment, Interest, and Money* (1936), Keynes challenged classical economic assertions that natural market forces would always produce full employment and that savings would always be invested. As monopolies, which tend to develop in capitalism, take control of production, wages and prices are not likely to decline even during economic downturns. This is because there is no competition between firms. If prices do not drop, only two other results are possible in an economic decline—inflation or unemployment. Keynes argued that vigorous government intervention through deficit spending (that is, government spending that exceeded tax revenues) was necessary to maintain high levels of employment. The government could become the employer of last resort. The state could spend money on social welfare, which could raise economic demand and smooth the ups and downs of business cycles. Thus the harsh effects of unemployment could be reduced. Many Western nations today follow policies of deficit spending and/or tax cuts in an effort to maintain consumer demand and hence high levels of employment. Such policies increase the amount of money in circulation.

### Criticisms of Capitalism

Capitalism has been criticized for the way it distributes wealth and income unequally in the population, for its tendencies toward monopolies (which encourage price fixing and an end to competition), and for its periodic unemployment.

Karl Marx's criticisms of capitalism go deeper than these, however. He argued that human beings are alienated from their labor and from themselves under capitalist forms of production. People, he stated, produce goods only through their own labor, and those goods may be valued according to the amount of labor it takes to produce them. Under capitalism, the worker is not paid for part of the value of the goods produced (the "surplus value"). Instead, the surplus value is taken away from the worker and turned into a profit for the capitalist at the expense of the worker. Alienation is furthered by work in very large organizations, where each person does a very small, specific job, as on an assembly line, never seeing how his or her work helps to create the final product (for instance, a car). People may forget that these products are humanly created, and the way they are produced tends to lead to their being viewed with awe and adoration. Through this process people lose their humanity, Marx felt.

## Welfare-State Economies

Welfare-state economies represent a somewhat modified version of capitalist market economies. They temper the operation of market mechanisms with state programs of taxation and spending. Welfare-state economies include many of the advanced industrial democracies of western Europe, including West Germany, the Netherlands, Sweden, Denmark, France, Italy, and Great Britain. Since World War II, the national governments of those countries have developed and run a series of programs, based on Keynesian economic principles, designed to guarantee workers a basic standard of living (Quadagno, 1987; Myles, 1984). These include family allowances, unemployment benefits, old-

*Welfare-state programs in state socialist societies such as West Germany, the Netherlands, Sweden, and Denmark provide family allowances, unemployment benefits, old-age pensions, educational benefits, and health insurance. The United States has fewer such programs.*

age pensions, educational benefits, and health insurance.

Neo-Marxists see welfare-state programs as ways of curbing the excesses of capitalism and resolving some of the contradictions between capitalism and democracy. Welfare programs lead workers to accept the legitimacy of the capitalist system, because investment and profitability is needed to generate the surplus to support welfare-state spending. Capitalists accept welfare benefits because they help to ensure a healthy and satisfied working class (Offe, 1984). State welfare programs also spread over the wider population the costs of social expenses that capitalists might otherwise have to pay themselves (O'Connor, 1973; Olson, 1982).

The benefits of welfare-state economies are that they provide a floor below which workers cannot fall. As a result, there are fewer homeless persons and less of an urban underclass in the cities of societies with welfare-state economies. The disadvantages of welfare-state economies are seen in the higher proportion of national GNP that is spent by the state, the correspondingly higher levels of taxation, and concerns that these policies and programs sap people's incentives to work. There are some suggestions that, because of the higher rate of taxation, there is more cheating on income-tax returns in such economies and greater activity in the black market (discussed in the box at the end of the chapter). There is also a growing awareness of the

"fiscal crisis of the state"—that is, the inability of national governments to continue paying for ever more costly benefits.

## Centrally Planned Economies

Various centrally planned economies have tried to apply some of Marx's economic ideas. One of the major points of difference between capitalist and centrally planned economies arises from basic assumptions concerning the right to own and control productive resources and the surplus generated from them. In state **socialist societies,** productive resources are owned and controlled by the state, not by individuals.

In its pure form, the **centrally planned economy** includes public ownership of or control over all productive resources, including mines, factories, transportation, communications, and labor. The economic activity of the entire system is planned by individuals in the government. The plan allocates a fixed amount of resources to particular organizations and sets production quotas. The planners issue commands that production managers must follow. The government sets prices in ways that have nothing to do with production costs. It does this as a deliberate social policy in keeping with the belief that everyone should have food, medical care, housing, and education before some people have luxury goods (for example, videotapes or cars). For this reason, many consumer goods are extremely expensive, whereas essentials such as food, housing, and medical care are inexpensive by Western standards—to the degree that they are available. One nation that practices central economic planning is the Soviet Union.

### The Soviet Economy

In the USSR the state owns the means of production, including land, mines, and factories. The state has decided that defense and heavy industry are most important and that consumer goods have a lower priority. So political decisions within the government and the ensuing allocation of state resources favor heavy industry, military equipment, electric generating and distribution systems, transportation systems, chemical and fertilizer production, and agriculture.

Earning more money has limited value for workers in Soviet society. Certain key goods, like access to better housing, are determined by political influence rather than by economic market factors. Money is further devalued by the shortages of some consumer goods and the very high prices of others.

About 15 percent of the USSR's GNP went for military spending in 1987 (McCauley, 1988b). Soviet leader Mikhail Gorbachev seemed to realize that Soviet arms spending pushed up U.S. and NATO defense spending. If he could cut Soviet spending, he thought that might stimulate defense cuts in the West. It would also free badly needed resources for the civilian economy. In 1989 the Soviet newspaper *Izvestia* began running U.S. advertisements for consumer goods.

On May 1, 1988, a new "individual labor"

*In 1988 the Soviet Union began allowing trade with the United States, and U.S. entrepreneurs began setting up businesses there.*

law went into effect in the Soviet Union. It allowed individuals to set up their own businesses but not to hire others to work for them. Individuals had to buy licenses from their local governments and pay income taxes on their gross earnings. Some enterprises that had been illegal (such as selling foreign-made blue jeans) suddenly became legal (McCauley, 1988a). Individual artisans could also make and sell their wares. The law may help increase the production of some food supplies, but it promises to do little to address the acute housing shortages in the USSR.

There is considerably more diversity in state socialist societies than the Soviet example suggests. As part of the "Four Modernizations" begun in 1977, China declared new government policies that encourage individuals to develop their own money-making projects. In the first six years, Chinese peasants increased crop production every year and doubled their annual cash income (to $125 per year). China also became a net exporter of grain. Chinese leader Deng Xiaoping warned that China must "combat the corrosive influence of capitalist ideas" (Iyer, 1985, p. 44). He appeared to be aware of the tension between market-driven and state-controlled economies. Party officials have no legitimate way to increase their wealth and may fear they will lose control (Iyer, 1985, p. 55). The challenge is one of controlling capitalist excesses and preventing reactionary opposition to reforms. So far, only about 3 percent of the Chinese economy is involved in private enterprises. Most of these are in rural areas. As this book went to press, it was not yet clear what effect the 1989 student and worker protests would have on the Chinese economy.

In Poland and Yugoslavia, on the other hand, agriculture was never collectivized on the same scale as in the Soviet Union, and some 75 percent of farming is privately owned. Bulgaria has some companies that offer bonuses or other incentives to workers if profits are high enough.

### Criticisms of Centrally Planned Economies

In centrally planned economies, economic and political power tends to become concentrated in the hands of one group whose authority is based on party position. Strikes, unwillingness to work overtime, or similar worker actions are considered disloyal to the state. Workers are controlled politically as well as economically. Many questions can be asked about the incentive system in state socialist economies. If essential goods or services like food and medical care are subsidized by the state and the user does not pay their full cost, will users consume more than they would if they had to pay the full costs themselves? If producers of such goods or services are protected from competition and assured of continued government subsidies, will they be blind to user needs and preferences? Will a "black market" of luxury goods develop? Critics of centrally planned economies, in short, raise questions about how much freedom individual workers have and about the effectiveness of central planning and collective rather than individual incentives.

Are these different types of economies becoming more alike over time? Most of the major centrally planned economies have introduced changes in recent years that make them hybrid economies of one sort or another. Yugoslavia began experimenting with a hybrid economy even earlier.

## Hybrid Economies—Yugoslavia

Critics of state socialist economic systems say that centralized political planning is an inefficient way to manage a geographically dispersed economic system. Yugoslavia attempts to solve some of these problems with a **hybrid economy** that blends features of both planned and market economies.

Yugoslavia broke with the Soviet Union in 1948 to follow a new path to socialism involving "self-management." In the Yugoslav system, the workers in a factory form a workers' council and the council elects or hires its own managers. The members of this group decide, on the basis of what they think will sell, what products they will make. They can try to borrow money from a central pool or from suppliers of raw materials, who are often located in other countries. If the organization generates a profit—that is, has money left over after paying its costs, including the wages it has agreed to pay—the workers' council decides what to do with it. The council may decide to reinvest it in the organization in order to fund research, development, and future growth. Or it may pay it out in the form of

bonuses to all the members. Workers have considerable decision-making power within the limits placed on them by market influences on prices, profitability, and the incentive structure needed to motivate wage earners. The Yugoslav system of self-management relies much more on market forces than on central planning.

## Are Various Economies Converging?

It remains to be seen how extensive and long-lasting the adoption of incentive systems within centrally planned economies will be. Capitalist economies have also adopted a number of state-supported welfare policies. Although the United States has been among the slowest to adopt such measures and has the least adequate welfare programs, it does have some welfare-state programs. Hence there is some evidence that the various types of economic organization are becoming somewhat more alike.

## WHERE WORK GETS DONE

Societies differ with respect to where people work. A very basic distinction is one that sees the economy as consisting of primary, secondary, and tertiary sectors. The United States, especially, has experienced dramatic shifts over time in the proportion of its population that is engaged in each of these sectors. We can say that societies have primarily agricultural, industrial, or service economies depending on the proportion of their population that works in each sector.

## Primary, Secondary, and Tertiary Sectors

In all societies work occurs in three main sectors. In the **primary economic sector** people farm, fish, fell trees, and extract ores and other resources such as coal from the ground. All the activities of this sector deal with the collection of natural resources. In the **secondary economic sector** people work with the raw materials to turn them into manufactured goods.

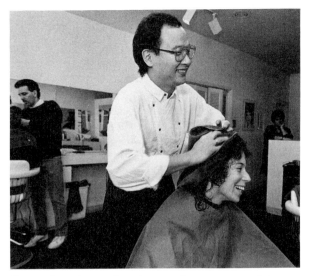

*Personal services such as beauty shops are part of the tertiary, or service, sector of the economy. This sector also includes business services such as banking, insurance, and communications; social services like education and health care; and other personal services.*

They smelt and roll steel, build cars, freeze foods, weave and sew clothing, produce chemicals, and pour concrete. This is the industrial or manufacturing sector of a society's economy. The **tertiary economic sector** involves services to manufacturers such as those provided by banking, transportation, insurance, and communications, as well as such social services as education, medicine, welfare, and personal services like hotels, restaurants, household service, barber and beauty shops, cleaning, laundering, and repair services. Within a given society the proportion of people working in each sector depends on how well endowed the society is with natural resources and energy and on its level of industrial development.

In most societies agriculture occupies most of the people working in the primary sector. The proportion of the population in agriculture is significant, because it indicates how many people remain available to produce other goods and services. A subsistence economy is one in which nearly every member of a society is engaged in gathering or producing the basic necessities of life. If the people producing food, clothing, and other essentials are able to provide such goods for more people than just themselves, it becomes possible for a society to support other activities—for example, full-time religious lead-

ers, full-time toolmakers, storytellers, builders, and musicians. In Figure 13.1, selected nations in the world are ranked according to the proportion of their population in agriculture; their average per capita income is also indicated. In general, the smaller the proportion of the population in agriculture, the higher the per capita income.

Technology helps to explain the wide variation among nations in the size of the agricultural sector. As farming is mechanized, fewer people can produce more food. In some societies work in the primary sector still involves very simple hand-operated technologies. Hoes, axes, picks, or fishnets owned jointly by groups of people may be used. In other societies a great deal of expensive and elaborate farming or mining equipment is used. The mechanization of farming in the United States, for example, has led to the production of enough food for its population and the generation of a surplus for export to other nations. At the same time, the percentage of the American labor force engaged in farming has dropped dramatically, from 72 percent in 1820 to 3 percent in 1984. Food production ability, however, is not necessarily a sign of wealth. A few very rich nations (such as Kuwait) cannot produce all the food they con-

*In subsistence economies, nearly every member of society works to produce the basic necessities of life, and most of the population is engaged in farming, like this woman and child who are growing cabbages.*

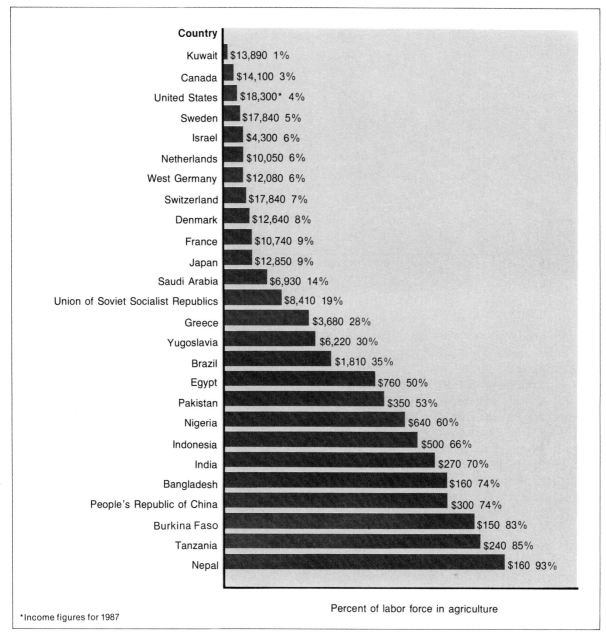

**Figure 13.1    Percentage of Labor Force in Agriculture and
Per Capita Income in U.S. Dollars in 1986.**

The poorest societies tend to have a larger proportion of their
population working in agriculture than do more affluent societies.

*Sources: Britannica Book of the Year,* 1989; World Almanac, 1988.

sume, but they have other valuable resources,
like oil, which they can trade for food.

    The secondary, or manufacturing, sector of
the U.S. economy expanded dramatically from
1820 to 1920 (as Figure 13.2 shows), but it has
remained stable at about one-third of the labor
force since 1920. As late as 1860, three out of
five Americans in the labor force worked in
farming. After the Civil War, however, industries that had responded to wartime needs in-

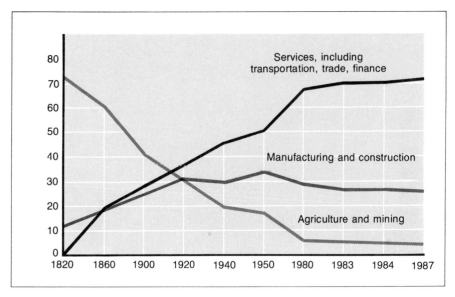

**Figure 13.2 Percentage of Labor Force in Major Economic Sectors in the United States, 1820–1984.**

In the United States the proportion of the population working in agriculture has steadily declined since 1820, the proportion working in manufacturing increased until 1950 when it began a gradual decline, and the proportion working in services has increased dramatically.

*Source:* U.S. Bureau of the Census, 1975; 1985a, p. 404; 1989a; p. 391.

creased their productivity. This was especially true in textiles and shoe manufacturing. The first transcontinental railroad was completed in 1869, spurring the prospects for national trade. The oil and steel industries also grew tremendously in the closing decades of the nineteenth century. By 1900 the United States was the most productive industrial nation in the world. The manufacturing portion of the work force continued to grow. The number of factory workers, for example, rose steadily as a percentage of the work force until 1950, when it peaked. The percentage has been declining ever since.

By 1950 half the labor force was working in the *service sector* of the economy. This sector includes people who do not produce food or goods, but may aid production by providing financial, information, education, marketing, transportation, communication, or other services needed by people in the primary and secondary sectors. As machines have been developed to perform more and more agricultural and manufacturing activities, per capita productivity in those areas has increased and more people have been freed to move into the tertiary sector of the economy. As Figure 13.2 shows, the service sector jumped from 19 percent of the U.S. labor market in 1860 to 71 percent in 1987. This sector represents a larger percentage of the labor market in the United States than it does in Japan or West Germany (Singelmann, 1978).

## The Dual Economy: Core, Periphery, and State Sectors

Another way to analyze economic activity is in terms of the dual economy. The term **dual economy** refers to the division of the private sector of the economy into (1) a core, or monopoly, sector and (2) a periphery, or competitive, sector (Averitt, 1968; O'Connor, 1973).

Firms in the **economic core** have large numbers of employees, large total assets and annual sales, and generally high profits. Core enterprises are distinguished from peripheral ones by their greater size, more complex structures, more advanced technologies, and greater market dominance (Baron and Bielby, 1984). Their operations and sales are national or international. They usually produce many different products. The major oil, automobile, chemical, steel, electronics, food, soap, tobacco, and drug companies are prime examples of core industries. The core sector of the economy employs about one-third of the labor force, with the largest proportion in manufacturing and mining. The markets of core firms are generally concentrated, meaning that a few very large firms sell most of what the market buys. The cash flow and credit ratings of these firms are usually very high. They tend to have more capital invested per worker than peripheral firms and to have higher productivity. Unionization is well developed in this sector, and wages are relatively high. New competitors are generally kept out through state regulations (for example, in the banking and insurance industries), by high capital requirements (as in automobile manufacturing or mining), by high overhead costs, or by heavy advertising and brand loyalty (for instance, in the soap and tobacco industries).

The people who work in the core sector of the economy constitute what has been called the primary labor market (Piore, 1975). The primary labor market contains jobs with relatively high wages, good working conditions, considerable job security, opportunities for advancement, and work rules and procedures based on due process. On-the-job training is available and may be necessary for moving up the career ladder.

In the **economic periphery,** firms are relatively small. They tend to be located in one geographic region, to produce only a small line of related products, and to have markets that are normally local or regional in scope. Their cash flow is much smaller, their credit ratings are poorer, and they pay higher interest rates on borrowed funds than do core firms. Productivity is relatively low. They have less capital invested per worker, and because they are not capital-intensive, it is relatively easy for competitors to set up in business. Examples include the textile and apparel industries, meat-packing firms, restaurants, drug and grocery stores, automotive supply companies, and other small manufacturers.

Many competitive sector firms produce or sell in markets that are seasonal, subject to sudden changes in fashion or style, or are unstable for other reasons. As a result, work in these industries is seasonal and irregular, and wages are low. People who cannot find work in the core sector are more likely to accept the lower pay and poorer working conditions of the peripheral sector. Union organization is weak in this sector because of the social characteristics of the labor force and because there are large numbers of small, local firms. In addition, highly competitive markets and small profit margins make it costly for employers to recognize unions. So workers in this sector tend not to be organized, with some exceptions in the garment industry and among foundry workers (O'Connor, 1973).

Competitive industries employ about one-third of the U.S. labor force, with the largest proportion working in services or distribution. Most of the new jobs in the United States in the last ten years were in the peripheral sector.

The competitive-sector labor market differs from the core-sector labor market. The more disadvantaged groups, such as racial minorities, women, young or old workers, are the ones most likely to end up in this market. In addition to characteristics of workers in the secondary labor market, it is important to consider issues of power and social relations on the job (Hodson and Kaufman, 1982). Jobs in this sector tend to be unstable and to have short or nonexistent mobility chains. These features—combined with low wages, poor working conditions, and little job security—discourage job stability (Edwards, 1979; Sokoloff, 1980). No matter how long or hard employees work at jobs in the secondary labor market, there are no established paths for advancing to better jobs (Gordon, 1972). The influence of the sector on the career mobility of men was especially evident in the latter part of their careers (Tolbert, 1982).

The **state sector** of the economy can be divided into (1) goods and services produced by the state itself (for example, education, public health, welfare and other social services, and military service, excluding the production of arms) and (2) production organized by private industries under contract with the state. The latter includes military equipment and supplies and building and highway construction. Today nearly one-third of the U.S. labor force is employed in direct or contractual state sector activities (including local, state, and federal governments; O'Connor, 1973).

Productivity in the state sector is relatively low and increases slowly. The demand for labor in this sector was relatively stable and increasing during the 30 years after World War II, but in the late 1970s and 1980s, public employees began being laid off. The large size of work units and relatively low turnover among employees foster the growth of labor unions in state industries, but the diversity of the work force (young, old, blacks, whites, men, women, handicapped, nonhandicapped) is an inhibiting factor. Occupational distinctions and civil service rankings also limit unionization. Because increased labor costs in the state sector tend to force up taxes, government agencies generally try to discourage the development of unions. In recent years the state sector has become more highly organized than the competitive sector but less organized than the core sector (O'Connor, 1973). See Table 13.2 for a comparison of the three sectors.

## Large Corporations

The core or monopoly sector of economic activity consists of relatively few large corporations. Assets, sales, and jobs are concentrated in the hands of a few corporate owners and managers. In 1987 the 200 largest industrial corporations in the United States owned 86 percent of all corporate assets (U.S. Bureau of the Census, 1989a). This helps to explain the unequal distribution of wealth noted in Chapter 9. The four largest firms in the breakfast food, automobile, aluminum, and vacuum cleaner industries control 75 percent or more of the sales in those industries, not counting imports; other industries are nearly as concentrated. Although there are more than 350,000 manufacturing firms in the United States, the top 500 U.S. industrial firms employed 67 percent of the manufacturing labor force in 1987 (U.S. Bureau of the Census, 1989a).

This tremendous concentration of economic power and resources offers financial advantages, advertising and brand-name recognition, and political power to the large corporations in the core sector. Such firms can limit the develop-

**Table 13.2**   *General Characteristics of Core, Periphery, and State Sectors of the Economy*

| | Core or Monopoly Sector | Periphery or Competitive Sector | State Sector |
|---|---|---|---|
| | (Oil, auto, chemical, and drug industries; big, prosperous multinationals) | (Textiles, auto industry suppliers, meat-packing, restaurants; smaller local firms) | (Teachers, social workers, sanitation workers, federal, state, and local government workers) |
| **Wage and Salary Levels** | High | Low | Medium to high |
| **Job Stability** | High | Low | High |
| **Degree of Labor Force Unionization** | High | Low | Intermediate |
| **Wages and Salaries Determined by** | Productivity and cost of living; negotiations | Supply and demand | Political bargaining |
| **Working Conditions** | Relatively good | Poor | Good |
| **Employee Benefits** | Generally good | Poor | Good |
| **Percentage of White Males** | High | Low | Medium |
| **Percentage of Females** | Low | High | Low at upper ranks; high at lower ranks |
| **Percentage of Nonwhites** | Low | High | Equals percentage of minorities in the work force |

*Sources:* Averitt, 1968; Barclay, 1981; Edwards, 1979; Fusfeld, 1973; O'Connor, 1973.

ment of new products, resist the adoption of new technologies, and ignore new ways of organizing the work process. They are fairly effectively protected from serious competition. They may restrict the options available to consumers, keep prices high, resist new technology that is more efficient in the long run, and persist in organizing work in ways that produce boredom and alienation. The few people who control more than 80 percent of the productive assets can decide what investments they will make, what new products or services they will develop, where they will build plants or offices, and whom they will hire.

These firms do not operate in a competitive market. Instead, they constitute an **oligopoly,** a market composed of a few sellers. The products they sell are close substitutes for one another, and it is difficult for new competitors to enter the market. All firms are influenced by the pricing actions of other firms in the industry (Averitt, 1968). Because they are not operating in a competitive market, these firms can set "administered" prices, which consumers must pay unless they are willing to do without the goods or services. It is difficult, for instance, to live without home heating oil in zero-degree weather, so most consumers pay the higher administered prices oligopolies charge. (Although growing numbers of families are installing wood-burning furnaces, they still represent a small portion of the total market.)

Such firms have considerable political power, not only because they can make large political contributions and have people who are well-connected politically on their boards but also because their production, jobs, and taxes are considered valuable national resources (Evans and Schneider, 1981). Their political power is enhanced by the ability of the large firms to cooperate. Besides sharing many directors in common (Dooley, 1969; Levine, 1972; Mizruchi, 1982; Zeitlin, 1974) and having many social and intellectual ties (Domhoff, 1983, 1967, 1970; Moore, 1979; Useem, 1984, 1980, 1979, 1978), large firms are bound together by overlapping ownership. The Mellon family and bank, for example, not only have a dominant position in Alcoa Aluminum but are also among the largest shareholders in IBM, General Electric, Atlantic Richfield, Standard Oil of California, Exxon,

AT&T, Caterpillar Tractor, K Mart, Sears, Roebuck, Eastman Kodak, U.S. Steel, and Jones and Laughlin Steel. And the banking industry is itself very concentrated.

Corporations and banks are increasing their assets and sales and the percentage of market share they control; in addition, they are taking over other corporations to form conglomerates that operate simultaneously in many industries. ITT, for example, produces food and electrical equipment, runs hotels, and owns publishing houses. Besides light bulbs and refrigerators, General Electric makes medical systems, plastics, aircraft engines, and nuclear reactors; it also sells coal, oil, gas, and uranium.

## DIFFERENT TYPES OF WORK

Sociologists see work as consisting of human effort interacting with physical nature, other people, or both (Freidson, 1980). As a result, the world of physical nature, social considerations, and the state of technology all set limits on how work can be conducted and subdivided.

All the work that we do is located in a global economy; within a national economy; in the extractive, manufacturing, or service sectors; and within the dual economy. These locations affect the nature of the work we do and influence changes in that work.

### Occupations and Professions

Occupations and professions involve the technical activities associated with particular positions in the world of work. An **occupation** is a position that calls for specialized technical knowledge and activities. A **profession** is a position that, in addition to specialized technical knowledge and activities, requires background and training in a body of knowledge and often some form of degree or credential. These concepts illuminate the nature of work and the connections between individuals and the economy through jobs, income, and unemployment.

In the last 100 years, not only have jobs shifted from the agricultural and manufacturing sectors to sales and services (as Figure 13.2

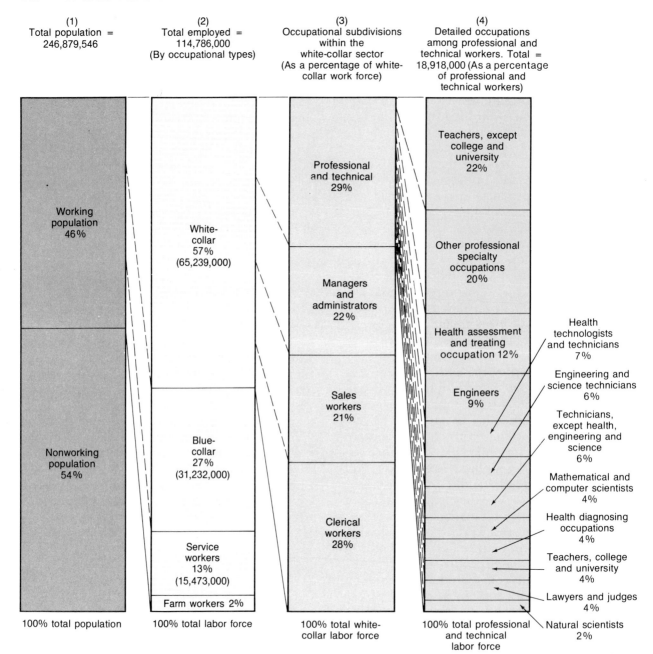

**Figure 13.3  Analyzing the U.S. Labor Force, 1989.**

Column 1 shows the proportion of the U.S. population that is working (slightly less than half). Column 2 shows the proportions of the working population in various types of occupations (more than half are in white-collar occupations). Column 3 shows the composition of the white-collar work force in more detail, and column 4 provides a more refined breakdown of professional and technical occupations in the United States in 1989.

*Source:* Adapted from Montagna, 1977, U.S. Department of Labor, 1989a, p. 1.

shows) but the number of occupational specialties has also grown tremendously. The latest edition of the *Dictionary of Occupational Titles,* for example, lists nearly 21,000 occupational specialties, including air analyst, perfumer, fish culturist, tissue technician, floral designer, lease buyer, sound mixer, magazine keeper, swatch clerk, fingerprint classifier, pickler, airbrush artist, and stripper (U.S. Department of Labor, 1977, 1986). (This government handbook lists only legitimate occupations, of course; it does not mention numbers runners, purse snatchers, pool sharks, pimps, prostitutes, drug pushers, and hired guns.)

### The Division of Labor

In broad terms, the world of work is broken down by government record keepers into *white-collar, blue-collar, service,* and *farm work* (see Figure 13.3, column 2). As indicated in column 1, 46 percent of the population was working in 1989. Among those working, 57 percent were in occupations classified as white-collar. The white-collar category includes professional and technical workers like teachers and engineers, managers and administrators, sales workers, and clerical workers such as secretaries (column 3, Figure 13.3). Many of these occupations can be performed in the primary, secondary, or tertiary sectors. Table 13.3 shows the shift in the percentage of people working in white-collar, blue-collar, service, and farm occupations from 1900 to 1987. In this case, the term **division of labor** refers to subdividing work into specialized tasks.

Blue-collar workers include skilled craft workers such as carpenters and toolmakers; operatives such as drillers, crane operators, and assembly-line workers; and other nonfarm laborers such as garbage collectors and zookeepers. Service workers care for children; do cleaning, prepare and serve food; work as bank tellers, insurance salespersons, nursing aides or orderlies; and provide protective functions like firefighting and police protection. The final occupational type listed is that of farm workers, who may work on farms as managers or laborers. White-collar occupations are broken down in Figure 13.3 into occupational subdivisions in column 3, and the professional and technical subdivision is presented in even more detail in column 4.

### Professions and Professionalization

If all occupations share the interplay among knowledge and skill, nature, and other people, what is different about the professions? Sociologists such as Goode (1960) have defined the traditional professions as the ministry, law, and medicine. More recently, sociologists have included as professionals college professors, engineers, and scientific researchers. Professions are characterized as resting on a theoretical body of knowledge, not simply on the application of technical procedures. Professions, presumably, call for considerable knowledge, skill, and expertise, as well as problem-solving and decision-making abilities. Knowledge and expertise require specialized training, which is generally recognized by some form of degree or creden-

**Table 13.3** *Percentage of Labor Force in Various Occupations, 1900–1980*

| | Type of Occupation | 1900 (%) | 1920 (%) | 1940 (%) | 1970 (%) | 1980 (%) | 1987 (%) |
|---|---|---|---|---|---|---|---|
| White-collar | Professional and technical | 4 | 5 | 8 | 14 | 16 | 16 |
| | Managers, officials, and proprietors | 6 | 7 | 7 | 11 | 11 | 12 |
| | Clerical | 3 | 8 | 10 | 17 | 19 | 16 |
| | Sales | 5 | 5 | 7 | 6 | 6 | 12 |
| Blue-collar | Craftsmen and foremen | 11 | 13 | 12 | 13 | 13 | 12 |
| | Operatives | 13 | 16 | 18 | 18 | 14 | 11 |
| | Nonfarm laborers | 13 | 12 | 9 | 5 | 5 | 4 |
| Service | Service workers, except private household | 4 | 5 | 7 | 10 | 13 | 13 |
| | Private household workers | 6 | 3 | 5 | 2 | | 1 |
| Farm | Farmers and farm managers | 20 | 15 | 10 | 2 | 3 | 3 |
| | Farm laborers and foremen | 18 | 12 | 7 | 2 | | |

*Sources:* U.S. Bureau of the Census, 1975; 1981a, p. 401; 1989a, pp. 388–389.

tial. Although almost anyone can claim to be a gardener, not everyone can claim to be a psychiatrist or a lawyer.

Professionals operate in situations where the stakes are high—salvation, jail, death. All involve considerable risks and uncertain outcomes. Therefore, not only technical knowledge and skill but also symbolic and interpersonal skills are important. Finally, professionals claim the need for relative autonomy in the conduct of their work on the grounds that only professionals can decide the best way to perform the work, since only they have the specialized knowledge needed to make the decisions. In return for their relative autonomy, professionals claim to regulate themselves through professional associations and self-imposed ethical standards. One form this regulation takes is restricting the supply of new members in the profession so there will not be an excessive number of people competing for the available work. They also regulate and certify the training of new members, partly to restrict the number of entrants and keep their own fees high.

In recent years workers in many occupations (for example, chiropractors, accountants, and various therapists) have tried to become more "professional" by raising educational requirements and sometimes installing state licensing procedures to certify members. This trend reflects in part the desire of clients to have "genuine" practitioners perform work for them and

*Professionals, like these lawyers conferring on a case, often work in situations where the stakes are high. They may work long hours to meet the needs of the clients who pay for their services.*

in part the efforts of members of an occupation to control the number of people eligible to perform certain tasks. This effort grows out of the concern shared by many who undergo expensive training that there will be jobs available when they complete their educations.

In 1776, 80 percent of the American working population were independent artisans, farmers, and professionals. By 1880, this was down to 33 percent; today, it is around 10 percent. Independent artisans are not free of market pressures, of course, but they do have some flexibility with respect to when they will work and how they will do a particular job. Moreover, if they work efficiently, they benefit directly from their efforts.

What awaits the 90 percent of the work force who work for others? What is the nature of work in modern industrial and service societies today? Much has been written about the mindless monotony of assembly-line industrial production as well as about the petty paper pushing that occurs in large-scale white-collar bureaucracies. Is work as boring, repetitive, dehumanizing, dulling, alienating, fragmented, or dangerous as critics suggest? Here we consider the working situations of managerial, white-collar, and blue-collar employees.

## Managerial Work

As business and government become larger, they require more supervisors and managers to coordinate the many people in their organizations. Although managerial work is highly varied, it does share some common features. Much of the work involves data, information, problem solving, and dealing with people. Sales managers need to collect and analyze sales data to see which salespeople are succeeding, to help those whose sales are lagging, or to develop new products.

Managers need to monitor and control the work of others. They often face conflicting demands—for example, between the personal needs of workers and the productivity demands of a firm. They may be called on to fire people they know and like. They may face frustration because they lack the power to solve a problem, yet they are often blamed if things go wrong and seldom appreciated when things go well.

Their productivity and the quality of their work may be difficult for others to assess clearly. Many work long hours without overtime pay, and they often take problems from work home.

As managers move higher in an organization, their responsibilities increase along with the job benefits and satisfactions. Especially in the core sector, high-level managers receive high salaries, generous fringe benefits, bonuses, and stock options. In part, these rewards are based on their ability to control the work force and work situation so as to produce a profit. Where they have some autonomy to carry out projects, they may get a sense of accomplishment and satisfaction from their work as well.

## White-Collar Work

While managers are white-collar workers, the term also includes many clerical occupations. Clerical jobs in many large organizations today may be impersonal, routine, almost robotlike, and offer little prestige. Educational credentials have been raised for many jobs, but the content of the jobs, the responsibility or autonomy they afford, and their prestige and status have not increased along with the educational requirements. Workers often perform highly fragmented jobs whose connection to the larger purposes of the organization is obscure. As a result, many white-collar workers feel estranged from the goals of their organizations (U.S. Department of Health, Education, and Welfare [HEW], 1973).

Even middle managers have become increasingly discontented with their work. Traditionally they were strong supporters of their organizations and their policies, but there has been growing receptivity to unionization in their ranks. One in three middle managers indicates some willingness to join a union (HEW, 1973). Without unionization, many middle managers find themselves earning less than unionized blue-collar workers. One compensation was that such workers always believed their jobs were secure as long as they performed them well. But in recent years large numbers of middle managers have been laid off in the auto industry, insurance, and publishing (Bennett, 1980). People who have invested 20 or 30 years in the same organization may find themselves

White-collar work also includes many clerical occupations, which are increasingly becoming computerized.

suddenly without a job, too young to retire and yet too old to move into another job with ease.

Many white-collar workers have little influence over organizational policies and decisions. They are often called on to implement programs they have not designed, a chore that leads to feelings of frustration or alienation.

## Blue-Collar Work

The term "blue-collar blues" refer to the feelings of depression and unhappiness many blue-collar workers feel about their work. Their dissatisfaction may be expressed in high rates of absenteeism, wildcat strikes, or sabotage of the product they are making (for example, failing to tighten an important screw or scratching the side of new car). Because of their effects, the "blue-collar blues" have been much discussed in recent years. Even adequate pay along with reasonable security, safety, comfort, and convenience on the job do not protect workers against the blues, according to Seashore and Barnowe (1972). In addition, workers need a chance to perform their work well, a chance to increase their competence, to achieve, and to contribute something personal and unique to their work. Workers whose jobs measure high on variety, autonomy, and the chance to use their skills score lower on measures of political and personal alienation (Sheppard and Herrick, 1972).

Over the last 100 years, increasing numbers of blue-collar workers have come to labor in shops and plants owned and controlled by others rather than in their own organizations. One result of this trend has been a struggle between workers and managers over the control of work. As owners and managers have increased their control over the organization of work, workers have tended to lose autonomy (Edwards, 1979). A number of social observers have commented on the trend toward **"deskilling"** among blue-collar craft workers and sometimes among white-collar workers as well (Braverman, 1974; Carchedi, 1977; Cooley, 1980; Crompton and Gubbay, 1977; Kraft, 1977, 1985; Wallace and Kalleberg, 1982). By this they mean that jobs are broken up into segments that are less complex and require less knowledge and judgment on the part of workers. The result, they argue, is that work is simplified and routinized to such a degree that semiskilled workers and machinery can do jobs that could once be done only by people with high skill and craftsmanship.

But deskilling jobs as an employer strategy for controlling the labor process may occur less often than some have suggested (Whalley, 1984). In the desire for greater efficiency, employers may grant more job discretion to employees (Burawoy, 1979). The loyalty of some occupational groups—for example, engineers—may be secured other ways, and their performance may require greater independence (Whalley, 1984).

Blue-collar workers also complain that white-collar employees have privileges they do not, such as not being required to punch a time clock and having paid vacations, sick leave, and pensions. The benefits blue-collar workers receive depend largely on whether they work in the core, competitive, or state sectors of the economy. Blue-collar workers may also feel that work rules are often enforced in a paramilitary fashion and that bosses often fail to listen to

*Blue-collar workers like these foundry workmen at a steel mill often face higher physical risks on the job. Blue-collar jobs at decent wages have been rapidly disappearing in the United States during the last two decades.*

suggestions they have for better ways to do their jobs (U.S. Department of HEW, 1973).

Blue-collar complaints about work tend to target four major objective areas of discontent: compensation, health and safety hazards, work settings, and job security (Shostak, 1980). One's view of one's pay depends on a number of factors, including comparison with previous years. Between 1946 and 1956, the average real take-home pay of blue-collar workers increased 2 percent a year; from 1956 to 1966 it increased 1.4 percent a year; and from 1966 to 1976 it increased only 0.3 percent a year, and most of this went for increased local taxes. Since 1976, in the face of increased inflation, there has been an actual drop in real, after-tax income for blue-collar workers. In blue-collar occupations especially, inflation brings the additional fear of rising unemployment.

Health and safety hazards are often the result of shortsighted pressures to increase productivity and profitability. U.S. Department of Labor figures suggest that each year there are 14,000 deaths from industrial accidents, 100,000 persons are permanently disabled, and about 100,000 people die from industrial diseases. An additional 300,000 may become disabled annually from occupationally related diseases. Dangerous machinery, chemicals, radiation, heat, pesticides, noise levels, and toxic fumes and dust are some of the culprits of work-related illness for blue-collar workers. Since the passage in 1970 of the Occupational Safety and Health Act (OSHA), safety regulations and inspections may have provided some relief (Shostak, 1980).

Related to the health and safety of work conditions are the more general conditions under which blue-collar work is done. The setting is often dirty, smelly, uncomfortable, noisy, and barren of any comfort. Outdoor workers face the harsh heat of summer and cold of winter. Blue-collar workers are continually irritated by broken pay phones, coin-operated vending machines, and toilets; by filthy or nonexistent factory windows and poor ventilation systems. Work sites are seldom clean, tidy, comfortable, warm in winter or air conditioned in summer— a situation that is particularly annoying when those conditions are compared to the settings in which office workers perform their jobs.

Another negative point of comparison with white-collar work hangs on the issue of job security. The general lack of growth in the blue-collar occupational sector increases anxiety about being laid off. Seniority is some defense, but even that fails to help in an economic downturn. Even when workers are reemployed elsewhere, they lose the seniority and benefits (such as more than two weeks vacation) they had slowly worked up to in a previous job.

Despite all the drawbacks associated with blue-collar work, there are some positive features. Some workers report they are doing "real work" in contrast with paper pushing, which many of them scorn as nonwork. The results of their work are often tangible and in some way objectively measurable. For craft workers and for unionized workers in profitable industries, the pay is quite good. Overtime work results in overtime pay. Long years of education (sometimes seen as boring or expensive) are not necessary to get the job. In difficult or dangerous occupations (for example, mining, steel foundry work, high steel construction, or fire fighting), strong bonds of friendship and solidarity develop among workers. Groups that face danger together seem to share a more intense capacity for laughter, living, and loving as compared to more sheltered workers (Schrank, 1978). Moreover, blue-collar workers seem better at shedding their work concerns at day's end than do managers, engineers, and other white-collar workers (Schrank, 1978). In his study of workers on high steel buildings, however, Cherry (1974) found that the constant danger and fear they faced tended to result in escapist activities outside work—like drinking—for at least some.

All types of work—blue-collar, white-collar, managerial, and professional—present various frustrations and satisfactions. But some jobs are better than others. Jencks, Perman, and Rainwater (1988) developed a single measure of a job's desirability. They included pay but also nonmonetary features like fringe benefits (vacation time, pension, medical insurance, sick days), hours worked, training and promotion opportunities, prestige (using some of the scales discussed in Chapter 9), hazards, educational requirements, technical characteristics, autonomy, authority, and the organizational setting. They found that earnings were the single most important determinant of a job's desirability. However, all the nonmonetary job characteristics together were twice as important for determining a job's desirability as earnings. When they took nonmonetary job characteristics into account, they found that women and blacks experienced even greater labor-market inequality than they faced based on income alone (Jencks et al., 1988). Labor-market success may be related to the ways people get jobs.

## IMPLICATIONS

### Getting Jobs

Individuals are never more directly affected by economic sectors and occupational subdivisions than when they try to find jobs. On the one hand stands a job market that consists of openings in various economic and occupational sectors and on the other a labor market that consists of individuals with varying experience, education, and personal qualities. The nature of these markets is shaped by structures (such as capitalism or state socialism), resources (such as mineral and energy supplies), and policy decisions. Both in the creation of job markets and in the nature of defining various "eligible" or "appropriate" labor pools, human agents and organizations make decisions and take actions that shape the opportunities open to individuals. Processes of social channeling (and excluding) send large numbers of educated white males into

## *Job Prospects for College Graduates, 1990–2000*

Various sectors of the economy are expected to experience different rates of growth between 1990 and 2000. For college graduates, the biggest percentage increases in jobs are expected in marketing and sales occupations, technical jobs such as computer programmers and health technologists, managerial jobs, and professional occupations (Sargent, 1988).

Figure 13.4 shows the percentage of college graduates entering professional, technical, and managerial jobs between 1962–1969

and in 1986. College graduates have a lower unemployment rate than high school graduates. In 1988 the unemployment rate for all college graduates was 1.7 percent. High school graduates, however, had an unemployment rate of 5.4 percent in 1988 (U.S. Bureau of the Census, 1989a).

In 1990 competition for entry-level jobs will drop, as the number of workers aged 16 to 24 declines. The bulge in the labor market in 1990 will come with the workers aged 25 to 54.

The earnings advantage of college graduates over high school graduates has increased. In 1969 college graduates earned nearly 50 percent more than high school graduates, but in 1986 they earned nearly 70 percent more on the average. High school graduates earned $19,844, on the average in 1986, compared to college graduates, who earned $33,443 on the average (U.S. Department of Labor, 1987).

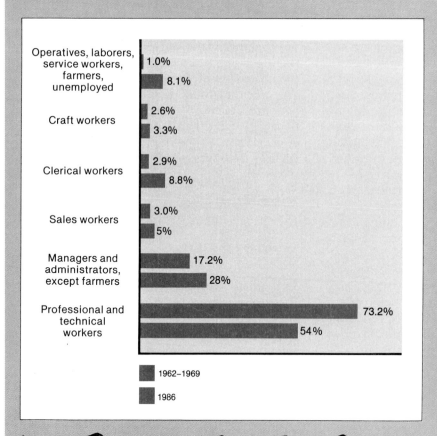

**Figure 13.4   Where College Graduates Got Jobs, 1962–1969 and 1986, by Major Occupational Group.**

College graduates are most likely to become professional and technical workers after graduation, although their proportions in those occupations were somewhat smaller in 1986 compared to 1962–1969. College graduates were somewhat more likely to become sales workers, clerical workers, or operatives in 1986 than in 1962–1969.

*Source:* U.S. Department of Labor, winter 1979, p. 6; Sargent, 1984, p. 4.

the core sector of the economy, which has the best wage and salary rates, the best benefits, and the best promotion opportunities. (See the discussion of job prospects for college graduates in the years 1990–2000 in the box.)

The process of finding a job may be broken down into three parts. First, there are positions in the job market. These positions exist in the extractive, manufacturing, or service divisions and in the core, competitive, or state sectors of the economy. They may call for people with training or experience in particular occupations. Second, there are individuals in the labor market who have various qualifications for doing different types of work based on education, experience, or skills. Most economists stop analyzing the process at this point. Sociologists add the social *processes* that link individuals to particular positions. Linkages come to life immediately when we think about how people hear about positions. Less than one job in five is filled through help-wanted listings in newspapers or by employment agencies (Lathrop, 1977). Moreover, the more interesting, responsible, and higher-paying jobs with greater potential are less likely to be advertised (Becker, 1977; Bolles, 1977; Granovetter, 1974).

To understand how individuals find jobs, we need to know how they form networks and how those networks operate to provide links with jobs (see Chapter 3 for more on networks). By including the three elements of individual characteristics, characteristics of positions, and the links between them, sociologists are able to offer an inclusive framework for viewing how individuals actually get jobs.

In finding jobs, young people rely on the assistance of acquaintances and relatives even more than older workers do. They also find work by applying directly to employers, and this method is used in all occupations (Becker, 1977). Blacks and whites use somewhat different strategies for getting jobs, with blacks more likely to use public employment services, whereas whites successfully use newspaper ads and private agencies (Becker, 1977). Whites are also more likely to hear about jobs from family or friends than are blacks. For various reasons, whites are more likely than blacks to find work in the monopoly sector. As a result, whites are likely to continue to fill many of the jobs in that sector.

Women and minorities, who may not receive the help from informal networks that white males get, are more likely to end up in the competitive (and lower-paying) economic sector unless their job-finding strategies are able to overcome the social channeling and discrimination that have traditionally occurred. Moreover, the labor market operates differently in that sector. Education, for example, seems to provide little return to workers in the secondary market but to give good returns to workers in the primary market (Edwards, 1979, p. 166).

## Factors Affecting Income

Some of the same features that affect how individuals get jobs also influence how much they are paid to do those jobs. The extent of what is possible depends primarily on market factors in a capitalist economy and primarily on political factors in a state socialist economy. In capitalism, the economic rewards available for a position depend on whether it exists in the monopoly or competitive sector and on the political power of the occupation (including professional associations and unions). The total salary pool is greater in the monopoly than in the competitive sector of the economy.

There are differences in what determines earnings even within capitalist economies, however. In the United States, manufacturing employees' earnings are heavily influenced by job characteristics, positions in the authority system, and (among workers) union representation. But in Japan, earnings are much more influenced by life-cycle features such as age and by firm patterns of seniority, promotions, and training (Kalleberg and Lincoln, 1988).

Within a particular corporation, certain occupational groups have greater leverage than others. The salaries paid to lawyers, accountants, and doctors who work for an automobile company, for example, are set by the bargaining terms established by their occupational groups. Craft workers and assembly-line workers in the auto industry are represented by highly organized labor unions that have helped to negotiate what salaried workers at various levels should be paid. The pay for certain positions may depend on proximity to key resources within or outside the organization as well as on the wage priorities set by a particular firm. Sales and financial managers, who are close to key resources, are often paid more than personnel managers, for example. Ceilings may be set on certain clerical job categories. The historical scarcity of individuals for a particular position may also be related to the income levels attached to certain jobs—for example, computer programming.

All the features of positions mentioned above—economic sector, occupational power, labor organization, and scarcity—affect the salaries paid for various positions. This analysis of positions differs from the approach taken by human capital theorists. They believe that individual characteristics such as intelligence, industry, skill, training, experience, attitudes, and other qualities determine the salaries individuals are paid in the marketplace. This is only partly true. People with greater technical skill sometimes do earn more than people with less proficiency. However, two-thirds of the variation in income occurs *within* occupational groups (Jencks et al., 1972). Differences in human capital do not explain all of that variation. Instead, much of the difference in salaries within occupations seems to be explained better by location in the monopoly or competitive sectors and by union organization.

In addition to knowledge, skill, and experience, other individual characteristics influence where people work and how much they are paid. These can be considered the bargaining resources individuals bring to the labor market. Educational credentials, for example, have become increasingly important in the competition for certain positions. Traditionally, race, sex, socioeconomic status, attitudes, demeanor, appearance, and other personal qualities have been bargaining chips as well. Job candidates are often sorted on the basis of social traits like race and sex into lesser positions and lower incomes within the organizations that employ them.

This discussion refers to individuals who actually reach the point of entry into particular organizations and are hired. But a series of channeling operations occurs prior to the point of entry into an organization. The channeling of individuals into positions with various incomes resembles the *linking* process in getting jobs.

What determines who gets matched with jobs that offer the possibility of high earnings? Are there general or ethnic barriers to certain types of jobs? Who gets through such barriers and how? What part do networks of contacts and geographic location play in that process? These are some of the questions sociologists ask about the linkages among individuals, positions, and

incomes (Granovetter, 1979a). They are quite different from the questions economists ask.

## Unemployment

Perhaps the most important link between individuals and the economy is whether or not one has a job at all. The issue of unemployment has become an important one in recent years. In the United States, unemployment rates exceeded 10.8 percent in 1982, when 12 million people were out of work. These figures represented the highest rate of unemployment since the Great Depression. By 1989, unemployment had dropped to 5.2 percent nationally.

Because of employment shifts caused by individual illness, recent college graduations, and job changes, no society has a zero unemployment rate (although state socialist societies claim to). About 2 percent unemployment is considered nearly full employment in most industrial societies. In the United States, only people who have actively looked for work in the last four weeks and have not worked at all are defined as *unemployed*. People who have worked part-time or who have given up looking for work are not considered unemployed. For these reasons, official rates of unemployment understate the actual rates.

Unemployment rates are presented as a national average, although unemployment is not distributed evenly throughout the population, as Figure 13.5 shows. Teenagers and minorities are hardest hit. Although 4.6 percent of white-collar employees were unemployed in the 1981–1982 recession, that rate was much lower than the 18 percent rate among construction workers, or the 29 percent among auto workers (Kelly, 1982). These unemployment patterns mean that certain regions—the manufacturing Midwest, the construction-related Northwest, and urban centers with large numbers of minority teenagers—had particularly high rates of unemployment.

Unemployment occurs more often and with greater severity in the peripheral rather than in the core sector of the economy. During the 1981–1982 recession, for example, Marina Whitman, vice-president and chief economist at General Motors, estimated that for every one auto

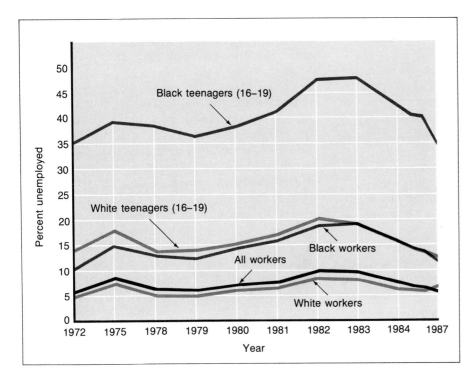

**Figure 13.5   Unemployment Rates Among Various Groups of U.S. Workers, 1972–1987.**

Unemployment is not evenly distributed in the U.S. work force. Teenagers and black workers are most likely to be unemployed, whereas white adult workers are least likely to be unemployed.

*Source:* U.S. Bureau of the Census, 1985a, p. 406; 1989a, p. 393.

worker who was laid off, there were three unemployed workers in firms that supply the auto industry. Core firms are not always immune to economic recessions, but the effects of such downturns are felt much more severely in the competitive sector.

Losing a job and being unable to find a job affect individuals in negative ways. Economic hardships were cushioned in the 1973–1975 recession by unemployment benefits received by more than 75 percent of the jobless. But in the 1981–1982 recession, only one-third of those out of work received unemployment compensation, as a result of budget cuts engineered by the Reagan administration.

People with home mortgages and other debts to pay off are especially hard hit because they cannot subsist on a meager income. For white-collar and professional workers who have never had the experience of losing their jobs, the psychological blow may be personally devastating. Virginia Hall, a job counselor for professionals in Atlanta, Georgia, observed: "All these people have mortgages and are committed to certain life-styles. . . . This is their first experience of losing a job, and they are stunned. They have no idea of how to cope" (Kelly, 1982, p. 27).

Sociological studies of the unemployed reveal a tremendous loss of self-esteem, feelings of powerlessness, and a sense of lost identity (Jahoda, Lazarsfeld, and Zeisel, 1971; Komarovsky, 1940; Maurer, 1979). These feelings may be expressed in withdrawal or depression, alcoholism, or in anger and abuse directed at family members. The personal and interpersonal costs are not captured by the statistics that make headlines. Besides affecting those without jobs, unemployment increases the anxiety and lowers the morale of those who do have jobs, making them reluctant to push for their rights on the job. High rates of unemployment are also associated with higher rates of part-time employment and **underemployment**—that is, people taking jobs that are not customarily filled by individuals with their levels of experience or education. Drama majors waiting on tables or journalism graduates collecting trash are two examples of underemployment.

One source of unemployment is the globalization of the world economy. Investment capital is leaving the United States for regions where labor and raw material costs are lower and where governments offer more favorable tax treatment and less regulation (Barnet and

Muller, 1974; Vernon, 1977). Markets and production used to be confined within regions or within nations. Now, however, both consumers and producers have begun to look all over the world for better prices and profits. The result is that manufacturing jobs in the United States are declining.

## Money in a Global Economy

Imagine that you have just landed on the earth from the planet Mars. You see people go into a building and talk to someone who brings them hamburgers and french fries. In return they give the person little plastic cards. You find some plastic on the street, which you give to the salesclerk in the hope of getting some food. But the clerk simply looks at you as if you were crazy. You are very puzzled. Why are some pieces of plastic accepted in exchange for food or other goods and services, whereas others are not?

It is now possible to use a little plastic rectangular card to buy goods and services in many countries around the world. Money or money substitutes rest on social conventions and shared symbols. At various times and places, different items have served as money, including the wampum (beads made from shells) used by Native Americans, cowries (pretty shells) in India, whales' teeth in Fiji, woven mats in the Trobriand Islands, large stone slabs on the Pacific Island of Yap, tobacco among early North American settlers and prisoners, gold and silver coins, and pieces of colored paper.

Because money and credit are social creations, the meaning and value people attach to them depend on their social experiences. The social meaning of money and credit is apparent in two major conditions that have affected economic systems since the creation of money: inflation and depression. Each of these conditions is at least partially influenced by social factors and each has important social consequences. Both are related, in different ways, to economic growth. **Economic growth** is an increase in the amount of goods and services that are produced with the same amount of labor and resources. For example, when Japanese management took over an electronics plant in Chicago, it nearly doubled the plant's output and reduced

quality rejects by 96 percent, to a nearly zero level (Bond, 1981). The result of these efforts was economic growth.

### Inflation

**Inflation** is an increase in the supply of money in circulation, so that it exceeds the rate of economic growth. When the supply of money rises relative to the available goods and services, the same amount of money will buy fewer goods or services. Consumers see the result in the form of rising prices. In sociological terms, inflation may be considered the social recognition that money is worth less in relation to various goods and services. Inflation occurs when money itself is debased; it has occurred in situations where governments print paper money faster than economic productivity increases. We think of inflation as an economic phenomenon, but it is actually created by social and political processes, and it has major social repercussions.

Inflation does not affect all social groups in society equally. In general, inflation benefits borrowers (because they can repay their loans with "cheaper" dollars later) but hurts lenders and pinches people living on fixed incomes. People who have little discretionary income (the poor) and those who have some money but no property lose ground. Those who own property gain, since real estate and other property generally increase in value in inflationary times. As the biggest borrowers, governments benefit from inflation. Taxpayers, meanwhile, are pushed into higher tax brackets with incomes that buy fewer goods and services. It has been suggested that inflation undermines the traditional virtues of hard work and thrift. Certainly those virtues have less payoff in an inflationary context.

Clearly, inflation influences the attitudes and behaviors of people. During inflationary times, people save less money and tend to adopt a "spend or borrow now, repay later" approach. Such behavior reflects a response to the declining value of money and savings in an inflationary era. The high cost of borrowing money makes it difficult for people to buy homes or to start businesses.

Sociologists tend to view the market economy as constantly tending to unbalance the society in which it operates. This view has been advanced by functionalist sociologists such as Durkheim and Parsons as well as by Karl Marx and Daniel Bell (1976). The destabilizing effects of a market economy can only be offset by shared values and norms in a society, such as a belief in equal opportunity, or by some type of forced coordination ultimately backed by force, such as a military dictatorship. Economists, on the other hand, tend to view the market economy as inherently stable or at least as able to be stabilized by the skillful management of economic policies. Inflation in such a system is viewed as a problem that can be fixed, since the system itself is healthy (Goldthorpe, 1978).

Extreme inflation has severe social consequences, as can be seen in countries currently experiencing very high rates of inflation. They include Chile, Bolivia, Mexico, and Argentina. Long-term lending at fixed rates of interest almost stops, and people hold little money. Rapid inflation encourages residential building, since an apartment or house is considered a good hedge against inflation. At the same time, it discourages public utility development because people are reluctant to commit their funds to long-term investments.

None of the Latin American nations has matched the hyperinflation and resulting social chaos that occurred in Germany between 1921 and 1923. In a **hyperinflation**—an extreme form of inflation—prices accelerate very rapidly and people resist using the currency as much as possible. In the German hyperinflation after World War I, the printing press was used on a massive scale to create money. In part this was a response to the massive reparations (war payments) Germany had to pay England, France, and the United States. People collected their wages in suitcases or wheelbarrows and rushed out to spend them immediately, before the money became totally worthless.

Hyperinflation is a good example of the limits of the social construction of reality and of the self-fulfilling prophecy in action. Once growth in the money supply loses any relation to increases in the production of goods and services, it becomes more and more difficult to sustain the socially constructed view of the money's value. A negative self-fulfilling prophecy occurs when people lose confidence in the medium of exchange, which speeds the medium's circulation and increases the use of other forms of exchange.

### Recession and Depression

Just as runaway inflation can have dire consequences for the social fabric, the other extreme, that of economic deflation and depression, also has severe social consequences. In a depression, economic productivity declines. The Great Depression of the 1930s was worldwide and profoundly affected the individuals who lived through it. They had quite different attitudes toward work, money, and the world from those of the generation that preceded or followed them. By 1933 average income in the United States had dropped to half of what it was in 1928. Ninety thousand businesses had failed, and the banking system was on the verge of collapse. Fifteen million people, or about a quarter of the working population, were unemployed.

In addition, the decade of the 1930s was a time of drought and crop failures in the Great Plains states. Farmers were uprooted from their farms and homes. In Kentucky and other Appalachian states, coal miners literally had nothing but dandelions and blackberries to eat. In major cities across the country, people stood in bread lines and went to soup kitchens, and many were malnourished (Bird, 1966). When they lost their homes or apartments, people formed shantytowns or "Hoovervilles," named after President Herbert Hoover, who was in office when the Depression struck. There were no federal programs of unemployment insurance, bank insurance, or welfare until President Roosevelt pushed the Federal Emergency Relief Act through Congress in 1933. Private charities, churches, and city and state governments tried to keep people from starving, but their limited resources quickly proved inadequate. Most of the people who lived through those times subsequently had a terrible fear of debt, valued job security very highly, and have remained cautious and conservative in their social and economic behavior.

One consequence of the increasingly global nature of the economy is that inflation or recession in one country will affect the economic health of other countries. That, in turn, has ma-

# The Underground Economy

*Richard Lawson is a 34-year-old financial executive with an ascending career at a big New York corporation, an Ivy League pedigree, and Hollywood looks. He lives on Manhattan's West Side in a brownstone that he bought four years ago when it seemed a candidate for the wrecker's ball and has since renovated the building with his own money and toil. He is a runner, doesn't smoke, and prefers Perrier to stronger libations. A friend describes him as "upbeat, positive, a straight-arrow type." [Lohr, 1981, p. 3-1]*

Even though he is a "straight arrow," Lawson participates in what economists and sociologists call the underground economy. He reports only two-thirds of the rental money he makes on his apartment building. The underground economy is work done or goods that are exchanged "off the books," for cash or barter, with no records kept. It exists all over the world. The French call it *travail au noir*, the Italians *lavoro nero*, the Germans *schwarzarbeiter* and the British name it *fiddling* (Malabie Jr., 1981). The phenomenon is growing in the United States, and it has important social and economic implications.

*People who don't partake tend not to notice it. But it is there, in the neighborhood laundry without a cash register, in the doctor who asks that checks be made out to cash, in the moonlighting carpenter or plumber, in the waiter or taxi driver pocketing tips, in the bar owner "skimming" cash from the till, in the dress shop that records as "inventory losses" items that it sold but didn't ring up. Then, too, there is money from criminal activity that goes unrecorded, from the drug trade in Miami to the black market for stolen art in New York. [Lohr, 1981, p. 3-1]*

Several economists have come up with a way of estimating the underground economy because they realized that the official gross national product (that is, legal money transactions) is quite a bit less than the amount of money in circulation, due to underground economic activity, according to economists Peter Gutmann and Edgar Feige. In the early 1960s the underground economy was just a few percentage points of total GNP.

Today the underground economy accounts for 8 to 10 percent of GNP concludes Mattera

(1985), or about $330 billion in 1983.

The underground economy has significant social and economic implications. From a policy point of view, "official" government figures become less and less accurate as the underground economy grows. The underground economy affects the fiscal condition of the state because many nations are running major deficits in their budgets. These deficits would be reduced substantially if people paid the unpaid taxes due on legal and illegal income (Thurow, 1985a).

Perhaps the most serious implication of the underground economy is the way it reflects a loss of what Thurow calls "civic virtue." Dishonest societies are by their nature inefficient ones, in which individual incomes tend to decline.

To the degree that the underground economy reflects increasing dishonesty in society, it represents a problem that threatens to undermine civic commitment and economic efficiency. A similar loss of civic virtue presaged the fall of the Roman Empire (Thurow, 1985).

jor implications for the employment and income prospects of individuals.

## Growth of the Informal or "Underground" Economy

The informal or **underground economy** involves activities that occur outside the arena of the normal, regulated economy, and therefore escape official record keeping. The activities themselves are not criminal, although illegal action may occur if employers and employees do

not pay the required taxes on their activities. Informal economic activity has been growing in the United States in recent years. This growth seems to be due to several changes (Portes and Sassen-Koob, 1987). The global recession beginning in the mid-1970s and the increased competition it created for firms seem to have made firms willing to be more flexible in their labor practices. It also helped create high rates of unemployment and massive international migrations. Those conditions made workers more willing to enter the informal economy. In its wages and benefits, the informal economy resembles an even poorer version of the secondary or competitive sector of a dual-labor economy. People may work in the informal economy because they lack alternatives and because the "off the books" nature of the work makes it slightly more attractive than a minimum-wage job in the formal economy. The informal economy may also have increased because state and local officials "look the other way" and do not try to stop its growth (Portes and Sassen-Koob, 1987). (See the box for more on the underground economy.)

## SUMMARY

1. The term "economic institution" refers to the socially patterned ways that people produce and exchange goods and services.

2. The move toward a global economy is reflected in the changing nature of markets from places to networks, the internationalization of capital, the growing importance of multinational corporations, and the growth of world trade.

3. Societies differ with respect to the degree of state control of the economy. Western-type capitalist market economies draw heavily on the social and economic ideas of Adam Smith and John Maynard Keynes. Critics of capitalism stress the way it exploits and alienates the individuals working in it and the way it distributes wealth and income unequally among the population.

4. Welfare-state economies offer welfare benefits to workers, including family allowances, unemployment benefits, old-age pensions, educational benefits, and health insurance. While they do benefit workers, critics suggest they reduce incentives for work.

5. Centrally planned economies depend on state officials rather than on market factors or private ownership to decide where resources and profits should go. The Soviet Union is probably the purest case of a centrally planned economy. The USSR and China have recently introduced some capitalist-type incentives into their economies in small ways.

6. Critics of planned economies question the amount of freedom workers have and whether planned economies are as efficient as capitalist ones.

7. Hybrid economies like Yugoslavia's try to decentralize power in the participatory democratic control of workers over production, and they try to have the market rather than the state determine supply and demand.

8. There seems to be some evidence that centrally controlled and capitalist market economies are becoming somewhat more alike.

9. Economic activity has been roughly classified into three major sectors: the primary sector, where people grow or extract food and resources; the secondary sector, where raw materials are converted into products; and the tertiary sector, which provides both business and social services.

10. In the world today, most people in most societies work to produce food. In the United States, the proportion of the population in farming has declined dramatically, from 72 percent in 1820 to 3 percent in 1987. As a result, many people are free to produce other goods and services.

11. In the United States the secondary, or manufacturing, sector grew dramatically between 1820 and 1920. Since then it has declined to about one-quarter of the labor force.

12. In the United States, the chief growth area has been the service sector, which has grown from 19 percent of the labor market in 1860 to 71 percent in 1987.

13. The term "dual economy" refers to the division of the economy into a core or monopoly sector, a periphery or competitive sector, and a state sector. The core is characterized by large, oligopolistic firms that are national or multinational in scope. The periphery or competitive sector consists of small, local, barely profitable firms like textile mills and automobile suppliers. The state sector includes federal, state,

and local government workers. The labor markets in these sectors differ in terms of pay scales, job security, benefits, promotion opportunities, and the social characteristics of the people in them.

14. The large corporations that comprise the core sector of the economy control the majority of corporate assets, sales, and employees. Their annual sales exceed the GNP of many nation-states. As a result, they have a high and concentrated degree of economic, political, and social power.

15. Nearly 21,000 legal occupations are listed in the *Dictionary of Occupational Titles*. The type of work people do is sometimes described as blue-collar, white-collar, service, or farm work. White-collar work in general, and the professions in particular, have expanded in recent years. Professions rest on a theoretical body of knowledge and expertise acquired through specialized training. Blue-collar workers include skilled craft workers such as carpenters and tool-makers; operatives such as drillers, crane operators, and assembly-line workers; and other nonfarm laborers such as trash collectors and zookeepers. Services workers care for children, serve food, and are bank tellers, salespersons, hospital orderlies, or fire fighters.

16. The nature of work is affected by the type of work and by the declining number of jobs for independent artisans. "Blue-collar blues" refers to the discontent blue-collar workers feel because of the monotonous, boring, and non-challenging nature of their work and because of their unhappiness over the compensation, health and safety hazards, work settings, and security of their jobs. White-collar workers often complain that their work lacks real challenge, interest, prestige, or future prospects. Professional and managerial workers are relatively well rewarded but may face conflicting demands and frustrations.

17. Getting a job involves the characteristics of individuals and those of jobs and the processes that link the two together. Interpersonal networks are important in that process.

18. Like jobs, income is affected by the nature of the job being done, the traits of the individuals doing it, and market and linking factors.

19. Unemployment has been a major problem in Western economies during the past decade, with rates exceeding 10 percent occurring in the United States. Unemployment hit the hardest in the industrial Midwest and the Pacific Northwest. It has been especially hard on teenagers, minorities, and other workers in the competitive sector of the economy.

20. Money is a social invention. It survives because people accept it in exchange for goods and services. Social processes may produce situations where the money supply and economic growth are out of balance. These result in inflation, deflation, or depression, conditions that have important social implications and that affect various social groups in different ways.

21. The informal, or underground, economy has grown in recent decades. Its growth appears to be related to changes in the global economy, including recession, unemployment, and labor migrations.

## KEY TERMS

capitalism (p. 327)
centrally planned economy (p. 329)
deskilling (p. 342)
division of labor (p. 339)
dual economy (p. 334)
economic core (p. 334)
economic growth (p. 348)
economic institution (p. 323)
economic periphery (p. 335)
global economy (p. 323)
hybrid economy (p. 331)
hyperinflation (p. 349)
inflation (p. 348)
Keynesian economics (p. 328)
laissez-faire economics (p. 328)
multinationals (p. 325)
occupation (p. 337)
oligopoly (p. 337)
primary economic sector (p. 331)

profession (p. 337)
secondary economic sector (p. 331)
socialist societies (p. 329)
state sector (p. 335)
tertiary economic sector (p. 332)
underemployment (p. 347)
underground economy (p. 350)

## SUGGESTED READINGS

Barnet, Richard J., and Ronald E. Muller. 1974. *Global Reach: The Power of the Multinational Corporations.* New York: Simon & Schuster. A highly readable account of the immense power exercised by large multinational corporations.

Edwards, Richard. 1979. *Contested Terrain: The Transformation of the Workplace in the Twentieth Century.* New York: Basic Books. A major study by a young radical economist describing how workers have lost autonomy and impersonal bureaucracies have developed to legitimate hierarchy and enhance the employer's control over workers.

Farber, Henry S. 1987. "The Recent Decline of Unionization in the United States." *Science* 238: 915–920. Explores reasons for the dramatic decline in unionization during the last decade, including increased foreign and nonunion domestic competition for jobs and wages.

Jencks, Christopher, Lauri Perman, and Lee Rainwater. 1988. "What Is a Good Job? A New Measure of Labor-Market Success." *American Journal of Sociology* 93: 1322–1357. Discusses how the authors developed their measure of "good jobs" and analyzes who is most likely to get them.

Miller, S. M., and Donald Tomaskovic-Devey. 1983. *Recapitalizing America: Alternatives to the Corporate Distortion of National Policies.* Boston: Routledge & Kegan Paul. A critical examination of the current emphasis on the policy of "recapitalizing" America that challenges the belief that increasing the power and profitability of private capital will solve the structural problems of a faltering economy.

# Politics and Power

*"Look hard for ways to make little moves against destructiveness." This was the message preached in his sermons by a Protestant minister in southern France in the late 1930s, as the Nazis were gaining power in neighboring Germany. When France fell to Nazi Germany on June 22, 1940, his mission to resist the Nazis became increasingly important. Andre Trocmé, pastor in the small French village of Le Chambon, helped his town develop ways of resisting the dominant evil they faced. Together they established first one, and then a number of "safe houses" where Jewish and other refugees seeking to escape the Nazis could hide. These houses received contributions from International Quaker, Catholic, American Congregationalist, Jewish, and World Council of Churches groups, and from the national governments of Sweden and Switzerland, to buy food and supplies for the fleeing refugees. Many private families also took in children whose parents had been shipped to concentration camps in Germany. Trocmé refused to accept the definitions of those in power. "We do not know what a Jew is. We know only men," he said when asked by the authorities to produce a list of the Jews in the town. [Hallie, 1979, p. 103]*

*Between 1940 and 1944 when World War II ended in Europe, Trocmé estimated that about 2500 Jewish refugees were saved by the tiny village of Le Chambon, because the people refused to give in to what they considered to be the illegitimate legal, military, and police power of the Nazis.*

---

**Power** is the capacity of an individual or group to control or influence the behavior of others even in the face of opposition. A person or group is powerful in relation to someone else. For this reason, power is relational; it involves at least two parties. Possessing power is a matter of degree: almost nobody is totally without power, although some people may be relatively powerless. As the story of Le Chambon shows, even very powerful groups can be resisted, especially if that power is considered to be illegitimate.

Power is considered **legitimate** when those who exercise it are accepted as having the right to do so. When this "rightness" is absent, power is illegitimate and may be seen as immoral, il-

legal, lacking popular support, or unscientific. Legitimate power is often referred to by sociologists as **authority.** In Chapter 1 we considered several types of authority, including traditional, charismatic, and rational-legal. To persist over a long period of time, the exercise of power must to some extent be legitimized. Relying solely on force and coercion may require people to submit for a time, but it will not gain their allegiance and will break down in the long run.

When people's genuine needs and wishes are seriously taken into account and they are allowed to participate in decisions that concern them, they are more likely to accept an authority structure as legitimate. Participating in the decision-making process is sometimes referred to by applied social scientists, such as organizational consultants, as "owning the decision." In work organizations major decisions such as the taking on of new projects, the organization of operating procedures, and the trimming of costs will be more acceptable if there is input from all levels of the work force (and perhaps compromises in the process), rather than if they are simply imposed from the top down. At the family level, parents gain more enthusiastic acceptance of plans if they involve children in making decisions rather than just telling them what to do.

Power operates at all levels of social life—in interactions among individuals, family members, and friends; within organizations and institutions; at the state and national levels; and in the international arena. In this chapter we consider the sources and expressions of power, the organization of power in the state, how functionalists and conflict theorists differ in their views of the political order, the structure of power in the United States, and, finally, how political change occurs.

## THE SOURCES AND EXPRESSIONS OF POWER

### Sources of Power

The amount of power any individual has depends heavily on the resources he or she commands. These resources can be material, coercive, or normative. *Material* power accompanies advantages such as the ownership or control of property, services, and privileges. *Coercive* resources provide the ability to injure someone else physically or mentally—at the personal level, this includes verbal abuse, intimidation, and guns; at the societal level, it includes military force, police, and weaponry. *Normative* or symbolic resources confer public honor, prestige, and love (Lehman, 1977). Knowledge can also be a source of power, especially if it is used to apply other resources more effectively.

How do people acquire these resources? Most of them depend on the position of the individual in the social structure. Some of the advantages of high economic and social standing are wealth,

the control of effective organizations, access to a network of people and opportunities, high moral standing, and influence over the legal structure. These advantages confer power, which in turn can be used to maintain and increase economic and social inequality. This permits the accumulation of even more power. There are other sources of power: control of or access to critical resources that are in demand, whether they be money, raw materials, supplies, information, or personnel; personal charisma or magnetism that elicits the support of others, especially important in political and religious realms; and characteristics such as charm, wit, and graciousness, which can confer power in personal relations.

Another means to power is having a particular skill or talent. Someone who can do something extremely well will exercise power in situations where that skill or talent is useful. On the soccer field the best players have the most power. In financial transactions those with superior talent for investment may have the edge. Of course, acquiring competence and skills depends on having access to information and knowledge.

The different sources of power are not mutually exclusive: any and all of them may operate in any given situation. Furthermore, power in one situation often carries over into other areas. The skilled athlete may sometimes be able to translate power on the playing field into other

*Charisma is an important source of power and influence in the religious realm. Charisma may partly explain the leadership of Bishop Desmond Tutu (left) and Bishop Manas Buthelezi in South Africa.*

avenues of advancement, such as business or politics. The carryover of power poses problems for certain groups, particularly women and minorities, that have traditionally been excluded from power in many areas. The lower status generally accorded them by society may undercut their authority in organizational decision making. High-level managers, whose primary concern is making sure their organizations run effectively and as smoothly as possible, have generally favored hiring white, educated, middle- or upper-class males in middle- and upper-management positions, in part because they already bring with them certain symbols of authority that reinforce their ability to give orders and have them accepted.

A final source of power is the desire for it, the burning ambition present in some to work their will, for good or bad, in a larger context. To what degree does the exercise of power depend on the willingness to use any means necessary or possible? Are people such as airport terrorists, who are willing to ignore moral or legal restraints and use violence, torture, murder, or deception, able to wield more power than those who are unwilling to ignore such restraints? Under what conditions? What prevents power contests from going to the extreme use of force? Why does this work in some cases and not in others? These questions can be partially answered by examining the ways in which power is exercised.

## The Exercise of Power

We have already noted that the nature of power requires that there be at least two parties involved. It makes little sense to say that "Courtney has power," but it does make sense to say that "Courtney has power over Chris." Power is also interactional. That is, Courtney may exercise power in various ways; Chris may or may not choose to comply. Let's look more closely at the ways power is exercised and complied with (see Table 14.1).

In the first case in Table 14.1 power is exercised with "taken-for-granted" authority by Courtney when he or she has complete confidence in the right to do so. If Chris accepts this authority in an equally taken-for-granted man-

**Table 14.1    *Levels in the Exercise of Power and Compliance to It***

After each of these actions and reactions has occurred, Chris still has the ultimate possibility of refusing to comply with Courtney's power and authority. Herein lies the ultimate limit on Courtney's power.

| Courtney Can Exercise Power over Chris by: | Chris May Show Courtney Various Kinds of Compliance |
|---|---|
| 1. Acting with a taken-for-granted power and authority | 1. Assumed or taken-for-granted compliance |
| 2. Stating his or her wishes or desires | 2. Thought-about but willing compliance |
| 3. Negotiating with or trying to persuade Chris | 3. Negotiated or exchanged compliance |
| 4. Exercising coercion or violence toward Chris | 4. Forced or coerced compliance |

ner, the operation of power in the situation may be almost invisible to the participants. This situation, where certain attitudes and behaviors are assumed and no one thinks of challenging them, occurs often in everyday life. Consider the case of a mother and child crossing the street. The mother is holding the child's hand and suddenly pulls back, saying "Wait!" because a car is approaching. The mother is exercising power and authority in the situation, but most likely neither she nor her child will think of it in these terms. They have a common interest in not being hit by the car, and the mother's experience and concern for her child makes the operation of authority in this case taken for granted.

The second situation in Table 14.1 may be called "willing compliance." Here Chris may be aware that Courtney is exercising power over him or her, but for any of a number of reasons (for example, the desire to please) may be willing to comply on a voluntary basis. This level of conscious, willing compliance often takes place among friends, colleagues, and family members.

At the third level in Table 14.1, Chris may resist Courtney's initial use of authority, and Courtney may then try to persuade or negotiate with Chris. Persuasion or negotiation occurs when authority is not taken for granted, there is no voluntary compliance, and coercion is inappropriate or illegitimate. Within the realm of civilized human interaction, negotiation is common and required in a broad range of situations. An important reason is that there are many sources of power among people, and—even though some sources are stronger than others—even weak power sources usually cannot be completely ignored.

When Courtney tries to exercise power over Chris and fails to obtain compliance through negotiations, he or she may resort to coercion or force, the fourth case in Table 14.1. Coercion involves the application of sanctions. These may be economic, such as losing one's job, having to pay fines, or going out of business; legal, such as arrests, trials, and lawsuits; social, such as being shunned by others, solitary confinement, gossip, or nasty remarks; or physical. Violence is the most extreme form of coercion. In most societies the state is the only entity legally empowered to use violence, and it is confined within certain limits. Still, the monopoly on violence is frequently violated.

When individuals claiming legitimate authority coerce others into doing their will, they usually cover the "iron fist" of coercion with some kind of "velvet glove," or ideology, that seeks to explain why the superior power and authority of the dominant person or group should be obeyed.

The lower the level of legitimacy is in a society, the greater will be the degree of coercion necessary to exercise power. If people are held back only by the threat of force, they will rebel when the opportunity presents itself. Ultimately, the use of coercion is limited. There is only so much that one person can force another to do. Courtney may kill Chris for noncompliance, but if Chris values noncompliance with Courtney's demands more than life, he or she can refuse to obey. Moreover, coercion is inefficient. The slave labor employed in Nazi armament plants during World War II, for ex-

ample, was notoriously unproductive, and U.S. coal miners have a slogan that underscores the same point, "You can't dig coal with a bayonet."

In the final analysis, therefore, the successful exercise of power and authority requires enlisting the willing and voluntary compliance of those on whom it is exercised. Such compliance can be of at least two different kinds. The first is called attitudinal compliance, when someone obeys because he or she accepts or "buys into" the values of the authority system. The second is behavioral conformity, in which someone obeys without necessarily believing in what is being done. In most simple cases, behavioral conformity is sufficient; in more complex situations such as political allegiance, the question of whether or not those being ruled share the values of the rulers can be of crucial importance.

This analysis of different levels of power and compliance describes theoretical and ideal kinds of behavior. In the real world, power is like an onion, with layers of habit, interpersonal social relations, and negotiation and persuasion, beneath which there is generally a capacity to reward or punish. All layers may operate at the same time in any given situation. The exercise of power at the interpersonal level is discussed by Collins (1975), who fuses a conflict and an interactionist perspective. One indication of occupational power, Collins suggests, is the amount of talk that occurs. Manual work involves little talk, skilled labor involves somewhat more, and administrative, business, and professional work consists almost entirely of talk, especially if written communication is included. The content of talk also reflects power. People not only need to know the names of various equipment, processes, or people but also how to use those words in appropriate ways. Third, individuals with more power have more people reporting to them and report less often to someone above them. Individuals with less power report more often (or are constantly supervised) and have few or no people reporting to them. Succeeding in one's authority relations involves understanding what forms of personal demeanor, tone, timing, and vocabulary are called for in a particular situation (Collins, 1975). These are some of the interpersonal ways in which power is reflected and exercised.

## THE STATE

The clearest expression of power, authority, and force occurs in the political arena at the national and international levels. The **state** is an institutionalized way of organizing power within territorial limits. Its legal authority is backed by force, and it is accepted as legitimate, exclusive, and supreme, at least passively, by most of its citizens. The state is distinguished from government, which refers to the leaders (elected or otherwise) and bureaucracy of the state. Members of governments can and do change, but unless there is a new constitution or a revolution, the state remains the same.

### The Modern Nation-State

**Sovereignty** is perhaps the most distinctive feature of the modern state. It is the theory by which the state legitimizes its ability to create, interpret, and enforce a legal system, uses coercive power to secure obedience, and maintains its independence from other states. The concept of the state as a political unit for organizing society is relatively recent. Many date it to the writing of *The Prince* by the Italian Niccolò Machiavelli in 1513. The earlier classical Greek unit, the *polis,* was not only much smaller than the modern state but also included in its definition a social, religious, and cultural way of life.

A **nation** is a relatively autonomous political grouping that usually shares a common language and a particular geography. National loyalty can help to create a state. Despite the fact that there was no Polish state during the nineteenth century, its idea was kept alive by the Polish nation, and the state was re-created after World War I. On the other hand, the experience of being a state, including being ruled by the same authority and laws, can help instill a sense of nationhood in citizens of different cultures and language backgrounds. To varying degrees, this national identification has occurred in the United States and in Israel. The fact that diverse cultures can be melded into a state suggests how powerful the state is as a principle of social organization.

The **nation-state,** where political authority overlaps a cultural and geographic community, is a concept that goes back to the eighteenth century. It is the primary unit of organization of societies in the world today, although even in the most firmly established nation-states there will be opposition and even resistance by certain segments. For a long time, for example, the southern part of the United States defied the laws of the country against segregations until legal sanctions imposed by the federal government began to break down such resistance.

The state is a political, legal, and geographic entity within which power and force are organized. The **political order** is the institutionalized system of acquiring and exercising power. Sociologists are concerned with the question of when and why people accept the authority of the state as legitimate. Whether one considers a state legitimate often depends on one's view of why the state is needed and how it came about. Functionalists emphasize the need for the state to maintain order and security. Conflict theorists, on the other hand, argue that the state is used as a tool by privileged classes to support their own interests and that it emerged with the rise of private property.

### Functionalist Approaches to the State

The problem of social order was clearly posed by the seventeenth-century English philosopher Thomas Hobbes, who lived in England during a time of civil war and turmoil. Hobbes's view of human nature led him to believe that an absolutely powerful sovereign and state were necessary. He saw the "natural condition" of humanity as "solitary, poor, brutish, and short" and humans as naturally selfish and competitive. For Hobbes, only a state ruled by someone with absolute authority could prevent the unattractive prospect of continual strife. If the sovereign, however, was unable to fulfill the function of maintaining public order and protecting subjects, then subjects were no longer obligated to obey.

Functionalists begin with the assumption that social order is necessary and desirable and that the state is necessary to secure this order. They focus on the positive functions of the state. If it provides these functions adequately, it is likely to be perceived as legitimate. These functions include the protection of life, liberty, and property; enforcement of norms in a formal way; regulation of conflict; the conduct of relations with other nations; and the planning, coordination, and regulation of activities conducted by various groups. In Western democracies, certain political values—such as due process, contested elections, and human rights—must also be perceived as existing in everyday life.

### Protecting Life, Liberty, and Property

In large industrial societies, people rely on the state to keep the peace, prevent gangs from rampaging through the streets, enforce traffic regulations, and control robbery, murder, and other crimes. The state also has the task of protecting its borders from armed invasion and illegal entry of foreigners. To perform these functions, the state sets up police forces, military services, and immigration agencies. Only the state is empowered to use force against others, although the law does allow a person to act in his or her own self-defense. Most people would agree that the state is better suited to perform these tasks than are private individuals or groups. Still, certain private groups may attempt to take matters into their own hands in the name of justice, for private gain, or when state services are seen as inadequate. Most would also agree that the state should exercise its power only within the law, although again this is not always what happens.

### Enforcing Norms in a Formal Way

All members of a small tribal society know the norms—the rules, values, and customs—of that society. As society becomes more complex and multicultural, there is less agreement on what the norms are and therefore less willingness to enforce many of them personally. In parts of Africa today, even in cities, if a burglar is caught breaking into someone's home, he will be beaten by the neighbors who apprehend him and may have to be rescued by the police to avoid being badly injured or killed. In societies like the United States, individuals who see a burglary in progress are likely to call the police rather than involve themselves in the situation.

When people are unclear about the norms operating in certain situations, the state steps in to codify behavior into formal laws. It also assumes the responsibility for enforcing these laws, although, as we saw in Chapter 7, it is only partially effective in doing so.

### Regulating Conflict

By writing laws to indicate which norms will prevail and when, the state sets the "rules of the game." In order to regulate and contain conflicts, it also plays the role of umpire, arbitrating disputes among the individuals and groups. This role involves establishing procedures and practices for resolving disputes. The state succeeds in its role as arbitrator to the degree that it is perceived to be fair and impartial and not "in the pocket" of any particular interests.

### Conducting Relations with Other Nations

If citizens independently worked out their own special agreements with foreign governments, the conduct of foreign affairs would become chaotic. Individuals with differing amounts of power would strike different bargains. The state, therefore, is empowered to work out uniform political and military relationships with other nations, which its citizens are supposed to obey. This power includes the capacity to declare war on another nation. (See the box on the sociology of nuclear war.) The state also tries to protect its citizens when they travel abroad. Despite theories of free-market capitalism in the United States, the power of the state also extends to regulating certain economic activities. American wheat sales to the Soviet Union depend as much on political realities at a given time as they do on market relations. Products with strategic military importance, such as certain computers, cannot freely be sold to all countries. As nation-states throughout the world have become more interdependent economically, the power of the state to regulate the behavior of its citizens has increased.

### Planning, Coordinating, and Regulating the Activities of Various Groups

The complexity of the modern world has increased the need for planning, coordination, and regulation. Air traffic, highway construction, television broadcasting, health care delivery, pension plans, environmental protection, human resource development, occupational safety,

*National leaders such as President George Bush of the United States and President Mikhail Gorbachev of the Soviet Union are expected to represent their countries in foreign affairs. These statesmen have brought new dimensions to Soviet-American relations.*

and interstate commerce are only some of the activities that would be chaotic if there were not some coordination and standardization of effort to avoid duplication, omissions, conflicting operations, and harmful side effects.

The enforcement of these efforts may call for a great degree of state regulation. In the United States the number of state regulations has come under attack by those who cite the time and expense needed to comply with them. Clearly, there are cases of excessive regulation that need to be brought under control. In New York City, for example, local public schools must fill out more than 125 forms annually, many of which relate to compliance with federally mandated programs and practices that are compulsory, and many of them asking for the same information. However, if industries did not bear the costs of complying with safety and pollution regulations, the costs of noncompliance would be felt in the air people breathe and the water they drink; it would be borne by innocent members of society. The state must balance the costs of enforcing regulations against the need of society for uniform, fair, and safe policies.

Newer state functions involve "social goods" that cannot be satisfied by the operation of free markets, which regulate only "individual goods"—goods individuals can produce, purchase, and enjoy. Clean air and water, for example, are social goods. From the standpoint of the market, such goods are irrational. For any firm to introduce pollution equipment without others doing likewise is unlikely, because the cost of the equipment would handicap the firm economically vis-à-vis its competitors. Only a centralized authority can make decisions regarding collective goods (Zaret, 1981).

## A Conflict View of the State

The functionalist view of the state suggests that it is equally in everyone's interest to form a state to preserve law and order. The conflict view claims that the state was formed and continues to exist primarily to protect the positions of privileged members of society. That is, the state safeguards those who have property and position from those who do not.

### Rousseau

Functionalists draw upon Hobbes and his formulation of the "problem of order." Conflict theorists are influenced by the eighteenth-century Swiss philosopher Jean-Jacques Rousseau, whose view of human nature was diametrically opposed to that of Hobbes. According to Rousseau, people in their natural state were "naturally good" and free. They pursued their own interests, primarily self-preservation, in isolation without desiring to gain unfair advantage over others. The introduction of private property, however, ended this state of tranquil equality. The existence of property stirred new conflicts and wars. Because the rich were the most concerned about protecting their property, Rousseau (1750) believed that they created the idea of a unified social state to protect life and property. He thought this development gave "new fetters to the weak and new strength to the rich, permanently destroyed natural freedom, established the law of property and inequality forever, turned adroit usurpation into an irrevocable right, and for the advantage of a

# The Sociology of Nuclear War

Ironically, although nuclear war poses the threat of destroying human society as we know it, there is rather little sociological research on the subject. In fact, in American sociology, there has been little research on war in general between 1936 and 1984 (Bock, 1955; Garnett, 1988). Existing research tends to fall into three categories: (1) the study of social attitudes toward nuclear war, (2) the analysis of peace movements as social movements, and (3) the specialty of military sociology and the sociology of the state.

## Social Attitudes

Social psychologists often study people's attitudes about a social phenomenon in the belief that attitudes are related to behavior. For instance, one set of researchers wondered how U.S. residents' attitudes toward nuclear war have changed from 1945 to 1982. They found a modest increase in personal fears over that time. In 1958, 14 percent of the people in a Gallup poll reported that they were "very worried" about the possibility of nuclear war. By 1961, 22 percent were. A 1982 Los Angeles *Times* survey asked, "How often do you worry about the possibility of nuclear war?" and 28 percent of the sample said they worried often or a great deal (Kramer et al., 1983, p. 21). The authors point out that it is still only a minority who report high levels of worry. A majority (74 percent), however, of those polled in 1982 report that they favor a freeze on the production of nuclear weapons in both the United States and the Soviet Union (Kramer et al., 1983, Table 4, p. 16). This attitude may be due in part to an increasing percentage who

perceive that if the United States continues to make arms, the Soviet Union will follow suit.

Social psychologists have also assessed how adolescents perceive the threat of nuclear war and how they feel about such prospects. As early as the 1960s, researchers found that 70 percent of children in the United States felt that widespread war with nuclear weapons was a likely possibility (Escalona, 1965). As a result, they felt quite pessimistic about their futures. Subsequent research shows similar concerns (Beardslee and Mack, 1982; Blackwell and Gessner, 1983; Schwebel, 1982; Zweigenhaft, 1985).

## Peace Movements

Other researchers have investigated how people's attitudes toward the threat of nuclear war are related to their actions. Two groups of people that have responded differently to the threat of nuclear war are nuclear freeze activists and survivalists. Tyler and McGraw compared members of those groups with a sample of respondents in the general public, to see if the underlying attitudes of the three groups differed (1983). They wanted to understand why some people decided to act in response to a perceived threat while others did nothing. Among those who acted, they wondered, what influenced the direction of their actions? They found four factors related to whether or not people became involved and the type of action they took. The four factors were (1) perceived risk, (2) demographics, (3) efficacy judgments, and (4) a person's moral attitudes toward the issue.

Perceived risk was related to prevention behaviors such as

joining a disarmament organization or writing to public officials. It also led to support for disarmament policies such as a weapons freeze, but not to survival behaviors such as building shelters or stockpiling food (Tyler and McGraw, 1983, p. 35). An analysis of demographic factors revealed that people with high levels of education and income were more likely to become involved than those with the lowest levels (although this was not a random sample).

Efficacy judgments also played a role (that is, whether people thought war was preventable or not). For example, those who thought war was preventable were more likely to engage in prevention behavior, less likely to engage in survival behavior, and more likely to support disarmament policies. The reverse was true for beliefs about survivability. Those who viewed nuclear war as survivable were more likely to engage in survival behavior but less likely to engage in prevention behavior and less likely to support disarmament policies. In short, the view that war is preventable but not survivable fueled antinuclear activism, while the belief that war is survivable but not preventable spurred survival behaviors (Tyler and McGraw, 1983, pp. 36–37).

The belief that war has a moral component is importantly related to preventive behaviors as well. In fact, it was found to be even more importantly related to preventive behaviors than the rational calculation of whether the preventive behaviors will succeed. In other words, many people think about, and act, on the basis of what they believe they should be doing, even if they are not convinced they will eventually succeed. For these people, working to oppose nuclear war is worthwhile even if the chances of preventing it seem small.

## Sociological Specialties

Scholars interested in social movements consider questions such as how peace movements are organized, what influences their capacity to enlist members and mobilize resources, and what impact they have on public policy and national behavior. An example of studying a peace movement as a social movement is found in Chapter 19.

Military sociology examines the social organization of the military, the role of the military in history, and the effects of modern warfare and military institutions on advanced industrial societies and on sociopolitical change. Sociologists also consider whether military participants are stratified by race and class and examine the postwar adjustment of veterans.

The focus of military sociology is primarily on the analysis of the military as a social institution and its relations with other social institutions. The issue of the social factors that promote or inhibit war has not been fully addressed by military sociologists. Moreover, in modern societies the state has almost total control over issues of war and peace. (For example, individuals cannot and do not build or buy nuclear weapons for their own arsenals.) Thus, sociologists who are interested in questions of war and peace need to consider the state. To what degree do the governments of the Western democracies respond to democratic and civilian control? What social conditions might influence a nation to use nuclear weapons? These are questions that sociologists might fruitfully

explore, but to my knowledge little work is being done in the area.

Kurtz argues that "we are trapped in a nuclear cage" (1988, p. xiii). He suggests that this situation can be understood in terms of three sociological concepts: reciprocity, bureaucracy, and ritual. Reciprocity involves an exchange between two parties. Each party feels obliged to repay any good or harm received from the other party. The risk is that reciprocity can lead to escalation. The person who receives one blow may give several in return. Thus the exchange and escalation become very difficult to end. The nuclear arms race has taken on this character. Each action or even potential action elicits a stronger reaction (Kurtz, 1988, p. 75). Thus each side is locked into responding to the perceived threat from the other side.

Bureaucracies tend to expand and maintain secrecy, which can intensify the arms race. Individuals pursuing careers in such organizations develop new weapons systems, develop winning-case scenarios, and insulate themselves from the negative consequences of their plans (Kurtz, 1988, p. 76). A ritual is a "regularly repeated, traditional, and carefully prescribed set of behaviors that symbolizes a value or a belief" (Kurtz, 1988, p. 76). Many aspects of the arms race can be seen as rituals, suggests Kurtz, including the stockpiling of weapons, military exhibitions, and civil defense drills.

Kurtz suggests that "Concrete steps for reducing the fears on both sides produced by the arms race include a reduction in the level of negative rhetoric, the creation of institutional measures that reinforce the common inter-

ests of the superpowers, and the institutionalization of ongoing personal contacts and economic exchanges . . ." (p. 203). In addition, a solution requires comprehensive and verifiable arms control agreements. Some of these steps appear to be starting.

A few sociologists have wondered why research on such questions seemingly has such a low priority. Garnett (1988) did a content analysis of three major U.S. sociological journals, two English journals, and one German journal at six-year intervals. In the U.S. journals, he found that in 1936, 0.8 percent of the articles dealt with war; 15.4 percent did in 1942, 2.9 percent in 1948, 0.7 percent in 1972, 0.6 percent in 1978, and 1.3 percent in 1984 (Garnett, 1988, p. 275). Only 0.6 percent of English and German articles from 1948 onward dealt with war (p. 279). The writing on war that was published in U.S. journals "was very narrowly focused. With few exceptions, these articles dealt with the effects of war on a particular aspect of society or with specific issues, such as antiwar protests. There were no articles [dealing] with the causes of war or with war as a social process" (Garnett, 1988, p. 281). He concludes that the seeming lack of interest in war suggests that "other concerns are seen as more important in the discipline or more amendable to research and publication (on which careers depend)" (Garnett, 1988, p. 281).

Another member of the discipline suggests that sociology has failed to address the causes of war and militarism because the discipline functions "as a legitimator of unjust socioeconomic and political systems" (Flynn, 1983, p. 1). If a critical tradition were completely lacking in sociology, that might be a valid criticism of the discipline, but it is not lacking. Grimshaw suggests that sociologists, like many others, are overwhelmed by the magnitude of the problem or are stunned into apathy (1984). I agree that many sociologists feel overwhelmed by the problem and have not yet been able to find a way to isolate and study some meaningful aspect of it. There is no strongly developed research tradition to follow. Nevertheless, there are some signs, such as the work of Tyler and McGraw that has already been cited, that sociological efforts to study the problem of nuclear war are beginning.

few ambitious men, subjected all others to unending work, servitude, and poverty" (p. 186). For Rousseau, the primary purpose of the state was thus to protect the interests of the rich.

### Marx

Karl Marx also believed that the state served the interests of the privileged. He understood the state to be a part of the superstructure of society, along with religion, morality, and culture. The base of this superstructure lay in the social relationships of economic life. Marx, like Rousseau, viewed the state as an instrument of class rule that helped to rob ordinary people of their freedom. He saw the law, police, prisons, and the army as designed to maintain existing economic relationships, including control over surplus wealth.

According to Marx, throughout history different forms of social and economic organization have been accompanied by different forms of political organization. Like earlier forms of economic organization, capitalism generates internal contradictions, thereby developing the thrust for its own revolutionary overthrow. The next stage of economic development, he suggested, will be the socialist revolution. Workers will seize the means of production and gain economic as well as political control. Because former property owners would keep their old attitudes, this stage requires the retention of the machinery of the state, which would operate under what Engels and later Lenin called "a dictatorship of the proletariat."

In the final stage of social organization, the communist stage, there would be no need for a state or for laws, because in a free and classless society everyone voluntarily seeks the good of the entire society instead of trying to advance the interests of a narrow group of owners. Un-der such conditions the state would gradually "wither away." In a communist society, persons will no longer need to be governed. Instead, only services will need to be administered and the processes of production directed. Economic life still will be organized and rules will guide social and economic life, but there will be no need for formal laws or for agents of social control like the police. Everyone will obey the rules willingly, since they will know that the rules benefit everyone equally rather than being used by one group to advance their interests at the expense of others.

In their projections about the role of the state in future societies, Marx, Engels, and Lenin departed from the role of social analysts and became social prophets. They moved from an analysis of the way the state actually operates to a prediction about its role in a different type of society.

## Pluralist and Neo-Marxist Views of the Capitalist State

### The Pluralist View

Pluralists stress the existence of different interest groups that struggle to influence concrete political decisions. An **interest group** is a group of people who work to influence political decisions affecting them. Interest groups may form temporary coalitions, depending on the specific issues being considered. Farmers, for example, may join with labor unions to oppose the high interest rates supported by bankers. The same farmers, however, may form a coalition with business people and bankers to support investment tax credits. Pluralists point to the facts that some individuals and groups have the ability to influence political decisions and that at different times different groups seem to have relatively more influence than others. They see this as evidence that American political affairs are subject to competing interest groups rather than to domination by a particular elite (Dahl, 1961; Greeley, 1974; Riesman, 1961). The pluralist perspective stresses shared values, political consensus, and the peaceful, evolutionary nature of political change (Alford and Friedland, 1985).

Critics suggest that the pluralist approach overlooks "structural conditions that keep some issues from being raised" (Kasinitz, 1983). They also suggest that pluralists have a "one-dimensional view of power" (Lukes, 1974). Neo-Marxists analyze the role the state has played in the persistence of capitalism. Neo-Marxists include "instrumentalists," who view the state as

*Farmers in the United States often constitute a special-interest group working to advance certain political positions. They may demonstrate in Washington and threaten not to grow certain important crops in an effort to persuade others to support their concerns.*

an instrument of certain social classes, and structuralists, who stress the relative autonomy of the modern state (Mollenkopf, 1975; Skocpol, 1980). Each of these views is worth examining more closely.

### The Instrumentalist View

A group of neo-Marxist theorists seeks to refute pluralist theories of politics and the state. They argue that the upper class tends to dominate the state and uses this dominance to shape the economy politically as needed. C. Wright Mills, for example, saw the **power elite** as a closely connected group of the corporate rich, political leaders, and military commanders who decide most key political and social issues. These leaders all operate in institutional spheres that are relatively independent at the base of their institutional pyramids but closely interconnected at the top. Figure 14.1 illustrates this view that, at the highest echelons of U.S. society, the top military men, the president, cabinet members, and heads of large corporations and banks confer frequently over national and international policy matters. Farther down the organizational hierarchies in each sphere, civil servants, rank-and-file military officers, and corporate staff members operate quite independently of one another.

Power-structure researchers such as G. William Domhoff (1970, 1976, 1979), focus on upper-class cohesion and influence. They try to show how a power elite rather than competing interest groups dominate political decisions. Domhoff sees the "power elite as the leadership group or operating arm of the ruling class" (1979, pp. 13–14). This approach tends to focus heavily on individuals, which is both its strength and its limitation. It provides concrete demonstrations of social interaction among individuals defined as members of the "higher circles" and documents upper-class persons in government positions. For example, 90 percent of U.S. cabinet members in this century were members of the social or business elite (Mintz, 1975, p. 135). Clearly, elites are overrepresented, but do they also dominate the outcomes of political conflicts? Labor and other interest groups may gain major concessions from the state, especially in times of social and economic upheaval (Kasinitz, 1983). Power-elite theorists may underestimate

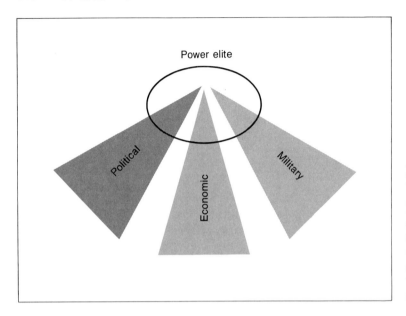

Power elite

Political

Economic

Military

**Figure 14.1   Mills's View of the Power Elite.**

In Mills's view, the top leadership of the military, economic, and political realms are in frequent contact with each other and make up a large portion of what he called the "power elite."

the possibility that state bureaucracies can develop some degree of autonomy from class interests.

### The Structuralist View

Structuralists focus on the relative autonomy of state bureaucracies. Two distinct types of structuralism are the political position of Nicos Poulantzas and the "class struggle" position represented by Fred Block (1977b, 1981). Poulantzas sees the state as a "relatively autonomous power center." It is not completely independent because class factors ultimately influence its direction. The state can, however, act independently of the wishes of individual capitalists. But since the state's interests coincide with the interests of the dominant class, members of the ruling class do not need to participate in state organizations (Poulantzas, 1972). It is better for capitalism if "the ruling class is not the politically governing class" (Poulantzas, 1972). Poulantzas goes to the other extreme from Domhoff. Highly impersonal and deterministic states, rather than active individuals, operate to maintain capitalism (Kasinitz, 1983). Thus, Poulantzas effectively rules out the possibility that class struggle might change the direction of state action.

Fred Block does not assume that the state always acts in the interests of capitalism. He asks instead why the state tends to act in those interests. He asserts that state officials have their own goals—of maintaining political stability and their rule, collecting revenue, and expanding their departments (Kasinitz, 1983). The state seeks economic stability because it needs steady revenues to continue its programs. Capitalists generally have more potential to threaten political stability than does labor, because they can simply refuse to invest in a particular nation-state. As a result, states are usually more responsive to capitalists. Only during major depressions or war are states more likely to respond to labor (Kasinitz, 1983). In such cases, class struggle is brought into state policies.

## THE STRUCTURE OF POWER IN THE UNITED STATES

How is power organized in the United States? Is there one small group of people who exercise power over all aspects of life in the society, or are there many competing groups? Do the leaders of the major institutions come together on important issues? How we, as social scientists and citizens, answer these questions goes a long way toward shaping our opinions about whether power is being exercised legitimately in society, whether we feel U.S. society is democratic, and therefore whether we feel major social and political changes are necessary or desirable. So it is not surprising that the question of how power is structured in the United States is a hotly debated issue among social scientists.

How does business, for example, achieve the unity to carry out the coordinated political action that Domhoff and others have documented? Financial decisions set the stage on which policy-formation bodies operate (Mintz and Schwartz, 1985). These include the decisions to pursue certain investment options rather than others (for example, nuclear energy rather than solar energy) and to develop some industries but not others (military technologies rather than consumer electronics). These decisions set up a system of opportunities and limitations within which policy-setting bodies and government operate.

## Direct Business Influence over Politics

Lindblom documents the "disproportionate influence of business in interest-group, party and electoral politics" (1977, p. 202). He notes that business does this through contributions, organizational strength, ready access to government leaders, and the molding of citizen attitudes. To compare the political contributions of private citizens to those of business is "to compare a mouse to a mountain" (Lindblom, 1977, p. 196). Businesses can act directly and through their associations. The *Encyclopedia of Organizations in the United States* fills 256 pages with the names of national business associations, 17 pages with labor organizations, 60 with public affairs organizations, and 71 with scientific and technical organizations (Lindblom, 1977, p. 197). Business leaders are known to government officials and can readily gain their ear. This access is aided by the frequent movement of government officials into corporations (Nader and Green, 1973; Engler, 1961; Mintz and Cohen, 1971). Labor unions do not have this ready access (Lindblom, 1977). Business shapes attitudes, for example, by providing teaching materials to the public schools. The goal is to get citizens to take for granted the privileged position of business (Lindblom, 1977). They also try to "remove grand issues from politics," so that

there will be "political silence on them" (Lindblom, 1977, p. 204–205).

Useem (1984) analyzes further the way business influence is exercised. He notes the emergence of a new "classwide principle of organization" based on linked networks of corporate ownership and direction (Useem, 1984, p. 194). A select group of business leaders, usually those who serve on the boards of multiple corporations, help run the affairs of the United States and Britain (Silk and Silk, 1980; Useem, 1984). They do this by guiding the major business associations (like the Business Roundtable and the Conference Board), by providing advice to high-level government officials, and by governing cultural organizations, universities, foundations, and other nonprofit organizations (Useem, 1984).

Another study found that bank directors who served on the "Save St. Louis" committee with other citizens did not change their banks' policy of lending most of their money to large outside corporations instead of providing mortgages within the city limits (Ratcliff, 1980). Additional evidence suggests that representatives of the capitalist class do coordinate their activities and statements in regard to public policies—for example, in first opposing and then supporting proposals for mass transportation in California from 1962 to 1974 (Whitt, 1980).

Given this evidence for the existence and relative cohesiveness of an inner group of the capitalist class, can we say that members of this group operate to benefit their own interests as a class rather than working to serve "the common good"? At this writing, clear evidence that they operate in their own interests and to the detriment of other class groups is beginning to emerge. The possibility for such action exists, and the potential for the persistent exercise of organized power by a small group in society for its own benefit remains.

## The Exclusion of Key Decisions from the Political Arena

The capacity of business to mobilize and act in the political world is not the only way that business influences social policy (Mintz and Schwartz, 1985). This is because many major decisions are made outside the political arena and are therefore neither public nor democratic. Instead, major decisions made in the business world influence social policy. This happens because major banks select projects to which they will commit major national resources—for example, loaning money to Third World nations, stimulating leasing as a way of acquiring capital goods, and financing private rather than public transportation (Mintz and Schwartz, 1985). In short, the dominance of financial institutions permits business to develop a unified position in relation to government and allows a "massive independent policy making capacity" to exist within business (Mintz and Schwartz, 1985).

## POLITICAL CHANGE

Political changes occur in a variety of different ways, depending on the structure of a particular state and on the depth and breadth of the commitment to change. Small groups of people who are highly committed to social change may use terrorism to try to change an existing situation.

*Decisions made by banks and other corporate enterprises influence social policies in major ways. If banks decide to finance new construction in a neighborhood, for example, and to finance the mortgages for people to buy homes in the area, such decisions support jobs and increase the prospect of neighborhood stability. If banks decide not to lend money in a particular neighborhood, however, that decision can have very negative effects on the area.*

When a state tries to suppress efforts at peaceful political change, people sometimes accept injustice or suffering; at other times, they rebel against it. Sometimes such rebellions lead to revolutionary political changes. Political changes also occur more gradually, through a process of evolution. Sociologists want to know what conditions are associated with the various kinds of political change.

### Terrorism as a Form of Opposition

Some individuals and groups are so completely opposed to an existing state or society that they want nothing to do with it. They do not consider working to change the laws gradually or getting their representatives elected to be an effective or satisfying strategy. If they feel strongly enough about their cause, they may use terrorism as a strategy for trying to gain power and further their goals. Terrorism is a weapon of the politically powerless or disenfranchised. **Terrorism** refers to an attack on individuals in order to frighten society into doing one's will. It includes hijacking airplanes, throwing grenades, shooting, bombing abortion clinics, kidnapping, and murdering for political reasons. Sometimes political terrorists demand money to support their activities, but their avowed aims are political goals rather than personal ones. Therefore it is particularly important to terrorists that they receive the right publicity for their actions.

Because terrorists are politically motivated, one person's terrorist may be another's freedom fighter. Terrorists often have supporters within a society. They may also have foreign sympathizers, including foreign governments, who supply money, arms, and sanctuary for them. Both the Irish Republican Army (IRA) and the Palestine Liberation Organization (PLO) have international supporters—the IRA among some Irish-Americans, and the PLO within Arab and some European nations. Support for terrorists makes it more difficult to find and stop them.

Television magnifies the impact of terrorists by personalizing their violence and bringing it into the homes of millions of people. Seeing the tearful families of victims or hostages talking to us from every TV screen makes it more difficult for governments to remain firm in the face of terrorists' demands. Television can also fan the fear aroused by terrorism and lead to harsh repression. The stifling of dissent, however, may push more citizens toward sympathy with the terrorists and "make a society more brittle and vulnerable to attack" (Clutterbuck, 1977, p. 115). Terrorist violence is less likely to lead to revolutionary change than to repression and rigidity in a society. At times, if they seek to undermine the legitimacy of the state, this may be the aim of certain terrorist groups.

## State Terrorism

Some totalitarian governments use state terror and torture to intimidate and control citizens. It is often used by states seeking to resist political change. Hitler used terror in Nazi Germany, as did Stalin in the Soviet Union. It disappeared in Germany with the collapse of Nazism and has declined in the Soviet Union (Amnesty International, 1975). It has reappeared in recent decades in Argentina, Bolivia, Brazil, Chile, Ecuador, Guatemala, Paraguay, Uruguay, and elsewhere. Political regimes there use psycho-

logical and physical torture, death squads, and disappearances as part of a campaign of "effective intimidation" (Amnesty International, 1975; Herman, 1982, p. 8). The regimes share these features, according to Herman:

*(1) they represent a small elite interest, including the multinational corporation, which they treat kindly; (2) they all use terror, including modern forms of torture, to keep the majority unorganized, powerless, and as a means to local elite and multinational corporate ends; (3) the leadership of these states are almost invariably venal; (4) they have allowed already highly skewed income distributions to become still more unequal, and have caused a large fraction of their populations to be kept in a state of extreme deprivation. [1982, p. 2]*

State terrorism allows terror to become a relatively permanent part of state activity. It aims to prevent political, social, and economic change and to control wages and welfare spending (Herman, 1982). A major consequence is the generation of a "culture of fear" (Corradi, 1982–1983, p. 63). Between 1960 and 1980, hundreds of thousands have been tortured (Herman, 1982, p. 115). At the same time that state terror has become widespread in many of these countries,

*Individual terrorists, like these in Northern Ireland, seek to change social policy, often by attacking other individuals who represent the government being resisted. State terrorism, on the other hand, seeks to intimidate and control citizens, by arresting, torturing, or killing them.*

U.S. banks have been investing billions of dollars there, at high rates of return (between 15 and 20 percent annual return as a minimum; Whichard, 1981). The United States has also been pouring hundreds of millions of dollars of military assistance, armaments, and police aid into these countries (Herman, 1982, p. 129). Herman argues that U.S. economic interests benefit from this state terror, and that those benefits explain why the U.S. government continues to aid military dictatorships.

## Conditions Generating Obedience and Revolt

Strategies of peaceful protest, efforts to change the law, and even terrorism are difficult to use in a totalitarian society like South Africa, where the state or an arm of the state (like a prison camp or a mental institution) may use oppression and terror to control a large population. In such a situation, when do people accept injustice and suffering, and when do they rebel against it? In situations where a cultural explanation of suffering as part of the cosmic order prevails, people may believe injustice to be inevitable and justified. Such a cultural explanation narrows human visions about how people can respond to the reality around them. This general explanation applies to experiences in Nazi concentration camps and instances where social injustice has been explained by religions that emphasize that the poor or oppressed will be reincarnated or otherwise enjoy a higher status in an afterworld.

Based on a close look at concentration camps, Moore (1978) noted four social processes that tend to suppress cooperative efforts to identify, reduce, or resist oppression. First, victims were more likely to unite against a single rebel in their midst because they observed how one defiant member could cause an entire group to be punished. Second, prior family, religious, or community ties were destroyed among sufferers, leaving individuals without social support. Cooptation was the third social process that undermined collective resistance to an oppressor. Since the dominant individuals or groups usually controlled vital resources, such as food,

some people were willing to conform to obtain those rewards. Fourth, fragmentation occurred when an oppressed population was split into two or more competing groups, each with a distinctive way of life. Divisions may occur along religious, ethnic, national, or occupational lines. In the concentration camps, criminals were put with lawyers, Russians with Germans. Prior social antagonisms were intensified, and the result was heightened conflict between groups. These four processes tended to stifle the impulse to rebel; they created a sense of the inevitability of oppression and an aura of moral authority around the suffering. Once people see the situation in this way, resistance is unlikely.

Whereas certain social processes sap the will to resist, others fuel it. Even a small degree of social support can shatter the illusion that oppression is part of the natural order of things and nurture the development of a critical rather than an obedient response to a situation. Even one person who differs from the majority can nurture the independent judgment of others. Milgram's experiments on obedience identify some conditions that lead humans to disobey even an apparently legitimate authority.

To study people's willingness to harm others while following orders, Milgram brought 40 men from various occupations into his laboratory to participate in what he called a learning experiment. Lots were drawn, apparently, and subjects were assigned the role of "teacher" or "pupil." The pupil was strapped into a chair, with an electrode attached to his wrists. Teachers faced an electrical control panel of dials, gauges, and switches. Switches were labeled in volts, from 15 to 315, and some had signs like "Extreme-Intensity Shock," "Danger—Severe Shock," and "XXX." The teacher read a list of word pairs to the pupil and asked him to match them up. Whenever the learner made a mistake, the experimenter instructed the teacher to throw one of the switches, beginning with the mildest, to shock the pupil. Although the teachers could not see the pupils in the next room, they could hear them through an open door.

As the experiment continued, teachers were asked to give even more severe shocks, until the pupil was screaming for mercy and begging for the experiment to end. Many teachers paused at this point, but were told by the experimenter that it was important to continue giving the shocks. After a while, the pupils began kicking the wall between the rooms while continuing to scream. Finally, when teachers read the list and asked for pupil responses, there was only silence in the other room. The experimenter said that no answer should be considered an error and that the next higher shock should be administered. This continued until the "XXX" shock at the top of the dial had been given. Of the first 40 subjects, none refused to give the shocks until the pupil began to kick the wall. Then 5 out of 40 refused. Other teachers balked between there and the end of the experiment, but 26 out of 40 continued giving shocks up to the final point.

A slight change in social conditions greatly increased the resistance to authority. When two "teachers" refused to obey the experimenter's order to administer increasingly severe shocks, most other "teachers" gladly rebelled against the authority of the experimenter. Added social support effectively undercut the experimenter's authority. More subjects also refused to obey the experimenter's commands when they had to administer the punishment through direct physical contact with the "student-victim." When they had to press the victim's hand onto a shock plate, only 30 percent obeyed, compared to 65 percent who obeyed when the victim was out of sight in the next room; the size of the shock they were willing to administer was also much less under these conditions (Milgram, 1969).[1] Apparently, physical closeness increases identification with a victim and also diminishes the willingness to obey cruel authority.

Every attempt at oppression tends to dehumanize and distance the victims of oppression. Language and beliefs paint the victim as subhuman, stupid, lazy, unfeeling, or evil, as reflected in such terms as "gooks" (to refer to the Vietnamese who fought Americans), "niggers" (to allude to American blacks), or "bitch" (to describe a woman men consider too assertive). To throw off oppression, victims must refuse to accept the labels, beliefs, and orders issued by their oppressors. To do so requires counter-definitions and social support.

The opposition or rebellion discussed here occurs when resisters lack the power to make basic changes in the leadership structure itself. These forms of resistance or revolt differ from the broader process of **revolution,** which involves a large-scale change in the political leadership of a society and the restructuring of major features of that society. (The term "revolution" is also used to refer to any major occurrence in society that causes basic changes—for example, industrial revolution, scientific revolution, or agricultural revolution.) Although **rebellion** involves opposition to authority, it does not usually result in leadership changes. It may force an existing regime to change its policies in some way, but it is not considered a revolution unless it successfully overthrows an existing set of rulers.

## Revolution

When people become angry about social conditions and are organized enough to overturn existing institutions, they may create a political revolution. By comparing a number of revolutions, social thinkers have identified several common conditions that appear to precede revolutionary upheavals (Brinton, 1965; de Tocqueville, 1856; Graham, 1979; Saikal, 1980; Skocpol, 1979).

Brinton (1965) tentatively identified five common features in the revolutions he studied in England, America, France, and Russia. First, revolution is very often preceded by some improvements in social and economic conditions, as occurred before the French Revolution, the American Revolution, and the Iranian revolution of 1978. Such improvements lead to **rising expectations**—that is, a situation in which people feel that past hardships should not have to be suffered in the future.

Revolutionary movements seem to originate in the discontents of reasonably comfortable people who feel restrained and annoyed rather than those of people facing crushing oppression (Brinton, 1965). The rulers in power, however, try to control and limit the changes they allow,

---

[1] As you may know, the shocks were fake and only the "teacher" was a real subject in the experiment. There was no actual harm done to the "pupils." The experiment was designed to test willingness to obey, even to the point of apparently injuring or killing someone.

thus adding to the frustration of the populace. This situation is accompanied by a growing sense that the existing government is illegitimate. Power is seen as being arbitrary, and the distribution of wealth may be seen as unfair. Discontents of this kind certainly helped to fuel the American, French, Russian, and Iranian revolutions.

Second, prerevolutionary societies have bitter class antagonisms. Revolutions seem more likely when classes are more alike in circumstances rather than very different (Brinton, 1965). A country that has high levels of inequality and a political regime that is in between a democratic structure and a totalitarian structure seems to be more likely to experience political instability than countries with less economic inequality and either a democratic or a totalitarian structure (Muller, 1985).

Third, there is what Brinton calls the "transfer of allegiance of the intellectuals" (Brinton, 1965, p. 251). Fourth, the government is ineffective and fails to change old institutions. Fifth, individuals of the old ruling class lose faith in the traditions of their class and join the attacking group or become immoral, dissolute, or politically inept.

Existing rulers are also viewed as being weak and possibly divided internally. A crisis of confidence in the prevailing leadership builds. Many leading citizens become highly critical of the existing order. Nobles in France and Russia, just before those revolutions began, started doubting that the existing political regime would survive. Some even joined and helped to lead the revolutions. The signers of the Declaration of Independence in the United States, for example, were hardly wild-eyed rebels; many came from prominent colonial families. Given these doubts at the upper levels of society, government is often hesitant to sanction its critics strongly. Gradually the social institutions supporting the state begin to crumble, leaving only the military and the police. In the advanced stages of a revolution members of the military often join the revolutionary forces, further weakening the government's position.

The aftermath of a revolution may also be choppy, as new political leaders try to gain power and legitimacy. Old rulers are usually executed or banished. Contending factions may fight among themselves, sometimes bringing about further violence and rapid shifts in leadership. Those who achieve power are often the ones who are most ruthless in suppressing their opposition. Revolutions are often followed by dictatorships that rule by terrorizing all who might oppose them. As they gain legitimacy, they may loosen the political reins somewhat and restore certain civil liberties.

## Evolution

In the United States there are a number of mechanisms to allow change to occur gradually in an evolutionary rather than a revolutionary way. Some of these vehicles include the existence of more than one political party, regularly scheduled elections, and an inclusive stance toward political participation.

### Political Parties

A **political party** is an organized group of people that seeks to control or influence political decisions through legal means. In some societies political parties are active groups that individuals join and support regularly by paying dues. These parties may sponsor lectures, publications, youth groups, and other educational efforts to involve the masses in political life. The United States does not follow this pattern. The Democratic and Republican parties in the United States have few formal members. Instead of one national organization for each party, there are 50 or more distinct Republican and Democratic parties, with at least one in each state.

Most of the activity of political parties in the United States is centered around local, state, and federal election campaigns. There is a national committee for each party, but its control is loose and decentralized. There is no unified political program that everyone in a political party supports, and there are no formal ways of controlling the behavior of party officeholders once they are elected. Why, then, are political parties important at all? Their significance rests on the fact that they control the pathways to political office. Political parties determine who will be the candidates for political positions. This function gives them their political power.

Party membership in the United States is not as clearly tied to social class as it is in other countries, although the lower and working classes are more likely to vote Democratic, whereas upper-middle-class and upper-class voters are more likely to vote Republican. However, even these tendencies have weakened somewhat in recent elections. In the United States political parties have always been less important than individual political candidates, especially at the national level.

In 1986, only 4 percent of the population belonged to a formal political club or organization (Gans, 1988). The mass media may also undermine party importance. (See the debate on the role of mass media in a democracy.) Political coverage and advertisements enable candidates to solicit contributions and votes directly from voters without depending on the party organization.

### Voting Behavior

Citizens can participate in government processes in various ways. Voting in elections is often taken as an important indicator of participation. Nonvoting does not necessarily mean people are not interested in politics, however. It may be that they are interested but that they do

*Although voting is an important right of citizenship, many Americans do not vote in either local or national elections. Middle-aged and older voters, college graduates, whites, the well-to-do, and professionals are more likely to vote than younger, less-educated, black, low-income, and working-class voters. Such voting patterns inevitably affect elections results.*

not like the choices or that they are reasonably satisfied with either possibility or that they were sick, too busy, or out of town on election day. In general, younger, less educated, black, low-income, working-class voters and those with no party preference are less likely to vote in national elections. Republicans, the middle-aged, college graduates, the well-to-do, and professionals are overrepresented among voters, giving them more impact on elections (*Public Opinion*, 1980).

The first systematic research on American voting patterns was conducted by Paul F. Lazarsfeld, Bernard Berelson, and Hazel Gaudet (1944) and reported in the famous book *The People's Choice*. They found that certain social statuses were closely related to political party preference and to voting behavior. Protestants, upper-class individuals, and rural dwellers were most likely to be Republicans; whereas Catholics, the working class, and urban dwellers were more often Democrats. People with two or three of these characteristics were more likely to vote for the expected party than people with mixed statuses, such as lower-class Protestant urban dwellers. People with mixed status characteristics made up the "swing" voters who decided late in a campaign, were more likely to switch political preferences during a campaign, and were least likely to vote at all.

Other voting studies (Berelson et al., 1954; Campbell et al., 1954) tended to confirm Lazarsfeld's original findings. Recent research confirms the trend that the number of swing voters with mixed status characteristics (such as highly educated Catholics) has been growing in recent years. Seemingly as a result, we have witnessed in recent years fairly rapid shifts in political allegiances, uncertain political outcomes, and a decline in the percentage of the voting-age population who are voting, even in presidential elections, from 63 percent in 1960 to an estimated 49 percent in 1988 (U.S. Bureau of the Census, 1985a; *New York Times*, 1988).

### The Gender Gap

In the last few presidential elections, a new phenomenon called the "gender gap" has arisen. Until then, there were few differences in the way women and men voted. The term **gender gap** refers to the difference in the way men and women vote. In 1976 women favored Ford over

One of the key issues in the study of mass communication is the question of how media technologies affect public life and political culture. Concern about these effects has accompanied the introduction of each new technology and inspired considerable social research. Early in the twentieth century, the infant motion picture industry faced widespread local opposition because of its supposed corrupting influence upon youth. The ensuing controversy led in the 1920s to the Payne Fund Studies, the first large-scale sociological research on the social effects of any communication technology. In 1938, when Orson Welles's dramatic broadcast of *The War of the Worlds* caused outbreaks of panic from coast to coast, Hadley Cantril at Princeton University's Office of Radio Research responded with an "emergency" study, funded by the Rockefeller Foundation, to find out why some people believed the broadcast invasion from Mars to be real. What new and powerful forces were set loose in society when a new medium could command such credibility?

Throughout the 1930s radio was put to two very different political uses. In the United States, weekly radio broadcasts ("fireside chats") by Franklin Roosevelt brought the American people into unprecedentedly close contact with their president, and his soothing and cultured voice reassured a nation deeply shaken by the Great Depression. In Germany, by contrast, Adolph Hitler used radio broadcasts to whip up racial hatred and mass hysteria.

With the diffusion of television and more advanced media technologies after 1945, sociological concern about their political and

## Do Communication Technologies Promote or Undermine Democracy?

cultural influence has continued to grow. Views on whether the media technologies are "good" or "bad" for democracies anchor at two extremes of the spectrum.

### The Pessimistic View

Pessimists see media technologies as a powerful tool of political control and oppression, irresistibly tempting to political and economic elites. They regard the public as a "mass audience," highly vulnerable to manipulation, and media technologies as susceptible to domination by centralized powers. The most famous exponent of the pessimistic viewpoint was George Orwell, who envisioned, in his novel *Nineteen Eighty-Four,* a society enslaved by the omnipresent telescreen—a technology that droned incessant propaganda and scrutinized the individual's every movement and word. In Orwell's horrific tale, the government was able to use a powerful media technology to enforce a singular pattern of thought and action on every citizen.

Though Orwell's gloom might seem to border on paranoia, a similar pessimism has informed the work of many social scientists who study the media. For example, studies such as those by Hannah Arendt (1951) and William Kornhauser (1959) have explained the rise of totalitarianism in Europe in the 1930s as partly a consequence of the demagogic manipulation of mass media—a manipulation that was particularly effective in Germany because traditional authority had

been severely undermined by the First World War and its aftermath. By this account, the mass media became an instrument of propaganda that provided pseudoauthority and pseudocommunity to an anxious population.

More recent works in the "pessimistic" school have focused particularly on the effects of television. Such analysts as Jacques Ellul (1964), Herbert Marcuse (1964), and Neil Postman (1985) have argued that the mass media, both in programming and in advertising, support the status quo by promoting our common myths, simplifying complex realities, and constantly reassuring us that everything is all right; in their view, the mass media serve as a mass opiate. Other pessimists, such as Ben Bagdikian (1983) and George Gerbner (1972), have denounced the media (particularly television) for their negative influences on culture and society—especially on children. By their account, the media inculcate superficial, acquisitive, materialistic values, desensitize us to real-world violence, and trivialize political life. Finally, other critics, working both in neo-Marxist and in European structuralist traditions, argue that mass media institutions neutralize social conflicts and reinforce the hegemony of bourgeois culture (e.g., Gitlin, 1980; Schudson, 1984; Allen, 1987).

### The Optimistic View

Optimists counter that communication technologies are actually very good for democracies because they distribute information more widely and freely than ever before. Thinkers in this tradition begin by pointing to the revolutionary impact of Gutenberg's printing press—an inven-

**DEBATING SOCIETY'S ISSUES**

tion that broke the monastic monopoly on the production and interpretation of the holy scriptures and was thereby crucial to the Protestant Reformation. Since that time, according to the optimists, every advance in communication technology has allowed humankind to expand its knowledge base and reduce ignorance and superstition—trends that are not only congenial but also indispensable to democracy. In the optimist's view, the mass media are technologies of freedom, not of domination.

While Orwell was imagining the horrors of the telescreen, MIT's Vannevar Bush (1945) was correctly foretelling the advent of the personal computer—a device that would give each individual access to the entire store of the world's accumulated knowledge and culture; permit a person to calculate or manipulate words, images or data; and allow instantaneous worldwide communication. To Bush and other optimists (e.g., Innis, 1951;

McLuhan, 1964; Pool, 1983), communication technologies almost always lead to wider distribution of information; thus they inherently are the enemies rather than the instruments of totalitarian domination. Though dictators usually take over the television stations soon after seizing power, citizens can pick up broadcasts from beyond their nations' borders. Though governments may try to suppress information, copying machines, telephones, and computer networks all encourage "leaks," since they inherently distribute information. Even if one channel of communication is temporarily closed to the political opposition, other channels serve as replacements; for example, the Shah of Iran's attempt to keep the revolutionary speeches of Ayatollah Khomeini out of Iran during the 1970s was foiled by the widespread smuggling of audiocassette tapes.

With today's proliferation of cable-carried television channels

and satellite broadcasts, it is nearly impossible for despots to monopolize information. Thus, to such "optimists" as Daniel Bell (1973), John Naisbett (1982), Alvin Toffler (1980), W. Russell Neuman (1986), Yoneji Masuda (1980), and Simon Nora and Alain Minc (1980), communication technologies are inherently pluralistic. They tend to decentralize the flow of information and undermine the foundations of bureaucratic centralization. They are also thought to reinforce democracy by fostering literacy and the widest possible diffusion of information. Even television, the bête noire of the pessimists, is held by the optimists to be beneficial because it permits much wider dissemination and diversity of information than was possible before.

Written by Scott C. McDonald, Director of Research, Time Inc. Magazines, and Adjunct Professor of Sociology, New York University.

Carter 51 to 48 percent, but they were 9 percent more likely to favor Carter than men were in 1980, 7 percent more likely to favor Mondale than men were in 1984, and 8 percent more likely to favor Dukakis than men were in 1988 (Figure 14.2). In 1988, women were crucial to Dukakis's victories in most of the states he carried. In Iowa, for example, men split their votes, giving 49 percent of the total to each candidate. Women voted for Dukakis 60 percent to 39 percent, giving him the margin of victory there (Dionne, 1988, p. B6).

Women represented 52 percent of all voters in 1988, so their participation rates have increased slightly over time as well. Women are more likely to oppose the use of force than men are, both in foreign affairs and in dealing with urban problems (Lansing and Baxter, 1980). As

more women enter higher education, we would predict that their rate of voting will continue to increase. This may have increasingly important consequences for political outcomes.

Voting rates are lower in the United States than in most other industrialized countries. Rates of voting are particularly low among 18- to 20-year-olds. Governments with higher voting rates are usually parliamentary systems (Wills, 1988). In such a system, smaller and more focused parties can appeal more strongly to voters. The two-party system in the United States favors political compromise to such a degree that many voters tend to lose interest.

Another explanation that has been offered for the declining voter turnout, especially among younger voters, is a growing sense of political alienation and apathy. If people feel alienated

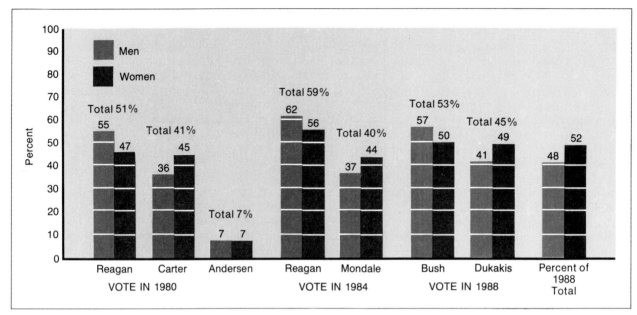

**Figure 14.2    The Gender Gap and Voting Behavior.**

The gender gap in men's and women's voting behavior appeared
in the last three presidential elections.

*Source:* The New York Times/CBS News Poll, 1988.

from the political process, they are less likely to
vote in elections. Political apathy among many
voters means that special-interest groups stand
a better chance of influencing the outcome of an
election and that a candidate without majority
support can be elected.

### Class Bias in Voting

Less than one-quarter of the population had
family incomes of $50,000 or more in 1988. But
about half of those who voted in the 1988 presidential election had incomes of $50,000 or more
(Dionne, 1988, p. B6). Very large proportions
of the well-to-do vote compared with the poor.
Those with family incomes under $25,000 com-
prised only one-third of 1988 voters. "For any
politician calculating the economic interests of
his or her constituents, these figures of relative
voting strength are of key importance" (Edsall,
1984, p. 183). This growing class bias in voting
has had significant consequences for the making
of economic policy (Edsall, 1984, p. 185).

One reason for this class bias in voting is the
way local governments in the United States
have made it difficult to register and to vote,
particularly for certain portions of the population (Piven and Cloward, 1988). People must
reregister every time they move. The times and
places of registration are often poorly publicized
and frequently changed. The result over the past
decade has been the shrinking capacity of the
political system to represent the interests of the
bottom two-thirds of society (Edsall, 1984).

The higher their social class, the more likely
individuals are to participate in politics in additional ways besides voting. These include working in local political organizations, campaigning
for particular candidates, contacting an elected
official about an issue or problem, or contributing money to a party or a candidate (Campbell
et al., 1964; Verba and Nie, 1972). People are
more likely to participate in various political
activities when they believe they can influence
politicians and political events, when they trust

the political order and politicians, and when they know about political events and discuss them with others (Orum, 1978).

### Lobbying Groups

One way that people influence the political process is through organized groups that represent their special interests. The American Medical Association (AMA), National Education Association, National Rifle Association (NRA), Right to Life, and United Auto Workers are among the thousands of interest groups that try to influence political decisions affecting their members. All these groups try to change the course of state and national political events in line with their members' interests through a process called **lobbying.** The larger and better-organized their membership is and the more financial and media resources they command, the greater their influence is likely to be. Many groups form Political Action Committees (PACs). These PACs contributed $132.7 million to Congressional campaigns in 1985–1986.

Lobbying occurs once people are elected. But a major way PAC managers buy influence is by contributing money to political incumbents,

Lobbying efforts such as this one by people supporting state aid to public libraries are visible efforts by interest groups to try to gain support for their concerns. But most efforts at political influence are not so visible. Powerful political action committees (PACs) raise millions of dollars annually, which they contribute to cooperative political incumbents.

particularly those with influential posts in Congress and those who have good chances of being reelected (Stern, 1988). Most political candidates are obsessed with political contributions. The result is the emergence of the "special-interest state" (Drew, 1983). The voters' range of choice is limited by PAC contributions, many of them from outside the candidate's district (Wills, 1988).

These groups hire full-time lobbyists to supply information, favors, and entertainment to lawmakers. They may offer bribes, run advertisements, pledge money and votes to candidates, threaten lawsuits, organize letter-writing campaigns, or talk directly with legislators. In recent years right-to-life groups have been effective in using computerized national lists of voters and contributors to oppose certain political candidates whose opinions differ from their own. For years the AMA has blocked federal health insurance, and the NRA has prevented the control or registration of guns, including handguns, despite popular support for both issues.

Interest groups are especially effective in promoting issues so complex or technical that members of the general public have little knowledge about them. Specific features of the tax law, for example, may greatly benefit certain interest groups, while costing the government millions of dollars in revenues. If citizens' groups do not understand the technical details of such proposals, they are unlikely to oppose them effectively. Interest groups funnel millions of dollars each year to selected members of the Senate and Congress. Given the high costs of political campaigning and media advertising, the well-financed interest groups are likely to remain powerful forces in political life. Sometimes this lobbying is done with government agencies rather than with lawmakers. (See the box entitled "Federal Policy Formation.")

A 1981 Gallup poll found that 13 percent of respondents said they had joined an "interest group," such as one protecting wildlife, an antiabortion group, an anti–gun-control group, or groups defending the rights of Vietnam veterans or blacks. Another 23 percent said they had given money to such a group. College or professional-school graduates were more likely to

## Federal Policy Formation

The executive director of a major petroleum-industry trade association was leafing through the *Federal Register*, his daily ritual of scanning the Washington scene. Buried in the fine print was an apparently innocuous announcement by the Federal Aviation Administration of its intent to promulgate new regulations that would require detailed flight plans to be filed by pilots of noncommercial aircraft. Recently, several planes had gone down and search-and-rescue efforts had been hampered by lack of information on the pilots' intended routes. The trade-association director muttered, "We've got a problem" and spent a frantic morning on the phone alerting his group's membership to apply pressure on the FAA to set aside the regulation. The executive realized that, once detailed flight plans were on record with the FAA, the open disclosure provisions of the Freedom of Information Act would allow anyone to learn where his member companies' planes were flying on their aerial explorations for oil, gas, and minerals. The alert director's quick mobilization of collective response saved the corporations potentially millions of dollars of secret data that might have fallen into the laps of their competitors.

This incident dramatically encapsulates several important features of State policy-making: the centrality of large formal organizations; the significance of policy interests in narrowly focused events; the great value of timely and trustworthy information; the activation of policy participants through communication networks; and the mobilization of influence resources to bear upon the formal authorities. State policies are the product of complex interactions among governmental and nongovernment organizations, each seeking to influence the collectively binding decisions about events that have consequences for their interest.

Quoted from Laumann et al., 1985, p. 1.

be members than high school or grade school graduates (Gans, 1988).

## SUMMARY

1. Power is the capacity of a person or group to achieve a specific goal, even in the face of opposition from others.

2. Authority is power that is accepted as legitimate; that is, the people exercising it are seen as having the right to do so.

3. The amount of power people have depends on the material, coercive, and normative resources they command. Some of these resources are inherited; others are earned.

4. Power is relational; that is, it becomes evident in relation to other people. Sometimes power differences are taken for granted; sometimes people comply willingly; sometimes they must be persuaded.

5. Power, authority, and force appear in their most distilled form in the state. In the nation-state, political authority and sovereignty overlap with a cultural and geographic unit.

6. Functionalists stress the usefulness of such state roles as protection, enforcing norms, regulating conflict, dealing with other nations, and coordinating the actions of other groups. Conflict theorists, on the other hand, suggest that the state arose as a tool to serve the interests of privileged classes. Each perspective captures part of the essence of the state.

7. Pluralists stress the existence of different interest groups that struggle to influence concrete political decisions. They emphasize shared values; political consensus; and the peaceful, evolutionary nature of political change.

8. Neo-Marxists analyze the role the state has played in the persistence of capitalism. They include instrumentalists, who view the state as an instrument of certain social classes, and structuralists, who stress the relative autonomy of the modern state.

9. Business influences politics through contributions, organizational strength, ready access

to government leaders, and the molding of citizen attitudes. A select group of business leaders, usually those who serve on the boards of multiple corporations, help run the affairs of the United States and Britain. In addition, financial decisions set the stage on which policy-making bodies operate. Many of these decisions occur outside the political arena.

10. Terrorism is a strategy used by groups that totally reject the legal order of a society or by states resisting social change. It consists of attacking or torturing a few individuals in an effort to frighten many others and force them to do the terrorists' will.

11. Opposition of any kind is likely to occur in societies where there is a cultural explanation of suffering and oppression. The impulse to rebel is also stifled when the whole group is punished for one defiant individual, when communal ties are torn, when certain individuals are coopted by the authorities, and when groups are split into warring factions.

12. Opposition is more likely when social supports exist and when oppressors must come into direct physical contact with their victims.

13. Revolutions involve the rapid and dramatic overthrow of political institutions. They are often preceded by some improvements in social conditions that raise peoples' expectations and fuel their discontent with the existing situation. Revolution is more likely in societies with bitter class antagonisms. Intellectuals withdraw their support from the existing regime.

14. Constitutional democracies attempt to provide mechanisms for peaceful evolutionary change in the political order. These means include the existence of rival political parties, elections, other forms of political participation, and the operation of interest groups. All of these allow participation by some members of society in the political process, although it is sometimes questionable as to how open these avenues are to the general public.

15. There is growing evidence of a gender gap and a class bias in the electoral process.

## KEY TERMS

authority (p. 355)
gender gap (p. 373)
interest group (p. 364)
legitimate (p. 355)
lobbying (p. 377)
nation (p. 359)
nation-state (p. 359)
political order (p. 359)
political party (p. 372)
power (p. 355)
power elite (p. 365)
rebellion (p. 371)
revolution (p. 371)
rising expectations (p. 371)
sovereignty (p. 359)
state (p. 359)
state terrorism (p. 369)
terrorism (p. 368)

## SUGGESTED READINGS

Domhoff, G. William. 1978. *Who Really Rules? New Haven and Community Power Reexamined.* New Brunswick, NJ: Transaction Books. This important book challenges the conclusions of Robert A. Dahl in his book *Who Governs?* by reexamining the data used by Dahl to conclude that key political decisions result from competition among a number of competing groups in a pluralistic society.

Gans, Herbert J. 1988. *Middle American Individualism: The Future of Liberal Democracy.* New York: Free Press. Gans sees middle Americans as the nation's pink-, white-, and blue-collar workers of all ethnicities who live modestly in suburbs, small towns, or ethnic neighborhoods in big cities. Gans feels that political institutions must encourage their participation.

Kurtz, Lester R. 1988. *The Nuclear Cage: A Sociology of the Arms Race.* Englewood Cliffs, NJ: Prentice Hall. One of the only sociological efforts to understand the nuclear arms race and what might be done to avoid nuclear holocaust.

Lehman, Edward W. 1977. *Political Society: A Macro-sociology of Politics*. New York: Columbia University Press. Suggests that large-scale groups including political parties, business corporations, labor unions, ethnic and religious groups, and branches of the state are the crucial elements shaping our political life.

Mills, C. Wright. 1956. *The Power Elite*. New York: Oxford University Press. A classic argument about how the business, military, and political elites are connected at the top, in what Mills calls the "power elite."

Useem, Michael. 1984. *The Inner Circle: Large Corporations and the Rise of Business Political Activity in the U.S. and U.K.* New York: Oxford University Press. A thorough, careful analysis of business leaders in England and the United States and their growing, classwide role in national political affairs. Winner of the 1985 C. Wright Mills award.

# *Education*

*Ollie Taylor is 11 years old. He lives with his family in Boston. They are very poor even though his father works almost 50 hours a week. For this boy failure is an inevitability. Almost every action he takes ends in convincing him that he is, in his own words, worthless. And from speaking with him for three years, I know that feeling can be traced directly to his school, not to his family, from whom he receives encouragement, love, and respect.*

*"The only thing that matters in my life is school and there they think I'm dumb and always will be. I'm starting to think they're right. . . . Every word those teachers tell me, even the ones I like most, I can hear in their voice that what they're really saying is, 'All right you dumb kids. I'll make it as easy as I can, and if you don't get it then, then you'll never get it. Ever.' That's what I hear every day, man. From every one of them. Even the other kids talk that way to me too."*

*"You mean the kids in the upper tracks?" I asked, barely able to hold back my feelings of outrage.*

*"Upper tracks? Man, when do you think I see those kids? I never see them. Why should I? Some of them don't even go to class in the same building with me. If I ever walked into one of their rooms they'd throw me out before the teacher even came in. They'd say I'd only be holding them back from their learning." [Cottle, 1974, pp. 23–24]*

---

Every September, more than 5 million American children enter school for the first time, joining some 58 million more who are returning (U.S. Bureau of the Census, 1989a, p. 124). While all of them may not have as dramatic an encounter with schools as Ollie Taylor did, almost no one in the United States grows up without going to school.

In the United States the number and proportion of children attending school has increased dramatically. As Figure 15.1 shows, the percentage of young people (aged 14 to 17) attending high school leapt from 2 percent in 1870 to 95 percent in 1986. College attendance has increased almost as strikingly, from 2 percent in 1870 to 39 percent in 1986. More money is spent on education than on any other activity in the United States except health care, with the amount rising faster than the number of students in school. In 1988 the United States spent $308 billion (or about 7 percent of the gross national product) on all levels of public and private education. Clearly, Americans value education.

**Education** can be defined as the process, in school or beyond, of transmitting a society's knowledge, skills, values, and behaviors. Every society seeks to educate its young members, to prepare them for adult roles. Formal education is one way many societies prepare newcomers for membership, so education is one form of socialization. In small tribal societies, fathers taught sons how to fish or hunt; mothers taught daughters how to farm or make pottery. More specialized occupations, like medicine or black-smithing, were learned from a parent or another member of the tribe. As tribal life became more complex, and especially with the growth of written language, communities began to appoint someone to teach reading and writing to a number of village children at the same time. Often such early formal education was started and supervised by religious leaders who wanted children to be able to read sacred writings. Thus began the first schools.

Especially in recent times, Americans have stressed formal education, called **schooling** by sociologists. In colonial American society, schooling was not compulsory. After 1875, states such as Massachusetts and Connecticut began to require primary education for everyone, in response to growing numbers of immigrants and a more mobile labor force. From 1918 to 1940, secondary education expanded and the compulsory school-leaving age was raised to the teens in most states.

In the last 30 years, higher education has grown enormously. Consider the case of Charles Smith. When he graduated from high school in 1960, only about 24 percent of his age group went to college. Today more than 34 percent of high school graduates enroll in college. Most people have more years of schooling than they did in Charles Smith's time, and more and more employers require at least some college education as a condition for employment. As a result, what happens in school takes on profound importance for a student's future, much more so than in Charlie's day. Today students not only receive an education but are also labeled and slotted within the educational system in a way that affects their future. For these reasons, the relation between education and society, the effects of schooling, what happens inside schools, and the part schools play in

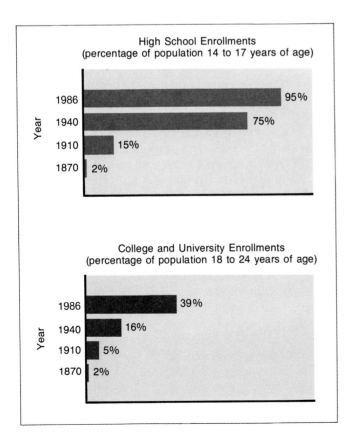

**Figure 15.1   Changes in High School and College Attendance, 1870–1986.**

Between 1870 and 1986, the proportion of the U.S. population in high school and college increased substantially, with more than nine out of ten young people being in high school and two out of five young adults attending college.

*Source:* Dearman and Plisko, 1979, p. 61; Trow, 1966; U.S. Bureau of the Census, 1989a, pp. 27, 128, *U.S. Department of Commerce News,* 1986, p. 1.

reducing or enhancing inequalities have important consequences for all of us. We consider each of these issues in turn.

# THE RELATION BETWEEN SCHOOLS AND SOCIETY

## The Functions of Education

Why do societies support schools? Sociologists have identified a number of school functions: (1) cultural transmission and socialization of the young; (2) selection for adult positions; and (3) support for the discovery of new knowledge, especially in higher education. Some people suggest additional latent functions of education, which will not be discussed here, such as keeping young people off the streets, providing an appropriate "marriage market" for mate selection, and serving as an agent of social reform (Goslin, 1965). Functionalist and conflict sociologists differ in the way they view these activities.

### Cultural Transmission and Socialization

Education is important for passing on the social and cultural heritage of one generation to the next. The knowledge, values, beliefs, and norms that adult members of society think young members should learn are transmitted partly through education. Schools try to per-

*In every society schools seek to transmit culture and to socialize the young for their adult roles. In this Chinese nursery, children are learning songs of their culture as well as how to behave in a group situation.*

form this task by providing experiences that instill knowledge (of history, say), skills (such as reading), attitudes (school loyalty, for example), and values (like punctuality) in their students—in other words, through *socialization*. Functionalists stress that the knowledge and skills students acquire in this process are central for obtaining and performing adult occupational roles. Functionalists tend to assume, however, that education provides the same benefits and opportunities for everyone in society. Conflict sociologists suggest that certain groups benefit more than others, partly because different social classes, races, and sexes receive different socialization in schools. They also suggest that mental skills are not so important for occupational attainment and income as functionalists claim they are.

Functionalists view education as a means of integrating society through common cultural and political socialization—for example, many children learn the pledge of allegiance in elementary school. Conflict sociologists emphasize that education is a resource used by groups competing for domination, legitimacy, power, income, or status within a society. Educational degrees may be used to exclude people from certain jobs, even when the content of the required education is unrelated to the job.

### Selection and Allocation to Adult Positions

Complex societies that do not pass on adult positions by simple inheritance need a system for assigning people to various positions. Traditionally (and frequently still today), family background, race, religion, birth order, and sex determine the position an individual holds in society. In industrial societies, schools have the power to place individuals in the running for specific life positions. Schools are granted that power by state legislatures and government departments of education, which grant colleges and universities the right to award certain types of degrees. These degrees, in turn, make people eligible to be considered for certain jobs and occupations. Meyer (1977) sees schools as obtaining special **charters** to "define people as graduates and as therefore possessing distinctive rights and capacities in society." Schools therefore affect life chances through the degrees they can award.

*State governments grant certain colleges and universities the right to confer different types of degrees. These degrees, in turn, enhance a person's life chances. Such consequences help to explain the happiness of this mother and son at his graduation.*

Both functionalist and conflict sociologists agree that schools are becoming increasingly important in determining an individual's life chances. But they differ in their assessment of whether this process is fair and desirable. Functionalists argue that the growing complexity of society and the jobs in it underscore the importance of individuals occupying positions for which they are "well suited." So, to functionalists, individual ability and achievement are the most important criteria for allocating people to various curricula and occupations. Functionalists and conflict sociologists both note that schools do not always ignore the class, sex, or race of students, however.

Conflict sociologists challenge the underlying assumptions of the functionalist view. They doubt that most jobs are becoming more complex and technical; instead, they see many jobs as getting simpler. They note that test scores and school grades are unrelated to job performance, suggesting that such measures are poor indicators of "merit." Conflict sociologists see schools as allocating individuals to highly unequal positions in society and legitimizing that allocation on the basis of test scores or grades that may not be valid indicators of merit (Bourdieu, 1971; Bowles and Gintis, 1976).

### Education as a Knowledge-Generating Institution

Schools also affect us through the knowledge they produce. In keeping with their view of a homogeneous society, functionalists tend to see the knowledge produced in educational institutions as equally valuable to all members of society. Conflict sociologists (such as Touraine, 1974) argue that the pursuit of knowledge in the United States has consistently been exploited by powerful elites in order to pursue the science and technology (for example, defense hardware) that benefits their position in society, often to the detriment of other groups. Touraine links this development to the student rebellions of the 1960s, when affluent students at some of the most selective universities in the nation began to challenge the role of the university in society.

The conflict perspective leads us to ask who supports the production of certain kinds of knowledge rather than others, and who benefits from it? For example, who supports research on missile systems, and who benefits from it? What are the consequences of some rather than other knowledge—for example, knowing how to treat cancer with chemicals once people have it, or knowing how to avoid getting cancer? We can ask such questions about the kinds of cancer research that are supported or the issues that get defined as "social problems."

## Educational Expansion

Why has education expanded so dramatically in the United States? Functionalists argue that education expanded in response to the increasing complexity of the division of labor and the need for a more highly educated work force. Marxians such as Bowles and Gintis (1976) suggest that education expanded because of the need for capitalist owners to maintain control over an unruly labor force.

However, as Hurn (1978) points out, a need, whether of society or of a group of capitalists, does not necessarily translate directly into social practice. He believes that education expanded in the United States because people believed education would be useful to them in their own lives and because groups were competing for status and prestige. Education was a useful symbolic resource in that competition. Hurn's position is supplemented by Collins's comparative study of the expansion of education. Collins (1977) suggests that there are three different demands for education—practical, status, and bureaucratic. These three have shaped the educational systems of various countries. The functionalist interpretation suggests that education in the United States grew to meet demands for practical or technical skills, but Collins says this was not the major reason people demanded more education. Much of modern education is not very practical, the number of years of school and grades earned are not related to work performance, and most people learn on the job much of what they need to know to do the job. Reading and writing are among the few practical skills that are taught in school. For these reasons, Collins argues that technical demands were not a major reason for expanding education.

Instead, Collins believes, American education expanded as a result of status-group competition. Education motivated by the desire for status-group membership is notable in ceremonies dramatizing the unity of the educated group and its status compared to that of outsiders. The content of such education reflects cultural ideals, usually impractical ones. Status-group membership is defined primarily by leisure and consumption activities, not by productive work. A common culture is central for the creation of a status-group community. Collins (1979) cites the great emphasis on fraternities and sororities in U.S. colleges as evidence for status-group concerns in education. Historically, Collins indicates, education has been used more often to define status groups than for other purposes.

Other factors in addition to status-group competition seem to have contributed to the expansion of education. These include immigration (Ralph and Rubinson, 1980), increasing technical efficiency in the economy (Rubinson and Ralph, 1984), changes in the occupational structure, and the presence or absence of available work opportunities for young adults (Walters, 1984).

Finally, education that develops in the process of bureaucratization reflects efforts of elites to promote impersonal methods of control. The content of education is irrelevant, Collins (1979) suggests, but the central feature is the structure of grades, ranks, degrees, and formal credentials.[1] This kind of education serves some of the control purposes suggested by Bowles and Gintis (1976). Mass education, at least, may be considered an effort to ensure labor and social discipline. But, says Collins, although modern education may discipline the lower social classes, the demand for labor discipline does not explain why some industrial societies have large mass education systems whereas others have small ones. The United States has a very large educational system, and the Soviet Union's and Japan's are quite large, but Britain, France, and Germany all have smaller systems of higher education. These are all highly industrialized societies. Why should some have massive educational systems whereas others do not?

Capitalists may have pushed for mass education in some societies, as the Marxian view suggests, but compulsory education developed in Prussia and Japan prior to industrialization. Collins (1977) suggests that the expansion of education arises from the existence of a bureaucratic state. The state imposes compulsory education on groups considered threats to state control. Those economic classes, sometimes including capitalists, may influence who the state defines as needing control. So, Collins (1977) concludes, mass compulsory education was created first to impose military and political discipline. Only later, perhaps, was it adopted to further industrial discipline.

In our system of higher education, elements of all three demands for education exist. We see some stress on practical skills, such as computer programming, laboratory, or business courses; we see strong residues of classical or humanistic education and ritualized ceremonies like fraternity hazing and graduation, which are the cultural aspects of attaining membership in certain status groups; and, finally, we see increasing specialization, stress on grades, ranks, degrees,

---

[1] The bureaucratic form of control that sometimes operates in education is illustrated by the World War II army experience of a German-speaking recruit. The Army gave a test to see who should become a translator. The German-speaking recruit was labeled "overqualified" based on his test performance.

and formal bureaucratically recognized credentials.

## EFFECTS OF SCHOOLING ON INDIVIDUALS

People hope for different gains from education. Some seek to develop their minds and to learn more about their world, their culture, and themselves. Others hope to get an interesting or prestigious job. Some want to make a lot of money. Probably all these motives operate in each person to varying degrees. Are people's hopes in what education can do for them justified? Does education, especially higher education, make a difference?

### Knowledge and Attitudes

Two major studies (Coleman et al., 1966; Jencks et al., 1972) concluded that schools have little effect on the knowledge students possess (as measured by scores on an achievement test) that can be statistically separated from the influence of the students' homes. In other words, students who score well on an academic achievement test appear to do so because they live in socially and economically advantaged families rather than because of the schools they attend. One result of this is that differences in academic achievement within the same school tend to be greater than the differences between schools.

Some people have interpreted these studies as saying that "schools make no difference in what students learn." One of the problems in proving that schools make a difference is finding children who do not go to school in a society where schooling is compulsory until the age of 14 or more. One relevant example occurred in Prince Edward County in Virginia in the 1960s. Rather than integrate the public schools, the community closed them. Private schools were opened for white children, but black children were unable to attend school for four years. As a result, they knew much less than children who began first grade on schedule (Green et al., 1964). The children who had never attended school did not know who George Washington, Thomas Jefferson, or Abraham Lincoln was, how many states

there are in the United States, how to do simple arithmetic, or how to read. This situation suggests that children learn a great deal from even the poorest schools in the United States.

One researcher (Wiley, 1976) suggests that the actual amount of time in school is related to the amount learned. The more hours of schooling there are, the more pupils learn (as measured by standardized tests). Another study (Heyns, 1978) found that sixth- and seventh-grade students who went to summer school, used the library, and read a lot in the summer made greater gains in knowledge than pupils who did not have such educational exposures during the summer. The impact of schooling was particularly dramatic for disadvantaged and minority students. These studies strongly suggest that schools do influence the knowledge and skills that pupils gain.

Education also influences the general knowledge, habits, and attitudes of those who obtain it. Education is thought to prepare people for a lifetime of learning, and more educated people do indeed make greater use of printed media (newspapers, books, magazines). Better-educated individuals have wider and deeper general knowledge than those who are less educated years after they finish school (Hyman and Wright, 1979; Hyman, Wright, and Reed, 1975). These differences persist even when many possible confounding factors—including sex, religion, social origins, and adult social position—are controlled. Education (especially college attendance) is related to adult interest in politics and public affairs, to keeping abreast of health news, and to taking adult education courses. Moreover, education makes people more skeptical of traditional institutions and is associated with more liberal political and social attitudes (Feldman and Newcomb, 1969; Ladd, 1978; Martire and Clark, 1982; Weil, 1985).

On the other hand, however, a comprehensive analysis of the intergroup beliefs, feelings, desire for personal contact, and policy orientations of men toward women, of whites toward blacks, and of the nonpoor toward the poor, failed to support the view that education is significantly related to more liberal attitudes (Jackman and Muha, 1984). Instead, they argue that educated people have simply developed more subtle forms of an ideology that supports their group's dominant position in society.

Although high schools make a substantial contribution to the creation of a better-informed citizenry, college graduates know even more, read more, and have different attitudes and behaviors than nongraduates. People with more education are also more likely to participate in the political process (Jennings, 1981). In general, education is related to a greater sense of well-being and higher self-esteem (Hyman, Wright, and Reed, 1975). Students' chances for self-directed educational activities increase their capacity for self-direction in adulthood. They also help their chances for getting better jobs (Miller, Kohn, and Schooler, 1986).

## Getting a Job

Education is also the single most important factor in getting a job. As we saw earlier, theorists differ on why this is true, but they agree that for most people, at least some higher education is necessary for a professional or managerial position. Most Americans now work in large organizations (whether business, government, schools, or hospitals), and the larger and more nationally oriented these organizations are, the more they require high levels of education for white-collar, managerial, or administrative jobs (Collins, 1974). About half of all college graduates hold professional or technical positions. They work as scientists, engineers, doctors, teachers, pilots, and accountants. About one in five college graduates have managerial or administrative jobs.

The percentage of recent college graduates entering professional and technical jobs is smaller than in the past, but the absolute number is larger. As Figure 13.4 shows, about 54 percent of the 8 million college graduates in 1986 entered professional and technical jobs, compared to 73 percent of the 4 million graduates who entered such jobs between 1962 and 1969. Thus today's college graduates are less likely to obtain a professional or technical job than were their counterparts in the 1960s. A larger proportion of college graduates is now entering occupations as managers and administrators, sales workers, clerical workers and operatives, service workers, and farm workers than was the case in the 1960s (Clogg and Shockey, 1984; Rumberger,

1981; Sargent, 1984). This situation occurred because the number of college graduates grew faster than the number of professional and technical jobs (Freeman, 1976). A college education is no longer sufficient to get a good job, but it is all the more necessary (Smith, 1986).

## Job Performance

Although most social scientists concur that education is necessary to get many jobs, there is less agreement on whether it helps a person do that job well. No one denies that most jobs today require people to be able to read, write, and do simple arithmetic. At issue is the assumption that more education produces skills that are required to perform increasingly technical and complex jobs, such as those of nurses, air traffic controllers, or police officers. Research suggests that education is not related to job performance (Berg, 1970; Collins, 1974; Folger and Nam, 1967). Berg (1970), for example, studied factory workers, maintenance workers, department store clerks, technicians, secretaries, bank tellers, engineers, industrial research scientists, military personnel, and federal civil service employees and found that the more highly educated employees performed their jobs no better than less educated ones. Despite this evidence, schools are increasingly becoming the "gatekeepers" of adult positions. Whereas once people could go out and get a job "on their own," they now need a credential awarded by a school even to be considered (Faia, 1981). An educational **credential** is a degree or certificate used to determine a person's eligibility for a position. This gives the schools a much more powerful role in society.

## Education and Income

Do educated people earn more than less educated ones? Broadly speaking, yes: the more education one has, the higher one's total lifetime earnings will be. The association between education and income needs further examination, however. There is a wide range of incomes for people at each level of education. Many earn less than the average and some earn more. Social factors other than education, notably race and sex, affect income. Figure 15.2 shows the in-

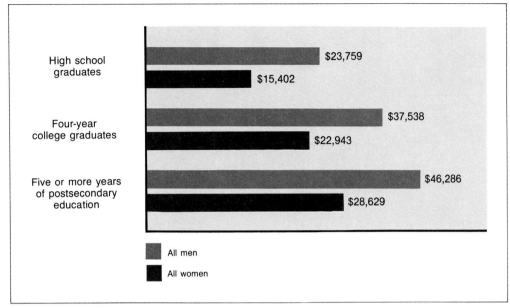

**Figure 15.2   Median Income of Men and Women 18 Years Old and Over, Working Full Time and Year Round in 1986.**

The median income in 1986 of full-time men and women workers was related to their educational attainment, but men high school graduates still earned more than women college graduates.

*Source:* U.S. Bureau of the Census, 1989a, p. 450.

come of men and women with different amounts of education who work full time. The returns on education for women are much lower than the returns for men. Females earn less than males at every level of education; indeed, on the average, female college graduates earn less than male high school graduates. The disparity is due partly to occupational segregation by sex and to interruptions in employment, but pay discrimination appears to play a role as well.

Young black males who are highly educated may earn as much as or more than their white male counterparts, according to some research (Freeman, 1977; Smith and Welch, 1978). Whether they continue to hold their own throughout their careers remains to be seen.

Other factors—such as type of employer, region, age, union membership, and social class background—also affect how much one earns. In one analysis, Mincer (1974) concluded that level of education explained only about one-third of the variation in the earnings of white nonfarm males. Even for this group, for whom education has the greatest association with in-

come, two-thirds of the variation in earnings was due to other factors.

The economic benefits of college have been hotly debated in recent years. Some social scientists (Freeman, 1976) argue that the cost of college plus the income lost while studying will never be earned back by graduates. Others (Witmer, 1976) counter that college definitely is worth what it costs. In 1986, the relative earnings of college graduates were at a 25-year high. Most agree that the economic payoffs of college are keyed to the economy, with higher gains coming in good years and lower ones during recessions.

## Education and Mobility

The relationship between education, jobs, and income varies by social class. Among the upper class (including owners of productive resources, high-level managers, and professionals), social origin is more important than education for achieving high position (as well as for inheriting

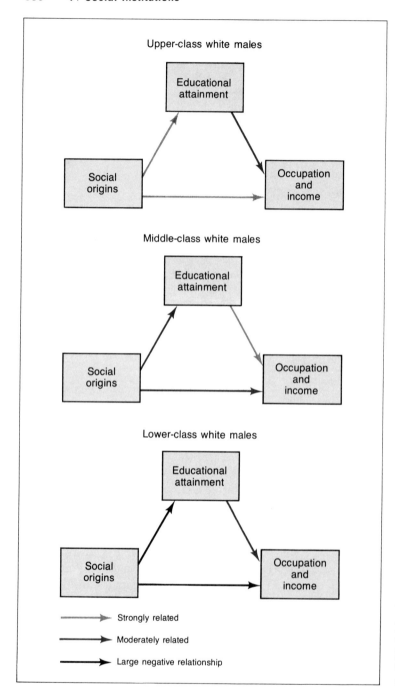

**Figure 15.3 Schematic Portrayal of the Relationships Between Social Origins, Education, and Adult Occupation and Income.**

For upper-class white males, social background is strongly related to the education they obtain. Their occupations and income depend to some degree upon their education but are also influenced by their social connections and wealth. For middle-class white males, social origins are related to the education they obtain, and educational background explains more of the variation in their occupations and incomes than does social background. Lower-class white males attain less education, in general, than males of the middle or upper class. Even when they do obtain more education, however, they are less likely than their middle- and upper-class contemporaries to enter high-status and high-income occupations.

wealth and gaining access to power). Class plays a large part in protecting the upper class from downward mobility and blocking the lower class from upward mobility (Figure 15.3). Education is used by the upper class to avoid downward mobility. Every effort is made to ensure high academic achievement and many years of school attendance. One way the upper class often does this is by sending its children to elite private schools (Cookson and Persell, 1985a).

Among the white middle class (which includes professionals, managers, supervisors, and some highly skilled manual workers), the education of children is related to the social positions they achieve. That is, the more education they get, the more likely they are to achieve higher status and somewhat higher-paying jobs within the middle class (Bielby, 1981; Blau and Duncan, 1967; Jencks et al., 1972). They have limited chances of gaining upper-class positions, however. Thus, for white middle-class males, there is some evidence that education is related to better jobs and higher incomes. Among the lower class (including semiskilled and unskilled manual workers and the perennially unemployed), even a college education offers poor odds for achieving a prestigious occupation (Boudon, 1973; Tinto, 1978).

Sociologists suggest at least three models that show the relationship between education and social mobility in industrial societies. The **sponsored mobility** pattern, Turner (1960) says, occurs in Great Britain. There, children are selected at an early age for academic and university education, and few get chosen. (This may be even more true of Germany today, because Great Britain has abandoned the tests given to 11-year-olds that determined their futures.) Children are selected early for elite status or are fated for a life of nonelite status. Turner contrasts this situation with that in the United States, where he sees a pattern of **contest mobility.** Here, selection is delayed and students go to school together for a long period of time. They are urged to compete with one another all along the way, in the hope that someday they may achieve a high position. A third model, presented by Rosenbaum (1976), identifies a process of **tournament selection** operating in American high schools. As in a sports playoff, you play a round and winners have the right to go on to the next round. If you lose, you are out of the running. Rosenbaum's view is based on actual practice in American society. In the tournament there is a continual process of selection, but selection works in only one direction—out. You can be eliminated, but winning one round does not make you a permanent winner.

Further research confirms that early academic success does not guarantee later success and that early academic failure strongly predicts later failure. It is also possible, however, for some people who are unsuccessful at one point to reenter the academic game at a later time (Temple and Polk, 1986).

Rosenbaum accurately describes the selection process in American society today. Competitors may be compared with the players on major league baseball teams. They are preoccupied with their standings in the league, so much so that they may mistakenly think that theirs is the "only game in town." However, perhaps unknown to them, there are sand-lot players (the lower class), most of whom will never be allowed into league competition. Only one or two of their members may make it into the major leagues. Behind the scenes are the upper-class individuals who own the teams but who do not compete themselves. Educational credentials may be likened to an invitation to try out for the teams in the league. Most lower-class members will not get those invitations. Most middle-class members will.

Within this model, it is possible for some individuals to experience occupational mobility through education, although the individual does not move upward in class. For example, the son of a pharmacist may become a dentist, thus achieving occupational mobility, but both positions are "middle-class." Although individuals may move slightly up or down on the hierarchy of occupational prestige, the underlying class structure of society has not changed.[2] This helps to explain why the expansion of educational opportunity has not noticeably reduced social inequality. Social inequality is based on occupational prestige, life-style, income, and wealth ownership, and the range of inequality in society is relatively unchanged by examples of individual mobility.

Functional and conflict sociologists agree that schools have powerful socialization and certification effects on individuals. They differ with respect to whether education promotes social opportunity via "merit" or serves to reproduce and legitimate existing inequalities in society. Part of their difference stems from functional sociologists' stress on individual mobility within the existing class structure. Conflict sociologists note that the relative positions of groups have not changed and urge the reduction of social and economic inequality within society. Both

[2] Recall from Chapter 9 that "class" refers to position in the system of production or to the control some positions exercise over others in the production process. "Occupation" refers to the technical division of labor in a society, and "occupational prestige" refers to the social respect given to various positions in society. Questions of occupation and occupational prestige do not tap the issues of wealth, ownership, and control.

views raise questions about school organization and processes and their consequences.

## INSIDE THE SCHOOLS

In the 1950s the United States was surprised by the launching of the world's first space satellite by the Soviet Union. The fact that we had been "beaten" by the Soviet Union led to great agitation and to the conclusion that we had somehow fallen behind in the development of science and technology. A considerable commotion occurred in education. Leaders such as James Conant (1959), a former president of Harvard University, began to focus on what happens inside schools. Sociologists have also been interested in the organizational aspects of schools. Some features—like curriculum, teacher activities, teacher expectations, and student peer groups—may influence what individuals learn in school and how well they do. Other organizational features—including school size, governance, bureaucracy, and classroom organization—have been found to affect how children feel about their schools, whether or not they feel alienated, and whether or not they drop out or become violent. Pupil learning, feelings, and behaviors may influence the effects of schooling on individuals and may be related to social inequalities if lower-class or minority children are more likely to attend bureaucratic or unresponsive schools or to have teachers who hold lower expectations for them. For these reasons, what occurs in schools is important to understand, both for the light it sheds on a major social institution and for its implications for the larger society.

### Curriculum

Did you ever wonder why you study what you do in school? At one time everyone who went to school studied the same subjects. Beginning in the nineteenth century and more so in the 1920s, students began taking different courses. Today in public secondary schools in the United States about 36 percent of students take what is called an "academic" curriculum (college pre-

paratory English, history, science, math, and foreign language); 20 percent take a vocational program (such as printing or auto mechanics); and 43 percent follow a general curriculum (with English, accounting, and clerical courses) (Fiske, 1983, p. C8). In private and parochial schools nearly everyone pursues an academic curriculum (Coleman et al., 1982).

One of the curricular changes the Conant Report (1959) recommended was that students take more math, physics, and chemistry. This report is a dramatic illustration of how events outside the schools may influence what happens inside them. Once in schools that offer particular choices of curriculum, students may study certain subjects because they find them socially prestigious (the classics) or because the next level of education requires them for admission (math) or because they believe they may be useful in the future (computer programming). There are patterned variations in who studies what, according to race, sex, and social class. Middle- and upper-class white pupils are more likely than lower-class and minority students to take an academic program. Females are less likely than males to study science and math and more likely to study language and literature. These curricular choices may help to reproduce social inequalities, since high school curriculum is the single biggest determinant of college attendance (Jaffe and Adams, 1970; Lee and Bryk, 1988) and influences choice of college major. College curriculum increasingly determines what graduate and professional education one may pursue, and hence to a growing degree what occupations are open to individuals.

### Teacher Activities

Teachers implement curriculums. Although the formal mandate of teachers is to teach, sociologists have observed that they spend a great deal of time doing other things. Classrooms are crowded places, and a class is a collection of individuals who vary in background, interests, and concentration spans. There are 20 to 40 children in most elementary school classrooms, and only one or at most two teachers. Jackson (1968) found teachers had as many as a thousand interpersonal contacts each day with children in their

*Teachers spend a great deal of their day interacting with their students. One study found that teachers had as many as a thousand interpersonal contacts with children each day.*

classrooms. Because of the large number of children, teachers often function as official time-keepers, supply sergeants, traffic cops, and judges. One result is that students spend a lot of time waiting, denying their desires, being interrupted in what they are doing, and being distracted by other people (Jackson, 1968). These features of school life may resemble the adult world, but they may also make learning difficult for many children.

Teachers function as employees in a bureaucratic organization even as they attempt to nurture young minds. Teachers are organizational spokespersons, required to take attendance, read daily announcements, collect lunch money, and administer various tests. They serve as organizational enforcers, disciplinarians, and protectors of public morality. In many schools, children are chastised for swearing or for wearing only their undershirts. In their role as evaluators, teachers continually assess the performance, character, and conformity of students (Schlechty, 1976).

## Teacher Expectations

Teachers may lose sight of the fact that they sometimes hold unequal expectations for children. Yet one of the most dramatic ways teachers can affect students is through their own expectations of them. Many social scientists have examined whether the expectations teachers hold for children influence what they learn in school. Rosenthal and Jacobson (1968) were among the first to do so. They told teachers in an elementary school in California that certain children in their class were likely to have a mental "growth spurt" that year. Actually, the children had been given a type of intelligence test that could reveal nothing about future mental growth. The names given to the teachers had been selected randomly. At the end of the year the researchers returned to the school and gave another test to see which children had improved. All the children in the school improved somewhat, but those labeled "spurters" made greater gains than the "nonspurters," especially in the first and second grades.

The effect of the labels that had randomly been assigned is an example of the self-fulfilling prophecy. The **self-fulfilling prophecy** is a belief or prediction about a person or situation that influences that person or situation in such a way that the belief or prediction comes true. In this case, if teachers expect children to make gains and treat them accordingly, they may be more likely to make such gains, thus confirming the prophecy.

This example of "mind over matter" does not operate in all realms, but there is a growing body of data since the Rosenthal and Jacobson study that suggests how the process operates in classrooms. Although it is probably subconscious, teachers call more often on students for whom they hold high expectations. They talk to them more and tend to show more praise and acceptance of them and their ideas. Teachers may make more eye contact and show greater warmth and friendliness toward favored students. Students or classes highly esteemed by the teacher may be given more opportunities to respond, thus gaining personal confidence and reinforcing the teacher's already high expectations. Often teachers actually teach more to pupils or classes for whom they have higher expectations, and they may teach them different material as well. Not surprisingly, when teachers taught more and praised students more, the students learned more. Students also felt better about themselves and about school (Persell, 1977). Teacher expectations can be a positive or a negative force in a student's academic career, depending on what expectations teachers hold.

Teachers tend to hold lower expectations for students of ethnic minorities and lower social classes more often than the students' test scores warrant. In addition, young, minority, and lower-class students often appear more susceptible to a teacher's influence. It is possible that teachers' expectations for minority and lower-class pupils may account in part for their lower school achievement.

Some teachers hold lower expectations for the reading progress of boys, especially in the first grade (Palardy, 1969). Boys learned to read more slowly when they had teachers who expected exactly that to happen, but not when they had teachers who believed that boys and girls are equally likely to learn to read. Other research suggests that teachers generally have higher expectations for girls than for boys (Clifton et al., 1986; Dusek and Joseph, 1983). Although we do not know how widespread different expectations by sex are, we do know that all through elementary school more boys have learning "problems" than girls.

The expectations of teachers we have been discussing are not due to personality flaws or weak character; teachers simply reflect the prevailing conditions and ideas of a society. Society often undervalues minorities or places caste barriers in their path, and underrates lower-class individuals. The lower expectations for boys may be rooted in educational literature that describes their growth cycle as somewhat behind that of girls. Educational practices may help to create and exaggerate differences between children in a teacher's mind. Finally, teachers may form expectations based on who a student's friends are.

## Student Peer Groups

The values and behaviors of the student's peer group may be more important for explaining adolescent behavior than are the values of the student's school or parents, suggests Coleman (1961) in his book *The Adolescent Society*. He argues that adolescents are segregated from adult society, leading to the development of a youth subculture distinct from and opposed to the culture of the adult world. Popularity

among peers depends more on athletic prowess among boys and looks or personality among girls than on academic performance. Hence the student subculture may be at odds with what teachers and schools are trying to do.

Other research supports Coleman's view that there is a somewhat distinct youth culture in the United States but questions how opposed that culture is to adult society. Riley (1961), for example, found that students feel pulled between parental demands for academic success and peer pressures for engaging in social life. Most students combine elements of both into their self-images; they tend to see themselves as successful students who are not "nerds," who are friendly and popular, but who are also realistic about the relationship between schoolwork and their adult futures.

Some peer groups provide social support for delinquency or violence. Stinchcombe (1964) learned that students who joined a rebellious subculture were those inclined to be most pessimistic about their futures and the part school could play in brightening those futures. Whatever their social origins, students in vocational courses and those headed toward low-status jobs were most likely to join a rebellious subculture.

Both visions of their adult futures and social origin seem to shape college student subcultures. Katz (1968) noted that a student might "try out" more than one subculture. Generally college students from working-class back-

*As children grow older, their peer groups may be more important influences on them than either their parents or schools. Schools seldom take this into account in their social organization.*

grounds are more likely to form subcultures valuing vocational goals, whereas middle-class students tend to enter groups stressing fun or favoring scholastic achievement, report Clark and Trow (1966). Another subculture observed was a nonconformist one.

A study of Stanford University students found four major types of students: careerists, intellectuals, strivers, and the unconnected (Katchadourian and Boli, 1986). *Careerists* were from different ethnic backgrounds but mainly from upper-middle and middle-class homes. They felt pressures to be successful in careers, earned few academic honors, tended to lose confidence during college, and felt only average satisfaction with their college experience.

*Intellectuals* were likely to come from upper-class families and were seldom ethnic minorities. Many of their fathers held doctorates, and were professors, doctors, or corporate executives. They found it hard to focus on a career, often majored in the humanities, were involved in political and volunteer extracurricular activities, and earned many academic honors. They left college with self-confidence and felt very satisfied with their college experience.

*Strivers* were most likely to be members of minority groups and from families of modest social and economic status. They often earned relatively low grades; leaned toward careers in business, law, and engineering; and left with strongly positive feelings about college.

The *unconnected* were equally likely to be men or women, were from all ethnic groups, and were likely to be of quite high or quite low social and economic status rather than middle-class. They tended to major in the humanities or sciences and avoided extracurricular activities. As a group they were the least satisfied with their college experience. It remains to be discovered whether or not these four types appear on other college campuses as well.

## Bureaucracy in Schools

If you attend a school of more than 500 students, you have probably encountered its bureaucratic authority system (see Chapter 6 for more discussion of bureaucracy). Bureaucracy is a type of organization with a hierarchy of offices, standardized rules and regulations to govern the conduct of affairs, and numerous records. Most public schools and universities rely on this type of organizational authority.

Advocates of bureaucracy and largeness cite several advantages. First, larger organizations with correspondingly higher budgets can provide certain facilities and programs—for example, an Olympic-size swimming pool or classes in Chinese—that would be too costly for small schools with few students. Second, teachers in one study reported a greater sense of power in schools that were more rather than less bureaucratic (Moeller and Charters, 1970). The bureaucratic schools gave teachers a sense that policies were directed and consistent rather than capricious and varied. Finally, some students say they like the feeling of anonymity they get in a large place. As long as they do what they have to do, no one bothers them. In short, some teachers and administrators find that hierarchy and standardized rules help them to run a school well. This situation may not bother some students, although other students complain that large bureaucratic schools are impersonal and alienating, and some research bears this out (Anderson, 1973).

In the public sector, smaller schools are disappearing at all levels of education. Only by sending children to private schools can parents obtain a small, intimate environment. Of course, such a course of action is generally available only to parents with the ability to pay the costs of private education.

## Student Alienation and Violence

As schools have grown in size and in degree of bureaucratization, there has also been an increase in the number of violent incidents in schools. Such incidents have escalated sharply in the last few years. Students attack not only each other in increasing numbers but there has also been a dramatic increase in the number of serious assaults on teachers, including rapes, beatings, and even murder. The American Federation of Teachers attributes this increase to the problems underpaid teachers face in overcrowded classrooms, where they cannot keep order. A hundred years ago, however, miserably paid teachers taught much larger classes of lower-class and immigrant minority pupils and maintained a high degree of order. So it seems that the decline in order in today's schools reflects a deeper problem. Students today are increasingly unwilling to accept the authority of teachers and administrators, suggests Katz (1977).

The growth of violence may reflect a fundamental challenge to the legitimacy of the school as a social institution. There are other indicators of this crisis of legitimacy as well. Parents and citizens are voting down school bond issues and cutting taxes; parents are challenging the school's definition of failure as residing in the child and holding the school accountable when it fails to teach a child to read. Absenteeism and truancy are increasing. Although largeness and bureaucracy have not been proved to cause increased violence in the schools, the two trends have developed together, suggesting the possibility that they are related.

## EDUCATION AND INEQUALITY

### Differences by Ethnicity and Class

Many individual lower-class and minority children do as well as or better than upper- and middle-class white children in school. But when groups are compared, socially disadvantaged children tend to get lower test scores and poorer grades and to drop out sooner. Why is social background so strongly related to school achievement? Many explanations have been offered: genetic deficits, cultural gaps, inadequate schools, tracking, segregation, and societal opportunities.

#### *Genetic Deficits*
Academic achievement is influenced by academic ability and prior performance (Hauser and Featherman, 1976; Jencks, Crouse, and Mueser, 1983). Some have searched for genetic explanations of academic ability. In 1969 the view that certain groups might have "inferior" genes was revived by Arthur Jensen, an educational psychologist at the University of California at Berkeley. He speculated that black children might be doing poorly in school because

of their genetic backgrounds. Much of the evidence he used for his hypothesis, however, was apparently faked by Sir Cyril Burt in England. Jensen and Burt aside, the "genetic deficit" argument falters because race is a social category in the United States, not a biological one (many whites and blacks are genetically mixed). Further, no one has ever identified the specific gene or genes that transmits "intelligence." So most social scientists reject an explanation of genetic deficit for racial differences in school achievement.

Sociologists also challenge the way intelligence itself is measured. It is often measured by an **IQ (intelligence quotient) test,** which is a standardized paper-and-pencil test of verbal and numerical knowledge and reasoning. IQ tests do not measure originality, interpersonal sensitivity, motivation, energy, or scientific and artistic talent. In fact, no one knows exactly what they do measure. Despite the claims of some test designers that they have developed culture-free tests, most sociologists claim that IQ tests are culture-bound—that is, they require knowledge and language skills possessed by a particular cultural group. In fact, a "culture-free" test is an impossibility, since every test requires background in some culture in order to take it. What thoughtful test designers mean by "culture-free" is a test composed of items that are no more likely to be missed by members of one group (say, blacks) than by members of another (whites).

Members of various groups are often at a disadvantage in taking IQ tests. (See, for example, the box containing the Barriology exam. How well did you do on it? Do you consider the test a fair indication of your innate ability? If a ghetto child does not know that a cup goes on a saucer rather than on a table, how does that lack of knowledge reflect innate ability?) Many IQ tests, then, measure culturally acquired knowledge and skills based on white, middle-class culture. IQ scores may be related to school success because scores are often used for tracking students (that is, grouping students by ability) into various programs, but they are not related to success in life. The way tests are used may generate self-fulfilling prophecies of academic success or failure and thus affect life chances.

# BARRIOLOGY EXAM   *By Barriologist Emeritus Antonio Gómez*

The cultural content of IQ tests may be evident in the Barriology exam based on knowledge of Mexican-American cultural mores.

1. Laurel and Hardy were popularly known in the barrio as _____.

2. Duck _____ describes a hairstyle worn by barrio dudes in the 50s.

3. According to baby care practices of barrio women, tickling a baby will produce what defect?

4. Barrio tradition among youth has often demanded that students

    A. excel in school
    B. do poorly in school
    C. keep the group norm
    D. none of the above is applicable

5. *Pedichi* and *moocher* have what in common?

6. Eating watermelon and drinking beer simultaneously is, according to barrio lore,

    A. sexually stimulating
    B. bad for one's stomach
    C. good for hangovers

    D. not an ethnic diet

7. What slang name refers to the older barrio dudes?

8. Large brown market bags have been used in barrio households for what purpose? How about 1/2 gallon milk cartons?

9. Complete the following children's chant:

> *De tin marin*
> *de do pinque*
> *cucara macara*

_____

10. Lowered, channeled, chopped, primed all refer to what barrio art form?

_____

## ANSWERS TO BARRIOLOGY EXAM

1. El gordo y el Flaco.
2. Ducktail.
3. A speech defect.
4. C. Keep the group norm.
5. Both describe one who asks for handouts.
6. B. Bad for one's stomach.
7. *Veteranos*—adults who have been through barrio warfare and usually no longer take part in gang hassles.
8. Trash bags and garbage containers.
9. *Tiere fue*—a chant used by children to select players for a game—similar to "one potato, two potato," etc.
10. A customized car.

## RATE YOURSELF ON THE CON SAFOS BARRIOLOGY QUOTIENT SCALE

*Barriology Examination Questions answered correctly:*

7 to 10   Chicano Barriologist, *o muy de aquellas.*

5 or 6   High Potential, *o ya casi*

2 to 4   *Vendido, o culturally deprived*

0 or 1   *Pendejo*

*Source:* Ludwig and Santibanez (Eds.), *The Chicanos*, Baltimore: Penguin, 1971, pp. 149–153.

## Cultural Gaps

Standing in apparent opposition to the "genetic deficit" explanation of unequal school achievement is the "cultural gap" view. It suggests that poor children do badly in schools because their lives are marked by emptiness at best or, at worst, by limitations in family structure, child-rearing patterns, values, attitudes, or language exposure, all of which impair intellectual development. But close studies of minority children find them to be "bathed in verbal stimulation," to be skilled users of their language (Labov, 1973), and to be marked by family strengths such as helpful extended-family ties (Hill, 1971). The family differences that do appear are rooted in the economic, political, and ethnic inequalities of the society, not in the failings of individuals. Moreover, existing differences have not been pinpointed as causes of school failure. So this view does not provide a convincing explanation of unequal school achievement. Indeed, where lower-class or minority children are taught by teachers who assume they can learn and who take responsibility for teaching them, they do learn, sometimes better than white middle-class children (Brookover and Schneider, 1975).

Cultural background is related to the grades high school students in the United States get, perhaps because it influences the way students interact with their teachers. The concept of **cultural capital** is defined as "symbolic wealth socially designated as worthy of being sought and possessed" (Bourdieu and Passeron, 1977).

DiMaggio (1982) used student self-reports of involvement in art, music, and literature as indicators of how much cultural capital they possessed. He thought that teachers would communicate more easily with students who participated in elite status cultures and would give them more attention and special assistance. As a result, he hypothesized that students with more cultural capital would receive higher grades in high school, which they did. This effect occurred even when family background and a student's measured academic ability were statistically controlled. The results were different for girls and boys, however. Cultural capital was most strongly related to getting higher grades among girls whose fathers were college graduates, and weaker effects occurred for girls whose fathers had less education. For boys the opposite was true. The impact of cultural capital on grades was greatest for sons of less-educated men and least for sons of college graduates (DiMaggio, 1982). Although the relationship between cultural capital and grades is complex, it does seem to exist.

### Societal Opportunities

Ogbu (1978) suggests that the generally lower academic achievement of minority children is due to the barriers they face in the larger society. He studied members of inferior castes in six societies around the world and found they all shared inferior education and a job ceiling based on caste rather than on training or ability. Children see the barriers to their full participation in adult society and become disillusioned with hard work and school success. Ogbu's work is especially interesting because it attributes lower school performance to caste status rather than to race. In only three of the six societies (the United States, Britain, and New Zealand) were the minority castes racially different. In the other three societies (Japan, Israel, and India) they belonged to the same race but were stigmatized as an inferior caste by geographic origin, ancestry, or other traits. In some cases persons facing caste barriers performed very well when they moved away from the society where they were stigmatized. This significant finding suggests that social rather than personal factors explain the poorer school performance of some groups relative to others.

### Inadequate Schools

American public schools reflect their geographic locations. In practice this would make no difference if all areas were similar, but anyone who has traveled from a downtown urban area to a suburban or rural area knows that such areas may differ immensely. Residential segregation based on income, occupation, and race abounds. Such segregation results in area schools that tend to be economically and ethnically homogeneous. As a result, Black and Hispanic youth had less access to educational resources, teachers, and counselors than did whites. This increased their educational deficits over time (Orfield and Paul, 1988).

In addition to geographic distinctions, American education is divided into public and private sectors. Although only about 10 percent of the population attends private elementary and secondary schools, that group differs dramatically from the other 90 percent of the population, and their schools differ also. More than 85 percent of private and Catholic school seniors are white, compared with 78 percent of public school seniors (Coleman, Hoffer, and Kilgore, 1982, p. 39). The average family income of private-school students is considerably higher than that of public-school families (Baird, 1977; Cookson and Persell, 1985b). Elite private schools spend about $20,000 per year on each child, compared to about $3,100 spent per child nationally in public schools. The schools also differ in goals, financial base, and size, with private schools more likely to be small and wealthy.

*Research comparing Catholic schools with public schools found that the former enroll more of their students in an academic curriculum and that more of their students graduate, with a larger percentage going on to college.*

Students in private schools, including Catholic schools, are more likely to attend college after graduation and to attend four-year and private colleges rather than two-year and public colleges. Catholic-school students are also less likely to drop out. A major national study found that 24 percent of public high school students dropped out compared to 12 percent of Catholic-school students (Coleman, Hoffer, and Kilgore, 1982). This is partly explained by differences in family background, academic ability, educational hopes, and curriculum of public- and private-school students. However, private-school students are 7.5 percent more likely to enter college than are public-school students, even when their background differences and curriculums are statistically controlled (Falsey and Heyns, 1984). Elite private-school graduates overwhelmingly attend prestigious private colleges (Cookson and Persell, 1985b, chap. 9) and are very likely to end up in high-level business, financial, professional, or cultural positions (Useem, 1984).

Students who start in four-year colleges are more likely to graduate than those who start in two-year colleges (Velez, 1985), suggesting another way that class-linked educational opportunities help the advantaged and hurt the disadvantaged (Hearn, 1984). Spatial divisions, then, are one way students are separated during schooling. However, even within the same school, there are administrative devices for dividing students. Sometimes student athletes are separated, for example, from other students. (For the impact of athletics on academic careers, see the box in Chapter 22.)

### Tracking

Further segregation by race and income (and sometimes sex) occurs within most schools through the practice of tracking. **Tracking** refers to the grouping of students by ability or curriculum, often both at the same time. Students may be assigned to the academic or the vocational curriculum based on academic abilities (Alexander and Cook, 1982; Lee and Bryk, 1988). Once in a particular curriculum, they may be tracked further by ability into several levels within the curriculum. Test scores are a primary basis for track placement in many schools; because test scores are highly correlated with race and social class, school classes based on such scores tend to be highly segregated by race and class (Alexander and McDill, 1976; Metz, 1978; Oakes, 1982, 1985; Vanfossen, Jones, and Spade, 1987). Hence, even within a mixed school, students may go to class only with students who are remarkably like themselves in important social ways. Tracking is particularly widespread in large urban school systems that are racially and economically diverse (Persell, 1977). Moreover, teachers compete for higher-status students in ways that shape and maintain the system of tracking (Finley, 1984).

As practiced today, tracking is widespread, particularly in large, diverse school systems and in schools serving primarily lower-class students (Findley and Bryan, 1970). It is less prevalent and less rigid when it occurs in upper-middle-class suburban and private schools and in parochial schools (Jones, Vanfossen, and Spade, 1985). The results of tracking are clear.

A study of ability grouping in 34 elementary school classes found that students in different groups learned different amounts. This was due to their unequal opportunities for learning and the differing instructional climates. "High-ability" groups spent more class time on actual teaching activities. Also, teachers used more interesting teaching methods and materials (Hallinan, 1987). In secondary schools, college-track students consistently received better teachers, class materials, laboratory facilities, field trips, and visitors than did their lower-track peers (Oakes, 1985; Goodlad, 1984). The different track experiences affect cognitive development (Oakes, 1985; Rosenbaum, 1979; Shavit and Featherman, 1988).

Tracking helps to legitimate structural inequalities in the larger society, argue Bowles and Gintis (1976), by teaching students to accept inequality and hierarchy in schools and society and to blame themselves if they fail. In a national study of 139 junior and senior high school English and math classes, Oakes (1982, 1985) found some evidence that supported Bowles and Gintis's hypothesis. Lower-track classes were more likely to be characterized by alienation, distance, and more authoritarian teachers than were high-track classes. Teachers in lower-track classes spent more time on discipline; students there felt teachers were more punitive and less concerned about them; and lower-track students more often felt their classmates were unfriendly than did students in higher-track classes (Oakes, 1982). Such a pattern of attitudes, Oakes concluded, tends to reinforce and legitimate inequality.

### Desegregation

In 1954 the Supreme Court ruled in the case of *Brown* v. *Board of Education* that "separate but equal" educational facilities for black and white children are unconstitutional. Since the decision, considerable attention has been devoted to the issue of desegregated education. In fact, the overwhelming majority (85 percent) of the American population believes black and white children should go to the same schools (Golladay and Noell, 1978).

What has become controversial in the past decade is the use of court-ordered busing to achieve racial balance in schools. The underlying concern of parents, children, and teachers is the way desegregation occurs. So it seems useful to consider what we know from social research about the conditions under which desegregation has been relatively successful.

The goals of desegregation include equal educational opportunity, equal achievement, reduced prejudice between members of different races, equal self-esteem, and increased respect among members of different races. Not all studies measure all these goals. Relatively successful desegregation (on one or more of these goals) has occurred in communities where parents, school leaders, and teachers have worked together to develop plans for desegregation, and where racial conflict has not occurred (St. John, 1975). Black students have made achievement gains in open-enrollment schools, which allow students to attend schools beyond their neighborhoods, and in central schools, where attendance zones have been broadened.

In desegregation, what happens after pupils get off the bus is particularly important. Schools that show significant gains from integration are those that have good multiracial instructional materials, an experienced staff that holds favorable racial attitudes, racially mixed classrooms, work and play groups, and clearly cooperative classroom situations. Desegregation is less suc-

cessful when parents and teachers are violently opposed to it.

The age of the children when desegregation begins seems to affect their achievement, according to Crain and Mahard (1978). Reviewing 10 studies of desegregation among first- and second-graders, they found 8 that showed black achievement gains and 2 that showed no effect. When desegregation began in the third and fourth grades, only 9 of 21 studies reported improved black achievement. The higher the grade is at which desegregation occurred, the lower is the chance that academic gains would result. Whites were unaffected by the grade at which integration occurred.

The first long-term study of the effects of school desegregation traced the educational, economic, and social development of 661 black first- and second-grade pupils who were in a desegregation experiment in Hartford, Connecticut, in 1966. Almost half (318) were randomly selected to attend largely white schools in the suburbs and the other 343 remained in predominantly black city schools. The young people were followed until 1981. All of the pupils were from a lower-income black community with a high crime rate and numerous abandoned buildings. Despite their similar backgrounds, however, those who attended racially mixed schools differed in seven major ways from those who did not attend these schools:

1. They were more likely to graduate from high school.
2. They were more likely to attend mainly white colleges and to complete more years of college.
3. They perceived less discrimination in college and in other areas of adult life in Hartford.
4. They were involved in fewer incidents with the police and got into fewer fights as adults.
5. They have closer and more frequent social contact with whites as adults, are more likely to live in desegregated neighborhoods, and have more friends in college.
6. They are more likely to work in occupations with smaller percentages of blacks, such as sales and professional-managerial jobs.
7. Women in the group were less likely to have

a child before they were 18 years old (Brad-dock et al., 1984).

The first six conclusions were more true of the men than of the women. Why the women did not get as much education as the men in the program is a problem that remains to be explained and remedied. Even so, the results suggest that black students who attended an integrated suburban school benefited greatly. Society also gained because such graduates pay higher taxes, have fewer involvements with the police, and have lower rates of teen pregnancy.

Although critics of desegregation have claimed that simply putting black and white children together does not produce social acceptance and equality, this study shows that desegregation can lead to such changes. Although the study did not discuss the effects of desegregation on white children, it may well be that they also feel more comfortable in an interracial environment as a result of attending a desegregated school. In short, in the middle of intense public debate about school desegregation, social researchers have begun to identify where desegregation is working more and less effectively and why.

## How Schools Affect Boys and Girls

Racial differences are not the only ones that affect education. From an early age, males and females are educated somewhat differently as well. Generally, girls begin school intellectually ahead of boys. Girls tend to speak, read, and count sooner, and in the early grades of school they are better in math. Somewhere in high school, girls' performance on ability tests begins to sag, and males show greater IQ gains from youth to adulthood (Maccoby, 1966). Even so, females earn higher grades in high school than males, but they are less likely to believe they can do college work (Cross, 1968). Even when women attend prestigious colleges and earn the same grades as men, they have lower self-esteem and lower aspirations than men (*New York Times,* December 10, 1978).

Why do educational declines occur among females? Clearly, schools alone do not depress the

aspirations of women. Parents, peers, the media, and general societal influences play a major part in shaping gender roles, as we saw in Chapter 11. And a number of school features may influence how girls feel about themselves and what they can do.

### Gender Composition of Faculty and Staff

Although many women enter education as a career, they are not equally represented at all levels. As Figure 15.4 illustrates, the majority of elementary school teachers are female; a slight majority of secondary teachers are male. School administrators are mainly male. Women who become administrators wait longer to move up than do men. School boards are also composed mainly of males. How might these figures affect schoolchildren? Two researchers, Frazier and Sadker (1973), suggest several ways:

*Whenever an issue is too big or troublesome for the teacher (usually female) to handle, the principal (usually male) is called upon to offer the final decision, to administer the ultimate punishment or reward. And children, so alert to body cues, so sensitive to messages transmitted through the silent language, must detect the teacher's change in demeanor, the slight shift in posture that transforms confidence into deference and respect. It would be hard to misinterpret the relationship. The teacher is the boss of the class; the principal is the boss of the teacher. And the principal is a man. In the child's mind associations form. When a woman functions professionally, she takes orders from a man, and the image of female inferiority and subservience begins to come across. [pp. 99–100]*

Hence the gender of individuals employed in the schools conveys a subtle but powerful message.

### Teachers as Gender-Role Socializers

Teachers may contribute to gender-role stereotypes in various ways. For example, teachers behave differently toward boys and girls. Boys tend to receive more attention (both good and bad) than girls (Cherry, 1975; Sears and Feldman, 1966; Serbin et al., 1973). Teachers may ask boys to carry bundles and girls to pour juice, thereby adding to gender-role typing in chil-

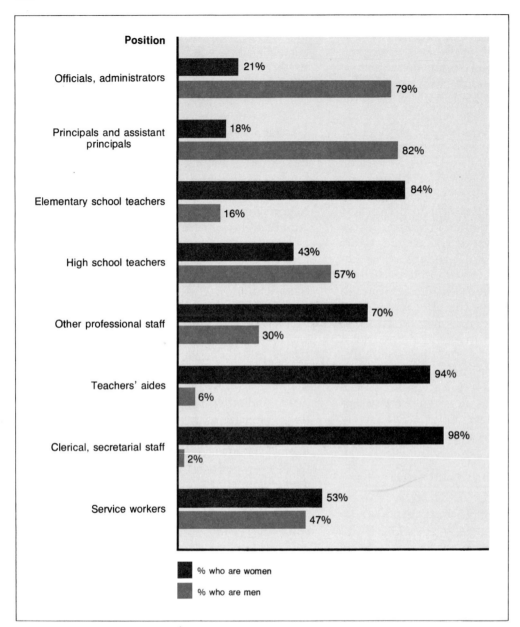

**Figure 15.4   Proportion of Elementary and Secondary School Staff Who Are Men and Women, 1980.**

Men are much more likely to be educational administrators and principals than are women and much less likely to be elementary school teachers. High school teachers are slightly more likely to be men. Almost all teacher aides and clerical staff in schools are women.

*Source:* U.S. Bureau of the Census, 1985a, p. 140.

dren's lives. Like teachers, guidance counselors sometimes reflect the gender-role biases of their society (Pietrofesa and Schlossberg, 1974). Adolescent girls may be advised to become legal secretaries instead of lawyers, nurses rather than doctors, laboratory technologists rather than engineers.

One reason for continued gender-role biases

may be that although sex bias in education has been discussed since the 1960s and Title IX of the Higher Education Amendments was passed in 1972, a content analysis of the 24 top-selling teacher education textbooks published between 1973 and 1978 did not reflect those concerns. Twenty-three of the books devoted less than 1 percent of their space to the issue of sexism or sex equity, and one-third of the books failed to mention the topic at all. Most of those failing to include it were texts on teaching mathematics and science, the areas in which girls have traditionally experienced difficulties (Sadker and Sadker, 1980).

Under the Reagan administration, the Justice Department took the position that prohibitions on sex discrimination need to exist only in those programs that receive federal funds directly. Before the *Grove City College* v. *Bell* decision, such prohibitions applied to an entire institution when it received federal funds. If this policy were applied extensively, most students would not be protected by antibias laws. The Reagan administration consistently tried to abolish the Women's Educational Equity Act (WEEA), the sex equity program in the Education Department, and Title IV which funded antidiscrimination programs through the 1964 Civil Rights Act, although Congress resisted those efforts (Lewis, 1984). Women educators have worked to resist such efforts, for example, by publishing the *Handbook for Achieving Sex Equity Through Education* (Klein, 1985).

### Gender and College Attendance

Women have begun attending all types of colleges in equal or higher proportions than men (Figure 15.5). However, women are less likely than men to attend four-year rather than two-year colleges and less likely to attend selective colleges (Persell, Catsambis, and Cookson, 1989). Employers may use these differences in college attendance patterns to hire women for different types of jobs, pay them less, or promote them more slowly.

Also, social background (such as race, mother's education, and parental aspirations for the student) still influence women's college attendance more than men's. For men, academic curriculum, academic ability, and grades are more important for college attendance and selective college attendance than they are for women

(Persell et al., 1989). Thus, gender differences exist in the types of college attended and in the influences on college attendance. Despite the seeming female advantage in Figure 15.5, gender inequalities in higher education persist.

### Schools as Arbitrators of Gender

Some sociologists are analyzing how the "school is actively engaged in constructing gender" (Kessler et al., 1985, p. 42). There isn't just one sex-role pattern that is imposed on boys and one on girls. One school, for example, had both a football hero version of masculinity and a brainier version of male accomplishment; another had girls who were aiming to become professionals as well as an older style of "socialite" girls. They suggest that the school is an arena in which new kinds of masculinity and femininity are being arbitrated. Knowledge and curriculum, as well as the kinds of gender behaviors that are allowed, encouraged, or discouraged, are related to the patterned power relations of gender in the larger society (Kessler et al., 1985). Although this research was done in Australia, it has great relevance for the United States, England, and numerous other societies.

Certain extracurricular activities may also influence the male and female adolescent cultures. Male athletes, for example, learn to compete and achieve. Female cheerleaders learn the importance of appearance and the management of emotions (Eder and Parker, 1987).

*Although women have recently begun attending all types of colleges in equal or greater proportions than men, women are less likely than men to attend four-year colleges and selective colleges.*

### *Teaching Materials as Gender-Role Socializers*

Teaching materials in American schools have portrayed gender roles in very limited and stereotypical ways. Children's elementary school readers surveyed in 1972 (134 books published by 14 major companies) revealed some startling trends. In these books, male characters greatly outnumbered female characters—by 5 to 2. Boys were creative, built things, and used their wits. Girls did very little and often appeared limp and dull. Clever boys appeared 131 times, clever girls only 33 times. Men lived exciting lives and did all kinds of work. Women mostly stayed home and were mothers *or* workers (but not both), and then usually only teachers, librarians, or nurses (Jacobs and Eaton, 1972). Not surprisingly, perhaps, several studies show that the self-esteem of girls drops the longer they are in school and as their vision of available options narrows (Minuchin, 1966).

The stories read in the early grades, the race and sex of major characters, what they do, how they live—all these aspects of school curriculum have come under increasing scrutiny as minority and feminist groups have underscored the importance of images and roles in school materials for the development of identities. There is some indication that sex-role stereotypes have declined recently in curricular material. But there are competing currents in our society. The moral majority, for example, favors traditional gender roles, whereas other groups favor more equal presentation of gender-role possibilities. So race, class, and gender—the major social cat-

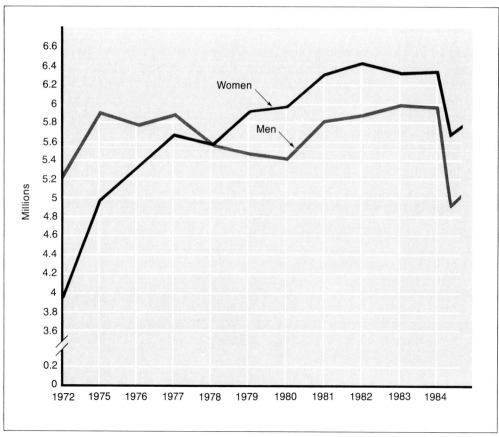

**Figure 15.5   U.S. College Enrollment by Sex, 1972–1986.**

In 1979 the number of women enrolled in college surpassed the number of men for the first time in U.S. history, and that trend has continued.

*Source:* U.S. Bureau of the Census, 1989a, p. 148.

egories of our society—seem to impinge on educational ideas and processes and to contribute to unequal school achievement.

## SUMMARY

1. Education is an organized way of passing a society's culture to a new generation. Schools have become increasingly important gatekeepers for jobs and social rewards.

2. Education affects learning, attitudes, getting a job, and earnings, but it seems to be somewhat more helpful for white middle-class males than it is for nonwhites, females, and members of the lower class.

3. Students study different subjects, even in high school, and such curricular placements determine college attendance, college majors, and eventually occupational options.

4. Teachers may have a thousand or more interactions with students each day and serve as organizational representatives as well as instructors. They may be unaware of the expectations they hold for different children, but these expectations affect how students learn and how they feel about school.

5. Peer groups gain importance in adolescence. They tend to value popularity somewhat more than achievement but may not be too far removed from adult values. Some peer groups may be rebellious or even violent.

6. The size of schools and school districts has increased greatly in the last 25 years, leading to greater bureaucracy and sometimes student alienation.

7. The roots of school violence go beyond the peer group and reflect a growing crisis in the legitimacy of the school's authority.

8. Differences in educational achievement are not adequately explained by genetic or cultural deficits. Instead, unequal societal opportunities, geographic and racial segregation, tracking, and

teacher expectations begin to explain unequal school achievement by race and class.

9. Gender-role socialization helps to explain why female educational achievement and aspirations begin to sag in high school. Women are still somewhat less likely than men to attend four-year colleges and selective colleges.

## KEY TERMS

charters (p. 384)
contest mobility (p. 391)
credential (p. 388)
cultural capital (p. 397)
education (p. 382)
IQ (intelligence quotient) test (p. 396)
schooling (p. 383)
self-fulfilling prophecy (p. 393)
sponsored mobility (p. 391)
tournament selection (p. 391)
tracking (p. 399)

## SUGGESTED READINGS

Collins, Randall. 1979. *The Credential Society*. New York: Academic Press. An historical sociological explanation for the expansion of educational opportunities and requirements in the United States that includes a close look at professional education in law, medicine, and engineering.

Cookson, Peter W., Jr., and Caroline Hodges Persell. 1985. *Preparing for Power: America's Elite Boarding Schools*. New York: Basic Books. A lively and comprehensive study of America's boarding schools that draws upon in-depth interviews with students, headmasters, teachers, and alumni to analyze the complex ways in which elite schools prepare students for success and power.

Kozol, Jonathan. 1985. *Illiterate America*. Garden City, NY: Anchor Press/Doubleday. An exploration of adult illiterates in the United States, who may comprise as much as one-third of the population. Also considers what might be done about the problem.

Persell, Caroline Hodges. 1977. *Education and Inequality: The Roots and Results of Stratification in America's Schools.* New York: Free Press. A synthesis of theory and research showing how educational structures such as neighborhood schools and tracking, concepts such as IQ testing, and processes such as teachers' expectations contribute to unequal educational outcomes.

Rist, Ray. 1970. "The self-fulfilling prophecy in ghetto education." *Harvard Educational Review* 40: 411–451. A moving account of how first-grade students are grouped and ranked in the early days of school according to their social backgrounds.

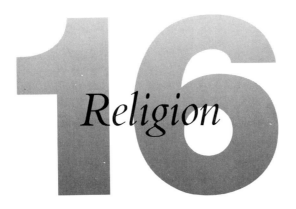

# 16
## *Religion*

*I was finding value in the wrong things. I used to get high on marijuana, acid and cocaine every week. . . . Now I am going in a definite direction instead of constantly changing.*

*I was drifting. I had no sense of purpose. The major difference in my life since joining the Church is that I have a clearer idea of what I want to accomplish for myself and others. [Bromley and Shupe, 1979, p. 189]*

These words of a young convert to the Unification Church (popularly known as the "Moonies") express something of the meaning religious commitment has in his life. **Religion** is a set of beliefs about ultimate meanings that often includes a belief in the existence of the supernatural. In this chapter we examine first the institution of religion in American society and some of its social consequences. With this background, we consider how sociologists view religion, religious organizations, and religious change, and how they analyze the place of religion in other societies around the world.

## RELIGION IN THE UNITED STATES

The United States is distinct from other societies because of its many different religious communities. The variety of these communities creates unique cultural groupings, social networks, and forms of social organization.

### Civil Religion

American life is notable for the way it interweaves religious and political symbols in what sociologist Robert Bellah (1967) calls a **civil religion.** We are one nation "under God," according to the pledge of allegiance. Presidents are sworn into office with their hands on the Bible. Printed on our currency are the words "In God We Trust." A major theme of public life is the vision of America as a redeemer nation and Americans as a chosen people. This vision is not rooted in any single denomination. Instead, it embraces the pluralism of American religious life. Although this tendency may seem to promote self-worship, it also operates to subject American behavior and values to moral scrutiny (Bellah, 1967).

Although the U.S. Constitution separates church and state and there is no official state religion, the political realm draws heavily on religious themes. A person who was openly irreligious would have little or no chance of being elected president, for example. Several presidents in recent years, as well as congressional leaders, have publicly proclaimed their participation in prayer groups in addition to their church attendance.

Despite the continued connection between political leadership and religious imagery, Bellah (1975) believes that in recent years American civil religion has become "an empty and broken shell," because individualism has taken over as the dominant American ethos. Individuals busily pursue private material goals. Their selfishness, suggests Bellah, may have destroyed the sense of covenant between God and a religious community. Bellah sees the present religious ferment as an effort to re-create a new moral community and replace the decaying civil religion.

In the recent book *Habits of the Heart,* Bellah and his associates (1985) voice the concern that our problems as a nation today are not just economic or political but moral problems that deal with the meaning of life. An exclusive concern for material accumulation will not build a meaningful common life, they argue. They continue:

*Perhaps the truth lies in what most of the world outside the modern West has always believed, namely that there are practices of life, good in themselves, that are inherently fulfilling. Perhaps work that is intrinsically rewarding is better for human beings than work that is only extrinsically rewarded. Perhaps enduring commitment to those we love and civic friendship toward our fellow citizens are preferable to restless competition and anxious self-defense. Perhaps common worship, in which we express our gratitude and wonder in the face of the mystery of being itself, is the most important thing of all. [Bellah et al., 1985, p. 295]*

In their view, a society without religious commitment may falter.

## Is Religion Declining?

Since 1965, membership in mainline Protestant churches declined slowly but steadily in the United States, leading some analysts to conclude that religion was on the wane (Ostling, 1989). But church membership is increasing in the more evangelical Christian denominations (*New York Times*, June 19, 1985, p. A20; Ost[ling], 1989). There is other evidence as well to suggest that religion is not dying. The percentage of Americans who believe that religion is "very important in their personal life" increased in 1980, after declining since 1952 (Gallup Organization, 1977). Hundreds of new religious sects and cults are forming in the United States (Stark and Bainbridge, 1985, p. 431). Finally, the majority of those who grew up in nonreligious homes now belong to a Christian denomination, often a traditional one (Stark and Bainbridge, 1985, chap. 1).

## Denominational Membership

In public opinion surveys over the last three decades in the United States, between 92 and 98 percent of the population indicated a preference for some religion. This finding has remained remarkably stable for more than thirty years. Only 9 percent of Americans indicate that they have no religious preference. The denomination mentioned most frequently after Roman Catholicism is Baptist, by about 21 percent of the population. Methodists are the third largest group (about 10 percent), followed by Presbyterians (5 percent), Lutherans (3 percent), United Church of Christ (3 percent), Episcopalians (3 percent), and all other Protestant denominations. About one-quarter of the U.S. population (or 49 million people in 1973) indicated that they were members of the Roman Catholic Church. About 6 million people in the population indicated that they were members of a Jewish congregation (Carroll et al., 1979; *Public Opinion,* 1979).

Roman Catholics are the easiest religious group to count, because their highly centralized organization keeps them from splintering into competing groups. Central registration also aids in keeping count. Catholics are found in most counties of the United States, but they tend to be concentrated in the Northeast (particularly in large cities), the Great Lakes states, the Louisiana delta country, and parts of the Southwest, including southern Texas.

Although most European settlers to North America came from societies where there was

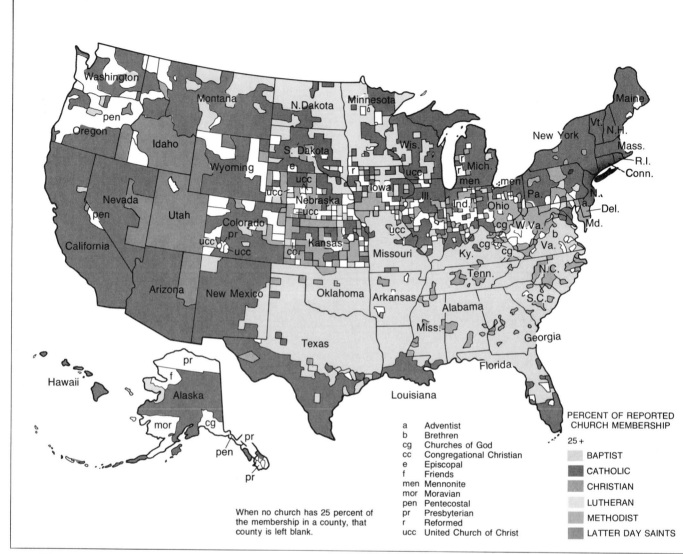

Figure 16.1   **Major Religious Denominations by Counties of the United States, 1980.**

Both the diversity and concentration of Christian denominations are evident in this figure. Many different denominations exist in the United States, and in a number of counties more than 25 percent of the population belongs to one particular denomination. Among non-Christian religions, only Judaism has a significant concentration, in Manhattan and Dade County, Florida.

*Source:* Quinn et al, 1980.

little separation of church and state, many had fled to escape religious persecution. Once here, they wanted to find a way to protect various religious denominations.

Although we think of the United States as the home of many religious denominations, three—Catholics, Baptists, and Methodists—account for three-fifths of the total population. The addition of Lutherans, Presbyterians, and Episcopalians, includes three-fourths of the population. About 2 percent say they are Jewish, about 18 percent are "other Protestants," 4 percent preferred "other," and 9 percent preferred "none" (Riche, 1985, p. 38). Although the religious makeup of the population is diverse, there are definite patterns of religious predominance by region (see Figure 16.1).

## Characteristics of Various Denominations

The largest single denomination, Roman Catholic, has become middle-class with respect to the education, occupation, and economic achievement of many of its members (Greeley, 1972; Riche, 1985). Catholics report the highest rates of church attendance of any denomination, with more than two-thirds reporting that they attend mass weekly.

The major Protestant denominations are divided internally. The Baptist Church, for instance, has at least 16 different bodies, the largest of which is the Southern Baptists. Southern Baptists are more likely than other Baptists to be fundamentalist in their theology and con-

*Some Christian denominations still practice baptism by immersion for new members.*

servative politically. A quarter of all Baptists are blacks. Traditionally, the Baptist churches attracted the lower classes and the dispossessed; they still minister to many poor people in the South. In recent years, however, some Baptist churches have become prosperous, since the South has become increasingly affluent. Many members follow both the otherworldly religious Gospel and an affluent personal life-style. Baptists comprise more than 50 percent of the population of many southern counties; it is not unusual for these communities to be dominated by a Baptist "culture."

Early Baptists believed in immersing adults in water when they were baptized and in trying to live a simple life patterned after the moral codes of early Christianity (Marty, 1976). Even today, many southern Baptists are against smoking, drinking, swearing, gambling, dancing, and card-playing. In many towns, the recreation facilities, including the swimming pool and gymnasium, are owned and operated by the church, and church youth groups provide the hub of teenage social life. Evangelistic rallies are major cultural events in many areas. In such places, non-Baptists have little chance of being elected to political office.

Methodism is in many ways a mainstream American denomination. It is fairly evenly spread throughout the United States, although in most counties members do not comprise a majority of the population. Methodism followed settlers westward, and its democratic theology (which stressed member participation and no hierarchy of church officials) appealed to frontier villages. Methodist preaching was emotional as well as intellectual and succeeded in drawing many converts. Among workers newly arrived in the cities, Methodism appealed to those who were put off by the seemingly stodgy styles of worship practiced by Episcopalians and Congregationalists.

Methodists have long been interested in bringing Christian principles into the social order and have played an active role in public affairs. Methodists are middle-class in education, occupation, and income and average in church attendance.

Social class is correlated with denominational preferences and memberships. The groups with the largest proportion of upper-class or white-collar members are Jews, Episcopalians, Unitarians, Presbyterians, Christian Scientists, and Congregationalists.

Considerable sociological research suggests that people of higher socioeconomic backgrounds are less likely to hold orthodox religious beliefs, less likely to practice private religious acts such as prayer, and less likely to feel they have had a personal religious experience (Davidson, 1977; Fukuyama, 1961; Stark, 1972).

At the other extreme, Baptists, Mormons, Eastern Orthodox, and Fundamentalists (including Seventh Day Adventists, Pentecostals, Church of God, and Jehovah's Witnesses) have relatively more members from the lower social classes (Alston, 1973; Lauer, 1975; Moberg, 1962; Nelsen and Snizek, 1976; Riche, 1985; Schneider, 1952; and Warren, 1970).

More deprived individuals place greater stress on religion. Wimberley (1984) reports that people with more education and higher occupational prestige see religion as less significant than do those with less education and status. How much income people earned was not, however, related to the relevance of religion in their lives. From this he concluded that the significance of religion may be a response to social rather than economic deprivation (p. 234).

Denominations show a great deal of variation among their members, even though there are patterned differences among denominations on a national scale. Within various denominations, social class is correlated with church attendance (Glock and Stark, 1965; Greeley, 1972). Those who have done better with respect to the world's ranking systems appear to be more able or willing to attend church. Certain cultural and social traits also characterize various denominations. Mormons, for example, tend to be socially and politically conservative. They do not believe in having women as religious leaders, they believe in tithing (that is, contributing one-tenth of their income to the church), and they frown on drinking and smoking. When practiced, these religious beliefs help to create a more austere life-style than that of many Americans and something of a distinct cultural community.

Like Baptists, Lutherans comprise more than 50 percent of the population in a number of counties. Lutherans have the highest rates of church attendance of any Protestant denomination. They tend to be middle-class with respect to education, occupation, and income. Their cultural contributions include the founding of a number of excellent colleges and the building of some architecturally distinctive contemporary churches. Their representation in politics and other public spheres has been low compared to the size of their membership.

In 1957 the Evangelical and Reformed churches merged with the Congregational Christian churches to form the United Church of Christ (UCC). The Congregational branch had been strong in New England in colonial times. The low-key, quiet civility of Congregational evangelism did not compete very well with the fervor of the revivalists when it came to gaining converts among frontier settlers. Although their numbers did not grow rapidly, Congregationalists did found excellent colleges. The UCC does not have a numerical majority in any of the nation's counties. As a result, it has not created a cultural style that it might impose on nonmembers.

Presbyterians, Episcopalians, and Congregationalists have more college-educated, business, professional, and well-to-do members than do other Christian denominations. Jews, however, are more highly educated and of higher occupational status and income than even Episcopalians and Presbyterians. All these religious groups have considerably more influence on American society than their numbers would suggest, because of their high educational levels, their economic and social status, and their geographic locations.

## CONSEQUENCES OF RELIGION

Religious denomination and participation are related to political participation, political tolerance and, under some conditions, to the incidence of juvenile delinquency.

### Political Participation

There are denominational variations in political participation in the United States. There is a larger proportion of Protestants, for example, in the U.S. Senate than in the American adult

Ritual contributes to the third characteristic of religion, which is the existence of a special community of members and worshipers. Durkheim stressed that religious beliefs belong to a group. They do not exist in a vacuum or even simply inside the heads of individuals. Individuals in the group feel united by their common faith, rituals, and the way in which they divide the world into the sacred and the profane. They put their common ideas into common practices in what is called a church. In short, **religion** is a set of beliefs and rituals commonly shared by a special community and focusing on the sacred.

Religion differs from magic in that *magic* is "a practical art consisting of acts which are only means to a definite end expected to follow"; religion, on the other hand, is a "body of self-contained acts being themselves the fulfillment of their purpose" (Malinowski, 1948). Religion does not need to cause any specific result; the experience itself is sufficient. Part of what makes the experience of religion unique and satisfying, Durkheim suggests, is its shared foundation. This sharing separates it from magic. Magic does nothing to bind together those who practice it or to forge them into a group leading a common life.

Sociology focuses on the social contexts, consequences, and meanings of religion in society.

## The Functions of Religion

Humans are symbol-using animals who need beliefs and language systems to provide meaning in their lives. If each individual had to devise his or her own unique beliefs from which to take comfort when people get sick or die, or if each person had to create totally new social practices to deal with births, weddings, or funerals, we would all face tremendous strain. For many individuals and groups, religious beliefs, practices, and communities provide an ongoing system of shared customs that offers purpose. Whether the purpose stems from a sense of shared social support and community or from a shared set of beliefs or both, we see an important function of religion in modern and simple societies.

Religion may also function to *integrate* a society. It can provide shared values and beliefs that help bind people into a community. Religious beliefs may transcend differences of economic class or ethnicity that divide a society, as the Roman Catholic Church did in medieval Europe.

Religion often serves as an important source of *social control* by providing sacred support for many social values and norms. Relations between the sexes, races, and parents and children, for instance, are codified and reinforced by religious doctrines and practices. Biblical writings in the Old and New Testament have supported traditional sex roles by calling for wives to submit to their husbands. Durkheim suggests that religion helps uphold the structure of society. This happens because religious practices reflect the organization of authority in a group or society. A hierarchical religious organization, for example, tends to support a ranked social structure in which authority and decision making are concentrated at the upper levels.

Religion may also function as a *source of moral leadership* in society, suggesting that a supernatural being will be displeased with a person who lies or steals, for example. Religions provide moral canons against which social realities can be compared. They often provide ideological fuel for social movements. White and black clergy provided major leadership to the civil rights movement of the 1950s and 1960s and the antinuclear protests of the 1970s and 1980s. The Moral Majority has crusaded against sex and violence on television. These are all examples of movements pushing for social changes on the basis of religious justification.

A fifth function of religion is to provide *personal support* to individuals. Religious beliefs and rituals help to relieve anxiety, define personality, and support family and other social identities (Mol, 1976). Religion provides ceremonies to celebrate or mourn major events—birth, puberty, marriage, and death—through baptisms, bar mitzvahs, weddings, and funerals. These ceremonies provide social support and community acceptance for the individuals involved. Religion provides responses that are hallowed by tradition and by their ties with the transcendent, suggests Peter Berger (1967, 1969), thus giving individuals some meaning in an otherwise chaotic and frightening world that is being shaken by a profound crisis of belief.

*Religious ceremonies help to celebrate or mourn major life events such as birth, puberty, marriage, and death. Young Jewish males have traditionally had a Bar Mitzvah to celebrate their becoming men, and increasing numbers of Jewish girls are having Bat Mitzvahs to celebrate their becoming women.*

## Conflict Views of Religion

In contrast with the cohesive features of religion stressed by functionalism, a conflict perspective emphasizes the way religion helps to preserve groups and collectivities or to protect and reinforce the position of privileged groups in society. When groups differ religiously, as Protestants and Catholics do in Northern Ireland, and they are also divided along political and economic lines, the potential for serious conflict between them increases tremendously. In such a case religion may maintain the distinct cultural and social identities of each group, thereby tending to increase conflict between them rather than reducing it.

### Karl Marx: Religion as Delusion

Karl Marx tended to minimize the religious differences between groups of people. Instead, he stressed that the ruling ideas of a society, including religion, reflected the interests of the ruling class. In his view (1844), religion supported the economic dominance of the industrial owners (capitalists) by focusing the attention of workers on the rewards of a better life in the hereafter, away from the misery of their actual working and living conditions. He called religion the "opium of the people" and claimed

that it deluded workers from perceiving their true interests and inhibited them from working for political and economic change. In medieval Europe, for example, the Roman Catholic Church directed people's attention to rewards in the next life rather than toward inequalities in their earthly lives. In addition, it taught that one must accept one's worldly "station" in order to obtain heavenly rewards. For these reasons, Marx saw religion as a force opposed to social change.

### Max Weber: Religion and Rationality

Weber studied religion in many different societies. One of the themes he explored was the growth of rationality in all aspects of modern life, including religion. For Weber, "rationality" meant a systematic relation of means to ends. Rationality appears to flourish in complex, heterogeneous environments. There, people can more easily make comparisons and learn what actions produce what consequences (Wuthnow, 1988, p. 490).

In his study of inner-worldly asceticism and most specifically Puritan Calvinism, Weber explored the possible connection between religious beliefs and the rise of capitalism. Calvinism imposed highly systematized ideas about ethical behavior on people (Schluchter, 1981).

Ascetic Protestantism developed the idea that the way of living acceptably to God was by fulfilling the obligations imposed by one's position in the world or *calling* (Weber, 1904, p. 80). There was a religious value to "restless, continuous, systematic work in a worldly calling" (Weber, 1904, p. 172). Pursuing wealth as "an end in itself was highly reprehensible," but if people attained wealth as a result of their efforts in a calling, it was considered "a sign of God's blessing" (Weber, 1904, p. 172). These views were compatible with the kinds of complex calculations that fueled the expansion of capitalism in the seventeenth century (Wuthnow, 1988, p. 490).

Protestant asceticism restricted consumption, especially of luxuries. So, in Weber's view, the religious idea of a worldly calling—coupled with hard work, rationality, and limited consumption—all contributed to the growth of what he called "the spirit of capitalism" and furthered the development of surplus, savings, and investment. Weber did not argue that Protestant asceticism was the only way that capitalism could develop but rather that it seemed to contribute in that instance. Also, by emphasizing the importance of spiritual beliefs for the development of economic and material forms, Weber did not deny that material conditions could also influence spiritual forms. Instead, he suggested that at particular moments we may see the possible influence of culture on history (Weber, 1904, p. 183). The rise of religious rationalism also appears to have supported the growth of rational experimental procedures in the natural sciences (Merton, 1938/1970).

# RELIGIOUS ORGANIZATIONS AND THE ROOTS OF RELIGIOUS CHANGE

All religious organizations and movements may be defined in terms of the degree to which they accept their social environment or are in tension with it (Johnson, 1963, p. 542). Churches and denominations tend to be in a relatively low state of tension with their social environment, whereas sects and cults may be in much greater tension. In this section we consider the somewhat more established religious institutions of churches and denominations and then consider the relatively more innovative religious movements that are evident in sects and cults.

## Religious Institutions

*Religious institutions,* like other institutions, have a known cluster of roles, norms, values, and activities related to the performance of key religious functions, such as sanctifying marriages or burying the dead. Religious institutions include churches and well-established denominations.

### Churches
A **church** is a formally organized, highly institutionalized religious organization with established religious doctrine, beliefs, and practices. An official or established church, such as the Church of England, is linked in some way with the state. Such an official church may count all citizens in the society as members. These features tend to make the church socially conservative. Religious practices are traditional and formalized in most churches. As a result, they tend to be predictable. Church clergy are almost always professionally trained and formally recognized. Churches are likely to be hierarchically organized and to have formal statements of belief and dogmas.

### Denominations
A **denomination** is a religious organization that emerges in a society that has no official state church and permits various social or ethnic groups to practice their own religions (Greeley, 1972). Denominations tend to be relatively tolerant of one another; they may be relaxed about the intensity of commitment required of members; and they usually have professionally trained clergy (Niebuhr, 1929).

Churches and denominations tend to be predictable and relatively unthreatening to other institutions in society, to their members, and to members of other churches or denominations. Their very formality, tradition, and relative lack of fervor may provoke some members to break off into a more religiously active movement. Unlike established churches and denominations, religious movements are not satisfied with things as they are and seek to change them.

## Religious Movements

A **religious movement** is an organized religious group with the primary goal of changing existing religious institutions. All religious institutions and churches began as small religious movements, which means that they were often in considerable tension with their environment.

### Origins of New Religions
The great religions of the world all began in periods of rapid economic, social, and cultural upheaval. (See the final section of this chapter for more on the origins and nature of those religions.) Conditions of plague, war, famine, flood, and economic collapse often cause people to lose confidence in existing faiths and encourage religious innovation (Cohn, 1961; Harris,

1981; Wilson, 1975). Although there are always religious prophets who proclaim that they have found a new answer to the traditional problems that people face, people listen and follow only when existing religions fail to meet their needs. Usually these new movements have *charismatic leaders;* that is, men or women with special gifts and powers. These new movements grow when they can recruit new members through existing social networks with nonmembers (Heirich, 1977; Lofland, 1966; Lofland and Stark, 1965; Stark and Bainbridge, 1980).

**Cults** do not claim cultural continuity with existing churches or religious traditions; instead, they represent something new in relation to the other religious bodies in the society (Stark and Bainbridge, 1985, p. 25). In its early stages a new cult is likely to be in considerable tension with its environment. Members may separate themselves from the rest of society (for example, by moving to the wilderness), they may actively preach against what they see as the evils of the world (for example, by urging that certain books be burned), and they may call for their members to behave in more moral ways than the rest of society (for example, by not drinking, smoking, or dancing). These strict religious movements often appeal to the most deprived members of society. The millenarian movements are examples of religious movements that began as cults.

### Millenarian Movements

**Millenarian movements** are social movements based on the expectation that society will be suddenly transformed through a supernatural intervention. Movements based on a transforming vision have occurred throughout Christian history and among the cargo cult believers in New Guinea and the Sioux Indians of the American plains. Millenarian movements are focused on a millennium—that is, a thousand-year era beginning with a day when a sudden supernatural event will radically change the lives of members of the movements. Among Christians, Seventh Day Adventists and Jehovah's Witnesses are millenarians.

These religious movements tend to arise in conditions of hardship and strain. Often members have lost a more favorable position in the social order, either to colonial invaders or because of the rise of new, more affluent social classes. Traditional values and norms did not help them in the new situation. Neither reasoned effort nor traditional rituals helped them to deal with the crisis (Cohn, 1961, p. 311). Their only hope appeared to be the intervention of a supernatural being to change the world in which they lived. If millenarian movements do not destroy their followers through some misplaced faith, they may provide hope and a sense of purpose and serve as the basis for political organization. As a result, they may sometimes lead to dramatic social change (Cohn, 1961).

The *cargo cults* of New Guinea began to develop in the late nineteenth century and became more widespread after World War I. They were based on the idea that great cargo ships filled with flour, rice, cloth, tools, and weapons were created by the ancestors for the people of New Guinea and the surrounding islands. By sending in the cargo, prophets said, the ancestors were showing their support for the living. The cargo, however, was taken over by European colonists. With the help of the spirits and the cargo, the prophets told the people they could kill or drive out the European settlers and live at the same high standard the Europeans enjoyed. The cargo cults are considered millenarian movements because they expect a day when a sudden supernatural event will transform the members' lives.

The *Ghost Dance cult* represented an effort by native Americans in the western United States to restore traditional cultures that had been shattered by white conquest. In 1890 it reached the Sioux at about the time of the battle of Wounded Knee in South Dakota. The cult was wrongly blamed for that uprising. The ghost shirts that the prophet had promised would protect against the army's bullets failed to protect their wearers, and many were massacred (Mooney, 1965; Utley, 1963).

## SECULARIZATION, SECTS, AND CULTS

Despite the foregoing examples of intense religious movements, many social scientists, pointing to the trend toward increasing secularization, have wondered if religion is declining in

*These Cargo Cult believers in the New Hebrides have formed a social movement based on the belief that a sudden supernatural event will radically change the lives of members of the movement.*

importance as a social institution. In this section we examine secularization and consider the interesting work of two sociologists, Rodney Stark and William Bainbridge (1985), who have been studying religious changes for nearly twenty years. They suggest that secularization produces various forms of religious revival and innovation in the form of new sects and cults. They suggest that religion in various forms is flourishing rather than dying as a social institution.

## Secularization

Most cults or sects that flourish are likely to become more worldly and more institutionalized over time, a tendency called secularization. **Secularization** refers to the erosion of belief in the supernatural and is associated with modernization and industrialization (Stark and Bainbridge, 1985, p. 429). It includes a respect for values of rationality, cultural and religious pluralism, tolerance of moral ambiguity, faith in education, and belief in civil rights, the rule of law, and due process. A secularized religion accepts the rights of people to hold different beliefs and follow different practices instead of requiring them to conform to an established religious norm. A secularized society also tends to accept religion as one of a number of beliefs and activities that engage people, rather than an all-enveloping and dominating set of beliefs and practices that affects everything one does.

At the institutional level, the forces of secularization tend to make religion simply one institution among many. Other institutions—such as education, medicine, science, and the economy—take over many of the functions formerly filled by religion, and their goals may conflict with religious beliefs. Religious concerns, such as vowing to live in poverty, are not always compatible with economic values, such as making money. Science may offer explanations—for example, of how life on earth originated—that compete with religious explanations. The increasing narrowness of religion as one institution among many, along with the existence of religious pluralism, allows people to choose among competing beliefs. For large numbers of people, secularization has weakened religion because it undermines faith in the transcendent. As a result, Berger (1977) suggests that secularization frustrates the human desire for meaning and hope, because only a belief in the transcendent can offer such hope.

## Sects

Secularization appeals to those who are concerned with worldly success, but members of a religion who have otherworldly and spiritual concerns may break away to form new sects. A **sect** is usually a small, demanding, and intense religious group. Sect formation happens in the early stages of secularization and occurs in areas with strong religious traditions. It is an effort to breathe life back into an existing religious

tradition, according to Stark and Bainbridge (1985). At this early stage, sects are often in considerable tension with their environment, just as early cults are. As is evident in Table 16.1, sects and cults are more likely to be in greater tension with their environment than are major churches or denominations.

Stark and Bainbridge (1985) suggest that sect formation is most likely to occur in those parts of the United States, Canada, and Europe where existing religious traditions are relatively strong. In the United States, sects are most likely to form in states where church membership is relatively high rather than where it is relatively low (p. 446). In Europe, sect activity seems to be centered in areas where conventional churches are strongest—for example, in Poland and Spain (p. 502).

### Fundamentalism

Many times sects are formed in an effort to get back to the more basic, or fundamental,

**Table 16.1**  *Degree of Tension with Environment of American Churches, Denominations, Sects, and Cults*

| Degree of Tension | Characteristics | Examples |
|---|---|---|
| 1. Low | Well accommodated to environment | Protestant Episcopal Church, United Church of Christ (UCC), Methodist, Presbyterian |
| 2. Moderate | More than #1 but still low tension | American Lutheran Church, American Baptist Church, Catholic Church |
| 3. Somewhat high | Noticeable tension, but groups are considered respectable | Southern Baptist Convention, Lutheran Church-Missouri Synod |
| 4. High | Have lowered original level of tension but it is still somewhat high | Church of the Nazarene, Seventh-Day Adventist Church |
| 5. Very high | Experience considerable friction with society | Pentecostal groups that speak in tongues and claim divine gifts of healing |
| 6. Extreme | Experience ridicule or serious antagonism from society; often face legal challenges. May be physically remote and/or wear distinctive dress | Amish and Mennonites, snake-handling groups, polygamous Mormon communes, strong millenarian groups (e.g., Jehovah's Witnesses), cult movements such as Rev. Moon's Unification Church |

*Source:* Adapted from Stark and Bainbridge, 1985, p. 135.

teachings of the religion from which the members come.

**Fundamentalism** is a form of religious traditionalism that insists that the faithful allow every part of their lives to be dominated by religion (Marty, 1980). Christianity, Islam, Hinduism, and Judaism have seen the growth of fundamentalism. In many areas, such as Iran and the United States, religious fundamentalism has become a force for political change. It is able to do this in part because it focuses all of a person's energies on what is considered a holy cause.

Fundamentalism is typically characterized by the literal interpretation of religious texts or teachings, by a conception of an active supernatural, and by clear-cut distinctions between sin and salvation. It is often inspired by direct religious experiences, such as thoses of "born again" Christians who feel that Christ has entered their lives in a very personal way and has offered them salvation.

Two recent forms of fundamentalism include the New Christian Right and Islamic fundamentalism in Iran. The New Christian Right includes politically organized religious groups, such as the Religious Roundtable, the Christian Voice, and the Moral Majority. Members of these groups tend to be from traditional Protestant denominations, such as Baptists.

Fundamentalist political groups direct their attention to working for the defeat of certain liberal candidates for Congress and the support of conservatives. They gave important support to Ronald Reagan in the 1980 and 1984 presidential campaigns. Organizers focus on what they see as a moral decline in national life. They feel that God has been removed from the public schools, and they want to reestablish the right to pray in public schools. They seek to remove the teaching of evolution in schools and to prevent the spread of pornography (Marty, 1981).

The fundamentalist movement seems to gain power from the anger people feel about the changing moral climate and those who help foster change. It offers the hope of defeating "humanists" and liberals in church and state (Marty, 1981). However, fundamentalist positions frequently conflict with traditions of American democracy, such as strict separation of church and state, and fundamentalists often ignore the rights of others to differ philosophically and to follow other practices.

Although some Islamic scholars deny any similarities between Islamic movements and Christian fundamentalism, the two do share some similarities. They both deplore godlessness and material concerns that push out spiritual concerns. Both seek to put religious faith into the center of people's lives, and both are relatively intolerant of those who do not share their beliefs. They also differ in a number of respects. The Islamic movements in Saudi Arabia, Libya, and Iran denounce westernization and describe the West as exploitative and imperialist. Especially in Libya, but also in Iran, the Islamic movement is advancing a form of collectivism that its members say differs from Soviet forms of socialism but advocates sharing equally the wealth generated by society. Islamic fundamentalists contrast a utopian view of life in the first century of Islam with present conditions of poverty, squalor, and oppression. That belief, together with modern methods of communication and propaganda, may move a number of Arab nations farther and farther away from effective relations with the West (Kedourie, 1980).

### Evangelicalism

If American religious life has appeared to be torn between fundamentalism on the one hand and secularism on the other, these two tendencies may have overshadowed another very significant religious movement, the evangelicals. Billy Graham is one example of an evangelical religious leader. Evangelicals see themselves as more moderate religiously and politically than either fundamentalists or secularists. They tend to see fundamentalists as narrow-minded and reactionary and to view those with secular views as beset with uncertainty and lack of faith.

**Evangelicalism** is a form of Protestantism that stresses the preaching of the gospel of Jesus Christ, the validity of personal conversion experiences, biblical Scripture as the basis for faith, and active preaching of the faith in one's home country and abroad. In the early part of the twentieth century, they were often equated with fundamentalists; but in more recent years, evangelicals have become increasingly distinct. They are more open to science, rationality, and the concerns of the Reformation. In nineteenth-century America, evangelicalism was characterized by strong support for democracy, in keeping with the Reformation doctrine that individuals did not need priests or other intermediaries between themselves and God but were equal in the eyes of God. They were optimistic that people and societies could change for the better with God's support. Today's evangelicals see themselves as part of the same tradition.

## Cults

Because cults do not claim cultural continuity with existing churches and religious traditions, Stark and Bainbridge (1985) predict that cult activity will flourish in the later stages of secularization and in those regions where church membership is lowest. In their studies of church membership in the United States and Canada, they found that residents of California, Oregon, and Washington are least likely to belong to established churches, perhaps because they move around more often than people in other regions do. These three states are the ones with the largest amount of cult activity (Stark and Bainbridge, 1985).

Even in the Canadian province of Quebec, where 90 percent of the population is Catholic, cults thrive in little niches where the church is somewhat weaker. Stark and Bainbridge's (1985) theory is also supported in Europe; cults abound in the northern European countries, such as Denmark, Finland and Sweden, which have the lowest church attendance.

Stark and Bainbridge (1985) define three types of cults, depending on how tightly they are organized: *Audience cults* have the least social organization, since they reach their audience through magazines, newspapers, television, radio, and books, and membership may be seen as a consumer activity. (See the debate on televangelism.) *Client cults*—such as est, rolfing, and witchcraft—deal primarily in magic or therapeutic services, not religion, and do not bind their clients into stable organizations. Only *social-movement cults*—such as the members of Jim Jones's cult who committed "mass suicide" in a jungle clearing in Guyana in November 1978, the "Children of God," the Alamo Foundation, the Unification Church of Reverend Sun Myung Moon ("Moonies"), and the Hare Krishna—make the claim to be full-fledged religious organizations that attempt to satisfy all the religious needs of converts. As such, they come close to being sects. Members cannot belong to other faiths, and converting others is a primary goal of members.

These groups tend to be organized as "total institutions" that seek to isolate their members from contact with outsiders, including friends and members of their own families. In doing so, they recognize a basic sociological principle that if you want to change people's attitudes and behaviors, immersion in a total environment away from competing alternatives is often an effective way to proceed. At the same time, these techniques have been criticized for breaking up families and as designed to brainwash converts (Robbins and Anthony, 1978). Such charges, and the resulting lawsuits by parents seeking to free their children from such movements, have raised serious questions about the separation of church and state, religious persecution by the state, and the rights of young adults living with religious cults.

Who actually joins cults? Are the people who join marginal, deprived, or disturbed individuals, or are they people who have been "brainwashed" into joining? Stark and Bainbridge (1985) predict that individuals who do not belong to a church or who belong to a relatively more secularized denomination will be more likely to become involved in such cultic activities as yoga, transcendental meditation, Eastern religions, and mysticism. Their prediction is supported by Gallup poll data (Figure 16.2). Similarly, people who were not raised in religious homes are more likely to join Hare Krishna, Scientology, witches, or the Moonies (Stark and Bainbridge, 1985, p. 401). People who join cults have more education than people who do not join and they are more likely to have experimented with psychedelic drugs. A search for social ties with existing members is a major reason that people join (Heirich, 1977; Stark and Bainbridge, 1985, p. 423).

Both sect and cult formation, according to Stark and Bainbridge (1985), may be seen as responses to increasing secularization. Sect formation reflects the revival of a weakened but still existing religious tradition, whereas cult activity represents an innovative response to secularization.

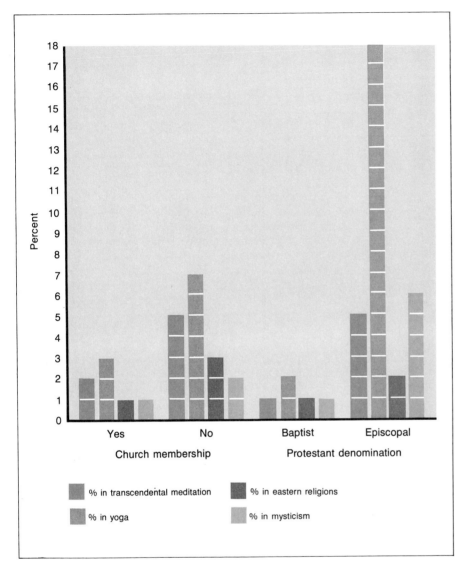

**Figure 16.2   Cultic Activity by Denomination.**

People who do not belong to institutionalized churches are more likely to report involvement in transcendental meditation, yoga, eastern religions, and mysticism than are church members. People who belong to more secularized Protestant denominations, for example, Episcopalians, were much more likely to report involvement in such activities than were members of less secularized denominations such as Baptists.

*Source:* Gallup, 1977, cited in Stark and Bainbridge, 1985, p. 400.

## Explanations for Religious Forms

Religious forms may vary due to differences in their social environments, because the production of various religious innovations is an example of cultural adaptation (Wuthnow, 1988). Several explanations for the rise of fundamentalism focus on relations with the social environment. Some suggest that fundamentalism develops as a reaction to certain modernizing tendencies. For example, it may be due to increasing emphasis on higher education and the growing importance of the national state (Antoun and Hegland, 1986). Others think that fun-damentalism is accommodating to modernity but is losing some of its unique qualities in the process (Hunter, 1983, 1986). Yet others see the growth of fundamentalism as a response to the way liberal denominations have abandoned ultimate religious concerns for social activism (Kelly, 1972). A fourth view is that fundamentalism has grown simply because its members have high fertility rates (Bibby and Brinkerhoff, 1983). On balance, fundamentalism appears to do best among groups of similar people where the connections between basic beliefs and lifestyles can remain unexamined (Wuthnow, 1988).

## DEBATING SOCIETY'S ISSUES

For growing numbers of people, religious contact occurs through the electronic church, where a new type of televangelist, or pastor of "Pray TV," beams out a combination of personality, gospel messages, dramatic personal stories, and rhythmic music. Will these televangelists hurt traditional churches?

As recently as 1957, TV evangelists filled only half the air time devoted to religious programming; but by 1980, they had a strong monopoly. Mainline religions are now a minor presence on TV (Ostling, 1986, pp. 67, 69).

There were 221 television, 7 cable TV, and 1370 radio stations broadcasting mostly religious programming in the United States in 1987. Preachers also bought time on hundreds of commercial stations (Martz and Carroll, 1988).

A 1984 Gallup survey estimated that 13.3 million people, or 6.2 percent of the national TV audience, are regular viewers of various religious shows. A 1985 Nielsen survey that included cable viewers showed that 21 percent of the nation's TV households tune in to Christian TV for at least six minutes in a month. This means that 61 million people, or about one-quarter of the U.S. population, gets at least minimal exposure to a TV evangelist.

Sociologist Jeffrey Hadden, coauthor with Charles Swann of *Prime Time Preachers* (1981), finds that these preachers now "have greater unrestricted access to media than any other interest group in America." Fueled by TV evangelism, he predicts, the Christian right "is destined to become the major social movement in America" during the late twentieth century (quoted in Ostling, 1986, p. 63).

### Will Televangelists Hurt Traditional Churches?

A series of events in 1987 and 1988 rocked the rise of the televangelists, however. First, Oklahoma evangelist Oral Roberts prophesied that God might call him home in death if his supporters did not contribute $8 million by a certain date. While he raised the money by the deadline, other evangelists criticized his tactics. Then South Carolina evangelist Jim Bakker, head of the "Praise the Lord" (PTL) organization, confessed to an extramarital sexual encounter with a church secretary, Jessica Hahn. Ms. Hahn revealed that PTL promised to pay her $265,000 in ministry funds to remain silent about the affair. When PTL invited rival evangelist Jerry Falwell in to rescue it, including the $172 million television and "theme park" enterprise, a "holy war" broke out among evangelists. PTL was charged with massive financial mismanagement. Jim and his wife Tammy were accused of personal aggrandizement, and the Assemblies of God defrocked Bakker as one of their ministers. Competing evangelist Jimmy Swaggart was the one who leaked the PTL sex and financial scandals to the press. Bakker turned against Falwell, who resigned from PTL after it declared bankruptcy.

Within less than a year, Swaggart was himself accused of strange, secret involvements with prostitutes in cheap motels. He confessed to these sins in a nationally televised sermon. A month later, the national leaders of his church ordered him not to preach from the pulpit or on his television show for at least a year, while he was rehabilitated from

"moral failure." Local church leaders in Louisiana recommended a more lenient punishment but were overruled. Swaggart's ministry was reaping more than $140 million per year and employed 1200 people on its $11.5 million annual payroll. It was the largest contributor to the National Assemblies of God, donating $12 million of the $48 million spent each year on foreign missionary activities (Associated Press, 1988). Many observers felt that Swaggart was the most effective of all the televangelists.

Since the PTL affair, the other televangelists all experienced sharply declining revenues (Ostling, 1988). Swaggart complained of losing $50,000 per day after the Bakker scandal. The Bakker incident involved more than a sinner slipping on the slippery slope of sex. It involved the misuse of financial contributions.

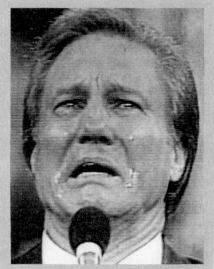

*Televangelists such as Jim Bakker and Jimmy Swaggart raised millions of dollars from their television viewers, but both had their electronic ministries cut short by public revelations of alleged financial scandals or sexual misconduct. Swaggart publicly confessed his sins on TV (above).*

It attracted the attention of the Internal Revenue Service, which began investigating whether the PTL deserved tax-exempt status as a nonprofit organization. The Bakkers had taken money from their ministry to buy a fleet of automobiles, including Mercedes-Benzes, Cadillacs, and a vintage Rolls-Royce. They also bought several multimillion-dollar houses. The one near Heritage U.S.A., their religious theme park, had three kitchens and an air-conditioned doghouse. There were also vacation condominiums in Florida and California (Martz and Carroll, 1988). Of the major televangelists, only Billy Graham and Robert Schuller were unscathed by the scandals.

Many billions of dollars move through religious channels in the United States. Churches are still the greatest recipients of voluntary financial gifts. The PTL and Swaggart scandals appeared to hurt other televangelists but did not seem to hurt local congregations or other religious institutions (Marty, 1988, pp. 294–295).

What is the appeal of television ministry? "Everybody thinks the TV preacher is doing a number on people," says the Rev. Ben Armstrong, a Presbyterian who has run the National Religious Broadcasters (NRB) association for 20 years. People who hope TV Gospel will fade when today's stars are gone, says Armstrong, "do not understand that the real key is grass-roots people, dying for personal religion and traditional values" (quoted in Ostling, 1986, p. 64).

"There is little doubt that many Americans are yearning for meaning and moral anchorage, which evangelical religion has ardently and successfully provided. Critics add that people find it easier to acquire simple answers to complex personal and social ills via television than to commit themselves to solving real-life troubles" (Ostling, 1986, p. 64). The message seems to appeal to people buffeted by social and economic ills over which they have little control. The majority (two-thirds or three-quarters) of the viewers are 50 years old or older and about two-thirds are women. In general, viewers tend to be somewhat poorer and less edu-cated than nonviewers (Hadden and Swann, 1981).

In 1987, 65 percent of the sampled public had a "not favorable" opinion of most television evangelists. Only 6 percent of "nonviewers" had a favorable opinion, and half of the viewers even had a "not favorable" opinion, according to a *New York Times/CBS News* Poll (Frankl, 1987).

Aside from the appeal of their message, TV evangelists use the latest electronic technology, including video recording equipment and computerized files to consolidate their mailing lists of supporters and potential contributors. They ask for viewer responses through WATS lines and by mail, offering books, calendars, lapel pins, records, other mementoes, personal help or service, healing, or success to those who contribute.

The people who watch are mostly those who are already committed to evangelical religion. Gospel TV does not seem to reduce attendance and contributions at local churches. The biggest competition for Gospel TV is secular TV.

---

Another form that emerged during the Great Transformation (see Chapter 1) is religious individualism. **Individualism** is a belief in individual rights and responsibilities. While present to some degree in all the doctrines of the Protestant Reformation, religious individualism may be most pronounced in English Puritanism. Puritanism placed high priority on personal salvation and left the individual accountable to God directly. It also diminished the authority of clergy and sacraments. Individuals were on their own to make the ethical decisions on which their salvation might depend. The growth of market conditions appears to be historically related to the growth of religious individualism (Wuthnow, 1988). A new version of individualism has appeared in contemporary culture. Different writers have described it as narcissism, civil privatism, expressive individualism, and individuality (Bellah et al., 1985; Habermas, 1975, pp. 75–92; Lasch, 1979; Sennett, 1974; Turner, 1983, p. 162). Whereas religious individualism focuses on the moral responsibility of one person to others, individuality focuses on the responsibility of the individual toward his or her own self (Wuthnow, 1988, p. 488). In its extreme form, this individuality can be captured by the sayings, "Do your own thing" and "anything goes" (Wuthnow, 1988, p. 485).

Several features of modern life may account for the growth of individuality. One is that modern bureaucracies are so highly organized that it is hard for individuals to feel any sense of free choice and moral responsibility. As a result, people seeking moral responsibility focus increasingly on private matters of the self, since these are more within their control (Wuthnow, 1988, p. 489). Another possible source is the greater role flexibility required in higher-level management and professional jobs (Bell, 1977; Swanson, 1980; Yankelovich, 1981). With so many roles, individuals may have trouble forming a stable sense of self and therefore become preoccupied with self-scrutiny. The result could be a limited role for religious or moral values in public issues and debates. Several scholars have wondered how this might affect the stability of modern society (Bellah, 1982; Bellah et al., 1985; Neuhaus, 1984).

## RELIGION WORLDWIDE

Nearly 60 percent of the people in the world belong to one or another of the seven major world religions (Table 16.2). These religions influence both individual lives and world events. Religious beliefs and practices are tightly interwoven with culture, with the world views that prevail in a society, with political actions, and with attitudes toward social change. Religion has influenced many of the major social movements in our society, as well as in societies around the world. Religions form the basis for many social networks that extend beyond the family (as noted in Chapter 4). Religious beliefs influence eating habits, concepts of honor and shame, business practices, and marriage relationships. Because the various religions are so central to many people's social lives, it is important to know something about some of the major ones, including their beliefs, rituals, the nature of their community, and where they are most widely practiced.

### Major World Religions

#### Christianity

Christianity in all its forms appears to be the most widely practiced religion in the world today (see Table 16.2). Nearly one billion people are considered Christians, and more than half of them are Catholics. Christians are widely spread

**Table 16.2** *Major Religions of the World*

| Religion | Number of Members (millions) |
|---|---|
| Total Christian | 1,669.5 |
|    Roman Catholic | 951.8 |
|    Protestant | 337.4 |
|    Eastern Orthodox | 161.8 |
|    Anglicans | 70.3 |
|    Other Christians | 148.1 |
| Muslim | 880.6 |
| Hindu | 663.5 |
| Buddhist | 311.8 |
| Confucian | 6.2 |
| Shinto | 3.4 |
| Judaism | 18.2 |

*Source:* Condensed and adapted from Barrett, 1989, p. 299.

around the globe, with about one-third living in Europe, about one-quarter in North America, about 15 percent in South America, 13 percent in Africa, and 10 percent in Asia.

Aside from the central belief in Christ as the saviour who brings the good news of salvation after death, forms of Christian belief and practice vary widely. Individual and family prayers are important in many denominations, as are formal church services. Some stress formalized prayers designed to instill the correct doctrines, while others value spontaneous prayers created by members. Prayers generally seek to praise God, to give thanks for what has been received, or to ask God to intercede in the world to help those who need it. The Bible is the single most important document in Christianity. More copies of the Bible have been sold than of any other book in the world. It has been translated into all languages of the world, and into many remote dialects as well. The Bible is believed by Christians to contain the literal word of God or at least to be divinely inspired. The role of an ordained clergy, the organizational structure of the church, and type of church service differ widely in various forms of Christianity. But in all denominations, the major events in human experience—birth, becoming a member of the church, marriage, death—are given special significance through the meanings imposed by Christian beliefs and rituals.

The existence of different denominations within Christianity has probably strengthened it around the world because in its various forms it can appeal to a wide variety of national and ethnic groups, who can find or adapt compatible beliefs. Like other major religions, Christianity often forged bonds with music (Johann Sebastian Bach), art (Michelangelo and Raphael), literature (Milton's *Paradise Lost*), and, more recently, television (Robert Schuller), to reach new and existing members. Sometimes it also formed partnerships with political and secular forces, as in the Crusades conducted in the Middle Ages to recover the Holy Land.

### Islam

After Christianity, Islam is the largest world religion. Muslims (believers of Islam) are heavily concentrated in North Africa, the Middle East, and parts of Asia. (See Figure 16.3 for a map of the distribution of Islam worldwide.) The religion was founded in the seventh century by the prophet Muhammad. It emphasizes an uncompromising belief in one supreme being (monotheism) and strict adherence to certain religious practices, such as observing five daily prayers, the profession of faith, payment of a welfare tax, fasting, and a pilgrimage to Mecca. Like Christianity, Islam has many sects and movements, but all followers of Islam are bound by certain shared beliefs and the overarching sense of belonging to a single common community.

The Arabic word "islam" means "to surrender" and contains the fundamental religious idea of Islam—namely, that believers surrender to the will of Allah, the unique God, creator, sustainer, and restorer of the world. Allah's will is given in the book of Islamic scriptures, the Qur'an (often spelled Koran), which was revealed to Allah's messenger, Muhammad. Muhammad is believed to be the last in a long line of prophets that includes Adam, Noah, Moses, and Jesus. The Muslim confession of faith makes it clear where Muhammad stands in this procession: "There is no god but Allah and Muhammad is His Prophet."

### Judaism

Judaism is the religion of the Jews, who live all over the world but have a homeland in the state of Israel. Essentially, Jews believe in one deity—known as Jehovah, Yahweh, or God—who cares for the world and for His chosen people, the Jews. As a religion, Judaism focuses on a continual interaction between God and people, with God continually being unwilling to turn His back on man, despite repeated violations of the covenant by man. God reveals His divine presence through history. Despite God's actions (for example, in presenting the commandments), however, humans are constantly falling short of His expectations. As a result,

*After Christianity, Islam is the second largest religion in the world. Here the Saudi Arabian king's honor guard kneels in prayer for one of the five daily prayers observed by practicing Muslims.*

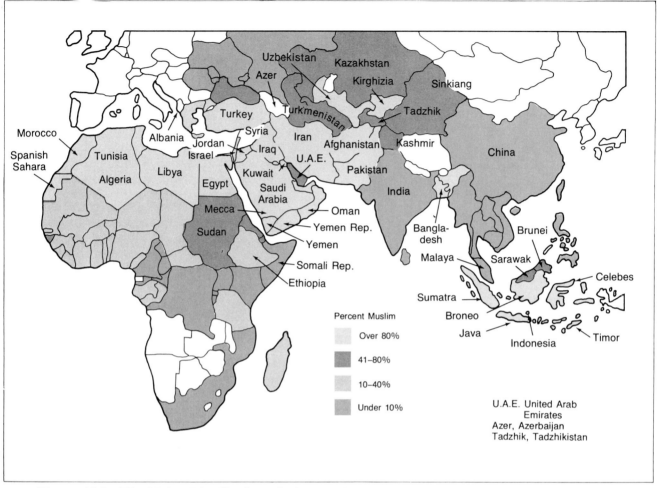

**Figure 16.3    The Major Distribution of Islam in the World.**

*Source:* Adapted from Wickens, 1976, p. 2.

prophets have appeared from time to time to bring Jews back to right practices.

The actions of God, such as leading the Israelites out of Egypt, are confirmed in the Torah, which means "to point the way," or the law. The writings of the Torah confirm the events that are acts of God. They also prescribe a series of behaviors for all aspects of social life. These include table blessings, observance of the Sabbath, celebration of the Feast of Tabernacles, the seder Passover meal, Yom Kippur, the Feast of Dedication (Hanukkah), and regular worship in the synagogue. Notable events recognized by religious ritual include circumcision of male babies, naming of female babies in the synagogue, the Bar Mitzvahs of 13-year-old boys (some girls have Bat Mitzvahs) symbolizing their religious coming of age, marriage, and death and burial.

Although Jews in Europe, the Middle East, and the United States have widely different racial and national origins, Judaism provides shared beliefs and practices that help to create a common culture and way of life. Moreover, Judaism is a powerful political force in the Middle East.

### Hinduism

Hinduism is found in India, parts of Pakistan, Sri Lanka, Nepal, and Sikkim. There are also smaller Hindu communities in parts of Southeast Asia, East and South Africa, Surinam, and on such islands as Fiji and Mauritius. The umbrella community of Hindus spans a wide range of doctrines, cults, and ways of life, ranging from animal worship and worship of personal gods to mysticism and abstract theological systems. Hinduism is a kaleidoscope of many pieces, with no single founder, central hierarchy, or final authority. Other religious doctrines, forms of worship, and gods may be considered "incomplete," but they are not considered wrong or undesirable. As a result, Hindus can follow non-Hindu religious practices without losing their Hindu identity.

Part of Hinduism is a belief in the spiritual and social superiority of the Brahmins, or noble class. Other members of society rank below Brahmins in prestige. The social status into which they are born is believed to be determined by how they behaved in prior lives. Although the rigid ranking of social castes in India has been weakened in modern times, particularly in northern India, some traces remain in other parts of the country. The term "Brahmin" has been used widely outside Hindu society to refer to members of a social group whose moral and social superiority is widely acknowledged.

Hinduism is an all-embracing religion. It has religious, social, economic, literary, and artistic implications. Its inclusiveness makes it acceptable to many who also practice their own local religions. Thus it is a religion that tends to flourish in areas of extensive migration. Its doctrine of "reincarnation," or rebirth in new bodies, tends to justify social and economic inequalities on earth as the result of one's purity or sinfulness in an earlier incarnation. Such a view deflects attention from attempting to change life on earth and directs it toward living virtuously in the hope of achieving a better situation the next time around. It borders on fatalism and may tend to depress efforts for social change.

### Buddhism

Buddhism was founded in India in the sixth century B.C. by Siddhartha Gautama, a reformer, known as the Buddha (meaning the awakened one). The religion spread from India to Central and Southeast Asia, China, Korea, and Japan and has influenced the spiritual, cultural, and social life of much of Asia. Buddha stressed the impermanence of all things and for-

*Buddhists seek to eliminate the craving for pleasure, and they emphasize the values of sympathy, compassion, and joyful participation in the good created by others. They also promote socially useful efforts such as hospitals, shelters, and irrigation projects. Here a woman is giving rice to a group of young Buddhist monks in Rangoon, Burma.*

mulated the Four Noble Truths: (1) misery is a major feature of life; (2) misery originates from within ourselves from the craving for pleasure; (3) this craving can be eliminated; and (4) this elimination can occur by diligently following a specific path. Spiritual liberation is achieved by meditation and by following the Noble Eightfold Path, which involves right seeing, thinking, speech, action, living, effort, mindfulness, and meditation. The ultimate goal is to achieve a state of Nirvana, or salvation. Buddhism appealed to many followers of Hinduism because Buddhism was open to all regardless of caste position.

Traditional Buddhist ethics prohibit killing, stealing, sexual misconduct, lying, and drinking liquor. Despite the transitory nature of existence, Buddhism emphasizes the values of sympathy, compassion, and joyful participation in the good created by others. Buddhists promote socially useful activities such as the building of irrigation projects, bridges, hospitals, and shelters for the benefit of people and animals. Moral energy and perseverance in the struggle for the common good are highly valued. Believers tend to develop a spirit of social cooperation and active participation in society. Buddhist society fosters participation by both men and women. All these features tend to strengthen the sense of human solidarity in Buddhist communities.

Buddhism has become a significant political force in efforts to establish national independence in modern Asia in such countries as Burma, Sri Lanka, Thailand, Vietnam, Cambodia, Laos, and Tibet. In South Vietnam in the 1960s and 1970s, numerous Buddhist monks committed suicide by setting themselves on fire as a protest against the war being fought there. They were dedicated to Buddha's ideal of peace, and they sacrificed themselves to stimulate resistance to the war.

## Religion in Totalitarian Societies

Religious groups do not always support the dominant institutions in a society. Sometimes they operate openly or quietly in opposition to major institutions. Even when the official state policy is one of religious suppression, it may not succeed. People often cling all the more tightly to their cherished religious beliefs in the face of state opposition.

When the Communist party took power in the Soviet Union in 1917, it adopted "scientific atheism" as the official state policy. For six decades the regime has been trying to stamp out the "prerevolutionary remnants" of religion. Large numbers of people still practice Russian orthodoxy, religious art and icons are highly valued in the underground economy, dissident writers often have religious content in their works, and there are a number of signs that a religious revival is under way. This revival is occurring in the face of state repression. Not only Soviet Jews but also Baptists, Pentecostals, and even Russian Orthodox believers have been severely persecuted. Nearly 500 serious religious protest demonstrations in the Soviet Union over a 13-year period were documented by Kowalewski (1980). Often the demonstrators were injured, detained, or sentenced to prison, yet the demonstrations continued to occur, along with more secret protests such as unsigned leaflets, banners, and slogans. In Poland religious opposition to the state is even more open. Striking Polish workers hung banners of the Virgin Mary on their factories and mines. Stark and Bainbridge (1985) suggest that repressive states increase individual suffering and thus fuel religious impulses. Religion may be most potent when it is underground, because it is then not tainted by worldly concerns.

## Liberation Theology and the Impetus for Social Change

Priests have been assassinated or expelled from the Church in Latin America for their religious and political teachings. What can explain such violent reactions to religious leaders? Historically, the Catholic church was often the ally of powerful political leaders. But the recent history of Catholicism, especially in Poland and many Central and Latin American countries, contradicts the image of the church as the mainstay of tradition and the establishment.

There are many liberation theologies that address various forms of oppression, whether by politics, race, class, gender, or sexuality. "All liberation theologies represent what Michel Foucault called 'the insurrection of subjugated knowledges' and all insist that justice is the moral test of God-claims and spirituality. They are profoundly oriented to public life and they push for the kind of Christian faith that would help end massive suffering" (Rasmussen, 1988, p. 180).

The Second Vatican Council (1962–1965) emphasized the social role of the church in pursuing justice and peace. In 1968 Latin American church leaders met in Bogotá, Colombia, and

*Despite the Communist party's efforts to abolish religion, religious communities flourish in many communist countries. In Poland, the Catholic Church has been a rallying point for opposition to the Communist party. This picture, taken May 10, 1988, shows the final day of a strike by Solidarity members in Gdansk, Poland. They are using religious symbols to help gain support for their cause.*

wrote the now famous Medellin Documents, stating their commitment to participate in Latin American social and economic affairs. They noted that poverty in Latin America is well documented and is rooted in the relation between rich and poor in each nation and in the dependent relation between Latin America and the developed world. From the theological viewpoint, they wrote, this is a "sinful situation."

Instances abound of church involvement in the social, political, and economic life of Latin America. In El Salvador, for example, Archbishop Romero was a strong critic of the state terror, intimidation, and violence shown by the Salvadoran government security forces and army to workers, peasants, nuns, and priests. He also spoke out against the violence of leftist guerrillas. On March 24, 1980, he was shot and killed while officiating at a Mass in the chapel of a hospital he had started for cancer patients. In Nicaragua, Fernando Cardenal was expelled by the Jesuit Order for being a minister in the left-wing Nicaraguan government. These and other examples did not go unnoticed by Vatican leaders. In recent years the Catholic church in many parts of Brazil has taken on the role of defending human rights and dignity in the face of repression by the military.

What is remarkable about these developments is the way the church has moved from being a defender of the status quo toward being a force for challenging the political and economic conditions that produce malnutrition and poverty.

## SUMMARY

1. Religion is a set of beliefs about ultimate meanings, including a belief in the supernatural.

2. America is considered to have a civil religion, according to sociologist Robert Bellah, who points out how American political life is interlaced with religious symbols and rituals.

3. In the United States, church membership declined steadily from 1960 to 1983, when membership suddenly increased. Other indicators as well suggest that religion is not a waning institution.

4. Catholics are the largest religious denomination in the United States, followed by all types of Baptists. Catholics, Baptists, and Mormons tend to live in geographically concentrated areas where church membership may overlap with ethnicity. The major social and cultural activities of such areas are often run by the church of the majority.

5. Social class is related to religious denomination in the United States. Jews, Episcopalians, Unitarians, Presbyterians, Christian Scientists, and Congregationalists have a larger proportion of members with higher-status occupations and higher incomes; Roman Catholics, Baptists, Mormons, Eastern Orthodox, and fundamentalists have a larger proportion of members of lower social classes. Social class is also related to religious beliefs and practices.

6. Studies of political participation by religious groups show that Methodists, Episcopalians, Unitarians, and Jews are overrepresented in political offices relative to their numbers in the population, whereas Lutherans and Baptists are underrepresented. This may have to do with the stress that the former groups place on public as well as private morality.

7. Religious denominations also vary in their degree of political tolerance. Although generally more secularized denominations are the most tolerant, Mormons and Jehovah's Witnesses are relatively more tolerant than might be predicted by their level of secularization, perhaps because they have experienced religious intolerance themselves.

8. Religion is related to how often teenagers commit delinquent acts. If young people go to church themselves and live in a community where the majority of young people also go to church, they are less likely to be delinquent than young people who live in a relatively "unchurched" community.

9. The French sociologist Emile Durkheim noted several features that characterize all religions, including a sense of the divine or holy, the practice of established rites, and the existence of a community of worshippers.

10. Functionalist sociologists stress the integrative functions of religion in society, such as

shared systems of belief, accepted moral leadership, and personal support for individuals.

11. Karl Marx, on the other hand, deplored the way religion diverted people's attention from their economic plight. Max Weber explored the rise of rationality and possible connections between religious beliefs and the rise of capitalism.

12. Religious institutions such as churches and established denominations have known roles, values, and activities. Religious movements seek to change existing practices in religion or other institutions.

13. New religions begin in periods of social upheaval, when charismatic leaders are able to attract loyal followers. Early religious movements may be in considerable tension with their social environment.

14. Millenarian movements that predict dramatic supernatural intervention in the world followed by a thousand years of peace have arisen throughout religious history. Followers of these movements have often been socially displaced by newly dominant groups or classes and see little practical way of improving their plight.

15. Over time religions tend to become more secularized and lose some of their emphasis on the supernatural. As a result, some members may break away to revive the original fervor, by forming a new sect. Sect formation occurs most often in regions with relatively strong religious traditions. Fundamentalist sects often stress literal interpretation of religious texts and the centrality of religion in a person's life.

16. Cults represent an innovative response to secularization, and cult formation is highest in regions where church membership is lowest. Social movement cults are most likely to be joined by relatively well-educated young people, some of whom have experimented with psychedelic drugs.

17. Changes in social environments may influence religious innovations. Fundamentalism appears to flourish in homogeneous settings.

Religious individualism seems to develop in situations where market conditions are expanding. Acute forms of individuality have become more frequent in modern society and may have negative consequences.

18. Around the world, about 60 percent of all people belong to one of the seven largest religions: Christianity, Islam, Hinduism, Buddhism, Confucianism, Shintoism, and Judaism.

19. Despite official efforts to repress religion in a number of state socialist societies such as the Soviet Union, religious revival appears to be occurring there.

20. Religious leaders have also spoken out against violent state regimes in many parts of Latin America, as part of a movement termed "liberation theology." Liberation theology is aimed at public rather than private concerns, and seeks to end oppression and suffering of various kinds.

## KEY TERMS

church (p. 417)
civil religion (p. 408)
cults (p. 418)
denomination (p. 417)
evangelicalism (p. 421)
fundamentalism (p. 421)
individualism (p. 425)
millenarian movements (p. 418)
religion (p. 415)
religious movement (p. 417)
ritual (p. 414)
sect (p. 420)
secularization (p. 419)

## SUGGESTED READINGS

Bellah, Robert N., Richard Madsen, William M. Sullivan, Ann Swidler, and Steven M. Tipton. 1985. *Habits of the Heart.* Berkeley: University of California Press. A noteworthy study of middle-class Americans' search for meaning and commitment in the 1980s.

Bromley, David G., and Anson D. Shupe, Jr. 1979. *"Moonies" in America: Cult, Church, and Crusade.* Beverly Hills, CA: Sage. A sociological analysis of the Unification Church, one of the major "cult" movements in the United States.

Hadden, Jeffrey K., and Charles E. Swann. 1981. *Prime Time Preachers: The Rising Power of Televangelism.* Reading, MA: Addison-Wesley. Explores the growing phenomenon of electronic religion.

Stark, Rodney, and William Sims Bainbridge. 1985. *The Future of Religion: Secularization, Revival, and Cult Formation.* Berkeley: University of California Press. A major sociological analysis of religious changes and reactions, drawing on more than a decade of research by the authors.

Weber, Max. 1904/1958. *The Protestant Ethic and the Spirit of Capitalism.* New York: Scribner's. A clear and classic analysis of the possible connections between religious beliefs and the rise of capitalism.

Wright, Robin. 1985. *Sacred Rage: The Crusade of Modern Islam.* New York: Simon & Schuster. A journalist's account and analysis of the rise and significance of modern-day Islamic revolutionaries.

# Science and Technology

The first public warning was dangerously high levels of radiation in Sweden, Finland, Norway, and Denmark early on the morning of April 28, 1986. By evening, Moscow television made a brief announcement. The full text of it was: "An accident has taken place at the Chernobyl power station, and one of the reactors was damaged. Measures are being taken to eliminate the consequences of the accident. Those affected by it are being given assistance. A government commission has been set up" (Greenwald, 1986, p. 39). Over the weekend, a nuclear power reactor had melted down and exploded. It killed 3 people immediately, and another 28 died soon after from acute radiation poisoning (Barringer, 1988). The long-term health and environmental damage is still being assessed.

We cannot go through a day without noticing the importance of science. Bridges and elevators, antibiotics and telephones, videotapes and artificial hearts, vacuum cleaners, space shuttles, jet planes, polyester, and new ways of organizing the social relations of work—all these result from the social institution we call science.

The development of science is one of the most distinctive features of modern industrial society. Here the term **science** refers to the approach used to obtain reliable knowledge about the physical and social worlds, based on systematic empirical observation. Science has helped to increase agricultural productivity, encourage economic growth, control disease, and increase life expectancy. Because it is an intense form of social discovery and invention, science is a constant source of social change both within itself and in relation to other social institutions. Science has a dark side as well. It poses major threats to life and health in the chemical, thermal, genetic, and radioactive harm it may do to us and to our environment, and it has been used to create an unsurpassed array of destructive weapons. As a result of the intense positive and negative implications of science, it is a major source of social tension and controversy.

The **institution of science** comprises the social communities that share certain theories and methods aimed at understanding the physical and social worlds. The word "science" may also refer to the knowledge obtained by those communities. The goal of science is to determine general principles that underlie natural and social events. It does not matter that these principles may not have any immediate practical utility.

Scientists are concerned with understanding the physical and social world; engineers, technologists, and managers seek to use the knowledge gathered by scientists to solve practical problems and make things work. Much of what we think of as science is actually the result of **technology,** or the practical application of scientific knowledge.

Science has flourished in only a few times and places in history. Some observers suggest that our current scientific flowering is due to the happy bonding of science and technology in our society (Sklair, 1973). Science and technology have accomplished some remarkable things in the last century. Diseases such as smallpox, diphtheria, whooping cough, scarlet fever, polio, and pneumonia have been reduced or wiped out through medical research. Crop yields have soared as the result of plant research and the development of chemical fertilizers and pesticides.

For a time, the marvels of science and technology were considered an unquestioned good; but in recent years, that confident appraisal has faltered. By reducing infant mortality and extending life expectancy, the same booming crop yields and medical advances also unleashed the worst population explosion in the world's history, a slowly ticking bomb that confronts millions with the prospect of starvation before the century ends. The result of spraying bugs with the pesticide DDT was that the hazardous chemical began appearing in well water, lakes, and oceans. Changes in the production of steel and electricity produce pollutants in the American

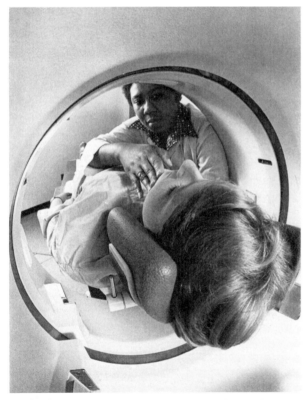

*Technology, or the practical application of scientific knowledge, has produced many benefits including new techniques of medical diagnosis. Here a computerized axial tomography (or CAT scan) will produce hundreds of X-ray pictures which are fed into a computer. The computer combines those pictures to reveal highly detailed images of body structure. CAT scans help to diagnose or rule out damage from a stroke, the existence of a brain tumor, and other conditions.*

Midwest and Northeast that blow north, fall as acid rain, and kill the fish in Canadian lakes. Scandinavian countries face the same problem from industrial Europe. Einstein's theories and atom-splitting physicists have produced nuclear wastes no one wants and nuclear weapons that can destroy life on this planet.

In the first section of this chapter, we consider why and how science has become institutionalized in the modern world. We also consider the different kinds of questions functionalists and conflict sociologists raise about science as an institution. The next three sections examine the internal operations of science. Any social activity generates certain social norms that suggest how people should behave; science is no exception. Sociologists study the norms of science and the conditions under which those norms may be violated.

Sociologists also study the processes of creativity and productivity within science to see how social factors affect productivity. Creative discoveries may provoke change in science. Sociologists are interested in how scientists react to new discoveries and theories, particularly when they challenge existing ideas. The final section of the chapter returns to the relation between science and society to consider (1) how science affects economic productivity, (2) the state of science in the United States today, (3) controversies in science policy, and (4) issues in the democratic governance of scientific activity.

## THE RISE AND INSTITUTIONALIZATION OF SCIENCE

### The Rise of Modern Science

Science existed in some form even in the very earliest human societies. But modern science as we know it today was inspired by the Italian Renaissance of the fifteenth century, during which the cultural heritage of Greek and Roman antiquity was rediscovered. Included in this revival of ancient scholarship were numerous scientific works written in Greek and Latin; these gave a new impetus to the development of Western thought. The invention of the printing press by Gutenberg in 1439 slowly made books more widely available, thus helping to transform learning and culture. The exploration of the world's oceans and lands placed new demands on astronomy and mathematics. Some of these developing techniques were also used by officers, military surgeons, and engineers in the wars of the Protestant Reformation. These events lowered the class barriers to such applied practical knowledge.

In the seventeenth century there was a revolution in the way people thought about the natural world, and this did a great deal to help scientific investigation. Nature was stripped of its spiritual and human properties and became open to objective investigation. Reflected in the views of Francis Bacon in England (born 1561), René Descartes in France (born 1596), and Galileo Galilei in Italy (born 1564), this approach saw nature as something that could be explored using sensory data, disciplined observation, and reasoning. There was a growing awareness that cooperative efforts were needed to collect and test data about the natural world. The first scientific society, the Royal Society in London, was founded in 1662 to encourage the exchange of observations about the natural world and to ensure that scientists received credit for their original discoveries. These societies founded the first scientific journals to share discoveries and theories.

In this early period, science was conducted on a very small scale by gentlemen of independent means or by engineers or physicians who conducted experiments in their spare time. Benjamin Franklin, for example, carried on electrical experiments while pursuing a career as a printer, publisher, author, and statesman. Only a few universities (for example, Edinburgh in Scotland and Leiden in The Netherlands) offered serious instruction in science. The idea of a full-time career dedicated to the pursuit of scientific work or of large laboratories with teams of many scientists working on projects was unknown.

The tradition of the gentleman scholar persisted longer in England than elsewhere because there were few full-time jobs for scientists there. Meanwhile, in the nineteenth century, Germany was building a strong university system. At a number of different centers, research and teaching were joined; students received research training in the university laboratory. With this institutional support and a strong system of scholarly journals and handbooks, German science took the lead in many fields between 1830 and 1880. Science in the United States during the nineteenth century was highly dependent on Europe; the major American universities were not deeply involved in basic research. Around the turn of the century, many Americans studied in Germany and returned with ideas about how to transplant features of the German system to the United States. In the 1930s, American science was greatly strengthened by the influx of refugee scholars fleeing from the Nazis. Many "American" Nobel prize-winning scientists were actually born and trained in Germany before moving to the United States. Since the end of World War II, there has been an unparalleled explosion of scientific achievements as nations have poured resources into the search for deeper understanding of the physical universe.

As Price (1963) noted, the growth of science has been exponential, which means that science has grown at an increasingly rapid rate. One way of expressing that growth is in the number of years it takes for scientific activity to double. Whatever measure is used—for example, the number of people in science or the number of publications—it tends to double within 10 to 12 years (Price, 1963, 1975). This rate of development means that at any given time, half the scientific papers ever published have appeared in the past decade. The result is that science appears (and to some degree is) continually new (Price, 1975). Nearly 90 percent of all the scientists who ever worked are alive today. This tendency also means that most of the scientists working at any given time are quite young— that is, in the first decade of their work. So most scientific discoveries are made by young scientists simply because there are more of them.

## The Institutionalization of Science

In order for science to survive and flourish, careers for practicing scientists need to be established in major social institutions. This process is called the **institutionalization of science.** It is described by Ben-David (1971). Careers and positions in science need historical continuity and some commitment of social resources if they are to stay healthy. When such institutionalized positions exist, people can train for and pursue lifetime careers as scientists. Otherwise, the pursuit of scientific activity is restricted to the independently wealthy or to hobbyists.

Today there are 4.7 million scientists and engineers in the United States, and less than one in five of them works in research and development (U.S. Bureau of the Census, 1989a). Most research scientists work on teams in large centers connected with universities or corporations. Part of the research process consists of writing proposals to obtain funding as well as conducting and writing up the results of the group's research. The lone scientist working in an attic or basement is rare today. The occasional one that appears (such as Stephen Jobs, who invented the Apple computer in his garage) may be given wide media coverage precisely because he or she is unusual.

Studies of occupational prestige in a number of major industrial societies show that scientific occupations are generally rated quite highly. Within the scientific community, those conducting and publishing original research are most highly esteemed (Cole and Cole, 1973). Nearly three-quarters of the scientists and engineers employed in research and development (R&D) worked in industry in 1987, 15 percent worked in colleges and universities, 8 percent for the federal government, and 4 percent for independent research and development centers. This is close to the proportions in 1960 (U.S. Bureau of the Census, 1989a). Within the R&D group, the highly productive units tend to be concentrated in relatively few university departments and in industrial, government, and nonprofit research laboratories.

## Functional and Conflict Approaches to Science

Functionalists see science as a major source of social change. Indeed, it is one of their major explanations for such change. Robert K. Merton, one of the leading sociologists of science, stresses that the relationship between science and other institutions does not move in only one direction. Science not only influences and changes other social institutions, such as the family (for example, through birth-control technology), religion (by challenging a literal interpretation of scripture), or the economy (by enhancing economic growth) but is itself influenced by social institutions. Merton's research on science in seventeenth-century England found that there was an interplay between institutional spheres. Science was affected by industrial, trade, military, and religious concerns, as well as having powerful consequences for those institutions (1970).

The conflict perspective focuses on how the distribution of power and resources affects science—for instance, by influencing the direction scientific inquiry takes. The influence of oil, gas, and nuclear industries may shift scientific research toward ways of extracting oil from shale and away from exploring small-scale windmill or solar sources of energy (Etzkowitz, 1984). To the degree that large corporations shape the direction of scientific research, they are likely to sponsor work in areas that will produce the greatest profits rather than in those that may have social and ecological value on a large scale. Conflict theorists would therefore be likely to ask: Who benefits from a particular line of research and who does not?

Some sociologists would go even further and suggest that science and the scientific method are a central part of the domination of weaker groups or nations by stronger ones (Habermas, 1970). Rationality, science, and technology have become for many Western peoples the only way of dealing with reality and other people. But although rationality may offer a valuable approach to many problems, it should not be forgotten that rationality may support the interests of certain groups (manufacturing and military interests) more than others (tribal societies, landed aristocracy, or unemployed ghetto residents), and that it may not be the best approach to all situations.

In examining the relationship between science and other institutions in society, functionalists and conflict theorists raise different types of questions. They also consider different issues within science itself. Functionalists, as we see in the next section of this chapter, examine the norms of science and how they are functional for the conduct of scientific research. Conflict theorists tend to focus on instances where those norms are violated (for example, in cases of scientific fraud), and ask whether they were violated because of the interests of one rather than another special group. Both approaches raise interesting and important questions about science as a social institution.

## THE NORMS OF SCIENCE

Merton (1957) suggests that certain norms prevail in science because they are functional for science as an institution. These norms include universalism, "communism," disinterestedness, and organized skepticism. If these norms did not operate, Merton indicates, science would not survive and flourish.

*Universalism* suggests that scientific statements are to be evaluated in terms of already existing scientific criteria, rather than in terms of the race, sex, religion, class, or fame of the person proposing them. The importance of this norm for the health of science was revealed in Nazi Germany when it rejected non-Aryan, especially Jewish, physics. German scientists at that time did not take Einstein's theories seriously and were unable to pursue lines of development stemming from those ideas.

*Communism* in science refers to the joint production, ownership, and utilization of scientific ideas by the entire scientific community. Even those making major discoveries that are named after them (for example, Newton's laws, Pasteur's pasteurization process for milk, Salk's vaccine, Einstein's theory of relativity), do not own those contributions. The ideas become part of the common property of the scientific community. One aspect of this norm is the opposition to secrecy in the conduct of scientific work. One's ideas are to be shared fully and readily with anyone who is interested.

The norm of *disinterestedness* requires scientists to put scientific truth above personal considerations. Merton (1957) suggests that the strong presence of this norm within the institution of science helps to explain the relative rarity of fraud in the history of science, "which appears exceptional when compared with the record of other spheres of activity . . ." (p. 559). He suggests that it is not the personal qualities of scientists that affect the likelihood of fraud but the structural contexts in which they work (pp. 286–324). Sociologists ask: What structural and cultural conditions promote or dampen violations of these norms? Merton (1973a) suggests that scientific deviance can be explained in a similar way to other forms of deviance, namely, as a response to the intensified emphasis on original discovery in the culture of science in the face of the very real difficulty of making an original discovery (p. 323). Faced with a situation where available means and desirable goals are not well matched, scientists may respond in various ways (described in Table 7.3). Not all of these adaptations are consistent with the norms of science (Merton, 1973a, p. 323; Zuckerman, 1977, pp. 87–138).

It is permissible for scientists to be motivated by the desire for recognition for their scientific contributions or the desire to benefit humanity, but those motives must never take priority over scientific integrity.

*Organized skepticism* requires scientists to scrutinize all statements in terms of the evidence that supports them and their logic. No belief is too sacred not to be viewed skeptically until the evidence is in. The norm is built into the institution of science through the standards of evidence and inference that are taught to new scientists as they are trained and in the way scientific papers are reviewed before being accepted for publication by scientific journals.

Although these norms may very well reflect the beliefs, behaviors, and attitudes of most members of the scientific community, they do not give us the whole picture. We must look at actual practice in science for a complete understanding of it as a social institution. Examples exist where these norms are violated (Broad and Wade, 1982). Famous scientists, especially Nobel prize winners, for example, are more likely to get their work accepted for publication and noticed once it is published than are little-known scientists (Zuckerman and Merton, 1971). Similarly, work by people at major research institutions may receive more attention than work by people from lesser-known places. In *The Double Helix,* James Watson (1968) tells how he visited the laboratories of other researchers to learn about the DNA research they were doing while telling them little about his own work. By using the willingness of others to share in order to advance his own work (which, with that of Francis Crick and Rosalind Franklin, led to the discovery in 1953 of the structure of the DNA molecule), he may have violated the norms of communism and disinterestedness.

Violations of the norms of science may come from pressures on individuals to achieve rapid research success. A scientist at the Sloan-Kettering Institute, for example, painted dark patches on white mice to convince his colleagues that he had learned how to make successful skin grafts between non-twins (Rensberger, 1977). Other cases of fraudulent research have been discovered in recent years. And allegations of fraudulent or careless research by laboratories testing new drugs on animals especially concern scientists and health administrators.

Sir Cyril Burt was a British psychologist who worked from the 1930s to the 1950s on intelligence. His results showed the dominance of genetic rather than environmental influences on intelligence and provided the "scientific" rationale for the wide use of IQ tests in the British school system. They were also the basis for Arthur Jensen's claims that the lower IQ scores of black children, compared to those of whites, may be due to genetic differences (Jensen, 1969). In recent years Burt's studies of separated identical twins have been severely criticized. An American psychologist, Leon Kamin (1974) of Princeton University, found that Burt's work was filled with verbal contradictions and arithmetical inconsistencies as well as failure to provide information about crucial procedural details. The medical correspondent of the London *Sunday Times* was unable to locate any evidence that the coauthors of Burt's later papers (Margaret Howard and J. Conway) had ever existed (Wade, 1976). Later the *London Times* reported that a Ms. Howard had been a faculty member at London University during the 1930s, but doubts remain about the other coauthor and about the validity of Burt's data.

Fraudulent claims waste the time and money of other scientists who try to replicate the falsified results. Careless or fraudulent research flagrantly violates the norms of disinterestedness and organized skepticism. Such violations may occur more often than people realize. One Brit-

ish scientist writes: "Although scientists in general are very critical of untested assumptions, the assumption of scientific impartiality is almost completely untested" (cited in Rensberger, 1977, p. 44). The pressure on young scientists for quick and successful results, rapid publication, and grant-seeking success may overpower the norm of disinterestedness. The goal of scientific discovery may be replaced by the desire for publications and grant support.

As has been noted (Merton, 1984), some science journalists maintain that fraud in science is commonplace. "Thus, William Broad and Nickolas Wade write (1982) of 'the cases of fraud that occur quite regularly in the elite institutions of science,'—this, on the basis of a grand total of 34, 'known or suspected cases of scientific fraud,' since 200 B.C. listed in their appendix." But, there is no census of deviant (including fraudulent) behavior by scientists (Merton, 1973), so relative frequency cannot be determined. Moreover, violations do not deny the existence of norms. The scientific community's vigorous opposition to fraudulent behavior suggests the existence of strong norms.

One indication of the scientific community's commitment to the norms against fraud is the fact that *Science* magazine, the official publication of the American Association for the Advancement of Science, publishes exposés of such incidents. Like any other profession seeking to maintain its autonomy, science as a profession must convince others that it is actively policing itself and that it stands ready to repudiate wrongdoers.

## CHANGE AND RESISTANCE TO CHANGE IN SCIENCE

### Kuhn and the Structure of Scientific Revolutions

If the norms of science call for scientists to be open-minded and always on the lookout for evidence that seems to undermine the theories they believe, the history of science tells a different story. The stormy process whereby scientific theories are challenged, defended, and ultimately overthrown is vividly described by

Kuhn (1970). People generally believe that scientific knowledge advances like a highway being built—research experiments gradually but steadily add to the unfolding ribbon of knowledge called science. This view of how science advances is close to what Kuhn calls "normal science." However, Kuhn challenged this view with his notion of "scientific revolutions," which he saw as contrasting sharply with normal science.

By **normal science** Kuhn meant research based on one or more past scientific achievements that are accepted as a useful foundation for further practice. The achievements that form the foundation must be new enough to attract a group of scientists who want to work within it, yet open-ended enough to leave a number of unresolved problems to work on. Kuhn uses the term **paradigm** to refer to a coherent tradition of scientific laws, theory, applications, assumptions, and measurement that forms a distinct approach to problems. The paradigms we call Copernican astronomy, Newtonian physics, or Einsteinian physics have distinguishable concepts, methods, and practices. Most scientists work in "normal science," solving puzzles that can be answered within a given paradigm. When scientists are trained, they are introduced to the prevailing assumptions and practices within the dominant paradigm of their field. They do not learn all the paradigms that have been discarded throughout the history of scientific investigation or even alternative contemporary paradigms that are regarded as "wrong." Such exposure would be considered a waste of time.

Sociologists of science are becoming increasingly aware that the development of theoretical paradigms may be influenced by social and cultural factors. For example, Darwin's concept of natural selection as a key mechanism in the process of evolution was influenced by Thomas Malthus's argument that population growth will be checked only as the "poor and inept" are eliminated by the ruthless agencies of hunger and disease (Mulkay, 1979; Schon, 1963). But this theoretical idea of Darwin's was very general, since he could not specify the laws of variation or the way that variations were preserved (Young, 1971, p. 469). Metaphors from outside science may shape the content of scientific ideas, especially in the case where there is "interpretive failure," that is, where scientific insights cannot

fully explain what is occurring (Mulkay, 1979, p. 109).

Without a guiding paradigm, researchers in a given field would find it difficult to define the important problems in the field and to determine the best way of solving them. The existence of a healthy paradigm does a great deal to further the advance of knowledge through normal science. The stage becomes set for a scientific revolution when increasing numbers of problems cannot be solved by the existing paradigm and when scientific observations begin to contradict the paradigm. Called **anomalies,** such examples are set aside and ignored for a while, as long as there are other problems that can be fruitfully explored within the paradigm and as long as no better paradigm comes along.

At such a time a scientific field may be in crisis, but scientists will not abandon their guiding paradigm until an alternative that explains more than the old one is proposed. Even when a new paradigm is offered, not all scientists will accept it immediately. Kuhn suggests that sometimes a paradigm must wait for a new generation of scientists who are not wedded to the old tradition before it is fully accepted. If a new paradigm does enable scientists to work fruitfully on more new problems, it will eventually triumph. Kuhn believes that the usual developmental pattern of mature science appears in the successive transition from one paradigm to another via revolution.

For example, in the eighteenth century, the prevailing paradigm in chemistry explained fire in terms of the escape of a substance called phlogiston. But the phlogiston theory could not explain why some materials gained weight after they burned. It was in such a context that Lavoisier offered his oxygen theory of combustion, which did take into account the greater weight of some substances after they burned. Similarly, Ptolemy's theory that the earth was the center of the universe led to imprecise predictions of planetary positions and gradually gave way to the Copernican view that the sun was at the center, despite violent opposition from religious groups. In another example, the wave theory of light was challenged by the particle theory, and today a hybrid paradigm describes light as photons, entities that exhibit some characteristics of waves and some of particles (Kuhn, 1970). These examples reveal that the development of science is not like the orderly succession of democratic governments but instead does sometimes resemble a **scientific revolution**—that is, the dramatic overthrow of one intellectual regime (or paradigm) by another.

## How Paradigms Affect Scientific Observations

The provisional nature of science is underscored by the philosopher of science Karl Popper (1959), who suggests that science can never establish the truth of scientific laws with absolute finality. All it can do is to advance a theory as possibly true until it is demonstrated to be false. With respect to paradigm shifts, Popper's view poses problems for Kuhn. The reason is that once you step outside a theory, you lose the shared operating assumptions and accepted methods of observation and interpretation that guide the conduct of science. It then becomes impossible to test the absolute truth or falsity of a scientific theory as Popper urges. This does not mean Kuhn believes that all theories are equally valid or that "anything goes" in science. Even though the absolute validity of a scientific theory may be impossible to determine, the relative value of one rather than another theory may be certainly judged by seeing how well the paradigm solves a number of problems in science and by considering its usefulness for suggesting further avenues of inquiry.

A strong paradigm in science may make it difficult for scientists to "see" an occurrence that is an anomaly within the paradigm. The problem partly stems from the fact that our perceptions are guided by what we believe, as demonstrated in an experiment by Bruner and Postman (1949). They asked subjects to identify a series of playing cards. Many of the cards were normal, but some had been made anomalous—for example, there was a red six of spades and a black four of hearts (in a normal deck, spades are black and hearts are red). Single cards were exposed to subjects, and after each one subjects were asked what they had seen. Even the anomalous cards were identified, without hesitation or puzzlement, as normal. The black four of hearts might, for example, be identified as a four of spades or of hearts. People were unaware that it was different and were readily able to place it in one of the categories supplied by prior experience.

If scientific theories are likened to such prior experience, the role they play in actually organizing our perceptions of the world becomes more apparent. This is why it is sometimes difficult to identify phenomena that challenge a theory. Similarly, the decision to use a certain type of apparatus or measuring instrument carries several assumptions—for example, that only certain circumstances will arise and that the apparatus or measure being used will tap everything important about a phenomenon. If you took a thermometer to a radioactive dump, you might conclude there was nothing unusual there.

## Constructing Scientific "Facts"

A recent development in the sociology of science focuses on the content of scientific knowledge. Specifically, the concern is "in what sense and to what degree . . . is knowledge . . . rooted in social life" (Knorr-Cetina and Mulkay, 1983, p. 6). Phrased differently, the concern is "with what comes to count as scientific knowledge and how it comes to count" (Collins, 1983, p. 267). Researchers such as Knorr-Cetina (1981) and Latour and Woolgar (1986) have done detailed field studies of biological laboratories and the scientists who work in them. They note that much laboratory work involves elaborate equipment that collates and analyzes information rather than simply reflecting nature. Scientists spend considerable time discussing and arguing about what they have "seen" before they reach agreement about what it is. Knowledge does not simply spring straightforwardly out of an experiment (Knorr-Cetina, 1983, p. 162). Moreover, a major activity of scientists is the writing and rewriting of papers for publication. The purpose is to produce "publications designed to persuade others that what they are saying is true, important, worthy of support, and dictated by an external reality" (Zuckerman, 1988, p. 554). The work of Latour, Woolgar, and Knorr-Cetina suggests that the content of scientific ideas or findings emerges from so-

cial interaction. However, they do not deny the existence of an independent reality that scientists try to understand (Restivo, 1988).

Other researchers have examined the possible connection between interest groups in society and the direction of certain scientific work. For example, studies of the development of statistics in Britain from 1865 to 1930 suggest that the eugenics movement may have influenced the kinds of problems addressed by leading British statisticians (MacKenzie, 1981; Stigler, 1986). While social beliefs may have affected what they studied, it is less clear that those beliefs shaped what they found (Zuckerman, 1988, p. 551). These new developments in the sociology of science are significant because they focus on the process of producing scientific knowledge. Previous work devoted more effort to the products of science (Star, 1988).

## Resistance to New Ideas

History is full of examples of scientific ideas being rejected by the society in which the scientist operates. Galileo was tried by the medieval Catholic Church for his heretical astronomy. Charles Darwin's ideas were strongly opposed by religious bodies in his day—and religious resistance to them persists now—on the grounds that evolutionary theory runs counter to biblical accounts of the creation. Somewhat more surprising, perhaps, is the fact that resistance to ideas occurs within the scientific community itself. Scientists, after all, strongly value open-mindedness and view as illegitimate moral, political, or religious influences on the acceptance or rejection of a theory. But values such as open-mindedness, no matter how strongly held, do not fully explain human behavior. Cultural and social factors may reinforce or limit the expression of values in behavior (Barber, 1961). In other words, cultural blinders may operate in science as they do in other social realms.

As we noted earlier, theoretical ideas or methods of measuring phenomena may lead scientists to overlook or reject discoveries they or others make. Some scientists like theory; others prefer experiments or observations. Some like theories to be put into models. Some scientists want a particularly mathematical analysis, whereas others reject such an approach. Any of these preferences may provide a source of resistance to innovation.

A scientist's ideas may also be rejected because he or she is unknown in the community of science. A striking example was the case of the Austrian monk Gregor Mendel, whose research on inheritance of specific physical characteristics eventually created a paradigm revolution in genetics. Mendel first announced his theory in

1865, and it was published in the scientific proceedings of his time. But his discovery languished until his work was rediscovered and replicated in 1900. His work was ignored despite the fact that Mendel sent his paper to one of the most distinguished botanists of the day, Carl von Nageli of Munich. Von Nageli and other prominent scientists of the time dismissed Mendel's ideas as preposterous partly because they differed from von Nageli's and partly because Mendel seemed "an insignificant provincial" to them (Barber, 1961). As science has become more organized and bureaucratized, the possibility exists that innovative ideas by unknowns will not be published.

Professional specialization among scientists may lead to the rejection of new ideas that come from people outside a particular specialty. An interesting example comes from the history of medicine. Pasteur's germ theory of disease generated violent resistance from the medical men of his time. They continued to operate with dirty hands and instruments, causing countless patients to die of infection.

## SOCIAL PROCESSES AFFECTING SCIENTIFIC PRODUCTIVITY

Despite the resistance to ideas, a great deal of innovation does occur within science. **Innovation** refers to the discovery or invention of new ideas, things, or methods. Innovation tends to stimulate further innovation. Besides sometimes blocking scientific developments, social processes may also encourage and increase innovation, leading to greater productivity.

Numbers of scientists and research funds are important for scientific productivity (Price, 1971). By themselves, however, they do not seem to ensure success. Sociologists studying science have tried to identify what social features of scientific groups contribute to their greater or lesser productivity. **Scientific productivity** means making new discoveries, confirming or disconfirming theoretical hypotheses through experimentation and other types of research, and publishing the results of that research. At the national level, the relatively small British, German, and Swiss scientific communities have won Nobel prizes and produced scientific papers

at a disproportionately high rate for their numbers and financing since 1950 (Collins, 1975). There are many cases of one research laboratory, with financial and staff resources similar to another, producing many more inventions and discoveries than others. Such occurrences suggest that although adequate resources are necessary for scientific and technological advances, they do not guarantee results.

Several other factors seem to enhance productivity. Where there is maximum competition between research centers innovation will be greater, assuming that all rewards are not controlled by a single organization (Collins, 1975). This permits a number of alternative approaches to be pursued. Innovations are also more likely to occur where independent disciplines come into contact or where an individual is trained in one field but takes a job teaching or doing research in a different but related field. This has happened when people trained in biology moved into psychology and when mathematicians shifted into sociology. Laboratories that are organized in a hierarchical rather than a decentralized democratic way limit scientific productivity in a field by crimping the career chances of younger scientists (Ben-David and Zloczower, 1962) or by inducing premature conformity to ways of solving problems.

These general principles are illustrated by the case of the University of California at Berkeley's work in microelectronics. The founders of that program established a situation in which experimental facilities and equipment are shared among faculty people, a setup that is uncommon in American universities and virtually unknown in other countries. This arrangement means not only that together the researchers have better facilities than any one of them could have singly but also that they communicate and learn from one another as they pursue their own work. These factors appear to have contributed to the worldwide leadership of that department in microelectronics (Hodges, 1979).

In an industrial setting, technological innovations are encouraged by companies that not only reward successful new ideas but also avoid punishing failures. Innovation flourishes when the producer of an unsuccessful idea is encouraged to try a second and often even a third time to come up with something new. In addition, scientific productivity is high in organizations in which ideas are solicited from everyone, from top executives to middle managers to customers, without regard to the rank of the originator (Ingrassia, 1980).

Certain patterns run through a number of major industrial innovations, including the development of the IBM 360 computer, the introduction of the Xerox 914, the development of synthetic rubber by the petrochemical industry during World War II, and Data General's creation of the MV/8000 computer introduced in 1980 (Kidder, 1981; Quinn, 1979). The facilitating conditions in all those situations include these:

1. Strong incentives for successful development at the corporate level, whether from gains in market share or increased profits.
2. For those doing work, the goals of the project needed to be clear to all and to inspire fervent commitment. Making more money rarely brings this level of commitment, but creating a significant technical advance can spur people to new efforts.
3. Although the goal needed to be clearly defined by management, the people working on the project needed to have important roles in finding the particular technologies or solutions for meeting those needs.
4. These firms encouraged multiple competing approaches at both the basic research and the development stages. J. Thomas West of Data General heightened a dispute among engineers into almost a blood feud, but in the process he raised performance to new peaks.
5. The companies also involved the people who would eventually use, make, install, or service the product or system they were designing.
6. At the corporate level, there was a longer than usual time horizon on the major innovation (ten to twenty years or longer). Data General was an exception in that an unusually short time (18 months) was available. In that case the time limit was part of the challenge.
7. There was support for risky projects from top management.

One problem with technological innovation in organizations is the concern for profits. Many companies purposely keep research expenditures low so that they will not eat into profits. Such corporate behavior may keep profits sound in the short run but hurt them in later years, when the lack of research results in fewer new products to sell. One solution is for organizations to mix short-range and long-range projects. One company expects to get 25 percent of its total sales each year from products that did not exist five years earlier. Other companies have a special fund to finance long-shot projects. At Texas Instruments, which has such a fund, about half the projects fail, a record that leaves the company unperturbed. Another company offers cash incentives to inventors and enables top scientists to earn more than the managers to whom they report. The incentives show that technical creativity is highly valued and will be rewarded (Ingrassia, 1980).

In one study, creative ability, as measured by social researchers, was not necessarily related to scientific productivity (Pelz and Andrews, 1966). Instead, the study showed the significance of the delicate interplay between personal characteristics and the social organization of scientific work. Several work situations seemed to encourage high levels of productivity from the scientists' creative abilities, including working on a project or specializing in an area for a relatively short time, working on a team that was not too tightly coordinated, having the opportunity to influence important decisions, and having the facilities to communicate new ideas to others (Pelz and Andrews, 1966). Highly creative scientists who worked in environments where new ideas were not valued tended to become frustrated and to produce less than moderately creative scientists in better settings.

Scientific productivity has important implications for economic development, controversies over science policies, and the democratic governance of science. In other words, the relationship between science and society affects and is affected by scientific productivity.

## SCIENCE AND SOCIETY

Factors within as well as outside science may influence its direction. Wars and revolutions, famine and plague, sea exploration, economic booms and busts, religious revivals, and secular ideologies will affect staffing, social support for science, the material apparatus, and even the areas considered important for research. Just as events and institutions outside science may affect what happens within it, so also may science influence the position of one nation relative to others—for example, by accelerating the economic growth of a society or by increasing its military prowess. Within a society, controversies over the safety and desirability of various science policies may provoke public debate and protest. Such controversies raise serious issues about the place of knowledge and participation in the creation of science policy in a democracy.

## Science and Economic Productivity

Like a robust worker in the prime of life, American productivity seemed healthy for nearly twenty years after World War II. The annual rate of increase in labor productivity (output per hour) averaged 3.2 percent in the period from 1948 to 1965, slowed to 2.3 percent in the 1965 to 1973 period, and tumbled to only 1.2 percent in the 1973 to 1978 period (Federal Reserve Bank of San Francisco, 1980). By 1978 the rate had dropped to 0.5 percent. In 1979 and 1980, American productivity *declined*, but in 1982 it began increasing again.

The past economic productivity of the United States may have drawn heavily on scientific and technological innovation. **Research and Development (R&D)** refers to investments in basic research and in the practical application of basic research discoveries. Some economists estimate that nearly half of the economic growth of the United States between 1929 and 1969 was due to technical innovation (Tesar, 1978). Can this trend continue? The possibilities for scientific advances include computers that think like humans and mechanical robots that work better than humans. Gene-splicing techniques for recombining the DNA building blocks of cells are creating new organisms that can fight ailments like hoof-and-mouth disease, which afflicts cattle. Soon it may be possible to isolate the genes of molds that produce the soil nitrates needed by plants, so that these genes can be spliced into the genetic structure of the plants, thus eliminating the need for chemical fertilizers. Tiny

man-made organisms may be able to digest oil spills like the one caused by the oil tanker Valdez, thus minimizing damage to the environment. The energy crisis may be partially solved by technologies such as silicon photovoltaic cells that can convert sunlight directly into electricity. With developments in superconductivity, it may become possible to store electricity and then send it long distances at low cost. Materials-intensive technologies may also be dramatically improved. For example, 100 pounds of optical fibers in a cable can send as many telephone or other messages as a ton of copper wire (Bell, 1987). Such discoveries suggest that we stand on the brink of further technological transformations.

Which societies are in the best position to capitalize on these tremendous scientific developments? Japan, Germany, and Great Britain, at least, are making a concerted effort to capture some of the new electronic developments. A five-year program is under way in Japan, financed by $250 million in government and industrial money, to develop microelectronic technologies and production equipment. The British government has invested at least $90 million in a new company to develop and manufacture large-scale integrated circuits used in computers and other electronic devices. The Japanese, the Germans, and the Soviets have increased the proportion of GNP earmarked for R&D. The United States has been reducing its investment. The development and application of science requires resources and supportive settings. The basic research support that the U.S. government has been providing in recent years has not kept pace with inflation. Although business support for basic research has been increasing, it has not been rising fast enough to close the gap.

An estimated $117.8 billion of federal and private money was spent on R&D in the United States in 1987. This represents 2.6 percent of the total gross national product and is down from 3 percent of GNP in 1964 (U.S. Bureau of the Census, 1989a, p. 578).

The real growth rate of R&D spending declined sharply in the early 1980s. After a brief increase in 1984, the growth rate leveled off (Figure 17.1). About 80 percent of U.S. government-supported R&D is for military pur-

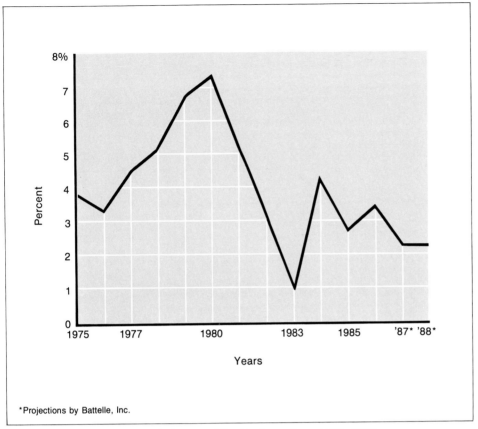

**Figure 17.1   Real Growth Rate of R&D Spending 1975–1988 (percentage increase from prior year).**

Since 1984, the growth rate of R&D spending in the United States has leveled off.

poses, economists estimate, and nearly one-third of U.S. scientists and engineers are in military R&D (Clark and Malabre, 1988). As a result, the United States trails Germany and Japan in its expenditures, as a percent of GNP, on nondefense R&D (Figure 17.2).

One consequence of this decline in funding may be the decrease in the number of patents issued to Americans for new inventions. In 1987, foreign inventors received nearly half of all U.S. patents, compared with only one-third in 1975 (Figure 17.3). In 1987, for the first time in history, no U.S. company was among the top three recipients, which were all Japanese: Canon Inc., Hitachi Ltd., and Toshiba Corp.

These are some signs that U.S. innovation may be declining. No one knows how much money for R&D is enough. Furthermore, legislators, members of the public, and business leaders need to believe that more money spent on R&D will result in a stronger economy and more jobs.

## The State of Science in the United States

Sociologists have offered several explanations for the declining rate of scientific development in the United States. These include a shortage of faculty to teach science and engineering, the rapid exportation of new technological breakthroughs by multinational corporations, and the diversion of existing scientific and technological personnel into military R&D.

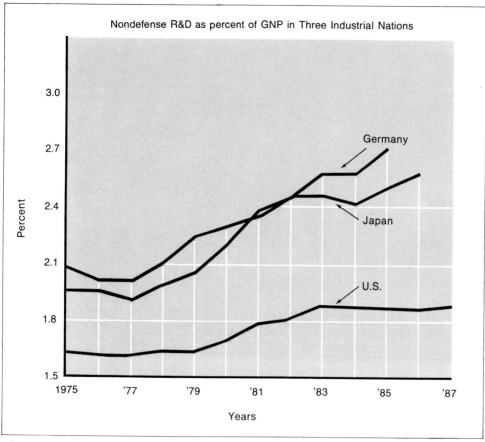

**Figure 17.2   Nondefense R&D as a Percent of GNP in Three Industrial Nations.**

In recent years the United States has spent a smaller percentage of its GNP on nondefense R&D than has Germany or Japan.

*Source:* National Science Board.

Japan, with half the population of the United States, graduated 19,257 electrical engineers with bachelor's and master's degrees or doctorates in 1977, whereas the United States produced a total of 14,290. An estimated one-third to one-half of engineering doctoral students in the United States are from foreign countries. High salaries for students graduating with a bachelor's degree in engineering serve to diminish the number who are interested in pursuing graduate degrees. The result is a major shortage of faculty to teach engineering students, making it difficult to expand research and the training of new engineers. Countries that are able to expand their training programs (or send their students to the United States for training) will be in a better position to maximize technological developments.

In addition to not keeping pace with the demand for well-trained scientific personnel, the United States has changed its policy about exporting technology. As recently as the late 1960s, firms in the United States would not sell their most advanced (called "front-end") technology to other countries because they would lose their competitive advantage by doing so. Now many U.S. firms have overseas subsidiaries that are using the newest technologies. Sometimes the latest technology is licensed to a foreign company, as when the Amdahl Corporation licensed its state-of-the-art computer technology to Fujitsu, a Japanese computer

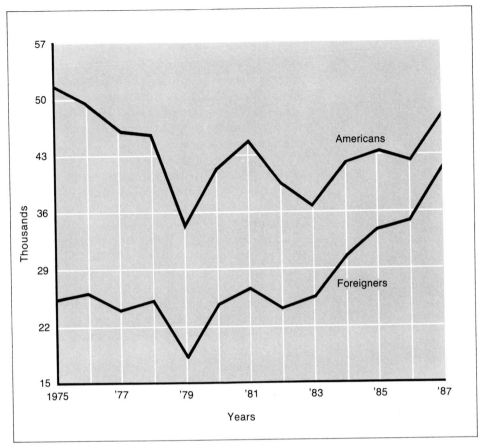

**Figure 17.3   Number of U.S. Patents Issued to Americans and Foreigners, 1975–1987.**

The number of U.S. patents received by other nationals has become nearly as large as the number received by Americans.

*Source:* U.S. Patent and Trademark Office.

maker (Blumberg, 1980). Well-developed foreign firms are then able to save the R&D costs that went into producing a given level of technology and to use that technology as a springboard for further advances. Such a step may accelerate the R&D of foreign technology, but it does nothing for the state of science and technology in the United States. (Such sales or licensing agreements do a great deal for the short-term balance sheets of multinational corporations, however.)

The third, and perhaps most significant, explanation for the slowing growth of American science and technology is the more than $2000 billion the United States has spent on military activities since 1946. Since World War II ended,

the United States has spent a larger share of its GNP on the military than any other advanced capitalist nation. (This does not include the Soviet Union.) The United States has spent about 9 percent of its GNP on the military, compared to Japan's less than 1 percent (Symanski, 1973). Some of these expenditures have been directed at scientific R&D, but usually they tend to be quite specifically applied to military or space efforts and do not support basic research in a broad variety of fields. Considerable scientific talent and resources have been devoted to research on nerve gas but rather little to sickle cell anemia. It has been argued by some that one reason the Japanese, for example, can spend so little on defense is because the United States has

Science and technology may have declined in the United States because so much of it has been directed toward military efforts such as the development of these nuclear missiles rather than toward more broadly useful scientific research.

stood ready to defend them should it become necessary.

A permanent military economy soaks up large numbers of scientists and technologists, drawing them away from other forms of research; moreover, the results of their research tend to be unproductive for improving human life or enhancing economic prosperity (Blumberg, 1980; Melman, 1974). This is not to say that life-enhancing scientific or technical breakthroughs never occur as the result of military research and development but simply that the same amount of money spent on more general scientific investigations would probably have many more productive and useful applications.

## Controversial Issues in Science

A number of controversies have swirled around science policy in the United States in recent years, but most of them have not dealt with how much money should be spent on the military compared to basic scientific research or training. Instead, the public has tended to become concerned about close-to-home issues like the teaching of evolutionary theory and the disposal of radioactive and poisonous waste products. These issues affect people in their own backyards, and they have generated considerable public discussion and protest.

### Evolutionary Theory Versus Creationism

For decades, Darwinian theories of the evolution of human life have clashed with **creationism,** which sees all major types of living things, including people, as having been made by the direct creative action of God in six days, as described in the biblical book of Genesis (Nelkin, 1977). Two points where the controversy came to a head were in challenges to state laws regarding the teaching of evolutionary theory and in conflicts over the content of textbooks that were adopted for public school biology classes. These controversies may be analyzed sociologically in terms of how they reveal ideological and organizational strategies used by science to establish itself as a profession (Gieryn et al., 1985).

In 1925 Tennessee passed a law forbidding any teacher to teach that "man has descended from a lower order of animals." Thomas Scopes was a young science teacher and coach in Dayton, Tennessee. Like most science teachers in the state, he had violated the new law because the official biology text—Hunter's *Civic Biology,* in use since 1909—contained elements of Darwin's theory of evolution. Scopes agreed to help challenge the law and allowed himself to be arrested for breaking it. This set the stage for the famous Scopes trial, which was an effort to challenge the constitutionality of that Tennessee law (Eldredge, 1982; Furniss, 1954). At the heart of Scopes's defense was the argument that "if the Bible were reasonably interpreted in a non-literal way, its account of creation is *compatible* with scientific theories of evolution" (Gieryn et al., 1985, p. 395). The strategy of scientists was to advance an image of science as practically useful for technical progress in industry and agriculture and as distinct from, but not incompatible with, religion. The jury convicted Scopes, but an appeal led to his effective acquittal. As a result, there was no chance to bring the issue to the Supreme Court and try to challenge the Tennessee law's constitutionality.

Furthermore, the Scopes trial did not establish scientists' authority over what was taught in science textbooks. Evolution virtually disappeared from the science textbooks published in the decade after the trial, and publishers continued to avoid evolution in many science texts throughout the 1950s (Grabiner and Miller, 1974; Muller, 1959).

In the post-Sputnik efforts to reform science education, the National Science Foundation gave $7 million to the American Institute of Biological Sciences to produce new biology textbooks. These were ultimately adopted in about half of American high schools (Gieryn et al., 1985; Nelkin, 1983). Perhaps as a response, creationists struggled to get science education to "respect beliefs that are outside the dominant scientific culture" (Nelkin, 1982, p. 175). In many states, creationists gained remarkable influence on local school boards, state curriculum committees, and state legislatures (Nelkin, 1977). In the 1970s and 1980s, some states passed laws requiring equal time for creation theory in biology courses. Tennessee passed such a law in 1973, but it was struck down as unconstitutional two years later. In 1981 Arkansas passed Act 590, calling for the balanced presentation of both creation-science and evolution-science views in biology classes in Arkansas public schools.

This act was one of many attempts by national and local creationist organizations to prevent the *exclusive* teaching of evolutionary theory (Gieryn et al., 1985). It was challenged two months later in the *Rev. Bill McLean et al.* v. *Arkansas Board of Education* case. The judge ruled in favor of those challenging Act 590 on the grounds that "creation-science is not science because it is not falsifiable and not confined to natural law . . ." (Gieryn et al., 1985, p. 401).

According to Gieryn and his associates:

*Success was achieved, in part, through effective boundary work: an image of science was constructed at the trial that placed a boundary between science and creation-science, one that excluded creation-science as pseudoscientific religious apologetics. Boundary work by "professional" scientists at McLean emphasized four distinctive features of science.*

*1. Science is the domain of experts, whose specialized training and accomplishments enable them alone to decide the validity of knowledge about nature. Creation-scientists lack professional credentials and so they are denied the authority to speak as "genuine" scientists. . . .*

*2. Genuine scientists are skeptical, tentative and cautious about claims to knowledge, in contrast to the dogmatic faith in Biblical inerrancy attributed to creation-scientists. . . .*

*3. Scientists reach consensus over facts or theories that are accorded at least the provisional status of truth. . . . Creation-scientists' unwillingness to conform to prevailing scientific opinion on even uncontroversial knowledge-claims is presented as further evidence that they are outside the boundaries of "real" science. . . .*

*4. Science is the disinterested search for knowledge. . . . Creation-science has a hidden agenda: its ulterior motive is to advance religious teaching in public schools under the guise of scientific objectivity. . . . [pp. 401–403]*

*For the scientific community, it is essential that scientific and religious goals be separated; whereas for creation-scientists those goals are inseparable. If science and religion are not separate, government support of science is of questionable Constitutionality. [1985, p. 404]*

The battle over boundaries and professional authority did not end with the *McLean* trial, however. It continued in the arena of textbook publishing and adoption. Not until 1984 did the Texas state school board drop a policy that evolution could only be taught as one of several theories on how life came to be. In 1985 the California school board notified eight publishers that it would not accept their junior high science texts in their current form. The state's 16-member curriculum committee charged that the books systematically excluded human reproduction, ethics (for example, in discussing pollution), and, most glaringly, evolution (Bowen, 1985). Since California buys 12 percent of all U.S. schoolbooks (and more than any other state), their call for full text treatment of such key features of evolutionary theory as natural selection, mutation, and adaptation is likely to have a major impact on publishers. Scientists and educators try not to define this controversy as requiring a choice between science and religion. It is very much, however, a contest over what definition of science gets accepted.

## Biological Testing

New developments in genetics and the neurosciences allow for more refined testing and prediction. For example, prenatal tests can predict the transmission of cystic fibrosis, Down's syndrome, hemophilia, Tay-Sachs disease, and many others in the early months of pregnancy. Genetic tests that detect the presence of certain markers in a person's DNA can reveal a predisposition to a host of other conditions, including certain mental illnesses. New imaging technologies—such as positron emission tomography (PET) and computer assisted tomography (CAT) scans as well as more sophisticated electroencephalograms (EEGs)— can detect subtle differences in the way people's brains function (Nelkin and Tancredi, 1989). Such detection techniques are useful in clinical settings for diagnostic and remedial purposes. But what happens when insurance companies, schools, courts, or employers start to use predictive tests? Such institutions have powerful economic incentives to obtain and use information about the biological traits of employees and clients. What rights and safeguards exist for the people involved? The issues surrounding these new technologies are explored in the book *Test and Control: The Power of Biological Information* (Nelkin and Tancredi, 1989). It considers such issues as the definition of normal and abnormal, whose measuring rods should be used, and the social implications of policies that increase the number of biologically stigmatized people who may be unemployable or uninsurable. The issue of biological testing centers on the control and use of new scientific technologies. A related issue addresses the ownership of scientific research.

## Ownership of Scientific Discoveries

In recent years scientists have cracked the genetic code and learned how to cut, splice, and synthesize DNA molecules. As a result, new forms of life can be created. One sociological consequence is a dramatic change in the relationships between university scientists and private industries. Individual scientists have a long history of consulting with commercial firms, especially in engineering departments and med-

*Sophisticated genetic tests can predict that a man's or woman's DNA carries certain diseases. Here a genetic counselor discusses the possibility of chromosome irregularities with a pregnant woman about to undergo such tests.*

ical schools. Some drug and chemical firms have funded university research with long-term contracts. The founding of venture-capital start-up companies by university scientists is a recent development, however. Such arrangements can undermine the academic enterprise. Many scientists starting companies continue to hold academic positions. Since different members of a department may be connected to competing firms, they may shift from the open sharing of scientific ideas and results to secrecy. Thus commercial commitments can squeeze out professorial duties. Students may be exploited for commercial purposes and public monies may finance private projects (Kenney, 1986). Revenue considerations rather than scientific significance and quality may dominate research decisions.

When the Massachusetts Institute of Technology (MIT) founded the Whitehead Institute as a vehicle for channeling industry money into basic research, there was a furor over the role the institute would play in the appointment of university faculty. (The institute has considerable influence over new faculty appointments.) MIT's role in connection with Whitehead is a new one and it undermines the authority of senior faculty, department heads, and deans.

As Nelkin notes (1989), as such liaisons between science and industry increase, it will become more difficult for the scientific institution to project an image of purity and neutrality. Thus, "its moral authority as a trusted source of unbiased information" is eroded (Nelkin, 1989). Moral concerns about the scientific enterprise are not new, as the creationism controversy shows. Religious conservatives have consistently opposed abortion, fetal research, and in vitro fertilization (IVF) procedures. Another indication of the erosion of support for science may be seen in the increasingly evident and vocal social movement opposed to the use of animals in laboratory experiments. Activists compare scientific laboratories with slaughterhouses and Nazi prison camps. Such analogies suggest serious public concern about the morality of scientists (Nelkin, 1989).

The animal-rights movement has already had an effect. In 1988, a professor at Cornell Medical College gave up a $600,000 federal grant and shut down an unfinished 14-year study, using cats, of barbiturate addiction (Lyall, 1988). Animal-rights activists have successfully recruited allies and focused media attention on the use of laboratory animals. This suggests that the legitimacy of science rests on its moral authority as well as upon social contributions and technical breakthroughs (Nelkin, 1989). There has also been a growth in such "new age" values as enthusiasm for crystals. These developments indicate that "questioning of instrumental rationality and doubts about the value of a scientific way of thinking extend well beyond the creationists and the religious right to the educated middle class" (Nelkin, 1989, p. 11). If Nelkin is right, the association of science with corporate interests may undermine its moral authority as an unbiased, disinterested institution.

## Implications for Democratic Governance

These examples show that the practice of science and public policy are coming together at increasingly important decision points. Any society with great scientific capabilities faces the problem of how to regulate and control scientific and technological innovations. Science is one social institution we cannot ignore. If people do not like the institution of the family, they can choose not to re-create it in their adult lives. If they dislike the institutional forms of religion, they can remain unaffiliated. If they dislike the political institutions of a given state, they can move to another nation or work to elect another party. The institution of science, however, may affect us in ways that we cannot escape. If the water or air becomes polluted, there may be no alternatives available. If a deadly virus escapes and ravages the world, there may be no safe haven. If the temperature of the earth is raised and more of the polar ice cap melts, the East and West Coasts of the United States may be under 30 feet of water. A small drop in the earth's temperature could set the world on the path to another ice age. Unleashing even a small percentage of the world's nuclear weapon arsenal could destroy life as we know it.

*Animal rights movements have gained momentum in recent years. One of their targets is the use of animals in laboratory research.*

These examples illustrate how powerfully science may affect our lives. In many ways scientific and technological developments have outrun the forms of social organization we have for creating an orderly and democratic means to debate and decide what policies to pursue. The people who will be affected have little chance to learn about, discuss, and decide what to do about a particular development.

Public forums to discuss science policies require that several conditions be met. People need to be educated and informed about scientific issues. Lay persons, including leaders of public agencies and elected officials, are often unable to assess the competing scientific evidence and arguments in a policy issue. Such a situation poses serious probl ms for governance and decision making in a democracy: How can participatory democracy be maintained when people do not understand the scientific principles on which a debate hinges? At the very least, nonscientists need to receive a good science education in school and have continuing education in science through books, magazines, television, and other media. They need to be willing to educate themselves about the key issues being decided.

Scientists themselves are frequently divided on the risks involved in various procedures and how they evaluate those dangers. These scientists need to be able to explain the issues to nonscientists and indicate the benefits and dangers of various courses of action. Scientists and nonscientists need to discuss and decide issues of science policy. As things stand presently, laypersons can only protest or obstruct already decided policies, such as decisions to build a nuclear power plant or an industrial waste dump. There is no social mechanism for debating and voting on policies before they are decided.

The scientific community is understandably wary about the possible tyranny of ignorance that might result from debating science issues in a political arena. The dangers of unbridled political control over scientific thought are well documented. In the Soviet Union, for instance, Lysenkoism was the only form of genetics that could be taught in universities or used in agricultural experiments. This body of doctrine denied the existence of genes and believed that an organism could be changed by its environment and that those changes could be passed on to its offspring. This politically determined position dominated Soviet agriculture and education from the 1930s to the 1960s, when it was discredited. Another example occurred in Nazi Germany, where the state declared the genetic superiority of the Aryan race in an effort to provide some scientific legitimacy for the persecution of others.

These examples show what happens when scientific evidence is overruled by political power. Clearly, scientific theories and research results cannot be determined by popular vote. What is done with those theories and research findings, however, may affect many people in a society. Science policies are more likely to be viewed as legitimate and science will receive more public support if the people who are affected have a voice in forming the policies. Without such participation, a society runs the risk that certain avenues of scientific research and development (nuclear power and weapons or sugar-coated cereals) are vigorously pursued, whereas others (soil erosion or preventive medicine) are neglected. The lack of citizen participation in issues of science policy also runs the risk of developing a technocratic elite that loses touch with the concerns of the general population and is no longer able to weigh those concerns when making decisions.

For all its professional concern with objectivity, science is a social institution. Social factors influence scientific productivity and science may be engaged in social conflicts with other institutions. Sociology helps to illuminate the distinctively social aspects of science.

## SUMMARY

1. The results of scientific activities affect us on a daily basis. "The institution of science" refers to the community devoted to developing theories and methods for understanding the physical and social world. The term "science" is also used to refer to the knowledge produced by that community.

2. Technology refers to the practical applications of scientific knowledge. Science applications have produced far-reaching benefits, but they have also raised concerns about possible negative effects.

3. The rise of modern science as we know it began in the fifteenth century. Scientific de-

velopment was spurred on by the printing press, the lowering of class barriers between theoretical and practical knowledge, and new approaches to understanding the physical world. The start of scientific societies and journals, and subsequent development of university instruction in science, all contributed to the institutional support for science as an activity.

4. Today nearly 4.7 million scientists and engineers work in the United States, and 20 percent are doing research and development work.

5. In order to flourish in a society, science needs to have continuity and commitment within that society. Resources need to be allocated on a predictable basis, so that people can develop careers in science.

6. The functionalist approach to science emphasizes the interdependence of science with various other social institutions, stresses that science is a major source of social change, and realizes that there may be positive as well as negative consequences of scientific activity.

7. The conflict approach stresses how the unequal distribution of power and resources in society or within science may shape the direction that scientific development takes. It asks which specific groups do and do not benefit from particular policies and practices.

8. Science as a social activity is governed by the norms of universalism, communism, disinterestedness, and organized skepticism. Although they are sometimes violated in practice, scientists' strong reaction to such violations suggests the existence of the norms Merton identified.

9. Sociologists have studied productivity within the scientific community and identified a number of conditions that enhance it, including competition between universities, cooperation within organizations, a "safe" environment for innovation, and the chance to influence decisions.

10. Kuhn's work on the nature of scientific revolutions suggests that major scientific paradigms do not change gradually in an evolutionary fashion but abruptly in a revolutionary way.

11. Popper suggests that scientific views may be tentatively considered true until proved false, but Kuhn indicates that the paradigm guiding a scientist's work may make it difficult to see contradictory evidence. Lay persons and scientists alike may resist new discoveries for a variety of social reasons.

12. Recent work in the sociology of science focuses on the content of scientific knowledge and how social interactions and discussions may shape what scientists have "seen." This does not deny the existence of some independent reality. Instead, it suggests that the interpretation of that reality is socially constructed.

13. Scientific productivity has contributed to the economic development of industrialized countries. Flagging economic productivity in the United States in recent years has generated new concerns about scientific research and development, particularly in relation to other industrialized nations.

14. Sociologists suggest that the declining rate of scientific development in the United States is due to a shortage of science and engineering faculty, the rapid exportation of new technologies, and the diversion of scientific personnel and resources into military research and development.

15. Controversial science policies are often those that affect individuals in their own neighborhoods. Theories of evolution being taught in the schools, biological testing, and the ownership of scientific discoveries are three issues that have aroused considerable public controversy.

16. New links between science and industry, the success of the animal-rights movement, and the popularity of "new age" values all suggest that the moral authority of science is facing new challenges.

## KEY TERMS

anomalies (p. 441)
creationism (p. 450)
innovation (p. 444)
institution of science (p. 435)
institutionalization of science (p. 437)
normal science (p. 441)
paradigm (p. 441)
research and development (R&D) (p. 446)
science (p. 435)
scientific productivity (p. 444)
scientific revolution (p. 442)
technology (p. 435)

## SUGGESTED READINGS

Etzkowitz, Henry. 1984. "Solar versus nuclear energy: Autonomous or dependent technology?" *Social Problems* 31: 417–434. Considers the technical, economic, and political factors affecting the use of solar technology in the United States and analyzes solar and nuclear technologies in light of competing theories about autonomous and dependent technology.

Keller, Evelyn Fox. 1985. *Reflections on Gender and Science*. New Haven, CT: Yale University Press. Thoughtful essays by a mathematical biophysicist, suggesting that conceptions of masculinity and science may have become fused in modern science and calling for a reclamation of science as a human rather than a masculine project.

Knorr-Cetina, Karin D., and Michael Mulkay (eds.). 1983. *Science Observed: Perspectives on the Social Study of Science*. Beverly Hills, CA: Sage. A collection of papers showing some of the ways sociologists have studied the institution of science.

Kuhn, Thomas S. 1970. *The Structure of Scientific Revolutions*. Chicago: University of Chicago Press. A book that changes the way we think about the world, in this case the world of scientific development.

Latour, Bruno, and Steve Woolgar. 1986. *Laboratory Life,* ed. 2. Princeton, NJ: Princeton University Press. An ethnographic study of a scientific laboratory.

Merton, Robert K. 1973. *The Sociology of Science.* Chicago: University of Chicago Press. A collection of classic papers spanning a 40-year period by the preeminent American sociologist of science.

# P A R T 5

# SOCIAL CHANGES AND ISSUES

**M**ajor social changes stimulated the development of sociology, and significant social changes continue to occur today. Chapter 18 considers shifts in the size and age of the U.S. population, particularly the impact of the "baby boom" generation and the growth of the elderly population. Food production, distribution, and health care affect world population trends. Chapter 19 considers other sources of social change, including deliberate efforts to create change through organized social movements and modernization. The chapter contrasts collective behavior and social movements. Chapter 20 examines changes in urban, suburban, and rural communities, and considers the roots and results of such shifts. Sex and sexuality have a heavily social component that is considered in Chapter 21. Cross cultural comparisons show the social nature of teenage sexual behavior and responses to homosexual behavior. Leisure and sport are interesting subjects in their own right, but they also provide rich opportunities for applying the sociological imagination to the social world. Chapter 22 shows how leisure and sport have different social meanings in various societies, and considers how stratification by race, gender, and class affects sport.

# Population, Health, and Aging

**18**

*In 1976 a 26-year-old woman in an African village said she wanted as many as 20 children. By 1985, she was the mother of seven children. When reminded of her earlier desire, she laughed and said, "I have rejected that proposal, because there is not enough food to meet the demand" [Quoted in Tierney, 1986, p. 16].*

*Such thinking may explain why worldwide fertility rates are dropping.*

Population changes powerfully affect the course of human events. Large changes in the number of eligible marriage partners, young workers coming into the job market, or elderly people in need of special social and medical services can have a dramatic impact on a society. Birth and death rates can change. These changes, in turn, affect social institutions such as health care, housing, and education. These are national problems facing most societies.

There are also international implications to great shifts in population size and distribution. Will world population continue to explode? Will increasing population pressures lead to famine, starvation, terrorism, war, and the onset of economic collapse? Or, can we control population growth in such a way as to reduce rather than increase human suffering? What might the social, political, and economic consequences be of preventing continued growth in world population? These are immediate and real questions that the governments of the world must face today.

This chapter begins by considering world population changes and world food production

in order to illuminate the issue of population explosion and its significance. Then we explore certain social features of health and health care. The chapter concludes with a section on age and aging, especially in societies with increasing numbers of elderly persons.

## WORLD POPULATION CHANGES

In early human history, in fact for the first 99 percent of the time humans have been on the earth, population growth was very slow, as Figure 18.1 shows. **Population** refers to all the people living in a given geographic area. Death rates, particularly among infants and young children, were so high that even high birth rates led to only a gradual increase in the population. With the agricultural revolution beginning about 8000 B.C., the population gradually increased. Initially, death rates probably increased in agricultural societies because of poor sanitation and increased disease problems in the growing urban areas. Fertility rates also rose, how-

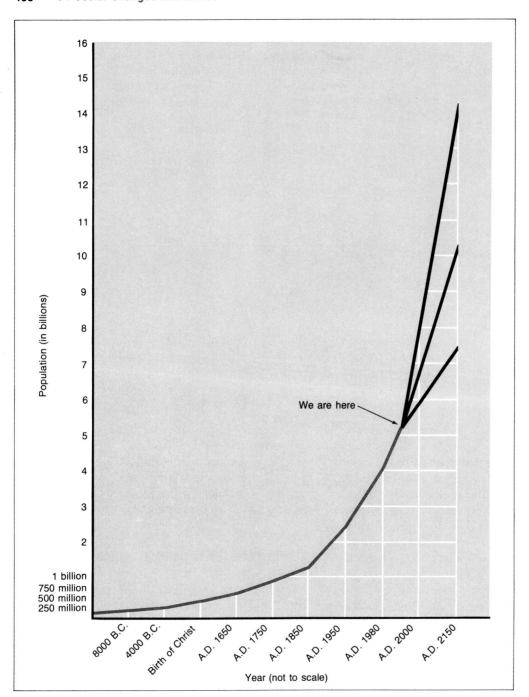

**Figure 18.1 World Population Explosion, Three Scenarios.**

World population has been growing geometrically at least since 1850. World population projections to the year 2100 vary, depending upon the assumptions that are made about future birth rates. The United Nations has made three projections from 1950, shown here. The middle series assumes that world fertility will decline to about two children per woman by the year 2035. If that happens, the world population in 2100 will be 10.2 billion, exactly twice what it is today. If the "two-child family" average is reached by 2010, as in the low series, world population would reach 7.5 billion by 2100. If it is not reached until 2065, as in the high series, then world population would reach 14.2 billion by 2100.

*Sources:* Deevey, 1960; Heer, 1975; Population Reference Bureau, 1988.

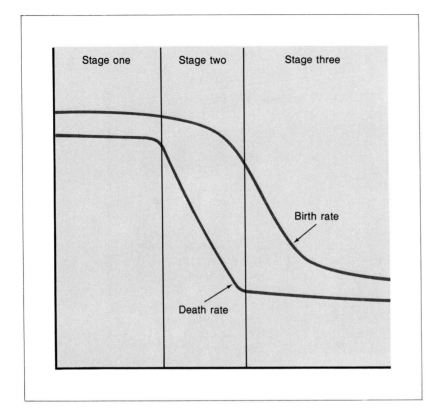

**Figure 18.2   The Demographic Transition.**

The demographic transition theory sees three population stages. In stage one, both birth and death rates are high. In stage two, the death rate drops (because of improved health and sanitation measures and industrialization) before the high birth rate does, leading to rapid population growth. In stage three, the birth rate drops to about the same level as the death rate, leading ultimately to a relatively stable population. Western Europe has followed this pattern, but it is not yet clear whether the industrializing nations of the world will make a similar demographic transition.

ever, because the improved diet increased the ability of women to conceive and bear children.

## The Demographic Transition

The rate of population growth accelerated after 1750. With the onset of the industrial revolution, death rates dropped dramatically because of increased food production, better transportation (which improved the distribution of food), and improved sanitation. Since the time of the industrial revolution, western Europe and North America have undergone what has been called a **demographic transition:** that is, the birth rate has declined so that it is about equal to the death rate. As shown in Figure 18.2, the three stages in a demographic transition are, first, the stage of high birth and high death rates, especially among children. Before the industrial revolution, this was the stage most societies were in. In the second stage, improved food production and distribution, the discovery of bacteria and antiseptics, and better sanitation produce a sharp decline in death rates, but birth

rates remain high. This second stage occurred in Europe in the early stages of industrialization and is happening in many developing nations today. In the third stage, birth rates drop so they are once again in balance with death rates.

Why does this happen? **Demography** (the study of population trends) suggests that in an agrarian society, children are an economic advantage. There is plenty of work for children to do on a farm, and there is usually enough food for them. They also represent old-age insurance for their parents, since they are expected to care for their elders in later life. Industrialization changes children from income producers to income consumers. As a result, industrial families tend to have fewer children. This has been the trend for the past 200 years, since well before reliable methods of contraception were developed. One exception to this trend was the post–World War II "baby boom" in the United States (see the box on the effects of the baby boom on life in the United States).

In the late nineteenth century, breakthroughs in germ theory, vaccination against infectious diseases, and improved sanitation lowered mor-

# The Effects of the "Baby Boom" on Life in the United States

Along with the massive immigration to the United States between 1880 and 1910, the so-called "baby boom" is probably the most significant demographic event in American history. The **baby boom** comprises those people born between 1946 and 1965 (see bulge in Figure 12.5). They represent a sharp increase in both the birth rate and the absolute number of births compared to pre-1946 levels. Totaling more than 79 million people, the baby-boom generation (called a **cohort** by demographers) is slightly more than one-third of the entire population of the United States. This cohort stands between two much smaller generations and numerically dominates those older and younger than themselves. See Figure 18.3. To see how a major demographic change like the baby boom influences many aspects of social life, we look at some of the highlights of this cohort as it moves through the life cycle.

In the late 1940s and early 1950s, as the baby boom cohort was in its infancy, there was a tremendous increase in the sale of baby food, washing machines, diaper services, and toys, and Dr. Benjamin Spock's book on baby and child care became a major bestseller. Growing families moved to new homes in the suburbs, leading to a doubling of the suburban population between 1950 and 1970. Sales of cars, barbecues, hot dogs, and lawn furniture took off.

In 1952 those born in 1946 entered first grade, and the schools began to feel the baby boom's impact. There was a 38 percent increase in the number of first-graders in that year alone. When the baby boomers became teenagers, popular record sales quadrupled in six short years between 1954 and 1960, and sales of blue jeans and acne medicines soared.

Today the members of the baby-boom cohort are in their mid-twenties to mid-forties. They fill the ranks of what have been termed "Yuppies," or young urban professionals. They buy fewer jeans but more hair coloring products, and they join health clubs. They made *Jane Fonda's Workout Book* a best-seller and made a big hit of films such as *The Big Chill* which deal with the changes experienced by members of the baby-boom cohort. Baby boomers have experienced intense competition from their numerous peers in the search for good educations, jobs, and housing. Since about 1975, when baby boomers began having children of their own (humorously called "yuppie puppies" by some journalists), the number of births has generally been increasing (Figure 12.5). As a result, the United States faces the prospect of another smaller baby boom 30 years later (the so-called "echo effect" after the first boom).

In the 1990s the baby-boom cohort will be middle-aged and will fill middle management and the upper levels of leadership in all major American institutions. At an earlier period in their life cycle, the median age in the United States was 25 in the 1960s (when the political slogan, "Don't trust anyone over the age of 30," was coined). The large numbers of young people under 25 at that time helps to explain the youthful rebellions of the 1960s. By 1987 the median age was 32, which may help to explain the shift toward political, economic, social, and sexual conservatism today, since some people become more conservative as they get older. By the year 2030, the median age is projected to be over 40.

When they reach 65 the baby-boom cohort will swell the already expanded ranks of retirees and put additional strains on pension, housing, and health and nursing programs for the elderly. They should continue to strengthen the already considerable political clout of those over 65. Labor shortages and federal budget deficits may combine to provide additional incentives for people to continue working after they reach retirement age.

The so-called "birth dearth" cohort, born from 1965 to 1975, will experience different life situations from those of the baby-boom cohort. They will see many colleges and graduate schools eagerly advertising for them to attend, they will find themselves being wooed by employers who are faced with a shortage of entry-level workers, and they will discover a good supply of first homes becoming available as the baby boomers move on to bigger ones. A heavy economic burden will fall on this birth cohort, however. They will have to earn enough to pay the Social Security of those who retire and will have to support their own children as well. Not surprisingly, increasing numbers of married women will join the work force. The number of working women has increased since 1950, when only 20 percent of married women worked, to 1984, when 53 percent did. By 2000 more than 75 percent of married women are expected to be working.

In these and other ways the baby boom is having major social consequences for many aspects of American life and will continue to affect the economy, politics, education, medicine, and leisure.

*Sources:* Brown, 1984; Jones, 1980; Kennedy, 1989; Robey, 1982.

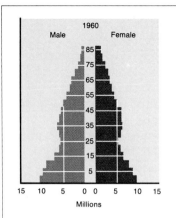

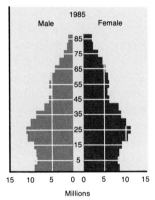

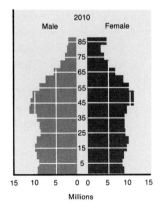

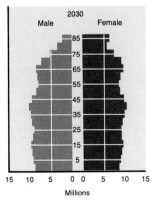

**Figure 18.3    Age and Sex Composition of the U.S. Population: 1960, 1985, 2010, 2030.**

In 1960, the "baby boom" cohort was concentrated at age 15 and below. In 1985, it was age 20 to 35. In 2010, it is projected to be age 45 to 60. By 2030, it will be swelling the ranks of those over 65.

*Source:* U.S. Bureau of the Census, 1989a.

tality rates still further. At first, these developments lowered mortality only in Europe and the United States; but after World War II (1945), medical and public health advances spread all over the world, lowering death rates in many other countries as well. Within one or two generations after the death rate began to decline in Europe and North America, the fertility rate also began to decline, but more slowly. Although the physical factors that reduce death rates may change fairly quickly, the social norms that value high birth rates change more slowly. The result is that births increase until gradually industrial and urban life weakens the pressure for large families. Total world population growth therefore slowed, but growth continues in developing nations.

## A Population Vocabulary

### Fertility

In order to study population issues, we need to understand several technical terms. The **crude birth rate** indicates the total number of live births per 1000 persons in a population within a particular year. People who think about how the birth rate is calculated often come up with an objection: Suppose one society had lots of women of childbearing age and another society had relatively few women in that age bracket, shouldn't that difference somehow be reflected in the statistics? If you were thinking along these lines, you are absolutely right, and demographers agree with you. They have developed what they call a **total fertility rate,** which relates the birth rate to the number of women of childbearing age. It uses information about the number of women in each age group and the birth rates of those women to figure out the average number of children that would be born to each woman over her reproductive life if current age-specific birth rates remained constant.

The total fertility rate permits comparisons of societies that may have very different age and sex structures. "The age and sex structure of a society" is another way of referring to the proportion of the population that is a particular age or sex. (For an example of contrasting age and sex structures in more industrialized regions of the world compared with less industrialized regions, see Figure 18.4.) Different societies have different age structures, and these can profoundly affect social life. A society in which much of the population is under the age of 20 (for example, Mexico) will have to spend a great deal on food and education and will have relatively few people in the work force to generate a surplus for supporting those needs. Such a society also has more potential for increasing its numbers, because there are so many young people moving into their reproductive years. At the other extreme, a society like the United States, with a relatively large proportion of retirement-age people, will have other problems, such as health care for the elderly and adequate pensions. Knowing the existing age structure of a society and projecting that structure into the future helps make social forecasts about issues and opportunities.

## Mortality

The other critical element in world population growth is the death rate, or **mortality rate.** Like fertility rates, there are several ways mortality rates can be calculated. The **crude death rate** is the number of deaths per 1000 persons occurring within a one-year period in a particular population. Crude death rates tell us little about the probability of death at any given age, however, since the age structure of a population can dramatically influence the crude death rate. In 1967 the crude death rate in West Berlin was 18, whereas in West Germany it was 11, suggesting that mortality was much higher in West Berlin. Yet a female baby had nearly a 90 percent chance of surviving to be 55 in both places. Mortality probabilities were the same, despite different crude death rates; the difference in the crude death rates was undoubtedly affected by the fact that 21 percent of West Berliners were 65 or older (and therefore more likely to die), compared to only 12 percent of West Germans (Weeks, 1981).

To capture the essence of a society's mortality experience while considering the age and sex structure of that society, we can compute an average **life expectancy,** which gives the average years of life remaining to people born in a particular year. Such an estimate is derived

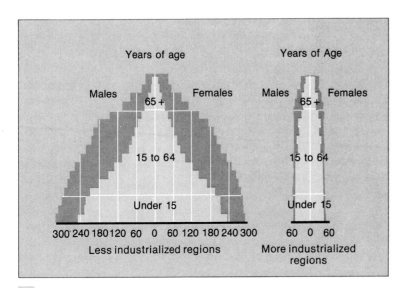

Population in 1985 (millions)

Increase 1985 to 2025

**Figure 18.4  Age and Sex Composition of the World's Population in More and Less Industrialized Regions, 1985 and 2025 (projected).**

Industrialized regions of the world have roughly equal numbers of people at all age levels of their populations, except for the very old. Less industrialized regions have many more babies, children, and young adults in their populations, giving them a much younger age profile. As a result, their populations are likely to grow much faster. About 37 percent of their populations are below age 15, compared to 23 percent in more industrialized regions.

*Source:* Population Reference Bureau, 1988.

from a **life table.** Life tables require a system of registering vital statistics, especially deaths by age and sex, and an accurate census showing the number of people in each age and sex category. They summarize the mortality experience of a particular population. Insurance companies use life tables to compute life insurance premiums. Life expectancies are good summary statistics for comparing societies or subgroups within a society. As noted in earlier chapters, the life expectancy of blacks and whites in the United States is quite different, as is that of males and females. When such differences are known, then sociological, biological, or medical hypotheses about possible causes can be investigated.

Another important measure used by population experts is the **rate of natural increase,** which is the difference between birth and death rates, excluding immigration. **Migration** refers to the relatively permanent movement of people from one area to another. The rate of natural increase and the total fertility rate are used to consider the question of whether the world population is continuing to explode, is stabilizing, or may ultimately decline.

*The Chinese government has stringent policies to control population growth, including the one-child family policy. There are incentives for those who follow the policy and sanctions against those who do not. In this case social policy often collides with individual desires.*

## World Population Trends

Although the rate of world population growth has slowed somewhat in recent years, the number of people in the world is still increasing at a staggering rate. A middle range projection suggests that the world population will double (to 10.2 billion) by 2100 (Population Reference Bureau, 1988). The world population growth rate reached a high of 2.4 percent a year in the 1960s and is now 1.7 percent a year. Much of this drop is due to the success of efforts to control population in China, the world's most populous country, where the annual rate of increase is only 1.4 percent a year (Figure 18.5). India's rate of 2.0 percent a year remains high and is likely to make India the most populous country in the world by 2050, with a projected 1.7 billion people in that country alone. Moreover, sub-Saharan Africa's population is growing at a rate of 2.7 percent or more per year.

Fertility (and hence the rate of growth) has been reduced in developing nations by breast-feeding babies longer (mothers who are nursing their babies usually do not ovulate and hence do not get pregnant), by marrying at a later age, by using contraception, and by performing abortions (World Bank, 1984, p. 115). Around the world, many married women with families do not want to bear and rear more children than they already have, whereas many men—whether for reasons of machismo, a desire for security in old age, or tribal or national pride—favor having many sons (Gupte, 1984; Jacobson, 1988).

China has effectively reduced fertility. One-child families receive many positive incentives, including substantial pay increases, better housing, longer maternity leaves, and priority access to education. Couples who have more than one child face heavy fines and social criticism. Urban couples especially must follow the policy, but rural couples (about 80 percent of the population) may have two or sometimes more children (Jacobson, 1988, p. 166). There have been news reports about forced abortions and sterilizations in China, which Gupte asked about when he interviewed Chinese officials. They acknowledged that such abuses had occurred but insisted that offenders had been punished and abuses stopped. Although the measures adopted by China are strong ones, Gupte writes: "The

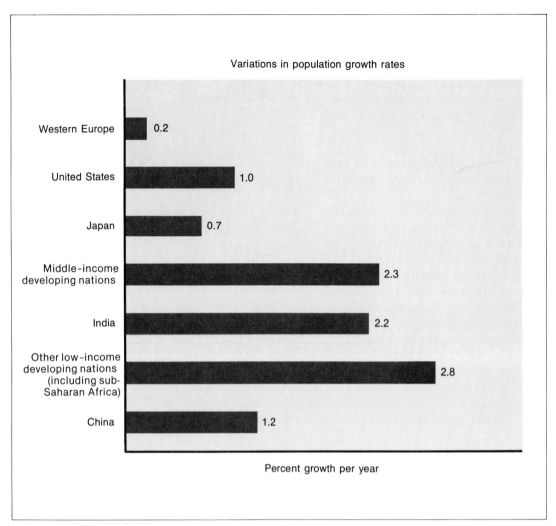

**Figure 18.5 Variations in Population Growth Rates, 1980–1986.**

Population growth rates are generally much higher in middle- and low-income developing nations than in higher-income regions such as western Europe, the United States, and Japan. China, however, is a notable exception to this pattern, with a population growth rate that is much lower than that of other low-income developing nations.

*Source:* World Bank, 1988, pp. 274–275; Population Reference Bureau, 1988.

Chinese have quite clearly decided that their population problem is so enormous that its solution justifies the severe restriction of individual liberties for the good of the community" (1984, p. 182).

The reports of coerced abortions in China have fueled the efforts of people opposed to birth control of any kind. They have mounted a campaign to cut off American aid to all agencies working in any country said to allow forced abortions—even if the agencies do not use American dollars in those countries. Such a step would hamstring countries seeking to reduce the rate of population growth.

## Trends in Industrial Nations

The more industrialized nations—including western European countries, the USSR, and the United States—have been experiencing dramatically declining fertility rates for even longer than have the developing nations. These declining fertility rates are reflected in the low growth rates in industrialized nations (Figure 18.3). Indeed, some of the world's developed nations have reached zero population growth.

**Zero population growth** (ZPG) occurs when the population of a nation or the world remains the same from one year to the next. That is, the number of people remains stable. It does not mean that no new babies are born but only that the number of births does not exceed the number of deaths. The United Kingdom is approaching equilibrium; that is, births and deaths are about equal. If current fertility trends continue, Belgium, Czechoslovakia, Norway, and Sweden will reach zero growth in a few years, as will Bulgaria, Finland, Greece, Italy, and Switzerland. Denmark, West Germany, and Hungary already have more deaths than births each year, resulting in declining populations.

If present trends persist, the population of Europe as a whole will begin to decline by the year 2000. Westoff (1978) argues that declining fertility is part of a long-term trend and that a number of factors favor its continuation.

The two biggest reasons for the decline in fertility in industrialized nations are interrelated. First, more women are in the labor force. This means that the economic costs of having children are magnified. The second reason for the decline in fertility is the decreasing frequency of marriage, since women who work are less tied to having their economic needs met through marriage. Birth rates are also reduced by the high divorce rates among those who do marry and by the declining rate of remarriage among divorced persons.

## Consequences of Trends

Although prior efforts to predict future population trends have not been very successful, it seems reasonable to expect that populations in western Europe *will* stop growing in the next 30 years. Meanwhile, the world population will continue to grow, although at a slower rate than in the past. If these predictions come true, what are the likely consequences?

At present more than three-quarters of the world's production and hence consumption of resources occurs in the industrialized nations of the world, where only a quarter of the world's people live. The remaining 21 percent of production and consumption is distributed among the other three-quarters of the world's people. There are both ethical and practical reasons for people in developed nations to be concerned about this situation. Ethically, many people and groups feel that if something can be done to lessen human suffering, it should be. Practical concerns focus on how such an unbalanced situation might rock world stability (Clark, 1984). In an age when terrorists may threaten an industrial nation with nuclear blackmail, no industrial nation can safely ignore the gross suffering and inequities in the world.

Within industrial societies and especially in the United States, there is the possibility of a "top-heavy" age structure by about 2030. Most college students of today will be in their late sixties or seventies by then, and they will be affected by changes in the elderly dependency ratio that are expected to occur between now and then. The **elderly dependency ratio** relates the size of the elderly population (65 years and over) to the working-age population (ages 18 to 64). Unless another baby boom or a surge of immigration occurs, the elderly dependency ratio will rise steadily and then climb sharply around the year 2010, as shown in Figure 18.6. In 1970 there were 17 elderly per 100 working-age people. By the year 2040 there are expected to be 40 elderly per 100 working-age people (Kennedy, 1989, p. 127).

Since social security payments, in particular, are financed out of the payments of *current* workers, this shift in the dependency ratio means that many more people will be collecting benefits and many fewer will be supporting the system. An increase in the elderly dependency ratio places a heavier burden on those who are working and makes it even more essential that they be as productive as possible. To accomplish this, society must invest in the care and education of the young in order to prepare them for their working years. The burden of the elderly dependency ratio will be eased to some degree by the growing proportion of women in the work force. By the year 2000, 75 percent of working-age females are expected to be in the labor force.

Assuming that regional migrations continue in the United States, some areas will experience growth, whereas others will lose residents. If, for example, cities retain large numbers of dependent elderly and children, they will be strained to provide the health and educational services such populations require. Other areas, such as sunbelt suburbs, may experience the growing pains of traffic congestion and inadequate sewers even though they are gaining relatively affluent workers in their prime years.

Societies experiencing low or zero growth rates may be more receptive to immigration from beyond their borders. The United States has a long history of immigration that has dramatically changed its population size, age structure, and ethnic composition. Since 1924, immigration has been restricted considerably by legislation; but immigration policies can be used to affect overall population size. Gaining population through immigration may lead to other problems, however. Westoff (1978), for example, feels that countries with major immigra-

tions seem to experience problems sooner or later due to differences in language, customs, religion, or race. Some northern European countries have admitted workers from other countries for limited stays by issuing work permits or temporary visas. The practice has supplied labor to industrial societies and provided work (usually of a menial kind) to unemployed laborers from more populous countries. In periods of economic contraction, however, workers are often sent home, placing the burden of unemployment on them and their home countries rather than on the countries that received the benefit of their labor. International migration probably cannot fully counteract the effects of a stationary or declining national growth rate (Westoff, 1978). So the likely issues stemming from current population trends need to be addressed.

Most of the rest of the world is in a situation exactly opposite that of the United States and western Europe. Even with declining rates of growth, world population is expected to continue growing for the foreseeable future. What are the implications of this growth for the globe? Does the world have enough food, air, water, energy, and other resources to support nearly twice as many people as now live here, or will overpopulation lead to wars, massive migra-

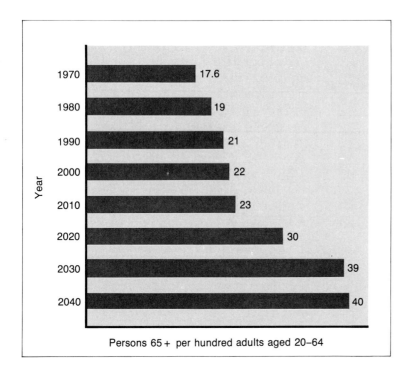

**Figure 18.6  Elderly Dependency Ratio in the United States, 1970–2040.**

By the year 2040, there are expected to be 40 persons in the United States aged 65 or older for every 100 adults between the ages of 20 and 64. Since Social Security is financed by current workers, this change in the elderly dependency ratio creates a major challenge for the system.

*Source:* Morrison, 1978, p. 23; Kennedy, 1989; Wade, 1986.

tions, or more millions dying of starvation within our lifetime?

## Malthus and Marx on Population Pressures

The consequences of population growth have been hotly debated since an English clergyman and professor, Thomas Robert Malthus, published his now famous *An Essay on Population* in 1798. Malthus believed that humans, like plants and animals, were "impelled" to reproduce and that they would multiply to an "incalculable" number in the future if there were no checks on population growth. The ultimate check was the lack of food, and Malthus saw population growing more rapidly than the food supply could expand. The result of these two tendencies would be poverty and eventual starvation, unless people took action. Malthus personally approved of only one way of limiting population growth, and that was use of "moral restraint." People were to remain chaste until they could support a family, and only then were they to marry. He considered contraception, abortion, and sterilization "improper means" of birth control. Malthus practiced what he preached (as far as we know). He waited to marry and have his children until he had obtained a secure job as a college professor, even though it meant putting off marriage until he was 39. Although people have given him a "bad press" by suggesting that he had 11 children, he actually had only 3 (Nickerson, 1975).

Germany was one state that, in the nineteenth century, took Malthus's advice by legislating against marriages in which the father could not guarantee that his family would avoid welfare (Glass, 1953). As a result, many out-of-wedlock children were born in Germany at the time. Growing up in Germany then, Karl Marx and Friedrich Engels were strongly influenced by the effects of Malthus's ideas, particularly by the way they increased the number of children on welfare. Marx and Engels saw this trend as an outrage against humanity (Weeks, 1981). In particular, they rejected Malthus's view that poverty was the fault of the poor. Instead, they saw poverty as due to the capitalist organization of production. They viewed the human condition as a result of social and economic arrangements. In the kind of society they envisioned, popula-

tion growth would lead to greater economic production and well-being. Science and technology could enhance food production to keep pace with population expansion.

The Malthusian perspective remains alive today and shapes much of the debate and action over world population. Malthus's ideas have been developed and modified by Paul Ehrlich in his book *The Population Bomb* (1968), and in the Club of Rome's report *The Limits to Growth* (Meadows et al., 1972).[1] These books have helped to raise public consciousness in the United States and western Europe about the negative effects of recent population growth. Ehrlich advocates all methods of birth control, since he foresees a calamitous war, famine, or other dire consequence if something is not done quickly.

The Marxian perspective has been modified in recent decades, but it continues to place the locus of the population issue in a different place than does the Malthusian view. Prior to the 1960s, Marxians tended to take the ideological position that a well-organized society should be able to handle any population growth that occurs (Sauvy, 1969). More recently, Marxians have tempered this position. Both the Soviet Union and China, countries whose social philosophy draws on Marxist principles, permit contraception and abortion.

## WORLD FOOD PRODUCTION

Every second of every day almost 5 babies are born somewhere in the world, on the average. If it took you 4 seconds to read these sentences, 20 new lives appeared on earth during that time. This means almost 400,000 per day and 144 million per year. One reason for this growth, despite the declining rate of fertility, is the very young age structure of most developing nations

[1] The Club of Rome is an informal international association of economists, industrialists, academics, and scientists devoted to studying the interdependent economic, political, natural, and social elements of the global system. It first met in 1968 in Rome. Members share the conviction that the major problems facing the world are so complex and interrelated that traditional institutions and policies are no longer able to deal with them.

in the world, as can be seen in Figure 18.4. Even with major declines in fertility, the large numbers of young people reaching childbearing age means the world will soon need to provide food for at least another 2 *billion* people. Can it produce enough food to meet this demand?

One of the factors affecting the amount of food that can be produced is the amount of land available for growing crops. About 11 percent of the world's land surface lends itself well to farm production, and most of it is already in use (Weeks, 1981). No major untapped areas comparable to the Great Plains of North America lie awaiting the plow. The Amazon Basin and other jungle areas appear to have rather shallow layers of topsoil, so they provide little hope. Also, like other areas that are not now under cultivation, they would require massive effort and expense to clear and make usable.

Not only is it unlikely that we can use much more of the world's land for growing crops but we are actually losing some of the suitable land to erosion, urbanization, and desertification—the gradual transformation of farmland into desert. It follows that if our usable land base is shrinking, the only hope is to raise the yield per acre on the land that is available.

## The Green Revolution

The development and use of new forms of grain to improve crop yields led to the so-called **green revolution.** Hybrid wheat and rice with shorter stems but more grain-producing stalks were developed by agricultural scientists in the 1940s and 1950s. By 1971 about 50 million acres were sown with high-yield varieties (HYV) of wheat (Brown, 1973). When these seeds were planted, harvests soared. In Mexico, for instance, wheat production jumped from 3 metric tons per hectare to 6 or 8 tons (Chandler, 1971). Similar gains in rice production were obtained in India, Pakistan, the Philippines, Indonesia, and South Vietnam. This transformation of agricultural productivity has been called the "green revolution." In 1987 and 1988, however, global grain production fell sharply (Brown, 1989).

In order to produce, these seeds need much more water, fertilizer, and pesticides than did existing varieties. Fertilizers and pesticides are

*High technology has increased crop yields dramatically. This computerized sensor monitors the rate of water flow in the Colorado River, a river that is used to irrigate farm lands in 14 different states.*

usually petroleum-based, and irrigation systems need to be pumped by fuel, usually oil. So the potential of these new seeds was much greater in the 1960s, when the price of oil was lower than it is today. The green revolution and other forms of intensive agriculture have other costs. Many pesticides and fertilizers are either poisonous or carcinogenic (cancer-producing). They not only contaminate the produce and the soil, but they are washed by the rain into rivers and lakes, where they affect drinking-water supplies and build up as concentrated residues in the bodies of fish, farm animals, and people. Large plantings of genetically similar types of plants such as rice or corn are also likely to fall victim periodically to massive crop failures due to insect pests or disease. This happened to the potato crop in Ireland in the nineteenth century and could happen today to U.S. wheat or corn crops or to Asian rice. Over time, the pressure to increase crop yields may seriously (and permanently) affect the quality of farmland and water supplies.

Extensive irrigation may deplete underground water supplies more rapidly than they can be replenished. In the long run, overusing those areas may cause them to dry up and become unfit for farming. Soil erosion is seriously reducing crop yields in many parts of the United States, and basic agricultural research has been cut back by the government (Crittenden, 1981). On balance, although the green revolution has led to dramatic gains in productivity, it does not seem to offer an easy solution to the problems of world food production, at least not in the next two decades.

In another 20 years or so great potential for major innovations in agriculture may come from recombinant DNA research ("gene splicing"). Disease- and stress-resistant plants may be developed, as well as new hybrids that can use sunlight more effectively. Such developments could increase crop yields in the future (Crittenden, 1981; Hager, 1988), although dramatic production gains are not likely (Brown, 1989).

## The Seas

What about the food potential of the sea? Can we catch more fish or grow and harvest kelp, algae, plankton, or other sea life to enhance our food supply? From 1950 to 1970 the annual catch of fish grew from 22 to 70 million tons (Brown, 1975), and it seemed as if the supply of fish was endless. Since 1970, however, the amount of fish caught has declined, perhaps due to overfishing. Also, since the sea is the ultimate repository of all pollutants, dangerous quantities of DDT, mercury, and radioactive particles have begun to appear in some seafood. As a result, the oceans no longer appear to offer a major source of food for a growing world population.

## Stemming Waste

At this point in history, technology seems unable to raise food production in substantial ways. This limitation suggests the vital importance of conservation and the changing of eating habits. It has been estimated that people in wealthy nations discard as much as 25 percent of the food they buy (*Newsweek*, 1974). People in certain nations tend to overeat and to suffer from obesity and diseases related to obesity. Certain types of food, especially beef, require more acres to produce a pound of protein than do other kinds of food, such as grains and poultry. It takes several pounds of grain to produce one pound of beef, whereas the same amount of protein can be produced much more efficiently in peanuts, peas, soybeans, and beans. If Americans and western Europeans reduce their intake of red meat and increase their intake of more efficient forms of protein, they will stretch the world's food supplies. Food patterns and preferences are deeply rooted cultural features, however, and usually change quite slowly, although changes along these lines have begun, apparently in response to both price and health concerns.

## Food Distribution

About half of the world's food is based on grain (rice, wheat, and corn). In 1988, worldwide drought caused the sharpest one-year drop ever in international grain reserves. Grains fell from a 101-day supply to a 54-day supply at the end of 1988. Government actions and falling water

*Major droughts result in low crop yields and shrink international grain reserves.*

tables have reduced the world's grain-growing areas by 7 percent since 1981 (Hager, 1988). Unless crop yields improve dramatically, grain costs could soar and famine increase.

In the 1980s the major grain exporters included the United States, Canada, France, Australia, and Argentina. Most other areas in the world had to import grain. Although the United States represents only 5 percent of the world's population and American farmers comprise only 3 percent of the labor force, they produced 44 percent of the world's corn and 11 percent of the world's wheat in 1986 (U.S. Bureau of the Census, 1989a, p. 643). American farmers are by far the most effective in the world; each one can feed 59 people, on the average—a much higher ratio than occurs in other countries (see Figure 18.7). In the last two decades the rest of the world has become increasingly dependent on American exports to feed people. Rich nations, such as Kuwait, import food to improve or vary their diets; poorer, faster-growing nations such as Bangladesh and the Philippines require imported food to avoid massive starva-

tion. The latter countries, which may also lack valuable natural resources such as oil or copper, are the very ones that find it most difficult to pay for the food they so desperately need.

The issue of whether food is a commodity to be bought and sold or traded for, or whether it is a human right more important than economic or political concerns, came to be more than simply an academic debate in the 1970s and early 1980s, when millions of people began starving to death in the Sahel (the region south of the Sahara Desert in Africa), Bangladesh, Cambodia, Ethiopia, and Somalia. The world is facing the moral, social, and political question of whose responsibility it is to feed people. Do those with control over large food surpluses have the right to withhold food from people who need it simply because they cannot pay for it?

There are strong feelings on both sides of this question. The Environmental Fund, a research center and "think-tank" in Washington, D.C., takes one stance toward the problem of world hunger. It argues, for example, that American

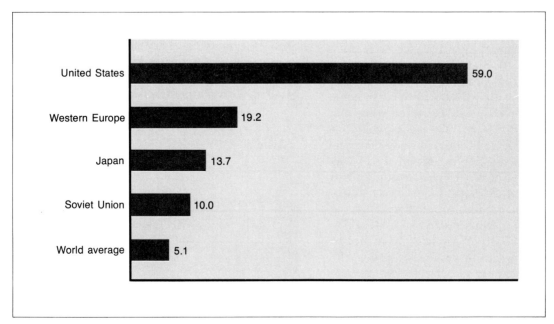

**Figure 18.7   Number of People Fed per Farmer.**

Farmers in the United States are the most efficient food producers in the world, because of their highly industrialized operations and their fertile land.

*Source: Time,* November 6, 1978, p. 95.

aid merely encourages less developed nations to "have as many children as they please," whereas "others have the responsibility to feed them" (Environmental Fund, 1976, p. 2). In their view, the real crisis is population growth. They are staunchly in the neo-Malthusian camp and demand that less developed nations cut their birth rates in response to food shortages.

Other groups, such as Bread for the World, adopt a position of moral responsibility. They believe that as long as nations that have been blessed by nature and location have a food surplus, they have an obligation to share that food with others. The only way for individuals in poorer nations to limit family size voluntarily is for them to see that the children they do have will survive and grow up. In agricultural societies, children are still the only form of old-age insurance people have. This being the case, people will not limit their childbearing unless they can be sure their children will not die of starvation or nutrition-related diseases. This position stresses the point that the present hunger problem is more of a distribution problem than a production problem.

A third and more drastic position is called *triage*. The term "triage" is taken from wartime medical work, where the wounded were classified into those who would definitely benefit from medical attention, those who might, and those who were too badly injured to gain from care. In responding to world hunger, a triage approach involves the determination, by nations with surplus food, of those needy nations that are most likely to survive. Then donor nations concentrate existing food surpluses on them while ignoring the others (Environmental Fund, 1976).

Whatever the short-term actions nations take to deal with the world population and hunger problem, the only immediately visible way to avert world starvation on a major scale for the longer term seems to be population control. With the reduction of death rates on a worldwide basis, the growth of population has far exceeded gains in agricultural productivity. We are staring at a crisis of global proportions. Unless technology produces some dramatic and rapid changes, we may be approaching the limits of existing subsistence strategies.

## HEALTH AND SOCIETY

Life expectancy and illness are strongly influenced by ecological and social factors. The way people respond to and treat different illnesses varies from country to country and for different groups within one society. The same physical ailment may be treated by witchcraft, prayer, the laying on of hands, or radiation and chemotherapy, or some combination of these, depending on the culture in which the illness occurs.

In addition, people in different societies around the world die of very different causes. In preindustrial and developing societies, people may weaken and die of tuberculosis, starvation, and parasites such as tapeworms. Many young children die of malnourishment, typhoid, or diphtheria. In industrial societies, most of these causes of death have been eliminated. Moreover, previously stubborn diseases such as smallpox, polio, German measles, tetanus, diphtheria, mumps, and measles have been controlled.

People in industrial societies generally live to be much older, on the average, and die of quite different causes than people in preindustrial societies. Cancer, heart disease, and stroke are the chief killers in industrial societies.

### The Health of Americans

American health patterns are consistent with these trends. Americans are much more likely to die from chronic illness now than they were at the turn of the century (Figure 18.8). Deaths from infectious diseases have dropped over the last 80 years. Accidents continue to account for about 10 percent of deaths, and these are particularly likely to involve Americans under age 30. Wide differences remain within the United States in death rates and types of illness according to social class, race, and sex. There also are cultural differences in reaction to pain, with some cultural groups such as those of Anglo Saxon or Asian origin talking less about their pain than other cultural groups (Zborowski, 1981). As noted in Chapters 10 and 11, whites have a longer life expectancy than blacks, and women live longer than men. The life expectancy of women has increased dramatically in the last 60 years. It was 56, only two years longer than that for men, in 1920, but by 1987 it was 78.3, seven years longer than men's (U.S. Bureau of the Census, 1989a).

How can we explain the dramatic drop in mortality rates, the shift in the causes of death, and the persistence of gender, race, and social-class differences in death and disease in the United States? A likely answer seems to be the progress and availability of modern, scientific medical care. Throughout this century, medical practitioners armed with increasingly powerful tools and techniques have attacked and wiped out many diseases. But because some social groups have not had access to physicians or hospitals, they have been more likely to get sick and to die at younger ages.

This explanation is only a small part of the answer, however. Social rather than medical reasons appear to play a more important role in increased life expectancy (McKinlay and McKinlay, 1986). Death rates for four of the infectious diseases plaguing the United States dropped sharply before modern physicians discovered the vaccine or cure for each disease (Figure 18.9). A rising standard of living enabled people to buy more nutritious food, which increased resistance to disease and the chances that they would survive illness. Improvements in public sanitation (i.e., cleaning up water and sewage systems) reduced people's exposure to infection.

Continued differences in health and death rates for different groups in the United States today result from both social and medical causes. People in higher social classes tend to be healthier than those in lower social classes. This phenomenon seems to be due to better nutrition, lower likelihood of smoking, lower exposure to health hazards and stressful situations, more knowledge about health, and greater access to superior health care (Kitagawa, 1972;

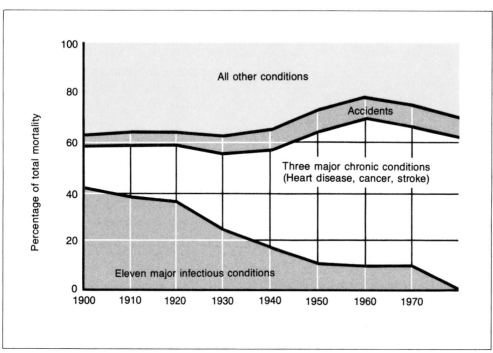

**Figure 18.8   The Changing Contribution of Chronic and Infectious Conditions to Total Mortality (Age- and Sex-Adjusted), in the United States, 1900–1973.**

In this century, increasing numbers of people have died from chronic conditions rather than infections.

*Source:* McKinlay and McKinlay, 1986, p. 16.

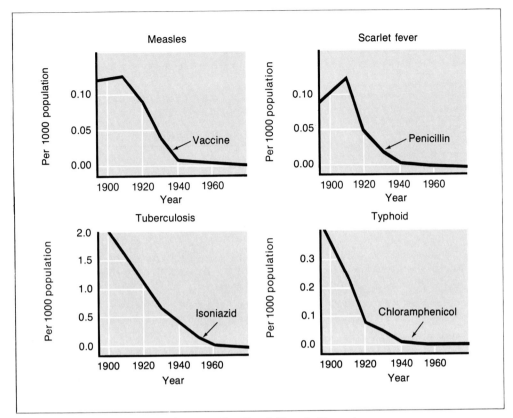

**Figure 18.9    The Fall in the Standardized Death Rate (per 1000 Population) for Four Common Infectious Diseases in Relation to Specific Medical Measures, for the United States, 1900–1973.**

Mortality from these diseases had already dropped dramatically before vaccines or treatments were discovered.

*Source:* McKinlay and McKinlay, 1986, p. 20.

Syme and Berkman, 1981). Both medical and social factors seem to affect gender differences as well. Among young adults, males are more likely to succumb to accidents. At older ages, heart and kidney diseases and lung cancer contribute to the higher mortality of men. Women, in turn, have become less likely to die in childbirth or of uterine cancer in recent years (Waldron, 1981). Cultural factors play a role in the lower mortality rates among married rather than single or widowed males, particularly from such causes as cirrhosis of the liver (associated with heavy drinking). Gove (1973) argues that married men receive better physical care than single ones and have a greater sense of psychological well-being.

Diseases that are on the increase in the United

States also appear to have important social causes. More than 53 million people in the United States—over one-quarter of the population—will develop some form of cancer. Why, in the face of improved techniques of identifying and treating cancer, has the rate of death due to this disease increased? Some argue that rising levels of industrial chemicals in our environment and the exposure of large numbers of people to those chemicals over the last four decades are related to these increases (Epstein, 1981). Experts suggest that up to 90 percent of human cancers are environmentally induced.

This conclusion is supported by evidence showing that the incidence of cancer varies geographically (Epstein, 1981). It is already known that about 50 percent of long-time asbestos-in-

*Life expectancy is related to a rising standard of living which enables people to buy more nutritious food. Better nutrition, in turn, increases resistance to disease and the chances of surviving illness.*

sulation workers die of cancer; the rates of bladder cancer are very high in dye and rubber industry workers; lung cancer is up in uranium miners of Colorado and coke-oven workers. Other cancers are associated with certain occupations: skin cancer in shale-oil workers, nasal sinus cancer in woodworkers, liver cancer in workers making polyvinyl chloride, leukemia in benzene workers, and cancer of the pancreas in organic chemists. Lung cancer is demonstrably higher in smokers than in nonsmokers and possibly in their spouses and children as well.

Such cancers are ultimately preventable if the specific causes can be pinpointd. Spotting cancer-causing agents is sometimes difficult because cancers crop up 15 or 20 years after workers or residents are exposed to the agents (Selikoff, 1980). Not only are workers exposed, but vast areas of the world are in danger of contamination from the chemical wastes produced by many manufacturing processes (Magnuson, 1980). Industry seems unconcerned with the issue. When additional regulatory standards limiting environmental and occupational exposure to toxic agents are proposed, industries often respond by forecasting major economic distress and unemployment as a result of the regulations. Such calculations overlook the fact that the economic (not to mention the human) costs of cancer are at least $15 billion a year (Epstein, 1981). The scourge of cancer calls for major social, economic, and political solutions at least as much as medical ones.

Other serious diseases, such as AIDS, have no known medical cures. Changes in social behavior are the only available ways to prevent infection. (See box in Chapter 21 for more on AIDS.)

## The Medical Profession in America

Why, if social features appear to be so important in health and illness, do Americans tend to think primarily in terms of physicians, hospitals, and medical cures? Perhaps the reason lies in what we see around us. We see large hospitals with sophisticated technology like CAT scanners, doctors trained in rigorous medical schools, and a host of supporting professions and personnel. Although these aspects of care are taken for granted today, doctors have not always offered effective cures or had an exclusive monopoly on medicine. Less than 100 years ago, they offered bleeding and strong emetics or purgatives as their major forms of treatment. Until the latter part of the nineteenth century, various groups, including midwives, shared medical practice with doctors. But by the 1920s, virtually only M.D. physicians had the legal right to practice medicine in the United States (Conrad and

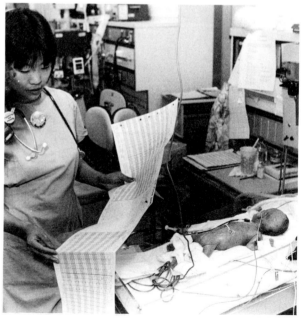

*Sophisticated medical technologies can help sustain the lives of very premature babies such as this one.*

## The Social Transformation of American Medicine

American medicine has not always enjoyed the prosperity and professional esteem that have marked its position since the middle of this century. In his award-winning book *The Social Transformation of American Medicine,* Paul Starr (1982) traces the roller coaster history of the medical profession since the nineteenth century.

### The Nineteenth Century

In this period physicians had an insecure and ambiguous status and received low pay. The lack of a sound scientific base for diagnosis and treatment meant they could do little to help the sick other than to offer reassurance and moral support. The field of medicine was in a state of uncertainty and disagreement.

### The Early Twentieth Century

After the Flexner Report in 1910, medical education was completely revamped to bridge the gap between scientific knowledge and medical practice. Medical education came to be rooted in basic science, research, and clinical instruction. Students were expected to have some college training or even a college degree before attending medical school. Medical graduates had to pass a licensing exam. As admission to the profession became increasingly restricted, the number of physicians dropped and their social characteristics changed. In particular, the number of black and women's medical schools plummeted in this period (Ehrenreich and English, 1978; Morantz-Sanchez, 1985). In 1900, 20 percent of doctors in some American cities had been women (Walsh, 1977), but as recently as 1960 women received only 5.5 percent of all medical degrees (U.S. Bureau of the Census, 1985a, p. 159). Although the Flexner report and the ensuing certification requirements for doctors enhanced the scientific status of medicine, they also generally restricted access to a medical career to white males.

### 1945 to 1965

The post–World War II years saw the growth of an immense medical research establishment, the expansion of scientifically advanced hospitals, and a tremendous increase in the size of the medical work force and the amount of health care expenditures. Physicians became prosperous, socially privileged, and highly influential professionals who completely dominated the health care market. University medical schools became tied in with major hospital systems in large metropolitan areas. Power was held by "chairmen-chiefs" who chaired the major medical school departments and were chiefs of medicine, surgery, and other departments in the teaching hospitals.

### 1970s and 1980s

Along with many other American institutions in the 1970s, medicine experienced a stunning loss of public confidence. Scientific progress in medicine captured public attention at mid-century, but by the 1970s and 1980s people were increasingly concerned about costs and moral problems. The women's movement raised questions about the authority and power of doctors, particularly in regard to childbirth practices and cancer surgery. As Starr notes, physicians found their political influence, economic power, and cultural authority all being challenged.

At least four developments will strongly affect the medical system for the rest of this century: the increasing supply of physicians, the continuing effort by government and employers to control the growth of medical expenditures, the rising cost of medical malpractice insurance, and the growth of corporate enterprise in health services. Changes such as these will limit the medical profession's control of markets and health organizations, and they will affect their standards of judgment too.

As Starr (1982) suggests: "In the future, more doctors will be in group practice; more hospitals will be in multihospital systems; and more insurance companies will be directly involved in providing medical care through HMOs" (p. 440).

Kern, 1981). Their monopoly extends over the right to define illness and its treatment, the right to limit and evaluate other medical care workers, and the supervision of childbirth.

In the United States, the medical profession also has a very strong influence over the financing and planning of health services. (See the box entitled "The Social Transformation of American Medicine" for more about how the practice of medicine has changed over time in the United States and how the profession has faced its challenges.)

The American medical profession is among the most independent and powerful of its kind in the world, and the organization of American health care is characterized by the monopolistic control physicians have over medical practice. Doctors have an exclusive state-supported right, apparent in the licensing of physicians, to practice medicine. They are the only ones who are legally entitled to prescribe restricted drugs, cut into the human body, and sign a certificate giving the cause of death. While each country grants slightly different privileges to its physicians, the medical profession in all modern countries stands in a dominant and influential position. In the United States, however, the professional's rise to dominance brought considerable control over the organization and financing of medical care. This was not typical of other countries.

### Financing Medical Care

Perhaps the most striking feature of health care organization in the United States is the way it is financed. Medical care is considered a service available to those who can pay for it or who have insurance to do so—just as, say, the services of an auto body shop are available to people who can afford them. The price of medical care depends on market forces. This market model of medical care stands in sharp contrast to the organization of medical services elsewhere. In virtually all other industrial countries, medical care is viewed more as a right of citizenship than a service to be purchased. Health care systems received subsidies from the state. Hence, the kind and quality of the medical care received may depend on the nature of the illness, not on a person's income (Freidson, 1978). In recent years, financial barriers to adequate medical care in the United States have fallen considerably (Dutton, 1978; Rundall and Wheeler, 1979).

A team of medical researchers at Harvard was surprised to find that a significantly higher proportion of white people admitted to Massachusetts hospitals have coronary bypass operations and other heart surgery than do blacks (Stevens, 1989). This difference in medical treatment by race existed even when the study took into account other factors such as income, age, sex, and insurance status. The authors urged caution about concluding that black patients are underserved, however, suggesting that whites might undergo more unnecessary procedures than do blacks. Other researchers have found that black Americans significantly underuse medical care in the United States, and other studies report that blacks and women are less likely than white men to receive kidney transplants, even if they have similar incomes, insurance coverage, or states of health (Stevens, 1989). Such results suggest the need for further research on how social factors and health care are interrelated.

### Problems in the Health Care System

The high level of professional autonomy and reliance on market forces has created problems in the U.S. health care system. As early as 1970, then-President Nixon announced that there was a "health care crisis" in the United States. This included the inability of many Americans to obtain medical care; the spiraling costs for people and government; and concerns about the success, priorities, and methods of medical treatment.

For example, the market model and the relative autonomy of doctors have led to problems in the distribution and type of doctors available. Physicians are very unevenly distributed throughout the nation. In 1985, Washington, D.C., had 573 active physicians per 100,000 population, compared to 119 per 100,000 in Mississippi (U.S. Bureau of Census, 1987a). Thousands of towns and counties in America have no doctor at all.

Another difficulty has been the increasing specialization of modern medicine. Until World War II, most physicians were family doctors, practicing general medicine and making house calls. Now, all but 14 percent of the nation's doctors are specialists (U.S. Bureau of the Census, 1989a). This specialization may lead to higher costs, loss of perspective on a whole human being, and lack of continuity of treatment. This specialization, some argue, leads to higher costs, loss of perspective on the patient as a "whole person," and a lack of continuity in medical care for the individual.

Even when medical care is available, many Americans delay seeking care because of its high cost. Although 87 percent of the population had some kind of private health insurance in 1985, that still left 13 percent of Americans without any coverage at all (U.S. Bureau of the Census, 1989a). Moreover, many who have coverage find that it is limited as to the kind and amount of payment. The result is that some people can pay high prices to see private physicians, whereas many have only crowded public clinics and hospital outpatient facilities. Some even use the emergency room as a last resort when their medical condition worsens.

Even the staunchest defenders of the medical profession express concern about runaway med-ical costs. Although the cost of medical care in the United States is higher than almost any-where in the world, we do not have the lowest infant mortality rates or the lowest death or disability rates. Health care costs increased more than 35 times between 1950 and 1986, as Figure 18.10 shows. In the latter year, they were about $458 billion (or 10.9 percent of the GNP). This was up from $13 billion (4.5 percent of GNP) in 1950 (U.S. Bureau of the Census, 1989a).

Another major consequence of the current or-ganization of health care is the relatively greater

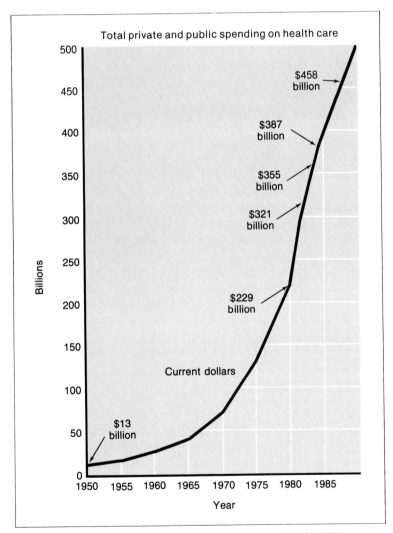

**Figure 18.10   Rising Costs of Health Care, 1950–1986.**

Health care expenditures in the United States rose steadily be-tween 1950 and 1986; in 1986, they represented 11 percent of the GNP.

*Source:* U.S. Bureau of the Census, 1982a, p. 101; 1989a, p. 92.

emphasis on the treatment rather than the prevention of illness. Yet some activities actively create illness and injury; for example, occupations such as logging, mining, chemical handling, or professional football have much higher rates of illness or injury than do many other occupations. Certain behaviors—such as being competitive, aggressive, and impatient—may be encouraged and rewarded in our society and yet be linked to higher rates of heart attack and high blood pressure. Various foods and drugs are widely advertised around the world (for instance, sugar-rich soft drinks, alcohol, coffee, cigarettes, and tranquilizers), although growing evidence suggests that they may be harmful to our health.

Despite the overwhelming hints that environmental causes of cancer might be a fruitful area for further investigation, the National Cancer Institute's expenditures on environmental cancer agents have been estimated at only 5 to 20 percent of the total (Epstein, 1981). Medical treatment has been very effective in preventing and treating acute infectious diseases such as pneumonia, which lends itself to treatment with antibiotics. But long-term chronic illnesses such as heart disease, cancer, and stroke are more likely to affect people in industrial societies. Therefore, an improved understanding of ways to prevent these diseases may produce more benefits (Torrens, 1978).

### Responses to the Problems

Responses to the growing problems in American medical care have come from the public, "alternative" healers, the government, health care insurance companies, and the medical community itself.

Opposition to the rising costs of health care has been growing, both among private health insurance companies and in the federal government. Blue Cross and Blue Shield, among the largest private health insurance programs, set limits on the fees they will pay to doctors and hospitals. In 1983 Medicare (the government-sponsored health insurance program for the elderly) began paying hospitals a preset amount based on the problem a patient was diagnosed as having, rather than simply reimbursing hospitals for itemized daily charges. Under this DRG (diagnostic related groups) system, hos-

pitals face a cap on the amount they will receive for each patient. Therefore hospitals have urged physicians to cut unnecessary diagnostic tests and prescribe only essential care. This places physicians in a precarious position, because they also face increased pressure, from the rising number of malpractice suits, to run diagnostic tests. Despite the American Medical Association's bitter opposition, the government began in the 1970s to reimburse charges by chiropractors through Medicare and Medicaid (government-sponsored medical insurance for the poor).

**HMOs.** The development of **health maintenance organizations** (HMOs) represents another organizational effort to trim health care costs. Members of an HMO pay a set fee each year to belong. In return, they receive a full range of health services. Some HMOs have been criticized for denying membership to poor health risks, so the reductions in cost may be offset by social costs.

**HOSPICES.** Hospices were started as a way of responding more humanely to the needs of terminally ill people, first in England and then in the United States (DuBois, 1980). The goal of a **hospice** is to help people with fatal diseases spend their last days in as little pain and as much comfort as possible and to provide them and their loved ones with emotional support. They may also help to reduce health care costs. Hospices may be part of a hospital or they may be independent. Some are mobile units of doctors, nurses, and social workers that help families care for dying patients at home. In general, hospices are designed to be as homelike as possible. Pain-killing drugs are used as needed for relief, and no extraordinary efforts (such as resuscitation) are made to prolong the process of dying. Dying is treated as a natural part of the life cycle rather than as a "failure."

The U.S. public has not passively accepted problems in the medical care system. As early as the mid-seventies, a substantial portion of the American population was willing to question the authority and medical expertise of physicians (Haug and Lavin, 1983, p. 69). Americans also gave more negative evaluations to government efforts in the medical-care system than did the citizens of six European countries (Pescosolido, Boyer, and Tsui, 1985). A growing consumerism in medicine has led to increased interest in self-care, other types of medical practitioners (for example, acupuncturists), and physical fitness. In recent years, many residents of industrial societies, especially the United States, have joined health clubs, taken up exercise programs, or embarked on programs to ensure better nutrition.

Three changes in the delivery of health care have challenged physicians' professional dominance. The first two have already been mentioned. They are the greater involvement of the government because of Medicare and Medicaid and the rise of consumerism in health care. The third is the corporate takeover by business conglomerates of a significant portion of the health market (Starr, 1982). By the mid-1980s, one out of five U.S. hospitals was owned by for-profit corporations (Cockerham, 1988, pp. 592–593).

Analyzing and changing the social origins of illness requires a different approach than that practiced by the health profession. It involves efforts to understand and change the ecological, political, and social forces affecting health and disease in our society.

The kind of medical care needed in a society depends partly on its age structure. A society's population, age structure, health care, and food production are all interrelated. When children do not regularly die of malnutrition or disease, parents tend to have fewer children. If such a decline follows a period of numerous births and life expectancy increases, the proportion of elderly in the population will increase. Such an increase has occurred in the United States, and it has numerous significant social consequences.

## AGE AND AGING

Ellen's 85-year-old grandmother, Mary Sargent, has lived alone for the last ten years, ever since her husband died. Since she never worked, she subsists on her widow's Social Security benefits and the modest income from the savings and investments she and her husband made. She lives in a fully paid-for house, but finds that rising costs are a growing burden. Her health

has been good until recently, but now her family is beginning to worry about letting her live alone, since lately she has had several dizzy spells and falls.

In many ways, Mary Sargent reflects a significant social change. In 1900, the average life expectancy in the United States was 47, but today it is 75. Moreover, women outlive men by 7 years, on the average. In 1988, more than 12 percent, or 30 million Americans, were 65 or older, compared to 8 percent in 1950. By the year 2030 those 65 and over are expected to total 68 million persons, or nearly one-quarter of the total population.

The enormous increase in the number and percentage of older people has led to increased interest in age. The aging of the population is a historically new social phenomenon. Sociologists examine how social factors affect living longer and how age is evaluated; they also consider the social consequences of increasing numbers of older people in a society.

## How Social Factors Affect Life Expectancy

Pure water, safe milk, and better sewers helped to control such diseases as cholera and typhoid. The social acceptance of the germ theory of disease helped to fight other diseases and infections. Women began to die much less often in childbirth, thereby extending their life expectancy. In recent years the earlier detection and treatment of high blood pressure, diabetes, heart disease, and some forms of cancer—as well as a decline in the health-threatening practice of cigarette smoking—have helped to extend life expectancy.

Other social factors are also related to life expectancy. People who are involved in a satisfying network of social relations and who enjoy life are likely to live longer than those who are not involved and do not enjoy life. One social loss, namely, being widowed, seems to affect men and women differently. Bereaved women are more likely than men to report new or worsened illnesses (Thompson et al., 1984). Men are dramatically more likely to die after losing their wives, whereas the death of a husband has almost no effect on women's mortality rates (Helsing, Szklo, and Comstock, 1981). Widowers do not die immediately, as though from the shock of losing their mates, but rather, the researchers found that the shock of losing a spouse is a great deal harder on men than on women. The mortality rate of widowers is 26 percent higher than that for married men, whereas the rate for widows is only 3.8 percent higher than that for married women. Young widowers fare the worst; the mortality rate of those aged 55 to 64 is 61 percent higher than that for married men. For widowers who remarry, however, the death rate is 70 percent lower than for those who do not.

Widowed men and women who move into a retirement or nursing home because they are ill or unable to live with other family members have three or four times the mortality rate of those who do not go into a retirement or nursing home. Those living alone also have higher mortality rates (Helsing, Szklo, and Comstock, 1981). Clearly, social as well as physical factors are related to life expectancy.

## How Is Age Valued?

Every society is stratified one way or another by age (Riley, Foner, and Waring, 1988). In a traditional tribal society, much of the tribe's knowledge and wisdom is stored in the memories of tribal elders. They may remember which other tribes were friendly or aggressive in the past, where water was found, or how to deal with a plague of locusts. Since subsistence in such societies is drawn from the land, the elders provide a smooth and legitimate means of controlling use of the land, thereby avoiding conflict. Therefore they represent a valuable resource in the society's efforts to survive, and valuing age and elders is functional for the society. There are also fewer elders in such societies, and they do not live as long.

In industrial societies, in contrast, the economic activity of most members is not centered around the land. Individuals can subsist independently of their elder kin. Moreover, the knowledge and technology that support their activities are changing rapidly. Often the younger generations know how to do more things than do the older ones. As a result, it is not functional for such a society to rely heavily on its older generations for social and economic guidance.

The conflict perspective stresses that the way a society is arranged depends on the relative power and resources of various groups in it. In industrial societies, the elderly lose power and resources, since for many people their power and resources are rooted in jobs rather than in the land. Because there are more people who want to work than there are jobs available, the more numerous middle-aged people set age limits on who can work. As a result, both the young and the old in industrial societies tend to be squeezed out of opportunities for work, money, and status.

Symbolic interactionism approaches the issue of aging somewhat differently. One approach that interactionists might take is to examine the age of cultural heroes. When the median age of the American population was 25, in the 1960s, the cultural heroes were very young people. One of the slogans of the era was "Don't trust anyone over 30!" By the time the median age hit 32 in 1986, that slogan had disappeared and a number of important cultural heroines were over 40 or even 50, for example, Jane Fonda, Meryl Streep, and Elizabeth Taylor. Fashion magazines featured "great women over the age of 40" on their covers. Changes in the median age are correlated with changes in the social

*Women who lose their husbands are more likely to experience new or worsened illnesses afterwards, whereas men who lose their wives are dramatically more likely to die. Many more women outlive their husbands than men outlive their wives.*

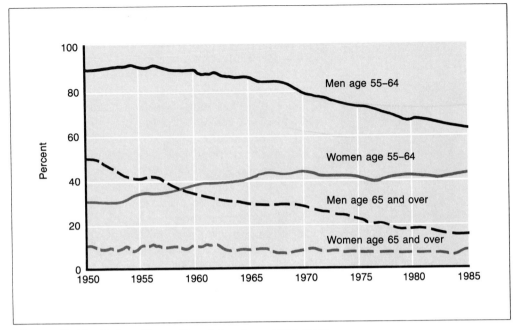

**Figure 18.11  Labor Force Participation, 1950–1985.**

The labor-force participation of older men has generally declined since 1950, while that of women aged 55 to 64 has increased.

*Source:* U.S. Bureau of the Census and Bureau of Labor Statistics; Soldo and Agree, 1988, p. 25.

definitions of attractiveness. Although the age of cultural heroines appears to have increased in recent years and movies such as *Cocoon* featured older people as central characters, the question remains: How are older persons (those 65 and over) faring today?

## Economic Status of the Elderly

Older Americans have an average household income of $14,334, about 55 percent of the average U.S. household income of $25,986 (U.S. Bureau of the Census, 1989a). About 12 percent of older Americans hover around the "poverty line." Those in the poverty category are more likely to be female, and older than those above the line. More Americans over 65 today receive Social Security benefits than ever before (92 percent), but Social Security provides only 40 percent of the total income available to older Americans (Soldo and Agree, 1988, p. 27). Their next largest source of income is earnings from assets, equal to 26 percent of total income. In 1987 only

16.3 percent of men 65 and over were working, compared to 48 percent in 1947.

There was a steady decline in the proportion of older men working between 1950 and 1985 (Figure 18.11). The proportion of women aged 55 to 64 who are working has increased, however, while early retirement has become more popular among men. Among those receiving private retirement benefits, almost two-thirds stopped working before their sixty-fifth birthday (U.S. Senate, 1988a, vol. 1).

Younger workers (those 16 to 19 years old) are also much more likely to be unemployed and to earn lower wages than middle-aged workers. Some older persons are better off in one respect; namely, they are more likely to own their own homes. Among older persons, more than 75 percent owned their own homes in 1987, compared to 66 percent of the entire population. Of those, 75 percent have paid off their mortgages (Soldo and Agree, 1988, p. 28).

There are, of course, variations in the elderly population. Those aged 65 to 75, especially when they are white married couples, generally

*Many people over the age of 65 are more active, healthy, and adventurous than younger people realize.*

fare quite well, both in terms of financial security and health. If one or both of them held well-paying jobs throughout their adult lives, they generally have pensions and sometimes supplemental health insurance. They are likely to own a home and a car and are not economically or socially dependent on others. They are in the best position to enjoy their retirement years. The majority of those aged 76 to 85 are women, since men have shorter life expectancies. If only their husbands worked, they may lose any pension support they had been receiving, and their health problems are likely to increase with age. Those over 85 are the most needy and powerless. They may be unable to take advantage of many existing programs for the elderly. There are many more women in this category; they are more likely to have serious medical problems and expenses and to be poor.

## Health Care and the Elderly

The elderly are more likely than younger people to suffer from chronic ailments for which there are no medical "cures." However, individuals may develop programs for dealing with their heart disease, high blood pressure, diabetes, Parkinson's disease, hearing or sight loss, or the effects of a stroke. These conditions call for regular medical supervision and often careful monitoring of medications. Among people 65 and over, however, 60 percent are generally quite well (Moore, 1983). Those with serious health problems tend to be considerably over 65.

While about 80 percent of older persons have at least one chronic condition, only half need to restrict their activities because of those conditions. Only about 5 percent of the elderly are in institutions at any given time (Soldo and Agree, 1988, p. 30). Acute health conditions—such as pneumonia or a heart attack—are severe but of short duration. Chronic conditions are usually less severe but cannot be eliminated. The elderly are most likely to suffer from such chronic conditions as arthritis, hypertension, heart conditions, and hearing loss.

Some of the elderly need nursing care if they lose the capacity to control their mobility or other bodily functions. The needs of the medical staffs of nursing facilities shift as well. They are able to "cure" relatively few patients. They need to focus instead on the goal of enhancing the quality of life available to patients, a process that takes many mundane forms such as a clean bed or a caring manner, without offering opportunities for major improvements. Such medical needs lead to an increased need for good nursing homes rather than hospitals and suggest that there will be a major demand for people trained in geriatric nursing, medicine, and social work.

Long-term health care is the biggest problem facing the elderly, particularly as they age. The problem will grow as the number of elderly in the population increases. In 1980 an estimated 5.6 million needed long-term care. This figure is projected to increase to 9 million by 2000 and to 18 million by 2040 (Liu and Manton, 1987). Most (78 percent) of the elderly disabled currently live in the community rather than in nursing homes (U.S. Senate, 1987, vol. 3, p. 11). Most (72 percent) of caregivers for the disabled elderly are women (daughters, wives, and other women). The nursing home population, however, will probably grow rapidly over the next decades. The average annual cost of residence in a nursing home in 1987 was $22,000 (Soldo and Agree, 1988, p. 36). One out of every three elderly who spend any time in a nursing home will end up poor. The majority end up poor within one year (U.S. Senate, 1988b, vol. 3, p. 29). When poor, they may become eligible for **Medicaid,** a federal-state matching program that provides medical assistance to certain low-income persons. Each state sets the payment rates for Medicaid services. Nearly half of all nursing-home residents receive Medicaid. **Medicare** is a federal health insurance program. Eligibility and benefits are uniform throughout the United States. Individuals are eligible if they receive Social Security benefits, federal disability benefits, or sometimes if they have end-stage kidney disease. Older Americans paid an average of $728 to enroll in Medicare in 1987 (Soldo and Agree, 1988). Coverage is aimed more at acute rather than chronic care. Thus, it covers hospital and surgical care and recovery from surgery. Critics suggest that both Medicaid and Medicare stress institutional rather than home-care solutions to long-term-care needs (Soldo and Agree, 1988, p. 32).

In 1988 the U.S. Congress passed the Catastrophic Loss Prevention Act. It represents the most significant expansion of Medicaid since it began in 1965. The bill helps persons who have

*Only about 5 percent of the elderly are in institutions at any given time. As more of the population becomes elderly, however, the number of those needing institutional care is likely to increase.*

a major accident or acute illness. However, it provides minimal coverage for long-term care. The only relevant provision is coverage of up to 80 hours per year of home health services as "respite" for caregivers tending dependent older people (Soldo and Agree, 1988, p. 34). The lack of legislative action on long-term care may have brought the issue to the fore in health policy debates (U.S. Senate, 1987, vol. 3, p. 55). In the age of massive federal budget deficits, new programs need to pay for themselves. Benefits from the new Catastrophic Loss Prevention Act are to be financed by increased Medicare premiums and higher payroll taxes for workers earning more than $45,000 per year. Congress defeated a proposed Medicare Long-Term Home Care Catastrophic Protection Act in 1988, but it may reintroduce the bill. It would provide, for the first time, at least partial Medicare coverage for long-term home care.

## SUMMARY

1. For a long time in human history, population growth (birth rates minus death rates) remained constant at a steady replacement level. The demographic transition occurred in three stages. First, with the agricultural revolution, birth rates rose sharply, probably from improved nutrition, whereas death rates remained constant or rose only slightly. Population size began to increase.

2. Second, with the advent of the industrial revolution, death rates dropped sharply in western Europe, whereas birth rates remained high for a while. As a result, the population began to increase noticeably.

3. Within two generations, the fertility rate also began declining in Europe and North America. At the same time, disease control reduced mortality in the rest of the world, resulting in a major worldwide population explosion. The big question for the future of our planet is whether birth rates will drop in the rest of the world the way they have in western Europe and North America. The rate of growth in world population has declined recently, especially in China. But since there are more than 5 billion

people already living on earth, a much greater decline is needed if the population is to be stabilized.

4. With current knowledge, there is little that can be done to improve food production markedly. Some steps can be taken to minimize waste, change habits so that people eat more efficient forms of protein, and improve distribution. Since the time of the great agricultural empires, however, the control of a food surplus has tended to mean other forms of control and subordination as well. How surplus world food is managed will be one of the great social, moral, and political issues of our era.

5. Social factors influence life expectancy and the types of illnesses people contract. Developing nations have high death rates from starvation, infection, and parasites, whereas industrial nations have eliminated many infectious diseases. Environmental substances and dietary habits contribute to high mortality from heart disease, cancer, and strokes in industrialized societies.

6. Social factors explain much of the decline in rates of infectious disease. Social class and gender are also related to health and morbidity.

7. More than one American in four will develop some form of cancer. Some experts believe that as much as 90 percent of human cancer is environmentally induced. This underscores the importance of investigating the social and occupational factors related to cancer if the disease is to be controlled.

8. Health care systems are organized differently in various societies. The United States contrasts with other industrial societies because medical care delivery is based on a free-market model. This means that health care is considered a service available to those who can pay for it. Most other industrial societies view medical care as a right rather than a service.

9. U.S. health care faces a number of problems, including the uneven distribution of doctors, increasing specialization, and rapidly rising costs.

10. Several factors may affect the professional dominance of doctors in the United States. These include the growing involvement of government, the rise of consumerism among patients, and corporate takeovers of hospitals.

11. Although as Americans age they generally experience a decline in social position and an increase in health problems, an extensive and growing program of social services is in place to help them. As the numbers of elderly increase and they become an ever-larger percentage of the total population, we can expect great social changes to occur in response to their numbers and needs.

12. Long-term health care is the biggest single problem facing the elderly.

## KEY TERMS

baby boom (p. 462)
cohort (p. 462)
crude birth rate (p. 463)
crude death rate (p. 464)
demographic transition (p. 461)
demography (p. 461)
elderly dependency ratio (p. 467)
green revolution (p. 470)
health maintenance organizations (HMOs) (p. 480)
hospice (p. 480)
life expectancy (p. 464)
life table (p. 465)
Medicaid (p. 485)
Medicare (p. 485)
migration (p. 465)
mortality rate (p. 464)
population (p. 459)
rate of natural increase (p. 465)
total fertility rate (p. 463)
zero population growth (ZPG) (p. 467)

## SUGGESTED READINGS

Easterlin, Richard A. 1987. "The New Age Structure of Poverty in America: Permanent or Transient?" *Population and Development Review* 13(2): 195–208. Suggests that opposing trends in poverty rates of children and the elderly are due to two different and independent causes. He argues that the market forces responsible for the growing number of children in poverty will change by the year 2000.

Jacobson, Jodi. 1988. "Planning the Global Family." In Lester R. Brown et al., *State of the World, 1988.* New York: W. W. Norton, pp. 151–169. A readable account of world population prospects.

Kennedy, Robert E., Jr. 1989. *Life Choices: Applying Sociology,* ed. 2. New York: Holt, Rinehart and Winston. Designed to help readers improve their life prospects by applying sociological knowledge, particularly population projections, to their own lives.

Preston, Samuel H. 1984. "Children and the elderly in the U.S." *Scientific American* (December) 251: 44–49. An important statement about how and why children in the United States have been losing ground.

Soldo, Beth J., and Emily M. Agree. 1988. "America's Elderly," *Population Bulletin* 43(3): 1–51. An excellent overview of the aging of the U.S. population and its implications.

Starr, Paul. 1982. *The Social Transformation of American Medicine.* New York: Basic Books. A Pulitzer prize-winning sociological analysis of the dramatic changes that have occurred in American medicine between 1760 and the present.

# Social Change, Collective Behavior, and Social Movements

*A recent issue of* Inuit Today *titled "Alcoholism: A Northern Dilemma," carries a cartoon of an Eskimo holding a bottle saying "This is the life!" The remainder of the issue is devoted to the theme that "booze can seriously destroy your health, and even kill you if taken in large enough amounts, but that's just one side of the story about the damaging effects of alcohol abuse on your health. The fights and accidents caused by too much drinking are another going concern." [Inuit Today, 1978, p. 68, cited in Klausner and Foulks, 1982, pp. 105–106]*

*The way alcohol is used in a society opens a window to that society, a direct vista on its personal, religious, and family life. Drinking in North Village [the place they studied] is part of drinking in Alaska, which in turn is part of drinking in the contiguous states. In this respect, too, core and peripheral societies are bound together. [Klausner and Foulks, 1982, p. 107]*

*Eskimos are distributed in the territories of, and [are] politically and economically "peripheral" to, four nations: the United States, Canada, Greenland, and the Soviet Union. The increasing production of petroleum and other minerals, found in abundance in arctic regions, has resulted in accelerating social and economic changes. The Eskimos themselves have become part of technological civilization. The communities of northern Alaska have suddenly become wealthy, and some individual Eskimos have profited politically and economically from these changes. They struggle to maintain themselves and their leadership as they become actors on a world stage. Others, however, have not been able to come to terms with their new role in the modern system. The distress of both types of individuals is evidenced by increasing rates of suicide and alcohol-related deaths. [Klausner and Foulks, 1982, p. 1]*

---

Rapid social changes, especially ones that are largely beyond the control of those experiencing them, may have major effects on the lives of individuals and communities. Among the Eskimos of the North Slope, alcoholism runs as high as 72 percent; violence, particularly suicide, is the leading cause of death; and the rate of homicide is four times higher than for other Alaskans (and Alaska has one of the higher rates in the United States). Other times people respond to major social changes by working together to guide or oppose the changes.

**Social change** is a significant modification or transformation of the way a society is organized. It includes changes in social institutions such as the economy or the family, changes in social stratification, changes in social roles (for example, the relations between blacks and whites or men and women), and social or political revolutions. The term "social change" refers to significant and major changes in patterned social behaviors at the institutional or societal level rather than to little changes within a small group. This chapter considers social changes both within industrialized nations and in the developing areas of the world. It begins by examining three major sources of social change and several theories of social change.

Collective behavior includes apparently spontaneous social behavior and more organized social movements. Social movements may be a mechanism by which people work together to promote or suppress particular social changes. The second and third sections in the chapter examine the nature of collective behavior and social movements, why they occur, why people participate, what forms they take, and why they succeed or fail.

One of the major sources of social change in many nations of the world today is the press toward modernization. Theorists have differing views about changes in developing nations. These issues are explored briefly in the final section of the chapter.

At times in human history the children of one generation grew up and lived a life very similar to that of their grandparents. Today, however, we cannot assume that our lives will be lived in an unchanging world. A major series of social changes accompanied the transformation of agricultural societies into industrial societies. That

*Major earthquakes are a type of environmental upheaval that can cause significant social change. This picture was taken in January 1989, about a month after the massive earthquake in Leninakan, Soviet Armenia's second largest city. More than 40,000 of the city's 290,000 inhabitants were killed, and 80 percent of the city was destroyed. This woman has found her home shattered by the earthquake, but her dog is alive, still attached to its garden chain.*

transition was marked by a declining proportion of people who were needed in agriculture, by the growth of railroads, and by the rise of such industries as steelmaking, oil refining, chemical production, and manufacturing. The process was accompanied by the growth of monopoly capitalism, the rise of nation-states and political centralization within them, and demands for expanded political participation. A demographic transition also occurred: Societies moved from high birth and death rates to high birth rates and low death rates, and then to a condition of both low birth and death rates. (These social changes are described in Chapter 3; the changes in where people work are shown in Table 13.3; and the demographic transition was discussed in Chapter 18.)

## SOURCES AND THEORIES OF SOCIAL CHANGE

Major environmental changes, technological developments, and collective social action can all be sources of significant social change. The first two are discussed in this section. The third is so important that the last three sections of the chapter are devoted to various forms of it.

### Environmental Factors

No one can predict precisely how a particular change in the physical environment will affect social life, but we do know that major physical changes such as a volcano or earthquake may produce certain short- and long-term social changes. Floods, typhoons, hurricanes, earthquakes, volcanic eruptions, and coal-mine cave-ins all tend to produce a concerted social effort against a common threat in the physical environment. People cooperate and groups form to rescue individuals who are trapped and to dig out survivors and property.

#### The Ice Age Recedes
About 13,000 years ago, the temperature of the world gradually increased and the thick glaciers that had covered much of North America and northern Europe began melting away. As

the ice receded, forests gradually took over most of the grassy plains, where large animals such as the woolly mammoth, woolly rhinoceros, steppe bison, giant elk, and numerous types of goats had grazed. The reduction of grasslands combined with a steady growth in the human population produced a crisis. Many large animals were hunted into extinction. By 7000 B.C., 32 genera of large animals became extinct in North America, including horses, oxen, elephants, camels, ground sloths, and giant rodents. Gradually, the various tribes began to rely on plants for ever-greater amounts of their food. The extinction of large meat animals triggered the shift to an agricultural form of food production in both the Old and the New Worlds (Harris, 1977). Changes in the physical world gradually transformed social life.

Prolonged droughts may also generate changes. The great drought in the American Plains in the 1930s drove thousands of farmers off the land. Oklahoma was especially badly hit. Crops never came up or shriveled on the stalk. Farmers couldn't pay their mortgages, and many lost their homes and their land. Nearly half a million migrated to California, where they eked out livings as migrant laborers. Their arrival on the West Coast produced a series of social conflicts and changes. Homeless people without jobs drifted from place to place, putting up shantytowns wherever they could, to the distress of existing residents. Local wages sagged below their already low rates. This example shows how two separate sources of social change—environmental changes and population shifts—interact to produce marked social changes.

### The "Greenhouse Effect"

The "earth stands on the brink of a global temperature increase unprecedented in the history of human civilization" (Kerr, 1988, p. 23). The source of this temperature increase is carbon dioxide ($CO_2$) emissions. It comes from cars, factories, the burning of coal, chlorofluorocarbons (CFCs) from plastic foam and coolants in refrigerators and air conditioners, and other sources. Like the glass windows of a greenhouse, $CO_2$ holds in some of the sun's heat that is reflected off the earth. The more $CO_2$, the more heat is retained. If the environment warms between 3° and 8° Fahrenheit by the year 2050, as some scientists predict, heat waves, droughts, floods, and hurricanes like those of 1988 could become increasingly frequent (Lemonick, 1989).

The effects of global warming would not be uniformly bad around the world, since colder countries like Canada and the USSR might enjoy warmer climates. But many areas might warm up in serious ways. Chicago's summers could become as warm as New Orleans's are now (Kerr, 1988). There could be hordes of environmental refugees "dwarfing the numbers of the Dust Bowl era or the boat people," warns Thomas Lovejoy of the Smithsonian Institute (Lemonick, 1989, p. 37).

Although not everyone agrees about how much warming will occur, no one argues that $CO_2$ levels are rising. Three major international organizations—the United Nations Environment Program (UNEP), the World Meteorological Organization (WMO), and the International Council of Scientific Unions—have called for immediate worldwide action. They urge governments to encourage energy conservation and develop solar energy and other alternatives to fossil fuels. Other possible solutions include tapping methane gas more widely at garbage landfills, slowing rates of deforestation, and planting many new trees to help absorb $CO_2$. Environmental changes such as the warming of the earth could cause massive social changes unless concerted action is taken to slow this process.

### Geography and Population

The physical environment of a society may also influence the rate of social change by the way geography encourages or discourages contact between societies. Countries such as Yugoslavia, which have been invaded and occupied by various different tribes, reflect such social encounters in their languages, customs, and cooking. Relatively isolated societies, protected by oceans or mountains from other social groups, over time develop their own languages and customs that tend to distinguish them from other societies. Such societies are not exposed to new ways, so they have little chance for change as a result of cultural diffusion from other societies. Physically isolated societies are likely to experience social change from dramatic physical events, such as an earthquake or volcano, or through their own invention and discovery. Unless they face major new problems needing solution, however, their rate of invention may be slow. Invention is encouraged by other inventions and by new needs, for example, from rising population.

The total number of people in a society, birth and death rates, the relative size of different age groups, and patterns of migration and settlement within their geographic territory all influence social changes.

When adequate food is available, populations tend to increase in size. As they grow, they need to find better ways to produce more food to feed ever-larger numbers of people. This need may produce agricultural innovations, which in turn may require new forms of social organization. Large-scale farming such as that practiced on the American Plains requires considerable technology, capital, and planning both for producing food and for distributing it.

If existing land and technology are unable to support the population, one of three social changes will almost certainly occur. People will starve in large numbers; there will be struggle and conflict and perhaps even war in order to obtain food; or large numbers of people will migrate to what they hope will be more hospitable areas. In the last decade we have witnessed all three of these responses to hunger in places as far afield as Southeast Asia, East Africa, and Haiti.

## Scientific and Technological Developments

There is always an interplay between technical and social changes. Without a social and cultural climate that permits change, the pace of technical change slows. Once technological developments occur, their potential for social change is enormous. The jet engine, for example, underwent a long development from 1930, when the first patent was filed by the British engineer Frank Whittle, to 1942, when the first usable engine was built (Ziman, 1976). Spurred by the war effort, Britain raced to try to build a jet fighter plane. In Germany, meanwhile, engineers were working on a jet plane as well, but the German Air Ministry was committed to piston airplanes and failed to support the effort adequately. The German Air Ministry was able to resist technical changes. As a result, Germany was unable to gain air superiority with a fast jet fighter during World War II (Ziman, 1976).

History is filled with instances of social changes set in motion by technological changes. The European conquest of the world in the sixteenth to eighteenth centuries, for instance, was made possible by the three-masted sea-going galleons and the use of cannons. Several technical developments in agriculture, including the horseshoe, the shoulder harness, the iron-tipped plow, and a system of three-crop rotation, produced widespread social changes. The increased crop yields resulting from these developments raised the peasants' standard of living and allowed them to buy manufactured goods. The production of surplus food allowed the growth of cities. The rise of cities created a new social class—merchants and skilled artisans—who helped to create capitalism. The invention of the steam engine and the development of ways of using it to power spinning and weaving operations enabled the industrial revolution to occur when and where it did (White, 1964).

More recently the development of jet aircraft broke down the social isolation of many regions in the world, accelerating exposure to new peoples and ideas, just as years earlier the automobile did the same for many regions in the United States. Movies and television have spread certain cultural ideas around the world by making people aware of lives and experiences far different from their own.

In medicine, technical advances have changed the definition of death. In the past, someone who had stopped breathing and whose heart had ceased to beat was considered dead. Now, with ways of stimulating the heart to resume beating and respirators to aid breathing, the medical definition of death has been changed to the cessation of brain waves. This has resulted in a number of cases involving individuals who were "dead" with respect to everything except their brain waves. Serious ethical controversies swirl around the issue of whether their respirators should be disconnected and who has the authority to make such a decision. Furthermore, who should bear the tremendous expense of sustaining life in such a form? As these issues are resolved, they will lead to further social changes arising from various medical technologies. Beyond sustaining life on a mechanical basis, technical medical developments have lengthened life expectancy and cut the death rates in industrial societies, resulting in much older populations. At the other end of the age spectrum, test-tube babies have become a reality and eggs and sperm can be frozen for use in the future.

### Technological Determinism

Technological developments unquestionably cause social changes. Some sociologists go so far as to argue that there is a kind of **technological determinism** that shapes social life in rather fixed ways. Such a view of word processing on computers, for instance, suggests that technology will inevitably lead to certain social arrangements, such as the greater independence of machine operators. In fact, however, work involving such technology may be socially organized in a variety of ways, only some of which result in greater worker autonomy. Thus, although technical developments undoubtedly influence social life, it is not possible to predict exactly what form the social changes will take. As the American automobile was rising in importance, a social observer might have predicted that cars would influence culture and be used to express social status but could not have said exactly how this would occur. Most forms of technological development allow for several possible forms of social response.

### Culture Lag

Cultural values and practices change more slowly than technical developments. Humans tend to accept new tools and technological inventions more rapidly than they embrace cultural changes and new ideas. William Ogburn (1922) called this process **culture lag** between material innovations and cultural practices. For example, rapidly growing populations in early stages of modernization reflect a cultural lag. The ideal of large families persists even though changing economic conditions make children an economic liability rather than an asset.

Some observers suggest that for each technical advance, there is a compensatory cultural development. Naisbitt (1981) calls this the "high tech/high touch" syndrome. He believes that when any major technology is introduced into a society, there is a counterbalancing human response or else the technology is rejected. Television, for example, has been accompanied by the growth of group therapy, personal growth, and human potential movements. In medicine, the expansion of new life-sustaining equipment has heightened interest in the human quality of death and the hospice movement. Personal family doctors are increasingly valued at the same time that heart transplants and brain scanners have emerged. The growth of computerized word processing has enhanced the value of handwritten notes and letters.

Although communication satellites, long-distance telephone connections, home computer terminals, and FAX machines mean that people could stay home and do almost all their work and shopping from there, they are not going to want to, suggests Naisbitt. The increasing development and use of non-face-to-face communication will mean that more and more people are going to want to talk and meet directly together. The increased use of the telephone and the jet plane has been accompanied by more conferences and meetings.

## Ideas and Ideology as Sources of Change

There are times when ideas or ideologies seem to be a major force behind social change. For example, in writing about the French Revolution, Alexis de Tocqueville (1856) observed a revolution of rising expectations that he saw as a major force pushing for revolution. People whose lives had been unchanged for generations suddenly witnessed major social upheavals and reacted by thinking, "Why not me? Why can't I make my life different?" The resulting image of a possible alternative did much to fuel the French Revolution and uprisings in other European countries in the nineteenth century.

The major religions in the world also illustrate the importance of ideas as possible sources of social change. See, for example, Weber's analysis of ascetic Protestantism and the spirit of capitalism in Chapter 16.

## Sources of Cultural Change

Culture, as we saw in Chapter 3, consists of customs, values, ideas, and artifacts, including language, religion, strategies for obtaining food, and the tools that are used. **Cultural change** refers to modifications in any of these aspects of a culture. Such cultural changes may produce social changes—that is, changes in the way a society is organized. Cultural changes can occur in several ways. **Innovation** refers to a new way of doing something. They may result from the **discovery** of something that already exists, like uranium, or the **invention** of something new, like plastic. **Diffusion** refers to the spread of a cultural innovation to other people or even to another society. Discoveries or inventions produce social change only when they are widely used in a society.

Invention, discovery, and diffusion may all influence the course of a cultural innovation. Penicillin, for instance, was discovered by Alexander Fleming in 1928, and his findings were published in a scientific journal. The quiet Fleming was unable to secure the financial and biochemical resources that were needed to isolate and purify the substance in any quantity, so the discovery slept for ten years. Then a team of scientists at Oxford, England, began refining penicillin. Considerable invention was required to find ways to produce the drug in useful amounts. The team took the idea to the United States in 1941 to get the backing of the American pharmaceutical industry. In the beginning, it took six months of laboratory work to get enough active penicillin to treat one case (Ziman, 1976). The diffusion of the initial ideas encouraged further invention, which increased diffusion, and so on. As a cure for pneumonia and other life-threatening diseases, penicillin did much to lower death rates. Its strength against veneral disease helped to pave the way for the sexual revolution of this century. Thus the discovery, invention, and diffusion of a single cultural innovation—penicillin—has facilitated far-reaching social changes.

## Theories of Social Change

Some sociologists have tried to describe and explain social changes in more general theoretical terms. Evolutionary theories, functionalist theories, cyclical theories, and conflict theories of social change have been advanced. Each of these is worth considering briefly, because they help us to think about social changes more broadly.

### Evolutionary Theories
**Evolutionary theories** begin with the observation that some societies are simple, whereas others are more complex. They suggest that societies have a tendency to become more complex because of innovation or diffusion as they learn more elaborate subsistence strategies. Although they do not argue that social change will occur in the same way in every society, they do see a tendency for societies to evolve from simpler forms to more complex ones. This perspective risks an implicit bias that more complex societies are superior to less complex ones—that is, they represent a higher order of development in some sense. Such a belief may be used to justify the domination of simpler societies by more complex ones.

### Functionalist Theories
As discussed in Chapter 1, functionalists see society as a stable and balanced collection of interdependent parts, like an organism in that it tries to reestablish its equilibrium, or balance, after an unsettling event occurs. In 1988 massive earthquakes in Armenia killed tens of thousands of people. A major hurricane destroyed more than a quarter of the homes on the Caribbean island of Jamaica and seriously damaged Texas and Louisiana. In the face of these disasters, people tried to get their lives back to normal. Functionalism has been criticized because it has difficulty explaining *why* social changes occur if the social order is basically balanced. When pressed by critics, Parsons (1937, 1951) and other functionalists stress that no one or two single sources of change are primary in social systems. Instead, several sources of social change are possible.

First, changes can occur from strains within a society—for example, when young people do not see society the same way their parents do. Social changes can also originate from the outside, through cultural diffusion, physical events, or military invasion. Examples of the first two sources of change from the outside were presented earlier in this section. With respect to military action, it is safe to say that major social changes have occurred in Afghanistan as a result of the Soviet invasion. A third way that functionalists explain social change is in terms of the ever-increasing differentiation of social institutions as societies become more complex. Gradually, for instance, schools have taken over many of the socialization functions once performed by the family. Now more specialization is occurring within schools as they provide learning specialists, psychologists, career counselors, health aides, and nutritionists.

Functionalism seems to be best suited for explaining evolutionary social changes within institutions and is less able to explain massive social changes such as social movements or revolutions.

### Cyclical Theories

**Cyclical theories** such as those of Spengler (1945) and Toynbee (1947) suggest that societies, or civilizations, follow a certain life course. According to Spengler, they are vigorous, innovative, and idealistic in youth. In middle age the rate of innovation declines and they become more materialistic. As they reach full maturity, their capacities decline more severely. Toynbee holds out the hope that civilizations can learn from the errors of earlier societies and thus be able to count on an effective response to the challenges they face, whether from the environment or from internal or external opponents.

Although both Spengler's and Toynbee's theories bear some resemblance to the rise and fall of various civilizations in history, neither of them identifies the social processes that help or limit the rise or decline of a civilization. Their ideas present broad descriptive patterns and are elegant in their formulation, but they do little to explain why social changes occur when and where they do.

Paul Kennedy (1987) argues that the critical relationship of economic to military power af-
fects the rise and fall of empires. Nations extend their military power on the basis of their economic resources and defend their economic interests. But, over time, the cost of maintaining that military power exceeds the resources of even the largest economies. The result has been "the fall of Great Powers." He traces this argument from 1500 and projects it to the year 2000. Unlike Spengler and Toynbee, he does develop the social processes that contribute to the rise and decline of civilizations.

### Social Conflict Theories

Social conflict theories do not explain social change so much as they expect change as an integral part of social life. The tendency of individuals and social groups to compete for scarce resources or for prestige may be a major source of social change, suggest Lenski (1966) and Collins (1975). Competing groups may be formed on the basis of ethnic, national, cultural, or religious bonds. For Marx, **class conflict** was the most important source of cleavage and conflict in society—that is, conflict between those who own the means of production and those who have nothing to exchange with owners except their labor power.

The potential for class conflict exists in any society with an unequal class structure, but that conflict is not always expressed, nor does it always lead to social change. The same is true among ethnic or religious groups. Although they may be competing for scarce resources, their competition may or may not erupt into open conflict and may or may not lead to social change. Thus social conflict theories, like other theories of social change, do not fully explain why social changes occur when and where they do. Instead, they suggest conditions that may contribute to change. Sometimes social changes emerge from collective behavior or social movements.

## COLLECTIVE BEHAVIOR

Fads such as "streaking" (running naked in public) and riots are both examples of what sociologists call collective behavior. Views about collective behavior have changed over time. At the

*Fads and fashions include behaviors and styles that spread rapidly. They may be embraced enthusiastically but remain popular for only a short time. Sometimes they signify membership in a social group or a subculture.*

beginning of this century, prominent social theorists felt threatened by social change, and their ideas about collective behavior reflected their unease. They tended to define collective behavior as the relatively spontaneous and unstructured behavior of unorganized collections of people who were responding to a common influence. Today a number of activist researchers study collective behavior with an eye to encouraging social change. One result of this shift has been more emphasis on the study of social movements than on less organized forms of collective behavior such as fads, fashions, rumors, mass hysteria, and riots (Marx and Wood, 1975). In this section we consider the apparently more spontaneous forms of collective behavior, and the following section treats social movements.

## Spontaneous Forms of Collective Behavior

### Fads

**Fads** are striking behaviors that spread rapidly, are embraced enthusiastically, yet remain popular for only a short time. Examples include Halley's Comet T-shirts with special slogans, "punk" hairstyles, and "streaking."

### Fashion

**Fashion** is a socially approved but temporary style of appearance or behavior, such as wearing cowboy boots in the city or drinking white wine or Perrier water in place of beer or hard liquor. Commercial interests support fashion changes through advertising and media coverage. Following fashions of various kinds can be a form of *conspicuous consumption,* that is, the consumption of resources, goods, or services primarily for display purposes with the aim of enhancing one's social status (Veblen, 1899). By following fashions one shows that he or she can afford to stay current (Blumer, 1968, 1969b). The study of fashions may reveal important clues about social networks, diffusion of innovations, and other forms of collective behavior.

### Rumor

A **rumor** is a report that is passed informally from one person to another without firm evidence. Rumors often develop in highly charged social situations where accurate information is absent or lacks credibility. Any account that seems plausible or fits the prejudices of the people involved may be seized on and passed along to others. For example, the Watts riots in 1965 were fueled in part by the rumor that white police officers had beaten a pregnant black woman. Hence, rumor may be a part of other, more complex forms of collective behavior.

### Panics and Mass Hysteria

A **panic** is a frightened response to an immediate threat by an aggregate of people. They become irrational and may act in uncooperative ways that increase their risk. Panics may occur when there is a fire in a theater or a hotel and people trample each other in their haste to escape. Panics also occur in financial markets, for example, in the stock market crash of 1929, the sudden fall in stock prices in 1988, and when banks close suddenly. (See the debate about the panic at the "Who" concert.)

**Mass hysteria** involves widely felt fear and anxiety, often based on some erroneous belief or information. In 1938, H. G. Wells's novel *The War of the Worlds* was broadcast over a New York radio station. Although the program began with an announcement that the program was a fictional dramatization, some people tuned in late and others were fooled by an announcer who interrupted the music to say that strange disturbances had been observed in New Jersey. Soon the music was again interrupted by

# DEBATING SOCIETY'S ISSUES

*On December 3, 1979, eleven young people were killed in a crush entering Riverfront Coliseum in Cincinnati, Ohio for a concert by the British rock group The Who. The incident was immediately labeled as a "stampede" by the local media, and commentators were quick to condemn the "mob psychology" which precipitated the seemingly selfish, ruthless behavior of participants. Crowd members were thought to have stormed over others in their rush for good seats within the arena, leading a national columnist (Royko, 1979) to refer to the crowd of young people as barbarians who "stomped 11 persons to death [after] having numbed their brains on weeds, chemicals, and Southern Comfort . . ." and a local editor to write of the "uncaring tread of the surging crowd" [Burleigh, 1979]. . . .*

*Those who interpreted the incident in this way and labeled it as a "stampede" recognized that other features contributed, such as the unreserved seating and the late opening of an inadequate number of doors. The unreserved or "festival" seating prompted many in the crowd to arrive several hours early to compete for the choicest locations within the building. During the hours before the doors were opened, the large crowd became so tightly packed outside the arena doors that some people who wanted to withdraw could not do so, and*

### Did Panic Behavior Kill Eleven People at the 1979 "Who" Concert in Cincinnati?

*policemen patrolling the area could not see the problems that were developing near the doors. [Johnson, 1987, p. 362]*

Sociologists distinguish between two forms of panics. One is an "acquisitive panic" (Brown, 1965) or "craze" (Smelser, 1963), where participants rush toward a desired gratification or valued commodity. The other is a classic "escape panic" where people rush to get away from something—for example, the flight from a burning building (Johnson, 1987, p. 363). Was the above scene an example of an acquisitive panic? Did callous, unregulated competition for a seat at the concert take precedence over people's lives, as press accounts suggest? Norris Johnson, a sociologist at the University of Cincinnati, set out to learn what happened. Analyzing police files and transcripts of interviews with witnesses and victims, he found no evidence of unregulated competition. Instead, cooperative and helping behavior continued throughout the course of the event. Small groups of friends stayed

together and tried to help each other. Strangers also tried to help those who had fallen. Smaller women were more likely to fall in the crowd, and larger men were the most likely ones to try to help them. "While those near the rear of the crowd did continue to push forward in order to enter the concert, the only behavior that resembled panic occurred nearer the front among those who were trying to escape an entrapping situation." (Johnson, 1987, p. 370). Here and in other cases studied, there is surprisingly little evidence of unregulated competition (Johnson, 1987). Johnson suggests another conclusion: Most crowds consist of small, often primary, groups, not unattached individuals. "Group bonds constrain totally selfish behavior, even when the situation seems life-threatening; thus, the type of unregulated competition generally labeled as panic occurs very infrequently" (Johnson, 1987, p. 371). He thinks that the evidence from the study of the "Who" concert "is more than sufficient to discount popular interpretations of 'The Who Concert Stampede' which focus on the hedonistic attributes of young people and the hypnotic effects of rock music" (Johnson, 1987, p. 371).

an apparent eyewitness account of a strange meteorite that had landed and from which a monster emerged. Various "experts," "scientists," and "public officials" made comments. Then the station announced that the Martian invaders had destroyed an army unit and moved on to New York City where it had overcome the population with poison gas. By the time of the half-hour station break, panic had struck. Phone lines were swamped, crowds swarmed into bus and

train stations, people hid in cellars or jumped into their cars and drove away.

The dramatization was so vivid that people did not search for additional evidence, for example, by turning their radio dial to another station. The level of anxiety in this period of depression just prior to World War II was sufficiently high that mass hysteria flourished (Cantril et al., 1940; Herzog, 1955; Houseman, 1948).

In 1983 a similar incident occurred. A TV movie, *Special Bulletin,* showed an unnervingly realistic account of terrorists staging a nuclear attack on Charleston, S.C. The two-hour drama was presented as a network television news special that had interrupted regular programming. Aware of the panic that followed *War of the Worlds* in 1938, NBC ran notices reminding viewers that they were watching a movie. In addition, during the climactic explosion, they flashed the word, "DRAMATIZATION" on the screen. Nevertheless, the network heard from panic-stricken callers who feared that Charleston was being destroyed. Many viewers who knew it was fictional still felt terrified, perhaps because the movie showed something that could really happen.

### Riots

**Riots** are destructive and sometimes violent collective outbursts. Antidraft riots occurred in New York City in 1863 when white laborers protested efforts to draft them into the Union army. (More affluent whites could buy their way out of the draft.) Race riots in which whites rampaged through the black sections of Chicago took place in 1919 and in Detroit in 1943. The black ghetto riots of the mid-1960s in Cleveland, Detroit, the Watts section of Los Angeles, and Rochester, New York, were aimed not at people so much as at the stores and businesses owned by whites from outside the ghetto.

Riots differ from mass movements because they are more likely to be violent, they may be relatively more spontaneous, and they may be aimed less at attaining a particular goal. One way of including both riots and social movements in a common frame for analysis would be to focus on the larger context in which the behavior occurs and to examine meanings and symbols that participants share.

Riots might be classified in terms of two dimensions, suggests Gary Marx (1970): Does the riot have a specific goal or not, and does it have a unifying belief or not? (See Table 19.1.) The riots in cell A of Table 19.1 may come very close to revolutions or social movements. Because these types of collective behavior are relatively enduring and may have far-reaching consequences for the social order, they are treated in more detail in the next section.

## Theories of Collective Behavior

Theories of collective behavior seek to explain all forms of such behavior, from social movements to revolutions to panics and fads. These theories try to address the questions: Why does collective behavior occur and what direction will it take? At least four major theories have been offered.

### Le Bon's "Contagion" Theory

The French thinker Gustave Le Bon was one of the early theorists who were alarmed by collective behavior. In his classic book *The Crowd,*

**Table 19.1    *Types of Riots***

| | | Goal Oriented? | |
|---|---|---|---|
| | | **Yes** | **No** |
| **Unifying Belief?** | Yes | A<br>Change-oriented riots: draft riots, food riots, revolutionary mobs | B<br>Hate and/or destruction riots: lynching parties, cross-burnings |
| | No | C<br>Situational riots: prison riots, looting | D<br>Issueless riots: at sports events or rock concerts |

*Source:* Marx, 1970.

written in 1895, he suggested that people turn from rational individuals into violent, crazed animals when they are part of a crowd. This happens because the anonymity people feel in a crowd gives them a sense of power. Emotions sweep through a crowd like a contagious virus (hence the name of his theory). As a result, people become more susceptible to the suggestions of fanatical leaders. Le Bon's work has been criticized for its aristocratic bias, for its failure to explain calm collective behavior such as peace vigils, and for its inability to explain why contagion may or may not spread through a crowd. Not everyone accepts Le Bon's view that joining a crowd infects a person with irrational desires.

### Convergence Theory

**Convergence theory** suggests that certain crowds attract particular people, who may be inclined toward behaving in specific irrational ways. This theory helps to explain lynch mobs and rock star fans who crowd into concerts. The theory does not explain shifts in the middle of a collective action, for example, when a mob calms down or when it decides to loot rather than to go home.

### Emergent-Norm Theory

**Emergent-norm theory** offers a more sociological explanation for collective behavior. Rather than suggesting, as Le Bon does, that collective behavior is due to some contagious irrationality in a crowd or to the emotional predispositions the way convergence theory does, emergent-norm theory suggests that collective behavior shares many similarities with more institutionalized forms of social life, including emergent norms, values, social relations, and patterns of communication (Turner and Killian, 1987). A rigorous study of the streaking fad on college campuses examined these ideas about collective behavior (Aguirre, Quarantelli, and Mendoza, 1988). It showed that the streaking incidents were heterogeneous rather than homogeneous (that is people streaked on bicycles, skis, or by parachute as well as on foot). Most examples involved extensive planning (no one wanted to streak without an audience and a way to escape) and normative limits (it was generally taboo to streak in classes having exams). They

also found that adoption of the fad was a product of group life. Often fraternities or sororities organized the event. Moreover, streaking had positive benefits for group life. Not only was it amusing and fun for students, but small groups and residents of dorms used it as a way to compete for social status. The event served to increase social solidarity among student social groups. Hence, the adoption of the fad was more utilitarian than some early descriptions of fads suggest is true of a fad. The positive consequences of participation may help to explain why neighboring schools adopted the fad. Moreover, "the greater the social reactions and sanctions evoked by previous streaking episodes," the more likely neighboring schools were to adopt the fad (Aguirre et al., 1988, p. 579). Apparently the deterrence effect of such sanctions was weaker than the perceived benefits of excitement and social solidarity. The researchers conclude that fads are not odd, irrational, or inconsequential. In addition, understanding fads better furthers our understanding of other forms of collective behavior such as panics and social movements.

### Value-added Theory

Smelser's (1963) **value-added theory** suggests that many instances of collective behavior represent efforts to change the social environment. Collective behavior develops through six stages, each one of which contributes to the process:

1. *Structural conduciveness* refers to the social conditions that allow collective behavior to occur. In the *Invasion from Mars* incident people were anxious about the war scare in Europe (Herzog, 1955). They were also accustomed to having radio programs interrupted with real news bulletins.
2. *Structural strains* are social conditions that fail to fit people's expectations about how things should be. Hence there are discrepancies, conflicts, or ambiguities in the social order. When people think their social and economic conditions should be improving but they are not, there is a structural strain that may lead to collective behavior. The theory is weak on indicating when strain leads to collective behavior and when it does not.

3. *Generalized belief* refers to a shared definition of a situation and what needs to be done about it. Injustice and indignity alone do not lead to collective behavior unless they are defined as unacceptable and worthy of resistance. Not everyone involved may share exactly the same beliefs.

4. *Precipitating factors* are dramatic behaviors that give the generalized beliefs concrete substance. When Mrs. Rosa Parks refused to move to the back of the bus, that action was a significant precipitating factor in the Birmingham Bus Boycott that helped to focus the civil rights movement.

5. *Mobilization for action* refers to the way participants in collective behavior become organized for further action. For Mrs. Parks's gesture to be a precipitating factor, it had to be used as a rallying cry for further action.

6. *Social control* may limit or add to the emergence of collective behavior. Even when these five stages have been experienced, collective behavior may or may not occur because of the amount of social control that is exercised. The actions of the police, national guard, mass media, institutional authorities, and others may serve to weaken or magnify a collective behavior. Sometimes police action contains a riot whereas other times it fires it up.

When collective behavior is focused, sustained, and aimed at social changes, it takes the form of a social movement.

## SOCIAL MOVEMENTS

Cultural innovations may be started by a single individual, but they depend on larger social groups or organizations to be diffused and to create social changes. Many social changes are due to organized, collective efforts by groups of people who are consciously committed to making changes in society. Such efforts are **social movements.** These movements are not simply temporary "flashes in the pan" but have some permanence—they develop leaders and followers, and they involve deliberate planning to mobilize more members, public opinion, and other resources. Social-movement scholars have raised two important sets of questions: Under what social conditions do social movements occur? Why do individuals participate in collective behavior?

## Why Social Movements Occur

From slave revolts in ancient Egypt and Rome through the French Revolution and contemporary antinuclear protests, people have joined forces throughout history to try to shape the direction of their lives and societies. Ground Zero, Right to Life, the Moonies, the Grey Panthers—these are just a few of the many social movements that exist in American society today.

Social movements are a bit like volcanoes in that they do not usually erupt without giving warning rumbles. The first step is the growing feeling among individuals or groups that something is wrong with the social order. The feeling of discontent or deprivation usually has two parts, an objective basis and subjective perceptions of that reality (Lauer, 1976). Take the nuclear arms freeze–disarmament movement, for instance. In Pella, Iowa, "the movement" began in February 1982 with an advertisement in the local paper that read: "Wanted: People Who Don't Want to Die in a Nuclear Holocaust." As Fialka (1982a) reports:

*There were already isolated pockets of nuclear angst growing in this rural, conservative and stubbornly prosperous town of 8000 people in central Iowa. What that ad provided was the spark, the catalyst that brought parishioners out of some of the local churches, teachers from the town's two high schools, and students and faculty from Central College. Together, they sat down to map out a week of activism designed to teach people about the horrors of nuclear war. [p. 1]*

People may endure horrible conditions for centuries because they consider them to be inevitable. Their perceptions influence their feelings about the correctness of existing conditions and about whether they can or should be changed. But once perceptions shift and the conditions begin to seem unjust or the possibility

*Social movements against the nuclear arms race exist in Europe as well as in the United States. Here members of the Peace Committee wear death masks as they march through the streets of Geneva, Switzerland, to protest the nuclear arms race.*

of change occurs, social movements may arise.

As we have said, one of the roots of mobilization is a rising sense of injustice: Existing conditions begin to seem wrong to growing numbers of people, social arrangements are seen to violate the norms and values of a society, and people begin to have an alternative vision or rising expectations of how things might be. Then the possibility of organizing into a social movement arises.

## Necessary Conditions for a Social Movement

To emerge as a social movement, an issue or group needs leadership, members, and the mobilization of resources.

### Leadership

To be successful, social movements need effective leaders who can create shared visions of what people are working for and mobilize the resources needed to accomplish their common goals. The Ground Zero group, one example of an antinuclear organization, was started by Roger C. Molander, a 41-year-old physicist who had been advising the White House on nuclear targeting strategies. Mr. Molander and

his brother Earl, a Harvard Business School professor, decided in 1981 to establish a new organization aimed at people who had not been in movements before. "We wanted to be in the mainstream," says Roger Molander (Fialka, 1982a, p. 1). Since he and his brother were so established in the mainstream of society themselves, they were well suited to lead a mainstream movement.

Leaders help with the symbolic task of redefining a situation as unjust, identifying the source of the problem, and proposing solutions to it. Early demonstrators in the Ground Zero Movement carried signs that read, "If This Were Ground Zero, a One Megaton Nuclear Explosion Would Totally Destroy Virtually Everything within Two Miles of This Spot—Instantly." Signs such as that one began to rouse people's awareness of the issue.

Leaders perform other functions for a social movement as well: They help to formulate a movement's ideology; they arouse the commitment of members and potential members; they articulate the movement's position to the larger society; and they decide the strategies to pursue. Often there is more than one leader in a movement, because no single person has all the skills such a movement needs. As a movement develops, different leadership needs may arise. The early stages seem to call for agitators who stir things up and prophets who spread the news and generate enthusiasm. As a social movement becomes more formally organized, its need for administrators increases, as does the need for strong leadership in the larger community (Spector and Kitsuse, 1973, 1977). The civil rights movement illustrates all these types of leadership. In 1961 the Congress of Racial Equality sent "Freedom Riders" of both races through the South on public buses to challenge segregation laws in interstate transportation. These Freedom Riders were perceived by some to be agitators. The Student Nonviolent Coordinating Committee helped to fill the role of prophet by spreading word of the movement across college campuses and by generating support from people of all ages who were pleased to see students involved. Efforts at voter registration throughout the South called for administrative leadership. Getting the civil rights bill through Congress in 1964 required strong leadership within the larger society from President Lyndon B. Johnson.

Outside leadership may be particularly important in getting a social movement started (McCarthy and Zald, 1977; Zald and McCarthy, 1979). The civil rights movement, for example, was greatly helped by the leadership of Martin Luther King, Jr. What might have been a single incident, the arrest of Mrs. Rosa Parks for refusing to move to the Negro section of a bus in Montgomery, Alabama, on December 5, 1955, was transformed by Martin Luther King, Jr., into a major resistance movement. A boycott staged against the bus company resulted in the desegregation of its facilities. After that success the methods of picketing and boycotting spread rapidly to other southern communities. The Rev. King's Southern Christian Leadership Conference provided moral and practical support for the protest movement. In addition to being a powerful preacher and speaker who could rally people around a shared vision (for example, with his "I have a dream" speech at the 1963 Civil Rights March on Washington, D.C.), the Rev. King was adept at building bridges with other church leaders and with leaders in labor, government, and education.

The antinuclear movement was also supplemented by significant outside support. A growing number of Catholic bishops began pushing the church to take a pro-freeze stance, and many church leaders spoke about the topic from the pulpit. Many mass movements have been organizationally rooted in churches (McAdam, McCarthy, and Zald, 1988). The antinuclear drive also picked up substantial strength in Congress, where Democratic Senator Edward Kennedy of Massachusetts and Republican Senator Mark Hatfield of Oregon led a bipartisan effort. They introduced a resolution in Congress calling for a freeze on the testing, production, and further deployment of nuclear weapons by both the United States and the Soviet Union. Considerable financial support was donated by younger members of the Rockefeller family (Fialka, 1982a; Fialka, 1982b). It is important to realize, however, that outside agitators can do little to mobilize a social movement if conditions do not need improvement and if people have not already begun to perceive the need for a change. Outside leadership may be helpful in the beginning stages of a social movement, but few movements can flourish without strong local leaders and members.

### Membership

Any significant social movement needs to recruit large numbers of committed members. Support for a nuclear freeze swelled in 1982. Citizens in more than 400 American towns and numerous state legislatures passed resolutions endorsing a nuclear weapons freeze. Activists in California collected some 500,000 signatures to put the issue on the state ballot in November (Fialka, 1982a, p. 1).

For a long time sociological research on social movements focused on the values, attitudes, and grievances of participants in an effort to explain why people did or did not join particular movements. The individual social psychology of participants is one aspect of the phenomenon, but more recent analyses of social movements have emphasized political, sociological, and economic theories more than social psychological ones (Gamson, 1975; McCarthy and Zald, 1977). This shift has resulted from research suggesting little or no relationship between personal deprivation and willingness to participate in social movements (Bowen et al., 1968; Crawford and Naditch, 1970; Mueller, 1972; Snyder and Tilly, 1972). Mobilization theory views members as one of several key resources needed for a social movement to succeed. Rapid mobilization of members does not occur by recruiting large numbers of solitary individuals, but by tying in with existing groups of people who are already organized (Oberschall, 1973). A major way that a movement gains strength is by forming organizational networks. (This presumes, of course, that the organizations share common goals.)

### Mobilization of Resources

The **resource mobilization theory** of social movements considers how a social movement seeks to marshal key resources, how it tries to establish connections with other groups, what outside support it needs, and how external authorities may try to control or coopt it (McCarthy and Zald, 1977; Tilly, 1975; Tilly, Tilly, and Tilly, 1975). The resources available to social movements include the number of people committed to a movement's goals and the intensity of their commitment; the verbal and visual communications skills of leaders and members, including their access to mimeographing machines, printing presses, photographs, audio and videotapes, music, and the mass media; the organizational skills of leaders or the services of professional organizers; the legal and financial skills of members; and the ability to tap millions of dollars in contributions to support their goals.

Resource mobilization theory suggests that social movements are affected by the total amount of discretionary resources available, by the way social movements are organized (for example, having many isolated supporters or a series of local chapters), and by the number of social organizations competing for the total resources available to social movements (McCarthy and Zald, 1977).

Resource mobilization theory stresses the importance of preexisting social organizations and planning. Some social movements, such as the civil rights movement, show that spontaneity (a classical feature of collective behavior) helps to explain what occurred (Killian, 1984).

The antinuclear movement, including groups such as Ground Zero, has been extremely effective in tapping significant financial, organizational, and communications resources. Many major religious denominations and large donors have given important support. Numerous effective teaching devices—including films such as *The Last Epidemic, Eight Days to Zero, Atomic Café, The Day After,* and *War Without Winners*—have been developed and shown on national television and also at hundreds of church and community rallies around the United States. Jonathan Schell's book *The Fate of the World* (1982) has had a powerful impact, with its suggestion that a nuclear war would destroy life on earth.

In March of 1979 more than 150,000 residents of communities in central Pennsylvania, near Harrisburg, evacuated their homes and towns when the nearby Three Mile Island (TMI) nuclear power station began leaking radiation (Flynn, 1979). Sociologists Edward Walsh and Rex Warland set out to study people's reactions to this event (1983).

Many meetings were held after the accident to help educate and/or mobilize citizens regarding TMI issues. One issue was the proposed restarting of the TMI nuclear power Unit 1 (which happened to be closed down for routine refueling at the time of the accident). A second major issue was monitoring the extensive and dangerous cleanup operations of TMI-2. The anti-TMI community groups aimed to shut down TMI-1 permanently and wanted to monitor the cleanup of TMI-2 carefully (Walsh, 1981, 1983).

Although thousands of people had been evacuated during the emergency, only a small proportion of them became involved in an anti-TMI social movement as a result. Instead, large numbers of people in the area were "free riders" on both sides of the TMI issue; that is, they did not join one of the social movements even though they agreed with the goals advanced by one or the other of them. Only 12 percent of those who defined themselves as discontented with the situation contributed *any* time or money to organized efforts by fellow citizens. The most frequently mentioned reason for nonparticipation was lack of knowledge about their local social movement organization (by 26 percent); familial and personal preoccupations were the second most frequently mentioned reason (by 18 percent; Walsh and Warland, 1983, p. 774).

Walsh and Warland's research suggests why some people actively opposed restarting the plant and others remained neutral. Both structural variables such as educational background and relationships with other activists, suggested by resource mobilization theories, and social or psychological attitudes such as ideology and discontent help to explain why some people join and others do not join social movements (Walsh and Warland, 1983, p. 778). The relative importance of structural and ideological factors may vary from one situation of collective action to another; that is, what was found at TMI may not apply in all other situations.

## Individual Recruitment to Activism

### Rational Choice Explanations

What leads individuals to get involved with collective action? Some social-movement theorists suggest that individuals calculate the likely costs and benefits of various actions (Friedman,

1983; Oberschall, 1973). If the costs of participating in a social movement are high, few individuals will join. If the benefits are likely to be high, many will join. Rational calculation would lead few individuals to collective action because, if the movement were a success, they could expect to get the benefits of it whether or not they were active (Olson, 1965). This is the "free rider problem" (Olson, 1965). Rational choice theorists think that there must be selective incentives for participants and sanctions on nonparticipants, to compensate for the low benefits relative to costs. Persons with more interest in the incentives offered by collective-action organizations are likely to take more active roles and to contribute more time and money (Knoke, 1988).

### Social Structural Explanations

Rational choice and individual incentives may not be a sufficient explanation for participation, however. Considerable social research suggests four structural features that are related to individual participation in social movements. These are: (1) prior contact with a movement member, (2) membership in other organizations, (3) a prior history of social activism, and (4) availability (that is, an absence of social constraints, such as full-time work and marriage and family responsibilities). The first three increase the chances that individuals will get hooked into social-movement activity. The fourth lowers barriers to participation.

### Ideology

There is another essential element behind individuals' participation in social movements, and that is the way they think about, or frame, the issues (Snow et al., 1986). Social movements must provide ideological rationales for what they are trying to do. Groups of people "jointly create the meanings" of current and future events (Edelman, 1971, p. 32). In order to recruit people, a social movement needs to help them see the problems they face as external to themselves, and as something they can influence through collective action (Ferree and Miller, 1985). Movement ideology plays a key role in the recruitment process. By ideology, Ferree and Miller mean "a flexible structure of beliefs about the nature of social relationships, one's

position in the social structure, and the causes and consequences of social action" (1985, p. 42).

## Types of Social Movements

It is possible that some types of social movements rely more on ideology while others may depend more on rational choice for recruiting members. The four social structural explanations may be relevant regardless of the type of social movement. One type is utilitarian or interest-based movements, such as the labor movement or the civil rights movement. This type may depend more upon rational choice than upon ideology, although ideology may also be important. Other social movements, such as religious movements or the animal rights movement (mentioned in Chapter 17), may be considered moralist social movements. Group ties and ideology may be more important than rational choice for participation in such social movements.

Different types of social movements may also select different strategies and tactics. **Revolutionary movements** are so dissatisfied with society that they want to overhaul it completely and replace present social forms with others of their own design. When a revolutionary movement succeeds, as those in China and Cuba did, it creates widespread social changes. Because they feel no allegiance to the existing social system, members may be willing to use warfare, murder, bombings, ambushes, or other violence to advance their goals. Some revolutions, however, such as Gandhi's in India, are based totally on nonviolent protest. They differ markedly from a **reform movement,** which basically accepts the status quo but seeks certain specific changes. The antidraft movement, the antinuclear movement, and the gay rights movement are all examples of reform movements. Tactically they tend not to favor the use of violence or of strategies that might alienate the mainstream institutions of society, since they continue to hope for support from other social groups. Instead, they favor public demonstrations and marches, efforts to change legislation, and educational strategies. These strategies may lead to violence, as the history of labor organizing in the United States shows.

A **regressive movement,** such as the Islamic resurgence in the Middle East in recent years or the Moral Majority in the United States, aims to move the social world back to where it is seen to have been at an earlier time. Islamic fundamentalists drove the shah of Iran from political power and tried to restore religious rule in the form of an Ayatollah. Such social movements may use both violence and persuasion to gain control.

## Success or Failure of Social Movements

When social movements are able to mobilize many members as well as considerable resources and when they have effective leaders, they have the potential for success. Success, however, ultimately depends on wise strategy decisions and the effective use of the resources members have been able to mobilize. At the time of this writing, the antinuclear movement has been very successful in terms of leadership, mobilizing resources, and membership. It was able to mount the largest disarmament demonstration in U.S. history on June 12, 1982, in New York City, consisting of more than 750,000 people who traveled from all over the world in support of the United Nations second special session on disarmament. The ultimate test of any movement, of course, is whether or not it can make the social changes it desires. The goal of the antinuclear movement is to educate the public to the true horrors of nuclear war and to put pressure on the president and Congress to negotiate a cutback in nuclear arms with the Soviet Union.

When Mikhail Gorbachev was in the United States in 1988, he announced that the USSR was going to cut back on its nuclear weapons in Europe. We cannot say that these outcomes are due to antinuclear movements. In general, "demonstrating the independent effect of collective action on social change is difficult" (McAdam, McCarthy, and Zald, 1988, p. 727). In their efforts to recruit new members, social movements may take credit for such outcomes, however.

The success of a social movement may also be affected by how those opposed to it respond, as Smelser noted. In cities where the southern civil rights movement met violent resistance, it was relatively more successful than in cities where white officials used quasi-legal means of opposition and avoided violence. Violence resulted in greater northern sympathy and federal action and helped civil rights forces to succeed. When compared to cities where violence occurred, cities that were able to avoid violence (through frequent, although questionable, arrests, high bail, and court proceedings that lacked due process) were able to retain some measure of legitimacy for segregationist policies and so could stifle criticism. The resulting legal problems helped to defeat civil rights forces (at least temporarily) in those cities (Barkan, 1984).

Mothers Against Drunk Driving (MADD) is a social movement organized in 1980 by Candy Lightner, a mother whose daughter had been killed by an intoxicated driver. Mrs. Lightner received several grants to help organize local chapters of her organization. In addition, early in its history, MADD employed a direct-mail solicitation firm in Los Angeles to raise funds. Soon money began pouring in (Reinarman, 1985). From the start, MADD aimed to get maximum media attention, and it succeeded in that effort.

The evolution of MADD is explained both by its successful resource mobilization and by what Smelser calls the "structural conduciveness" of that particular historical moment. As Reinarman (1985) notes, at least three features of that historical moment set the stage for

*Students Against Driving Drunk (SADD) is a social movement aimed at developing peer support for safe driving.*

MADD's rise: growing health consciousness in the American population, more emphasis in the alcohol field on prevention rather than just treatment of alcohol-related problems, and a national political culture that stressed individual responsibility while avoiding any analysis of structural sources or corporate interests that might lie behind drinking and driving problems.

The objective of MADD was to reduce alcohol-related auto fatalities. Without doubt, MADD's activities have spurred the arrests of intoxicated drivers, often led to increased criminal penalties for such drivers, raised the legal drinking age in many states, and resulted in hundreds of new alcohol-control statutes in various states (Reinarman, 1985). It is less clear that it has reduced alcohol-related auto fatalities. In 1985, when MADD and the anti–drunk-driving movement may have been at their peak influence and when harsh new laws and sentencing patterns were taking effect, highway deaths increased (Reinarman, 1985). Despite such questions about MADD's ultimate effectiveness, however, its evolution as a social movement is explained by both structural conduciveness and by its capacity to offer leadership, attract members, and mobilize key resources, especially money and the media.

Unsuccessful movements begin the same way as successful ones do, with members trying to gain public support for their aims. What happens, however, is that their appeals may fall on deaf ears, they may make claims that others do not believe, they may be powerless members of society to whom others will not listen, or their strategies may alienate rather than enlist supporters.

## MODERNIZATION

Collective behavior and technological developments together contribute to modernization in many of the developing nations of the world. **Industrialization** refers to the shift within a nation's economy from a primarily agricultural base to steel production, oil refining, and other forms of manufacturing. The transformation from an agricultural to an industrial society is accompanied by more productive agriculture, more specialized division of labor, greater urbanization, higher rates of literacy, and improved systems of transportation (such as railroads, highways, or canals) and communication (such as postal service, telephone and telegraph networks, radio and television broadcasting). Today countries such as India, South Korea, and Mexico are struggling to make the transition from an agricultural to an industrial society.

Some sociologists use the term **"modernization"** to describe the major shift from a traditional agricultural society to a highly industrialized society. Modernization affects many areas of social life, undermining traditional religious systems, family ties, village loyalties, and customs. Some traditionalists and nationalists in modernizing countries equate modern practices with Western domination. But even they realize that feeding and educating their populations and keeping them healthy and housed requires some industrialization. Their hope is to try to control the process of development so that traditional values are not destroyed by it.

Modernization has a number of interrelated social consequences, including the transfer of culture through television and films from one society to another (Barnet and Muller, 1974; Smith, 1980); the possibility of permanent personality change (Inkeles and Smith, 1974); the growing importance of large bureaucratic organizations such as the army or the national government rather than family, village, or ethnic groups; and declining death rates.

Considerable research has been done to investigate how modernization may change personalities. Inkeles and Smith (1974) surveyed 6000 men from six developing countries and found that some of them had what they called a "modern personality," characterized by a strong future orientation, confidence in the effectiveness of human action in the world, and an openness to new ideas. Such "modern" attitudes were more likely to be found in educated men who had worked in a factory-type setting than in farmers, other nonfactory workers, or those with little education, suggesting that "modern" attitudes grow out of a person's educational and work experiences.

Social thinkers hold competing views of the dynamics behind economic development, and

*Developing nations such as South Korea face issues of integrating old and modern traditions. Here in Seoul, South Korea, the old Bigag Pavilion is reflected in the glass windows of the new Kyobo Building.*

those views have important social consequences in the world. United States foreign policy with regard to Vietnam and other developing countries has been guided by what American policymakers assume about the way development occurs. For these reasons, it is important to consider briefly two different views of modernization—convergence theory and dependency theory.

## Convergence Theory

**Convergence theory** suggests that modernizing nations come to resemble one another more and more closely over time (their individual characteristics will *converge*). They will shed their unique cultural traditions and begin thinking and acting more like one another and more like already developed societies (Lerner, 1968). They will become more alike with respect to labor-force structure, technology, level of development, and occupational prestige rankings (Lenski and Lenski, 1987; Inkeles and Rossi, 1956; Moore, 1963).

*Stage theories* of economic development are considered one form of convergence theory. Stage theories, proposed by such economic thinkers as W. W. Rostow (1960), view nations as going through various stages on the path to development. One of these stages is called the *takeoff,* suggesting that economic development occurs only after a critical level of economic activity has been reached. The stages are assumed to be somewhat similar in all developing societies.

Convergence theory suggests that developing nations desire to become more like Western nations in every respect and ignores the role Western nations may play in pushing them in this direction in order to exploit their natural resources, labor, or potential markets. Critics of convergence theory argue that nations are following different developmental paths, depending on their cultural, political, or environmental situation (Odum, 1971; Horowitz, 1966).

## Dependency Theory

Developing nations do not operate in a world vacuum. Other, more powerful, and highly developed nations have a stake in how they develop. An early proponent of **dependency theory,** André Gunder Frank (1966), challenged the stage theory of economic development advanced by convergence theorists. He saw the major industrial nations as the "metropolitan centers" of a world in which developing nations were the rural hinterlands. The center takes advantage of the cheap labor and raw materials of the outer regions to produce a surplus controlled by the center. Such an arrangement makes the center reluctant to encourage industrial development in outer areas because not only would the center not control it, but the outer areas might end up competing with the center's production. In Frank's view, those nations that are least involved with the major industrial powers have the greatest chance of becoming industrialized.

Many developing nations have a single major cash crop or raw material, such as sugar, coffee, copper, or bananas, that they export to industrialized nations. Local leaders who want to encourage the industrial development of their countries need advanced technologies, people who can run them, and money to invest. Where can they get these resources? Major sources are the already strong multinational corporations, the international banking community (dominated by American, Japanese, and Western European banks), the International Monetary

Fund, private (generally Western) investors, or the World Bank. Although many of these sources are eager to lend money to developing nations, they do so on terms favorable to themselves. Not only are their interest rates high, but they often demand a voice in national policies dealing with taxation, military spending, and other internal affairs. As a result, the developing nations lose some control over the direction of their development. Western backers may be concerned that the country be an open market for their own manufactured goods, including such consumer items as toasters and cars. Industrialized nations do not want other nations to become self-sufficient with respect to such goods, because they want to control the market. Nor do they want such goods banned or highly taxed (Frank, 1967, 1979, 1980; Magdoff, 1978; Mytelka, 1979; Rodney, 1974).

Dependency theory questions convergence theory's assumption that developing nations are simply at an earlier stage of development and will eventually reach the same "advanced" stage as industrial capitalist countries. Instead, dependency theory suggests that the needs of developing nations for external financing, technology, and personnel, and their history of domination by colonial powers makes their prospects for development quite different from those of already industrialized nations.

## World Systems Analysis

**World systems analysis** takes into account current and historical relationships between nations and societies. For example, Immanuel Wallerstein (1974) considers a social system as largely self-contained, with the dynamics of development stemming mainly from internal sources. Given this definition, he sees only two genuine types of social systems in the world: small, self-contained tribes and world systems.

World systems consist of sets of interconnected societies, and they contain many diverse cultures and a highly refined division of labor. Wallerstein believes that only two types of world systems have ever existed: world empires and world economies. In a world empire there is a single political and military system controlling the physical area of the system. Charle-

magne's Europe, the Roman Empire, and the British Empire are all examples of world empires. World economies incorporate a wide variety of cultures and lands into a trading network, but they are not bound by a common political and military authority. The modern world economy, based on a capitalist form of economic organization, has prevailed for the last 400 years without becoming a world empire. Modern capitalism has taken advantage of the absence of a single system of political control to maneuver the system advantageously. Different sets of political boundaries and rules mean, for example, that the cheap labor of one area may be combined with the favorable tax situation in another area to maximize profits, as noted in our earlier discussion of multinational corporations.

Wallerstein sees world economies as divided into core states and peripheral areas. The core states consist of the advantaged areas of the world economy, which have strong, integrated state machinery and national cultures. In the twentieth century, these are the highly industrialized, militarily powerful nations, such as the United States and the Soviet Union. These nations tend to dominate peripheral areas, which have weak state machinery, weaker economic activities, and less cultural consistency. These include developing nations in Africa, Central America, and countries such as Afghanistan. Semiperipheral areas operate as buffers and traders between core and peripheral areas. They are trying to industrialize and diversify their economies. They are less likely than peripheral areas to be manipulated by core states. Countries like Iran or Spain might be considered semiperipheral. As such, they mute some of the political opposition that might otherwise be directed at the core.

A recent research study focuses on convergence and divergence in economic development and relates it to world systems theory (Peacock, Hoover, and Killian, 1988). World systems theory can incorporate the possibility of convergence within each of the three zones—core, semiperiphery, and periphery—and divergence between zones. Peacock et al. found that convergence (i.e., declining economic inequality between nations) occurred only within the core, not in the semiperiphery or periphery. Within the semiperiphery, they found divergence (increasing inequality between nations from 1950 to 1980). In the periphery, they found a slow movement toward divergence. Peacock et al. found that inequality between zones was increasing, although some of that increase was due to faster population growth among low-income countries.

Wallerstein's ideas suggest that the more powerful positions of core states will enable them to shape the direction of social change in the future. As much as they might like to change, peripheral areas will find it difficult to do so. The strength of OPEC in the 1970s, however, suggests that when peripheral areas control vital resources like oil and become socially and politically organized, they may create considerable social change in the core states.

Sociologists are beginning to understand the processes of social change, collective behavior, social movements, and modernization. More research is needed to further illuminate these complex processes. This is an important area of research because we face increasingly rapid change, whether the source is the environment, technology, or collective action.

## SUMMARY

1. Social change is a change in the way a society is organized, and it is one of the striking features of the era in which we live.

2. Social changes may result from shifts in the physical environment (such as the "greenhouse effect"), scientific and technological developments, and collective action.

3. "Culture lag" refers to the fact that inventions and technology are changed more rapidly and easily than cultural practices.

4. Cultural changes may involve discoveries or inventions of technology or cultural practices. Unless they are diffused to other people, such innovations do not lead to social changes.

5. At least four theoretical efforts have been made to explain social change in general terms. These include evolutionary, functionalist, cyclical, and conflict theories. Each offers some insight into the nature of social change, but no one alone explains why social changes occur when or where they do.

6. "Collective behavior" refers to relatively spontaneous behavior by collections of people who may be more or less organized. The types of behavior studied range from fads and fashions through rumors, panics, mass hysteria, riots, and social movements.

7. Four major theories of collective behavior are considered—Le Bon's "contagion" theory, convergence theory, emergent-norm theory, and Smelser's value-added theory.

8. Smelser's theory suggests that collective behavior develops through six stages, each of which contributes to the process. The stages are structural conduciveness, structural strains, generalized belief, precipitating factors, mobilization for action, and social control.

9. Social movements represent organized efforts to promote or retard social changes. Realizing they can do more together than alone, people have come together in social movements all through history.

10. Conditions necessary for the growth of social movements are a sense of injustice over current conditions, good leadership, and the mobilization of resources, such as members, money, and media. Success or failure depends on all these factors. The process is illustrated by the current antinuclear movement in the United States.

11. People join social movements because of rational choices, structural factors, and collectively defined ideologies and beliefs. The first reason may be more important for utilitarian movements, while the last one may be more important for moralist movements.

12. Revolutionary, reform, and regressive movements differ in their goals.

13. Modernization is one form of social change that is brewing in many areas of the

world. Convergence theory sees this process as gradual and evolutionary; developing nations steadily become more like contemporary industrial ones. Divergence theory expects increased inequality between nations of the world.

14. Dependency theory and world systems analysis stress the historical relations between dominant and developing nations and argue that the latter cannot simply follow the path trod by early industrializers. They may need new models if they are to break away from their dependence on dominant world states.

## KEY TERMS

class conflict (p. 495)
contagion theory (p. 498)
convergence theory (p. 499, 507)
cultural change (p. 494)
culture lag (p. 493)
cyclical theories (p. 495)
dependency theory (p. 507)
diffusion (p. 494)
discovery (p. 494)
emergent-norm theory (p. 499)
evolutionary theories (p. 494)
fads (p. 496)
fashion (p. 496)
industrialization (p. 506)
innovation (p. 494)
invention (p. 494)
mass hysteria (p. 496)
modernization (p. 506)
panic (p. 496)
reform movement (p. 504)
regressive movement (p. 505)
resource mobilization theory (p. 502)
revolutionary movement (p. 504)
riots (p. 498)
rumor (p. 496)
social change (p. 489)
social movement (p. 500)
technological determinism (p. 493)

value added theory (p. 499)
world systems analysis (p. 509)

## SUGGESTED READINGS

Bell, Daniel. 1987. "The World and the United States in 2013." *Daedalus* 116: 1–31. A fascinating effort by a leading sociologist to analyze the U.S. role in the world in 2013.

Evans, Peter B., and John D. Stephens. 1988. "Development and the World Economy." In Neil J. Smelser (ed.), *Handbook of Sociology*. Beverly Hills, CA: Sage, pp. 739–773. A good review of the emergence of development as a field and some of the current issues in the area.

Gribben, John. 1982. *Future Weather and the Greenhouse Effect*. New York: Delacorte Press. Explores the devastating effects that rapid global warming will have on most third-world nations.

McAdam, Doug, John D. McCarthy, and Mayer N. Zald. 1988. "Social Movements." In Neil J. Smelser (ed.), *Handbook of Sociology*. Beverly Hills, CA: Sage, pp. 695–737. A broad and thoughtful overview of recent research in the area of social movements.

Piven, Frances Fox, and Richard Cloward. 1971. *Poor People's Movements: Why They Succeed, How They Fail*. New York: Vintage. An analysis of how poor people have sometimes been able to mobilize and effect social changes.

Spector, Malcolm, and John I. Kitsuse. 1973. *Constructing Social Problems*. Menlo Park, CA: Cummings. Analyzes how the definition of a social problem is socially negotiated.

Ziman, John. 1976. *The Force of Knowledge*. New York: Cambridge University Press. A fascinating and well-illustrated account of how science and technology have influenced the social world.

# Communities and Ecology

*Jackie R. is in her mid-sixties and for the past eight years she has been without a place to live. She came home to her one-room furnished apartment in one of America's largest cities one day to find the front door chained shut. All her personal possessions were in boxes on the street. She saved what she could carry in two shopping bags and was forced to leave the rest. Her landlord had sold the building to someone who planned to convert it to condominiums, and the new owner decided to evict the tenants in a hurry. The problems faced by Jackie R. are one of the human costs of large-scale changes in where and how people live.*

Within the last several centuries, human society has shifted from small agricultural communities to large urban metropolises. The term **community** has been used in various ways by sociologists. At the least it refers to a collection of people in a geographical area. It may also include the idea that those collections of people have a social structure, that is, that they are in some kind of relationship to each other. Sometimes the term includes, as well, a sense of community spirit or belonging (Abercrombie et al., 1984, p. 47). Like most communities, large cities change and grow over time. A major social issue today is the direction that urban growth and change will take. Political and economic forces often propel the changes, and the effects on people are immediate and dramatic. Urban dwellers may be forced out of their apartments when a building is converted into condominiums or coops, neighborhoods may decline when banks stop investing money in them, other neighborhoods may become too expensive for long-term residents to continue living there. Rapid urban growth in "Sunbelt" cities such as Phoenix raises real estate values but also creates traffic, pollution, educational, and other social prob-

lems. People seek pleasant and safe places to live, but they must compete for the land with those who want to use it for maximum economic gain. Sociologists try to understand the social and economic forces that influence the use of land in urban, suburban, and rural areas.

The first section of this chapter examines alternative theories of urban growth. These ideas are then applied to suburban growth and rural development in the next two sections. Ecology is considered in the fourth section. The last section examines the makeup of communities and how the type of community in which people live may affect the way they feel and behave.

## URBAN GROWTH AND DECLINE

### The Growth of Cities

For most of human history, people lived in small clusters, bands, or communities that were often temporary. They hunted, gathered, or raised their own food. A city contrasts sharply with such an arrangement, since a **city** is a relatively permanent settlement of large numbers of people who do not grow or gather their own food. Within the last several centuries human society has shifted from a small community base to being urban-centered.

In large areas of the world today—including North and South America, Europe, Australia–New Zealand, and the Soviet Union—more than half the population lives in urban centers. Only in Africa and parts of Asia and Oceania[1] does less than half of the population live in cities. The growth of cities, or **urbanization,** as it is called, is one of the largest changes in the organization of human society. Although we tend to take cities for granted, they did not always exist. Sociologists have considered why cities developed in the places and times that they did. Three major factors have contributed to the rise of cities in various parts of the world: the development of agriculture, trade, and industrialization.

Cities developed first in areas that were favorable to agriculture. Rich agricultural areas were able to produce a surplus of food that could support some nonfarmers. Since transporting large quantities of food very far was difficult in earlier times, settlements tended to grow up near agricultural areas. The first cities developed about 5000 years ago in the Middle Eastern valley of the Tigris-Euphrates Rivers, in Egypt along the Nile, along the Yellow River Valley in China, and the Indus River Valley in Pakistan. All these areas had rich soil, a favorable climate, and plenty of water. The rivers provided transport routes for trade, and many cities grew larger because they were trading centers.

As cities grow, they require increasingly complex systems of social organization and control. Such systems must extend to the surrounding agricultural areas in order to draw in the agricultural surplus. This requires religious, political, and military organizations to extract taxes or tribute from the food-producing areas and transfer them to the central power in cities. The importance of political and military organization was particularly apparent in the way the Roman Empire used agricultural surpluses to build cities. As the Roman legions conquered new lands, they set up systems of tax collection which they used to build aqueducts, sewer systems, and public buildings in their cities. These cities would probably not have been built without political and social systems for extracting or exchanging surpluses from agricultural areas.

World trade was a second major impetus to the development of cities. In the seventeenth and eighteenth centuries, many new port cities sprang up, including New York and Boston in North America, Capetown in South Africa, Bombay in India, and Rio de Janeiro in Brazil. All these cities were centers of trade and colonial rule.

Industrialization was a third major source of urbanization, along with agricultural and trading importance. As factories expanded in Great Britain, people migrated to cities in search of work. British cities such as Birmingham, Leeds, and Manchester and younger American cities including Rochester, Detroit, Minneapolis–St. Paul, and Chicago, all grew in response to industrialization.

In many Third World countries today, large numbers of rural people migrate from the farms and villages to the cities, pursuing the dream of a better life. Mexico City, for example, has experienced a major population explosion in recent years, due to the migration of landless farm workers. For many, however, there are no jobs, and they end up living in makeshift shanties or tents around the fringes of the urban center. As a result, some developing nations are labeled "overurbanized" by sociologists.

In the United States both trade and industrialization contributed to the rise of cities. Between 1850 and 1970, urbanization increased, first in the Northeast, then in the South, and more recently in the West and Southwest. One way the urban areas handled their increasing populations was by expanding outward from their centers, in what has been called urban sprawl or suburbanization. This tendency began around 1900 in older cities like New York and Philadelphia and became very pronounced all over the country after World War II ended in 1945—for instance, north of Chicago; in Houston, Texas; and in California's Orange County.

---

[1] Oceania is the collective name for the more than 10,000 islands scattered throughout most of the Pacific Ocean, including Australia and New Zealand, Polynesia, and Micronesia.

## Living Patterns, U.S.A.

Knowing where people live and what the trends in their living patterns are is important for selling goods or services, for real estate development, and for planning transportation, park-lands, health services, education, or other social services. To meet these needs, the federal Office of Management and the Budget (OMB) has established certain definitions that it uses to collect data about where people live. In order to understand the reports, we need to know their code.

As Figure 20.1 shows, three-quarters of the population in the United States live in metropolitan areas. A metropolitan area is made up of a large population center, along with the bordering communities that are integrated economically and socially with that center (U.S. Bureau of the Census, 1989a, p. 3). Formally defined, a **Metropolitan Statistical Area (MSA)** must have (1) one city with 50,000 or more residents or (2) a census-defined urban area of at least 50,000 inhabitants *and* a total population of at least 100,000 (except in New England where the required total is 75,000).

There is also a category of "supercities," or what the OMB calls **Consolidated Metropolitan Statistical Areas (CMSAs).** They have more than a million people apiece and meet certain other criteria. The supercities are indicated by the initials CMSA. The population density of those cities is evident in Figure 20.2. Figure 20.3 lists the largest 25 metropolitan areas in the United States.

Although nonmetropolitan areas grew faster than metropolitan areas for a brief period in the 1970s, their growth rate had slowed by 1980. Since then, metropolitan areas have been growing faster. The nation's metropolitan population grew 3.5 percent between 1980 and 1983,

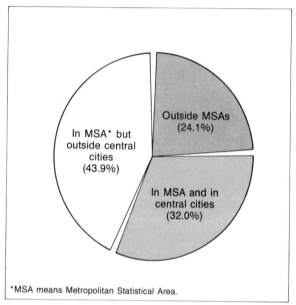

*MSA means Metropolitan Statistical Area.

**Figure 20.1 Proportions of U.S. Population in MSAs and in Central Cities, in MSAs but Outside Central Cities, and Outside MSAs.**

Three-quarters of the U.S. population lived in central cities or their suburbs and only one-quarter lived outside Metropolitan Statistical Areas (MSAs) in 1985.

*Source:* U.S. Bureau of the Census, 1985a, p. 19.

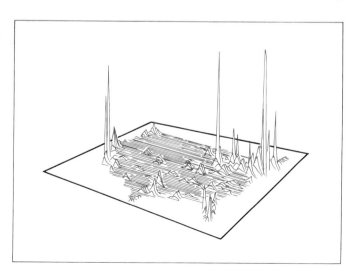

**Figure 20.2 Population Density in the United States, 1979.**

In this three-dimensional graph drawn by a computer, the density of a population is illustrated by the height of the peaks. Thus it provides a pictorial representation of the information in Figure 20.3.

*Source:* Produced by Harvard University Laboratory for Computer Graphics Mapping Service.

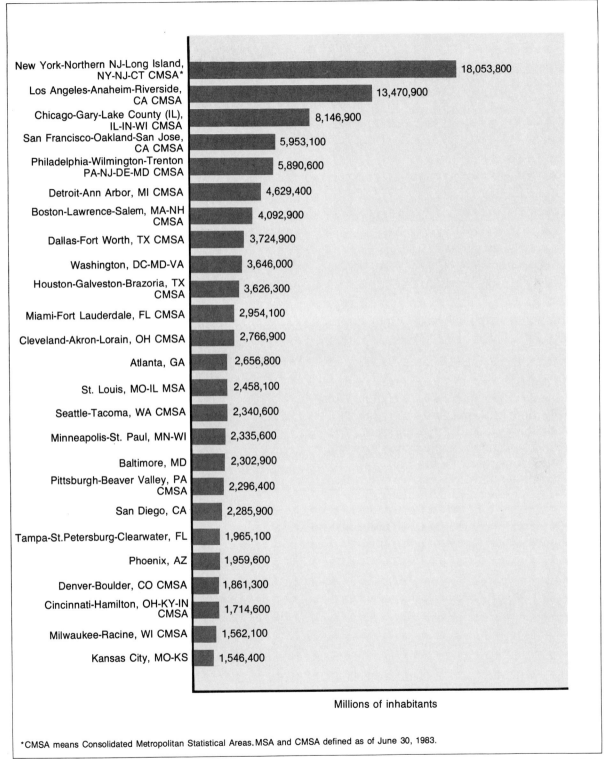

| Metropolitan Area | Population |
|---|---|
| New York-Northern NJ-Long Island, NY-NJ-CT CMSA* | 18,053,800 |
| Los Angeles-Anaheim-Riverside, CA CMSA | 13,470,900 |
| Chicago-Gary-Lake County (IL), IL-IN-WI CMSA | 8,146,900 |
| San Francisco-Oakland-San Jose, CA CMSA | 5,953,100 |
| Philadelphia-Wilmington-Trenton PA-NJ-DE-MD CMSA | 5,890,600 |
| Detroit-Ann Arbor, MI CMSA | 4,629,400 |
| Boston-Lawrence-Salem, MA-NH CMSA | 4,092,900 |
| Dallas-Fort Worth, TX CMSA | 3,724,900 |
| Washington, DC-MD-VA | 3,646,000 |
| Houston-Galveston-Brazoria, TX CMSA | 3,626,300 |
| Miami-Fort Lauderdale, FL CMSA | 2,954,100 |
| Cleveland-Akron-Lorain, OH CMSA | 2,766,900 |
| Atlanta, GA | 2,656,800 |
| St. Louis, MO-IL MSA | 2,458,100 |
| Seattle-Tacoma, WA CMSA | 2,340,600 |
| Minneapolis-St. Paul, MN-WI | 2,335,600 |
| Baltimore, MD | 2,302,900 |
| Pittsburgh-Beaver Valley, PA CMSA | 2,296,400 |
| San Diego, CA | 2,285,900 |
| Tampa-St.Petersburg-Clearwater, FL | 1,965,100 |
| Phoenix, AZ | 1,959,600 |
| Denver-Boulder, CO CMSA | 1,861,300 |
| Cincinnati-Hamilton, OH-KY-IN CMSA | 1,714,600 |
| Milwaukee-Racine, WI CMSA | 1,562,100 |
| Kansas City, MO-KS | 1,546,400 |

Millions of inhabitants

*CMSA means Consolidated Metropolitan Statistical Areas. MSA and CMSA defined as of June 30, 1983.

**Figure 20.3   Top 25 Metropolitan Areas in the United States.**

Forty-three percent of the U.S. population lived in the top 25 Metropolitan Statistical Areas in 1980, the largest of which were the New York MSA, Los Angeles MSA, and the Chicago MSA.

*Source:* U.S. Department of Commerce, 1988b.

*The Metropolitan Statistical Area (MSA) of Bakers-field, California, had about 150,000 inhabitants in 1986. It has grown rapidly since 1970, and many new housing developments like this one have sprung up.*

whereas the nonmetropolitan population grew only 2.7 percent (Engels and Forstall, 1985, p. 23).

Despite the growth of many metropolitan areas, their central cities are often losing jobs, population, and tax revenues. Who remains? As middle-aged, more affluent whites move to the suburbs or the Sunbelt, often it is the poor, the young, the old, and the nonwhite who are left behind. Some urban residents have no place to live. (See the box on homelessness.) Some cities or sections decay, whereas others flourish in a process of "gentrification." Most urban dwellers can easily observe such changes. Sociologists have developed several explanations for why they occur.

## Why and How Cities Grow

Sociologists offer two major paradigms—the ecological and the political economy—to explain living patterns, land use, and growth or decline of geographical areas.

### The Ecological Paradigm

The **ecological paradigm** examines the interplay between economic functions (such as the shift from trade to factory production); geographical factors, such as harbors or rivers; demographic factors, including migrations and the replacement of one group by another (what is

called **ecological succession**); and transportation technologies, such as buses or subways. Urban ecologists concentrate heavily on describing the spatial characteristics of urban areas. For example, the **concentric zone theory** was developed by Park, Burgess, and McKenzie (1925) on the basis of their study of Chicago. This theory shows how zones grow out from the center, like the rings formed by a pebble dropped into a pond. In each zone, land is used in a different way. The innermost zone is the *central business district*, which contains department stores, banks, hotels, theaters, business offices, rail and bus centers, and government buildings. The next concentric circle forms the *zone in transition*, which represents mixed residential and commercial land use. Often, this zone is where earlier residents of a city once lived. As commercial activities began to spread, newly arrived immigrants settled there in crowded dwellings that often became slums. If groups stay in such areas long enough, they often develop cohesive social networks. Little Italies and Chinatowns may develop in such areas.

Third is the *zone of workers' homes*, consisting of aging but often quite stable residential areas, where workers' families can afford to live and may do so for several generations. The fourth circle makes up the *middle-class residential zone* and contains many single-family dwellings where white-collar workers and professionals live. Fifth is a band of upper-class residences. Sixth is the *commuter zone*, where upper-middle and upper-class administrators, executives, and professionals live. In most places this zone consists of suburban areas.

Some concentric zone theorists include outlying agricultural areas: first, those that produce milk, eggs, and butter; second, even farther afield, areas that provide produce and meat. Although it is useful for describing urban development, the concentric zone theory does not explain why some cities simply do not correspond to zones. Nor does it explain why growth patterns vary over time.

The **sector theory** helps to deal with changes in the way cities develop. Hoyt (1939) described urban growth as following major trolley lines or waterways and expanding away from overcrowded areas. According to this theory, cities will not develop in full rings but in wedge-

# Homeless in America

Jackie R., who was mentioned at the beginning of this chapter, is only one of an estimated 250,000 to 3 million people in the United States who have no homes in which to escape the killing cold of winter, much less to enjoy safety and privacy. The homeless wander through all of the large urban centers in the United States. Why do they exist and why are their numbers increasing? A recent report to the U.S. Congress (Committee on Government Operations, 1985) analyzes the causes of homelessness, discusses its crisis proportions, considers the effect of federal programs on the situation, and recommends strategies for dealing with the emergency.

Although the causes of homelessness are complex, the growing shortage of reasonably priced housing is the single most important cause. The supply of such housing is shrinking due to urban redevelopment, conversion of existing low-quality housing to luxury condominiums, reduced construction, increased demand for luxury housing, and the virtual elimination of federal funds for the construction of new, subsidized housing. During the 1970s the United States lost as many as 1 million single room occupancy (SRO) units, which is nearly half of the total supply in the country.

Several other factors have contributed as well. In the past 20 years hundreds of thousands of mentally ill persons were released from mental institutions. They were supposed to be treated in community mental health centers, but too few mental health centers were opened. As a result, many people were released into the streets.

At the same time, unemployment rose dramatically in the United States, reaching a high of 10.8 percent in 1982. High unemployment is a symptom of the loss of jobs in basic industry, the so-called "deindustrialization" of America. It frequently happens that the newly unemployed must give up their homes.

But even those who have jobs may not earn enough to afford shelter. By the end of 1983 the rate of poverty in the United States was at its highest level in 18 years, partly as a direct result of cuts in federal programs such as Aid to Families with Dependent Children (AFDC) and Food Stamps. Many homeless people who are eligible for Veterans Administration benefits or Social Security benefits cannot receive them because they do not have a fixed address.

Although no one has done a complete count of the homeless population, two trends are very clear: the homeless population is increasing each year and the homeless exist in epidemic proportions, according to the Congressional Report. One governor noted, "never since the Great Depression have there been so many people without shelter." On any given night in the United States, well over 100,000 people do not have access to a shelter. Not only are the numbers of homeless increasing, but they include more families, women, and children than was true in the past.

For people who get into shelters, conditions are often not that much better. In a typical shelter in Washington, D.C., there is one shower for every 300 people and one toilet for every 150 people (Committee on Government Operations, 1985, p. 10). In Phoenix, Arizona, the only public shelter is an outdoor, fenced-in lot. On the day the congressional subcommittee toured the shelter it was cold and rainy. While city officials looked on, homeless men and women huddled under wet blankets and garbage bags to try to keep warm and escape the rain.

The Congressional Report offers nine recommendations to deal with homelessness:

1. The president should issue an Executive Order declaring homelessness a national emergency.
2. Federal agencies with benefit programs should make a nationwide outreach effort to seek out and help homeless Americans.
3. The federal government should expand low-income housing programs.
4. Model community health programs should be developed and established to help the persons released from mental health institutions.
5. The Federal Emergency Food and Shelter Program should be expanded, and the restriction on the use of funds for creating new shelters should be lifted.
6. The Department of Defense should identify vacant military buildings that could be used as emergency shelters and work with local governments to encourage the use of military facilities as shelters.
7. The U.S. Department of Defense should provide surplus food from military commissaries to food banks for the hungry and homeless.
8. The Public Health Service should provide medical services to the homeless.
9. Congress should fund demonstration shelter projects to explore the most effective ways of helping the homeless.

shaped patterns that follow transport systems. This pattern explains how some downtown areas, such as Boston's Beacon Hill or Manhattan's Park and Fifth Avenues, remain fashionable and vital regardless of what else happens around them. The theory fails to recognize, however, that development does not always occur in similar areas.

Not all cities have a central downtown area, or core, in relation to which zones or sectors grow. Many cities in the United States have a number of business centers as well as residential and industrial sections. The **multiple-nuclei theory,** proposed by Harris and Ullman (1945), takes into account the way land use tends to become specialized around certain functions—for instance, an area of artists' galleries and lofts; a meat-cutting center; the so-called tenderloin section with its sex shops, pornographic movies, and vice operations; a printing area; and a financial center. Different activities thus cluster around different nuclei within a city; they are not all concentrated in one downtown area. Some cities also have overlapping nuclei. A section of Philadelphia, for example, contains stores selling religious garments by day next to those selling pornographic movies by night.

Urban ecologists tend to see newer cities as "catching up" with older cities as part of a tendency toward equilibrium in the United States. They focus attention on changes in the shape of cities and in who lives where.

Contemporary analysts in the ecological tradition stress recent trends, especially since 1970, toward the diffusion of urban population and industry. This trend includes the diffusion of urban industries, consumer goods and services, and life-styles to previously isolated rural communities (Kasarda, 1980). The result is a new form of "polycentric urbanism," in which economic and social exchanges are structured around advanced transportation and communications technologies (Frisbie and Kasarda, 1988). "Within this new, more diffuse form of polycentric urbanization, networks of information flows are increasingly substituting for product and people flows" (Frisbie and Kasarda, 1988, p. 636). Cities are increasingly becoming the centers of coordination and control activities (financial, legal, marketing, and public relations efforts) rather than centers of manufacturing or

retail sales. Metropolitan centers interconnect with other regional, national, and sometimes world centers.

These trends have major implications for the changing populations of metropolitan areas. As middle- and upper-income residents tend to move to the suburbs and lower-income minorities partially replace them (Kasarda, 1984; Long, 1981), there is a growing gap between the educational backgrounds of residents and the requirements of new urban employment opportunities. One result is high rates of structural unemployment and welfare dependency (Frisbie and Kasarda, 1988; Kasarda, 1985).

Is "gentrification" likely to reverse these trends? **Gentrification** is the movement of middle- and upper-middle-class (usually white) persons into lower-income, sometimes minority urban areas, where they often buy and refurbish declining housing stock (see Laska and Spain, 1980). For several reasons, gentrification has not reduced the trend toward urban population dispersion. One explanation for gentrification is the desire to get closer to important activities, especially as energy and transportation costs increase. But as the centers of important activity become more dispersed, moving "closer to the action" may mean moving to a new activity center in a suburb (Edmonston and Guterbock, 1984). Another reason is that when a middle-class family buys a four-story building housing

*"Gentrification" is the movement of middle- and upper-middle-class (usually white) persons into lower-income, often minority urban areas, where they often buy and renovate declining houses. The process may displace lower-income and minority families.*

four or more families and converts it into a one-family house, the population density declines. Cities experiencing extensive gentrification in the last decade or two have often lost population at the same time.

### Political Economy Paradigm

The second major paradigm is the **political economy model.** Also called "critical theorists," the political economy theorists have faulted urban ecology for downplaying or ignoring the role of the state (for example, its zoning policies, tax subsidies, public works, or protectionist legislation) and for taking too positive a view of urban changes.

The political economy paradigm takes several forms. Gordon (1977), for example, has advanced a comprehensive theory that links the development of cities with the stage of economic production they are experiencing at the time of their major growth. He suggests that there are three types of contemporary cities: commercial, industrial, and corporate. The form they take depends on the process of capital accumulation that was dominant at the time the cities developed to maturity.

### Commercial Cities

Commercial cities began in favorable natural harbors and waterways and developed as merchant capitalists bought and sold commodities. From the outset in the American colonies, political controls were placed on where ships could land and unload. The chosen cities received a powerful advantage over others. In the North only Boston, New York, Philadelphia, and later Baltimore were officially sanctioned commercial ports where British merchants could unload. These limits aided resident merchants by sharply limiting competition from other places.

In the early commercial cities, most people owned their own property. Many worked in the same building where they lived, since most businesses were small. People of many different backgrounds and occupations lived and worked in close quarters in central city districts. There was an active neighborhood street life (Warner, 1968). The hub of commercial cities was the wharf areas where streets were narrow and zigged and zagged in unexpected patterns. The outer ring of these cities consisted of the transient poor, who stayed in temporary shanties or roominghouses (Gordon, 1977). When urban land speculation boomed, new streets and buildings were mapped out in regular rectangles (Mumford, 1961). This pattern of development is evident in Manhattan above Houston Street and contrasts sharply with the irregular streets in lower Manhattan and the Wall Street area. Philadelphia shows a similar pattern.

### Industrial Cities

The industrial city was exemplified by Chicago. Early factories were built along river banks because water power was their source of energy. Once coal replaced water as the major energy source, factories could be built anywhere. Economists suggest that large cities were chosen as the sites for major factories because they offered (1) larger numbers of workers, (2) markets for their goods, (3) major rail and water transportation, and (4) other factories that produced needed supplies. Gordon (1977) feels that large cities also offered desirable conditions for controlling labor.

The growth of the industrial city changed the commercial urban forms. Huge factories were built downtown near rail or water transportation centers, and working-class housing was built nearby. The middle and upper classes began moving out of the center of town, although major shopping districts were still located downtown. These developments led to major residential segregation by economic class and the separation of jobs and residences.

In his analysis of why cities developed the way they did, Gordon adds the dimension of social class, a factor that was not included in ecological models of how cities develop. Economic and class considerations also help to explain the rise of corporate headquarters cities.

### Corporate Cities

The corporate city is characterized by towering skyscrapers housing corporate headquarters and banking and legal services. In such cities industrial activity has moved rapidly away from the center of the city, sometimes outside the city altogether. They include some older industrial cities like New York that have shifted away from manufacturing activity toward the financial, communications, and business services

**Figure 20.4   The American Sunbelt.**

Many people talk about the *Sunbelt* in describing changes in American society. This map shows one analyst's definition of the **Sunbelt** as following the 37th parallel across the United States, from Southern California to North Carolina. Clark County in Nevada, which contains Las Vegas, is included as well. In California the upper boundaries of the Sunbelt are formed by San Bernardino, Kern, and San Luis Obispo counties, according to Rice (1981).

needed by corporate headquarters. They also include some newer cities such as Houston, San Diego, and Denver, which have grown up as the centers of energy, electronics, and defense corporations.

The growth of corporate cities may have been spurred by efforts to control labor more effectively, suggests Gordon (1977). If labor became too militant in a particular region, an industry could simply move to a different location out of the city or the state. Increasingly, manufacturing and administrative functions were separated, with plant managers handling manufacturing at regionally dispersed plants while central corporate headquarters were built downtown. This division of functions increased the growth of corporate cities.

The political boundaries of cities and how they changed over time are also related to capitalist development. Although manufacturing concerns were operating in center cities, industry favored annexing outlying regions as people moved out to them to spread the tax base. (The *tax base* refers to the boundaries within which a political unit has the power to tax.) But when manufacturing began to move out to avoid the taxing authority of central cities, cities began to stop their policies of annexation, suggests Gordon (1977). One result is that today's city is politically fragmented, with hundreds of distinct urban and suburban jurisdictions trying to tax and govern single metropolitan areas. Whereas older industrial cities had been dominated by shopping areas downtown, corporate headquar-

ters now began to dominate some cities. The new corporate cities were described as the "fragmented metropolis" (Fogelson, 1967), since they have no center at all. They are one step beyond the multiple-nuclei city, which consisted of a number of clusters around various centers.

Several other developments contributed to the recent physical and economic growth of new corporate cities in the **Sunbelt**.[2] The auto, oil, and highway construction industries promoted automobile transportation, which led to the sprawling development so characteristic of new cities like San Diego, Los Angeles, and Houston. When cars are the major means of transportation, housing can be built anywhere people can drive, rather than growing out along existing rail lines, for instance. Meanwhile, their economic development has been fueled by military spending on missiles, space shuttles, jet aircraft, and weapons.

Others sharing Gordon's political economy approach stress the importance of the economic and political decisions made by business and government leaders. For example, real estate developers, construction companies, industries, and political leaders strongly shape urban development. Corporate decisions about where to build or move new offices and factories affect job opportunities in the surrounding neighborhoods and tax revenues for urban areas. The

[2] The term "Sunbelt" does not always refer to the same states when it is used by different writers, but a useful definition is suggested in Figure 20.4.

growing number of government employees is another factor that has influenced the growth of certain urban areas such as Washington, D.C. (Carroll and Meyer, 1982). The decision by business and political leaders in some cities (such as Houston) to rely on auto transport rather than on a mass transit system determined how Houston grew and the problems it faced (Snell, 1979). Transportation issues remain hotly debated political issues today. (See the debate on raising the gasoline tax.)

Analysts taking a political economy approach note that the development of cities is quite uneven; certain northern "Frostbelt" cities are decaying, whereas many Sunbelt cities are expanding (Perry and Watkins, 1977; Sale, 1976). Within cities, some areas flourish due to gentrification, but poorer residents suffer as their neighborhoods change (Fainstein and Fainstein, 1982, p. 166).

A broader political economy approach to explaining urban growth stresses the global context rather than the regional or national context alone. Feagin (1985) suggests that the rise and fall of at least some cities depend heavily on their role in the world economy. Houston grew and, more recently, faced recession, because it provided technology and equipment to a global oil industry. Similarly, Los Angeles and New York serve international banking needs. On the other hand, a city like Detroit has been hurt by the relative decline of the American auto business in the world economy. Although this view sees the fate of many cities as rooted in the global economy, it also emphasizes the importance of government, especially national government, in helping local business and political leaders to foster growth. Such decisions influence the uneven growth of different regions (see Figure 20.5).

The post–World War II growth of the West, and especially California, stemmed from the rapid growth of aerospace, defense, solid-state electronics, and other advanced-technology industries (Biggar, 1979; Castells, 1985; Frisbie and Kasarda, 1988). The South's economy grew because of new interstate highways and airports (which improved access to national and international markets), more modern industrial plants, its favorable climate, improved universities, and tax and wage rates attractive to corporations (Frisbie and Kasarda, 1988). Southern states and communities also adopted aggressive progrowth attitudes (Biggar, 1979; Cobb, 1982). The booming economies of the West and South attracted national and international migrants. The result is that, together, the South and the West made up more than 90 percent of the nation's 14.5 million population increase from 1980 to 1986 (U.S. Bureau of the Census, 1987a, p. 21). It appears that both ecological and political economy factors lie behind the disparities in regional growth.

The ecological and political economy theories of urban growth are summarized and compared in Table 20.1. Although the theories focus on

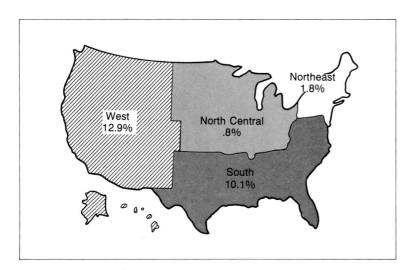

**Figure 20.5  Population Changes in Major Regions of the United States, 1985–1988.**

Between 1985 and 1988, population growth was greater in the West and South than in the North Central and Northeast regions.

*Source:* U.S. Department of Commerce, 1988c, p. 3.

**Table 20.1**    *A Comparison of Ecological, Conflict, and World Economy Theories of Urban Growth*

|  | Impetus for Growth | Role of Government | Pattern of Urban Development |
|---|---|---|---|
| **Ecological Theory (See Berry and Kasarda, 1977; Guest 1984; Hawley, 1981; Poston, 1984)** | Free market forces, cheap land, cheap labor, migration, transportation and communication technologies. "Better business climate," i.e., less regulation | Minimal in market-directed societies, decentralized. Should combat crises | Newer "Sunbelt" cities are thought to be "catching up" with older northern cities, as part of a tendency toward equilibrium in the United States |
| **Political Economy (Conflict Approach)** | Political and economic decisions by business and government leaders. Technologies depend on those decisions | Government is considered more important for urban development. Local links among government, private capital, and cities are stressed (Molotch, 1976; Domhoff, 1983) | Uneven development, e.g., growth in Sunbelt, decay in Frostbelt. Cities are moving apart (Perry and Watkins, 1977; Sale, 1976) |
| **World Economy Theory** | World market trends, specialization of a particular city in the global context. Earlier stages of urban economic and political development are building blocks for later stages of growth or decline | Federal government is very important, despite free-enterprise and antigovernment ideology. Local governments have to deal with the social costs of rapid development. Local growth coalitions are important | Some cities take on a specialized function within the global economy. These cities that have a vital role in the world economy will prosper, whereas others will decline |

*Source:* Adapted from Feagin, 1985, pp. 1204–1230.

different features of urban growth, it is helpful to think of them as complementing rather than excluding each other. After all, some of the factors that ecologists examine, such as ecological succession or transportation technologies, have interesting consequences, but they depend on the political economy characteristics of the city.

These macro-level theories tend to minimize the importance of cultural and social groups, but social and symbolic factors cannot be overlooked when one is trying to understand urban development. Although the values and wishes of people living in an area are often less powerful than large economic and political interests, they may help to explain why certain neighborhoods resist plans for urban development (Suttles, 1984) or why urban restoration occurs in some sections of a city rather than in others (Firey, 1947).

## SUBURBAN DEVELOPMENT

Suburbs began developing in the United States around 1900. They may be small villages or good-sized towns, but all suburbs have in common that they are within commuting range of the central city in their Metropolitan Statistical

# DEBATING SOCIETY'S ISSUES

*Should Congress Raise the Gasoline Tax?*

At the beginning of 1989, as this book was going to press, the federal gasoline tax was 9.1 cents a gallon. The last raise had been 5 cents per gallon in 1982. Most advocates of a higher tax favored a 10- to 25-cent increase per gallon, but some urged as much as 50 cents to a dollar. Supporters of some increase included Alan Greenspan, the chairman of the Federal Reserve Board; Representative Dan Rostenkowski, Democrat of Illinois and chairman of the House Ways and Means Committee; and Drew Lewis, the Republican cochairman of the National Economic Commission (Hershey, 1988). Opponents include road builders, tourism interests, farm groups, state officials, the oil industry, the American Automobile Association, truckers, insurers, and members of Congress from the West and other areas where there is little public transportation (Hershey, 1988).

## PRO:

1. A tax increase would help to conserve fuel.

2. This would add to U.S. energy security by reducing the need for foreign oil.

3. It would also help to narrow the U.S. trade deficit.

4. Reduced fuel consumption would help to reduce environmental pollution.

5. Gas is still much cheaper in the United States than in western Europe or Japan. Those regions charge a tax of about $2 per gallon, which has not seemed to hurt their economies.

6. The new tax could raise revenues that could help to balance the U.S. budget deficit. Government and private analysts estimate that each penny of increase would yield the U.S. Treasury $1 billion.

7. Past research shows that higher cost does lower fuel consumption.

8. Such a tax would be easy to administer. It would preserve the income tax rate reductions.

9. The regressive burden of the tax could be lightened by annual rebates to low-income consumers.

## CON:

1. Such a tax is hardest on working people in remote areas, who may have little choice over how much they drive.

2. Distances are much greater in the United States than in western Europe or Japan. Public transportation is often not available.

3. Such a tax is hard on lower-income people who cannot afford to buy new, more fuel-efficient cars. For these reasons, the tax is class-biased and regressive.

4. Research also shows that values about conservation as well as higher costs help to lower fuel consumption. It is unclear that higher taxes alone would change people's values about conservation.

5. The tax selectively hurts certain businesses—tourism, salespersons, truckers, airlines. Is it fair that certain groups have to bear a disproportionate share of the burden of solving the nation's economic problems?

6. Such an increase could fuel regional animosities. "A top official of a leading oil industry trade group said the opponents of a tax increase would not hesitate to make use of regional animosities. 'What you're saying is that the good-living folks in Wyoming should pay for the deficit of all those yuppies up in New York,' he said. . . . 'And don't think that we're not going to encourage that' conception as a way to defeat gasoline-tax legislation" (Hershey, 1988).

## FURTHER DISCUSSION:

What do you think about an increased gasoline tax? How do you think it would affect people in your part of the country? Would it affect all groups the same way? Why or why not?

Area (MSA). In fact, suburbs include all the localities in an MSA that are not central cities. In this section we trace the history of their growth and then look at sociological explanations for changes in suburban development. There has been a steady increase in the suburban population since 1900. **Suburbs** are fairly small communities that develop near central cities. As streetcar lines were built, people gradually moved farther away from where they worked, seeking more space, yards, and sunshine. Research by Guterbock (1976) and Marshall (1979) suggests that people move to the suburbs because of the lure suburban life has for them rather than because they are fleeing unattractive features of city life.

By 1920, about 17 percent of the population already lived in suburbs. The rise in automobile use in the 1920s contributed greatly to the continued growth of suburbs. During the Depression and World War II suburban growth slowed, but it leapt upward after the war, as tract homes began to be produced on a mass scale. By 1983, 44 percent of the population lived in suburbs, and business had begun to move there as well. The biggest growth areas in the early 1980s were the suburbs around large Sunbelt metropolitan areas, particularly Houston, Texas; Dallas–Fort Worth, Texas; Phoenix, Arizona; and Tampa-St. Petersburg–Clearwater, Florida. In general, suburban areas all over the United States gained 5.5 percent in their population between 1980 and 1983 (Engels and Forstall, 1985, p. 23).

The recent growth of suburbs and even small towns has been facilitated by technological developments, especially in the areas of transpor-

tation and communications. The development of highways, cars, and trucks along with the telephone, radio, television, and even cable and satellite TV meant that people could live farther away from where they worked and still keep in touch or get to work. The possibilities of earning a living in small towns are enhanced by emerging computer and FAX technologies that permit the electronic transfer of messages and access to distant sources of information. In addition, the shift in the economy away from heavy manufacturing toward service, communications, and information "industries" increases the possibilities for ever greater decentralization. Suburban borders of urban centers continue to expand as people search for desirable or affordable property.

## Ecological Explanations

The ecological and political economy theories that were developed to explain urban growth may also be applied to suburban development. The *persistence model,* in the ecological tradition, suggests that high-status suburbs will grow faster than others because newcomers will select communities to match their own status levels and because newer suburbs may require undesirably long commutes. Such a growth pattern would lead to the persistence of the relative status levels of different suburbs (Logan and Schneider, 1981). An *ecological succession model* suggests that suburbs with originally high status will decline as higher-status families move to newer, less deteriorated suburbs (Burgess, 1967; Choldin et al., 1980). Such a model suggests major changes in the relative growth and status of different suburbs.

## Political Economy Explanations

A *political economy model* expects that inequalities will increase among suburbs. It sees high-status communities (measured by median household income) using the superior economic and political resources of their residents to reinforce their relatively advanced position, whereas low-status communities deteriorate unless new industries and jobs enter the picture.

*Many suburban borders of urban centers continue to expand as people search for desirable or affordable homes.*

Logan and Schneider (1981) found some support for the persistence, ecological, and political economy models. In metropolitan areas with high rates of suburban growth, the status rank of suburbs was fluid between 1960 and 1970. This was especially true in southern suburbs and supports the ecological succession model. In the North, suburbs were more likely to develop antagonistic political relationships with central cities and to use exclusionary zoning to preserve their advantages. Thus there was some evidence for the persistence model within certain metropolitan areas. The political economy model was supported by findings that inequalities between suburbs declined when jobs moved into formerly poor suburbs. The splintering of political power among many municipal governments is also somewhat related to increasing stratification.

The trend toward suburbanization was encouraged by several ecological factors, including cheaper land, fewer zoning restrictions, and the economies of mass production. Federal programs such as low-interest FHA (Federal Housing Authority) and GI mortgages, federally financed highways, and the deductibility of home mortgage interest on income taxes also encouraged the development of suburbs.

Thus we see how economic and political factors affect the fate of cities and suburbs. Large metropolitan areas are more likely to attract private capital. The age, occupation, and wealth of inhabitants play a role in how much public capital is invested in metropolitan development. Political decisions such as zoning regulations may restrict the size of building lots (in some communities as much as two acres may be required for a one-family house), which, in turn, affects who can afford to live in such suburbs.

## RURAL DEVELOPMENT

The settlement of the American West was also influenced by both ecological factors and the political economy. People settled first in areas with the best farmland and water, where there was the least resistance from native Americans. The passage of the Homestead Act by Congress in 1862 further encouraged westward migration. The act stated that any head of a family or any adult who had not borne arms against the government (the Civil War had begun in 1861) could become an owner of 160 acres of public land. He had to live on it, cultivate it for five years, and pay a small fee to record his ownership. The extension of the railroad—encouraged by federal and state assistance in the form of land, money, and guaranteed loans—also stimulated rural settlements.

The same year, 1862, Congress also passed the Morrill Act, which gave a generous grant of public land to each state for the purpose of establishing a college to teach agriculture. About 70 "land grant" colleges were founded or helped under the Morrill Act. The U.S. Department of Agriculture was also established by the federal government in 1862. These political events encouraged the growth of more scientific methods of farming, and farm productivity increased. Farm prices, however, fell, and many farmers, in debt to buy farm equipment, lost their farms. Before the Civil War (1861–1865), most farmers owned their own farms, but by 1900 about one-third had lost them.

Between 1890 and 1930, there was extensive capital investment in agriculture, mostly to buy farm equipment, and the value of American farm equipment increased 700 percent in that period. Gasoline-driven tractors replaced horses, freeing millions of acres for cultivation that had previously been used to graze the horses. Aided by county agents and supported by federal and state governments, scientific agriculture resulted in improved varieties of plants and animals; ways of fighting plant diseases; soil improvement; and better methods of plowing, planting, and harvesting.

Farm prices soared in World War I but fell afterward, as production increased and world demand dropped or was cut off by protective tariffs. Wheat, corn, and cotton prices in 1932 tumbled far below pre–World War I prices. The average farmer could not meet his obligations. Many mortgages were foreclosed, and farmers became tenants on land they had owned. Between 1927 and 1932, 10 percent of American farm property was sold at auction to meet unpaid mortgages. By 1935, 42 percent of farmers were tenants.

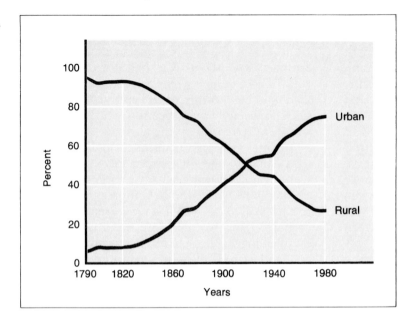

**Figure 20.6  U.S. Urban★ and Rural Population, 1790–1980 (as percent of population).**

Between 1790 and 1980 the proportion of the U.S. population living in urban areas has climbed consistently, whereas the proportion in rural areas has dropped steadily and sharply.

*Source:* U.S. Bureau of the Census, as cited in Whittingham, 1982, p. 134.

★ The urban population comprises all persons living in urbanized areas and in places of 2,500 inhabitants or more outside urbanized areas. An urbanized area consists of a central city, or twin cities, with a total population of 50,000 or more, together with contiguous closely settled territory.

Under the New Deal, President Franklin D. Roosevelt established the Farm Credit Administration (FCA). The FCA refinanced 20 percent of all farm mortgages in the United States. Even so, the drought, dust storms, and low world prices drove many farmers off their land. Some became tenant farmers while others migrated, often to California or Oregon. Wheat and corn prices were set in a world market, then as now, with the result that global events affected the number of people who could stay on farms. All during this period, and particularly after World War II, the proportion of the population in rural areas declined, whereas the percent in urban areas was rising (Figure 20.6).[3]

Today American agriculture, and hence rural and small town life, is experiencing another transformation. The number of family farms continues to decline, whereas the number of commercial-size farms (that is, those with sales over $100,000) is increasing. These commercial-size farms include only 14 percent of all farmers but account for nearly three-quarters of farm sales (U.S. Bureau of the Census, 1989a, p. 635). Between 1981 and 1983, 200,000 farmers

went bankrupt or out of business, a trend that continues today. Besides low prices, farmers have been hurt by high interest rates and the inflationary spiral of farmland prices in the early 1980s, all related to trends in the global economy.

These global trends have reduced the number of farms, the number of family-owned farms, and the number of people who live on farms. They have also served to undermine small-town institutions such as local banks, farmers' cooperatives, and equipment dealers (Hershey, 1985; Wall, 1984). What happened to many family-owned and -run business operations between 1890 and 1920 seems to be happening to farming today. The owner-manager is increasingly being replaced by a manager who farms land owned by national or international investors. Some of the same forces that rearrange the ownership and use of land in urban and suburban areas also seem to be influencing the use of rural land and treatment of the environment.

## ECOLOGY

**Ecology** is the study of how organisms relate to one another and to their environments. An **ecosystem** is the system formed by the interaction of a community of organisms with their environment. In the broadest sense, the human

[3] Because the population was increasing, the absolute number of farmers fell more slowly than did their proportion in the national population. Thus, in 1930, the total farm population was 30,529,000, which was 24.9 percent of the population. By 1987, the farm population was 4,986,000, which was 2.0 percent of the population (U.S. Bureau of the Census, 1989a, p. 627).

ecosystem is the planet earth. The study of ecology has become increasingly important in recent years, as people have begun to feel the effects of a century of industrialization on the environment and as they realize they may be doing irreversible damage to that environment and to themselves. (See also Chapters 18 and 19.)

Attitudes toward the natural environment have varied widely through time. Many preliterate tribal societies have a religious attitude toward nature and treat everything in it with respect. Native Americans, for example, saw plants and animals as containing spirits as vital as the human spirit. As a result, they did not feel they could impose their wishes on nature. They could take what they needed in an attitude of respectful gratitude but were not to waste anything they took or in any way spoil nature.

The attitude of Native Americans contrasts sharply with that held by Western industrializers, who tend to see themselves as apart from nature and to view nature as a collection of resources to be exploited. Such a view sees nature as existing to meet human needs and desires. Short-term profit and productivity are the only things to consider. Long-term consequences are ignored, or it is assumed that technology can be developed to deal with them. Human desires are seen as the only important force in determining how the environment is shaped. Ponds may be drained for housing, rivers dammed, and highways carved into the sides of mountains. People even try to turn back the tides in an effort to keep shorefront property from eroding.

The more nature is manipulated, the more technology and human intervention are needed to sustain the results. New breeds of animals need constant human attention to survive. The new hybrid grains that produced the green revolution require irrigation, chemical fertilizers, and pesticides to flourish. The more the environment is exploited, the more intensified become the two major threats faced by our ecological system: pollution and depletion of natural resources.

## Environmental Principles

In recent years environmental exploitation has been challenged by many people, including Barry Commoner (1971), a biologist and ecological crusader. He offers four principles of ecology. First, everything is related to everything else. Because all organisms are interconnected, if even one gets out of balance, it will affect the balance of the others. Second, everything must go somewhere, meaning that there is no safe place to hide poisons. If they go into the air, they will be brought down to earth by rain and snow, be picked up by plants and animals, and eventually reach humans. One dramatic illustration of this principle is that today mother's milk contains ten times more of the insecticide DDT than is permitted in dairy milk sold in stores.

Third, "nature knows best." This means that whenever people try to change or "improve" a natural system, they will harm that system. Every organic substance produced by a living organism has a counterpart somewhere in nature that can break it down. This principle ensures that recycling occurs. In nature there is no such thing as waste. People and animals, for example, exhale carbon dioxide, and plants use it as nourishment. Plants, in turn, give off oxygen, which is needed by animals and humans. Organisms or enzymes break down decaying organic mat-

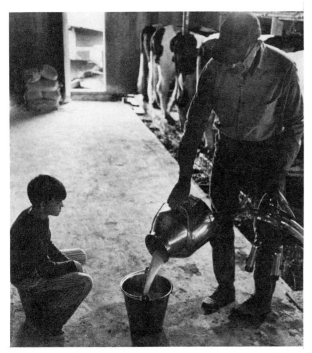

*Global trends are reducing the number of family farms and the number of Americans who live on farms.*

ter into simpler elements that further the growth of other things. But the synthetic fibers and plastics we have invented in recent years cannot be broken down by nature into reusable forms. This is what is meant when we say that something is not biodegradable. If it does not break down naturally, it must be burned, thereby creating pollution, or it piles up. Heavily populated areas are running out of space in which to dump their "disposable" diapers, Styrofoam cups, plastic tampon applicators, and polyester fabrics.

Fourth, "there is no such thing as a free lunch." In ecology, every gain has some cost. Because all things are interdependent, that cost can be delayed, but it cannot be avoided. We are reaching the point where we are beginning to pay those costs.

## Pollution

The air, water, and soil are seriously polluted in many areas of the world. The air in urban and industrial areas stings people's eyes, burns their lungs, and strains their hearts. Fumes from auto exhaust, steel and paper mills, oil refineries, in-

*Pollution of the groundwater used for drinking in many locales is an increasingly serious problem in the United States.*

cinerators, and electric generating plants are affected by sunlight and form smog, a substance that not only clouds landscapes but shortens lives. Chemically created fertilizers are applied in heavy doses to raise crop yields on American farms. What growing plants do not consume does not break down into simpler compounds. Instead, it runs off into local streams, rivers, and lakes. There the chemicals promote the growth of so much algae that fish cannot survive. The result is that the balance of nature is upset.

We have already mentioned that certain pesticides like DDT do not break down into simpler, safe compounds. Fertilizers and pesticides represent a small fraction of some 50,000 chemical compounds that have been created and marketed in the United States in the past generation. About three-quarters of these are considered by the Environmental Protection Agency to be surely or possibly harmful to human health. Many contribute to the increase in the number of cancer cases in this country. The rate at which these hazardous compounds are produced has soared. In 1941, the American petrochemical industry produced 1 billion pounds of synthetic chemicals. By 1977 production had skyrocketed to 350 billion pounds. Many of these chemicals are useful and even vital in our daily lives, but they have heavy ecological costs. For example, plastic fishnet, bottle tops, toys, and other plastic products are killing millions of ocean fish, seabirds, seals, whales, and sea turtles each year by choking or entangling them (Webster, 1984). This process could eventually destroy much of the world's ocean life unless steps are taken to halt the trend.

Another major cause for concern is that chemical wastes are seeping into groundwater that has been stored slowly over the centuries in porous places underground, threatening to contaminate the water supplies of more than half the nation's population. Millions of barrels of chemical waste have been disposed of, often in the dark of night, in unmarked and unsafe containers. These barrels are ticking time bombs. Nobody knows where all the "skeletons" are buried. The EPA estimates that there are about 231,000 sites and "lagoons" where chemicals have been dumped, and as many as 2000 of these dumps may pose serious risks.

In the wake of disasters in Times Beach, Missouri; Love Canal at Niagara Falls, New York; and parts of Europe where residential areas have been contaminated by poisonous refuse, toxic waste disposal is becoming a big business. In 1983 less than $5 billion was spent in the United States on toxic waste disposal. By 1990 an estimated $12 billion will be spent, according to the U.S. Office of Technology Assessment (OTA). Economic recessions, however, cut into the amount spent on toxic waste disposal and tend to put illegal "midnight dumpers" of toxic waste back on the road (Elkington, 1984).

Although proper disposal of toxic wastes costs money in the short run, it is much cheaper and safer in the longer term. It might have cost $2 million to dispose of the Love Canal wastes properly in the first place, but cleaning up the site will cost at least $100 million, plus, according to the OTA, the cost of settling some $2 billion in lawsuits, in addition to the incalculable human costs involved.

To stop pollution, we need to go to the source and change the technologies of production that create it (Commoner, 1988). Lead pollution in the air was reduced 90 percent by removing lead from gasoline. We could power electric cars with solar photovoltaic cells or a stratified charge engine and avoid the nitrous oxide and smog that high-compression gasoline engines produce (Commoner, 1988).

In addition to calling attention to the health risks related to the things people pour into the air, water, and soil, the study of ecology also draws attention to the use of nonrenewable resources. Some sources of energy—like sunlight, wind power, and hydroelectric power—are constantly renewing themselves. Other resources are part of an ever-dwindling supply.

## Resource Depletion

Until the Middle Eastern oil crises in 1973–1974 and 1979, most people had never thought that the world might run out of certain resources. The world's supply of clean air and water, oil, iron, aluminum, natural gas, gold, silver, and copper somehow seemed limitless. Those crises, and the gas station lines that accompanied them, showed that the supply of natural resources had

physical and political limitations. As Figure 20.7 indicates, at current projected rates of consumption, many key resources are expected to last only a few more years. Each year Americans discard 16 billion "disposable" diapers, 1.6 billion pens, 2 billion razors and blades, and 220 million tires. They throw away enough aluminum to replace all the U.S. commercial airlines every three months (Langone, 1989).

Energy production throughout the world consumes a great deal of oil, coal, and natural gas, all of which are nonrenewable resources. Optimists argue that new supplies of resources will be discovered or that substitutes will be invented. More pessimistic forecasts—like the *Limits to Growth* report by Meadows et al. (1972)—suggest that resource depletion, pollution, population growth, food production, and industrial growth are headed for collision and ultimate collapse if present trends continue. Although the assumptions and computations in the report by Meadows et al. have been questioned, it is becoming increasingly apparent that the planet has limited resources and that only so much pollution can be tolerated. Such realizations have prompted people to begin exploring alternative patterns of resource use.

## Alternatives

Conservation, changed patterns of consumption, home production of simple foods, and recycling are some of the strategies individuals and communities are exploring to cut costs and avoid resource depletion. When the costs of oil and natural gas skyrocketed, people tried to find ways to conserve energy. Many people drove less, used more fuel-efficient vehicles, turned down their thermostats, added insulation and storm windows to apartments or homes, explored solar sources of energy, built "earth houses" partially underground, and constructed smaller dwellings. As a result, between 1973 and 1985 U.S. per capita energy consumption fell 12 percent (*Time*, 1989, p. 65). But in the last several years, as oil prices have dropped, people began once again to buy bigger and more powerful cars and to use more energy.

Conservation of resources seems to be encouraged when individuals benefit directly from

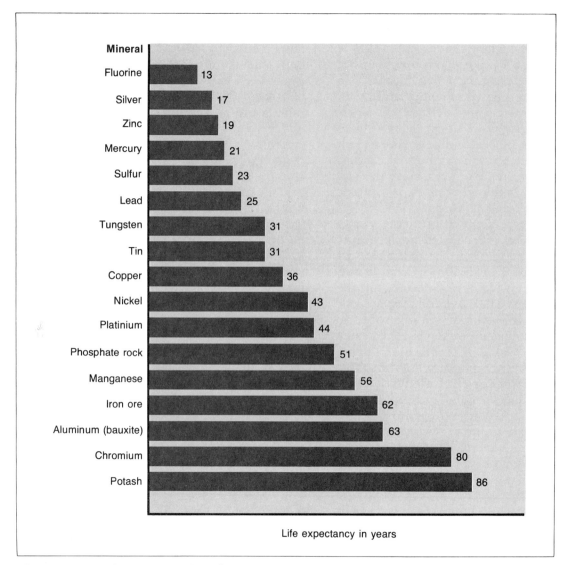

**Figure 20.7   Life Expectancies of 1976 World Reserves of Selected Minerals.★**

Reserves of certain minerals (such as fluorine) were expected to be depleted by 1989, whereas other minerals have somewhat longer but still not endless life expectancies.

*Source:* Barney, 1980, p. 29.

★ Assumes no increase in 1976 reserves and assumes that usage increases at the amount projected in the Global 2000 Technical Report, Table 12-2.

the consequences of their efforts. When tenants pay their own utility bills, they use less gas and electricity than when landlords pay the utilities and simply pass along the costs in higher rents. Recycling centers are also on the increase, as towns and cities run out of landfill areas. But the U.S. recycles only 10 percent of its garbage annually, compared with about 30 percent in western Europe and 50 percent in Japan (Langone, 1989).

New forms of recycling are being explored, including ways of turning garbage into energy.

Some of these alternatives are discussed by Schumacher (1973) in his book *Small Is Beautiful*.

The environmentalist and antigrowth movements have been populated by a mixture of young activists (some veterans of the peace or civil rights movements of the 1960s and 1970s) and professionals and managers in service or in "high-technology" occupations whose economic interests do not depend on exploiting the local environment (see Dunlap and Gale, 1972; Faich and Gale, 1971; Molotch, 1976; Nash, 1967).

The so-called natural foods movement stresses growing crops by using organic fertilizers and natural pest repellents, and it encourages people to produce more of their own food. Home gardening is on the increase, and even city dwellers are more and more likely to have a tub of tomatoes in a sunny window or to grow their own alfalfa or mung bean sprouts.

Ecology epitomizes the conflict between the need for a clean, safe environment and the push to maximize economic gains. Values, norms, and social and economic interests all contribute to the ecological crisis the world now faces. One source of ecological problems is the powerful and profitable petrochemical industry. But people who eagerly purchase its products are responsible as well. Our culture is part of the problem, and people need to change their values and attitudes if they are going to become part of the solution. These solutions lie beyond the power of technical innovations. They require changes in underlying attitudes and behaviors, tax structures, and the social organization of agriculture and industry. Existing institutions must change so that they support the ecosystem rather than undermine it. We face a race against time to see whether we can change our attitudes and institutions before we destroy our ecological support system.

## Explanations

Since ecological pollution is clearly not in the best interest of our planet or the people living on it, we need an explanatory framework to help understand why it happens. If we extend the urban ecology perspective to the more general issues of ecology, we see that certain areas develop because of the presence of natural resources (such as oil in Texas, copper in Montana, or iron ore in Michigan and Minnesota). Illegal dumping of toxic waste and pollution might be explained by urban ecologists in terms of market forces and the absence of government regulation.

A political economy perspective directs attention to links between private economic interests and political decision makers. Thus it suggests that problems are created when particular individuals rather than impersonal market forces make specific economic decisions. For example, in 1980 the United States launched its "superfund" hazardous-waste cleanup program to clean up what may be as many as 10,000 sites. But, after nearly five years, states and the Environmental Protection Agency (EPA) have started cleanups at only 62 sites (Taylor, 1985). The program faces technical, political, and economic problems. In 1983 the Reagan administration was shaken by an embarrassing scandal when it was discovered that the EPA had made "sweetheart deals" with industrial waste disposers (Elkington, 1984, p. 364). In Louisiana much of the water supply in southern counties is polluted with toxic heavy metals used in oil drilling and then dumped into an estimated 13,000 ground pits in the state. Statewide cancer deaths are 9.1 percent higher than the U.S. average,

*Although its recycling efforts have increased in recent years, the United States still lags behind Western Europe, which recycles about 30 percent of its trash, and Japan, which recycles about 50 percent.*

and in New Orleans they are 21 percent above the U.S. average. But when a recent editor of the Louisiana "state of the state" report included cancer-rate data and warned about "serious problems of air, water, and ground pollution," his bosses in Baton Rouge relieved him of his duties and never published the report (Petzinger, Jr., and Getschow, 1984). These examples suggest that pollution must be understood in the framework of a political economy.

Moreover, a political economy perspective shows how some technologies are encouraged whereas others are ignored by political and business leaders (Etzkowitz, 1984; Snell, 1979). A global context directs attention to corporate moves to escape restrictions and controls by building dirty manufacturing operations outside the United States if possible. More than 95 percent of industrial disasters like the one in Bhopal, India, occur in developing nations like Mexico, Brazil, and India.

## WHERE AND HOW PEOPLE LIVE

### Urban Life

American literature and art have traditionally found value in rural life and have viewed city life as corrupt, evil, crowded, unhealthy, and dirty. Gallup polls within the past decade suggest that many Americans still hold these views. At least three features of urban life seem to produce negative reactions in people: the physical congestion, noise, dirt, and pollution of city life; suspicion of the minorities and different cultures that live in cities; and the excessive social stimulation or isolation that cities produce.

Central cities have attracted large numbers of immigrants, beginning with Europeans and continuing more recently with blacks from the southern United States, Hispanics from the Caribbean and Mexico, and Asians. Most of these immigrants were poor; when they arrived, many affluent and educated residents moved to larger homes in less crowded areas on the outer rims of cities. Nationally, three-quarters of the people who now live in central cities are white and about one-quarter are black (Long and DeAre, 1981). In 1980, 56 percent of all blacks

*Central cities in the United States have attracted large numbers of immigrants since earliest times. Later immigrants often move into areas that earlier immigrants once occupied in a process called "residential succession."*

in the United States lived in central cities. Other ethnic groups such as Hispanics, Chinese, and Japanese comprise significant percentages in certain cities as well.

Some city dwellers who move out cite the attractions of newer homes with yards and driveways as pulling them away from the city, whereas others mention noise, dirty streets, crime, or crowding inside and outside their homes as negative features pushing them out. Respondents to surveys do not necessarily say they left a neighborhood because its racial or ethnic composition was changing, although they may say that other people move for those reasons. So-called white flight from cities or at least from urban schools because of school integration has been a hotly debated issue among sociologists, with some saying that whites leave urban schools when large-scale school desegregation occurs (Coleman, Kelly, and Moore,

1975). Others argue that whites leave even in districts that do not desegregate (Farley, Richards, and Wurdock, 1980). Whites may leave for better housing or more space rather than because of racial integration in the schools.

Whatever the reasons that Americans in general have often viewed life in central cities with distaste, sociologists writing about urban life have sometimes tended to see cities as having a negative effect on the social life of their inhabitants. A number of critical studies of cities were done by American sociologists at the University of Chicago. Many of the ideas found in these studies are distilled in a well-known paper by Louis Wirth (1938) entitled "Urbanism as a Way of Life." Wirth emphasized the size, density, and diversity of urban populations and suggested that they bombard individuals with more stimuli than they can handle. As a result, people escape into an impersonal, unfriendly, and distant style of relating to others.

*Sociologists such as Louis Wirth have suggested that the excessive stimulation of city life drives people into impersonal and unfriendly styles of relating to others. But Wirth overlooked the opportunities cities provide for people to find others like themselves with whom they can form friendships.*

Such defenses, Wirth said, are only partly effective, and people become tense and anxious as a result. City life also leads people to relate to each other only in terms of some specific task or role—as a newspaper vendor, bank teller, dry cleaner, or grocery clerk—rather than as more complete human beings. Most of these roles involve economic relationships, so that rules of the marketplace rather than of friendship and community prevail. This means, according to Wirth, that city dwellers have few true friends who can help them in times of personal need.

City life also promotes highly specialized activities that are distinctly separate. As a result, people belong to many groups, and no single group has the undivided allegiance of the individual. This situation, according to Wirth, weakens primary groups like the family. This weakening results in individual behavior that is less controlled by membership in any single social group and is less predictable. The close concentration of different individuals in cities tends to make them more tolerant of others who think and behave differently from the way they do. By promoting diversity rather than solidarity, cities permit more individual freedom. But that very freedom may lead to a condition of *anomie*, or normlessness, which individuals find very difficult to tolerate.

Different groups may demand conflicting behaviors or values of individuals. One group of friends, for example, may expect an individual to stay out late drinking on a Saturday night, whereas another group may expect to see the same individual ushering at an early church service the next morning. These different and even competing demands may cause individuals to feel inner turmoil. The existence of a wide variety of subgroups may even lead individuals to form bonds with a deviant group that commits illegal acts, suggests Wirth.

Not every sociologist accepts Wirth's description and analysis of urban life. One critic, Herbert Gans (1962a), suggests that Wirth was contrasting urban life with a folk society rather than with rural life in an industrial society. As we saw in Chapter 3, individuals in a folk or tribal society have strong primary bonds with virtually everyone in their group or community. Most individuals are tightly integrated into such societies, and informal social controls operate effectively in such a situation. Even in rural areas of large-scale industrial societies, many of these strong primary-group ties are weakened or broken. Gans goes further and states it is unreasonable to suggest that people behave the way they do because of where they live rather than because of other features of their social life. He argues that there are at least five types of urban residents, each of whom follows a different lifestyle. They do not all behave in the way that Wirth described as typical of city dwellers.

### Urban Populations

The five types of urban residents that Gans (1962a) describes are the cosmopolites, the unmarried or childless, the ethnic villagers, the deprived, and the trapped. The *cosmopolites* are artists, writers, musicians, students, intellectuals, and professionals. They live in the city to be near cultural facilities that only a city can support. Many are unmarried or childless. If they are affluent, they may have children and hire servants or governesses to help with their care. This group normally includes some of the richest and most powerful city residents. The life-style of one cosmopolite segment is vividly depicted in Tom Wolfe's novel *The Bonfire of the Vanities* (1987).

The *unmarried or childless* may be temporarily or permanently in that status. Those who are temporarily alone may come to the city as young adults and share an apartment with friends until they marry and have children. The large numbers in this group—resulting from the postwar baby boom—has led, since Gans wrote, to the coining of a special word for them, "yuppies," which stands for "young urban professionals."

The *ethnic villagers* live in such ethnic enclaves as Little Italy in New York, Chinatown in many cities, and Koreatown in Los Angeles. Their lives center around primary groups such as their families. Except on their jobs, they may have little to do with the life of the city around them. Their lives are very different from those described by Wirth, because they live what resembles a village life set within the borders of large cities. Secondary groups and formal organizations such as political clubs tend to be weak within their communities, and they are suspicious of anything and anyone from outside the neighborhood.

The three groups just discussed are likely to have chosen to live in the city; the final two types described by Gans have no choice. The *deprived* include the very poor, the physically or mentally handicapped, victims of racial prejudice, and people lacking assistance from their families. The *trapped* are unable to move when a neighborhood changes. Many of these people are old and live in rent-controlled or low-rent apartments or in homes purchased many years ago. Most lack the money or the energy to move.

Gans (1962a) suggests that Wirth's characterization of city life as the same for everyone is too simple. Instead, Gans indicates that the social structure and cultural patterns the ethnic villagers bring with them to the city or the cosmopolites develop by living in the city protect individuals from the feeling of not belonging anywhere that Wirth described.

### Social Networks in Cities

A third student of urban life, Claude Fischer (1976), uses features of the work of Gans and Wirth to illuminate the ways in which urbanism influences personal lives. Like Wirth, he believes that population size does affect social life, but in a positive way by creating and strengthening social groups. In a large aggregate of people as found in a city, individuals are more likely to find others like themselves with whom they can form a subculture centered around their special interests. Where else but in a large city could, for example, bassoonists, hot air balloonists, tap

*Cities provide many groups where people can pursue a wide variety of interests. These adults are taking a Japanese cooking course together.*

dancers, Ukrainian nationalists, sadomasochists, and diamond dealers form common groups? Cities provide the numerical and financial base to support such specialization and to allow individuals to form networks with others who share their own special interests. As noted in Chapter 4, a social network is a specific set of relationships among individuals (Fischer et al., 1977). Some of these networks may seem "deviant" in the eyes of other groups, but the diversity of city life enhances the tolerance for networks that differ from one's own.

By bringing together large numbers of people, cities promote the development of specialized occupations. If you repair computers, for example, you must be in a settlement large enough to have people needing your service. So a computer fixer might thrive in a city but not in a village.

Economic and political power tend to be concentrated in urban areas. This was as true of the cities of ancient Egypt or the Rome of the Roman Empire as it is of the investment and banking centers in New York and Zurich, Switzerland, and the political centers of Washington, D.C., or Ottawa, Canada, today. National cities like Paris reveal the political, cultural, and economic concentration of urban life in its most intense form. In France, for example, virtually all cities have a rail link to Paris, but many of those cities have no rail connections with each other. Cultural and political activities are similarly concentrated in the national city.

Because cities concentrate power, people, and other resources, they increase the chances of communication, stimulation, and exchange among city dwellers. Cities bring people into face-to-face contact, enabling them to think, discuss, and act together. Such contact and communication are important for decision making and the exercise of power. Such exposure may lead to further opportunities and may increase the power of the people there. Because of their central locations, urbanites may also have superior communication and transportation links with people in other cities within a country or around the world. Urban centers have always served as the hubs of major transportation networks—first as seaports and rail centers, and now as centers for air transport. Most of the major urban centers around the world are linked by nonstop plane connections.

As a result, cities act as magnets, drawing ambitious and talented people, especially people involved in finance, law, politics, communications, and the arts. Cities are the source of much of a society's "high culture" as well as popular music, records, tapes, movies, books, and big-time sports. Today, with television and other forms of mass media also concentrated in cities, these cultural products are beamed all through a society, reaching even very remote areas.

### Is City Life Alienating?

In further research, Fischer (1981a, 1981b) set out to explain two conflicting sets of findings: one, suggested by Wirth (1938) and others (Karp et al., 1977; Lofland, 1973; Milgram, 1970), that urban life is alienating; and the other, supported by the work of Gans (1962a and 1962b) and others, that it is not alienating. Fischer explains these conflicting sets of findings by distinguishing between the public and private realms of social behavior. The urban alienation thesis is supported by his finding that urban dwellers were somewhat less likely than others to be helpful to a stranger (that is, to let the interviewer inside their homes). This finding was largely explained by their fear of crime. If urban dwellers did let the interviewer in, they were just as likely to be helpful as people in smaller communities. The more urban the community was, the more likely people were to be aware of distinct social groups (such as "old people" or "rich snobs") and of possible tensions between them.

Urban dwellers were no more likely than other people to report feeling upset, nervous, depressed, angry or unhappy unless they felt their neighborhood was unsafe. Furthermore, most urban dwellers were not socially isolated. Instead, they had extensive friendship and kinship networks. Fischer (1981) concludes that urban dwellers have as close ties with family and friends—their private world—as do residents of smaller towns. They are more likely, however, to distrust the inhabitants of the "world of strangers" in their city.

### Urban Crowding and Mental Health

Besides studying the possibly alienating features of urban life, sociologists consider whether the density of what may be called the macroenvironment (that is the number of people per acre) affects people badly. Fischer et al. (1975) conclude that it does not. Density, however, can also be examined at the micro level—for example, in terms of crowding within the home. Interviewing a sample of 2035 people, Gove et al. (1979, pp. 59–80) found that both objective crowding (measured by the number of persons per room) and the subjective sense of being crowded (indicated by feelings that social demands are excessive and that there is a lack of privacy) were strongly related to poor mental health, poor social relationships in the home, poor child care, and poor physical health. Crowding in the home was a more important factor in mental health than the combined effects of gender, race, education, income, age, and marital status. The more specific conclusions of Gove et al. were:

1. The higher the number of persons per room in the home, the greater the social demands and the more people felt they had no privacy.
2. Crowding leads to physical withdrawal, psychological withdrawal, a lack of effective planning, and a general feeling of being "washed out."
3. People in crowded homes had more mental health problems than those in less crowded homes.
4. They also had more family fights, and husbands and wives were less satisfied with their marriages.
5. People in crowded homes were relieved when their children were out of the home; they knew less about their children's activities and their children lacked a place to study. In these ways crowding hurt the quality of child care.
6. People in more crowded homes had more physical problems because they got less sleep, caught more diseases, were unable to get a good rest when sick, and had chores to do even when they were sick (Gove et al., 1979, p. 78).

## Suburban Life

Suburbs look different from most central cities. They have fewer high-rise buildings; they are less densely built and populated; they usually have more lawns, trees, and flowers and many more single-family and free-standing houses. There are fewer apartment buildings in suburbs than in central cities, although there may be some. The suburb is not unique, however. Outer urban areas often resemble suburbs with their lawns, patios, driveways, and less dense housing.

### Types of Suburbs

Suburbs vary considerably according to the social class, race, and even religion of their residents (Fernandez et al., 1982; Muller, 1981). Muller identified four major types of mainly white suburbs: the exclusive upper-income suburb, the middle-class family suburb, working-class suburbs, and suburban cosmopolitan centers.

*Exclusive upper-income suburbs*—such as Grosse Pointe, Michigan; Beverly Hills, California; Middleburg, Virginia; or Old Greenwich, Connecticut—are characterized by large homes built on spacious grounds screened by huge old trees and situated near elegant private schools, established churches, and exclusive country clubs. Newcomers are screened first for their financial and social traits by real estate brokers. If they are able to move in, their social credentials are screened by long-time residents before they are admitted to social clubs and networks.

Traditional organizations are less important in such *middle-class family suburbs* as Levittown, Long Island; Balboa Park, California; and Skokie, Illinois. Many of the families expect to live there only a short time as they pursue their aspirations for better jobs and homes. Much of their social contact focuses on family-oriented organizations such as the PTA, Little League, or Scouts. The other social networks of these families extend well beyond the borders of their suburban town, and most social activity occurs outside the local neighborhood (Michelson, 1976). These "communities of limited liability" require only minimal involvement with local affairs (see Suttles, 1972, pp. 44–81).

*Working-class suburbs*—such as Union City, New Jersey; Cicero, Illinois; and Milpitas, California—have steadily multiplied since 1945. Especially when these communities are ethnically homogeneous, their social life centers around churches, bingo parlors, taverns, street corners, or front stoops. Residents value having neighbors like themselves and easy social relationships

*Working-class and middle-income neighborhoods, such as this one in Jersey City, New Jersey, are often stable and relatively permanent.*

among people who know each other well (Michelson, 1976; Rainwater, 1966). Working-class suburbanites see little possibility for social or geographical mobility, so they see their present homes and communities as relatively permanent (Berger, 1971).

*Suburban cosmopolitan centers*—such as Ann Arbor, Michigan; Boulder, Colorado; Stanford, California; or Princeton, New Jersey—provide many of the cultural attractions of urban life, including universities, industrial research parks, theater, music, and arts facilities. The fine restaurants that appeal to cosmopolitans in the cities—as well as such suburban attractions as larger homes, yards, and space for sports—can also be found.

People who live in the suburbs—as opposed to cities—are more likely to be married couples between the ages of 30 and 50 with children and less likely to be single, divorced, or retired persons. They are also likely to be more homogeneous with respect to race, occupation, education, income, recreational activities, and perhaps with respect to social and political views as compared to city dwellers. As a general rule, then, suburbs tend to bring together people who share many social and behavioral traits and to do this in smaller and somewhat more self-contained social communities. These differences between urban and suburban dwellers are intensified among higher-status residents. Educated suburbanites are much more likely than educated urban dwellers to own a house, have children, or be housewives (if they are women) as well as to live in an economically and racially homogeneous neighborhood (Fischer and Jackson, 1977).

### How Suburban Living Affects People

Suburbanites are more locally oriented than city dwellers. This means that in their leisure activities, suburbanites tend to be more involved in home pursuits, such as gardening and entertaining. People living in town tend to go out more often to theaters and museums. Suburbanites also talk more frequently on a casual basis with their neighbors, visit in one another's homes, and participate in neighborhood organizations (Lopata, 1972). Finally, suburbanites are more likely to draw their friends from among their neighbors than are urban dwellers (Fischer et al., 1977). These features are considered indicators of *localism,* or interest in one's neighbors.

Differences between urban and suburban residents remain when such personal characteristics as having children, social class, employment status of women in the household, and years of residence are controlled (Fischer and Jackson, 1977). If these differences do not seem to be due to personal factors, what is it about suburbs that might encourage localism? Both single-family homes and compatible neighbors appear to encourage the greater localism of suburbanites. Homeowners spend more time around their homes than apartment dwellers do, which may lead to greater localism. Being around other people who are locally oriented seems to encourage people who move to the suburbs to become more involved locally and even to act together—for example, by forming a neighborhood association (Fischer and Jackson, 1977).

### How Suburbs Affect Special Populations

Immobile or special populations appear to be more isolated in suburbs than their neighbors or people like them who live in cities (Abu-Lughod and Foley, 1960; Gans, 1967; Tomeh, 1964). Considerable research has been done on this issue with respect to women, the aged, and minorities, three groups that may face isolation in the suburbs.

**SUBURBS AND WOMEN.** Suburbs affect women and men differently (Fava, 1978). Wives are more likely than their husbands to feel isolated from relatives and friends. Quite often they can overcome their feelings of isolation by becoming socially involved with their neighbors, but if they do not find compatible neighbors, they may be lonely (Fava, 1975; Fischer et al., 1977).

The growth of suburbs after World War II paralleled the return of women to full-time domesticity. Some might argue that such a result was another instance of what Rose Coser calls using physical space to regulate social relations (1975). The geographic dispersion and low population density of suburban areas seem designed to support the role of full-time housewife and mother for women. Because of time and travel costs, suburban life makes it more difficult for women to form support groups, find stimulating activities, and get rewarding jobs. The extensive needs of the home, yard, and cars; dispersed shopping; and the chauffeuring of children to various activities all make it more difficult for women in the suburbs to be anything but housewives and mothers. It is no accident that the return of many wives and mothers to the labor force has coincided with the resettlement of many urban areas.

**SUBURBS AND THE AGED.** By 1980, for the first time in American history, more people over the age of 65 lived in suburban areas (10.1 million) than in central cities (8.1 million) (Fitzpatrick and Logan, 1985, p. 106). One result of this trend has been that segregation of the elderly has been declining, largely because suburban residents are "aging in place"; that is, they are unlikely to move because there are few places where they can live as cheaply (Golant, 1978; Palmore and Whittington, 1971). One exception is certain southern suburbs, where age segregation increased, probably because of the migration of older persons to the area. Although the majority of communities with high proportions of elderly residents have lower home values and more moderate rents than suburbs with younger residents, there are some suburbs with many elderly residents that have the highest home values and rents, suggesting that some elderly suburbanites are able to afford high-cost

housing even though their current incomes are low (Fitzpatrick and Logan, 1985).

A consequence of declining segregation of the elderly in northern suburbs is that the need for special social services for the elderly (such as home health aides, hot meal programs, or transportation) is spread more thinly across a wider range of communities. Although this may help to disperse the economic costs, it may reduce the political power of elderly constituencies in any one community (Logan, 1984).

A social consequence of the aging in place of suburban residents is that fewer suburban houses are on the market, keeping house prices high and making it very difficult for young families with children to afford them. Many suburban communities have closed some of their schools because the number of children has dropped so sharply. The suburbs may offer the elderly more physical safety from crime, but automobile transportation—a necessity in most suburbs—becomes increasingly difficult for many of the elderly to manage, as does home maintenance. Many communities are devising ways to help older residents and attract more younger persons. Some have changed their zoning to permit "accessory apartments" in single-family homes, thus providing the elderly with needed income. Others help arrange home-sharing by unrelated individuals so that older homeowners can trade unneeded empty rooms for needed maintenance work (Lublin, 1984, p. 1).

*Suburban living becomes increasingly difficult as people age. Driving and home maintenance may become problems for the elderly.*

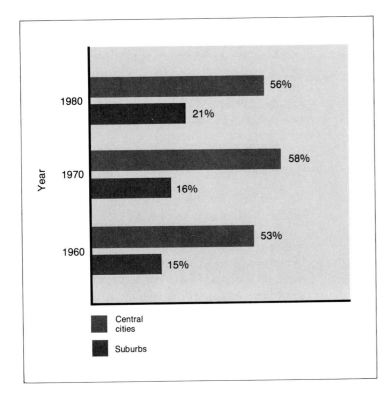

**Figure 20.8  Percentage of Blacks Who Live in Central Cities and Suburbs, 1960–1980.**

The percentage of blacks who live in suburbs increased slowly but steadily from 15 percent in 1960 to 21 percent in 1980.

*Source:* Long and DeAre, 1981, p. 19.

The financial and physical problems of the elderly make them relatively immobile. Several studies have found that the farther from the center of town elderly people lived, the fewer friends they had, the less socially active they were, and the lonelier they said they were (Bourg, 1975; Cantor, 1975; Carp, 1975).

**SUBURBS AND MINORITIES.** Besides having some negative features for women and the elderly, suburbs also affect minorities and whites differently. Traditionally, blacks were largely excluded from the suburbs by real estate covenants, although that picture has begun to change somewhat in the last decade. As shown in Figure 20.8, the 1980 Census revealed that the percentage of blacks living in central cities declined for the first time in many decades, whereas the percentage of blacks living in the suburbs increased from 15 percent in 1960 to 21 percent in 1980 (Long and DeAre, 1981). The proportion of Hispanics living in suburbs is also up, to 37 percent in 1980 (Herbers, 1981a).

The suburban black population increase of the 1970s is not evenly distributed throughout all suburbs, however (Logan and Schneider, 1984). Blacks are moving to suburban communities where blacks already live and where whites are moving away. The result is that many suburbs are increasingly being divided along racial lines, rather than being integrated (Lake, 1981, pp. 239–240), although in the South some black suburbs lost black residents (Logan and Schneider, 1984). Race influences where blacks live, with whom they are likely to associate socially once there, and how much the value of their homes will increase (Lake, 1981, p. 239). Blacks are more likely to move to more crowded suburbs, which are closer to the central city, have more residential instability, a weak tax base, and high tax rates (Logan and Schneider, 1984). Logan and Schneider conclude that there is a continuing pattern of segregation and inequality in black suburbanization.

## Rural Life

People in small towns or rural areas tend to be more like their neighbors in their ethnic, religious, and social backgrounds than are many urban dwellers. As a result, they know more about each other and they often share common values. They are more likely to experience the close, *gemeinshaft* relationships described in Chapter 3 and are usually neighborly, friendly, and helpful to the people in their communities. In many small towns and farms today people still leave their doors and windows unlocked except perhaps when they go on vacation.

On the other hand, they are more likely than urban dwellers to be narrow-minded and intolerant of people who are different from themselves (Wilson, 1985). Atheists, gays, pacifists, communists, or others who hold different values from their own may be shunned or persecuted. The names of people getting tickets for speeding or drunk-driving are published in some small-town newspapers, and in general, people know much more about the lives and businesses of their neighbors than is true in urban or even some suburban areas.

Rural social norms and mores are gradually changing as a result of changes in the wider society (see Vidich and Bensman, 1958). The social isolation of the farms and small towns of America has been pierced forever by radio, the interstate highway system, television (especially satellite TV today), movies, records, and tapes, in short, by rural exposure to the people and culture of mass society.

## Summary

1. Land use highlights the clash between the desire for economic gain and other social values.

2. Urbanization represents one of the biggest changes in the way human society has been organized over time. A city is a large, long-term settlement of people who do not produce their own food.

3. The first cities arose in favorable agricultural and trading centers. The rise of cities is accompanied by an increasingly complex system of social organization and control.

4. In the United States, urbanization continued to spread after 1850 up until the 1970s, when small towns and rural areas began to grow faster than urban areas for the first time.

5. Sociologists offer two major paradigms for explaining how urban areas develop—the

ecological paradigm and the political economy paradigm. Within the ecological paradigm, the concentric zone theory suggests that cities grow out from their center like the rings of a tree trunk. The sector theory indicates that cities grow in specialized districts following transportation systems. The multiple-nuclei theory recognizes that not all cities have a single center. Instead, there may be various nuclei, depending on the function being served.

6. Within the political economy paradigm, Gordon suggests that cities develop according to the stage of economic production they are in when they do most of their growing. Commercial, industrial, and corporate cities each take different forms. The political economy paradigm may be extended to include the global political economy as a factor in the growth or decline of particular cities.

7. Although ecological and structural processes are very important, so are the social and symbolic meanings that people bring to neighborhood life and culture.

8. Suburban and rural development, as well as urban development, can be analyzed with the ecological and political economy paradigms.

9. Ecology focuses on our social and physical environment in the broadest sense. Simple tribal societies tend to accept nature as they find it; Western industrializers view nature as something to be dominated and changed. Ecologists suggest that all organisms on earth are interdependent, that nature knows best, and that everything taken from nature has some cost.

10. Two major ecological problems are pollution of air, water, and earth and depletion of key natural resources.

11. A political economy perspective suggests the existence of links between private economic interests and political decision makers, technological decisions, and the handling of toxic wastes.

12. The city has been viewed negatively in American culture. Wirth felt that cities produced distant, impersonal, and unfriendly personal re-

lationships. Gans challenged Wirth's view and suggested there were at least five types of urban life-styles: cosmopolites, the childless and single, the ethnic villagers, the deprived, and the trapped. Fischer feels that urban life creates and strengthens social networks, which in turn enrich the lives of urban residents.

13. Fischer found that urban dwellers divided their social worlds into a private social world of friends and kin with whom they had close relationships, and a "world of strangers" whom they kept at a distance.

14. Gove and his associates studied the effects of crowding within the home and found many negative personal and social consequences of crowding.

15. Suburban life is quite varied and includes exclusive upper-income suburbs, middle-class family suburbs, working-class suburbs, and suburban cosmopolitan centers.

16. Suburban residents are more homogeneous than urban dwellers with respect to race, occupation, education, income, and recreational activities. They are also more likely to socialize with their neighbors than are city residents.

17. The physical setting of suburbs seems to influence women, whose social and occupational opportunities may be limited by the low density of suburbs, and the elderly, who may not be able to drive or to find compact housing.

18. Minorities have begun moving to suburbs in greater numbers in the past decade, but a continuing pattern of segregation and inequality lies beneath this trend.

19. Rural life is often more neighborly, but also more intolerant of social variations. Rural isolation has been changed forever by the interstate highway and other transportation systems and by the mass media.

## KEY TERMS

city (p. 513)
community (p. 512)

concentric zone theory (p. 516)
Consolidated Metropolitan Statistical Area (CMSA) (p. 514)
ecological paradigm (p. 516)
ecological succession (p. 516)
ecology (p. 526)
ecosystem (p. 526)
gentrification (p. 518)
Metropolitan Statistical Area (MSA) (p. 514)
multiple-nuclei theory (p. 518)
political economy model (p. 519)
sector theory (p. 516)
suburb (p. 524)
Sunbelt (p. 520)
urbanization (p. 513)

## SUGGESTED READINGS

Fainstein, Norman I., and Susan S. Fainstein. 1982. "Urban policy under capitalism." *Urban Affairs Annual Reviews* 22. Beverly Hills, CA: Sage. A clear statement of the political economy in urban development.

Feagin, Joe R. 1985. "The global context of metropolitan growth: Houston and the oil industry." *American Journal of Sociology* 90: 1204–1230. A study of the city of Houston, showing how its rise and fall can best be understood in the context of an international political economy.

Fischer, Claude S. 1981. *To Dwell Among Friends: Personal Networks in Town and City.* Chicago: University of Chicago Press. Undercuts the "urban alienation" theory somewhat by exploring the social networks that urban dwellers have.

Levine, Adeline Gordon. 1982. *Love Canal.* Lexington, MA: Lexington Books. An exemplary sociological case study, this book chronicles the efforts of citizens living in the Love Canal area of Niagara Falls to secure the resources they needed to escape homes poisoned by chemical wastes.

Whyte, William H. 1980. *The Social Life of Small Urban Spaces.* Washington, DC: The Conservation Foundation. An excellent example of applied sociology, showing how people use open spaces in New York City and the resulting new city codes for the use of open space.

# 21 *Sex and Sexuality*

*Most pro-lifers think that people, regardless of their station in life, ought to be chaste—this means chaste also for married people. . . . I think this is because [pro-lifers], much more than pro-abortion people, are in reverence of sexuality and believe it literally to be a sacred thing. . . . [But] if you do think this way, [sex] is something very special, it's the means by which two people can express their union with one another, spiritual and physical. [Luker, 1984, p. 164]*

*Pro-choice people believe that sexual activity is good as an end in itself. For much of a lifetime at least, its main purpose is not to produce children (or to remind them of that possibility) but to afford pleasure, human contact, and, perhaps most important, intimacy. Whereas for pro-life people sex is inherently transcendent— because a new life may be created at any time—for pro-choice people, it is potentially transcendent, and its spiritual meaning is a goal to be pursued rather than a fact to be faced. Despite the claims of some pro-life people, pro-choice people do believe that sex can be sacred, but it is a different kind of sacredness that they have in mind. For them, sex is sacred when it is mystical, when it dissolves the boundaries between self and other, when it brings one closer to one's partner, and when it gives one a sense of the infinite. [Luker, 1984, p. 178]*

As these views of individuals who are pro-life and pro-choice in the abortion controversy show, there were major differences in the way people in the United States in the 1980s viewed sex and sexuality. These differences were deeply rooted in differing religious and moral values and in conflicting world views. Sexuality is a focal point for major social differences and conflicts.

Sexuality is a term that encompasses biological reproduction; sexual gratification; and the values, feelings, and human relationships that surround those processes. Sexuality is very important to individuals, since the biological drive that develops with maturity is a strong one. Sexuality is tied in with people's personalities, their images of themselves, and their responses to others. Sexual feelings, fantasies, and behaviors occupy large spaces in people's personal and leisure lives. Relationships with others may be highly charged with sexual overtones. Even when a person is trying to do something else— perhaps study in the library—sexual feelings and thoughts may creep into awareness.

Individuals are not left to decide on their own how they will express their sexuality. Instead, all societies actively regulate, direct, and shape the sexuality of their members. Society sets limits on when, how, and with whom sexual relations can occur. The social aspects of sexuality are at least as important as the biological ones. Sexuality finds expression through and is shaped by social relationships. Sexuality involves erotic needs and attachments, emotional needs and involvements, and sexual behavior, all of which find expression through, are shaped by, or are frustrated by social relationships.

Even the biological expression of sexual behavior is influenced by social relationships and cultural values and norms. The forms and sources of sexual gratification, the meanings given to various kinds of sexual relationships, and the significance and desirability of sex are shaped by the customs and meanings of the culture or subculture to which an individual belongs and by the way those cultural features interact with an individual's particular social experiences. Sexual behavior may involve physiological release, emotional relationships and satisfactions, reproduction, and economic exchange. At some times and in some settings it may have political or religious overtones as well.

Sexual expression has been widely institutionalized within marriage. In most societies, marriage includes the sexual union of husband and wife with the full blessing and support of religious and political institutions. This sexual and social bond forms the bedrock on which the institution of the family is built, and the family is the basic unit of all societies. Most families seek to create the next generation, produce legitimate heirs, and provide care and socialization for the young. Further, families desire to pass on the family name and other ascribed characteristics such as nationality, and to transmit whatever property the family owns from one generation to the next. Since a sexual relationship underlies this vital institution, it is not surprising that society takes such a deep interest in the sexual activities of individual members.

## SOCIAL ASPECTS OF HUMAN SEXUALITY

Although a biological sex drive appears to be innate in humans, sexual feelings and behaviors are socially learned. Society defines for us what it considers to be normal and acceptable with respect to sexuality. Its definitions and rules vary over time, by place, and with changes in political and social power. Chapter 3 noted how the rules governing sexual behavior in restrictive

and permissive societies differ. Yet the influence of society and culture extends beyond such rules, to the point of coloring what we consider to be sexually attractive or stimulating and our capacity to express our sexuality.

The social molding of sexual expression is apparent in the reports on children raised in extreme isolation. They tend to masturbate a great deal, suggesting that they did not learn how to express their sexuality through interactions with other people. The social nature of sexuality is visible in the way sexual practices and feelings vary across cultures and over time within the same culture. Every child is taught about sex, whether directly or indirectly, but each culture teaches different lessons. It is the social patterning of sexuality that makes sex a concern of sociological inquiry.

### Sexuality Throughout the World

Much of what is known about sexuality in other societies throughout the world is based on Ford and Beach's (1951) extensive review of anthropological reports of 190 societies whose locations range from the edge of the Arctic Circle to the southern tip of Australia. Their work showed them, for example, that physical appearance is an important aspect of sexual attractiveness in all societies. Male attractiveness, however, tends to be based more on the man's skills and prowess than on his facial appearance, whereas physical beauty seems to be a more important consideration in female attractiveness in most societies. The idea of physical beauty varies widely, however. More cultures consider a plump woman more attractive than a slim one, and many prefer women with a broad pelvis and wide hips. In a few cultures, breasts are important criteria of sexual attractiveness, but while small, upright breasts are preferred in some places, long, pendulous ones are favored in others. The shape of the nose, mouth, eyes, or ears may be particularly important in determining sexual attractiveness in different cultures. In addition, personal cleanliness is stressed as a necessary element of attractiveness in many cultures, as is youthfulness.

Once an attractive partner has been found, cultures teach widely differing ways to stimulate

*The idea of physical beauty varies from one society to another. Here a Japanese woman prepares for her wedding in Nagoya, Japan (left), a young man in Egypt smiles for the camera, and two young Fulani women from noble families gather along the Niger River in Mali. In each case they have adorned themselves in ways considered attractive by their culture, but the results are quite different.*

that person sexually. In many societies, kissing precedes and accompanies sexual intercourse. But among some peoples, kissing appears to be unknown, as in the case with the Siriono of Eastern Bolivia. Among the Tinguian people of the Philippine Islands, lovers place their lips near their partner's face and then suddenly inhale.

In general, cultures differ greatly with respect to the amount and kinds of sexual foreplay practiced. Even within some cultures, such as ours, couples vary greatly in their use of foreplay. Some engage in extensive genital stimulation prior to intercourse, whereas others move immediately to coitus itself.

Handling, stroking, and rubbing one's partner's genitals is practiced in many cultures, with both manual and oral stimulation widely used. Such contact is forbidden in a few cultures such as the Tikopia, on a Pacific island east of the Solomons, and the Wogeo, off New Guinea. In some societies, sexual excitement is expressed or enhanced by scratching, biting, hair-pulling, and other behaviors that cause pain. Bruises or red marks may be signs of sexual status or may arouse jest among one's peers in certain cultures, such as the Toda of India. In other cultures, there is no association of pain with sexual arousal and satisfaction. In such cultures the ex-

perience of pain in a sexual context detracts from sexual activity and enjoyment.

Humans in a wide variety of cultures seem to prefer privacy for sexual intercourse. In some societies, suitable privacy is found indoors, so that is where sexual behavior occurs. In others, dwellings are crowded places, and couples prefer finding a secluded outdoor spot. Some peoples, including such Native American tribes as the Kwakiutl, Hopi, and the Crow, consider night and darkness to be the only proper time for sexual relations. Where there is no cultural proscription, either night or day may be chosen. Some peoples, such as the Rucuyen, in the mountains of Brazil, and the Yapese, in the Caroline Islands in the Pacific, have a definite preference for daylight, and the Chenchu of India believe that children conceived in the dark will be blind.

Many cultures place limitations on when intercourse can occur, even within marriage. Menstruating, pregnant, or lactating women are not considered appropriate sexual partners among a number of peoples. In some cultures, anyone who is ill is forbidden to have intercourse, and sometimes, as with the Chewa of Central Africa, this prohibition extends to all the relatives of a sick person. In many cultures, widows are expected to abstain from sexual relationships far longer than widowers. Religious celebrations may be accompanied by sexual restraints. Hunting, gardening, and warfare are sometimes surrounded with sexual taboos at certain critical times. Some coaches still urge players to abstain from sexual relations for a day or two before big games, in the belief that sexual denial will sharpen their prowess on the field.

Relatively few social customs restrict marital coitus in the United States. Frequency of sexual relations may be determined by the desire, health, and availability of both partners. However, although there are relatively few customs applying to all social groups in industrial societies, some customs and practices have been found to vary by social class and educational levels. Lower- and working-class partners are more likely to prefer having intercourse with the lights off, whereas upper-middle and upper-class couples prefer some illumination in the room. How much clothing people wear while engaged in sexual activities also seems to vary by social class, with higher-class couples in general preferring more nudity than lower-class couples.

Similarly, oral genital sexual stimulation appears to vary with the educational level of couples, with more educated persons more likely to report experiencing or performing such behaviors than less educated ones (Hunt, 1974).

## Sexuality in Western Societies

Attitudes toward sexuality have changed dramatically over the last several hundred years, moving from the view of sex as sin to sex as acceptable pleasure and everywhere in between. Whenever major changes in attitudes occur, it is likely that some groups will retain the values of an earlier era. This is clearly the case today with respect to sexuality.

### Sex and Religion

Since its early years, the Christian church tried to control sexual behavior. Christianity, along with a number of other religions, tended to divide the world into the godly, spiritual portion and the carnal, material world. This division was captured by the struggle between the spirit that aspired to escape the world and the flesh that was bound to the world. Sex epitomized the flesh and was thus considered the enemy of the spirit. The Mosaic law is a clear instance of the way both Judaism and Christianity attempted to regulate sexuality by injecting sex with a strong moral dimension. Six of the Ten Commandments, for example, deal with human relationships, and two of these address sex directly ("Thou shalt not commit adultery" and "Thou shalt not covet thy neighbor's wife"). These commandments firmly forbid extramarital relationships.

Christian teachings did not stop there. Even within marriage, sex was often viewed as an unfortunate necessity for reproduction but not as a pleasure to be enjoyed. Sex as basically a sinful activity is reflected in St. Paul's statement that it was "better to marry than to burn." By saying this, he was indicating that sexual activity outside of marriage was grounds for eternal damnation, so it was better to get married in order to avoid hellfire. He felt that it was better still to remain celibate, if possible.

For centuries, the official Christian doctrine on sex was that it was a necessary evil, to be permitted for purposes of procreation within marriage but not an experience to be celebrated or enjoyed for its own sake. In the early centuries of Christianity, women were viewed as spiritually weak creatures, quick to yield to fleshly impulses. Much of the blame for sexual weakness was placed on women. Like Eve, women were cast as evil temptresses who seduced men to sin.

Even in the nineteenth century, reproduction was the major legitimate purpose of sex for Christians, although religious support for this purpose was sometimes supplemented by appeals for the need to increase the population of the nation, society, or species (Rosow and Persell, 1980). A different view of women and sexuality gradually emerged. Increasingly women were portrayed as essentially without sexual feelings.

Changes in sexual values and practices in recent years have not gone unnoticed by religious authorities. Today there is less unity among religious leaders over issues of sexuality than there was in the past. Some leaders reaffirm traditional values, whereas others seek to open themselves to new directions. In 1976 the Vatican issued its "Declaration on Certain Questions Concerning Sexual Ethics," which reaffirmed traditional teachings condemning premarital sex, homosexuality, and masturbation. In 1980 the Fifth World Synod of Roman Catholic Bishops issued "A Message to Christian Families in the Modern World," in which the bishops vehemently opposed contraception, sterilization, abortion, and euthanasia and reaffirmed that the bond of marriage must be both permanent and indissoluble (*New York Times,* October 26, 1980, p. 18). In both these statements the church continues to uphold a view of sexuality and marriage as religiously imbued and subject to religious authority.

A somewhat different perspective was presented in 1977, when the Catholic Theological Society of America published a book entitled *Human Sexuality.* In it, theologians suggested the need for pastoral guidelines that emphasize the goodness and sacredness of human sexuality as a creative and integrative force. They seem to be suggesting that sexuality can be a positive force in individual lives and can encourage the building of good relationships between people. The differences between the two schools of thought is evident in their treatment of masturbation. In 1976 the Vatican declared "masturbation is an intrinsically and serious disordered act." In contrast, the American theologians stressed the complex meaning of masturbation and deplored extreme views that either condemned it as immoral or treated it very casually, thereby failing to do justice to its complex nature and significance.

Religious authorities face the difficulty of maintaining moral leadership over a diverse body of members. These competing positions indicate that some leaders are trying to be the source of norms and values even in the face of challenges from their members and others are responding to the changing norms, values, and behaviors of their members.

### Sex as Recreation

The recommendations of religious leaders no doubt reflect a trend that has been noted by such sociologists as John Gagnon (1977). He suggests that as our society has moved from a religious to an individual justification for much of what

we do, there has been a movement away from the social justifications of sexual conduct to more personal ones. He believes that sexuality has come increasingly to be defined in terms of individual desires and preferences. As a result, the importance of sexuality as love, play, and joy has received more emphasis. (Witness the popularity of the book *The Joy of Sex* by Alex Comfort.) The purpose of sexuality in our society now, Gagnon suggests, is essentially recreation rather than procreation. This shift is evident in the 1985 Gallup poll that found, for the first time in the nearly two decades that the question has been asked, that more than half of American adults consider premarital sex acceptable (Belkin, 1985). This trend has encouraged greater tolerance of birth control, abortion, premarital sexual relationships, and homosexuality.

### Sex and the Law

Religion generally endorsed customs and laws governing sexuality. Some religious views were gradually incorporated into state codes. The Napoleonic Code broke with some religious traditions and permitted somewhat greater sexual tolerance than earlier laws. Laws against homosexual behavior between consenting adults in private, for example, were dropped. No such break occurred in English and American sex laws. Most sex laws differ from other laws in that they are aimed directly at maintaining morality rather than at preserving and protecting individual or property rights.

Some sex laws do seek to protect individuals; they deal with the notion of consent in sexual relations. Individuals who are deemed unable to give consent—including minors, mental retardates, and the insane—are legally protected. This means that the law assumes they are unable to give consent in a legally binding way because they are under age or mentally incompetent and are considered to lack the right or the ability to give such consent. There is considerable consensus in many societies against sexual conduct involving force and violence and against the sexual exploitation of children. Beyond that, there is less agreement about what the law should or should not prohibit (MacNamara and Sagarin, 1977).

Despite the lack of consensus about how the law should regulate sexual behavior, another kind of sex law aims at preventing offense to public sensibilities. Laws, for example, prohibit public sexual actions, exhibitionism, and offensive sexual solicitations. Other sex laws seek to maintain sexual morality as defined by state legislators. The United States, in sharp contrast to western Europe, has extensive laws relating to sexual conduct and morality.

Laws in some states in the United States prohibit homosexuality, **prostitution** (the selling of sexual favors), incest, and intercourse with animals. Laws that attempt to maintain morality are extremely difficult to enforce, particularly when the behavior being legislated occurs in the privacy of a person's home.

### Rape

Rape is a crime of violence. In most penal codes, **rape** is defined as a completed sexual assault by a male upon a female (MacNamara and Sagarin, 1977), although males may also rape other males, as has often occurred within the U.S. prison system (Davis, 1970). Rape represents "a sexual invasion of the body by force, an incursion into the private, personal inner space without consent—in short, an internal assault from one of several avenues and by one of several methods [that] constitutes a deliberate violation of emotional, physical and rational integrity . . ." (Brownmiller, 1975, p. 422).

Rape is a particularly repugnant crime because it may use an organ of sexual intimacy as a weapon to inflict injury and degradation on another person. Although it is a terrible thing to be stabbed or shot, knives or guns are not used on other occasions as instruments of lovemaking. As a result, someone who is raped is not only injured (and quite often killed as well) but also traumatized. In many cultures the victim of rape is also shamed. The defilement is used to stigmatize—a classic instance of blaming the victim. Even if the culture does not stigmatize someone for being raped, the victim has to shed the terrible memories of being violated and hurt.

Sociologists have tried to understand the causes of rape, its frequency, how society reacts to it, and its consequences. Not all modern societies have such high rates of rape. The United States is among the most rape-prone of all (Scully and Marolla, 1985). In 1980 the U.S. rate was eighteen times higher than that of En-

gland and Wales (West, 1983). Rape may be viewed as an act of violence and social control serving to "keep women in their place" (Scully and Marolla, 1985). Males learn to associate power, dominance, strength, virility, and superiority with masculinity; conversely, they tend to associate submissiveness, passivity, weakness, and inferiority with femininity (Scully and Marolla, 1985). This cultural context may be seen as a predisposing factor to rape. In a culture seemingly prone to rape, what do rapists gain from sexual aggression and violence? To address this question, Scully and Marolla interviewed 114 convicted, imprisoned rapists. They found

*. . . that some men used rape for revenge or punishment while, for others, it was an "added bonus" . . . while committing another crime. In still other cases, rape was used to gain sexual access to women who were unwilling or unavailable, and for some it was a source of power and sex without any personal feelings. Rape was also a form of recreation, a diversion or an adventure and, finally, it was something that made these men "feel good." [Scully and Marolla, 1985, p. 254]*

While some rapists may be psychologically disturbed, it is not necessary to use pathological motives to explain rape. Instead, rape can be viewed as an extreme example of more general sexual aggression that rewards men and victimizes women. Most of the rapists interviewed did not expect to go to prison. They saw rape as a rewarding, low-risk act (Scully and Marolla, 1985).

Differences in the rates of rape in different states in the United States are related to gender inequality, social disorganization, the circulation of pornography, economic inequality, and percent unemployed (Baron and Straus, 1987). Campus gang rapes also appear to be increasing (Brozan, 1986).

Research has helped to explain why some men in the United States commit rape. A macro-level study comparing societies found that societies with more exploitative modes of production produce greater sexual inequality and sexual violence (Schwendinger and Schwendinger, 1983).

In another paper, Scully and Marolla explore the justifications and excuses convicted rapists use to explain themselves and their crimes (1984). They found five themes running through the accounts rapists gave in an attempt to deny their rapes. These were: (1) "women as seductresses" who lured them into sexual action; (2) "women mean 'yes' when they say 'no,'" (3) "most women eventually relax and enjoy it," (4) "nice girls don't get raped," and (5) "I was only a little bit wrong"; for example, "I'm guilty of sex and contributing to the delinquency of a minor, but not rape" (p. 537). These accounts overlooked the use of a knife or other weapon by assailants and denied the existence of a victim. Scully and Marolla stress that deniers "did not invent these justifications" (1984, p. 542). Instead, they reflect a belief system that victimizes women with myths that women enjoy and help cause their own rapes. Therefore, understanding the causes of rape behavior requires us to examine the cultural contexts within which individual actions occur.

Other convicted rapists admitted they were guilty and that rape was a repulsive crime. They offered excuses to show that there was no intent or that their responsibility was impaired. Some said they were under the influence of drugs or alcohol. Others said they had emotional problems that led them to commit rape. They used these excuses to try to negotiate a new moral identity for themselves. They expressed regret and sorrow for their victims and sometimes apologized repeatedly. In this way they tried to present an image of themselves as "nice guys." They admitted guilt while suggesting that what they did should not be considered an indication of what they were really like (Scully and Marolla, 1984).

The rate of forcible rape cases reported to the police increased steadily between 1967 and 1980, declined slightly from 1981 to 1983, increased 5.9 percent from 1983 to 1986, and declined in 1987 (see Figure 21.1). It is impossible to tell the degree to which these changes are due to the willingness of victims to report what has happened to them and how much is due to changes in the number of rapes committed. Forcible rape is probably "the most underreported crime" (McGarrell and Flanagan, 1985).

What constitutes force is a debatable issue in our society. Is someone like an employer, professor or doctor who uses his position of authority to sway a woman to have intercourse with him using force? Is a male who forcibly undresses a woman on a date and makes her submit to sexual intercourse committing forcible rape? Since some women are taught to "play hard to get" even when they are willing to have intercourse with a man and some men are taught to be insistent in pushing themselves on a woman, there is room for ambiguity and misunderstanding in such a situation.

There are some similarities in the way societies react to rape and some differences over time. Rape is a legal crime in all modern European and American countries and is widely banned in preindustrial societies as well (Brown, 1952; Schwendinger and Schwendinger, 1983). As recently as two decades ago in the United States, male police officers, judges, and juries would doubt a rape victim's claims. One study found that juries were less likely to convict accused rapists than were judges (Kalven and Zeisel, 1966). It was not unusual for a victim to be cross-examined by the defense attorney for the

*Rape rates are higher in the United States than in many other societies, perhaps reflecting attempts to put women down. Here college students seek to educate each other about ways to prevent rape.*

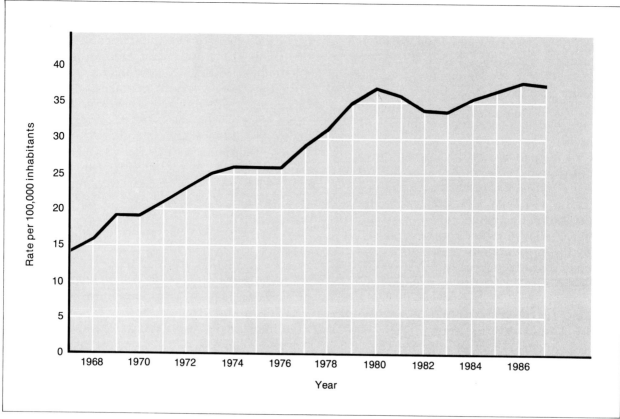

**Figure 21.1   Rate of Forcible Rape per 100,000 Inhabitants in the U.S., 1967–1987.**

The rate of forcible rape generally increased between 1967 and 1987.

*Source:* U.S. Bureau of the Census, 1980, p. 182; 1981a, p. 174; 1985a, p. 166; 1989a, p. 169.

alleged rapist, who might try to argue that the victim was a prostitute or did something to encourage the rapist.

While a rape trial can still be traumatic for a victim, feminists' efforts have brought reforms into the handling of rape complaints by the police. The percentage of convicted rapists who are sent to prison is higher than for that of persons convicted of aggravated assault, and the sentences are on the average longer (Greenberg, 1988a). This also represents some change from the recent past, when rape convictions were difficult to obtain.

### Incest

Most societies have taboos against incest. This does not mean that it never happens. Like rape, incest was also nearly taboo as a subject of schol-

arly investigation until quite recently. While clinical cases were reported and discussed, few studies based on systematic probability samples were done. Perhaps the first was *The Secret Trauma: Incest in the Lives of Girls and Women* (1986), by Diana E. H. Russell. She found that 16 percent of the San Francisco women sampled reported that they had been sexually abused by a relative before the age of 18, and 4.5 percent reported that they had been sexually abused by their fathers before age 18 (1986). Her view, and that of others, is that incest is rarely consensual, since there are usually power differentials in the relationship, whether of age, position, size, or authority. Usually implicit or explicit coercion is involved, and the victims generally have negative reactions, ranging from mild dislike to intense trauma. Because incest involves family members, it means a violation of the deepest bonds of trust people can have; sometimes too, it involves elements of rape. There is often a "conspiracy of silence" surrounding the event (Butler, 1978). If and when victims decide to confide in someone else about what happened, they may experience further humiliation and trauma. They may not be believed, they may be considered disgusting, or they may be reviled. Incest can have long-term consequences. There is a strong relationship between incest abuse in childhood or adolescence and later experiences of victimization and self-destructive behavior (Russell, 1986).

What sociological explanations are there for the occurrence of incest? Russell examined the related social background factors. Her most startling finding was that girls from high-income families were more frequently victimized by incest than girls in lower-income families (Russell, 1986). This finding differs from those of most nonprobability studies of incest. Russell found few differences by race or ethnicity. There were, however, enormous differences in the vulnerability of girls raised by stepfathers as opposed to biological fathers. Among women raised by stepfathers in the first 14 years of life, 17 percent were sexually abused by them in those years, compared to only 2 percent of women raised by their biological fathers. This finding is consistent with that of Finkelhor (1984) as well. Russell suggests that stepfathers may feel less bound by the incest taboo than biological fathers do, and she also suggests that some men who become stepfathers may do so to gain access to children.

## TEENAGE SEXUAL ACTIVITY

### Changes in Teenage Sexual Behavior

In the 1940s about 20 percent of American women reported that they had had premarital intercourse before the age of 19 (Kinsey et al., 1953).

A 1982 study found that 43 percent of 17-year-olds had already had intercourse (Wallis, 1985). However, a survey of high school juniors and seniors selected in 1983 from *Who's Who*

*Among American High School Students* found that only 25 percent of these high-achieving students had experienced sexual intercourse. A similar survey in 1971 revealed that 40 percent were no longer virgins (Leo, 1983, p. 76). Although sexual activity is not the same among all groups of teenagers, there has been a general change in the premarital sexual activity of teenage women over the last 40 years. At the same time, the sexual behavior of male American teenagers has remained constant, with nearly three-quarters experiencing coitus before the age of 19 (Kinsey et al., 1948; Zelnik and Kantner, 1980).

The relative constancy of male sexual activity combined with increased female premarital sexual experience has several implications. Apparently in the late 1940s and early 1950s quite a large number of males were having sexual intercourse with relatively few females. Such a pattern of sexual relations magnified the great divide in the social landscape between those few girls who engaged in sexual intercourse and the overwhelming majority of girls with whom a male could not have sexual relations before marriage. Such a social division intensified the **double standard** of sexual conduct for males and females, a standard that considered premarital sex to be acceptable for men but not for women. As more women have become involved in sexual relationships, often with the person whom they expect to marry, the negative view of such behavior in women has declined.

Only a small percentage of boys or girls now feel that it is desirable for either men or women to be virgins when they marry. Among 17- to 18-year-old boys, 17 percent agreed that a girl should be a virgin when she marries and less than one in ten felt that a boy should be. Among girls of the same age, one-quarter felt that a girl should be a virgin, whereas one in six felt a boy should be (Hass, 1979). This evidence suggests that attitudes have changed more than behaviors, since the percentages of males and females who are still virgins is higher than the percentage who think it is important to be a virgin. The evidence also suggests that lingering traces remain of the double standard of normative conduct governing the sexual behavior of males and females. Although the numbers are small, both males and females are more likely to think females rather than males should be virgins at marriage.

# *Reactions to AIDS*

"I just found out that I have AIDS. You are a wonderful girl and I am deeply sorry that our special night together has put you at risk." This note, in a lost wallet found at Christmas recently, brings out both the personal pain of AIDS and its social nature.

By the beginning of 1989, at least 350,000 cases of AIDS (or acquired immune deficiency syndrome) had occurred worldwide, according to the World Health Organization (WHO), and 1 million more cases were expected by 1992 (Heise, 1989). The disease has already struck 85,000 Americans, more than half of whom have died (Altman, 1989). An estimated 1 to 1.5 million additional individuals in the United States are infected with the virus (Heise, 1989). While gay men account for the majority of existing AIDS cases, new cases are increasingly appearing among intravenous drug users, their sex partners, and their babies (Altman, 1989). New cases among gay men appear to be declining, while new cases among heterosexual intravenous drug users are increasing (Figure 21.2).

There is now no known medical cure for AIDS, and it seems to be almost certainly fatal. Until there is a medical solution, it is critical that AIDS be addressed in social terms. Except for blood recipients and infants, most of the people who have AIDS were exposed through consensual sexual behavior or sharing needles. The disease is not transmitted through coughing or other casual contact. Instead, AIDS seems to be transmitted by the exchange of certain body fluids, specifically semen and blood. It is a socially transmitted disease and therefore changes in social behaviors can curb its spread.

The number of AIDS victims so far is small compared with other major historical epidemics, such as the bubonic plague or "black death" that killed about 75 million people in Europe in the fourteenth century, the epidemic of syphilis in Europe in the sixteenth century, the great London plague of 1665, the influenza outbreak of 1918–1919 that killed as many as 50 million people worldwide (including more than 500,000 Americans), and polio, which infected nearly 600,000 Americans, of whom 10 percent died before a vaccine was developed. Nevertheless, the reactions to this illness share some similarities to earlier plagues. Faced with an incurable and fatal disease, people tend to blame either the "wrath of God" or to seek out handy human scapegoats. Both of these reactions have surfaced in response to AIDS.

In 1983 the conservative fundamentalist preacher Jerry Falwell combined both reactions

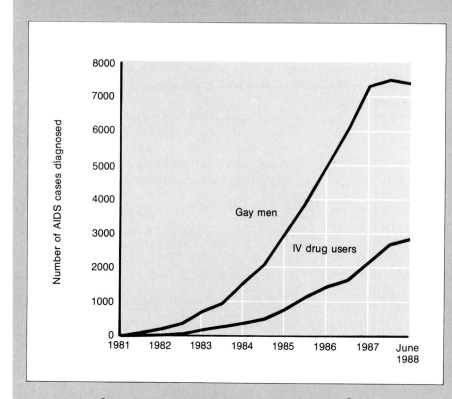

**Figure 21.2   Number of New AIDS Cases, Among Gay Men and Intravenous Drug Users in Each Six-Month Period, 1981–1988.**

Among homosexual men who do not use drugs, the number of new AIDS cases seems to be declining. The number of new cases among heterosexual intravenous drug users is rising, however.

*Source:* Centers for Disease Control, as cited in the *New York Times,* February 5, 1989, p. 28.

when he described AIDS as divine retribution on homosexuals. He has become alarmed at the discovery that the disease is not confined to those who he thinks "deserve it."

Many of the social reactions to AIDS have combined panic with varying degrees of scapegoating—for example, boycotting gay restaurants and other businesses; talk by insurance companies of refusing coverage to gays as a group, rather than just to individuals with the disease; landlords who have evicted tenants with AIDS; doctors, dentists, and morticians who have refused to provide professional service to people with AIDS; talk of a quarantine for life for people who carry the virus; a reported change for the worse in the attitudes of about one-third of the population toward homosexuals; and boycotts of schools by thousands of children when their parents heard that one child with AIDS had been admitted to the New York City public schools. Neither panic nor scapegoating helps those who suffer or works to stem the course of the disease.

The federal government, especially, has been faulted for failing to teach people how to protect themselves from getting the virus. Since gay sex is illegal in about half the states in the country, the government was not about to issue brochures about it, noted a gay political activist. In late 1983 and 1984 in San Francisco, the AIDS Foundation began devising explicit educational materials, in a move to "eroticize safe sex." Standing-room-only crowds attended safe-sex lectures and forums at neighborhood churches and social clubs on subjects like learning how to make condoms a "turn-on as well as protection from the AIDS virus." Men talked about having "re-er-

oticized" (Leishman, 1985, p. 24).

Statistical studies in San Francisco show that this "safe-sex" advice is being followed. One indicator is the way the rate of rectal gonorrhea has plummeted, falling more than 75 percent in recent years, suggests Mervyn Silverman, director of health for San Francisco from 1977 to 1985 (Forum, 1985, p. 45). This suggests that effective educational programs can change social behaviors in important ways.

As more has been learned about how AIDS is transmitted, fear about contagion has lessened, especially among the more educated and people of higher socioeconomic status. The announcement in 1985 that the actor Rock Hudson had AIDS, from which he soon died, seemed to bring the illness out of the closet and into the forum of public debate. Support for medical research on AIDS and media coverage has increased. In 1982 and 1983 the Reagan administration set aside nothing for AIDS research. Congress appropriated some $33 million. For the 1986 budget, the House voted $190 million, the Senate $221 million (Lieberson, 1986, p. 45).

Health care institutions, particularly in California, New York, and Florida, have already begun dealing with an influx of AIDS patients. San Francisco General Hospital has a busy AIDS center, Ward 5B. New York City municipal hospitals, especially Bellevue, face financial and morale problems as their intensive care wards fill with indigent, dying AIDS patients. New York State plans to create a system of hospital-based AIDS centers that stress hospice care and home services rather than long-term hospital stays.

As another step toward prevention, gays have been urged to

form long-term, monogamous relationships. Such a suggestion ignores the fact that the prejudice against homosexuals in American society makes it difficult, in many parts of the country, for two gay men to settle down and live publicly together. Sociologists ask: To what degree do the barriers and stigmas of society against gays contribute to the life-style and behaviors that might increase the spread of the disease?

A similar question may be raised with respect to the spread of the AIDS virus among drug users. In the United States, new, sterile hypodermic needles cannot be purchased without a doctor's prescription so as to make it more difficult for drug users to obtain them. The result is that addicts share dirty, used needles among themselves, thus passing on the virus.

An experimental program in New York City in 1988 to give free, new needles to addicts did not solve the problem. Neighborhood groups, parents, and school officials deplored the greatly increased number of used needles that were left lying around for children to pick up and perhaps to infect themselves with.

Human society has a stake in limiting the dissemination of the AIDS virus. We need to examine the social beliefs and behaviors that contribute to its spread. If people concentrate on blaming the victims, they lose the chance to help those who suffer and to apply informed thought to checking the disease.

*Sources:* Adler et al., 1985; Barron, 1985; Bishop, 1985; Forum, 1985; Leishman, 1985; Lieberson, 1986; McGrath, 1985; Morrow, 1985; *New York Times*, 1985a; *News Roundup*, 1985a, 1985b; Serrill, 1985; Sullivan, 1985a, 1985b; Tanne, 1985; and Trippett, 1985.

There is some recent evidence suggesting that sexual activity may have leveled off. Although no one knows for sure why such a development might be happening—whether it is the increase in untreatable sexually transmitted diseases (STDs) such as AIDS or an increasing seriousness among young people—sexual behavior seems to be moving in a somewhat more conservative direction for both males and females. (See the box on reactions to AIDS.) For example, a July 1983 reader survey by *Psychology Today* found that half of those under age 22 felt that sex without love is unenjoyable or unacceptable (Leo, 1984, p. 76).

Sexual values and activity have personal and social meanings for the individuals involved. Sorenson (1973) studied the personal values and sexual behavior of 13- to 19-year-olds in the United States and found that adolescents receive a great deal of satisfaction from their sex lives. A majority of boys and girls claim that they do what they want to do regardless of what society thinks. The majority disagree that the most important aspect of their sexual relationships is the physical pleasure it provides. Instead, they suggest that they value sex because it is something in their lives that they make decisions about; it makes a relationship with someone else seem more important than a mere friendship; it enhances communication with members of the op-

posite sex; and it may compensate for the painful, irrational, or unnecessary aspects of life such as parents who fight, racial injustice, or world conflict (Sorenson, 1973). The personal meanings and satisfactions teenagers gain from their sexual experiences provide a better context for understanding the large-scale social trends described earlier.

## Masturbation as Social Behavior

The social context and meanings of sexual behaviors shape their significance. The social importance of sex and sexuality is evident in such acts as masturbation, or self-stimulation. Although masturbating is no longer considered dangerous to one's health (it is no longer purported to cause blindness or to make one's hand fall off), it is still the cause of some embarrassment. One study of teenage sexuality found that young people (like adults) were more reluctant to discuss masturbation than most other forms of sexual activity (Hass et al., 1979). So there does seem to be some residual social stigma attached to the act of masturbating. Despite lingering embarrassment about the subject, most 17- to 18-year-olds think it is all right for a boy or a girl their age to masturbate, with 85 percent of the boys and 72 percent of the girls expressing this belief. Moreover, they are also quite likely to practice it themselves, with 80 percent of males and 59 percent of females indicating that they do so.

In their interviews with teenagers, Hass and his associates (1979) found instances where masturbation served as a physical release while enabling individuals to behave socially in ways that met their own expectations. For example, one 17-year-old girl reported, "After I lost my virginity I read the *Hite Report* and I found there were other ways of releasing my sexual emotions through masturbation without jumping into bed with every guy I meet. Now I do it when my desire is great and so I won't become promiscuous" (p. 91). Another comment suggests that masturbation represents a form of social-sexual learning that will prepare one for sexual relations with others in the future, as in the remark by an 18-year-old boy who said: "I wondered what happened during intercourse so

*Teenage sexual attitudes and behavior have changed in recent decades, with more young women becoming sexually active than was true in the past. Behavioral changes still lag behind attitudinal changes, however.*

I tried to reenact what happens in order to find out" (Hass, 1979, p. 90).

The socially conditioned nature of sexual feelings, responses, and behaviors is revealed in masturbation. Teenagers report having social and interpersonal fantasies while they are masturbating, and some report masturbating with others. Physical satisfaction is tied in with social relationships and meanings, whether real or imagined. Sometimes sexual fantasies allow individuals to think about situations that would be unacceptable for them to carry out socially, such as incestuous relations, prostitution, "kinky" sex, sexual relations with movie stars, or sex with someone admired from a distance. The freedom to imagine what they might do sexually enables individuals to behave socially in the more restrained ways they may feel are necessary. In this way, sexual fantasies and masturbation may offer ways for individuals to reconcile personal feelings and desires with social expectations and conventions. Not all teenage sexual activity remains in the realm of fantasy or masturbation, however, as the high rate of teenage pregnancy makes clear.

## TEENAGE PREGNANCY

Amy was 15 when, as a worker in a fast-food restaurant, she became pregnant as a result of a brief amorous relationship with her already married boss. As her pregnancy became visible, she was embarrassed to continue attending school in her small midwestern town so she dropped out of high school. However, she went on living with her parents, both of whom worked. When the baby was born, she had to stay out of school to care for him. All of her former friends were either in school or working; thus she was very lonely at home all day. Both her social and her economic prospects are dim at this point. In this respect she is not very different from many young teenage mothers.

Social policymakers and sociologists alike have pondered the high rate of teenage pregnancy and their research provides a number of insights. The increase in premarital sexual activity among teenagers has been accompanied by an increasing number of out-of-wedlock preg-

It's like being grounded for eighteen years.

Having a baby when you're a teenager can do more than just take away your freedom, it can take away your dreams.

*The rise in out-of-wedlock teenage birth rates has prompted efforts to prevent teen pregnancies. Posters such as this one have been used in an effort to make teen pregnancy a national concern.*

nancies. In 1970, 10.7 percent of all births were to unmarried women. By 1986, 23.4 percent were (U.S. Bureau of the Census, 1989a, p. 66).

Although the number of sexually active teenage girls has increased, the percentage among unmarried teenagers who say that they want to get pregnant has declined from 25 percent in 1971 to 9 percent in 1980[1] (Jones et al., 1985, p. 56).

Of all teenagers who do not want to get pregnant, only about one in three ever use contraceptives, meaning that more than two-thirds risk becoming pregnant. One reason for not using contraceptives may be the fact that more than half of the pregnancies among unwed teenagers occur within six months of their first intercourse and one in five occurs within the first month of sexual activity (Zabin, 1981). Among teenagers who never used contraceptives, the pregnancy rate jumped, perhaps because they

[1] Reasons unmarried teenagers give for wanting to get pregnant include wanting to get out of their parents' house, having a baby to love, getting on welfare, and being like their friends or relatives.

# Teenage Pregnancy—Why Is it So Much Higher in the United States Than in Other Countries?

A study of early teenage pregnancy rates in 30 countries by the Alan Guttmacher Institute shows that only Hungary had a higher rate of early teenage pregnancy than the United States (Westoff et al., 1983, p. 105). The United States was compared in detail with five other industrialized Western countries. Although American adolescents were no more sexually active than their counterparts in these countries, nor did they begin having intercourse any sooner, they were found to be many times as likely to become pregnant. Moreover, the United States is the only country where the incidence of teenage pregnancy has been increasing in recent years. Whereas black teenagers in the United States have a higher pregnancy rate than whites, whites alone had nearly double the rate of their British and French peers and six times the rate of the Dutch (see Figure 21.3).

In 1957 the teenage birth rate in the United States (like all birth rates for women at that time) was higher than it is today, but nearly a quarter of 18- and 19-year-old women were married then. If an unwed teenage became pregnant, a "shotgun wedding" was likely. If that was impossible, a girl disappeared for a while to have her baby and the child was quietly put up for adoption. Abortion was not a likely option for most until 1973, when the Supreme Court ruled that it could not be outlawed. As recently as 1970, fewer than one-third of the teenage mothers were unmarried.

Today, many fewer pregnant teenagers marry. Forty five percent of them have abortions. Of the rest, more than half have their babies without being married, and in some areas more than three-quarters of teenage mothers are not married. "Unwed motherhood has become so pervasive that 'we don't use the term illegitimate any more,' notes Sister Bertille Prus, executive director of Holy Family Services, a Los Angeles adoption agency for pregnant teens" (Wallis, 1985, p. 80).

This historical shift in attitudes and behaviors does not seem sufficient to explain the dramatic differences between the United States and other countries. Comparing the United States with five other countries reveals a number of other sharp differences that may go further to explain widely varying rates of teenage pregnancy.

1. The United States appears to have the lowest level of contraceptive practice among teenagers of all six countries. In particular, the pill is less likely to be used.

2. Contraceptives, including condoms, are much more accessible to teenagers in countries other than the United States. Reproductive clinics are also much more available in the other countries than in the United States.

3. Abortion servies are more readily available and cheaper in the other countries than in the United States, although they are used less than in the United States in three out of five of the countries. Most women in the United States must pay for an abortion procedure themselves, whereas it is free in Sweden, France, and England, and the cost is low in the Netherlands.

4. Sex education is part of the official curriculum in all Swedish schools. The program emphasizes contraception and human and sexual relationships. Starting at age 7, every child in the country receives a thorough grounding in reproductive biology and by the age of 10 or 12 has been introduced to the various types of contraceptives. "Teachers are expected to deal with the subject whenever it becomes relevant, irrespective of the subject they are teaching," says Annika Strandell, the Swedish board's specialist in sex education. "The idea is to dedramatize and demystify sex so that familiarity will make the child less likely to fall prey to unwanted pregnancy and venereal disease" (Wallis, 1985, p. 82). There has also been a close link between schools and contraceptive clinic services for adolescents since 1975, and adolescent abortion rates have declined since then, whereas adult rates have changed little (Jones et al., 1985, p. 58).

5. The national governments in England and Wales, Netherlands, France, and Sweden see teenage childbearing as undesirable and feel they should help teenagers avoid pregnancies and births. Therefore, rather than focusing on the morality of teenage sexual activity, they have aimed to prevent pregnancies and births. A larger study of 38 nations found that openness about sex was importantly related to lower rates of adolescent pregnancy.

6. Religiosity is greater in the United States than in Europe and fundamentalist religious groups are more numerous and vocal in public life (see Chapter 16). "Both the nature and the intensity of religious feeling in the United States serve to inject an emotional quality into public debate dealing with adolescent sexual behavior that seems to be generally lacking in the other countries" (Jones et al., 1985, p.

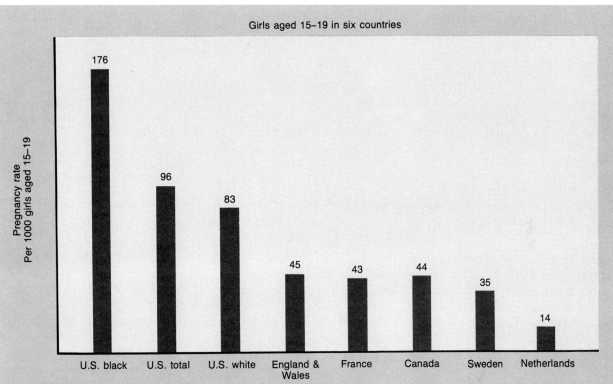

Girls aged 15–19 in six countries

Pregnancy rate
Per 1000 girls aged 15–19

176 U.S. black
96 U.S. total
83 U.S. white
45 England & Wales
43 France
44 Canada
35 Sweden
14 Netherlands

**Figure 21.3   Pregnancy Rate per 1000 Girls Aged 15–19 in Six Countries.**

In the United States, girls between 15 and 19, black and white combined, are more than twice as likely to become pregnant as girls in England, Wales, France, and Canada and nearly seven times as likely as teenagers in the Netherlands.

*Source:* Jones et al., 1985, p. 55.

59). Some people feel that teaching children about birth control is close to condoning promiscuity. Sex-education classes are simply "sales meetings" for abortion clinics, says Phyllis Schlafly, a leading antiabortionist. In addition, she claims, there is no way to tell youngsters about contraception "without implicitly telling them that sex is O.K. You've put your Good Housekeeping seal on it" (Wallis, 1985, p. 89). Although 78 percent of American adults favor sex education in the schools, including information about birth control, minority opposition views such as those of Ms. Schlafly often shape public policy.

7. Although young people in all six countries studied were worried about getting jobs, other countries were more likely than the United States to offer youth job training, unemployment insurance, and other support.

8. The overall extent and nature of poverty is much greater in the United States than in the other five countries studied. "In every country, when respondents were pressed to describe the kind of young woman who would be most likely to bear a child, the answer was the same: adolescents who have been deprived, emotionally as well as economically, and who unrealistically seek gratification and fulfillment in a child of their own. Such explanations are also given in the United States, but they tend to apply to a much larger proportion of people . . ." (Jones et al., 1985, p. 60). Moreover, the 37-nation study found that countries with more equally distributed family incomes had lower rates of teenage pregnancy, at least among younger teenagers.

The relationship between poverty and teenage pregnancies is

evident in the higher rates for blacks, many more of whom are poor. Poor teenagers of both races are much more likely to have not only one but several out-of-wedlock births. The socioeconomic roots of some teenage pregnancy in the United States may stem from the sense of hopelessness and worthlessness felt by many girls mired in poverty. "The girls tell me, 'before I was pregnant, I was nothing. Now I am somebody. I'm a mother.' " says Sharon Watson, Executive Director of the Crittenton Center in Los Angeles, which offers contraceptive counseling programs for teenagers (Wallis, 1985, p. 90).

Many American teenagers do not want to become pregnant, however, and they are in the majority, even among the poor. They are all too often unable to obtain the information or the contraceptives needed to avoid unwanted pregnancy. Political and religious opposition to giving teenagers access to the means of avoiding pregnancies and births serves, whether or not the result is intended, to hurt the young, the poor, women, and ethnic minorities. It has longer-term costs as well for the rest of society, such as welfare costs and the problems teenagers have raising babies.

*Sources:* Jones et al., 1985; Wallis, 1985; Westoff et al., 1983.

---

were having intercourse more frequently. But pregnancies were also up among teenagers who said they always used contraceptives. This increase may be due to the declining use of the pill or the IUD and the rise in the use of less effective methods of contraception, especially withdrawal before ejaculation, a decidedly risky method (Zelnik and Kantner, 1980).

Having sexual relations without using contraception, even though one does not want to get pregnant, may be explained by several factors. Teenagers may lack knowledge about how pregnancy occurs and how to avoid getting pregnant. They may lack access to effective methods of contraception. To procure the most effective methods, medical examinations and prescriptions are required. Such a requirement may pose too many problems and too great an expense for teenagers to manage. In certain areas, the availability of contraceptive information and materials, especially to teenagers, is limited by law. (See the box on teenage pregnancy rates in the United States and other countries.)

The beliefs of teenagers themselves may also contribute to high pregnancy rates. One survey revealed that nearly one-third of all adolescents believed that "If a girl truly doesn't want to have a baby, she won't get pregnant, even though she may have sex without taking any birth-control precautions" (Sorenson, 1973); "girls cannot become pregnant the first time they have sex, if they have sex only occasionally, or if they have it standing up" (Kisker, 1985).

The fact that these beliefs are mistaken is vividly revealed in the large numbers of premarital pregnancies and births among unmarried teenagers (see Figure 21.4).

In an age of economic uncertainty, high technology, and increasingly stringent educational requirements for jobs, early parenthood places significant social, educational, and economic strains on teenagers. Teenage mothers are also more likely to have miscarriages, stillborn babies, low-birthweight babies, or babies with birth defects than are mothers in their twenties, partly because only one in five pregnant teenagers under the age of 15 receives any prenatal care.

The educational attainments and aspirations of teenage mothers and fathers suffer as a result of early marriage and early parenthood (Furstenberg et al., 1981; Haggstrom et al., 1981). Only half of those who give birth before age 18 complete high school, compared to 96 percent of those who postpone childbearing.

Youths (and their parents) may be increasingly aware of how teenage parenthood jeopardizes educational and career plans. Extramaritally pregnant teenagers are less likely to get married than ever before, and those who do not marry are increasingly likely to terminate their pregnancies with induced abortions. About one-third of all abortions performed in the United States are performed for teenage women. Another three out of ten teenagers indicated that they wanted and needed abortions but were unable to obtain them. The 160,000 teenagers who

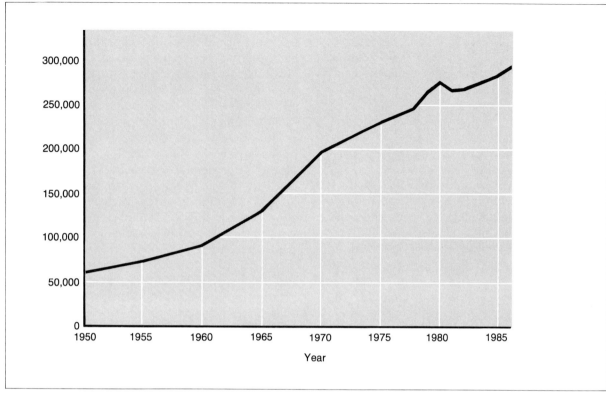

**Figure 21.4    Number of Babies Born to Unwed U.S. Mothers 19 Years of Age or Younger, 1950–1986.**

Between 1950 and 1986, the number of babies born annually to young unwed mothers in the United States increased nearly six-fold, from about 60,000 to nearly 300,000. Fewer babies are put up for adoption today as well, so many more unwed teenagers have babies to raise.

*Source:* U.S. Bureau of the Census, 1982a, p. 66; 1985a, p. 62; 1989a, p. 66.

indicated this represented about 60 percent of all unintended births among teenagers (Alan Gutt-macher Institute, 1981).[2]

## THE GAY WORLD— HOMOSEXUALITY AND LESBIANISM

A sociological analysis of homosexuality and lesbianism raises additional general issues about the social definitions of sexuality. Understanding the gay world requires us to define several

terms. "Straight" is the word used to refer to **heterosexual** individuals whose preferred partner for erotic, emotional, and sexual interaction is someone of the opposite sex. A **homosexual** is someone who is emotionally, erotically, and physically attracted to persons of the same sex. Some people are exclusively attracted to people of the same sex, some are exclusively heterosexual, and some have mixed same-sex and heterosexual experiences (see Figure 21.5).

**Lesbians** are women who are attracted to women; homosexuals are men who are drawn to men. Some people use the term "homosexual" to include both men and women who are attracted to same-sex individuals. Some lesbians, however, wish to distinguish themselves from men and therefore prefer the term "lesbian" to "homosexual." The term "gay" refers

[2] This means that if abortion is again declared illegal in many states, the likelihood that out-of-wedlock teenage pregnancies will increase is very great.

to both men and women. A gay identity goes one step further, in a social sense, to include cultural and social affiliation with a homosexual or lesbian community (Warren, 1974). Being a member of the gay community helps to neutralize the stigma the larger society may attach to homosexuality because the gay community does not accept the stigmatizing social definitions of homosexuality as sick, sinful, or weird. Instead, it helps individuals to accept a homosexual identity as positive and good.

Within the gay community, two major strategies for dealing with gayness in relation to the outside world have developed. *Secret gays* segregate their lives by time, place, and relationships into gay and straight. When operating in the straight world, they try to conceal their sexual identity from those around them. *Gay liberationists,* in contrast, actively bring their gay identity into all aspects of their life experiences. Secret gays seek to avoid the efforts of straight society to stigmatize them, whereas gay liberationists try to confront and transform the stigma (Humphreys, 1972).

Gay people face at least three types of oppression in our society: legal-physical, in which certain kinds of behavior practiced by a stigmatized group are declared illegal and people practicing them are subject to arrest; occupational-financial, in which opportunities for jobs, advancement, and income are limited for gay people; and ego-destructive, in which stigmatized individuals are made to feel sick, sinful, or otherwise despicable (Humphreys, 1972).

The negative effects of such social stigmatization are apparent in the cases of people who have attempted to change their homosexual orientation by aversive behavior modification—for example, by getting electric shocks while viewing erotic pictures of same-sex individuals (Riordon, 1979). The results of such "treatment" seem to be influenced by how strongly an individual wants to change, by how long he or she has been a homosexual, and by the nature of the heterosexual experiences the individual has had. Other gays have sought less drastic "cures" through psychotherapy. With the advent of gay liberation and intensive debates within the American Psychiatric Association, there seems to be increasing rejection of aversive therapies and a growing sense among both gays and psychiatrists that changing one's sexual orientation is unnecessary, difficult, and undesirable. Instead, therapy should be directed at helping individuals accept themselves and function well as they are (Katchadourian and Lunde, 1972).

Whether individual gays choose an openly gay life-style and a gay liberationist stance or pursue a secret gay life-style may depend to a considerable degree on occupation and where one works. Some occupations and organizations practice overt discrimination against gays, refusing to hire or promote them or firing them when their identities are discovered (Levine, 1979). Until such discriminatory practices are eliminated, gay people working in such situations seem to be faced with the difficult choice

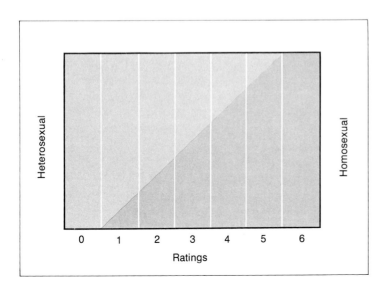

**Figure 21.5 Kinsey's Heterosexual-Homosexual Rating Scale.**

Some people have completely heterosexual histories (the leftmost column in the diagram); others have exclusively same-sex histories; and a great many people are in between, with some mixture of heterosexual and same-sex experiences.

*Source:* Alfred C. Kinsey et al., *Sexual Behavior in the Human Female,* 1953, p. 470.

of keeping their gay identities secret or endangering their careers.

Similar life-style distinctions exist within the lesbian community. What Wolf (1979) calls the "old gay life" centered around lesbian bars, which were the only public places where a woman could go to meet other lesbians. Yet the bars represented a kind of social ghetto, "a place where the stigmatized were hemmed in and allowed to socialize" (p. 46). The social life that centered around bars was often superficial, based on role playing and encouraging its own form of depression and isolation. This depression may have resulted in large part from the fact that participants tended to accept the negative stereotype of lesbianism held by the larger society. They tended to accept a stigmatized identity and to feel they did not deserve any better.

Wolf sees a second sociohistorical era in lesbian life emerging with the rise of homophile organizations in the 1950s. Such groups include the Daughters of Bilitis for women and the Mattachine Society for men. They serve as civil rights and educational organizations for gays working within the norms of the larger society. They do research, try to change the attitudes of society and gay people about their identities, sponsor consciousness-raising groups, and form political coalitions with other groups to achieve common goals.

The third historical development Wolf notes is the rise of militant lesbian feminism, which had its counterpart in the more militant male gay liberationists. This approach aimed to transform society rather than to work for moderate change within it. Lesbian feminism, for instance, proudly defines lesbianism in positive terms and sees it as leading the way toward a feminist future in which both selves and society would be redesigned (Wolf, 1979). In the male gay community, one manifestation of gay liberation is "radical drag," in which a man wears an evening dress and gloves with boots, a beard, and a hairy chest (Warren, 1974). Such a display is designed to shock the straight world and to challenge conventional definitions of sexuality and appearance.

The goal of gay liberation movements is to change an oppressive system, thereby destroying old patterns of dominance and exploitation (Wolf, 1979). One result has been that the self-esteem of gays has increased tremendously. Another result is that in some areas—such as San Francisco, California, and Greenwich Village, New York—gay rights are taken seriously by politicians. In brief, social roles both within and beyond the gay community are beginning to be redefined as a result of the gay rights and liberation movements (Wolf, 1979).

## Historical Views of Homosexuality and Lesbianism

Do views of homosexuality vary by place and time? Are there sociological explanations for these differences? In a major new study, David Greenberg (1988b) analyzes the nature of homosexual activity and societal reactions to it in tribal kinship societies, ancient Greece and Rome, other ancient societies, and western Europe and the United States up to the present. His goal is to explain why persecution of homosexuality waxed and waned. The approach he takes can be applied to a sociological analysis of sexuality more generally, not just to homosexuality.

He finds that homosexuality is not a uniform phenomenon across time. Furthermore, social beliefs about homosexuality stem from identifiable social features in the societies in which they are found. In tribal kinship societies lacking a centralized political authority, the most negative reaction to homosexual activity is that it is foolish, but no one considers interfering with the people involved in it (Greenberg, 1988b, p. 77).

In feudal society, the social organization of military combat among the aristocracy was conducive to male homosexuality. This was evident in England, Italy, France, Germany, Sicily, and Normandy (Greenberg, 1988b, p. 259). Since the aristocracy made secular law, it is not surprising, Greenberg suggests, that there were few measures against homosexuality in European secular law until the middle of the thirteenth century. The relationship between military organization and sexual customs was also evident in feudal Japan (Greenberg, 1988b, p. 260).

During the twelfth and thirteenth centuries, hostility toward homosexuality intensified. The church and the state were gaining in their capacity to carry out repression as more of Europe converted to Christianity and political power became increasingly centralized (Greenberg, 1988b, pp. 268–279). Continuing church-state conflict was one of the social sources of greater repression in this period. Although marriage of clergy had been prohibited since the fifth century, the prohibition was widely ignored and many clergy were married. One of the problems this posed was the inheritance of some clerical positions and churches by sons from their fathers. Secular rulers were also meddling in church affairs—for example, by buying ecclesiastical offices. If the church did not have the power to appoint and remove clergy, it could not maintain effective discipline over priests and monks. It could also do little to improve the sexual incontinence and low reputations of many clergy. Papal ambitions for a clergy loyal only to the church made the elimination of priestly marriage even more important. However, the elimination of heterosexual opportunities for priests could only increase homoerotic feelings (Greenberg, 1988b, p. 283). Thus, one source of the fear and loathing of homosexuality that developed in the Middle Ages may have been "the inner conflict created by the imposition of clerical celibacy and the rigid repression of all sexual expression" (Greenberg, 1988b, p. 289). In the Byzantine Empire, where priestly marriage was allowed, antihomosexual feelings were not as strong as they were in the West under Catholicism. In short, "growing preoccupation with homosexuality was an indirect and unanticipated consequence of the efforts of church reformers to establish sacerdotal [i.e., priestly] celibacy" (Greenberg, 1988b, p. 280).

The second source of increased hostility toward homosexuality was growing class conflict. As class divisions widened, "popular hostility toward homosexuality was part of a broader middle-class morality that became increasingly forceful in its opposition to a life-style of luxury and excess" (Greenberg, 1988b, p. 280). In fact, "complaints about homosexuality were beginning to serve as a vehicle for the expression of popular discontent with the growing social gap between the court and the rest of the population" (Greenberg, 1988b, p. 293). The middle classes supported reform-minded monks, who practiced their vows of poverty and moral restraint. One result, in the middle of the thirteenth century in Italy, was new antisodomy legislation (Greenberg, 1988b, p. 298).

"From the fourteenth to the beginning of the nineteenth century, homosexuality continued to be described as a sin or crime contrary to nature" (Greenberg, 1988b, p. 302). A notable feature of this period is that "involvement in homosexual relations did not become the basis for self-identification: participants probably did not think of themselves as 'buggers' or 'sodomites.' Their genders—that is, their identification of themselves as male—were conventional" (Greenberg, 1988b, p. 330).

In the nineteenth and twentieth centuries, new ideas about homosexuality and new methods of social control emerged. Three developments shaped the modern response: the growth of competitive capitalism, the rise of modern science, and the spread of bureaucratic principles of social organization. While the effects of these developments were contradictory, the general result was to fortify antihomosexual beliefs and attitudes (Greenberg, 1988b, p. 347). The new capitalist order intensified competition between men, sharpened the sexual division of labor, strengthened the ideology of the family, and stimulated the invention of medical explanations (Greenberg, 1988b, p. 356). Self-control becomes increasingly important in market economies because entrepreneurs feel torn between spending their money and investing it (Greenberg, 1988b, p. 360). The growth of bureaucratic organizations encouraged the socialization by parents of appropriate personality traits in children. The "bureaucratic personality" has been defined by Merton as "methodical, rational, prudent, disciplined, unemotional, and preoccupied with conformity to expectations" (Greenberg, 1988b, p. 446). It requires the suppression of affective emotional responses by males toward other males.

Doctors became increasingly involved in the definition and control of homosexuality. Why did this happen? "Physicians came primarily from the middle class and would have shared the general sexual ideology of that class" (Greenberg, 1988b, p. 401). The medicalization of homosexuality was one example of a number of social problems that medical leaders claimed as part of their province in the late nineteenth and early twentieth centuries. In an era of rapid social change and immigration, physicians "had become a kind of secular clergy" (Greenberg, 1988b, p. 403). Medical definitions included psychiatric evaluations of homosexuals as "disturbed personalities" (p. 429). In 1973, under pressure from gay-liberation activists, the American Psychiatric Association removed homosexuality from its listing of mental illnesses in the *APA Diagnostic and Statistical Manual of Psychiatric Disorders*. It did not change the thinking of most psychiatrists (nearly 70 percent opposed the removal), nor did it stimulate a rethinking of the theory of sexual preferences (Greenberg, 1988b, p. 430).

By the late 1960s, resistance to homosexuality began to weaken. Why did this happen? Greenberg traces some of the social and economic changes that lie behind this shift. A long period of economic prosperity led to less emphasis on self-discipline and self-restraint in child rearing compared to earlier times (pp. 459–460). The economy required spending to forestall recession. The nature of work and the labor force were changing, creating new demands for women workers. Gender differences began to weaken. "As rigid gender stereotypes weakened, so did resistance to homosexuality" (pp. 460–461). England and Sweden experienced parallel trends (p. 462). "While some psychiatrists continued to regard homosexuality as a form of psychopathology," others abandoned that idea and some even branded the irrational fear of, or anger toward, homosexuality as "homophobia,"a condition one psychologist termed "a disease" (Greenberg, 1988b, p. 463).

But not everyone favors reducing opposition to homosexuality. Efforts to block the expansion of gay rights have been led by Orthodox Jewish rabbis, significant members of the Roman Catholic Church's hierarchy, and more conservative Protestant denominations (p. 467). In national social surveys, "respondents from the South, from small towns, and from rural areas, who are older, poorer, and less well-educated, are more likely to think homosexuality morally wrong and to oppose gay rights, but religion is a more powerful predictor [of opposition to homosexuality] than any other individual trait" (Greenberg, 1988b, p. 468). One reason for their opposition is fear that homosexuality will undermine the family. The threat of

gay liberation is "not just homosexuality; but its validation" (p. 473). One user of an earlier edition of this textbook objected that the amount of space devoted to homosexuality seems to legitimate homosexual behavior. Greenberg notes that moral conservatives see various sex and gender issues as linked. Permissiveness about homosexuality therefore implies permissiveness on abortion, premarital and extramarital sex, pornography, and the role of women in society. "For many Americans, adherence to conventional values and standards was a major component of their claim to respectability" (p. 473). For those with other sources of self-regard, conventional morality may be less important. But for some, especially those whose material success is limited, moral respectability is very important psychologically (Greenberg, 1988b, p. 473).

The continued importance of bureaucracies in postindustrial societies and the social pressures facing the lower middle classes will not disappear, suggests Greenberg. As a result, the full acceptance of homosexuality is unlikely (p. 475).

## Frequency of Homosexuality and Lesbianism

Although their sample was not representative, the research of Kinsey and his associates in the 1940s suggests that sexuality cannot always be neatly categorized as heterosexual or homosexual. Instead, sexual behavior should be thought of as a wide range of behaviors from exclusively homosexual to exclusively heterosexual, as Figure 21.5 shows. Most people are not at the extremes but somewhere in between. In addition, many people have experienced a variety of feelings and behaviors along the range.

When Kinsey set out to determine the number of people with same-sex experiences, he excluded any such behavior that occurred before puberty. Even with this limitation, he learned that by the time they were 45 years old, 37 percent of males had experienced at least one homosexual contact leading to orgasm. Among women, this was true of 13 percent. Single people were more likely to report such contact, with 50 percent of single males and 26 percent of single females indicating such experience by age 45. Another 13 percent of males had felt homosexual desires or attractions but had not acted on them. Other studies in the United States, as well as research in Germany and Sweden, confirm the Kinsey figures that about 4 percent of the white, college-educated adult male population is predominantly homosexual (Gebhard, 1972). This represents about 4 million American males over the age of 21 who are predominantly homosexual in attitudes and behaviors. About 1 percent of women are predominantly same-sex in their preferences and behaviors (Gebhard, 1972). This suggests that at least 1 million women are interested primarily in other women.

A recent study using a national probability sample of males interviewed by telephone found that 3.7 percent of males reported that they were homosexual or bisexual. This national probability sample revealed that members of certain groups were underrepresented in previous samples drawn from the gay world. These included men who are less educated, married, older, living in small towns, or members of minority groups (Harry, 1988).

Research on sexuality faces problems of classification as well as sampling. "Gay" and "straight" are not clear-cut dichotomies. Definitions must include physical behavior, emotional attraction, and erotic attraction. As Figure 21.5 clearly shows, most people experience some mixture of heterosexual and homosexual behaviors.

More recent studies by Kinsey's Institute for Sex Research suggest that the earlier estimates still hold. Lay persons and sex researchers, both assuming a gradual loosening of sexual mores, had quite different expectations concerning the effects on same-sex behavior. Many people feared that the greater visibility of same-sex relations in our society would increase such contacts. Sex researchers, in contrast, expected that the general loosening of mores would reduce same-sex relations because heterosexual experiences could be obtained earlier and more easily. Neither expectation has been supported, and the rates of same-sex contact have remained quite constant over the years (Tripp, 1979).

Of perhaps greater sociological interest is how people classify themselves. Clearly not everyone who has one or even more than one homosexual experience takes on the identity of a lesbian or homosexual. As Greenberg's research (1988b) suggests, people have different categories of identities available to them in different societies and at different times. Also, some people's self-definitions change over time. One researcher studying lesbians and gay men asked a lesbian if she had told her ex-husband during their marriage that she was a lesbian. She said, "No, I wasn't one then" (Whisman, 1986).

## Explanations of Same-Sex Orientation

For the reasons noted above, explanations of same-sex orientation and behavior are bound to be difficult. Biological, psychological, and sociological explanations have been offered to explain why some individuals are attracted to others of the same sex. Few research studies, however, have attempted to analyze all three types of explanations together. One major study based on about 1500 heterosexual and homosexual individuals attempted to do precisely that. Bell, Weinberg, and Hammersmith (1981) of the Institute for Sex Research at Indiana University were startled to find that many traditional notions about the causes and development of same-sex orientation were not supported by their research.

The widely accepted psychological theories suggesting that homosexuality is due to certain parental behaviors, such as dominant mothers and weak fathers, were not supported. Moreover, lack of peer acceptance while a person is growing up seems to be an unimportant factor in homosexual development. The sociological theory that homosexuality results from being labeled as sexually different is not supported, because such labels appear to be the result of a developing homosexual orientation rather than a cause of it. Frightening experiences such as being raped by someone of the opposite sex do not seem to direct women toward lesbianism, nor does being seduced by an older person of one's own sex cause someone to become a homosexual. Although homosexuals do sometimes have experiences such as those noted previously, they are no more likely to have them than are heterosexuals. How, then, is sexual orientation determined?

Bell and his associates (1981) suggest that sexual orientation is likely to be already determined before boys and girls reach adolescence, even though they have not yet been active sexually. People experience homosexual feelings about three years before they experience any homosexual activity. The existence of these feelings was more importantly related to adult sexual orientation than were prior homosexual behaviors. The feelings were experienced by males around the age of 13 and by females about the age of 16. Participation in homosexual activities occurred several years later and grew out of the homosexual feelings rather than being the source of such feelings. Homosexuals had about as many heterosexual experiences while growing up as did heterosexuals, but they differed in that they did not find such experiences gratifying.

Gender nonconformity during childhood and adolescence is related to a homosexual orientation, but only about half of the homosexual respondents showed atypical gender traits while growing up. A person's childhood and adolescent sexual feelings (and to a lesser extent behaviors) continue in that person's adult sexual orientation. The continuity may reflect either very strong conditioning situations that teach boys and girls to respond homosexually or the emergence of a deep-seated propensity toward either homosexuality or heterosexuality that begins in childhood and continues into adulthood. In sum, Bell, Weinberg, and Hammersmith (1981) feel they have identified "a pattern of feelings and reactions within the child that cannot be traced back to a single social or psychological root" (pp. 183–192). Furthermore, they suggest that their findings are not inconsistent with what they would expect to find if there were a biological basis for sexual preference.

The nature of a society may affect the frequency of same-sex orientations among its members. Societies that applaud bravery and courage tend to idealize and eroticize male attributes. Such societies—like the Tanganyikan Nayakyusa, the warrior Mohave Indians of the Southwest, or the Algerian Kabyles—tend to involve most males in some forms of homosexual activity (Katchadourian and Lunde, 1972; Tripp, 1979). When heterosexuality and homosexuality are defined by a culture as mutually exclusive identities, people seem to be less willing to define themselves as homosexuals if they also experience heterosexual attractions and behaviors (Duberman, 1974). Other societies, such as certain contemporary Arab states, offer the possibility of bisexuality, enabling people to form an identity that recognizes their multifaceted sexuality.

The social creation of homosexual identities is apparent in the lives of individuals who occasionally engage in homosexual activity yet also lead conventional working- or middle-class lives that include marriage and parenthood. They see themselves as "not really homosexual" (Miller, 1979). Young male prostitutes who allow older male homosexuals to fellate them in exchange for money do not define themselves as homosexuals either. Instead, they consider what they do as simply a way of making money (Hoffman, 1979; Reiss, 1961). Studies of homosexuality in prisons suggest that not all the participants are considered homosexuals by their peers. Only those who take the role of the other sex are viewed as homosexuals. The sexual aggressors, considered to be "voluntary aggressors," are tagged "wolves" or "jockers." They are seen as playing the conventional masculine role and thus may often be defined by their peers as heterosexuals even when their aim is sexual gratification through homosexual acts. The submissive partners, or involuntary recruits, are dubbed "fags," "fairies," "effeminates," "queens," or "punks." They are thought to have lost their masculinity, even if they are raped (Kirkham, 1971; Lindner, 1951; Lockwood, 1979; Sagarin, 1976; Sykes, 1958).

## Same-Sex Behaviors and Life-Styles

Much of our knowledge about same-sex behaviors is based on research by Bell and Weinberg (1978) of the Institute for Sex Research. They conducted extensive interviews with nearly 5000 black and white males and females who engage in same-sex behavior. Although their research suffers from the same problems that most studies of sexual behavior do—namely, the use of non-random samples that may not be typical of an entire population—nevertheless they have made a significant effort to describe and analyze same-sex behavior in the United States.

The single most striking result of their research is the diversity of behaviors that exist. The range of behaviors is extensive and shows the degree to which generally held stereotypical views of homosexual behavior are mistaken. There is no single life-style, set of sexual behaviors, or type of relationship that appears among all homosexuals and lesbians.

Both men and women who engage in same-sex relations tend not to adopt a single role, such as that of the active or the passive partner in the sex act. Unlike prison studies, where such role typing frequently occurs, individuals in the sample interviewed by Bell and Weinberg alternated between initiating and receiving overtures. Individuals do not limit themselves to a single sexual technique or practice but tend to experience a variety of forms of sexual contact. Younger people tend to have more varied sexual repertoires than older people. Some of the variation in sexual techniques may result from the lack of cultural approval for homosexual and lesbian behavior in general (Tripp, 1979). Tripp suggests that since no forms of sexual behavior are especially prescribed, individuals are freer to experiment and devise their own.

As is true among heterosexuals, sexual behaviors and preferences are correlated with race, social class, and sex. Fellatio (oral sexual contact) was the most frequently reported technique among black and white homosexuals. Among white males, mutual masturbation was the technique next most frequently used, whereas black males were more likely to engage in anal intercourse (Bell and Weinberg, 1978). Body rubbing to orgasm was used by only a few and was more commonly reported by lower-status men. The most desired activities were receiving fellatio (27 percent) and performing anal intercourse (26 percent).

Among women, mutual masturbation was the most frequently used technique (40 percent), with cunnilingus (oral sexual contact) next. About 25 percent of white lesbians and 50 percent of black lesbians performed cunnilingus once a week or more. Such activity was more frequent among younger women. About 20 percent of white lesbians and 40 percent of black ones achieved orgasm through body rubbing. As with males, this practice was more frequent among members of lower-status occupations. Cunnilingus was the sexual activity most preferred by lesbians.

Just as the roles and techniques experienced in same-sex relations vary considerably, the appearance of the participants is quite diverse. Many people tend to assume they can detect a homosexual or lesbian by the way he or she looks. However, even the trained sex researchers in the Kinsey group could recognize only 15 percent of homosexuals and 5 percent of lesbians, despite cues on the basis of dress and whether a known homosexual or lesbian had referred the respondent to them. Many masculine-looking males are gay, as are a number of feminine-looking females. Similarly, not all effeminate-appearing males or masculine-appearing females are attracted to members of their own sex.

Another important area of variation in same-sex life-styles occurs with respect to the types of relationships that are formed. In their research, Bell and Weinberg (1978) found five types that they termed close-coupled, open-coupled, functional, dysfunctional, and asexual. Close-coupled individuals had long-term, marriagelike relationships with a single partner. Men and women in this group had fewer sexual problems and did much less cruising (that is, visiting bars to meet other gays) than the other people interviewed. Females in this group had less regret over being lesbians, were more active sexually, and used more sexual techniques than other female respondents. The open-coupled people had regular same-sex partners, but they had more sexual problems, spent more time cruising, or had more outside relationships than did the close-coupled ones. Women showed these characteristics to a lesser extent than did men.

The functional gays were not coupled, but they were sexually active and had little regret over their same-sex preferences. None of the dysfunctionals were coupled. Although most of them were sexually active with numerous partners, they had more regrets about their sexual preferences and reported more sexual problems. Not many women were classified as dysfunctional, but those who were tended to be younger than the men and to think of themselves as lacking in sex appeal to other women. The asexuals were low in level of sexual activity, number of partners, amount of cruising; they reported relatively more sexual problems. Both male and female asexuals were older, on the average, than other respondents.

Some gay men and lesbian women may follow life-styles that differ from those of heterosexuals (DeVall, 1980; Harry, 1984). But there is no single life-style that everyone follows. For many, it may be that a preference for one sex or another as an object of emotional and erotic choice is the only major difference between homosexuals and heterosexuals. Beyond that preference, gays and lesbians may show the same range of behaviors that heterosexuals do with respect to life-styles and emotional commitments.

## SUMMARY

1. Sexuality is important to both individuals and societies.

2. Social norms and structures influence what sexual behavior is considered acceptable and what individuals find attractive. Societies place limits on when and with whom sexual relations can occur.

3. For centuries Judaism and Christianity were antisexual, accepting sex only for its role in procreation. In recent decades the joyous aspects of sexuality have been more widely affirmed.

4. Rape is a crime of violence. It may be encouraged by a society and culture in which women are dominated by men and sexual exploitation of women is taken for granted. Rape rates are higher in the United States than in many other industrial societies. This may be due to cultural factors that suggest potential gains from rape and offer justifications and excuses to individual rapists. To understand rape, we need to understand its social and cultural context.

5. Like rape, incest has been a taboo topic for research in the United States until quite recently. Sixteen percent of women in a probability sample in one western city reported that they had experienced incest abuse before the age of 18. Such incidents were more prevalent in

higher-income than in lower-income homes and much more likely with stepfathers than with biological fathers.

6. Sexual activity among teenagers, especially white teenagers, has increased dramatically in the last 40 years. Two out of five American teenage girls have experienced premarital intercourse, as have about three-quarters of American teenage boys. The double standard of sexual morality for boys and girls seems to be declining, but it is not completely gone. The social meaning of sexuality is evident even in solitary behaviors like masturbation.

7. Premarital pregnancies are on the increase. Teenagers are not beginning sexual relations at an earlier age, on the average, but they are engaging in them more frequently. Half of premarital teenage pregnancies occur within six months of first intercourse. Although more teenagers now as compared to earlier years say they do not want to get pregnant, their use of the relatively more effective methods of birth control has declined. Early parenthood depresses the educational and occupational aspirations and attainments of teenage boys and girls.

8. In the gay world, the term "straight" refers to heterosexuals. Homosexuals are emotionally, erotically, and physically attracted to persons of the same sex. Homosexuals are men who are drawn to other men, lesbians are women attracted to other women. A gay identity includes membership in a social community of homosexuals or lesbians. Secret gays feel they must not divulge their gay identity to the straight world, whereas gay liberationist males and lesbian feminists seek to change the oppressive straight society.

9. Same-sex behaviors have been widely practiced in different societies and viewed in varied ways in those societies. General attitudes in Western society toward sexuality have been reflected in social mores regarding homosexuality and lesbianism. The concept of homosexuality has changed through time, as have official reactions to it. Hostility increased in the twelfth and thirteenth centuries, because of changes in the structure of western European society. New

ideas emerged in the nineteenth and twentieth centuries, largely due to the development of capitalism, modern science, and bureaucratic organizations. In the latter part of the twentieth century, structural changes in the economy and work may have lowered resistance to homosexuality. According to Greenberg, the existence of counterpressures suggests that full acceptance of homosexuality is unlikely.

10. Despite these shifts in societal reactions to same-sex behavior, its frequency seems to have remained stable over the last 40 years, with about 4 percent of the male and about 1 percent of the female population being exclusively interested in same-sex relationships. One of Kinsey's major findings was that most people are not exclusively homosexual or heterosexual but experience some mixture of same- and opposite-sex attractions and behaviors. Of sociological interest is the process of how individuals assume a heterosexual or homosexual identity.

11. Recent research suggests that sexual orientation is determined early in life, but existing evidence does not support sociological labeling theory explanations of homosexuality or psychological theories of family interaction.

12. Sociological explanations for the frequency of same-sex behavior stress two features of a society. The degree to which masculinity is idealized may be related to how eroticized maleness becomes and hence to the frequency of homosexual relations between males. Cultural definitions and group memberships influence how sexual behaviors are linked to particular sexual identities.

13. Same-sex behaviors are not all alike. Homosexuals and lesbians vary considerably with respect to taking the passive or active role with a sexual partner, sexual techniques, appearance and mannerisms, and types of relationships.

## KEY TERMS

double standard (p. 551)
heterosexual (p. 559)
homosexual (p. 559)
lesbian (p. 559)
prostitution (p. 548)
rape (p. 548)

## SUGGESTED READINGS

Bell, Alan P., Martin S. Weinberg, and Sue Kiefer Hammersmith. 1981. *Sexual Preference*. Bloomington: Indiana University Press. Reports a major research study on the origins of sexual preferences.

Furstenberg, F. F., Jr., R. Lincoln, and J. Menken (eds.). 1981. *Teenage Sexuality, Pregnancy and Childbearing*. Philadelphia: University of Pennsylvania Press. Examines the consequences, many of them negative, of early teenage pregnancy.

Greenberg, David F. 1988. *The Construction of Homosexuality*. Chicago: University of Chicago Press. An ambitious book for an ambitious student. A masterpiece of scholarship.

Jones, Elise F., et al. 1985. "Teenage pregnancy in developed countries: Determinants and policy implications." *Family Planning Perspectives* 17: 53–63. A cross-national study that considers why teenage fertility and abortion rates are so much higher in the United States than in other developed countries.

Russell, Diana E. H. 1986. *The Secret Trauma: Incest in the Lives of Girls and Women*. New York: Basic Books. An interview study based on a probability sample of women who did and did not experience incest abuse in their childhoods.

Wolf, Deborah Coleman. 1979. *The Lesbian Community*. Berkeley: University of California Press. A sensitive field study of lesbian life-styles and some of the problems they involve.

# Leisure and Sport

*The expedition members scaling such lofty giants as Mount Everest are clearly engaged in climbing a mountain, but in other instances the distinction is not always clear. Is the ascent of 6800-foot Strawberry Peak in the San Gabriel range near Los Angeles mountain climbing? Are the wintertime skiers who ascend Mount Whitney, California's highest peak, mountain climbing? Are the rock gymnasts inching their way up some vertical face in the Yosemite Valley mountain climbing? [Mitchell, 1983, p. 1]*

*Mountain climbing is a technical process with a social meaning and morality of its own. Understanding the experience of climbing requires attention to the social context in which it occurs. Without an investigation of the social component of the climber's world, mountaineering is reduced to makeshift engineering, to a manipulation of tools for no purpose. No climber would long tolerate such a reduction. Climbing is least of all simply getting to the top of mountains and other awkward locales. It is, most centrally, a social event, a deed done usually with others and always with others in mind.*

*The vital importance of social definitions in mountaineering is made clear when one considers that the awesome importance ascribed to mountains is largely a social construction. . . . For some, mountaineering symbolizes certain quintessential human qualities— plucky striving and courage in the face of adversity and danger; achievement, conquest, self-actualization. For others, it is the epitome of foolishness and waste, a dim-witted, plodding exercise that ends in dreadful falls. . . .*

*The sociological study of mountaineering is important. It complements the sociologist's perennial concern for work and vocations with additional knowledge of a rapidly increasing aspect of American social life—leisure. More time is now spent in leisure pursuits than in any other social activity, including family and personal care and employment. . . .*

*For sociology to retain its utility and relevance, understanding the ways in which leisure activity is selected and the gratifications and challenges it offers is of vital importance. [Mitchell, 1983, pp. xii–xv]*

Leisure and sport may seem to be less weighty subjects than some of the other social processes and institutions discussed in this book. However, sport and leisure activities excite human interest and passions, and people spend a lot of time and money on them. So, although they may seem less significant, leisure and sport engage the hearts of millions of people. In addition, they illustrate important sociological and societal features, including the ways in which various angles of sociological vision—functionalism, conflict theory, and symbolic interactionism—raise different questions about the world. Finally, they provide new insights into social life.

In this chapter we examine some of the questions sociologists have raised about leisure and sport, consider the tremendous growth of leisure time that has occurred in Western societies in the past two decades, and examine sport in relation to society generally and as it reflects social stratification.

## THE RELATION BETWEEN LEISURE AND SOCIAL LIFE

As is the case with other individual tastes and preferences, leisure and sport activities are influenced by social values, norms, culture, and social structure. At the same time, leisure and sport reveal self-aware individuals who carve out some areas of choice for themselves. In this way leisure and sport bring into sharp relief the dual elements of social forces and individual will. Yes, we are influenced by social forces outside ourselves, but we also select and choose from among those forces what we will affirm, reject, or modify.

### The Interplay Between Life and Leisure

Sociologists differ in the ways they see sport and leisure. Some see them as an extension of the values and skills people use in their occupations (Parker and Smith, 1976). Others suggest that how people experience their everyday world influences the leisure activities they pursue. People select activities that contrast with or complement their regular affairs, suggest Mitchell (1983) and Ball (1972). When everyday life is routine, limiting, and tightly structured, people seek variety and personal challenge in recreation. They hunger for situations where the results depend on their own choices (Mitchell, 1983). In mountain climbing, for example, people use their own skills and strategies to influence outcomes such as falling or staying alive. Ball (1972) calls this *control-oriented* action.

Controlled risk taking—reflected in activities such as skiing, scuba diving, skydiving, hang-gliding, and mountain climbing—is more likely to occur in societies whose routine affairs are marked by safety and stability. Numerous mountaineers, for example, come from Britain, France, Germany, Switzerland, Japan, and the United States; relatively few are from Uganda, Ethiopia, Turkey, Peru, Pakistan, Nepal, Vietnam, or Cambodia. Their origins do not depend totally on the availability of mountains or of wealth (Mitchell, 1983). Within the United States mountaineers are well-educated, secure, middle- and upper-class individuals, many of whom are engineers and applied scientists (Mitchell, 1983).

*Acceptance-oriented* action differs from control-oriented action, and is reflected in such activities as "fair" dice games or watching TV, suggests Ball (1972). An individual's skill does not affect the result of acceptance-oriented action. Social groups that regularly cope with risks and uncertainties in their daily lives, people with hazardous or insecure jobs, with little education or political influence, and with relatively little control over their own lives and experience, do not usually seek to exercise control in the face of uncertainty. Instead, they seek leisure activities that require no effort on their part but only the acceptance of their fate. They escape responsibility and blame, yet still have the chance to win against the odds or to relax from grueling daily activities. Ball's theory helps to explain why different activities may be more popular in some societies than others and why various social groups within a society may be more or less likely to participate in various types of leisure.

### The Concept of Flow

Successful leisure is characterized by **flow,** an experience of total involvement in one's activities. In flow experiences, people do not feel the need to intervene consciously. Instead, the action of one movement flows smoothly into the next action (Csikszentmihalyi, 1974; Mitchell, 1983). Action characterized by flow is freely chosen, self-rewarding, and contains an uncertainty of outcomes that allows for creativity.

In activities characterized by flow, the self does not need to function in its role as negotiator. In much of social life the self serves to negotiate and reconcile the needs of individuals, on the one hand, and the demands of social groups and society, on the other hand. Flow experiences differ from other social life because the self can go "off-duty" for a time. As a result, experiences of flow are immensely rewarding and restorative in and of themselves, without regard to any objective accomplishment they produce. Although the condition of flow may be most purely experienced in something like mountaineering or soccer, it is possible that flow experiences may occur in everyday life—for example, in conversation, lovemaking, cake baking, gardening, carpentry, dancing, choir practice, or other satisfying efforts in school or on the job (Mitchell, 1983).

Although individuals experience flow as a psychological condition, it is also possible to describe the social conditions under which flow experiences can occur. Mitchell defines flow as occurring in the middle ground between alienation and anomie. He sees anomie and alienation as opposite poles on a spectrum ranging from certainty to uncertainty in the way social life is experienced by individuals. People experience alienation when they can predict how they will

*Gardening is a highly satisfying leisure activity for millions of Americans. It may provide a flow experience similar to that encountered by some while mountain climbing, playing soccer, or white-water rafting.*

behave based on the social world they inhabit. Every possibility for creativity or spontaneity is stifled by social rules and regulations. Life in prisons, concentration camps, military academies, or on the assembly line may provide so much certainty that it is viewed as alienating by individuals. Individuals may feel powerless and unable to do anything they find personally rewarding (Mitchell, 1983).

Anomie stands at the other extreme. Individuals feel anomie when they do not know what to expect in most or all their social interactions—for example, when a social encounter differs from anything previously experienced and when known rules do not help to predict how others will behave. The lives of secret agents, homeless urban dwellers, confidence game artists, or lone shipwreck victims in foreign lands may contain considerable uncertainty about the results of their actions and produce anomie in individuals, suggests Mitchell (1983).

Flow occurs at a point of balance between the extremes of anomie and alienation. "Flow emerges in circumstances which are perceived as both problematic and soluble" (Mitchell, 1983, p. 188). Certain social conditions reduce the chances that flow will occur. These include the overrationalization of life, leisure, and sport. Examples might be white-water rafting trips where people become passengers rather than participants in the situation, or professional sports where winning, records, and standings become much more important than the process itself. The more rationalized play becomes, the more self-conscious the participants are and the less the chances of having a flow experience (Mitchell, 1983).

## LEISURE

### Is Leisure Increasing in Industrial Societies?

From the beginning of the twentieth century to 1960, the number of hours worked has declined from about 60 hours per week to 38.6 hours per week. But, between 1960 and 1985, there was no further decline. People worked an average of 38.7 hours per week in 1985, slightly more than the hours worked in 1960. Despite the fact that

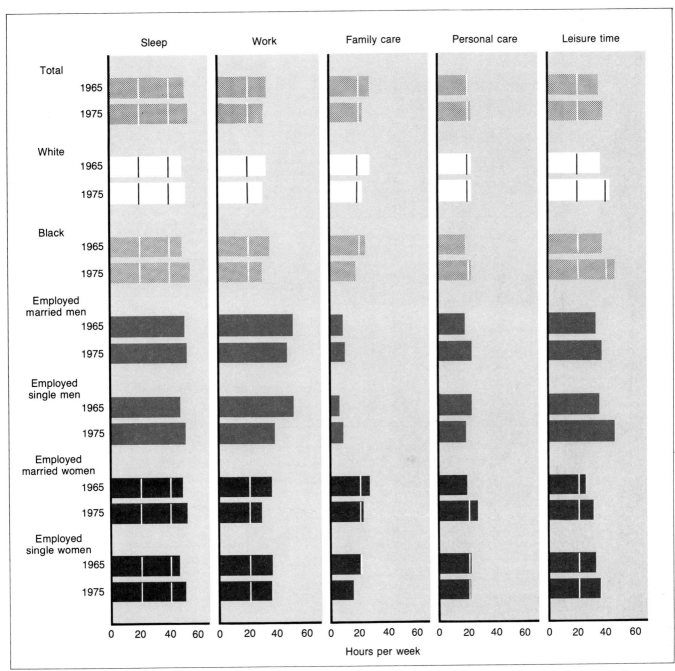

**Figure 22.1    Average Hours per Week Spent in Major Types of Activities by Selected Urban Population Groups, 1965 and 1975.**

Employed married men spent more hours per week on work than anyone else except employed single men, not much more time on family care than em-

ployed single men, and considerably less time than employed married women. Employed married women spent fewer hours on leisure than any other group, and employed single men in 1975 spent the most time on leisure.

*Source:* U.S. Department of Commerce, 1980, p. 544.

leisure has not increased in the last 25 years, people still have a considerable amount of "leisure" time (McAdams, 1989; Robinson, 1987).

As Figure 22.1 shows, except for work by married men, people now spend more time on leisure pursuits than on any other social activity,

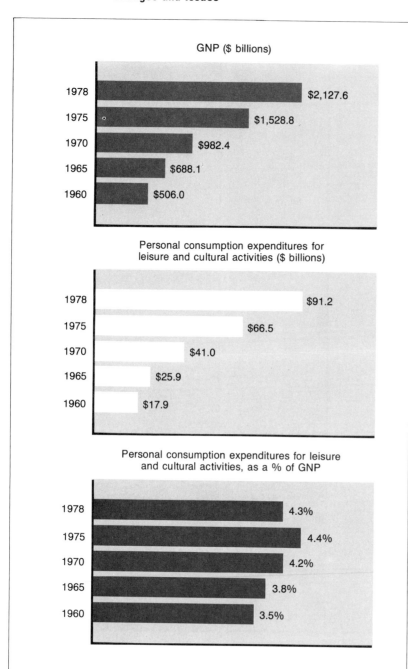

**GNP ($ billions)**

| | |
|---|---|
| 1978 | $2,127.6 |
| 1975 | $1,528.8 |
| 1970 | $982.4 |
| 1965 | $688.1 |
| 1960 | $506.0 |

**Personal consumption expenditures for leisure and cultural activities ($ billions)**

| | |
|---|---|
| 1978 | $91.2 |
| 1975 | $66.5 |
| 1970 | $41.0 |
| 1965 | $25.9 |
| 1960 | $17.9 |

**Personal consumption expenditures for leisure and cultural activities, as a % of GNP**

| | |
|---|---|
| 1978 | 4.3% |
| 1975 | 4.4% |
| 1970 | 4.2% |
| 1965 | 3.8% |
| 1960 | 3.5% |

**Figure 22.2   Gross National Product and Personal Consumption Expenditures for Leisure and Cultural Activities, Selected Years, 1960–1978.**

Although the dollar value of expenditures for leisure activities increased steadily between 1960 and 1978, the percent of GNP represented by those expenditures dipped slightly in 1978.

*Source:* U.S. Department of Commerce, 1980, p. 553.

including family, personal care, and employment. As Mitchell (1983) notes, in the past two decades life expectancy has increased, retirement age has decreased, health has improved, and paid vacations for plant and office workers have doubled in number and increased in length. Peo-

ple now have time, energy, money, and inclination to participate in leisure activities.

People are also spending heavily on their leisure pursuits. As Figure 22.2 reveals, personal expenditures on leisure activities have been increasing since 1960, both in terms of the absolute dollar amounts and as a percentage of gross national product (except for slight dips in 1978 and 1980). Such spending totaled $18 billion in 1960. By 1987 it had soared to $223 billion, more than a twelvefold increase. The amount comes close to the $282 billion spent on national defense in 1987. When social observers speak of the "leisure explosion," they are referring to the expansion of nonwork time and to growing expenditures on leisure activities.

The dollars Americans spend on recreation and sporting equipment may be at an all-time high. However, they represent no larger a share of household expenditures than they did 20 years ago (Robinson, 1987, p. 34).

The amount American families spend on sporting equipment may be at an all-time high. This family is heavily involved in sports, as is evident from the wall full of team pictures and memorabilia, as well as from their collection of sports equipment and shoes, only part of which is shown here.

## How People Spend Their Leisure

How do you like to spend your leisure time? Do you enjoy sitting around doing nothing, going to a friend's house, playing a sport or watching one, playing music or listening to it, walking in the park, swimming, or climbing a mountain? If you ask your classmates what their preferred leisure activities are, you will probably get many different kinds of answers. This is not to say that there are no patterns to people's preferred leisure activities. Many of the leisure activities people enjoy are socially learned. If you took a Bushman from Southwest Africa—like the one in the movie *The Gods Must Be Crazy*—to a baseball game, he might not enjoy it very much. Nor would everyone necessarily like opera the first time they attended one.

The problems social scientists have dealing with a world that is both objectively present yet subjectively defined and interpreted is evident in the phenomenon of leisure. Some social scientists deal with this problem by focusing only on an effort to measure leisure objectively. Thus, for example, some define leisure as free or unobligated time. Thus leisure is simply the residual time left over after required activities have been attended to—work, housekeeping, child care, shopping, personal care (including eating and sleeping), study, participation in various organizations, and the travel associated with all these activities (Robinson, 1977). This approach reflects an attitude among some social scientists that leisure is neither as relevant nor as interesting as other forms of social activities. How about you? Are your leisure activities simply the residual of time allotted to more important tasks? Or are they of major importance to you?

There is the additional issue that some needed activities are pleasurable. Playing with their children is enjoyable to many people, even though that may be tagged by a social researcher as a necessary activity—child care. Others may enjoy using their "leisure" time to wash their cars or the windows of their homes.

The various meanings of time and the activities that fill it make a tidy sociological study of leisure very difficult. Nevertheless, in order to understand more fully why people in a society do certain things they consider leisure activities, we need to know both the meaning of the activity for the individual participant and the significance attributed to the activity by sociologists. The study of the ways in which people spend their leisure time is of interest to sociologists who view leisure activities as an indicator of cultural values and possibly even "national character." It is also of interest to government policymakers, social planners, and businesspeople.

One "objective" approach to the study of leisure is simply to ask people what kinds of leisure activities they frequently engage in. As Figure 22.3 indicates, the activity mentioned by the largest percentage was eating, followed by watching television, listening to the radio, reading books, listening to music at home, and fixing things around the house (ABC News-Harris Survey, 1979). Social activities like parties, eating out, or dancing were mentioned by one-quarter of the respondents, as was having sex. Fewer than a quarter mentioned participating in church or club activities, outdoor activities such as hiking, fishing, hunting or boating, or participation in sports like swimming, tennis, and golf. The activities most often reported as being done frequently require little effort, and most can be done at home.

When people were asked in another survey, "What is your *favorite* leisure activity?" television finished first, followed by reading, and staying home with family. (Sex was not listed as a choice.) These activities need not exclude each other, since you can stay home with your family and watch television at the same time. Less than 4 percent indicated participating in sports or indoor hobbies as their favorite activity (Gallup Poll, 1977, in U.S. Department of Commerce, 1980, p. 556). Interestingly, most of the indicated activities require little active participation. Despite the much-touted fitness boom in this country, more than four out of five Americans do not participate in sports according to one survey, and less than 4 percent do according to another survey. The increase in sports and fitness activities (or at least the surging sales of running shoes) may be due to the growing number of young adults aged 18 to 35.

While 17 percent of the adult population own jogging shoes, less than half of those owners (or 8 percent of the total U.S. population) jog more than once a year and only 17 percent of them (3 percent of the population) jog more than once a week. Similarly, about half of the bicycle owners and owners of weight-lifting equipment never use it (Brooks, 1988, p. 30). As the baby boomers have been aging, "couch potatoes" (people who spend their leisure on the sofa in front of the TV or VCR) are becoming more numerous (Pereira, 1989).

It is surprising to hear what people consider to be "outdoor or physical activities." Most frequently mentioned, as being done five or more times a year, are driving for pleasure and walking or jogging (57 percent each), followed by swimming or sunbathing at a pool and picnicking (40 percent each), and attending a sports event (44 percent). Even in the realm of outdoor activity, a clear picture comes forward: Americans are not engaged in strenuous outdoor physical activity with great frequency or in great numbers. They appear much more likely to spend their leisure time in relatively quiet and passive activities such as watching television. Some sociologists suggest that despite the pervasive emphasis on physical fitness in our culture, people are actually getting less exercise than they did 50 years ago. Instead of walking half an hour daily as many people used to, a small number go jogging for seven minutes once or twice a week. The rest have cut down their walking time without substituting other physical activities. Auto use per capita, for instance, has more than doubled in the last 30 years (Mitchell, 1981).

## Functionalist Views of Leisure

Functionalist views raise questions about an activity's significance for major social institutions such as the family or for societal integration. In families shared leisure is associated with open communication and with higher marital satisfaction scores (Orthner, 1976; Presvelou, 1971; West and Merriam, 1970).

Shared leisure time was related to marital stability (Hill, 1988) and to marital quality (Kingston and Nock, 1987). However, Hill found that not all types of leisure activities were equally important. Shared leisure spent on "church attendance, visiting friends, attending parties, going to the movies, reading newspapers, household conversations, "and just relaxing . . .

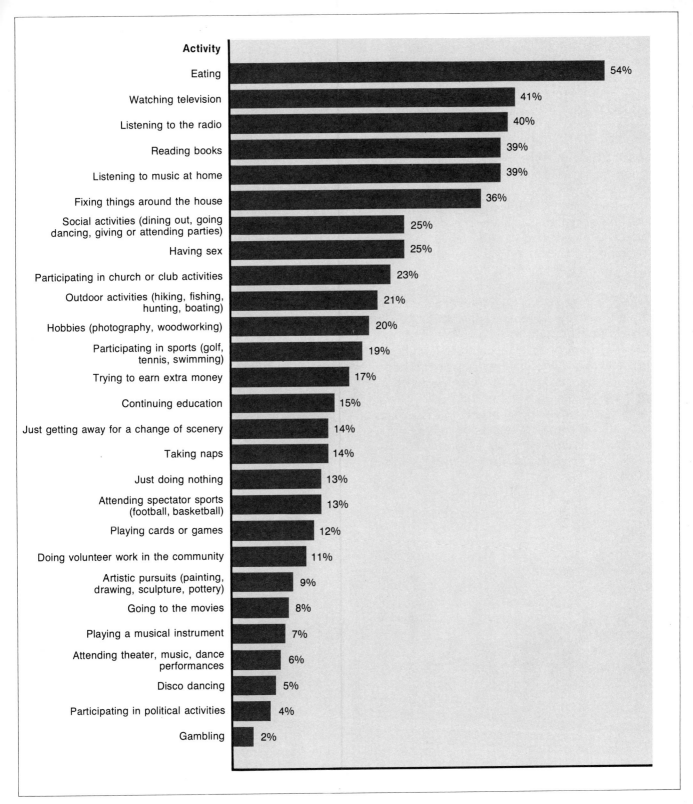

**Figure 22.3  Leisure Activities of the U.S. Population.**

The favorite leisure activities of adults in the United States are eating, watching television, listening to the radio, reading books, listening to music at home, and fixing things around the house.

*Source:* The *Chicago Tribune, ABC News–Harris Survey,* January 1, 1979, p. 1.

had no statistically significant effect on marital disruption" (Hill, 1988, p. 14). Only participatory leisure pursuits—such as active sports, outdoor activities, card games, and travel—were positively related to marital stability (Hill, 1988, p. 14).

Functionalist research emphasizes the positive or negative functions of leisure for other institutions in society, or for society itself. Functionalist theory suggests that leisure helps to hold societies together by motivating individuals to fill their social roles. They may work so that they can afford to go to the big game on the weekend, or they may work overtime to purchase a desired recreational vehicle. Certain other leisure activities may serve to promote societal cohesiveness. Examples are the reopening of the Statue of Liberty, Thanksgiving, Bastille Day celebrations in France, May Day in the Soviet Union, or special parades celebrating the heritage of a particular ethnic group, like St. Patrick's Day or Columbus Day parades. Such leisure activities may mute the degree of class conflict within a society. In shared leisure activities, such as company picnics or softball games, owners and workers may develop a sense of unity that seems to transcend their economic differences.

On the other hand, recreational pursuits sometimes openly conflict with work. In certain parts of the country, absenteeism from work runs high when the hunting or fishing season opens. And the major cause of absenteeism from work is alcohol consumption, which is another form of leisure activity (Mitchell, 1981).

## Leisure as Cultural Competition

Conflict theorists focus on leisure activities as resources in the cultural competition between groups. Leisure activities may be indicators of cultural membership or nonmembership. If someone plays *bocce* (the Italian bowling game) or squash, rides horseback, or collects pre-Colombian art or early American antiques, such activities or souvenirs serve as a set of cultural badges that may be revealed at appropriate times to verify membership in a particular group (Burdge, 1969; Clark, 1956; White, 1955). Because leisure activities are not necessarily prescribed by occupational demands, they are more open-ended, and they are expected to reflect one's "true personality" more fully. Since part of one's personality is tastes and pleasures cultivated through childhood and family exposure,

*People sharing an interest in the outdoors may bring widely different cultural values to that experience. On the left are people who travel to recreational areas in their RVs, which they park close together. They then may travel around on motorcycles, which they brought on their RVs. Others seek to escape from the crowds and noise of urban life. They prefer simple, remote campsites, accessible only on foot.*

they are presumably a significant indicator of class and status background.

Cultural differences arise among various users of the outdoors and national parks (DeVall and Harry, 1978). Backpackers and wilderness buffs differ from people who stay in heated cabins, and both groups see themselves as different from people who drive up to a campsite in their RVs (recreational vehicles), plug into running water, gas, and electricity, and turn on their television sets. All of them may go to a national park for the same general purpose, to enjoy the outdoors in some form, but how they become involved with nature reflects cultural differences among various groups. Picnics may have similar cultural content, depending on whether the fare is hot dogs, potato chips, and beer or French paté, strawberries, and white wine. The meaning that different cultural groups attach to various menus varies widely. The conflict perspective goes beyond simply noticing individual or group differences in cultural style to suggest that sometimes such variations become resources in status competitions between groups.

Sometimes leisure competition moves out of the realm of cultural tastes and into direct competition over scarce resources such as land in national parks or recreational waters. At any given moment the existence of limited facilities means that people will compete for their use. Ethnic groups may compete over city basketball courts, and social classes may compete over how parklands are allocated among wilderness areas, developed campgrounds, RV stations, or concessions. Are resources allocated in a way everyone considers fair, or do some groups get special access? Access to publicly supported national parks is supposedly allocated on a first-come, first-served basis, but there is evidence that socially or politically powerful people have easier access (Langley, 1981). The worlds of leisure and recreation are not insulated from the realities of stratification.

## SPORT AND SOCIETY

The sports a society glorifies may be an important indicator of that society's structure and essence. With this in mind, we will discuss the historical changes sports have undergone in En-

gland and the United States and will compare American sports to those played by other societies. We will also examine the ways in which sports reflect the inequalities that exist within a society, whether those inequalities are based on race, gender, or social class.

## Definitions of Sport

Play, games, and sport sound like the same activities to most of us, but sociologists of sport use those terms for different and specific activities. **Play** refers to spontaneous activity, undertaken freely for its own enjoyment, not designed to accomplish any productive end, yet governed by rules and often characterized by an element of make-believe. **Games** are one form of play, although not all forms of play are games. Games involve competitive or cooperative interaction in which the outcome is determined by physical skill, strength, strategy, or chance. **Sport** is a form of game in which the outcome is affected by physical skill and prowess (Loy, 1968; Loy, McPherson, and Kenyon, 1978). Chess, for example, is a game but not a sport, whereas kite flying may be considered a sport.

**Athletics,** by way of contrast, is associated with occupations, and is part work. When sports are performed for pay, elements of work are likely to be more important than the playful aspects of the activity. College players on athletic scholarships often mention that in high school they played ball for fun, but in college it is work (Coakley, 1982; Sack, 1977; Underwood, 1980). The links among these aspects of sport are portrayed schematically in Figure 22.4. Modern sport may be seen as being at the center of a band between work and play. At the same time, the dotted lines in Figure 22.4 suggest that work may have elements of play within it, just as play may have some elements of work in it.

The interconnection between sport and society is revealed in three kinds of evidence: first, how sports evolved historically in the United States and England; second, sport in the United States compared with sport in other societies; and third, views of sport as reflecting a larger debate about the nature of American society and how it is studied and evaluated.

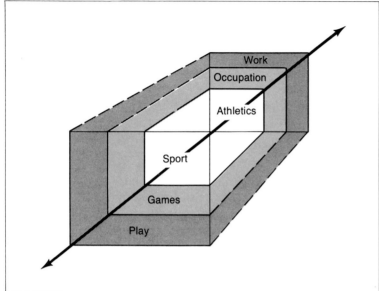

**Figure 22.4    Sport on a Play-Work Band.**

Play is a spontaneous activity, games are a more organized form of play, sport is a form of game where skill and strength affects the result, and athletics are closer to the world of occupations and work.

*Source:* Adapted from Loy, McPherson, and Kenyon, 1978, p. 23.

## The Historical Evolution of Sport in England and the United States

American attitudes toward sport and games were influenced by two trends: the English royalist tradition that favored sports and gaming on the one hand, and the Puritan tradition that actively opposed play, sport, and all forms of "frivolous" activity (Dulles, 1965). The English aristocracy always enjoyed gaming and sports, but the middle-class Puritan leaders of the American colonies in their early years stood in opposition to the worldliness of the established Church of England and the pleasures of the rich, landed nobility. They detested idleness and saw pleasure as sinful (Dulles, 1965). In 1611 Sir Thomas Dale forbade bowling on the green in Jamestown, Virginia. About the same time, Governor Endicott of the Massachusetts Bay Colony cut down the Maypole at Merry Mount. The early settlers did have a practical need to promote industry and frugality, but the Puritan leaders went far beyond those practical needs in their efforts to stifle play.

The publication in England of *Tom Brown's Schooldays* in 1857 by Thomas Hughes may have helped to provide a moral justification for sport even to Puritans. That author praised games for the way they built character (Goodhart and Chataway, 1973). The claim that sport enhanced virtue gave it new respectability in the eyes of the Puritan middle classes, who could use their ca-

pacity to rationalize activities to develop organized sport. Shortly thereafter, the modern forms of rugby, football, hockey, and swimming contests were developed. Lawn tennis began spreading around the world, polo staged a comeback, and golf competitions began. Various other sports such as badminton, court tennis, squash, and croquet were all newly organized (Goodhart and Chataway, 1973).

Along with changing attitudes toward sport, attitudes toward work were also easing somewhat. By the mid-nineteenth century many English workers had Saturday afternoons free from work. The shift in the moral conception of sport and the organizational efforts of the middle class, along with improved communications, more leisure, and growing urbanization, all contributed to the growth of mass spectator sports. Similar transformations occurred in the United States.

In eighteenth- and nineteenth-century American society, sporting events consisted of foot, boat, and horse races, log splitting, shooting, horse pulling, and plowing contests, and sometimes cockfighting. Except for the last activity, these sports involve skills that were functionally related to the challenges of a rural environment. They generally had an individual rather than a team winner. Such events were often staged at county fairs or local gatherings, with some spectators watching. There was nothing akin to the large masses of spectators who today crowd gigantic sports stadiums or follow sport through the mass media. Sport in that earlier era was neither highly organized nor centralized.

Major demographic, economic, and technological changes that occurred in the United States transformed the social context of sport. Huge waves of immigration and growing American industry greatly increased the number of urban dwellers. The invention of light bulbs in 1897 and the development of railroads meant that teams could travel to other cities to play and that athletic contests could be held at night. Stadiums—ever larger—were built. Baseball's National League was founded in 1876, the National Hockey League in 1917, the National Football League in 1922, and the National Basketball Association in 1946. Newspapers began adding sport coverage in the late 1890s. The growth of radio after 1900 meant that even people who could not attend could follow the games.

More recently, the advent of jet aircraft and television has intensified this growth. Television really fueled the expansion of professional sport because it provides huge TV audiences, high advertising fees, gigantic profits for the networks, and huge revenues to the leagues. In 1960 there were 42 professional sport franchises; by 1970 there were 87 franchises, and by 1985 there were 98. Television has affected the content as well as the expansion of sport. Some rules have been changed—for example, the use of tie breakers in tennis so that a set cannot drag on endlessly; there are commercial timeouts; and games are scheduled to fill prime-time hours.

All these developments enhanced the growth of professional athletics, spurred the rise of sport figures as cultural heroes, and shaped the direction of professional sport organizations. Today's athletic teams are organized as large-scale monopoly organizations involved in regional rivalries that sometimes become quite intense. Big-time professional football, baseball, basketball, and hockey are large-scale business operations.

## Comparisons with Other Societies

The sports that are popular in a society seem to reflect the values that predominate in a particular society, and those values in turn may reflect underlying economic and cultural practices. Sport in the United States is characterized by competition rather than cooperation, high levels of violence, and spectatorship rather than participation on the part of most adults. If we considered only the United States, it would be easy to assume that all sport is competitively organized with the goal of producing winners and losers. The sport of other societies reflects some of the different values of those societies, however.

The Tangu people of Oceania play a game called *taketak*. Two opposing teams try to throw a spinning top made from a dried fruit rind and touch a group of palm branches that have been driven into the ground. Each team tries to hit exactly the same number of stakes as the other team. The object of the game is to demonstrate the similarity of the teams, not the superiority of one team over another one. In this way the game reflects the cultural message that people are morally equivalent. This value is also reflected in the fact that the Tangu exchange food and other essentials (Burridge, 1957).

In another society sport is used as a substitute for warfare. In the Gahaku tribe of New Guinea a sporting contest is set up to redress a grievance one tribe has against another. The team from the tribe believed to have committed an offense enters the contest with a score of 1. The object of the encounter is to "even the score." When that has been done, the game is over and the grievance is settled (Read, 1965). Competition is not considered an end in itself, but a means for resolving preexisting conflicts between groups.

In Switzerland, a society characterized by decentralized economic production and diverse cultural groups, large-scale national sport competitions are less popular than family outings that involve hiking, skiing, or swimming (Clinard, 1978). Rather than stressing competitive games among professional teams, the Swiss place relatively greater stress on sharing their enjoyment of nature and maintaining good health.

Americans and Europeans seem to value spectator sports with distinctly different characteristics. Americans value skill and teamwork in situations that are tightly bound by space and time limitations, as reflected in football, baseball, basketball, and hockey. Europeans place greater value on individual exploits in the face of exhaustion, danger, or suffering, such as occurs in the 22-day, 2600-mile Tour de France bicycle race, speed skiing, and car racing (Daley, 1963). Why these different preferences exist is explained by sociologists such as Ball (1972) and Mitchell (1983) in terms of the way they complement the everyday lives of participants and spectators.

Europeans in general may feel less opportunity to take risks and find challenges as individuals, whereas many Americans may find daily challenges but have little chance to experience the fruitful combination of teamwork and skill within a finite time and space. Sport also reflects the amount of violence in a society and how violence is viewed. The United States, with the highest per capita homicide rate in the world, also exhibits a high degree of violence in sport, especially among players. Other Western countries are less likely to experience violence among players, but more likely to have violent episodes among spectators.

How do we explain different levels of violence in sport, and what are their consequences for society? Some sport, for example football, clearly encourages violent behavior among the players, whether in tackling, blocking, or protecting the quarterback. As a result, many players are injured. The National Football League found that each season the 1040 players in the league suffered an average of 1101 injuries so severe that they were unable to return to the game or to a subsequent game or practice. Each year about 13 percent of all players undergo surgery (Surface, 1974).

*Different societies value different sports. Fans in the United States value sports such as football, which requires skill and teamwork in situations tightly bound by space and time.*

U.S. sports also reveal the power of large organizations over individuals and the stress on winning, suggests MacAloon (1987). He notes that "60 to 80 percent of NFL players dangerously abuse steroids, and in some teams, apparently, are blackballed if they insist on remaining drug-free" (1987, p. 111).

Canadian and American ice hockey are especially known for the physical abuse of players and numerous fights. Aggressive body checking and physical domination are considered necessary for winning. As a result, a "subculture of violence" develops, even among young amateur players (Smith, 1979). Fans realize the place of violence in the game, and often favor more aggressive players over more skillful ones. Although player attitudes and values supportive of violence are related to violent behavior in the game, Smith found that they were poor predictors of how often these same players got into fights in their private lives. In the USSR ice hockey players are valued more for their skating ability and their good passing than for their prowess as fighters, suggesting that even in the same sport cultural factors influence which aspects are emphasized.

Why do violent sports thrive in some societies but not in others? Some theories suggest that sport serves as a form of a social safety valve, allowing individuals to vent their seething aggressions, and thereby lowering the chances of war or other forms of violence. The **tension release theory** seems to rest on the assumption that some degree of aggression is innate and that frustration produces further aggressive feelings, which somehow accumulate in individuals or societies until released. It is argued that when too much aggressive tension is bottled up inside individuals or societies, interpersonal conflict or war results.

A competing theory termed the **culture pattern theory** suggests that sport does not provide an emotional release from aggression. The theory further suggests that aggression and violence are learned—not innate—behaviors. Societies that are already strongly aggressive will promote competitive and aggressive sport, whereas those that are more cooperative will promote peaceful or cooperative sport. Exposure to one kind of sport or the other will increase the violent or peaceful tendencies that already exist in a society.

*European societies value individual exploits in the face of exhaustion, danger, or suffering, as in long-distance bicycle races such as the 2600-mile Tour de France.*

A direct test of these competing theories was made by Sipes (1973), who randomly selected 20 tribal societies to see if warlike societies had combative sport. Nine out of ten warlike societies had combative sport, whereas only two out of ten peaceful societies had combative sport. These findings provide strong support for the culture pattern model. Sipes also examined the relative popularity of combative sport in the United States between 1920 and 1970 and found that combative sports such as football and hunting were more popular in times of war, whereas baseball, a sport without violence, was less popular during wartime. This analysis also tends to support the culture pattern model, Sipes suggests. Perhaps during wartime the levels of aggression in an entire society are raised, yet most of the population cannot engage in actual warfare. This excessive aggression might need some tension release through violent sport. Also Sipes's analysis supports the culture pattern theory, it does not fully refute the competing tension release model. Combative sport, whatever its cause, may still serve as a safety valve or release for the members of a particular society (Eitzen, 1979b).

Further support for the learned nature of violence, however, is found by researchers who examine the effects on spectators of watching violent sports (Goldstein and Arms, 1971; Green and Berkowitz, 1966; Turner, 1968). Several kinds of violence occur among spectators at sporting events. The term "rowdyism" refers to generalized interpersonal violence or property destruction. It appears to be unrelated to what is happening on the playing field, but reflects instead the anger of people who come to games with the idea of having a good fight or destroying the place.

In England rowdy behavior is a growing problem at soccer matches (Taylor, 1972). Incidents are also increasing in the United States. Spectators may run onto the playing field, throw beer or solid objects at players, set off firecrackers, or rip out the seats. Fimrite (1974) suggests both societal and sport-related reasons for the growing frequency of such behavior, including increased drinking at games; greater permissiveness in raising the young, who feel they can vent their emotions however they like; growing contempt for established institutions; and a widening breach between fans and players as professional athletes command ever-higher salaries and are willing to strike or move to another city when it suits them.

Sport riots may occur as a new form of victory celebration. A *riot* is a destructive and sometimes violent collective outburst. Quite often the spectators on the winning side tear down the opponents' goal posts (Klein, 1981). In a somewhat more extreme example, when the New York Mets won the World Series in 1969, the fans stripped the stadium of anything they could break loose and carry away, including signs, bases, grass, seats, and wood. Other sport riots reflect hostility rather than jubilation. Societies with major ethnic, class, religious, political, or economic cleavages are likely to have riots when the members of groups already at odds meet in a sports contest. Riots have erupted, for example, when black lower-class high schools have played affluent white schools in football playoffs or when countries that are having border skirmishes meet in a soccer contest.

Riots do not always occur under such conditions, however, and sociologists try to analyze what makes riots more or less likely to occur. One factor is the absence of other avenues for expressing grievances. In societies that lack effective means of political protest, violence associated with sporting events may be more severe. This interpretation is supported by the violent riots that occur in Latin American countries. A soccer riot in Lima, Peru, resulted in the death of 293 fans and the injury of more than 500 others. Fans in relatively poor countries may identify strongly with players who come from humble backgrounds similar to their own. Such identification seems greatly to intensify the feelings of the fans. Under such conditions, riots may occur if there is a precipitating event, such as a fight between spectators, a contested call by officials, or violence or injury among the players (Eitzen, 1979b). The severity of the riot may be affected by the importance of the contest, the intensity of the traditional rivalry between competing teams, and the violence of the sport being watched, suggests Lewis (1975).

## Theoretical Views of Sport and Society

Large numbers of people in the United States seem to believe that sport contributes to the well-being of society and the individuals in it. In fact, 75 percent of the respondents in a midwestern urban area agreed that sport is "particularly important for the well-being of our so-

ciety," and 71 percent agreed that "sports are valuable because they help youngsters to become good citizens" (Spreitzer and Snyder, 1975). General Douglas MacArthur felt that sport stimulated the pride and genius of the American people and renewed their national spirit.

In one sense, the way people view sport reflects the way they view and evaluate American society. Those who are basically satisfied with the nature and structure of American society will be similarly uncritical of sport. They will see sport as compatible with the basic values of society and as contributing to social stability. Those who are critical of the structure of American society are more likely to see sport as a means of diverting the masses from their frustrations and a way of making a profit from the efforts of athletes. Each of these views is limited, but both direct our attention to important questions about sport and society.

## The Functionalist View of Sport

Functionalist sociologists have considered how sport helps a society to meet the functional needs of pattern maintenance and tension management, integration, goal attainment, and adaptation. We will define these terms and explain the ways in which sport promotes them—in the view of functionalists.

Social patterns are *maintained* when individuals become motivated to support the structures and values of a particular society. If sport teaches loyalty to a team, unselfishness to teammates, and the desire to work hard, achieve, and win, all within a rule-bound structure, those values and motives and the willingness to accept the existing structure all contribute to the maintenance of that structure. Furthermore, players learn limits on ways they can express anger or disappointment within a particular social setting, thus learning ways of managing tension.

Compared to nonathletes, students who participate in high school sport are more likely to accept school norms and traditions (Schafer and Philips, 1970) and are more conservative in their political attitudes (Rehberg and Cohen, 1976). There is no evidence, however, that such values result directly from participation in sport or that such values are the most functional ones for young people to learn. Regarding the motivations sport is assumed to teach, it may be that more people are discouraged from working hard and achieving as a result of their experiences than are encouraged. Since the structure of sport allows for few winners, those who do not make the team or who regularly lose despite their best efforts may end up believing that hard work and effort are not enough to win. Instead, they may come to feel that people need to be exceptional in order to be successful—for example, very tall (like Manute Bol in basketball) or very large (like William "Refrigerator" Perry in football). Most people may conclude that their own efforts cannot influence the outcome or that illicit means are justified—cheating, use of drugs, or injuring other players. Such a result would not be functional for a society.

*Integration* involves the acceptance of certain common values and motives. It also involves the effective coordination and communication of various members of society, even if they belong to different racial, religious, or social class groups. With its emphasis on coordinated teamwork, sport is presumed to develop interpersonal skills in individuals, which will help achieve integration. Business organizations often sponsor company teams on the assumption that people who play together will work together better in the office. At a community level sport has been suggested as a major means of integrating members of a town, city, or region without regard to the class, racial, or religious divisions that might otherwise be prominent.

International competitions are stressed as a mechanism for enhancing national solidarity or promoting mutually beneficial relationships between countries. The same might be true within a nation as well. Interscholastic sports or regional competitions might promote travel, exchange, contacts, and other forms of communication among schools or regions that could provide a basis for greater integration. Whether or not sport will achieve such results probably depends on the severity of other social cleavages—political, racial, or economic—between competing groups. Sport may enhance integration, but it may also heighten conflicts and rivalries. It is not always clear why sport sometimes fosters social cohesiveness and at other times does not.

All societies need to know how to attain goals such as producing food in order to survive. In a general way, *goal attainment* in a society is helped by sport, functionalists suggest, because sport stresses a goal-oriented model of behavior; it develops mental and physical fitness and encourages self-discipline. These experiences are considered useful for the various goal-attainment activities of a society. No studies have proved that sport helps a society to attain its goals, however, so this assertion should be considered an idea to be tested rather than a statement of fact.

All social systems need to adapt to their ecological and social space on earth, and sport is seen as fulfilling this need for *adaptation* in several ways. In simple societies, sport stresses the physical skills and dexterities that are directly useful in hunting or in battle. By publicly displaying and valuing such skills through sport, a society can encourage their development. In modern industrial societies, it is less clear how sport may help a society adapt to its environment, although it may contribute to the general level of health in a society. In his extensive study, the writer James Michener (1976) suggests that sport has two major justifications: improving the overall physical health of the individuals in a society throughout their lifetimes and providing entertainment to players and spectators. The former may be considered a form of physical adaptation, whereas the latter may improve the mental health of individuals.

Several sociologists have suggested that, even in industrial societies, sport can serve as preparation for combat readiness (Wohl, 1970). State laws making physical education programs in American schools mandatory grew out of the increased pressure to be prepared militarily after World War I. World War II gave physical education and organized sports a similar boost (Cozens and Stumpf, 1953). It is not apparent that the Korean or Vietnamese wars had the same results, however. Within a competitive society sports programs may teach people how to manage losing and failure, since most people and teams do not win. The idea that sport helps societies adapt can also be considered a hunch to be tested with careful research.

## Conflict Perspectives on Sport

Although sport may under certain conditions promote the social functions functionalists claim it does, it may also have dysfunctional consequences. Because conflict theorists stress the unequal power and resources of various groups in society, they raise questions about whether sport might serve the interests of some groups more than others. Big-time athletics, for example, may benefit a few individuals in society while actually exploiting many others, including players and spectators. Within a society, critics contend, sport may serve as an *opiate*—that is, as something that takes people's minds off problems but does nothing to solve those problems (Hoch, 1972). In this view, sport is the great distractor. Sport keeps workers, for example, from realizing how boring and alienating their jobs are. Besides distracting people, sport operates in ways that fortify the position of the powerful elite groups of society. Specifically, popular violent sports like football, hockey, and boxing make official, rule-governed violence appear acceptable and even part of a package of idealized masculinity. Seeing that violence is acceptable within the world of sport may help to make it seem more acceptable in other realms.

Sport, according to conflict theorists, also encourages the belief that hard work is a necessary and a sufficient cause of success. Such a belief tends to legitimate the positions of people who control more resources in society, since it suggests that people occupy positions on the basis of their own talents and efforts.

Conflict theorists also suggest that sport has shifted away from being an activity to be enjoyed for its own sake to a product to be consumed. This means that instead of going out and having a good time playing a sport with one's friends, sport has become an important commodity that is promoted, marketed, and sold so that certain groups can make a profit. Team owners promote a phony loyalty to their teams in an effort to fill the stands with supporters. What was fun when played by amateurs loses its enjoyment, and winning becomes much more important than having a good time.

In such a situation, the intrinsic satisfactions that are derived from flow experiences are replaced by the pursuit of external goals such as prestige or profits. "The purpose of play shifts from the achievement of immediate enjoyment to earning ultimate successes, from means to ends" (Mitchell, 1983, pp. 13–38).

A study of Little League baseball, for example, found that while coaching begins as an effort to build character and skills, it becomes the strategic management of resources to win games (Fine, 1987). Rationality begins to influence even play, with growing efforts to improve it through calculation, regimen, and control. In Little League, this means the activity is judged more by statistics (runs, hits, errors, RBIs, and so forth) and wins than by how much the boys enjoyed themselves (Fine, 1987; Mitchell, 1989).

A Marxian conflict analysis of sport tends to lump all forms of sporting activity into the same category. Little League baseball and professional boxing tend to be treated similarly in that they are seen as serving the same interests. Such treatment is clearly an oversimplification. Another problem is that Hoch's analysis of sport as an opiate assumes that the people who are involved in sports as players or spectators would be involved in critically analyzing and reforming

*Rationality, calculation, and control seem to be increasingly replacing the intrinsic satisfactions of sports as a game. This can be seen, for example, in highly organized Little Leagues where success is emphasized more than having a good time.*

American social structure if it were not for their involvement in sports.

Given the composition and attitudes of those people who are sports fans—namely, solid middle-class, working-class, and some upper-middle-class people, all of whom tend to support the political, economic, and social status quo—it seems unlikely that most of them would be involved in challenging the system in any case. We do not know if the existence of sports increases their general level of satisfaction with the status quo or whether people who pursue occupations in which goal attainment and achievement are important are drawn to sports. Without studies of the long-term effects of sports involvement on one's political and social behavior and beliefs, we cannot tell whether or not Hoch's view is supported.

## An Interactionist View of Sport

We have already seen sport as viewed by conflict and functionalist analysts. We can also consider it from an interactionist perspective. This approach places greater emphasis on the meanings attached to sport by interacting individuals. The perspective stresses the active role of players and spectators in shaping the social organization, conduct, and interpretation of sport.

Mountain climbing clearly reveals the importance of human agency and social definitions in the conduct and interpretation of sport. Take the issue of accidents, which can fatally affect a climber. When a slip occurs, mountaineers spend hours discussing it, trying to figure out what happened and why. The mountains are not dangerous places, they say, and events are controllable by human agents. If something goes wrong in the mountains, it is because people failed to follow the clear rules climbers are supposed to obey. Determining the degree to which a seasoned climber should know something and seeing whether or not proper procedures were followed enables other climbers to define an event as an avoidable accident. Thus people remain the masters of their fates (Mitchell, 1981, 1983). In these ways mountain climbing illustrates features of all sports—namely, events by themselves have no set meaning until the participants and spectators define and interpret those events. People define a "good sport," a "good player," or an "avoidable accident."

By drawing on both an interactionist and a Marxian perspective, we may raise some questions. Who has relatively greater power and resources in a particular sport? Who is therefore able to have their definitions and rules prevail? In privately owned professional sports leagues the owners, the media, and the spectators are influential in creating or modifying the rules and definitions. In a sport such as mountain climbing there are no owners and there is little media intrusion. Under such conditions the definitions of participants and their peers prevail. Even in rigid traditional sports, however, there may be borderline rules or definitions that are open to negotiation, depending on how strongly various participants feel about changing them.

## SPORT AND STRATIFICATION

Do sports provide upward mobility for talented youngsters regardless of race, sex, or social class? This is a controversial question in professional sports in the United States. Supporters of the American social structure stress the openness of the system to talent and effort. They extol the opportunities sport offers to proficient youngsters, however humble their backgrounds. Black athletes are highly visible in basketball, football, and baseball. As a result, the belief that sport provides blacks with "a ladder to success and a passport to a better life" is widely held (Miller and Russell, 1971). The widespread assertion that sport is "color-blind," however, needs closer examination to see if it fits social facts.

### Race and Sport

Critical commentators suggest that the visibility of blacks in a few sports actually masks the racial cleavages that exist within the institution. They note that blacks are involved in only a few sports—football, basketball, baseball, boxing, and track. There are many other sports with few or no black participants, including hockey, tennis, golf, swimming, polo, mountain climb-

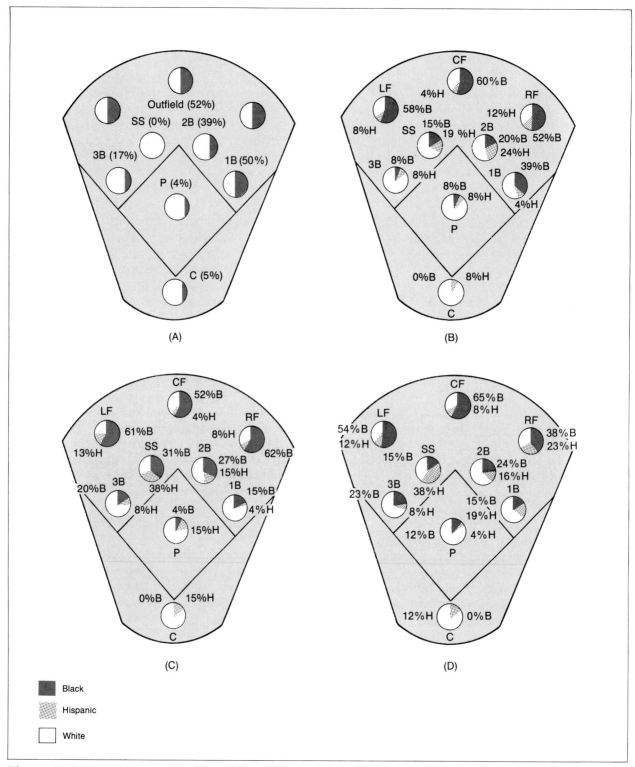

**Figure 22.5** **(A) Percentage of Black Players in Major League Baseball Starting Positions in 1975; (B) Percentage of Black and Hispanic Players in Major League Baseball Starting Lineups in 1982; (C) Percentage of Black and** **Hispanic Players in Major League Baseball Starting Lineups in 1986; (D) Percentage of Black and Hispanic Players in Major League Baseball Starting Lineups in 1989.**

*Figure legend follows on top of page 589.*

Between 1975 and 1982 the percentage of black players in the outfield increased slightly, as did the percentage of black players at shortstop and pitcher. The percentage of black players declined, however, in the positions of first, second, and third bases, and catcher. Black players remain much more likely to play outfield positions than to play infield positions. In 1986 blacks and Hispanics had made major gains at shortstop and had become even more numerous in the outfield. In 1989 blacks stayed even at first base (with 15 percent) and catcher (at 0 percent); made small gains in center field, third base, and pitcher; and lost ground in other positions. In 1982, 1986, and 1989, there were no black catchers, a position that has often led to future coaching jobs. In 1989 Hispanics made noteworthy gains at right field and first base, a small gain at center field, lost ground at catcher and pitcher, and stayed about even in the other positions. Overall, whites were the biggest gainers in 1989.

*Sources:* (A) Coakley, 1978, p. 284; Eitzen and Yetman, 1979, p. 391; (B) Persell, 1982; (C) Persell and Haft, 1986; (D) Persell, 1989.

ing, skiing, car racing, horse racing, sailing, figure skating, and gymnastics. It seems unlikely that the absence of blacks from these sports is due to lack of athletic ability so much as to lack of opportunity to learn and practice a particular sport. Mitchell goes even further than this to suggest that the absence of blacks and other minorities from certain sports is a commentary on their perception of their own position in society, not just an indication of their access to tools, techniques, and resources (Mitchell, 1982).

In those sports that do have a high proportion of blacks, critical commentators focus on three examples of discrimination within them: the assignment of playing positions, rewards and promotions within sports, and performance standards (Eitzen and Yetman, 1979). Black players tend to be assigned by professional coaches and managers to particular positions, such as outfielders in baseball (see Figure 22.5). In that way they do not compete against whites in all positions, including pitcher. Position assignment has been explained by the importance of a position for social interaction on a team. Sociologists suggest that the more central the position is, the greater is the chance that it will be filled by whites (Loy and McElvogue, 1970). In football the central positions are quarterback, center, offensive guard, and linebacker; in baseball they are pitcher, catcher, and infielders. These are the positions that are filled by whites rather than blacks. Between 1960 and 1975 the proportion of blacks in baseball increased dramatically, but almost all their gains were in the noncentral positions (Eitzen and Yetman, 1979). This was true between 1975 and 1982 as well, when shortstop and second base were the only positions to gain significantly more minority representation (as shown in Figure 22.5). By 1989, the proportion of whites in a number of positions increased (Figure 22.5).

Others suggest that the spatial centrality of the position is less important than the degree of leadership responsibility and the chance to influence the outcome of the game that the position represents (Brower, 1973; Edwards, 1969). This assertion is supported by the small number of blacks in the key positions of quarterback, place-kick holder, and kicker (Eitzen and Yetman, 1979). In baseball this is reflected in the small proportion of minorities who play catcher (see Figure 22.5). Edwards suggests that the absence of blacks in leadership positions is due to the persistence of negative stereotypes in the sports world about black intellectual and leadership abilities. Although racial "stacking" by position existed in college basketball in 1972, it had disappeared in both college and professional basketball by 1974 (Eitzen and Yetman, 1979).

Position assignment by race affects the rewards blacks and whites receive in sports. About one-third of the most highly paid baseball players in 1982 were either pitchers or catchers and one-quarter played one of the bases, positions that minorities are less likely to play than are whites (see Figure 22.5). Although black superstars with high salaries are frequently in the sports news and the mean salaries of black players often equal or exceed those of white players, the salaries of black players do not match their exemplary performance records (Eitzen and Yetman, 1979; Scully, 1971). If all black players were paid in a way that reflected their achievements, and if blacks were more likely to play the more lucrative positions, then it is likely that they would earn more than white players in general. Also, earnings of black players from commercials, endorsements, and off-season jobs often do not equal those of white players.

After their sports careers end, blacks are less likely than whites to obtain well-paying sportscasting jobs. Coaching jobs are disproportionately held by white rather than black former athletes. Part of the reason for few black coaches at all levels may rest on the positions they held while players. In baseball between 1968 and 1971, 68 percent of all managers were former infielders (Eitzen and Yetman, 1979). Because blacks have traditionally lacked the leadership experience of these positions, they may have been hindered in their chances of becoming coaches right from the start.

The blacks who do play professional sports seem to have higher performance records than whites, at least in baseball and football (Pascal and Rapping, 1970). In baseball black batting averages are 20 points higher than those of whites (Eitzen and Yetman, 1979; Rosenblatt, 1967). Blacks are more likely than whites to be on the starting teams in football and basketball, although basketball players on all teams are more likely to be black. This evidence suggests that to play professional sports, blacks need to be good enough to make the starting team, whereas there are many more jobs for whites as average players who may spend part of their time "sitting on the bench."

This evidence suggests that sport is not color-blind, that discrimination against black athletes exists with respect to their assignment to positions and to the rewards they receive. If racial discrimination exists in sports, where clearly measurable performance is presumably the only criterion for advancement and reward, then no arena of American life can be assumed to be free of discrimination, suggest Eitzen and Yetman (1979). Sport, then, becomes a crucial test of whether a society treats all members fairly.

## Gender and Sport

Women, like blacks, have been stereotyped in sport. Women have been barred by law or social custom at least since the Olympic Games began in 776 B.C. in ancient Greece. For some time, a series of myths about the physical nature of

*The extent and type of sports participation available to women has been historically limited by legal or social sanctions. Even the tennis clothes women had to wear around the turn of the century (on the left) were much more restrictive than the ones worn today.*

women suggested that women would endanger their childbearing capacity if they played sports. More recently biological research shows that those myths are just that and are quite unfounded in fact. Another restraint on the participation of women in sport has been the social definitions of masculinity and femininity that prevailed in American society and in industrial societies generally. Women were supposed to be passive rather than active. Certain forms of activity were considered appropriate for females: figure skating, dance, diving, horseback riding, skiing, golf, archery, bowling, badminton, and volleyball. Some of these activities, such as riding and skiing, are restricted to women of sufficient economic resources. In others, the degree of face-to-face competition is limited, as is the size of the physical object that needs to be moved by the application of force (Metheny, 1965).

Until recently both the extent and the type of sports participation available to women were limited by legal or social sanctions. It was always acceptable, however, for women to be active supporters and spectators of vigorous male sports activities—for example, by being cheerleaders. The struggle to redefine and reassign power in sport reflects an underlying struggle to redefine gender rules and relationships in all areas of society (Heide, 1978). At the high school and college level, if sport develops the self-confidence, teamwork, strength, perseverance, and physical health that its supporters claim, why should girls and women be denied these positive outcomes? Leadership at the national level, combined with pressure from the women's movement, has led to a shift in the view of sport as training for masculinity to sport as training for achievement by either sex.

The push for sexual equality in sport received major support from the passage of the so-called Title IX legislation of 1972, which reads: "No person in the United States shall, on the basis of sex, be excluded from participation in, be denied the benefits of, or be subjected to discrimination under any education program or activity receiving Federal financial assistance." Title IX seems to have influenced the participation of women in sport. In 1970–1971 (before Title IX) high school girls were 7 percent of all high school athletes; by 1976–1977 they were 28 percent (Grett, 1978). Moreover, in 1974, 60 colleges offered athletic scholarships to women; by 1978, 500 colleges offered them (Pogge, 1978).

## Social Class and Sport

Ever since Veblen (1899) declared that sport and leisure are used by their participants to proclaim economic and cultural distinctiveness, the possible link between social class and sport has been suggested. Generally, sociologists have analyzed two types of issues: First, how is social class related to the sports that people play? Second, does sports participation affect an individual's chances for social mobility?

The sports played by individuals are clearly related to social class background. The higher classes are much more likely to participate in sailing, riding, skiing, golf, racquet games, swimming, crew, and fencing. Members of the lower social classes are much more likely to be involved in boxing, wrestling, football, and baseball (Loy, 1969). Class differences are fairly easily explained in terms of what sports are taught in schools, the availability of public recreational facilities, and the need for expensive equipment and professional instructors.

Leaving aside for the moment the class-linked nature of participation in many sports, let us examine whether participation in the relatively open sports of boxing, basketball, football, and baseball increases an individual's chances of upward social mobility. The rags to riches tales of some players, such as Babe Ruth, O. J. Simpson, Muhammad Ali, and Fernando Valenzuela, suggest this possibility. Moreover, the highly publicized second careers of sports heroes as movie stars (Jim Brown), sports commentators (Frank Gifford), or politicians (Bill Bradley and Jack Kemp) support the view of sports as a social aid. Most of these stories overlook three things. The rags to riches stories describe players at the peaks of their careers. They do not always show them in their retirement or describe how far their sport celebrity carries them in later life. They do not indicate how many hopefuls there are for every successful star. Finally, most of the success stories fail to spell out how these people used their sports fame to achieve success.

Four ways that participation in sport might help upward social mobility are suggested by

Loy (1969). We will mention each of them and then consider the relevant evidence. First, sports skills may help a player to enter professional sports. But what are the odds of this happening? For every 200,000 high school seniors who play basketball, there are only 5700 college seniors who play. Of those, 211 are drafted by the pros, and only 55 are actually signed (Durso, 1975). This means that most young players will be disappointed. These odds are seldom perceived by lower-class or minority youngsters and their parents. For these reasons, black leaders like Roscoe C. Brown, president of Bronx Community College, and the tennis player Arthur Ashe urge young people to spend two hours in the library for every one hour they spend on the athletic field.

Second, Loy suggests that sports may enhance an individual's educational aspirations and attainment. When compared to nonathletes, high school athletes are likely to get slightly better grades (especially if they have blue-collar parents), are less likely to become delinquents, and are more likely to be upwardly mobile (Phillips and Schafer, 1971). Athletics may raise the aspirations for kids who would not otherwise go to college (Snyder and Spreitzer, 1978). This assertion is confirmed by a study of former Notre Dame college football players. Members of the team were more likely to be from lower-status backgrounds than the regular college students (Sack and Thiel, 1979). The relatively small numbers of athletic scholarships compared to the number of hopefuls means that not everyone will get one, but the existence of such scholarships may raise the educational aspirations of some students and actually help a few to go to college who might not otherwise have gone. On the other hand, participating in "big-time" athletics may pull students away from academic success. (See the box on college athletics.)

Third, success in college or professional sports may result in a former athlete being sought after and sponsored for a position in business. One's fame as a starring college or professional ballplayer is traded for a high-paying job in business. But although fame may open doors, education and socioeconomic background is related to subsequent advancement on the job (Haerle, 1975), suggesting that the convertibility of sports fame for lower-class or mi-

nority players might be somewhat limited. A study of Notre Dame football players found that 41 percent of former first-team football players were making $50,000 or more annually 14 to 34 years after graduation from college, compared to 30 percent of second-team players, 24 percent of nonteam members, and 13 percent of reserve players (Sack and Thiel, 1979). This finding is consistent with the sponsorship view of sport and mobility.

The fourth way sports may help individuals achieve social mobility is by teaching attitudes and behaviors that have value off the field. This interpretation is also consistent with the Notre Dame study, which suggests that the interpersonal skills and character traits that produce successful athletes may be precisely the same ones that make successful entrepreneurs. "Athletes who rise to the top in the often brutal competition of big time college football may be best suited for careers in business" (Sack and Thiel, 1979, p. 65). This suggests that individuals who perform well under stress and who are strivers and achievers in sport may perform the same way in business situations. Sack and Thiel did not measure the personality characteristics of team members, compared to regular graduates, so this interpretation cannot be tested definitively with the available data.

One somewhat disturbing finding they do report is the fact that football players are more likely to report that they cheated on their schoolwork while in college than are regular students—69 percent of ballplayers reported cheating, compared to 43 percent of regular students (Sack and Thiel, 1979). The possibility also exists that players learn attitudes and behaviors that are not particularly helpful for social mobility. Total devotion to their sport may not help them if they are cut from the team or if they must face the prospect of an early retirement. (All athletes face early retirement; the only question is how early.) Players devoted to sports may face a major identity crisis when they are cut. As Wayne Embry, the former general manager of the Milwaukee Bucks basketball team noted, "I see that every year—the guys who have gone to school and never thought of having a vocation to fall back on. You tell them they have been cut and they can't believe you" (quoted in Snyder and Spreitzer, 1978, p. 84).

## The Impact of Big-Time Athletics on College Athletes' Academic Careers

To see how participation in a university athletic program affected athletes, sociologist Peter Adler did field observations of a "big-time" college basketball program over a four-year period (1980–1984), which he and Patricia A. Adler analyzed and wrote up together (Adler and Adler, 1985).

They found that most athletes came to the university feeling optimistic about their academic experience and their chances of graduating. The longer they were in school, however, the more structural problems they faced and the more cynical they became. First, they realized how *professionalized* sport was in college as compared to high school. As one senior said, "college athletics . . . take over you [sic] mind" (p. 244). Practices, games, road trips, and athletic-related media and social functions took a great deal of their discretionary time. Coaches actively *intervened* in the athletes' academic lives, declaring their majors, registering them for courses, adjusting their schedules, and contacting their professors. As one athlete said, "it kinda make you feel like you not involved in it . . ." (p. 244). At the same time, athletics gave athletes more positive *reinforce-*ment than their academic work did.

Socially the athletes were isolated from the other students on campus, because they were housed in the athletes' dorm in a remote part of campus and because of their greater size and build as compared to other students. As a result, they forged tight bonds with each other, which led to the formation of common attitudes and beliefs about their college experiences. In general, the peer culture they shared was anti-intellectual and anti-academic and tended to discourage academic effort. Negative classroom experiences with professors or the content of their classes helped to push some athletes further away from the academic side of college.

Roughly a quarter of the athletes were able to realize their original academic goals. The others either shifted out of pre-professional programs into easier majors or faced the prospect that they might not graduate. As a result, "athletes became increasingly cynical about and uninterested in academics" (p. 248).

Adler and Adler see several policy implications in their research:

1. Universities should reinstitute the ban on freshmen eligibility to help protect athletes from the "enticing whirlwind of celebrity" (p. 249).
2. Separate dorms for athletes should be abolished to help athletes become more integrated into the larger university culture.
3. Athletes should be offered more academic role models and advisers, rather than having athletic personnel act as academic advisers.

What do you think? Do you think athletes should have separate facilities? Do you think their coaches should be involved in their academic lives? What are some of the contextual pressures on coaches and athletes to devote so much time to their athletics?

This research by Adler and Adler is consistent with a number of other studies suggesting that big-time college athletes have lower GPAs, higher attrition rates, and lower chances of graduating than other students (Cross, 1973; Edwards, 1984; Nyquist, 1979; Purdy, Eitzen, and Hufnagel, 1982; Sack and Thiel, 1979).

---

Some Ivy League athletes never go beyond their days of glory as gridiron heroes (Page, 1969).

## SUMMARY

1. Leisure and sport illustrate a number of sociological and societal features. They may extend or complement the values and skills people use in their daily occupations.

2. Successful leisure is characterized by flow. A flow experience is freely chosen; it totally involves the self; it is self-rewarding; and it contains an uncertainty of outcomes that allows for creativity. Flow experiences are inhibited by self-consciousness and overrationalization.

3. Leisure time has increased dramatically for Americans in this century, and now exceeds the amount of time most people spend working or with their families. Leisure expenditures have increased tenfold in the last two decades. Watching television is the leisure activity people mention most frequently. Despite the much publicized "fitness craze," Americans do not appear

to be spending a great deal of time on strenuous physical activity.

4. Functionalist views of leisure stress the consequences of leisure activities for family or societal cohesiveness.

5. Conflict theorists suggest that leisure activities and resources may be used by groups in cultural competition with one another.

6. Sport is a form of game in which the outcome is affected by physical skill and prowess. Sport in America has been influenced by English royalty, which loved games, and by the Puritans, who frowned on idle pleasures.

7. Early sport in the United States represented individual competitions in some skill that was useful for dealing with the environment.

8. Urbanization, immigration, and industrialization swelled the populations in a given city or region who could cheer a sports team. Demographic and technological changes encouraged the growth of big-time sports beginning in the early twentieth century and continuing to the present.

9. Some societies favor less competitive or less violent sport than does the United States. Two different theories have been offered to explain why violent sport thrives in some societies but not in others, the culture pattern theory and the tension release theory. Sipes's analysis supports the former interpretation, but the existence of violent sport in a violent society does not prove that one causes the other.

10. Violence among spectators has also increased in recent years, and several sociological explanations have been offered to explain its incidence, including greater societal permissiveness, growing contempt for social institutions, and a widening gap between fans and highly paid athletes.

11. People's views of sport tend to mirror their views of American society in general. Some see sport as positive and functional for the maintenance, integration, goal attainment, and adaptation of society. Others argue that sport

distracts people from examining the social roots of their problems. Sport also tends to justify the use of violence as an acceptable means of attaining certain ends and to legitimate the existence of large-scale inequalities of wealth and power. Functionalist and Marxian analyses of sport both direct our attention to interesting questions about sport.

12. Symbolic interactionists add a further dimension to the understanding of sport, specifically the insight that events and rules in sport, as in all forms of social life, are socially created by the various participants in the situation. Some participants in that process may control greater power and resources than others, however.

13. Racial inequalities occur within sport with respect to the sports played by blacks and whites, the stacking of blacks into particular positions in baseball and football, and the relative rewards blacks and whites receive in sports.

14. Like blacks, women have been excluded and stereotyped in sports. In recent years Title IX has provided some impetus for more opportunities for women athletes.

15. The sports individuals play are related to class backgrounds. Sport has been touted as an avenue of upward mobility for talented members of the lower classes. Rags-to-riches tales of superstars neglect the thousands of hopefuls who do not achieve stardom; they do not follow the stars beyond their short-lived careers; and they fail to indicate how sport may help social mobility. Four ways that sport may aid mobility include using one's skills to become a professional player; the possibility that sports success might increase educational aspirations and attainment through athletic scholarships; the sponsorship of a former athlete in business; and the learning of attitudes and behaviors through sport that are useful in later life.

## KEY TERMS

athletics (p. 579)
culture pattern theory (p. 582)
flow (p. 571)

games (p. 579)
play (p. 579)
sport (p. 579)
tension release theory (p. 582)

## SUGGESTED READINGS

Adler, Peter, and Patricia A. Adler. 1985. "From idealism to pragmatic detachment: The academic performance of college athletes." *Sociology of Education* 58: 241–250. A sociological field study of college basketball players and their problems at a university trying to move into "big-time" athletics.

Fine, Gary Alan. 1987. *With the Boys*. Chicago: University of Chicago Press. An excellent ethnographic study of Little League baseball. It may distress those who subscribe to the idea of the character-building nature of competitive team sport, yet it will not uphold the worst fears of Little League critics.

Mitchell, Richard G., Jr. 1983. *Mountain Experience: The Psychology and Sociology of Adventure*. Chicago: University of Chicago Press. Although the site is mountain climbing, the subject is much broader and includes sociological reflections on leisure, challenge, and life.

Nelson, Linden L., and Spencer Kagan. 1972. "Competition: The star-spangled scramble." *Psychology Today* (September): 53–54ff. An experimental study showing that competition is more important than goal achievement for many Americans.

Sack, Allen L., and Robert Thiel. 1979. "College football and social mobility: A case study of Notre Dame football players." *Sociology of Education* 52: 60–66. A research study that traces what happens to a group of first-, second-, and third-string players on the Notre Dame football team.

# Glossary

**Absolute poverty**  The condition of having too little income to buy the necessities—food, shelter, clothing, health care.

**Achieved status**  A social position (status) obtained through an individual's own talents and efforts.

**Affirmative action**  The requirement that employers make special efforts to recruit, hire, and promote qualified members of previously excluded groups, including women and minorities.

**Aggregate**  A collection of unrelated people who do not know one another but who may occupy a common space—for example, a crowd of people crossing a city street.

**Agrarian societies**  Societies in which large-scale cultivation, using plows and draft animals, is the primary means of subsistence.

**Alienation**  The separation, or estrangement, of individuals from themselves and from others.

**Amalgamation**  The biological as well as cultural assimilation (merging) of racial or ethnic groups.

**Anomalies**  In science, observations or problems that cannot be explained or solved in terms of a prevailing paradigm.

**Anomie**  A breakdown or confusion in the norms, values, and culture of a group or a society. A condition of relative normlessness.

**Anomie theory**  The theory suggesting that deviance and crime occur when there is an acute gap between cultural norms and goals and the socially structured opportunities for individuals to achieve those goals.

**Anticipatory socialization**  The process of taking on the attitudes, values, and behaviors of a status or role one expects to occupy in the future.

**Apartheid**  The policy of racial separation in South Africa enforced by legal, political, and military power.

**Ascribed status**  A social position (status)—such as sex, race, and social class—that a person acquires at birth.

**Assimilation**  The merging of minority and majority groups into one group with a common culture and identity.

**Association**  A group of people bound together by common goals and rules, but not necessarily by close personal ties.

**Athletics**  A form of sport that is closer to work than to play.

**Authority**  Power regarded as legitimate.

**Autocracy**  Rule or government concentrated in a single ruler or group of leaders who are willing to use force to maintain control.

**Baby boom**  The people who were born in the United States between 1946 and 1965. This group represented a sharp increase in birth rates and in the absolute number of births compared to pre-1946 levels.

**Bias**  The influence of a scientist's personal values and attitudes on scientific observations and conclusions.

**Bicultural**  The capacity to understand and function well in more than one cultural group.

**Birth rate**  Number of births per year per 1000 women 15 to 44 years old.

**Bureaucracy**  A large-scale, formal organization with centralized authority, a hierarchical chain of command, explicit rules and procedures, and an emphasis on formal positions rather than on persons.

**Calling**  The idea in certain branches of ascetic Protestantism that one can live acceptably to God by fulfilling the obligations imposed by one's secular position in the world.

**Capitalism**  A form of economic organization in which private individuals accumulate and invest capital, own the means of production, and control profits.

**Caste system**   A closed system of social stratification in which prestige and social relationships are based on hereditary position at birth.

**Centrally planned economy**   An economic system that includes public ownership of or control over all productive resources and whose activity is planned by the government.

**Charisma**   The exceptional mystical or even supernatural quality of personality attributed to a person by others. Literally, "the gift of grace."

**Charismatic leader**   An individual who enlists the strong emotional support of followers through personal and seemingly supernatural qualities.

**Charter**   The capacity of certain schools to confer special rights on their graduates.

**Church**   A formally organized, institutionalized religious organization with formal and traditional religious doctrine, beliefs, and practices.

**City**   A relatively permanent settlement of large numbers of people who do not grow or gather their own food.

**Civil law**   The branch of law that deals largely with wrongs against the individual.

**Civil religion**   The interweaving of religious and political symbols in public life.

**Class**   Position in a social hierarchy based on prestige and/or property ownership.

**Class conflict**   The struggle between competing classes, specifically between the class that owns the means of production and the class or classes that do not.

**Class consciousness**   The sense of common class position and shared interests held by members of a social class.

**Class system**   A system of stratification based primarily on the unequal ownership and control of economic resources.

**Closed system**   In organizational theory, the degree to which an organization is shut off from its environment.

**Coercion**   A form of social interaction in which one is made to do something through the use of social pressure, threats, or force.

**Cognitive development**   The systematic improvement of intellectual ability through a series of stages.

**Cognitive development theory**   Suggests that individuals try to pattern their lives and experiences to form a reasonably consistent picture of their beliefs, actions, and values.

**Cohort**   Persons who share something in common, usually being born in the same year or time period.

**Commitment**   Willingness of members of a group to do what is needed to maintain the group.

**Community**   A collection of people in a geographical area; may also include the idea that the collection has a social structure and a sense of community spirit or belonging.

**Comparable worth**   A policy of equal pay for men and women doing similar work, even if the jobs are labeled differently by sex.

**Competition**   A goal-directed form of social interaction in which the goals or objects pursued are limited, so not all competitors can attain them. Competitive behavior is governed by rules and limitations (restraints).

**Complementary marriages**   Marriages in which husband and wife take distinctly separate family roles.

**Concentric-zone theory**   A theory of urban development holding that cities grow around a central business district in concentric zones, with each zone devoted to a different land use.

**Concept**   A formal definition of what is being studied.

**Conflict**   A form of social interaction involving direct struggle between individuals or groups over commonly valued resources or goals. Differs from competition because individuals are more interested in defeating an opponent than in achieving a goal.

**Conflict approach**   One of the major theoretical perspectives in sociology: emphasizes the importance of unequal power and conflict in society. *Weberian conflict theorists* stress inequality and conflict based on class, status, power; *Marxian theorists* emphasize conflict and inequality based on ownership of the means of production.

**Conformity**   Going along with the norms or behaviors of a group.

**Conjugal family**   A form of family organization centered around the husband-wife relationship rather than around blood relationships.

**Consolidated Metropolitan Statistical Area (CMSA)**    A "supercity" with more than one million people. There were 21 such cities in the United States in 1984.

**Contact hypothesis**    The theory that people of different racial groups who became acquainted would be less prejudiced toward one another.

**Contagion theory**    Le Bon's theory that the anonymity people feel in a crowd makes them susceptible to the suggestions of fanatical leaders, and that emotions can sweep through such a crowd like a virus.

**Content analysis**    A research method used to describe and analyze in an objective and systematic way the content of literature, speeches, or other media presentations. The method helps to identify cultural themes or trends.

**Content of socialization**    The ideas, beliefs, values, knowledge, and so forth that are presented to people who are being socialized.

**Contest mobility**    The educational pattern in which selection for academic and university education is delayed and children compete throughout their schooling for high positions.

**Context of socialization**    The setting or arena within which socialization occurs.

**Continued subjugation**    The use of force and ideology by one group to retain domination over another group.

**Control group**    A group that is not exposed to the independent variable of interest to a researcher but whose members' backgrounds and experience are otherwise like those of the experimental group that is exposed to the independent variable.

**Controlling for**    In research, the effort to hold constant factors that might be influencing observed changes in the dependent variable.

**Convergence theory**    A theory suggesting that modernizing nations come to resemble one another over time. In collective behavior, a theory suggesting that certain crowds attract particular types of people, who may behave irrationally.

**Cooperation**    A form of social interaction involving collaborative effort among people to achieve a common goal.

**Cooptation**    A social process by which people who might otherwise threaten the stability or existence of an organization are brought into the leadership or policy-making structure of that organization.

**Correlation**    An observed association between a change in the value of one variable and a change in the value of another variable.

**Counterculture**    A subculture whose norms and values sharply contradict the dominant norms and values of the society in which it occurs.

**Creationism**    A theory that sees all major types of living things, including people, as having been made by the direct creative action of God in six days.

**Credential**    The educational degree or certificate used to determine a person's eligibility for a position.

**Crime**    A behavior prohibited by law.

**Criminal law**    Law enacted by recognized political authorities that prohibits or requires certain behaviors.

**Criteria for inferring causality**    Evidence that two variables are correlated and that the hypothesized cause preceded the hypothesized effect in time, as well as evidence eliminating rival hypotheses.

**Crude birth rate**    The total number of live births per 1000 persons in a population within a particular year.

**Crude death rate**    The number of deaths per 1000 persons occurring within a one-year period in a particular population.

**Cult**    A loosely organized group of people who together act out religious feelings, attitudes, and relationships; may focus on an unusual form of worship or belief.

**Cultural capital**    Symbolic wealth socially defined as worthy of being sought and possessed.

**Cultural change**    Modifications or transformations of a culture's customs, values, ideas, or artifacts.

**Cultural determinism**    The view that the nature of a society is shaped primarily by the ideas and values of the people living in it.

**Cultural division of labor**    A situation in which a person's place in the occupational world is determined by his or her cultural markers (such as ethnicity).

**Cultural imposition** The forcing of members of one culture to adopt the practices of another culture.

**Cultural relativism** The view that the customs and ideas of a society must be viewed within the context of that society.

**Cultural revolution** The repudiation of many existing cultural elements and the substitution of new ones.

**Cultural universals** Cultural features, such as the use of language, shared by all human societies.

**Culture** The common heritage shared by the people of a society, consisting of customs, values, language, ideas, and artifacts.

**Culture lag** The time difference between the introduction of material innovations and resulting changes in cultural practices.

**Culture of poverty** A distinctive culture thought to develop among poor people and characterized by failure to delay gratification, fatalism, and weak family and community ties.

**Culture pattern theory** In the sociology of sport, a theory that explains aggression and violence in sport as learned behavior that mirrors the degree of aggression and violence in the society.

**Cyclical theories** Theories of social change suggesting that societies follow a certain life course, from vigorous and innovative youth to more materialistic maturity and then to decline.

**Deduction** Reasoning from the general to the specific.

**Defining the situation** The socially created perspective that people apply to a situation.

**Democracy** A form of political organization in which power resides with the people and is exercised by them.

**Democratic-collective organization** An organization in which authority is placed in the group as a whole, rules are minimized, members have considerable control over their work, and job differentiation is minimized.

**Demographic transition** The demographic change experienced in Western Europe and North America since the industrial revolution in which the birth rate has declined so that it is about equal to the death rate.

**Demography** The scientific study of population size, composition, and distribution as well as patterns of change in those features.

**Denomination** One of a number of religious organizations in a society with no official state church. Has some formal doctrines, beliefs, and practices, but tolerates diverse religious views.

**Dependency theory** A theory about the place of developing nations in the world economy suggesting that major industrial nations take advantage of the cheap labor and raw materials of developing nations and hence are reluctant to see them become industrialized.

**Dependent variable** The variable that occurs or changes in a patterned way due to the presence of, or changes in, another variable or variables.

**Descriptive study** A research study whose goal is to describe the social phenomena being studied.

**Deskilling** The process of breaking down jobs into less complex segments that require less knowledge and judgment on the part of workers.

**Deterrence theory** The view that certain qualities of punishment—such as certainty, swiftness, and severity—will help prevent others from committing crimes that have been so punished.

**Deviance** Behaviors or characteristics that violate important social norms.

**Deviant career** The regular pursuit of activities regarded by the individual and by others as deviant.

**Differential association** A theory that attributes the existence of deviant behavior to learning from friends or associates.

**Differentiation, functional** The division of labor or of social roles within a society or an organization.

**Differentiation, rank** The unequal placement and evaluation of various social positions.

**Diffusion** The spread of inventions and discoveries from one group or culture to another on a voluntary basis; a source of cultural change.

**Discovery** The uncovering of something that

existed but was unknown; a source of cultural change.

**Discrimination**    The unequal and unfair treatment of individuals or groups on the basis of some irrelevant characteristic, such as race, ethnicity, religion, sex, or social class.

**Division of labor**    The assignment of specialized tasks to various members of a group, organization, community, or society.

**Dominant status**    One social position that overshadows the other social positions an individual occupies.

**Domination**    The control of one group or individual by another.

**Double standard**    A set of social norms that allows males greater freedom of sexual expression, particularly before marriage, than females.

**Dramaturgical analysis**    An approach to social situations developed by Erving Goffman in which they are examined as though they were theatrical productions.

**Dual-career families**    Families in which both husband and wife have careers.

**Dual-career responsibilities**    The responsibilities of women who are wives as well as workers—often used to explain why women earn less.

**Dual economy**    The conceptual division of the private sector of the economy into monopoly (core) and competitive (periphery) sectors.

**Dyad**    A group composed of two people.

**Dysfunction**    Any consequence of a social system that disturbs or hinders the integration, adjustment, or stability of the system.

**Ecological paradigm**    A theory of land use and living patterns that examines the interplay among economic functions, geographical factors, demography, and the replacement of one group by another.

**Ecological succession**    In urban sociology, the replacement of one group by another over time.

**Ecological view**    An approach to the study of culture or other social phenomena that emphasizes the importance of examining climate, food and water supplies, and existing enemies in the environments.

**Ecology**    The scientific study of how organisms relate to one another and to their environments.

**Economic core**    The sector of the economy characterized by large, generally very profitable, oligopolistic firms that are national or multinational in scope; also called the monopoly sector.

**Economic growth**    An increase in the amount of goods and services produced with the same amount of labor and resources.

**Economic institution**    The pattern of roles, norms, and activities organized around the production, distribution, and consumption of goods and services in a society.

**Economic periphery**    The sector of the economy characterized by small, local, barely profitable firms; also called the competitive sector.

**Ecosystem**    A system formed by the interaction of a community of organisms with its environment.

**Education**    The process, in school or beyond, of transmitting a society's knowledge, skills, values, and behaviors.

**Egalitarian marriage**    A family in which husband and wife share equally in family decision making.

**Ego**    In Freudian theory, a concept referring to the conscious, rational part of the personality structure, which mediates between the impulses of the id and the rules of society.

**Elderly dependency ratio**    The ratio between the number of the elderly (65 and over) and the number of working-age people (ages 18 to 64).

**Emergent norm theory**    A theory of collective behavior suggesting that people move to form a shared definition of the situation in relatively normless situations.

**Emotion work**    An individual's effort to change an emotion or feeling to one that seems to be more appropriate to a given situation.

**Equilibrium**    In functionalist theory, the view that the parts of a society fit together into a balanced whole.

**Ethnic group**    A group that shares a common cultural tradition and sense of identity.

**Ethnocentrism**    The tendency to see one's own culture as superior to all others.

**Ethnography**    A detailed study based on actual observation of the way of life of a human group or society.

**Ethnomethodology**  The study of the methods used by individuals to communicate and make sense of their everyday lives as members of society. Many ethnomethodologists focus on the study of language and everyday conversation.

**Evangelicalism**  A form of Protestantism that stresses the preaching of the gospel of Jesus Christ, the validity of personal conversion, the Bible as the basis for belief, and active preaching of the faith.

**Evolutionary theories**  Theories of social change that see societies as evolving from simpler forms to more complex ones. In biology, the theory that living organisms develop new traits that may aid their adaptation or survival.

**Exchange**  A form of social interaction involving trade of tangibles (objects) or intangibles (sentiments) between individuals.

**Exchange theory**  An interpretive perspective that explains social interaction on the basis of the exchange of various tangible or intangible social rewards.

**Experiment**  A carefully controlled situation where the independent variable is manipulated while everything else remains the same; the aim is to see whether the dependent variable will change.

**Experimental group**  In research, the group of individuals exposed to the independent variable that is being introduced by the experimentor.

**Explanatory study**  A research study with the goal of explaining how or why things happen the way they do in the social world.

**Expressive**  A type of role that involves the showing of emotional feelings or preferences in interpersonal relationships.

**Expressive leader**  A group leader whose role in the group is to help maintain stability through joking, mediating conflicts, and otherwise reducing tension.

**Extended family**  A family in which relatives from several generations live together.

**Face-work**  A term used by Goffman to refer to the actions taken by individuals to make their behavior appear consistent with the image they want to present.

**Fads**  Striking behaviors that spread rapidly and that, even though embraced enthusiastically, remain popular for only a short time.

**Family**  Two or more persons who are related by blood, marriage, or adoption and who live together. They usually form an economic unit, and adult members care for the dependent children.

**Fashion**  A socially approved but temporary style of appearance or behavior.

**Flow**  An experience of total involvement in one's present activity.

**Folkways**  Social norms to which people generally conform, although they receive little pressure to do so.

**Formal organizations**  Highly structured groups with specific objectives and usually clearly stated rules and regulations.

**Formal sanction**  A social reward or punishment that is administered in an organized, systematic way, such as receiving a diploma or getting a fine.

**Functional approach**  A theoretical approach that analyzes social phenomena in terms of their functions in a social system.

**Functional equivalent**  A feature or process in society that has the same function (consequence) as some other feature or process.

**Functions**  The consequences of social phenomena for other parts of society or for society as a whole.

**Fundamentalism**  A form of religious traditionalism characterized by the literal interpretation of religious texts, a conception of an active supernatural, and clear distinctions between sin and salvation.

**Game**  A form of play involving competitive or cooperative interaction in which the outcome is determined by physical skill, strength, strategy, or chance.

**Gemeinschaft**  A term used by Tönnies to describe a small, traditional, community-centered society in which people have close, personal, face-to-face relationships and value social relationships as ends in themselves.

**Gender**  The traits and behaviors that are socially designated as "masculine" or "feminine" in a particular society.

**Gender differences**   Variations in the social positions, roles, behaviors, attitudes, and personalities of men and women in a society.

**Gender gap**   Differences in the way men and women vote.

**Gender-role expectations**   People's beliefs about how men and women should behave.

**Gender stratification**   The hierarchical ranking of men and women and their roles in terms of unequal ownership, power, social control, prestige, and social rewards.

**Generalized other**   A general idea of the expectations, attitudes, and values of a group or community.

**Genocide**   The destruction of an entire population.

**Gentrification**   The movement of middle-class and upper-middle-class persons (usually white) into lower-income, sometimes minority urban areas.

**Gesellschaft**   A term used by Tönnies to describe an urban industrial society in which people have impersonal, formal, contractual, and specialized relationships and tend to use social relationships as a means to an end.

**Global economy**   An economy in which the economic life and health of one nation depends on what happens in other nations.

**Green revolution**   The improvement in agricultural production based on higher-yielding grains and increased use of fertilizers, pesticides, and irrigation.

**Groups**   Collections of people who share some common goals and norms and whose relationships are usually based on interactions.

**Groupthink**   The tendency of individuals to follow the ideas or actions of a group.

**Health maintenance organizations (HMOs)**   Organizations that people pay a fee to join in return for access to a full range of health services.

**Heterosexual**   A person whose preferred partner for erotic, emotional, and sexual interaction is someone of the opposite sex.

**Hierarchy**   The arrangement of positions in a rank order, with those below reporting to those above.

**Hispanics**   A general term referring to Spanish-speaking persons. It includes many distinct ethnic groups.

**Homosexual**   Someone who is emotionally, erotically, and physically attracted to persons of his or her own sex.

**Horizontal mobility**   Movement from one social status to another of about equal rank in the social hierarchy.

**Horticultural societies**   Societies in which the cultivation of plants with hoes is the primary means of subsistence.

**Hospice**   An organization designed to provide care and comfort for terminally ill persons and their families.

**Human-capital explanation**   The view that the earnings of different workers vary because of differences in their education or experience.

**Hunting and gathering societies**   Societies that obtain food by hunting animals, fishing, and gathering fruits, nuts, and grains. These societies do not plant crops or have domesticated animals.

**Hybrid economy**   An economic system that blends features of both centrally planned and capitalist (market) economies.

**Hyperinflation**   An extreme form of inflation.

**Hypothesis**   A tentative statement asserting a relationship between one factor and something else (based on theory, prior research, or general observation).

**Id**   In Freudian theory, a concept referring to the unconscious instinctual impulses—for instance, sexual or aggressive impulses.

**Ideal values**   Values that people say are important to them, whether or not their behavior supports those values.

**Identification theories**   Views suggesting that children learn gender roles by identifying with and copying the same-sex parent.

**Ideology**   A system of ideas that reflects, rationalizes, and defends the interests of those who believe in it.

**Impression management**   A term used by Goffman to describe the efforts of individuals to influence how others perceive them.

**Incest**   Sexual intercourse with close family members.

**Incest taboo**   The prohibition of sexual intercourse between fathers and daughters, mothers and sons, and brothers and sisters.

**Income**   The sum of money wages and salaries (earnings) plus income other than earnings.

**Independent variable**   The variable whose occurrence or change results in the occurrence or change of another variable; the hypothesized cause of something else.

**Individualism**   A belief in individual rights and responsibilities.

**Induction**   Reasoning from the particular to the general.

**Industrialization**   The shift within a nation's economy from a primarily agricultural base to a manufacturing base.

**Industrialized societies**   Societies that rely on mechanized production, rather than on human or animal labor, as the primary means of subsistence.

**Inflation**   An increase in the supply of money in circulation that exceeds the rate of economic growth, making money worth less in relation to the goods and services it can buy.

**Informal sanction**   A social reward or punishment that is given informally through social interaction, such as an approving smile or a disapproving frown.

**Innovation**   The discovery or invention of new ideas, things, or methods; a source of cultural change.

**Instinct**   A genetically determined behavior triggered by specific conditions or events.

**Institution of science**   The social communities that share certain theories and methods aimed at understanding the physical and social worlds.

**Institutionalization of science**   The establishment of careers for practicing scientists in major social institutions.

**Institutionalized**   Social practices that have become established, patterned, and predictable and that are supported by custom, tradition, and/or law.

**Institutions**   The patterned and enduring roles, statuses, and norms that have formed around successful strategies for meeting basic social needs.

**Instrumental**   A type of role that involves problem-solving or task-oriented behavior in group or interpersonal relationships.

**Instrumental leader**   A group leader whose role is to keep the group's attention directed to the task at hand.

**Interest group**   A group of people who work to influence political decisions affecting them.

**Intergenerational mobility**   A vertical change of social status from one generation to the next.

**Interlocking directorates**   The practice of overlapping memberships on corporate boards of directors.

**Intermittent reinforcement**   In learning theory, the provision of a reward sometimes but not always when a desired behavior is shown.

**Internalization**   The process of taking social norms, roles, and values into one's own mind.

**Interpretive approach**   One of the major theoretical perspectives in sociology; focuses on how individuals make sense of the world and react to the symbolic meanings attached to social life.

**Intragenerational mobility**   A vertical change of social status experienced by an individual within his or her own lifetime.

**Invention**   An innovation in material or nonmaterial culture, often produced by combining existing cultural elements in new ways; a source of cultural change.

**"I" portion of the self**   In George Herbert Mead's view, the spontaneous or impulsive portion of the self.

**IQ (intelligence quotient) test**   A standardized set of questions or problems designed to measure verbal and numerical knowledge and reasoning.

**"Iron law of oligarchy"**   In Robert Michels's view, the idea that power in an organization tends to become concentrated in the hands of a small group of leaders.

**Keynesian economics**   The economic theory advanced by John Maynard Keynes, which holds that government intervention, through deficit spending, may be necessary to maintain high levels of employment.

**Kinship**   Socially defined family relationships, including those based on common parentage, marriage, or adoption.

**Labeling theory**   A theory of deviance that focuses on the process by which some people are labeled deviant by other people (and thus take on deviant identities) rather than on the nature of the behavior itself.

**Labor-market segmentation**  The existence of two or more distinct labor markets, one of which is open only to individuals of a particular gender or ethnicity.

**Laissez-faire economics**  The economic theory advanced by Adam Smith, which holds that the economic system develops and functions best when left to market forces, without government intervention.

**Language**  Spoken or written symbols combined into a system and governed by rules.

**Latent function**  The unintended and/or unrecognized function or consequence of some thing or process in a social system.

**Law**  The system of formalized rules established by political authorities and backed by the power of the state for the purpose of controlling or regulating social behavior.

**Learning theory**  In psychology, the theory that specific human behaviors are acquired or forgotten as a result of the rewards or punishments associated with them.

**Legal protection**  The protection of minority-group members through the official policy of a governing unit.

**Legitimate**  In reference to power, the sense by people in a situation that those who are exercising power have the right to do so.

**Lesbian**  A woman who is emotionally, erotically, and physically attracted to other women.

**Life chances**  The probabilities of an individual having access to or failing to have access to various opportunities or difficulties in society.

**Life course**  The biological and social sequence of birth, growing up, maturity, aging, and death.

**Life-course analysis**  An examination of the ways in which different stages of life influence socialization and behavior.

**Life expectancy**  The average years of life anticipated for people born in a particular year.

**Life-style**  Family, child-bearing, and educational attitudes and practices; personal values; type of residence; consumer, political, and civic behavior; religion.

**Life table**  A statistical table that presents the death rate and life expectancy of each of a series of age-sex categories for a particular population.

**Line job**  A job that is part of the central operations of an organization rather than one that provides support services for the operating structure.

**Lobbying**  The process of trying to influence political decisions so they will be favorable to one's interests and goals.

**Location**  In Kanter's view, a person's position in an organization with respect to having control over decision making.

**Looking-glass self**  The sense of self an individual derives from the way others view and treat him or her.

**Macro level**  An analysis of societies that focuses on large-scale institutions, structures, and processes.

**Magic**  According to Malinowski, "a practical art consisting of acts which are only means to a definite end expected to follow."

**Manifest function**  The intended function or consequence of some thing or process in a social system.

**Marriage**  A social institution that recognizes and approves the sexual union of two or more individuals and includes a set of mutual rights and obligations.

**Marriage rate**  Number of marriages in a year per 1000 single women 15 to 44 years old.

**Marriage squeeze**  A situation in which the eligible individuals of one sex outnumber the supply of potential marriage partners of the other sex.

**Marxian approach**  A theory that uses the ideas of Karl Marx and stresses the importance of class struggle centered around the social relations of economic production.

**Mass hysteria**  Widely felt fear and anxiety.

**Mass media**  Widely disseminated forms of communication, such as books, magazines, radio, television, and movies.

**Matthew effect**  The social process whereby one advantage an individual has is likely to lead to additional advantages.

**Mean, arithmetic**  The sum of a set of mathematical values divided by the number of values; a measure of central tendency in a series of data.

**Median**   The number that cuts a distribution of figures in half; a positional measure of central tendency in a series of data.

**Medicaid**   A federal-state matching program that provides medical assistance to certain low-income persons.

**Medicare**   A federal health insurance program. Individuals are eligible if they receive Social Security benefits, federal disability benefits, or sometimes if they have end-stage kidney disease.

**"Me" portion of the self**   In George Herbert Mead's view, the portion of the self that brings the influence of others into the individual's consciousness.

**Method of comparison**   An approach that compares one subgroup or society with another one for the purpose of understanding social differences.

**Methodology**   The rules, principles, and practices that guide the collection of evidence and the conclusions drawn from it.

**Metropolitan Statistical Area (MSA)**   A geographical area containing either one city with 50,000 or more residents or an urban area of at least 50,000 inhabitants and a total population of at least 100,000 (except in New England where the required total is 75,000).

**Micro level**   An analysis of societies that focuses on small-scale process, such as how individuals interact and how they attach meanings to the social actions of others.

**Migration**   The relatively permanent movement of people from one area to another.

**Millenarian movements**   Social movements based on the expectation that society will be suddenly transformed through supernatural intervention.

**Minority group**   Any recognizable racial, religious, ethnic, or social group that suffers from some disadvantage resulting from the action of a dominant group with higher social status and greater privileges.

**Mode**   The value that occurs most often in a series of mathematical values.

**Modeling**   Copying the behavior of admired people.

**Modernization**   The economic and social transformation that occurs when a traditional agricultural society becomes highly industrialized.

**Monopoly**   The exclusive control of a particular industry, market, service, or commodity by a single organization.

**Mores**   Strongly held social norms, a violation of which causes a sense of moral outrage.

**Mortality rate**   The number of deaths per thousand in a population.

**Multinational corporation**   A corporation that locates its operations in a number of nations.

**Multiple-nuclei theory**   A theory of urban development holding that cities develop around a number of different centers, each with its own special activities.

**Nation**   A relatively autonomous political grouping that usually shares a common language and a particular geography.

**Nation-state**   A social organization in which political authority overlaps a cultural and geographical community.

**Negative sanctions**   Actions intended to deter or punish unwanted social behaviors.

**Negotiation**   A form of social interaction in which two or more parties in conflict or competition arrive at a mutually satisfactory agreement.

**Network**   See *Social network*.

**Nomadic**   Societies that move their residences from place to place.

**Nonverbal communication**   Visual and other meaningful symbols that do not use language.

**Norm**   A shared rule about acceptable or unacceptable social behavior.

**Normal science**   A term used by Kuhn to describe research based on one or more past scientific achievements that are accepted as a useful foundation for further study.

**Nuclear family**   A family form consisting of a married couple and their children.

**Objectivity**   Procedures researchers follow to minimize distortions in observation or interpretation due to personal or social values.

**Occupation**   A position in the world of work that involves specialized knowledge and activities.

**Occupational segregation**   The concentration of workers by gender or ethnicity into certain jobs but not others.

**Oligarchy** The rule of the many by the few.

**Oligopoly** The control of a particular industry, market, service, or commodity by a few large organizations.

**Open system** In organizational theory, the degree to which an organization is open to and dependent on its environment.

**Operationalization** In research, the actual procedures or operations conducted to measure a variable.

**Opportunity** In an organization, the potential that a particular position contains for the expansion of work responsibilities and rewards.

**Organization** A social group deliberately formed to pursue certain values and goals.

**Organizational level** Social life in groups and organizations.

**Organizational ritualism** A form of behavior in organizations, particularly in bureaucracies, in which people follow the rules and regulations so closely that they forget the purpose of those rules and regulations.

**Organizational waste** The inefficient use of ideas, expertise, money, or material in an organization.

**Panic** A frightened response by an aggregate of people to an immediate threat.

**Paradigm** In the sociology of science, a coherent tradition of scientific law, theory, and assumptions that forms a distinct approach to problems.

**Parallel marriage** When husband and wife both work and share household tasks.

**Participant observation** A research method in which the researcher does obervation while taking part in the activities of the social group being studied.

**Pastoral societies** Societies in which the raising and herding of animals such as sheep, goats, and cows is the primary means of subsistence.

**Patriarchal family** A form of family organization in which the father is the formal head of the family.

**Peer group** Friends and associates of about the same age and social status.

**Play** Spontaneous activity undertaken freely for its own sake yet governed by rules and often characterized by an element of make-believe.

**Pluralism** In ethnic relations, the condition that exists when both majority and minority groups value their distinct cultural identities, and at the same time seek economic and political unity. In political sociology, the view that society is composed of competing interest groups, with power diffused among them.

**Policy research** Research designed to assess alternative possibilities for public or social action, in terms of their costs and/or consequences.

**Political economy model** A theory of land use that emphasizes the role of political and economic interests.

**Political order** The institutionalized system of acquiring and exercising power.

**Political party** An organized group of people that seeks to control or influence political decisions through legal means.

**Population** In demography, all the people living in a given geographic area. In research, the total number of cases with a particular characteristic.

**Population exclusion** The efforts of a society to prevent ethnically different groups from joining it.

**Population transfer** The efforts of a dominant ethnic group to move or remove members of a minority ethnic group from a particular area.

**Positive sanctions** Rewards for socially desired behavior.

**Positivist** An approach to explaining human action that does not take into account the individual's interpretation of the situation.

**Postindustrial society** A term used by Bell (1973) to refer to societies organized around knowledge and planning rather than around industrial production.

**Power** The capacity of an individual group to control or influence the behavior of others, even in the face of opposition.

**Power elite** According to Mills, a closely connected group of the corporate rich, political leaders, and military commanders who decide most key social and political issues.

**Prejudice** A "prejudged" unfavorable attitude toward the members of a particular group, who are assumed to possess negative traits.

**Prestige** A social recognition, respect, and deference accorded individuals or groups based on their social status.

**Primary deviance** Deviant behavior that is

invisible to others, short-lived, or unimportant and therefore does not contribute to the public labeling of an individual as being deviant.

**Primary economic sector** The sector of an economy in which natural resources are gathered or extracted.

**Primary group** A social group characterized by frequent face-to-face interaction, the commitment and emotional ties members feel for one another, and relative permanence.

**Principle of cumulative advantage** A process whereby the positive features of some institutions help to generate further benefits for them.

**Privatization** The tendency of families in industrial societies to turn away from the community and workplace toward a primary focus on privacy, domesticity, and intimacy.

**Processes of socialization** Those interactions that convey to persons being socialized how they are to speak, behave, think, and feel.

**Profession** An occupation that rests on a theoretical body of knowledge and thus requires specialized training usually recognized by the granting of a degree or credential.

**Projection** A psychological process of attributing one's own unacceptable feelings or desires to other people to avoid guilt and self-blame.

**Property** The rights and obligations a group or individual has in relation to an object, resource, or activity.

**Proposition** A statement about how variables are related to each other.

**Prostitution** The selling of sexual favors.


**Race** A classification of humans into groups based on distinguishable physical characteristics that may form the basis for significant social identities.

**Racism** The institutionalized domination of one racial group by another.

**Random sample** A sample of units drawn from a larger population in such a way that every unit has a known and equal chance of being selected.

**Range** The total spread of values in a set of figures.

**Rank** Place in a social hierarchy.

**Rank differentiation** See *Differentiation, rank.*

**Rape** A completed sexual assault by a male, usually upon a female, although sometimes upon another male.

**Rate of natural increase** The difference between birth and death rates, excluding immigration.

**Rationalization** The process of subjecting social relationships to calculation and administration.

**Real values** The values people consider truly important, as evident in their behavior and how they spend their time and money.

**Rebellion** In anomie theory, a form of deviance that occurs when individuals reject culturally valued means and goals and substitute new means and goals. In political sociology, the expression of opposition to an established authority.

**Reference group** A social group whose standards and opinions are used by an individual to help define or evaluate beliefs, values, and behaviors.

**Reform movement** A type of social movement that accepts the status quo but seeks certain specific social reforms.

**Regressive movement** A type of social movement whose aim is to move the social world back to where members believe it was at an earlier time.

**Relative poverty** The condition of having much less income than the average person in society, even if one can afford the necessities of life.

**Religion** A set of shared beliefs and rituals common to a special community and focusing on the sacred and supernatural.

**Religious movement** An organized religious group with the primary goal of changing existing religious institutions.

**Research and development (R&D)** Investments in basic research and in the practical application of basic research discoveries.

**Research design** The specific plan for conducting a research study, including sampling, measurement, and data analysis.

**Resocialization** The process of socializing people away from a group or activity in which they are involved.

**Resource mobilization theory** The theory that social movements are affected by their ability to marshal various key resources.

**Retreatism** In anomie theory, a form of deviance that occurs when individuals abandon culturally valued means and goals.

**Revolution**    A large-scale change in the political leadership of a society and the restructuring of major features of that society.

**Revolutionary movement**    A type of social movement whose aim is to reorganize existing society completely.

**Riot**    A destructive and sometimes violent collective outburst.

**Rising expectations**    A situation in which people feel that past hardships should not have to be suffered in the future.

**Ritual**    In the sociology of religion, the rules of conduct concerning behavior in the presence of the sacred. Intended to produce feelings of reverence, awe, and group identity.

**Ritualism**    In anomie theory, a form of deviance in which individuals lose sight of socially valued goals but conform closely to socially prescribed means.

**Rival hypothesis**    An explanation that competes with the original hypothesis in a study.

**Role**    To functionalists, the culturally prescribed and socially patterned behaviors associated with particular social positions. For interactionists, the effort to mesh the demands of a social position with one's own identity.

**Role accumulation**    Adding more statuses and roles to the ones an individual already has.

**Role conflict**    A situation in which two or more social roles make incompatible demands on a person.

**Role exit**    The process of leaving a role that is central to one's identity and building an identity in a new role while also taking into account one's prior role.

**Role expectations**    Commonly shared norms about how a person is supposed to behave in a particular role.

**Role performance**    The behaviors of a person performing a certain social role.

**Role set**    The cluster of roles that accompanies a particular status.

**Rowdyism**    Generalized interpersonal violence or property destruction occurring at spectator events.

**Ruling class**    A small class that controls the means of economic production and dominates political decisions.

**Rumor**    A report that is passed informally from one person to another without firm evidence.

**Sample survey**    A systematic method of collecting information from respondents, using personal interviews or written questionnaires.

**Sanction**    A social reward or punishment for approved or disapproved behavior; can be positive or negative, formal or informal.

**Scapegoating**    Blaming a convenient but innocent person or group for one's trouble or guilt.

**Schooling**    Formal education.

**Science**    An approach used to obtain reliable knowledge about the physical and social worlds, based on systematic empirical observations; the knowledge so obtained.

**Scientific productivity**    Making new discoveries, confirming or disconfirming theoretical hypotheses through experimentation and other types of research, and publishing the results of that research.

**Scientific revolution**    The dramatic overthrow of one intellectual paradigm by another.

**Secondary deviance**    Behavior discovered by others and publicly labeled by them as deviant.

**Secondary economic sector**    The sector of an economy in which raw materials are turned into manufactured goods.

**Secondary group**    A social group bound together for the accomplishment of common tasks, with few emotional ties among members.

**Sect**    An exclusive, highly cohesive group of ascetic religious believers. Sects usually last longer and are more institutionalized than cults.

**Sector theory**    A theory of urban development explaining that cities develop in wedge-shaped patterns following transportation systems.

**Secularization**    The erosion of belief in the supernatural. Includes a growing respect for rationality, cultural and religious pluralism, tolerance of moral ambiguity, faith in education, and belief in civil rights, the rule of law, and due process.

**Self-fulfilling prophecy**    A belief or prediction about a person or situation that influences that person or situation in such a way that the belief or prediction comes true.

**Sex** The biological distinction of being male or female.

**Sibling** A brother or sister.

**Social categories** Groups of people who may not interact but who share certain social characteristics or statuses.

**Social change** A modification or transformation in the way society is organized.

**Social class** A group's position in a social hierarchy based on prestige and/or property ownership.

**Social construction of reality** The process of socially creating definitions of situations so that they appear to be natural.

**Social control** The relatively patterned and systematic ways in which society guides and restrains individual behaviors so that people act in predictable and desirable ways.

**Social forces** The social structures and culture individuals face in a society.

**Social inequality** The existence of unequal opportunities or rewards for people in different social positions.

**Social interaction** The ways people behave in relation to one another by means of language, gestures, and symbols.

**Socialist societies** Societies in which productive resources are owned and controlled by the state rather than by individuals.

**Socialization** The process of preparing newcomers to become members of an existing social group by helping them to learn the attitudes and behaviors that are considered appropriate.

**Social learning theory** A form of learning theory suggesting that people learn through observation and imitation, even though they are not rewarded or punished for certain behaviors.

**Social mobility** The movement from one status to another within a stratified society.

**Social movement** A group of people who work together to guide or suppress particular changes in the way society is organized.

**Social network** A set of interdependent relations or links between individuals.

**Social psychology** The scientific study of how individual behavior is socially influenced.

**Social relations of production** The organization of economic life on the basis of owning or not owning the means of production, purchasing or selling labor power, and controlling or not controlling other people's labor power.

**Social sciences** Related disciplines that study human activity and communication.

**Social stratification** The fairly permanent ranking of positions in a society in terms of unequal power, prestige, or privilege.

**Social structure** Recurrent and patterned relationships among individuals, organizations, nations, or other social units.

**Society** A group of people with a shared and somewhat distinct culture who live in a defined territory, feel some unity as a group, and see themselves as distinct from other peoples.

**Sociobiology** The scientific study of the biological basis for human behavior.

**Socioeconomic status (SES)** An index of social status that considers a person's occupation, education, and income as measures of social status.

**Sociology** The study and analysis of patterned social relationships in modern societies.

**Sovereignty** The authority claimed by a state to maintain a legal system, use coercive power to secure obedience, and maintain its independence from other states.

**Sponsored mobility** A pattern in which certain children are selected at an early age for academic and university education and are thus helped to achieve higher social status.

**Sport** A form of game in which the outcome is affected by physical skill.

**Staff job** In an organization, an advisory or administrative job that supports the manufacturing, production, selling, or other primary activities of the organization.

**Stage theory** A theory suggesting that nations go through various systematic stages of development.

**State** The institutionalized, legal organization of power within territorial limits.

**State sector** The sector of the economy controlled by local, state, or federal governments that supplies goods and services under direct contract to that state.

**State terrorism** The use of torture, death

squads, and disappearances by political states to intimidate citizens.

**Status**    A socially defined position in society that carries with it certain prescribed rights, obligations, and expected behaviors.

**Status-attainment model**    A view of social mobility suggesting the importance of father's education, father's occupation, son's education, and son's first job for a man's adult status.

**Status group**    People who share a social identity based on similar values and life-styles.

**Status inconsistency**    May occur when an individual occupies two or more unequal statuses in a society.

**Stigmatization**    The process of spoiling a person's identity by labeling him or her in a negative way.

**Structural change**    Demographic, economic, and rank-order changes in a society.

**Structural-functional perspective**    One of the major theoretical perspectives in sociology, developed by Talcott Parsons: focuses on how the various parts of society fit together or adjust to maintain the equilibrium of the whole.

**Subculture**    A distinguishable group that shares a number of features with the dominant culture within which it exists while also having unique features such as language, customs, or values.

**Subjective meanings**    The values and interpretations individuals place on their life situations and experiences; may vary from person to person.

**Subjective social class**    A person's own perception of his or her class position.

**Suburb**    A fairly small community within an urban area that includes a central city.

**Sunbelt**    The area south of the 37th parallel in the United States, including Clark County in Nevada.

**Superego**    In Freudian theory, the part of the personality structure that upholds the norms of society.

**Symbol**    Any object or sign that evokes a shared social response.

**Symbolic interaction**    Interaction that relies on shared symbols such as language.

**Symbolic interactionism**    An interpretive perspective, inspired by the work of George Herbert Mead, saying that individuals learn meanings through interaction with others and then organize their lives around these socially created meanings.

**Taboo**    A strongly prohibited social practice; the strongest form of social norm.

**Technological determinism**    The belief that technological development shapes social life in rather fixed ways.

**Technology**    The practical applications of scientific knowledge.

**Tension release theory**    A theory suggesting that sport serves as a form of social safety valve, allowing individuals to vent their seething aggressions.

**Terrorism**    An attack on people designed to frighten society and force it to meet the terrorists' demands.

**Tertiary economic sector**    The sector of an economy that offers services to individuals as well as to business.

**Theoretical approach**    A set of guiding ideas.

**Theory**    A system of orienting ideas, concepts, and relationships that provides a way of organizing the observable world.

**Theory X**    A view of organizational behavior suggesting that people hate their jobs, want to avoid responsibility, resist change, and do not care about organizational needs.

**Theory Y**    A view of organizational behavior suggesting that people have the desire to work, to be creative, and to take responsibility for their jobs and for the organization.

**Theory Z**    A form of organizational culture that values long-term employment, trust, and close personal relationships between workers and managers.

**Total fertility rate**    An estimate of the average number of children that would be born to each woman over her reproductive life if current age-specific birth rates remained constant.

**Total institution**    A place where people spend 24 hours of every day for an extended part of their lives, cut off from the rest of society and tightly controlled by the people in charge.

**Totalitarianism**    A form of autocracy that involves the use of state power to control and regulate all phases of life.

**Tournament selection** An educational pattern in which a continual process of selection serves to weed out candidates; winners move on to the next round of selection and losers are eliminated from the competition.

**Tracking** The practice of grouping students by ability, curriculum, or both.

**Triad** A group composed of three people.

**Underemployment** The hiring of people in jobs that are not customarily filled by individuals with their relatively high levels of experience or education.

**Underground economy** Exchanges of goods and services that occur outside the arena of the normal, regulated economy and therefore escape official record keeping.

**Unit of analysis** Who or what is being studied in a piece of social research.

**Urbanization** The growth of cities.

**Value-added theory** A theory suggesting that many instances of collective behavior represent efforts to change the social environment.

**Values** Strongly held general ideas that people share about what is good and bad, desirable or undesirable; values provide yardsticks for judging specific acts and goals.

**Variable** A logical set of attributes with different degrees of magnitude or different categories. For example, age is a variable on which people can be classified according to the number of years they have lived.

**Verstehen** The effort to understand social behavior in terms of the motives individuals bring to it.

**Vertical integration** A form of business organization that attempts to control the business environment by assuming control of one or more of its resources or business outlets.

**Vertical mobility** Movement of an individual or a group upward or downward, from one social status to another.

**Wealth** The total value (minus debts) of what is owned.

**Weberian approach** The views held by conflict theorists who, using the ideas of Max Weber, stress the significance of conflict in social life, especially conflict among status groups such as those based on occupation, ethnic background, or religion.

**White-collar crime** Crimes committed by "respectable" individuals, often while they practice their occupations—for example, embezzling money or stealing computer time.

**White ethnics** White Americans who value and preserve aspects of their ethnic heritage.

**World systems analysis** A form of sociological analysis that stresses understanding national behavior in terms of historical and contemporary relationships among nations and societies.

**Zero population growth (ZPG)** The situation that occurs when the population of a nation or the world remains stable from one year to the next.

# REFERENCES

**ABC News–Harris Survey.** 1979. "Leisure Time Activities." New York: Chicago Tribune–New York News Syndicate, Inc. (January 1).

**Abercrombie, Nicholas, Stephen Hill, and Bryan S. Turner.** 1984. *The Penguin Dictionary of Sociology.* Harmondsworth, England: Penguin.

**Abu-Lughod, J. and M. M. Foley.** 1960. "The Consumer Votes by Moving." and "Consumer Preferences: The City Versus the Suburb." Pp. 134–214 in *Choices and Housing Constraints,* edited by N. N. Foote et al. New York: McGraw-Hill.

**Adams, Robert McCormick, et al.** 1984. *Behavioral and Social Science Research: A National Resource.* Washington, DC: National Academy Press.

**Adler, Freda.** 1975. *Sisters in Crime.* New York: McGraw-Hill.

**Adler, Jerry et al.** 1985. "The AIDS Conflict." *Newsweek* (September 23):18–24.

**Adler, Peter and Patricia A. Adler.** 1985. "From Idealism to Pragmatic Detachment: The Academic Performance of College Athletes." *Sociology of Education* 58:241–50.

**Aguirre, Benigo E., Enrico L. Quarantelli, and Jorge L. Mendoza.** 1988. "The Collective Behavior of Fads: The Characteristics, Effects, and Career of Streaking." *American Sociological Review* 53:569–84.

**Akers, Ronald L.** 1964. "Socioeconomic Status and Delinquent Behavior: A Retest." *Journal of Research in Crime and Delinquency* 1:38–46.

**Alba, Richard D. and Mitchell B. Chamlin.** 1983. "A Preliminary Examination of Ethnic Identification among Whites." *American Sociological Review* 48:240–47.

**Aldous, Joan.** 1982a. "From Dual-Earner to Dual-Career Families and Back Again." Pp. 11–26 in *Two Paychecks: Life in Dual-Earner Families,* edited by Joan Aldous. Beverly Hills, CA: Sage.

**Aldous, Joan, ed.** 1982b. *Two Paychecks: Life in Dual-Earner Families.* Beverly Hills, CA: Sage.

**Alexander, Karl L. and Martha A. Cook.** 1982. "Curricula and Coursework: A Surprise Ending to a Familiar Story." *American Sociological Review* 47:626–40.

**Alexander, Karl L. and E. L. McDill.** 1976. "Selection and Allocation within Schools: Some Causes and Consequences of Curriculum Placement." *American Sociological Review* 6:963–80.

**Alford, Robert R. and Roger Friedland.** 1985. *Powers of Theory: Capitalism, the State, and Democracy.* New York: Cambridge University Press.

**Allen, Robert C.** 1987. *Channels of Discourse: Television and Contemporary Criticism.* Chapel Hill: University of North Carolina Press.

**Allport, Gorden.** 1958. *The Nature of Prejudice.* New York: Doubleday.

**Alston, Jon P.** 1973. "Aggregate Social Mobility among Major Protestant Denominations and Major Religious Groups, 1939–1969." *Sociological Analysis* 34 (fall):230–35.

**Altman, Lawrence K.** 1989. "Who's Stricken and How: AIDS Pattern Is Shifting." *New York Times* (February 5):1, 28.

**Alwin, Duane F.** 1984. "Trends in Parental Socialization Values: Detroit, 1958–1983." *American Journal of Sociology* 90:359–82.

**Alwin, Duane and Philip Converse.** 1984. "Living Alone." *IRS Newsletter:* 3–6. Ann Arbor: Institute for Social Research, University of Michigan.

**American Indian Fund.** 1981. "How About 'Human Rights' for This American, Too?" Letter to potential contributors. New York: Association on American Indian Affairs, Inc.

**Amnesty International.** 1975. *Report on Torture.* New York: Farrar, Straus and Giroux.

**Anderson, Barry D.** 1973. "School Bureaucratization and Alienation from High School." *Sociology of Education* 46:315–34.

**Antonovsky, Aaron.** 1960. "The Social Meaning of Discrimination." *Phylon* 21:13–19.

**Antoun, Richard and Mary Hegland (eds.).** 1986. *Religious Resurgence in Comparative Perspective.* Syracuse, NY: Syracuse University Press.

**Archer, Dane and Rosemary Gartner.** 1984. *Violence and Crime in Cross-National Perspective.* New Haven, CT: Yale University Press.

**Arendt, Hannah.** 1951. *The Origins of Totalitarianism.* New York: Harcourt Brace.

**Ariés, Philippe.** 1962. *Centuries of Childhood.* R. Baldick (trans.). New York: Knopf.

**Aronoff, Joel and William D. Crano.** 1975. "A Re-examination of the Cross-Cultural Principles of Task Segregation and Sex Role Differentiation in the Family." *American Sociological Review* 40(February): 12–20.

**Asch, Solomon E.** 1952. *Social Psychology.* Englewood Cliffs, NJ: Prentice-Hall.

**Associated Press.** 1988. "Swaggart Is Barred from Pulpit for One Year." *New York Times* (March 30): A1, A25.

**Astin, Alexander W., Kenneth C. Green, William S. Korn, and Marilynn Schalit.** 1985. *The*

*American Freshman: National Norms for Fall 1985.* University of California, Los Angeles: Higher Education Research Institute, Graduate School of Education.

———. 1987. *The American Freshman: National Norms for Fall 1987.* University of California, Los Angeles: Cooperative Institutional Research Program, American Council on Education.

**Astin, Helen S.** 1985. "The Meaning of Work in Women's Lives: A Sociopsychological Model of Career Choice and Work Behavior." *The Counseling Psychologist* 12:117–28.

**Averill, James R.** 1980. "A Constructivist View of Emotions." Pp. 305–39 in *Theories of Emotion,* edited by Robert Plutchik and Henry Kellerman. New York: Academic Press.

**Averitt, Robert.** 1968. *The Dual Economy.* New York: Norton.

**Bachman, J. G.** 1967. *Youth in Transition.* Ann Arbor: Institute for Social Research, University of Michigan.

**Bagdikian, Ben H.** 1983. *The Media Monopoly.* Boston: Beacon.

**Bahr, Stephen and Richard Galligan.** 1984. "Teenage Marriage and Marital Stability." *Youth and Society* 15:387–400.

**Bainbridge, William Sims.** 1978. *Satan's Power: A Deviant Psychotherapy Cult.* Berkeley: University of California Press.

**Baird, John S., Jr.** 1980. "Current Trends in College Cheating." *Psychology in the Schools* 17:515–22.

**Baird, Leonard L.** 1977. *The Elite Schools.* Lexington, MA: Lexington Books.

**Baker, Mary Anne et al.** 1980. *Women Today: A Multidisciplinary Approach to Women's Studies.* Monterey, CA: Brooks/Cole.

**Bales, Robert F. and Philip E. Slater.** 1954. "Role Differentiation in Small Decision Making Groups." Pp. 259–306 in *Family Socialization and Interaction Process Analysis,* edited by Talcott Parsons and Robert F. Bales. New York: Free Press.

**Bales, Robert F. and Fred L. Strodbeck.** 1951. "Phases in Group Problem Solving." *Journal*

*of Abnormal and Social Psychology* 46:485–95.

**Ball, Donald.** 1972. "What the Action Is:" A Cross-Cultural Approach." *Journal for the Theory of Social Behavior* 2(October): 121–43.

**Baltzell, E. Digby.** 1964. *The Protestant Establishment: Aristocracy and Caste in America.* New York: Random House.

———. 1979. *Puritan Boston and Quaker Philadelphia.* New York: Free Press.

**Bandura, Albert.** 1969. *Principles of Behavior Modification.* New York: Holt, Rinehart and Winston.

———. 1977. *Social Learning Theory.* Englewood Cliffs, NJ: Prentice-Hall.

**Bandura, Albert and Richard H. Walters.** 1963. *Social Learning and Personality Development.* New York: Holt, Rinehart and Winston.

**Banfield, Edward.** 1960. *The Unheavenly City.* Boston: Little, Brown.

**Bank, S. and M. D. Kahn.** 1975. "Sisterhood-Brotherhood Is Powerful: Sibling Subsystems and Family Therapy." *Family Process* 14:311–37.

**Baratz, Joan and Stephen Baratz.** 1970. "Early Childhood Intervention: The Social Scientific Basis of Institutionalized Racism." *Harvard Educational Review* 39:29–50.

**Barber, Bernard.** 1961. "Resistance by Scientists to Scientific Discovery." *Science* 134 (September 1): 596–602.

**Barclay, Bill.** 1981. "The Economy: Who Benefits?" Pp. 189–216 in *Political Economy,* edited by Scott G. McNall. Glenview, IL: Scott, Foresman.

**Barkan, Steven E.** 1984. "Legal Control of the Southern Civil Rights Movement." *American Sociological Review* 49:552–65.

**Barnet, Richard and Ronald Muller.** 1974. *Global Reach: The Power of the Multinational Corporations.* New York: Simon & Schuster.

**Barnett, Rosalind C. and Grace K. Baruch.** 1987. "Determinants of Fathers' Participation in Family Work." *Journal of Marriage and the Family* 49:29–40.

**Barney, Gerald O.** 1980. *The Global 2000 Report to the President.* Vol. 1.

Washington, DC: U.S. Government Printing Office.

**Baron, James N. and William T. Bielby.** 1980. "Bringing the Firms Back in: Stratification, Segmentation, and the Organization of Work." *American Sociological Review* 45:737–65.

———. 1982. "Workers and Machines: Dimensions and Determinants of Technical Relations in the Workplace." *American Sociological Review* 47:175–88.

———. 1984. "The Organization of Work in a Segmented Economy." *American Sociological Review* 49:454–73.

**Baron, Larry and Murray A. Straus.** 1987. "Four Theories of Rape: A Macrosociological Analysis." *Social Problems* 34:467–89.

**Barrett, David B.** 1989. "World Religious Statistics." P. 299 in *Britannica Book of the Year.* Chicago: Encyclopaedia Britannica.

**Barringer, Felicity.** 1988. "Review of Final Warning: The Legacy of Chernobyl, by Robert Peter Gale and Thomas Hauser." *New York Times Book Review* (August 31).

**Barron, James.** 1985. "Insurers Study Screening for AIDS." *New York Times* (September 26): B12.

**Barry, Herbert III, Irvin Child, and Margaret Bacon.** 1959. "Relation of Child Training to Subsistence Economy." *American Anthropologist* 61:51–63.

**Barton, Allen H. and Bo Anderson.** 1966. "Change in an Organizational System: Formalization of a Qualitative Study." Pp. 400–18 in *Complex Organizations,* edited by Amitai Etzioni. New York: Holt, Rinehart and Winston.

**Baruch, Grace K. and Rosalind Barnett.** 1983. *Lifeprints: New Patterns of Love and Work for Today's Women.* New York: McGraw-Hill.

**Batra, Ravi.** 1987. "Are the Rich Getting Richer? An Ominous Trend to Greater Inequality." *New York Times* (May 3):2.

**Battersby, John D.** 1988. "Pretoria Pass Law Dies, but Spirit Lives." *New York Times* (June 27): A1, A9.

**Baumgartner, Alice.** 1983. "My Daddy Might Have Loved Me: Student Perceptions of Differences Between Being Male and Being Female." Paper published by the

Institute for Equality in Education, Denver, CO.

**Beardslee, W. and J. Mack.** 1982. "The Impact on Children and Adolescents of Nuclear Development." *American Psychiatric Association Task Force Monograph #20 (Psychological Aspects of Nuclear Development)*:64–93.

**Beatty, Kathleen Murphy and Oliver Walter.** 1984. "Religious Preference and Practice: Reevaluating Their Impact on Political Tolerance." *Public Opinion Quarterly* 48:318–29.

**Becker, Ernest.** 1973. *The Denial of Death.* New York: Free Press.

**Becker, Gary.** 1968. "Crime and Punishment: An Economic Approach." *Journal of Political Economy* 75:169–217.

**Becker, Gary, Elisabeth Landes, and Robert Michael.** 1977. "An Economic Analysis of Marital Instability." *Journal of Political Economy* 85:1141–87.

**Becker, Henry Jay.** 1977. "How Young People Find Career-Entry Jobs: A Review of the Literature." Report No. 241, Center for Social Organization of Schools, Johns Hopkins University.

**Becker, Howard S.** 1963. *Outsiders.* New York: Free Press.

———. 1973. "Labeling Theory Reconsidered." In *Outsiders.* Revised edition. New York: Free Press.

**Becker, Howard S., Blanche Geer, Everett C. Hughes, and Anselm L. Strauss.** 1961. *Boys in White: Student Culture in Medical School.* Chicago: University of Chicago Press.

**Belkin, Lisa.** 1985. "Poll Finds Liberalized Sex Views." *New York Times* (May 16): C8.

**Bell, Alan P. and Martin S. Weinberg.** 1978. *Homosexualities: A Study of Diversities among Men and Women.* New York: Touchstone.

**Bell, Alan P., Martin S. Weinberg, and Sue Kiefer Hammersmith.** 1981. *Sexual Preference.* Bloomington: Indiana University Press.

**Bell, Daniel.** 1973. *The Coming of Post-Industrial Society.* New York: Basic Books.

———. 1976. *The Cultural Contradictions of Capitalism.* New York: Harper & Row.

———. 1977. "Beyond Modernism, Beyond Self." Pp. 213–53 in *Art, Politics, and Will: Essays in Honor of*

*Lionel Trilling,* edited by Quentin Anderson, Stephen Donadio, and Steven Marcus. New York: Basic Books.

———. 1987. "The World and the United States in 2013." *Daedalus* 116:1–31.

**Bellah, Robert N.** 1967. "Civil Religion in America." *Daedalus 96* (winter):1–21.

———. 1975. *The Broken Covenant.* New York: Seabury.

———. 1982. "Cultural Pluralism and Religious Particularism." Pp. 33–52 in *Freedom of Religion in America: Historical Roots, Philosophical Concepts, and Contemporary Problems,* edited by Henry B. Clark, Jr. New Brunswick, NJ: Transaction Books.

**Bellah, Robert N., Richard Madsen, William M. Sullivan, Ann Swidler, and Steven M. Tipton.** 1985. *Habits of the Heart.* Berkeley: University of California Press.

**Belsky, J.** 1979. "The Interrelation of Parental and Spousal Behavior During Infancy in Traditional Nuclear Families: An Exploratory Analysis." *Journal of Marriage and the Family* 41:62–68.

**Bem, Sandra Lipsitz.** 1983. "Gender Schema Theory and Its Implications for Child Development: Raising Gender-Aschematic Children in a Gender-Schematic Society." *Signs* 8:598–616.

**Ben-David, Joseph.** 1971. *The Scientist's Role in Society.* Englewood Cliffs, NJ: Prentice-Hall.

**Ben-David, Joseph and A. Zloczower.** 1962. "Universities and Academic Systems in Modern Societies." *European Journal of Sociology* 3:45–85.

**Benedict, Ruth.** 1934. *Patterns of Culture.* Boston: Houghton Mifflin.

**Bennett, Amanda.** 1980. "Detroit Distress: White-Collar Workers Are Singing the Blues in the Auto Industry." *Wall Street Journal* (May 1):1, 35.

———. 1986. "American Culture Is Often a Puzzle for Foreign Managers in the U.S." *Wall Street Journal* (February 12):33.

**Bennett, Neil G., Ann Klimas Blanc, and David E. Bloom.** 1988. "Commitment and the Modern Union: Assessing the Link between Premarital Cohabitation and Subsequent Marital Stability."

*American Sociological Review* 53:127–38.

**Benson, Michael L. and Esteban Walker.** 1988. "Sentencing the White-Collar Offender." *American Sociological Review* 53:294–302.

**Berelson, Bernard, Paul Lazarsfeld, and William McPhee.** 1954. *Voting: A Study of Opinion Formation in a Presidential Campaign.* Chicago: University of Chicago Press.

**Berg, Eric N.** 1985. "Practical Traveler: Help from the Home Computer." *New York Times* (January 20):3.

**Berg, Ivar E.** 1970. *Education and Jobs: The Great Training Robbery.* New York: Praeger.

**Berger, Bennett M.** 1971. "Suburbs, Subcultures, and Styles of Life." Pp. 165–87 in *Looking for America: Essays on Youth, Suburbia, and Other American Obsessions,* edited by Bennett M. Berger, Englewood Cliffs, NJ: Prentice-Hall.

**Berger, Peter L.** 1967. *The Sacred Canopy: Elements of a Sociological Theory of Religion.* Garden City, NY: Doubleday.

———. 1969. *Rumor of Angels: Modern Society and the Rediscovery of the Supernatural.* Garden City, NY: Doubleday.

———. 1977. *Facing up to Modernity: Excursions in Society, Politics, and Religion.* New York: Basic Books.

**Bergmann, Barbara R.** 1986. *The Economic Emergence of Women.* New York: Basic Books.

**Berk, Richard A., Kenneth J. Lenihan, and Peter H. Rossi.** 1980. "Crime and Poverty: Some Experimental Evidence from Ex-offenders." *American Sociological Review* 45:766–86.

**Berk, Sarah Fenstermaker.** 1985. *The Gender Factory.* New York: Plenum.

**Berkowitz, S. D.** 1982. *An Introduction to Structural Analysis: The Network Approach to Social Research.* Toronto: Butterworths.

**Berman, Phyllis W.** 1980. "Are Women More Responsive Than Men to the Young? A Review of Developmental and Situational Variables." *Psychological Bulletin* 88:668–95.

**Bernard, Jessie.** 1972. *The Future of*

*Marriage.* New York: Bantam.

———. 1975. *Women, Wives, Mothers: Values and Options.* Chicago: Aldine.

———. 1981a. "Facing the Future." *Transaction* 18:53–59.

———. 1981b. *The Female World.* New York: Free Press.

———. 1982. *The Future of Marriage.* New Haven, CT: Yale University Press.

Bernstein, Paul. 1976. *The Dynamics of Bureaucracy.* Chicago: University of Chicago Press.

Berry, Brian J. L. and John D. Kasarda. 1977. *Contemporary Urban Ecology.* New York: Macmillan.

Best, Raphaela. 1983. *We've All Got Scars: What Boys and Girls Learn in Elementary School.* Bloomington: University of Indiana Press.

Bianchi, Suzanne M. and Daphne Spain. 1986. *American Women in Transition.* New York: Russell Sage Foundation.

Bibby, R. and M. Brinkerhoff. 1983. "Circulation of the Saints Revisited: A Longitudinal Look at Conservative Church Growth." *Journal for the Scientific Study of Religion* 22:253–62.

Bielby, Denise D. and William T. Bielby. 1988. "She Works Hard for the Money: Household Responsibilities and the Allocation of Work Effort." *American Journal of Sociology* 93:1031–59.

Bielby, William T. 1981. "Models of Status Attainment." Pp. 3–26 in *Research in Social Stratification and Mobility,* edited by Donald Treiman and Robert Robinson. Greenwich, CT: JAI Press.

Bielby, William T. and James N. Baron. 1986. "Men and Women at Work: Sex Segregation and Statistical Discrimination." *American Journal of Sociology* 91:759–99.

Biggar, Jeanne C. 1979. "The Sunning of America: Migration to the Sunbelt." *Population Bulletin* 34.

Bird, Caroline. 1966. *The Invisible Scar.* New York: David McKay.

Birnbaum, Judith Abelew. 1975. "Life Patterns and Self-esteem in Gifted Family-oriented and Career-committed Women." Pp. 396–419 in *Women and Achievement: Social and Motivational Analyses,* edited by Martha T. Shuch Mednick, Sandra Schwartz Tangri, and Lois Wladis Hoffman. New York: Halsted Press.

Bishop, Katherine. 1985. "Ward 5B: A Model of Care for AIDS." *New York Times* (December 14): 10.

Black, Donald. 1976. *The Behavior of Law.* New York: Academic Press.

———. 1983. "Crime as Social Control." *American Sociological Review* 48:34–45.

Blackburn, McKinley L. and David E. Bloom. 1985. "What Is Happening to the Middle Class?" *American Demographics* 7:18–25.

Blackwell, Patricia L. and John C. Gessner. 1983. "Fear and Trembling: An Inquiry into Adolescent Perceptions of Living in the Nuclear Age." *Youth and Society* 15: 237–55.

Blair, William G. 1984. "Inmate Cost Is Put at $40,000 a Year." *New York Times* (December 27): A1, B10.

Blake, Judith. 1981. "Family Size and the Quality of Children." *Demography* 18:421–22.

———. 1985. "Number of Siblings and Educational Mobility." *American Sociological Review* 50:84–93.

Blake, Judith and J. H. del Pinal. 1981. "The Childlessness Option: Recent American Views of Nonparenthood." Pp. 235–61 in *Predicting Fertility: Demographic Studies of Birth Expectations,* edited by G. E. Hendershot and P. J. Placek. Lexington, MA: Lexington.

Blalock, Hubert M., Jr. 1967. *Toward a Theory of Minority-Group Relations.* New York: Wiley.

Blau, Judith R. and Peter M. Blau. 1982. "The Cost of Inequality: Metropolitan Structure and Violent Crime." *American Sociological Review* 47:114–29.

Blau, Peter. 1968. "Interaction, IV: Social Exchange." In *International Encyclopedia of the Social Sciences 7,* edited by David L. Sills. New York: Free Press.

Blau, Peter M. and Otis Dudley Duncan. 1967. *The American Occupational Structure.* New York: Wiley.

Blau, Peter M. and Joseph E. Schwartz. 1984. *Crosscutting Social Circles: Testing a Macrostructural Theory of Intergroup Relations.* Orlando, FL: Academic Press.

Blauner, Robert. 1969. "Internal Colonialism and Ghetto Revolt." *Social Problems* 16:393–408.

———. 1972. *Racial Oppression in America.* New York: Harper & Row.

Block, Fred L. 1977a. *The Origins of International Economic Disorder.* Berkeley: University of California Press.

———. 1977b. "The Ruling Class Does Not Rule: Notes on the Marxist Theory of the State." *Socialist Revolution* 33:6–28.

———. 1981. "Beyond Relative Autonomy: State Managers as Historical Subjects." *New Political Science* 2:33–49.

Blossfeld, Hans-Peter. 1987. "Labor-Market Entry and the Sexual Segregation of Careers in the Federal Republic of Germany." *American Journal of Sociology* 93:89–118.

Blum, David J. 1980. "Black Politicians Fear They Can't Do Much to Help Their People." *Wall Street Journal* (October 29):1, 18.

Blum, Linda M. 1987. "Possibilities and Limits of the Comparable Worth Movement." *Gender & Society* 1:380–99.

Blumberg, Paul. 1980. *Inequality in an Age of Decline.* New York: Oxford University Press.

Blumer, Herbert. 1968. "Fashion." Pp. 341–45 in *International Encyclopedia of the Social Sciences 5,* edited by David V. Sills. New York: Macmillan.

———. 1969a. *Symbolic Interactionism.* Englewood Cliffs, NJ: Prentice-Hall.

———. 1969b. "Fashion: From Class Differentiation to Collective Behavior." *Sociological Quarterly* 10 (winter): 275–91.

Blumstein, Philip and Pepper Schwartz. 1983. *American Couples: Money/Work/Sex.* New York: Morrow.

Bock, Kenneth E. 1955. "The Study of War in American Sociology." *Sociologus* 5:104–13.

Boland, Walter R. 1973. "Size, External Relations, and the Distribution of Power: A Study of Colleges and Universities." Pp. 428–41 in *Comparative Organizations,* edited by Wolf V. Heydebrand. Englewood Cliffs, NJ: Prentice-Hall.

Bolles, Richard Nelson. 1977. *What Color Is Your Parachute?* Revised edition. Berkeley: Ten Speed Press.

**Bolter, J. David.** 1984. *Turing's Man: Western Culture in the Computer Age.* Chapel Hill: University of North Carolina Press.

**Bonacich, Edna.** 1972. "A Theory of Ethnic Antagonism: The Split Labor Market." *American Sociological Review* 37:547–59.

**Bond, Nicholas A., Jr.** 1981. "The Psychological Component in Productivity." *Wall Street Journal* (March 10): 35.

**Boorman, Scott A.** 1975. "A Combinatorial Optimization Model for Transmission of Job Information through Contact Networks." *Bell Journal of Economics* 6:216–49.

**Booth, Alan, David R. Johnson, Lynn White, and John N. Edwards.** 1984. "Women, Outside Employment, and Marital Instability." *American Journal of Sociology* 90:567–83.

**Boserup, Ester.** 1965. *The Conditions of Agricultural Growth.* Chicago: Aldine.

**Bott, Elizabeth.** 1971. *Family and Social Network.* Second edition. London: Tavistock.

**Boudon, Raymond.** 1973. *Education, Opportunity, and Social Inequality.* New York: Wiley.

**Bourdieu, Pierre.** 1971. "Systems of Education and Systems of Thought." Pp. 189–207 in *Knowledge and Control,* edited by M. F. D. Young. London: Collier-Macmillan.

**Bourdieu, Pierre and Jean-Claude Passeron.** 1977. *Reproduction: In Education, Society, and Culture.* Beverly Hills, CA: Sage.

**Bourg, C. J.** 1975. "Elderly in a Southern Metropolitan Area." *The Gerontologist* 15(February): 15–22.

**Bowen, D., E. Bowen, S. Gawiser, and L. Masotti.** 1968. "Deprivation, Mobility, and Orientation toward Protest of the Urban Poor." Pp. 187–200 in *Riots and Rebellion: Civil Violence in the Urban Community,* edited by L. Mascotti and D. Bowen. Beverly Hills, CA: Sage.

**Bowen, Ezra.** 1985. "The Publishers Flunk Science." *Time* (September 30):86.

**Bowers, William J.** 1964. *Student Dishonesty and Its Control in College.* New York: Bureau of Applied Social Research.

———. 1974. *Executions in America.* Lexington, MA.: Lexington.

**Bowers, William J. and G. L. Pierce.** 1980. "Deterrence or Brutalization: What Is the Effect of Executions?" *Crime and Delinquency* 26:453–84.

**Bowles, Samuel and Herbert Gintis.** 1976. *Schooling in Capitalist America.* New York: Basic Books.

**Box, Steven and Chris Hale.** 1983. "Liberation and Female Criminality in England and Wales." *British Journal of Criminology* 23:35–49.

**Braddock, Jomills Henry, II, Robert L. Crain, and James M. McPartland.** 1984. "A Long-Term View of School Desegregation: Some Recent Studies of Graduates as Adults." *Phi Delta Kappan* (December):259–64.

**Braithwaite, John.** 1979. *Inequality, Crime, and Public Policy.* London and Boston: Routledge & Kegan Paul.

———. 1981. "The Myth of Social Class and Criminality Reconsidered." *American Sociological Review* 46:36–57.

**Braithwaite, John and V. Braithwaite.** 1978. "Unpublished Cross-Tabulations from Data Reported in 'An Exploratory Study of Delinquency and the Nature of Schooling.'" *Australian and New Zealand Journal of Sociology* 14:25–32.

———. 1980. "The Effect of Income Inequality and Social Democracy on Homicide." *British Journal of Criminology* XX:45–53.

**Braverman, Harry.** 1974. *Labor and Monopoly Capital.* New York: Monthly Review Press.

**Brenner, Johanna.** 1987. "Feminist Political Discourses: Radical Versus Liberal Approaches to the Feminization of Poverty and Comparable Worth." *Gender & Society* 1:447–65.

**Brenner, M. Harvey.** 1973. *Mental Illness and the Economy.* Cambridge, MA: Harvard University Press.

**Brickman, P.** 1974. *Social Conflict.* Lexington, MA: Heath.

**Bridges, W. P.** 1982. "The Sexual Segregation of Occupations: Theories of Labor Stratification in Industry." *American Journal of Sociology* 88:270–95.

**Brinton, Crane.** 1965. *The Anatomy of Revolution.* New York: Vintage.

**Brinton, Mary C.** 1988. "The Social-Institutional Bases of Gender Stratification: Japan as an Illustrative Case." *American Journal of Sociology* 94:300–34.

*Britannica Book of the Year.* 1989. Chicago: Encyclopaedia Britannica, Inc.

**Broad, William and Nicholas Wade.** 1982. *Betrayers of the Truth: Fraud and Deceit in the Halls of Science.* New York: Simon & Schuster/Touchstone.

**Brody, Elaine.** 1985. "Parent Care as a Normative Family Stress." *The Gerontologist* 35:19–29.

**Bromley, David G. and Anson D. Shupe, Jr.** 1979. *"Moonies" in America: Cult, Church, and Crusade.* Beverly Hills, CA: Sage.

**Bronfenbrenner, Urie.** 1970. *Two Worlds of Childhood: U.S. and U.S.S.R.* New York: Basic Books–Russell Sage Foundation.

———. 1981. "Children and Families: 1984?" *Transaction* 18:38–41.

**Brookover, Wilbur B. and Jeffrey M. Schneider.** 1975. "Academic Environments and Elementary School Achievement." *Journal of Research and Development in Education* 9:82–91.

**Brooks, Christine M.** 1988. "Armchair Quarterbacks." *American Demographics* 10:29–31.

**Brophy, I. N.** 1945. "The Luxury of Anti-Negro Prejudice." *Public Opinion Quarterly* 9:456–66.

**Brower, J. J.** 1973. "The Black Side of Football: The Salience of Race." Unpublished doctoral dissertation. Santa Barbara: University of California.

**Brown, Barbara.** 1984. "How the Baby Boom Lives." *American Demographics* 6(5):35–37.

**Brown, Bernard.** 1983. "Stress in Children and Families." Paper presented at the annual meeting of the American Association for the Advancement of Science, Detroit.

**Brown, G.** 1976. "The Social Causes of Disease." In *An Introduction to Medical Sociology,* edited by D. Tuckett. London: Tavistock.

**Brown, Julia S.** 1952. "A Comparative Study of Deviations from Sexual Mores." *American Sociological Review* 17:134–46.

**Brown, Lester R.** 1973. "Population and Affluence: Growing Pressures on World Food Resources." *Population Bulletin* 29:1–31.

———. 1975. "The World Food Prospect." *Science* 190:1053–59.

———. 1989. "Reexamining the World Food Prospect." Pp. 41–58 in *State of the World 1989*, edited by Lester R. Brown, et al. New York: Norton.

**Brown, Roger.** 1965. *Social Psychology.* New York: Free Press.

**Brownmiller, Susan.** 1975. *Against Our Will: Men, Women and Rape.* New York: Bantam.

**Brozan, Nadine.** 1986. "Gang Rape: A Rising Campus Concern." *New York Times* (February 17):B8.

**Bruner, Jerome S. and Leo Postman.** 1949. "On the Perception of Incongruity: A Paradigm." *Journal of Personality* 18:206–23.

**Bumpass, Larry.** 1984a. "Some Characteristics of Children's Second Families." *American Journal of Sociology* 90:608–23.

———. 1984b. "Children and Marital Dissolution." *Demography* 21:71–82.

**Bumpass, Larry and Ronald Rindfuss.** 1979. "Children's Experience of Marital Disruption." *American Journal of Sociology* 85:49–65.

**Bumpass, Larry L. and J. A. Sweet.** 1972. "Differentials in Marital Instability: 1970." *American Sociological Review* 37:754–66.

**Burawoy, Michael.** 1979. *Manufacturing Consent.* Chicago: University of Chicago Press.

**Burdge, Rabel J.** 1969. "Levels of Occupational Prestige and Leisure Activity." *Journal of Leisure Research* 3:262–74.

**Burgess, Ernest W.** 1967. "The Growth of the City." Pp. 47–62 in *The City,* edited by R. E. Park, E. W. Burgess, and R. D. McKenzie. Chicago: University of Chicago Press.

**Burgess, Robert L. and Ted L. Huston (ed.).** 1979. *Social Exchange in Developing Relationships.* New York: Academic Press.

**Burleigh, William R.** 1979. "Editor's Notebook: At Death's Door." *Cincinnati Post* (December 8).

**Burridge, K. O. L.** 1957. "Disputing in Tangu." *American Anthropologist* 56:143–46.

**Burrough, Bryan.** 1987. "Broken Barrier: More Women Join Ranks of White-Collar Criminals." *Wall Street Journal* (May 27):B1.

**Burt, Ronald S.** 1983. *Corporate Profits and Cooptation: Networks of Market Constraints and Directorate Ties in the American Economy.* New York: Academic Press.

**Bush, Diane Mitsch.** 1985. "The Impact of Changing Gender Role Expectations upon Socialization in Adolescence: Understanding the Interaction of Gender, Age, and Cohort Effects." Pp. 269–97 in *Research in the Sociology of Education and Socialization.* Vol. 5, edited by Alan C. Kerckhoff. Greenwich, CT: JAI Press.

**Bush, Vannevar.** 1945. "As We May Think." *Atlantic Monthly* (July):101–108.

**Butler, Sandra.** 1978. *Conspiracy of Silence: The Trauma of Incest.* San Francisco: New Glide Publications.

**Butterfield, Fox.** 1977. "Taiwan Bridges the Income Gap While Maintaining High Growth." *New York Times* (April 12): 25, 26.

**Cain, Pamela Stone.** 1985. "Prospects for Pay Equity in a Changing Economy." Pp. 137–65 in *Comparable Worth: New Directions for Research,* edited by Heidi I. Hartmann. Washington, DC: National Academy Press.

**Campbell, Angus, Philip E. Converse, Warren E. Miller, and Donald D. Stokes.** 1964. *The American Voter—An Abridgement.* New York: Wiley.

**Campbell, Angus, Gerald Gurin, and W. E. Miller.** 1954. *The Voter Decides.* Evanston, IL: Row, Peterson.

**Cantor, David and Kenneth C. Land.** 1985. "Unemployment and Crime Rates in the Post-World War II United States: A Theoretical and Empirical Analysis." *American Sociological Review* 50:317–32.

**Cantor, M. H.** 1975. "Life Space and the Social Support System of the Inner City Elderly of New York." *The Gerontologist* 15(February):23–26.

**Cantril, Hadley, Herta Herzog, and Hazel Gaudet.** 1940. *The Invasion from Mars.* Princeton, NJ: Princeton University Press.

**Caplow, Theodore.** 1959. "Further Development of a Theory of Coalitions in the Triad." *American Journal of Sociology* 64 (March): 488–93.

**Caplow, Theodore and Howard M. Bahr.** 1979. "Half a Century of Change in Adolescent Attitudes: Replication of a Middletown Survey by the Lynds." *Public Opinion Quarterly* 43:1–17.

**Carchedi, Guglielmo.** 1977. *On the Economic Identification of Social Classes.* London: Routledge and Kegan Paul.

**Carnoy, Martin and Henry M. Levin.** 1985. *Schooling and Work in the Democratic State.* Stanford, CA: Stanford University Press.

**Carp, F. M.** 1975. "Life-Style and Location within the City." *The Gerontologist* 15 (February): 27–33.

**Carroll, Glenn R. and John W. Meyer.** 1982. "Capital Cities in the American Urban System: The Impact of State Expansion." *American Journal of Sociology* 88:565–78.

**Carroll, Jackson W., Douglas W. Johnson, and Martin E. Marty.** 1979. *Religion in America: 1950 to the Present.* New York: Harper & Row.

**Castells, Manuel.** 1985. "High Technology, Economic Restructuring and the Urban-Regional Process in the United States." Pp. 11–40 in *High Technology, Space, and Society,* edited by Manuel Castells. Beverly Hills, CA: Sage.

**Centers, Richard.** 1949. *The Psychology of Social Classes.* Princeton, NJ: Princeton University Press.

**Chagnon, N. A.** 1968. *Yanomamö: The Fierce People.* New York: Holt, Rinehart and Winston.

**Chambliss, William J.** 1969. *Crime and the Legal Process.* New York: McGraw-Hill.

**Chandler, Robert F.** 1971. "The Scientific Basis for the Increased Yield Capacity of Rice and Wheat and Its Present and Potential Impact on Food Production in the Developing Countries." Pp. 25–43 in *Food Population and Employment: The Impact of the Green Revolution,* edited by Thomas T. Poleman and Donald K. Freebain. New York: Praeger.

**Charters, W. W., Jr.** 1974. "Social Class Analysis and the Control of Public Education." Pp. 98–113 in *The Education Establishment,* edited by Elizabeth L. Useem and Michael Useem. Englewood Cliffs, NJ: Prentice-Hall.

Cherlin, Andrew and Frank F. Furstenberg, Jr. 1983. "The American Family in the Year 2000." *The Futurist* 17 (June): 7–14.

———. 1986. *The New American Grandparent: A Place in the Family, a Life Apart.* New York: Basic Books.

Cherlin, Andrew and Pamela Barnhouse Walters. 1981. "Trends in United States Men's and Women's Sex-Role Attitudes: 1972 to 1978." *American Sociological Review* 46:453–60.

Cherlin, Andrew J. 1977. "The Effects of Children on Marital Dissolution." *Demography* 14:265–72.

———. 1978. "Remarriage as an Incomplete Institution." *American Journal of Sociology* 84:634–50.

———. 1979. "Work Life and Marital Dissolution." Pp. 151–66 in *Divorce and Separation*, edited by G. Levinger and O. Moles. New York: Basic Books.

———. 1983. "Recent Research on Aging and the Family." Pp. 5–23 in *Aging in Society*, edited by M. W. Riley, B. Hess, and K. Bond. Hillsdale, NJ: Erlbaum.

Cherry, L. 1975. "Teacher-Child Verbal Interaction: An Approach to the Study of Sex Differences." Pp. 172–83 in *Language and Sex: Difference and Dominance*, edited by B. Thorne and N. Henley. Rowley, MA: Newbury House.

Cherry, Mike. 1974. *On High Steel.* New York: Ballantine.

Chesney-Lind, M. 1980. "Rediscovering Lilith: Misogyny and the 'New Female Criminality.'" In *The Female Offenders*, edited by C. Taylor Griffiths and M. Nance. Vancouver, BC: Simon Fraser University.

Childe, V. Gordon. 1964. *What Happened in History*. Baltimore, MD: Penguin.

Chinoy, E. 1955. *Automobile Workers and the American Dream*. Boston: Beacon.

Chodorow, Nancy. 1978. *The Reproduction of Mothering*. Berkeley: University of California Press.

Choldin, Harvey M., Claudine Hanson, and Robert Bohrer. 1980. "Suburban Status Instability." *American Sociological Review* 45:972–83.

Cicourel, Aaron V. 1968. *The Social Organization of Juvenile Justice.* New York: Wiley.

Clark, Alfred C. 1956. "The Use of Leisure and Its Relation to Occupational Prestige." *American Sociological Review* 21:301–07.

Clark, Burton R. and Martin Trow. 1966. "The Organizational Context." Pp. 17–70 in *College Peer Groups: Problems and Prospects for Research*, edited by Theodore M. Newcomb and Everett K. Wilson. Chicago: Aldine.

Clark, Lindley H., Jr. and Alfred L. Malabre, Jr. 1988. "Eroding R&D: Slow Rise in Outlays for Research Imperils U.S. Competitive Edge." *Wall Street Journal* (November 16): A1, A10.

Clark, William. 1984. "More Means Less." (Review of P. Gupte's book, *The Crowded Earth*.) *New York Times Book Review* (September 30): 32.

Clifton, Rodney A., Raymond P. Perry, Karen Parsonson, and Stella Hryniuk. 1986. "Effects of Ethnicity and Sex on Teachers' Expectations of Junior High School Students." *Sociology of Education* 59:58–67.

Clinard, Marshall B. 1978. *Cities with Little Crime: The Case of Switzerland.* Cambridge, England: Cambridge University Press.

Clingempeel, W. Glenn and N. Dickon Reppucci. 1982. "Joint Custody After Divorce: Major Issues and Goals for Research." *Psychological Bulletin* 9L:102–27.

Clogg, Clifford C. and James W. Shockey. 1984. "Mismatch between Occupation and Schooling: A Prevalence Measure, Recent Trends and Demographic Analysis." *Demography* 21:235–57.

Clogg, Clifford C. and Theresa A. Sullivan. 1983. "Labor Force Composition and Underemployment Trends, 1969–1980." *Social Indicators Research* 12:117–52.

Clutterbuck, Richard Lewis. 1977. *Guerrillas and Terrorists.* London: Faber & Faber.

Coakley, Jay J. 1978. *Sport in Society*. St. Louis, MO: Mosby.

———. 1982. *Sport in Society*. Second edition. St. Louis, MO: Mosby.

Cobb, James C. 1982. *The Selling of the South: The Southern Crusade for Industrial Development, 1936–1980.* Baton Rouge: Louisiana State University Press.

Cockerham, William C. 1988. "Medical Sociology." Pp. 575–99 in *The Handbook of Sociology*, edited by Neil J. Smelser. Beverly Hills, CA: Sage.

Coe, Richard D. and Greg Duncan. 1985. "Welfare: Promoting Poverty or Progress?" *Wall Street Journal* (May 15): 30.

Cohen, Lawrence E. and Kenneth C. Land. 1987. "Age Structure and Crime: Symmetry Versus Asymmetry and the Projection of Crime Rates through the 1990s." *American Sociological Review* 52:170–83.

Cohn, Norman. 1961. *The Pursuit of the Millennium*. New York: Harper & Row.

Cole, Jonathan R. and Stephen Cole. 1973. *Social Stratification in Science*. Chicago: University of Chicago Press.

Coleman, James. 1961. *The Adolescent Society*. New York: Free Press.

Coleman, James S., Ernest Q. Campbell, Carol J. Hobson, James McPartland, Alexander M. Mood, Frederic D. Weinfeld, and Robert L. York. 1966. *Equality of Educational Opportunity*. Washington, DC: U.S. Government Printing Office.

Coleman, James S., Thomas Hoffer, and Sally Kilgore. 1982. *High School Achievement*. New York: Basic Books.

Coleman, James S., Sara D. Kelly, and John A. Moore. 1975. *Trends in School Segregation, 1968–1973*. Washington, DC: The Urban Institute.

Coleman, James William. 1987. "Toward an Integrated Theory of White-Collar Crime." *American Journal of Sociology* 93:406–39.

Coles, Robert. 1967. *Migrants, Sharecroppers, Mountaineers*. Vol. II of *Children of Crisis*. Boston: Little, Brown.

———. 1977. *Privileged Ones*. Vol. V of *Children of Crisis*. Boston: Little, Brown.

Collins, Glenn. 1984. "Experts Debate Impact of Day Care on Children and on Society." *New York Times* (September 4): B11.

Collins, Harry M. 1983. "An

Empirical Relativist Programme in the Sociology of Scientific Knowledge." Pp. 85–113 in *Science Observed*, edited by K. Knorr-Cetina and M. Mulkay. Beverly Hills, CA: Sage.

**Collins, Randall.** 1974. "Where Are Educational Requirements for Employment Highest?" *Sociology of Education* 47:419–42.

———. 1975. *Conflict Sociology.* New York: Academic Press.

———. 1977. "Some Comparative Principles of Educational Stratification." *Havard Educational Review* 47:1–27.

———. 1979. *The Credential Society.* New York: Academic Press.

**Coltrane, Scott.** 1988. "Father-Child Relationships and the Status of Women: A Cross-Cultural Study." *American Journal of Sociology* 93:1060–95.

**Colvin, Mark and John Pauly.** 1983. "A Critique of Criminology: Toward an Integrated Structural-Marxist Theory of Delinquency Production." *American Journal of Sociology* 89:513–51.

**Committee on Government Operations.** 1985. "The Federal Response to the Homeless Crisis." Third Report, to the 99th Congress, 1st Session, House Report 99–47. Washington, DC: U.S. Government Printing Office.

**Commoner, Barry.** 1971. *The Closing Circle.* New York: Knopf.

———. 1988. Talk given at New York University. New York. March 18.

**Comstock, George, Steven Chaffee, Natan Katzman, Maxwell McCombs, and Donald Roberts.** 1978. *Television and Human Behavior.* New York: Columbia University Press.

**Conant, James B.** 1959. *The American High School Today: A First Report to Interested Citizens.* New York: McGraw-Hill.

**Condry, John and Sharon Dyer.** 1976. "Fear of Success: Attribution of Cause to the Victim." *Journal of Social Issues* 32:63–83.

**Congressional Budget Office.** 1984. Washington, DC: U.S. Government Printing Office.

**Connor, Jane M. and Lisa A. Serbin.** 1977. "Behaviorally Based Masculine- and Feminine-Activity-Preference Scales for Pre-

schoolers: Correlates with Other Classroom Behaviors and Cognitive Tests." *Child Development* 48:1411–16.

**Conrad, Peter and Rochelle Kern (eds.).** 1981. *The Sociology of Health and Illness.* New York: St. Martin's Press.

**Conrad, Peter and Joseph W. Schneider.** 1980. *Deviance and Medicalization: From Badness to Sickness.* St. Louis, MO: Mosby.

**Cookson, Peter W., Jr. and Caroline Hodges Persell.** 1985a. "English and American Residential Schools: A Comparative Study of the Reproduction of Social Elites." *Comparative Education Review* 29:283–98.

———. 1985b. *Preparing for Power: America's Elite Boarding Schools.* New York: Basic Books.

**Cooley, Charles Horton.** 1902/1922. *Human Nature and the Social Order.* New York: Scribner's.

**Cooley, Mike.** 1980. *Architect or Bee? The Human/Technology Relationship.* Boston: South End Press.

**Coombs, R. H. and P. S. Powers.** 1975. "Socialization for Death: The Physician's Role." *Urban Life* 4:250–71.

**Corradi, Juan E.** 1982–83. "The Mode of Destruction: Terror in Argentina." *Telos* 54:61–76.

**Coser, Lewis A.** 1956. *The Functions of Social Conflict.* New York: Free Press.

———. 1967. *Continuities in the Study of Social Conflict.* New York: Free Press.

**Coser, Rose Laub.** 1975. "Stay Home Little Sheba: On Placement, Displacement and Social Change." *Social Problems* 22 (April): 470–80.

**Cottle, Thomas J.** 1974. "What Tracking Did to Ollie Taylor." *Social Policy* 5:21–24.

**Covello, Vincent T.** 1979. "Inequality and Opportunity: Occupational Mobility and Educational Attainment in Five Nations." Unpublished paper, National Science Foundation.

**Cozens, F. and F. Stumpf.** 1953. *Sports in American Life.* Chicago: University of Chicago Press.

**Crain, Robert L. and Rita E. Mahard.** 1978. "Desegregation and Black Achievement: A Case-Survey of the Literature." *Law and*

*Contemporary Problems* 42(summer): 17–56.

**Crandall, Virginia C.** 1969. "Sex Differences in Expectancy of Intellectual and Academic Reinforcement." Pp. 11–45 in *Achievement-Related Motives in Children*, edited by Charles P. Smith. New York: Russell Sage Foundation.

**Crawford, T. J. and M. Naditch.** 1970. "Relative Deprivation, Powerlessness and Militancy: The Psychology of Social Protest." *Psychiatry* 33 (May): 208–23.

**Crittenden, Ann.** 1981. "U.S. Farm Productivity May Be Leveling Off." *New York Times* (September 7): A1, D2.

**Crompton, Rosemary and Jon Gubbay.** 1977. *Economy and Class Structure.* New York: St. Martin's Press.

**Cross, H. M.** 1973. "The College Athlete and the Institution." *Law and Contemporary Problems* 38:151–71.

**Cross, Patricia.** 1968. "College Women: A Research Description." *Journal of the National Association of Women Deans and Counselors* 32:12–21.

**Crystal, John C. and Richard N. Bolles.** 1974. *Where Do I Go from Here with My Life?* New York: Seabury.

**Csikszentmihalyi, Mihaly.** 1974. *Flow: Studies of Enjoyment.* Chicago: University of Chicago Press.

**Cummings, Scott and Del Taebel.** 1978. "The Economic Socialization of Children: A Neo-Marxist Analysis." *Social Problems* 26:198–210.

**Curtiss, Susan.** 1977. *Genie.* New York: Academic Press.

**Dahl, Robert A.** 1961. *Who Governs?* New Haven, CT: Yale University Press.

———. 1967. *Pluralist Democracy in America.* Chicago: Rand-McNally.

**Dahrendorf, Ralf.** 1958. "Out of Utopia: Toward a Reorientation of Sociological Analysis." *American Journal of Sociology* 64:115–27.

———. 1959. *Class and Class Conflict in Industrial Society.* Stanford, CA: Stanford University Press.

**Daley, Robert.** 1963. *The Bizarre World of European Sports.* New York: Morrow.

**Dannefer, Dale.** 1984. "Adult Development and Social Theory: A Paradigmatic Reappraisal." *American Sociological Review* 49:100–16.

**Dannefer, Dale and Russell K. Schutt.** 1982. "Race and Juvenile Justice Processing in Court and Police Agencies." *American Journal of Sociology* 87:1113–32.

**Darnton, Nina.** 1985. "Women and Stress on Job and at Home." *New York Times* (August 8): C1, C6.

**Darwin, Charles.** 1859/1958. *The Origin of Species.* New York: Mentor.

**Davidson, James D.** 1977. "Socioeconomic Status and Ten Dimensions of Religious Commitment." *Sociology and Social Research* 61:462–85.

**Davies, Mark and Denise B. Kandel.** 1981. "Parental and Peer Influences on Adolescents' Educational Plans: Some Further Evidence." *American Journal of Sociology* 87:363–87.

**Davis, Alan J.** 1970. "Sexual Assaults in the Philadelphia Prison System." Pp. 107–24 in *The Sexual Scene,* edited by John H. Gagnon and William Simon. Chicago: Transaction/Aldine.

**Davis, James A.** 1983. *General Social Survey Cumulative File, 1972–1982.* 1st ICPSR ed. Ann Arbor, MI: Interuniversity Consortium for Political and Social Research.

**Davis, Kingsley.** 1940. "Extreme Social Isolation of a Child." *American Journal of Sociology* 45:554–64.

———. 1947. "Final Note on a Case of Extreme Isolation." *American Journal of Sociology* 50(March): 432–37.

**Davis, Kingsley and Wilbur E. Moore.** 1945. "Some Principles of Stratification." *American Sociological Review* 10:242–49.

**Day, Robert C.** 1972. "The Emergence of Activism as a Social Movement." Pp. 506–32 in *Native Americans Today: Sociological Perspectives,* edited by Howard M. Bahr, Bruce A. Chadwick, and Robert C. Day. New York: Harper & Row.

**Dearman, Nancy B. and Valena White Plisko.** 1979. *The Condition of Education.* 1979 edition. Washington, DC: National Center for Education Statistics, U.S. Department of Health, Education and Welfare.

———. 1980. *The Condition of Education.* Washington, DC: National Center for Education Statistics.

**Deevey, Edward S., Jr.** 1960. "The Human Population." *Scientific American* 203:195–204.

**Della Fave, L. Richard.** 1980. "The Meek Shall Not Inherit the Earth: Self-evaluation and the Legitimacy of Stratification." *American Sociological Review* 45:955–71.

**Della Fave, L. Richard and George A. Hillery, Jr.** 1980. "Status Inequality in a Religious Community: The Case of a Trappist Monastery." *Social Forces* 59:62–84.

**Deloria, Vine, Jr.** 1981. "Native Americans: The American Indian Today." *The Annals of the American Academy of Political and Social Science* 454 (March): 125–38.

**Deloria, Vine, Jr. (ed.).** 1985. *American Indian Policy in the Twentieth Century.* Norman: University of Oklahoma Press.

**Deutsch, Martin, Theresa J. Jordan, and Cynthia P. Deutsch.** 1985. "Long-Term Effects of Early Intervention: Summary of Selected Findings." Xeroxed report, New York University, Institute for Developmental Studies.

**DeVall, William.** 1980. "Leisure and Lifestyles among Gay Men: An Exploratory Essay." Pp. 44–60 in *Homosexuality in International Perspective,* edited by Joseph Harry and Man Singh Das. New Delhi, India: Vikas.

**DeVall, William and Joseph Harry.** 1978. "Who Hates Whom in the Great Outdoors: Recreation Equipment and the Microecology of Leisure Settings." Paper presented at the annual meeting of the American Sociological Association, San Francisco.

**DeVore, Irven.** 1965. *Primate Behavior: Field Studies of Monkeys and Apes.* New York: Holt, Rinehart and Winston.

**Dickson, Paul.** 1975. *The Future of the Workplace.* New York: Weybright & Tally.

**Digest.** 1985. "Little or No Change in Attitudes on Abortion." *Family Planning Perspectives* 17:76–78.

**DiMaggio, Paul.** 1982. "Cultural Capital and School Success: The Impact of Status Culture Participation on the Grades of U.S. High School Students." *American Sociological Review* 47:189–201.

**DiMaggio, Paul and Michael Useem.** 1978. "Cultural Property and Public Policy—Emerging Tensions in Government Support for Arts." *Social Research* 45:356–89.

**Dionne, E. J., Jr.** 1988. "G.O.P. Hope of Dominance Is Delayed." *New York Times* (November 10): A1, B6.

**DiPrete, Thomas A. and Whitman T. Soule.** 1988. "Gender and Promotion in Segmented Job Ladder Systems." *American Sociological Review* 53:26–40.

**Doerner, William R.** 1985. "Asians: To America with Skills." *Time* (July 8): 42–44.

**Domhoff, G. William.** 1967. *Who Rules America?* Englewood Cliffs, NJ: Prentice-Hall.

———. 1970. *The Higher Circles.* New York: Vintage.

———. 1974. *The Bohemian Grove and Other Retreats.* New York: Harper & Row.

———. 1976. "I Am Not an Instrumentalist." *Kapitalstate* 4:221–24.

———. 1978. *Who Really Rules? New Haven and Community Power Reexamined.* New Brunswick, NJ: Transaction Books.

———. 1979. *The Powers That Be.* New York: Vintage.

———. 1983. *Who Rules America Now?* Englewood Cliffs, NJ: Prentice-Hall.

**Dooley, P. C.** 1969. "The Interlocking Directorate." *American Economic Review* 59:314–23.

**Drew, Elizabeth.** 1983. *Politics and Money—The New Road to Corruption.* New York: Macmillan.

**Duberman, Martin.** 1974. "The Bisexual Debate." *New Times* 2: 34–41.

**Dubin, Steven C.** 1987. "Symbolic Slavery: Black Representations in Popular Culture." *Social Problems* 34:122–40.

**DuBois, Paul M.** 1980. *The Hospice Way of Death.* New York: Human Sciences Press.

**Dulles, F. R.** 1965. *A History of Recreation.* Englewood Cliffs, NJ: Prentice-Hall.

**Duncan, B. and O. D. Duncan.** 1969. "Family Stability and Occupational Success." *Social Problems* 16:273–83.

**Duncan, Greg J.** 1983–1984. "Poverty Turnover High." *ISR Newsletter* 11:3–5.

**Dunlap, R. E. and R. P. Gale.** 1972. "Politics and Ecology: A Political Profile of Student Eco-activists." *Youth and Society* 3:379–97.

**Durkheim, Emile.** 1893/1933. *The Division of Labor in Society.* Glencoe, IL: Free Press.

———. 1897/1951. *Suicide.* Glencoe, IL: Free Press.

———. 1915. *The Elementary Forms of the Religious Life.* Glencoe, IL: Free Press.

**Durso, Joseph.** 1975. *The Sports Factory: An Investigation into College Sports.* New York: Quadrangle.

**Dusek, J. B. and G. Joseph.** 1983. "The Bases of Teacher Expectancies: A Meta-Analysis." *Journal of Educational Psychology* 75:327–46.

**Dutton, Diana B.** 1978. "Explaining the Low Use of Health Services by the Poor: Costs, Attitudes, or Delivery Systems." *American Sociological Review* 43:348–68.

**Duvall, E.** 1971. *Family Development.* Philadelphia: J. B. Lippincott.

**Easterlin, Richard A.** 1980. *Birth and Fortune: The Impact of Numbers on Personal Welfare.* New York: Basic Books.

———. 1987. "The New Age Structure of Poverty in America: Permanent or Transient?" *Population and Development Review* 13:195–208.

**Ebaugh, Helen Rose Fuchs.** 1988. *Becoming an EX: The Process of Role Exit.* Chicago: University of Chicago Press.

**Eccles (Parsons), Jacquelynne.** 1982. "Sex Differences in Math Achievement and Course Enrollment." Paper presented at the annual meeting of the American Educational Research Association, New York.

**Edelman, Murray.** 1971. *Politics as Symbolic Action.* New York: Academic Press.

**Eder, Donna and Stephen Parker.** 1987. "The Cultural Production and Reproduction of Gender: The Effect of Extracurricular Activities on Peer-Group Culture." *Sociology of Education* 60:200–13.

**Edmonston, Barry and Thomas M. Guterbock.** 1984. "Is Suburbanization Slowing Down? Recent Trends in Population Deconcentration in U.S. Metropolitan Areas." *Social Forces* 62:905–25.

**Edsall, Thomas Byrne.** 1984. *The New Politics of Inequality.* New York: Norton.

**Edwards, Harry.** 1969. *The Revolt of the Black Athlete.* New York: Free Press.

———. 1984. "The Collegiate Arms Race: Origins and Implications of the 'Rule 48' Controversy." *Journal of Sport and Social Issues* 8:4–22.

**Edwards, Richard.** 1979. *Contested Terrain: The Transformation of the Workplace in the Twentieth Century.* New York: Basic Books.

**Ehrenreich, Barbara and Deirdre English.** 1978. *For Her Own Good: 150 Years of the Experts' Advice to Women.* Garden City, NY: Doubleday/Anchor.

**Ehrlich, Issac.** 1974. "Participation in Illegitimate Activities: An Economic Analysis." Pp. 68–134 in *Essays in the Economics of Crime and Punishment,* edited by G. S. Becker and W. M. Landes. New York: Columbia University Press.

———. 1975. "The Deterrent Effect of Capital Punishment: A Question of Life and Death." *American Economic Review* 65 (June): 397–417.

———. 1977. "Capital Punishment and Deterrence: Some Further Thoughts and Additional Evidence." *Journal of Political Economy* 85:741–88.

**Ehrlich, Paul.** 1968. *The Population Bomb.* New York: Ballantine.

**Eitzen, D. Stanley.** 1979a. "Sport and Deviance." Pp. 73–87 in *Sport in Contemporary Society,* edited by D. Stanley Eitzen. New York: St. Martin's Press.

———. 1979b. "The Structure of Sport and Society." Pp. 41–46 in *Sport in Contemporary Society,* edited by D. Stanley Eitzen. New York: St. Martin's Press.

**Eitzen, D. Stanley and Norman R. Yetman.** 1979. "Immune from Racism?" Pp. 388–408 in *Sport in Contemporary Society,* edited by D. Stanley Eitzen. New York: St. Martin's Press.

**Ekman, P. and W. V. Friesen.** 1969. "The Repertoire of Nonverbal Behavior: Categories, Origins, Usage, and Coding." *Semiotica* 1: 49–98.

**Elder, Glen H., Jr.** 1974. *Children of the Great Depression.* Chicago: University of Chicago Press.

———. 1978. "Family History and the Life Course." Pp. 17–64 in *Transitions: The Family and the Life Course in Historical Perspective,* edited by Tamara K. Hareven. New York: Academic Press.

**Eldredge, Niles.** 1982. *The Monkey Business.* New York: Washington Square Press.

**Elkin, A. P.** 1954. *The Australian Aborigines.* Third edition. Sydney: Angus and Robertson.

**Elkington, John.** 1984. "Poisons to Burn—or Bury." Pp. 364–65 in *1984 Book of the Year.* Chicago: Encyclopaedia Britannica.

**Elliott, Delbert S. and Suzanne S. Ageton.** 1980. "Reconciling Race and Class Differences in Self-reported and Official Estimates of Delinquency." *American Sociological Review* 45 (February): 95–110.

**Ellis, Godfrey J., Gary R. Lee, and Larry R. Petersen.** 1978. "Supervision and Conformity: A Cross-Cultural Analysis of Parental Socialization Values." *American Journal of Sociology* 84:386–403.

**Ellul, Jacques.** 1964. *The Technological Society.* New York: Random House.

**Ellwood, David T. and Mary Jo Bane.** 1984. "The Impact of AFDC on Family Structure and Living Arrangements." *Working paper prepared for the U.S. Department of Health and Human Services under grant no. 92A–82.* Springfield, VA: U.S. Department of Commerce, National Technical Information Service.

**Emerson, Joan P.** 1970. "Behavior in Private Places: Sustaining Definitions of Reality in Gynecological Examinations." Pp. 74–97 in *Recent Sociology* No. 2, edited by Hans Peter Dreitzel. New York: Macmillan.

**Empey, LaMar Taylor.** 1978. *American Delinquency.* Homewood, IL: Dorsey Press.

**Encyclopaedia Britannica.** 1977. "Productivity, Economic." *Macropaedia* 15:30.

**Engels, Friedrich.** 1884/1972. *The Origin of the Family, Private Prop-*

*erty, and the State.* New York: Pathfinder Press.

**Engels, Richard A. and Richard L. Forstall.** 1985. "Metropolitan Areas Dominate Growth Again." *American Demographics* 7:22–25, 45.

**England, Paula.** 1981. "Assessing Trends in Occupational Sex Segregation, 1900–1976." Pp. 273–95 in *Sociological Perspectives on Labor Markets,* edited by Ivar Berg. New York: Academic Press.

**England, Paula, George Farkas, Barbara Stanek Kilbourne, and Thomas Dou.** 1988. "Explaining Occupational Sex Segregation and Wages: Findings from a Model with Fixed Effects." *American Sociological Review* 53:544–58.

**Engler, Robert.** 1961. *The Politics of Oil.* Chicago: University of Chicago Press.

**Ennis, Philip H.** 1967. "Criminal Victimization in the U.S.: A Report of a National Survey." *Field Survey II, President's Commission on Law Enforcement and Administration of Justice.* Washington, DC: U.S. Government Printing Office.

**Environmental Fund.** 1976. *World Hunger: Too Little Food or Too Many People?* Washington, DC: Environmental Fund.

**Epstein, Cynthia Fuchs.** 1983. *Women in Law.* Garden City, NY: Doubleday/Anchor.

———. 1988. *Deceptive Distinctions: Sex, Gender and the Social Order.* New Haven, CT: Yale University Press.

**Epstein, Samuel S.** 1981. "The Political and Economic Basis of Cancer." Pp. 75–82 in *The Sociology of Health and Illness,* edited by Peter Conrad and Rochelle Kern. New York: St. Martin's Press.

**Erikson, Kai T.** 1966. *Wayward Puritans: A Study in the Sociology of Deviance.* New York: Wiley.

**Escalona, S.** 1965. "Children and the Threat of Nuclear War." In *Behavioral Science and Human Survival,* edited by M. Schwebel. Palo Alto, CA: Behavioral Science Press.

**Espenshade, Thomas J.** 1983. "Black-White Differences in Marriage, Separation, Divorce and Remarriage." Paper presented at the annual meeting of the Population Association of America,

———. 1984. *Investing in Children.* Washington, DC: Urban Institute.

**Etheridge, Carolyn F.** 1974. "The Dynamics of Changing Sex-Roles: An Integrating Theoretical Analysis." Paper presented at the annual meeting of the American Sociological Association, Montreal.

———. 1978. "Equality in the Family: Comparative Analysis and Theoretical Model." *International Journal of Women's Studies* 1:50–63.

**Etienne, Mona and Eleanor Leacock (eds.).** 1980. *Women and Colonization.* New York: Praeger/Bergin.

**Etzioni, Amitai.** 1965. "Dual Leadership in Complex Organizations." *American Sociological Review* 30:688–98.

**Etzkowitz, Henry.** 1984. "Solar Versus Nuclear Energy: Autonomous or Dependent Technology?" *Social Problems* 31:417–34.

**Evans, Peter B. and Steven A. Schneider.** 1981. "The Political Economy of the Corporation." Pp. 216–41 in *Political Economy: A Critique of American Society,* edited by Scott G. McNall. Glenview, IL: Scott, Foresman.

**Eve, Raymond A. and David G. Bromley.** 1981. "Scholastic Dishonesty Among College Undergraduates: Parallel Tests of Two Sociological Explanations." *Youth and Society* 13:3–22.

**Faia, Michael A.** 1981. "Selection by Certification: A Neglected Variable in Stratification Research." *American Journal of Sociology* 86:1093–1111.

**Faich, R. G. and R. Gale.** 1971. "Environmental Movement: From Recreation to Politics." *Pacific Sociological Review* 14:270–87.

**Fainstein, Norman I. and Susan S. Fainstein.** 1982. "Urban Policy under Capitalism." *Urban Affairs Annual Reviews* 22. Beverly Hills, CA: Sage.

**Falsey, Barbara and Barbara Heyns.** 1984. "The College Channel: Private and Public Schools Reconsidered." *Sociology of Education* 57:111–22.

**Farber, Henry S.** 1987. "The Recent Decline in Unionization in the United States." *Science* 238:915–20.

**Farley, Reynolds and Walter R.**

**Allen.** 1987. *The Color Line and the Quality of Life in America.* New York: Russell Sage Foundation.

**Farley, Reynolds, Toni Richards, and Clarence Wurdock.** 1980. "School Desegregation and White Flight: An Investigation of Competing Models and Their Discrepant Findings." *Sociology of Education* 53(July): 123–39.

**Farrell, Warren.** 1976. "Women's Liberation as Men's Liberation: Twenty-one Examples." Pp. 278–90 in *The Forty-Nine Percent Majority: The Male Sex Role,* edited by Deborah S. David and Robert Brannon. Reading, MA: Addison-Wesley.

**Fava, Sylvia F.** 1975. "Beyond Suburbia." *Annals of the American Academy* 422 (November): 10–24.

———. 1978. "Women's Place in the New Suburbia." Paper presented at the annual meeting of the American Sociological Association, San Francisco.

**Feagin, Joe R.** 1972. "Poverty: We Still Believe That God Helps Those Who Help Themselves." *Psychology Today* 6:101ff.

———. 1975. *Subordinating the Poor: Welfare and American Beliefs.* Englewood Cliffs, NJ: Prentice-Hall.

———. 1985. "The Global Context of Metropolitan Growth: Houston and the Oil Industry." *American Journal of Sociology* 90:1204–30.

**Featherman, David L. and Robert M. Hauser.** 1978. *Opportunity and Change.* New York: Academic Press.

**Feldman, Kenneth A. and Theodore M. Newcomb.** 1969. *The Impact of College upon Students.* San Francisco: Jossey-Bass.

**Fernandez, Judith, John Pincus, and Jane Peterson.** 1982. *Troubled Suburbs: An Exploratory Study.* Santa Monica, CA: Rand Corporation.

**Ferree, Myra Marx and Frederick D. Miller.** 1985. "Mobilization and Meaning: Toward an Integration of Social Psychological and Resource Perspectives on Social Movements." *Sociological Inquiry* 55:38–61.

**Ferriss, Abbott L.** 1988. "The Changing U.S. Household: More Are Living Alone." *Social Indicators Network News* (February): 1, 5.

**Fialka, John J.** 1982a. "Ground

Zero: Town of Pella, Iowa, Talks of Little Other than Nuclear Attack." *Wall Street Journal* (April 16): 1, 22.

———. 1982b. "Atom-Weapons Issue Stirs Divisive Debate in the Catholic Church." *Wall Street Journal* (June 9): 1, 20.

**Fimrite, Ron.** 1974. "Take Me Out to the Brawl Game." *Sports Illustrated* (June 17): 10–13.

**Findley, Warren G. and Miriam M. Bryan.** 1970. *Ability Grouping: 1970—I. Common Practices in the Use of Tests for Grouping Students in Public Schools.* Athens: The Center for Educational Improvement, University of Georgia.

**Fine, Gary Alan.** 1987a. *With the Boys: Little League Baseball and Preadolescent Culture.* Chicago: University of Chicago Press.

———. 1987b. "One of the Boys: Women in Male-Dominated Settings." Pp. 131–47 in *Changing Men,* edited by Michael S. Kimmel. Beverly Hills, CA: Sage.

**Finkelhor, David.** 1979. *Sexually Victimized Children.* New York: Free Press.

———. 1984. *Child Sexual Abuse: New Theory and Research.* New York: Free Press.

**Finkelman, J. J.** 1966. "Maternal Employment, Family Relationships and Parental Role Perception." Unpublished doctoral dissertation, Yeshiva University, Israel.

**Finley, Merrilee K.** 1984. "Teachers and Tracking in a Comprehensive High School." *Sociology of Education* 57:233–43.

**Firebaugh, Glenn and Kenneth E. Davis.** 1988. "Trends in Antiblack Prejudice, 1972–1984: Region and Cohort Effects." *American Journal of Sociology* 94:251–72.

**Firey, Walter.** 1947. *Land Use in Central Boston.* Cambridge, MA: Harvard University Press.

**Fischer, Claude S.** 1976. *The Urban Experience.* New York: Harcourt Brace Jovanovich.

———. 1981a. "The Public and Private Worlds of City Life." *American Sociological Review* 46:306–19.

———. 1981b. *To Dwell among Friends: Personal Networks in Town and City.* Chicago: University of Chicago Press.

**Fischer, Claude S., Mark Baldas-**

sare, and Richard Ofshe.** 1975. "Crowding Studies and Urban Life: A Critical Review." *Journal of the American Institute of Planners* 41: 406–18.

**Fischer, Claude S. and Robert Max Jackson.** 1977. "Suburbanism and Localism." Pp. 117–38 in *Networks and Places,* edited by Claude S. Fischer et al. New York: Free Press.

**Fischer, Claude S., Robert Max Jackson, C. Ann Stueve, Kathleen Gerson, Lynn McCallister Jones, with Mark Baldassare.** 1977. *Networks and Places: Social Relations in the Urban Setting.* New York: Free Press.

**Fiske, Edward B.** 1983. "High Schools Stiffen Diploma Requirements." *New York Times* (October 9): 1, 68.

———. 1984. "Earlier Schooling Is Pressed." *New York Times* (December 17): A1, B15.

**Fitzpatrick, Kevin M. and John R. Logan.** 1985. "The Aging of the Suburbs, 1960–1980." *American Sociological Review* 50:106–17.

**Flanagan, Timothy J. and Katherine M. Jamieson (eds.).** 1988. *Sourcebook of Criminal Justice Statistics—1987.* Washington, DC: U.S. Department of Justice.

**Flanagan, Timothy J., David J. van Alstyne, and Michael R. Gottfredson (eds.).** 1982. *Sourcebook of Criminal Justice Statistics—1981.* Washington, DC: U.S. Department of Justice, Bureau of Justice Statistics, U.S. Government Printing Office.

**Flynn, Charles P.** 1983. "Militarism, Means of Coercion, and the Sociological Construction of Reality." *Humanity and Society* 7:1–9.

**Flynn, Cynthia.** 1979. "Three Mile Island Telephone Survey: Preliminary Report on Procedures and Findings." Report submitted to the U.S. Nuclear Regulatory Commission. Seattle, WA: Social Impact Research.

*Focus.* 1985. "Are We Losing Ground?" University of Wisconsin-Madison, Institute for Research on Poverty, *Focus* 8:1–12.

**Fogelson, Robert.** 1967. *The Fragmented Metropolis: Los Angeles, 1850–1930.* Cambridge, MA: Harvard University Press.

**Folger, John D. and Charles B.**

Nam.** 1967. *Education of the American Population.* Washington, DC: U.S. Bureau of the Census, U.S. Government Printing Office.

**Ford, Clellan S. and Frank A. Beach.** 1951. *Patterns of Sexual Behavior.* New York: Harper Torchbooks.

**Ford, W. Scott.** 1973. "Interracial Public Housing in a Border City: Another Look at the Contact Hypothesis." *American Journal of Sociology* 78:1426–47.

**Form, W. H.** 1976. *Blue Collar Stratification.* Princeton, NJ: Princeton University Press.

**Forste, Renata T. and Tim B. Heaton.** 1988. "Initiation of Sexual Activity among Female Adolescents." *Youth and Society* 19:250–68.

*Fortune.* 1988. "The World's 50 Biggest Industrial Corporations." *Fortune* (August 1): D3, D4.

*Forum.* 1985. "AIDS: What Is to Be Done?" *Harper's* (October): 39–52.

**Foucault, Michel.** 1972. *The Archaeology of Knowledge.* New York: Random House.

**Fowles, Jib.** 1988. "The 1950s Revisited. Coming Soon: More Men than Women." *New York Times* (June 5): D3.

**Frank, André Gunder.** 1966. "The Development of Underdevelopment." *Monthly Review* 18 (September): 3–17.

———. 1967. *Capitalism and Underdevelopment in Latin America.* New York: Monthly Review Press.

———. 1979. *Dependent Accumulation and Underdevelopment.* New York: Monthly Review Press.

———. 1980. *Crisis in the World Economy.* New York: Holmes & Meier.

**Frankl, Razelle.** 1987. *Televangelism: The Marketing of Popular Religion.* Carbondale: Southern Illinois University Press.

**Franklin, Clyde W.** 1984. *The Changing Definition of Masculinity.* New York: Plenum.

**Frazier, Nancy and Myra Sadker.** 1973. *Sexism in School and Society.* New York: Harper & Row.

**Freedman, Daniel G.** 1974. *Human Infancy: An Evolutionary Perspective.* Hillsdale, NJ: Erlbaum.

**Freeman, Jo.** 1975. *The Politics of Women's Liberation.* New York: David McKay.

**Freeman, Richard B.** 1976. *The*

*Over-Educated American*. New York: Academic Press.

———. 1977. *Black Elite: The New Market for Highly Educated Black Americans*. New York: McGraw-Hill.

**Freidson, Eliot.** 1978. "The Prospects for Health Services in the United States." *Medical Care* 16: 971–83.

———. 1980. "Conceiving of Divisions of Labor." Paper presented at the annual meeting of the American Sociological Association, New York.

**Freitag, Peter.** 1975. "The Cabinet and Big Business: A Study of Interlocks." *Social Problems* 23:137–52.

**Friedl, Ernestine.** 1975. *Women and Men: An Anthropologist's View*. New York: Holt, Rinehart and Winston.

**Friedman, Debra.** 1983. "Why Workers Strike: Individual Decisions and Structural Constraints." Pp. 250–83 in *The Microfoundations of Macrosociology*, edited by Michael Hechter. Philadelphia: Temple University Press.

**Frieze, Irene H.** 1975. "Women's Expectations for and Causal Attributions of Success and Failure." Pp. 158–71 in *Women and Achievement: Social and Motivational Analyses*, edited by Martha T. S. Mednick, Sandra Schwartz Tangri, and Lois Wladis Hoffman. Washington, DC: Hemisphere.

**Frisbie, W. Parker and John D. Kasarda.** 1988. "Spatial Processes." Pp. 629–66 in *Handbook of Sociology*, edited by Neil J. Smelser. Beverly Hills, CA: Sage.

**Fukuyama, Yoshio.** 1961. "The Major Dimensions of Church Membership." *Review of Religious Research* 2:154–61.

**Furniss, Norman F.** 1954. *The Fundamentalist Controversy, 1918–1931*. New Haven, CT: Yale University Press.

**Furstenberg, Frank F., Jr. and Christine Winquist Nord.** 1985. "Parenting Apart." *Journal of Marriage and the Family* 47:893–904.

**Furstenberg, Frank F., Jr. and Graham Spanier.** 1984. *Recycling the Family*. Beverly Hills, CA: Sage.

**Furstenberg, Frank F., Jr., R. Lincoln, and J. Menken (eds.).** 1981. *Teenage Sexuality, Pregnancy and Childbearing*. Philadelphia: University of Pennsylvania Press.

**Furstenberg, Frank F., Jr., Christine Winquist Nord, James L. Peterson, and Nicholas Zill.** 1983. "The Life Course of Children of Divorce: Marital Disruption and Parental Contact." *American Sociological Review* 48:656–68.

**Fusfeld, Daniel.** 1973. *The Basic Economics of the Urban Racial Crisis*. New York: Holt, Rinehart and Winston.

**Gagnon, John H.** 1977. *Human Sexualities*. Glenview, IL: Scott, Foresman.

**Gallup Opinion Index.** 1977. *Religion in America 1977–78*. Princeton, NJ: American Institute of Public Opinion.

**Gamson, William A.** 1975. *The Strategy of Protest*. Homewood, IL: Dorsey Press.

**Gamson, William A., Bruce Fireman, and Steven Rytina.** 1982. *Encounters with Unjust Authority*. Homewood, IL: Dorsey Press.

**Gans, Herbert J.** 1962a. "Urbanism and Suburbanism as Ways of Life: A Reevaluation of Definitions." Pp. 625–48 in *Human Behavior and Social Processes*, edited by Arnold Rose. Boston: Houghton Mifflin.

———. 1962b. *The Urban Villagers*. New York: Free Press.

———. 1967. *The Levittowners*. New York: Free Press.

———. 1971. "The Uses of Poverty: The Poor Pay All." *Social Policy* 2:21–23.

———. 1988. *Middle American Individualism: The Future of Liberal Democracy*. New York: Free Press.

**Garabedian, Peter G.** 1963. "Social Roles and Processes of Socialization in the Prison Community." *Social Problems* 11:139–52.

**Gardner, Robert W., Bryant Robey, and Peter C. Smith.** 1983. *Asian Americans: Growth, Change and Diversity*. Washington, DC: Population Reference Bureau.

**Garfinkel, Harold.** 1956. "Conditions of Successful Degradation Ceremonies." *American Journal of Sociology* 61:420–24.

———. 1967. *Studies in Ethnomethodology*. Englewood Cliffs, NJ: Prentice-Hall.

**Garfinkel, I. and Sara McLanahan.** 1986. *Single Mothers and Their Children: A New American Dilemma*. Washington, DC: Urban Institute.

**Garnett, Richard A.** 1988. "The Study of War in American Sociology: An Analysis of Selected Journals, 1936 to 1984." *The American Sociologist* 19:270–82.

**Gebhard, Paul H.** 1972. "Incidence of Overt Homosexuality in the United States and Western Europe." Pp. 22–29 in *National Institute of Mental Health Task Force on Homosexuality: Final Report and Background Papers,* edited by John M. Livingood. Washington, DC: U.S. Government Printing Office.

**Gecas, Viktor.** 1979. "The Influence of Social Class on Socialization." Pp. 365–404 in *Contemporary Theories about the Family,* edited by Wesley R. Burr, Reuben Hill, F. Ivan Nye, and Ira L. Reiss. New York: Free Press.

**Gelles, Richard J.** 1974. *The Violent Home: A Study of Physical Aggression between Husbands and Wives*. Beverly Hills, CA: Sage.

———. 1979. *Family Violence*. Beverly Hills, CA: Sage.

**Gelles, Richard J. and Murray A. Straus.** 1979. "Determinants of Violence in the Family: Toward a Theoretical Integration." Pp. 549–81 in *Contemporary Theories about the Family,* edited by Wesley R. Burr et al. Vol. I. New York: Free Press.

**Gerbner, George.** 1972. "Violence in Television Drama." Pp. 28–187 in *Television and Social Behavior,* edited by G. A. Comstock and E. A. Rubenstein. Washington, DC: U.S. Government Printing Office.

**Gerbner, George and Nancy Signorielli.** 1979. "Women and Minorities in Television Drama 1969–1978." The Annenberg School of Communications, University of Pennsylvania.

**Geronimus, Arline T.** 1987. "On Teenage Childbearing and Neonatal Mortality in the United States." *Population and Development Review* 13:245–79.

**Gerson, Kathleen.** 1983. "Changing Family Structure and the Position of Women: A Review of the Trends." *American Planners' Association Journal* (spring): 138–48.

———. Forthcoming. *The Price of Privilege*. New York: Basic Books.

Gerstein, Dean R., R. Duncan Luce, Neil J. Smelser, and Sonja Sperlich (eds.). 1988. *The Behavioral and Social Sciences: Achievements and Opportunities*. Washington, DC: National Academy Press.

Gerstel, Naomi. 1988. "Divorce, Gender, and Social Integration." *Gender & Society* 2:343–67.

Gerstel, Naomi, Catherine Kohler Riessman, and Sarah Rosenfield. 1985. "Explaining the Symptomatology of Separated and Divorced Women and Men: The Role of Material Resources and Social Networks." *Social Forces* 64:84–101.

Giacquinta, Joseph B., Margot Ely, and Trika Smith-Burke. 1984. *Educational Microcomputing at Home: A Comparative Analysis of 20 Families*. New York: New York University School of Education, Health, Nursing, and Arts Professions.

Giddens, Anthony. 1982. *Sociology: A Brief but Critical Introduction*. New York: Harcourt Brace Jovanovich.

———. 1987. *Social Theory and Modern Sociology*. Stanford, CA: Stanford University Press.

Giele, Janet Zollinger. 1978. *Women and the Future: Changing Sex Roles in Modern America*. New York: Free Press.

———. 1988. "Gender and Sex Roles." Pp. 291–323 in *Handbook of Sociology*, edited by Neil J. Smelser. Beverly Hills, CA: Sage.

Gieryn, Thomas F., George M. Bevins, and Stephen C. Zehr. 1985. "Professionalization of American Scientists: Public Science in the Creation/Evolution Trials." *American Sociological Review* 50:392–409.

Gilligan, Carol. 1977. "In a Different Voice: Women's Conception of the Self and of Morality." *Harvard Education Review* 47:481–517.

———. 1982. *In a Different Voice*. Cambridge, MA: Harvard University Press.

———. 1985. "Two Perspectives on Child Development." Talk given at New York University, November 6, 1985.

Gilmartin, Brian G. 1979. "The Case Against Spanking." *Human Behavior* (February):18–23.

Gitlin, Todd. 1980. *The Whole World Is Watching*. Berkeley: University of California Press.

———. 1983. *Inside Prime Time*. New York: Pantheon.

Glass, D. V. (ed.). 1953. *Introduction to Malthus*. New York: Wiley.

Glick, Paul C. 1988. "The Role of Divorce in the Changing Family Structure." Pp. 3–34 in *Children of Divorce: Empirical Perspectives on Adjustment*, edited by Sharlene A. Wolchik and Paul Karoly. New York: Gardner.

Glick, Paul C. and Arthur J. Norton. 1979. "Marrying, Divorcing, and Living Together in the U.S. Today." *Population Bulletin* 32:3–38.

Glick, Paul C. and Sung-Ling Lin. 1986. "Recent Changes in Divorce and Remarriage." *Journal of Marriage and the Family* 48:737–47.

Glock, Charles and Rodney Stark. 1965. *Religion and Society in Tension*. Chicago: Rand McNally.

Goffman, Erving. 1959. *The Presentation of Self in Everyday Life*. Garden City, NY: Doubleday/Anchor.

———. 1961. *Asylums*. Garden City, NY: Doubleday.

———. 1963. *Behavior in Public Places*. New York: Free Press.

———. 1967. *Interaction Ritual: Essays on Face-to-Face Behavior*. Garden City, NY: Doubleday.

———. 1971. *Relations in Public*. New York: Basic Books.

———. 1974. *Frame Analysis*. Cambridge, MA: Harvard University Press.

———. 1979. *Gender Advertisements*. Cambridge, MA: Harvard University Press.

Golant, Stephen M. 1978. "Residential Concentrations of the Future Elderly." *The Gerontologist* 15:16–23.

Gold, Martin. 1970. *Delinquent Behavior in an American City*. Belmont, CA: Brooks/Cole.

Goldscheider, Frances Kobrin and Linda J. Waite. 1986. "Sex Differences in the Entry into Marriage." *American Journal of Sociology* 92:91–109.

Goldstein, Jeffrey H. and Robert L. Arms. 1971. "Effects of Observing Athletic Contests on Hostility." *Sociometry* 34 (March): 83–90.

Goldstein, Joseph and Jay Katz. 1965. *The Family and the Law*. New York: Free Press.

Goldthorpe, John H. 1978. "The Current Inflation: Towards a Sociological Account." Pp. 186–214 in *The Political Economy of Inflation*, edited by Fred Hirsch and John H. Goldthorpe. London: Martin Robertson.

Golladay, Mary A. and Jay Noell (eds.). 1978. *The Condition of Education*. Washington, DC: National Center for Education Statistics.

Goode, William J. 1960. "Encroachment, Charlatanism, and the Emerging Profession: Psychology, Medicine, and Sociology." *American Sociological Review* 25:902–14.

———. 1977. *Principles of Sociology*. New York: McGraw-Hill.

Goode, William J., Elizabeth Hopkins, and Helen M. McClure. 1971. *Social Systems and Family Patterns: A Propositional Inventory*. New York: Bobbs-Merrill.

Goodhart, Philip and Christopher Chataway. 1973. "The Rise of Sports." Pp. 211–17 in *The Other Side of Western Civilization: Readings in Everyday Life*. Vol. II: *The Sixteenth Century to the Present*, edited by Peter N. Stearus. New York: Harcourt Brace Jovanovich.

Goodlad, John I. 1984. *A Place Called School*. New York: McGraw-Hill.

Gordon, David M. 1972. *Theories of Poverty and Unemployment: Orthodox, Radical, and Dual Labor Market Perspectives*. Lexington, MA: Lexington Books.

———. 1977. "Capitalism and the Roots of Urban Crisis." Pp. 82–112 in *The Fiscal Crisis of American Cities*, edited by Roger E. Alcaly and David Mermelstein. New York: Vintage.

Gordon, Milton. 1964. *Assimilation in American Life*. New York: Oxford University Press.

Gordon, Robert K. 1983. "Casualties of History: Making Amends to Japanese-Americans." *New Republic* 189 (August 15): 11.

Goring, Charles. 1913. *The English Convict*. London: His Majesty's Stationery Office.

Goslin, David A. 1965. *The School

*in Contemporary Society.* Glenview, IL: Scott, Foresman.

**Gove, Walter R.** 1972. "The Relationship between Sex Roles, Marital Status, and Mental Illness." *Social Forces* 51:34–44.

———. 1973. "Sex, Marital Status, and Mortality." *American Journal of Sociology* 79:45–67.

**Gove, Walter R., Michael Hughes, and Omer R. Galle.** 1979. "Overcrowding in the Home: An Empirical Investigation of Its Possible Pathological Consequences." *American Sociological Review* 44:59–80.

**Gove, Walter R. and Jeanette F. Tudor.** 1973. "Adult Sex Roles and Mental Illness." *American Journal of Sociology* 78:812–32.

**Grabiner, Judith V. and Peter D. Miller.** 1974. "Effects of the Scopes Trial." *Science* 185 (September 6): 832–37.

**Graham, Robert.** 1979. *Iran: The Illusion of Power.* New York: St. Martin's Press.

**Granovetter, Mark S.** 1974. *Getting a Job: A Study of Contacts and Careers.* Cambridge, MA: Harvard University Press.

———. 1979a. "Toward a Sociological Theory of Income Differences." Paper presented at the annual meeting of the American Sociological Association, Boston.

———. 1979b. "The Idea of 'Advancement' in Theories of Social Evolution and Development." *American Journal of Sociology* 85:489–515.

———. 1986. "Labor Mobility, Internal Markets and Job-Matching: A Comparison of the Sociological and the Economic Approaches." Pp. 3–39 in *Research in Social Stratification and Mobility,* edited by Robert V. Robinson. Greenwich, CT: JAI Press.

**Greeley, Andrew.** 1972. *The Denominational Society.* Glenview, IL: Scott, Foresman.

———. 1974. *Building Coalitions: American Politics for the 1970s.* New York: Watts.

**Green, Robert L., Louis J. Hoffmann, Richard J. Morse, Marilyn E. Hayes, and Robert F. Morgan.** 1964. "The Educational Status of Children in a District Without Public Schools." Cooperative Research Project 2321.

Washington, DC: U.S. Office of Education.

**Green, Russell and Leonard Berkowitz.** 1966. "Name-mediated Aggressive Cue Properties." *Journal of Personality* 34:456–65.

**Greenberg, B. S. and B. Dervin.** 1970. *Use of the Mass Media by the Urban Poor.* New York: Praeger.

**Greenberg, David F.** 1976. "On One-dimensional Marxist Criminology." *Theory and Society* 3:610–21.

———. 1977a. "Delinquency and the Age Structure of Society." *Contemporary Crises* 1:189–223.

———. 1977b. "The Dynamics of Oscillatory Punishment Processes." *Journal of Criminal Law and Criminology* 68:643–51.

———. 1977c. "The Correctional Effects of Corrections: A Survey of Evaluations." Pp. 111–48 in *Corrections and Punishment,* edited by David F. Greenberg. Beverly Hills, CA: Sage.

———. 1985. "Age, Crime, and Social Explanation." *American Journal of Sociology* 91:1–21.

———. 1988a. Personal communication, New York University.

———. 1988b. *The Construction of Homosexuality.* Chicago: University of Chicago Press.

———. **(ed.).** 1981. *Crime and Capitalism.* Palo Alto, CA: Mayfield.

**Greenberg, David F. and Marcia H. Bystryn.** 1978. "Social Sources of the Prohibition against Male Homosexuality." Paper presented at the annual meeting of the Society for the Study of Social Problems, San Francisco, CA.

**Greenberg, David F., Ronald C. Kessler, and Charles H. Logan.** 1977. "Crime Rates and Arrest Rates: A Causal Analysis." *American Sociological Review* 44:843–50.

**Greenberg, Ellen and Robert Nay.** 1982. "The Intergenerational Transmission of Marital Instability Reconsidered." *Journal of Marriage and the Family* 44:335–48.

**Greenstein, Robert.** 1985. "Losing Faith in Losing Ground." *New Republic* (March 25): 12.

**Greenwald, John.** 1986. "Deadly Meltdown." *Time* (May 12):38–52.

**Grett, Wayne.** 1978. "More Sports." *Des Moines Tribune* (April 5): 34.

**Gribben, John.** 1982. *Future Weather*

*and the Greenhouse Effect.* New York: Delacorte Press.

**Grimshaw, Allen D.** 1984. *Teaching War as a Social Problem.* Washington, DC: American Sociological Association, Teaching Resources Center.

**Guest, Avery M.** 1984. "The City." Pp. 277–322 in *Sociological Human Ecology,* edited by M. Micklin and H. M. Choldin. Boulder, CO: Westview.

**Gupte, Pranay.** 1984. *The Crowded Earth: People and the Politics of Population.* New York: Norton.

**Guterbock, Thomas M.** 1976. "The Push Hypothesis: Minority Presence, Crime and Urban Deconcentration." Pp. 137–61 in *The Changing Face of the Suburbs,* edited by Barry Schwartz. Chicago: University of Chicago Press.

**Guttentag, Marcia and Paul F. Secord.** 1983. *Too Many Women? The Sex Ratio Question.* Beverly Hills, CA: Sage.

**Guttmacher (Alan) Institute.** 1981. *Teenage Pregnancy: The Problem That Hasn't Gone Away.* New York: Alan Guttmacher Institute.

**Haas, Linda.** 1980. "Domestic Role-Sharing in Sweden." Paper presented at the annual meeting of the American Sociological Association, New York.

**Habermas, Jürgen.** 1970. *Toward a Rational Society.* Boston: Beacon.

———. 1975. *Legitimation Crisis.* Boston: Beacon.

**Hacker, Andrew.** 1980. "Creating Inequality in America." *New York Review of Books* (March 20): 20–27.

———. 1984. "Women Vs. Men in the Work Force." *New York Times Magazine* (December 9): 123ff.

———. 1988. "Getting Rough on the Poor." *New York Review* (October 13):12ff.

**Hacker, Helen.** 1951. "Women as a Minority Group." *Social Forces* 30: 60–69.

**Hadden, Jeffrey K. and Charles E. Swann.** 1981. *Prime Time Preachers: The Rising Power of Televangelism.* Reading, MA: Addison-Wesley.

**Haerle, Rudolph D., Jr.** 1975. "Education, Athletic Scholarships, and the Occupational Career of the Professional Athlete." *Sociology of*

*Work and Occupations* 2 (November): 373–403.

**Hagan, John.** 1974. "Extra-Legal Attributes and Criminal Sentencing: An Assessment of a Sociological Viewpoint." *Law and Society Review* 8:357–83.

———. 1975. "The Social and Legal Construction of Criminal Justice: A Study of the Presentencing Process." *Social Problems* 22:620–37.

**Hagan, John and Celesta Albonetti.** 1982. "Race, Class, and the Perception of Criminal Injustice in America." *American Journal of Sociology* 88:329–55.

**Hagan, John and Patricia Parker.** 1985. "White-Collar Crime and Punishment: The Class Structure and Legal Sanctioning of Securities Violations." *American Sociological Review* 50:302–16.

**Hagan, John, John Simpson, and A. R. Gillis.** 1987. "Class in the Household: A Power-Control Theory of Gender and Delinquency." *American Journal of Sociology* 92:788–816.

**Hager, Mary.** 1988. "The Threat of a Global Grain Drain." *Newsweek* (August 15): 36.

**Haggstrom, Gus W., Thomas J. Blaschke, David E. Kanouse, William Lisowski, and Peter A. Morrison.** 1981. *Teenage Parents: Their Ambitions and Attainments.* Santa Monica, CA: Rand Corporation.

**Hallie, Philip.** 1979. *Lest Innocent Blood Be Shed.* New York: Harper & Row.

**Hallinan, Maureen T.** 1987. "Ability Grouping and Student Learning." Pp. 41–69 in *The Social Organization of Schools: New Conceptualizations of the Learning Process,* edited by Maureen T. Hallinan. New York: Plenum.

**Hampton, Robert.** 1979. "Husband's Characteristics and Marital Disruption in Black Families." *Sociological Quarterly* 20:255–66.

**Hardt, R. H.** 1968. "Delinquency and Social Class: Bad Kids or Good Cops?" Pp. 132–45 in *Among the People: Encounters with the Poor,* edited by I. Deutscher and E. Thompson. New York: Basic Books.

**Hare, A. Paul.** 1976. *Handbook of Small Group Research.* Second edition. New York: Free Press.

**Hareven, Tamara K.** 1982. *Family Time and Industrial Time.* Cambridge, England: Cambridge University Press.

**Harlow, Harry F.** 1963. "The Maternal Affectional System." Pp 3–33 in *The Determinants of Infant Behavior,* edited by B. M. Foss. New York: Wiley.

**Harlow, Harry F. and M. K. Harlow.** 1965. "The Affectional Systems." Pp. 287–334 in *Behavior of Nonhuman Primates,* edited by S. Schrier, H. F. Harlow, and F. Stollnitz. Vol. II. New York: Academic Press.

**Harp, John and Philip Taietz.** 1966. "Academic Integrity and Social Structure: A Study of Cheating among College Students." *Social Problems* 13:365–73.

**Harris, Chauncey D. and Edward L. Ullman.** 1945. "The Nature of Cities." *The Annals of the American Academy of Political and Social Science* 242:7–17.

**Harris, M. W.** 1972. "The Child as Hostage." In *Children of Separation and Divorce,* edited by I. R. Stuart and L. E. Abt. New York: Grossman.

**Harris, Marvin.** 1974. *Cows, Pigs, Wars, and Witches: The Riddles of Culture.* New York: Random House.

———. 1977. *Cannibals and Kings: The Origins of Cultures.* New York: Vintage.

———. 1979. *Cultural Materialism: The Struggle for a Science of Culture.* New York: Random House.

———. 1981. *America Now: The Anthropology of a Changing Culture.* New York: Simon & Schuster.

**Harry, Joseph.** 1984. *Gay Couples.* New York: Praeger.

———. 1988. "A Probability Sample of Gay Males." Paper presented at the annual meeting of the American Sociological Association, Atlanta.

**Hartley, Wynona S.** 1968. "Self-conception and Organizational Adaptation." Paper presented at the annual meeting of the Midwest Sociological Association.

**Hartmann, Heidi.** 1987. "Comparable Worth and Women's Economic Independence." Pp. 251–58 in *Ingredients for Women's Employment Policy,* edited by Christine Bose and Glenna Spitze. Albany, NY: SUNY Press.

**Hartmann, Heidi I., Patricia A. Roos, and Donald J. Treiman.** 1985. "An Agenda for Basic Research on Comparable Worth." Pp. 3–33 in *Comparable Worth: New Directions for Research.* Washington, DC: National Academy Press.

**Hass, Aaron.** 1979. *Teenage Sexuality.* New York: Macmillan.

**Hatt, Paul K. and Cecil C. North.** 1947. "Jobs and Occupations: A Popular Evaluation." *Opinion News* 9 (September): 1–13.

**Haug, Marie and Bebe Lavin.** 1983. *Consumerism in Medicine: Challenging Physician Authority.* Beverly Hills, CA: Sage.

**Hauser, Robert M. and Donald L. Featherman.** 1976. "Equality of Schooling: Trends and Prospects." *Sociology of Education* 49:99–120.

**Hauser, Robert M. and William Sewell.** 1985. "Birth Order and Educational Attainment in Full Sibships." *American Educational Research Journal* 22:1–23.

**Hawley, Amos.** 1981. *Urban Society: An Ecological Approach.* Second edition. New York: Wiley.

**Hayghe, Howard.** 1982. "Dual-Earner Families: Their Economic and Demographic Characteristics." Pp. 27–40 in *Two Paychecks: Life in Dual-Earner Families,* edited by Joan Aldous. Beverly Hills, CA: Sage.

**Hearn, James C.** 1984. "The Relative Roles of Academic, Ascribed, and Socioeconomic Characteristics in College Destinations." *Sociology of Education* 57:22–30.

**Hechter, Michael.** 1978. "Group Formation and the Cultural Division of Labor." *American Journal of Sociology* 84:293–318.

**Heer, David M.** 1975. *Society and Populations.* Second edition. Englewood Cliffs, NJ: Prentice-Hall.

———. 1985. "Effect of Sibling Number on Child Outcomes." Pp. 27–47 in *Annual Review of Sociology,* edited by Ralph Turner and James F. Short, Jr. Palo Alto, CA: Annual Reviews.

**Heide, Wilma.** 1978. "Feminism for a Sporting Future." Pp. 195–202 in *Women and Sport: From Myth to Reality,* edited by Carole A. Oglesby. Philadelphia: Lea & Febiger.

**Heidensohn, Frances.** 1985. *Women and Crime: The Life of the Female Offender.* New York: New York University Press.

**Heirich, Max.** 1977. "Change of Heart: A Test of Some Widely Held Theories about Religious Conversions." *American Journal of Sociology* 83:653–77.

**Heise, Lori.** 1989. "Responding to AIDS." Pp. 113–31 in *State of the World 1989,* edited by Lester R. Brown et al. New York: Norton.

**Helsing, Knud J., Moyses Szklo, and George W. Comstock.** 1981. "Factors Associated with Mortality after Widowhood." *American Journal of Public Health* 71:802–08.

**Henshaw, Stanley K., Nancy J. Binkin, Ellen Blaine, and Jack C. Smith.** 1985. "A Portrait of American Women Who Obtain Abortions." *Family Planning Perspectives* 17:90–96.

**Henshaw, Stanley K., Jacqueline Darroch Forrest, and Ellen Blaine.** 1984. "Abortion Services in the United States, 1981 and 1982." *Family Planning Perspectives* 16:119–27.

**Henslin, James and Mae A. Briggs.** 1971. "Dramaturgical Desexualization: The Sociology of the Vaginal Examination." In *Studies in the Sociology of Sex,* edited by James M. Henslin. New York: Appleton-Century-Crofts.

**Herbers, John.** 1981a. "Hispanic Gains in Suburbs Found." *New York Times* (June 28): 1, 36.

———. 1981b. "Blacks Returning to Southern Cities." *New York Times* (July 5): 1, 9.

**Herman, Edward S.** 1982. *The Real Terror Network: Terrorism in Fact and Propaganda.* Boston: South End Press.

**Hershey, Robert D., Jr.** 1985. "Kansas Farm Banker's Pain." *New York Times.* (July 10): D1, D5.

———. 1988. "Fight Over a Gasoline Tax Rise." *New York Times* (December 30): D1, D3.

**Hertz, Rosanna.** 1986. *More Equal Than Others: Women and Men in Dual Career Marriages.* Berkeley: University of California Press.

**Herzog, A. Regula and Jerald G. Bachman.** 1982. "Sex Role Attitudes among High School Seniors: Views about Work and Family Roles." Ann Arbor, MI: Institute for Social Research.

**Herzog, Herta.** 1955. "Why Did People Believe in the 'Invasion from Mars'?" Pp. 420–28 in *The Language of Social Research,* edited by Paul F. Lazarsfeld and Morris Rosenberg. New York: Free Press.

**Hess, Beth and Joan Waring.** 1978. "Parent and Child in Later Life." Ch. 9 in *Child Influences on Marital and Family Interaction: A Life-Span Perspective,* edited by Richard M. Lerner and Graham B. Spanier. New York: Academic Press.

**Hess, Robert D. and Judith V. Torney.** 1967. *The Development of Political Attitudes in Children.* Chicago: Aldine.

**Hewlett, Sylvia.** 1986. *A Lesser Life: The Myth of Women's Liberation in America.* New York: Morrow.

**Heyns, Barbara.** 1978. *Summer Learning and the Effects of Schooling.* New York: Academic Press.

**Hill, Martha.** 1988. "Marital Stability and Spouses' Shared Time: A Multidisciplinary Hypothesis." *Journal of Family Issues* 9:427–51.

**Hill, Robert.** 1971. *The Strengths of Black Families.* New York: Emerson Hall.

**Hindelang, Michael J.** 1976. *An Analysis of Victimization Survey Results from the Eight Impact Cities.* U.S. Department of Justice, Law Enforcement Assistance Administration. Washington, DC: U.S. Government Printing Office.

**Hindelang, Michael J., Michael R. Gottfredson, and Timothy J. Flanagan (eds.).** 1981. *Sourcebook of Criminal Justice Statistics—1980.* U.S. Department of Justice, Bureau of Justice Statistics. Washington, DC: U.S. Government Printing Office.

**Hindelang, Michael J., Travis Hirschi, and Joseph C. Weis.** 1979. "Correlates of Delinquency: The Illusion of Discrepancy between Self-report and Official Measures." *American Sociological Review* 44:995–1014.

**Hirsch, Paul M.** 1986. "From Ambushes to Golden Parachutes: Corporate Takeovers as an Instance of Cultural Framing and Institutional Integration." *American Journal of Sociology* 91:800–37.

**Hirschi, Travis.** 1969. *Causes of Delinquency.* Berkeley: University of California Press.

**Hirschi, Travis and Michael Gottfredson.** 1983. "Age and the Explanation of Crime." *American Journal of Sociology* 89:552–84.

———. 1985. "Age and Crime, Logic and Scholarship: Comment on Greenberg." *American Journal of Sociology* 91:22–27.

**Hirschi, Travis and Rodney Stark.** 1969. "Hellfire and Delinquency." *Social Problems* 17:202–13.

**Hirschman, Charles and Morrison G. Wong.** 1984. "Socioeconomic Gains of Asian Americans, Blacks, and Hispanics: 1960–1976." *American Journal of Sociology* 90:584–607.

**Hoch, Paul.** 1972. *Rip Off the Big Game.* Garden City, NY: Doubleday.

**Hochschild, Arlie Russell.** 1973a. "A Review of Sex Role Research." *American Journal of Sociology* 78:249–67.

———. 1973b. *The Unexpected Community.* Englewood Cliffs, NJ: Prentice-Hall.

———. 1975. "The Sociology of Feeling and Emotion." Pp. 280–307 in *Another Voice,* edited by Marcia Millman and Rosabeth Moss Kanter. Garden City, NY: Doubleday/Anchor.

———. 1979. "Emotion Work, Feeling Rules, and Social Structure." *American Journal of Sociology* 85:551–75.

———. 1981. "Power, Status, and Emotion: A Review of a Social Interactional Theory of Emotions, by Theodore D. Kemper." *Contemporary Sociology* 10:73–77.

———. 1983. *The Managed Heart: Commercialization of Human Feeling.* Berkeley: University of California Press.

———. 1985. "Housework and Gender Strategies for Getting Out of It." Paper presented at the annual meeting of the American Sociological Association, Washington, DC.

**Hodge, Robert W., Paul M. Siegel, and Peter H. Rossi.** 1966. "Occupational Prestige in the United States: 1925–1963." Pp. 322–34 in *Class, Status, and Power,* edited by Reinhard Bendix and Seymour Martin Lipset. Second edition. New York: Free Press.

Hodge, Robert W. and Donald J. Treiman. 1968. "Class Identification in the United States." *American Journal of Sociology* 73:535–47.

Hodge, Robert W., Donald J. Treiman, and Peter H. Rossi. 1966. "A Comparative Study of Occupational Prestige." Pp. 309–21 in *Class, Status, and Power,* edited by Reinhard Bendix and Seymour Martin Lipset. Second edition. New York: Free Press.

Hodges, David A. 1979. "The Microelectronics Revolution." Testimony before the University of California Board of Regents.

Hodson, Randy and Robert L. Kaufman. 1982. "Economic Dualism: A Critical Review." *American Sociological Review* 47:727–39.

Hoffman, Lois W. 1963. "The Decision to Work." In *The Employed Mother in America,* edited by F. I. Nye and L. W. Hoffman. Chicago: Rand McNally.

———. 1977. "Fear of Success in 1965 and 1974: A Follow-up Study." *Journal of Consulting and Clinical Psychology* 45:310–21.

Hoffman, Lois W. and F. I. Nye (eds.) 1974. *Working Mothers.* San Francisco: Jossey-Bass.

Hoffman, Martin. 1979. "The Male Prostitute." Pp. 275–84 in *Gay Men,* edited by Martin P. Levine. New York: Harper & Row.

Hohenstein, William F. 1969. "Factors Influencing the Police Disposition of Juvenile Offenders." Pp. 138–49 in *Delinquency: Selected Studies,* edited by Thorsten Sellin and Marvin E. Wolfgang. New York: Wiley.

Homans, George C. 1950. *The Human Group.* New York: Harcourt Brace Jovanovich.

Hood, Jane C. 1983. *Becoming a Two-Job Family.* New York: Praeger.

Hope, Keith. 1982. "A Liberal Theory of Prestige." *American Journal of Sociology* 87:1011–31.

Horner, Matina. 1969. "Fail: Bright Women." *Psychology Today* 3:36ff.

Horowitz, Irving Louis. 1962. "Consensus, Conflict, and Cooperation." *Social Forces* 41:177–88.

———. 1966. *Three Worlds of Development.* New York: Oxford University Press.

Houseman, John. 1948. "The Men from Mars." *Harper's Magazine* 197 (December): 78–82.

Hoyt, Homer. 1939. *The Structure and Growth of Residential Neighborhoods in American Cities.* Washington, DC: Federal Housing Authority.

Huber, Bettina J. 1985. "Weitzman's Research Plays Key Role in New Legislation." *Footnotes* 13 (November): 1, 9.

Huber, Joan and William H. Form. 1973. *Income and Ideology: An Analysis of the American Political Formula.* New York: Free Press.

Huber, Joan and Glenna Spitze. 1980. "Considering Divorce: An Expansion of Becker's Theory of Marital Instability." *American Journal of Sociology* 86:75–89.

———. 1988. "Trends in Family Sociology." Pp. 425–48 in *Handbook of Sociology,* edited by Neil J. Smelser. Beverly Hills, CA: Sage.

Hubert, M. 1976. "Scientist is Hopeful on World Resources." *New York Times* (December 2): A27.

Hughes, Everett C. 1945. "Dilemmas and Contradictions of Status." *American Journal of Sociology* 50 (March): 353–59.

Humphreys, Laud. 1970. *Tearoom Trade: Impersonal Sex in Public Places.* Chicago: Aldine.

———. 1972. *Out of the Closets: The Sociology of Homosexual Liberation.* Englewood Cliffs, NJ: Prentice-Hall.

Hunt, Chester L. and Lewis Walker. 1974. *Ethnic Diversity.* Homewood, IL: Dorsey Press.

Hunt, Morton M. 1974. *Sexual Behavior in the 1970s.* Chicago: Playboy Press.

Hunter, James Davison. 1983. *American Evangelicalism: Conservative Religion and the Quandary of Modernity.* Chicago: University of Chicago Press.

———. 1986. *Evangelicalism: The Coming Generation of America.* Chicago: University of Chicago Press.

Hurn, Christopher J. 1978. *The Limits and Possibilities of Schooling.* Boston: Allyn & Bacon.

Hyman, Herbert H. and Charles R. Wright. 1979. *Education's Lasting Influence on Values.* Chicago: University of Chicago Press.

Hyman, Herbert H., Charles R. Wright, and John Shelton Reed. 1975. *The Enduring Effects of Education.* Chicago: University of Chicago Press.

Hymowitz, Carol and Thomas F. O'Boyle. 1984. "Pittsburgh's Evolution from Steel to Services Sparks a Culture Clash: Hungry Jobless Grow Bitter as Young Professionals Pursue Lives of Fashion." *Wall Street Journal* (August 21): 1, 12.

Illinois Institute for Juvenile Research. 1972. *Juvenile Delinquency in Illinois.* Chicago: Illinois Department of Mental Health.

Ingrassia, Lawrence. 1980. "Taking Chances: How Four Companies Spawn New Projects by Encouraging Risks." *Wall Street Journal* (September 18): 1, 19.

Inkeles, Alex and Peter H. Rossi. 1956. "National Comparisons of Occupational Prestige." *American Journal of Sociology* 61:329–39.

Inkeles, Alex and David H. Smith. 1974. *Becoming Modern.* Cambridge, MA: Harvard University Press.

Innis, Harold A. 1951. *The Bias of Communication.* Toronto: University of Toronto Press.

Iyer, Pico. 1985. "The Second Revolution." *Time* (September 23): 42–46ff.

Izraeli, Dafna. 1983. "Sex Effects or Structural Effects? An Empirical Test of Kanter's Theory of Proportions." *Social Forces* 62:153–65.

Jackman, Mary R. and Robert W. Jackman. 1982. *Class Awareness in the United States.* Berkeley, CA: University of California Press.

Jackman, Mary R. and Michael J. Muha. 1984. "Education and Intergroup Attitudes: Moral Enlightenment, Superficial Democratic Commitment, or Ideological Refinement?" *American Sociological Review* 49:751–69.

Jackson, Philip W. 1968. *Life in Classrooms.* New York: Holt, Rinehart and Winston.

Jackson, Robert Max. 1989. "The Reproduction of Parenting." *American Sociological Review* 54:215–32.

———. 1990. *The Subordination of Women.* New York: Cambridge University Press.

Jacobs, Carol and Cynthia Eaton.

1972. "Sexism in the Elementary School." *Today's Education* 61:20–22.

**Jacobson, Jodi.** 1988. "Planning the Global Family." Pp. 151–69 in *State of the World*, edited by Lester R. Brown et al. New York: Norton.

**Jaffe, A. J. and W. Adams.** 1970. "Academic and Social Factors Related to Entrance and Retention at Two- and Four-Year Colleges in the Late 1960s." New York: Bureau of Applied Social Research, Columbia University.

**Jahoda, Marie, Paul Lazarsfeld, and Hans Zeisel.** 1971. *Marienthal: The Sociology of an Unemployed Community.* Chicago: Aldine/Atherton.

**Jedlicka, Davor and Ira E. Robinson.** 1987. "Fear of Venereal Disease and Other Constraints on Occurrence of Premarital Coitus." *Journal of Sex Research* 23:390–400.

**Jencks, Christopher.** 1985. "How Poor Are the Poor?" *New York Review of Books* (May 9): 41–49.

———. 1987. "Genes and Crime." *New York Review* (February 12): 33–41.

**Jencks, Christopher, Susan Bartlett, Mary Corcoran, James Crouse, David Eaglesfield, Gregory Jackson, Kent McClelland, Peter Mueser, Michael Olneck, Joseph Schwartz, Sherry Ward, and Jill Williams.** 1979. *Who Gets Ahead? The Determinants of Economic Success in America.* New York: Basic Books.

**Jencks, Christopher, J. Crouse, and P. Mueser.** 1983. "The Wisconsin Model of Status Attainment: A National Replication with Improved Measures of Ability and Aspirations." *Sociology of Education* 56:3–19.

**Jencks, Christopher, Lauri Perman, and Lee Rainwater.** 1988. "What Is a Good Job? A New Measure of Labor-Market Success." *American Journal of Sociology* 93:1322–57.

**Jencks, Christopher, Marshall Smith, Henry Acland, Mary Jo Bane, David Cohen, Herbert Gintis, Barbara Heyns, and Stephan Michelson.** 1972. *Inequality: A Reassessment of the Effect of Family and Schooling in America.* New York: Basic Books.

**Jennings, M. Kent.** 1981. *Generations and Politics: A Panel Study of Young Adults and Their Parents.* Princeton, NJ: Princeton University Press.

**Jennings, M. Kent and Richard G. Niemi.** 1968. "Patterns of Political Learning." *Harvard Educational Review* 38 (summer): 443–67.

**Jensen, Arthur R.** 1969. "How Much Can We Boost I.Q. and Scholastic Achievement?" *Harvard Educational Review* 39:1–123.

**Jensen, Gary and Raymond Eve.** 1976. "Sex Differences in Delinquency." *Criminology* 13 (February): 427–48.

**Joffe, Carole.** 1979. "Symbolic Interactionism and the Study of Social Services." Pp. 235–56 in *Studies in Symbolic Interaction.* Vol. 2, edited by Norman K. Denzin. Greenwich, CT: JAI Press.

**Johnson, A. G. and W. F. Whyte.** 1977. "The Mondragon System of Worker Production Cooperatives." *Industrial and Labor Relations Review* 31:18–30.

**Johnson, Benton.** 1963. "On Church and Sect." *American Sociological Review* 28:539–49.

**Johnson, Norris R.** 1987. "Panic at 'The Who Concert Stampede': An Empirical Assessment." *Social Problems* 34:362–73.

**Johnson, Sheila K.** 1971. "Sociology of Christmas Cards." *Society* 8:27–29.

**Jones, Elise F. et al.** 1985. "Teenage Pregnancy in Developed Countries: Determinants and Policy Implications." *Family Planning Perspectives* 17:53–63.

**Jones, James D., Beth E. Vanfossen, and Joan Z. Spade.** 1985. "Curriculum Placement: Individual and School Effects Using the High School and Beyond Data." Paper presented at the annual meeting of the American Sociological Association, Washington.

**Jones, Landon Y.** 1980. *Great Expectations: America and the Baby Boom Generation.* East Rutherford, NJ: Coward, McCann & Geoghegan.

**Joyce, James Avery.** 1961. *Capital Punishment: A World View.* New York: Grove Press.

**Jump, Teresa L. and Linda Haas.** 1987. "Fathers in Transition: Dual-Career Fathers Participating in Child Care." Pp. 98–114 in *Changing Men: New Directions in Research on Men and Masculinity*, edited by Michael S. Kimmel. Beverly Hills, CA: Sage.

**Kadushin, Charles.** 1977. Remarks made at the annual meeting of the American Association for the Advancement of Science.

**Kalleberg, Arne L. and Larry J. Griffin.** 1980. "Class, Occupation, and Inequality in Job Rewards." *American Journal of Sociology* 85:731–68.

**Kalleberg, Arne L. and James R. Lincoln.** 1988. "The Structure of Earnings Inequality in the United States and Japan." *American Journal of Sociology* 94:S121–53.

**Kalven, Harry and Hans Zeisel.** 1966. *The American Jury.* Boston: Little, Brown.

**Kamerman, Sheila B.** 1979. "Parenting in an Unresponsive Society." Notes: Program in Sex Roles and Social Change, Center for the Social Sciences, Columbia University (spring): 1–2.

**Kamerman, Sheila B. and Alfred J. Kahn (eds.).** 1978. *Family Policy: Government and Families in Fourteen Countries.* New York: Columbia University Press.

**Kamin, Leon J.** 1974. *The Science and Politics of I.Q.* Hillsdale, NJ: Erlbaum.

**Kandel, D. B. and G. S. Lesser.** 1972. *Youth in Two Worlds.* San Francisco: Jossey-Bass.

**Kanter, Rosabeth Moss.** 1972. *Commitment and Community: Communes and Utopias in Sociological Perspective.* Cambridge, MA: Harvard University Press.

———. 1976. "The Impact of Hierarchical Structure on the Work Behavior of Women and Men." *Social Problems* 23:415–30.

———. 1977a. *Men and Women of the Corporation.* New York: Basic Books.

———. 1977b. *Work and Family in the United States: A Critical Review and Agenda for Research and Policy.* New York: Russell Sage Foundation.

———. 1979. "Complex Organizations." Paper presented at the annual meeting of the American Sociological Association, Boston.

**Karier, Clarence J.** 1973. "Testing

for Order and Control in the Corporate Liberal State." Pp. 108–37 in *Roots of Crisis: American Education in the Twentieth Century,* edited by Clarence J. Karier, Paul Violas, and Joel Spring. Chicago: Rand McNally.

**Karp, D. A., G. P. Stone, and W. C. Yoels.** 1977. *Being Urban.* Lexington, MA: Heath.

**Kasarda, John.** 1980. "The Implications of Contemporary Redistribution Trends for National Urban Policy." *Social Science Quarterly* 61:373–400.

———. 1984. "Hispanics and City Change." *American Demographics* 6:25–29.

———. 1985. "Urban Change and Minority Opportunities." Pp. 33–67 in *The New Urban Reality,* edited by Paul E. Peterson. Washington, DC: Brookings Institute.

**Kasinitz, Philip.** 1983. "Neo-Marxist Views of the State." *Dissent* 30:337–46.

**Katchadourian, Herant A. and John Boli.** 1986. *Careerism and Intellectualism among College Students.* San Francisco: Jossey-Bass.

**Katchadourian, Herant A. and Donald T. Lunde.** 1972. *Fundamentals of Human Sexuality.* New York: Holt, Rinehart and Winston.

**Katz, Marlaine L.** 1972. "Female Motive to Avoid Success: A Psychological Barrier or a Response to Deviance?" Unpublished manuscript, School of Education, Stanford University.

**Katz, Michael B.** 1977. "Education and Inequality: An Historical Perspective." Paper presented for Russell Sage Foundation project on history and social policy, New York.

**Kedourie, Elie.** 1980. "Islam Resurgent." Pp. 58–63 in *Britannica Book of the Year.* Chicago: Encyclopaedia Britannica.

**Kelly, Dean M.** 1972. *Why Conservative Churches Are Growing.* New York: Harper & Row.

**Kelly, James.** 1982. "Unemployment on the Rise." *Time* (February 8): 22–29.

**Kelly, Joan Berlin.** 1986. "Divorce: The Adult Perspective." Pp. 304–08 in *Family in Transition,* edited by Arlene Skolnick and Jerome Skolnick. Boston: Little, Brown.

**Kemper, Theodore D.** 1978. *A Social Interactional Theory of Emotions.* New York: Wiley.

———. 1981a. "Power, Status, and Emotions: Kemper's Reply." *Contemporary Sociology* 10:719–21.

———. 1981b. "Social Constructionist and Positivist Approaches to the Sociology of Emotions." *American Journal of Sociology* 87:336–62.

———. 1983. "Predicting the Divorce Rate: Down?" *Journal of Family Issues* 4:507–24.

**Keniston, Kenneth and Carnegie Council on Children.** 1977. *All Our Children.* New York: Harcourt Brace Jovanovich.

**Kennedy, Paul.** 1987. *The Rise and Fall of the Great Powers.* New York: Random House.

**Kennedy, Robert E.** 1989. *Life Choices: Applying Sociology.* Second Edition. New York: Holt, Rinehart and Winston.

**Kenney, Martin.** 1986. *Biotechnology: The University-Industrial Complex.* New Haven, CT: Yale University Press.

**Kephart, William M.** 1950. "A Quantitative Analysis of Intragroup Relationships." *American Journal of Sociology* 60:544–49.

———. 1957. *Racial Factors and Urban Law Enforcement.* Philadelphia: University of Pennsylvania Press.

**Kephart, William M. and Davor Jedlicka.** 1988. *The Family, Society, and the Individual.* Sixth Edition. New York: Harper & Row.

**Kerbo, Harold R.** 1983. *Social Stratification and Inequality: Class Conflict in the United States.* New York: McGraw-Hill.

**Kerckhoff, Alan C., Richard T. Campbell, and Idee Winfield-Laird.** 1985. "Social Mobility in Great Britain and the United States." *American Journal of Sociology* 91:281–308.

**Kerr, Norman D.** 1964. "The School Board as an Agency of Legitimation." *Sociology of Education* 38:34–59.

**Kerr, Richard A.** 1988. "Report Urges Greenhouse Action Now." *Science* 241 (July 1): 23–24.

**Kesselman, Mark.** 1982. "Prospects for Democratic Socialism in Advanced Capitalism: Class Struggle and Compromise in Sweden and France." *Politics & Society* 11:397–438.

**Kessler, Ronald C. and James A. McRae, Jr.** 1982. "The Effect of Wives' Employment on the Mental Health of Married Men and Women." *American Sociological Review* 47:216–27.

**Kessler, S., D. J. Ashenden, R. W. Connell, and G. W. Dowsett.** 1985. "Gender Relations in Secondary Schooling." *Sociology of Education* 58:34–48.

**Keynes, John Maynard.** 1936/1973. *The General Theory of Employment, Interest and Money.* New York: Cambridge University Press.

**Kidder, Tracy.** 1981. *The Soul of a New Machine.* Boston: Atlantic/Little, Brown.

**Killian, Lewis M.** 1984. "Organization, Rationality and Spontaneity in the Civil Rights Movement." *American Sociological Review* 49:770–83.

**Kimmel, Michael (ed.).** 1987. *Changing Men: New Directions in Research on Men and Masculinity.* Beverly Hills, CA: Sage.

**King, K., J. McIntyre, and L. J. Axelson.** 1968. "Adolescent Views of Maternal Employment as a Threat to the Marital Relationship." *Journal of Marriage and the Family* 30:633–37.

**Kingston, Paul William and Steven L. Nock.** 1987. "Time Together among Dual-Earner Couples." *American Sociological Review* 52:391–400.

**Kinsey, Alfred C., Wardell B. Pomeroy, and Clyde E. Martin.** 1948. *Sexual Behavior in the Human Male.* Philadelphia: Saunders.

**Kinsey, Alfred C., Wardell B. Pomeroy, Clyde E. Martin, and Paul H. Gebhard.** 1953. *Sexual Behavior in the Human Female.* Philadelphia: Saunders.

**Kirkham, George Lester.** 1971. "Homosexuality in Prison." Pp. 325–49 in *Studies in the Sociology of Sex,* edited by James M. Henslin. New York: Appleton-Century-Crofts.

**Kisker, E. E.** 1985. "Teenagers Talk about Sex, Pregnancy and Contraception." *Family Planning Perspectives* 17:83.

**Kitagawa, Evelyn M.** 1972. "Socioeconomic Differences in Mortality in the United States and Some Implications for Population Policy." In *Demographic and Social*

*Aspects of Population Growth and the American Future.* Vol 1, edited by Charles F. Westoff and Robert Parke Jr. Washington, DC: Commission on Population Growth and the American Future.

**Kitano, Harry H. L.** 1981. "Asian-Americans: The Chinese, Japanese, Koreans, Filipinos, and Southeast Asians." *The Annals of the American Academy of Political and Social Science* 454 (March): 125–38.

**Kitson, Gaye, Karen Benson-Babri, and Mary Joan Roach.** 1985. "Who Divorces and Why: A Review." *Journal of Family Issues* 6:255–94.

**Klausner, Samuel Z. and Edward F. Foulks.** 1982. *Eskimo Capitalists: Oil, Alcohol and Politics.* Totowa, NJ: Allanheld, Osmun.

**Kleck, Gary.** 1981. "Racial Discrimination in Criminal Sentencing: A Critical Evaluation of the Evidence with Additional Evidence on the Death Penalty." *American Sociological Review* 46 (December): 783–805.

**Klein, Heywood.** 1981. "Goal Posts Tumble Like Tackled Backs at College Stadiums." *Wall Street Journal* (November 3): 1, 23.

**Klein, Susan S. (ed.).** 1985. *Handbook for Achieving Sex Equity through Education.* Baltimore, MD: Johns Hopkins University Press.

**Kleinman, Carol.** 1981. *Women's Networks: The Complete Guide to Getting a Better Job, Advancing Your Career and Feeling Great as a Woman through Networking.* New York: Ballantine.

**Kluckhohn, Clyde.** 1954. *Mirror for Man.* New York: McGraw-Hill.

**Kluegel, James R. and Eliot R. Smith.** 1982. "Whites' Beliefs about Blacks' Opportunities." *American Sociological Review* 47:518–32.

**Knoke, David.** 1988. "Incentives in Collective Action Organizations." *American Sociological Review* 53:311–29.

**Knorr-Cetina, Karin.** 1981. *The Manufacture of Knowledge: An Essay on the Constructivist and Contextual Nature of Science.* New York: Pergamon.

———. 1983. "New Developments in Science Studies: The Ethnographic Challenge." *Canadian Journal of Sociology* 8:153–77.

**Knorr-Cetina, Karin and Michael J. Mulkay.** 1983. "Emerging Principles in Social Studies of Science." Pp. 1–17 in *Science Observed,* edited by K. Knorr-Cetina and M. Mulkay. Beverly Hills, CA: Sage.

**Koenig, Thomas, Robert Gogel, and John Sonquist.** 1979. "Models of the Significance of Interlocking Corporate Directorates." *American Journal of Economics and Sociology* 38:173–86.

**Koepp, Stephen.** 1987. "For Sale: America." *Time* (September 14): 52ff.

**Kohn, Melvin L.** 1969. *Class and Conformity.* Homewood, IL: Dorsey Press.

———. 1976. "Social Class and Parental Values: Another Confirmation of the Relationship." *American Sociological Review* 41:538–45.

**Kohn, Melvin L. and Carmi Schooler.** 1973. "Occupational Experience and Psychological Functioning: An Assessment of Reciprocal Effects." *American Sociological Review* 38:97–118.

———. 1978. "The Reciprocal Effects of the Substantive Complexity of Work and Intellectual Flexibility: A Longitudinal Assessment." *American Journal of Sociology* 84:24–52.

———. 1983. *Work and Personality.* Norwood, NJ: Ablex.

**Kollock, Peter, Philip Blumstein, and Pepper Schwartz.** 1985. "Sex and Power in Interaction: Conversational Privileges and Duties." *American Sociological Review* 50:34–46.

**Komarovsky, Mirra.** 1940/1971. *The Unemployed Man and His Family.* New York: Octagon Books.

———. 1962. *Blue-Collar Marriage.* New York: Vintage.

———. 1982. "Female Freshmen View Their Future: Career Salience and Its Correlates." *Sex Roles* 8:299–314.

———. 1985. *Women in College: Shaping New Feminine Identities.* New York: Basic Books.

———. 1988. "The New Feminist Scholarship: Some Precursors and Polemics." *Journal of Marriage and the Family* 50:585–93.

**Kornhauser, William.** 1959. *The Politics of Mass Society.* New York: Free Press.

**Korte, Charles and Stanley Milgram.** 1970. "Acquaintance Links between White and Negro Populations: Applications of the Small World Method." *Journal of Personality and Social Psychology* 15:101–108.

**Kowalewski, David.** 1980. "Trends in the Human Rights Movement." Pp. 150–81 in *Soviet Politics in the Brezhnev Era,* edited by Donald R. Kelly. New York: Praeger.

**Kozol, Jonathan.** 1985. *Illiterate America.* New York: Doubleday.

**Kraft, Philip.** 1977. *Programmers and Managers: The Routinization of Computer Programmers in the U.S.* New York: Springer-Verlag.

———. 1985. *A Review of Empirical Studies of the Consequences of Technological Change on Work and Workers in the United States.* Washington, DC: National Academy Press.

**Kramer, Bernard M., S. Michael Kahck, and Michael A. Milburn.** 1983. "Attitudes toward Nuclear Weapons and Nuclear War: 1945–1982." *Journal of Social Issues* 39:7–24.

**Kramer, Cheris.** 1975. "Women's Speech: Separate but Unequal?" Pp. 43–56 in *Language and Sex: Difference and Dominance,* edited by Barrie Thorne and Nancy Henley. Rowley, MA: Newbury House.

**Kraus, Henry.** 1947. *The Many and the Few.* Los Angeles: Plantin Press.

**Krosnick, Jon A. and Charles M. Judd.** 1982. "Transitions in Social Influence at Adolescence: Who Induces Cigarette Smoking?" *Developmental Psychology* 18:359–68.

**Kübler-Ross, Elisabeth.** 1969. *On Death and Dying.* New York: Macmillan.

**Kuhn, Manford H. and Thomas S. McPartland.** 1954. "An Empirical Investigation of Self-attitudes." *American Sociological Review* 19 (February): 68–76.

**Kuhn, Thomas S.** 1970. *The Structure of Scientific Revolutions.* Second edition, enlarged. Chicago: University of Chicago Press.

**Kurtz, Lester R.** 1988. *The Nuclear Cage: A Sociology of the Arms Race.* Englewood Cliffs, NJ: Prentice-Hall.

**Kuttner, Robert.** 1985. "Haves and Have-nots: Some Reflections." Washington, DC: Trend Analysis

Program, American Council of Life Insurance.

**Labov, William.** 1973. "The Logic of Nonstandard English." Pp. 21–66 in *The Myth of Cultural Deprivation,* edited by N. Keddie. Harmondsworth, England: Penguin.

**Ladd, Everett, Jr.** 1978. "The New Lines Are Drawn: Class and Ideology in America." *Public Opinion* (July–August): 48–53.

**Lake, Robert W.** 1981. *The New Suburbanites: Race and Housing in the Suburbs.* New Brunswick, NJ: Center for Urban Policy Research, Rutgers University.

**Lamb, Michael E.** 1977. "Father-Infant and Mother-Infant Interaction in the First Year of Life." *Child Development* 48:167–81.

**Landry, Bart.** 1987. *The New Black Middle Class.* Berkeley: University of California Press.

**Lane, R. E.** 1962. *Political Ideology: Why the American Common Man Believes as He Does.* New York: Free Press.

**Langley, Monica.** 1981. "Perks at Parks Help Perk Up Vacations of Federal VIPs." *Wall Street Journal* (June 14): 1, 16.

**Langone, John.** 1989. "Waste: A Stinking Mess." *Time* (January 2): 44–47.

**Lansing, Marjorie and Sandra Baxter.** 1980. *Women and Politics: The Invisible Majority.* Ann Arbor: University of Michigan Press.

**Lapidus, Gail Warshofsky.** 1978. *Women in Soviet Society.* Berkeley: University of California Press.

**Lasch, Christopher.** 1979. *Haven in a Heartless World: The Family Besieged.* New York: Basic Books.

**Laska, Shirley Bradway and Daphne Spain (eds.).** 1980. *Back to the City: Issues in Neighborhood Renovation.* New York: Pergamon.

**Laslett, Peter (ed.).** 1974. *Household and Family in Past Time.* Cambridge, MA: Harvard University Press.

**Latané, Bibb and John M. Darley.** 1970. *The Unresponsive Bystander: Why Doesn't He Help?* Englewood Cliffs, NJ: Prentice-Hall.

**Lathrop, Richard.** 1977. *Who's Hiring Who.* Berkeley, CA: Ten Speed Press.

**Latour, Bruno and Steve Woolgar.** 1986. *Laboratory Life.* Second edition. Princeton, NJ: Princeton University Press.

**Lauer, Jeanette and Robert Lauer.** 1985. "Marriages Made to Last." *Psychology Today:* 23–26.

**Lauer, Robert H.** 1975. "Occupational and Religious Mobility in a Small City." *Sociological Quarterly* 16:380–92.

———. 1976. "Afterward: Summary and Directions for the Future." Pp. 259–64 in *Social Movements and Social Change,* edited by Robert H. Lauer. Carbondale: Southern Illinois University Press.

**Laumann, Edward O., David Knoke, and Yong-Hak Kim.** 1985. "An Organizational Approach to State Policy Formation: A Comparative Study of Energy and Health Domains." *American Sociological Review* 50:1–19.

**Lawrence, Paul and Jay Lorsch.** 1967. *Organization and Environment.* Cambridge, MA: Harvard University Press.

**Lazarsfeld, Paul, Bernard Berelson, and Hazel Gaudet.** 1944. *The People's Choice.* New York: Columbia University Press.

**Leavitt, H. J.** 1964. *Managerial Psychology.* Chicago: University of Chicago Press.

**Lee, Carmen J.** 1984. "Rise in Networking among Blacks Is Yielding Sizable Career Benefits." *Wall Street Journal* (October 12): 33.

**Lee, Richard.** 1969. "Kung Bushman Subsistence: An Input-Output Analysis." In *Environment and Cultural Behavior,* edited by A. Vayda. Garden City, NY: Natural History Press.

**Lee, Richard and I. DeVore.** 1968. *Man the Hunter.* Chicago: Aldine.

**Lee, Valerie E. and Anthony S. Bryk.** 1988. "Curriculum Tracking as Mediating the Social Distribution of High School Achievement." *Sociology of Education* 61:78–94.

**Lee, Valerie E. and Norma C. Ware.** 1985. "Factors Predicting College Science Major Choice for Men and Women Students." Paper presented at the annual meeting of the American Educational Research Association, Chicago.

**Lehman, Edward W.** 1977. *Political Society: A Macrosociology of Politics.* New York: Columbia University Press.

**Leishman, Katie.** 1985. "A Crisis in Public Health." *The Atlantic Monthly* (October): 18–41.

**Lelyveld, Joseph.** 1985. *Move Your Shadow.* New York: Penguin.

**Lemonick, Michael D.** 1989. "Global Warming: Feeling the Heat." *Time* (January 2): 36–39.

**Lengermann, Patricia Madoo and Ruth A. Wallace.** 1985. *Gender in America: Social Control and Social Change.* Englewood Cliffs, NJ: Prentice-Hall.

**Lenski, Gerhard E.** 1966. *Power and Privilege: A Theory of Social Stratification.* New York: McGraw-Hill.

———. 1979. "Marxist Experiments in Destratification: An Appraisal." *Social Forces* 57:364–83.

**Lenski, Gerhard E. and Jean Lenski.** 1978. *Human Societies: An Introduction to Macrosociology.* Third edition. New York: McGraw-Hill.

———. 1987. *Human Societies.* New York: McGraw-Hill.

**Leo, John.** 1984. "The Revolution Is Over." *Time* (April 9): 74–83.

**Leonard, Eileen B.** 1982. *Women, Crime and Society.* London: Longman.

**Lerner, Daniel.** 1968. "Modernization: Social Aspects." In *International Encyclopedia of the Social Sciences.* Vol. 10, edited by D. L. Sills. New York: Free Press.

**Lever, Janet.** 1976. "Sex Differences in the Games Children Play." *Social Problems* 23:478–87.

———. 1978. "Sex Differences in the Complexity of Children's Play and Games." *American Sociological Review* 43:471–83.

**Levin, Henry M.** 1985. "The Educationally Disadvantaged: A National Crisis." The State Youth Initiatives Project, Working Paper No. 6, Philadelphia, PA: Public/Private Ventures.

**Levine, Joel H.** 1972. "The Sphere of Influence." *American Sociological Review* 37 (February): 14–27.

**Levine, Martin P. (ed.).** 1979. *Gay Men.* New York: Harper & Row.

**Levinger, George.** 1965. "Marital Cohesiveness and Dissolution: An Integrative Review." *Journal of Marriage and the Family* 27:19–28.

**Lévi-Strauss, Claude.** 1956. "The Family." Pp. 142–70 in *Man, Culture, and Society,* edited by Harry L. Shapiro. New York: Oxford University Press.

**Levitan, Sar A. and Richard S. Belous.** 1981. *What's Happening to the American Family?* Baltimore, MD: Johns Hopkins University Press.

**Levitan, Saul A. and C. M. Johnson.** 1984. *Beyond the Safety Net: Reviving the Promising of Opportunity in America.* Cambridge, MA: Ballinger.

**Levy, Frank.** 1988. "Income Distribution: A Growing Gap between Rich and Poor." *New York Times* (May 1): 3.

**Levy, Frank and Richard C. Michel.** 1985. "Are Baby Boomers Selfish?" *American Demographics* 7:38–41.

**Levy, Robert I.** 1973. *Tahitians.* Chicago: University of Chicago Press.

**Lewis, Anne C.** 1984. "Me President, You Jane: The Administration's Sex Equity Policy." *Phi Delta Kappan* (January): 307–08.

**Lewis, Gordon H.** 1972. "Role Differentiation." *American Sociological Review* 37:424–34.

**Lewis, Jerry M.** 1975. "Sports Riots: Some Research Questions." Paper presented at the annual meeting of the American Sociological Association, San Francisco.

**Lewis, Oscar.** 1965. *La Vida.* New York: Random House.

**Lichter, Daniel T.** 1988. "Racial Differences in Underemployment in American Cities." *American Journal of Sociology* 93:771–92.

**Lieberson, Jonathan.** 1986. "The Reality of AIDS." *New York Review of Books* XXXII (January 16): 43–48.

**Lieberson, Stanley.** 1961. "A Societal Theory of Race and Ethnic Relations." *American Sociological Review* 26:902–10.

**Lin, Nan, Walter M. Ensel, and John C. Vaughn.** 1981. "Social Resources and Strength of Ties: Structural Factors in Occupational Status Attainment." *American Sociological Review* 46 (August): 393–405.

**Lincoln, James R. and Arne L. Kalleberg.** 1985. "Work Organization and Workforce Commitment: A Study of Plants and Employees in the U.S. and Japan." *American Sociological Review* 50:738–60.

**Lindblom, Charles E.** 1977. *Politics and Markets: The World's Political-Economic Systems.* New York: Basic Books.

**Lindner, Robert.** 1951. "Sex in Prison." *Complex* 6:5–20.

**Lindsey, Robert.** 1984. "Increased Demand for Day Care Prompts a Debate on Regulation." *New York Times* (September 2): 1, 52.

**Lipset, Seymour Martin and Reinhard Bendix.** 1959. *Social Mobility in Industrial Society.* Berkeley: University of California Press.

**Lipton, Douglass, Robert Martinson, and Judith Wilks.** 1975. *The Effectiveness of Correctional Treatment: A Survey of Treatment Evaluation Studies.* New York: Praeger.

**Liska, A. E. and M. Tausig.** 1979. "Theoretical Interpretations of Social Class and Racial Differentials in Legal Decision-Making for Juveniles." *The Sociological Quarterly* 20:197–207.

**Little, Marilyn.** 1982. *Family Breakup.* San Francisco: Jossey-Bass.

**Liu, Korbin and Kenneth G. Manton**. 1987. *Long-term Care: Current Estimates and Projections.* DHH Pub. PHS 88-1214. Washington, DC: U.S. Department of Health and Human Services, U.S. Government Printing Office.

**Lizotte, Alan J.** 1978. "Extra-legal Factors in Chicago's Criminal Courts: Testing the Conflict Model of Criminal Justice." *Social Problems* 25:564–80.

**Lockwood, Daniel.** 1979. *Prison Sexual Violence.* New York: Elsevier.

**Lofland, John.** 1966. *Doomsday Cult.* Englewood Cliffs, NJ: Prentice-Hall.

**Lofland, John and Rodney Stark.** 1965. "Becoming a World-Saver: A Theory of Conversion to a Deviant Perspective." *American Sociological Review* 30:862–75.

**Lofland, L.** 1973. *A World of Strangers.* New York: Basic Books.

**Logan, John R.** 1984. "The Graying of the Suburbs." *Aging* 345:4–8.

**Logan, John R. and Mark Schneider.** 1981. "The Stratification of Metropolitan Suburbs, 1960–1970." *American Sociological Review* 46:175–86.

———. 1984. "Racial Segregation and Racial Change in American Suburbs, 1970–1980." *American Journal of Sociology* 89:874–88.

**Lohr, Steve.** 1981. "How Tax Evasion Has Grown." *New York Times* 3(March 15): 1, 15.

**Lombroso, Cesare.** 1911/1968. *Crime: Its Causes and Remedies.* Henry P. Horton (trans.). Montclair, NJ: Patterson Smith.

**Long, John F.** 1981. *Population Deconcentration in the United States.* Washington, DC: U.S. Bureau of the Census.

**Long, Larry and Diana DeAre.** 1981. "The Suburbanization of Blacks." *American Demographics* 3: 16–21, 44.

**Lopata, Helena Z.** 1972. *Occupation: Housewife.* New York: Oxford University Press.

———. 1973. *Widowhood in an American City.* Cambridge, MA: Schenkman.

**Lopreato, J. and L. Hazelrigg.** 1972. *Class, Conflict, and Mobility.* San Francisco: Chandler.

**Loy, John W., Jr.** 1968. "The Nature of Sport: A Definitional Effort." *Quest,* Monograph 10 (May): 1–15.

———. 1969. "The Study of Sport and Social Mobility." Pp. 101–19 in *Aspects of Contemporary Sport Sociology,* edited by .G. S. Kenyon. Chicago: The Athletic Institute.

**Loy, John W., Jr. and J. F. McElvogue.** 1970. "Racial Segregation in American Sport." *The International Review of Sport Sociology* 5:5–23.

**Loy, John W., Jr., Barry D. McPherson, and Gerald Kenyon.** 1978. *Sport and Social Systems.* Reading, MA: Addison-Wesley.

**Lublin, Joann S.** 1984. "Growing Older: Suburban Population Ages, Causing Conflict and Radical Changes." *Wall Street Journal* (November 1): 1, 25.

**Ludwig, Ed and James Santibanez (eds.).** 1971. *The Chicanos: Mexican American Voices.* Baltimore, MD: Penguin.

**Luker, Kristin.** 1984. *Abortion & the Politics of Motherhood.* Berkeley: University of California Press.

**Lukes, Steven.** 1974. *Power: A Radical View.* London and New York: Macmillan.

**Lyall, Sarah.** 1988. "Pressed on Animal Rights, Researcher Gives Up Grant." *New York Times* (November 22): B1, B5.

**Lyle, J. and H. R. Hoffman.** 1972. "Children's Use of Television and Other Media." Pp. 129–256 in *Television and Social Behavior.* Vol. 4: *Television in Day-to-Day Life: Patterns of Use,* edited by E. A. Rubinstein, G. A. Comstock, and J. P. Murray. Washington, DC: U.S. Government Printing Office.

**Lyman, Stanford M.** 1977. *The Asian in North America.* Santa Barbara, CA: American Bibliographical Center–Clio Press.

**Lynd, Robert S. and Helen Merrell Lynd.** 1929. *Middletown: A Study in American Culture.* New York: Harcourt Brace Jovanovich.

**McAdam, Doug, John D. McCarthy, and Mayer N. Zald.** 1988. "Social Movements." Pp. 695–737 in *Handbook of Sociology,* edited by Neil J. Smelser. Beverly Hills, CA: Sage.

**McAdams, Jonathan.** 1989. Personal Communication on AT&T Consumer Behavior Time Diary Project.

**MacAloon, John J.** 1987. "An Observer's View of Sport Sociology." *Sociology of Sport Journal* 4:103–15.

**McArthur, Leslie Zebrowitz.** 1982. "Television and Sex Role Stereotyping: Are Children Being Programmed?" *The Brandeis Quarterly* 2:12–13.

**McCall, George J. and J. L. Simmons.** 1966. *Identities and Interactions.* New York: Free Press.

**McCarthy, John D. and Mayer N. Zald.** 1977. "Resource Mobilization and Social Movements: A Partial Theory." *American Journal of Sociology* 82:1212–41.

**McCarthy, John E.** 1980. "The Boat People." Pp. 594–96 in *Britannica Book of the Year.* Chicago: Encyclopaedia Britannica.

**McCauley, Martin.** 1988a. "Special Report: U.S.S.R: Perestroika and Glasnost—A Progress Report." Pp. 474–75 in *1988 Britannica Book of the Year.* Chicago: Encyclopaedia Britannica.

———. 1988b. "Union of Soviet Socialist Republics." Pp. 473, 476–77 in *1988 Britannica Book of the Year.* Chicago: Encyclopaedia Britannica.

**McCleery, Richard H.** 1966. "Policy Change in Prison Management." Pp. 376–400 in *Complex Organizations: A Reader,* edited by Amitai Etzioni. New York: Holt, Rinehart and Winston.

**Maccoby, Eleanor E.** 1966. "Sex Differences in Intellectual Functioning." Pp. 25–55 in *The Development of Sex Differences,* edited by Eleanor Maccoby. Stanford, CA: Stanford University Press.

**Maccoby, Eleanor E. and Carol N. Jacklin.** 1974. *The Psychology of Sex Differences.* Stanford, CA: Stanford University Press.

**McGarrell, Edmund F. and Timothy J. Flanagan (eds.).** 1985. *Sourcebook of Criminal Justice Statistics—1984.* U.S. Department of Justice, Washington, DC: USGPO.

**McGrath, Ellie.** 1985. "The AIDS Issue Hits the Schools." *Time* (September 9): 61.

**McGregor, Douglas.** 1960. *The Human Side of Enterprise.* New York: McGraw-Hill.

**MacKenzie, Donald A.** 1981. *Statistics in Britain, 1865–1930. The Social Construction of Scientific Knowledge.* Edinburgh: Edinburgh University Press.

**McKinlay, John B. and Sonja M. McKinlay.** 1986. "Medical Measures and the Decline of Mortality." Pp. 10–23 in *The Sociology of Health and Illness: Critical Perspectives,* edited by Peter Conran and Rochelle Kern. New York: St. Martin's Press.

**Macklin, Eleanor D.** 1983. "Cohabitation in the United States." Pp. 62–78 in *Current Issues in Marriage and the Family,* edited by J. Gipson Wells. New York: Colliers Macmillan.

**McLanahan, Sara.** 1985. "Family Structure and the Reproduction of Poverty." *American Journal of Sociology* 90:873–901.

**McLanahan, Sara and Julia Adams.** 1987. "Parenthood and Psychological Well-being." Pp. 237–57 in *Annual Review of Sociology,* edited by W. Richard Scott and James F. Short, Jr. Palo Alto, CA: Annual Reviews.

**McLanahan, Sara, Glen Cain, Michael Olneck, Irving Piliavin, Sheldon Danziger, and Peter Gottschalk.** 1985. "Losing Ground: A Critique." University

of Wisconsin-Madison: Institute for Research on Poverty, Special Report No. 38.

**McLuhan, Marshall.** 1964. *Understanding Media.* New York: New American Library.

**MacNamara, Donal E. J. and Edward Sagarin.** 1977. *Sex, Crime, and the Law.* New York: Free Press.

**McPherson, J. Miller and Lynne Smith-Lovin.** 1982. "Women and Weak Ties: Differences by Sex in the Size of Voluntary Organizations." *American Journal of Sociology* 87:883–904.

———. 1986. "Sex Segregation in Voluntary Associations." *American Sociological Review* 51:61–79.

**McQueen, Michel.** 1988. "Even with Good Pay, Many Americans are Unable to Buy a Home." *Wall Street Journal* (February 2): 1, 8.

**Magdoff, H.** 1978. *Imperialism: From the Colonial Era to the Present.* New York: Monthly Review Press.

**Magnuson, Ed.** 1980. "The Poisoning of America." *Time* (September 22): 58–69.

**Malabie, Alfred L., Jr.** 1981. "Off-the-Books Business Booms in Europe." *Wall Street Journal* (August 24): 1.

**Malinowski, Bronislaw.** 1948. *Magic, Science and Religion.* Garden City, NY: Doubleday/Anchor.

**Malthus, Thomas R.** 1798/1965. *An Essay on Population.* New York: Augustus Kelley, Bookseller.

**Manis, Jerome G. and Bernard N. Meltzer.** 1978. *Symbolic Interaction: A Reader in Social Psychology.* Boston: Allyn & Bacon.

**Mankoff, M.** 1970. "Power in Advanced Capitalist Society: A Review Essay on Recent Elitist and Marxist Criticism of Pluralist Theory." *Social Problems* 17:418–29.

**Mann, M.** 1970. "The Social Cohesion of Liberal Democracy." *American Sociological Review* 35:423–39.

**Marantz-Sanchez, Regina Markell.** 1985. *Sympathy and Science: Women Physicians in American Medicine.* New York: Oxford University Press.

**Marcuse, Herbert.** 1964. *One-Dimensional Man.* Boston: Beacon.

**Mare, Robert D. and Christopher Winship.** 1984. "The Paradox of Lessening Racial Inequality and Joblessness among Black Youth:

Enrollment, Enlistment, and Employment, 1964–1981." *American Sociological Review* 49:39–55.

**Maren, Michael.** 1988. "Pretoria's Iron Curtain—II: The Peace Talk Propaganda Show." *The Nation* (June 16): 854–56.

**Markham, William T. et al.** 1985. "Gender and Opportunity in the Federal Bureaucracy." *American Journal of Sociology* 91:129–50.

**Markoff, John.** 1988. "Wider Threat to Privacy Seen as Computer Memories Grow." *New York Times* (June 1): C1, C10.

**Marshall, Harvey.** 1979. "White Movement to the Suburbs: A Comparison of Explanations." *American Sociological Review* 44:975–94.

**Marshall, Victor W.** 1975. "Socialization for Impending Death in a Retirement Village." *American Journal of Sociology* 80:1124–44.

**Martin, Douglas.** 1988. " 'I Started to Keep a Knife under the Pillow.' " *New York Times* (November 5): 29.

**Martin, Patricia Yancey.** 1985. "Group Sex Compositions in Work Organizations: A Structural-Normative Model." Pp. 311–49 in *Research in the Sociology of Organizations*, edited by Samuel Bacharach and S. Mitchell. Greenwich, CT: JAI Press.

**Martin, Susan E.** 1978. "Sexual Politics in the Workplace: The Interactional World of Policewomen." *Symbolic Interaction* 1:44–60.

———. 1980. *Breaking and Entering: Policewomen on Patrol*. Berkeley: University of California Press.

———. 1982. Personal Communication (February 1).

**Martinson, Robert.** 1974. "What Works? Questions and Answers about Prison Reform." *Public Interest* 10:22–54.

**Martire, Gregory and Ruth Clark.** 1982. *Anti-Semitism in the United States: A Study of Prejudice in the 1980s*. New York: Praeger.

**Marty, Martin E.** 1976. *A Nation of Behavers*. Chicago: University of Chicago Press.

———. 1980. "Resurgent Fundamentalism." Pp. 606–07 in *Britannica Book of the Year*. Chicago: Encyclopaedia Britannica.

———. 1981. "The New Christian Right." Pp. 605–06 in *Britannica Book of the Year*. Chicago: Encyclopaedia Britannica.

———. 1988. "Religion, Television, and Money." Pp. 294–95 in *Britannica Book of the Year*. Chicago: University of Chicago Press.

**Martz, Larry and Ginny Carroll.** 1988. *Ministry of Greed: The Inside Story of the Televangelists and Their Holy War*. New York: Weidenfeld & Nicolson.

**Marwell, Gerald.** 1975. "Why Ascription? Parts of a More or Less Formal Theory of the Functions and Dysfunctions of Sex Roles." *American Sociological Review* 40:445–55.

**Marx, Gary T.** 1970. "Issueless Riots." *Annals of the American Academy of Political and Social Science* 391 (September): 12–33.

**Marx, Gary T. and James L. Wood.** 1975. "Strands of Theory and Research in Collective Behavior." Pp. 363–428 in *Annual Review of Sociology*. Vol. 1, edited by Alex Inkeles, James Coleman, and Neil Smelser. Palo Alto, CA: Annual Reviews.

**Marx, Karl.** 1844/1963. *Introduction to a Critique of the Hegelian Philosophy of Right*. T. B. Bottomore (trans.). New York: McGraw-Hill.

———. 1867–1895/1967. *Capital*. New York: International.

**Marx, Karl and Friedrich Engels.** 1846/1947. *The German Ideology*. Parts I and II. R. Pascal (ed.). New York: International.

**Masaoka, Mike**. 1972. "The Evacuation of the Japanese Americans and Its Aftermath." Pp. 186–95 in *Minority Problems*, edited by Arnold Rose and Caroline Rose. New York: Harper & Row.

**Masnick, George and Mary Jo Bane.** 1980. "The Nation's Families: 1960–1990." Cambridge, MA: Joint Center for Urban Studies, MIT and Harvard University.

**Mason, Karen O., John L. Czajka, and Sara Arber.** 1976. "Change in U.S. Women's Sex-Role Attitudes, 1964–1974." *American Sociological Review* 81:573–96.

**Mason, Karen O. and Yu-Hsia Lu.** 1988. "Attitudes toward Women's Familial Roles: Changes

in the United States, 1977–1985." *Gender & Society* 2:39–57.

**Masters, William Howell and Virginia Johnson.** 1979. *Homosexuality in Perspective*. Boston: Little, Brown.

**Masuda, Yoneji.** 1980. *The Information Society as Post Industrial Society*. Bethesda, MD: World Future Society.

**Matsueda, Ross L. and Karen Heimer.** 1987. "Race, Family Structure, and Delinquency: A Test of Differential Association and Social Control Theories." *American Sociological Review* 52:826–40.

**Mattera, Marianne Dekker.** 1980. "Female Doctors: Why They're on an Economic Treadmill." *Medical Economics* 57 (February 18): 98–110.

**Mattera, Philip.** 1985. *Off the Books: The Rise of the Underground Economy*. New York: St. Martin's Press.

**Matthews, Mervyn.** 1978. *Privilege in the Soviet Union: A Study of Elite Life-Styles under Communism*. London: George Allen & Unwin.

**Matthews, Sarah and Jetse Sprey.** 1984. "Divorce Impact on Grandparenthood." *The Gerontologist* 24:41–47.

**Matza, David.** 1969. *Becoming Deviant*. Englewood Cliffs, NJ: Prentice-Hall.

**Maurer, Harry.** 1979. *Not Working: An Oral History of the Unemployed*. New York: Holt, Rinehart and Winston.

**Mauss, Marcel.** 1954. *The Gift*. New York: Free Press.

**Mayer, Martin.** 1974. *The Bankers*. New York: Ballantine.

**Mead, George Herbert.** 1934. *Mind, Self, and Society*. Chicago: University of Chicago Press.

**Mead, Lawrence M.** 1986. *Beyond Entitlement: The Social Obligations of Citizenship*. New York: Free Press.

**Mead, Margaret.** 1935. *Sex and Temperament in Three Primitive Societies*. New York: Morrow.

**Meadows, D. H., D. L. Meadows, J. Randers, and W. Behrens III.** 1972. *The Limits to Growth*. New York: New American Library.

**Meier, H. C.** 1972. "Mother-Centeredness and College Youth's Attitudes toward Social Equality for

Women: Some Empirical Findings." *Journal of Marriage and the Family* 34:115–21.

Meiselman, K. 1978. *Incest.* San Francisco: Jossey-Bass.

Melman, Seymour. 1974. *The Permanent War Economy: American Capitalism in Decline.* New York: Simon & Schuster.

Merton, Robert K. 1957. *Social Theory and Social Structure.* New York: Free Press.

———. 1968. "The Matthew Effect in Science." *Science 159* (January 5): 56–63.

———. 1970. *Science, Technology and Society in Seventeenth-Century England.* New York: Harper & Row. (Original work published 1938.)

———. 1973a. *The Sociology of Science: Theoretical and Empirical Investigations.* Chicago: University of Chicago Press.

———. 1973b. "The Matthew Effect in Science." Pp. 439–59 in *The Sociology of Science: Theoretical and Empirical Investigations,* edited by Robert K. Merton. Chicago: University of Chicago Press.

———. 1982. *Social Research and the Practicing Professions.* Cambridge, MA: Abt Books.

———. 1984. "Scientific Fraud and the Fight to Be First." *Times Literary Supplement* (November 2): 1265–66.

Merton, Robert K. and Paul F. Lazarsfeld. 1954. "Friendship as a Social Process: A Substantive and Methodological Analysis." Pp. 18–66 in *Freedom and Control in Modern Society,* edited by Monroe Berger, Theodore Abel, and Charles Page. New York: Van Nostrand.

Messner, Steven F. 1980. "Income Inequality and Murder Rates: Some Cross-National Findings." Pp. 185–98 in *Comparative Social Research.* Vol. 3, edited by Richard Tomasson. Greenwich, CT: JAI Press.

———. 1982. "Societal Development, Social Equality, and Homicide: A Cross-National Test of a Durkheimian Model." *Social Forces* XX:225–40.

Metheny, Eleanor. 1965. *Connotations of Movement in Sport and Dance.* Dubuque, IA: William C. Brown.

Metz, Mary Haywood. 1978.

*Classrooms and Corridors: The Crisis of Authority in Desegregated Secondary Schools.* Berkeley: University of California Press.

Meyer, John. 1977. "Education as an Institution." *American Journal of Sociology* 83 (July): 55–77.

Michael, Robert T., Victor R. Fuchs, and Sharon R. Scott. 1980. "Changes in the Propensity to Live Alone: 1950–1976." *Demography* 17:39–56.

Michels, Robert. 1911/1967. *Political Parties.* New York: Free Press.

Michelson, William H. 1976. *Man and His Urban Environment.* Second edition. Reading, MA: Addison-Wesley.

Michener, James A. 1976. *Sports in America.* New York: Fawcett Crest.

Middleton, Russell. 1976. "Regional Differences in Prejudice." *American Sociological Review* 41:94–117.

Milgram, Stanley. 1969. *Obedience to Authority.* New York: Harper & Row.

———. 1970. "The Experience of Living in Cities." *Science* 167: 1461–68.

Milgram, Stanley and John Sabini. 1978. "On Maintaining Urban Norms: A Field Experiment in the Subway." Pp. 31–40 in *Advances in Environmental Psychology.* Vol. 1. *The Urban Environment,* edited by A. Baum, J. Singer, and S. Valins. Hillsdale, NJ: Erlbaum.

Miller, Brian. 1979. "Unpromised Paternity: Life Styles of Gay Fathers." Pp. 239–52 in *Gay Men,* edited by Martin P. Levine. New York: Harper & Row.

Miller, D. M. and K. R. E. Russell. 1971. *Sport: A Contemporary View.* Philadelphia: Lea & Febiger.

Miller, Joanne, Carmi Schooler, Melvin L. Kohn, and Karen A. Miller. 1979. "Women and Work: The Psychological Effects of Occupational Conditions." *American Journal of Sociology* 85:66–94.

Miller, Jon. 1980. "Access to Interorganizational Networks." *American Sociological Review* 45:479–96.

Miller, Karen A., Melvin L. Kohn, and Carmi Schooler. 1986. "Educational Self-direction and Personality." *American Sociological Review* 51:372–90.

Miller, Rita Sieden. 1978. "The Social Construction and Reconstruction of Physiological Events: Acquiring the Pregnancy Identity." Pp. 181–204 in *Studies in Symbolic Interaction.* Vol. 2, edited by Norman K. Denzin. Greenwich, CT: JAI Press.

Miller, S. M. and Donald Tomaskovic-Devey. 1983. *Recapitalizing America: Alternatives to the Corporate Distortion of National Policies.* Boston: Routledge & Kegan Paul.

Mills, C. Wright. 1956. *The Power Elite.* New York: Oxford University Press.

Mincer, Jacob. 1974. *Schooling, Experience and Earnings.* New York: Columbia University Press.

Mintz, Beth. 1975. "The President's Cabinet, 1897–1972: A Contribution to the Power Structure Debate." *Insurgent Sociologist* 4:131–48.

Mintz, Beth and Michael Schwartz. 1985. *The Power Structure of American Business.* Chicago: University of Chicago Press.

Mintz, Morton and Jerry S. Cohen. 1971. *America, Inc.* New York: Dial Press.

Minuchin, Patricia. 1966. "Sex Differences in Children: Research Findings in an Educational Context." *National Elementary Principal* 46:45–58.

Mirande, Alfredo. 1985. *The Chicano Experience.* Notre Dame, IN: University of Notre Dame Press.

Mitchell, Arnold. 1983. *The Nine American Lifestyles.* New York: Macmillan.

Mitchell, Richard G., Jr. 1981. Personal communication.

———. 1982. Personal communication (January 12).

———. 1983. *Mountain Experience: The Psychology and Sociology of Adventure.* Chicago: University of Chicago Press.

———. forthcoming. "Review of Gary Fine's *With the Boys.*" *European Sport Journal.*

Mizruchi, Mark S. 1982. *The American Corporate Network: 1904–1974.* Beverly Hills, CA: Sage.

Moberg, David O. 1962. *The Church as a Social Institution.* Englewood Cliffs, NJ: Prentice-Hall.

Moeller, G. H. and W. W. Charters, Jr. 1970. "Relation of Bureaucratization to Sense of Power among Teachers." Pp. 638–55 in *Learning in Social Settings*, edited by Matthew W. Miles and W. W. Charters, Jr. Boston: Allyn & Bacon.

**Mol, Hans J.** 1976. *Identity and the Sacred*. New York: Free Press.

**Mollenkopf, John.** 1975. "Theories of the State and Power Structure Research." *Insurgent Sociologist* 4:245–64.

**Molotch, Harvey.** 1976. "The City as a Growth Machine: Toward a Political Economy of Place." *American Journal of Sociology* 82:309–32.

**Monaghan-Leckband, Kathleen.** 1978. "Role Adaptations of Single Parents: A Challenge to the Pathological View of Male and Female Single Parents." Unpublished doctoral dissertation, New York University.

**Money, John and Anke A. Ehrhardt.** 1972. *Man and Woman: Boy and Girl*. New York: Mentor.

**Montagna, Paul D.** 1977. *Occupations and Society: Toward a Sociology of the Labor Market*. New York: Wiley.

**Moodie, T. Dunbar.** 1975. *The Rise of Afrikanerdom: Power, Apartheid, and the Afrikaner Civil Religion*. Berkeley: University of California Press.

**Mooney, James.** 1965. *The Ghost-Dance Religion and Sioux Outbreak of 1890*. Chicago: University of Chicago Press.

**Moore, Barrington, Jr.** 1978. *Injustice: The Social Bases of Obedience and Revolt*. White Plains, NY: M. E. Sharpe.

**Moore, Didi.** 1983. "America's Neglected Elderly." *New York Times Magazine* (January 30): 30–32ff.

**Moore, Gwen.** 1979. "The Structure of a National Elite Network." *American Sociological Review* 44:673–92.

**Moore, Joan W. and Harry Pachon.** 1985. *Hispanics in the United States*. Englewood Cliffs, NJ: Prentice-Hall.

**Moore, Kristin and Linda Waite.** 1981. "Marital Dissolution, Early Motherhood and Early Marriage." *Social Forces* 60:20–40.

**Moore, Wilbert E.** 1963. "Industrialization and Social Change." Pp. 299–370 in *Industrialization and Society*, edited by B. F. Hoselitz and Wilbert E. Moore. Paris: UNESCO.

**Morantz-Sanchez, Regina Markell.** 1985. *Sympathy and Science: Women Physicians in American Medicine*. New York: Oxford University Press.

**Morgan, Michael.** 1982. "Television and Adolescents' Sex Role Stereotypes: A Longitudinal Study." *Journal of Personality and Social Psychology* 43:947–55.

**Morgan, Philip and Ronald Rindfuss.** 1985. "Marital Disruption." *American Journal of Sociology* 90:1055–77.

**Morrow, Lance.** 1985. "The Start of a Plague Mentality." *Time* (September 23): 92.

**Mott, Frank and Sylvia Moore.** 1979. "The Causes of Marital Disruption among Young American Women." *Journal of Marriage and the Family* 41:355–65.

**Moynihan, Daniel Patrick.** 1967. *The Negro Family: The Case for National Action*. In *The Moynihan Report and the Politics of Controversy*, edited by Lee Rainwater and William L. Yancey. Cambridge, MA: MIT Press.

———. 1986. *Family and Nation*. San Diego: Harcourt Brace Jovanovich.

**Mueller, E.** 1972. "A Test of a Partial Theory of Potential for Political Violence." *American Political Science Review* 66 (September): 928–59.

**Mulkay, Michael.** 1979. *Science and the Sociology of Knowledge*. Boston: Allen & Unwin.

**Muller, Edward N.** 1985. "Income Inequality, Regime Repressiveness, and Political Violence." *American Sociological Review* 50:47–61.

**Muller, Hermann J.** 1959. "One Hundred Years without Darwinism Are Enough." *The Humanist* XIX(3):139–49.

**Muller, Peter O.** 1981. *Contemporary Suburban America*. Englewood Cliffs, NJ: Prentice-Hall.

**Mumford, Lewis.** 1961. *The City in History*. New York: Harcourt, Brace & World.

**Murdock, George.** 1967. *Ethnographic Atlas*. Pittsburgh: University of Pittsburgh Press.

**Murray, Charles.** 1984. *Losing Ground: American Social Policy, 1950–1980*. New York: Basic Books.

**Mydans, Seth.** 1987. "From Forest to Manila, Stranger in a Strange Land." *New York Times* (December 27): 16.

**Myles, J.** 1984. "The Retirement Wage in Post-War Capitalist Democracies." Paper presented at the annual meeting of the American Sociological Association, San Antonio.

**Mytelka, L. K.** 1979. *Regional Development in a Global Economy*. New Haven, CT: Yale University Press.

**Nader, Ralph and Mark Green (eds.).** 1973. *Corporate Power in America*. New York: Grossman.

**Naisbitt, John.** 1981. "The Bottom-up Society: American between Eras." *Public Opinion* (April–May): 18–19, 54–57.

———. 1982. *Megatrends*. New York: Warner Books.

**Nance, John.** 1975. *The Gentle Tasaday*. New York: Harcourt Brace Jovanovich.

**Nash, R.** 1967. *Wilderness and the American Mind*. New Haven, CT: Yale University Press.

**National Academy Press.** 1982. *Behavioral and Social Science Research: A National Resource*. Washington, DC.

**National Center for Education Statistics.** 1988. *American Education at a Glance*. Washington, DC: Office of Educational Research and Improvement, U.S. Department of Education.

**National Center for Health Statistics.** 1986. *Monthly Vital Statistics Report*. Washington, DC: U.S. Department of Health and Human Services.

———. 1988. *Advanced Report of Final Marriage Statistics, 1985*. Monthly Vital Statistics Report, 1985. Vol. 37, 1 (April 29). Washington, DC: U.S. Department of Health and Human Services.

**Nelkin, Dorothy.** 1977. "Creation Vs. Evolution: The Politics of Science Education." Pp. 265–87 in *The Social Production of Scientific Knowledge*, edited by Everett Mendelsohn, Peter Weingart, and Richard Whitley. Dordrecht-Holland: D. Reidel.

———. 1982. *The Creation Controversy: Science or Scripture in the Schools.* New York: Norton.

———. 1983. "From Dayton to Little Rock: Creationism Evolves." Pp. 74–85 in *Creationism, Science and the Law,* edited by Marcel C. LaFollette. Cambridge, MA: MIT Press.

———. 1989. "Science Studies in the 1990s." Talk presented at New York University (January).

Nelkin, Dorothy and Lawrence Tancredi. 1989. *Test and Control: The Power of Biological Information.* New York: Basic Books.

Nelsen, Hart M. and William E. Snizek. 1976. "Musical Pews: Rural and Urban Modes of Occupational and Religious Mobility." *Sociology and Social Research* 60:279–89.

Neuhaus, Richard John. 1984. *The Naked Public Square: Religion and Democracy in America.* Grand Rapids, MI: Eerdmans.

Neuman, W. Russell. 1986. *The Paradox of Mass Politics.* Cambridge, MA: Harvard University Press.

Newman, Barry. 1985. "Structured Society: A Briton Needn't Pay Much Heed to Class; He Knows His Place." *Wall Street Journal* (May 6): 1, 26.

Newman, Katherine S. 1988. *Falling from Grace: The Experience of Downward Mobility in the American Middle Class.* New York: Free Press.

News Roundup. 1985a. "As Fear of AIDS Spreads, People Change Ways They Live and Work." *Wall Street Journal* (October 10): 35.

———. 1985b. "AIDS Costs: Employers and Insurers Have Reasons to Fear Expensive Epidemic." *Wall Street Journal* (October 18): 1, 12.

*Newsweek.* 1974. "The World Food Crisis: Bumper Crop to Empty Bowls: How to Ease the Hunger Pangs." (November 11): 56–61, 67.

*New York Times.* 1978. "College Women and Self-esteem." (December 10): 85.

———. 1980. "Fifth World Synod of Roman Catholic Bishops: Excerpts from Bishops' 'Message to Christian Families in the Modern World.'" (October 26): 18.

———. 1985a. "Church Rolls Up; Long Decline Ends." (June 19): A20.

———. 1985b. "37% in Poll Say AIDS Altered Their Attitude to Homosexuals." (December 15): 41.

———. 1988. "Those Who Chose to Vote." (November 10): B6.

Nickerson, J. 1975. *Homage to Malthus.* Port Washington, NY: National University Publications.

Niebuhr, H. Richard. 1929. *The Social Sources of Denominationalism.* New York: Holt.

Nielsen, Joyce McCarl. 1978. *Sex in Society: Perspectives on Stratificatiion.* Belmont, CA: Wadsworth.

Nisbet, Robert A. 1966. *The Sociological Tradition.* New York: Basic Books.

Noel, Donald L. 1968. "How Ethnic Inequality Begins." *Social Problems* 16:157–72.

Nora, Simon and Alain Minc. 1980. *The Computerization of Society.* Cambridge, MA: MIT Press.

NORC. 1978. "General Social Survey." National Opinion Research Center, University of Chicago. Cited in *Public Opinion,* 1980.

Nyden, Phillip W. 1985. "Democratizing Organizations: A Case Study of a Union Reform Movement." *American Journal of Sociology* 90:1179–203.

Nye, F. Ivan, James F. Short, Jr., and Virgil J. Olson. 1958. "Socioeconomic Status and Delinquent Behavior." *American Journal of Sociology* 63:381–89.

Nyquist, E. B. 1979. "Wine, Women and Money: College Athletics Today and Tomorrow." *Educational Review* 60:376–93.

Oakes, Jeannie. 1982. "Classroom Social Relationships: Exploring the Bowles and Gintis Hypothesis." *Sociology of Education* 55:197–212.

———. 1985. *Keeping Track: How Schools Structure Inequality.* New Haven, CT: Yale University Press.

Oberschall, Anthony. 1973. *Social Conflict and Social Movements.* Englewood Cliffs, NJ: Prentice-Hall.

O'Brien, John E. 1971. "Violence in Divorce Prone Families." *Journal of Marriage and the Family* 33 (November): 692–98.

O'Connor, James. 1973. *The Fiscal Crisis of the State.* New York: St. Martin's Press.

Odum, Howard T. 1971. *Environment, Power, and Society.* New York: Wiley.

Offe, Claus. 1984. *Contradictions of the Welfare State.* Cambridge, MA: MIT Press.

Ogbu, John U. 1978. *Minority Education and Caste.* New York: Academic Press.

Ogburn, William F. 1922. *Social Change: With Respect to Culture and Original Nature.* New York: B. W. Huebsch.

Ollman, Bertell. 1971. *Alienation: Marx's Critique of Man in Capitalist Society.* Cambridge, England: Cambridge University Press.

Olson, L. 1982. *The Political Economy of the Welfare State.* New York: Columbia University Press.

Olson, Mancur, Jr. 1965. *The Logic of Collective Action.* Cambridge, MA: Harvard University Press.

Oppenheimer, Valerie Kincade. 1970. *The Female Labor Force in the United States.* Westport, CT: Greenwood Press.

———. 1982. *Work and the Family: A Study in Social Demography.* New York: Academic Press.

———. 1988. "A Theory of Marriage Timing." *American Journal of Sociology* 94:563–91.

Orfield, G. and F. Paul. 1988. "Patterns of Decline in Minority Access to Higher Education in Five Metropolitan Areas." *Educational Record* 69:52–56.

Orthner, D. 1976. "Patterns of Leisure and Marital Interaction." *Journal of Leisure Research* 8:98–111.

Orum, Anthony M. 1978. *Introduction to Political Sociology: The Anatomy of the Body Politic.* Englewood Cliffs, NJ: Prentice-Hall.

Ossowski, S. 1963. *Class Structure in the Social Consciousness.* Sheila Patterson (trans.). New York: Free Press.

Ostling, Richard N. 1986. "Power, Glory–And Politics." *Time* (February 17): 62–69.

———. 1988. "Now It's Jimmy's Turn." *Time* (March 7): 46–48.

———. 1989. "Those Mainline Blues: America's Old Guard Protestant Churches Confront an Unprecedented Decline." *Time* (May 22): 94–96.

Ostrander, Susan A. 1984. *Women of the Upper Class.* Philadelphia: Temple University Press.

**Ouchi, William G.** 1981. *Theory Z: How American Business Can Meet the Japanese Challenge.* New York: Avon.

**Pachon, Harry P. and Joan W. Moore.** 1981. "Mexican Americans." *The Annals of the American Academy of Political and Social Science* 454 (March): 111–24.

**Page, Charles H.** 1969. "Symposium Summary, with Reflections upon the Sociology of Sport as a Research Field." Pp. 189–209 in *Aspects of Contemporary Sport Sociology*, edited by Gerald S. Kenyon. Chicago: The Athletic Institute.

**Palardy, J. Michael.** 1969. "What Teachers Believe—What Children Achieve." *Elementary School Journal* 69:370–74.

**Palmer, John L. and Isabel V. Sawhill.** 1984. *The Reagan Record.* Cambridge, MA: Ballinger.

**Palmore, Erdman and Frank Whittington.** 1971. "Trends in the Relative Status of the Aged." *Social Forces* 50:84–90.

**Parelius, Ann Parker and Robert J. Parelius.** 1978. *The Sociology of Education.* Englewood Cliffs, NJ: Prentice-Hall.

**Parenti, Michael.** 1967. "Political Values and Religious Culture: Jews, Catholics, and Protestants." *Journal for the Scientific Study of Religion* 7 (fall): 259–69.

**Park, Robert E., Ernest W. Burgess, and Roderick D. McKenzie.** 1925. *The City.* Chicago: University of Chicago Press.

**Parke, R. D.** 1981. *Fathers.* Cambridge, MA: Harvard University Press.

**Parker, Stanley R. and Michael A. Smith.** 1976. "Work and Leisure." Pp. 37–64 in *Handbook of Work Organization and Society*, edited by Robert Dubin. Chicago: Rand McNally.

**Parkin, Frank.** 1971. *Class Inequality and Political Order.* New York: Praeger.

**Parsons, J. E., D. N. Ruble, K. L. Hodges, and A. W. Small.** 1976. "Cognitive-Developmental Factors in Emerging Sex Differences in Achievement-related Expectancies." *Journal of Social Issues* 32:47–61.

**Parsons, Talcott.** 1937/1949. *The Structure of Social Action.* Glencoe, IL: Free Press.

———. 1951. *The Social System.* Glencoe, IL: Free Press.

**Parsons, Talcott and Robert F. Bales.** 1953. *Family, Socialization and Interaction Process.* Glencoe, IL: Free Press.

**Pascal, A. H. and L. A. Rapping.** 1970. *Racial Discrimination in Organized Baseball.* Santa Monica, CA: Rand Corporation.

**Patchin, Robert I.** 1983. *The Management and Maintenance of Quality Circles.* Homewood, IL: Dow Jones–Irwin.

**Patterson, Orlando.** 1982. "Persistence, Continuity and Change in the Jamaican Working Class Family." *Journal of Family History* 7:135–61.

**Pawelczynska, Anna.** 1979. *Values and Violence in Auschwitz: A Sociological Analysis.* Catherine S. Leach (trans.). Berkeley: University of California Press.

**Peacock, Walter Gillis, Greg A. Hoover, and Charles D. Killian.** 1988. "Divergence and Convergence in International Development: A Decomposition Analysis of Inequality in the World System." *American Sociological Review* 53:838–52.

**Pearlin, Leonard I.** 1971. *Class Context and Family Relations: A Cross-National Study.* Boston: Little, Brown.

**Pelton, L.** 1981. *Social Context of Child Abuse and Neglect.* New York: Human Sciences Press.

**Pelz, Donald C. and Frank M. Andrews.** 1966. *Scientists in Organizations.* New York: Wiley.

**Pepitone-Rockwell, Fran (ed.).** 1980. *Dual-Career Couples.* Beverly Hills, CA: Sage.

**Pereira, Joseph.** 1989. "The Exercise Boom Loses Its Strength." *Wall Street Journal* (January 9): B1.

**Perrow, Charles.** 1979a *Complex Organizations: A Critical Essay.* Second edition. Glenview, IL: Scott, Foresman.

———. 1979b. "Organizational Theory in a Society of Organizations." Paper presented at the annual meeting of the American Sociological Association, Boston.

**Perry, David C. and Alfred J. Watkins.** 1977. "Regional Change and the Impact of Uneven Urban Development." Pp. 19–54 in *The Rise of the Sunbelt Cities,* edited by David C. Perry and Alfred J. Watkins. Beverly Hills, CA: Sage.

**Perry, Stewart E.** 1978. *San Francisco Scavengers.* Berkeley: University of California Press.

**Persell, Caroline Hodges.** 1977. *Education and Inequality.* New York: Free Press.

———. 1981. "Genetic and Cultural Deficit Theories." *Journal of Black Studies* 12:19–37.

———. 1982. "Percentage of Blacks and Hispanics in 1982 Baseball Starting Lineup." Unpublished study.

**Persell, Caroline Hodges, Sophia Catsambis, and Peter W. Cookson, Jr.** 1989. "Gender, School Type and Selective College Attendance: Comparing Status Attainment and Status Allocation Theories of Stratification." Paper presented at the annual meeting of the American Sociological Association, San Francisco.

**Persell, Caroline Hodges and Peter W. Cookson, Jr.** 1985. "Chartering and Bartering: Elite Education and Social Reproduction." *Social Problems* 33:114–29.

**Persell, Caroline Hodges and Timothy Haft.** 1986. "Racial Composition of Baseball Players by Position, 1986." Unpublished paper, New York University.

**Pescosolido, Bernice A., Carol A. Boyer, and Wai Ying Tsui.** 1985. "Medical Care in the Welfare State: A Cross-National Study of Public Evaluations." *Journal of Health and Social Behavior* 26:276–97.

**Peterson, Ruth D. and John Hagan.** 1984. "Changing Conceptions of Race: Towards an Account of Anomalous Findings of Sentencing Research." *American Sociological Review* 49:56–70.

**Pettigrew, Tom.** 1981. "Race and Class: An Interactive View." *Daedalus* 110:233–55.

**Petzinger, Thomas, Jr. and George Getschow.** 1984. "Oil's Legacy: In Louisiana, Pollution and Cancer are Rife in the Petroleum Area." *Wall Street Journal* (October 23): 1, 24.

**Phillips, John C. and Walter E. Schafer.** 1971. "Consequences of Participation in Interscholastic

Sports: A Prospectus and Review." *Pacific Sociological Review* (July): 328–38.

**Pietrofesa, John J. and Nancy K. Schlossberg.** 1974. "Counselor Bias and the Female Occupational Role." Pp. 148–50 in *Sociology of Education,* edited by William M. Cave and Mark A. Chesler. New York: Macmillan.

**Piliavin, Irving, Rosemary Gartner, Craig Thornton, and Ross L. Matsueda.** 1986. "Crime, Deterrence, and Rational Choice." *American Sociological Review* 51:101–19.

**Pines, Maya.** 1981. "The Civilizing of Genie." *Psychology Today* 15:28–34.

**Piore, Michael J.** 1975. "Notes for a Theory of Labor Market Stratification." Pp. 125–50 in *Labor Market Segmentation,* edited by R. C. Edwards, M. Reich, and D. M. Gordon. Lexington, MA: Heath.

**Piven, Frances Fox and Richard A. Cloward.** 1971. *Regulating the Poor: The Functions of Public Welfare.* New York: Vintage.

———. 1977. *Poor People's Movements: Why They Succeed, How They Fail.* New York: Vintage.

———. 1988. *Why Americans Don't Vote.* New York: Pantheon.

**Pleck, Joseph H.** 1985. *Working Wives/Working Husbands.* Beverly Hills, CA: Sage.

**Plisko, Valena White and Joyce D. Stern.** 1985. *The Condition of Education 1985.* National Center for Education Statistics, U.S. Department of Education, Washington, DC: U.S. Government Printing Office.

**Poewe, Karla O.** 1980. "Universal Male Dominance: An Ethnological Illusion." *Dialectical Anthropology* 5:111–25.

**Pogge, Mariann.** 1978. "From Cheerleader to Competitor." *Update* (fall): 18.

**Polanyi, Karl.** 1944. *The Great Transformation.* New York: Rinehart.

**Polgar, Steven (ed.).** 1975. *Population, Ecology and Social Evolution.* Chicago: Aldine.

**Poloma, Margaret M., Brian F. Pendleton, and T. Neal Garland.** 1982. "Reconsidering the Dual-Career Marriage: A Longitudinal Approach." Pp. 173–92 in

*Two Paychecks: Life in Dual-Earner Families,* edited by Joan Aldous. Beverly Hills, CA: Sage.

**Pool, Ithiel de Sola.** 1983. *Technologies of Freedom.* Cambridge, MA: Harvard University Press.

**Popper, Karl.** 1959. *The Logic of Scientific Discovery.* New York: Basic Books.

**Population Reference Bureau, Inc.** 1988. *1988 World Population Data Sheet.* Washington, DC: Population Reference Bureau.

**Portes, Alejandro and Saskia Sassen-Koob.** 1987. "Making It Underground: Comparative Material on the Informal Sector in Western Market Economies." *American Journal of Sociology* 93:30–61.

**Portes, Alejandro and Cynthia Truelove.** 1987. "Making Sense of Diversity: Recent Research on Hispanic Minorities in the United States." Pp. 359–85 in *Annual Review of Sociology,* edited by W. Richard Scott and James F. Short, Jr. Palo Alto, CA: Annual Reviews.

**Postman, Neil.** 1985. *Amusing Ourselves to Death: Social Discourse in the Age of Show Business.* New York: Viking.

**Poston, Dudley L.** 1984. "Regional Ecology." Pp. 323–82 in *Sociological Human Ecology,* edited by M. Micklin and H. M. Choldin. Boulder, CO: Westview.

**Poulantzas, Nicos.** 1972. "The Problem of the Capitalist State." Pp. 238–53 in *Ideology in the Social Sciences,* edited by Robin Blackburn. London: Fontana.

**Presthus, Robert.** 1962. *The Organizational Society.* New York: Vintage.

**Preston, Samuel H.** 1984. "Children and the Elderly in the U.S." *Scientific American* (December) 251:44–49.

**Presvelou, C.** 1971. "Impact of Diferential Leisure Activities in Intraspousal Dynamics." *Human Relations* 24:565–74.

**Price, Derek J. de Solla.** 1963. *Little Science Big Science.* New York: Columbia University Press.

———. 1971. "Measuring the Size of Science." Cited in Joseph Ben-David, *The Scientist's Role in Society.*

———. 1975. "The Productivity of Research Scientists." Pp. 408–21 in

*Yearbook of Science and the Future.* Chicago: Encyclopaedia Britannica.

***Public Opinion.*** 1979. "Religious Preference." March–May: 34.

———. 1980a. "Psephological Psouffle." April–May: 34.

———. 1980b. "The 70's: Decade of Second Thoughts." December–January: 19–42.

———. 1985. "Opinion Roundup: Defining Woman's Place." February–March: 40.

**Purdy, D. A., D. S. Eitzen, and R. Hufnagel.** 1982. "Are Athletes Also Students? The Educational Attainment of College Athletes." *Social Problems* 29:439–48.

**Putnam, R. D.** 1976. *The Comparative Study of Political Elites.* Englewood Cliffs, NJ: Prentice-Hall.

**Quadagno, Jill.** 1987. "Theories of the Welfare State." Pp. 109–28 in *Annual Review of Sociology,* edited by W. Richard Scott and James F. Short, Jr. Palo Alto, CA: Annual Reviews.

**Quinn, Bernard, Herman Anderson, Martin Bradley, Paul Goetting, and Peggy Shriver.** 1982. *Churches and Church Membership in the United States: 1980.* Atlanta, GA: Glenmary Research Center.

**Quinn, James Brian.** 1979. "Technological Innovation, Entrepreneurship, and Strategy." *Sloan Management Review* (spring): 19–30.

**Quinney, Richard.** 1970. *The Social Reality of Crime.* Boston: Little, Brown.

———. 1974. *Critique of Legal Order: Crime Control in Capitalist Society.* Boston: Little, Brown.

**Radin, N. and G. Russell.** 1983. "Increased Father Participation and Child Development Outcomes." Pp. 191–218 in *Fatherhood and Family Policy,* edited by M. Lamb and A. Sagi. Hillsdale, NJ: Erlbaum.

**Rainwater, Lee.** 1966. "Fear and the House-as-Haven in the Lower Class." *Journal of the American Institute of Planners* 32:23–30.

———. 1969. "The Problem of Lower-Class Culture and Poverty-War Strategy." In *On Understanding*

*Poverty,* edited by Daniel Moynihan. New York: Basic Books.

**Rallings, E. M. and F. I. Nye.** 1979. "Wife-Mother Employment Family, and Society." Pp. 203–26 in *Contemporary Theories about the Family.* Vol. 1. *Research-Based Theories,* edited by W. R. Burr, R. Hill, F. I. Nye, and I. L. Riess. New York: Free Press.

**Ralph, John H. and Richard Rubinson.** 1980. "Immigration and the Expansion of Schooling in the United States, 1890–1970." *American Sociological Review* 45:943–54.

**Rapoport, Robert and Rhonda Rapoport.** 1976. *Dual-Career Families Reexamined: New Integrations of Work and Family.* New York: Harper & Row.

**Rasmussen, Larry.** 1988. "New Dynamics in Theology." *Christianity and Crisis* 48 (May 16): 178–83.

**Ratcliff, Richard E.** 1980. "Banks and Corporate Lending: An Analysis of the Impact of the Internal Structure of the Capitalist Class on the Lending Behavior of Banks." *American Sociological Review* 45:553–70.

**Ratner, Ronnie Steinberg (ed.).** 1980. *Equal Employment Policy for Women: Strategies for Implementation in the United States, Canada, and Western Europe.* Philadelphia: Temple University Press.

**Read, Kenneth.** 1965. *The High Valley.* New York: Scribner's.

**Rees, C. Roger and Mady Wechsler Segal.** 1980. "Role Differentiation in Groups: The Relationship between Instrumental and Expressive Leadership in Two College Football Teams." Paper presented at the annual meeting of the American Sociological Association, New York.

**Rehberg, R. A. and M. Cohen.** 1976. "Political Attitudes and Participation in Extracurricular Activities." In *Social Problems in Athletics,* edited by Daniel M. Landers. Urbana: University of Illinois Press.

**Reinarman, Craig.** 1985. "Social Movements and Social Problems: 'Mothers Against Drunk Drivers,' Restrictive Alcohol Laws and Social Control in the 1980s." Paper presented at the 35th annual meeting of the Society for the Study of Social Problems, Washington, DC.

**Reiss, Albert J., Jr.** 1961. "The Social Integration of Peers and Queers." *Social Problems* 9:102–20.

**Reiss, Albert J., Jr., Otis D. Duncan, Paul K. Hatt, and Cecil C. North.** 1961. *Occupational and Social Status.* New York: Free Press.

**Reiss, Ira L.** 1967. *The Social Context of Premarital Sexual Permissiveness.* New York: Holt, Rinehart and Winston.

**Reiss, Spencer.** 1988. "South Africa's Big Chill: Two Years of Emergency Rule by the Whites Have Taken the Heat Out of a 'Revolutionary Climate.'" *Newsweek* (June 20): 39.

**Rensberger, Boyce.** 1977. "Fraud in Research Is a Rising Problem in Science." *New York Times* (January 23): 1, 44.

**Reskin, Barbara F.** 1988. "Bringing the Men Back In: Sex Differentiation and the Devaluation of Women's Work." *Gender & Society* 2:58–81.

**Reskin, Barbara F. and Heidi I. Hartmann (eds.).** 1986. *Women's Work, Men's Work: Sex Segregation on the Job.* Washington, DC: National Academy Press.

**Reskin, Barbara F. and Patricia A. Roos.** 1990. *Job Queues, Gender Queues: Explaining Women's Gains in Male Occupations.* Philadelphia: Temple University Press.

**Restivo, Sal.** 1988. "Modern Science as a Social Problem." *Social Problems* 35:206–25.

**Retine, Nancy and Joan Huber.** 1974. "The Demography of Poverty: Trends in the Sixties." In *The Sociology of American Poverty,* edited by Joan Huber and Peter Chalfant. Cambridge, MA: Schenkman.

**Reynolds, Morgan O.** 1971. "Crime for Profit: The Economics of Theft." Ph.D. Dissertation, University of Wisconsin.

**Rice, Bradley R.** 1981. "Searching for the Sunbelt." *American Demographics* 3:22–23.

**Rice, David G.** 1979. *The Dual-Career Marriage.* New York: Free Press.

**Richards, Bill.** 1986. "They Have Jobs Again in La Porte, but Work Doesn't Pay So Well." *Wall Street Journal* (March 12): 1, 31.

**Riche, Martha Farnsworth.** 1985. "Religion's New Demographics." *American Demographics* (December): 38–41.

**Rieder, Jonathan.** 1985. *Canarsie: The Jews and Italians of Brooklyn against Liberalism.* Cambridge, MA: Harvard University Press.

**Riesman, David.** 1961. *The Lonely Crowd.* New Haven, CT: Yale University Press.

**Riley, Matilda White, Anne Foner, and Joan Waring (eds.).** 1988. *Sociology of Age.* Beverly Hills, CA: Sage.

**Riordon, Michael.** 1979. "Notes of a Willing Victim." Pp. 78–99 in *Gay Men,* edited by Martin P. Levine. New York: Harper & Row.

**Robbins, Thomas and Dick Anthony.** 1978. "New Religions, Families and Brainwashing." *Society* 15 (May–June): 77–83.

**Robey, Bryant.** 1982. "A Guide to the Baby Boom." *American Demographics* (September): 16–21.

**Robinson, Ira E. and Davor Jedlicka.** 1982. "Changes in Sexual Attitudes and Behavior of College Students from 1965 to 1980: A Research Note." *Journal of Marriage and the Family* 44:237–40.

**Robinson, John P.** 1976. "Changes in America's Use of Time, 1965–1975." Report of Communication Center, Cleveland State University.

———. 1977. *How Americans Use Their Time: A Social-Psychological Analysis of Everyday Behavior.* New York: Praeger.

———. 1987. "Where's the Boom?" *American Demographics* (March): 36–7, 56.

**Rodney, W.** 1974. *How Europe Underdeveloped Africa.* Washington, DC: Howard University Press.

**Roethlisberger, Fritz J. and William J. Dickson.** 1939. *Management and the Worker.* Cambridge, MA: Harvard University Press.

**Rollins, Judith.** 1985. *Between Women: Domestics and Their Employers.* Philadelphia: Temple University Press.

**Roos, Patricia A.** 1985. *Gender and Work: A Comparative Analysis of In-*

*dustrial Societies*. Albany, NY: SUNY Press.

**Roper Organization.** 1980. *The 1980 Virginia Slims American Women's Opinion Poll*. New York.

**Rosaldo, M. Z. and L. Lamphere.** 1974. *Woman, Culture and Society*. Stanford, CA: Stanford University Press.

**Rosenbaum, James E.** 1976. *Making Inequality*. New York: Wiley.

———. 1979. "Organizational Career Mobility: Promotion Chances in a Corporation during Periods of Growth and Contraction." *American Journal of Sociology* 85:21–48.

**Rosenblatt, A.** 1967. "Negroes in Baseball: The Failure of Success." *Transaction* 4:51–53.

**Rosenfeld, Rachael A.** 1978. "Women's Employment Patterns and Occupational Achievements." *Social Science Research* 7:61–80.

———. 1980. "Race and Sex Differences in Career Dynamics." *American Sociological Review* 45:583–609.

**Rosenfield, Sarah.** 1980. "Sex Differences in Depression: Do Women Always Have Higher Rates?" *Journal of Health and Social Behavior* 21:33–42.

**Rosenthal, Robert and Lenore Jacobson.** 1968. *Pygmalion in the Classroom*. New York: Holt, Rinehart and Winston.

**Rosow, Kenneth and Caroline Hodges Persell.** 1980. "Sex Education from 1900 to 1920: A Study of Ideological Social Control." *Qualitative Sociology* 3:186–203.

**Ross, Catherine E., John Mirowsky, and Joan Huber.** 1983. "Dividing Work, Sharing Work, and In-between: Marriage Patterns and Depression." *American Sociological Review* 48:809–23.

**Ross, Heather and Isabel Sawhill.** 1975. *Time of Transition: The Growth of Families Headed by Women*. Washington, DC: The Urban Institute.

**Ross, James B. and Mary M. McLaughlin (eds.).** 1949. *The Portable Medieval Reader*. New York: Viking.

**Rossi, Alice S.** 1972. "Sex Equality: The Beginnings of Ideology." Pp. 344–53 in *Toward a Sociology of Women,* edited by Constantina

Safilios-Rothschild. Lexington, MA: Xerox College Publishing.

———. 1983. *Seasons of a Woman's Life*. University of Massachusetts, Amherst: Social and Demographic Research Institute.

**Rossides, Daniel.** 1976. *The American Class System*. Boston: Houghton Mifflin.

**Rostow, W. W.** 1960. *The Stages of Economic Growth: A Non-Communist Manifesto*. New York: Cambridge University Press.

**Rothschild, Joyce and Raymond Russell.** 1986. "Alternatives to Bureaucracy: Democratic Participation in the Economy." Pp. 307–28 in *Annual Review of Sociology,* edited by Ralph H. Turner and James F. Short, Jr. Palo Alto, CA: Annual Reviews.

**Rothschild, Joyce and J. Alan Whitt.** 1986. *The Cooperative Workplace: Potentials and Dilemmas of Organizational Democracy and Participation*. New York: Cambridge University Press.

**Rothschild-Whitt, Joyce.** 1976. "Conditions Facilitating Participatory-Democratic Organizations." *Sociological Inquiry* 46:75–86.

———. 1979. "The Collectivist Organization: An Alternative to Rational-Bureaucratic Models." *American Sociological Review* 44 (August): 509–27.

**Rousseau, Jean-Jacques.** 1750/1974. *Discourse on the Origin of Inequality*. Lowell Bair (trans.). New York: New American Library.

**Royal Commission on the Distribution of Income and Wealth.** 1980. *An A to Z of Income and Wealth*. London: Her Majesty's Stationery Office.

**Royko, Mike.** 1979. "The New Barbarians: A Glimpse of the Future." *Cincinnati Post* (December 4).

**Rubin, Lillian Breslow.** 1976. *Worlds of Pain: Life in the Working-Class Family*. New York: Basic Books.

**Rubinson, Richard and John Ralph.** 1984. "Technical Change and the Expansion of Schooling in the United States, 1890–1970." *Sociology of Education* 57:134–52.

**Rumberger, Russell W.** 1981. *Overeducation in the U.S. Labor Market*. New York: Praeger.

**Rundall, Thomas G. and John R. C. Wheeler.** 1979. "The Effect of Income on Use of Preventive Care: An Evaluation of Alternative Explanations." *Journal of Health and Social Behavior* 20:397–406.

**Russell, Diana E. H.** 1986. *The Secret Trauma: Incest in the Lives of Girls and Women*. New York: Basic Books.

**Russell, Josian Cox.** 1972. *Medieval Regions and Their Cities*. Bloomington: Indiana University Press.

**Russell, Raymond, Art Hochner, and Stewart Perry.** 1977. "San Francisco's Scavengers Run Their Own Firm." *Working Papers for a New Society,* 5:30–36.

**Ryan, William.** 1971. *Blaming the Victim*. New York: Random House.

**Sack, Allen L.** 1977. "Big Time College Football: Whose Free Ride?" *Quest* 27:87–97.

**Sack, Allen L. and Robert Thiel.** 1979. "College Football and Social Mobility: A Case Study of Notre Dame Football Players." *Sociology of Education* 52 (January): 60–66.

**Sadker, Myra Pollack and David Miller Sadker.** 1980. "Sexism in Teacher-Education Texts." *Harvard Educational Review* 50:36–46.

**Sagarin, Edward.** 1976. "Prison Homosexuality and Its Effects on Post-prison Sexual Behavior." *Psychiatry* 39:245–57.

**Saikal, Amin.** 1980. *The Rise and Fall of the Shah*. Princeton, NJ: Princeton University Press.

**St. John, Nancy Hoyt.** 1975. *School Desegregation*. New York: Wiley.

**Sale, Kirkpatrick.** 1976. *Power Shift*. New York: Random House.

**Sallach, D.** 1974. "Class Domination and Ideological Hegemony." *Sociological Quarterly* 15:39–50.

**Salzman, Harold and G. William Domhoff.** 1979–1980. "Corporations, Non-profit Groups and Government: Do They Interlock?" *The Insurgent Sociologist* IX (2–3):121–35.

**Sampson, Robert J.** 1986. "Effects of Socioeconomic Context on Official Reaction to Juvenile Delinquency." *American Sociological Review* 5:876–85.

———. 1987. "Urban Black Violence: The Effect of Male Jobless-ness and Family Disruption." *American Journal of Sociology* 93:348–82.

**Sanday, Peggy R.** 1981. *Female Power and Male Dominance: On the Origins of Sexual Inequality.* Cambridge, England: Cambridge University Press.

**Sargent, Jon.** 1984. "The Job Outlook for College Graduates through the mid-1990's. *Occupational Outlook Quarterly* (summer): 2–7.

———. 1988. "A Greatly Improved Outlook for College Graduates: A 1988 Update to the Year 2000." *Occupational Outlook Quarterly* (summer): 3–8.

**Sauvy, A.** 1969. *General Theory of Population.* New York: Basic Books.

**Sawin, Douglas B. and Ross D. Parke.** 1979. "Fathers' Affectionate Stimulation and Caregiving Behaviors with Newborn Infants." *Family Coordinator* 28:509–13.

**Scanzoni, John.** 1972. *Sexual Bargaining: Power Politics in American Marriage.* Englewood Cliffs, NJ: Prentice-Hall.

**Scarf, Maggie.** 1980. *Unfinished Business: Pressure Points in the Lives of Women.* New York: Ballantine.

**Scarr, Sandra.** 1984. *Mother Care/ Other Care.* New York: Basic Books.

**Scarr-Salapatek, Sandra and Richard A. Weinberg.** 1975. "When Black Children Grow Up in White Homes." *Psychology Today* 9:80–82.

**Schafer, W. E. and J. C. Phillips.** 1970. "The Athletic Subculture: A Preliminary Study." Paper presented at the annual meeting of the American Sociological Association, Washington, DC.

**Schell, Jonathan.** 1982. *The Fate of the World.* New York: Knopf.

**Schlechty, Phillip C.** 1976. *Teaching and Social Behavior: Toward an Organizational Theory of Instruction.* Boston: Allyn & Bacon.

**Schlegel, Alice (ed.).** 1977. *Sexual Stratification: A Cross-Cultural View.* New York: Columbia University Press.

**Schluchter, Wolfgang.** 1981. *The Rise of Western Rationalism: Max Weber's Developmental History.*

Berkeley: University of California Press.

**Schneider, Herbert.** 1952. *Religion in 20th Century America.* Cambridge, MA: Harvard University Press.

**Schon, D. A.** 1963. *Displacement of Concepts.* London: Tavistock.

**Schrank, Robert.** 1978. *Ten Thousand Working Days.* Cambridge, MA: MIT Press.

**Schudson, Michael.** 1984. *Advertising, the Uneasy Persuasion.* New York: Basic Books.

**Schumacher, E. F.** 1973. *Small Is Beautiful.* New York: Harper & Row.

**Schur, Edwin M.** 1965. *Crimes without Victims.* Englewood Cliffs, NJ: Prentice-Hall.

———. 1968. *Law and Society: A Sociological View.* New York: Random House.

———. 1979. *Interpreting Deviance: A Sociological Introduction.* New York: Harper & Row.

———. 1980. *The Politics of Deviance: Stigma Contests and the Uses of Power.* Englewood Cliffs, NJ: Prentice-Hall.

———. 1982. Personal communication.

———. 1984. *Labeling Women Deviant: Gender, Stigma, and Social Control.* New York: Random House.

**Schvaneveldt, Jay D. and Marilyn Ihinger.** 1979. "Sibling Relationships in the Family." Pp. 453–67 in *Contemporary Theories about the Family.* Vol. I, edited by Wesley R. Burr et al. New York: Free Press.

**Schwartz, Barry.** 1975. *Queuing and Waiting.* Chicago: University of Chicago Press.

**Schwebel, M.** 1982. "Effects of the Nuclear War Threat on Children and Teenagers: Implications for Professionals." *American Journal of Orthopsychiatry* 52:608–18.

**Schweinhart, Lawrence J. and David P. Weikart.** 1987. "Evidence of Problem Prevention by Early Childhood Education." Pp. 87–101 in *Social Intervention: Potential and Constraints,* edited by Klaus Hurrelmann, Franz-Xaver Kaufmann, and Friedrich Lösel. Berlin and New York: De Gruyter.

**Schwendinger, Herman and Julia Siegel Schwendinger.** 1985. *Ad-*

*olescent Subcultures and Delinquency.* New York: Praeger.

**Schwendinger, Julia R. and Herman Schwendinger.** 1983. *Rape and Inequality.* Beverly Hills, CA: Sage.

**Scott, Hilda.** 1984. *Working Your Way to the Bottom: The Feminization of Poverty.* Boston: Routledge & Kegan Paul, Pandora Press.

**Scully, Diana and Joseph Marolla.** 1984. "Convicted Rapists' Vocabulary of Motive: Excuses and Justifications." *Social Problems* 31:530–44.

———. 1985. " 'Riding the Bull at Gilley's': Convicted Rapists Describe the Rewards of Rape." *Social Problems* 32:251–63.

**Scully, G. W.** 1979. "Discrimination: The Case of Baseball." Pp. 365–87 in *Sport in Contemporary Society,* edited by D. Stanley Eitzen. New York: St. Martin's Press.

**Sears, Pauline and David Feldman.** 1966. "Teacher Interactions with Boys and Girls." *National Elementary Principal* 46:30–35.

**Seashore, Stanley E. and J. Thad Barnowe.** 1972. "Demographic and Job Factors Associated with the 'Blue Collar Blues.' " Mimeo.

**Seay, B., B. K. Alexander, and H. F. Harlow.** 1964. "Maternal Behavior of Socially Deprived Rhesus Monkeys." *Journal of Abnormal and Social Psychology* 69:345–54.

**See, Katherine O'Sullivan and William J. Wilson.** 1988. "Race and Ethnicity." Pp. 223–42 in *Handbook of Sociology,* edited by Neil J. Smelser. Beverly Hills, CA: Sage.

**Selikoff, Irving.** 1980. "The Toxicity Connection." *Time* (September 22): 63.

**Selznick, Philip.** 1948. "Foundations of the Theory of Organizations." *American Sociological Review* 13:25–35.

———. 1966. *TVA and the Grass Roots.* New York: Harper Torchbooks.

**Semler, H. Eric.** 1988. "What Technology Can Do for the Disabled." *New York Times* (June 5).

**Sennett, Richard.** 1970. *The Uses of Disorder.* New York: Vintage.

———. 1974. *The Fall of Public Man.* New York: Vintage.

**Sennett, Richard and Jonathan**

**Cobb.** 1973. *The Hidden Injuries of Class.* New York: Vintage.

**Serbin, Lisa A. and Jane M. Connor.** 1979. "Sex-Typing of Children's Play Preferences and Patterns of Cognitive Performance." *Journal of Genetic Psychology* 134:315–16.

**Serbin, Lisa A., K. D. O'Leary, R. N. Kent, and I. J. Tonick.** 1973. "A Comparison of Teacher Response to the Preacademic and Problem Behavior of Boys and Girls." *Child Development* 44:796–804.

**Serrill, Michael S.** 1985. "A Scourge Spreads Panic." *Time* (October 28): 50–52.

**Sewell, William, A. O. Haller, and G. W. Ohlendorf.** 1970. "The Educational and Early Occupational Status Attainment Process: A Replication and Revision." *American Sociological Review* 35:1014–27.

**Shaver, Phillip.** 1976. "Questions Concerning Fear of Success and Its Conceptual Relatives." *Sex Roles* 2:305–20.

**Shavit, Yossi and David L. Featherman.** 1988. "Schooling, Tracking, and Teenage Intelligence." *Sociology of Education* 61:42–51.

**Shaw, Clifford.** 1930. *The Jack-Roller.* Chicago: University of Chicago Press.

**Sheppard, Harold L. and Neal Q. Herrick.** 1972. *Where Have All the Robots Gone? Worker Dissent in the Seventies.* New York: Free Press.

**Shkilnyk, Anastasia M.** 1985. *A Poison Stronger Than Love.* New Haven, CT: Yale University Press.

**Shostak, Arthur B.** 1980. *Blue-Collar Stress.* Reading, MA: Addison-Wesley.

**Shott, Susan.** 1979. "Emotion and Social Life: A Symbolic Interactionist Analysis." *American Journal of Sociology* 84:1317–34.

**Sieber, Sam D.** 1974. "Toward a Theory of Role Accumulation." *American Sociological Review* 39 (August): 567–78.

**Silk, Leonard and Mark Silk.** 1980. *The American Establishment.* New York: Simon & Schuster.

**Simirenko, Alex.** 1972. "From Vertical to Horizontal Inequality: The Case of the Soviet Union." *Social Problems* 20:150–61.

**Simmel, Georg.** 1905/1955. *Conflict and the Web of Group Affiliations.* Kurt H. Wolff and Reinhard Bendix (eds.). New York: Free Press.

———. 1950. *The Sociology of Georg Simmel.* Kurt H. Wolff (ed.). Glencoe, IL: Free Press.

———. 1956. *Conflict and the Web of Group Affiliation.* Kurt H. Wolff (trans.). Glencoe, IL: Free Press.

**Simmons, Jerry L.** 1969. *Deviants.* Berkeley, CA: Glendessary Press.

**Simmons, Roberta G., Dale A. Blyth, Edward Van Cleave, and Diane Mitsch Bush.** 1979. "Entry into Early Adolescence: The Impact of Puberty, School Structure, and Early Dating on Self-esteem." *American Sociological Review* 44:948–67.

**Simon, Rita J.** 1975. *Women and Crime.* Lexington, MA, and London: Lexington.

———. 1979. "Arrest Statistics." Pp. 101–13 in *The Criminology of Deviant Women,* edited by Freda Adler and Rita James Simon. Boston: Houghton Mifflin.

**Simonds, Wendy.** 1988. "Confessions of Loss: Maternal Grief in 'True Story.' " *Gender & Society* 2:149–71.

**Simpson, George E. and J. Milton Yinger.** 1972. *Racial and Cultural Minorities: An Analysis of Prejudice and Discrimination.* Fourth edition. New York: Harper & Row.

**Simpson, R.** 1956. "A Modification of the Functional Theory of Stratification." *Social Forces* 35: 132–37.

**Singelmann, Joachim.** 1978. *From Agriculture to Services: The Transformation of Industrial Employment.* Beverly Hills, CA: Sage.

**Sipes, Richard G.** 1973. "War, Sports and Aggression: An Empirical Test of Two Rival Theories." *American Anthropologist* 75 (January): 64–86.

**Sjoquist, David.** 1971. "Property Crime as an Economic Phenomenon." Ph.D. dissertation, University of Minnesota.

**Skelly, Florence R.** 1978. "Emerging Values of the Young Worker." Talk given at the 28th annual meeting, the Seagram Family Association, La Costa Hotel, California, April 4.

**Sklair, Leslie.** 1973. *Organized Knowledge.* St. Albans, Herts: Paladin.

**Skocpol, Theda.** 1979. *States and Social Revolutions.* New York: Cambridge University Press.

———. 1980. "Political Response to Capitalist Crises: Neo-Marxist Theories of the State and the New Deal." *Politics and Society* 10:155–201.

**Smelser, Neil J.** 1963. *Theory of Collective Behavior.* New York: Free Press. Originally published 1962.

**Smith, Adam.** 1776/1976. *The Wealth of Nations.* New York: Oxford University Press.

**Smith, Anthony.** 1980. *The Geopolitics of Information: How Western Culture Dominates the World.* New York: Oxford University Press.

**Smith, Douglas A. and Christy A. Visher.** 1980. "Sex and Involvement in Deviance/Crime: A Quantitative Review of the Empirical Literature." *American Sociological Review* 45:691–701.

**Smith, G.** 1975. "Leisure, Recreation and Delinquency." Master's thesis, Department of Anthropology and Sociology, University of Queensland.

**Smith, Herbert L.** 1986. "Overeducation and Underemployment: An Agnostic Review." *Sociology of Education* 59:85–99.

**Smith, James P. and Finis Welch.** 1978. *Race Differences in Earnings: A Survey and New Evidence.* Santa Monica, CA: Rand Corporation.

**Smith, Michael D.** 1979. "Hockey Violence: A Test of the Violent Subculture Hypothesis." *Social Problems* 27 (December): 235–47.

**Snell, Bradford.** 1979. "American Ground Transport." Pp. 241–66 in *The Urban Scene,* edited by Joe R. Feagin. New York: Random House.

**Snow, David A., E. Burke Rocheford, Jr., Steven K. Worden, and Robert D. Benford.** 1986. "Frame Alignment Processes, Micromobilization, and Movement Participation." *American Sociological Review* 51:464–81.

**Snow, David A., Louis A. Zurcher, Jr., and Sheldon Ekland-Olson.** 1980. "Social Networks and Social Movements: A Microstructural Approach to Differential Recruitment." *American Sociological Review* 45:787–801.

**Snyder, David, Mark D. Hayward, and Paula M. Hudis.** 1979. "The Location of Change in the Sexual Structure of Occupations, 1950–1970: Insights from Labor Market Segmentation Theory." *American Journal of Sociology* 84:706–17.

**Snyder, David and Charles Tilly.** 1972. "Hardship and Collective Violence in France." *American Sociological Review* 37 (October): 520–32.

**Snyder, Eldon E. and Elmer Spreitzer.** 1978. *Social Aspects of Sport.* Englewood Cliffs, NJ: Prentice-Hall.

**Sokoloff, Natalie.** 1980. *Between Money and Love: The Dialectics of Women, Home and Market Work.* New York: Praeger.

**Soldo, Beth J. and Emily M. Agree.** 1988. "America's Elderly." *Population Bulletin* 43:1–51.

**Soref, Michael.** 1976. "Social Class and a Division of Labor within the Corporate Elite." *Sociological Quarterly* 17:360–68.

**Sorenson, Robert C.** 1973. *Adolescent Sexuality in Contemporary America.* New York: World.

**South, Scott J. and Katherine Trent.** 1988. "Sex Ratios and Women's Roles: A Cross-National Analysis." *American Journal of Sociology* 93:1096–115.

**Spanier, Graham and Linda Thompson.** 1984. *Parting.* Beverly Hills, CA: Sage.

**Spector, Malcolm and John I. Kitsuse.** 1973. "Social Problems: A Re-formulation." *Social Problems* 21:145–59.

———. 1977. *Constructing Social Problems.* Menlo Park, CA: Cummings.

**Speiglman, Richard.** 1977. "Prison Drugs, Psychiatry, and the State." Pp. 149–71 in *Corrections and Punishment,* edited by David F. Greenberg. Beverly Hills, CA: Sage.

**Spengler, Oswald.** 1945. *The Decline of the West.* 2 vols. New York: Knopf.

**Spiegel, J.** 1971. *Transactions.* New York: Science House.

**Spitz, Rene A.** 1972. "Hospitalism: An Inquiry into the Genesis of Psychiatric Conditions in Early Childhood." (Originally copyrighted 1945 and 1946.) Pp. 202–23 in *Influences on Human Development,* edited by Urie Bronfenbrenner. Hinsdale, IL: Dryden Press.

**Spreitzer, Elmer and Eldon E. Snyder.** 1975. "The Psychosocial Functions of Sport as Perceived by the General Population." *International Review of Sport Sociology* 3–4:87–93.

**Sprey, Jetse.** 1969. "The Family as a System in Conflict." *Journal of Marriage and the Family* 31 (November): 722–31.

**Stack, Carol B.** 1974. *All Our Kin: Strategies for Survival in a Black Community.* New York: Harper Colophon.

**Star, Susan Leigh.** 1988. "Introduction: The Sociology of Science and Technology." *Social Problems* 35:197–203.

**Stark, Rodney.** 1972. "The Economics of Piety: Religious Commitment and Social Class." Pp. 483–503 in *Issues in Social Inequality,* edited by Gerald Thielbar and Saul Feldman. Boston: Little, Brown.

**Stark, Rodney and William Sims Bainbridge.** 1980. "Networks of Faith: Interpersonal Bonds and Recruitment to Cults and Sects." *American Journal of Sociology* 85: 1376–95.

———. 1985. *The Future of Religion: Secularization, Revival, and Cult Formation.* Berkeley: University of California Press.

**Starr, Bernard D. and Marcella Bakur Weiner.** 1980. *The Starr and Weiner Report on Sex and Sexuality in the Mature Years.* New York: Paddington.

**Starr, Paul.** 1982. *The Social Transformation of American Medicine.* New York: Basic Books.

**Steffensmeier, Darrel J.** 1978. "Crime and the Contemporary Woman." *Social Forces* 57:566–84.

**Stein, Peter J.** 1976. *Single.* Englewood Cliffs, NJ: Prentice-Hall.

**Steinberg, Ronnie.** 1987. "Radical Challenges in a Liberal World: The Mixed Success of Comparable Worth." *Gender & Society* 1:466–75.

**Steinberg, Stephen.** 1981. *The Ethnic Myth: Race, Ethnicity and Class in America.* New York: Atheneum.

**Steinmetz, Suzanne K.** 1971. "Occupation and Physical Punishment: A Response to Straus." *Journal of Marriage and the Family,* 33 (November): 664–66.

———. 1974. "Occupational Environment in Relation to Physical Punishment and Dogmatism." Pp. 166–79 in *Violence in the Family,* edited by Suzanne K. Steinmetz and Murray A. Straus. New York: Dodd, Mead.

**Steinmetz, Suzanne K. and Murray A. Straus (eds.).** 1974. *Violence in the Family.* New York: Harper & Row. (Originally published by Dodd, Mead, 1974.)

**Stephens, John D.** 1979. "Class Formation and Class Consciousness: A Theoretical and Empirical Analysis with Reference to Britain and Sweden." *British Journal of Sociology* 30:389–414.

**Stephens, William N.** 1963. *The Family in Cross-Cultural Perspective.* New York: Holt, Rinehart and Winston.

**Stern, Daniel.** 1977. *The First Relationship: Infant and Mother.* Cambridge, MA: Harvard University Press.

**Stern, Philip M.** 1972. "Uncle Sam's Welfare Program for the Rich." *New York Times Magazine* (April 16).

———. 1988. *The Best Congress Money Can Buy.* New York: Pantheon.

**Sternglanz, Sarah H. and Lisa A. Serbin.** 1974. "Sex Role Stereotyping in Children's Television Programs." *Developmental Psychology* 10:710–15.

**Stevens, William K.** 1989. "Racial Differences Found in Care Heart Patients Obtain at Hospitals." *New York Times* (January 13): A1, D18.

**Stigler, Stephen M.** 1986. *The History of Statistics: The Measurement of Uncertainty Before 1900.* Cambridge, MA: Belknap Press.

**Stinchcombe, Arthur L.** 1963. "Some Empirical Consequences of the Davis-Moore Theory of Stratification." *American Sociological Review* 28:805–08.

**Stoller, Eleanor Palo.** 1983. "Parental Caregiving by Adult Children." *Journal of Marriage and the Family* 45:851–58.

Straus, Murray A. 1971. "Some Social Antecedents of Physical Punishment: A Linkage Theory Interpretation." *Journal of Marriage and the Family* 33 (November): 658–63.

———. 1976. "Sexual Inequality, Cultural Norms, and Wife-Beating." *Victimology* 1:54–76.

———. 1977–1978. "Wife Beating: How Common and Why?" *Victimology* 2:443–58.

———. 1979. "Family Violence Research Program." University of New Hampshire. Mimeo.

Straus, Murray A. and Richard J. Gelles. 1986. "Societal Change and Change in Family Violence from 1975 to 1985 as Revealed by Two National Surveys." *Journal of Marriage and the Family* 48:465–79.

Straus, Murray A., Richard J. Gelles, and Suzanne K. Steinmetz. 1979. *Behind Closed Doors: Violence in the American Family.* Garden City, NY: Doubleday/Anchor.

Stryker, Sheldon. 1980. *Symbolic Interactionism: A Social Structural Version.* Menlo Park, CA: Benjamin/Cummings.

Sudnow, David. 1967. *Passing On: The Social Organization of Dying.* Englewood Cliffs, NJ: Prentice-Hall.

Sullerot, Evelyn. 1971. *Woman, Society and Change.* New York: World University Library.

Sullivan, Ronald. 1985a. "AIDS: Bellevue Tries to Cope with Disease It Cannot Cure." *New York Times* (December 23): A1, B8.

———. 1985b. "State to Propose Centers for AIDS." *New York Times* (December 24): A1, B2.

Sullivan, Walter. 1979. "A Tough New Drive on Births in China." *New York Times* (October 10): C1.

Surface, Bill. 1974. "Pro Football: Is It Getting Too Dirty? *Reader's Digest* (November): 151–54.

Sutherland, Edwin H. 1937. *The Professional Thief.* Chicago: University of Chicago Press.

———. 1949/1983. *White Collar Crime: The Uncut Version.* New Haven, CT: Yale University Press.

Sutherland, Edwin H. and Donald R. Cressey. 1978. *Criminology.* New York: Lippincott.

Suttles, Gerald D. 1972. *The Social Construction of Communities.* Chicago: University of Chicago Press.

———. 1984. "The Cumulative Texture of Local Urban Culture." *American Journal of Sociology* 90:283–304.

Swanson, Guy E. 1980. "A Basis of Authority and Identity in Post-Industrial Society." Pp. 190–217 in *Identity and Authority: Explorations in the Theory of Society,* edited by Roland Robertson and Burkart Holzner. New York: St. Martin's Press.

Swidler, Ann. 1979. *Organization without Authority.* Cambridge, MA: Harvard University Press.

Sykes, Gresham M. 1958. *The Society of Captives: A Study of a Maximum Security Prison.* Princeton, NJ: Princeton University Press.

———. 1978. *Criminology.* New York: Harcourt Brace Jovanovich.

Syme, S. Leonard and Lisa F. Berkman. 1981. "Social Class, Susceptibility, and Sickness." Pp. 35–44 in *The Sociology of Health and Illness,* edited by Peter Conrad and Rochelle Kern. New York: St. Martin's Press.

Szymanski, Albert. 1973. "Military Spending and Economic Stagnation." *American Journal of Sociology* 79 (July): 1–14.

Tanne, Janice Hopkins. 1985. "The Last Word on Avoiding AIDS." *New York* (October 7): 28–34.

Tavris, Carol and Carole Wade. 1984. *The Longest War.* Second edition. San Diego: Harcourt Brace Jovanovich.

Taylor, Ian. 1972. " 'Football Mad': A Speculative Sociology of Football Hooliganism." Pp. 352–77 in *Sport: Readings from a Sociological Perspective,* edited by Eric Dunning. Toronto: University of Toronto Press.

Taylor, Ian, Paul Walton, and Jock Young. 1973. *The New Criminology: For a Social Theory of Deviance.* New York: Harper & Row.

Taylor, Robert E. 1985. "Toxic-

Waste Cleanup Is Expensive and Slow and Tough to Achieve." *Wall Street Journal* (May 16): 1, 20.

Teal, D. 1971. *The Gay Militants.* New York: Stein & Day.

Temin, Carolyn Engel. 1979. "Discriminatory Sentencing of Women Offenders." Pp. 273–86 in *The Criminology of Deviant Women,* edited by Freda Adler and Rita James Simon. Boston: Houghton Mifflin.

Temple, Mark and Kenneth Polk. 1986. "A Dynamic Analysis of Educational Attainment." *Sociology of Education* 59:79–84.

Terry, R. M. 1968. "Discrimination in the Handling of Juvenile Offenders by Social-Control Agencies." *Journal of Research in Crime and Delinquency* 4:218–30.

Tesar, Delbert. 1978. "Mission-Oriented Research for Light Machinery." *Science* 201 (September): 880–87.

Thernstrom, Stephan. 1964. *Poverty and Progress: Social Mobility in a Nineteenth-Century City.* Cambridge, MA: Harvard University Press.

Thernstrom, Stephan, Ann Orlov, and Oscar Handlin (eds.). 1980. *Harvard Encyclopedia of American Ethnic Groups.* Cambridge, MA: Harvard University Press.

Thoits, Peggy A. 1983. "Multiple Identities and Psychological Well-Being: A Reformulation and Test of the Social Isolation Hypothesis." *American Sociological Review* 48 (April): 174–87.

Thomas, Melvin, E. and Michael Hughes. 1986. "The Continuing Significance of Race: A Study of Race, Class, and the Quality of Life in America, 1972–1985." *American Sociological Review* 51:830–41.

Thompson, Larry W., James N. Breckenridge, Dolores Gallagher, and James Peterson. 1984. "Effects of Bereavement on Self-perceptions of Physical Health in Elderly Widows and Widowers." *Journal of Gerontology* 39:309–14.

Thornberry, Terence P. and R. L. Christenson. 1984. "Unemployment and Criminal Involvement: An Investigation of Reciprocal

Causal Structures." *American Sociological Reviews* 47:398–411.

**Thornberry, Terence P. and Margaret Farnworth.** 1982. "Social Correlates of Criminal Involvement: Further Evidence on the Relationship between Social Status and Criminal Behavior." *American Sociological Review* 47:505–18.

**Thorne, Barrie, Cheris Kramarae, and Nancy Henley (eds.).** 1983. *Language, Gender and Society.* Rowley, MA: Newbury House.

**Thornton, Arland.** 1978. "Marital Instability Differentials and Interactions: Multivariate Contingency Table Analysis." *Sociology and Social Research* 62:570–95.

———. 1985. "Changing Attitudes toward Separation and Divorce: Causes and Consequences." *American Journal of Sociology* 90:856–872.

**Thornton, Arland, Duane F. Alwin, and Donald Camburn.** 1983. "Causes and Consequences of Sex-Role Attitudes and Attitude Change." *American Sociological Review* 48:211–27.

**Thornton, Arland and Deborah Freedman.** 1982. "Changing Attitudes toward Marriage and Single Life." *Family Planning Perspectives* 14:297–303.

**Thurow, Lester.** 1975. *Generating Inequality.* New York: Basic Books.

———. 1984. "The Disappearance of the Middle Class: It's Not Just Demographics." *New York Times* (February 5): F3.

———. 1985. "The Dishonest Economy." *The New York Review* XXXII (November 21): 34–37.

**Tienda, Marta, Shelley A. Smith, and Vilma Ortiz.** 1987. "Industrial Restructuring, Gender Segregation, and Sex Differences in Earnings." *American Sociological Review* 52:195–210.

**Tierney, John.** 1986. "The Population Crisis Revisited." *Wall Street Journal* (January 20): 16.

**Tilly, Charles.** 1975. "Revolution and Collective Violence." Pp. 483–555 in *Handbook of Political Science.* Vol. 3: *Macro Political Theory,* edited by F. Greenstein and N. Polsky. Reading, MA: Addison-Wesley.

**Tilly, Charles, L. Tilly, and R.**

**Tilly.** 1975. *The Rebellious Century: 1830–1930.* Cambridge, MA: Harvard University Press.

**Tilly, Louise.** 1981. "Paths of Proletarianization: Organization of Production, Sexual Division of Labor, and Women's Collective Action." *Signs* 7:400–17.

*Time.* 1978. "The American Farmer." (November 6): 95.

———. 1989. "Planet of the Year." *Time* (January 2): 65.

**Tinto, Vincent.** 1978. "Does Schooling Matter? A Retrospective Assessment." Pp. 201–35 in Lee S. Shulman (ed.), *Review of Research in Education* 5, 1977. Itasca, IL: Peacock.

**Titmuss, Richard M.** 1971. *The Gift Relationship.* New York: Random House.

**Tittle, Charles R. and Wayne J. Villemez.** 1977. "Social Class and Criminality." *Social Forces* 56:475–502.

**Tittle, Charles R., Wayne J. Villemez, and Douglas A. Smith.** 1978. "The Myth of Social Class and Criminality." *American Sociological Review* 43:643–56.

**Toby, Jackson.** 1981. "Deterrence without Punishment." *Criminology* 19:195–209.

**Tocqueville, Alexis de.** 1835/1954. *Democracy in America.* Vols. 1 and 2. New York: Vintage.

———. 1856/1955. *The Old Regime and the French Revolution.* Stuart Gilbert (trans.). Garden City, NY: Doubleday.

**Toffler, Alvin.** 1980. *The Third Wave.* New York: Morrow.

**Tolbert, Charles M. II.** 1982 "Industrial Segmentation and Men's Career Mobility." *American Sociological Review* 47:457–77.

**Tomeh, A. K.** 1964. "Informal Group Participation and Residential Pattern." *American Journal of Sociology* 70 (July): 28–35.

**Tönnies, Ferdinand.** 1887/1957. *Community and Society.* New York: Harper Torchbooks.

**Toren, Nina and Vered Kraus.** 1987. "The Effects of Minority Size on Women's Position in Academia." *Social Forces* 65:1090–100.

**Torrens, Paul R.** 1978. *The American Health Care System: Issues and Problems.* St. Louis, MO: Mosby.

**Touraine, Alain.** 1974. *The Academic System in American Society.* New York: McGraw-Hill.

**Toynbee, Arnold J.** 1947. *A Study of History.* 10 vols. Oxford, England: Oxford University Press.

**Travers, Jeffrey and Stanley Milgram.** 1969. "An Experimental Study of the Small World Problem." *Sociometry* 32:425–43.

**Treas, Judith.** 1977. "Family Support Systems for the Aged." *The Gerontologist* 17:486–91.

———. 1987. "The Effect of Women's Labor Force Participation on the Distribution of Income in the United States." Pp. 259–88 in *Annual Review of Sociology,* edited by W. Richard Scott and James F. Short, Jr. Palo Alto, CA: Annual Reviews.

**Treiman, Donald J.** 1977. *Occupational Prestige in Comparative Perspective.* New York: Academic Press.

**Treiman, Donald J. and Heidi I. Hartmann (eds.).** 1981. *Women, Work, and Wages: Equal Pay for Jobs of Equal Value.* Washington, DC: National Academy Press.

**Treiman, Donald J. and Patricia A. Roos.** 1983. "Sex and Earnings in Industrial Society: A Nine-Nation Comparison." *American Journal of Sociology* 89:612–50.

**Treiman, Donald J. and Kermit Terrell.** 1975. "The Process of Status Attainment in the United States and Great Britain." *American Journal of Sociology* 81 (November): 563–83.

**Tresemer, David.** 1974. "Fear of Success: Popular, but Unproven." *Psychology Today* (March): 82–85.

———. 1976. "Do Women Fear Success?" *Signs* 1 (summer): 863–74.

**Tripp, Clarence A.** 1979. "An Interview by Philip Nobile." *New York* (June 25): 36–41.

**Trippett, Frank.** 1985. "A Gala with a Grim Side." *Time* (September 30): 30, 32.

**Troll, Lillian, Sheila Miller, and Robert Atchley.** 1979. *Families in Later Life.* Belmont, CA: Wadsworth.

**Trow, Martin.** 1966. "The Second Transformation of American Secondary Education." Pp. 437–49 in *Class, Status and Power,* edited by

Reinhard Bendix and Seymour M. Lipset. New York: Free Press.

**Tullock, Gordon.** 1974. "Does Punishment Deter Crime?" *The Public Interest* 36:103–11.

**Tumin, Melvin M.** 1953. "Some Principles of Stratification: A Critical Analysis." *American Sociological Review* 18:387–94.

**Turkle, Sherry.** 1984. *The Second Self: Computers and the Human Spirit.* New York: Simon & Schuster.

**Turnbull, Colin M.** 1972. *The Mountain People.* New York: Simon & Schuster.

**Turner, Bryan S.** 1983. *Religion and Social Theory.* London: Heinemann.

**Turner, Edward T.** 1968. "The Effects of Viewing College Football, Basketball and Wrestling on the Elicited Aggressive Responses of Male Spectators." Pp. 325–28 in *Contemporary Psychology of Sport,* edited by Gerald Kenyon. Chicago: The Athletic Institute.

**Turner, Jonathan.** 1978. *The Structure of Sociological Theory.* Revised edition. Homewood, IL: Dorsey Press.

**Turner, Ralph H.** 1960. "Modes of Social Ascent through Education: Sponsored and Contest Mobility." *American Sociological Review* 25:121–39.

———. 1976. "The Real Self: From Institution to Impulse." *American Journal of Sociology* 81:989–1016.

**Turner, Ralph and Lewis Killian.** 1987. *Collective Behavior.* Englewood Cliffs, NJ: Prentice-Hall.

**Tyack, David B. and Myra H. Strober.** 1981. "Women and Men in the Schools: A History of the Sexual Structuring of Educational Employment." Report presented to the National Institute of Education, Washington, DC.

**Tyler, Tom R. and Kathleen M. McGraw.** 1983. "The Threat of Nuclear War: Risk Interpretation and Behavioral Response." *Journal of Social Issues* 39:25–40.

**Underwood, J.** 1980. "The Writing Is on the Wall." *Sports Illustrated* 21:36–71.

**United Nations, Department of Economic and Social Affairs.** 1972. *Demographic Yearbook, 1971.* New York: United Nations.

**U.S. Bureau of the Census.** 1975. *Historical Statistics of the United States, Colonial Times to 1970.* Bicentennial edition, Part 2. Washington, DC: U.S. Government Printing Office.

———. 1980. *Statistical Abstract of the United States: 1980.* Washington, DC: U.S. Government Printing Office.

———. 1981. *Statistical Abstract of the United States: 1981.* Washington, DC: U.S. Government Printing Office.

———. 1982a. *Statistical Abstract of the United States: 1982–83.* Washington, DC: U.S. Government Printing Office.

———. 1982b. Money Income of Households, Families and Persons in the United States: 1980. *Current Population Reports,* Series P–60, No. 132. Washington, DC: U.S. Government Printing Office.

———. 1983. Population Profile of the United States: 1982. *Current Population Reports,* Series P–23, No. 130. Washington, DC: U.S. Government Printing Office.

———. 1984. *Statistical Abstract of the United States: 1985.* Washington, DC: U.S. Government Printing Office.

———. 1985a. *Statistical Abstract of the United States 1986.* Washington, DC: U.S. Government Printing Office.

———. 1985b. Money Income and Poverty Status of Families and Persons in the United States: 1984. *Current Population Reports,* Series P–60, No. 149. Washington, DC: U.S. Government Printing Office.

———. 1985c. After Tax Money Income Estimates of Households: 1983. *Current Population Reports,* Series P–23, No. 143. Washington, DC: U.S. Government Printing Office.

———. 1985d. Households, Families, Marital Status, and Living Arrangements: March 1985 (Advance Report). *Current Population Reports,* Series P–20, No. 402. Washington, DC: U.S. Government Printing Office.

———. 1986a. Current Population Reports, Series P–20, No. 411, *Household and Family Characteristics: March 1985.* Washington, DC: U.S. Government Printing Office.

———. 1986b. Current Population Reports, Series P–25, No. 968, *Projections of the Number of Households and Families: 1986–2000.* Washington, DC: U.S. Government Printing Office.

———. 1987a. *Statistical Abstract of the United States 1988.* Washington, DC: U.S. Government Printing Office.

———. 1987b. *Fertility of American Women: June 1986.* Current Population Reports. P–20, No. 421 (June). Washington, DC: U.S. Government Printing Office.

———. 1987c. *Who's Minding the Kids? Child Care Arrangements: Winter 1984–85.* Current Population Reports, P–70, Household Economic Studies. Washington, DC: U.S. Government Printing Office.

———. 1988. *Who's Helping Out: Support Networks among American Families.* Washington, DC: U.S. Bureau of the Census.

———. 1989a. *Statistical Abstract of the United States: 1989.* Washington, DC: U.S. Government Printing Office.

———. 1989b. Current Population Reports, Series P–60, No. 162, *Money Income of Households, Families and Persons in the United States: 1987.* Washington, DC: U.S. Government Printing Office.

**U.S. Department of Commerce.** 1977. *Social Indicators 1976.* Washington, DC: U.S. Government Printing Office.

———. 1980. *Social Indicators III: Selected Data on Social Conditions and Trends in the United States.* Washington, DC: U.S. Government Printing Office.

———. 1986. "Elementary and High School Enrollment Down." *News* (January 9). Washington, DC: Bureau of the Census.

———. 1988a. "Median Family Income Up, No Significant Change in Poverty Rate." *News* (August 31). Washington, DC: U.S. Bureau of the Census.

———. 1988b. "About Half of the U.S. Population Lives in Metro Areas of a Million or More, Census Bureau Reports." *News* (September 30): 1–6.

———. 1988c. "Midwest Population Begins Growing Again, Census Bureau Reports." *News* (December 30): 1–3.

———. 1989. "U.S. Population Totals 246.9 Million as 1989 Begins, Census Bureau Says." *News* (January 1): 1–2.

**U.S. Department of Health and Human Services.** 1983. Advance Report, Final Divorce Statistics, 1980. *Monthly Vital Statistics,* Report 32 (June): 1. Washington, DC: National Center for Health Statistics.

———. 1985. Births, Marriages, Divorces, and Deaths for 1984. *Monthly Vital Statistics,* Report 33 (March 26): 1. Washington, DC: National Center for Health Statistics.

**U.S. Department of Health, Education and Welfare.** 1973. *Work in America.* MA: MIT Press.

**U.S. Department of Justice.** 1984. *Uniform Crime Reports: Crime in the United States.* Washington, DC: U.S. Government Printing Office.

——— 1987. *Uniform Crime Reports for the United States: 1987.* Washington, DC: Federal Bureau of Investigation.

**U.S. Department of Labor.** 1977. *Dictionary of Occupational Titles.* Washington, DC: U.S. Government Printing Office.

———. 1979. The Job Outlook for College Graduates through 1990. *Occupational Outlook Quarterly.* (winter): 2–7.

———. 1985. *Dictionary of Occupational Titles.* Washington, DC: U.S. Government Printing Office.

———. 1986. *Supplement to the Dictionary of Occupational Titles.* Washington, DC: U.S. Government Printing Office.

———. 1987. *Occupational Outlook Quarterly* 31 (fall).

**U.S. Department of Labor, Bureau of Labor Statistics.** 1986a. *Employment and Earnings* (January). Washington, DC: U.S. Government Printing Office.

———. 1986b. *Employment and Earnings* (February). Washington, DC: U.S. Government Printing Office.

———. 1989a. *Employment and Earnings.* 36 (January). Washington, DC: U.S. Government Printing Office.

———. 1989b. *Employment and Earnings.* 36 (February). Washington, DC: U.S. Government Printing Office.

———. 1989c. *Employment and Earnings.* 36 (March). Washington, DC: U.S. Government Printing Office.

**U.S. Senate, Special Committee on Aging.** 1988a. *Developments in Aging: 1987.* Vol. 1. Washington, DC: U.S. Government Printing Office.

———. 1988b. *Developments in Aging: 1987.* Vol. 3 (February 29). Washington, DC: U.S. Government Printing Office.

**Useem, Michael.** 1978. "Inner Group of the American Capitalist Class." *Social Problems* 25 (February): 225–40.

———. 1979. "The Social Organization of the American Business Elite and Participation of Corporation Directors in the Governance of American Institutions." *American Sociological Review* 44 (August): 553–72.

———. 1980. "Corporations and the Corporate Elite." Pp. 41–77 in *Annual Review of Sociology,* edited by Alex Inkeles, Neil J. Smelser, and Ralph H. Turner. Palo Alto, CA: Annual Reviews.

———. 1984. *The Inner Circle: Large Corporations and the Rise of Business Political Activity in the U.S. and U.K.* New York: Oxford University Press.

**Utley, Robert M.** 1963. *The Last Days of the Sioux Nation.* New Haven, CT: Yale University Press.

**Valentine, Charles A.** 1971. "Deficit, Difference, and Bicultural Models of Afro-American Behavior." *Harvard Educational Review* 41:137–57.

**Van den Berghe, Peter.** 1963. "Dialectic and Functionalism: Toward a Theoretical Synthesis." *American Sociological Review* 28:695–705.

**Van den Haag, Ernest.** 1975. *On Punishing Criminals: Concerning an Old and Very Painful Question.* New York: Basic Books.

**Vanfossen, Beth E.** 1979. *The Structure of Social Inequality.* Boston: Little, Brown.

**Vanfossen, Beth E., James D.** Jones, and Joan Z. Spade. 1987. "Curriculum Tracking and Status Maintenance." *Sociology of Education* 60:104–22.

**Vanneman, Reeve D.** 1980. "U.S. and British Perceptions of Class." *American Journal of Sociology* 85:769–90.

**Veblen, Thorstein.** 1899/1967. *The Theory of the Leisure Class.* New York: Penguin.

**Velez, William.** 1985. "Finishing College: The Effects of College Type." *Sociology of Education* 58:191–200.

**Verba, Sidney and Norman Nie.** 1972. *Participation in America: Political Democracy and Social Equality.* New York: Harper & Row.

**Vernon, Raymond.** 1977. *Storm over the Multinationals: The Real Issues.* Cambridge, MA: Harvard University Press.

**Veroff, Joseph, Elizabeth Douvan, and Richard Kulka.** 1981. *Mental Health in America: Patterns of Help-Seeking from 1957–1976.* New York: Basic Books.

**Vidich, Arthur J. and Joseph Bensman.** 1958. *Small Town in Mass Society.* Princeton, NJ: Princeton University Press.

**Vogel, S. R., I. K. Broverman, D. M. Broverman, F. E. Clarkson, and P. S. Rosenkrantz.** 1970. "Maternal Employment and Perception of Sex Roles among College Students." *Developmental Psychology* 3:384–91.

**Voss, Harwin L.** 1966. "Socioeconomic Status and Reported Delinquent Behavior." *Social Problems* 13:314–24.

**Wade, Alice.** 1986. *Social Security Area Population Projections, 1986.* Actuarial Study No. 97. SSA Pub. No. 11–11544 (October). Washington, DC: Office of the Actuary, Social Security Administration.

**Wade, Nicholas.** 1976. "IQ and Heredity: Suspicion of Fraud Beclouds Classic Experiment." *Science* 194 (November 26): 916–19.

**Waite, Linda J. and Sue E. Berryman.** 1986. "Job Stability among Young Women: A Comparison of Traditional and Nontraditional Occupations." *American Journal of Sociology* 92:568–95.

**Waite, Linda J., Gus Haggstrom, and David Kanouse.** 1985. "The Consequences of Parenthood for the Marital Stability of Young Adults." *American Sociological Review* 50:850–57.

**Waldron, Ingrid.** 1981. "Why Do Women Live Longer than Men?" Pp. 45–66 in *The Sociology of Health and Illness,* edited by Peter Conrad and Rochelle Kern. New York: St. Martin's Press.

**Wall, Wendy L.** 1984. "Life on the Land: New Breed of Farmers Focus on Bottom Line and Defy Traditions." *Wall Street Journal* (November 13): 1, 19.

**Wallace, Michael and Arne L. Kalleberg.** 1982. "Industrial Transformation and the Decline of Craft: The Decomposition of Skill in the Printing Industry, 1931–1978." *American Sociological Review* 47:307–24.

**Wallace, Ruth A. and Alison Wolf.** 1980. *Contemporary Sociological Theory.* Englewood Cliffs, NJ: Prentice-Hall.

**Wallace, Walter L.** 1971. *The Logic of Science in Sociology.* Chicago: Aldine/Atherton.

**Wallerstein, Immanuel.** 1974. *The Modern World-System.* New York: Academic Press.

**Wallerstein, Judith S. and Joan Berlin Kelly.** 1980. *Surviving the Breakup: How Children and Parents Cope with Divorce.* New York: Basic Books.

**Wallis, Claudia.** 1985. "Children Having Children." *Time* (December 9): 78–90.

**Walsh, Edward J.** 1981. "Resource Mobilization and Citizen Protest in Communities around Three Mile Island." *Social Problems* 29:1–21.

———. 1983. "Three Mile Island: Meltdown of Democracy?" *Bulletin of the Atomic Scientists* 39:57–60.

**Walsh, Edward J. and Rex H. Warland.** 1983. "Social Movement Involvement in the Wake of a Nuclear Accident: Activists and Free Riders in the TMI Area." *American Sociological Review* 48:764–80.

**Walsh, M. R.** 1977. *Doctors Wanted: No Women Need Apply.* New Haven, CT: Yale University Press.

**Walters, Pamela Barnhouse.** 1984. "Occupational and Labor Market Effects on Secondary and Postsecondary Educational Expansion in the United States: 1922 to 1979." *American Sociological Review* 49:659–71.

**Walum, Laurel Richardson.** 1977. *The Dynamics of Sex and Gender: A Sociological Perspective.* Chicago: Rand McNally.

**Warner, Sam Bass.** 1968. *The Private City.* Philadelphia: University of Pennsylvania Press.

**Warner, W. Lloyd, Marchia Meeker, and Kenneth Eels.** 1949. *Social Class in America.* Chicago: Science Research Associates.

**Warren, Bruce L.** 1970. "Socioeconomic Achievement and Religion: The American Case." Pp. 130–55 in *Social Stratification,* edited by Edward O. Laumann. Indianapolis: Bobbs-Merrill.

**Warren, Carol A.** 1974. *Identity and Community in the Gay World.* New York: Wiley.

**Watson, James D.** 1968. *The Double Helix.* New York: Atheneum.

**Wax, Murray L. and Rosalie Wax.** 1971. "Cultural Deprivation as an Educational Ideology." Pp. 127–39 in *The Culture of Poverty: A Critique,* edited by Eleanor B. Leacock. New York: Simon & Schuster.

**Webb, Eugene J., Donald T. Campbell, Richard D. Schwartz, and Lee Sechrest.** 1966. *Unobtrusive Measures: Nonreactive Research in the Social Sciences.* Chicago: Rand McNally.

**Weber, Max.** 1904/1958. *The Protestant Ethic and the Spirit of Capitalism.* New York: Scribner's.

———. 1920/1968. *Economy and Society.* Gunther Ross (ed.). New York: Bedminster.

———. 1922/1963. *The Sociology of Religion.* Boston: Beacon.

———. 1925a/1958. *From Max Weber: Essays in Sociology.* Hans Gerth and C. Wright Mills (eds.). New York: Oxford University Press.

———. 1925b/1947. *The Theory of Social and Economic Organization.* Glencoe, IL: Free Press.

———. 1978. *Economy and Society.* Guenther Roth and Claus Wittich (eds.). Berkeley: University of California Press.

**Webster, Bayard.** 1984. "Deadly Tide of Plastic Waste Threatens World's Oceans and Aquatic Life." *New York Times* (December 25): 33–34.

**Weeks, John R.** 1981. *Population: An Introduction to Concepts and Issues.* Second edition. Belmont, CA: Wadsworth.

**Weil, Frederick D.** 1985. "The Variable Effects of Education on Liberal Attitudes: A Comparative-Historical Analysis of Anti-Semitism Using Public Opinion Survey Data." *American Sociological Review* 50:458–74.

**Weitzman, Lenore J.** 1979. *Sex Role Socialization.* Palo Alto, CA: Mayfield.

———. 1985. *The Divorce Revolution: The Unexpected Social and Economic Consequences for Women and Children in America.* New York: Free Press.

**Welch, Mary Scott.** 1980. *Networking: The Great New Way for Women to Get Ahead.* New York: Harcourt Brace Jovanovich.

**Wellman, Barry.** 1983. "Network Analysis: Some Basic Principles." Pp. 155–200 in *Sociological Theory 1983,* edited by Randall Collins. San Francisco: Jossey–Bass.

**Wentworth, William M.** 1980. *Context and Understanding: An Inquiry into Socialization Theory.* New York: Elsevier.

**West, Donald J.** 1983. "Sex Offenses and Offending." Pp. 1–30 in *Crime and Justice: An Annual Review of Research,* edited by Michael Tonry and Norval Morris. Chicago: University of Chicago Press.

**West, P. and L. C. Merriam, Jr.** 1970. "Outdoor Recreation and Family Cohesiveness: A Research Proposal." *Journal of Leisure Research* 2:251–59.

**Westoff, Charles F.** 1978. "Marriage and Fertility in the Developed Countries." *Scientific American* 239:51–57.

**Westoff, Charles F., G. Calot, and A. D. Foster.** 1983. "Teenage Fertility in Developed Nations." *Family Planning Perspectives* 15:105

**Whalley, Peter.** 1984. "Deskilling Engineers? The Labor Process, Labor Markets, and Labor Segmentation." *Social Problems* 32:117–32.

**Wharton, Amy S. and James N. Baron.** 1987. "So Happy Together? The Impact of Gender Segregation on Men at Work." *American Sociological Review* 52:574–87.

**Wheeler, Stanton, David Weisburd, and Nancy Bode.** 1982. "Sentencing the White-Collar Offender: Rhetoric and Reality." *American Sociological Review* 47:641–59.

**Whichard, Obie.** 1981. "U.S. Direct Investment Abroad in 1980." *Survey of Current Business* (August): 20–27.

**Whicker, Marcia Lynn and Jennie Jacobs Kronenfeld.** 1986. *Sex Role Changes: Technology, Politics, and Policy.* New York: Praeger.

**Whisman, Vera.** 1986. "The Social Construction of Homosexual Identity." Paper presented at the annual meeting of the American Sociological Association, New York.

**White, Burton L., Barbara T. Kaban, and Jane S. Attanucci.** 1979. *The Origins of Human Competence.* Lexington, MA: Heath.

**White, Lynn, Jr.** 1964. *Medieval Technology and Social Change.* New York: Oxford University Press.

**White, Lynn, Jr. and Alan Booth.** 1985. "The Quality and Stability of Remarriages: The Role of Step-Children." *American Sociological Review* 50:689–98.

**White, R. Clyde.** 1955. "Social Class Differences in the Use of Leisure." *American Journal of Sociology* 61:145–50.

**Whiting, Beatrice and Carolyn Pope Edwards.** 1973. "A Cross-Cultural Analysis of Sex Differences in the Behavior of Children Aged 3 through 11." *Journal of Social Psychology* 91:171–88.

**Whitt, J. Allen.** 1980. "Can Capitalists Organize Themselves?" *Insurgent Sociologist* 9:51–59.

**Wideman, John Edgar.** 1984. *Brothers and Keepers.* New York: Holt, Rinehart and Winston.

**Wilensky, H. L.** 1961. "Orderly Careers and Social Participation: The Impact of Work History on Social Integration in the Middle Mass." *American Sociological Review* 26:521–39.

**Wiley, D. E.** 1976. "Another Hour, Another Day: Quantity of Schooling, a Potent Path for Policy." Pp. 225–65 in *Schooling and Achievement in American Society,* edited by W.

H. Sewell et al. New York: Academic Press.

**Will, Jerrie A.** 1978. "Neonatal Cuddliness and Maternal Handling Patterns in the First Month of Life." *Dissertation Abstracts International* 38(12–B):6128–29.

**Willard, Myra.** 1967. *History of the White Australia Policy to 1920.* London: Melbourne University Press.

**Williams, Jay R. and Martin Gold.** 1972. "From Delinquent Behavior to Official Delinquency." *Social Problems* 20 (fall): 209–29.

**Williams, Raymond.** 1976a. *Keywords: A Vocabulary of Culture and Society.* New York: Oxford University Press.

———. 1976b. "Developments in the Sociology of Culture." *Sociology* 10:497–506.

**Williams, Robin M., Jr.** 1960. *American Society: A Sociological Interpretation.* New York: Knopf.

———. 1966. "Some Further Comments on Chronic Controversies." *American Journal of Sociology* 71:717–21.

**Williams, T. H.** 1972. "Educational Aspirations: Longitudinal Evidence on Their Development in Canadian Youth." *Sociology of Education* 45:107–33.

**Willie, Charles V.** 1979. *Caste and Class Controversy.* New York: General Hall.

**Wills, Garry.** 1988. " 'New Votuhs.' " *New York Review* (August 18): 3–5.

**Wilsnack, Richard W. and Randall Cheloha.** 1987. "Women's Roles and Problem Drinking across the Lifespan." *Social Problems* 34:231–48.

**Wilson, Bryan.** 1975. *Magic and the Millennium.* Frogmore, England: Paladin.

**Wilson, Edward O.** 1975a. *Sociobiology: The New Synthesis.* Cambridge, MA: Harvard University Press.

———. 1975b. "Human Decency Is Animal." *New York Times Magazine* (October 12): 38–50.

**Wilson, James Q. and Richard J. Herrnstein.** 1987. *Crime and Human Nature.* New York: Simon & Schuster.

**Wilson, Thomas C.** 1985. "Urbanism and Tolerance: A Test of Some Hypotheses Drawn from Wirth

and Stouffer." *American Sociological Review* 50:117–23.

**Wilson, William Julius.** 1978. *The Declining Significance of Race.* Chicago: University of Chicago Press.

———. 1987. *The Truly Disadvantaged: The Inner City, the Underclass, and Public Policy.* Chicago: University of Chicago Press.

**Wimberley, Dale W.** 1984. "Socioeconomic Deprivation and Religious Salience: A Cognitive Behavioral Approach." *Sociological Quarterly* 25:223–38.

**Winn, Marie.** 1977. *The Plug-in Drug: Television, Children and the Family.* New York: Viking.

**Wirth, Louis.** 1938. "Urbanism as a Way of Life." *American Journal of Sociology* 44 (July): 3–24.

**Wise, Nancy B.** 1967. "Juvenile Delinquency among Middle Class Girls." Pp. 179–188 in *Middle-Class Juvenile Delinquency,* edited by Edmund W. Vaz. New York: Harper & Row.

**Witkin, Herman A. et al.** 1976. "Criminality in XYY and XXY Men." *Science* 193:547–55.

**Witmer, David R.** 1976. "Is the Value of College-Going Really Declining?" *Change* 8 (December): 46–47, 60–61.

**Wohl, Andrzej.** 1970. "Competitive Sport and Its Social Functions." *International Review of Sport Sociology* 5:117–24.

**Wolf, Deborah Coleman.** 1979. *The Lesbian Community.* Berkeley: University of California Press.

**Wolf, Wendy and Neil Fligstein.** 1971. "Sex and Authority in the Work Place: The Causes of Sexual Inequality." *American Sociological Review* 44:235–52.

**Wolfe, Tom.** 1987. *The Bonfire of the Vanities.* New York: Bantam.

**Women on Words and Images.** 1975. "Channeling Children: Sex Stereotyping in Prime Time TV." Princeton, NJ: Women on Words and Images.

**Woodrum, Eric.** 1981. "An Assessment of Japanese American Assimilation, Pluralism, and Subordination." *American Journal of Sociology* 87:157–69.

**World Almanac.** 1988. *World Almanac and Book of Facts.* New York: Pharos Books.

**World Bank.** 1984. *World Develop-*

*ment Report 1984.* Washington, DC: The World Bank.

———. 1988. *World Development Report 1988.* New York: Oxford University Press.

Wright, Erik Olin. 1978. "Race, Class, and Income Inequality." *American Journal of Sociology* 83:1368–88.

Wright, Erik Olin, Cynthia Costello, David Hachen, and Joey Sprague. 1982. "The American Class Structure." *American Sociological Review* 47:709–26.

Wright, Erik Olin and Luca Perrone. 1977. "Marxist Class Categories and Income Inequality." *American Sociological Review* 42 (February): 32–55.

Wright, J. 1976. *The Dissent of the Governed: Alienation and Democracy in America.* New York: Academic Press.

Wright, Robin. 1985. *Sacred Rage: The Crusade of Modern Islam.* New York: Simon & Schuster.

Wrong, Dennis. 1961. "The Oversocialized Conception of Man in Modern Sociology." *American Sociological Review* 26:183–93.

Wuthnow, Robert J. 1988. "Sociology of Religion." Pp.473–509 in *Handbook of Sociology,* edited by Neil J. Smelser. Beverly Hills, CA: Sage.


Yaeger, Matthew G. 1979. "Unemployment and Imprisonment." *Journal of Criminal Law and Criminology* 70:586–88.

Yankelovich, Daniel. 1981. *New Rules: Searching for Self-fulfillment in a World Turned Upside Down.* New York: Bantam.

Yankelovich, Skelly, and White Survey. 1977. "Views on Morality." *Public Opinion* (December–January): 27.

Yanowitch, Murray. 1977. *Social and Economic Inequality in the Soviet Union.* New York: Macmillan.

Yarrow, Marian Radke, Charlotte Green Schwartz, Harriet S. Murphy, and Leila Calhoun Deasy. 1955. "The Psychological Meaning of Mental Illness in the Family." *Journal of Social Issues* 11:12–24.

Yinger, J. Milton. 1977. "Counterculture and Social Change." *American Sociological Review* 42:833–53.

Young, R. M. 1971. "Darwin's Metaphor: Does Nature Select?" *The Monist* 55:442–503.


Zabin, Laurie Schwab. 1981. "The Impact of Early Use of Prescription Contraceptives on Reducing Premarital Teenage Pregnancies." *Family Planning Perspectives* 13:72–74.

Zablocki, Benjamin D. and Rosabeth Moss Kanter. 1976. "The Differentiation of Life-Styles." Pp. 269–98 in *Annual Review of Sociology,* edited by Alex Inkeles, James Coleman, and Neil Smelser. Palo Alto, CA: Annual Reviews.

Zald, Mayer N. and John D. McCarthy (eds.). 1979. *The Dynamics of Social Movements.* Cambridge, MA: Winthrop.

Zaret, David. 1981. Review of *Understanding Society* manuscript for Harper & Row.

Zaretsky, Eli. 1976. *Capitalism, the Family, and Personal Life.* New York: Harper & Row.

Zaslavsky, Victor. 1980. "Socioeconomic Inequality and Changes in Soviet Ideology." *Theory and Society* 9:383–407.

Zatz, Marjorie. 1982. Personal communication.

Zborowski, Mark. 1981. "Cultural Components in Responses to Pain." Pp. 126–38 in *The Sociology of Health and Illness,* edited by Peter Conrad and Rochelle Kern. New York: St Martin's Press.

Zeitlin, Irving M. 1967. *Marxism: A Reexamination.* New York: Van Nostrand.

Zeitlin, Maurice. 1974. "Corporate Ownership and Control: The Large Corporation and the Capitalist Class." *American Journal of Sociology* 79:1073–119.

Zelditch, Morris, Jr. 1955. "Role Differentiation in the Nuclear Family: A Comparative Study." Ch. 2 in *Family, Socialization and Interaction Process Analysis,* edited by Talcott Parsons and Robert F. Bales. New York: Free Press.

Zelnik, Melvin and John F. Kant-

ner. 1980. "Sexual Activity, Contraceptive Use and Pregnancy among Metropolitan-Area Teenagers: 1971–1979." *Family Planning Perspectives* 12:230–31, 233–37.

Ziman, John. 1976. *The Force of Knowledge.* New York: Cambridge University Press.

Zimbardo, Philip G. 1972. "Pathology of Imprisonment." *Society* 9 (April): 4–8.

Zimmer, Lynn. 1988. "Tokenism and Women in the Workplace: The Limits of Gender-Neutral Theory." *Social Problems* 35:64–77.

Zimmerman, Don H. and D. Lawrence Wieder. 1970. "Ethnomethodology and the Problem of Order: Comments on Denzin." Pp. 287–95 in *Understanding Everyday Life,* edited by Jack Douglas. Chicago: Aldine.

Zinn, Maxine Baca and D. Stanley Eitzen. 1987. *Diversity in American Families.* New York: Harper & Row.

Zonana, Victor F. 1984. "Is the U.S. Middle Class Shrinking Alarmingly? Economists Are Split." *Wall Street Journal* (June 20): 1, 27.

Zuckerman, Harriet. 1977. "Deviant Behavior and Social Control in Science." Pp. 87–138 in *Deviance and Social Change,* edited by Edward Sagarin. Beverly Hills, CA: Sage.

———. 1988. "The Sociology of Science." Pp. 511–74 in *Handbook of Sociology,* edited by Neil J. Smelser. Beverly Hills, CA: Sage.

Zuckerman, Harriet and Robert K. Merton. 1971. "Patterns of Evaluation in Science: Institutionalisation, Structure and Functions of the Referee System." *Minerva* 9:66–100.

Zukin, Sharon. 1984. *Loft Living: Culture and Capital in Urban Change.* Baltimore, MD: Johns Hopkins University Press.

Zurcher, Louis A., Jr. 1977. *The Mutable Self: A Self-concept for Social Change.* Beverly Hills, CA: Sage.

Zweigenhaft, Richard L. 1985. "Students Surveyed about Nuclear War." *Bulletin of the Atomic Scientists* (February): 26–27.

# *Acknowledgments*

## Text Credits

The following material is being reprinted with permission:

*Pages 122–123*, Quotation from Henry Kraus, *The Many and the Few*, Los Angeles: Plantin, 1947, pp. 48–54, beginning with the words, "The whistle blew," and ending with the words, "The moment tingled with expectancy."; *page 192*, Table 8.1 from Arthur L. Stinchcombe, "Some Empirical Consequences of the Davis-Moore Theory of Stratification." *American Sociological Review*, 28 (October 1963), p. 808; *page 325*, Table 13.1 from FORTUNE (August 1, 1988), pp. D3, D4. © 1988 Time Inc. All rights reserved; *page 349*, Quotation from Steve Lohr, "How Tax Evasion Has Grown," *New York Times*, March 15, 1981, pp. C1, C15. © 1981 by The New York Times Company. Reprinted by permission; *page 560*, Figure 21.4 from Alfred C. Kinsey, Wardell B. Pomeroy, Clyde E. Martin, and Paul H. Gebhard, *Sexual Behavior in the Human Female*, Philadelphia: Saunders, 1953, p. 470; *page 580*, Figure 22.4 from Loy, McPherson, Kenyon, *Sport and Social Systems*, © 1978, Addison-Wesley Publishing Co., Inc., Reading, Massachusetts. Adapted from p. 23. Reprinted with permission of the publisher.

## Photo Credits

*Pages 3, 4*, Jean-Marie Simon/Taurus; *page 8*, David M. Grossman/Photo Researchers; *page 9*, Mary Evans Picture Library/Photo Researchers; *page 11*, Culver; *pages 12, 13*, Topham/The Image Works; *page 15*, Eric Kroll/Taurus; *page 17*, Ulrike Welsch/Photo Researchers; *page 19*, Eric Kroll/Taurus; *page 26*, Hugh Rogers/Monkmeyer; *page 29*, Ellis Herwig/The Picture Cube; *page 36*, Bob Daemmrich/The Image Works; *page 39*, Y. B. Rabeuf/The Image Works; *page 41*, David S. Strickler/Monkmeyer; *page 47*, David Hiser/Photographers Aspen; *page 48*, Peter Menzel/Stock, Boston; *page 51, top*, DeVore/AnthroPhoto, *bottom*, James Holland/Stock, Boston; *page 53*, Jean-Claude Lejeune/Stock, Boston; *page 55*, NASA/The Image Works; *page 56*, Robert A. Isaacs/Photo Researchers; *page 58*, Tom Hollyman/Photo Researchers; *page 59*, Cary Wolinsky/Stock, Boston; *page 61*, Eric Kroll/Taurus Photos; *page 63*, John Griffin/The Image Works; *page 64*, Steve Kagan/Photo Researchers; *page 75, left*, Hazel Hankin/Stock, Boston, *right*, Alan Carey/The Image Works; *page 76, top*, Deborah Kahn/Stock, Boston, *bottom left*, Roberta Hershenson/Photo Researchers, *bottom right*, Michael Greco/Stock, Boston; *page 77*, Owen Franken/Stock, Boston; *page 80*, Rhoda Sidney/Monkmeyer; *page 81*, Barbara Alper/Stock, Boston; *page 82*, Paul Conklin/Monkmeyer; *page 85*, Hazel Hankin/Stock, Boston; *page 87*, Barnes/Southern Light; *page 89*, Paul Sequeira/Photo Researchers; *page 90*, Michael Hayman/Stock, Boston; *page 98*, Mark Antman/The Image Works; *page 99*, Peter G. Aitken/Photo Researchers; *page 100*, Chester Higgins, Jr./Photo Researchers; *page 102, top,* Alan Carey/The Image Works; *pages 102, bottom, 104, both,* Elizabeth Crews/The Image Works; *page 105*, Neil Goldstein/Stock, Boston; *page 106*, Arlene Collins/Monkmeyer; *page 108*, Jean Claude Lejeune/Stock, Boston; *page 111*, Sponholz/Monkmeyer; *page 117*, Mark Antman/The Image Works; *page 123*, UPI/Bettmann Newsphotos; *page 124, top*, Margot Granitsas/The Image Works, *bottom*, Will McIntyre/Photo Researchers; *page 127*, Julie O'Neil/Stock, Boston; *page 130*, Alan Carey/The Image Works; *page 132*, Eric Kroll/Taurus; *page 133*, Shmuel Thaler/Jeroboam; *page 137*, Boleslaw Edelhadjt/Gamma Liaison; *page 144*, Eric Kroll/Taurus; *page 149*, David Wells/The Image Works; *page 154*, Michael Weisbrot/Stock, Boston; *page 155*, Eric Kroll/Taurus; *page 161*, Charles Gatewood/The Image Works; *page 167*, Bob Daemmrich/The Image Works; *page 170, top*, Jim Pickerell/Stock, Boston; *page 170, bottom*, David Powers/Stock, Boston; *page 179*, Topham/The Image Works; *page 181*, Bohdan Hrynewych/Stock, Boston; *page 183, top*, Patrick Ward/Stock, Boston; *page 183, bottom*, J.P. Laffont/Sygma; *page 186, both*, William Campbell/Sygma; *pages 188, 194*, UPI/Bettmann Newsphotos; *page 197*, Ballard/EKM-Nepenthe; *page 201*, Barbara Rios/Photo Researchers; *page 203, top*, Cary Wolinsky/Stock, Boston; *page 203, bottom*, Nancy J. Pierce/Photo Researchers; *page 214, top*, Bill Owens; *page 214, right*, Allan Tannenbaum/Sygma; *page 218*, Wu/Jeroboam; *page 219*, Arthur Grace/Stock, Boston; *page 221, top*, Bryce Flynn/Stock, Boston, *bottom*, Olive R. Pierce/Stock, Boston; *pages 224, 232*, UPI/Bettmann Newsphotos; *page 233, left*, Alan Carey/The Image Works; *pages 233, right, 234*, Katrina Thomas/Photo Researchers; *page 236*, Randy Taylor, Sygma; *page 240*, Sandra Weiner, The Image Works; *page 244*, Bob Adelman/Magnum; *page 245*, Jean Claude Lejeune/Stock, Boston; *page 249*, Library of Congress; *page 250*, Lionel Delevinge/Stock, Boston; *page 252*, Peter Menzel/Stock, Boston; *page 254*, Eric Kroll/Taurus; *page 260*, Cary Wolinsky/Stock, Boston; *page 264, left*, Bob Daemmrich/The Image Works, *right*, Mark Antman/The Image Works; *page 267*, Alan Carey/The Image Works; *page 272*, UPI/Bettmann Newsphotos; *page 277, left*, Jon Chase/Stock, Boston, *right*, Alan Carey/The Image Works; *page 281*, Bronstein; *page 293*, Brady/Monkmeyer; *page 294*, Barbara Alper/Stock, Boston; *page 295*, Michael Greco/Stock, Boston; *page 297*, Photofest; *page 300*, Michael Weisbrot/Stock, Boston; *page 301*, Elizabeth Crews/The Image Works; *page 308*, Donald Dietz/Stock, Boston; *page 316*, Elizabeth Crews/Stock, Boston; *page 323*, Bob Adelman/Magnum; *page 324*, Paul Sequeira/Photo Researchers; *page 325*, Dion Ogust/The Image Works; *page 329*, Tom McHugh/Photo Researchers; *page 330*, Reuters/Bettmann Newsphotos; *page 332, left*, Roberta Hershenson/Photo Researchers, *right*, Bernard Pierre Wolffe/Photo Researchers; *page 340*, W. Marc Bernsau/The Image Works; *page 341*, Lorraine Rorke/The Image Works; *page 342*, Mark Antman/The Image Works; *page 355*, Hallie, *Lest Innocent Blood Be Shed*, Harper & Row, © 1979; *page 356*, Reuters/Bettmann; *page 361*, Jean Louis Atlan/Sygma; *page 365*, Paul Conklin/

Monkmeyer; *page 368*, Catherine Ursillo/Photo Researchers; *page 369, both*, Topham/The Image Works; *page 373*, Paul Conklin/Monkmeyer; *page 377*, Alan Carey/The Image Works; *page 382*, Bruce Roberts/Rapho/Photo Researchers; *page 384*, Paul Conklin/Monkmeyer Press; *page 385*, Elaine Rebman/Photo Researchers; *page 393*, Gabor Demjen/Stock, Boston; *page 394*, Paul Conklin/Monkmeyer; *page 398*, Rick Kopstein/Monkmeyer; *page 403*, Bob Daemmrich/The Image Works; *page 408*, Bettina Cirrone/Photo Researchers; *page 411*, Bruce Roberts/Rapho/Photo Researchers; *page 413*, Laimute E. Druskis/Taurus; *page 416*, Bill Aron/Photo Researchers; *page 419;* Muller/Woodfin Camp; *page 424*, UPI/Bettmann; *page 427*, Alain Nogues/Sygma; *page 429*, Fujihira/Monkmeyer; *page 431*, Gamma-Liaison; *page 435*, Novosti/Gamma-Liaison; *page 436*, Richard Wood/Taurus; *page 443, New York Times*, January, 17, 1982; *page 450*, Ira Wynman/Sygma; *page 452*, Alan Carey/The Image Works; *page 453*, Bettye Lane/Photo Researchers; *page 459*, Paul Conklin/Monkmeyer; *page 465*, Eric Kroll/Taurus; *page 470*, Lowell Georgia/Photo Researchers; *page 471*, Atlan/Sygma; *page 476, top*, Ellis Herwig/Taurus; *page 476, bottom* and *page 482*, Peter Menzel/Stock, Boston; *page 484*, Thomas Hopker/Woodfin Camp; *page 485*, Jim Harrison/Stock, Boston; *page 489*, All-Stock; *page 490*, G. Pinkhassov/Magnum; *page 496*, Margot Granitsas/The Image Works; *page 501*, Peter Marlow/Magnum; *page 505*, Frank Siteman/Stock, Boston; *page 507*, Pamela Hasegawa/Taurus; *page 512*, Ann Marie Rousseau/The Image Works; *page 516*, Peter Menzel/Stock, Boston; *page 518*, Frederik C. Bodin/Stock, Boston; *page 524*, Alan Carey/The Image Works; *page 527*, Mark Antman/The Image Works; *page 528*, Alexander Lowry/Photo Researchers; *page 531*, J. Berndt/Stock, Boston; *page 532*, Paul Fusco/Magnum; *page 533*, Ken Gaghan/Jeroboam; *page 534*, Laimute E. Druskis; *page 537*, Barbara Rios/Photo Researchers; *page 538*, Tom Check/Stock, Boston; *page 543*, Robin Wishna/Picture Group; *page 545, left*, David Austen/Stock, Boston, *center*, Owen Franken/Stock, Boston, *right*, Richard Wood/Taurus; *page 549*, Jane Scherr/Jeroboam; *page 554*, Alan Carey/The Image Works; *page 555*, Children's Defense Fund; *page 570*, Ed Buryn/Jeroboam; *page 572, top*, Alan Carey/The Image Works, *bottom*, Keith Gunnar/Photo Researchers; *page 575*, Nancy J. Pierce/Photo Researchers; *page 578, left*, Bob Krueger/Rapho/Photo Researchers, *right*, Keith Gunnar/Photo Researchers; *page 582*, Dan Chidester/The Image Works; *page 583*, Kirschenbaum/Stock, Boston; *page 590, left*, Culver, *right*, UPI/Bettmann Newsphoto.

## Color Insert Credits

*Page 2-2, top*, Joe Sohm/The Image Works, *center*, Bob Daemmrich/The Image Works, *bottom*, Hugh Rogers/Monkmeyer; *page 2-3, top left*, Catherine Ursillo/Photo Researchers, *top right*, Margot Granitsas/The Image Works, *center*, Paolo Koch/Photo Researchers, *bottom*, The Museum of The American Indian, Heye Foundation; *page 3-1, top*, Margaret Bourke-White, The New York Public Library Picture Collection, *center*, Irvin Saulowitz/Taurus, *bottom*, Grant LeDuc/Monkmeyer; *page 3-2, top left*, The New York Public Library Picture Collection, *top center*, Lisa Law/The Image Works, *top right*, Mark Antman/The Image Works, *bottom left*, Culver, *bottom right*, Ken Levinson/Monkmeyer; *page 3-3, top*, David Campione/Taurus, *center*, Van Bucher/Photo Researchers, *bottom*, Michal Heron/Monkmeyer; *page 3-4, top, bottom right*, Dan McCoy/Rainbow, *bottom left*, Hank Morgan/Rainbow; *page 4-1, top*, Bob Daemmrich/The Image Works, *center, bottom*, Owen Franken/Stock, Boston; *page 4-2, top left*, Marvin E. Newman/Woodfin Camp, *top center*, Christiana Dittmann/Rainbow, *top right*, Robert Frerck/Woodfin Camp, *bottom left*, David Austen/Stock, Boston, *bottom center*, Rick Smolan/Stock, Boston, *bottom right*, Mark Antman/The Image Works, *page 4-3, top*, Eastcott/Mamatiuk/The Image Works, *bottom*, John Moss/Photo Researchers; *page 4-4, top left*, Richard Pasley/Stock, Boston, *top right*, Bill Stanton/Rainbow, *center*, Dan McCoy/Rainbow, *bottom*, Ellis Herwig/Taurus; *page 9-1, left*, Tracy/FPG, *right*, Bob Daemmrich/Stock, Boston; *page 9-2, top*, Eric Kroll/Taurus, *center*, Billy E. Barnes/Stock, Boston, *bottom*, Elaine Wicks, O.S.F./Taurus; *page 9-3, top*, Don & Pat Valenti/Taurus, *bottom*, Anne McQueen/Stock, Boston; *page 9-4, top*, Richard Hutchings/Photo Researchers, *bottom*, Joan Menschenfreund/Taurus; *page 9-5, top left*, Jeff Lowenthal/Woodfin Camp, *top right*, Dan McCoy/Rainbow, *bottom* Christiana Dittmann/Rainbow; *page 9-6, top left*, Alan Carey/The Image Works, *top right*, Steven R. Kraus/Stock, Boston, *center*, Sybil Shackman/Monkmeyer, *bottom*, Audrey Gottlieb/Monkmeyer; *page 9-7, top*, Hugh Rogers/Monkmeyer, *center*, Hank Morgan/Rainbow, *bottom*, © Griffin/The Image Works; *page 9-8*, Mazzaschi/Stock, Boston; *page 11-1, top, bottom*, Dan McCoy/Rainbow, *center*, Michal Heron/Woodfin Camp; *page 11-2, top left*, Michal Heron/Woodfin Camp, *top right*, Joseph Schuler/Stock, Boston, *center*, Donald Dietz/Stock, Boston, *bottom left*, Nancy Dudley/Stock, Boston, *bottom right*, Berndt/Stock, Boston; *page 11-3, top left*, Hank Morgan/Rainbow, *top right*, Jeff Persons/Stock, Boston, *bottom*, Bob Daemmrich/Stock, Boston.

# NAME INDEX

# SUBJECT INDEX